STRATEGIC MANAGEMENT

Strategy Formulation and Implementation

The Irwin Series in Management and The Behavioral Sciences
L. L. Cummings and E. Kirby Warren   Consulting Editors

STRATEGIC MANAGEMENT

Strategy Formulation and Implementation

John A. Pearce II
School of Business Administration
George Mason University

Richard B. Robinson, Jr.
College of Business Administration
University of South Carolina

1988   Third Edition

IRWIN
Homewood, Illinois 60430

To David Donham Pearce, Mark McCartney Pearce, Katherine Elizabeth Robinson, John Braden Robinson—wonderful young people and our much beloved children

© RICHARD D. IRWIN, INC., 1982, 1985, and 1988

Acquisitions editor: William R. Bayer
Project editors: Jean Roberts and Karen Smith
Production manager: Bette Ittersagen
Compositor: Arcata Graphics/Kingsport
Typeface: 10/12 Century Schoolbook
Printer: R. R. Donnelley & Sons Company

ISBN 0-256-06236-6

Library of Congress Catalog Card No. 87-82169

Printed in the United States of America

1 2 3 4 5 6 7 8 9 0 DO 5 4 3 2 1 0 9 8

PREFACE

The third edition of this book is the culmination of 10 years of diligent work on the part of many people. This preface is designed to provide you with an overview of the content of the third edition and to recognize the many contributors to it. To do this we have divided the preface into three sections. The first section is addressed to the student and is designed to give this first-time user a concise overview of the structure and content of the book. The second section is addressed to the instructor and is designed to give the person familiar with our previous editions a sense of what is new. The third section acknowledges the many contributors to this ongoing project.

To the Student

Strategic Management: Strategy Formulation and Implementation, third edition, is a book designed to introduce you to the critical business skills of planning and managing strategic activities. It incorporates three teaching approaches: text, cohesion cases, and business case studies.

The text portion of this book provides you with a readable, up-to-date introduction to the management of strategy in the business enterprise. We have tried to integrate the work of strategic management theorists, practitioners, and researchers with a strong emphasis on real-world applications of strategic management concepts. To further this aim, we have included **Strategy in**

Action reports across 13 chapters which give current examples of the application of key concepts by well-known business firms.

The structure of the text material is guided by a comprehensive model of the strategic management process. The model will help you acquire an executive-level perspective on strategy formulation and implementation. It provides a visual display of the major components of the entire process and shows both how they are conceptually related and how they are sequenced through the process.

The major components of the model are each discussed in depth in separate chapters, thereby enabling you to acquire detailed knowledge and specific skills within a broad framework of strategic management. The use of the model is also extended to the cohesion cases and the business case studies, where you will be guided in your case analyses to pursue disciplined, systematic, and comprehensive studies of actual strategic dilemmas.

The **Cohesion Case** offers a particularly unique feature designed to aid both the student and the teacher of strategic management and business policy. We have taken a well-known, multi-industry firm—Holiday Inns, Inc.—and used it as the basis of an in-depth case study to illustrate in detail the application of the text material. To do this, we provide a cohesion case section at the end of each chapter which applies the chapter material to the company. The Holiday Inns, Inc., case offers a clear illustration of the corporate, business, and functional levels of strategy—so important to the understanding of strategic management in today's corporate environment.

The Cohesion Case offers several benefits to the reader:

It provides a continuous illustration of the interdependence of the various parts of the strategic management process by using the same enterprise throughout the chapters.

It provides a useful aid in understanding the text material when the primary emphasis in the course is to be on case studies or other nontext analysis.

It provides a useful aid in preparing for the case analysis component of the course, in the event that the instructor prefers to emphasize the conceptual material.

It offers an in-depth basis for class discussion of strategic management concepts, application, and ideas for any classroom pedagogy.

The **business case studies and industry notes** developed and chosen for this book offer you wide exposure to a systematically selected cross section of strategic management situations. All 34 cases and industry notes represent pertinent, relevant, factual, and, we hope, interesting and challenging opportunities to develop and test your skills as strategic managers. The rich diversity among these exciting cases and industry notes is described in greater detail later in this preface.

To the Instructor

This third edition of *Strategic Management: Strategy Formulation and Implementation* provides a thoroughly revised, state-of-the-art treatment of the critical business skills of planning and managing strategic activities. We have reorganized our treatment of strategic management into 13 chapters; added critical pedagodical features; condensed the material into fewer pages; expanded the number of "real-world" examples; condensed and updated the Cohesion Case; and further incorporated the work of contemporary scholars into our coverage of strategic management. We feel confident you will find the material well organized, laden with current examples, and reflective of new contributions in the strategic management literature while retaining a structure guided by our time-tested model of the strategic management process.

We have selected 34 cases and industry notes for this edition; 30 are new, and the remaining 4 carry-overs from the second edition were unanimously selected to remain in the third edition in a nationwide poll of professors currently using this book. The cases are grouped into four sections. Nine cases introduce students to strategic management and the process of strategy formulation; nine cases place students in the role of implementing basic strategies; eight cases allow students to experience the challenges of monitoring and controlling implemented strategies; and eight cases and industry notes allow you to cover industry analysis and strategic management across an integrated set of cases and industry notes. We are very excited about the case selection for this edition—they are contemporary, interesting situations students will recognize, enjoy, and learn from.

We have revised and condensed the Cohesion Case while retaining Holiday Inns, Inc., as the company that we examine. We have been pleased with the response of both students and instructors to this innovative, pedagogical feature we pioneered in this book. While the Cohesion Case has been recognized by many as one of the unique pedagogical advances in business policy this decade, we have endeavored to add still more self-teaching aids to this edition.

We have expanded our strategic management teaching package for this edition. In our second edition, we pioneered the use of computer-assisted strategic analysis with the introduction of *Strategic Analyst* to accompany our textbook. *Strategic Analyst* allowed the student to conduct a computer-based, systematic analysis of the strategic options available to a business and do so with built-in linkages to our text. *Strategic Analyst* is still available with this third edition. We are excited about our second computer-assisted offering to accompany our third edition. Selected cases in the third edition have Lotus templates available for use by the students.

Other components of our teaching package include a totally revised and enhanced *Instructor's Manual;* a set of four-color teaching transparencies; a computerized version of our test bank; *Formulating and Implementing Com-*

petitive Strategy, a paperback offering text-only coverage of strategic management identical to that in this book; *Company and Industry Cases in Strategy and Policy,* and a paperback offering 28 cases and industry notes. Each of these components of our teaching package offers the instructor optimal, integrated flexibility in designing and conducting the strategic management course.

Changes to Our Text Material

The literature and research comprising the strategic management field has been developing at a rapid pace in recent years. We have endeavored to create a third edition that incorporates major developments in this literature while keeping our focus centered on a simple, understandable framework through which students can begin to grasp the complexity of strategic management. Several text revisions or additions you should be aware of are described below:

- A new chapter has been added covering international issues and strategic management in an international setting.
- The three-chapter set on external analysis has become four chapters plus a supplement on sources of industry data. Separate chapters now cover the nature of external environments, environmental forecasting, industry analysis, and the international business setting. While the number of chapters is expanded, the material has been condensed and streamlined, affording a concise, practical treatment.
- A major new section has been added on the topic of "strategic control." Three basic types of strategic control and ways to use them are highlighted in this material.
- Organizational culture as a central dimension of strategy implementation has received significantly greater attention in Chapter 12 of this edition. Several useful analytical concepts and techniques that aid identification and management of the strategy–culture interface are incorporated to aid the student in understanding the culture concept.
- Two useful supplements now accompany our text material. A revised guide to financial analysis is provided following Chapter 8—Internal Analysis. It provides perhaps the most thorough and easy-to-use guide to quantitative analysis of financial and operating information available in any strategic management text. A guide to industry information sources follows Chapter 5—Environmental Forecasting. It has been revised and updated for this edition. Students will find it most helpful in rapidly orienting them to where and how to get company and industry data.
- We have increased the number of **Strategy in Action Illustration Capsules** by 30 percent. The text material now contains 43 of these illustra-

tion vignettes, 35 of which are new to this edition. Each Strategy in
Action provides a contemporary business example of a key chapter topic
to interest the student and aid learning.

- Our popular **Cohesion Case** feature has received considerable attention
  this edition. We have continued the use of a well-known, multi-industry
  firm—Holiday Corporation (Holiday Inns, Inc.)—as an in-depth case
  study to illustrate in detail the application of the text material. We also
  continue to provide cohesion case sections at the end of each chapter,
  which apply chapter material to the Holiday situation. We have updated
  the material about Holiday Corporation, and we have streamlined and
  shortened its presentation, making this feature even more appealing and
  useful.

- Our survey of over 200 adopters and "almost adopters" of the second
  edition told us they wanted maximum material to aid students unsure
  about the case method, what they need to do in preparing a case, and
  maintaining a strategic point of view. We have added a major section
  in this edition that is solely intended to aid students in understanding
  case method pedagogy and to prepare them to analyze a case. The first
  part of this section provides a thorough, detailed description of the case
  method format; what to expect in each class session; and how to analyze
  a case, prepare it for class, and participate in class discussion. The second
  part offers a short case accompanied by a useful example of former students' analysis and preparation of it. These two supplements, combined
  with the revised Cohesion Case illustrating each step of strategic analysis,
  provide the most thorough package available in any strategy textbook
  to ensure that students understand and benefit from the case method
  pedagogy.

In conclusion, we are confident you will find the text material in this third
edition well organized, concise, filled with current examples, and consistent
with the current theory and practice of strategic management.

Cases in the Third Edition

We are very excited about the 34 cases and industry notes available in this
edition. Thirty cases and notes are new to this edition. Four cases were retained based on the unanimous preference expressed in our survey of current
adopters. We are confident you will find this case collection does an excellent
job of meeting your classroom needs for several reasons:

- The collection offers a rich diversity of recognizable domestic, foreign,
  and international companies and industries.
- The collection presents very current situations. All the cases involve situations in the 1980s with most focusing on 1985 or later.

- Contemporary, recognizable, interest-piquing situations abound: New Coke, Pepsi and the cola wars; Federal Express's ZapMail decision; Citicorp and Merrill Lynch; Manville and A.H. Robins' product liability dilemma; Tylenol and capsule tampering; Goodyear and South Africa; People Express and the airlines; international truck competition among Mercedes Benz, Volvo, and Mack Truck; Wendy's growth and maturity; Wal-Mart's retailing success—all situations our tests have shown motivate student interest.

- The nature of the firms provides varied exposure. We have included 7 small companies in either family or rapid growth phases; 5 foreign (non-U.S.) companies; 15 companies with international operations; 6 of the top companies in America; 2 nonprofit organizations; and 4 industry sets providing 2 or more companies in competition with each other.

- Three industry notes with matching cases provide a rich basis for teaching industry analysis. With the Coke and PepsiCo cases comprising a fourth industry set, you have a variety of domestic and international industry settings at different stages of evolution and spanning manufacturing, services, and consumer products.

- This collection provides the variety instructors expect in a superior case offering. Cases are present that span the basic types of business (retail, wholesale, service, manufacturing, etc.), companies in market leadership positions, companies falling out of leadership, high-tech companies, start-up companies, chapter 11 companies, exporters, importers, and diversifying companies.

- We have also given significant attention to case length. A major effort has been made to ensure that a majority of the cases are short to medium in length. We still include several long cases, "two-day" cases, and two-part cases. The instructor's needs in this regard are further supplemented by information in the *Instructor's Manual*.

Finally, we have endeavored to ensure a collection of cases that are flexible in their course sequencing, yet able to offer exposure to distinct management challenges associated with strategy formulation, implementation, or control. Because our survey found this to be one of the key demands and concerns of strategic management professors worldwide, this case collection was developed with this need upmost in our minds. Students will see Wendy's managers formulating a new strategy for entering the competitive fast-foods industry, Mercedes Benz and Volvo reformulating their strategies in the mature and concentrated worldwide truck industry. They can study Citicorp implementing international expansion, Sharpco consolidating growth, and Merrill Lynch implementing its financial supermarket strategy. They can experience strategic control at Tylenol, Union Carbide, and Payless Cashways—and experience strategic decisions like Goodyear's choices in South Africa, Manville's chapter 11, and Coke's "New Coke."

Overall, we think you will find this case collection interesting and motivating for your students, representative and varied in the application of strategic problems and analytical applications, flexible in terms of course sequencing, and comfortably teachable.

Acknowledgments

We have repeatedly benefited from the help of many people in the evolution of this book over three editions. Students, adopters, colleagues, and reviewers have provided literally hundreds of insightful comments, suggestions, and contributions that have progressively enhanced this package. We are certainly indebted to several researchers, writers, and practicing managers who have accelerated the development of the literature on strategic management. And we are likewise indebted to the talented case researchers who have produced several cases used in this book as well as the growing network of case researchers encouraging the revitalization of case research as important academic endeavor. The discipline of strategic management is eminently more teachable when current, well-written, well-researched cases are available. We encourage every opportunity to reinforce proper recognition and reward for first-class case research—it is a major avenue through which top strategic management scholars should be recognized.

The following strategic management scholars have provided the results of their case research in the creation of this exciting third edition:

Paul E. Arney, Bradley University
Franz X. Bea, University of Tubingen, West Germany
John M. Bryson, University of Minnesota
William K. Carter, University of Virginia
James J. Chrisman, University of South Carolina
DeAnn Chappell, University of Virginia
Julio DeCastro, University of South Carolina
J. Kim DeDee, University of Wisconsin at Oshkosh
David W. Gillen, Wilfred Laurier University
John H. Grant, IMEDE, Lausanne, Switzerland
John M. Gwin, University of Virginia
Benjamin Harrison, Georgia State University
Manfred Heubner, Georgia State University
Per V. Jenster, University of Virginia
Richard C. Johanson, University of Arkansas
J. Kay Keels, University of South Carolina
Paula J. King, University of Minnesota
Harry R. Knudson, University of Washington
Alfred Kotzle, University of Tubingen, West Germany
Stewart C. Malone, University of Virginia
Patricia P. McDougall, Georgia State University

Jon Morris, Georgia State University
Lorraine Norian, University of Virginia
Tae H. Oum, University of British Columbia
Brian Pauleen, University of Virginia
Betty R. Ricks, Old Dominion University
William D. Roering, University of Minnesota
John A. Seeger, Bentley College
Arthur Sharplin, McNeese University
Kellen Smith, University of Virginia
Marie Smith, University of Virginia
Neil H. Snyder, University of Virginia
Linda E. Swayne, University of North Carolina at Charlotte
Patricia A. Timms, Georgia State University
Michael W. Tretheway, University of British Columbia
E. K. Valentin, Weber State College
Andrew H. Van de Ven, University of Minnesota
Robert P. Vichas, Florida Atlantic University
Yaakov Weber, University of Kentucky
Frank L. Winfrey, University of Wisconsin at Parkside

We have personally ensured that the Dean at each of their resepctive institutions is aware of the value their case research efforts have added to the profession's ability to teach strategic management.

The development of this book through three editions has been greatly enhanced by the generous commitment of time, energy, and ideas from the following people:

Sonny S. Ariss, University of Toledo
Robert Earl Bolick, Metropolitan State University
William E. Burr II, University of Oregon
E. T. Busch, Western Kentucky University
Richard Castaldi, San Diego State University
Larry Cummings, Northwestern University
William Davig, Auburn University
Peter Davis, University of Oregon
Greg Dess, University of Texas at Arlington
Marc J. Dollinger, University of Kentucky
Liam Fahey, Northwestern University
Elizabeth Freeman, Portland State University
Diane J. Garsombke, University of Maine
J. Michael Geringer, Southern Methodist University
Peter G. Goulet, Hawkeye Consultations and University of Northern
   Iowa
Don Hambrick, Pennsylvania State University
Richard C. Hoffman, College of William and Mary

Troy Jones, University of Central Florida
Jon G. Kalinowski, Mankato State University
Kay Keels, University of South Carolina
Michael Koshuta, Valparaiso University
Myroslaw J. Kyj, Widener University of Pennsylvania
Joseph W. Leonard, Miami University, Ohio
Edward L. McClelland, Roanoke College
Patricia McDougall, Georgia State University
John G. Maurer, Wayne State University
S. Mehta, San Jose State University
Richard R. Merner, University of Delaware
Cynthia Montgomery, University of Michigan
Stephanie Newell, Bowling Green State University
Kenneth Olm, University of Texas at Austin
Benjamin Oviatt, Clemson University
Joseph Paolillo, University of Mississippi
G. Norris Rath, Shepherd College
Paula Rechner, University of Illinois
Les Rue, Georgia State University
J. A. Ruslyk, Memphis State University
Scott Snell, Michigan State University
James S. Snyder, North Adams State College
Arien A. Ullman, SUNY at Binghamton
William C. Waddell, California State University, Los Angeles
Bill Warren, College of William and Mary
Kirby Warren, Columbia University
Michael White, University of Tulsa
Frank Winfrey, University of Wisconsin
Robley Wood, Virginia Commonwealth University

The valuable ideas, recommendations, and support of these outstanding scholars and teachers have added quality to this book.

Because we are affiliated with two separate universities, we have two sets of co-workers to thank.

The growth and dynamic environment at George Mason University have contributed directly to the development of this edition. Valuable critiques and helpful recommendations have been made by strategic management faculty Carolyn Erdener, Keith Robbins, and Shaker Zahra, and by colleagues Bill Bolce, Debra Cohen, Joe English, Ellen Fagensen, Freda Hartman, Eileen Hogan, Ken Kovach, Steve Patrick, and Hank Sims. For his gracious support and personal encouragement, we also wish to thank Coleman Raphael, Dean of George Mason University's School of Business Administration and Chairman of the Board of Atlantic Research, Inc. For their excellent secretarial assistance, we most sincerely appreciate the work of Debbie McDanial, Sondra Patrick, and Luci Rosinski.

We are especially grateful to LeRoy Eakin, Jr., and his family for their generous endowment of the Eakin Endowed Chair in Strategic Management at George Mason University that Jack holds. The provisions of the Chair have enabled Jack to continue his dual involvements with this book and strategic management research.

The stimulating environment at the University of South Carolina has contributed to the development of this book. Thought-provoking discussions with strategy colleagues Alan Bauerschmidt, Carl Clamp, Jim Chrisman, Herb Hand, John Logan, Bob Rosen, Bill Sandberg, and David Schweiger gave us many useful ideas. We also want to recognize the important input of doctoral candidates Kay Keels, Frank Winfrey, Jacob Weber, Lanny Herron, and Julio DeCastro in the development, class testing, and refinement of selected business case studies. Likewise, we want to thank James F. Kane, Dean of the College of Business Administration; James G. Hilton, our Associate Dean; and Joe Ullman, Program Director in Management, for their interest and support. Our sincere appreciation also goes to Sandra Murrah for her help in preparing this manuscript and in solving endless logistical problems.

In using this text, we hope that you will share our enthusiasm both for the rich subject of strategic management and for the learning approach that we have taken. We value your recommendations and thoughts about our materials. Please write Jack at the School of Business Administration, George Mason University, Fairfax, Virginia 22030, or Richard at the College of Business Administration, University of South Carolina, Columbia, South Carolina 29208.

Jack Pearce

Richard Robinson

ABOUT THE AUTHORS

John A. Pearce II, Ph.D., is the holder of the Eakin Endowed Chair in Strategic Management in the School of Business Administration at George Mason University (Fairfax, VA 22030, 703-323-4361) and Chairman of the school's Management Department.

Professor Pearce has published more than 100 journal articles, invited book chapters, and professional papers in outlets that include *Academy of Management Executive, Academy of Management Journal, Academy of Management Review, California Management Review, Journal of Business Venturing, Sloan Management Review,* and the *Strategic Management Journal*. He has served on the editorial boards of four journals, and he is currently the Consulting Editor in Strategic Management for the *Journal of Management*. Professor Pearce is also the coauthor or coeditor of 17 texts, proceedings, and supplements for publishers that include Richard D. Irwin, Inc., McGraw-Hill, Random House, and the Academy of Management.

Elected to more than a dozen offices in national and regional professional associations, Professor Pearce has served as Chairman of the Academy of Management's Entrepreneurship Division, Strategic Management and Entrepreneurship Track Chairman for the Southern Management Association, and Strategy Formulation and Implementation Track Chairman for the Decision Sciences Institute. He is also the 1989 President-elect of the Southern Management Association.

An active consultant and management trainer, Professor Pearce specializes in helping executive teams to develop and activate their firms' strategic plans.

Richard B. Robinson, Jr., Ph.D., is currently Professor of Strategy and Entrepreneurship in the College of Business Administration at the University of South Carolina (Columbia, SC 29208, 803-777-5961).

Professor Robinson has published more than 100 journal articles, invited chapters, and professional papers in outlets that include the *Academy of Management Journal, Strategic Management Journal, Academy of Management Review, Journal of Business Venturing, Journal of Small Business Management,* and the *Personnel Administrator.* He is also coauthor or coeditor of 16 texts, proceedings, and supplements for publishers that include Richard D. Irwin, Inc., McGraw-Hill, Random House, and the Academy of Management.

Professor Robinson is the recipient of several awards in recognition of his work in strategic management and entrepreneurship. Sponsors of these awards include the Heizer Capital Corporation, the Academy of Management, the Center for Family Business, the National Association of Small Business Investment Companies, the Southern Business Administration Association, the Small Business Administration, the National Venture Capital Association, and Beta Gamma Sigma. He has also held offices in the Academy of Management, the Southern Management Association, and the International Council on Small Business. Professor Robinson is an active consultant in strategic management of growth-oriented ventures.

CONTENTS

of the Model: *Holistic. Analytic versus Prescriptive. Nonpolitical. Evolutionary.* Summary.
Cohesion Case Illustration: Strategic Management Framework for Holiday Inns   65

Problems for the Multinational Firm. Multinational Strategic Planning: *Multidomestic Industries and Global Industries*. *The Multinational Challenge*. Multinationalization of the Corporate Mission: *The MNC Mission Statement*. *Components of the Corporate Mission Revisited*. Summary. Appendix: Components of the Multinational Environment. Cohesion Case Illustration: The Multinational Environment of Holiday Inns, Inc.   170

PART THREE
Strategy Implementation   323

Evaluating Deviations. Reward Systems: Motivating Execution and
Control. Summary.
Cohesion Case Illustration: Guiding and Evaluating the Strategy at
Holiday Inns, Inc. 433
Epilogue: A Summary of Key Decisions Made by Holiday Inn
Executives in Positioning the Company for the 1990s 439

Guide to Strategic Management Case Analysis 443
The Case Method. Preparing for Case Discussion: *Suggestions for
Effective Preparation.* Participating in Class: *The Student as Active
Learner. Your Professor as Discussion Leader.* Assignments: *Written
Assignments. Oral Presentations. Working as a Team Member.*
Summary.
Sample Case: Pennsylvania Movie Theatres, Inc. 450
Sample Case Analysis: Pennsylvania Movie Theatres, Inc. 455

**PART FOUR
Cases 467**

STRATEGIC MANAGEMENT MODEL

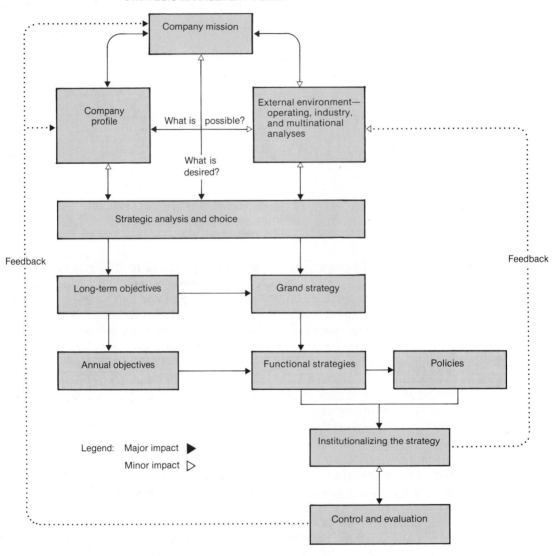

PART ONE

Overview of Strategic Management

The first two chapters of this text provide a broad introduction to strategic management. They describe the nature, need, benefits, and terminology of the processes for producing and implementing major plans directing business activities. Subsequent chapters then provide greater detail.

Chapter 1, The Nature and Value of Strategic Management, emphasizes the practical value of a strategic management approach for a business organization and reviews the actual benefits for companies that have instituted strategic management. The critical activities of strategic management are then presented as a set of dimensions that can be used to distinguish strategic decisions from other planning tasks of the firm.

Chapter 1 stresses the key point that, in many companies, strategic management activities are undertaken at three levels: corporate, business, and functional. The distinctive characteristics of strategic decision making at each of these levels are discussed; these characteristics will serve as the basis for later observations concerning the impact of activities at different levels on company operations.

The extent to which formality is desirable in strategic management is another key point in Chapter 1, as is the alignment of strategy makers with particular activities in the overall process of strategy formulation and implementation. It is shown that it is possible to assign areas of decision-maker responsibility, and an appropriate degree of formality in strategic activities is suggested. The factors determining these conclusions are discussed in detail.

A final section in Chapter 1 reviews the results of research in business organizations. The studies convincingly demonstrate that companies utilizing strategic management processes often enjoy financial and behavioral benefits that justify the additional costs involved.

Chapter 2 presents a model of the strategic management process. The model is representative of approaches currently used by strategic planners and will serve as an outline for the remainder of the book in that each subsequent chapter is devoted to an in-depth discussion of one of the major components of the model. Each of the individual components is carefully defined and explained in Chapter 2, as is the process by which the components are integrated to produce cohesive and balanced results. The chapter ends with a discussion of the practical limitations of the model and the advisability of tailoring the general recommendations suggested to the unique situations confronted in actual business practice.

1

The Nature and Value of Strategic Management

The complexity and sophistication of business decision making requires strategic management. Managing various and multifaceted internal activities is only part of the modern executive's responsibilities. The firm's immediate external environment poses a second set of challenging factors. This environment includes competitors whenever profits seem possible, suppliers of increasingly scarce resources, government agencies monitoring adherence to an ever-growing number of regulations, and customers whose often inexplicable preferences must be anticipated. A remote external environment also contributes to the general yet pervasive climate in which a business exists. This environment consists of economic conditions, social change, political priorities, and technological developments, each of which must be anticipated, monitored, assessed, and incorporated in top-level decision making. However, these influences are often subordinated to the fourth major consideration in executive decision making—the multiple and often mutually inconsistent objectives of the stakeholders of the business: owners, top managers, employees, communities, customers, and country.

To deal effectively with all that affects the ability of a company to grow profitably, executives design strategic management processes they feel will facilitate the optimal positioning of the firm in its competitive environment. Such positioning is possible because these strategic processes allow more accurate anticipation of environmental changes and improved preparedness for reacting to unexpected internal or competitive demands.

Broad-scope, large-scale management processes have become dramatically more sophisticated since the end of World War II, principally as a reflection of increases in the size and number of competing firms; of the expanded intervention of government as a buyer, seller, regulator, and competitor in the free enterprise system; and of greater business involvement in international trade. Perhaps the most significant improvement in management processes came in the 1970s as "long-range planning," "new venture management," "planning, programming, budgeting," and "business policy" were blended with increased emphasis on environmental forecasting and external as well as internal considerations in formulating and implementing plans. This all-encompassing approach is known as *strategic management* or *strategic planning*.[1]

Strategic management is defined as *the set of decisions and actions resulting in formulation and implementation of strategies designed to achieve the objectives of an organization.* It involves attention to no less than nine critical areas:

1. Determining the mission of the company, including broad statements about its purpose, philosophy, and goals.
2. Developing a company profile that reflects internal conditions and capabilities.
3. Assessment of the company's external environment, in terms of both competitive and general contextual factors.
4. Analysis of possible options uncovered in the matching of the company profile with the external environment.
5. Identifying the desired options uncovered when possibilities are considered in light of the company mission.
6. Strategic choice of a particular set of long-term objectives and grand strategies needed to achieve the desired options.
7. Development of annual objectives and short-term strategies compatible with long-term objectives and grand strategies.
8. Implementing strategic choice decisions based on budgeted resource allocations and emphasizing the matching of tasks, people, structures, technologies, and reward systems.
9. Review and evaluation of the success of the strategic process to serve as a basis for control and as an input for future decision making.

As these nine areas indicate, strategic management involves the planning, directing, organizing, and controlling of the strategy-related decisions and actions of the business. By strategy, managers mean their *large-scale, future-oriented plans for interacting with the competitive environment to optimize*

---

[1] In this text the term *strategic management* refers to the broad overall process because to some scholars and practitioners the term *strategic planning* connotes only the formulation phase of total management activities.

achievement of organization objectives. Thus, a strategy represents a firm's "game plan." Although it does not precisely detail all future deployments (people, financial, and material), it does provide a framework for managerial decisions. A strategy reflects a company's awareness of how to compete, against whom, when, where, and for what.

Dimensions of Strategic Decisions

What decisions facing a business are strategic and therefore deserve strategic management attention? Typically, strategic issues have six identifiable dimensions:

Strategic Issues Require Top-Management Decisions.   Strategic decisions overarch several areas of a firm's operations. Therefore, top-management involvement in decision making is imperative. Only at this level is there the perspective for understanding and anticipating broad implications and ramifications, and the power to authorize the resource allocations necessary for implementation.

Strategic Issues Involve the Allocation of Large Amounts of Company Resources.   Strategic decisions characteristically involve substantial resource deployment. The people, physical assets, or moneys needed must be either redirected from internal sources or secured from outside the firm. In either case, strategic decisions commit a firm to a stream of actions over an extended period of time, thus involving substantial resources.

Strategic Issues Are Likely to Have a Significant Impact on the Long-Term Prosperity of the Firm.   Strategic decisions ostensibly commit the firm for a long period of time, typically for five years; however, the time frame of impact is often much longer. Once a firm has committed itself to a particular strategic option in a major way, its competitive image and advantages are usually tied to that strategy. Firms become known in certain markets, for certain products, with certain characteristics. To shift from these markets, products, or technologies by adopting a radically different strategy would jeopardize previous progress. Thus, strategic decisions have enduring effects on the firm—for better or worse.

Strategic Issues Are Future Oriented.   Strategic decisions are based on what managers anticipate or forecast rather than on what they know. Emphasis is on developing projections that will enable the firm to select the most promising strategic options. In the turbulent and competitive free enterprise environment, a successful firm must take a proactive (anticipatory) stance toward change.

Strategic Issues Usually Have Major Multifunctional or Multibusiness Consequences.   A strategic decision is coordinative. Decisions about such factors as customer mix, competitive emphasis, or organizational structure necessarily involve a number of a firm's strategic business units (SBUs), functions, divisions, or program units. Each of these areas will be affected by the allocation or reallocation of responsibilities and resources related to the decision.

Strategic Issues Necessitate Considering Factors in the Firm's External Environment.   All business firms exist in an open system. They impact and are impacted by external conditions largely beyond their control. Therefore, if a firm is to succeed in positioning itself in future competitive situations, its strategic managers must look beyond the limits of the firm's own operations. They must consider what relevant others (e.g., competitors, customers, suppliers, creditors, government, and labor) are likely to do.

Three Levels of Strategy

The decision-making hierarchy of business firms typically contains three levels. At the top is the corporate level, composed principally of members of the board of directors and the chief executive and administrative officers. They are responsible for the financial performance of the corporation as a whole and for achieving the nonfinancial goals of the firm, for example, corporate image and social responsibility. To a large extent, orientations at the corporate level reflect the concern of stockholders and society at large. Particularly in multibusiness firms, one duty of those at the corporate level is to determine the businesses in which the company should be involved. Further, corporate officers set objectives and formulate strategies that span the activities of individual businesses in the corporation and the functional area of these businesses. By adopting a portfolio approach to strategic management, corporate-level strategic managers attempt to exploit their distinctive competencies within their industries while typically planning over a five-year time horizon.

The second rung of the decision-making hierarchy is the business level, composed principally of business and corporate managers. These managers must translate the general statements of direction and intent generated at the corporate level into concrete, functional objectives and strategies for individual business divisions or SBUs. In essence, business-level strategic managers must determine the basis on which a company can compete in the selected product–market arena. While so doing, they strive to identify and secure the most profitable and promising market segment. This market segment is the fairly unique piece of the total market that the business can claim and defend because of competitive advantages. Every corporation, even the largest multinational, depends on the strength of market segments for continuing viability.

The third rung is the functional level, composed principally of managers

Figure 1–1
Alternative strategic management structures

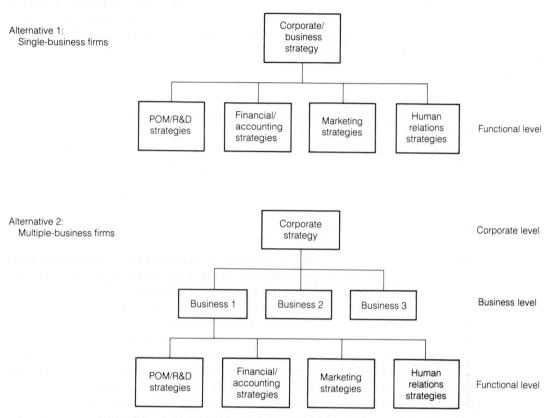

of product, geographic, and functional areas. It is their responsibility to develop annual objectives and short-term strategies in such areas as production, operations, and research and development; finance and accounting; marketing; and human relations. However, their greatest responsibilities are in the implementation or execution of a company's strategic plans. While corporate and business-level managers center their planning concerns on "doing the right things," managers at the functional level must stress "doing things right." Thus, they directly address such issues as the efficiency and effectiveness of production and marketing systems, the quality and extent of customer service, and the success of particular products and services in increasing their market shares.

Figure 1–1 depicts the three levels of strategic management as they are actually structured in practice. In alternative 1 the company is engaged in only one business and the corporate and business-level responsibilities are concentrated in a single group of directors, officers, and managers. This particular structure is nearly synonymous with the organizational formats of the

small businesses that constitute approximately 95 percent of all business organizations in the United States.

Alternative 2 is a classical corporate structure comprised of three fully
operative levels. The suprastructure is provided at the corporate level, with
the superstructure at the business level giving direction and support for functional-level activities.

The approach taken throughout this text is best depicted by alternative 2.
Thus, whenever appropriate, topics will be covered from the perspective of
each level of strategic management. In this way the text presents one of the
most comprehensive and up-to-date discussions of the strategic management
process.

Characteristics of Strategic Management Decisions

The characteristics of strategic management decisions vary with the level of
strategic activity considered. As shown in Figure 1–2, corporate-level decisions
tend to be value oriented, conceptual, and less concrete than those at the
business or functional level of strategy formulation and implementation. Corporate-level decisions are also characterized by greater risk, cost, and profit
potential, as well as by longer time horizons and greater needs for flexibility.
These characteristics are logical consequences of the more far-reaching futuris-
tic, innovative, and pervasive nature of corporate-level strategic activity. Examples of corporate-level decisions include the choice of business, dividend policies,
sources of long-term financing, and priorities for growth.

At the other end of the continuum, functional-level decisions principally
involve action-oriented operational issues. These decisions are made periodically and lead directly to implementation of some part of the overall strategy
formulated at the corporate and business levels. Therefore, functional-level
decisions are relatively short range and involve low risk and modest costs
because they are dependent on available resources. Functional-level decisions
usually determine actions requiring minimal companywide cooperation. These
activities supplement the functional area's present activities and are adaptable
to ongoing activities so that minimal cooperation is needed for successful implementation. Because functional-level decisions are relatively concrete and quantifiable, they receive critical attention and analysis even though their comparative profit potential is low.

Some common functional-level decisions include generic versus brand-name
labeling, basic versus applied R&D, high versus low inventory levels, general-
versus specific-purpose production equipment, and close versus loose supervision.

Bridging corporate- and functional-level decisions are those made at the
business level. As Figure 1–2 indicates, business-level descriptions of strategic
decisions fall between those for the other two levels. For example, business-
level decisions are less costly, risky, and potentially profitable than corporate-

Figure 1–2
Characteristics of strategic management decisions at different levels

	Level of strategy		
Characteristic	*Corporate*	*Business*	*Functional*
Type	Conceptual	Mixed	Operational
Measurability	Value judgments dominant	Semiquantifiable	Usually quantifiable
Frequency	Periodic or sporadic	Periodic or sporadic	Periodic
Adaptability	Low	Medium	High
Relation to present activities	Innovative	Mixed	Supplementary
Risk	Wide range	Moderate	Low
Profit potential	Large	Medium	Small
Cost	Major	Medium	Modest
Time horizon	Long range	Medium range	Short range
Flexibility	High	Medium	Low
Cooperation required	Considerable	Moderate	Little

level decisions, but they are more costly, risky, and potentially profitable than functional-level decisions. Some common business-level decisions involve plant location, marketing segmentation and geographic coverage, and distribution channels.

Formality in Strategic Management

The formality of strategic management systems varies widely among companies. *Formality* refers to the degree to which membership, responsibilities, authority, and discretion in decision making are specified. It is an important consideration in the study of strategic management because degree of formality is usually positively correlated with the cost, comprehensiveness, accuracy, and success of planning.

A number of forces determine the need for formality in strategic management. As shown in Figure 1–3, the size of the organization, its predominant management styles, the complexity of its environment, its production processes, the nature of its problems, and the purpose of its planning system all combine in determining an appropriate degree of formality.

In particular, formality is often associated with two factors: size and stage of development of the company. Methods of evaluating strategic success are also linked to degree of formality. Some firms, especially smaller ones, are *entrepreneurial*. They are basically under the control of a single individual and produce a limited number of products or services. With this mode, performance evaluation is very informal, intuitive, and limited in scope. At the other end of the spectrum, evaluation is part of a comprehensive, formalized,

Figure 1–3
Forces influencing design of strategic management systems

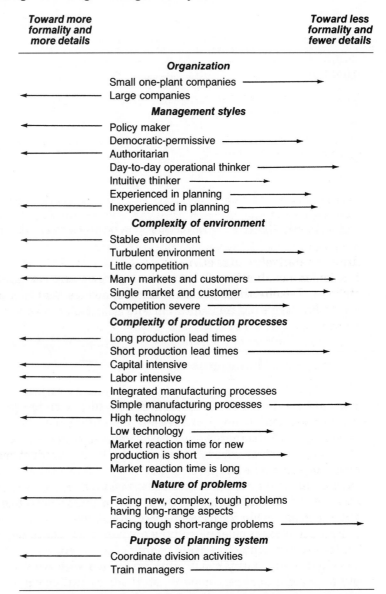

Toward more formality and more details   *Toward less formality and fewer details*

Organization

Small one-plant companies ⟶

⟵ Large companies

Management styles

⟵ Policy maker

Democratic-permissive ⟶

⟵ Authoritarian

Day-to-day operational thinker ⟶

Intuitive thinker ⟶

Experienced in planning ⟶

⟵ Inexperienced in planning ⟶

Complexity of environment

⟵ Stable environment

Turbulent environment ⟶

⟵ Little competition

⟵ Many markets and customers ⟶

Single market and customer ⟶

Competition severe ⟶

Complexity of production processes

⟵ Long production lead times

Short production lead times ⟶

⟵ Capital intensive

⟵ Labor intensive

⟵ Integrated manufacturing processes

Simple manufacturing processes ⟶

⟵ High technology

Low technology ⟶

Market reaction time for new production is short ⟶

⟵ Market reaction time is long

Nature of problems

⟵ Facing new, complex, tough problems having long-range aspects

Facing tough short-range problems ⟶

Purpose of planning system

⟵ Coordinate division activities

Train managers ⟶

Source: George A. Steiner, *Strategic Planning* (New York: Free Press, 1979), p. 54. Copyright © 1979 by the Free Press, a division of Macmillan Publishing Co., Inc. Reprinted with permission of Macmillan.

Figure 1–4
Hierarchy of objectives and strategies

Ends (What is to be achieved?)	Means (How it is to be achieved?)	Strategic decision makers			
		Board of directors	Corporate managers	Business managers	Functional managers
Mission, including goals and philosophy		√√	√√	√	
Long-term objectives	Grand strategy	√	√√	√√	
Annual objectives	Short-term strategy policies		√	√√	√√
Functional objectives	Tactics			√	√√

Note: √√ indicates a principal responsibility; √ indicates a secondary responsibility.

multilevel strategic planning system. This approach, which Henry Mintzberg called the *planning mode,* is used by large firms, such as Texas Instruments and General Electric. Mintzberg also identified a third mode (the *adaptive mode*) in the middle of this spectrum, which he associated with medium-sized firms in relatively stable environments.[2] For firms in the adaptive mode, identification and evaluation of alternative strategies are closely related to existing strategy. Despite these generalities, it is not unusual to find different modes within the same organization. For example, Exxon might adopt an entrepreneurial mode in the development and evaluation of its solar subsidiary's strategy, while the rest of the company follows a planning mode.

The Strategy Makers

The ideal strategic management process is developed and governed by a strategic management team. The team consists principally of decision makers at all three levels (corporate, business, and functional) in the corporation, for example, the chief executive officer (CEO), the product managers, and the heads of functional areas. The team also relies on input from two types of support personnel: company planning staffs, when they exist, and lower-level managers and supervisors. The latter provide data for strategic decision making and are responsible for implementing strategies.

Because strategic decisions have such a tremendous impact on a firm and because they require large commitments of company resources, they can only be made by top managers in the organizational hierarchy. Figure 1–4 indicates the alignment between levels of strategic decision makers and the kinds of objectives and strategies for which they are typically responsible.

---

[2] Henry Mintzberg, "Strategy Making in Three Modes," *California Management Review* 16, no. 2 (1973), pp. 44–53.

Figure 1–5
Responsibility relationships in strategic planning

Planning activities	Corporate responsibility		Business responsibility		Functional responsibility
	Top management	Corporate planning department	General management	Staff groups	Departmental planning groups
Establish corporate objectives	△				
Identify performance targets	●	●			
Setting planning horizon	●		●		
Organize and coordinate planning effort		●			●
Make environmental assumptions	△	●	△	●	
Collection information and forecast					
Forecast sales	△		△	●	
Assess firm's strength and weaknesses			△	●	
Evaluate competitive environment			△	●	
Establish business objectives	△		△	●	△
Develop business plans	△	○	△		△
Formulate alternative strategies		○		●	
Select alternative strategies		○	●		
Evaluate and select projects			△	●	
Develop tactics			△	●	
Revise objectives and plans if objectives are not met	△				
Integrate plans		●			
Allocate resources	△				
Review progress against the plan	●		●		
Evaluate plan's effectiveness		●			

Key: △ Approves.
   ○ Reviews, evaluates, and counsels.
   ● Does the work.

Source: Adapted from Ronald J. Kudla, "Elements of Effective Corporate Planning," *Long-Range Planning*, August 1976, p. 89.

The use of company planning staffs has increased considerably since the 1960s. In large corporations, the existence of planning departments, often headed by a corporate vice president for planning, is common. Medium-sized firms frequently employ at least one full-time staff member to spearhead strategic data-collection efforts. Even in smaller or less progressive firms, an officer or group of officers designated as a planning committee is often assigned to spearhead the company's strategic planning efforts.

Precisely what are managers' responsibilities in the strategic planning process at the corporate and business levels? Figure 1–5 provides some answers.

It shows that top management shoulders responsibility for broadly approving each of the six major phases of planning listed. They are assisted in the execution of these responsibilities by the corporate planning department, staff, or personnel, who actually prepare major components of the corporate plan. Top management also reviews, evaluates, and counsels on most major phases of the plan's preparation.

Figure 1–5 further shows that general managers at the business level have principal responsibilities for approving environmental analysis and forecasting, establishing business objectives, and developing business plans prepared by staff groups. The figure clearly indicates the pervasive and potentially powerful influence of corporate planners in the overall strategic management process.

One final, but perhaps overriding, point must be made about strategic decision makers: a company's president or CEO characteristically plays a dominant role in the process. In many ways this situation is desirable and reasonable. The principal duty of a CEO is often defined as giving long-term direction to the firm. The CEO is ultimately responsible for the success of the business and therefore of its strategy. Additionally, CEOs are typically strong-willed, company-oriented individuals with a high sense of self-esteem. Their personalities often prevent them from delegating substantive authority to others in formulation or approval of strategic decisions.

However, when the dominance of the CEO approaches autocracy, the effectiveness of the firm's strategic planning and management processes are likely to be greatly diminished. The advantages of a team-oriented, participative strategic system are obviously related inversely to the CEO's propensity to make major strategic decisions single-handedly. For these reasons, establishment of a strategic management system carries with it an implicit promise by the CEO to provide managers at all levels with the opportunity to play a role in determining the strategic posture of the firm. The degree to which the CEO fulfills this promise is often parallel to the degree of success enjoyed through the use of the strategic management process.

The Interactive and Iterative Flow of the Strategic Process

The strategic management process is sometimes misperceived as involving a unidirectional flow of objectives, strategies, and decision parameters from corporate- to business- to functional-level managers. In fact, the process is highly interactive, that is, designed to stimulate input from creative, skilled, and knowledgeable people throughout the firm. While the strategic process is certainly overseen by top managers—because they have a broad perspective on the company and its environment—managers at all levels have multiple opportunities to participate in various phases of the total process.

Figure 1–6 provides an example of the basic, typical, interactive flow. As indicated by the solid line, strategic management activities tend to follow a formalized pattern of top-down/bottom-up interactions involving planners at all three levels.

Figure 1–6
Strategic planning process cycle

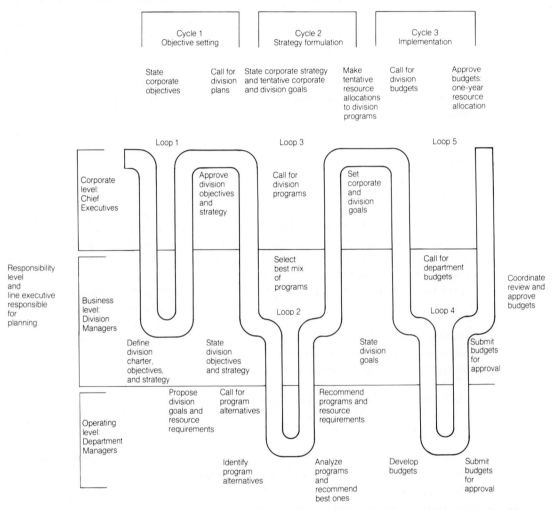

Source: Adapted from Richard F. Vancil and Peter Lorange, "Strategic Planning in Diversified Companies," by permission of the *Harvard Business Review*, January–February 1975.

As indicated by the five loops in Figure 1–6, the strategic management process is also iterative. This means strategic decisions are usually reached only after trial and error. Management expert Peter Lorange illustrates the five iterative loops as follows:

Loop 1: When the CEO receives inputs indicating where the businesses may be going, he or she may have to reconcile the emerging portfolio pictures with initial tentative objectives. As a result, the CEO may ask one or more of the businesses to revise their inputs, and may change the original tentative objectives as well. One or more iterations may be necessary before the loop is closed.

Loop 2: In formulating strategy, the business manager may frequently go back to the functional departments and request revisions so that individual programs fit into a more coherent package from the business strategy viewpoint.

Loop 3: When the CEO receives the portfolio of business strategies, he or she may have to recycle one or more of these for revisions to achieve the desired portfolio strategy.

Loop 4: During implementation, a business manager may have to recycle functional proposals so that the overall implementation plan has the desired strategic properties (i.e., becomes a near-term reflection of the longer-term strategy).

Loop 5: Similarly, the CEO might want revisions in one or more of the business implementation plans so that a final overall fit is achieved.[3]

The central point of this discussion is that the team concept is a critical and practiced feature in strategic processes. Managers at various levels have different responsibilities for various parts of the process, but they interact and are interdependent in achieving the final outcome.

Value of Strategic Management

Financial Benefits

The principal appeal of any managerial approach is the expectation that it will lead to increased profit for the firm. This is especially true of a strategic management system with a major impact on both the formulation and implementation of plans.

A series of studies of various business organizations actually measured the impact of strategic management processes on the bottom line. One of the first major studies was conducted by Ansoff, Avner, Brandenburg, Portner, and Radosevich in 1970.[4] In a study of 93 U.S. manufacturing firms, the authors found that formal planners who took a strategic management approach outperformed nonplanners in terms of financial criteria that measured sales, assets, sales price, earnings per share, and earnings growth. The planners were also more accurate in predicting the outcome of major strategic actions.

---

[3] P. Lorange, *Corporate Planning: An Executive Viewpoint* (Englewood Cliffs, N.J.: Prentice-Hall, 1980), p. 62.

[4] H. I. Ansoff, J. Avner, R. Brandenburg, F. E. Portner, and R. Radosevich, "Does Planning Pay? The Effect of Planning on Success of Acquisitions in American Firms," *Long-Range Planning* 3 (1970), pp. 2–7.

A second pioneering research effort was published in 1970 by Thune and House, who studied 36 firms in six different industries.[5] They found that formal planners in the petroleum, food, drug, steel, chemical, and machinery industries significantly outperformed nonplanners in the same fields. Additionally, planners improved their own performance significantly after the formal process had been adopted as compared to their financial performance during the nonplanning years.

Herold later (1972) reported a replication of part of the Thune and House research dealing with drug and chemical companies.[6] His findings supported the earlier study and, in fact, suggested that the disparity between the financial performance of planning and nonplanning firms was increasing over time.

In 1974 Fulmer and Rue published a study of the strategic management practices of 386 companies over a three-year period. The authors found that durable goods manufacturing firms with strategic management were more successful than those without.[7] Their findings did not hold for nondurable and service companies—probably, the authors suspected, because strategic planning among these firms was a recent phenomenon and its effects were not fully realized.

In 1974, Schoeffler, Buzzell, and Heany reported a study designed to measure the profit impact of market studies (PIMS).[8] This PIMS project involved the effects of strategic planning on a firm's return on investment (ROI). The researchers concluded that ROI was most significantly affected by market share, investment intensity, and corporate diversity. The overall PIMS model, which incorporated 37 performance variables, disclosed that up to 80 percent of the improvement possible in a firm's profitability is achieved through changes in the company's strategic direction.

An additional study of widespread impact was reported by Karger and Malik in 1975.[9] Their research—involving 90 U.S. companies in five industries—found that strategic long-range planners significantly outperformed nonformal planners in terms of generally accepted financial measures.

Finally, while most studies have examined strategic management in large firms, a 1982 report found that strategic planning had a favorable impact on performance in small businesses. After studying 101 small retail, service, and manufacturing firms over a three-year period, Robinson found a significant

---

[5] S. S. Thune and R. J. House, "Where Long-Range Planning Pays Off," *Business Horizons*, August 1970, pp. 81–87.

[6] D. M. Herold, "Long-Range Planning and Organizational Performance: A Cross-Validation Study," *Academy of Management Journal*, March 1972, pp. 91–102.

[7] R. M. Fulmer and L. W. Rue, "The Practice and Profitability of Long-Range Planning," *Managerial Planning* 22 (1974), pp. 1–7.

[8] S. Schoeffler, R. D. Buzzell, and D. F. Heany, "Impact of Strategic Planning on Profit Performance," *Harvard Business Review*, March–April 1974, pp. 137–45.

[9] D. W. Karger and Z. A. Malik, "Long-Range Planning and Organizational Performance," *Long-Range Planning*, December 1975, pp. 60–64.

improvement in sales, profitability, and productivity among those businesses engaging in strategic planning when compared to firms without systematic planning activities.[10]

The overall pattern of results reported in these seven studies clearly indicates the value of strategic management as gauged by a variety of financial measures.[11] Based on the evidence now available, organizations that adopt a strategic management approach do so with the strong and reasonable expectation that the new system will lead to improved financial performance.

Benefits of Strategic Management[12]

The strategic management approach emphasizes interaction by managers at all levels of the organizational hierarchy in planning and implementation. As a result, strategic management has certain behavioral consequences that are also characteristic of participative decision making. Therefore, an accurate assessment of the impact of strategy formulation on organizational performance also requires a set of nonfinancial evaluation criteria—measures of behavioral-based effects. In fact, it can be argued that the manager trained to promote the positive aspects of these behavioral consequences is also well positioned to meet the financial expectations of the firm. However, regardless of the eventual profitability of particular strategic plans, several behavioral effects can be expected to improve the welfare of the firm:

1. Strategy formulation activities should enhance the problem prevention capabilities of the firm. As a consequence of encouraging and rewarding subordinate attention to planning considerations, managers are aided in their monitoring and forecasting responsibilities by workers who are alerted to needs of strategic planning.

2. Group-based strategic decisions are most likely to reflect the best available alternatives. Better decisions are probable outcomes of the process for two reasons: first, generating alternative strategies is facilitated by group interaction; second, screening of options is improved because group members offer forecasts based on their specialized perspectives.

3. Employee motivation should improve as employees better appreciate the productivity–reward relationships inherent in every strategic plan. When employees or their representatives participate in the strategy formulation process,

---

[10] R. B. Robinson, Jr., "The Importance of 'Outsiders' in Small Firm Strategic Planning," *Academy of Management Journal,* March 1982, pp. 80–93.

[11] A few additional studies not discussed in the chapter reported mixed results. For a review of both sides of the issue, refer to J. A. Pearce II, E. B. Freeman, and R. B. Robinson, Jr., "The Tenuous Link between Formal Strategic Planning and Financial Performance," *Academy of Management Review,* in press.

[12] This section was adapted in part from J. A. Pearce II and W. A. Randolph, "Improving Strategy Formulation Pedagogies by Recognizing Behavioral Aspects," *Exchange,* December 1980, pp. 7–10, with permission of the authors.

a better understanding of the priorities and operations of the organization's reward system is achieved, thus adding incentives for goal-directed behavior.

4. Gaps and overlaps in activities among diverse individuals and groups should be reduced as participation in strategy formulation leads to a clarification of role differentiations. The group meeting format, which is characteristic of several stages of a strategy formulation process, promotes an understanding of the delineations of individual and subgroup responsibilities.

5. Resistance to change should be reduced. The required participation helps eliminate the uncertainty associated with change, which is at the root of most resistance. While participants may be no more pleased with their own choices then they would be with authoritarian decisions, their acceptance of new plans is more likely if employees are aware of the parameters that limit the available options.

Risks of Strategic Management

While involvement in strategy formulation generates behavior-based benefits for participants and for the firm, managers must be trained to guard against three types of unintended negative consequences. First, while it is readily recognized that the strategic management process is costly in terms of hours invested by participants, the negative effects of managers spending time away from work is considered less often. Managers must be trained to schedule their duties to provide the necessary time for strategic activities while minimizing any negative impact on operational responsibilities.

Second, if the formulators of strategy are not intimately involved in implementation, individual responsibility for input to the decision process and subsequent conclusions can be shirked. Thus, strategic managers must be trained to limit their promises to performance that can be delivered by the decision makers and their subordinates.

Third, strategic managers must be trained to anticipate, minimize, or constructively respond when participating subordinates become disappointed or frustrated over unattained expectations. Frequently, subordinates perceive an implicit guarantee that their involvement in even minor phases of total strategy formulation will result in both acceptance of their preferred plan and an increase in clearly associated rewards. Alternatively, they may erroneously conclude that a strategic manager's solicitation of their input on selected issues will extend to other areas of decision making. Sensitizing managers to these issues and preparing them with effective means of negating or minimizing such negative consequences will greatly enhance the overall potential of any strategic plan.

Executives' Views of Strategic Management

How do managers and corporate executives view the contribution of strategic management to the success of their firms? To answer this question a survey was conducted that included over 200 executives from the Fortune 500, Fortune

Strategy in Action 1–1
Executives' General Opinions and Attitudes

Item	Percent of respondents indicating		
	Agreement	Neutral	Disagreement
1. Reducing emphasis on strategic planning will be detrimental to our long-term performance.	88.7	4.9	6.4
2. Our plans today reflect implementation concerns.	73.6	16.9	9.5
3. We have improved the sophistication of our strategic planning systems.	70.6	18.6	10.8
4. Our previous approaches to strategic planning are not appropriate today.	64.2	16.2	19.6
5. Today's systems emphasize creativity among managers more than our previous systems do.	62.6	20.2	17.2
6. Our strategic planning systems today are more consistent with our organization's culture.	55.6	30.7	13.7
7. We are more concerned about the evaluation of our strategic planning systems today.	54.0	29.7	16.3
8. There is more participation from lower-level managers in our strategic planning.	56.6	18.0	25.4
9. Our tendency to rely on outside consultants for strategic planning has been on the decrease.	50.8	23.0	26.2
10. Our systems emphasize control more than before.	41.3	33.0	25.7
11. Planning in our company or unit is generally viewed as a luxury today.	15.0	13.0	72.0

Source: Adapted from V. Ramanujam, J. C. Camillus, and N. Venkatraman, "Trends in Strategic Planning," in *Strategic Planning and Management Handbook,* ed. W. R. King and D. I. Cleland (New York: Van Nostrand Reinhold, 1987), p. 619.

500 Service, and INC 500 companies.[13] Their responses are summarized in Strategy in Action 1–1.

Overall, the responses paint a very supportive picture of corporate America's view of strategic management. The process is generally seen as instrumental

[13] V. Ramanujam, J. C. Camillus, and N. Venkatraman, "Trends in Strategic Planning," in *Strategic Planning and Management Handbook,* ed. W. R. King and D. I. Cleland (New York: Van Nostrand Reinhold, 1987).

to high performance, evolutionary and perhaps revolutionary in its ever-increasing sophistication, increasingly pervasive throughout the firm, action oriented, and cost effective.

In the collective view of the responding executives, strategic management clearly is critical to their individual and organizational success.

Summary

Strategic management was defined as the set of decisions and actions resulting in the formulation and implementation of strategies designed to achieve the objectives of an organization. It was shown to involve long-term, future-oriented, complex decision making necessitating top-management action because of the resources required to formulate an environmentally opportunistic plan.

Strategic management was presented as a three-tiered process involving corporate-, business-, and functional-level planners, and support personnel. At each progressively lower level, strategic activities were shown to be more specific, narrow, short term, and action oriented with lower risks but fewer opportunities for dramatic impact.

The value of strategic management was demonstrated in a review of seven large-scale business studies. Using a variety of financial performance measures, each of these studies was able to provide convincing evidence of the profitability of strategy formulation and implementation. In addition, the chapter identified five major behavioral benefits for the team-oriented, strategic-management-directed firm. Despite some noteworthy behavioral costs, the net behavioral gains justify the approach, almost irrespective of the hope of improved financial performance.

Questions for Discussion

1. Find a recent copy of *Business Week* and read the "Corporate Strategies" section. Was the main decision discussed strategic? At what level in the organization was the key decision made?

2. In what ways do you think the subject matter in this strategic management/business policy course will differ from previous courses you have had?

3. Why do you believe the case method is selected as the best approach for learning the skills needed in strategy formulation and implementation?

4. After graduation you are not likely to move directly into a top-level management position. In fact, most members of your class may never reach that level. Why then is it important for all business majors to study the field of strategic management?

5. Do you expect that outstanding performance in this course will require a great deal of memorization? Why or why not?

6. You have undoubtedly read about individuals who seemingly single-handedly have given direction to their corporations. Is it likely that a participative strategic management approach might stifle or suppress the contributions of such individuals?

Bibliography

Fulmer, R. M., and L. W. Rue. "The Practice and Profitability of Long-Range Planning." *Managerial Planning* 22 (1974), pp. 1–7.

Herold, D. M. "Long-Range Planning and Organizational Performance: A Cross-Validation Study." *Academy of Management Journal,* March 1972, pp. 91–102.

Hofer, C. W., and D. Schendel. *Strategy Formulation: Analytical Concepts.* St. Paul, Minn.: West Publishing, 1978.

Karger, D. W., and Z. A. Malik. "Long-Range Planning and Organizational Performance." *Long-Range Planning,* December 1975, pp. 60–64.

Kudla, R. J. "Elements of Effective Corporate Planning." *Long-Range Planning,* August 1976, pp. 82–93.

Lorange, P. *Corporate Planning: An Executive Viewpoint.* Englewood Cliffs, N.J.: Prentice-Hall, 1980.

Mintzberg, H. "Strategy Making in Three Modes." *California Management Review* 16, no. 2 (1973), pp. 44–53.

Pearce, J. A., II; E. B. Freeman; and R. B. Robinson, Jr. "The Tenuous Link between Formal Strategic Planning and Financial Performance." *Academy of Management Review,* in press.

Pearce, J. A., II, and W. A. Randolph. "Improving Strategy Formulation Pedagogies by Recognizing Behavioral Aspects." *Exchange,* December 1980, pp. 7–10.

Robinson, R. B., Jr. "The Importance of 'Outsiders' in Small Firm Strategic Planning." *Academy of Management Journal,* March 1982, pp. 80–93.

Schoeffler, S.; R. D. Buzzell; and D. F. Heany. "Impact of Strategic Planning on Profit Performance." *Harvard Business Review,* March–April 1974, pp. 137–45.

Steiner, G. A. "The Rise of the Corporate Planner." *Harvard Business Review,* September–October 1970, pp. 133–39.

————. *Strategic Planning.* New York: Free Press, 1979.

Thune, S. S., and R. J. House. "Where Long-Range Planning Pays Off." *Business Horizons,* August 1970, pp. 81–87.

Vancil, R. F. ". . . So You're Going to Have a Planning Department!" *Harvard Business Review,* May–June 1967, pp. 88–96.

The Cohesion Case

A Unique Learning Aid to Understanding the Strategic Management Process

This section inaugurates a unique feature of this book, the *Cohesion Case* and 13 *Cohesion Case Illustrations*. The purpose of this unique feature is to help you understand the process and the concepts associated with strategic management, which are discussed throughout the 13 chapters in this book. As the word *cohesion* suggests, the objective of this learning aid is to "tie related parts together." Specifically, the objective is to tie together the strategic management concepts discussed in each chapter with an illustration of their practical application in an actual business firm.

To ensure continuity across the 13 chapters, each of the 13 Cohesion Case Illustrations will focus on the same company—Holiday Inns, Inc. This provides you with the added advantage of illustrating each part of the strategic management process within the same firm, thus offering an integrated, consistent picture of the formulation and implementation of a company's strategy. Over 200,000 people have used this Cohesion Case in the last six years as a learning aid in their study of strategic management. The overwhelming sentiment is that it provides a useful, easy-to-understand way of becoming familiar with strategic management.

Holiday Inns, Inc., is the world's leading hospitality company, with interests in hotels/motels, casino gaming, restaurants, and transportation. It was selected as the Cohesion Case for several reasons:

1. Holiday Inns, Inc., is a highly visible, well-known company.
2. Holiday Inns, Inc., is a multibusiness company. Only 54 percent of its revenues come from its lodging chain, with the remainder coming from gaming, restaurants, and transportation. The fact that Holiday Inns, Inc., is a multibusiness company provides the opportunity to apply strategic management concepts at three key levels—corporate strategy, business strategy, and operations strategy.
3. While Holiday Inns, Inc., is a multibusiness company, it is still a relatively simple, comprehendable enterprise. As a result, using this firm facilitates maximum focus on the application of text material and avoids wasting energy on simply trying to understand what the business is about.

The remainder of this section provides the Cohesion Case describing Holiday Inns, Inc. This case is the basis for understanding the Cohesion Case Illustrations. This material should be read thoroughly to gain a familiarity with Holiday Inns. As the remaining chapters (and accompanying Cohesion Case Illustrations) are covered, refer to this case material, occasionally rereading it. Doing this will ensure an adequate foundation for understanding how the components of strategic management, discussed in each chapter, are being applied to Holiday Inns in the respective illustrations.

The first objective in dealing with this Cohesion Case is to become more familiar with the total operation of Holiday Inns, Inc., and to think about the relevance of strategic management to this firm. An illustration is provided at the conclusion of the case to aid in applying the Chapter 1 material to Holiday Inns.

Your instructor may choose to use this Cohesion Case feature as a regular part of your class discussion related to coverage of the chapter materials. An equally viable option used by many instructors is to leave coverage of the Cohesion Case and the 13 Cohesion Case Illustration sections up to you as an optional aid in understanding strategic management. Both approaches work well, and the material is written to accommodate either one.

One final point: The case covers Holiday Inns, Inc., through early 1982. This date was chosen because the early 1980s represented a key decision point in the strategic posture of the firm. Thus, the Cohesion Case Illustrations allow the reader to assume the role of assistant to the president and executive committee at Holiday Inns with the assignment of formulating and implementing a strategy for the 1980s. An update of key actions at Holiday Inns, Inc., is provided at a later point in this book.

The Cohesion Case: Holiday Inns, Inc.

The Businesses of Holiday Inns, Inc.

1   When we think about Holiday Inns, we generally are only considering hotels and motels. However, Holiday Inns, Inc., is a $1.2 billion-per-year diversified multinational corporation. In fact, only 54 percent of total corporate revenues results from hotel operations. The company was structured into four divisions:

1. Hotel group.
   a. Parent company.
   b. Licensees.
   c. International.
2. Transportation group.
   a. Trailways, Inc.
   b. Delta Steamship Lines, Inc.
3. Restaurant group.
   a. Perkins Cake and Steak.
4. Casino gaming.
   a. Atlantic City.
   b. Las Vegas.

2   As Holiday Inns moved into the decade of the 1970s, top management sought to broaden its hotel-intensive earnings base. Under the leadership of Kemmons Wilson, Holiday Inns' founder, the mission was redefined from being a food-and-lodging company to a travel and transportation-related company. This definition led to the four business groups.

3   A reexamination and possible restructuring of the company's operations was being considered as the company's executives devised a strategy for the 1990s. The thrust of the reexamination involved both the basic mission of the company and the missions and appropriateness of its business groups. Exhibit 1 provides some insight into operations at Holiday Inns, Inc., from a financial perspective through 1981. The next several sections briefly describe the operations of the four business groups that make up Holiday Inns, Inc.

Hotel Group

4   Hotels that are part of Holiday Inns, Inc., are segregated into two groups. The hotels in the first group are company owned, and those in the second group are franchisee owned and operated. The Holiday Inns system continued to reflect the company's

---

This 1988 revised edition of the Holiday Inns, Inc., case was prepared by Richard Robinson, University of South Carolina. © Richard Robinson, 1988.

Exhibit 1
Financial information on each business group ($ millions)

	1979	*1980*	*1981*
Revenues			
Hotel	$ 784	$ 849	$ 853
Gaming	1	201	388
Restaurant	30	93	96
Transportation	278	377	413
Products and other	19	13	13
	$1,112	$1,533	$1,765
Operating income			
Hotel	$ 137	$ 155	$ 171
Gaming	1	24	56
Restaurant	3	4	6
Transportation	17	48	46
Products and other	11	7	11
	$ 169	$ 238	$ 290
Identifiable assets			
Hotel	$ 651	$ 712	$ 749
Gaming	30	451	573
Restaurant	98	97	92
Transportation	234	268	254
Products and other	226	152	147
	$1,239	$1,680	$1,815
Capital expenditures			
Hotel	$ 111	$ 122	$ 127
Gaming	—	61	29
Restaurant	12	11	2
Transportation	2	6	6
Products and other	8	7	6
	$ 133	$ 207	$ 170
Depreciation and amortization			
Hotel	$ 45	$ 49	$ 53
Gaming	—	10	18
Restaurant	1	5	4
Transportation	8	8	9
Products and other	2	2	3
	$ 56	$ 74	$ 87

original emphasis on franchising. In 1981, 82 percent of the system was operated by franchisees—independent businesspeople or companies—while Holiday Inns, Inc., operated the remaining 18 percent. The Holiday Inns system has maintained an approximately 80/20 franchised-to-company-owned ratio since the chain was started. Exhibit 2 shows a breakdown of the Holiday Inns system by these two groups.

Exhibit 2
Hotel group

	1979	1980	1981	5-year compound growth rate[†] (percent)	10-year compound growth rate[‡] (percent)
Hotels at year-end					
Company owned or managed	246	240	229	(4.5)%	(2.3)%
Licensed*	1,495	1,515	1,522	1.3	3.5
Total system	1,741	1,755	1,751	0.4	2.5
Rooms at year-end					
Company owned or managed	55,821	56,141	55,285	(1.1)	.7
Licensed	240,430	247,437	252,828	2.8	5.4
Total system	296,251	303,578	308,113	2.1	4.4
Occupancy (company owned)	73.8%	71.5%	69.2%	—	—
Average rate per occupied room (company owned)	$32.65	$36.80	$40.79	13.0	9.5

* Licensed means franchised.
[†] Since 1976.
[‡] Since 1971.

5   Holiday Inns' commitment to the ownership and operation of properties provided a basis for innovation and leadership in the marketplace; for example, company-operated hotels provided an extensive research base for the development of marketing information, operating procedures, and marketing techniques. The company claimed that its 200-plus properties provide a solid, diverse base from which to build and improve operating expertise.

6   As shown in Exhibit 2, the number of company-owned hotels has steadily decreased. This reflects Holiday Inns' emphasis on removing older properties from its system. Commenting on this trend, Roy Winegardner, chairman of the board, made the following observation in a December 1980 interview:

> By 1983, 217,000 rooms or 60 percent of the Holiday Inns hotel system will be new or extensively renovated. A major emphasis for company-owned hotels will be to move into destination and multiuser properties, such as airports, suburban, midtown, and downtown locations, which are expected to account for over 95 percent of all company-owned or -operated rooms.

Franchises

7   The 1,522 inns not operated by the company are owned by independent businesspeople called franchisees. The company carefully screened all applicants for franchises and placed a great deal of emphasis on the character, ability, and financial responsibility of the applicant, in addition to the appropriateness of the proposed location. Franchise

agreements, which were for a 20-year period, established standards for service and the quality of accommodations. The company trained franchise management personnel at Holiday Inn University near Memphis, Tennessee; made inspections of franchise operations three times a year; and provided detailed operational manuals, training films, and instructional aids for franchise personnel. During the initial period of 20 years, most franchises were terminated in certain circumstances by the franchisee. In the event of a franchisee's violation of the agreement, the company terminated the franchise. The company's policy in determining whether or not to renew a particular franchise agreement (after the initial 20 years) was in part to evaluate the overall desirability of retaining the franchisee's inn within the system.

8   Since Holiday Inns started franchising in 1955, 20-year renewal activity started becoming a regular issue by the late 1970s. Franchise expiration and renewal activity from 1977 through 1983 follow:

	Franchises expiring	*Number renewed*
1977	5	2
1978	6	2
1979	7	2
1980	34	32
1981	31	?
1982	41	?
1983	34	?

9   Commenting on the financial attractiveness of franchising, Holiday Inns' CFO Charles Solomonson said:

> [One of our] unique characteristic[s] is franchising. Using our hotel group as an example, with franchise fees normally tied to room revenues, this provides a "top line" inflation hedge. Our franchise revenues, which include both initial fees and ongoing royalty payments, totaled $63.6 million in 1980 and have grown at a very steady 18.2 percent compound rate since 1975.
>
> The outlook for continued franchise revenue growth is quite positive. Industry supply and demand trends in our segment are favorable, and our franchisees have aggressive development plans as well. In addition, starting in the mid-1980s through the end of the century, an average of about 100 franchises a year—or 6 to 7 percent of the currently existing franchise system—will come up for renewal. At renewal time the company not only requires that the units be refurbished to current standards, which helps upgrade the system, but in virtually all cases the new franchise fee will be well in excess of the old rate.

10   The fees required by newly issued or renewed franchise agreements have been increased from time to time. A comparison of requirements for new or renewed domestic franchise agreements is provided at the top of the next page.

Early 1980s	Mid-1980s
An initial payment of $5,000.	No initial payment.
A one-time fee of $150 per room ($20,000 minimum).	One-time fee of $300 per room ($30,000 minimum).
A royalty of 4 percent of gross sales paid monthly.	Same 4 percent royalty as in 1978.
Conversion of 2 percent of gross room sales for marketing and reservation services monthly.	Same conversion charge but with a minimum of 14 cents per room per night.

Multinational Operations

11 Foreseeing possible obstacles in the intensive expansion of hotels/motels in the United States, Holiday Inns, Inc., had been rapidly expanding hotel operations abroad. The company's international development strategy had been to build strong national chains within the country where it now operated, as well as to gradually expand into new markets. Holiday Inns, Inc., argued that this strategy differs from that of its competitors who had but one location in each major city overseas. At the same time, the company had emphasized multiuser, politically stable locations for company-owned hotels. For example, 18 of the 24 hotels in which the company had an ownership interest in 1980 were located in major European cities.

12 At the beginning of the 1980s the Holiday Inns system had 195 international locations in 55 countries (of which 161 were franchised) with well over 40,000 rooms. By 1981, the number of non–U.S. locations had increased to 226. International operations' performance information is provided below.

	International operations[*]		
	1979	**1980**	**1981**
Consolidated assets	$123,580	$134,117	$137,641
Consolidated equity	79,896	98,951	108,488
Revenues	129,698	143,244	129,219
Operating income	26,014	28,049	21,949

[*] In thousands of dollars.

13 International projects under way in 1981 nearly equaled domestic activity. By the end of 1981, Holiday Inns maintained an equity interest in only 18 international properties, as it sought to decrease its international asset exposure.

Key Operating Systems

14 Holiday Inns operated the Holidex reservation system, which linked over 17,000 terminals throughout the world, thus representing the largest reservation system in the hotel industry. The importance of a reservation system such as the Holidex network cannot be overstated. Approximately 70 percent of all room-nights at Holiday Inns were sold through advance reservations. The company invested over $20 million in the second generation of this system, Holidex II. It was not only an information system, providing accounting and room inventory services, but it also provided a marketing data base as well as information services at the unit location.

15   In 1980, the new Holidex II network booked about 33 million room-nights, more than a third of all system reservations, and several times more than competing hotel chains. Nonetheless, the number of room-nights booked was down 50 percent from mid-1970 levels.

16   In concert with expanded Holidex II computer capabilities, Holiday Inns' operations management system (OMS) was developed to improve profits at the hotel level. Consisting of weekly department forecast, energy control, staff scheduling, inventory control, industrial engineering, and quality assurance, the system was fully implemented in company-owned or -operated properties by 1981. The program helped improve margins on a consistent basis, even where occupancies declined temporarily.

17   Another new internal program—Inn-level business planning—called for careful monitoring of trends in the local market environment, including product competitiveness, rates, opportunities, and competitive developments. This market-by-market monitoring enabled each hotel to stay abreast of, and react quickly to, changing competitive situations.

18   Another technological system on which Holiday Inns placed major future importance was its HI-NET Satellite Communications Network. The HI-NET system provides low-cost, in-room entertainment that is free to the guest, as well as the capability to hold nationwide teleconferences linking over 150 Holiday Inn facilities. As an example of the capabilities of the HI-NET system for teleconferencing, Holiday Inns, Inc., held a 1981 teleconference meeting for its employees that was aimed at increasing employee involvement and ultimately improving productivity in all of its businesses. They were able to communicate directly with approximately 15,000 employees of Holiday Inns, Harrah's, Perkins, and Delta at over 130 locations throughout the United States.

Competitive Posture

19   President and CEO Mike Rose offered the following summary of the hotel group's 1980s mission:

> The current mission of the hotel group is to [increase] Holiday Inns' leadership position in the broad midscale segments of the lodging industry. This mission will be achieved by producing superior consumer satisfaction through increased emphasis on the quality of our product and further capitalization on our significant distributional advantages over all other competitors. We also intend to [increase] our consumer recognition as the preferred brand in the lodging industry.

20   The Holiday Inns hotel system led the lodging industry in terms of number of rooms (see Exhibit 3) as well as customer preference (see Exhibit 4). The sustained leadership of the Holiday Inn brand in the broad midpriced market segment, which accounts for approximately two thirds of all travelers, was attributable to the hotel group's focus on customer satisfaction, according to corporate executives. These

---

Exhibit 3
Leading lodging firms by number of rooms, 1981 (in thousands)

Holiday Inns	308
Best Western	204
Sheraton	109
Ramada	98
Hilton	76

---

executives cite hotel operating systems, extensive training, and emphasis on value for price paid as key elements of this focus. Marketing efforts reinforce this focus. For example, in 1981, the company introduced a "No Excuses" room guarantee program for all U.S. hotels, which promised guests would be satisfied with their rooms or their room charge for the night's stay would be refunded. The Holiday Inns hotel system was the only hotel chain to offer guests such a guarantee.

21 During the period from 1979 to 1983, the hotel group planned to increase the number of company-owned rooms by 72,000 and sell 75,000 new franchise rooms. Riding the crest of steady occupancy growth, the hotel system offered nearly twice as many rooms as its nearest competitor and sold one out of every three hotel chain room-nights in 1979. In the face of mounting competition from both the budget and luxury segments of the lodging industry, Holiday Inns executives did not expect occupancy to drop due to price or service competition. As Exhibit 2 shows, occupancy of Holiday Inns properties declined for the third year in a row to 69.2 percent in 1981, down from 71.5 percent in 1980, and 73.8 percent in 1979. General economic weakness, a decline in family disposable income, and rapidly increasing airline fares were given as primary reasons. Single occupancy, an indicator of business travel, remained virtually unchanged in 1981. Business travel accounts for approximately 60 percent of Holiday Inn hotel room-nights sold. Multiple occupancy, which the company felt reflects personal travel, was down in each of these years. Room rates increased 10.8 percent in 1981, compared with 12.7 percent in 1980 and 17.4 percent in 1979 (see Exhibit 2).

22 Some industry forecasters predicted that demand for hotel accommodations would grow faster than supply into the 1990s, with the middle-priced segment projected to account for the majority of this growth. Other analysts warned of potential overbuilding as the industry became increasingly segmented. Commenting on growth potential in different industry segments, president and CEO Mike Rose offered the following:

Holiday Inn® hotels are ideally positioned in the moderate-price market segment to take advantage of the large projected demand growth within this segment.
In simple terms, the lodging industry could be described in three major segments: the high-price or image segment, the moderate-price segment, and the low-price segment.
While we think the percentage growth of demand will be highest in the high-price or image segment, in absolute terms the demand for rooms in the moderate-

Exhibit 4
Hotel brand preference (percent)

	1979	1980	1981	1988 (projected)
Holiday Inns	40%	36%	38%	34%
Best Western	6	7	7	9
Hilton	6	5	6	7
Ramada	6	7	6	7
Sheraton	5	5	5	5
Days Inn	1	1	4	6
Hyatt	2	2	4	6
Mariott	2	2	3	6
Howard Johnson	3	3	2	2
Quality Inn	—	1	2	3
Motel 6 (and others)	—	1	2	12

price segment will grow three times faster than in either the high-price or low-price segments.

We are further encouraged that new room supply is being focused more and more at the high end of the market, and we can foresee an oversupply of hotel rooms in that segment during this decade. On the other hand, we think that most of our chain competitors in the moderate segment do not have the inherent strength to keep pace with the demand growth in the moderate-price segment, and that we will continue to [increase] our share of that segment during the next decade.

Our domestic parent company development will be predominantly in major metropolitan areas in locations where we serve multiple demand sources. For example, we would like to be in locations that serve both business and leisure travelers, that also serve small group meetings, and that serve people arriving by automobile and air.

23   While Holiday Inns sees enormous growth potential in the middle-priced segment, rumors were beginning to surface in early 1980 that Holiday Inns was considering entry (through acquiring existing chains and/or starting new ones) into both the high-priced and low-priced industry segments. The growth rates and profit margins reported by chains like Days Inns and La Quinta were twice those of Holiday Inns.

Transportation Group

24   The transportation group of Holiday Inns, Inc., consisted of two major units: Trailways (headquartered in Dallas, Texas), the second-largest intercity bus system, and Delta Steamship Lines. The transportation group accounted for 35 percent of Holiday Inns, Inc.'s revenue, with bus operations producing 22 percent and steamship operations producing 13 percent (see Exhibits 5 and 6).

Exhibit 5
Transportation group: Bus operations

Bus operating statistics

	1976	1977	1978	1985 (projected)
Bus operating revenues (000)	$ 226,568	$ 240,262	$ 254,495	$ 275,000
Bus-miles (000)	207,678	198,125	190,770	180,000
Number of intercity buses	2,312	2,203	2,158	2,100
Passenger-miles (000)	2,727,453	2,856,095	2,694,454	2,500,000
Bus occupancy (load factor)	36.4%	40.4%	39.5%	38%

Bus operations—financial performance ($ millions)

	1976	1977	1978
Passenger	$ 136.8	$ 141.9	$ 145.7
Charter	38.9	41.2	44.7
Express	44.9	51.3	58.8
Other	14.1	10.0	18.9
Total revenue	$ 234.7	$ 244.4	$ 268.1
Operating income	$ 15.4	$ 16.4	$ 19.7
Operating margin	6.5%	6.7%	7.4%
Capital expenditures	$ 13.1	$ 10.0	$ 21.4
Assets	165.5	171.3	177.0

Note: More current statistics are not available.

Exhibit 6
Transportation group: Steamship operations

Steamship operating statistics

	1979	1980	1981	1985 (projected)	Compound growth rates (percent) 5-year	10-year
Voyages completed	162	177	174	190	27.8%	11.6%
Tons of cargo (000)	2,635.2	3,183.6	3,264.2	4,000	29.1	15.3

Steamship operations—financial performance ($ millions)

	1979	1980	1981
Revenue	$278.1	$377.1	$413.2
Operating income	16.6	47.8	46.2
Operating margin	9.8%	20.1%	15.9%
Capital expenditures	1.4	5.7	6.4
Assets	233.5	268.4	258.0

25   Trailways' fundamental business was to provide intercity passenger service, charter bus service, and express package services. In 1979, the Trailways route system covered 70,000 miles, serving 5,000 cities and towns in 43 states.

26   J. Kevin Murphy, formerly president of Purolator Services, Inc., was president of the bus operations. Placing primary emphasis on new marketing approaches, Murphy streamlined the company's name from Continental Trailways to Trailways and adopted a sunburst logo. A new marketing program—Anywhere Program—was initiated. It allowed the traveler to go anywhere in the United States—from one origin city to a destination city—with unlimited stopovers for a low, fixed price. Advertising expenditures were increased on programs stressing the cost-saving aspects of bus travel as opposed to other transportation forms.

27   Greyhound (number one in the bus service industry) and Trailways began to experience increased competition from the newly deregulated airline industry for low-cost intercity travel. Travelers could often fly and arrive at a destination from 3 to 10 times faster for a fare only 15 to 25 percent above the cost of a bus ticket. Between 1974 and 1979, the number of scheduled passengers increased by 25 percent for airlines, while it declined over 32 percent for buses.

28   In an effort to combat discount fares offered by airlines on selected routes, the Trailways division announced a new series of low fares between major cities in the northeastern section of the United States. In addition to competing with the airlines, Trailways was trying to counteract Greyhound's discount offerings on interstate routes. These fares represented a reduction of 30 to 50 percent from regular fares and applied primarily to interstate trips averaging 775 miles (one way) or more. An article in *Fortune* concluded that Greyhound and Trailways' price war was hurting only each other's profitability, without producing any additional share of the long-haul business, which was dominated by the airlines at fares only 50 percent above the discount bus fares.

29   Trailways became the first intercity bus company to offer a discount to senior citizens, a group that made up 25 percent of its market. The idea was initiated as a result of a recommendation from Trailways' senior citizen advisory council. Holiday Inns corporate executives anticipated that Trailways' senior citizen and charter passengers would provide a convenient customer base for its hotel properties.

30   Two growing segments of bus services were charter operations and package express. Trailways' charter operations served 26 million passengers a year, representing 9 percent of the total charter market. During the last half of the 1970s, charter sales grew at a compounded annual rate of almost 13 percent.

31   Package express, the fastest-growing segment of the Trailways division, accounted for 22 percent of total revenues from bus operations. Package pickup and delivery were offered in more than 110 major U.S. cities. The package express and overnight delivery industry was growing at over 60 percent in the early 1980s. Federal Express, the industry leader, virtually created this industry and doubled its volume every six months between 1977 and 1981. The industry became very competitive, and telecommunication technology threatened to become a future basis for the overnight message service.

32   The company lobbied vigorously in favor of municipal ownership of bus terminals. Airplane terminals and other public transportation terminals (e.g., trains) are primarily municipally owned. This would have transferred the cost of bus terminal maintenance from the company to the taxpayer—a key savings for Trailways. Unfortunately, this effort met with little success. The movement in the passenger transportation industry, as evidenced by deregulation of airlines, was toward decreased government involvement. Business analysts forecast continued hard times for the intercity bus industry, which was caught between rising energy, labor, and maintenance costs on the one hand and increasing price competition, particularly with airlines, on the other. Top management was beginning to seriously question the strategic fit of Trailways in Holiday Inns, Inc.'s mission and business portfolio.

33   Delta Steamship Lines was acquired by Holiday Inns, Inc., in the 1960s. Delta operated a fleet of 24 vessels between Gulf ports, Central America, South America, and Africa.

34   In June 1978, Delta reached an agreement with Prudential Lines, Inc., to acquire 13 vessels and add five new trade routes (from the East and West coasts of the United States) over the next two years at a cost in excess of $71.5 million (see Exhibit 7). Approximately half of the Prudential acquisition cost was financed using Delta's capital construction fund, and the balance came through Delta assuming low-interest, government-guaranteed mortgages on the vessels.

35   The Prudential acquisition returned Delta to passenger service, in which the line had had no involvement since 1968. All four combination passenger/cargo vessels acquired from Prudential have first-class accommodations for 100 passengers.

36   Of greater importance to Holiday Inns' steamship operation, the acquisition doubled the number of Delta's Latin and South American trade routes to Pacific U.S. ports.

37   In 1973, Delta introduced LASH (light aboard ship) cargo containers in its operations. The LASH containers (they are found in all of Delta's fleet) were filled before the arrival of a ship to improve the scheduling of the ship's time in port. For example, the average length of a typical South American voyage was reduced from 84 to 42 days by using LASH containers.

38   While Delta's revenue nearly doubled in 1978, operating income dropped significantly (see Exhibit 6). Captain J. W. Clark, president of the Delta operation, offered the following reasons:

> For one thing, it took longer to absorb the Prudential Lines, Inc., operations than originally thought. This was due to start-up costs connected with the acquisition, the transfer of vessels to new routes, higher-than-anticipated maintenance costs required to bring the new fleet up to Delta standards, and a delay in closing the transaction [that] reduced the revenue base over which expenses could be spread. Unsettled political and economic conditions also affected Delta's West Africa Trade.

39   Though faced with heavy foreign competition, Delta, the major U.S.-flag cargo carrier in its trade routes, anticipated increased market share through effective vessel scheduling, LASH technology, and beneficial government subsidies of U.S. marine transport operations.[1]

---

[1] Delta operated under differential subsidy agreements (expiring in 1995 and 1997) in which the U.S. Maritime Administration compensated Delta for portions of certain vessel operating expenses that are in excess of those incurred by its foreign competitors. The subsidy recorded in 1980, 1979, 1978, and 1977 amounted to $60,419,000; $52,429,000; $33,666,000; and $15,035,000, respectively.

Exhibit 7
Delta Steamship Line, Inc.'s trade routes

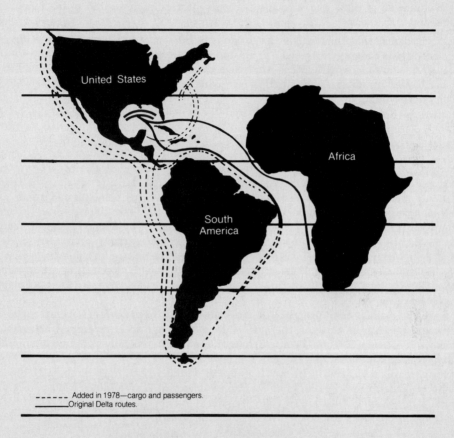

------ Added in 1978—cargo and passengers.
———— Original Delta routes.

40   By 1980, Delta Steamship Lines, Inc.'s operating income almost tripled to a record $47.8 million on a 35.6 percent revenue increase. This dramatic improvement was accompanied by the installation of a new management team. Fifty percent of the subsidiary's top 28 positions were filled by people new to the company. This revitalized management successfully instituted a number of marketing and operational programs, which contributed greatly to the 1980 improvement. Cargo tonnage increased by 15.4 percent through fleet deployment to trade routes that best utilized each vessel's capabilities. Better scheduling permitted a 6.8 percent improvement in completed voyages. This increased the frequency of port calls, a factor important to shippers and their customers. Fifty percent more containers for better cargo handling and inexpensive hardware modifications allowed Delta to provide more container equipment to customers while reducing its unit costs through this expanded LASH technology as well as through favorable lease arrangements.

41   While Delta's performance improved dramatically, top management was seriously questioning its fit in Holiday Inns, Inc.'s hospitality-oriented portfolio for the next decade. Some managers were arguing that Delta should be divested. Others agreed with chairman of the board Winegardner's perspective, summarized in the following comment:

> We recognize that Delta might not fit Holiday Inns' long-term objective of being a hospitality company, although . . . its improved performance provides significant cash flow to fund investment in our hospitality businesses. As a result, Delta has earned an important position in our plans to maintain leadership in the hospitality industry.

Restaurant Group

42   On April 18, 1979, Holiday Inns, Inc., acquired Perkins Cake and Steak, Inc., a privately held restaurant chain headquartered in Minneapolis. The decision to enter the free-standing restaurant business reflected significant research on demographic trends as well as a corporate desire to build a broader earnings base. The 20-to-45-year-old age group will grow to over 50 percent of the U.S. population by 1990. This group eats out frequently—an average of five meals per week. The number of women in the work force was projected to exceed 60 percent in 1990. The number of single households was also steadily increasing. Both trends were associated with more eating out. According to Holiday Inns' research, food away from home is increasingly viewed as a necessary convenience.

43   Based on Holiday Inns' prepurchase market research, two thirds of Perkins' customers were found to be between the ages of 18 and 49 and to have annual household incomes in excess of $25,000. Demographically, the Perkins customer profile was similar in many respects to that of a Holiday Inn hotel guest.

44   Perkins was positioned in the marketplace as a family restaurant. It offered a broad menu at moderate prices and table service in "pleasant surroundings." Most Perkins restaurants were open 24 hours a day. A typical Perkins restaurant built since 1977 seats 172 people in a 5,000-square-foot structure. About one third of the restaurants in the Perkins system in 1980 were less than four years old.

45   There were 270 franchised units and 71 company-owned units when Holiday Inns bought the chain in early 1979. By the end of 1979, the number of franchised units remained unchanged, while 23 new company-owned units were added. Exhibit 8 highlights Perkins' activity between 1979 and 1981. Commenting on future emphasis for Perkins' growth, one major Holiday Inns executive offered the following in late 1981:

> It is our intent [that] Perkins [grows] primarily through the franchise system, with corporate stores filling in those major markets where we have already established a strong presence. Obviously, Perkins can never become a large part of Holiday Inns, Inc., with such mammoth businesses as the hotel and casino

Exhibit 8
Perkins operating data ($ millions)

	1979	1980	1981
Revenues	$81.8	$93.2	$96.4
Operating profit	10.1	4.3	6.5
Food and labor cost as percent of sales	54.6%	55.6%	56.7%
Number of stores:			
Corporate units	94	106	101
Franchise units	270	269	242
Total units	364	375	343

businesses, but we do think it is a vehicle for percentage growth and high return on assets employed.

It is our intention that Perkins will continue to grow using only its own cash flow, so that it will not be competitive with the hotel or casino businesses for capital resources.

46   Perkins' initial performance since being acquired was disappointing. The average customer count at company-owned restaurants dropped annually since the acquisition. This trend and the change in average guest checks are shown below as a percent of change from the previous year:

Average company-owned restaurant	Percent change from previous year			
	1979	1980	1981	1982
Change in average customer count	(14.9)%	(13.3)%	1.4%	9.0%
Change in average guest check	6.8	5.4	3.8	0.4

47   In general, there was no clear nationwide leader among family restaurant chains. In 1980, Perkins' system sales represented 10 percent of total sales generated by the five largest family restaurant chains. Perkins was fifth in sales in the family restaurant category in which it competed.

48   Overall, the restaurant industry was becoming increasingly competitive. The family restaurant market segment represented about one fourth of total U.S. restaurant sales (see Exhibit 9). Holiday Inns' management expected this segment to have continued growth during the 1980s, with chains expanding at the expense of independent operators.

Exhibit 9
Family restaurant industry: 1980s

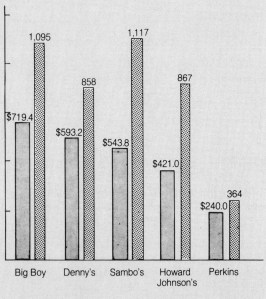

Diversified-menu family restaurant segment

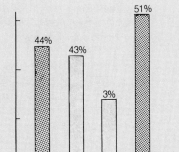

Overall customer satisfaction ratings*

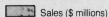 Sales ($ millions)   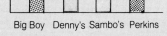 Number of stores

* Percentage giving an "excellent" or "very good" rating.
Source: *Institutions Magazine*.

49   Perkins competed in the large middle market and differentiated itself from the competition, according to company sources, by focusing on consistent high quality, as opposed to focusing on low price. Holiday Inns' consumer research showed that Perkins' customers preferred a quality dining-out experience in terms of food, service, ambience, and decor. Guest checks at company-owned Perkins restaurants averaged 10 percent to 25 percent higher than typical competitors' checks.

50   Mike Rose, president and CEO, had the following comment in late 1981: "While Perkins has frankly been a bit of a disappointment to us at this stage, we do strongly believe that we can rebuild head counts, continue to control costs, and expand on a regional basis to obtain sufficient market penetration."

51   In response to corporate concerns, Perkins management adopted a back-to-basics philosophy in its approach to operations, especially in service and food preparation, in 1981. The clarity and effectiveness of Perkins' long-term strategy appeared very much in question as top management started planning for the next decade.

Gaming Group

52   In 1979, the board of directors of Holiday Inns, Inc., expanded corporate policy to explore potential opportunities for hotel/casino operations in any area where such operations were legal.[2] While the company stressed that this decision implied no firm commitment toward a new development, it did indeed recognize the fact that the expansion in this area represented a natural extension of its current hotel operations. Previously, corporate policy restricted the expansion of hotel/casino operations to the state of Nevada and areas external to the United States.

53   Immediately following this announcement, the company approved a proposal to construct and manage a $75 million hotel/casino in Atlantic City, New Jersey.

54   Gaming was one industry that was examined when the company began researching future growth opportunities in the hospitality industry in 1975. Initial investigation revealed that most successful casino operations included hotels, a business in which the company was an acknowledged leader. Casinos also have sizable food and beverage operations, an area where the Holiday Inns system averaged more than $1 billion in annual revenues. Preliminary studies also indicated that the Holiday Inn hotel customer exhibited demographic characteristics similar to those of gaming participants (see the accompanying table). Of greater importance to Holiday Inns, customer surveys indicated that the overwhelming majority of Holiday Inn hotel guests had no objection to the company's becoming involved in the gaming business.

Demographic comparison: Holiday Inn versus Las Vegas

	Las Vegas casino visitor	Holiday Inn guest
Age 21–50	66%	66%
Family income: over $30,000	73	69
Occupation: professional, manager, white-collar	40	37

---

55   Holiday Inns' research showed that 80 percent of adults approve of gambling, and 60 percent participate in some form, ranging from casino visits to fund-raising raffles. Their conclusion: Gaming was truly a national pastime and was viewed by the public as a leisure activity. Of the 11 million people who visited Las Vegas, the average guest spent about $200 in nongaming expenditures and budgeted $300 for gaming.

56   Traditionally thought of as the exclusive domain of Nevada, the opening of Atlantic City to casino operations has given gaming a whole new outlook, and casino revenues

---

[2] This decision, however, was reached over considerable internal management dissention. Several key managers questioned the inappropriateness of gambling relative to the founding philosophy and mission of Holiday Inns. As evidence of the degree of top-management polarity, this decision triggered the resignation of the company president and chief executive officer, L. M. Clymer. Clymer said his resignation was incited by personal and religious opposition to this company decision.

were expected to more than double to between $5 billion and $7.5 billion nationwide by 1985.

57   Holiday Inns' extensive research led to the conclusion that it "needed outside expertise in gaming and big-name entertainment contracting. Careful control of the large volumes of cash handled requires well-run operations and specialized procedures. Thus, if we [Holiday Inns] were to succeed, we would need seasoned management in place."

58   In 1979, Holiday Inns formed a joint venture company with Harrah's (of Nevada) to develop, build, and operate all future gaming facilities for both companies. In September 1979, a merger agreement was approved by both firms. Under the merger, Harrah's will maintain its identity as a wholly owned subsidiary and will be the gaming operations arm of Holiday Inns, Inc.

59   Commenting on the merger with Harrah's, a Holiday Inns executive said: "We could not have picked a better company than Harrah's, a leader in the hotel/casino and entertainment industry. The control measures developed by Harrah's are now the standards for the industry. They provide seasoned expertise in gaming and big-name entertainment contracting. Their growth record has been superior."

60   U.S. casino gaming industry revenues reached $3 billion in 1980, compared to $2.4 billion in 1979, a 25 percent increase despite the impact of the 1980 recession and escalating transportation costs. In 1980, Atlantic City nearly doubled its 1979 casino revenues, winning more than $600 million. Forecasts made in 1976 (when casino gaming was first legalized in New Jersey) predicted the Atlantic City market would not reach $800 million in gaming revenues annually until 1988. Many industry experts expected Atlantic City to gross over $2 billion in gaming revenues in 1985. Part of their prediction was based on Atlantic City's location—one day's drive from one fourth of the U.S. population.

61   Some analysts were less sure about Atlantic City's potential. They pointed out that many Atlantic City gamblers only stayed one day and came back more often rather than staying for an extended period in a hotel facility. Also, Atlantic City had been slow in gaining convention traffic and gambling junkets, partially because of a much more heavily regulated situation than in Nevada.

62   Through its entry into casino gaming operations, Holiday Inns, Inc., kept pace with the spectacular industry growth. With the November 23, 1980, opening of Harrah's Marina hotel/casino in Atlantic City, Holiday Inns, Inc., became the largest U.S. gaming concern, operating alone or in partnership the most slot machines, 5,656; most table games, 439; and most casino space, 188,200 square feet. Holiday Inns, Inc., was the only company with properties in all four major U.S. gaming centers (see Exhibit 10). Casino gaming accounted for 13 percent of Holiday Inns' revenues in 1980 and 22 percent in 1981 (see Exhibit 10).

63   Commenting on Holiday Inns' rapid success in casino gaming, Holiday Inns President and CEO Mike Rose offered management's view of the gaming future:

Harrah's management depth and the strength of its operating programs and systems place Holiday Inns, Inc., in an excellent position to capitalize on the future growth of gaming. The company is already the largest in terms of facilities and has begun to successfully establish a nationally recognized brand name. These accomplishments, together with innovative marketing and planning, will

Exhibit 10
U.S. gaming industry: 1981–1985

A. Largest U.S.
gaming companies (1981)

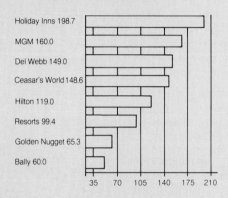

(Casino square feet in thousands—1981)

Holiday Inns 198.7

MGM 160.0

Del Webb 149.0

Ceasar's World 148.6

Hilton 119.0

Resorts 99.4

Golden Nugget 65.3

Bally 60.0

35 70 105 140 175 210

B. Gaming representation in major
U.S. markets

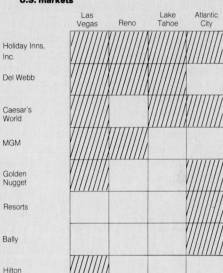

C. U.S. gaming revenues

($ billions)

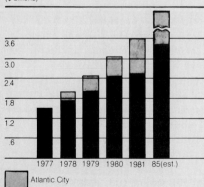

3.6
3.0
2.4
1.8
1.2
.6

1977 1978 1979 1980 1981 85(est.)

Atlantic City

Nevada

D. Holiday Inns, Inc.: Gaming group
market share by location (in percent of
market gaming revenues—1981)

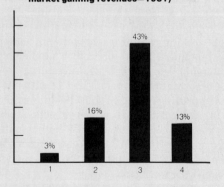

1. Las Vegas.
2. Reno.
3. Lake Tahoe.
4. Atlantic City.

Source: Nevada Gaming Control Board and New Jersey Casino Control Commission.

put the company in the same leadership position in gaming that it enjoys in the lodging industry.

64 Indeed, numerous traditional competitors share the same view. Hilton Hotels Corp. and Hyatt Corporation had already entered the field and were doing quite well. Gerald E. Hollier, chief operating officer at Ramada Inns, echoed Holiday Inns' optimism in a 1980 interview:

> As the gaming industry expands rapidly, smaller companies will have difficulty keeping up with market growth. Even established companies that are doing well in Nevada, such as Del Webb, Caesar's World, and Summa, don't have as good a chance as the big companies because they lack the base [from which] to expand. In the long run, it's the big companies like Holiday Inns, Ramada Inns, and Hilton which will do best, because they have the muscle.

65 Only two major lodging competitors, Best Western and Days Inn, were not pursuing casino gaming. Best Western President Robert Hazard saw gaming as "an infatuation that could burst like a bubble," while Days Inn executives considered gaming outside the concept and corporate philosophy underlying Days Inn.

Financial Perspective

66 Exhibit 11 provides a corporatewide summary of selected financial results at Holiday Inns, Inc., since 1976.

67 Cash flow from operations was $291.8 million in 1981. This provided a sizable source of internally generated funds Holiday Inns, Inc., could use to support future expansion. Capital expenditures corporatewide were $170.9 million and $207.1 million in 1981 and 1980, respectively. The company had available at year-end 1981 $225 million of prime-related, intermediate-term credit facilities and $43 million in unused, short-term credit facilities. Only $30 million of the intermediate-term credit was utilized at the end of 1981. Holiday Inns, Inc.'s customers were generally required to pay for the company's products and services at the time they were provided. Consequently, high working capital levels were not necessary. Furthermore, the size and nature of the company's assets offered a number of ways to finance expansion, including fee ownership, leasing, joint ventures, management contracts, and franchising.

68 Corporate management had traditionally been very concerned about maintaining and improving return on shareholders' equity. Shareholders' equity rose by $64.4 million or 9.1 percent in 1981, which reflects Holiday Inns, Inc.'s net income less its dividend payments *and* the effect of a 2-million-share repurchase program. Dividends in 1981 increased for the 18th consecutive year. Return on average shareholders' equity increased to 18.5 percent in 1981, up from 16.1 percent in 1980, and exceeding near-term corporate objectives.

69 The ratio of long-term debt to invested capital at the end of 1981 was 41.9 percent, up slightly from 1980's 41.3 percent, but still considerably higher than pre-1980 levels (see Exhibit 11). Corporate management considered this debt ratio conservative in view of the company's asset base. Holiday Inns, Inc., engaged an independent firm in

Exhibit 11
Selected financial results: Holiday Inns, Inc. (corporatewide)

	1979	1980	1981	5-year compound growth rate*	10-year compound growth rate†
Operating results ($ millions)					
Revenues	$1,112.6	$1,533.8	$1,765.1	12.8%	10.3%
Operating income	169.3	238.1	290.8	22.7	11.5
Income before income taxes	125.1	166.6	196.2	25.0	11.2
Pretax margin (percent)	11.2%	10.9%	11.1%	—	—
Tax rate (percent)	43.0%	35.0%	30.0%	—	—
Income	$ 71.3	$ 108.3	$ 137.4	28.5	13.0
Discontinued operations	(15.4)				—
Net income	$ 55.9	$ 108.3	$ 137.4	28.8%	13.7%
Common stock data					
Income per share	$1.76	$2.92	$3.66	23.6%	10.7%
Cost dividends declared per share	0.66	0.70	0.74	13.1	11.5
Book value per share	18.93	21.51	24.73	10.2	8.3
Price range of common	22⅞–15¼	33½–13¾	33¼–21⅛	—	—
Average number of common and outstanding (000)	31,704	39,278	39,449	5.2%	2.8%
Financial position ($ millions)					
Total assets	$1,227.3	$1,680.1	$1,815.4	13.6%	59.0%
Property and equipment (net)	737.1	1,147.7	1,323.3	14.3	10.4
Long-term debt	311.3	546.6	639.6	16.4	8.4
Shareholders' equity	624.5	708.0	772.4	10.6	8.6
Depreciation and amortization	56.3	74.6	87.3	9.2	n/a
Capital expenditures	133.4	207.1	170.9	19.5	—
Current ratio	1.4	0.9	0.8	—	—
Performance measures (percent)					
Return on sales	6.4%	7.1%	7.8%	—	—
Return on average invested capital	7.1	10.6	12.0	—	—
Return on average equity	9.5	16.1	18.5	—	—
Long-term debt to invested capital	30.1	41.3	41.9	—	—

* Base 1976.
† Base 1971.

1981 to appraise the appreciated value of the company's tangible assets and certain contract rights. The study indicated a market value of $1.86 billion, or nearly 2.5 times the $.77 billion reported shareholders' equity shown on its 1981 balance sheet. Corporate management believed this information provided a clearer definition of the true financial condition of Holiday Inns, Inc., showing the value of the company's contract income streams as well as the "real" benefits from the appreciation of its substantial real estate assets.

70   Holiday Inns, Inc., had two convertible subordinate debenture issues as a part of its long-term debt. The first, an 8 percent issue for which the company was making sinking fund payments to 1985, was convertible into common stock at $35 per share. The 1981 value of this issue was $5.85 million. The second issue, a 9⅝ percent debenture with sinking fund payments scheduled between 1991 and 2005, was convertible into common stock at $20 per share. This issue represented a $144.2 million long-term debt on Holiday Inns' 1981 balance sheet. The company was considering calling the 9⅝ percent debentures for redemption in 1982 to lower the debt-to-capital ratio (removing $144.2 from debt into capital would lower the ratio to 32.3 percent). The stock price hovered around $22 per share toward the end of 1981.

For the Future

71   Mike Rose, president and CEO, offered the following corporate philosophy to guide Holiday Inns in the 1980s:

> We are operating our businesses under a very simple and straightforward management philosophy. We have shared this philosophy with the entire rank and file of our company, and I would like to share it with you because it says a lot about our future success. Our philosophy is:
>
> We are *a forward-looking, innovative industry leader with clearly defined goals, producing superior products, services, and consistently high return for our shareholders.*
>
> We will *maintain integrity in both our internal and external relationships, fostering respect for the individual and open, two-way communications.*
>
> We will *promote a climate of enthusiasm, teamwork, and challenge, which attracts, motivates, and retains superior personnel and rewards superior performance.*

72   Charles Barnette, director of corporate public relations, succinctly summarized the perspective adopted by Holiday Inns, Inc., for the future. He stated, "We want to focus business activities on markets and market segments where we can excel, achieve competitive advantage, and be the cost-effective leader."

73   Some of the specifics that emerge from Barnette's statement are: (1) maintain a corporate debt ratio of 35 percent of invested capital; (2) increase corporate return on investment capital (ROIC) to over 13 percent; (3) grow at a rate of 15 percent or more per year; (4) achieve a dividend payment representing 35 percent of net income. While these corporatewide objectives offer a realistic challenge, the future contribution of different business groups could vary considerably.

74   To summarize their optimism about the future, Kemmons Wilson, founder and then retiring chairman of the board, placed all corporate objectives for the future in a concise framework. He stated:

> Now it's time to embark on a new era of growth and to continue the very favorable trends for our shareholders that we've seen in the past 10 years. The outlook on tourism in this country and worldwide has never been better. We are truly becoming a unified world where people are traveling farther, more frequently, and for more reasons.
>
> Twenty-seven years ago I had a dream. It has been fulfilled. But even in my wildest dreams I could not see the changes that were ahead. I never dreamed that so many people would travel between countries. Or that people would choose to spend a weekend in their own hometown, or that people would begin to eat more meals away from home than at home, or that forms of acceptable entertainment would change so dramatically.
>
> Today we have a better picture of the future, and at Holiday Inns, Inc., I am proud to say we're anticipating change. In fact, we welcome it. And we're determined to be out in front in whatever markets we are able to serve.

75   "Whatever markets we are able to serve" may have a double meaning for Holiday Inns as it moves toward the 1990s. Is it a challenge for further diversification of this travel-related company or a call for urgent reexamination of what its mission and business strategies should be? Is Holiday Inns' diversified group of businesses inspired by Mr. Wilson's desire for a broadened earnings base consistent with the perspective articulated above by Charles Barnette and Mike Rose? Can each separate business achieve the "cost-effective leadership" position Barnette talks about, or is such an accomplishment possible for only a few Holiday Inns, Inc., businesses? Are Holiday Inns' stockholders better served by diverse businesses or by a concentrated focus in the company's major leadership areas—lodging and gaming? Which focus represents the company's best chance to meet its ambitious, corporatewide goals [see paragraph 73]? These questions and more faced Holiday Inns executives as they met to shape a strategic plan for the 1990s.

Chapter 1 Cohesion Case Illustration

Strategic Management and Holiday Inns, Inc.

Chapter 1 provided a broad introduction to strategic management. What role does strategic management play (or could it play) at Holiday Inns? Based on the material in Chapter 1, this question can be answered by addressing four issues:

1. Is Holiday Inns facing a strategic decision?
2. What is Holiday Inns' strategy?
3. What value would strategic management offer Holiday Inns?
4. What strategic management structure is appropriate at Holiday Inns?

Is Holiday Inns facing a strategic decision? Yes! Lower-cost air travel (due to deregulation of the airline industry) led to fundamental changes in the travel practices of the American public. In the early 1980s, the lodging industry also had the largest oversupply of rooms since the 1930s. These are but a few key factors that significantly affect Holiday Inns and point out the need for sound strategic decisions.

Other issues foretell a need for strategic decisions. Budget motels are expanding. This threatens the hotel business in Holiday Inns' midpriced segment, which is Holiday Inns, Inc.'s key revenue generator. Holiday Inns is trying to diversify, but the percentage breakdown of revenues shows little change since 1974. Why? Is Holiday Inns' management not seriously pushing diversification? Is the necessary expertise lacking? The recent move into casino gaming represents a potentially major philosophical change for the company, as evidenced by the resignation of President L. M. Clymer. Is this to be a sideline operation or a serious future commitment? What ramifications, in light of Clymer's resignation, does this have for Holiday Inns' top-management structure and cohesion? With Holiday Inns still dependent on hotels/motels for 55 percent of its revenue, is there still room for growth, or is the domestic (and international) market becoming saturated? With the departure of Kemmons Wilson, has Holiday Inns completed the evolution from an entrepreneurially run company to a professionally managed one? Clearly, Holiday Inns faces a number of the strategic issues described in Chapter 1.

What is Holiday Inns' strategy? Holiday Inns appears to be pursuing steady growth through gradual, concentric diversification into hospitality- and transportation-related businesses. Its business portfolio is still dominated by the

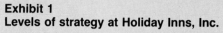

Exhibit 1
Levels of strategy at Holiday Inns, Inc.

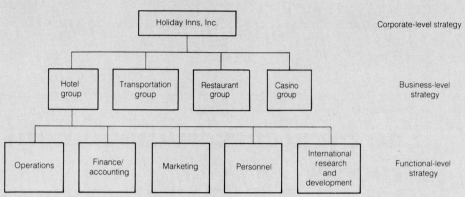

hotel division. But the transportation and other divisions now represent just under 50 percent of Holiday Inns' revenues. And the gaming industry is seen as a strong avenue for growth.

What value does strategic management offer Holiday Inns? With the numerous strategic issues facing Holiday Inns, systematic strategic management would appear essential for survival and prosperity. Holiday Inns' top management team is clearly interested in adopting a proactive rather than reactive strategic orientation. While its nonhotel divisions represent approximately 52 percent of Holiday Inns' revenue, this breakdown has not changed significantly since 1974, raising the question of whether its long-term strategy is just to supplement the hotel core or to actually reduce dependence on the traditional hotel side of its business.

Systematic strategic management clearly is needed to address this issue in looking to the 1990s. Holiday Inns' management also believes the need for strategic management is imperative, based on this comment in the 1981 annual report: "The strategic framework and management team of Holiday Inns, Inc., are in place, and we are well positioned for growth and accomplishment."

What strategic management structure is appropriate at Holiday Inns? Clearly, the multibusiness structure presented in Figure 1–1 is called for at Holiday Inns. It could be illustrated as shown in Exhibit 1.

2

The Strategic Management Process

Businesses vary in the processes they use to formulate and direct their strategic management activities. Sophisticated planning organizations, such as General Electric, Procter & Gamble, and IBM, have developed more detailed processes than similarly sized, less formal planners. Small businesses that rely on the strategy formulation skills and limited time of an entrepreneur typically exhibit very basic planning concerns when contrasted with larger firms in their industries. Understandably, firms with diverse operations due to their reliance on multiple products, markets, or technologies also tend to utilize more complex strategic management systems. However, despite differences in detail and degree of formalization, the basic components of the models used to analyze strategic management operations are very similar.[1]

Because of the similarity among general models of the strategic management process, it is possible to develop one eclectic model representative of the foremost thought in the area. Such a model was developed for this text and is

---

Portions of this chapter are from John A. Pearce II, "An Executive-Level Perspective on the Strategic Management Process," *California Management Review*, Spring 1982, pp. 39–48.

[1] Models by academics, typically developed from consulting experience and intended either for business or educational use, that reflect such similarity include those of Stevenson (1976), Rogers (1975), King and Cleland (1978), and numerous others. Models recommended for use by small businesses are almost identical to those recommended for larger firms, for example, those published by Gilmore (1973) and Steiner (1967). Finally, models that describe approaches for accomplishing strategic options contain elements similar to those included in general models; see, for example, Pryor (1964) on mergers and Steiner (1964) on diversification. The bibliography at the end of this chapter contains complete citations.

Figure 2–1
Strategic management model

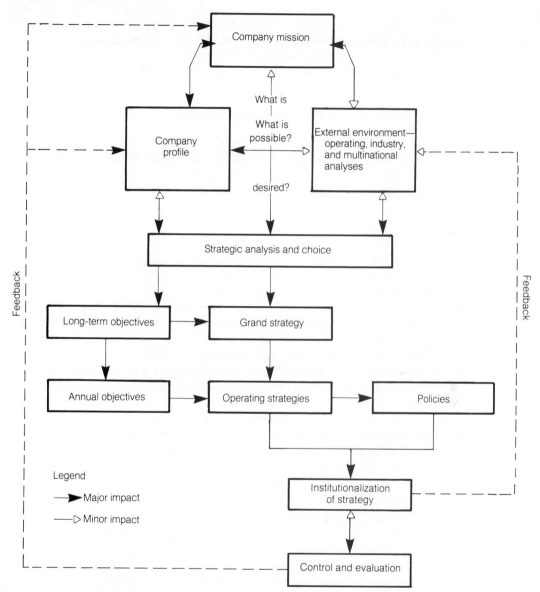

shown in Figure 2–1. This *strategic management model* serves three major functions. First, it provides a visual representation of the major components of the entire strategic management process. The model also shows how the components are related and how they are arranged in sequence throughout the process. Second, the model will serve as the outline for this text. After providing a general overview of the strategic management process in this chapter, the major components of the model will be used as the principal theme of subsequent chapters. Finally, the model is suggested for use in analyzing the case studies included in this text. In this context, the model enhances development of strategy formulation skills by guiding the analyst in a systematic and comprehensive study of each business situation.

Components of the Strategic Management Model

In this section the key components of the strategic management model will be defined and briefly described. Each will receive much greater attention in a later chapter. The intention here is simply to provide an introduction to the major concepts.

Company Mission

The mission of a business is the fundamental, unique purpose that sets it apart from other firms of its type and identifies the scope of its operations in product and market terms. The mission is a general, enduring statement of company intent. It embodies the business philosophy of strategic decision makers, implies the image the company seeks to project, reflects the firm's self-concept, and indicates the principal product or service areas and primary customer needs the company will attempt to satisfy. In short, the mission describes the product, market, and technological areas of emphasis for the business in a way that reflects the values and priorities of the strategic decision makers.

Because conceptualizing a company mission can be difficult, an excellent example is shown in Figure 2–2, the mission statement of Nicor, Inc., as abstracted from an annual report to its stockholders.

Company Profile

A firm's internal analysis determines its performance capabilities based on existing or accessible resources. From this analysis, a company profile is generated. At any designated point in time, the company profile depicts the quantity and quality of financial, human, and physical resources available to the firm. The profile also assesses the inherent strengths and weaknesses of the firm's management and organizational structure. Finally, it contrasts the historical successes of the firm and the traditional values and concerns of management with the firm's current capabilities in an attempt to identify the future capabilities of the business.

Figure 2–2
Mission statement of Nicor, Inc.

Preamble

We, the management of Nicor, Inc., here set forth our belief as to the purpose for which the company is established and the principles under which it should operate. We pledge our effort to the accomplishment of these purposes within these principles.

Basic purpose

The basic purpose of Nicor, Inc., is to perpetuate an investor-owned company engaging in various phases of the energy business, striving for balance among those phases so as to render needed satisfactory products and services and earn optimum, long-range profits.

What we do

The principal business of the company, through its utility subsidiary, is the provision of energy through a pipe system to meet the needs of ultimate consumers. To accomplish its basic purpose, and to ensure its strength, the company will engage in other energy-related activities, directly or through subsidiaries or in participation with other persons, corporations, firms, or entities.

All activities of the company shall be consistent with its responsibilities to investors, customers, employees, and the public and its concern for the optimum development and utilization of natural resources and for environmental needs.

Where we do it

The company's operations shall be primarily in the United States, but no self-imposed or regulatory geographical limitations are placed upon the acquisition, development, processing, transportation, or storage of energy resources, or upon other energy-related ventures in which the company may engage. The company will engage in such activities in any location where, after careful review, it has determined that such activity is in the best interest of its stockholders.

Utility service will be offered in the territory of the company's utility subsidiary to the best of its ability, in accordance with the requirements of regulatory agencies and pursuant to the subsidiary's purposes and principles.

External Environment

A firm's external environment consists of all the conditions and forces that affect its strategic options but are typically beyond the firm's control. The strategic management model shows the external environment as consisting of two interactive and interrelated segments: the operating environment and the remote environment.

The operating environment consists of the forces and conditions within a specific industry and a specific competitive operating situation, external to the firm, that influence the selection and attainment of alternative objective/ strategy combinations. Unlike changes in the remote environment, changes in the operating environment often result from strategic actions taken by the firm or its competitors, consumers, users, suppliers, and/or creditors. Thus, a consumer shift toward greater price consciousness, a loosening of local bank credit restrictions, a new entrant into the marketplace, the development of a substitute product, or the opening of a new wholesale outlet by a competitor are all likely to have direct and intentional positive or negative effects on a firm.

The remote environment refers to forces and conditions that originate beyond and usually irrespective of any single firm's immediate operating environment and provide the general economic, political, social, and technological framework within which competing organizations operate. For example, a company's strategic planners and managers may face spiraling inflation (economic), import restrictions on raw materials (political), demographic swings of population in the geographic areas they serve (social), or revolutionary technological innovations that make their production systems unexpectedly obsolete (technological).

Strategic Analysis and Choice

Simultaneous assessment of the external environment and company profile enables a firm to identify a range of possibly attractive interactive opportunities. These opportunities are *possible* avenues for investment. However, the full list must be screened through the criterion of the company mission before a set of possible and *desired* opportunities is generated. This process results in the selection of a *strategic choice*. It is meant to provide the combination of long-term objectives and grand strategy that will optimally position the firm in the external environment to achieve the company mission.

Consider the case when strategic managers feel that a firm is overly dependent on a single customer group, for example, a chain of record shops with principal customers 10 to 20 years old. The firm's interactive opportunities might include expanding the product line, heavily emphasizing related products, accepting the status quo, or selling out profitably to a competitor. While each of these options might be possible, a firm with a mission that stressed commitment to continued existence as a growth-oriented, autonomous organization might find that only the first two opportunities are desirable. In that case, these options would be evaluated on the basis of payoff and risk potential, compatibility with or capability for becoming the firm's competitive advantage, and other critical selection criteria.

A complicated subprocess is used to derive the strategic choice. Strategic analysis involves matching each of the possible and desirable interactive opportunities with reasonable long-term objectives and targets. In turn, these are matched with the most promising means—known as grand strategies—for achieving the desired results. Each of the sets of alternatives is then evaluated individually and comparatively to determine the single set or group of sets that is expected to best achieve the company mission. The chosen set (or sets) is known as the strategic choice.

Critical assessment of strategic alternatives initially involves developing criteria for comparing one set of alternatives with all others. As is the case in making any choice, a company's strategic selection involves evaluating alternatives that are rarely wholly acceptable or wholly unacceptable. The alternatives are therefore compared to determine which option will have the most favorable overall, long-run impact on a firm.

Among the criteria used in assessing strategic choice alternatives are strategic managers' attitudes toward risk, flexibility, stability, growth, profitability, and diversification. Other factors included in the decision-making process are volatility of the external environment, life-cycle stages of the evaluated products, and the company's current level of commitment to its organizational structure, access to needed resources, traditional competitive advantages, as well as the potential reaction of influential external or internal interest groups.

Long-Term Objectives

The results an organization seeks over a multiyear period are its *long-term objectives*.[2] Such objectives typically involve some or all of the following areas: profitability, return on investment, competitive position, technological leadership, productivity, employee relations, public responsibility, and employee development. To be of greatest value, each objective must be specific, measurable, achievable, and consistent with other objectives of the firm. Objectives are a statement of *what* is expected from pursuing a given set of business activities. Examples of common company objectives include the following: doubling of earnings per share within five years with increases in each intervening year; moving from third to second as a seller of commercial electrical fixtures in Oregon; and a decrease of 10 percent a year in undesirable employee turnover over the next five years.

Grand Strategy

The comprehensive, general plan of major actions through which a firm intends to achieve its long-term objectives in a dynamic environment is called the *grand strategy*. This *statement of means* indicates how the objectives or ends of business activity are to be achieved. Although every grand strategy is, in fact, a fairly unique package of long-term strategies, 12 basic approaches can be identified: concentration, market development, product development, innovation, horizontal integration, vertical integration, joint venture, concentric diversification, conglomerate diversification, retrenchment/turnaround, divestiture, and liquidation. Each of these grand strategies will be covered in detail in Chapter 9. Any of these grand, master, or business strategies are meant to guide the acquisition and allocation of resources over an extended period of time. Admittedly, no single grand strategy, or even several in combination, can describe in adequate detail the strategic actions a business will undertake over a long period. However, when a firm's strategic managers are committed to a fundamental approach for positioning the business in the competitive marketplace, it provides a galvanizing central focal point for subsequent decision making.

---

[2] Five years is the normal, but largely arbitrary, period of time identified as long term.

Some brief examples of grand strategies include Hewlett-Packard's technological innovation approach for capturing the high profit margins on new products, First Pennsylvania's retrenchment approach for avoiding bankruptcy despite $75 million in 1980 losses, and General Electric's concentric diversification approach allowing growth through acquisition of related business.

Annual Objectives

The results an organization seeks to achieve within a one-year period are *annual objectives*. Short-term or annual objectives involve areas similar to those entailed in long-term objectives. The differences between them stem principally from the greater specificity possible and necessary in short-term objectives. For example, a long-term objective of increasing companywide sales volume by 20 percent in five years might be translated into a 4 percent growth objective in year one. In addition, it is reasonable that the planning activities of all major functions or divisions of the firm should reflect this companywide, short-run objective. The research and development department might be expected to suggest one major addition to the product line each year, the finance department might set a complementary objective of obtaining the necessary $300,000 in funds for an immediate expansion of production facilities, and the marketing department might establish an objective of reducing turnover of sales representatives by 5 percent per year.

Functional Strategies

Within the general framework of the grand strategy, each distinctive business function or division needs a specific and integrative plan of action. Most strategic managers attempt to develop an operating strategy for each related set of annual objectives (for example, there will be a functional strategy to indicate how the marketing department's annual objectives will be achieved, one for the production department's objectives, and so on).

Operating strategies are detailed statements of the *means* that will be used to achieve objectives in the following year. The company's budgeting process is usually coordinated with the development of the operating strategies to ensure specificity, practicality, and accountability in the planning process.

Policies

Policies are directives designed to guide the thinking, decisions, and actions of managers and their subordinates in implementing the organization's strategy. Policies provide guidelines for establishing and controlling the ongoing operating processes of the firm consistent with the firm's strategic objectives. Policies are often referred to as *standard operating procedures* and serve to increase managerial effectiveness by standardizing many routine decisions and to limit the discretion of managers and subordinates in implementing operation strategies.

The following are examples of the nature and diversity of company policies:

A requirement that managers have purchase requests for items costing more than $500 cosigned by the controller.

The minimum equity position required for all new McDonald's franchises.

The standard formula used to calculate return on investment for the 43 strategic business units of General Electric.

A companywide decision that employees have their annual performance review on the anniversary of their hiring date.

Institutionalizing the Strategy

Annual objectives, functional strategies, and specific policies provide important means of communicating what must be done to implement the overall strategy. By translating long-term intentions into short-term guides to action, they make the strategy operational. But the strategy must also be *institutionalized*—must permeate the very day-to-day life of the company—if it is to be effectively implemented.

Three organizational elements provide the fundamental, long-term means for institutionalizing the firm's strategy: (1) structure, (2) leadership, and (3) culture. Successful implementation requires effective management and integration of these three elements to ensure the strategy "takes hold" in the daily life of the firm.

Control and Evaluation

An implemented strategy must be monitored to determine the extent to which objectives are achieved. The process of formulating a strategy is largely subjective despite often extensive efforts at objectivity. Thus, the first substantial reality test of a strategy comes only after implementation. Strategic managers must watch for early signs of marketplace response to their strategies. Managers must also provide monitoring and controlling methods to ensure their strategic plan is followed.

Although early review and evaluation of the strategic process concentrates on market-responsive modifications, the underlying and ultimate test of a strategy is ability to achieve its end—the annual objectives, long-term objectives, and mission. In the final analysis, a firm is only successful when its strategy achieves designated objectives.

Strategic Management as a Process

A *process* is an identifiable flow of information through interrelated stages of analysis directed toward the achievement of an aim. Thus, the strategic management model in Figure 2–1 depicts a process. In the strategic management process, the flow of information involves historical, current, and forecast data on the business, its operations, and environment, which are evaluated in light of the values and priorities of influential individuals and groups—often called *stakeholders*—who are vitally interested in the actions of the business. The interrelated stages of the process are the 12 components discussed in the last section. Finally, the aim of the process is the formulation and implementation of strategies that result in long-term achievement of the company's mission and near-term achievement of objectives.

Viewing strategic management as a process has several important implications. First, a change in any component will affect several or all other components. Notice that the majority of arrows in the model point two ways, suggesting that the flow of information or impact is usually reciprocal. For example, forces in the external environment influence the nature of the mission designed by a company's strategic managers and stakeholders. The existence of a given company with a given mission in turn legitimizes the environmental forces and implicitly heightens competition in the firm's realm of operation. A specific example is a power company persuaded, in part by governmental incentives, that its mission statement should include a commitment to the development of energy alternatives. The firm might then promise to extend its R&D efforts in the area of coal liquification. Obviously, in this example, the external environment has affected the firm's definition of its mission, and the existence of the revised mission signals a competitive condition in the environment.

A second implication of strategic management as a process is that strategy formulation and implementation are sequential. The process begins with development or reevaluation of the company mission. This step is associated with, but essentially followed by, development of a company profile and assessment of the external environment. Then follow, in order: strategic choice, definition of long-term objectives, design of grand strategy, definition of short-term objectives, design of operating strategies, institutionalization of the strategy, and review and evaluation. However, the apparent rigidity of the process must be qualified.

First, the strategic posture of a firm may have to be reevaluated in terms of any of the principal factors that determine or affect company performance. Entry by a major new competitor, death of a prominent board member, replacement of the chief executive officer, or a downturn in market responsiveness are among the thousands of changes that can prompt reassessment of a company's strategic plan. However, no matter where the need for a reassessment originates, the strategic management process begins with the mission statement.

Second, not every component of the strategic management process deserves equal attention each time a planning activity takes place. Firms in an extremely stable environment may find that an in-depth assessment is not required every five years.[3] Often companies are satisfied with their original mission

---

[3] Formal strategic planning is not necessarily done on a rigid five-year schedule, although this is most common. Some planners advocate planning on an irregular time basis to keep the activity from being overly routine.

statements even after decades of operation and thus need to spend only a minimal amount of time in addressing the subject. In addition, while formal strategic planning may be undertaken only every five years, objectives and strategies are usually updated each year, and rigorous reassessment of the initial stages of strategic planning is rarely undertaken at these points.

A third implication of strategic management as a process is the necessity of feedback from institutionalization, review, and evaluation to the early stages of the process. *Feedback* can be defined as postimplementation results collected as inputs for the enhancement of future decision making. Therefore, as indicated in Figure 2–1, strategic managers should attempt to assess the impact of implemented strategies on external environments. Thus, future planning can reflect any changes precipitated by strategic actions. Strategic managers should also carefully measure and analyze the impact of strategies on the need for possible modifications in the company mission.

A fourth and final implication of strategic management as a process is the need to view it as a dynamic system. *Dynamic* describes the constantly changing conditions that affect interrelated and interdependent strategic activities. Managers should recognize that components of the strategic process are constantly evolving, while formal planning artificially freezes the changing conditions and forces in a company's internal and external environments, much as an action photograph freezes the movement of a swimmer. In actuality, change is continuous, and thus the dynamic strategic planning process must be constantly monitored for significant changes in any components as a precaution against implementing an obsolete strategy.

Practical Limitations of the Model

It is important to understand the limitations of the strategic management model to gain an awareness of how the model can be properly used. This awareness will help ensure effective strategic management. Thus, in this section, three points will be stressed: the model is holistic, analytical, and nonpolitical.

Holistic

Users of the model believe strategic planning should be initiated by a company's top management. Thus, because of the broad perspective of these executives, the strategy-formulating process develops from general to specific. The business is first studied as a whole within the context of its competitive environment, then from the standpoint of individual functions or divisions, and eventually specific operational activities of the firm are involved in the process.

Some researchers have argued that in certain circumstances the holistic approach is inferior to a tactical approach in strategic planning.[4] With the tactical approach, strategic managers work "up" through the firm in their study of its potential. After obtaining an operational view of the firm's strengths and weaknesses, managers assess their firm's compatibility with its external environment.

The risk of using the holistic approach implicitly advocated in the strategic management model is that planning might be unrealistic because of the potential tendency to minimize the difficulties of implementation. The holistic approach can sometimes lead managers to gloss over details that may eventually be critical in making the firm's strategies operational.

On the other hand, the tactical approach poses far greater risks to strategic managers, first because planning may be inflexible. Managers risk emphasizing operational details and overstating the extent to which the firm is locked into the status quo. It is difficult to envision new interactive opportunities when initial planning activities stress narrow operational concerns. Second, the integration of planning activities is more difficult with the tactical approach. Because there is no overall planning framework, as is characteristic of the holistic method, the initial phases of planning are often disjointed, complicating development of a unified strategic plan. Third, and most damaging, the tactical approach leads to a concentration on the present rather than on the future, while strategic planning is specifically intended to be future oriented. With tactical planning, the emphasis is too often on improving current capabilities instead of on satisfying anticipated needs.

In the final analysis, the holistic approach of the strategic management model appears to be superior to tactical alternatives. However, users of the model should be alert to the shortcomings in planning that the strategic model fosters and should guard against them. Specifically, users of the model should continually monitor the data-gathering and implementation phases. In this context, it is important to remember that although middle- and lower-level managers seldom have a voice in the strategic choice process, they are a principal source of the operational data on which the ultimate decisions are largely based. Therefore, their advice and critiques should be actively sought and carefully considered in all phases of strategic management.

Analytic versus Prescriptive

A second major issue of concern in using the strategic management model is that it is analytical rather than prescriptive or procedural. The model generally describes the logical or analytical steps many businesses actually use in their strategic activities. However, it does not describe the procedures or routines necessary to carry out each step. Further, research has not proved that the model is *ideal*. In fact, while considerable evidence indicates that firms having

---

[4] For example, see George W. McKinney III, "An Experimental Study of Strategy Formulation Systems" (Ph.D. dissertation, Graduate School of Business, Stanford University, 1969).

formal strategic planning outperform nonplanners, somewhat different planning models were used by almost every business studied.[5] As a result, no model should be seen as providing a prescription for the way strategic planning should be done. Therefore, when the strategic management model is used it should be remembered that the model builders are recommending the general approach they believe will provide a sound basis for strategic planning, not a model they are certain will lead to the best results. It is important that users of the model be continually alert to the need for occasional additions or deletions. The model will be most valuable if it is treated as a dependable outline for construction of individualized planning systems.

Nonpolitical

The third major limitation of the model is that it is nonpolitical. A naive observer could therefore be misled into seeing strategic management as largely devoid of subjective assessments, biased interpretations, human error, self-serving voting by individual managers, intuitive decision making, favoritism, and other forms of political activity. In reality, most strategic management experts believe the opposite. Strategic management is a behavioral activity and, as such, is vulnerable to the same pitfalls as other "people" processes. It is truly a management process. People involved in all phases of strategy formulation and implementation must be skillfully organized, led, planned about, and controlled. For this reason, the behavioral implications of each phase of the strategic management process will be discussed extensively in this book. However, limitation of the strategic management model per se is that it presumes strategic planners are skilled managers who are sensitive to the people-related issues that continuously arise in every phase of the process.

The effects of political activity on the strategic management process are critical to its effective functioning and are a principal determinant of the plan's final composition. Effective strategic managers must be attentive to this aspect and attempt to skillfully manage the inevitable people-related concerns.

Evolutionary

The strategic management process undergoes continual assessment and subtle updating. While elements in the basic model rarely change, the relative emphasis each element receives varies with decision makers and the environments of their companies.

Strategy in Action 2–1 presents a recent update on the general trends in strategic management. In summarizing the responses of over 200 corporate

---

[5] See, for example, Ansoff et al. (1971), Burt (1978), Eastlock and McDonald (1970), Herold (1972), Karger and Malik (1975), Malik and Karger (1975), Rue and Fulmer (1972), Schoeffler et al. (1974), Thune and House (1970), and Wood and LaForge (1979), all listed in the bibliography in this chapter.

Strategy in Action 2–1
General Trends in Strategic Management

Item	Percent of respondents indicating		
	Increase	**No change**	**Decrease**
1. Overall emphasis on strategic planning systems.	81.2	7.7	11.1
2. Perceived usefulness of strategic planning.	82.0	10.2	7.8
3. Involvement of line managers in strategic planning activities.	75.2	21.4	3.4
4. Time spent by the chief executive in strategic planning.	78.7	17.8	3.5
5. Acceptance of the outputs of the strategic planning exercise by top management.	74.0	20.6	5.4
6. Perceived usefulness of annual planning.	53.9	38.7	7.4
7. Involvement of staff managers in the annual planning exercise.	52.9	39.3	7.8
8. Involvement of the board of directors in strategic planning.	51.4	47.0	1.6
9. Resources provided for strategic planning.	62.9	23.9	13.2
10. Consistency between strategic plans and budgets.	53.4	38.2	8.3
11. Use of annual plans in monthly performance review.	42.3	55.6	2.1
12. Overall satisfaction with the strategic planning system.	57.4	24.5	18.1
13. Number of planners (that is, those management personnel whose primary task is planning).	52.9	24.8	22.3
14. Attention to stakeholders other than stockholders.	32.8	63.0	4.2
15. Use of planning committees.	40.9	46.1	13.1
16. Attention to societal issues in planning.	33.2	59.8	7.0
17. The planning horizon (that is, the number of years considered in the strategic plan).	28.8	56.6	14.6
18. The distance between the CEO and the chief of planning.	13.3	45.1	41.5
19. Threats to the continuation of strategic planning.	12.0	47.0	41.0
20. Resistance to planning in general.	10.2	31.7	58.0

Source: Adapted from V. Ramanujam, J. C. Camillus, and N. Venkatraman, "Trends in Strategic Planning," in *Strategic Planning and Management Handbook,* ed. W. R. King and D. I. Cleland (New York: Van Nostrand Reinhold, 1987), p. 614.

executives, it shows an increasing emphasis on and appreciation for the value of strategic management activities throughout a company. It further provides evidence of increasing attention given by practicing managers to the needs for frequent and widespread involvement in the formulation and implementation phases of the strategic management process.

Finally, the report indicates that the potential negative consequences of instituting a vigorous strategic management process are overcome as managers and their firms gain knowledge, experience, skill, and understanding in how to design and manage their planning activities.

Summary

This chapter presented an overview of the strategic management process. The model provided will serve as the structure for understanding and integrating all of the major phases of strategy formulation and implementation. Although each of these phases is given extensive individual attention in subsequent chapters, it is important to acquire an early feeling for their nature.

The chapter stressed that the strategic management process centers around the belief that the mission of a firm can best be achieved through a systematic and comprehensive assessment of both a firm's resource capabilities and its external environment. Subsequent evaluation of the company's opportunities leads, in turn, to the choice of long-term objectives and grand strategies and, ultimately, to annual objectives and operating strategies, which must be implemented, monitored, and controlled.

The holistic approach of strategic management was preferable to a tactical one. However, three potential problems with the holistic method were discussed, as were the means by which their negative impact can be minimized.

Questions for Discussion

1. Think about the courses you have had in functional areas such as marketing, finance, production, personnel, and accounting. What is the importance of each of these areas to the strategic planning process?
2. Discuss with practicing business managers the strategic planning approaches used in their businesses. What are the similarities and differences between their models and the one in the text?
3. In what ways do you believe the strategic planning approach would differ in profit-oriented and not-for-profit organizations?
4. How do you explain the success of businesses that do not use a formal strategic planning process?
5. Think about your postgraduation job search as a strategic decision. How would the model be helpful to you in identifying and securing the most promising position?
6. Examine the collection of corporate annual reports in your school's library. Can you locate a report that includes a good mission statement? Does it exhibit the characteristics of a company mission described in this chapter?

Bibliography

Ansoff, H. Igor; R. Brandenberg; F. Portner; and R. Radosevich. *Acquisition Behavior of U.S. Manufacturing Firms, 1946–65.* Nashville, Tenn.: Vanderbilt University Press, 1971.

Burt, David. "Planning and Performance in Australian Retailing." *Long-Range Planning,* June 1978, pp. 62–66.

Eastlock, Joseph, Jr., and Philip McDonald. "CEO's Role in Corporate Growth." *Harvard Business Review,* May–June 1970, pp. 150–63.

Gilmore, Frank. "Formulating Strategy in Smaller Companies." *Harvard Business Review,* May–June 1971, pp. 75–85.

Glueck, William F. *Business Policy and Strategic Management.* 3rd ed. New York: McGraw-Hill, 1980.

Herold, David. "Long-Range Planning and Organizational Performance: A Cross Validation Study." *Academy of Management Review,* March 1972, pp. 91–102.

Karger, Delmar, and Zafar Malik. "Long-Range Planning and Organizational Performance." *Long-Range Planning,* December 1975, pp. 60–64.

King, William R., and David I. Cleland. *Strategic Planning and Policy.* New York: Van Nostrand Reinhold, 1978.

Malik, Zafar, and Delmar Karger. "Does Long-Range Planning Improve Company Performance?" *Management Review,* September 1975, pp. 27–31.

McKinney, George W., III. "An Experimental Study of Strategy Formulation Systems." Ph.D. dissertation, Graduate School of Business, Stanford University, 1969.

Pearce, John A., II. "An Executive-Level Perspective on the Strategic Management Process." *California Management Review,* Spring 1982, pp. 39–48.

Pryor, Millard H., Jr. "Anatomy of a Merger." *Michigan Business Review,* July 1964, pp. 28–34.

Rogers, David C. D. *Essentials of Business Policy.* New York: Harper & Row, 1975.

Rue, Leslie, and Robert Fulmer. "Is Long-Range Planning Profitable?" *Academy of Management Proceedings,* 1972.

Schoeffler, Sidney; Robert D. Buzzell; and Donald F. Heany. "Impact of Strategic Planning on Profit Performance." *Harvard Business Review,* March–April 1974, pp. 137–45.

Stagner, Ross. "Corporate Decision Making." *Journal of Applied Psychology,* February 1969, pp. 1–13.

Steiner, George A. "Why and How to Diversify." *California Management Review,* Summer 1964, pp. 11–18.

————. "Approaches to Long-Range Planning for Small Business." *California Management Review,* Fall 1967, pp. 3–16.

Stevenson, Howard H. "Defining Corporate Strengths and Weaknesses." *Sloan Management Review,* Spring 1976, pp. 51–68.

Thune, Stanley, and Robert House. "Where Long-Range Planning Pays Off." *Business Horizons,* August 1970, pp. 81–87.

Wood, D. Robley, Jr., and R. Lawrence LaForge. "The Impact of Comprehensive Planning on Financial Performance." *Academy of Management Journal* 22, no. 3 (1979), pp. 516–26.

Chapter 2 Cohesion Case Illustration

Strategic Management Framework for Holiday Inns, Inc.

Chapter 2 presented a framework for the strategic management process. How should it be applied at Holiday Inns, Inc.?

Holiday Inns, Inc., is a multibusiness firm. As such, it must have an overall corporate-level strategy for dealing with decisions involving its portfolio of businesses and for guiding strategic decisions made by key managers within each business group. In addition, *each* business group must formulate and implement a business-level strategy to guide resource deployment and pursuit of opportunity consistent with overall corporate objectives.

The purpose of Chapter 2 was to introduce a logical process for developing and implementing a strategy. Each component was briefly discussed in this chapter; the remaining 11 chapters will deal with each component in greater detail. Thus, the objective at this point is to broadly apply the strategic management paradigm to Holiday Inns, Inc.

As assistant to the president, how would one approach strategy development at Holiday Inns? (Illustrations of two possibilities are provided based on the material in Chapter 2.)

Looking to the 1990s, Holiday Inns must first address its corporate-level strategy. Exhibit 1 shows how to go about this. Strategy at this level is a critical issue for Holiday Inns. What should the company mission be? Is the company a travel business or a hospitality business? How does the current portfolio of business groups fit this overall mission? What do the trends in the competitive environment(s) suggest for each group and for the overall mission? What alternative portfolios are available? Which is best? What guidelines must be given to business groups to ensure that their strategy is consistent with and supportive of the corporate strategy chosen? These are some of the issues that must be addressed in designing the corporate-level side of strategic management for Holiday Inns.

Strategies generated for Holiday Inns must also deal with the formulation and implementation of business-level strategy for each business group. Exhibit 2 shows how one might apply the material in Chapter 2 to organize the strategic management of each business group. The mission of the hotel group may be quite different than that of the transportation group or the casino group. Each group has its own strengths and weaknesses. Their respective competitive environments present different opportunities and threats. Alternative strategies, generated through comparison of internal capacity and environmental

Exhibit 1
Corporate-level strategic management process

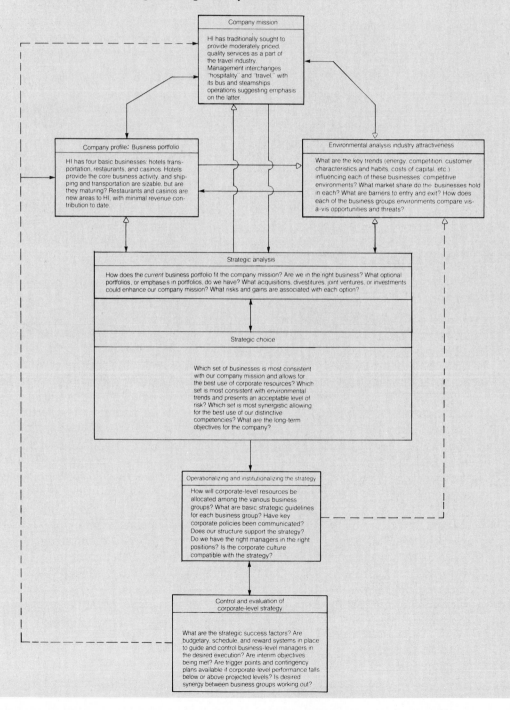

Exhibit 2
Business-level strategic management process

Company mission: HI's business groups

Hotel group: A strong hospitality focus providing moderately priced, quality food and lodging services to the traveling public.
Restaurant group: Build a national, freestanding restaurant business via franchise and company-owned Perkins restaurants.
Casino gaming: Build an HI presence in this hospitality-related market. Use Harrah's to build a leadership position in gaming markets by providing high-quality service at a high perceived value.

Company profile: internal analysis of each business group

What are distinct competencies within each of the businesses? What are the critical weaknesses? Identify both in light of the industry sectors and competitors the businesses face.

Environmental assessment for each business group

What are key external factors facing or influencing each business? Who are their competitors? What changes/trends are occurring that present major impacts on each business's future operations?

Strategic analysis

For each business group, what broad strategy options are suggested by comparing the respective environmental/internal analyses? How do they fit with the current mission? What are the risks and gains associated with each alternative? How compatible are alternatives for each business group, with corporate-level strategy and objectives?

Strategy choice

For each business group, which strategy offers the desired risk level and uses the business's key resource strengths to best exploit environmental opportunities? Is each chosen strategy within each business's realistic capacity to support? Are the choices compatible with corporate strategy and portfolio objectives?

Long-term objectives

For each business group, what are the objectives the strategy is meant to achieve (market shares, sales, ROI, social responsibility)? What is the time frame for accomplishment?

Grand strategy

For each business group, provide a clear, consistent, comprehensive statement of the business's long-term strategy. Ensure agreement with corporate management understanding and commitment from business's management.

Annual objectives

For each business group, what should these initial functional actions accomplish in the next year? What targets and timing are critical to insure the strategy is on track?

Functional strategies

For each business group, what critical actions must be taken in marketing, finance, operations, and personnel to initiate the grand strategy?

Policies

What specific policies need to be changed to be consistent with the new strategy? What new policies are essential to communicating and implementing the new strategy?

Institutionalizing the strategy

For each business group, is the current organization structure appropriate for the chosen strategy? Should it be adjusted or redesigned? Do we have the right managers in the critical assignments? Do the values and norms of managers and employees create a culture that "fits" the strategy?

Control and evaluation of strategy

For each business group, have key targets and milestones been set? Is an effective information system in place to provide timely feedback? Do we have trigger points and contingency plans for rapid adjustments in strategy or actions? For example, have we pre-planned responses if systemwide occupancy rates run 10 percent below or above current projections over the next six months? Are budgets prepared and communicated to enhance control? Have we scheduled the use of time-constrained and sequential physical and human resources? Is the reward system consistent with desired actions?

opportunities, must be evaluated for each business group. And for each business group, a strategy that stakes out the desired competitive position must be chosen, implemented, and controlled. This must also be consistent with the role of the business group as expressed in the corporate-level strategy.

The interactive nature of the strategic management process should also be apparent in Exhibits 1 and 2. If the content of one component of the model changes, then the other components will change as well.

STRATEGIC MANAGEMENT MODEL

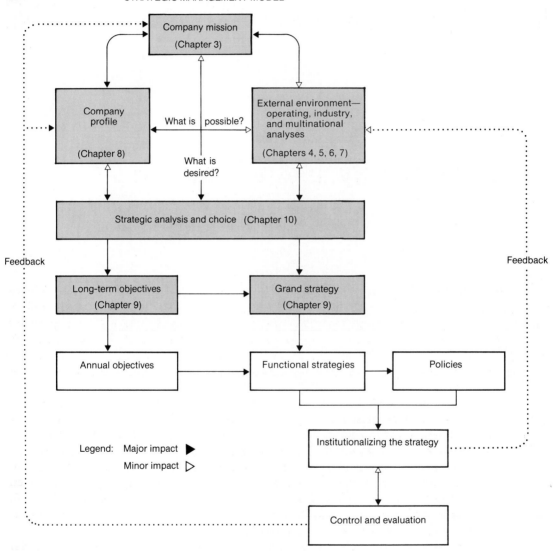

PART TWO

Strategy Formulation

Strategy formulation is designed to guide executives in defining the business their company is in, the aims it seeks, and the means it will use to accomplish these aims. Strategy formulation involves an improved approach to traditional long-range planning. As discussed in the following eight chapters, strategy formulation combines a future-oriented perspective with concern for a firm's internal and external environments in developing its competitive plan of action.

The process of strategy formulation begins with a definition of the company mission, as discussed in Chapter 3. In this chapter the purpose of business will be defined to reflect the values of a wide variety of interested parties.

Chapter 4 deals with the principal factors in a firm's external environment that must be assessed by strategic managers so that they can anticipate and take advantage of future business conditions. A recently popular approach to the strategic study of a firm's industry is the focal point of Chapter 5. This chapter systematically outlines and describes a five-force method of conducting a competitive industry analysis.

Chapter 6 describes the key differences between domestic and multinational firms in terms of the ways they impact on strategic planning and success. Special attention is given to the new vision of itself that a corporation must create when it multinationalizes, as is communicated in a revised mission statement.

Chapter 7 focuses on environmental forecasting—approaches currently used by strategic managers in assessing and anticipating changes in the external environment.

Chapter 8 shows how businesses evaluate their internal strengths and weaknesses to produce a company profile. Such profiles are used by strategic managers to target the competitive advantages they can emphasize and the competitive disadvantages they should correct or minimize.

In Chapter 9 attention turns to the types of long-range objectives set by strategic managers and to the qualities these objectives must have to provide a basis for direction and evaluation. The 12 grand strategies that companies use as broadly defined approaches for achieving long-range objectives are also highlighted.

Detailed comprehensive approaches to evaluation of strategic opportunities and to the final strategic decision are the focus of Chapter 10. The chapter deals with comparing strategic alternatives in a way that allows selection of the best available option for a firm, measured by potential for satisfying the company purpose.

CHAPTER

3

Defining the Company Mission

What Is a Company Mission?

Whether developing a new business or reformulating direction for an ongoing company, the basic goals, characteristics, and philosophies that will shape a firm's strategic posture must be determined. This *company mission* will guide future executive action. Thus, the company mission is defined as the fundamental, unique purpose that sets a business apart from other firms of its type and identifies the scope of its operations in product and market terms. As discussed in Chapter 2, the mission is a broadly framed but enduring statement of company intent. It embodies the business philosophy of strategic decision makers; implies the image the company seeks to project; reflects the firm's self-concept; indicates the principal product or service areas and primary customer needs the company will attempt to satisfy. In short, the mission describes the product, market, and technological areas of emphasis for the business. And it does so in a way that reflects the values and priorities of strategic decision makers.

Strategy in Action 3–1 presents an example of a good mission statement that incorporates major features and provides a broad framework. The statement is from an internal communication of the Zale Corporation, a company

Note: Portions of this chapter are adopted from John A. Pearce II, "The Company Mission as a Strategic Tool," *Sloan Management Review*, Spring 1982, pp. 15–24.

Strategy in Action 3–1
Zale Corporation—Summary Statement of Corporation Mission

Our business is specialty retailing. Retailing is a people-oriented business. We recognize that our business existence and continued success is dependent on how well we meet our responsibilities to several critically important groups of people.

Our first responsibility is to our customers. Without them we would have no reason for being. We strive to appeal to a broad spectrum of consumers, catering in a professional manner to their needs. Our concept of value to the customer includes a wide selection of quality merchandise, competitively priced and delivered with courtesy and professionalism.

Our ultimate responsibility is to our shareholders. Our goal is to earn an optimum return on invested capital through steady profit growth and prudent, aggressive asset management. The attainment of this financial goal, coupled with a record of sound management, represents our approach toward influencing the value placed on our common stock in the market.

We feel a deep, personal responsibility to our employees. As an equal opportunity employer we seek to create and maintain an environment where every employee is provided the opportunity to develop to his or her maximum potential. We expect to reward employees commensurate with their contribution to the success of the company.

We are committed to honesty and integrity in all relationships with suppliers of goods and services. We are demanding but fair. We evaluate our suppliers on the basis of quality, price, and service.

We recognize community involvement as an important obligation and as a viable business objective. Support of worthwhile community projects in areas where we operate generally accrues to the health and well-being of the community. This makes the community a better place for our employees to live and a better place for us to operate.

We believe in the free enterprise system and in the American democratic form of government under which this superior economic system has been permitted to flourish. We feel an incumbent responsibility to ensure that our business operates at a reasonable profit. Profit provides opportunity for growth and job security. We believe growth is necessary to provide opportunities on an ever-increasing scale for our people. Therefore, we are dedicated to profitable growth—growth as a company and growth as individuals.

with annual sales of $1 billion from four major lines: jewelry ($700 million), sporting goods, footwear, and drugs. Zale is best known for its 769 jewelry stores and enjoys operating profits of approximately $130 million per year.

The Need for an Explicit Mission

Defining the company mission is time consuming, tedious, and not required by any external body. The mission contains few specific directives, only broadly outlined or implied objectives and strategies. Characteristically, it is a statement of attitude, outlook, and orientation rather than of details and measurable targets.

What then is a company mission designed to accomplish? King and Cleland provide seven good answers:

1. To ensure unanimity of purpose within the organization.
2. To provide a basis for motivating the use of the organization's resources.
3. To develop a basis, or standard, for allocating organizational resources.
4. To establish a general tone or organizational climate, for example, to suggest a businesslike operation.
5. To serve as a focal point for those who can identify with the organization's purpose and direction, and to deter those who cannot from participating further in the organization's activities.
6. To facilitate the translation of objectives and goals into a work structure involving the assignment of tasks to responsible elements within the organization.
7. To specify organizational purposes and the translation of these purposes into goals in such a way that cost, time, and performance parameters can be assessed and controlled.[1]

Formulating a Mission

The process of defining the mission for a specific business can perhaps be best understood by thinking about a firm at its inception. The typical business organization begins with the beliefs, desires, and aspirations of a single entrepreneur. The sense of mission for such an owner-manager is usually based on several fundamental elements:

1. Belief that the *product* or *service* can provide benefits at least equal to its price.
2. Belief that the product or service can satisfy a *customer need* currently not met adequately for specific market segments.

---

[1] W. R. King and D. I. Cleland, *Strategic Planning and Policy* (New York: Van Nostrand Reinhold, 1978), p. 124.

3. Belief that the *technology* to be used in production will provide a product or service that is cost and quality competitive.

4. Belief that with hard work and the support of others the business can do better than just *survive,* it can *grow* and be *profitable.*

5. Belief that the *management philosophy* of the business will result in a favorable *public image* and will provide financial and psychological rewards for those willing to invest their labor and money in helping the firm to succeed.

6. Belief that the entrepreneur's *self-concept* of the business can be communicated to and adopted by employees and stockholders.

As the business grows or is forced by competitive pressures to alter its product/market/technology, redefining the company mission may be necessary. If so, the revised mission statement will reflect the same set of elements as the original. It will state the basic type of product or service to be offered, the primary markets or customer groups to be served, the technology to be used in production or delivery; the fundamental concern for survival through growth and profitability; the managerial philosophy of the firm; the public image sought; and the self-concept those affiliated with it should have of the firm. These components will be discussed in detail in this chapter. The examples shown in Strategy in Action 3–2 provide insights as to the way the components are actually handled by some major corporations.

Strategy in Action 3–2
Identifying Mission Statement Components: A Compilation of Excerpts from Actual Corporate Mission Statements

1.	Customer/ market	We believe our first responsibility is to the doctors, nurses, and patients, to mothers and all others who use our products and services. (Johnson & Johnson)
		To anticipate and meet market needs of farmers, ranchers, and rural communities within North America. (CENEX)
2.	Product/ service	AMAX's principal products are molybdenum, coal, iron ore, copper, lead, zinc, petroleum and natural gas, potash, phosphates, nickel, tungsten, silver, gold, and magnesium. (AMAX)

Continued on Page 77

Strategy in Action 3–2 *(concluded)*

3. Geographic domain	We are dedicated to the total success of Corning Glass Works as a worldwide competitor. (Corning Glass)
4. Technology	Control Data is in the business of applying microelectronics and computer technology in two general areas: computer-related hardware; and computing-enhancing services, which include computation, information, education, and finance. (Control Data)
	The common technology in these areas relates to discrete particle coatings. (NASHUA)
5. Concern for survival	In this respect, the company will conduct its operations prudently, and will provide the profits and growth which will assure Hoover's ultimate success. (Hoover Universal)
6. Philosophy	We are committed to improve health care throughout the world. (Baxter Travenol)
	We believe human development to be the worthiest of the goals of civilization and independence to be the superior condition for nuturing growth in the capabilities of people. (Sun Company)
7. Self-concept	Hoover Universal is a diversified, multi-industry corporation with strong manufacturing capabilities, entrepreneurial policies, and individual business unit autonomy. (Hoover Universal)
8. Concern for public image	We are responsible to the communities in which we live and work and to the world community as well. (Johnson & Johnson)
	Also, we must be responsive to the broader concerns of the public including especially the general desire for improvement in the quality of life, equal opportunity for all, and the constructive use of natural resources. (Sun Company)

Source: J. A. Pearce II and F. R. David, "Corporate Mission Statements: The Bottom Line," *Academy of Management Executive* 1, no. 2 (May 1987), pp. 109–16.

Basic Product or Service; Primary Market; Principal Technology

Three components of a mission statement are indispensable: specification of the basic product or service, primary market, and principal technology for production or delivery. The three components are discussed under one heading because only in combination do they describe the business activity of the company. A good example of these three mission components is to be found in the business plan of ITT Barton, a division of ITT. Under the heading of business mission and area served, the company presents the following information:

> The unit's mission is to serve industry and government with quality instruments used for the primary measurement, analysis, and local control of fluid flow, level, pressure, temperature, and fluid properties. This instrumentation includes flow meters, electronic readouts, indicators, recorders, switches, liquid level systems, analytical instruments such as titrators, integrators, controllers, transmitters, and various instruments for the measurement of fluid properties (density, viscosity, gravity) used for process variable sensing, data collection, control, and transmission. The unit's mission includes fundamental loop-

closing control and display devices, when economically justified, but excludes broadline central control room instrumentation, systems design, and turnkey responsibility.

Markets served include instrumentation for oil and gas production, gas transportation, chemical and petrochemical processing, cryogenics, power generation, aerospace, government and marine, as well as other instrument and equipment manufacturers.

This segment of the mission statement clearly indicates to all readers—from company employees to casual observers—the basic products, primary markets, and principal technologies of ITT Barton, and it was accomplished in only 129 words.

Often a company's most referenced public statement of selected products and markets is presented in "silver bullet" form in the mission statement; for example, "Dayton-Hudson Corporation is a diversified retailing company whose business is to serve the American consumer through the retailing of fashion-oriented quality merchandise."[2] Such a statement serves as an abstract of company direction and is particularly helpful to outsiders who value condensed overviews.

Company Goals: Survival, Growth, Profitability

Three economic goals guide the strategic direction of almost every viable business organization. Whether or not they are explicitly stated, a company mission statement reflects the firm's intention to secure its *survival* through sustained *growth* and *profitability*.

Unless a firm is able to survive, it will be incapable of satisfying any of its stakeholders' aims. Unfortunately, like growth and profitability, survival is such an assumed goal that it is often neglected as a principal criterion in strategic decision making. When this happens, the firm often focuses on short-term aims at the expense of the long run. Concerns for expediency, a quick fix, or a bargain displace the need for assessing long-term impact. Too often the result is near-term economic failure owing to a lack of resource synergy and sound business practice. For example, Consolidated Foods, makers of Shasta soft drinks and L'Eggs hosiery, sought growth in the 1960s through the acquisition of bargain businesses. However, the erratic sales patterns of their diverse holdings forced the firm to divest itself of more than four dozen of the companies in the late 1970s. The resulting stabilization cost Consolidated Foods millions of dollars and hampered its growth.

Profitability is the mainstay goal of a business organization. No matter how it is measured or defined, profit over the long term is the clearest indication of a firm's ability to satisfy the principal claims and desires of employees

---

[2] See W. Ouchi, *Theory Z* (Reading, Mass.: Addison-Wesley Publishing, 1981). Ouchi presents more complete mission statements of three of the companies discussed in this chapter: Dayton-Hudson, Hewlett-Packard, and Intel.

and stockholders. The key phrase in the sentence is "over the long term." Obviously, basing decisions on a short-term concern for profitability would lead to a strategic myopia. A firm might overlook the enduring concerns of customers, suppliers, creditors, ecologists, and regulatory agents. In the short term the results may produce profit, but over time the financial consequences are likely to be detrimental.

The following excerpt from the Hewlett-Packard Company's statement of corporate objectives (i.e., mission) ably expresses the importance of an orientation toward long-term profit:

> Objective: To achieve sufficient profit to finance our company growth and to provide the resources we need to achieve our other corporate objectives.
>
> In our economic system, the profit we generate from our operations is the ultimate source of the funds we need to prosper and grow. It is the one absolutely essential measure of our corporate performance over the long term. Only if we continue to meet our profit objective can we achieve our other corporate objectives.

A firm's growth is inextricably tied to its survival and profitability. In this context, the meaning of growth must be broadly defined. While growth in market share has been shown by the product impact market studies (PIMS) to be correlated with firm profitability, other important forms of growth do exist. For example, growth in the number of markets served, in the variety of products offered, and in the technologies used to provide goods or services frequently leads to improvements in the company's competitive ability. Growth means change, and proactive change is a necessity in a dynamic business environment. Hewlett-Packard's mission statement provides an excellent example of corporate regard for growth:

> Objective: To let our growth be limited only by our profits and our ability to develop and produce technical products that satisfy real customer needs.
>
> We do not believe that large size is important for its own sake; however, for at least two basic reasons continuous growth is essential for us to achieve our other objectives.
>
> In the first place, we serve a rapidly growing and expanding segment of our technological society. To remain static would be to lose ground. We cannot maintain a position of strength and leadership in our field without growth.
>
> In the second place, growth is important in order to attract and hold high-caliber people. These individuals will align their future only with a company that offers them considerable opportunity for personal progress. Opportunities are greater and more challenging in a growing company.

The issue of growth raises a concern about the definition of a company mission. How can a business specify product, market, and technology sufficiently to provide direction without delimiting unanticipated strategic options? How can a company define its mission so opportunistic diversification can be considered while at the same time maintaining parameters that guide growth decisions? Perhaps such questions are best addressed when a firm outlines its mission conditions under which it might depart from ongoing operations. The growth philosophy of Dayton-Hudson shows this approach:

> The stability and quality of the corporation's financial performance will be developed through the profitable execution of our existing businesses, as well as through the acquisition or development of new businesses. Our growth priorities, in order, are as follows:
>   1. Development of the profitable market preeminence of existing companies in existing markets through new store development or new strategies within existing stores;
>   2. Expansion of our companies to feasible new markets;
>   3. Acquisition of other retailing companies that are strategically and financially compatible with Dayton-Hudson;
>   4. Internal development of new retailing strategies.
>
> Capital allocations to fund the expansion of existing operating companies will be based on each company's return on investment, in relationship to its return-on-investment (ROI) objective and its consistency in earnings growth, and on its management capability to perform up to forecasts contained in capital requests.
>
> Expansion via acquisition or new venture will occur when the opportunity promises an acceptable rate of long-term growth and profitability, acceptable degree of risk, and compatibility with the corporation's long-term strategy.

Company Philosophy

The statement of a company's philosophy, often called a company creed, usually accompanies or appears as part of the mission. It reflects or explicitly states basic beliefs, values, aspirations, and philosophical priorities. In turn, strategic decision makers are committed to emphasizing these in managing the firm. Fortunately, company philosophies vary little from one firm to another. Thus, owners and managers implicitly accept a general, unwritten, yet pervasive code of behavior. Through this code, actions in a business setting are governed and largely self-regulated. Unfortunately, statements of philosophy are so similiar and are so full of platitudes that they look and read more like public relations statements than the commitment to values they are meant to be.

Despite similarities in these philosophies, strategic managers' intentions in developing them do not warrant cynicism. In most cases managers attempt, often successfully, to provide a distinctive and accurate picture of the firm's managerial outlook. One such valuable statement is that of Zale Corporation, whose company mission was presented earlier in this chapter. As shown in Strategy in Action 3–3, Zale has subdivided its statement of management's operating philosophy into four key areas: marketing and customer service, management tasks, human resources, and finance and control. These subdivisions allow more refinement than the mission statement itself. As a result, Zale has established especially clear directions for company decision making and action.

Strategy in Action 3–3
Zale Corporation—Operating Philosophy

1. Marketing and customer service.
   a. We require that the entire organization be continuously customer oriented. Our future success is dependent on meeting the customers' needs better than our competition.
   b. We expect to maintain a marketing concept and distribution capability to identify changing trends and emerging markets and effectively promote our products.
   c. We strive to provide our customers with continuous offerings of quality merchandise, competitively priced—stressing value and service.
   d. We plan to constantly maintain our facilities as modern, attractive, clean, and orderly stores that are pleasing and exciting places for customers to shop.
2. Management tasks.
   a. We require profitable results from operations—activity does not necessarily equate with accomplishment—results must be measurable.
   b. We recognize there are always better ways to perform many functions. Continuous improvement in operating capability is a daily objective of the entire organization.
   c. We expect all managers to demonstrate capabilities to plan objectives, delegate responsibilities, motivate people, control operations, and achieve results measured against planned objectives.
   d. We must promote a spirit of teamwork. To succeed, a complex business such as ours requires good communication, clearly understood policies, effective controls and, above all, a dedication to "make it happen."
   e. We are highly competitive and dedicated to succeeding. However, as a human organization we will make mistakes. We must openly acknowledge our mistakes, learn from them, and take corrective action.
3. Human resources.
   a. We must develop and maintain a competent, highly motivated, results-oriented organization.
   b. We seek to attract, develop, and motivate people who demonstrate professional competence, courage, and integrity in performing their jobs.
   c. We strive to identify individuals who are outstanding performers,

Continued on Page 82

Strategy in Action 3–3 *(concluded)*

provide them with continuous challenges, and search for new, effective ways to compensate them—utilizing significant incentives.

d. Promotion from within is our goal. We must have the best talent available and, from time to time, will have to reach outside to meet our ever-improving standards. We heartily endorse and support development programs to prepare individuals for increased responsibility. In like manner, we must promptly advise those who are not geared to the pace, in order that they make the necessary adjustments without delay.

4. Finance and control.
   a. We will maintain a sound financial plan that provides capital for growth of the business and provides optimum return for our stockholders.
   b. We must develop and maintain a system of controls that highlights potential significant failures early for positive corrective action.

The mission statement of the Dayton-Hudson Corporation is at least equally specific in detailing the firm's management philosophy, as shown in Strategy in Action 3–4. Perhaps most noteworthy is the delineation of responsibility at both the corporate and business levels. In many ways, the statement could serve as a prototype for the three-tiered approach to strategic management. This new approach argues that the mission statement must address strategic concerns at the corporate, business, and functional levels of the organization. To this end, Dayton-Hudson's management philosophy is a balance of operating autonomy and flexibility on the one hand, and corporate input and direction on the other.

Public Image

Particularly for the growing firm involved in a redefinition of its company mission, public image is important. Both present and potential customers attribute certain qualities to a particular business. Gerber and Johnson & Johnson make safe products; Cross Pen makes high-quality writing instruments; Aigner Etienne makes stylish but affordable leather products; Corvettes are power machines; and Izod Lacoste is for the preppy look. Thus, mission statements often reflect public anticipations, making achieving the firm's goals a more likely consequence. Gerber's mission should not open the possibility for diversification into pesticides, nor Cross Pen's into 39-cent brand-named disposables.

On the other hand, a negative public image often prompts firms to re-emphasize the beneficial aspects reflected in their mission. For example, as a result of what it saw as a disturbing trend in public opinion, Dow Chemical

Strategy in Action 3–4
Management Philosophy of Dayton-Hudson Corporation

The corporation will:
Set standards for return on investment (ROI) and earnings growth.
Approve strategic plans.
Allocate capital.
Approve goals.
Monitor, measure, and audit results.
Reward performance.
Allocate management resources.

The operating companies will be accorded the freedom and responsibility:
To manage their own business.
To develop strategic plans and goals that will optimize their growth.
To develop an organization that can ensure consistency of results and optimum growth.
To operate their businesses consistent with the corporation's statement of philosophy.

The corporate staff will provide only those services that are:
Essential to the protection of the corporation.
Needed for the growth of the corporation.
Wanted by operating companies and that provide a significant advantage in quality or cost.

The corporation will insist on:
Uniform accounting practices by type of business.
Prompt disclosure of operating results.
A systematic approach to training and developing people.
Adherence to appropriately high standards of business conduct and civic responsibility in accordance with the corporation's statement of philosophy.

undertook an aggressive promotional campaign to fortify its credibility, particularly among "employees and those who live and work in [their] plant communities." Dow's approach was described in its 1980 annual report:

All around the world today, Dow people are speaking up. People who care deeply about their company, what it stands for, and how it is viewed by others. People who are immensely proud of their company's performance, yet realistic enough to realize it is the public's perception of that performance that counts in the long run.

A firm's concern for its public image is seldom addressed in an intermittent fashion. While public agitation often stimulates greater response, a corporation is concerned about its image even when public concern is not expressed. The following excerpt from the mission statement of Intel Corporation is an example of this attitude:

> We are sensitive to our *image with our customers and the business community*. Commitments to customers are considered sacred, and we are upset with ourselves when we do not meet our commitments. We strive to demonstrate to the business world on a continuing basis that we are credible in describing the state of the corporation, and that we are well organized and in complete control of all things that determine the numbers.

Company Self-Concept

A major determinant of any company's continued success is the extent to which it can relate functionally to the external environment. Finding its place in a competitive situation requires the firm to realistically evaluate its own strengths and weaknesses as a competitor. This idea—that the firm must know itself—is the essence of the company's self-concept. This notion per se is not commonly integrated into theories of strategic management; however, scholars have appreciated its importance to an individual: "Man has struggled to understand himself, for how he thinks of himself will influence both what he chooses to do and what he expects from life. Knowing his identity connects him both with his past and the potentiality of his future."[3]

There is a direct parallel between this view of the importance of an individual's self-concept and the self-concept of a business. Fundamentally, the need for each to know the self is crucial. The ability of a firm or an individual to survive in a dynamic and highly competitive environment would be severely limited if the impact on others and of others is not understood.

In some senses, then, the organization takes on a personality of its own. Hall stated that much behavior in organizations is organizationally based, that is, a business acts on its members in other than individual and interacting ways.[4] Thus businesses are entities that act with a personality transcending those of particular company members. As such, the firm can be seen as setting decision-making parameters, based on aims different than and distinct from the individual aims of its members. The effects of organizational considerations are pervasive.

---

[3] J. Kelly, *Organizational Behavior* (Homewood, Ill.: Richard D. Irwin, 1974), p. 258.

[4] R. H. Hall, *Organization—Structure and Process* (Englewood Cliffs, N.J.: Prentice-Hall, 1972), p. 11.

Organizations do have policies, do and do not condone violence, and may or may not greet you with a smile. They also manufacture goods, administer policies, and protect the citizenry. These are organizational actions and involve properties of organizations, not individuals. They are carried out by individuals, even in the case of computer-produced letters, which are programmed by individuals—but the genesis of the actions remains in the organization.[5]

The actual role of the corporate self-concept has been summarized as follows:

1. The corporate self-concept is based on management perception of the way others (society) will respond to the corporation.
2. The corporate self-concept will function to direct the behavior of people employed by the company.
3. The actual response of others to the company will in part determine the corporate self-concept.
4. The self-concept is incorporated in statements of corporate mission to be explicitly communicated to individuals inside and outside the company, that is, to be actualized.[6]

A second look at the company mission of the Zale Corporation in Strategy in Action 3–1 reveals much about the business's self-concept. The strategic decision makers see the firm as socially responsive, prudent, and fiercely independent.

Characteristically, descriptions of self-concept per se do not appear in company mission statements. Yet, strong impressions of a firm's self-image are often evident. An example from Intel Corporation is given in Strategy in Action 3–5.

The Claimant Approach to Company Responsibility

In defining or redefining the company mission, strategic managers must recognize and acknowledge the legitimate claims of other stakeholders of the firm. These include both investors and employees as well as outsiders affected by the company's actions. Such outsiders commonly include customers, suppliers, governments, unions, competitors, local communities, and the general public. Each of these interest groups has justifiable reasons to expect, and often to demand, the company to act in a responsible manner in satisfying their claims. Generalizing, stockholders claim appropriate returns on their investment; employees seek broadly defined job satisfaction; customers want what they pay for; suppliers seek dependable buyers; governments want adherence to legis-

---

[5] Ibid., p. 13.

[6] E. J. Kelley, *Marketing Planning and Competitive Strategy* (Englewood Cliffs, N.J.: Prentice-Hall, 1972), p. 55.

Strategy in Action 3–5
Abstract of Intel's Mission-Related Information

Management Style.   Intel is a company of individuals, each with his or her own personality and characteristics.

Management is *self-critical.* The leaders must be capable of recognizing and accepting their mistakes and learning from them.

Open *(constructive) confrontation is encouraged* at all levels of the corporation and is viewed as a method of problem solving and conflict resolution.

Decision by *consensus* is the rule. Decisions once made are supported. Position in the organization is not the basis for quality of ideas.

A highly communicative, open management is part of the style.

A high degree of *organizational skills and discipline* are demanded.

Management must be ethical. Managing by telling the truth and treating all employees equitably has established credibility that is ethical.

Work Ethic/Environment

It is a general objective of Intel to line up individual work assignments with career objectives.

We strive to provide an *opportunity for rapid development.*

Intel is a *results-oriented* company. The focus is on *substance* versus form, *quality* versus quantity.

We believe in the principle that *hard work, high productivity* is something to be proud of.

The concept of *assumed responsibility* is accepted. (If a task needs to be done, assume you have the responsibility to get it done.)

Commitments are long term; if career problems occur at some point, reassignment is a better alternative than termination.

We desire to have *all employees involved and participative* in their relationship with Intel.

lation; unions seek benefits for members in proportion to contributions to company success; competitors want fair competition; local communities want companies to be responsible citizens; and the general public seeks some improvement in the quality of life resulting from the firm's existence.

However, when a business attempts to define its mission to incorporate the interests of these groups, broad generalizations are insufficient. Thus, four steps need to be taken:

1. Identification of claimants.
2. Understanding of specific claims vis-à-vis the company.
3. Reconciliation of claims and assigning them priorities.
4. Coordination of claims with other elements of the mission.

Identification.   The left-hand column of Figure 3–1 lists the commonly encountered claimants, to which the executive officer group is often added. Obviously though, every business faces a slightly different set of claimants, who vary in number, size, influence, and importance. In defining a mission, strategic managers must identify all claimant groups and weight their relative ability to affect firm success.

Understanding.   The concerns of principal claimants tend to center around the generalities in the right-hand column of Figure 3–1. However, strategic decision makers should understand the specific demands of each group. Then strategic managers will be better able to both appreciate these concerns and initiate clearly defined actions.

Reconciliation and Priorities.   Unfortunately, the concerns of various claimants often conflict. For example, the claims of governments and the general public tend to limit profitability, which is the central concern of most creditors and stockholders. Thus, claims must be reconciled. To achieve a unified approach managers must define a mission that resolves the competing, conflicting, and contradictory claims. For objectives and strategies to be internally consistent and precisely focused, mission statements must display a single-minded, though multidimensional, approach to business aims.

There are hundreds, if not thousands, of claims on any business—high wages, pure air, job security, product quality, community service, taxes, occupational health and safety (OSHA) and equal opportunity (EEOC) regulations, product variety, wide markets, career opportunities, company growth, investment security, high ROI, and many, many more. Although most, if not all, of these claims are desirable ends, they cannot be pursued with equal emphasis. Claims must be assigned priorities that reflect the relative attention the firm will give to each. Such emphasis is reflected by the criteria used in strategic decision making; by the company's allocation of human, financial, and physical resources; and by the long-term objectives and strategies developed for the firm.

Coordination with Other Elements.   Demands of claimant groups for responsible action by a company constitute only one set of inputs to the mission. Managerial operating philosophies and determination of the product-market

Figure 3–1
A claimant view of company responsibility

Claimant	Nature of the claim
Stockholders	Participation in distribution of profits, additional stock offerings, assets on liquidation; vote of stock; inspection of company books; transfer of stock; election of board of directors; and such additional rights as established in the contract with the corporation.
Creditors	Legal proportion of interest payments due and return of principal from the investment. Security of pledged assets; relative priority in event of liquidation. Subsume in some management and owner prerogatives if certain conditions exist within the company (such as default of interest payments).
Employees	Economic, social, and psychological satisfaction in the place of employment. Freedom from arbitrary and capricious behavior on the part of company officials. Share in fringe benefits, freedom to join union and participate in collective bargaining, individual freedom in offering up their services through an employment contract. Adequate working conditions.
Customers	Service provided with the product; technical data to use the product; suitable warranties; spare parts to support the product during customer use; R&D leading to product improvement; facilitation of consumer credit.
Suppliers	Continuing source of business; timely consummation of trade credit obligations; professional relationship in contracting for, purchasing, and receiving goods and services.
Governments	Taxes (income, property, etc.), fair competition, and adherence to the letter and intent of public policy dealing with the requirements of fair and free competition. Legal obligation of businessmen (and business organizations); adherence to antitrust laws.
Unions	Recognition as the negotiating agent for employees. Opportunity to perpetuate the union as a participant in the business organization.
Competitors	Norms established by society and the industry for competitive conduct. Business statesmanship on the part of peers.
Local communities	Place of productive and healthful employment in the community. Participation of company officials in community affairs, regular employment, fair play, purchase of reasonable portion of products of the local community, interest in and support of local government, support of cultural and charity projects.
The general public	Participation in and contribution to society as a whole; creative communications between governmental and business units designed for reciprocal understanding; bear fair proportion of the burden of government and society. Fair price for products and advancement of state-of-the-art technology which the product line involves.

Source: From William R. King and David I. Cleland, *Strategic Planning and Policy.* © 1978 by Litton Educational Publishing Inc., p. 153. Reprinted by permission of Van Nostrand Reinhold Company.

offering are the other principal components considered. The latter factors essentially pose a reality test the accepted claims must pass. The key question is: How can the company satisfy claimants and simultaneously optimize its success in the marketplace?

Social Responsibility

The various claimants on a company can be divided into two categories, as indicated by Figure 3–2. Insiders are individuals and groups who are stockholders or are employed by the firm. Outsiders are all other individuals or groups

Figure 3–2
Inputs to the development of the company mission

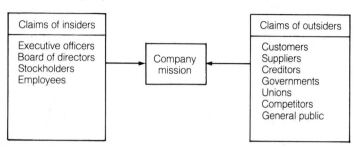

affected by the actions of the firm. This extremely large and often amorphous set of outsiders makes the general claim that the company be socially responsible.

Questions of social responsibility are perhaps the thorniest of all issues faced in defining a company mission. The claimant approach offers the clearest perspective on the problem. Broadly stated, outsiders often demand that the claims of insiders be subordinated to the greater good of the society, that is, to the greater good of the outsiders. They believe such issues as elimination of solid and liquid wastes, pollution, and conservation of natural resources should be principal considerations in strategic decision making. Also broadly stated, insiders tend to believe that the competing claims of the outsiders should be balanced against each other in a way that protects the company mission. For example, the consumers' need for a product must be balanced against the water pollution resulting from production, if the company cannot totally afford to eliminate the pollution and remain profitable. Additionally, some insiders argue that the claims of society, as activated by government regulation, provide tax money that is more than sufficient to eliminate unwanted business by-products, such as water pollution, if this is truly the wish of the general public.

The issues are numerous and complex, and the problems are contingent on the situation. Thus, rigid rules of conduct are not possible. Each business must decide on its approach in trying to meet its perceived social responsibility. Different approaches will reflect differences in competitive position, industry, country, environmental and ecological pressure, and a host of other factors. In other words, they will reflect both situational factors and differing priorities in the acknowledgment of claims.

Despite differences in approaches, most American companies now try to assure outsiders that they attempt to conduct business in a socially responsible manner. Many firms, including Abt Associates, Eastern Gas and Fuel Associates, and the Bank of America, have gone to the effort of conducting and publishing annual social audits. For example, the social audit of Eastern Gas and Fuel, as published in its 1981 annual report, is given in Strategy in

Action 3–6. These social audits attempt to evaluate the business from the perspective of social responsibility. They are often conducted for the firm by private consultants, who offer minimally biased evaluations on what are inherently highly subjective issues.

Strategy in Action 3–6
Social Audit of Eastern Gas and Fuel, 1981

Beyond Financial Concerns

Managing for profit is a common objective of all business, the cornerstone of the free enterprise system. However, business style varies widely. Eastern's philosophy is based on the premise that its performance objectives can be achieved in a manner that is responsive to the needs of Eastern's people—its shareholders, customers, employees, and the general public.

Corporate performance must be in line with shareholder expectations to justify their continued financial support. Service to Eastern's many customers must not be compromised. The selection and development of a highly skilled and motivated work force is essential. The work environment must be safe, healthy, and provide ample opportunity for self-improvement. The needs of the communities in which Eastern has a presence must also be addressed.

In striving to meet all of these objectives, Eastern has established proper business conduct as a top priority.

A. Health and Safety

	Incidence rate per 100 full-time workers*					
	Number of fatalities		Disabling injuries and illnesses		All injuries and illnesses	
	1981	1980	1981	1980	1981	1980
Coal	1	3	5.9	7.7	6.8	8.6
Coke	0	0	9.3	24.0	60.7	24.4
Gas	0	0	5.7	5.3	6.6	5.8
Marine	0	0	8.0	7.7	13.6	14.0
Total corporate	1	3	6.5	7.4	8.9	9.9

* The incidence rates represent Number of work-related injuries and illnesses × 200,000 (100 employees working 40 hours per week, 50 weeks per year) ÷ Total hours worked by employees.

Continued on Page 91

Strategy in Action 3–6 *(concluded)*

B. Charitable Giving

	Total charitable giving	
	1981	*1980*
Total contributions (000)	$770.3	$679.0
Percent of pretax income*	1.0%	1.0%
Dollar per employee	$ 82.83	$ 73.01
Cost per share, after income tax	1.8¢	1.6¢

* Five-year average pretax income.

C. Minority Employment

	Minority employment levels (December 31)			
	1981		*1978*	
	Number	*Percent of total*	*Number*	*Percent of total*
Officers and managers	35	2.6%	29	2.0%
Professional and technical	36	5.0	37	4.6
Clerical	94	10.2	89	9.6
Skilled	613	13.6	441	9.3
Unskilled	187	9.0	324	16.2
Total Eastern	965	10.0%	920	9.3%

D. Pensions

	Annual cost of pensions and welfare plans ($000)	
	1981	*1980*
Company-administered plans for salaried, nonunion, and certain union employees	$ 9,413	$ 8,991
Other union retirement and welfare plans	30,086	27,684
Total cost	$29,509	$36,675

Many other firms periodically report to both insiders and outsiders on their progress to reach self-set social goals. Primarily through their annual reports, companies such as Diamond Shamrock discuss their efforts and achievements in social responsibility. Strategy in Action 3–7 provides the 1980 Diamond Shamrock report.

Strategy in Action 3–7
Social Responsibility Report of Diamond Shamrock
(Excerpts from the 1980 Annual Report)

Concern for the safety and well-being of our employees and those communities in which we operate is an integral part of Diamond Shamrock's management philosophy. These concerns are translated into company policies, procedures, and programs, from planning and research to the production, sale, and distribution of our products.

Safety, Health, and the Environment

It is the policy of Diamond Shamrock to manufacture and market our products with care, exercising regard for potential hazards involved in their use and handling by our employees, customers, and the public in general.

During 1980, Diamond Shamrock improved its plant safety record for the 10th consecutive year. Thirty plants and facilities operated without a lost-time accident. Companywide, lost-time injuries were reduced 21 percent from 1979.

The company's highly trained staff of environmental specialists continues to establish an admirable record of meeting or exceeding standards established by local, state, and national regulatory agencies. Diamond Shamrock invested more than $19 million in new and replacement environmental equipment during 1980.

Diamond Shamrock administered 4,626 extensive physical examinations to employees in 1980 at no cost to [the employees]. These served as an integral part of Diamond Shamrock's computer-operated health and environmental surveillance system (COHESS). Developed at a cost of more than $2 million, COHESS is designed to compare workplace exposure, employee characteristics, and the results of physical examinations to help ensure that our industrial hygiene programs are effective and to identify unknown risks as quickly as possible. The company has made the program available to other corporations at reasonable cost.

In addition to our worker health and environmental control programs, Diamond Shamrock invested more than $4.1 million during 1980 to determine the potential health and environmental effects of our products and to communicate that information to employees and customers. The company not only participates actively in industrywide studies of its products but, through multidisciplinary functions, conducts extensive in-house toxicological and environmental studies through its research center and its health and environmental affairs department.

Continued on Page 93

Strategy in Action 3–7 *(concluded)*

Human Resources

Company-sponsored employee development spending exceeded $800,000 in 1980, with more than 1,500 individuals attending Diamond Shamrock training programs. These continuing programs have resulted in improved job performance and have assisted employees in achieving individual career goals.

Diamond Shamrock actively pursues equal opportunity, without regard to religion, race, or sex. In addition, the company participates in and supports programs for the handicapped, Vietnam era veterans, women, and minority students.

Diamond Shamrock's compensation and benefit programs are designed not only to be competitive with [those of] the best of our peer companies but to provide an environment that fosters and gives recognition to excellence. Individual employee compensation is based on performance measured against job goals mutually selected by employee and supervisor.

Public Affairs

Diamond Shamrock maintains a responsive attitude to the needs of those communities in which we operate and considers this an important management responsibility. Several community relations programs assisted us in addressing these concerns during 1980.

The company invested $1,289,005 in philanthropic funds to support public, nonprofit organizations addressing needs of critical importance to the company, our employees, shareholders, and individual communities in 1980, a 26 percent increase from 1979. Plans call for $1,409,000 in philanthropic spending in 1981.

Diamond Shamrock encourages its employees to become involved in community affairs. Through our Citizen-of-the-Year program, inaugurated in 1980, the company provides recognition for those employees who unselfishly invest personal time and [funds] for the betterment of their communities. Last year, 40 employees were recognized for their outstanding service to others.

Diamond Shamrock management also plays an important role in other local, state, and national affairs through advice and counsel offered to planning and zoning commissions, cooperation with various regulatory agencies, testimony before congressional review and policymaking committees, and regional task forces addressing significant social challenges.

Guidelines for a Socially Responsible Firm

After decades of debate on the topic of social responsibility, an individual firm still must struggle to determine the orientation reflected in its mission statement. However, public debate and business concern have led to a jelling of perspectives. One excellent summary of guidelines for a socially responsible firm, consistent with the claimant approach, was provided by Sawyer:

1. The purpose of the business is to make a profit; its managers should strive for the optimal profit that can be achieved over the long run.
2. No true profits can be claimed until business costs are paid. This includes all social costs, as determined by detailed analysis of the social balance between the firm and society.
3. If there are social costs in areas where no objective standards for correction yet exist, managers should generate corrective standards. These standards should be based on managers' judgment of what ought to exist and should simultaneously encourage individual involvement of firm members in developing necessary social standards.
4. Where competitive pressure or economic necessity precludes socially responsible action, the business should recognize that its operation is depleting social capital and, therefore, represents a loss. It should attempt to restore profitable operation through either better management, if the problem is internal, or by advocating corrective legislation, if society is suffering as a result of the way that the rules for business competition have been made.[7]

Summary

Defining a company mission is one of the most easily slighted tasks in strategic management. Emphasizing operational aspects of long-range management activities comes much more easily for most executives. But the critical role of the company mission as the basis of orchestrating managerial action is repeatedly demonstrated by failing firms whose short-run actions are ultimately found to be counterproductive to their long-run purpose.

The principal value of a mission statement is its specification of the ultimate aims of the firm. A company gains a heightened sense of purpose when its managers address the issues of: "What business are we in?" "What customer do we serve?" "Why does this organization exist?" Yet managers can undermine the potential contribution of the company mission when they accept platitudes or ambiguous generalizations in response to these questions. It is not enough to say that Lever Brothers is in the business of "making anything that cleans anything," or that Polaroid is committed to businesses that deal with "the interaction of light and matter." Rather, a firm must clearly articulate its long-term intentions. In this way, its goals can serve as a basis for shared expectations, planning, and performance evaluation.

When a mission statement is developed from this perspective, it provides managers with a unity of direction that transcends individual, parochial, and temporary needs. It promotes a sense of shared expectations among all levels

---

[7] G. E. Sawyer, *Business and Society: Managing Corporate Social Impact* (Boston: Houghton Mifflin, 1979), p. 401.

and generations of employees. It consolidates values over time and across individuals and interest groups. It projects a sense of worth and intent that can be identified and assimilated by company outsiders, that is, customers, suppliers, competitors, local committees, and the general public. Finally, it affirms the company's commitment to responsible action in symbiosis with the firm's needs to preserve and protect the essential claims of insiders—sustained survival, growth, and profitability.

Questions for Discussion

1. Reread the mission statement of the Zale Corporation in Strategy in Action 3–1. List five insights into the company you feel you gained as a result of knowing its mission.

2. Locate the mission statement of a company not mentioned in the chapter. Where did you find it? Was it presented as a consolidated statement or were you forced to assemble it yourself from various publications of the firm? How many elements of a mission statement outlined in this chapter did you find discussed or revealed in your company's mission?

3. Prepare a one- or two-page, typewritten mission statement for your school of business or for a company selected by your instructor.

4. List five potentially vulnerable areas for a business without a stated company mission.

5. The social audit shown in Strategy in Action 3–6 included only a few of the possible indicators of a firm's social responsibility performance. Name five additional potentially valuable indicators and describe how company performance in each could be measured.

6. Define the term *social responsibility*. Find an example of a company action that was legal but not socially responsible. Defend your example on the basis of your definition.

Bibliography

Ackoff, R. L. *A Concept of Corporate Planning*. New York: Wiley-Interscience, 1970.

Andrews, K. R. *The Concept of Corporate Strategy*. Homewood, Ill.: Dow Jones-Irwin, 1971.

Ansoff, H. I. *Corporate Strategy*. New York: McGraw-Hill, 1965.

Bender, M. "The Organizational Shrink." *New York Times,* March 5, 1972, p. 3.

Beresford, D., and S. Cowen. "Surveying Social Responsibility Disclosure in Annual Reports." *Business,* March–April 1979, pp. 15–20.

Cleland, D. I., and W. R. King. *Management: A System Approach*. New York: McGraw-Hill, 1972.

"Florida Developer to Refund $17 Million to Buyers." *New York Times,* September 14, 1974.

Hall, R. H. *Organization—Structure and Process*. Englewood Cliffs, N.J.: Prentice-Hall, 1972.

Harrison, R. "Understanding Your Organization's Character." *Harvard Business Review,* May–June 1972, pp. 119–28.

Kelley, E. J. *Marketing Planning and Competitive Strategy*. Englewood Cliffs, N.J.: Prentice-Hall, 1972.

Kelley, J. *Organizational Behavior*. Homewood, Ill.: Richard D. Irwin, 1974.

King, W. R., and D. I. Cleland. *Strategic Planning and Policy*. New York: Van Nostrand Reinhold, 1978.

Ouchi, W. *Theory Z*. Reading, Mass.: Addison-Wesley Publishing, 1981.

Pearce, J. A., II, and F. R. David. "Corporate Mission Statements: The Bottom Line." *Academy of Management Executive* 1, no. 2 (May 1987), pp. 109–16.

Pearce, J. A., II; R. B. Robinson, Jr.; and K. Roth. "The Company Mission as a Guide to Strategic Action." In *Strategic Planning and Management Handbook,* ed. W. R. King and D. I. Cleland. New York: Van Nostrand Reinhold, 1987.

Rogers, C. R. *Client-Centered Therapy*. New York: Houghton Mifflin, 1965.

Sawyer, G. E. *Business and Society: Managing Corporate Social Impact*. Boston: Houghton Mifflin, 1979.

Chapter 3 Cohesion Case Illustration

The Company Mission at Holiday Inns, Inc.

Chapter 3 described what is necessary for a good mission statement and why such a statement is needed. This Cohesion Case Illustration will first present mission statements of Holiday Inns, Inc., at the corporate and business levels. Afterward, a brief evaluation of the mission statements will be provided, as well as an examination of how these must be readdressed in the strategic management process at Holiday Inns, Inc. (See Exhibit 1.)

Several observations can be made about Holiday Inns' mission statements. The corporate statement gives a clear overview of products and services offered, primary customer attributes, fundamental concerns, and basic management philosophy. This statement emphasizes the hospitality side of the enterprise when identifying its technology for providing goods and services. This may reflect a lack of in-depth consideration of how parts of the product and transportation businesses fit into the overall corporate mission. With this exception, the business group missions otherwise adequately identify the product/market scope of each unit's operations and fit within the umbrella of the corporate mission.

While these mission statements appear adequate and useful, an underlying mission-related issue must be considered while moving through the strategic management process at Holiday Inns. That issue involves the fundamental purpose of defining company mission: "What businesses are (or should) Holiday Inns be in?" From its beginning until the early 1970s, Holiday Inns was in one business—full-service lodging facilities. Seeking a broader earnings base, Kemmons Wilson and senior management redefined the company as a travel- and transportation-related business. This definition is strongly reflected in the current corporate mission statement. That definition led to the Trailways and Delta Steamship acquisitions, and freestanding restaurants.

The company mission should provide long-term direction, but that does not mean the mission should be cast in stone. As the strategic management model in Chapter 2 indicated, the mission must be reconsidered in light of environmental analysis, the company profile, and the evaluation of alternative strategies. Thus, the underlying, mission-related issue of whether Holiday Inns should be in a travel- and transportation-related business, a travel-related business, or a hospitality-related business cannot be resolved until strategists begin to evaluate alternative strategies.

Exhibit 1
Holiday Inns, Inc., mission statements

Corporate mission

Holiday Inns, Inc. is a diversified, international corporation providing services in the lodging, food service, entertainment, and transportation industries. Hotel operations consist of both company-managed and franchised Holiday Inn hotels. Transportation operations include Trailways, Inc., the nation's second largest intercity busline, and Delta Steamship Lines, Inc., a major U.S.-flag shipping company. Freestanding restaurant operations include the Perkins 'Cake 'n Steak chain. Various product operations market institutional furnishings, design services, equipment, and supplies.

We are a forward-looking, innovative industry leader with clearly defined goals, producing superior products, services, and consistently high returns for our stockholders.

We are committed to leadership in marketing our products and services to the traveling and leisure-time public. Internal growth of our operations will continue to be emphasized. We are also closely monitoring changes in consumer needs and lifestyles so that we can develop or acquire new services to satisfy emerging trends. Pursuing these opportunities will supplement the growth that we anticipate from our existing lines of business.

Five basic tenets form our corporate philosophy. They are

1. Maintain high ethical standards.
2. Provide above-average growth in earnings.
3. Improve our return on invested capital (ROIC).
4. Maintain a strong balance sheet through prudent financial management.
5. People are our greatest asset. We will promote a climate of enthusiasm, teamwork, and challenge which attracts, motivates, and retains superior personnel and rewards superior performance.

Hotel group mission

The hotel group is committed to maintaining and expanding HI's leadership position in the lodging industry by staying ahead of its competitors in responding to the ever-changing needs of the traveling consumer. Through our company-owned and extensive franchise network HI will offer moderately priced full-service facilities in a manner that gives the customer the best price/value in the industry, provides for a superior return on stockholders' equity, and meets our social responsibilities to the communities in which we operate.

Restaurant group mission

The restaurant group is designed to provide a broader earnings base while transferring known skills—franchising, food service, freestanding locations in a brand new network—to the mid-priced restaurant industry. Through company-owned and extensive franchising, this group will grow the newly acquired Perkins chain to a national leadership position and also look for other restaurant acquisitions.

Transportation group mission

To provide a solid, profitable base for corporate diversification into travel-related areas. *Trailways'* To position HI as a market leader in providing innovative solutions to transportation (bus) industry problems through quality terminal facilities, better equipment utilization and reversing the industry decline in passenger miles. *Delta Steamships:* Delta is committed to becoming the leading U.S.-flag cargo carrier between U.S. ports and the growing markets of South America, West Africa, and the Caribbean through cost-effective management practices and state-of-the-art technology in cargo vessels.

New developments group mission

To build a broader base for future corporate earnings through diversification into hospitality-related businesses with exceptional growth potential. The customer profiles as well as the necessary operating expertise of these businesses should overlap HI's core capabilities in the food and lodging area. Primary focus in the near future should be on the casino/hotel business.

Note: This mission was prominent in 1977–78. By 1980–81, HI's gaming operations had become a *business group* with its own distinct mission—see paragraph 62.* This early mission statement is retained here to give you an example of a 'new development' mission statement.

* Numbers refer to paragraphs in the Cohesion Case at the end of Chapter 1.

4

Assessing the External Environment

A host of external and often largely uncontrollable factors influence a firm's choice of direction and action and, ultimately, its organizational structure and internal processes. These factors, which constitute the *external environment,* can be divided into two interrelated subcategories: those in the *remote* environment and those in the more immediate *operating* environment.[1] The aim of this chapter is to describe the complexities and necessities involved in formulating strategies that optimize a firm's opportunities in a highly competitive market within the overall business environment. Figure 4–1 suggests the interrelationship between the firm and the remote and operating environments.

Remote Environment

The remote environment is composed of a set of forces that originate beyond and usually irrespective of any single firm's operating situation—that is, political, economic, social, technological, and industry factors. It presents opportunities, threats, and constraints for the firm, while the organization rarely exerts any meaningful reciprocal influence. For example, when the economy slows and recession is threatening, an individual housing contractor is likely to

---

[1] Many authors refer to the operating environment as the *task* or *competitive* environment.

Figure 4–1
The firm's external environment

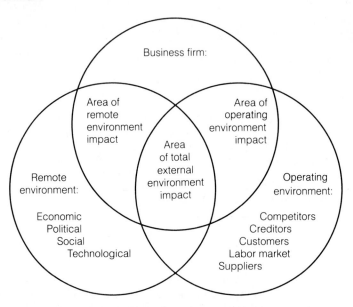

suffer a decline in business consistent with an industrywide decrease in construction starts. Yet that same contractor would be unable to reverse the negative economic trend even though it might be successful in stimulating local building activity. As a second example, political forces were operative in the trade agreements that resulted in improved relations between America and China in the mid-1970s. These agreements provided opportunities for individual U.S. electronics manufacturers to broaden their international bases of operation.

As a further example, Strategy in Action 4–1 describes the major conclusion of one firm in its pre-1984 assessment of the remote environment.

Economic Considerations

Economic considerations refer to the nature and direction of the economy in which the business operates. Because consumption patterns are affected by the relative affluence of various market segments, each firm must understand economic trends in the segments that affect its industry. On both national and international levels, a firm must consider the general availability of credit, the level of disposable income, and the propensity of people to spend. Prime interest rates, rates of inflation, and growth trends of the gross national product are additional economic factors that must be carefully considered in strategic planning.

Strategy in Action 4–1
External Factors Affecting the 1984 Strategy of Eastern Air Lines

Before determining its 1984 strategy, Eastern Air Lines conducted an assessment of its remote external environment. The following are the six major conclusions reached by Eastern's strategic planners:

The economic recovery is expected to continue.
GNP: +4.5%

Fuel prices should be stable.

The industry outlook is good:

Domestic passenger-miles:	+10.5%
Domestic yield:	+ 6.0%

New, low-cost carriers will continue to exert pressure on prices.
People Express, for example, is expected to take delivery of 18 B-727-200s by April 1984 and to more than double its capacity.

Extensive discounting of daytime fares will continue to limit our ability to establish night coach fare differentials and to increase night coach flying.

Schedule restrictions related to the PATCO (air controllers) strike are being removed. Slot restrictions at all but four airports will be removed by the end of 1983. Removal of restrictions at Denver and Los Angeles and an increase to at least prestrike levels at La Guardia and O'Hare are expected during the first quarter of 1984. (Quotas at La Guardia and O'Hare were in effect prior to the strike and may be retained.)

Until recently, the potential economic impact of international forces appeared to be severely restricted and was largely discounted. However, the emergence of new international power brokers has changed the focus of economic environmental forecasting. Three prominent examples of these new influences are the European Economic Community (EEC), the Organization of Petroleum Exporting Countries (OPEC), and coalitions of lesser-developed countries (LDC).

The EEC or Common Market was established by the Treaty of Rome in 1957, and its members include most Western European countries. Its purposes are elimination of quotas and establishment of a tariff-free trade area for industrial products. This unique example of intra-European cooperation has helped member countries compete more effectively in international markets.

Following the EEC precedent of economic cooperation, the United States, Canada, Japan, the EEC, and other countries conducted multilateral trade negotiations in 1979 to establish rules for international trade and conduct. The outcome of those negotiations had a profound, yet differential, effect on almost every aspect of business activity in the United States.

OPEC is among the most powerful international economic forces in existence today in terms of its impact on the United States. This cartel includes most major world suppliers of oil and gas, and its drastic increases in the price of energy supplied not only impeded U.S. recovery from the recession of the early 1970s but also fueled inflationary fires the world over. The U.S. automobile industry was particularly affected through an increase in user costs and the legislated redesign of engine sizes and performance standards.

Third World and Fourth World countries have recently assumed a greater role in international commerce, as a source of both threats and opportunities. Following the success of OPEC, these less developed countries have found it economically beneficial to directly confront the established powers. Since 1974, producers of primary commodities in the LDCs have formed or greatly strengthened their trade organizations to enforce higher prices and achieve larger real incomes for their members. On the other hand, developing countries offer U.S. firms huge new markets for foodstuffs and capital machinery.

Even countries not desiring or unable to form cartels exhibit the new aggressive attitude.

> The intense nationalism of the developing countries, with nearly three fourths of the world's population, represents perhaps the greatest challenge our industrialized society and multinational corporations will face in the next two decades. As one Third World expert puts it, "the vastly unequal relationship between the rich and poor nations is fast becoming the central issue of our time."[2]

Each of these international forces has the capacity to affect the U.S. business community's economic well-being—for better or worse, for richer or poorer. Consequently, companies must try to forecast major repercussions of actions taken in both the domestic and international economic arenas. Such forecasts are a critical part of the strategic management process.

Social Considerations

Social considerations involve the beliefs, values, attitudes, opinions, and lifestyles of those in a firm's external environment, as developed from their cultural,

---

[2] Richard Steade, "Multinational Corporations and the Changing World Economic Order," *California Management Review,* Winter 1978, p. 5.

ecological, demographic, religious, educational, and ethnic conditioning. As social attitudes change, so does demand for various clothing styles, books, leisure activities, and other products and services. As is true of other forces in the remote external environment, social forces are dynamic with constant change resulting from individuals' efforts to control and adapt to environmental factors to satisfy their desires and needs.

One of the most profound social changes in recent years is the large number of women entering the labor market. Not only have women affected the hiring and compensation policies and resource capabilities of firms employing them, they have also created or greatly expanded demand for a wide range of products and services necessitated by their absence from the home. Businesses that correctly anticipated or quickly reacted to this social change have profited by offering such products and services as convenience foods, microwave ovens, and day-care centers.

A second accelerating social change is consumer and employee interest in quality-of-life issues, even at the expense of greater affluence. Evidence of this change is seen in recent contract negotiations in that added to the traditional demand for increased salaries have been worker preferences for such benefits as sabbaticals, flexible hours or four-day workweeks, lump-sum vacation plans, and opportunities for advanced training.

A third important change in the social environment is the shift in national age distribution. Changing social values and increased acceptance of improved birth control methods have resulted in a rise in the mean age of the U.S. population from 27.9 in 1970 to an expected 34.9 years by the end of the 20th century. This trend will have an increasingly unfavorable impact on most producers of predominantly youth-oriented goods and will necessitate a shift in long-range marketing strategies. For example, producers of hair- and skin-care preparations have already begun to adjust research and development to reflect anticipated changes in the types of products demanded. One company that has recognized the potential impact is Procter & Gamble, as discussed in Strategy in Action 4–2.

A consequence of the changing population distribution is sharply increased demands from a growing senior citizen population. Constrained by fixed incomes, the elderly have demanded that arbitrary and rigid policies on retirement age be modified. They have successfully lobbied for tax exemptions and increases in social security benefits. Such changes have significantly altered the opportunity-risk equations of many firms—often much to the benefit of those businesses that anticipated the social impacts.

Translating social change into forecasts of business effects is a difficult process at best. Nevertheless, informed estimates of the impact of such alterations as geographic shifts in populations and changing work values, ethics, and religious orientation can only help a strategizing firm in its attempts to prosper.

Strategy in Action 4–2
Procter & Gamble

Procter & Gamble announced a new product on August 7, 1979, symbolizing a revolutionary era at the big Cincinnati company. The product was a medicinal cream for the treatment of skin lesions. Procter & Gamble had just begun a grand invasion of new markets, many of which were institutional and commercial fields well outside of its traditional haven in the nation's supermarkets. The first phalanx of these new products from P&G involved fanning out into such fields as prescription drugs, synthetic foods and food ingredients, and supplies for hospitals and nursing homes. Others, destined for the soft-drink and agriculture-chemicals markets, were laying in wait. These nonsupermarket offerings were forecast to account for as much as 20 percent of the company's business by the mid-1980s.

The broad intent of this strategy was clear. With birthrates declining and population growth leveling off, the demographic trends that fueled P&G's ascent over the decades of the 1960s and 1970s were reversing. Given this shift, the company decided to look elsewhere to continue expanding at its previous rate.

The diversification drive also involved huge, unexplored risks. In many of its new fields, such as drugs and chemicals, the company had to take on formidable competitors that were not much impressed by P&G's recognized preeminence in packaged goods. Although the company boasted an unequaled marketing network for consumer products, many rivals doubted its ability to sell to institutions, doctors, and pharmacists.

Still, P&G had clearly decided that the competitive risks did not outweigh the potential rewards of its new product campaign, nor did they eclipse the company's need to find new avenues of growth.

Based on the article "P&G's New New-Product Onslaught," from the October 1, 1979, issue of *Business Week*.

Political Considerations

The direction and stability of political factors is a major consideration for managers in formulating company strategy. Political considerations define the legal and otherwise governing parameters in which the firm must or may wish to operate. Political constraints are placed on each company through fair-trade decisions, antitrust laws, tax programs, minimum wage legislation, pollution and pricing policies, administrative jawboning, and many other actions aimed at protecting the consumer and the environment. These laws, practices, and regulations are most commonly restrictive, and as a result, they tend to reduce a firm's potential profits. However, other political actions are designed to benefit and protect a company. Examples include patent laws, government subsidies, and product research grants. Thus, political forces are both a limitation and a benefit to the firms they influence.

Political activity may also have a significant impact on three additional governmental functions influencing a firm's remote environment.

Supplier Function. Government decisions regarding creation and accessibility of private businesses to government-owned natural resources and national stockpiles of agricultural products will profoundly affect the viability of some firms' strategies.

Customer Function. Government demand for products and services can create, sustain, enhance, or eliminate many market opportunities. For example, in the same way that the Kennedy administration's emphasis on landing a man on the moon spawned the demand for literally thousands of new products in the 1960s, the Carter administration's emphasis on developing synthetic fuels temporarily created a similar demand for new skills, technologies, and products in the 1980s. And the Reagan administration's priority on a strategic defense initiative ("Star Wars" defense) sharply accelerated the development of laser technologies.

Competitor Function. The government can operate as an almost unbeatable competitor in the marketplace. Thus, knowledge of its strategies gained through assessment of the remote environment can help a firm to avoid unfavorable confrontation with government as a competitor. For example, forecasts that government will increase the number of nuclear power plants or communication facilities might simultaneously serve as a retreat signal to direct private competitors and as an invitation to private producers of services or associated activities.

Businesses are greatly affected by government decisions, as shown in Strategy in Action 4–3. Thus, continual assessment of government strategizing will help individual firms to develop complementary plans that anticipate and optimize environmental opportunities.

Technological Considerations

The final set of considerations in the remote environment involves technological advancements. To avoid obsolescence and promote innovation, a firm must be aware of technological changes that might influence its industry. Creative technological adaptations can affect planning in that new products may be suggested or existing ones improved; manufacturing and marketing techniques may also be improved.

Strategy in Action 4–3
A Major Threat in the CPA Firm's Environment

"These are our own ideas and opinions, our private notes," says Robert Hermann, a tax manager with the accounting firm of Deloitte Haskins & Sells. "They are none of the IRS's business."

The Internal Revenue Service disagrees, however, and the result is a bitter controversy.

The notes in question are those in which auditors spell out any doubts they have about a client's tax position. Accountants have always considered these confidential. But now, they say, recent IRS aggressiveness in seeking these papers has undermined their relationships with their corporate clients and has threatened to damage the quality of financial reports.

Says William Raby, a partner in Touche Ross & Co., "We've seen a drying up of the willingness of clients to discuss or even show data to their auditors. And the bottom line is that it isn't leading to good financial reporting."

When preparing and auditing financial statements, accountants include a reserve for taxes that might be payable if the IRS investigates. A company may take an investment tax credit, for instance, although it realizes that the IRS could disagree. [The company's] memos, and those of its auditors, would spell out the arguments on each side.

But the tax credit would likely be just one of many such items, and the IRS typically sees only the grand total reserve. If [the IRS] had access to the internal documents, it could see a breakdown of all the uncertain areas.

"It's a trail to the sensitive issues on the tax return," says William T. Holloran, a New York City lawyer and accountant. He says accountants try to dream up the worst possible scenarios, but "if the IRS sees that you wondered about something, they may just say 'Gee, there must be something wrong with it.'"

An IRS official takes a different view: "We feel that the information might throw light on the correctness of a taxpayer return." He says the memos are necessary because corporations usually are more open with accountants than with the government, "and we can't stay with a company for an unlimited period of time" ferreting out information. "The tax system shouldn't be viewed as a game of hide and seek. If we can get the papers, we can make a determination [of tax liability] much quicker, and not waste the taxpayers' money."

Most experts say that the only answer may rest with the IRS. "We can only hope that the IRS won't go bananas in this area," says Holloran. "On a normal audit, they have to show restraint."

A technological innovation can have a sudden and dramatic effect on the environment of a firm. A breakthrough may spawn sophisticated new markets and products or significantly shorten the anticipated life of a manufacturing facility. Thus, all firms, and most particularly those in turbulent growth industries, must strive for an understanding both of the present state of technological advancement affecting their products and services and of probable future innovations. This quasi science of attempting to foresee advancements and estimate their probable impact on an organization's operations is known as *technological forecasting*.

Technological forecasting can help protect and improve the profitability of firms in growing industries. It alerts strategic managers to both impending challenges and promising opportunities. As examples: (1) advances in xerography were a key to Xerox's success but caused major difficulties for carbon paper manufacturers; and (2) the perfection of transistors changed the nature of competition in the radio and television industry, helping giants like RCA while seriously weakening smaller firms with resource commitments that required products to continue to be based on vacuum tubes.

The key to beneficial forecasting of technological advancement lies in accurately predicting future capabilities and probable future impacts. A comprehensive analysis of the effect of technological change involves study of the expected impact of new technologies on the remote environment, on the competitive business situation, and on the business–society interface. In recent years, forecasting in the last area has warranted particular attention. For example, as a consequence of increased concern over the environment, businesses must carefully investigate the probable effect of technological advances on quality-of-life factors, such as ecology, aesthetics, and public safety.

Operating Environment

The operating environment involves factors in the immediate competitive situation that provide many of the challenges a particular firm faces in attempting to attract or acquire needed resources or in striving to profitably market its goods and services. Among the most prominent of these factors are a firm's competitive position, customer profile, reputation among suppliers and creditors, and accessible labor market. The operating environment, also called the competitive or task environment, differs from the remote environment in that it is typically subject to much more influence or control by the firm. Thus, when they consider conditions in the operating environment, businesses can be much more proactive (as opposed to reactive) in strategic planning than they are when dealing with remote factors.

Competitive Position

By assessing its competitive position, a business improves its chances of designing strategies that optimize environmental opportunities.

Development of competitor profiles enables a firm to more accurately forecast both its short- and long-term growth and profit potentials. Although the exact criteria used in constructing a competitor's profile are largely determined by situational factors in the environment, the following are often included:

1. Market share.
2. Breadth of product line.
3. Effectiveness of sales distribution.
4. Proprietary and key-account advantages.
5. Price competitiveness.
6. Advertising and promotion effectiveness.
7. Location and age of facility.
8. Capacity and productivity.
9. Experience.
10. Raw material costs.
11. Financial position.
12. Relative product quality.
13. R&D advantages/position.
14. Caliber of personnel.
15. General image.[3]

Once appropriate criteria have been selected, they are subjectively weighted to reflect their relative importance to a firm's success. Next, the competitor being evaluated is rated on the criteria. The rankings are multiplied by the weightings, and the resulting weighted scores are summed to yield a numerical profile of the competing business, as shown in Figure 4–2.

The type of competitor profile suggested is limited by the subjectivity of the criteria selection, weighting, and evaluation approaches employed. Nevertheless, this process is of considerable value in helping a business to explicitly define its perception of its competitive position. Comparing profiles of the firm and its competitors can further aid managers in identifying specific factors that might make a competitor vulnerable to alternative strategies the firm might choose to implement.

Customer Profiles

Perhaps the most valuable result of analyzing the operating environment is an understanding of the composition of a firm's customers. In developing a profile of present and prospective customers, managers are better able to plan the strategic operations of the firm, anticipate changes in the size of

---

[3] These items were selected from a competitive position assessment matrix proposed by Charles W. Hofer and Dan Schendel, *Strategy Formulation: Analytical Concepts* (St. Paul, Minn.: West Publishing, 1978), p. 76.

Figure 4–2
Competitor profile

Key success factors	Weight	Rating†	Weighted score
Market share	.30	4	1.20
Price competitiveness	.20	3	.60
Facilities location	.20	5	1.00
Raw materials cost	.10	3	.30
Caliber of personnel	.20	1	.30
	1.00*		3.30

* The total of the weights must always equal 1.00.

† The rating scale suggested is as follows: very strong competitive position (5 points), strong (4), average (3), weak (2), very weak (1).

markets, and allocate resources supporting forecast shifts in demand patterns. Four principal types of information are useful in constructing a customer profile: geographic, demographic, psychographic, and buyer behavior, as illustrated in Figure 4–3.

Geographic. It is important to define the geographic area from which customers do or could come. Almost every product or service has some quality that makes it variably attractive to buyers from specific locations. Obviously, a successful regional manufacturer of snow skis in Wisconsin should think twice about investing in a wholesale distribution center in South Carolina. On the other hand, advertising by a major Myrtle Beach (South Carolina) hotel in the Milwaukee *Sun-Times* could significantly expand the hotel's geographically defined customer market.

Demographic. Demographic variables are most commonly used for differentiating groups of customers. The term refers to descriptive characteristics that can be used to identify present or potential customers. Demographic information (such as sex, age, marital status, income, and occupation) is comparatively easy to collect, quantify, and use in strategic forecasting, and it is the minimum data used as the basis of a customer profile.

Psychographic. Customer personality and lifestyle are often better predictors of purchasing behavior than geographic or demographic variables. In such situations, a psychographic study of customers is an important component of the total profile. Recent soft-drink advertising campaigns by Pepsi-Cola ("the Pepsi generation"), Coca-Cola ("catch the wave"), and 7UP ("America's turning 7UP") reflect strategic management's attention not only to demographics but also to the psychographic characteristics of their largest customer segment—physically active, group-oriented nonprofessionals.

Figure 4–3
Customer profile considerations

Type of information	Typical breakdowns
Geographic	
Region	Pacific; Mountain; West North Central; West South Central; East North Central; East South Central; South Atlantic; Middle Atlantic; New England
County size	A, B, C, D
City or SMSA size*	Under 5,000; 5,000–19,999; 20,000–49,999; 50,000–99,999; 100,000–249,999; 250,000–499,999; 500,000–999,999; 1,000,000–3,999,999; 4 million or over
Density	Urban, suburban, rural
Climate	Northern, Southern
Demographic	
Age	Under 6, 6–11, 12–17, 18–34, 35–49, 50–64, 65+
Sex	Male/female
Family size	1–2, 3–4, 5+ persons
Family life cycle	Young, single; young, married, no children; young, married, youngest child under 6; young, married, youngest child 6 or over; older, married, with children; older, married, no children under 18; older, single; other
Income	Under $5,000; $5,000–$10,000; etc.
Occupation	Professional and technical; managers, officials, and proprietors; clerical, sales; craft workers, supervisors; operatives; farmers; retired; students, homemakers; unemployed
Education	Grade school or less, some high school, graduated from high school, some college, graduated from college
Religion	Catholic, Protestant, Jewish, other
Race	Caucasian, Negro, Oriental, other
Nationality	American, British, French, German, Eastern European, Scandinavian, Italian, Spanish, Latin American, Middle Eastern, Japanese, and so on
Social class	Lower-lower, upper-lower, lower-middle, middle-middle, upper-middle, lower-upper, upper-upper
Psychographic	
Compulsiveness	Compulsive/noncompulsive
Gregariousness	Extrovert/introvert
Autonomy	Dependent/independent
Conservatism	Conservative/liberal/radical
Authoritarianism	Authoritarian/democratic
Leadership	Leader/follower
Ambitiousness	High achiever/low achiever
Buyer behavior	
Usage rate	Nonuser, light user, medium user, heavy user
Readiness stage	Unaware, aware, interested, intending to try, trier, regular buyer
Benefits sought	Economy, status, dependability
End use	Varies with the product
Brand loyalty	None, light, strong
Marketing-factor sensibility	Quality, price, service, advertising, sales promotion

* SMSA stands for standard metropolitan statistical area.

Source: Adapted from Philip Kotler, *Marketing Management* (Englewood Cliffs, N.J.: Prentice-Hall, 1972), p. 170.

Buyer Behavior.   Buyer behavior data can also be used in constructing a customer profile. This includes a multifaceted set of factors used to explain or predict some aspect of customers' behavior with regard to a product or service. As shown in Figure 4–3, information on buyer behavior (such as usage rate, benefits sought, and brand loyalty) can significantly aid in designing more accurate and profitably targeted strategies.

Suppliers and Creditors: Sources of Resources

Dependable relationships between a business firm and its suppliers and creditors are essential to the company's long-term survival and growth. A firm regularly relies on its suppliers for financial support, services, materials, and equipment. In addition, a business is occasionally forced to make special requests of its creditors and suppliers for such favors as quick delivery, liberal credit terms, or broken-lot orders. Particularly at these times, it is essential for a business to have an ongoing relationship with its suppliers and creditors.

In addition to the strength of a firm's relationships with suppliers and creditors, several other factors should be considered in assessing this aspect of the operating environment. With regard to its competitive position with suppliers, a firm should address the following questions:

1. Are suppliers' prices competitive? Do suppliers offer attractive quantity discounts? How costly are their shipping charges?
2. Are vendors competitive in terms of production standards? In terms of deficiency rates?
3. Are suppliers' abilities, reputation, and services competitive?
4. Are suppliers reciprocally dependent on the firm?

With regard to its position with its creditors, the following questions are among the most important for the strategizing firm:

1. Is stock fairly valued and willingly accepted as collateral?
2. Do potential creditors perceive the firm as having an acceptable record of past payment? A strong working capital position? Little or no leverage?
3. Are creditors' current loan terms compatible with the firm's profitability objectives?
4. Are creditors able to extend the necessary line of credit?

Answers to these and related questions help a business forecast availability of the resources it will need to implement and sustain its competitive strategies. Because quantity, quality, price, and accessibility of financial, human, and material resources are rarely ideal, assessment of suppliers and creditors is critical to an accurate evaluation of the firm's operating environment.

Personnel: Nature of the Labor Market

The ability to attract and hold capable employees is a prerequisite for a firm's success. However, the nature of a business's operating environment most often influences personnel recruitment and selection alternatives. Three factors most affect a firm's access to needed personnel: reputation as an employer, local employment rates, and ready availability of needed knowledge and skills.

Reputation.   A business's reputation within its operating environment is a major element in its long-term ability to satisfy personnel needs. A firm seen as permanent in the community, at least competitive in its compensation package, and concerned with employee welfare, as well as respected for its product or service and appreciated for its overall contribution to general welfare, is more likely to attract and retain valuable employees than is a rival firm that either exhibits fewer of these qualities or emphasizes one factor to the detriment of others.

Employment Rates.   Depending principally on the stage of growth of a business community, the readily available supply of skilled and experienced personnel may vary considerably. A new manufacturing firm seeking skilled employees in a vigorous and established industrialized community obviously faces a more difficult problem than would the same firm if it were to locate in an economically depressed area where other similar firms had recently cut back operations.

Availability.   Some people's skills are so specialized that they may be forced to relocate to secure appropriate jobs and the impressive compensations their skills commonly command. Examples include oil drillers, experienced chefs, technical specialists, and industry executives. A firm seeking to hire such an individual is said to have broad labor market boundaries; that is, the geographic area within which the firm might reasonably expect to attract qualified candidates is quite large. On the other hand, an individual with more common skills would be less likely to relocate from considerable distance to achieve modest economic or career advancement. Thus, the labor market boundaries are fairly limited for such occupational groups as unskilled laborers, clerical personnel, and retail clerks.

Emphasis on Environmental Factors

This chapter has described the remote environment as encompassing four components—economic, political, social, and technological—and the operating environment five factors— competitors, creditors, customers, labor markets, and suppliers. While these descriptions are generally accurate, they may give the false impression that the components and factors are easily identified, mutually exclusive, and equally applicable in all situations. In fact, forces in the external environment are so dynamic and interactive that the impact of any single element cannot be wholly disassociated from the impact of other elements. For example, are increases in OPEC oil prices the result of economic, political, social, or technological changes? Or, are a manufacturer's surprisingly good relations with suppliers a result of competitors', customers', creditors', or the supplier's own activities? The answer to both questions is probably that a number of forces in the external environment have combined to create the situation. Such is the case in most studies of the environment.

Strategic managers are frequently frustrated in their attempts to anticipate the environment's changing influences. Different external elements affect different strategies at different times and with varying strengths. The only certainty is that the impact of the remote and operating environment will be uncertain until a strategy is implemented. This disconcerting reality leads many managers, particularly in comparatively less powerful, smaller firms, to minimize long-term planning, which requires a commitment of resources. Instead, they favor more flexibility, allowing managers to adapt to new pressures from the environment. While such a decision has considerable merit for many firms, there is an associated trade-off: namely, that absence of a strong resource and psychological commitment to a proactive strategy effectively bars the firm from assuming a leadership role in its competitive environment.

There is a final difficulty in assessing the probable impact of remote and operating environments on the effectiveness of alternative strategies. This involves collecting information that can be analyzed to disclose predictable effects. Except in rare instances, it is virtually impossible for any single firm to anticipate the consequences of a change in the environment, for example, the precise effect on alternative strategies of a 2 percent increase in the national inflation rate, a 1 percent decrease in statewide unemployment, or the entry of a new competitor in a regional market.

However, there is a real advantage in assessing the potential impact of changes in the external environment. In this way, decision makers are better able to narrow the range of available alternatives and eliminate options that are clearly inconsistent with forecast opportunities. Environmental assessment seldom identifies the best strategy, but it characteristically leads to the elimination of all but the most promising alternatives.

Designing Opportunistic Strategies

The process of designing business strategies is multifaceted, complex, and often principally dependent on fairly subjective and intuitive impact assessments (see Strategy in Action 4–4 for an example). The process is multifaceted because the decision maker must investigate independent and interactive influences from both the remote and operating environments. Such studies must

Strategy in Action 4–4
A Coal Industry Perspective

For the coal industry, 1979 was a bleak year. Spare capacity was as high as 20 percent, or 150 million tons. Miners were out of work, and mines were closing. Coal profits were off by more than 50 percent.

However, one segment of the industry appeared on the verge of remarkable gains—coal companies owned by oil companies. Eleven oil companies owned 25 percent of all the coal in the country in 1979, and had the future of coal in their grip. Moreover, oil companies planned to increase their 22 percent production share in 1979 to 50 percent by 1985.

In the past, during periods of slack demand, it was common for small mines to close; when prices firmed up, the mines reopened. In 1978, however, the growing cost and complexity of federal regulations made many such comebacks too expensive for small mines. Approximately 1,000 companies had left the coal business since the mid-1960s—about half of them since 1977.

But if costly regulation and a slack market spelled trouble to the small mines, their impact on big companies was just the opposite. "What oil companies contribute to their coal subsidiaries is staying power," said Hiram E. Bond, president of ARCO Coal Company. In fact, there was little evidence that the industry's slump in 1978 slowed big oil's plan for coal. Most of the country's top oil companies had major coal expansion programs under way. Increasingly, oil company money, technology, and management skills set the pace for coal's growth.

One reason the oil companies were banking on coal was a firmly held belief that utilities, the major coal consumers, had little choice about the fuel they burned in new plants—it had to be coal. The companies also believed coal would be a major beneficiary of the problems of nuclear energy.

There were some problems. These included environmental laws, such as the Clean Air Act, and reclamation regulations. In addition, new leasing regulations for federal coal mines slowed the industry's growth. Skyrocketing transportation costs were also a factor. However, the most troubling industry problem was another touchy political issue—the growing tide of sentiment against the oil industry could lead to antitrust action against energy conglomerates.

Based on the article "The Oil Majors Bet on Coal," from the September 24, 1979, issue of *Business Week*.

be conducted to prepare any systematic or comprehensive strategic decision. The process is complex because environmental forces have both individual and interactive effects on business generally and variable effects on a given business depending on the unique situation. Finally, most strategies are developed from fairly subjective and intuitive assessments of information gathered on the environment. Limited objectivity is an understandable consequence in that historical trends alone cannot be used to accurately predict future events, given constant changes in competitive external environments.

Designing a strategy to optimize opportunities identified by assessing the business environment is a difficult task:

> It usually means questioning old methods, exploring unfamiliar environmental waters, facing up to an objective evaluation of strengths and weaknesses, forcing important changes on people in the firm and [on] organizational arrangements, and taking high risks with the firm's capital. Moreover, it has to be done in a world of rapid change, and it has to be done continuously.[4]

As a result of the multifaceted, complex, and subjective nature of corporate strategy formulation, strategic managers should give special emphasis to four major design recommendations when developing their firm's plans: issue selection, data collection, conducting environmental impact studies, and planning for flexibility.

Issue Selection

An initial task is to determine the issues most likely to be critical to the success of the strategy. The identification of these issues will help to focus and prioritize data collection efforts.

In a recent study involving more than 200 company executives, the respondents were asked to identify key planning issues in terms of their recently increasing importance to strategic success. As shown in Strategy in Action 4–5, competitive domestic trends, customer or end-user preferences, and technological trends were the issues they selected.

Data Selection

Managers gather much of the forecasting information used to design strategies in the regular pursuit of business activities, for example, reading business and government publications, discussing competitive conditions with sales managers and clients, and serving on community councils and committees. However, such personal data collection is subject to considerable bias in interpretation, and its validity is often difficult to document and verify. Therefore, it is beneficial to systematically collect pertinent data from public sources. Such data are readily available, inexpensive, and, in general, comparatively reliable. Public data sources include annual reports, business literature indexes, business periodicals and reference services, government publications, trade publications, stockbroker reports, and many others. While all of these

---

[4] George A. Steiner, *Top-Management Planning* (New York: Macmillan, 1969), pp. 238–39.

Strategy in Action 4–5
Key Planning Issues

	Issue	Percent of respondents indicating		
		Increase	*No change*	*Decrease*
1.	Competitive (domestic) trends	83.6	13.5	2.9
2.	Customer or end-user preferences	69.0	29.1	2.0
3.	Technological trends	71.4	25.6	3.0
4.	Diversification opportunities	61.7	30.3	8.0
5.	Worldwide or global competition	59.4	34.4	6.3
6.	Internal capabilities	55.4	40.2	4.4
7.	Joint venture opportunities	56.6	36.7	6.6
8.	Qualitative data	55.9	38.1	5.9
9.	General economic and business conditions	46.4	47.3	6.3
10.	Regulatory issues	42.8	51.2	6.0
11.	Supplier trends	26.0	69.1	5.0
12.	Reasons for past failures	27.6	62.3	10.1
13.	Quantitative data	36.8	40.7	22.5
14.	Past performance	27.3	51.2	21.5

Source: Adapted from V. Ramanujam, J. C. Camillus, and N. Venkatraman, "Trends in Strategic Planning," in *Strategic Planning and Management Handbook,* ed. W. R. King and D. I. Cleland (New York: Van Nostrand Reinhold, 1987), p. 615.

sources may be examined to detect general environmental trends, managers must carefully select from among them when constructing a strategic data base. Relevance, importance, manageability, accessibility, variability, and cost must be considered in selecting or generating data to be used.

Impact Studies

The nature and magnitude of the predicted impact of new strategic action is a second important consideration in designing opportunistic strategies. After forecasting data is selected, a business must conduct impact studies to determine the overall consequences of implementing available alternative strategies. In the process, the firm will transform environmental data into situation-specific environmental information. A typical impact study involves a system view in assessing probable effects on the firm's strengths and weaknesses, operating environment, competitive position, and likelihood of achieving corporate objectives, grand strategies, and mission. Although impact studies are predominately subjective and intuitive, businesses attempt to develop objective estimates whenever possible. Firms increasingly employ such techniques as exponential smoothing, time trends, and adaptive forecasting to increase the objectivity of data analysis.

Flexibility

A third important consideration in the design of strategies is the need to incorporate flexibility. Because forecasting environmental conditions is uncertain, decision makers enhance their chances of profitability if they strive for an optimal level of flexibility in their strategic plans. Several approaches to increasing such flexibility can be suggested:

1. State a strategy in general terms so that those implementing it have some discretion in terms of their unique situations.
2. Review strategies frequently.
3. Treat strategies as rules with exceptions so that an aspect of a strategy can be violated if such action can be justified.
4. Keep options open.

While flexibility in a strategic plan will lessen the plan's benefits by increasing costs, shortening planning and action horizons, and increasing internal uncertainty, an overly rigid stance in support of a particular strategy can be devastating to a firm faced with unexpected environmental turbulence.

Summary

The external environment of a business consists of two interrelated sets of variables that play a principal role in determining the opportunities, threats, and constraints a firm faces. Variables originating beyond and usually irrespective of any single firm's operating situation (political, economic, social, and technological forces) form the remote environment. Variables influencing a firm's immediate competitive situation (competitive position, customer profiles, suppliers and creditors, and the accessible labor market) constitute the operating environment. These two sets of forces provide many of the challenges faced by a particular firm attempting to attract or acquire needed resources and striving to profitably market its goods and services. Environmental assessment is more complicated for MNCs because multinationals must evaluate several environments simultaneously.

Designing corporate strategies that will enable a firm to effectively interact with a dynamic external environment is multifaceted, complex, and often principally dependent on fairly subjective and intuitive assessments. Nevertheless, assessments of a firm's external environment can provide a valuable planning base, especially when three major recommendations are followed:

1. Environmental data should be collected for a meaningful range of factors. The personal perceptions of strategic managers should be combined with data from public sources.
2. Impact studies should be undertaken to convert the data into relevant information used in determining the overall consequences for the firm of implementing the available alternative strategies.
3. Flexibility should be incorporated in the strategy to allow for unexpected variations from the environmental forecasts.

Thus, designing opportunistic strategies is based on the conviction that a company able to anticipate future business conditions will improve its performance and profitability. Despite the uncertainty and dynamic nature of the business environment, an assessment process that narrows, if not precisely defines, future expectations is of substantial value to strategic managers.

Questions for Discussion

1. Briefly describe two important recent changes in the remote external environment of U.S. business in each of the following areas:
   a. Economic.
   b. Political.
   c. Social.
   d. Technological.
2. Describe two major anticipated environmental changes that you forecast as having a major impact on the wholesale food industry in the next 10 years.
3. Develop a competitor profile for your college and the one geographically closest to it. Next, prepare a brief strategic plan to improve the competitive position of the weaker of the two schools.
4. Assume a competitively priced synthetic fuel is invented that could supply 25 percent of U.S. energy needs within 20 years. In what major ways might the external environment of U.S. business be changed?
5. With the help of your instructor, identify a local business that has enjoyed great growth in recent years. To what degree and in what ways do you think this firm's success resulted from taking advantage of favorable conditions in its external remote and operating environments?

Bibliography

Capon, N.; J. Farley, Jr.; and J. Hulbert. "International Diffusion of Corporate and Strategic Planning Practices." *Columbia Journal of World Business,* Fall 1980, pp. 5–13.

Channon, D. F., and M. Jalland. *Multinational Strategic Planning.* New York: AMACOM, 1978.

Conover, Horbart H. "Meeting the New Social Concerns." *Management World,* May 1977, pp. 25–27.

Contractor, F. J. "The Role of Licensing in International Strategy." *Columbia Journal of World Business,* Winter 1981, pp. 73–83.

Cox, Joan G. "Planning for Technological Innovation." *Long-Range Planning,* December 1977, pp. 40–44.

Davidson, W. H. *Global Strategic Management.* New York: John Wiley & Sons, 1982.

Dymsza, W. A. *Multinational Business Strategy.* New York: McGraw-Hill, 1972.

Fayerweather, J., and A. Kapoor. *Strategy and Negotiation for the International Corporation.* Cambridge, Mass.: Ballinger, 1976.

Gerstenfeld, Arthur. "Technological Forecasting." *Journal of Business* 44 (1971), pp. 10–18.

Healey, Dennis F. "Environmental Pressures and Marketing in the 1970s." *Long-Range Planning,* June 1975, pp. 41–45.

Hout, T.; M. Porter; and E. Rudden. "How Global Companies Win Out." *Harvard Business Review,* September–October 1982, pp. 98–108.

Kiser, J. W. "Tapping Eastern Bloc Technology." *Harvard Business Review,* March–April 1982, pp. 85–93.

Neubauer, F. Fredrick, and Norman B. Solomon. "Managerial Approach to Environmental Assessment." *Long-Range Planning,* April 1977, pp. 13–20.

Perry, P. T. "Mechanisms for Environmental Scanning." *Long-Range Planning,* June 1977, pp. 2–9.

Pfeffer, Jeffery, and Gerald Salancik. *The External Control of Organizations.* New York: Harper & Row, 1978.

Preble, John. "Corporate Use of Environmental Scanning." *University of Michigan Business Review,* September 1978, pp. 12–17.

Ronstadt, R., and R. Kramer. "Getting the Most out of Innovation Abroad." *Harvard Business Review,* March–April 1982, pp. 94–99.

Sadler, Philip. "Management and the Social Environment." *Long-Range Planning,* April 1975, pp. 18–26.

Steade, Richard. "Multinational Corporations and the Changing World Economic Order." *California Management Review,* Winter 1978, pp. 5–12.

Steiner, George A. *Top-Management Planning.* New York: Macmillan, 1969.

Turner, Robert C. "Should You Take Business Forecasting Seriously?" *Business Horizons,* April 1978, pp. 64–72.

Watson, C. M. "Counter Competition Abroad to Protect Home Markets." *Harvard Business Review,* January–February 1982, pp. 40–42.

Chapter 4 Cohesion Case Illustration

Environmental Assessment at Holiday Inns, Inc.

Environmental assessment at Holiday Inns, Inc., must first involve evaluation of the remote and operating environments of each business group. Afterward, these evaluations would be synthesized to determine the environmental situation facing the overall corporate enterprise. This Cohesion Case Illustration will briefly analyze the remote and operating environments of the key business groups using a tabular format. To aid in this analysis, a scale from +10 to −10 will be used to identify the degree to which each environmental factor represents an opportunity or threat in the business's environment.

Comparing the remote environments in Exhibit 1, Holiday Inns' most favorable opportunities appear in the three hospitality-related businesses: hotels, restaurants, and casinos. Social factors in the remote environment are strongly favorable for all three businesses. The remote environment presents a moderate opportunity for the steamship operation but is inconsequential for the products group. The major remote environment threats appear in relation to the Trailways bus operation.

Exhibit 2 examines the operating environments of each business group. The operating environments presenting the greatest opportunity are those of the hotel and casino groups. The similarity of their competitive advantages (existing or potential) and favorable opportunities suggest strong synergy between the two groups from a corporate perspective. The operating environment of freestanding restaurants appears favorable, with several dimensions suggesting limited but clearly exploitable opportunities. Delta Steamship encounters selectively favorable opportunities, while Trailways' operating environment presents several formidable threats.

From a corporate perspective, the remote and operating environment analyses identify factors suggesting that the greatest opportunities exist in hospitality-related businesses, and the most pressing threats face the Trailways bus operation.

Exhibit 1
Assessment of remote environment factors

Business	Economy	Political	Social	Technology
Hotels	Reduced vacation travel during recessions/energy costs (21,22) (−4)	Political stability of international locations (11) (−2)	Increasing leisure time/older population/single travelers and smaller families/baby boom now 25–40 years old (42) (+8)	Electronic and computer technology in reservations and control systems/satellite communication/labor-saving technologies (14,17) (+6)
Trailways	Less travel during recession but bus is a low-priced alternative means of transportation (27,28) (+1)	Safety regulations/no government ownership of terminals/deregulation of airline industry (−5)	All of the factors in above hotel block applicable here, though considerably less beneficial (42) (−2)	Labor-saving and cost-saving technology only minimal benefits, other transportation areas more affected (32) (−3)
Delta Steamship	Recession can hurt exports and imports/energy costs (−3)	Emergence of Third World markets/U.S. subsidies of U.S.-flag carriers and low-interest loans (+5)	Increasing concern for U.S. international trade effectiveness (38) (+1)	Labor-saving (LASH) and energy-saving technologies (37) (+3)
Freestanding restaurants	Recessions generally have a limited impact on family restaurants/energy costs less severe (+2)	Legal challenges to franchising (−1)	Increasing pattern of eating out/baby boom now 25–40/number of single-member households rising/women in work force (42) (+8)	Labor-saving and energy-saving improvements/food preparation technology (+4)
Casino gaming	Recessionary impact on leisure travel/energy costs (60) (−2)	Regulation of casino gambling/limited legal gaming markets (62) (−2)	All the factors mentioned in the hotel block above/increasing social acceptance of gaming (42,54,55) (+8)	Similar to hotel above though with less impact (+3)

Note: Italicized numbers in parentheses at the end of the comments refer to paragraph numbers in the Cohesion Case at the end of Chapter 1. Each comment is based on the information provided in the paragraphs identified in italics.

Exhibit 2
Assessment of operating environment factors

Business	Competition	Customers	Labor	Creditors	Suppliers
Hotel group	Substantial increase in the number of budget-chain competitors/ no immediate threat to HI's leadership position but gap is narrowing, especially with budget-conscious traveler (21) (+3)	1 out of 6 American travelers stayed at HIs in 1978/research shows HI to be the preference of 40 percent of traveling public—high but declining since 1975/ages 24–49 with +$20,000 incomes most frequent guest/increasing number of single travelers and women travelers (25 percent in 1979)/ steady demand for HI franchise, with over 60 percent of new franchise locations sought by current franchisees (21) (+6)	Adequate labor supply, although HI's labor-sensitive operating margins hurt by minimum wage increases (+2)	Strong capital structure, undervalued real estate and leadership position make credit readily available (66) (+5)	Gasoline cost for customers is rising, which begins to curtail travel (−2)
Trailways	Powerful competition from Greyhound on price, facilities, size, etc./increasing competition from other transportation sectors, such as airlines, trains, and package delivery services/intensive price-cost squeeze (27,28) (−6)	Customer profile quite different than typical HI guest, especially in income/limited gains in passenger miles since 1975/no strong customer loyalty (26) (−2)	Labor cost rising though some labor-saving technology improvements (−1)	Weak capital structure in highly competitive industry lessens available credit (−2)	Energy costs, especially fuel, rising significantly (−3)

Exhibit 2 (concluded)

Delta Steamship	Stiff competition from foreign cargo vessels in all routes/LASH technology improving relative position/major U.S.-flag carrier (37,39) (+2)	Primarily agriculture and manufacturing importers and exporters at both ends of route structure/strong in Gulf ports area (36) (+2)	Severely dependent on independent longshore workers/decreasing labor intensity via LASH technology (37,40) (−2)	Legislation access to U.S. government low-interest loans and cost subsidies (39) (+5)	Energy costs, especially fuel, rising significantly (−3)
Freestanding restaurants	Stiff competition from several nationwide chains, but Perkins' position in northern United States rather strong/expanding primary demand, which negates, to some extent, competitive impact/opportunities for additional acquisition (48,49) (+1)	Customer's profile quite similar to typical HI guest/family-oriented image/good brand identity in current geographic locations/trend of increased outside dining and more single households quite favorable/substantial franchise network and interest (43) (+5)	Nonskilled labor positions/labor intensive/adequate supply, though profit margins sensitive to minimum wage (+1)	Adequate capital structure and operating history for outside credit/HI corporate resources (66) (+2)	Rising energy costs in operating units and in food products (−2)
Casino gaming	Growing competition in each of the four legalized gambling markets in United States/but no dominant competitor overall/rapidly growing primary demand related to increased leisure time and aging population (62) (+5)	Customer profile very similar to typical HI guest/HI name, image, and reputation should prove quite beneficial/changing population demographics—baby boom age, single households, increasing leisure time—are strongly favorable (54) (+8)	Temporary labor shortages but benefit by HI link in hotel, food, and lodging side/rising labor costs (54) (−2)	Impressive profit potential but too early to tell/HI corporate resources (55,56) (+1)	Fuel-sensitive business and energy-intensive facilities (−3)

Note: Italicized numbers in parentheses at the end of the comments refer to paragraph numbers in the Cohesion Case at the end of Chapter 1.

5

Industry Analysis

Foreword

Harvard Professor Michael E. Porter's book *Competitive Strategy* propelled the concept of industry analysis into the foreground of strategic thought and business planning. The cornerstone of the book is the following article from the *Harvard Business Review* in which Porter emphasized five forces that shape industry competition. His well-defined analytical framework helps strategic managers to understand industry dynamics and to correctly anticipate the impact of remote factors on a firm's operating environment.

The Authors

Overview

The nature and degree of competition in an industry hinge on five forces: the threat of new entrants, the bargaining power of customers, the bargaining power of suppliers, the threat of substitute products or services (where applicable), and the jockeying among current contestants. To establish a strategic agenda for dealing with these contending currents and to grow despite them, a company must understand how they work in its industry and how they affect the company in its particular situation. This chapter will detail how these forces operate and suggest ways of adjusting to them, and, where possible, of taking advantage of them.

How Competitive Forces Shape Strategy

The essence of strategy formulation is coping with competition. Yet it is easy to view competition too narrowly and too pessimistically. While one sometimes hears executives complaining to the contrary, intense competition in an industry is neither coincidence nor bad luck.

Moreover, in the fight for market share, competition is not manifested only in the other players. Rather, competition in an industry is rooted in its underlying economics, and competitive forces exist that go well beyond the established combatants in a particular industry. Customers, suppliers, potential entrants, and substitute products are all competitors that may be more or less prominent or active depending on the industry.

The state of competition in an industry depends on five basic forces, which are diagramed in Figure 5–1. The collective strength of these forces determines the ultimate profit potential of an industry. It ranges from intense in industries like tires, metal cans, and steel, where no company earns spectacular returns on investment, to mild in industries like oil-field services and equipment, soft drinks, and toiletries, where there is room for quite high returns.

In the economists' "perfectly competitive" industry, jockeying for position is unbridled and entry to the industry very easy. This kind of industry structure, of course, offers the worst prospect for long-run profitability. The weaker the forces collectively, however, the greater the opportunity for superior performance.

Whatever their collective strength, the corporate strategist's goal is to find a position in the industry where his or her company can best defend itself against these forces or can influence them in its favor. The collective strength of the forces may be painfully apparent to all the antagonists; but to cope with them, the strategist must delve below the surface and analyze the sources of competition. For example, what makes the industry vulnerable to entry? What determines the bargaining power of suppliers?

Knowledge of these underlying sources of competitive pressure provides the groundwork for a strategic agenda of action. They highlight the critical strengths and weaknesses of the company, animate the positioning of the company in its industry, clarify the areas where strategic changes may yield the greatest payoff, and highlight the places where industry trends promise to hold the greatest significance as either opportunities or threats.

Understanding these sources also proves to be of help in considering areas for diversification.

Figure 5–1
Forces driving industry competition

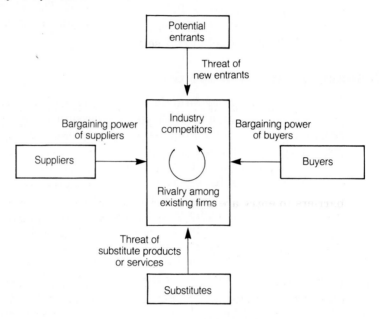

Contending Forces

The strongest competitive force or forces determine the profitability of an industry and so are of greatest importance in strategy formulation. For example, even a company with a strong position in an industry unthreatened by potential entrants will earn low returns if it faces a superior or a lower-cost substitute product—as the leading manufacturers of vacuum tubes and coffee percolators have learned to their sorrow. In such a situation, coping with the substitute product becomes the number one strategic priority.

Different forces take on prominence, of course, in shaping competition in each industry. In the ocean-going tanker industry the key force is probably the buyers (the major oil companies), while in tires it is powerful OEM buyers coupled with tough competitors. In the steel industry the key forces are foreign competitors and substitute materials.

Every industry has an underlying structure, or a set of fundamental economic and technical characteristics, that gives rise to these competitive forces. The strategist, wanting to position his company to cope best with its industry environment or to influence that environment in the company's favor, must learn what makes the environment tick.

This view of competition pertains equally to industries dealing in services and to those selling products. To avoid monotony in this article, I refer to both products and services as "products." The same general principles apply to all types of business.

A few characteristics are critical to the strength of each competitive force. They will be discussed in this section.

Threat of Entry

New entrants to an industry bring new capacity, the desire to gain market share, and often substantial resources. Companies diversifying through acquisition into the industry from other markets often leverage their resources to cause a shape-up, as Philip Morris did with Miller beer.

The seriousness of the threat of entry depends on the barriers present and on the reaction from existing competitors that the entrant can expect. If barriers to entry are high and a newcomer can expect sharp retaliation from the entrenched competitors, obviously he will not pose a serious threat of entering.

There are six major sources of barriers to entry:

1. Economies of Scale.   These economies deter entry by forcing the aspirant either to come in on a large scale or to accept a cost disadvantage. Scale economies in production, research, marketing, and service are probably the key barriers to entry in the mainframe computer industry, as Xerox and GE sadly discovered. Economies of scale can also act as hurdles in distribution, utilization of the sales force, financing, and nearly any other part of a business.

2. Product Differentiation.   Brand identification creates a barrier by forcing entrants to spend heavily to overcome customer loyalty. Advertising, customer service, being first in the industry, and product differences are among the factors fostering brand identification. It is perhaps the most important entry barrier in soft drinks, over-the-counter drugs, cosmetics, investment banking, and public accounting. To create high fences around their business, brewers couple brand identification with economies of scale in production, distribution, and marketing.

3. Capital Requirements.   The need to invest large financial resources in order to compete creates a barrier to entry, particularly if the capital is required for unrecoverable expenditures in up-front advertising or R&D. Capital is necessary not only for fixed facilities but also for customer credit, inventories, and absorbing start-up losses. While major corporations have the financial resources to invade almost any industry, the huge capital requirements in certain fields, such as computer manufacturing and mineral extraction, limit the pool of likely entrants.

4. Cost Disadvantages Independent of Size.   Entrenched companies may have cost advantages not available to potential rivals, no matter what their size and attainable economies of scale. These advantages can stem from the effects of the learning curve (and of its first cousin, the experience curve), proprietary technology, access to the best raw materials sources, assets purchased at preinflation prices, government subsidies, or favorable locations. Sometimes cost advantages are legally enforceable, as they are through patents. (For an analysis of the much-discussed experience curve as a barrier to entry, see Strategy in Action 5–1.)

Strategy in Action 5–1
The Experience Curve as an Entry Barrier

In recent years, the experience curve has become widely discussed as a key element of industry structure. According to this concept, unit costs in many manufacturing industries (some dogmatic adherents say in all manufacturing industries) as well as in some service industries decline with "experience," or a particular company's cumulative volume of production. (The experience curve, which encompasses many factors, is a broader concept than the better-known learning curve, which refers to the efficiency achieved over a period of time by workers through much repetition.)

The causes of the decline in unit costs are a combination of elements, including economies of scale, the learning curve for labor, and capital–labor substitution. The cost decline creates a barrier to entry because new competitors with no "experience" face higher costs than established ones, particularly the producer with the largest market share, and have difficulty catching up with the entrenched competitors.

Adherents of the experience curve concept stress the importance of achieving market leadership to maximize this barrier to entry, and they recommend aggressive action to achieve it, such as price cutting in anticipation of falling costs in order to build volume. For the combatant that cannot achieve a healthy market share, the prescription is usually, "Get out."

Is the experience curve an entry barrier on which strategies should be built? The answer is: not in every industry. In fact, in some industries, building a strategy on the experience curve can be potentially disastrous. That costs decline with experience in some industries is not news to corporate executives. The

Continued on Page 129

Strategy in Action 5–1 *(concluded)*

significance of the experience curve for strategy depends on what factors are causing the decline.

A new entrant may well be more efficient than the more experienced competitors; if it has built the newest plant, it will face no disadvantage in having to catch up. The strategic prescription, "You must have the largest, most efficient plant," is a lot different from "You must produce the greatest cumulative output of the item to get your costs down."

Whether a drop in costs with cumulative (not absolute) volume erects an entry barrier also depends on the sources of the decline. If costs go down because of technical advances known generally in the industry or because of the development of improved equipment that can be copied or purchased from equipment suppliers, the experience curve is not an entry barrier at all—in fact, new or less experienced competitors may actually enjoy a cost advantage over the leaders. Free of the legacy of heavy past investments, the newcomer or less experienced competitor can purchase or copy the newest and lowest-cost equipment and technology.

If, however, experience can be kept proprietary, the leaders will maintain a cost advantage. But new entrants may require less experience to reduce their costs than the leaders needed. All this suggests that the experience curve can be a shaky entry barrier on which to build a strategy.

While space does not permit a complete treatment here, I want to mention a few other crucial elements in determining the appropriateness of a strategy built on the entry barrier provided by the experience curve:

The height of the barrier depends on how important costs are to competition compared with other areas like marketing, selling, and innovation.

The barrier can be nullified by product or process innovations leading to a substantially new technology and thereby creating an entirely new experience curve. New entrants can leapfrog the industry leaders and alight on the new experience curve, to which those leaders may be poorly positioned to jump.

If more than one strong company is building its strategy on the experience curve, the consequences can be nearly fatal. By the time only one rival is left pursuing such a strategy, industry growth may have stopped and the prospects of reaping the spoils of victory long since evaporated.

5. Access to Distribution Channels.   The new boy on the block must, of course, secure distribution of his product or service. A new food product, for example, must displace others from the supermarket shelf via price breaks, promotions, intense selling efforts, or some other means. The more limited the wholesale or retail channels are and the more that existing competitors have these tied up, obviously the tougher that entry into the industry will be. Sometimes this barrier is so high that, to surmount it, a new contestant must create its own distribution channels, as Timex did in the watch industry in the 1950s.

6. Government Policy.   The government can limit or even foreclose entry to industries with such controls as license requirements and limits on access to raw materials. Regulated industries like trucking, liquor retailing, and freight forwarding are noticeable examples; more subtle government restrictions operate in fields like ski-area development and coal mining. The government also can play a major indirect role by affecting entry barriers through controls such as air and water pollution standards and safety regulations.

The potential rival's expectations about the reaction of existing competitors also will influence its decision on whether to enter. The company is likely to have second thoughts if incumbents have previously lashed out at new entrants or if:

The incumbents possess substantial resources to fight back, including excess cash and unused borrowing power, productive capacity, or clout with distribution channels and customers.

The incumbents seem likely to cut prices because of a desire to keep market shares or because of industrywide excess capacity.

Industry growth is slow, affecting its ability to absorb the new arrival and probably causing the financial performance of all the parties involved to decline.

Changing Conditions.   From a strategic standpoint there are two important additional points to note about the threat of entry.

First, it changes, of course, as these conditions change. The expiration of Polaroid's basic patents on instant photography, for instance, greatly reduced its absolute cost entry barrier built by proprietary technology. It is not surprising that Kodak plunged into the market. Product differentiation in printing has all but disappeared. Conversely, in the auto industry economies of scale increased enormously with post–World War II automation and vertical integration—virtually stopping successful new entry.

Second, strategic decisions involving a large segment of an industry can have a major impact on the conditions determining the threat of entry. For example, the actions of many U.S. wine producers in the 1960s to step up product introductions, raise advertising levels, and expand distribution nationally surely strengthened the entry roadblocks by raising economies of scale and making access to distribution channels more difficult. Similarly, decisions by members of the recreational vehicle industry to vertically integrate in order to lower costs have greatly increased the economies of scale and raised the capital costs barriers.

Powerful Suppliers and Buyers

Suppliers can exert bargaining power on participants in an industry by raising prices or reducing the quality of purchased goods and services. Powerful suppliers can thereby squeeze profitability out of an industry unable to recover cost increases in its own prices. By raising their prices, soft-drink concentrate producers have contributed to the erosion of profitability of bottling companies because the bottlers, facing intense competition from powdered mixes, fruit drinks, and other beverages, have limited freedom to raise their prices accordingly. Customers likewise can force down prices, demand higher quality or more service, and play competitors off against each other—all at the expense of industry profits.

The power of each important supplier or buyer group depends on a number of characteristics of its market situation and on the relative importance of its sales or purchases to the industry compared with its overall business.

A *supplier* group is powerful if:

It is dominated by a few companies and is more concentrated than the industry it sells to.

Its product is unique or at least differentiated, or if it has built up switching costs. Switching costs are fixed costs buyers face in changing suppliers. These arise because, among other things, a buyer's product specifications tie it to particular suppliers, it has invested heavily in specialized ancillary equipment or in learning how to operate a supplier's equipment (as in computer software), or its production lines are connected to the supplier's manufacturing facilities (as in some manufacture of beverage containers).

It is not obliged to contend with other products for sale to the industry. For instance, the competition between the steel companies and the aluminum companies to sell to the can industry checks the power of each supplier.

It poses a credible threat of integrating forward into the industry's business. This provides a check against the industry's ability to improve the terms on which it purchases.

The industry is not an important customer of the supplier group. If the industry is an important customer, suppliers' fortunes will be closely tied to the industry, and they will want to protect the industry through reasonable pricing and assistance in activities like R&D and lobbying.

A *buyer* group is powerful if:

It is concentrated or purchases in large volumes. Large-volume buyers are particularly potent forces if heavy fixed costs characterize the industry—as they do in metal containers, corn refining, and bulk chemicals, for example—which raise the stakes to keep capacity filled.

The products it purchases from the industry are standard or undifferentiated. The buyers, sure that they can always find alternative suppliers, may play one company against another, as they do in aluminum extrusion.

The products it purchases from the industry form a component of its product and represent a significant fraction of its cost. The buyers are likely to shop for a favorable price and purchase selectively. Where the product sold by the industry in question is a small fraction of buyers' costs, buyers are usually much less price sensitive.

It earns low profits, which create great incentive to lower its purchasing costs. Highly profitable buyers, however, are generally less price sensitive (that is, of course, if the item does not represent a large fraction of their costs).

The industry's product is unimportant to the quality of the buyers' products or services. Where the quality of the buyers' products is very much affected by the industry's product, buyers are generally less price sensitive. Industries in which this situation obtains include oil-field equipment, where a malfunction can lead to large losses; and enclosures for electronic medical and test instruments, where the quality of the enclosure can influence the user's impression about the quality of the equipment inside.

The industry's product does not save the buyer money. Where the industry's product or service can pay for itself many times over, the buyer is rarely price sensitive; rather, he is interested in quality. This is true in services like investment banking and public accounting, where errors in judgment can be costly and embarrassing, and in businesses like the logging of oil wells, where an accurate survey can save thousands of dollars in drilling costs.

The buyers pose a credible threat of integrating backward to make the industry's product. The Big Three auto producers and major buyers of cars have often used the threat of self-manufacture as a bargaining lever. But sometimes an industry engenders a threat to buyers that its members may integrate forward.

Most of these sources of buyer power can be attributed to consumers as a group as well as to industrial and commercial buyers; only a modification of the frame of reference is necessary. Consumers tend to be more price sensitive if they are purchasing products that are undifferentiated, expensive relative to their incomes, and of a sort where quality is not particularly important.

The buying power of retailers is determined by the same rules, with one important addition. Retailers can gain significant bargaining power over manufacturers when they can influence consumers' purchasing decisions, as they do in audio components, jewelry, appliances, sporting goods, and other goods.

Strategic Action.   A company's choice of suppliers to buy from or buyer groups to sell to should be viewed as a crucial strategic decision. A company can improve its strategic posture by finding suppliers or buyers who possess the least power to influence it adversely.

Most common is the situation of a company being able to choose whom it will sell to—in other words, buyer selection. Rarely do all the buyer groups a company sells to enjoy equal power. Even if a company sells to a single industry, segments usually exist within that industry that exercise less power (and that are therefore less price sensitive) than others. For example, the replacement market for most products is less price sensitive than the overall market.

As a rule, a company can sell to powerful buyers and still come away with above-average profitability only if it is a low-cost producer in its industry or if its product enjoys some unusual, if not unique, features. In supplying large customers with electric motors, Emerson Electric earns high returns because its low cost position permits the company to meet or undercut competitors' prices.

If the company lacks a low cost position or a unique product, selling to everyone is self-defeating because the more sales it achieves, the more vulnerable it becomes. The company may have to muster the courage to turn away business and sell only to less potent customers.

Buyer selection has been a key to the success of National Can and Crown, Cork and Seal. They focus on the segments of the can industry where they can create product differentiation, minimize the threat of backward integration, and otherwise mitigate the awesome power of their customers. Of course, some industries do not enjoy the luxury of selecting "good" buyers.

As the factors creating supplier and buyer power change with time or as a result of a company's strategic decisions, naturally the power of these groups rises or declines. In the ready-to-wear clothing industry, as the buyers (department stores and clothing stores) have become more concentrated and control has passed to large chains, the industry has come under increasing pressure and suffered falling margins. The industry has been unable to differentiate its product or engender switching costs that lock in its buyers enough to neutralize these trends.

Substitute Products

By placing a ceiling on prices it can charge, substitute products or services limit the potential of an industry. Unless it can upgrade the quality of the product or differentiate it somehow (as via marketing), the industry will suffer in earnings and possibly in growth.

Manifestly, the more attractive the price–performance trade-off offered by substitute products, the firmer the lid placed on the industry's profit potential. Sugar producers confronted with the large-scale commercialization of high-fructose corn syrup, a sugar substitute, are learning this lesson today.

Substitutes not only limit profits in normal times, they also reduce the bonanza an industry can reap in boom times. In 1978 the producers of fiberglass insulation enjoyed unprecedented demand as a result of high energy costs and severe winter weather. But the industry's ability to raise prices was tempered by the plethora of insulation substitutes, including cellulose, rock wool, and styrofoam. These substitutes are bound to become an even stronger force once the current round of plant additions by fiberglass insulation producers has boosted capacity enough to meet demand (and then some).

Substitute products that deserve the most attention strategically are those that (a) are subject to trends improving their price–performance trade-off with the industry's product or (b) are produced by industries earning high profits. Substitutes often come rapidly into play if some development increases competition in their industries and causes price reduction or performance improvement.

Jockeying for Position

Rivalry among existing competitors takes the familiar form of jockeying for position—using tactics like price competition, product introduction, and advertising slugfests. Intense rivalry is related to the presence of a number of factors:

Competitors are numerous or are roughly equal in size and power. In many U.S. industries in recent years foreign contenders, of course, have become part of the competitive picture.

Industry growth is slow, precipitating fights for market share that involve expansion-minded members.

The product or service lacks differentiation or switching costs, which lock in buyers and protect one combatant from raids on its customers by another.

Fixed costs are high or the product is perishable, creating strong temptation to cut prices. Many basic materials businesses, like paper and aluminum, suffer from this problem when demand slackens.

Capacity is normally augmented in large increments. Such additions, as in the chlorine and vinyl chloride businesses, disrupt the industry's supply-demand balance and often lead to periods of overcapacity and price cutting.

Exit barriers are high. Exit barriers, like very specialized assets or management's loyalty to a particular business, keep companies competing even though they may be earning low or even negative returns on investment. Excess capacity remains functioning, and the profitability of the healthy competitors suffers as the sick ones hang on. If the entire industry suffers from overcapacity, it may seek government help—particularly if foreign competition is present.

The rivals are diverse in strategies, origins, and "personalities." They have different ideas about how to compete and continually run head-on into each other in the process.

As an industry matures, its growth rate changes, resulting in declining profits and (often) a shakeout. In the booming recreational vehicle industry of the early 1970s, nearly every producer did well; but slow growth since then has eliminated the high returns, except for the strongest members, not to mention many of the weaker companies. The same profit story has been played out in industry after industry—snowmobiles, aerosol packaging, and sports equipment are just a few examples.

An acquisition can introduce a very different personality to an industry, as has been the case with Black & Decker's takeover of McCullough, the producer of chain saws. Technological innovation can boost the level of fixed costs in the production process, as it did in the shift from batch to continuous-line photo finishing in the 1960s.

While a company must live with many of these factors—because they are built into industry economics—it may have some latitude for improving matters through strategic shifts. For example, it may try to raise buyer's switching costs or increase product differentiation. A focus on selling efforts in the fastest-growing segments of the industry or on market areas with the lowest fixed costs can reduce the impact of industry rivalry. If it is feasible, a company can try to avoid confrontation with competitors having high exit barriers and can thus sidestep involvement in bitter price cutting.

Formulation of Strategy

Once the corporate strategist has assessed the forces affecting competition in his industry and their underlying causes, he can identify his company's strengths and weaknesses. The crucial strengths and weaknesses from a strategic standpoint are the company's posture vis-à-vis the underlying causes of each force. Where does it stand against substitutes? Against the sources of entry barriers?

Then the strategist can devise a plan of action that may include (1) positioning the company so that its capabilities provide the best defense against the competitive force; and/or (2) influencing the balance of the forces through strategic moves, thereby improving the company's position; and/or (3) anticipating shifts in the factors underlying the forces and responding to them, with the hope of exploiting change by choosing a strategy appropriate for the new competitive balance before opponents recognize it. Each strategic approach will now be considered in turn.

Positioning the Company

The first approach takes the structure of the industry as given and matches the company's strengths and weaknesses to it. Strategy can be viewed as building defenses against the competitive forces or as finding positions in the industry where the forces are weakest.

Knowledge of the company's capabilities and of the causes of the competitive forces will highlight the areas where the company should confront competition and where to avoid it. If the company is a low-cost producer, it may choose to confront powerful buyers while it takes care to sell them only products not vulnerable to competition from substitutes.

The success of Dr Pepper in the soft-drink industry illustrates the coupling of realistic knowledge of corporate strengths with sound industry analysis to yield a superior strategy. Coca-Cola and Pepsi-Cola dominate Dr Pepper's industry, where many small concentrate producers compete for a piece of the action. Dr Pepper chose a strategy of avoiding the largest-selling drink segment, maintaining a narrow flavor line, forgoing the development of a captive bottler network, and marketing heavily. The company positioned itself so as to be least vulnerable to its competitive forces while it exploited its small size.

In the $11.5 billion soft-drink industry, barriers to entry in the form of brand identification, large-scale marketing, and access to a bottler network are enormous. Rather than accept the formidable costs and scale economies in having its own bottler network—that, following the lead of the Big Two and of 7UP—Dr Pepper took advantage of the different flavor of its drink to "piggyback" on Coke and Pepsi bottlers who wanted a full line to sell to customers. Dr Pepper coped with the power of these buyers through extraordinary service and other efforts to distinguish its treatment of them from that of Coke and Pepsi.

Many small companies in the soft-drink business offer cola drinks that thrust them into head-to-head competition against the majors. Dr Pepper, however, maximized product differentiation by maintaining a narrow line of beverages built around an unusual flavor.

Finally, Dr Pepper met Coke and Pepsi with an advertising onslaught emphasizing the alleged uniqueness of its single flavor. This campaign built strong brand identification and great customer loyalty. Helping its efforts was the fact that Dr Pepper's formula involved lower raw materials cost, which gave the company an absolute cost advantage over its major competitors.

There are no economies of scale in soft-drink concentrate production, so Dr Pepper could prosper despite its small share of the business (6 percent). Thus, Dr Pepper confronted competition in marketing but avoided it in product line and in distribution. This artful positioning combined with good implementation has led to an enviable record in earnings and in the stock market.

Influencing the Balance

When dealing with the forces that drive industry competition, a company can devise a strategy that takes the offensive. This posture is designed to do more than merely cope with the forces themselves; it is meant to alter their causes.

Innovations in marketing can raise brand identification or otherwise differentiate the product. Capital investments in large-scale facilities or vertical integration affect entry barriers. The balance of forces is partly a result of external factors and partly in the company's control.

Exploiting Industry Change

Industry evolution is important strategically because evolution, of course, brings with it changes in the sources of competition. In the familiar product life-cycle pattern, for example, growth rates change, product differentiation is said to decline as the business becomes more mature, and the companies tend to integrate vertically.

These trends are not so important in themselves; what is critical is whether they affect the sources of competition. Consider vertical integration. In the maturing minicomputer industry, extensive vertical integration, both in manufacturing and in software development, is taking place. This very significant trend is greatly raising economies of scale as well as the amount of capital necessary to compete in the industry. This in turn is raising barriers to entry and may drive some smaller competitors out of the industry once growth levels off.

Obviously, the trends carrying the highest priority from a strategic standpoint are those that affect the most important sources of competition in the industry and those that elevate new causes to the forefront. In contract aerosol packaging, for example, the trend toward less product differentiation is now dominant. It has increased buyers' power, lowered the barriers to entry, and intensified competition.

The framework for analyzing competition can also be used to predict the eventual profitability of an industry. In long-range planning the task is to examine each competitive force, forecast the magnitude of each underlying cause, and then construct a composite picture of the likely profit potential of the industry.

The outcome of such an exercise may differ a great deal from the existing industry structure. Today, for example, the solar heating business is populated by dozens and perhaps hundreds of companies, none with a major market position. Entry is easy, and competitors are battling to establish solar heating as a superior substitute for conventional methods.

The potential of this industry will depend largely on the shape of future barriers to entry, the improvement of the industry's position relative to substitutes, the ultimate intensity of competition, and the power captured by buyers and suppliers. These characteristics will in turn be influenced by such factors as the establishment of brand identities, significant economies of scale or experience curves in equipment manufacture wrought by technological change, the ultimate capital costs to compete, and the extent of overhead in production facilities.

The framework for analyzing industry competition has direct benefits in setting diversification strategy. It provides a road map for answering the extremely difficult question inherent in diversification decisions: "What is the potential of this business?" Combining the framework with judgment in its application, a company may be able to spot an industry with a good future before this good future is reflected in the prices of acquisition candidates.

Multifaceted Rivalry

Corporate managers have directed a great deal of attention to defining their businesses as a crucial step in strategy formulation. Numerous authorities have stressed the need to look beyond product to function in defining a business, beyond national boundaries to potential international competition, and beyond the ranks of one's competitors today to those that may become competitors tomorrow. As a result of these urgings, the proper definition of a company's industry or industries has become an endlessly debated subject.

One motive behind this debate is the desire to exploit new markets. Another, perhaps more important, motive is the fear of overlooking latent sources of competition that someday may threaten the industry. Many managers concentrate so single-mindedly on their direct antagonists in the fight for market share that they fail to realize that they are also competing with their customers and their suppliers for bargaining power. Meanwhile, they also neglect to keep a wary eye out for new entrants to the contest or fail to recognize the subtle threat of substitute products.

The key to growth—even survival—is to stake out a position that is less vulnerable to attack from head-to-head opponents, whether established or new, and less vulnerable to erosion from the direction of buyers, suppliers, and substitute goods. Establishing such a position can take many forms—solidifying relationships with favorable customers, differentiating the product either substantively or psychologically through marketing, integrating forward or backward, or establishing technological leadership.

Questions for Discussion

1. Choose a specific industry and, relying solely on your impressions, evaluate the impact of the five forces that drive competition in that industry.
2. Repeat your analysis in question 1 but this time refer to published sources to provide more objective information on which to base your conclusions. (Hint: The appendix to Chapter 7 provides a helpful list of sources.)

3. Choose an industry in which you would like to compete. Use the five-forces method of analysis to explain why that industry is attractive to you.

4. Many businesses neglect industry analysis. When does this hurt them; when does it not?

5. The model below depicts industry forces analysis as a funnel that focuses on remote-factor analysis as a means of better understanding the impact of factors in the operating environment. Do you agree with this model? If not, how would you improve it?

6. Who in an organization should be responsible for industry analysis? Suppose there is no strategic planning department.

Bibliography

Caves, R. E., and M. E. Porter. "From Entry Barriers to Mobility Barriers: Conjectural Decisions and Contrived Deterrence to New Competition." *Quarterly Journal of Economics* 91 (1976), pp. 421–34.

Elzinga, K. G. "The Restructuring of the U.S. Brewing Industry." *Industrial Organization Review* 1 (1973), pp. 101–14.

Koch, J. V. "Industry Market Structure and Industry Price-Cost Margins." *Industrial Organization Review* 2 (1974), pp. 186–93.

Porter, M. E. "The Structure within Industries' and Companies' Performance." *Review of Economics and Statistics* 61 (1979), pp. 214–27.

Scherer, F. M. *Industrial Market Structure and Economic Performance.* 2nd ed. Skokie, Ill.: Rand McNally, 1980.

Weber, J. A. "Market Structure Profile Analysis and Strategic Growth Opportunities." *California Management Review* 20 (1977), pp. 34–46.

Chapter 5 Cohesion Case Illustration

Industry Analysis at Holiday Inns, Inc.

Industry analysis is a useful aid to the strategic management process at Holiday Inns, Inc. Each of Holiday Inns' business units must understand how the five basic competitive forces work in their industries and how they affect the business in its particular situation. In doing this, strategists are better prepared to establish an agenda for dealing with these contending forces. One business group—hotels—will be used to illustrate industry analysis at Holiday Inns, Inc. The technique is also necessary for the strategic management of each of Holiday Inns' remaining groups. Readers are encouraged to apply industry analysis to one or more of the other business groups.

Exhibit 1 is a diagram of basic forces driving competition in the lodging industry. It is useful to assess these forces to understand their relative influence on the lodging industry and ultimately to provide a basis for charting Holiday Inns' strategic course.

Threats of/Barriers to Entry. The lodging industry has created several strong barriers to entry. *Economies of scale* have been built via the existence of large, franchised networks for each of the major chains. This allows cost sharing in marketing, research, training, and technological services (like reservation systems). Interestingly, these networks have also facilitated the emergence of *product differentiation* as a barrier to entry. Brand identity and customer loyalty, particularly for firms like Holiday Inns, has been strongly established within the lodging industry. *Capital requirements,* particularly when the need for a network of locations is so important, is a substantial barrier to entry. Franchising has been one way to overcome this barrier, although the proliferation of franchises has lessened the viability of this strategy for newcomers to the industry. *Knowledge* of how to operate in the industry has become increasingly important as operating complexity increases. This in turn is becoming an entry barrier. *Access to distribution channels,* particularly in the sense of controlling prime locations (such as proximity to airports, downtown business centers, resorts, etc.) can create a substantial barrier to entry in several specific locations.

While entry barriers are increasing in this industry, the 1970s witnessed several entrants that overcame the barriers, particularly in the budget segment of the industry (e.g., Days Inn, La Quinta). Numerous individual investors aided this entrance as franchises. In the 1980s there appear to be potentially

Exhibit 1
Forces driving lodging-industry competition

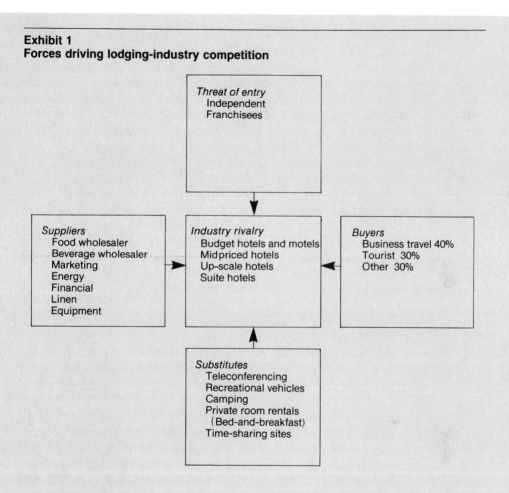

successful entrance strategies in the high-priced end of the industry. Predominantly located in large cities or resort locations, these "destination" entrants are successfully building positions in the industry by offering elaborate, expensive service to a narrow clientele.

Suppliers.   Typical *suppliers* to the lodging industry include equipment manufacturers, linen suppliers, food and beverage wholesalers, energy sources, financial suppliers and "people" resources. Generally, these suppliers are rather fragmented and do not offer unique products. Overall, there is very little threat of forward integration. Labor sources are generally not unionized, and the skill level required for entry positions is minimal. Training is provided by the industry. Finally, the lodging industry is usually an important, steady customer for most products and services offered by these suppliers. Therefore, the lodging industry is generally quite powerful relative to its suppliers.

Buyers.   The lodging industry is relatively powerful in relation to its *buyers*. First, buyers are primarily individuals, relatively small groups, and organizations—there is limited *concentration* of buying power. In some ways the service offered—bed, shower, TV, phone, food and beverage—can be seen as undifferentiated. Realistically, however, lodging services *are differentiated* by level of service, location of facilities, marketing efforts, brand identification, and the capacity of facilities (banquets, etc.). There is very little threat of backward integration. While buyers are fragmented, buyer power has manifest itself to some extent via the emergence of greater industry segmentation. To a sizable buyer segment—family businesses, salespeople on fixed allowances, families on limited budgets—lodging accommodations can represent a significant part of their "cost." Standard accommodation, not excess quality, is the key to the needs of these groups. Their "collective" power has led to the emergence of numerous chains providing budget accommodations.

Substitutes.   The services deserving the greatest strategic attention as potential *substitute products* are improving their price–performance trade-off with current lodging services, particularly when the services are produced by industries earning high profits. Teleconferencing and telecommunication are examples of this type of emerging potential substitute. Business and government employees, a major component of the lodging industry's customer base, have frequent travel needs (e.g., to attend meetings, call on people, demonstrate products). As satellite-based teleconferencing and telecommunications technology become steadily less expensive, they represent potentially cost-effective alternatives to travel and lodging services in some situations. Several major lodging firms, most notably Holiday Inns, have made significant commitments to expanding their teleconferencing capability so that this threat actually becomes a service advantage for their lodging network.

Competitive Rivalry.   Several factors are associated with intense *rivalry among competitors* in the lodging industry. Competitors have become numerous in virtually every segment of the lodging industry. While Holiday Inns is still recognized as the industry leader and has the largest number of rooms, other competitors have grown much more rapidly in the last 10 years. For example, Best Western actually has more locations in its system than does Holiday Inns.

Industry growth has slowed, particularly during the recession of 1981–82. Yet expansion-minded competitors are quite active, which should rapidly precipitate major market-share fights. The services offered, while somewhat differentiated, generally do not involve "switching costs" that tie buyers to one particular competitor.

Fixed costs (debt service and overhead) are high in the lodging industry, and the product ("one room-night") is *very* perishable in that it cannot be retained in inventory if it is not rented. This could create a strong temptation to cut prices if the capacity of lodging facilities expands too fast. Exit barriers can intensify the problem—who wants to buy a poorly performing motel? Industry participants have increasingly built their properties to purposely plan for office or condominum conversion so that exit options are greater.

The five-forces method of analysis suggests industry rivalry is the critical force shaping industry competition. Teleconferencing is emerging as the most important *potential* substitute. Neither suppliers nor buyers are very powerful, and barriers to entry are generally high. Increasing segmentation of buyers has increased industry rivalry and in some ways allowed selected entrants to successfully overcome entry barriers.

6

Evaluating the Multinational Environment

Strategic Considerations for Multinational Firms

Special complications confront a firm involved in international operations. Multinational corporations (MNCs) headquartered in one country with subsidiaries in others experience difficulties understandably associated with operating in two or more distinctly different competitive arenas.

Awareness of the strategic opportunities and threats posed and faced by MNCs is important to planners in almost every domestic U.S. industry. Among U.S.-headquartered corporations that receive more than 50 percent of their annual profits from foreign operations are Citicorp, the Coca-Cola Company, Exxon Corporation, the Gillette Company, IBM, Otis Elevator, and Texas Instruments. In fact, according to 1983 statistics, the 100 largest U.S. multinationals earned an average of 37 percent of their operating profits abroad. Equally impressive is the impact of foreign-based multinationals that operate in the United States. Their direct "foreign investment" in America now exceeds $70 billion, with Japanese, West German, and French firms leading the way. The extent of this foreign influence is evident in Strategy in Action 6–1.

Understanding the myriad and sometimes subtle nuances of competing in international markets or against multinational firms is rapidly becoming a prerequisite competency for strategic managers. Therefore, this section will focus on the nature, outlook, and operations of MNCs.

Strategy in Action 6–1
Multinational Corporation Ownership Test

In this test, you go down the alphabet and pick out the products that are foreign owned.

A   Airwick, Alka-Seltzer antacid, Aim toothpaste.
B   Baskin Robbins ice cream, Bactine antiseptic, Ball Park Franks.
C   Certain-Teed, Capitol records, Castrol oils.
D   Deer Park sparking water, Dove soap, Dunlop tires.
E   ENO antacids, Eureka vacuum cleaners, Ehler spices.
F   Four Roses whisky, French's mustard, First Love dolls.
G   Good Humor ice cream, Garrard turntables, Grand Trunk Railroad.
H   Humpty Dumpty magazine, Hires Root Beer, Hills Brothers coffee.
I   Imperial margarine, Instant potato mix, Indian Head textiles.
J   Juvena cosmetics, Jaeger sportswear, Jade cosmetics.
K   Knox gelatine, Kool cigarettes, Keebler cookies.
L   Libby's fruits and vegetables, *Look* magazine, Lifebuoy soap.
M   Magnavox, Massey-Ferguson tractors, Mr. Coffee.
N   Norelco appliances, Nescafé coffee, New Yorker Hotel.
O   Ovaltine drink mix, One-a-Day vitamins.
P   Panasonic, Pop Shoppes, Pepsodent toothpaste.
Q   Nestlé Quik chocolate mix, Quasar television sets, Quadra-Bar sedatives.
R   Ray-O-Vac batteries, Rinso, Rona Barret's gossip magazines.
S   Scripto pens, Seven Seas salad dressings, Slazenger tennis balls.
T   Tetley tea, Tic Tac Breath fresheners, Taster's Choice instant coffee.
U   Underwood typewriters, Urise antiseptics, Ultra Tears eye lotion.
V   Valium tranquilizers, Vogue pipe tobacco, Vim detergent.
W   Wish-Bone salad dressings, Wisk detergent, White Motor trucks.
X   Xam clock radios, Xylocaine salves, Xylee plastics.
Y   Yardley cosmetics, Yale locks, Yashica cameras.
Z   Zesta crackers, Zig-Zag cigarette papers, Zestatabs vitamins.

Answer: All of the companies (A through Z) are foreign owned.

Development of an MNC

The evolution of a multinational company often entails progressively involved strategies. The first strategy entails export–import activity but minimal effect on existing management orientation or product lines. The second levels involves foreign licensing and technology transfer but still little change in management or operation. The third level of strategy is characterized by direct investment in overseas operations, including manufacturing plants. This level requires large capital outlays as well as management effort in the development of international skills. At this point, domestic operations continue to dominate company policy, but the firm is commonly categorized as a true MNC. The most involved strategy is indicated by a substantial increase in foreign investment, with foreign assets comprising a significant portion of total assets. The company begins to emerge as a global enterprise with world approaches to production, sales, finance, and control.

While some firms downplay their multinational nature—so as never to appear distracted from their domestic operations—others highlight their international intentions. For example, General Electric's formal statement of mission and business philosophy includes the following commitment:

> To carry on a diversified, growing, and profitable worldwide manufacturing business in electrical apparatus, appliances, and supplies, and in related materials, products, systems, and services for industry, commerce, agriculture, government, the community, and the home.

A similar worldwide orientation is evident at IBM, which operates in 125 countries, conducts business in 30 languages and more than 100 currencies, and has 23 major manufacturing facilities in 14 different countries.

Why Companies Internationalize

The past 30 years has seen a dramatic decline in the technological advantage once enjoyed by the United States. In the late 1950s, over 80 percent of the world's major innovations were first introduced in the United States. By 1965 this figure had declined to 55 percent, and the decline continues today. On the other hand, France has made impressive advances in electric traction, nuclear power, and aviation. West Germany is a proclaimed leader in chemicals and pharmaceuticals, precision and heavy machinery, heavy electrical goods, metallurgy, and surface transport equipment. Japan leads in optics, solid-state physics, engineering, chemistry, and process metallurgy. Eastern Europe and the Soviet Union, the so-called COMECON (Council for Mutual Economic Assistance) countries, generate 30 percent of annual worldwide patent applications. However, the United States can regain some of its lost competitive advantages. Through internationalization U.S. firms can often reap benefits from emerging industries and evolutionary technologies developed abroad.

Multinational development makes sense as a competitive weapon in many situations. Direct penetration of foreign markets can drain vital cash flows from a foreign competitor's domestic operations. The resulting lost opportunities, reduced income, and limited production can impair the competitor's ability to invade U.S. markets. A case in point is the strategic action of IBM, which moved to establish a position of strength in the Japanese mainframe computer industry before two key competitors, Fiyitsue and Hitachi, could gain dominance. Once it had achieved an influential market share, IBM worked to deny its Japanese competitors the vital cash and production experience they needed to invade the U.S. market.[1]

Considerations prior to Internationalization

To begin their internationalizing activities, businesses are advised to take four steps:[2]

Scan the International Situation. Scanning includes reading journals and patent reports and checking other printed sources—as well as meeting people at scientific–technical conferences and/or in-house seminars.

Make Connections with Academia and Research Organizations. Enterprises active in overseas R&D often pursue work-related projects with foreign academics and sometimes form consulting agreements with faculty members.

Increase the Company's International Visibility. Common methods of attracting attention include participation in technological trade fairs, circulation of brochures illustrating company products and inventions, and hiring technology–acquisition consultants.

Undertake Cooperative Research Projects. Some multinational enterprises engage in joint research projects to broaden their contacts, reduce expenses, diminish the risk for each partner, or forestall entry of a competitor into the market.

In a similar vein, external and internal assessments may be conducted before a firm enters international markets.[3] External assessment involves

---

[1] C. M. Watson, "Counter Competition Abroad to Protect Home Markets," *Harvard Business Review,* January–February 1982, p. 40.

[2] R. Ronstadt and R. Kramer, "Getting the Most out of Innovation Abroad," *Harvard Business Review,* March–April 1982, pp. 94–99.

[3] J. Fayweather and A. Kapoor, *Strategy and Negotiation for the International Corporation* (Cambridge, Mass.: Ballinger, 1976).

careful examination of critical international environmental features with particular attention to the status of the host nation in such areas as economic progress, political control, and nationalism. Expansion of industrial facilities, balance of payments, and improvements in technological capabilities over the past decade should provide some idea of the host nation's economic progress. Political status can be gauged by the host nation's power in and impact on international affairs.

Internal assessment involves identification of the basic strong points of a company's present operations. These strengths are particularly important in international operations because they are often the elements valued most by the host nation and thus offer significant bargaining leverage. Both resource strengths and global capabilities must be analyzed. The resources to be examined in particular include technical and managerial skills, capital, labor, and raw materials. The global capability components include assessing the effectiveness of proposed product delivery and financial management systems.

A firm that gives serious consideration to internal and external assessment is Business International Corporation, which recommends that seven broad categories of factors be considered. As shown in Strategy in Action 6–2, these

Strategy in Action 6–2
Checklist of Factors to Consider in Choosing a Foreign Manufacturing Site

The following considerations were drawn from an 88-point checklist developed by Business International Corporation.

Economic factors:
1. Size of GNP and projected rate of growth.
2. Foreign exchange position.
3. Size of market for the company's products; rate of growth.
4. Current or prospective membership in a customs union.

Political factors:
5. Form and stability of government.
6. Attitude toward private and foreign investment by government, customers, and competition.
7. Practice of favored versus neutral treatment for state industries.
8. Degree of antiforeign discrimination.

Continued on Page 149

Strategy in Action 6–2 *(concluded)*

Geographic factors:

9. Efficiency of transport (railways, waterways, highways).
10. Proximity of site to export markets.
11. Availability of local raw materials.
12. Availability of power, water, gas.

Labor factors:

13. Availability of managerial, technical, and office personnel able to speak the language of the parent company.
14. Degree of skill and discipline at all levels.
15. Presence or absence of militant or Communist-dominated unions.
16. Degree and nature of labor voice in management.

Tax factors:

17. Tax rate trends (corporate and personal income, capital, withholding, turnover, excise, payroll, capital gains, customs, and other indirect and local taxes).
18. Joint tax treaties with home country and others.
19. Duty and tax drawbacks when imported goods are exported.
20. Availability of tariff protection.

Capital source factors:

21. Cost of local borrowing.
22. Local availability of convertible currencies.
23. Modern banking systems.
24. Government credit aids to new businesses.

Business factors:

25. State of marketing and distribution system.
26. Normal profit margins in the company's industry.
27. Competitive situation in the firm's industry; do cartels exist?
28. Availability of amenities for expatriate executives and families.

categories include economic, political, geographic, labor, tax, capital source, and business factors.

Complexity of the Multinational Environment

Multinational strategic planning is more complex than such purely domestic planning. There are at least five contributing factors:

1. The multinational faces multiple political, economic, legal, social, and cultural environments as well as various rates of change within each of them.

2. Interactions between the national and foreign environments are complex because of national sovereignty issues and widely differing economic and social conditions.

3. Geographical separation, cultural and national differences, and variations in business practices all tend to make communication between headquarters and the overseas affiliates difficult.

4. Multinationals face extreme competition because of differences in industry structures.

5. Multinationals are confronted by various international organizations, such as the European Economic Community, the European Free Trade Area, and the Latin American Free Trade Area, that restrict a firm's selection of its competitive strategies.

Indications of how these factors contribute to increased complexity in strategic planning and management are provided in Figure 6–1.

Control Problems for the Multinational Firm

An inherent complicating factor for many international firms is that financial policies of the multinational are typically designed to further the goals of the parent company with a minimum of attention paid to the goals of the host countries. This built-in bias creates conflict between the different parts of the organization, between the whole organization and its home and host countries, and between the home and host countries themselves. The conflict is accentuated by various schemes used to shift earnings from one country to another to avoid taxes, minimize risk, or achieve other objectives.

Different financial environments also make normal standards of company behavior concerning disposition of earnings, sources of finance, and the structure of capital more problematic. Thus, the performance of multinational divisions becomes increasingly difficult to measure.

In addition, important differences in measurement and control systems often exist. Fundamental to the concept of planning is a well-conceived, future-oriented approach to decision making based on accepted procedures and methods of analysis. Consistent approaches to planning throughout an organization are needed for effective review and evaluation by corporate headquarters. Such planning is complicated by differences in accounting conventions among countries, by attitudes about work measurement, and by different government requirements for disclosure of information.

Although such problems are more an aspect of the multinational environment than they are consequences of poor management, the problems are often most effectively reduced through increased attention to strategic management. Such planning aids in coordinating and integrating the company's future direction, objectives, and policies around the world. It enables the company to

Figure 6–1
Differences between U.S. and multinational operations that affect strategic management

Factor	U.S. operations	International operations
Language	English used almost universally	Local language must be used in many situations
Culture	Relatively homogeneous	Quite diverse, both between countries and within a country
Politics	Stable and relatively unimportant	Often volatile and of decisive importance
Economy	Relatively uniform	Wide variations among countries and between regions within countries
Government interference	Minimal and reasonably predictable	Extensive and subject to rapid change
Labor	Skilled labor available	Skilled labor often scarce, requiring training or redesign of production methods
Financing	Well-developed financial markets	Poorly developed financial markets. Capital flows subject to government control
Market research	Data easy to collect	Data difficult and expensive to collect
Advertising	Many media available; few restrictions	Media limited; many restrictions; low literacy rates rule out print media in some countries
Money	U.S. dollar used universally	Must change from one currency to another; changing exchange rates and government restrictions are problems
Transportation/ communication	Among the best in the world	Often inadequate
Control	Always a problem. Centralized control will work	A worse problem. Centralized control won't work. Must walk a tightrope between overcentralizing and losing control through too much decentralizing
Contracts	Once signed, are binding on both parties, even if one party makes a bad deal	Can be avoided and renegotiated if one party becomes dissatisfied
Labor relations	Collective bargaining; can lay off workers easily	Often cannot lay off workers; may have mandatory worker participation in management; workers may seek change through political process rather than collective bargaining
Trade barriers	Nonexistent	Extensive and very important

Source: R. G. Murdick, R. C. Moor, R. H. Eckhouse, and T. W. Zimmerer, *Business Policy: A Framework for Analysis,* 4th ed. (Columbus, Ohio: Grid, 1984), p. 275.

anticipate and better prepare for change. It facilitates the creation of programs to deal with worldwide developments. Finally, it helps the management of overseas affiliates become more actively involved in setting goals and in developing means to more effectively utilize the enterprise's total resources.

Multinational Strategic Planning

It should be evident from the previous sections that, as a company begins competing in the international marketplace, strategic decisions become increasingly complex and multidimensional. A manager cannot view the international operations as a set of independent decisions.[4] Rather, a manager is faced with trade-off decisions considering multiple products, country environments, resource sourcing options, corporate and subsidiary capabilities, and strategic options.[5]

Two recent trends, the globalization of industries and the increased activism of stakeholders, further add to this complexity of strategic planning for the multinational firm.[6] *Globalization* refers to a strategy of approaching worldwide markets with a standardized product. Such markets are most commonly created by end-consumers preferring a lower-priced, standardized product over higher-priced, customized products and by multinational corporations using their worldwide operations to compete in local markets.[7] *Stakeholder activism* refers to demands placed on the company by each foreign environment, principally foreign governments. This section provides a basic framework in which to analyze and better understand strategic decisions in this complex environment.

Multidomestic Industries and Global Industries

Michael E. Porter has developed a framework to view the basic strategic alternatives of a firm competing internationally.[8] The starting point of the analysis is understanding the industry or industries in which the firm competes. International industries can be characterized along a continuum from multidomestic to global.

Multidomestic Industries. A multidomestic industry is one in which the competition within the industry is essentially segmented from country to country. Thus, although multinational corporations are involved in the industry, competition in a country occurs independent of competition in other countries. Examples of such industries include retailing, insurance, and consumer finance.

---

[4] Yoram Wind and Susan Douglas, "International Portfolio Analysis and Strategy: The Challenge of the 80s," *Journal of International Business Studies,* Fall 1981, pp. 69–82.

[5] Thomas H. Naylor, "The International Strategy Matrix," *Columbia Journal of World Business,* Summer 1985, pp. 11–19.

[6] Balaj S. Chakravarthy and Howard V. Perlmutter, "Strategic Planning for a Global Business," *Columbia Journal of World Business,* Summer 1985, pp. 3–10.

[7] Theodore Levitt, "The Globalization of Markets," *Harvard Business Review,* September–October 1982, p. 92; and T. Hout, M. E. Porter, and E. Rudden, "How Global Companies Win Out," *Harvard Business Review,* September–October 1982, pp. 98–108.

[8] Michael E. Porter, "Changing Patterns of International Competition," *California Management Review* 28, no. 2 (Winter 1986), pp. 9–40.

In a multidomestic industry, the subsidiaries of an MNC should be managed as distinct entities; that is, each subsidiary should be rather autonomous, having independent decision-making authority to respond to local market conditions. Thus, in a multidomestic industry, an international strategy actually becomes the sum of the strategies developed by subsidiaries operating in different countries. The primary distinctions between a domestic firm and the multinational firm competing in a multidomestic industry are decisions related to what countries the company competes in and to how it conducts business abroad.

Factors determining the degree to which a market is multidomestic include:[9]

The need for customized products to meet the tastes or preferences of local customers.

A very fragmented industry with many competitors in each national market.

The lack of economies of scale in the functional activities of the business.

Distribution channels unique in each country.

A low technological dependence of each subsidiary on R&D provided by corporation.

Global Industries.   A global industry is one in which competition within the industry crosses national borders. A firm's strategic moves in one country can be significantly affected by its competitive position in another country. In fact, competition occurs on a world basis. Examples of global industries include commercial aircraft, automobiles, mainframe computers, and electronic consumer equipment.

In such industries, a multinational firm must link its subsidiaries together, maximizing its capabilities through a worldwide strategy. This necessitates a higher degree of centralized decision making in corporate headquarters so that trade-off decisions across subsidiaries can be made. Factors influencing the creation of global markets include:[10]

The presence of economies of scale in functional activities of the business.

A high level of R&D expenditures on products that require more than one market to recover development costs.

Predominantly multinational companies in the industry, who expect the same consistent product and service across markets.

Homogeneous product needs, which reduce the requirement of customizing the product for each market.

A small group of global competitors in the industry.

A low level of trade and foreign direct investment regulation.

---

[9] Yves Doz and C. K. Prahalad, "Patterns of Strategic Control within Multinational Corporations," *Journal of International Business Studies*, Fall 1984, pp. 55–72.

[10] Gary Harvel and C. K. Prahalad, "Managing Strategic Responsibility in the MNC," *Strategic Management Journal* 4 (1983), pp. 341–51.

The Multinational Challenge

Although industries can be characterized by the global–multidomestic distinction, few "pure" cases of either exist. Thus, a multinational competing in a global industry must, to some degree, also be responsive to local market conditions. Similarly, the multinational firm competing in a multidomestic industry cannot totally ignore opportunities to utilize intracorporate resources in competitive positioning. The question then becomes one of deciding which corporate functional activities should be performed where and what degree of coordination should exist between them.

Location and Coordination of Functional Activities.   Typical functional activities of a business include purchases of input resources, operations, research and development, marketing and sales, and after-sale service. A multinational corporation has a wide range of possible location options for each of these activities and must decide which set of activities will be performed in how many and which locations. A multinational corporation may desire each location to perform each activity, or it may have the activity centered in one location to serve the organization worldwide. For example, research and development may be centralized in one facility to serve the entire organization.

The multinational corporation must also decide the degree to which these activities are to be coordinated with each other across different countries. Coordination can be extremely low, allowing each location to perform each activity autonomously. Conversely, coordination can be extremely high, with the activities in different locations tightly linked together. For example, the Coca-Cola Company tightly coordinates R&D and marketing worldwide to offer a standardized brand name, concentrate formula, market positioning, and advertising theme. However, manufacturing is more adaptive to each location, with the artificial sweetener and packaging differing across countries.[11]

Location and Coordination Issues.   Figure 6–2 presents some of the issues related to the critical dimensions of location and coordination in international strategic planning. It also shows the different functional activities performed by the organization for each dimension. Given that a firm has a wide array of location and coordination options, Figure 6–2 highlights the different issues that address these basic options. For example, for the service activity, a company must decide where after-sale service should be performed throughout the world and the extent to which the service should be standardized.

Addressing these issues for a particular firm depends on the nature of the industry and the type of international strategy pursued by the firm. As dis-

---

[11] John A. Quelch and Edward J. Hoff, "Customizing Global Marketing," *Harvard Business Review,* May–June 1986, pp. 59–68.

Figure 6–2
Location and coordination issues by functional activity

Functional activity	Location issues	Coordination issues
Operations	Location of production facilities for components	Networking of international plants
Marketing	Product line selection	Commonality of brand name worldwide
	Country (market) selection	Coordination of sales to multinational accounts
		Similarity of channels and product positioning worldwide
		Coordination of pricing in different countries
Service	Location of service organization	Similarity of service standards and procedures worldwide
Research and development	Number and location of R&D centers	Interchange among dispersed R&D centers
		Developing products responsive to market needs in many countries
		Sequence of product introductions around the world
Purchasing	Location of the purchasing function	Managing suppliers located in different countries
		Transferring market knowledge
		Coordinating purchases of common items

Source: Adapted from Michael E. Porter, "Changing Patterns of International Competition," *California Management Review* 28, no. 2 (Winter 1986), pp. 9–40.

cussed earlier, the industry can be characterized along a continuum between multidomestic at one extreme and global at the other. In a multidomestic industry, competition occurs within each country; consequently, little coordination of functional activities across countries may be necessary. However, as the industry becomes increasingly global, the firm must begin to coordinate an increasing number of functional activities in order to effectively compete across countries.

International Strategy Options.   Figure 6–3 presents the basic international strategies derived from considering the location and coordination dimensions. If the firm is operating in a multidomestic industry, choosing a country-centered strategy implies low coordination of functional activities and geographical dispersion of organization activities. This allows each subsidiary to closely monitor the local market conditions it faces and the freedom to respond competitively.

A high coordination and geographical concentration of the multinational's activities results from choosing a pure global strategy. Although some activities, such as after-sale service, may need to be located in each market, the activities need to be tightly controlled so that standardized performance occurs

Figure 6–3
International strategy options

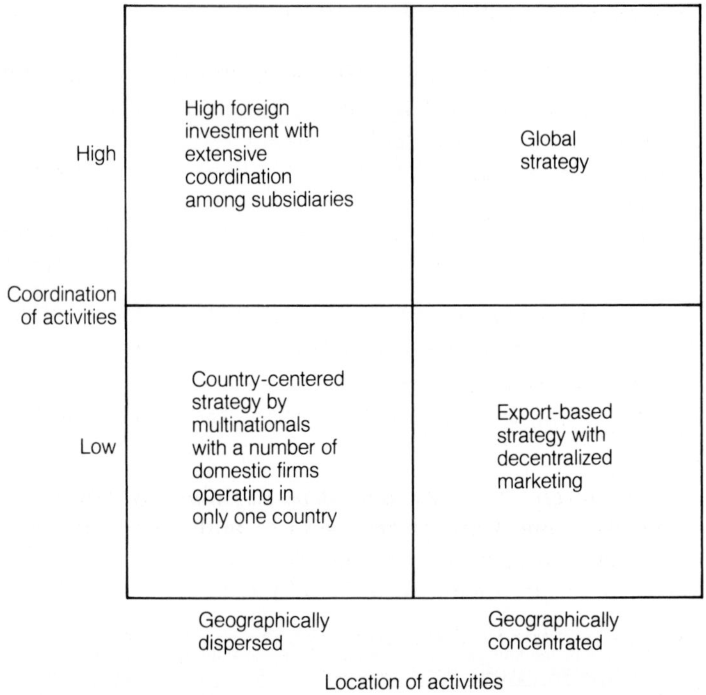

	Geographically dispersed	Geographically concentrated
High	High foreign investment with extensive coordination among subsidiaries	Global strategy
Low	Country-centered strategy by multinationals with a number of domestic firms operating in only one country	Export-based strategy with decentralized marketing

Coordination of activities

Location of activities

Source: Adapted from Michael E. Porter, "Changing Patterns of International Competition," *California Management Review* 28, no. 2 (Winter 1986), pp. 9–40.

worldwide. For example, IBM expects the same high level of marketing support and service for its customers, regardless of their location.

The final two types of strategies are a high foreign investment with extensive coordination among subsidiaries and an export-based strategy with decentralized marketing. These two strategies can represent the choice to remain at a particular stage, such as an exporter, or they can represent transition strategies as a multinational moves to a global strategy.

Multinationalization of the Corporate Mission[12]

Few strategic decisions bring about a more radical departure from the existing direction and operations of a company than the decision to expand internationally. Multinationalization subjects a company to a radically redefined and challenging set of environmentally determined opportunities, constraints, and risks. To prevent the company's direction from being dictated by these external

---

[12] The material in this section is taken from John A. Pearce II and Kendall Roth, "Multinationalization of the Corporate Mission," in press.

factors, top management must reassess the corporation's fundamental purpose, philosophy, and strategic intentions prior to multinationalization, thus ensuring that these basic values will continue as decision criteria in proactive planning.

Caterpillar Tractor's 1986 decline in market share and profitability highlight the purpose and need for multinationalization of a mission statement. Caterpillar's reversal can be primarily attributed to the strength of the U.S. dollar, in that the strong dollar made Caterpillar's products relatively more expensive in a global market. However, the impact of the dollar on Caterpillar's operations was anticipated and considered in declaring its long-term commitments. As shown in Strategy in Action 6–3, Caterpillar's corporate mission states that:

1. Subsidiaries should be located wherever in the world it is most economically advantageous to do so from a long-term standpoint.
2. Facility operations should be planned with the long term in mind in order to minimize the impact of sudden changes in the local work force and economy.

Adherence to these commitments helped synchronize the strategic and tactical decisions Caterpillar made in addressing the problems associated with the current currency imbalance. In the absence of such guidelines, Caterpillar actions could have possibly included:

Relocating facilities to gain short-term competitive production advantages.

Shifting production schedules radically throughout global operations regardless of the resultant impact on host country environments.

These actions would have redistributed production to weak-currency production locations, thereby enhancing Caterpillar's competitive pricing capabilities. However, they were not consistent with the more compelling motivations of the mission statement, which were to promulgate Caterpillar's commitment to high-quality products, stable operations, and corporate social responsibility. Consequently, irrespective of environmental aberrations, Caterpillar's mission provided for the corporation's broader, long-term strategic consistency.

The development of the corporate mission progresses through stages during the life of a company. At a company's inception and early stages of development, the mission is often the proprietary knowledge of the entrepreneur, who alone understands why the company exists and what purposes it serves—and this may be sufficient. As the company grows, it reaches a stage at which more formal mechanisms are required to coordinate increasingly complex and diverse organizational units. At this stage the mission statement needs to be made explicit so that it can be precisely communicated to organizational claimants.

For the remainder of this chapter, we will focus on a third developmental stage, at which the nature or character of the corporate mission is altered to encourage and encompass multinational expansion. A second-stage mission statement is usually designed with a domestic perspective, which does not recognize the added dimensions inherent in multinationalization. Thus, we will now look at the content of the domestic mission statement to determine appropriate modifications for a multinational corporation (MNC) that can help to ensure the resultant mission statement will continue to provide the necessary framework for strategic decision processes.

Strategy in Action 6–3
Mission Statement of Caterpillar Tractor Company

Business Purpose

The overall purpose of Caterpillar is to enhance the long-term interests of those who own the business—the shareholders.

This in no way diminishes the strong and legitimate claims of employees, dealers, customers, suppliers, governments, and others whose interests touch upon our own—nor, indeed, of the public at large. Nor is this to assert that profit should be maximized in any short-term framework of months, or even years, at the expense of other valid considerations.

Rather, it is to say we attempt to take a long-range view of things. We believe we can best serve the interests of shareholders and the long-term profitability of the enterprise by fair, honest, and intelligent actions with respect to all our constituencies.

With this in mind, our business aims are as follows:

1. Maintain corporate real growth at a rate not less than in the past, remain financially strong, and maximize long-term return on common stock equity.
2. Follow product and sourcing strategies that best utilize Caterpillar's strengths and resources . . . and that are consistent with users' needs and world economic, political, and social conditions.
3. Provide customers a total value—in terms of product quality and product support—that will maximize profit on their investment, as compared with competitive alternatives.
4. Work with suppliers, and those who sell our products, in upgrading their capabilities—to the end that each is the best available when judged by appropriate criteria.
5. Make wise and efficient use of energy and natural resources, and seek substitutes for those in critically short supply.
6. Remember that management is an acquired skill, not an intuitive art—and work continuously at improving the practice of management by objectives and judgment by results.

Continued on Page 159

Strategy in Action 6–3 *(concluded)*

7. Enhance our reputation for quality by pursuing excellence in all we do—in the belief that such is not only the best way to operate this business but also a key to personal satisfaction and happiness.

8. Improve our pursuit of goals, principles, and philosophies contained in this document.

Corporate Facilities

Caterpillar prefers to locate facilities wherever in the world it is most economically advantageous to do so, from a long-term standpoint.

Decisions as to location of facilities will, of course, consider such conventional factors as proximity to sources of supply, transportation, and sales opportunities; possibilities for volume production and resulting economies of scale; and availability of energy sources and a trained or trainable work force. Also considered will be political and fiscal stability, demonstrated governmental attitudes, industrial development plans, and other factors normally included in defining the local investment or business "climate."

We desire to provide functional, safe, attractive, efficient facilities that are harmonious with national modes. They are to be compatible with local environmental considerations, complement public planning, and reflect Caterpillar's commitment to conserve energy and other scarce resources.

Facility operations should be planned with the long term in mind, in order to minimize the impact of sudden change on the local work force and economy.

Source: Excerpted from "A Code of Worldwide Business Conduct and Operating Principles," Caterpillar Tractor Company.

The MNC Mission Statement

Expanding across national borders to secure new market or production opportunities may be initially viewed as consistent with a company's growth objectives as outlined in its existing mission statement. However, as multinationalization occurs, the direction of a company is inherently altered. For example, as a company expands overseas, its operations are physically relocated in foreign operating environments. Since strategic decisions are made in the context of some perception or understanding of the environment, information from new sources will be absorbed into planning processes as the environment becomes pluralistic, with revised corporate directions as a probable and desirable result. Thus, prior to the reconsideration of the corporate strategic choice, top management must reassess the mission statement and institute changes as required so that the appropriate environmental information is defined, collected, analyzed, and integrated into existing data bases.

Management must also provide a mission statement that continues to serve as a basis for evaluating strategic alternatives as this additional information is incorporated into the organization's system of decision-making processes.

Consider one component of the Zale Corporation's mission statement from this perspective:

> Our ultimate responsibilities are to our shareholders. Our goal is to earn an optimum return on invested capital through steady profit growth and prudent, aggressive asset management. The attainment of this financial goal, coupled with a record of sound management, represents our approach toward influencing the value placed upon our common stock in the market.

From a U.S. perspective this financial component seems quite reasonable. However, it could be unacceptable in a global context where financial goals are frequently divergent. Research has shown that financial goals are of differing importance in various countries.[13] Executives from France, Japan, and the Netherlands have displayed a clear preference for maximizing growth in after-tax earnings. Norwegian executives place a higher priority on maximizing earnings before interest and taxes. In contrast, the maximization of stockholder wealth has received little acclaim in any of these four countries. Thus, a mission statement specifying that a firm's ultimate responsibility is to its stockholders may or may not be appropriate as the basis for the company's financial operating philosophy when viewed from a global perspective. This illustrates the critical need for reviewing and revising the corporate mission prior to international expansion so that the mission statement maintains its relevance by overarching divergent situations and environmental factors.

Components of the Corporate Mission Revisited

Because multinationalization mandates change in strategic decision making, corporate direction, and strategic alternatives, the content of each mission component must be revised to incorporate multinational contingencies. The additional strategic capabilities that will result from internationalizing operations must continue to be encompassed by the corporate mission statement. Therefore, each basic component needs to be analyzed in light of specific considerations that serve to multinationalize the corporate mission.

Product or Service, Market, and Technology.   The mission statement defines the basic market need the company aims to satisfy. The essence of this definition is likely to remain intact in the MNC context in that the company has acquired competencies domestically that can be exploited as competitive advantages when transferred internationally. However, confronted with a multiplicity of contexts, some degree of prioritization and redefining the primary market and customer is necessary.

The MNC could define a global market, which would necessitate standardization in product and company responses, or it could pursue a "marketing concept" orientation by focusing on each national market's particular or unique de-

---

[13] A. Stonehill, T. Beekhuisen, R. Wright, L. Remmers, N. Toy, P. Pares, A. Shapiro, D. Egan, and T. Bates, "Financial Goals and Debt Ratio Determinants: A Survey of Practice in Five Countries," *Financial Management*, Autumn 1975, pp. 27–40.

mands. Thus, the mission statement must provide a basis for strategic decision making in this trade-off situation. For example, Hewlett-Packard's statement includes the directive that "HP customers must feel that they are dealing with one company with common policies and services," implying a standardized approach designed to provide comparable service to all customers. In contrast, Holiday Inns, Inc.'s corporate mission reflects the marketing concept "Basic to almost everything Holiday Inns, Inc. does is its interaction with its market, the consumer, and its consistent capacity to provide what the consumer wants, when, and where it is needed."

Subsequent to defining the company's target market, the mission statement should suggest the corresponding internal mechanisms required to support this definition. For example, if a company defines a global market, the mission statement may establish centralized corporate functions and activities that promote standardization. Illustrative of this example, the mission statement of Drew Chemical Corporation (shown in Strategy in Action 6–4) establishes three industry-defined divisions and one international division, which represents and supports the others. Thus, the international market is viewed as a standardized extension of the domestic divisions. To support this view, the mission statement creates economies of scale and product standardization across the industry division by specifying centralized research, production, and administrative operations to support the marketing organizations.

Company Goals: Survival, Growth, and Profitability.   The mission statement includes the company's intention to secure its future through growth and profitability. In the United States, growth and profitability are considered essentials for survival. Similarly, in environments relatively supportive of the free enterprise system, these priorities are widely acceptable. However, following international expansion, the firm may operate in economies not unequivocally committed to the profit motive. A host country may view social welfare and development goals as taking precedence over free market capitalism. For example, in Third World countries, employment and income distribution goals often take precedence over rapid economic growth.

Opposition to profit goals may also come from a nonphilosophical perspective; that is, even in environments that accept the profit motive, MNC profits are often viewed as having a unidirectional flow. At the extreme, the multinational is seen as a tool for exploiting the host country exclusively for the benefit of the parent's home country. Profits are the evidence of perceived corporate atrocities. Thus, in a multinational context, a corporate commitment to profits may not only fail to help secure survival, it may even increase the risk of failure.

Therefore, an MNC mission statement must reflect the firm's intention to secure its survival through dimensions that extend beyond growth and profitability. An MNC must develop a corporate philosophy that expresses the need for a bidirectional flow of benefits among the firm and its multiple environments. Such a view is expressed deftly by Gulf & Western Americas Corpora-

Strategy in Action 6–4
Drew Chemical Corporation Mission Statement

The Drew Chemical Corporation is a service-oriented chemical company that consists of four basic marketing organizations. Drew's assets are in people—not land, plant, or equipment.

Each of the operations is primarily concerned with the beneficiation of the world's most basic resource—water—through the use of performance.

The Water and Waste Treatment Division markets chemicals, equipment, and services for boiler and cooling water treatment and for use in waste disposal plants.

The Marine Division markets chemicals, equipment, and services for marine boilers and maintenance products and fuel oil additives for use aboard ships.

The Specialty Chemicals Division markets process additives and chemical specialties for the pulp and paper, paint and latex, textile, and chemical industries.

International Operations consist of 12 wholly owned subsidiaries. Eight subsidiaries are essentially sales agents for the Marine Division and licensees of the Water and Treatment and Specialty Chemicals Divisions. Drew Ameroid International is a tax shelter for Marine business outside of the United States. The other three subsidiaries function quite independently of the parent company, drawing on it mainly for technical support.

The marketing organizations are supported by centralized research, production, and administrative operations.

tion: "We believe that in a developing country, revenue is inseparable from mandatory social responsibility and that a company is an integral part of the local and national community in which its activities are based."[14] This statement illustrates a corporate attitude that acknowledges the intention of MNC contributions to the host country yet clearly maintains a commitment to firm profitability.

In a broader context, a company's mission must recognize not only economic dimensions but also an effectiveness dimension—where effectiveness is the ability to meet the desires of all major organizational claimants. This implies that effectiveness is in part an external standard, relative to and defined by each MNC context. Therefore, an MNC must identify which coalitions in each environment determine these external standards or, more important, the spe-

---

[14] See O. Williams, "Who Cast the First Stone?" *Harvard Business Review,* September–October 1984, pp. 151–61.

cific coalitions on which the MNC depends for its existence and prosperity. The organization must then include as an essential part of its corporate mission a "legitimization" element so as to proactively create and sustain this coalition support, thereby securing the organization's survival. For example, management of Caterpillar Tractor Company has stated:

> We affirm that Caterpillar investment must be compatible with social and economic priorities of host countries, and with local customs, tradition, and sovereignty. We intend to conduct our business in a way that will earn acceptance and respect for Caterpillar, and allay concerns by host country governments and others about multinational corporations.

The growth dimension of the mission statement continues to be closely tied to survival and profitability even in the MNC context. Multinationalization creates geographical dispersion of corporate resources and operations. This implies that strategic decision makers are no longer located exclusively at corporate headquarters, nor are they as easily and readily accessible to participate in collective decision-making processes. Therefore, some mechanism is required for recording the commitment to a unifying purpose, by which the cohesiveness of the organization is to be maintained. The mission statement can provide this basis for unification, tying together decision makers' perspectives with a common guiding thread of understanding and purpose.

Company Philosophy.   While an inclusive and detailed corporate philosophy may go unstated, the implicit understanding of the domestic environment results in a general uniformity of corporate values and behavior within the domestic setting. Few events that occur domestically will directly challenge a company to self-examine its espoused or actual philosophy to ensure that it is both properly formulated and implemented. Multinationalization is, however, clearly such an event. A corporate philosophy developed from a singular perspective cannot be assumed to maintain its relevance in variant cultures. Corporate values and beliefs are primarily culturally defined, reflecting the general philosophical perspective of the society in which the company operates. Thus, when a company extends into another social structure, it encounters a new set of accepted corporate values and preferences, which must be assimilated and incorporated into its own.

The critical concern for the MNC is to decide which values and philosophical needs will be given top priority, considering that multiple cultures are involved. The MNC has the basic choice of adopting a company philosophy for each operating environment or of defining an overarching, supranational corporate philosophy. Although each subsidiary must verify that its philosophy is not in direct conflict with existing cultural norms, the preferable choice for the MNC is usually the latter approach—striving to define an acceptable overall corporate philosophy not contingent on specific environments. The communication capabilities of modern society seldom allow exclusively subsidiary-defined corporate philosophies. For example, numerous U.S. multinational corporations have been subject to considerable criticism from U.S. special interest groups regarding the policies of their South African, Namibian, and Dominican Republic subsidiaries. The allegation of corporate social responsibility violations has, in general, not been instigated, motivated, or defined by coalitions within the host countries. Rather, values and beliefs regarding working standards and conditions have been directly transferred to each country by external coalitions from the United States, such as the Interfaith Center on Corporate Responsibility. Thus, though corporate philosophical preferences, values, and beliefs can be tailored to each host country, they cannot be fundamentally redefined because of the capability of concerned interest groups to selectively match or mismatch potentially conflicting positions. The result is a significantly enlarged external conscience to which the corporations must respond. Consequently, when expressing a corporate value system, the MNC's accountability to this collective conscience must be recognized in its entirety.

The mission statement must also provide for operationalizing the corporate philosophy to serve as a basis for strategic decision making and operational activities. The acquisition of corporate resources as well as their allocation and utilization must be consistent with the corporate value objectives. This necessitates a formal mechanism to assess contemplated corporate actions and ensure that value preferences will be implemented. For example, in responding to world criticism regarding the use of its infant formula, Nestlé established an independent audit committee to monitor its market practices and its compliance with the international code of the World Health Organization regarding infant formula marketing activities. Unfortunately, the committee was viewed by some critics as merely a public relations ploy. This criticism may have been avoided had the corporate philosophy provided for the committee prior to the infant formula crisis. Nevertheless, a committee is an example of a mechanism for monitoring the operationalization of the corporate philosophy on an ongoing basis.

Self-Concept.   The multinationalized self-concept is dependent on management's understanding and evaluation of the company's strengths and weaknesses as a competitor in each of its operating arenas. The firm's ability to survive in multiple dynamic and highly competitive environments is severely limited if strategic decision makers do not understand the impact the company has or could have on the environment and vice versa. They are, in fact, partially responsible for determining the environment to which they must subsequently respond; that is, a company may engage in actions to proactively select and impact its environments, or it may decide to take a reactive stance in which it responds and adapts to environmental changes once their impact is known with greater certainty. Activities by which management may proactively manage the environment include:

Developing leadership and innovation in products, marketing, and technology.

Securing monopolistic market or distribution positions.

Co-opting key environmental-determining coalitions.

Participating in environmental-determining political processes.

Joint venturing with environmental-determining coalitions.

Selecting particular portions of the environment to engage in competitively.

The mission statement must convey the overall corporate intentions and strategic orientation toward a proactive versus reactive choice. Subsidiaries cannot be allowed to determine their own environmental posture if the MNC is to fully capitalize on the potential advantages inherent in internationalized operations.

Public Image.   Domestically, the public image is often shaped from a marketing viewpoint. The firm's public image is considered a marketing tool that is managed with the objective of customer acceptance of the firm's product in the market. Although this dimension remains a critical consideration in the multinational environment, it msut be properly balanced with concern for organizational claimants other than the customer. The multinational firm is a major user of national resources and a major force in the socialization processes of many countries. Thus, the MNC must manage its image with respect to this larger context by clearly conveying its intentions to recognize the additional internal and external claimants resulting from multinationalization. The following excerpt from Hewlett-Packard's mission statement exemplifies this broadened public image: "As a corporation operating in many different communities throughout the world, we must assure ourselves that each of these communities is better for our presence. . . . Each community has its particular set of social problems. Our company must help to solve these problems." Through this statement, Hewlett-Packard conveys to the public an image of responsiveness to claimants throughout the world.

Summary

Managers need to recognize that different types of industry-based competition exist and that these differences are linked to an understanding of the strategic planning options available to a multinational corporation. Specifically, managers must identify their industry along the global versus multidomestic continuum and then consider the implications for their firm. This is the first step in developing a multinational strategy.

Global and multidomestic industries necessitate distinctive strategic emphasis as a result of the location and coordination of the corporation's functional activities. Consequently, once the industry is understood, managers must pursue a strategy consistent with the industry and supported through the functional activities. Specifically, managers must emphasize increased coordination and concentration of functional activities as the competition in the industry becomes global in nature.

The appendix at the end of this chapter lists many of the environmental components with which multinational companies must contend. This list is useful both in trying to comprehend the breadth of issues operating in the multinational environment and in evaluating the strategies of MNCs to determine their thoroughness.

As a starting point for international expansion, management needs to review and revise the corporate mission statement. A mission statement developed from a domestic perspective is often thought to continue encompassing and directing multinational activities. However, as multinational operations fundamentally alter corporate direction and strategic capabilities, the guiding purpose of the firm must be reclarified through multinationalization of the mission statement.

The multinationalized mission statement expresses the ultimate aim of the firm and provides a unity of direction that transcends both divergent managerial perspectives and geographically dispersed strategic decision makers. It provides a basis for strategic decision-making processes, particularly in situations where strategic alternatives may appear to conflict. It promotes the shared corporate values and commitments that extend beyond a single culture and can be identified and assimilated by internal and external organizational claimants. Finally, it asserts the legitimacy of the organization with respect to support coalitions in each of its operating environments, which is essential for the company to ensure and protect its survival.

Questions for Discussion

1. How does environmental analysis at the domestic level differ from a multinational analysis?
2. Which factors complicate environmental analysis at the multinational level? Which factors are making such analysis easier?
3. Do you agree with the suggestion that soon all industries will need to evaluate global environments?
4. Which industries operate almost devoid of international competition? Which inherent immunities do they enjoy?
5. Which components of a mission statement are most critical to revise when a corporation develops multinationally?
6. Obviously, multinationalization forces many changes in addition to those a corporation makes in its mission statement. Using the chapter appendix as a guide, develop a scheme for classifying the additional changes that should be considered.

Bibliography

Chakravarthy, Balaj S., and Howard V. Perlmutter. "Strategic Planning for a Global Business." *Columbia Journal of World Business,* Summer 1985, pp. 3–10.

Doz, Yves, and C. K. Prahalad. "Patterns of Strategic Control within Multinational Corporations." *Journal of International Business Studies,* Fall 1984, pp. 55–72.

Fayweather, J., and A. Kapoor. *Strategy and Negotiation for the International Corporation.* Cambridge, Mass.: Ballinger, 1976.

Harvel, Gary, and C. K. Prahalad. "Managing Strategic Responsibility in the MNC." *Strategic Management Journal* 4 (1983), pp. 341–51.

Hout, T.; M. E. Porter; and E. Rudden. "How Global Companies Win Out." *Harvard Business Review*, September–October 1982, pp. 98–108.

Levitt, Theodore. "The Globalization of Markets." *Harvard Business Review*, September–October 1982, p. 92.

Naylor, Thomas H. "The International Strategy Matrix." *Columbia Journal of World Business*, Summer 1985, pp. 11–19.

Pearce, John A., II, and Kendall Roth. "Multinationalization of the Corporate Mission." In press.

Porter, Michael E. "Changing Patterns of International Competition." *California Management Review 28*, no. 2 (Winter 1986), pp. 9–40.

Quelch, John A., and Edward J. Hoff. "Customizing Global Marketing." *Harvard Business Review*, May–June 1986, pp. 59–68.

Ronstadt, R., and R. Kramer. "Getting the Most out of Innovation Abroad." *Harvard Business Review*, March–April 1982, pp. 94–99.

Stonehill, A.; T. Beekhuisen; R. Wright; L. Remmers; N. Toy; P. Pares; A. Shapiro; D. Egan; and T. Bates. "Financial Goals and Debt Ratio Determinants: A Survey of Practice in Five Countries." *Financial Management*, Autumn 1975, pp. 27–40.

Watson, C. M. "Counter Competition Abroad to Protect Home Markets." *Harvard Business Review*, January–February 1982, p. 40.

Williams, O. "Who Cast the First Stone?" *Harvard Business Review*, September–October 1984, pp. 151–61.

Wind, Yoram, and Susan Douglas. "International Portfolio Analysis and Strategy: The Challenge of the 80s." *Journal of International Business Studies*, Fall 1981, pp. 69–82.

Appendix

Components of the Multinational Environment

Multinational companies must operate within an environment that has numerous components. These components include:

I. Government, laws, regulations and policies of home country (United States, for example).
   A. Monetary and fiscal policies and their effect on price trends, interest rates, economic growth, and stability.
   B. Balance-of-payment policies.
      1. Mandatory controls on direct investment.
      2. Interest equalization tax and other policies.
   C. Commercial policies, especially tariffs, quantitative import restrictions, and voluntary import controls.
   D. Export controls and other restrictions on trade with Eastern European and other Communist nations.
   E. Tax policies and their impact on overseas business.
   F. Antitrust regulations, their administration, and their impact on international business.

Source: W. A. Dymsza, *Multinational Business Strategy* (New York: McGraw-Hill, 1972), pp. 83–85.

      G. Investment guarantees, investment surveys, and other programs to encourage private investments in less developed countries.

      H. Export–import and governmental export expansion programs.

      I. Other changes in government policy that affect international business.

II. Key political and legal parameters in foreign countries and their projection.

      A. Type of political and economic system, political philosophy, national ideology.

      B. Major political parties, their philosophies, and their policies.

      C. Stability of the government.

          1. Changes in political parties.

          2. Changes in governments.

      D. Assessment of nationalism and its possible impact on political environment and legislation.

      E. Assessment of political vulnerability.

          1. Possibilities of expropriation.

          2. Unfavorable and discriminatory national legislation and tax laws.

          3. Labor laws and problems.

      F. Favorable political aspects.

          1. Tax and other concessions to encourage foreign investments.

          2. Credit and other guarantees.

      G. Differences in legal system and commercial law.

      H. Jurisdiction in legal disputes.

      I. Antitrust laws and rules of competition.

      J. Arbitration clauses and their enforcement.

      K. Protection of patents, trademarks, brand names, and other industrial property rights.

III. Key economic parameters and their projection.

      A. Population and its distribution by age groups, density, annual percentage increase, percentage of working age, percentage of total in agriculture, percentage in urban centers.

      B. Level of economic development and industrialization.

      C. Gross national product, gross domestic product, or national income in real terms and also on per capita basis in recent years and projections over future planning period.

      D. Distribution of personal income.

      E. Measures of price stability and inflation, wholesale price index, consumer price index, other price indexes.

      F. Supply of labor, wage rates.

      G. Balance-of-payments equilibrium or disequilibrium, level of international monetary reserves, and balance-of-payments policies.

H. Trends in exchange rates, currency stability, evaluation of possibility of depreciation of currency.

I. Tariffs, quantitative restrictions, export controls, border taxes, exchange controls, state trading, and other entry barriers to foreign trade.

J. Monetary, fiscal, and tax policies.

K. Exchange controls and other restrictions on capital movements, repatriation of capital, and remission of earnings.

IV. Business system and structure.

A. Prevailing business philosophy: mixed capitalism, planned economy, state socialism.

B. Major types of industry and economic activities.

C. Numbers, size, and types of firms, including legal forms of business.

D. Organization: proprietorships, partnerships, limited companies, corporations, cooperatives, state enterprises.

E. Local ownership patterns: public and privately held corporations, family-owned enterprises.

F. Domestic and foreign patterns of ownership in major industries.

G. Business managers available: their education, training, experience, career patterns, attitudes, and reputations.

H. Business associations and chambers of commerce and their influence.

I. Business codes, both formal and informal.

J. Marketing institutions: distributors, agents, wholesalers, retailers, advertising agencies, advertising media, marketing research and other consultants.

K. Financial and other business institutions: commercial and investment banks, other financial institutions, capital markets, money markets, foreign exchange dealers, insurance firms, engineering companies.

L. Managerial processes and practices with respect to planning, administration, operations, accounting, budgeting, control.

V. Social and cultural parameters and their projections.

A. Literacy and educational levels.

B. Business, economic, technical, and other specialized education available.

C. Language and cultural characteristics.

D. Class structure and mobility.

E. Religious, racial, and national characteristics.

F. Degree of urbanization and rural–urban shifts.

G. Strength of nationalistic sentiment.

H. Rate of social change.

I. Impact of nationalism on social and institutional change.

Chapter 6 Cohesion Case Illustration

The Multinational Environment of Holiday Inns, Inc.

Each of Holiday Inns, Inc.'s business groups could easily find itself facing international considerations associated with various strategic options that group managers might choose. The two groups with significant international involvement are the hotel group and the transportation (Delta Steamships) group. These two groups are used below to selectively illustrate issues associated with evaluating the multinational environment.

Differences between U.S. Operations and International Operations

Hotels are service businesses designed to meet the lodging, food, and entertainment needs of travelers and local customers. The service is highly personalized and takes place in each hotel location on a one-to-one basis.

Language, cultural, economic, political, and transportation/communication considerations vary from country to country. This variability makes it difficult for a hotel chain built on a guarantee of "no surprises" or differences in standards from place to place to ensure consistency and control across multinational locations. Holiday Inns established a separate international division, which is subdivided globally to facilitate recognition of such differences and to accommodate them in profitable ways at individual locations covering over 55 countries worldwide.

Delta Steamships confronts a wide array of differences when comparing its international markets (Latin America, South America, and Africa) with domestic ones. Port operations are more strongly controlled in each international setting. Government involvement often includes ownership of key competitors, control of loading facilities and dockworkers, and heavy taxation of Delta's revenue derived in that port.

Multidomestic Industries versus Global Industries

The worldwide lodging industry is steadily evolving from what was once a multidomestic industry to an increasingly global industry. With the speed of intercontinental travel, communication, and increased commerce, lodging services are increasingly open to nondomestic-based competition. And the concentration on heavy demand for lodging services in large, truly international cities worldwide has created fewer market differences for operating major hotels.

The ocean shipping business has been closer to a global industry for some time. Countries active in shipping and exporting for centuries have spawned sizable shipping enterprises that are knowledgeable and positioned to operate in all the major ports of the world.

Location and Coordination: Multinational Strategic Options

Figure 6–3 (presented earlier in Chapter 6) portrayed basic differences in the options available to multinational firms. These differences arise from the demands necessary to coordinate activities of the business and the location requirements to provide the firm's activities. Holiday Inns' hotel group and its Delta Steamship business are located on Figure 6–3 as follows:

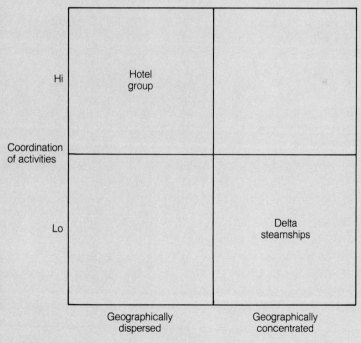

Following Figure 6–3's guidelines, Holiday Inns' multinational hotel business would face high foreign investment (each lodging facility must be built and run on foreign soil) and require extensive coordination (reservations, standards, and financial). The steamship business is much the opposite. It could follow an "export-based" strategy, meaning its main location could remain U.S. based while it emphasized decentralized marketing. The "decentralized marketing" suggests that Delta Steamship would need to market its transportation services within each port/country it serves.

Both suggestions emanating from Figure 6–3 are consistent with the international setting and options considered by these two business groups. The hotel business was concerned with the high foreign investment required to operate in foreign cities with non-U.S. governments. In addition to a heavy reliance on franchising, hotel group executives were considering moving extensively toward providing the Holiday Inn name and extended management services to foreign investors who would own the hotel facility rather than having any company-owned properties.

The steamship operation was more difficult to deal with. Extensive subsidy by foreign (host) governments to their respective merchant marine fleets was becoming increasingly impossible for Delta to compete with—even considering the new LASH technology.

CHAPTER

7

Environmental Forecasting

Importance of Forecasting

Change was rapid in the 1970s and early 1980s, with even greater changes and challenges forecast as the 80s come to a close. The crucial responsibility for managers will be ensuring their firm's capacity for survival. This will be done by anticipating and adapting to environmental changes in ways that provide new opportunities for growth and profitability. The impact of changes in the remote industry and task environments must be understood and predicted.

Even large firms in established industries will be actively involved in transitions. The $5.5 billion loss in the U.S. auto industry during 1980 and 1981 shows what can happen when firms fail to place a priority on environmental forecasting. The preceding decade saw a 20 percent penetration of the U.S. new car market by foreign competition; the oil embargo in 1973; rapidly climbing fuel prices; and uncertain future supplies of crude oil. Yet the long-term implications of these predictable factors on future auto sales were largely ignored by U.S. automakers. Because it was not open to changes in technology, Detroit was left without viable, fuel-efficient, quality-made alternatives for the American market. On the other hand, the Japanese anticipated the future need for fuel efficiency, quality, and service through careful market research

Note: Portions of this chapter are adopted from John A. Pearce II and Richard B. Robinson, Jr., "Environmental Forecasting: Key to Strategic Management," *Business*, July–September 1983, pp. 3–12.

and environmental forecasting. As a result, the Japanese gained additional market share at Detroit's expense. However, in the early 1980s, American automakers spent $80 billion on product and capital-investment strategies meant to recapture their lost market share. They realized that success in strategic decisions rests not solely on dollar amounts but also on anticipation of and preparation for the future.

Accurate forecasting of changing elements in the environment is an essential part of strategic management. One specific example is the case of National Intergroup described in Strategy in Action 7–1.

Strategy in Action 7–1
National Intergroup

In 1982 National Steel's sales dropped 26 percent to $3 billion, while the previous year's $86 million profit disintegrated into a massive $463 million loss. But long before the company reached this abyss, Chairman Howard M. Love, perplexed by the historically poor returns on steel, began to take a "cold, ungilded look" at every aspect of the company. This three-year analysis asked why the company's management did not perform better and culminated with the adoption of a new name that does not mention steel: National Intergroup Inc. (NII).

As the 1980s began National seemed mired, and its efforts to change were fizzling. Attempts to establish then-unproved quality circles at its Weirton, West Virginia, steel mill foundered because middle management—not labor—was unresponsive. With the help of Responsive Organizations, an Arlington, Virginia, consulting firm, National's top management came to realize that its managers lacked commonly held goals. To remedy that, 250 executives were involved for over a year in meetings meant to seek a consensus on the company's mission and to outline its financial, marketing, personnel, and social goals.

The company also set up task forces to study its strategic planning process and the system by which one unit, such as coal, charged another unit, such as steel, for its products. But the discussions "all began running up against a stone wall," said John A. McCreary, NII's vice president for human resources. The barrier, "an inappropriate organizational structure," focused too much on steel production.

So in 1982 the corporation was restructured into six autonomous business groups—steel, financial services, aluminum, distribution, energy, and diversified

Continued on Page 175

Strategy in Action 7–1 *(concluded)*

business. Each was a profit center with its own group president, and the new
corporate name reflected this change.

   National's studies showed that its two biggest markets—autos and cans—
were irrevocably reducing their use of steel. "The size of the steel company we
have now matches the markets we want to participate in," said Love. Future
capital investment could be concentrated on improving smaller plants. Consequently, Love believed, "we'll be significantly more profitable with less tons." In
early 1983 National showed this was no idle boast: It reported an operating
profit of $2 for each ton of steel it produced, while other major steel makers
lost from $17 to $32 per ton. The company's mills were running at 82 percent
of capacity, while industry as a whole was sputtering along at 56 percent.

   National's balance sheet was in much better shape than it had been in the
previous year. As of June 30, 1983, the company had $74 million in cash, three
times its holdings at year-end. Long-term debt was knocked down to $600 million
by September 30, 1983, or 36 percent of capitalization versus 41 percent the
previous year, and its stock had more than doubled in price in the same year.
"They've got their act together," said John C. Tumazos, an industry analyst
with Oppenheimer & Company, who in 1982 listed National as one of the steel
industry's financially weakest companies.

Source: Adapted from *Business Week,* September 26, 1983, p. 82.

   Forecasting the business environment for the second half of the 1980s has
led some firms, such as Sears, Roebuck, to expand. From 1980 to 1985, Sears
opened new financial centers in 250 retail stores.

   Other corporations have forecast a need for massive retrenchment. One
such firm is the Weyerhauser Company, which laid off 2,000 employees in
1982 to streamline its cost of doing business. Still other companies have cut
back in one area of operations to underwrite growth in another. In 1984 General
Electric decided to close 10 plants and reduce its work force by 1,600 employees
while simultaneously making a commitment to spend $250 million by 1986
to upgrade its facilities.

   These and many other examples indicate that strategic managers need to
develop skill in predicting significant environmental changes. To aid in the
search for future opportunities and constraints, the following steps should
be taken:

1. Select those environmental variables that are critical to the firm.
2. Select the sources of significant environmental information.
3. Evaluate forecasting approaches or techniques.
4. Integrate forecast results into the strategic management process.
5. Monitor the critical aspects of managing forecasts.

Select Critical Environmental Variables

Management experts have argued that the most important cause of the turbulent business environment is the change in population structure and dynamics. This change, in turn, produces other major changes in the economic, social, and political environments.

Historically, population shifts tended to occur over 40- to 50-year periods and, therefore, had little relevance to business decisions. However, during the second half of the 20th century, population changes have become radical, erratic, contradictory, and therefore of great importance.

For example, the U.S. baby boom between 1945 and the mid-1960s has had and will have a dramatic impact on all parts of society—from maternity wards and schools to the labor force and the marketplace. This population bulge is facing heavy competition for jobs, promotions, and housing, despite a highest-ever education level. Compounding this dilemma are the heightened demands of women and racial minorities. The lack of high-status jobs to fit the expectations of this large, educated labor force poses a potential for major social and economic changes. In addition, these workers encounter an increasingly aging labor force that finds it difficult to give up status, power, and employment when retirement programs are either not financially attractive or not available at the traditional age of 65. (See Figure 7–1 for comparative population growth projections.)

Obviously, the demands of these groups will have important effects on social and political changes in terms of lifestyle, consumption patterns, and political decisions. In economic terms, the size and potential affluence of these groups suggest increasing markets for housing, consumer products, and leisure goods and services.

Interestingly, the same shifts in population, life expectancy, and education have occurred in many developed nations. However, developing nations face the opposite population configurations. Although birthrates have declined, survival rates, because of medical improvements, have created a large population of people reaching adulthood in the 1980s. Jobs and food are expected to be in short supply. Therefore, many developing countries will face severe social and political instability unless they can find appropriate work for their surplus labor.[1]

The rates of population increase can obviously be of great importance, as indicated by the contrasting effects forecast above. If a growing population has sufficient purchasing power, new markets will be developed to satisfy their needs. However, too much growth in a country with a limited amount

---

[1] Peter M. Drucker, *Managing in Turbulent Times* (New York: Harper & Row, 1980), suggests that the practice of production sharing between developed and developing nations can be the economic integration needed by both groups of countries. Production sharing will include bringing together the abundant labor resources of the developing countries with the management, technology, educated people, markets, and purchasing power of the developed countries.

Figure 7–1
Population growth by age group (millions)

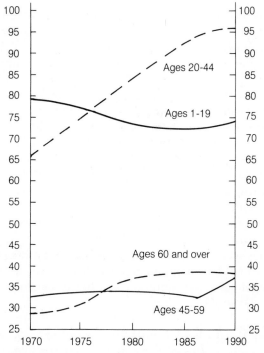

Source: Bureau of the Census, U.S. Department of Commerce, 1980.

or a drastic inequity in distribution of resources may result in major social and political upheavals and may pose substantial risks for businesses.

If forecasting were as simple as predicting population trends, strategic managers would only need to examine census data to predict future markets. But economic interpretations are more complex. Migration rates; mobility trends; birth, marriage, and death rates; and racial, ethnic, and religious structures complicate population statistics. In addition, resource development and its political use in this interdependent world further confuse the problem— as evidenced by the actions of some of the oil states (e.g., Saudi Arabia, Iraq, Libya, and Kuwait). Changes in political situations, technology, or culture add further complications.

Domestically, the turbulence is no less severe. Continually changing products and services, changing competitors, uncertain government priorities, rapid social change, and major technological innovations all add to the complexity of planning for the future. To grow, be profitable, at times even to survive in this turbulent world, a firm needs sensitivity, commitment, and skill in recognizing and predicting those variables that will most profoundly affect its future.

Who Selects the Key Variables?   Although executives or committees in charge of planning may assist in obtaining forecast data, responsibility for environmental forecasting usually lies with top management. This is the case at the Sun (oil) Company, where responsibility for the long-range future of the corporation is assigned to the chairman and vice chairman of the board of directors. One key duty of the vice chairman is environmental assessment. In this context, *environment* refers not to air, water, and land but rather to the general business setting created by the economic, technological, political, and social forces in which Sun plans to operate.

The environmental assessment group consists of Sun's chief economist, a specialist in technological assessment, and a public issues consultant—all reporting to the vice president of environmental assessment. The chief economist evaluates and forecasts the state of the economy; the technological assessment specialist covers technology and science; and the public issues consultant concentrates on politics and society.[2]

However, headquarters' capability and proficiency may be limited in analyzing political, economic, and social variables around the world. Therefore, on-the-spot personnel, outside consultants, or company task forces may be assigned to assist in forecasting.

What Variables Should Be Selected?   A list of key variables that will have make-or-break consequences for the firm must be developed. Some may have been crucial in the past, and others may appear to be important in the future. This list can be kept to manageable size by limiting key variables in the following ways:

1. Include all variables that would have a significant impact although their probability of occurrence is low (e.g., trucking deregulation). Also include highly probable variables regardless of impact (e.g., a minimal price increase by a major supplier). Delete others with little impact and low probabilities.

2. Disregard major disasters, such as nuclear war.

3. Aggregate when possible into gross variables (e.g., a bank loan is based more on the dependability of a company's cash flow than on the flow's component sources).

4. If the value of one variable is based on the value of the other, separate the dependent variable for future planning.[3]

---

[2] Eric Weiss, "Future Public Opinion of Business," *Management Review,* March 1978, p. 9.

[3] Robert E. Linneman and John D. Kennell, "Shirt-Sleeve Approach to Long-Range Plans," *Harvard Business Review,* March–April 1977, p. 145.

Limits of money, time, and skill in forecasting prevent a firm from predicting many variables in the environment. The task of predicting even a dozen variables is substantial. Often firms try to select a set of key variables by analyzing the environmental factors in the industry that are most likely to force sharp growth or decline in the marketplace. For the furniture, appliance, and textiles industries, housing starts are significant. Housing, in turn, is greatly affected by high interest rates.

Figure 7–2 identifies some of the key issues that may have critical impacts

---

Figure 7–2
Strategic forecasting issues

Key issues in the remote environment

Economy
Purchasing power depends on current income, savings, prices, and credit availability. The economic trends to be forecast often attempt to answer the following questions.

What are the probable future directions of the economies in the corporation's regional, national, and international markets? What changes in economic growth, inflation, interest rates, capital availability, credit availability, and consumer purchasing power can be expected?

What income differences can be expected between the wealthy upper-middle class, working class, and underclass in various regions?

What shifts in relative demand for different categories of goods and services can be expected?

Example. The record-setting high interest rates of 1980 and 1981 resulted in a general economic washout in the United States. Industries that depend on long- and short-term credit for their sales, such as housing and automobiles, were most severely affected. Despite the possibility that higher interest rates would be used to curtail the increasing inflation, little effort was made by loan institutions to develop innovative loan programs, such as variable-interest loans.

Society
In the rapidly changing social environment of the highly interdependent spaceship earth, businesses feel great pressure to respond to the expectations of society more effectively.

What effect do changes in social values and attitudes regarding childbearing, marriage, lifestyle, work, ethics, sex roles, racial equality, education, retirement, pollution, energy, and so on have on the firm's development? What effect will population changes have on major social and political expectations—at home and abroad? What constraints or opportunities will develop? What pressure groups will increase in power?

Example. The declining birthrate of the United States is a threat to some industries producing children's food, toys, clothes, and furniture. However, forecasting by trend extrapolation of birthrates in the late 1950s was so inaccurate that it created a severe threat to such firms as the Gerber Company. The six firms that survived or prospered into the 1980s were those that learned to recognize sociocultural value changes and to incorporate such changes in their strategic forecasts.

Politics
Although political forecasts are usually based on "soft" data, as compared to hard—attitudes and opinions—the impact of political issues and trends, as shown below, is frequently as important as economic or technological variables.

What changes in government policy can be expected regarding industry cooperation, antitrust activities, foreign trade, taxation, depreciation, environmental protection, deregulation, defense, foreign trade barriers, and other governing parameters? What success will a new administration have in achieving its stated goals? What effect will that success have on the firm?

Example. After the 1980 presidential election, major forecast adjustments were made to reflect the Reagan administration's new priorities in military defense, private sector growth, and reduced government spending.

Figure 7–2 (continued)

Will specific international climates be hostile or favorable? Is there a tendency toward instability, corruption, or violence? What is the level of political risk in each foreign market? What other political or legal constraints or support can be expected in international business (e.g., trade barriers, equity requirements, nationalism, patent protection)?

Example.   Despite the low political risk involved, several major U.S. firms discovered the importance of in-depth environmental forecasting when investing in Canada. Although aware of the Quebec separatist movement, ITT Rayonier dismissed its potential effect on construction of a $120-million pulp mill. ITT's use of English-speaking supervisors, supervisor conflict with the separatists, a power struggle between two labor federations, and a shortage of skilled labor more than doubled the construction cost to $250 million. Asbestos Corporation of America was also surprised when the province of Quebec nationalized its asbestos mines. Both firms underestimated the significance of growing nationalism.

Technology
Technological innovations can give the firm a special competitive advantage. Without continued product or service improvement, profitability and survival are often jeopardized.

What is the current state of the art? How will it change? What pertinent new products or services are likely to become technically feasible in the foreseeable future? What is the future impact of technological breakthroughs in related product areas? How will they interface with other remote considerations, such as economic issues, social values, public safety, regulations, and court interpretations?

Example.   Recent applications to telephone interconnections of sophisticated computer technology (such as PBX units) have developed an entire new industry seen as a first step toward the integrated electronic office of the future. In addition, decisions by the Federal Communications Commission curtailed previous monopolistic practices of AT&T that excluded the use of equipment from other than AT&T sources. The result has been the spin-off from AT&T of a marketing-oriented unit that will compete head on with firms seeking to relate computers to communication systems. Among the announced competitors are Xerox, IBM, Exxon, Volkswagen, ROLM Corporation, Northern Telecom, Mitel Corporation, and Nippon Electric Company.

Industry
At any given time in its life cycle, certain underlying forces in an industry operate to broadly define the potential for a company's success.

What is the degree of integration of major competitors? What is the industry's average percentage utilization of production capacity? What is the industry's vulnerability to new or substitute products? What, and how great, are the barriers to entry? What is the number and concentration of suppliers? What is the nature of the industry's customer base?

Example.   Head Ski began with a concentration strategy targeted at the high-quality/high-price niche of the snow ski market. With a quickly achieved 50 percent market share, the company faced only four major competitors. However, industry competition had changed dramatically. Head had diversified into new product markets, such as ski clothing, accessories, and archery equipment. It had also diversified geographically into Europe. Competitors had buttressed their resource bases through mergers with conglomerates such as Beatrice Foods. Head Ski followed suit when it was acquired by AMF. Thus, in just five years, the competitive industry composition had shifted from nondiversified, relatively small, single-industry businesses to large, multinational, multi-industry, diversified conglomerates.

Key issues in the operating environment

Competitive position
How probable is the entrance of important new competitors into the industry? Will they offer substitute or competing products? What strategic moves are expected by existing rivals—inside and outside the United States? What competitive advantage is necessary in selected foreign markets? What will be the competitors' priorities and their ability to change? Is their behavior predictable?

Example.   Employing a penetration strategy similar to that used in the auto, steel, shipbuilding, and television markets, Japanese medical electronics makers are gaining a niche with low-cost, stripped-down versions of competitors' equipment. American firms, like General Electric, dismissed the Japanese strategy by insisting that users of medical electronic equipment are concerned not with price but quality. However, as in past entry strategies, the Japanese researched the needs of

---

Figure 7–2 *(concluded)*

the market. They then began development of a three-dimensional scanner-monitor, which was a major technical breakthrough and may eventually give them a competitive edge in the marketplace.

Customer profiles and market changes
What is and will be considered as needed value by our customers? Is market research done, or do managers talk to each other to discover what the customer wants? Which customer needs are not being met by existing products? Why? Are R&D activities under way to develop means for fulfilling these needs? What is their status? What marketing and distribution channels should be used?

Example.   The Japanese research future customer needs and wants by interviewing those who own products of their major competitor, thereby identifying desired improvements. As an example, in the 1970s Japanese researchers identified Volkswagen's shortcomings by interviewing owners in the United States. They then designed Toyotas and Datsuns accordingly and consequently overcame the Beetle's dominance in the United States.

What demographic and population changes can be anticipated? What do they portend for the size of the market and sales potential? What new market segment or product might develop as a result of these changes? What will be our customer groups' buying power?

Example.   Because 95 percent of its $3.5 billion in revenues are generated from soft drinks and other beverages, Coca-Cola has become concerned about the aging of the prime soft drink population, 13- to 24-year-olds. Because Coke can identify the key population variables that will have make-or-break consequences for its product lines, it can more accurately forecast future market potential. As a result, Coke has decided to pursue the aging population bulge in the United States by diversifying into wines. By further expanding internationally with its soft drink products, Coke is also tapping growing youth markets in foreign countries.

Suppliers and creditors
What is the likelihood of major cost increases because of dwindling supplies of a needed natural resource? Will sources of supply, especially of energy, be reliable? Are there reasons to expect major changes in cost and availability of inputs as a result of money, people, or subassembly problems? Which suppliers and creditors can be expected to respond to special emergency requests?

Example.   As short-term interest rates skyrocketed to 20 percent in late 1979, hundreds of small firms fell into the marginal or money-losing categories. Officers of their banks often became alarmed and called in the loans. The resulting squeeze forced many of these businesses into bankruptcy.

Labor market
Are potential employees with desired skills and abilities available in the geographic areas involved? Are colleges and vocational–technical schools located near plant or store sites to aid in meeting training needs? Are labor relations in the industry conducive to expanding needs for employees?

Example.   The 1950s and 1960s were periods of business expansion into the southern states, where labor was plentiful and unions were comparatively weak. In the 1970s and 1980s, northern states regained a measure of attractiveness because they were able to offer unemployed or underemployed skilled workers and attractively priced industrial sites.

---

on a firm's future success. Examples of the importance of a few of these variables are also presented.

Select Sources of Significant Environmental Information

Before forecasting can begin in a formal way, appropriate sources of environmental information should be identified. Casual gathering of strategic information is part of the normal course of executive actions—reading, interactions, and meetings—but is subject to bias and must be balanced with alternative viewpoints. Although *The Wall Street Journal, Business Week, Fortune, Harvard Business Review, Forbes,* and other popular trade and scholarly journals are important sources of forecasting information, formal, deliberate, and structured searches are desirable. The appendix to this chapter lists published sources that can be used in forecasting. A review of these will help strategic managers identify sources that can help meet specific forecasting needs. If the firm can afford the time and expense, primary data should also be gathered in such areas as market factors, technological changes, and competitive and supplier strategies.

Evaluate Forecasting Techniques

Debate exists over the accuracy of quantitative versus qualitative approaches to forecasting (see Figure 7–3), with most research supporting quantitative models. However, the difference in predictions made using each type of approach is often minimal. Additionally, subjective or judgmental approaches may often be the only practical method of forecasting political, legal, social, and technological trends in the remote external environment. The same is true of several factors in the task environment, especially customer and competitive considerations.

Ultimately, the choice of technique depends not on the environmental factor under review but on such considerations as the nature of the forecast decision, the amount and accuracy of available information, the accuracy required, the time available, the importance of the forecast, the cost, and the competence and interpersonal relationships of the managers and forecasters involved.[4] Frequently, assessment of these factors leads to the selection of a combination of quantitative and qualitative techniques, thereby strengthening the accuracy of the ultimate forecast.

Techniques Available

Economic Forecasts.   At one time, only forecasts of economic variables were used in strategic management. These forecasts were primarily concerned with remote factors, such as general economic conditions, disposable personal income, the consumer price index, wage rates, and productivity. Derived from government and private sources, the economic forecasts served as the framework for industry and company forecasts. The latter forecasts dealt with task-environment concerns, such as sales, market share, and other pertinent economic trends.

---

[4] Steven C. Wheelwright and Darral G. Clarke, "Corporate Forecasting: Promise and Reality," *Harvard Business Review,* November–December 1976, p. 42.

Figure 7-3
Popular approaches to forecasting

Technique*	Short description†	Cost	Popularity‡	Complexity	Association with life-cycle stage§
Quantitative					
Causal					
Econometric models	Simultaneous systems of multiple regression equations	High	High	High	Steady state
Single and multiple regression	Variations in dependent variables are explained by variations in the independent one(s)	High/Medium	High	Medium	Steady state
Time series	Linear, exponential, S-curve, or other types of projections	Medium	High	Medium	Steady state
Trend extrapolation	Forecasts are obtained by linear or exponential smoothing or averaging of past actual values	Medium	High	Medium	Steady state
Qualitative or judgmental					
Sales force estimate‖	A bottom-up approach aggregating salespersons' forecasts	Low	High	Low	All stages
Juries of executive opinion	Marketing, production, finance, and purchasing executives jointly prepare forecasts	Low	High	Low	Product development
Customer surveys; market research	Learning about intentions of potential customers or plans of businesses	Medium	Medium	Medium	Market testing and early introduction
Scenario	Forecasters imagine the impacts of anticipated conditions	Low	Medium	Low	All stages
Delphi method	Experts are guided toward a consensus	Low	Medium	Medium	Product development
Brainstorming	Idea generation in a noncritical group situation	Low	Medium	Medium	Product development

* Only techniques discussed in this chapter are listed.
† Adapted in part from S. C. Wheelwright and S. Makridakis, *Forecasting Methods for Management*, 3rd ed. (New York: John Wiley & Sons, 1980), pp. 34–35.
‡ Adapted in part from S. C. Wheelwright and D. C. Clark, "Corporate Forecasting: Promise and Reality," *Harvard Business Review*, November–December 1976.
§ Adapted in part from J. C. Chambers, J. K. Mullick, and D. D. Smith, "How to Choose the Right Forecasting Technique," *Harvard Business Review*, July–August 1971. The associations shown are "most common," but most techniques can be used at most stages.
‖ For details see N. C. Mohn and L. C. Sartorius, "Sales Forecasting: A Manager's Primer," *Business*, May–June 1981 and July–August 1981.

Econometric Models.   With the advent of sophisticated computers, the government and some wealthy companies contracted with private consulting firms to develop "causal models," especially those involving *econometrics*. These models utilize complex simultaneous regression equations to relate economic occurrences to areas of corporate activity. They are especially useful when information is available on causal relationships and when large changes are anticipated. During the relatively stable decade of the 1960s and on into the 1970s, econometrics became one of the nation's fastest-growing industries. However, since early in 1979 the big three econometric firms—Data Resources (McGraw-Hill), Chase Econometrics (Chase Manhattan Bank), and Wharton Econometric Forecasting Associates (Ziff-Davis Publishing)—have fallen on hard times. The explosion of oil prices, inflation, and the growing interdependence of the world economy have created problems beyond the inherent limits of econometric models. And despite enormous technological resources, these models still depend on the judgment of the model builders. Recently, that judgment has not been dependable.[5]

Two more widely used and less expensive approaches to forecasting are *time series models* and *judgmental models*. Time series models attempt to identify patterns based on combinations of historical trend, seasonal, and cyclical factors. This technique assumes the past is a prologue to the future. Time series techniques, such as exponential smoothing and linear projections, are relatively simple, well known, inexpensive, and accurate.

Of the time series models, *trend analysis* is the most frequently used. This model assumes the future will be a continuation of the past, following some long-range trend. If sufficient historical data, such as annual sales, are readily available, a trend analysis can be done quickly and inexpensively.

In the trend analysis depicted in Figure 7–4, concern should focus on long-term trends, such as Trend C, which represents 10 years of fluctuating sales. Trend A, where three excellent years were used in the trend analysis, is too optimistic. Similarly, the four bad years depicted in Trend B represent a much too pessimistic outlook.

The major limitation of trend analysis is the assumption that all relevant conditions will remain relatively constant in the future. Sudden changes in the conditions upset the trend prediction.

Judgmental models are useful when historical data are not available or when they are hard to use. Examples of judgmental or qualitative approaches are *sales force estimates* and *juries of executive opinion*. Sales force estimates consolidate salespeople's opinions of customer intentions and opinions regarding specific products. These can be relevant if customers respond honestly and remain consistent in their intentions. Juries of executive opinion combine estimates made by executives from marketing, production, finance, and pur-

---

[5] "Where the Big Econometric Models Go Wrong," *Business Week,* March 30, 1981, pp. 70–73.

Figure 7–4
Interpretations in trend analysis

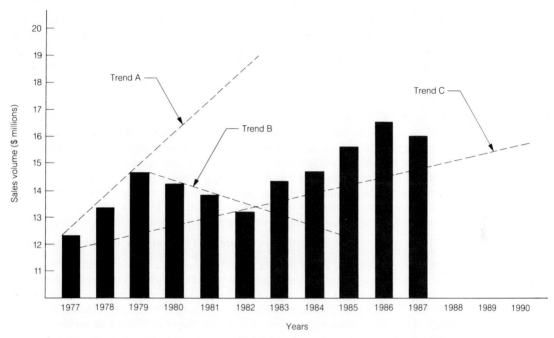

chasing and then average their views. No elaborate math or statistics are required.

Customer surveys may involve personal interviews or telephone questionnaires. The questions must be well stated and easily understood. Respondents are a random sample of the relevant population. Surveys can provide valuable in-depth information. They are often difficult to construct and time-consuming to administer, but many market research firms use such surveys. One strong advocate of judgmental approaches is a senior partner of Lord, Abbett Investment, as is discussed in Strategy in Action 7–2.

Social Forecasts. Relying only on economic indicators for strategic forecasting neglects many important social trends that can have a profound impact. Some firms have recognized this and forecast social issues as part of their environmental scanning to identify social trends and underlying attitudes. Social forecasting is very complex. Recent efforts have involved analyzing such major social areas as population, housing, social security and welfare, health and nutrition, education and training, income, and wealth and expenditures.

Strategy in Action 7–2
Lord, Abbett Investment

Development of investment strategies usually involves sophisticated econometric and mathematical models to forecast future investment values. However, John M. McCarthy, senior partner of Lord, Abbett Investment, a $3.6 billion investment company, has developed his own qualitative forecasting approach. As president of its $1.7 billion Affiliated Fund, McCarthy uses a subjective approach that examines events for tangible signs of pending changes in the economy. He believes that if you wait for the obvious to be discussed on TV, the process of solving the economic problem is already under way and it is too late to invest for important gains.

While numbers and graphs are sometimes combined in the jury of executive opinion approach, McCarthy feels that by the time the numbers of the key indicators reflect changes in the economy, it is too late to aid investment strategies. Instead, his forecasts tend to focus on fundamental changes such as interest rates, government investment incentives, and consumer trends. Among McCarthy's specific forecasts were a drop in interest rates in 1981, a probable return to the bond market, and a depressed consumer goods market until the mid-80s. He believes that President Reagan's savings and investment incentives will break the American habit of borrow and spend. Company and personal investment strategies will need to be fine-tuned, as these and other forecasts do or do not become reality.

Generally, McCarthy looks for the mainly unpopular investments. Often these are undervalued. An illustration of his unique but commonsense approach resulted in investment strategies of purchasing stocks that declined in price while interest rates climbed in 1980. Interest-sensitive issues, such as AT&T, utilities, and banks, account for about 18 percent of Affiliated's current portfolio.

Although this conservative strategy caused Lord, Abbett's growth rate to be below the averages of the Dow Jones Industrial Average and Standard & Poor's 500 during the brief bull market in 1980, McCarthy has focused on long-term results. This forecasting approach and investment strategy enabled Affiliated to grow 173.1 percent compared to 105.5 percent for the Dow during the period January 1975 through September 1980.

Lord, Abbett follows the same forecast method and investment strategy in managing its $1.5 billion of pension fund money.

A variety of approaches is used in social forecasting, including time series analysis and the judgmental techniques described earlier. However, a fourth approach, called *scenario development,* is probably the most popular of all techniques. Scenarios are imagined stories that integrate objective and subjective parts of other forecasts. They are designed to help managers anticipate changes. Because scenarios can be presented in an easily understood form, they have gained popularity in social forecast situations. Scenarios can be developed by the following process:

1. Prepare the background by assessing the overall social environment under investigation (such as social legislation).
2. Select critical indicators and search for future events that may affect the key trends (e.g., growing distrust of business).
3. Analyze reasons for past behavior for each trend (e.g., perceived disregard for air and water quality).
4. Forecast each indicator in at least three scenarios, showing the least favorable environment, the likely environment, and the most favorable environment.
5. Write the scenario from the viewpoint of someone in the future and describe conditions then and how they developed.
6. Condense the scenario for each trend to a few paragraphs.

Figure 7–5 presents an example of a "most likely" scenario for the future of business-government relations on social issues. Scenarios prepare strategic managers for alternative possibilities if certain trends continue, thus enabling them to develop contingency plans.

Political Forecasts.   Some strategic planners want to treat political forecasts with the same seriousness and consideration given to economic forecasts. They believe shifts toward or against a broad range of political factors—such as the size of government budgets, tariffs, tax rates, defense spending, the growth of regulatory bodies, and the extent of business leader participation in government planning—can have profound effects on business success.

Political forecasts for foreign countries are also important. Political risks increase the threat to businesses in any way dependent on international subsidiaries or suppliers for customers or critical resources. Increasing world interdependence makes it imperative for firms of all sizes to consider the international political implications of their strategies.

Because of the billions of U.S. dollars lost in the 1970s as a result of revolutions, nationalization, and other manifestations of political instability, multinational firms and consultants have developed a variety of approaches to international forecast. Some of the better known are listed on the following page.

Figure 7–5
Scenario on the future of business–government regulations: Social issues

The government–corporate relationship in the 1978–1987 period continued to develop along patterns established in previous decades, with no major discontinuities or radical surprises. The most far-reaching and substantial change occurred late in the period when Congress enlarged the planning authority of its budget office, setting 5- and 10-year national manpower, natural resource, and other economic goals. This legislation primarily affected federal fiscal policies and contained no authority to compel action on the part of the private sector to meet the indicated goals.

Nevertheless, following the lead of West Germany, the federal government did offer some incentives to companies that acted to meet certain national objectives—for example, locating new industrial facilities in certain areas for social reasons (such as environmental or employment reasons). During the decade, the government made a commitment to guaranteed jobs rather than guaranteed income.

In the environmental arena, economic incentives and penalties became the government's major tools for compliance. Effluent charges were established to internalize the costs of pollution. Other tax incentives and loans were made available to companies for the installation of pollution-control equipment. Congress also legislated a time limit for legal actions to block a construction project on environmental grounds.

In other regulatory areas, the government moved selectively, increasing requirements on some industries while reducing controls on others. For example, while moving to deregulate much of the air transport business, Congress at the same time passed a full-disclosure labeling act for prepared foods that requires the listing of all ingredients and the percentage of each ingredient. Congress also set a rule requiring that every proposal for new regulation be accompanied by a regulatory impact statement detailing the probable effects of the proposal on the economy.

Turning down proposals for federal chartering of corporations, Congress nevertheless acted to influence the internal governance of large corporations: it passed a full-disclosure law concerning most corporate activities and established a limit on the number of inside directors permitted to serve on the boards of directors. Legislation established due process and protection for whistle blowers (employees who report legal violations). The government placed stringent safeguards on corporate data banks containing information about employees and customers.

In the domain of social legislation affecting business, the minimum wage was indexed to the cost of living, and Congress passed a comprehensive national health plan in which employers pay a significant portion.

Source: James O'Toole, "What's Ahead for Business–Government Relationships," *Harvard Business Review,* March–April 1979, p. 100.

Haner's Business Environmental Risk Index, which monitors 15 economic and political variables in 42 countries.

Frost & Sullivan's World Political Risks Forecasts, which predicts the likelihood of various catastrophes befalling an individual company.

Probe International's custom reports for specific companies, which examine broad social trends.

Arthur D. Little's (ADL) developmental forecasts, which examine a country's progress from the Stone Age to the computer age.[6]

Of all the approaches, ADL's forecasting techniques may be the most ambitious and sophisticated. With computer assistance, they follow the progress of each country by looking at five criteria: social development, technological advancement, abundance of natural resources, level of domestic tranquility, and type of political system. When a country's development in any one of

---

[6] Niles Howard, "Doing Business in Unstable Countries," *Dun's Review,* March 1980, pp. 49–55.

these areas gets too far ahead of the others, tension builds and violence often follows. Using this system, political turbulence was forecast in Iran as early as 1972. ADL foresees that uneven development will likely produce similar turmoil in 20 other countries, such as Peru, Chile, Malaysia, and the Philippines. ADL believes the world is highly predictable if one asks the right questions. Unfortunately, too many executives fail to use the same logic in analyzing political affairs that they use in other strategic areas. Political analysis should be routinely incorporated into economic analyses. Ford, General Motors, Pepsi, Singer, Du Pont, and United Technologies are among the many companies that follow ADL's advice.

Technological Forecasts. Such rapidly developed and revolutionary technological innovations as lasers, nuclear energy, satellites and other communication devices, desalination of water, electric cars, and miracle drugs have prompted many firms to invest in technological forecasts. Knowledge of probable technological development helps strategic managers prepare their firms to benefit from change. To make technological forecasts, all of the previously described techniques, except econometrics, can be used. However, uncertainty of information favors use of scenarios and two additional forecasting approaches: brainstorming and the Delphi technique.

Brainstorming is used to help a group generate new ideas and forecasts. With this technique, analysis or criticism of contributions made by participants is postponed so that creative thinking is not stifled or restricted. Because there are no interruptions, group members are encouraged to offer original ideas and build on the innovative thoughts of other participants. The most promising ideas generated by this means are thoroughly evaluated at a later time.

The *Delphi* method involves a systematic procedure for obtaining a consensus from a group of experts. The procedure includes:

1. A detailed survey of expert opinion, usually obtained through a mail questionnaire.
2. Anonymous evaluation of the responses by the experts involved.
3. One or more revisions of answers until convergence is achieved.

The Delphi technique, although expensive and time-consuming, can also be successful for social and political forecasting.

Integrate Forecast Results into the Strategic Management Process

Once the techniques are selected and the forecasts made, the results must be tied into the strategic management process. For example, the economic forecast must be related to analyses of the industry, suppliers, the competition,

Figure 7–6
Task and remote environment impact matrix

Remote environments	Task environments			
	Key customer trends	*Key competitor trends*	*Key supplier trends*	*Key labor market trends*
Economic	*Example:* Trends in inflation and unemployment rates		*Example:* Annual domestic oil demand and worldwide sulfur demand through 1987	
Social	*Example:* Increasing numbers of single-parent homes			*Example:* Increasing education level of U.S. population
Political	*Example:* Increasing numbers of punitive damage awards in product liability cases		*Example:* Possibility of Arab oil boycotts	
Technological		*Example:* Increasing use of superchips and computer-based instrumentation for synthesizing genes	*Example:* Use of Cobalt 60 gamma irradiation to extend shelf life of perishables	
Industry		*Example:* Disenchantment with vertical integration; increases in large horizontal mergers		*Example:* Increasing availability of mature workers with experience in "smokestack" industries

and key resources. Figure 7–6 presents a format for displaying interrelationships between forecast remote environment variables and the influential task environment variables. The resulting predictions become part of the assumed environment in formulating strategy.

It is critical that strategic decision makers understand the assumptions on which environmental forecasts are based. An example is the experience of Itel, a computer-leasing firm. In 1978, Itel was able to lease 200 plug-in computers made by Advanced Systems and by Hitachi largely because IBM was unable to deliver its newest systems. Consequently, Itel made a bullish sales forecast for 1979, that it would place 430 of its systems—despite the rumor that IBM would launch a new line of aggressively priced systems in the first quarter of that year. Even Itel's competitors felt that customers would hold off their purchasing decisions until IBM made the announcement. However, Itel signed long-term purchase contracts with its suppliers and increased its marketing staff by 80 percent. This forecasting mistake and the failure to examine sales forecasts in relationship to actions of competitors and suppliers was nearly disastrous. Itel slipped close to bankruptcy within less than a year.

Forecasting external events enables a firm to identify the probable requirements for future success, to formulate or reformulate its basic mission, and to design strategies to achieve goals and objectives. If the forecast identifies any gaps or inconsistencies between the firm's desired position and its present position, strategic managers can respond with plans and actions.

Dealing with the uncertainty of the future is a major function of the strategic manager. The forecasting task requires systematic information gathering coupled with the ability to utilize a variety of forecasting approaches. A high level of intuitive insight is also needed to integrate risks and opportunities in formulating strategy. However, intentional or unintentional delays or lack of understanding of certain issues may prevent an organization from using insights gained in assessing the impact of broader environmental trends. Consistent sensitivity and constant openness to new and better approaches and opportunities are therefore essential.

Monitor the Critical Aspects of Managing Forecasts

Although almost all aspects of forecasting can be considered critical in specific situations, three aspects stand out over the lifetime of a business.

The first is identification of factors that deserve forecasting. Although literally hundreds of different factors might affect a firm, often a few factors of immediate concern (such as sales forecasts and competitive trends) are most important. Unfortunately, seldom are enough time and resources available for complete understanding of all environmental factors that might be critical to the success of a strategy. Therefore, executives must depend on their collective experience and perception of what is important in identifying factors worthy of the expense of forecasting.

The second critical aspect is whether reputable, cost-efficient sources are available outside the firm that can expand the company's forecasting database. Strategic managers should locate federal and state governments, trade and industry associations, and other groups or individuals that can provide data forecasts at reasonable costs.

The third critical aspect of forecast management arises with the decision to handle forecasting tasks in-house. Given the great credence often accorded formally developed forecasts—despite the inherent uncertainty of the data base—the selection of forecasting techniques is indeed critical. A firm beginning its forecasting efforts is well advised to start with less technical methods, such as sales force estimates and the jury of executive opinion, rather than highly sophisticated forecasting techniques, such as econometrics. With added experience and understanding, the firm can add approaches that require greater analytical sophistication. In this way, managers learn to cope with the inherent weaknesses as well as the variable strengths of forecasting techniques.

Summary

Environmental forecasting starts with identification of factors external to the firm that might provide critical opportunities or pose threats in the future. Both quantitative and qualitative strategic forecasting techniques are used to project the long-range direction and impact of these critical remote- and task environment factors. The strengths and weaknesses of the various techniques must be understood in evaluating and selecting the most appropriate forecasting approaches for the firm. Employing more than one technique is usually advised to balance the potential bias or errors individual techniques involve.

Critical aspects in the management of forecasting include the selection of key factors to forecast, the selection of forecast sources outside the firm, the selection of forecasting activities to be done in-house, and understanding between developers and users of the environmental forecasts.

Questions for Discussion

1. Identify five anticipated changes in the remote environment that you believe will affect major industries in the United States over the next decade. What forecasting techniques could be used to assess the probable impact of these changes?

2. Construct a matrix with forecasting techniques on the horizontal axis and at least five qualities of forecasting techniques across the vertical axis. Next, indicate the relative strengths and weaknesses of each technique.

3. Develop three *heuristics* (rules of thumb) to guide strategic managers in using forecasting.

4. Develop a two-page, typewritten forecast of a variable that you believe will affect the prosperity of your business school over the next 10 years.

5. Using prominent business journals, find two examples of firms that either profited or suffered from environmental forecasts.

6. Describe the background, skills, and abilities of the individual you would hire as the environmental forecaster for your $500-million-in-annual-sales firm. How would the qualifications differ for a smaller or larger business?

Bibliography

Drucker, P. M. *Managing in Turbulent Times*. New York: Harper & Row, 1980.

Fahey, L., and W. R. King. "Environmental Scanning for Corporate Planning." *Business Horizons,* August 1977, pp. 61–71.

Howard, Niles. "Doing Business in Unstable Countries." *Dun's Review,* March 1980, pp. 49–55.

Kast, F. "Scanning the Future Environment: Social Indications." *California Management Review,* Fall 1980, pp. 22–32.

La Bell, D., and O. J. Krasner. "Selecting Environmental Forecasting Techniques from Business Planning Requirements." *Academy of Management Review,* July 1977, pp. 373–83.

Linneman, R. E. *Shirt-Sleeve Approach to Long-Range Planning: For the Smaller, Growing Corporation*. Englewood Cliffs, N.J.: Prentice-Hall, 1980.

Linneman, R. E., and J. D. Kennell. "Shirt-Sleeve Approach to Long-Range Plans." *Harvard Business Review,* March–April 1977, pp. 141–50.

Madridakis, S., and S. Wheelwright. "Forecasting: Issues and Challenges for Marketing Management." *Journal of Marketing,* October 1977, pp. 24–38.

————, eds. *Forecasting*. New York: North Holland Publishing, 1979.

Weiss, E. "Future Public Opinion of Business." *Management Review,* March 1978, pp. 8–15.

Wheelwright, S. C., and D. G. Clarke. "Corporate Forecasting: Promise and Reality." *Harvard Business Review,* November–December 1976, pp. 40–64.

"Where the Big Econometric Models Go Wrong." *Business Week,* March 30, 1981, pp. 70–73.

Appendix

Sources for Remote Environmental and Operating Forecasts

Remote Environment

A. Economic considerations.
   1. *Predicasts* (most complete and up-to-date review of forecasts).
   2. National Bureau of Economic Research.
   3. *Handbook of Basic Economic Statistics.*
   4. *Statistical Abstract of the United States* (also includes industrial, social, and political statistics).
   5. Publications by the Department of Commerce agencies:
      a. Office of Business Economics (e.g., *Survey of Business*).
      b. Bureau of Economic Analysis (e.g., *Business Conditions Digest*).

Sources: Adapted with numerous additions from C. R. Goeldner and L. M. Kirks, "Business Facts: Where to Find Them," *MSU Business Topics,* Summer 1976, pp. 23–76, reprinted by permission of the publisher; Division of Research, Graduate School of Business Administration, MSU: F. E. deCarbonnel and R. G. Donance, "Information Source for Planning Decisions," *California Management Review,* Summer 1973, pp. 42–53; and A. B. Nun, R. C. Lenz, Jr., H. W. Landford, and M. J. Cleary, "Data Sources for Trend Extrapolation in Technological Forecasting," *Long-Range Planning,* February 1972, pp. 72–76.

      c. Bureau of the Census (e.g., *Survey of Manufacturers* and various reports of population, housing, and industries).

      d. Business and Defense Service Administration (e.g., *United States Industrial Outlook*).

  6. Securities and Exchange Commission (various quarterly reports on plant and equipment, financial reports, working capital of corporations).

  7. The Conference Board.

  8. *Survey of Buying Power.*

  9. *Marketing Economic Guide.*

 10. *Industrial Arts Index.*

 11. U.S. and national chambers of commerce.

 12. American Manufacturers Association.

 13. *Federal Reserve Bulletin.*

 14. *Economic Indicators,* annual report.

 15. *Kiplinger Newsletter.*

 16. International economic sources:

      a. *Worldcasts.*

      b. Master key index for business international publications.

      c. Department of Commerce.

        (1) Overseas business reports.

        (2) Industry and Trade Administration.

        (3) Bureau of the Census—*Guide to Foreign Trade Statistics.*

 17. Business Periodicals Index.

B. Social considerations.

  1. Public opinion polls.

  2. Surveys such as *Social Indicators* and *Social Reporting,* the annals of the American Academy of Political and Social Sciences.

  3. Current controls: Social and behavioral sciences.

  4. Abstract services and indexes for articles in sociological, psychological, and political journals.

  5. Indexes for *The Wall Street Journal, New York Times,* and other newspapers.

  6. Bureau of the Census reports on population, housing, manufacturers, selected services, construction, retail trade, wholesale trade, and enterprise statistics.

  7. Various reports from groups such as the Brookings Institution and the Ford Foundation.

  8. World Bank Atlas (population growth and GNP data).

  9. World Bank–World Development Report.

C. Political considerations.

  1. *Public Affairs Information Services Bulletin.*

  2. CIS Index (Congressional Information Index).

  3. Business periodicals.

4. Funk & Scott (regulations by product breakdown).
5. Weekly compilation of presidential documents.
6. *Monthly Catalog of Government Publications*.
7. *Federal Register* (daily announcements of pending regulations).
8. *Code of Federal Regulations* (final listing of regulations).
9. Business International Master Key Index (regulations, tariffs).
10. Various state publications.
11. Various information services (Bureau of National Affairs, Commerce Clearing House, Prentice-Hall).

D. Technological considerations.
1. *Applied Science and Technology Index*.
2. *Statistical Abstract of the United States*.
3. Scientific and Technical Information Service.
4. University reports, congressional reports.
5. Department of Defense and military purchasing publishers.
6. Trade journals and industrial reports.
7. Industry contacts, professional meetings.
8. Computer-assisted information searches.
9. National Science Foundation annual report.
10. *Research and Development Directory* patent records.

E. Industry considerations.
1. *Concentration Ratios in Manufacturing* (U.S. Bureau of the Census).
2. *Input-Output Survey* (productivity ratios).
3. *Monthly Labor Review* (productivity ratios).
4. *Quarterly Failure Report* (Dun & Bradstreet).
5. *Federal Reserve Bulletin* (capacity utilization).
6. *Report on Industrial Concentration and Product Diversification in the 1,000 Largest Manufacturing Companies* (Federal Trade Commission).
7. Industry trade publications.
8. Bureau of Economic Analysis, U.S. Department of Commerce (specialization ratios).

Operating Environment

A. Competition and supplier considerations.
1. Target Group Index.
2. U.S. Industrial Outlook.
3. Robert Morris annual statement studies.
4. Troy, Leo Almanac of Business & Industrial Financial Ratios.
5. Census of Enterprise Statistics.
6. Securities and Exchange Commission (10-K reports).
7. Annual reports of specific companies.

8. *Fortune 500 Directory, The Wall Street Journal, Barron's, Forbes, Dun's Review.*
9. Investment services and directories: Moody's, Dun & Bradstreet, Standard & Poor's, Starch Marketing, Funk & Scott Index.
10. Trade association surveys.
11. Industry surveys.
12. Market research surveys.
13. *County Business Patterns.*
14. *County and City Data Book.*
15. Industry contacts, professional meetings, salespeople.
16. *NFIB Quarterly Economic Report for Small Business.*

B. Customer profile.
1. *Statistical Abstract of the United States,* first source of statistics.
2. *Statistical Sources* by Paul Wasserman (a subject guide to data—both domestic and international).
3. *American Statistics Index* (Congressional Information Service Guide to statistical publications of U.S. government—monthly).
4. Office of the Department of Commerce.
   a. Bureau of the Census reports on population, housing, and industries.
   b. *U.S. Census of Manufacturers* (statistics by industry, area, and products).
   c. *Survey of Current Business* (analysis of business trends, especially February and July issues).
5. Market research studies (*A Basic Bibliography on Market Review,* compiled by Robert Ferber et al., American Marketing Association).
6. *Current Sources of Marketing Information: A Bibliography of Primary Marketing Data* by Gunther & Goldstein, AMA.
7. *Guide to Consumer Markets,* The Conference Board (provides statistical information with demographic, social, and economic data—annual).
8. *Survey of Buying Power.*
9. *Predicasts* (abstracts of publishing forecasts of all industries, detailed products, and end-use data).
10. *Predicasts Basebook* (historical data from 1960 to present, covering subjects ranging from population and GNP to specific products and services; series are coded by Standard Industrial Classifications).
11. *Market Guide* (individual market surveys of over 1,500 U.S. and Canadian cities; data includes population, location, trade area, banks, principal industries, colleges and universities, department and chain stores, newspapers, retail outlets, and sales).
12. *County and City Data Book* (includes bank deposits, birth and death rates, business firms, education, employment, income of families, manufacturers, population, savings, wholesale and retail trade).

13. *Yearbook of International Trade Statistics* (UN).
14. *Yearbook of National Accounts Statistics* (UN).
15. *Statistical Yearbook* (UN—covers population, national income, agricultural and industrial production, energy, external trade and transport).
16. *Statistics of (Continents): Sources for Market Research* (includes separate books on Africa, America, Europe).

C. Key natural resources.

1. *Minerals Yearbook, Geological Survey* (Bureau of Mines, Department of the Interior).
2. *Agricultural Abstract* (U.S. Department of Agriculture).
3. Statistics of electric utilities and gas pipeline companies (Federal Power Commission).
4. Publications of various institutions: American Petroleum Institute, U.S. Atomic Energy Commission, Coal Mining Institute of America, American Steel Institute, and Brookings Institution.

Chapter 7 Cohesion Case Illustration

Environmental Forecasting at Holiday Inns, Inc.

Holiday Inns, Inc., uses several of the forecasting techniques discussed in Chapter 7 to project changes in its remote and operating environments that are of major importance to the firm's future strategic position. The greatest emphasis, even at the corporate level, is on environmental forecasting for hospitality-related factors. The primary environmental variables emphasized include the following factors:

1. Customer.
2. Social.
3. Technological.
4. Competition.

Exhibit 1 summarizes some of the forecasting techniques in terms of their focus relative to these key environmental factors.

To help understand these forecasts and how they might be useful, a few items particularly relevant to the hotel business in Exhibit 1 are illustrated below.

In better managing properties on a weekly basis to ensure operating margins are maintained, projected occupancy cycles based on historical trends can be quite helpful from the corporate level (planning cash flows) to the individual hotel level (budgeting and scheduling). Exhibit 2 shows systemwide occupancy projections for 1982 relative to actual 1981 levels. The widely fluctuating, yet historically consistent, pattern can clearly accommodate weekly scheduling and budgeting of resources.

Trend analysis, surveys, and judgmental scenarios about changing customer profiles and social characteristics constitute the major forecasting emphasis at Holiday Inns. Using these techniques, the following forecasts have been made about customer and social characteristics:

Fewer and later marriages mean that HI's customer base has broadened to include a greater concentration of single persons, couples, and businesspeople with greater freedom to travel (42).[1]

---

[1] Numbers in parentheses refer to the appropriate paragraphs in the Cohesion Case at the end of Chapter 1.

Exhibit 1
Environmental forecasting at Holiday Inns, Inc.

Main environmental factors	Forecasting techniques		
	Trend analysis	*Surveys*	*Judgment/ scenarios*
Customers	Changing demographic profile Specific HI guest characteristics Historical occupancy rate cycles	Changing consumer preferences Perceptions and brand recognition of HI	Future travel patterns and destination areas
Social	Baby boom generation Household composition Women's changing role Use of leisure time	(little use)	Worldwide status of the travel industry
Technology	Energy-saving technology, especially in terms of automobile and hotel operation Gas prices and impact on vacation travel	(little use)	Future travel modes Computer usage in property management Communication, especially satellite, developments
Competition	Size and growth of competitors Location emphasis (regions? type of location?), key price/ value available from competition	Level of consumer name recognition Consumer image and brand preference	Which competitors represent key threats to aspects of HI operations

The demographic characteristics of the typical hotel, restaurant, and casino guest are virtually identical: age 24 to 49, income over $30,000, with a preference for reliable and quality service instead of the lowest price (42, 55).

In three out of four instances, HI guests were male, but the trend to more women travelers is steadily growing (42, 75).

The movement of the baby boom generation through the prime traveling age (25 to 45) over the next 15 years suggests unprecedented growth opportunity in the hospitality business (42, 75).

There are predictions that by the end of the century, as larger numbers of

Exhibit 2
Company-owned properties monthly domestic occupancy comparison,
1982 versus 1981 (percent)

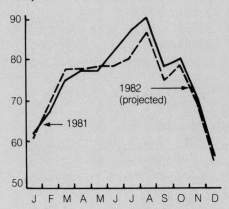

people pursue business and travel, the travel industry will have become the world's largest (74).

Using similar techniques regarding competition and technology, Holiday Inns, Inc., has developed such forecasts as:

Holiday Inn hotels will remain the brand preference of over one third of the traveling public through the 1990s (21).

Hospitality facilities located in multiuser locations will dominate industry growth and development in the 1990s (22).

Even with gasoline at $2 a gallon, highway driving habits will not change appreciably.

About 80 percent of U.S. adults approve of gambling, and 60 percent participate in some form. Gaming is fast becoming a national pastime and is viewed by the public as a leisure activity (55).

Most countries served by Delta Steamship are undergoing continued development and industrial expansion. This thrust provides a market for imports of high-value goods—of which U.S. industry is a major supplier (33, 34).

Are these forecasts accurate? Most seem plausible, although some have been previously questioned. At Best Western International, for example, a 17 percent cutback in auto travel if gas prices hit $2 a gallon is predicted. This view is shared by the American Petroleum Institute.

Holiday Inns executives disagree. They offer the following summary of their forecasts relative to the hospitality core of HI's business for the 1990s:

> The decade of the 1990s offers excellent potential for the hospitality industry. Business analysts see continued growth for travel through the end of the century.
>
> While temporary gasoline shortages have been a short-term negative factor in our operations twice in the past six years, we remain quite optimistic about gasoline availability for our customers. We expect occasional brief shortages, but by and large, we believe adequate supplies will be available.
>
> Our optimism is fostered by a significantly more efficient car fleet and rising energy prices. The 1988 auto fleet is 55 percent more fuel efficient than its 1978 counterpart. In 1990, the average car will travel 27.5 miles per gallon of gas, a 37.5 percent increase over 1980. As gasoline prices rise, we believe the consumer will be more selective. Conservation is already becoming the rule, and needless intracity travel is being curtailed. Our research tells us that our customers will continue to use their automobiles for intercity travel and vacations. Thus, we believe we are strongly positioned for the coming decade, especially as demand for our facilities will continue to outgrow supply.
>
> Our research shows us that the hospitality business is a good business and will remain so for as far as we can see. We look forward to the future and see continued growth, development, and profitability.

Two interesting factors that may receive increased attention at Holiday Inns for future forecasts are economic and political aspects. In the economic area, the 1981 recession was associated with poor performance years in Holiday Inns' hotel, restaurant, casino gambling, and transportation businesses. Although traditionally seen as somewhat "recession proof," these businesses are proving sensitive to economic cycles. Politically, as Holiday Inns concentrates on internal development, it will become more sensitive to such political factors as the situation in other countries and in terms of such concerns as currency exchange, regulation (of shipping, for example), and ownership restrictions.

8

The Company Profile: Internal Analysis of the Firm

Formulation of an effective strategy is based on a clear definition of company mission, an accurate appraisal of the external environment, and a thorough internal analysis of the firm. For a strategy to succeed, at least three ingredients are critical. First, the strategy must be *consistent* with conditions in the competitive environment. Specifically, it must take advantage of existing and/or projected opportunities and minimize the impact of major threats. Second, the strategy must place *realistic* requirements on the firm's internal resources and capabilities. In other words, pursuit of market opportunities must be based on key internal strengths and not only on the existence of such opportunity. Finally, the strategy must be *carefully executed*. The focus of this chapter is on the second ingredient for strategic success: realistic analysis of the firm's internal capabilities.

Internal analysis is difficult and challenging. An internal analysis that leads to a realistic company profile frequently involves trade-offs, value judgments, and educated guesses as well as objective, standardized analysis. Unfortunately, this dichotomy can lead managers to slight internal analysis by emphasizing personal opinion. But systematic internal analysis leading to an objective company profile is essential in the development of a realistic, effective strategy.

Internal analysis must identify the strategically important strengths and weaknesses on which a firm should ultimately base its strategy. Ideally, this purpose can be achieved by first identifying key internal factors (e.g., distribution channels, cash flow, locations, technology, and organizational structure) and second by evaluating these factors. In actual practice, the process is neither linear nor simple.[1] The steps tend to overlap, and managers in different positions and levels approach internal analysis in different ways. One major study found that managers even use different criteria for evaluating apparent strengths and potential weaknesses.[2] These findings will be examined in more detail later in this chapter.

While the process of internal analysis in most firms is not necessarily systematic, it is nonetheless recognized as a critical ingredient in strategy development. If only on an intuitive basis, managers develop judgments about what the firm does particularly well—its key strengths or distinct competencies. And based on the match between these strengths and defined or projected market opportunities, the firm ultimately charts its strategic course.

The Value of Systematic Internal Assessment

Before the components of internal analysis are discussed in greater detail, the impact of systematic internal analysis will be illustrated. The experiences of business firms, both large and small, suggest that thorough internal assessment is critical in developing a successful business strategy. Regardless of the favorable opportunities in the environment, a strategy must be based on a thorough consideration of internal strengths and weaknesses of the firm if such opportunities are to be maximized. Kalso Earth ® Shoes and Apple Computer Company illustrate the value of systematic internal analysis in shaping future strategies (see Figure 8–1).

Kalso Earth ® Shoes was a U.S. company that recently began making shoes based on the patented "negative-heel" design developed in Denmark by Ann Kalso. Earth ® Shoes were manufactured in Massachusetts and retailed by independent franchises throughout the United States.

Kalso Earth ® Shoes faced an impressive opportunity in the demand for its shoes among posture-conscious young professionals. Kalso's pursuit of this opportunity took precedence over *objective* internal analysis of production logistics, financial capacities, and dealer organization. The firm's single, large production facility in Massachusetts encountered difficulty in managing production runs and distribution to a nationwide network of small, franchised outlets. Each outlet ordered directly from the factory. Frequently, styles requested by outlets differed because of local market preferences. Therefore, the Kalso plant was constantly faced with the trade-off between small, inefficient production runs or, by holding orders until efficient runs were feasible, a slow response

---

[1] Howard H. Stevenson, "Defining Corporate Strengths and Weaknesses," *Sloan Management Review*, Spring 1976, pp. 51–68.

[2] Ibid., p. 65.

Figure 8–1
Kalso Earth® Shoe Company

Meet Anne Kalso . . .

We walk in a tough world. A world made of steel and concrete. A world without sympathy for our feet!

That's why Anne Kalso invented Earth® Shoes. They're designed to create underfoot the same natural terrain that existed before the earth was paved.

Patterned in the form of a healthy footprint in soft earth, the Earth® Shoe promises unsurpassed comfort and a new way of walking.

During her studies and experiments, Anne Kalso observed that by flexing the foot or lowering the heel, one could achieve a physical feeling similar to that attained in the Lotus or Buddah position of Yoga. Her further observations of foot imprints in sand, confirmed to her that nature intended people to walk with the weight of their bodies sunk low into the heels.

about the EARTH®
natural heel shoe.

Wearing the EARTH® Shoe, you will experience a completely new way of walking that might take some getting used to. Initially, you may feel off-balance because of the natural heel. This is normal so don't be alarmed. Young people adapt very quickly, older people take a little longer...

In effect, you are walking barefoot on the beach . . . or across summer fields . . . wherever you go. Because walking in EARTH® Shoes is a form of exercise, some may at first experience stiffness in the calves or thighs; some may find our unique arch may take getting used to; so moderate wear is advised in the beginning.

The uniquely contoured sole will allow you to walk in a gentle rolling motion. This helps to develop a more natural, graceful walk. There is no reason why you cannot interchange the use of other shoes with the EARTH® Shoes.

The human foot carries the entire weight load of our bodies and as we walk, this weight is constantly shifting.

The first point of contact, the heel ❶, takes the brunt of the load which then shifts to the outside of the foot ❷, and then across the metatarsal area to the ball ❸, and finally onto the large toe ❹ from which we spring into our next step.

The EARTH® Shoe is specifically designed to accommodate the shifting of weight load on our feet with the greatest ease and comfort.

Another feature of the EARTH® Shoe is the unique arch support.

Style 110 is the classic walking shoe. Our most popular all-around casual shoe. Available in sizes 6½ - 11 for women, and 7 - 11½ for men. Colors are Almond (medium brown) and Syrup (light tan).

Style 150 is a rugged, moccasin-toe oxford featuring an attractive closed-stitched design. Available in sizes 6½ - 11 for women, and 7 - 11½ for men. Colors are Almond and Sand Suede.

to consumer demand. Each outlet was an autonomous distributor/retailer linked directly to the Massachusetts production facility.

Kalso's financial structure presented additional difficulties. The company sought to finance increasing demand through short-term borrowing and the leveraging available through franchising. Kalso management wanted to maintain tight control over ownership of the firm, which they considered critical to maintaining the quality associated with its patented, negative-heel design. The popularity of its product and demand for franchises increased, but Kalso's pressed financial structure could not support such rapid growth.

As a result of Kalso's production logistics, distribution system, and emphasis on short-term debt, Kalso became overextended and failed. This happened even as the demand for its negative-heel design was escalating. Kalso Earth ® Shoes' strategy, even given an enviable market opportunity, was not based on a systematic objective analysis of its internal strengths and weaknesses.

IBM's meteoric rise in the personal computer market during the early 1980s raised significant challenges for Apple Computer Company. While it pioneered the personal computer industry, Apple saw its market share rapidly descend. Apple had grown rapidly, employing almost 5,000 people by the mid-1980s. These people were divided into product-centered divisions, with significant autonomy and a zealous independence reflecting the entrepreneurial personality of the company's youthful cofounder, Steven Jobs. Apple personnel succeeded in persuading Jobs to run a full-page ad in *The Wall Street Journal* when IBM brought out its IBM PC, welcoming IBM into the personal computer industry. Apple personnel were confident that their ingenuity, spirit, unique and growing product lines, and strong educational market position would keep them toe to toe with IBM.

By 1985, Apple found itself reeling from a series of heavy quarterly losses. Its two early attempts to attract business customers with the Apple III and Lisa computers had failed, and Macintosh (the product on which the company bet its future) shipments were running only 10,000 per month versus Apple's 80,000-per-month capacity to make the machine. John Sculley (see Figure 8–2), after replacing Jobs as chairman of Apple, sought to realistically identify internal key strengths around which Apple could rebuild its competitive position. Sculley saw four—its Macintosh computer, its desktop publishing software and peripherals to go with the Macintosh, its user-friendly product capabilities, and its strong position in the educational market. Sculley devised a careful strategy centered on these four strengths. Over 50,000 Macintosh publishing systems were sold in 1986 alone, and by 1988 Macintosh had become the de facto industry standard in news graphics and desktop publishing. This success, and its lock in the educational market, allowed Sculley to personally lead a marketing effort targeted toward large, personal service companies and technology-driven companies to make them aware of the user-friendly attributes of the product. Finally, he totally reorganized and centralized the company around functions rather than the old product-based fiefdoms, which eliminated

Figure 8–2

20 percent of Apple's overhead and provided greater consistency in the focus of Apple's marketing efforts. By 1988, Apple's sales were growing at twice the rate of the PC industry, and profit margins were triple those of the mid-1980s.

Apple faced a major threat to its survival as a serious player in the personal computer business. Its strategy was based on attributes representing emotionally charged feelings among executives and founders rather than on objectively assessed strengths and weaknesses. Its new chairman, John Sculley, focused objectively and intensely on rather limited internal strengths as a basis for Apple's subsequent strategy. And, just as some industry watchers were writing Apple's obituary as a serious player in the industry, Apple has reemerged as a major factor in both business and educational sectors of the personal computer industry.

Systematic internal analysis is particularly essential in small business firms. Small firms are continually faced with limited resources and markets. At the same time, these firms are flexible and capable of making specialized, uniquely catered responses to selected market needs. To effectively channel their limited resources in directions that maximize these limited market opportunities, small firms must frequently make objective internal analyses.

Given these brief illustrations of the value of systematic internal analysis, it is appropriate to examine the process in more detail.

Developing the Company Profile

A company profile is the determination of a firm's strategic competencies and weaknesses. This is accomplished by identifying and then evaluating strategic internal factors.

What are strategic internal factors? Where do they originate? How do we decide which are truly strategic factors that must be carefully evaluated? These questions might be raised by managers in identifying and evaluating key internal factors as strengths or weaknesses on which to base the firm's future strategy.

Identification of Strategic Internal Factors

A Function Approach.   Strategic internal factors are a firm's basic capabilities, limitations, and characteristics. Figure 8–3 lists typical factors, some of which would be the focus of internal analysis in most business firms. This list of factors is broken down along functional lines.

Firms are not likely to consider all of the factors in Figure 8–3 as potential strengths or weaknesses. To develop or revise a strategy, managers would rather identify the few factors on which success will most likely depend. Equally important, reliance on different internal factors will vary by industry, market segment, product life cycle, and the firm's current position. Managers are looking for what Chester Barnard calls "the strategic factors," those internal capabilities that appear most critical for success in a particular competitive area.[3] For example, strategic factors for firms in the oil industry will be quite different from those of firms in the construction or hospitality industries. Strategic factors can also vary between firms within the same industry. In the mechanical writing industry, for example, the strategies of BIC and Cross, both successful, are based on different internal strengths: BIC's on its strengths in mass production, extensive advertising, and mass distribution channels; Cross's on high quality, image, and selective distribution channels.

Strategists examine past performance to isolate key internal contributors to favorable (or unfavorable) results. What did we do well, or poorly, in marketing, operations, and financial management that had a major influence on past results? Was the sales force effectively organized? Were we in the right channels of distribution? Did we have the financial resources to support the past strategy? The same examination and questions can be applied to a firm's current situation, with particular emphasis on changes in the importance of key dimensions over time. For example, heavy advertising along with mass production and mass distribution were strategic internal factors in BIC's initial

---

[3] Chester Barnard, *Functions of the Executive* (Cambridge, Mass.: Harvard University Press, 1939), chap. 14.

Figure 8–3
Key internal factors: Potential strengths and weaknesses

Marketing

Firm's products/services; breadth of product line.

Concentration of sales in a few products or to a few customers.

Ability to gather needed information about markets.

Market share or submarket shares.

Product/service mix and expansion potential: life cycle of key products; profit/sales balance in product/service.

Channels of distribution: number, coverage, and control.

Effective sales organization; knowledge of customer needs.

Product/service image, reputation, and quality.

Imaginative, efficient, and effective sales promotion and advertising.

Pricing strategy and pricing flexibility.

Procedures for digesting market feedback and developing new products, services, or markets.

After-sale service and follow-up.

Goodwill/brand loyalty.

Finance and accounting

Ability to raise short-term capital.

Ability to raise long-term capital: debt/equity.

Corporate-level resources (multibusiness firm).

Cost of capital relative to industry and competitors.

Tax considerations.

Relations with owners, investors, and stockholders.

Leverage position: capacity to utilize alternative financial strategies, such as lease or sale and leaseback.

Cost of entry and barriers to entry.

Price–earnings ratio.

Working capital; flexibility of capital structure.

Effective cost control; ability to reduce cost.

Financial size.

Efficient and effective accounting system for cost, budget, and profit planning.

Production/operations/technical

Raw materials cost and availability; supplier relationships.

Inventory control systems; inventory turnover.

Location of facilities; layout and utilization of facilities.

Economies of scale.

Technical efficiency of facilities and utilization of capacity.

Effective use of subcontracting.

Degree of vertical integration; value added and profit margin.

Efficiency and cost/benefit of equipment.

Effective operation control procedures: design, scheduling, purchasing, quality control, and efficiency.

Costs and technological competencies relative to industry and competitors.

Research and development/technology/innovation.

Patents, trademarks, and similar legal protection.

Personnel

Management personnel.

Employees' skill and morale.

Labor relations costs compared to industry and competition.

Figure 8–3 *(concluded)*

Efficient and effective personnel policies.
Effective use of incentives to motivate performance.
Ability to level peaks and valleys of employment.
Employee turnover and absenteeism.
Specialized skills.
Experience.

Organization of general management

Organizational structure.
Firm's image and prestige.
Firm's record for achieving objectives.
Organization of communication system.
Overall organizational control system (effectiveness and utilization).
Organizational climate; culture.
Use of systematic procedures and techniques in decision making.
Top-management skill, capabilities, and interest.
Strategic planning system.
Intraorganizational synergy (multibusiness firms).

---

strategy for ballpoint pens and disposable lighters. With the product life cycle fast reaching maturity, BIC has currently determined that cost-conscious mass production is a strategic factor, while heavy advertising is not.

Analysis of past trends in sales, costs, and profitability is of major importance in identifying strategic internal factors. And this identification should be based on a clear picture of the nature of the firm's sales. An anatomy of past trends broken down by product lines, channels of distribution, key customers or types of customers, geographic region, and sales approach should be developed in detail. A similar anatomy should focus on costs and profitability. Detailed investigation of the firm's performance history helps isolate internal factors influencing sales, costs, profitability, or their interrelationships. These factors are of major importance to future strategy decisions. For example, one firm may find that 83 percent of its sales result from 25 percent of its products. Another firm may find that 30 percent of its products (or services) contribute 78 percent of its profitability. To understand such results, a firm may determine that certain key internal factors (e.g., experience in particular distribution channels, pricing policies, warehouse location, technology) deserve major attention in formulating future strategy.

Identifying strategic factors also requires an external focus. When a strategist isolates key internal factors through analysis of past and present performance, industry conditions/trends and comparisons with competitors also provide insight. BIC's identification of mass production and advertising as key internal factors is based as much on analysis of industry and competitive characteristics as on past performance of BIC itself. Changing industry conditions can lead to the need to reexamine internal strengths and weaknesses

Strategy in Action 8–1
Merrill Lynch's Strategic Internal Factors: Are They Strengths or Weaknesses?

As deregulation melds together the once-segmented financial service industries, Merrill Lynch faces increasing direct competition from Sears Roebuck, American Express, Citicorp, and other formidable companies outside the securities industry. While Merrill Lynch has proved itself the equal of anyone in innovating financial products and services, in the way it delivers them to consumers, in its compensation methods, and in its corporate culture, Merrill Lynch remains quintessentially a brokerage house.

Merrill Lynch's attempt to strike a balance between old Wall Street and the emergence of one-stop financial shopping has trapped it in a truly nasty dilemma. The company's greatest strength—its retail system of 431 branch offices and 8,763 brokers—may have become its greatest weakness. By funneling nearly all of its growing number of financial products through its brokers, Merrill Lynch generates huge sales volume. But because its brokers get a cut of all they sell, this approach is very expensive. And its inflexibility makes Merrill Lynch vulnerable at a time when discount brokering and other low-cost distribution methods are gaining market share.

But any attempt to tamper with Merrill Lynch's retail sales organization is perilous because the broker—not the company—typically commands customer loyalty. "My customers are my blanket," said one veteran Merrill Lynch broker. "I can just pick them up and walk away." Merrill Lynch has gingerly begun to walk a fine line between remaking its vaunted broker system and destroying it. The company has raised its performance standards for brokers and is beginning to weed out the laggards. It has also begun the delicate task of converting the broker into a financial adviser at the hub of a network of salaried sales assistants and professionals who specialize in insurance, lending, and tax matters.

Some veteran brokers are disillusioned by the trend toward one-stop financial shopping, while the performance crackdown stirs resentment among the newcomers. "Merrill Lynch is losing touch with its distribution system," claims a senior executive of a major Wall Street firm. "It's become a case of the home office proposing and the field disposing." The erosion of Merrill Lynch's legendary morale has made it easier for his company to lure away brokers, he says.

Merrill's vice president for human resources insists that the turnover rate among Merrill Lynch's sales force is "trending sideways at an acceptable level" and that most of those brokers who do leave are not top performers. Still, Merrill

Continued on Page 211

Strategy in Action 8–1 (*concluded*)

Lynch was one of the first firms to sue former brokers who allegedly violated pledges not to take their customers with them to other firms.

Especially at a time of internal tension, Merrill Lynch's monolithic retail distribution system is a cumbersome way of serving an unsettled market. Discount brokers, which do not pay commissions to their brokers, tripled their share of equity trading volume to 24 percent by the mid-1980s.

Meanwhile, many full-service brokers are expanding their branch systems at a furious pace. "The name of the game in the financial services industry is distribution," said James Settel, a senior vice president at Prudential Bache. "The more good distribution points you have, the better are your chances of picking up all the marbles."

Dean Witter Reynolds Inc., now part of Sears Roebuck & Company, plans to nearly double its branches and to increase its corps of brokers from 4,900 to 11,000 by 1991. About 280 of the offices will be in Sears stores.

Roger Birk, Merrill Lynch board chairman, recognized the difficulty in first identifying and acting on the brokerage firm's strengths and weaknesses in the changing financial services industry. Birk seems undaunted. "Who ever said it would be easy? It's not," he says. "This is a tough business—a very difficult business to manage."

Source: Based on the article "Merrill Lynch's Big Dilemma," from the January 6, 1984, issue of *Business Week*.

in light of newly emerging determinants of success in the industry. Strategy in Action 8–1 illustrates a strategic shift in Merrill Lynch's internal strengths and weaknesses based on changing determinants of success in the financial services industry. Furthermore, strategic internal factors are often chosen for in-depth evaluation because firms are contemplating expansion of products or markets, diversification, and so forth. Clearly, scrutinizing the industry under consideration and current competitors is a key means of identifying strategic factors if a firm is evaluating its capability to move into unfamiliar markets.

The "Value Chain" Approach. Diagnosing a company's key strengths and weaknesses requires the adoption of a disaggregated view of the firm. Examining the firm across distinct functional areas, as suggested above and in Figure 8–3, is one way to disaggregate the firm for internal analysis purposes. Another way to disaggregate the firm is to use a framework called the "value chain." Developed by Michael Porter in his book *Competitive Advantage*, a value chain is a systematic way of viewing the series of activities a firm performs to provide a product to its customers. Figure 8–4 diagrams a typical value chain. The value chain disaggregates a firm into its strategically relevant activities in order to understand the behavior of the firm's cost and its existing or

Figure 8–4
The value chain

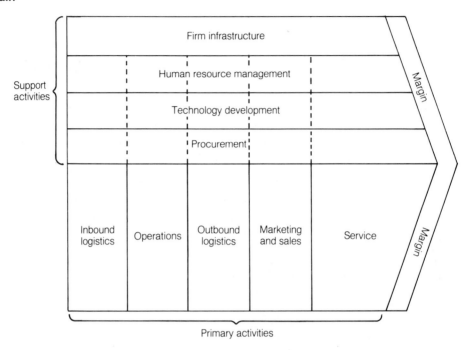

potential sources of differentiation. A firm gains competitive advantage by performing these strategically important activities—what we have called *key internal factors*—more cheaply or better than its competitors.

Every firm can be viewed (disaggregated) as a collection of value activities that are performed to design, produce, market, deliver, and support its product.

As portrayed in Figure 8–4, these activities can be grouped into nine basic categories for virtually any firm at the business unit level. Within each category of activity, a firm typically performs a number of discrete activities that may represent key strengths or weaknesses for the firm. Service activities, for example, may include such discrete activities as installation, repair, parts distribution, and upgrading—any of which could be a major source of competitive advantage or disadvantage. Through the systematic identification of these discrete activities, managers using the value chain approach can target potential strengths and weaknesses for further evaluation.

The basic categories of activities can be grouped into two broad types. *Primary* activities are those involved in the physical creation of the firm's product or service, its delivery and marketing to the buyer, and its after-sale support. Overarching each of these are *support* activities, which provide inputs or infrastructure allowing the primary activities to take place on an ongoing basis.

Identifying Primary Activities.   Identifying primary value activities requires the isolation of activities that are technologically and strategically distinct. Each of the five basic categories of primary activities is divisible into several distinct activities, such as the following:

Inbound Logistics: Activities associated with receiving, storing, and disseminating inputs to the product, such as material handling, warehousing, inventory control, vehicle scheduling, and returns to suppliers.

Operations: Activities associated with transforming inputs into the final product form, such as machining, packaging, assembly, equipment maintenance, testing, printing, and facility operations.

Outbound Logistics: Activities associated with collecting, storing, and physically distributing the product to buyers, such as finished goods warehousing, material handling, delivery vehicle operation, order processing, and scheduling.

Marketing and Sales: Activities associated with providing a means by which buyers can purchase the product and inducing them to do so, such as advertising, promotion, sales force, quoting, channel selection, channel relations, and pricing.

Service: Activities associated with providing service to enhance or maintain the value of the product, such as installation, repair, training, parts supply, and product adjustment.[4]

The primary activities most deserving of further analysis depend on the particular industry. For example, Holiday Inns may be much more concerned about operations activities—it provides its service instantaneously at each location—and marketing/sales activities than it is about outbound logistics. For a distributor, such as the food distributor PYA, inbound and outbound logistics are the most critical areas. After-sale service is becoming increasingly critical to automotive dealerships. Yet, in any firm, all the primary activities are present to some degree and deserve attention in a systematic internal analysis.

Identifying Support Activities.   Support value activities arise in one of four categories and can be identified or disaggregated by isolating technologically or strategically distinct activities. Often overlooked as sources of competitive advantage, these four areas can typically be distinguished as follows:

Procurement: Activities involved in obtaining purchased inputs, whether raw materials, purchased services, machinery, or so on. Procurement stretches

---

[4] Michael E. Porter, *Competitive Advantage* (New York: Free Press, 1985), pp. 39–40.

across the entire value chain because it supports every activity—every activity uses purchased inputs of some kind. Many discrete procurement activities are typically performed within a firm, often by different people.

Technology Development: Activities involved in designing the product as well as in creating and improving the way the various activities in the value chain are performed. We tend to think of technology in terms of the product or manufacturing process. In fact, every activity a firm performs involves a technology or technologies, which may be mundane or sophisticated, and a firm has a stock of know-how for performing each activity. Technology development typically involves a variety of discrete activities, some performed outside the R&D department.

Human Resource Management: Activities necessary to ensure the recruiting, training, and development of personnel. Every activity involves human resources, and thus human resource management activities cut across the entire chain.

Firm Infrastructure: Such activities as general management, accounting, legal, finance, strategic planning, and all others decoupled from specific primary or support activities but essential to the entire chain's operation.[5]

Using the Value Chain in Internal Analysis.   The value chain provides a useful approach to guide a systematic internal analysis of the firm's existing or potential strengths and weaknesses. By systematically disaggregating a firm into its distinct value activities across the nine activity categories, the strategist has identified key internal factors for further examination as potential sources of competitive advantage.

Whether using the value chain, an examination of functional areas, or both approaches, the strategist's next step in a systematic internal analysis is to compare the firm's status with meaningful standards to determine which value activities are strengths or weaknesses. Four sources of meaningful standards used to evaluate internal factors and value activities are discussed in the next section.

Evaluation of Strategic Internal Factors

Identification and evaluation of key internal factors have been separated for discussion, but in practice they are not separate, distinct steps. The objective of internal analysis is a careful determination of a firm's strategic strengths

---

[5] Michael Porter, "Changing Patterns of International Competition," *California Management Review* 28, no. 2 (1986), p. 14.

and weaknesses. An internal analysis that generates a long list of resources and capabilities has provided little to help in strategy formulation. Instead, internal analysis must identify and evaluate a limited number of strengths and weaknesses relative to the opportunities targeted in the firm's current and future competitive environment.

What are potential strengths and weaknesses? A factor is considered a strength if it is a distinct competency or competitive advantage. It is more than merely what the firm has the competence to do. It is something the firm does (or has the future capacity to do) particularly well relative to abilities of existing or potential competitors. A distinctive competence (strength) is important because it gives an organization a comparative advantage in the marketplace. For example, Kalso Earth ® Shoes' product image and patented design were two distinct competencies for that firm.

A factor is considered a weakness if it is something the firm does poorly or doesn't have the capacity to do although key rivals have the capacity. Centralized production facilities and lack of capital resources were major weaknesses for Kalso Earth ® Shoes in trying to compete with other shoe manufacturers on a nationwide basis. Scripto's outdated production facilities and lack of financial resources to support mass advertising were major weaknesses. The firm's management had to weigh these factors in deciding to challenge BIC in the ball-point segment of the writing implement industry.

How should strategists evaluate key internal factors and value activities as strengths or weaknesses? There are four basic perspectives: (1) comparison with the firm's past performance, (2) stage of product/market evolution, (3) comparison with competitors, and (4) comparison with key success factors in the firm's industry.

Comparison with Past Capabilities and Performance.   Strategists use the historical experience of the firm as a basis for evaluating internal factors. Managers are most familiar with their firm, its internal capabilities and problems, because they have been immersed over time in managing the firm's financial, marketing, production, and R&D activities. Not surprisingly, a manager's assessment of whether certain internal factors—such as production facilities, sales organization, financial capacity, control systems, and key personnel—are strengths or weaknesses will be strongly influenced by his or her internal experience. In the capital-intensive airline industry, for example, debt capacity is a strategic internal factor. Delta Airlines has a debt/equity ratio of less than 0.6, which is comparable to its past debt/equity ratio. Delta views this as a continued strength, representing significant flexibility to support Delta managers in deciding to invest in facilities or equipment. Yet Piedmont managers also view their 1.5 debt/equity ratio as a growing strength because it is down 100 percent from its 3.0 level in the early 1980s.

While historical experience can provide a relevant evaluation framework, strategists must avoid tunnel vision. Texaco management, for example, had long considered its large number of service stations (27,000 in 1980) a key strength. This strength (along with other perceived strengths) had "worked so well for so long [at Texaco] that even the thought of changing them was heretical to management."[6] But Shell, with just over 6,280 service stations, sold slightly more gasoline than Texaco.[7] Clearly, using only historical experience as a basis for identifying strengths and weaknesses can prove dangerously inaccurate.

Stages in Product/Market Evolution. The requirements for success in product/market segments evolve and change over time. As a result, strategists can use these changing patterns associated with different stages in product/market evolution as a framework for identifying and evaluating the firm's strengths and weaknesses.

Figure 8–5 depicts four general stages of product/market evolution and the typical changes in functional capabilities often associated with business success at each stage. The early development of a product/market, for example, entails minimal growth in sales, major R&D emphasis, rapid technological change in the product, operating losses, and a need for sufficient resources or slack to support a temporarily unprofitable operation. Success at this stage may be associated with technical skill with being first in new markets or with having a marketing advantage that creates widespread awareness. Radio Shack's initial success with its TRS-80 home computer was based in part on its ability to gain widespread exposure and acceptance in the ill-defined home computer market via the large number of existing Radio Shack outlets throughout the country.

The strengths necessary for success change in the growth stage. Rapid growth brings new competitors into the market. Such factors as brand recognition, product/market differentiation, and the financial resources to support both heavy marketing expenses and the effect of price competition on cash flow can be key strengths at this stage. IBM entered the personal computer market in the growth stage and was able to rapidly become the market leader with a strategy based on key strengths in brand awareness and the financial resources to support consumer advertising.

As the product/market moves through a "shakeout" phase and into the maturity stage, market growth continues but at a decreasing rate. The number of market segments begins to expand, while technological change in product design slows considerably. The result is usually more intense competition, and promotional or pricing advantages or differentiation become key internal

---

[6] "Texaco: Restoring Luster to the Star," *Business Week,* December 22, 1980, p. 54; and "Inside the Shell Oil Company," *Newsweek,* June 15, 1981, p. 74.

[7] "Texaco," p. 60.

Figure 8–5
Sources of distinctive competence at different stages of product/market evolution

Functional area	Introduction	Growth	Maturity	Decline
Marketing	Resources/skill to create widespread awareness and find acceptance from customers; advantageous access to distribution	Ability to establish brand recognition; find niche; reduce price; solidify strong distribution relations and develop new channels	Skill in aggressively promoting products to new markets and holding existing markets; pricing flexibility; skills in differentiating products and holding customer loyalty	Cost-effective means of efficient access to selected channels and markets; strong customer loyalty or dependence; strong company image
Production/ operations	Ability to expand capacity effectively; limit number of designs; develop standards	Ability to add product variants; centralize production or otherwise lower costs; improve product quality; seasonal subcontracting capacity	Improve product and reduce costs; ability to share or reduce capacity; advantageous supplier relationships; subcontracting	Ability to prune product line; cost advantage in production, location, or distribution; simplified inventory control; subcontracting or long production runs
Finance	Resources to support high net cash overflow and initial losses; ability to use leverage effectively	Ability to finance rapid expansion; still have net cash outflows but increasisng profits; resources to support product improvements	Ability to generate and redistribute increasing net cash inflows; effective cost control systems	Ability to reuse or liquidate unneeded equipment; advantage in cost of facilities; control system accuracy; streamlined management control
Personnel	Flexibility in staffing and training new management; existence of employee with key skills in new products or markets	Existence and ability to add skilled personnel; motivated and loyal work force	Ability to cost effectively reduce work force; increase efficiency	Capacity to reduce and reallocate personnel; cost advantage
Engineering and research and development	Ability to make engineering changes; have technical bugs in product and process resolved	Skill in quality and new feature development; state developing successor product	Reduce costs; develop variants to differentiate products	Support other growth areas or apply to unique customer needs
Key functional area and strategy focus	Engineering; market penetration	Sales; consumer loyalty; market share	Production efficiency; successor products	Finance; maximum investment recovery

Source: Adapted from Peter Doyle, "The Realities of the Product Life Cycle," *Quarterly Review of Marketing,* Summer 1976, pp. 1–6; Harold Fox, "A Framework for Functional Coordination," *Atlantic Economic Review,* November–December 1973; Charles W. Hofer, *Conceptual Constructs for Formulating Corporate and Business Strategy* (Boston: Intercollegiate Case Clearing House, 1977), p. 7; Philip Kotler, *Marketing Management* (Englewood Cliffs, N.J.: Prentice-Hall, 1988); and Charles Wasson, *Dynamic Competitive Strategy and Product Life Cycles* (Austin, Tex.: Austin Press, 1978).

strengths. Technological change in process design becomes intense as the many competitors seek to provide the product in the most efficient manner. Where R&D was critical in the development stage, efficient production has now become crucial to a business's continued success in the broader market segments. Chrysler has found efficiency a key strength in the maturing auto industry.

When products/markets move toward a saturation/decline stage, strengths and weaknesses center on cost advantages, superior supplier or customer relationships, and financial control. Competitive advantage can exist at this stage, at least temporarily, if a firm serves gradually shrinking markets that competitors are choosing to leave. Strategy in Action 8–2 describes Radio Shack's efforts to reexamine its strengths and weaknesses in the rapidly maturing consumer electronics market.

Figure 8–5 is a rather simple model of the stages of product/market evolution. These stages can and do vary. But it is important to realize, especially as illustrated in the preceding discussion, that the relative importance of various determinants of success differs across stages of product/market evolution. Thus, stage of evolution must be considered in internal analysis. Figure 8–5 suggests different dimensions that are particularly deserving of in-depth consideration when developing a company profile.

Comparison with Competitors.   A major focus in determining a firm's strengths and weaknesses is comparison with existing (and potential) competitors. Firms in the same industry often have different marketing skills, financial resources, operating facilities and locations, technical know-how, brand image, levels of integration, managerial talent, and so on. These different internal capabilities can become relative strengths (or weaknesses) depending on the strategy the firm chooses. In choosing strategy, a manager should compare the company's key internal capabilities with those of its rivals, thereby isolating key strengths or weaknesses.

In the major home appliance industry, for example, Sears and General Electric are major rivals. Sears' major strength is its retail network. For GE, distribution—through independent franchised dealers—has traditionally been a relative weakness. With the financial resources to support modernized mass production, GE has maintained both cost and technological advantages over its rivals, particularly Sears. This major strength for GE is a relative weakness for Sears, which depends solely on subcontracting to produce its Kenmore brand appliances. On the other hand, maintenance and repair service are important in the appliance industry. Historically, Sears has strength in this area because it maintains a fully staffed service component and spreads the costs over numerous departments at each retail location. GE, on the other hand, has had to depend on regional service centers and local contracting with independent service firms by its local, independent dealers.

In ultimately developing a strategy, distribution network, technological capabilities, operating costs, and service facilities are a few of the internal factors Sears and GE must consider. To ascertain whether their internal capabilities on these and other factors are strengths or weaknesses, comparison to key competitors can prove useful. Significant favorable differences (existing or expected) are potential cornerstones of the firm's strategy. Likewise, through comparison to major competitors, a firm may avoid strategic commitments it cannot competitively support.

Success Factors in the Industry.   Industry analysis involves identifying factors associated with successful participation in a given industry. As was

Strategy in Action 8–2
Internal Analysis at Radio Shack

After almost completely missing the VCR boom of the mid-1980s and also seeing its share of the personal computer market erode from 19 percent in the early 1980s to 8.6 percent by 1985, Radio Shack (Tandy) executives decided serious internal analysis was necessary if the highly successful electronics retailer was to regain its prominence in that industry. Radio Shack had been a profitable, resourceful retailer of electrical equipment (such as antenna wires, radios, electronic parts, telephones, stereos, CB radios, and radar) that entered the personal computer market at its infancy, taking prime advantage of its 6,800 locations in the United States and Canada. Executives arrived at the following assessment after six months of thorough analysis:

Strengths

1. 6,800 retail locations.
2. Fully integrated producer.
3. Low-cost capabilities.

Weaknesses

1. Poor market research (totally misprojected VCR demand; company sells 10 percent of all audio equipment in United States but 1 percent of VCRs; phone sales 150 percent below projections).
2. Poor computer brand name (TRS-80 known as "Trash-80").
3. Computers not IBM compatible; lack software.
4. Store appearance more suited to hobbyist.
5. Prices above industry median.

Radio Shack used this assessment as input for decisions about a new strategy. Elements of Radio Shack's new strategy include:

1. Sell low-priced, IBM-compatible computers to individuals and very small businesses.
2. Use the Radio Shack and Tandy brand names and provide retail store-based training service to computer customers.
3. Revamp store appearance to attract women shoppers.

Continued on Page 220

Strategy in Action 8–2 (*concluded*)

4. Focus on price-competitive versions of consumer electronic products in Radio Shack's traditional product areas.

5. Diversify into other discount electronics chains to take advantage of Tandy's highly integrated production capabilities.

true of the evaluation methods discussed above, the key determinants of success in an industry may be used to identify the internal strengths and weaknesses of a firm. By scrutinizing industry competitors, as well as customer needs, vertical industry structure, channels of distribution, costs, barriers to entry, availability of substitutes, and suppliers, a strategist seeks to determine whether a firm's current internal capabilities represent strengths or weaknesses in new competitive arenas. The previous discussion in Chapter 7 provides a useful framework—five industry forces—against which to examine potential strengths and weaknesses. General Cinema Corporation, the nation's largest movie theater operator, determined that its internal skills in marketing, site analysis, creative financing, and management of geographically dispersed operations provided key strengths relative to major success factors in the soft-drink bottling industry. This assessment proved accurate. Since entering the soft drink bottling industry in 1968, General Cinema has become the largest franchised bottler of soft drinks in the United States, handling Pepsi, 7UP, Dr Pepper, and Sunkist. Eastern Airlines, however, based its strategy on strengths and weaknesses derived from a historical comparison more so than an industry perspective. Strategy in Action 8–3 shows how this hurt Eastern in the long run.

Use of industry-level analysis to evaluate a firm's capacity for success and to help devise future strategy has become a popular technique.[8] Its relevance as an aid to comprehensive internal analysis is discussed more fully in a subsequent section of this chapter.

Quantitative versus Qualitative Approaches in Evaluating Internal Factors

Numerous quantitative tools are available for evaluating selected internal capabilities of a firm. These entail measurement of a firm's effectiveness vis-à-vis each relevant factor and comparative analysis of this measurement against both competitors (directly or through industry averages) and the historical experience of the firm. Ratio analysis is useful for evaluating selected financial, marketing, and operating factors. The firm's balance sheet and in-

---

[8] Michael E. Porter, *Competitive Strategy: Techniques for Analyzing Industries and Competitors* (New York: Free Press, 1980), offers broad, in-depth coverage of numerous techniques for evaluating the strengths and weaknesses of a firm and its competitors. Chapter 7 presents key aspects underlying Professor Porter's analytical approaches.

Strategy in Action 8–3
Eastern Airlines "Misses the Boat"

Eastern, seeking to calm nervous investors and employees, went to unusual lengths to communicate the basis for its 1984–85 corporate strategy. One key ingredient was its assessment of internal capabilities. Six key points were presented by Eastern management:

1. We will have the resources to substantially expand our operation.
   a. An average of 13 additional aircraft, primarily B-757s delivered in 1983, will be available for scheduled service.
   b. The pilot agreement permits additional hours to be flown with the existing work force. Similar productivity improvements are expected to limit the required increase in other personnel.
2. There are identified schedule opportunities at our established hubs for using the additional aircraft.
   a. Restoration of daytime service to the levels that preceded the air traffic controllers' (PATCO) strike at Atlanta and LaGuardia alone would effectively use the 13 aircraft.
3. Our position in the marketplace has been strong and improving.
   a. As measured by revenue per airplane seat-mile (ASM), we led all major airlines in 1982 and continued to outperform the industry in the first quarter of 1983.
4. Committed increases in employee compensation require increases in productivity that realistically can be achieved through both normal attrition and basic airline expansion.
   a. The pilot agreement includes improvements in productivity that are fundamental to our success. Similar improvements must be made elsewhere in the corporation.
5. In the aftermath of recent negotiations with the airline mechanics union, employee attitudes—morale and the willingness of different groups to work together—clearly are a major concern. Effectively addressing this issue is a major challenge for 1984.
6. Our balance sheet and cash situation require constant attention.

Eastern's management identified excess capacity as a key strength, ASM performance as an indicator of high customer demand (even though Eastern's high ASM is artificially high due to its New York-to-DC commuter service), financial position as a weakness, and morale/productivity as a pivotal question mark.

Continued on Page 222

Strategy in Action 8–3 (*concluded*)

But all of these were primarily based on Eastern's history rather than on comparison with competitors and changing requirements for success in the airline industry. The airline industry was rapidly changing, and competitive pressures were increasing. As a result, Eastern's strategy failed. Eastern subsequently avoided bankruptcy in late 1986 by selling out to Texas Air.

come statement are important sources from which to derive meaningful ratios. The appendix at the end of this chapter illustrates the use of these techniques for internal analysis.

Dun & Bradstreet and Robert Morris Associates regularly publish sets of ratios for a variety of industries.[9] Trade publications for specific types of firms are another source of comparative information. Information from these sources and from the firm's past performance are useful if ratio analysis is used to evaluate an internal factor. Examples of other quantitative or analytical tools include cash flow analysis, sensitivity analysis, and elasticity and variability analysis.[10]

Quantitative tools cannot be applied to all internal factors, and the normative judgments of key planning participants may be used in evaluation. Company or product image and prestige are examples of internal factors more amenable to qualitative evaluation. But, even though qualitative and judgmental criteria are used, identification and serious evaluation of this type of factor are necessary and important aspects of a thorough internal analysis. Research by Harold Stevenson found this to be particularly true in evaluating weaknesses.[11] Stevenson interviewed 50 executives in six medium to large firms and found the following criteria used to identify and evaluate strengths and weaknesses:

	Degree of use	
Type of criteria	Strengths	Weaknesses
Historical experience	90%	10%
Industry/competitor comparison	67	33
Normative judgment	21	79

[9] *Dun's Review,* published monthly by Dun & Bradstreet, N.Y.; RMA: *Annual Statement Studies* published annually by Robert Morris Associates, Philadelphia.

[10] O. M. Joy, *Introduction to Financial Management* (Homewood, Ill.: Richard D. Irwin, 1980), pp. 119–28, 207–9, provides a useful discussion of cash flow analysis and sensitivity analysis; C. W. Hofer and D. Schendel, *Strategy Formulation: Analytical Concepts* (St. Paul, Minn.: West Publishing, 1978), especially chap. 2, provides a discussion of sensitivity analysis, elasticity analysis, variability analysis, and the product life-cycle concept as tools for evaluating a business's strengths and weaknesses.

[11] Stevenson, "Defining Strengths," pp. 64–68.

While managers used past performance and competitive comparison in evaluating tentative strengths, they relied heavily on normative judgment (qualitative assessment and opinion) in evaluating probable weaknesses. Stevenson suggested that this was true because weaknesses often reflect competencies or areas in which the firm (and its managers) lack experience. And because they have no experience in these areas, managers must use qualitative assessment and opinion to evaluate the weakness. Stevenson's research probably does not reflect how all business firms evaluate strengths and weaknesses, but it provides a vivid illustration of how often typical managers employ normative judgments in internal analysis.

Summary: Viewing Internal Analysis as a Process

Figure 8–6 diagrams the development of a company profile as a four-step process you should find useful in guiding internal analysis. It also conveniently summarizes all that we have discussed in this chapter regarding internal analysis.

In step 1, managers audit and examine key aspects of the business's operation, seeking to target key areas for further assessment. Areas targeted are those deemed central to the firm's strategic direction. As such, they are called "strategic internal factors."

Step 2 has managers evaluating the firm's status on these factors by comparing their current condition with past abilities of the firm. This is where most managers start their planning efforts. How do we compare with last year? Have we improved over the last year? Are we better able to do key things than we were last year? Does each key factor represent a favorable or an unfavorable situation?

The third step is very critical. Managers seek some comparative basis—linked to key industry or product/market conditions—against which to more accurately determine whether the company's condition on a particular factor represents a potential strength or weakness. Managers use three perspectives to do this: (1) requirements for success across different product/market stages of evolution, (2) what competitors are capable of doing, and (3) perceived key requirements for success in the market/industry segments in which they compete.

The results of the third step should be a determination of whether key strategic internal factors are:

a. *Competitive advantages*—factors providing the company with an edge compared to its competitors, and therefore key factors around which to build the firm's strategy.

b. *Basic business requirements*—factors that are important capabilities for the firm to have but are also typical of every viable competitor; does not represent a potential source of any strategic advantage.

Figure 8–6
Steps in the development of a company profile*

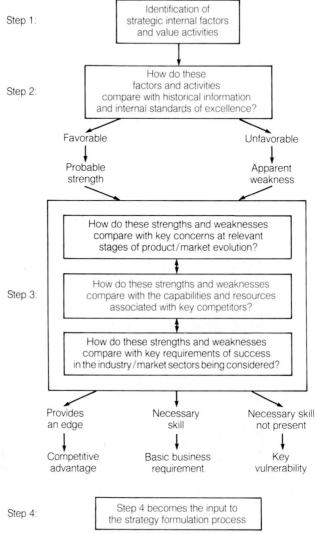

Step 1: Identification of strategic internal factors and value activities

Step 2: How do these factors and activities compare with historical information and internal standards of excellence?

Favorable → Probable strength

Unfavorable → Apparent weakness

Step 3:
How do these strengths and weaknesses compare with key concerns at relevant stages of product/market evolution?

How do these strengths and weaknesses compare with the capabilities and resources associated with key competitors?

How do these strengths and weaknesses compare with key requirements of success in the industry/market sectors being considered?

Provides an edge → Competitive advantage

Necessary skill → Basic business requirement

Necessary skill not present → Key vulnerability

Step 4: Step 4 becomes the input to the strategy formulation process

* The earlier work of Leslie Rue and Phyllis Holland, *Strategic Management* (New York: McGraw-Hill, 1986), provided an important foundation from which to portray these steps.

> c. *Key vulnerabilities*—factors on which the company currently lacks the necessary skill, knowledge, or resources to compete effectively. This assessment is also a key input into the strategic management process because managers will want to avoid choosing strategies that depend on factors in this category. And managers usually target key

vulnerabilities as areas for special attention so as to remediate and change this situation.

The final step in internal analysis is to provide the results, or company profile, as input into the strategic management process. This input is vital during the early, strategy formulation phase in the strategic management process.

While this summary and Figure 8–6 explain internal analysis as a process, it is important to remember that each step in the process often overlaps another step. Thus separating each step helps explain the process of internal analysis; but, in practice, efforts to distinguish each step are seldom emphasized because the process is very interactive.

The process of internal analysis, when matched with the results of management's environmental analyses and mission priorities, provides the critical foundation for strategy formulation. When the internal analysis is accurate, thorough, and timely, managers are in a better position to formulate effective strategies. The next chapter describes basic strategy alternatives any company may consider.

Questions for Discussion

1. Describe the process used to identify key internal factors in a firm's strategic management process. Why does this appear to be an important part of the strategic management process?

2. Apply the two broad steps of internal analysis to yourself and your career aspirations. What are your major strengths and weaknesses? How might these be used to develop your future career plans?

3. Select one business in your area that appears to be doing well and another that appears to be doing poorly. Form two small teams with the help of your instructor. Have each team take one of the businesses and schedule a brief interview with a key manager. Obtain a *specific* assessment of each firm's internal strengths and weaknesses. Compare the results in a subsequent class. Are there substantial differences? Is one more comprehensive and specific than the other? Do strengths and weaknesses vary by type of business?

4. Explain why a firm might emphasize historical experience over competitor comparison in evaluating its strengths and weaknesses. When would the reverse emphasis be more relevant?

Bibliography

Barnard, Chester. *Functions of the Executive*. Cambridge, Mass.: Harvard University Press, 1939, chap. 14.

Buchele, Robert B. "How to Evaluate a Firm." *California Management Review,* Fall 1962, pp. 5–17.

Doyle, Peter. "The Realities of the Product Life Cycle." *Quarterly Review of Marketing,* Summer 1976, pp. 1–6.

Dun's Review. New York: Dun & Bradstreet, published monthly.

Fox, Harold. "A Framework for Functional Coordination." *Atlantic Economic Review,* November–December 1973, p. 18.

Gilmore, Frank. "Formulating Strategy in Smaller Companies." *Harvard Business Review,* May–June 1971, pp. 71–81.

Henry, Harold W. "Appraising a Company's Strengths and Weaknesses." *Managerial Planning,* July–August 1980, pp. 31–36.

Joy, O. M. *Introduction to Financial Management.* Homewood, Ill.: Richard D. Irwin, 1980, pp. 119–28 and 207–9.

Kotler, Philip. *Marketing Management.* 6th ed. Englewood Cliffs, N.J.: Prentice-Hall, 1988.

Mintzberg, Henry. "Strategy Making in Three Modes." *California Management Review* 16, no. 2 (1973), pp. 44–53.

Porter, Michael E. *Competitive Advantage.* New York: Free Press, 1985.

RMA: *Annual Statement Studies.* Philadelphia: Robert Morris Associates, published annually.

South, Stephen E. "Competitive Advantage: The Cornerstone to Strategic Thinking." *Journal of Business Strategy* 1, no. 4 (1981), pp. 15–25.

Stevenson, Howard H. "Defining Corporate Strengths and Weaknesses." *Sloan Management Review,* Spring 1976, pp. 51–68.

Appendix

Using Financial Analysis

One of the most important tools for assessing the strength of an organization within its industry is financial analysis. Managers, investors, and creditors all employ some form of this analysis as the beginning point for their financial decision making. Investors use financial analyses in making decisions about whether to buy or sell stock, and creditors use them in deciding whether or not to lend. They provide managers with a measurement of how the company is doing in comparison with its performance in past years and with the performance of competitors in the industry.

Although financial analysis is useful for decision making, there are some weaknesses that should be noted. Any picture that it provides of the company is based on past data. Although trends may be noteworthy, this picture should not automatically be assumed to be applicable to the future. In addition, the analysis is only as good as the accounting procedures that have provided the information. When making comparisons between companies, one should keep in mind the variability of accounting procedures from firm to firm.

There are four basic groups of financial ratios: liquidity, leverage, activity, and profitability.

Depicted in Exhibit 8–1 are the specific ratios calculated for each of the basic groups. Liquidity and leverage ratios represent an assessment of the risk of the firm. Activity and profitability ratios are measures of the return

Prepared by Elizabeth Gatewood, University of Georgia. © Elizabeth Gatewood, 1985. Reprinted by permission of Elizabeth Gatewood.

Exhibit 8–1
Financial ratios

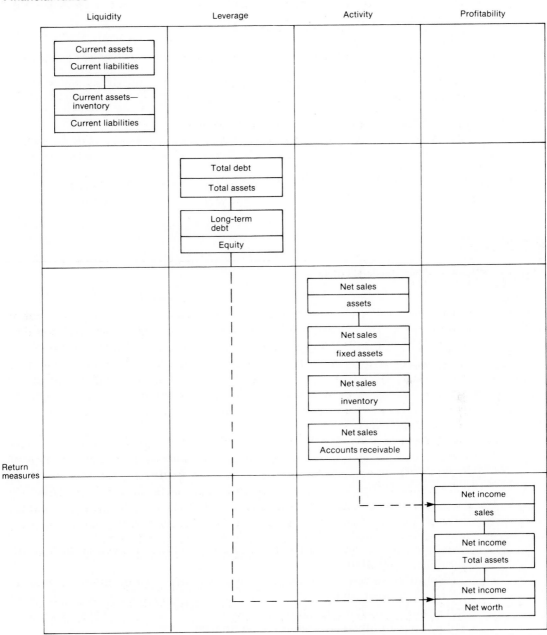

Exhibit 8–2

ABC COMPANY
Balance Sheet
As of December 31

	1989	1988
Assets		
Current assets		
Cash	$ 140,000	$ 115,000
Accounts receivable	1,760,000	1,440,000
Inventory	2,175,000	2,000,000
Prepaid expenses	50,000	63,000
Total current assets	4,125,000	3,618,000
Fixed assets		
Long-term receivables	1,255,000	1,090,000
Property and plant $2,037,000		$2,015,000
Less: Accumulated depreciation 862,000		860,000
Net property and plant	1,175,000	1,155,000
Other fixed assets	550,000	530,000
Total fixed assets	2,980,000	2,775,000
Total assets	$7,105,000	$6,393,000
Liabilities and Stockholders' Equity		
Current liabilities		
Accounts payable	$1,325,000	$1,225,000
Bank loans payable	475,000	550,000
Accrued federal taxes	675,000	425,000
Current maturities (long-term debt)	17,500	26,000
Dividends payable	20,000	16,250
Total current liabilities	2,512,500	2,242,250
Long-term liabilities	1,350,000	1,425,000
Total liabilities	3,862,500	3,667,250
Stockholders' equity		
Common stock (104,046 shares outstanding in 1985; 101,204 shares outstanding in 1984)	44,500	43,300
Additional paid-in capital	568,000	372,450
Retained earnings	2,630,000	2,310,000
Total stockholders' equity	3,242,500	2,725,750
Total liabilities and stockholders' equity	$7,105,000	$6,393,000

generated by the assets of the firm. The interaction between certain groups of ratios is indicated by arrows.

Typically two common financial statements are used in financial analyses: the balance sheet and the income statement. Exhibit 8–2 is a balance sheet and Exhibit 8–3 an income statement for the ABC Company. These statements will be used to illustrate the financial analyses.

Exhibit 8–3

ABC COMPANY
Income Statement
For the Years Ending December 31

		1989		1988
Net sales		$8,250,000		$8,000,000
Less: Cost of goods sold	$5,100,000		$5,000,000	
Administrative expenses	1,750,000		1,680,000	
Other expenses	420,000		390,000	
Total		7,270,000		7,070,000
Earnings before interest and taxes		980,000		930,000
Less: Interest expense		210,000		210,000
Earnings before taxes		770,000		720,000
Less: Federal income taxes		360,000		325,000
Earnings after taxes (net income)		$ 410,000		$ 395,000
Common stock cash dividends		$ 90,000		$ 84,000
Addition to retained earnings		$ 320,000		$ 311,000
Earnings per common share		$ 3.940		$ 3.90
Dividends per common share		$ 0.865		$ 0.83

Liquidity Ratios

Liquidity ratios are used as indicators of a firm's ability to meet its short-term obligations. These obligations include any current liabilities, including currently maturing long-term debt. Current assets move through a normal cash cycle of inventories—sales—accounts receivable—cash. The firm then uses cash to pay off or reduce its current liabilities. The best-known liquidity ratio is the current ratio: current assets divided by current liabilities. For the ABC Company, the current ratio is calculated as follows:

$$\frac{\text{Current assets}}{\text{Current liabilities}} = \frac{\$4,125,000}{\$2,512,500} = 1.64 \ (1989)$$

$$= \frac{\$3,618,000}{\$2,242,250} = 1.61 \ (1988)$$

Most analysts suggest a current ratio of 2 to 3. A large current ratio is not necessarily a good sign; it may mean that an organization is not making the most efficient use of assets. The optimum current ratio will vary from industry to industry, with the more volatile industries requiring higher ratios.

Since slow-moving or obsolescent inventories could overstate a firm's ability to meet short-term demands, the quick ratio is sometimes preferred to assess a firm's liquidity. The quick ratio is current assets minus inventories, divided by current liabilities. The quick ratio for the ABC Company is calculated as follows:

$$\frac{\text{Current assets} - \text{Inventories}}{\text{Current liabilities}} = \frac{\$1,950,000}{\$2,512,500} = 0.78 \text{ (1989)}$$

$$= \frac{\$1,618,000}{\$2,242,250} = 0.72 \text{ (1988)}$$

A quick ratio of approximately 1 would be typical for American industries. Although there is less variability in the quick ratio than in the current ratio, stable industries would be able to safely operate with a lower ratio.

Leverage Ratios

Leverage ratios identify the source of a firm's capital—owners or outside creditors. The term *leverage* refers to the fact that using capital with a fixed interest charge will "amplify" either profits or losses in relation to the equity of holders of common stock. The most commonly used ratio is total debt divided by total assets. Total debt includes current liabilities and long-term liabilities. This ratio is a measure of the percentage of total funds provided by debt. A total debt/total assets ratio higher than 0.5 is usually considered safe only for firms in stable industries.

$$\frac{\text{Total debt}}{\text{Total assets}} = \frac{\$3,862,500}{\$7,105,000} = 0.54 \text{ (1989)}$$

$$= \frac{\$3,667,250}{\$6,393,000} = 0.57 \text{ (1988)}$$

The ratio of long-term debt to equity is a measure of the extent to which sources of long-term financing are provided by creditors. It is computed by dividing long-term debt by the stockholders' equity.

$$\frac{\text{Long-term debt}}{\text{Equity}} = \frac{\$1,350,000}{\$3,242,500} = 0.42 \text{ (1989)}$$

$$= \frac{\$1,425,000}{\$2,725,750} = 0.52 \text{ (1988)}$$

Activity Ratios

Activity ratios indicate how effectively a firm is using its resources. By comparing revenues with the resources used to generate them, it is possible to establish an efficiency of operation. The asset turnover ratio indicates how efficiently management is employing total assets. Asset turnover is calculated by dividing sales by total assets. For the ABC Company, asset turnover is calculated as follows:

$$\text{Asset turnover} = \frac{\text{Sales}}{\text{Total assets}} = \frac{\$8,250,000}{\$7,105,000} = 1.16\,(1989)$$

$$= \frac{\$8,000,000}{\$6,393,000} = 1.25\,(1988)$$

The ratio of sales to fixed assets is a measure of the turnover on plant and equipment. It is calculated by dividing sales by net fixed assets.

$$\text{Fixed asset turnover} = \frac{\text{Sales}}{\text{Net fixed assets}} = \frac{\$8,250,000}{\$2,980,000} = 2.77\,(1989)$$

$$= \frac{\$8,000,000}{\$2,775,000} = 2.88\,(1988)$$

Industry figures for asset turnover will vary with capital-intensive industries, and those requiring large inventories will have much smaller ratios.

Another activity ratio is inventory turnover, estimated by dividing sales by average inventory. The norm for American industries is 9, but whether the ratio for a particular firm is higher or lower normally depends upon the product sold. Small, inexpensive items usually turn over at a much higher rate than larger, expensive ones. Since inventories are normally carried at cost, it would be more accurate to use the cost of goods sold in place of sales in the numerator of this ratio. Established compilers of industry ratios such as Dun & Bradstreet, however, use the ratio of sales to inventory.

$$\text{Inventory turnover} = \frac{\text{Sales}}{\text{Inventory}} = \frac{\$8,250,000}{\$2,175,000} = 3.79\,(1989)$$

$$= \frac{\$8,000,000}{\$2,000,000} = 4\,(1988)$$

The accounts receivable turnover is a measure of the average collection period on sales. If the average number of days varies widely from the industry norm, it may be an indication of poor management. A too low ratio could indicate the loss of sales because of a too restrictive credit policy. If the ratio is too high, too much capital is being tied up in accounts receivable, and management may be increasing the chance of bad debts. Because of varying industry credit policies, a comparison for the firm over time or within an industry is the only useful analysis. Because information on credit sales for other firms is generally unavailable, total sales must be used. Since not all firms have the same percentage of credit sales, there is only approximate comparability among firms.

$$\frac{\text{Accounts}}{\text{receivable turnover}} = \frac{\text{Sales}}{\text{Accounts receivable}} = \frac{\$8{,}250{,}000}{\$1{,}760{,}000} = 4.69 \text{ (1989)}$$

$$= \frac{\$8{,}000{,}000}{\$1{,}440{,}000} = 5.56 \text{ (1988)}$$

$$\text{Average collection period} = \frac{360}{\text{Accounts receivable turnover}}$$

$$= \frac{360}{4.69} = 77 \text{ days (1989)}$$

$$= \frac{360}{5.56} = 65 \text{ days (1988)}$$

Profitability Ratios

Profitability is the net result of a large number of policies and decisions chosen by an organization's management. Profitability ratios indicate how effectively the total firm is being managed. The profit margin for a firm is calculated by dividing net earnings by sales. This ratio is often called return on sales (ROS). There is wide variation among industries, but the average for American firms is approximately 5 percent.

$$\frac{\text{Net earnings}}{\text{Sales}} = \frac{\$410{,}000}{\$8{,}250{,}000} = 0.0497 \text{ (1989)}$$

$$= \frac{\$395{,}000}{\$8{,}000{,}000} = 0.0494 \text{ (1988)}$$

A second useful ratio for evaluating profitability is the return on invest-ment—or ROI, as it is frequently called—found by dividing net earnings by total assets. The ABC Company's ROI is calculated as follows:

$$\frac{\text{Net earnings}}{\text{Total assets}} = \frac{\$410{,}000}{\$7{,}105{,}000} = 0.0577 \text{ (1989)}$$

$$= \frac{\$395{,}000}{\$6{,}393{,}000} = 0.0618 \text{ (1988)}$$

The ratio of net earnings to net worth is a measure of the rate of return or profitability of the stockholders' investment. It is calculated by dividing net earnings by net worth, the common stock equity and retained earnings account. ABC Company's return on net worth, also called ROE, is calculated as follows:

$$\frac{\text{Net earnings}}{\text{Net worth}} = \frac{\$410,000}{\$3,242,500} = 0.1264 \,(1989)$$

$$= \frac{\$395,000}{\$2,725,750} = 0.1449 \,(1988)$$

It is often difficult to determine causes for lack of profitability. The Du Pont system of financial analysis provides management with clues to the lack of success of a firm. This financial tool brings together activity, profitability, and leverage measures and shows how these ratios interact to determine the overall profitability of the firm. A depiction of the system is set forth in Exhibit 8–4.

The right side of the figure develops the turnover ratio. This section breaks down total assets into current assets (cash, marketable securities, accounts receivable, and inventories) and fixed assets. Sales divided by these total assets gives the turnover on assets.

The left side of the figure develops the profit margin on sales. The individual expense items plus income taxes are subtracted from sales to produce net profits after taxes. Net profits divided by sales gives the profit margin on sales. When the asset turnover ratio on the right side of Exhibit 8–4 is multiplied by the profit margin on sales developed on the left side of the figure, the product is the return on assets (ROI) for the firm. This can be shown by the following formula:

$$\frac{\text{Sales}}{\text{Total assets}} \times \frac{\text{Net earnings}}{\text{Sales}} = \frac{\text{Net earnings}}{\text{Total assets}} = \text{ROI}$$

The last step in the Du Pont analysis is to multiply the rate of return on assets (ROI) by the equity multiplier, which is the ratio of assets to common equity, to obtain the rate of return on equity (ROE). This percentage rate of return could, of course, be calculated directly by dividing net income by common equity. However, the Du Pont analysis demonstrates how the return on assets and the use of debt interact to determine the return on equity.

The Du Pont system can be used to analyze and improve the performance of a firm. On the left, or profit, side of the figure, attempts to increase profits and sales could be investigated. The possibilities of raising prices to improve profits (or lowering prices to improve volume) or seeking new products or markets, for example, could be studied. Cost accountants and production engineers could investigate ways to reduce costs. On the right, or turnover, side, financial officers could analyze the effect of reducing investment in various assets as well as the effect of alternative financial structures.

There are two basic approaches to using financial ratios. One approach is to evaluate the corporation's performance over several years. Financial ratios are computed for different years, and then an assessment is made as to whether there has been an improvement or deterioration over time. Financial ratios

Exhibit 8–4
Du Pont's financial analysis

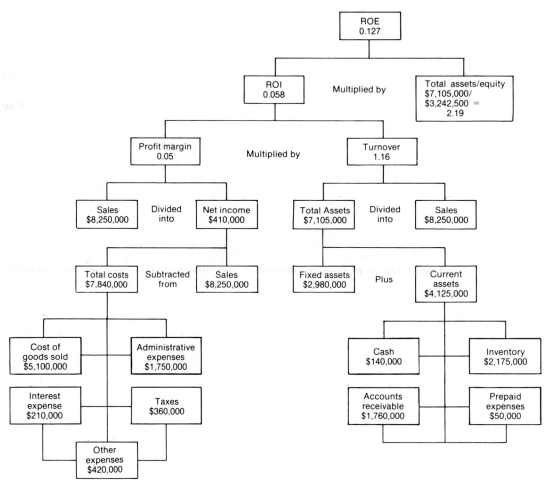

can also be computed for projected, or pro forma, statements and compared with present and past ratios.

The other approach is to evaluate a firm's financial condition and compare it with the financial conditions of similar firms or with industry averages in the same period. Such a comparison gives insight into the firm's relative financial condition and performance. Financial ratios for industries are provided by Robert Morris Associates, Dun & Bradstreet, and various trade association publications. (Associations and their addresses are listed in the *Encyclopedia of Associations* or the *Directory of National Trade Associations*.) Information about individual firms is available through *Moody's Manual,* Standard & Poor's manuals and surveys, annual reports to stockholders, and the major brokerage houses.

To the extent possible, accounting data from different companies must be standardized so that companies can be compared or so that a specific company can be compared with an industry average. It is important to read any footnotes of financial statements, since various accounting or management practices can have an effect on the financial picture of the company. For example, firms using sale-leaseback methods may have leverage pictures that are quite different from what is shown as debts or assets on the balance sheet.

Analysis of the Sources and Uses of Funds

The purpose of this analysis is to determine how the company is using its financial resources from year to year. By comparing balance sheets from one year to the next, one may determine how funds were obtained and the way in which these funds were employed during the year.

To prepare a statement of the sources and uses of funds it is necessary to (1) classify balance sheet changes that increase cash and changes that decrease cash, (2) classify from the income statement those factors that increase or decrease cash, and (3) consolidate this information on a sources and uses of funds statement form.

Sources of funds that increase cash are as follows:

1. A net decrease in any asset other than a depreciable fixed asset.
2. A gross decrease in a depreciable fixed asset.
3. A net increase in any liability.
4. Proceeds from the sale of stock.
5. The operation of the company (net income, and depreciation if the company is profitable).

Uses of funds include:

1. A net increase in any asset other than a depreciable fixed asset.
2. A gross increase in depreciable fixed assets.
3. A net decrease in any liability.
4. A retirement or purchase of stock.
5. Payment of cash dividends.

We compute gross changes to depreciable fixed assets by adding depreciation from the income statement for the period to net fixed assets at the end of the period and then subtracting from the total the net fixed assets at the beginning of the period. The residual represents the change in depreciable fixed assets for the period.

For the ABC Company, the following change would be calculated:

Net property and plant (1989)	$1,175,000
Depreciation for 1989	+ 80,000
	$1,255,000
Net property and plant (1988)	−1,155,000
	$ 100,000

To avoid double counting, the change in retained earnings is not shown directly in the funds statement. When the funds statement is prepared, this account is replaced by the earnings after taxes, or net income, as a source of funds and dividends paid during the year as a use of funds. The difference between net income and the change in the retained-earnings account will equal the amount of dividends paid during the year. The accompanying sources and uses of funds statement was prepared for the ABC Company.

A funds analysis is useful for determining trends in working-capital positions and for demonstrating how the firm has acquired and employed its funds during some period.

ABC COMPANY
Sources and Uses of Funds Statement
For 1989

Sources:	
Prepaid expenses	$ 13,000
Accounts payable	100,000
Accrued federal taxes	250,000
Dividends payable	3,750
Common stock	1,200
Additional paid-in capital	195,500
Earnings after taxes (net income)	410,000
Depreciation	80,000
Total sources	1,053,500
Uses:	
Cash	25,000
Accounts receivable	320,000
Inventory	175,000
Long-term receivables	165,000
Property and plant	100,000
Other fixed assets	20,000
Bank loans payable	75,000
Current maturities of long-term debt ...	8,500
Long-term liabilities	75,000
Dividends paid	90,000
Total uses	1,053,500

Exhibit 8–5
A summary of the financial position of a firm

Ratios and working capital	1985	1986	1987	1988	1989	Trend	Industry average	Interpretation
Liquidity: Current								
Quick								
Leverage: Debt/assets								
Debt/equity								
Activity: Asset turnover								
Fixed asset ratio								
Inventory turnover								
Accounts receivable turnover								
Average collection period								
Profitability: ROS								
ROI								
ROE								
Working-capital position								

Conclusion

It is recommended that you prepare a chart such as Exhibit 8–5 so that you can develop a useful portrayal of these financial analyses. The chart allows a display of the ratios over time. The Trend column could be used to indicate your evaluation of the ratios over time (for example, "favorable," "neutral," or "unfavorable"). The Industry Average column could include recent industry averages on these ratios or those of key competitors. These would provide information to aid interpretation of the analyses. The Interpretation column can be used to describe your interpretation of the ratios for this firm. Overall, this chart gives a basic display of the ratios that provides a convenient format for examining the firm's financial condition.

Finally, Exhibit 8–6 is included to provide a quick reference summarizing the calculation and meaning of ratios discussed earlier.

Exhibit 8–6
A summary of key financial ratios

Ratio	*Calculation*	*Meaning*
Liquidity ratios		
Current ratio	$\dfrac{\text{Current assets}}{\text{Current liabilities}}$	The extent to which a firm can meet its short-term obligations.
Quick ratio	$\dfrac{\text{Current assets—Inventory}}{\text{Current liabilities}}$	The extent to which a firm can meet its short-term obligations without relying upon the sale of its inventories.
Leverage ratios		
Debt-to-total-assets ratio	$\dfrac{\text{Total debt}}{\text{Total assets}}$	The percentage of total funds that are provided by creditors.
Debt-to-equity ratio	$\dfrac{\text{Total debt}}{\text{Total stockholders' equity}}$	The percentage of total funds provided by creditors versus by owners.
Long-term-debt-to-equity ratio	$\dfrac{\text{Long-term debt}}{\text{Total stockholders' equity}}$	The balance between debt and equity in a firm's long-term capital structure.
Times-interest-earned ratio	$\dfrac{\text{Profits before interest and taxes}}{\text{Total interest charges}}$	The extent to which earnings can decline without the firm becoming unable to meet its annual interest costs.
Activity ratios		
Inventory turnover	$\dfrac{\text{Sales}}{\text{Inventory of finished goods}}$	Whether a firm holds excessive stocks of inventories and whether a firm is selling its inventories slowly compared to the industry average.
Fixed assets turnover	$\dfrac{\text{Sales}}{\text{Fixed assets}}$	Sales productivity and plant and equipment utilization.
Total assets turnover	$\dfrac{\text{Sales}}{\text{Total assets}}$	Whether a firm is generating a sufficient volume of business for the size of its asset investment.
Accounts receivable turnover	$\dfrac{\text{Annual credit sales}}{\text{Accounts receivable}}$	(In percentage terms) the average length of time it takes a firm to collect credit sales.
Average collection period	$\dfrac{\text{Accounts receivable}}{\text{Total sales/365 days}}$	(In days) the average length of time it takes a firm to collect on credit sales.

Exhibit 8–6 (*concluded*)

Ratio	*Calculation*	*Meaning*
Profitability ratios		
Gross profit margin	$\dfrac{\text{Sales} - \text{Cost of goods sold}}{\text{Sales}}$	The total margin available to cover operating expenses and yield a profit.
Operating profit margin	$\dfrac{\text{Earnings before interest and taxes (EBIT)}}{\text{Sales}}$	Profitability without concern for taxes and interest.
Net profit margin	$\dfrac{\text{Net income}}{\text{Sales}}$	After-tax profits per dollar of sales.
Return on total assets (ROA)	$\dfrac{\text{Net income}}{\text{Total assets}}$	After-tax profits per dollar of assets; this ratio is also called return on investment (ROI).
Return on stockholders' equity (ROE)	$\dfrac{\text{Net income}}{\text{Total stockholders' equity}}$	After-tax profits per dollar of stockholders' investment in the firm.
Earnings per share (EPS)	$\dfrac{\text{Net income}}{\text{Number of shares of common stock outstanding}}$	Earnings available to the owners of common stock.
Growth ratios		
Sales	Annual percentage growth in total sales	Firm's growth rate in sales.
Income	Annual percentage growth in profits	Firm's growth rate in profits.
Earnings per share	Annual percentage growth in EPS	Firm's growth rate in EPS.
Dividends per share	Annual percentage growth in dividends per share	Firm's growth rate in dividends per share.
Price–earnings ratio	$\dfrac{\text{Market price per share}}{\text{Earnings per share}}$	Faster-growing and less risky firms tend to have higher price–earnings ratios.

Chapter 8 Cohesion Case Illustration

Internal Analysis at Holiday Inns, Inc.

At Holiday Inns, internal analysis must be conducted at both the business and corporate levels. To do this, strengths and weaknesses within each business group should be examined first. After these analyses have been completed, they should be pulled together in an integrated overview of the strengths and weaknesses of Holiday Inns as a multibusiness firm.

Exhibit 1
Hotel group: Internal analysis*

Strengths	Weaknesses
HI dominates the industry in number of rooms available. It has the largest market share of lodging revenue dollars. *(21)*	Increasing average age of the typical property suggests increased maintenance and renovation expense. *(6, 7)*
Name, image, and customer awareness. *(17, 20)*	Dependent on the traveling public, which faces increased gasoline prices. *(21, 22)*
Extensive and steadily growing franchise network (80 percent of all units), with franchise revenues inflation-immune because they are based on a percentage of gross revenues. *(4)*	Hotels/motels are energy wasters that can disturb margins in an era of rapidly increasing energy costs. *(16)*
Massive real estate holdings rising steadily in value, providing an expanding asset base. Also, older mortgage rates provide a relative advantage against the cost newer competitors must encounter. *(69)*	HI has become the moderate- to high-priced accommodation relative to the rapidly expanding budget chains. *(23)*
Accumulated lodging experience both domestically and abroad. Extensive managerial talent and resources as evidenced by franchisee Winegardner's move to the top. *(20)*	A maturing domestic lodging industry with limited expansion opportunities, as evidenced by the net decline in the number of company-owned facilities over the last five years. *(6)*
Generally stable occupancy rate, revenues per room, gross revenue, and profit margin. *(66)*	Sensitivity to economic downturns as people curtail pleasure travel. *(21, 22)*
Well-balanced locations for interstate, airport, resort, and downtown traveler needs. *(6, 20, 21, 75)*	Rapidly escalating price competition on the one end (Days Inn, Best Western) and quality competition (Hilton, Marriott, Hyatt) on the other cuts at HI's large middle market. Also, relative to price competition, HI's built-in overhead—like 16-hour restaurants, big lobbies, room service—limits flexibility in lowering operating margins. *(21, 22)*
Quality control system. *(17)*	
Food and lounge facilities at every location.	Cash drain on hotel group to support corporate-level overhead and ventures into new areas. Related attitude of franchisees regarding use of their fees to support this versus occupancy-enhancing activities. *(66)*
	Challenges to the franchise agreement and relative dependence on franchisees. *(9)*

* Italicized numbers in parentheses refer to appropriate paragraphs of the Cohesion Case in Chapter 1. Exhibits in vicinity of appropriate paragraphs may also support this point.

Exhibit 2
Transportation group: Internal analysis

Strengths	*Weaknesses*
Increasing cost of auto travel should bolster ridership on Trailways. Some executives feel that Trailways' riders could complement hotel operations, especially tour and charter services. *(73, 76)*	Major competition from Greyhound, the number one bus line, as well as from air and train transportation. *(27, 28)*
Second-largest domestic bus service. *(26)*	Unsure whether the typical Trailways passenger is the typical HI motel/hotel customer. *(29, 32)*
Steady increase in transportation group revenues, particularly package express services. *(31)*	Rising maintenance and energy-related costs, while at the same time engaging in a price war with Greyhound. *(29, 30)*
Steady increase in net bus income, although no improvement in income as percent of revenues and a major drop within the steamship component.	Privately owned and maintained terminal facilities instead of the municipally owned terminals airlines enjoy. *(32)*
Growing revenue in package express services and the existence of Trailways' already-established intercity bus network to provide these services. *(31)*	Condition and rising maintenance/replacement costs of Trailways bus terminals. *(32)*
	Growing popularity of airlines for both leisure and business travel based on a price/time in-transit comparison. *(27)*
Delta Steamship (cargo) represents an operating base not directly tied to vacation and business travel. *(35)*	Growing number and variety of companies providing package express services. The questionable ability of Trailways to deliver *anywhere* within 24 hours. *(31)*
Cargo business, with strong presence in South American and African routes, suggests a solid presence serving U.S. exports to Third World countries. *(35, 36)*	Extent of managerial expertise in transportation—bus and marine cargo—is rather limited. *(26, 38)*
LASH technology is a distinct cargo cost advantage. *(37)*	Heavy capital investment in marine cargo and ocean passenger business. *(66)*
Cruise ship passenger service is a high-margin business. *(37)*	Small market share in marine transport and ocean passenger markets. *(39)*
	Lack of clear synergy between Delta operations and Trailways or both and the hotel group. *(32)*

Hotel Group.   Clearly, this is the key business group for internal analysis. The hotel group is the core of Holiday Inns' diversified operations. It provides over 48 percent of total corporate revenues and over 59 percent of corporate income before taxes. Based on the Cohesion Case material, the strengths and weaknesses of the hotel group are shown in Exhibit 1.

Transportation Group.   This is a growing segment of Holiday Inns, Inc.'s overall corporate endeavor. Two rather different businesses make up the transportation group—Continental Trailways bus system and Delta Steamship. Trailways seeks to provide moderate- to low-priced domestic intercity travel, while Delta provides marine cargo service and, increasingly, ocean pleasure cruises. Based on the case material, the strengths and weaknesses of this business group are outlined in Exhibit 2.

Exhibit 3
Restaurant group: Internal analysis

Strengths	Weaknesses
Perkins provides an immediate presence in the freestanding restaurant business via 360 company-owned and franchised operations in 30 states.	Must be integrated into a growingly complex and diversely focused corporate management.
HI is experienced in restaurant operation.	Faces stiff competition from similar firms like Sambo's, Shoney's, Denny's, and fast-food firms like McDonald's, Burger King, and Wendy's. *(48)*
Perkins is positioned as a family restaurant with a customer profile quite similar to that of the HI hotel guest. *(43)*	Limited geographic emphasis—northern United States. *(42)*
It is a franchise-based business, again deriving synergy from past experiences and hotel expertise at HI. *(42)*	
Provides economy-of-scale advantage in purchasing and advertising with restaurant business. *(45)*	

Exhibit 4
Gaming group: Internal analysis

Strengths	Weaknesses
Most casinos include hotels and sizable food and beverage operations, a natural synergy with HI's core expertise. *(54)*	Philosophical contradiction with founding principles at HI, such as family environment. *(52)*
Casino gaming revenue is fast growing, and profitability is quite high. *(56)*	While HI has hospitality experience, it has little gambling experience. *(57)*
The demographic profile of the typical casino customer is quite similar to that of the typical HI hotel guest. *(54)*	Gambling is only legal in a few areas. *(52)*
	Because of lack of experience, the cost of entry (real estate, etc.) is quite high. *(53)*
	Compatibility with corporate image and organized crime inference. *(52)*

Restaurant and Casino Groups.   In late 1979, Holiday Inns, Inc., moved into the freestanding restaurant market with its purchase of Perkins Cake and Steak, Inc., and its joint venture into casino operations in Atlantic City and Las Vegas. Because these are relatively new business groups, the case material is rather limited. You are encouraged to seek outside information from such sources as *Moody's* and *Standard & Poor's Industry Surveys* to round out the assessment of strengths and weaknesses provided here. Tentative strengths and weaknesses are listed in Exhibits 3 and 4.

Exhibit 5
Corporate-level internal analysis

Strengths	*Weaknesses*
The hotel business provides an excellent cash generator to support growth areas.	Management capability to absorb a rapidly increasing number of businesses may be severely challenged, especially in the short term.
Substantial and appreciating real estate holdings enhance corporatewide debt capacity.	Hotels and now restaurants represent a major dependence of outside franchisees—with several threatening legal challenges in progress.
Synergy between the hotel core and restaurant (Perkins) and casino operations should produce a distinct advantage.	Questionable whether some operations (especially Trailways buses, ocean cruises, and, to some extent, institutional products) clearly fit with other businesses in a related diversification strategy.
Casino gaming and increasing resort emphasis within company-owned expansion provide a logical synergy.	Severity of the budget chain threat and eventual price/cost squeeze on the essential cash generator—the hotel group—during a time of rapid cash outflows to gain positions in other business arenas.
Delta Steamship provides an avenue for lessening the travel-based, cyclical exposure of other HI businesses.	Philosophical divisions among long-time managers over certain diversifications, especially casinos and restaurants, have corporatewide effect.
Restaurants, casinos, and possibly marine transport provide reasonable growth avenues as the lodging industry matures.	Revenues in the restaurant and gaming groups in 1980–81 indicate that these businesses may be more sensitive to recessionary business cycles than originally thought.
Franchising and marketing expertise across multiple businesses.	The debt/total capitalization ratio, at a 10-year low in 1978 (34.6 percent), stood at a comparative high (over 42 percent) in 1981.
The 9⅝ percent convertible subordinate debentures represent $144 million of potential equity if they can be converted. Management estimates a stock price of over $22 (in 1982) would be necessary to issue a successful call.	

Having completed a basic internal analysis of each business group, Holiday Inns, Inc.'s strengths and weaknesses must be examined from an overall corporate standpoint. The focus in Exhibit 5 is on the overall business portfolio and the strengths and weaknesses it provides as corporate management views internal corporate capabilities.

These are some of the key strengths and weaknesses facing Holiday Inns, Inc., at the business and corporate levels. Compared with the environment analyses in Chapters 4 through 7, this internal analysis provides the basis for generating alternative strategies. The Chapter 10 Cohesion Case Illustration will look at this comparison. Before leaving internal analysis, however, do you agree with the strengths and weaknesses identified? Are any key factors missing? Are any factors identified as strengths that could be weaknesses or vice versa?

9

Formulating Long-Term Objectives and Grand Strategies

The company mission was described (in Chapter 3) as encompassing the broad aims of the organization. The most specific statement of wants appeared as the goals of the firm. However, these goals, which commonly dealt with profitability, growth, and survival, were stated without specific targets or time frames. They were always to be pursued but could never be fully attained. So, while they gave a general sense of direction, goals were not intended to provide specific benchmarks for evaluating the company's progress in achieving its aims. That is the function of objectives.[1]

In the first part of this chapter, the focus will be on long-term objectives. These are statements of the results a business seeks to achieve over a specified period of time, typically five years. In the second part of the chapter, focus will shift to formulation of grand strategies. These provide a comprehensive general approach guiding major actions designed to accomplish long-term business objectives.

The chapter has two major aims: (1) to discuss in detail the concept of long-term objectives, the topics they cover, and the qualities they should exhibit and (2) to discuss in detail the concept of grand strategies, the 12 principal options available, and two approaches to grand strategy selection.

---

[1] Throughout this text the terms *goals* and *objectives* are each used to convey a special meaning, with *goals* being the less specific and more encompassing concept. Most writers agree with this usage of the terms. However, some authors use the two words interchangeably, while others reverse the definitions.

Long-Term Objectives

Strategic managers recognize that short-run profit maximization is rarely the best approach to achieving sustained corporate growth and profitability. An often-repeated adage states that if impoverished people are given food they will enjoy eating it but will continue to be impoverished. However, if they are given seeds and tools and shown how to grow crops, they will be able to permanently improve their condition. A parallel situation confronts strategic decision makers:

1. Should they eat the seeds by planning for large dividend payments, by selling off inventories, and by cutting back on research and development to improve the near-term profit picture, or by laying off workers during periods of slack demand?
2. Or should they sow the seeds by reinvesting profits in growth opportunities, by committing existing resources to employee training in the hope of improving performance and reducing turnover, or by increasing advertising expenditures to further penetrate a market?

For most strategic managers the solution is clear—enjoy a small amount of profit now to maintain vitality, but sow the majority to increase the likelihood of a long-term supply. This is the most frequently used rationale in selecting objectives.

To achieve long-term prosperity, strategic planners commonly establish long-term objectives in seven areas:

Profitability.   The ability of any business to operate in the long run depends on attaining an acceptable level of profits. Strategically managed firms characteristically have a profit objective usually expressed in earnings per share or return on equity.

Productivity.   Strategic managers constantly try to improve the productivity of their systems. Companies that can improve the input–output relationship normally increase profitability. Thus, businesses almost always state an objective for productivity. Number of items produced or number of services rendered per unit of input are commonly used. However, productivity objectives are sometimes stated in terms of desired decreases in cost. This is an equally effective way to increase profitability if unit output is maintained. For example, objectives may be set for reducing defective items, customer complaints leading to litigation, or overtime.

Competitive Position.   One measure of corporate success is relative dominance in the marketplace. Larger firms often establish an objective in terms of competitive position to gauge their comparative ability for growth and profitability. Total sales or market share are often used; and an objective describing competitive position may indicate a corporation's priorities in the long term. For example, in 1975 Gulf Oil set an objective of moving by 1981 from third to second place as a producer of high-density polypropylene. Total sales were to be the measure.

Employee Development.   Employees value growth and career opportunities in an organization. With such opportunities, productivity is often increased and expensive turnover decreased. Therefore, strategic decision makers frequently include an employee development objective in their long-range plans. For example, PPG has declared an objective of developing highly skilled and flexible employees, thereby providing steady employment for a reduced number of workers.

Employee Relations.   Companies actively seek good employee relations, whether or not they are bound by union contracts. In fact, a characteristic concern of strategic managers is taking proactive steps in anticipation of employee needs and expectations. Strategic managers believe productivity is partially tied to employee loyalty and perceived management interest in worker welfare. Therefore, strategic managers set objectives to improve employee relations. For example, safety programs, worker representation on management committees, and employee stock option plans are all normal outgrowths of employee relations objectives.

Technological Leadership.   Businesses must decide whether to lead or follow in the marketplace. While either can be a successful approach, each requires a different strategic posture. Therefore, many businesses state an objective in terms of technological leadership. For example, Caterpillar Tractor Company, which manufactures large earth movers, established its early reputation and dominant position in the industry on being a forerunner in technological innovation.

Public Responsibility.   Businesses recognize their responsibilities to customers and society at large. In fact, many actively seek to exceed the minimum demands made by government. Not only do they work to develop reputations for fairly priced products and services, but they also attempt to establish themselves as responsible corporate citizens. For example, they may establish objectives for charitable and educational contributions, minority training, public or political activity, community welfare, and urban renewal.

Qualities of Long-Term Objectives

What distinguishes a good objective from a bad one? What qualities of an objective improve its chances of being attained?

Perhaps the best answer to these questions is found in relation to seven criteria that should be used in preparing long-term objectives: acceptable, flexible, measurable over time, motivating, suitable, understandable, and achievable.

Acceptable.   Managers are most likely to pursue objectives that are consistent with perceptions and preferences. If managers are offended by the objectives (e.g., promoting a nonnutritional food product) or believe them to be inappropriate or unfair (e.g., reducing spoilage to offset a disproportionate fixed overhead allocation), they may ignore or even obstruct achievement. In addition, certain long-term corporate objectives are frequently designed to be acceptable to major interest groups external to the firm. An example might involve air-pollution abatement efforts undertaken at the insistence of the Environmental Protection Agency.

Flexible.   Objectives should be modifiable in the event of unforeseen or extraordinary changes in the firm's competitive or environmental forecasts. At the same time, flexibility is usually increased at the expense of specificity. Likewise, employee confidence may be tempered because adjustment of a flexible objective may affect their job. One recommendation for providing flexibility while minimizing associated negative effects is to allow for adjustments in the level rather than the nature of an objective. For example, an objective for a personnel department "to provide managerial development training for 15 supervisors per year over the next five-year period" can easily be adjusted by changing the number of people to be trained. In contrast, changing the personnel department's objective after three months to "assisting production supervisors in reducing job-related injuries by 10 percent per year" would understandably create dissatisfaction.

Measurable.   Objectives must clearly and concretely state what will be achieved and within what time frame. Numerical specificity minimizes misunderstandings; thus, objectives should be measurable over time. For example, an objective to "substantially improve our return on investment" would be better stated as "increase the return on investment on our line of paper products by a minimum of 1 percent a year and a total of 5 percent over the next three years."

Motivating.   Studies have shown that people are most productive when objectives are set at a motivating level—one high enough to challenge but not so high as to frustrate or so low as to be easily attained. The problem is that individuals and groups differ in their perceptions of high enough. A broad objective that challenges one group frustrates another and minimally interests a third. One valuable recommendation is to develop multiple objectives, some aimed at specific groups. More sweeping statements are usually seen as lacking appreciation for individual and somewhat unique situations. Such tailor-made objectives require time and involvement from the decision maker, but they are more likely to serve as motivational forces.

Suitable. Objectives must be suited to the broad aims of the organization, which are expressed in the statement of company mission. Each objective should be a step toward attainment of overall goals. In fact, objectives that do not coincide with company or corporate missions can subvert the aims of the firm. For example, if the mission is growth oriented, an objective of reducing the debt-to-equity ratio to 1.00 to improve stability would probably be unsuitable and counterproductive.

Understandable. Strategic managers at all levels must have a clear understanding of what is to be achieved. They must also understand the major criteria by which their performance will be evaluated. Thus, objectives must be stated so that they are understandable to the recipient as they are to the giver. Consider the potential misunderstandings over an objective "to increase the productivity of the credit card department by 20 percent within five years." Does this mean: Increase the number of cards outstanding? Increase the use of outstanding cards? Increase the employee workload? Make productivity gains each year? Or hope that the new computer-assisted system, which should automatically improve productivity, is approved by year five? As this simple example illustrates, objectives must be prepared in clear, meaningful, and unambiguous fashion.

Achievable. Finally, objectives must be possible to achieve. This is easier said than done. Turbulence in the remote and operating environments adds to the dynamic nature of a business's internal operations. This creates uncertainty, limiting strategic management's accuracy in setting feasible objectives. For example, the wildly fluctuating prime interest rates in 1980 made objective setting extremely difficult for 1981 to 1985, particularly in such areas as sales projections for consumer durable goods companies like General Motors and General Electric.

An especially fine example of long-term strategic objectives is provided in the 1981 to 1986 plan of Hawkeye Savings and Loan, a prominent financial organization in Iowa. Shown in Strategy in Action 9–1 are five of Hawkeye's major objectives for the period, specific performance targets for 1981 and 1982, and results from 1981. Hawkeye's approach is wholly consistent with the list of desired qualities for long-term objectives. In particular, Hawkeye's objectives are flexible, measurable over time, suitable, and understandable.

Grand Strategies[2]

Despite variations in implementing the strategic management approach, designers of planning systems generally agree about the critical role of *grand*

---

[2] Portions of this section are adapted from John A. Pearce II, "Selecting among Alternative Grand Strategies," *California Management Review,* Spring 1982, pp. 23–31.

Strategy in Action 9–1
Long-Range Objectives of Hawkeye Savings and Loan, 1981–1985

Objective 1. Hawkeye should earn, after taxes, not less than 15 percent on average stockholder equity annually and, by December 31, 1985, be earning up to 20 percent on average stockholder equity. Per-share earnings should increase 10 percent annually.

	1981 objectives	1981 results	1982 objectives
Average stockholder equity	$84.5 million	$86.3 million	$110.0 million
Return on equity	16.3%	15.5%	14.6%
Earnings per share	2.75	2.50	2.56

Objective 2. Hawkeye will grow from $1 billion in assets to $2 billion by December 31, 1985. This will be accomplished by: (a) acquiring $100 million in assets annually and (b) internal growth of 8 percent per annum.

	1981 objectives	1981 results	1982 objectives
Beginning assets	$1,100 million	$1,153 million	$1,408 million
Acquisitions	100	146	100
Internal growth	80	109	112
Ending assets	$1,280 million	$1,408 million	$1,620 million

Objective 3. Hawkeye will maintain capital and reserves in subsidiary banks in an amount not less than 7 percent of assets, realizing regulatory authorities may require amounts in excess of that amount. The parent company will maintain a debt ratio under 35 percent of total capitalization and 40 percent of stockholders' equity.

	1981 objectives	1981 results	1982 objectives
Year-end stockholders' equity	$97.0 million	$105.2 million	$115.0 million
Parent company debt	39.0 million	39.6 million	46.0 million
Average subsidiary bank capital and reserves-to-asset ratio	8.0%	8.7%	8.0%

Continued on Page 250

Strategy in Action 9–1 (*concluded*)

Objective 4.   Hawkeye's basic mission of "helping Iowans achieve their financial goals" requires that member banks be willing to loan funds. The willingness of Hawkeye's banks to loan funds also requires the bank to collect funds loaned.

	1981 objectives	*1981 results*	*1982 objectives*
Total loans	$650 million	$696 million	$708 million
Of the average total loans, total loan loss not to exceed	0.15%	0.242%	0.15%
Classified loans not to exceed	2.00%	1.750%	2.00%
Credit card delinquencies not to exceed	10.00%	6.790%	10.00%
Loan-to-deposit ratio not to exceed	73.50%	62.900%	73.50%

Objective 5.   The Financial Services Group will expand the number and variety of financial services offered in keeping with Hawkeye Bancorporation's mission to build a regional financial corporation. These activities will account for an increasing share of Hawkeye profits.

	After-tax earnings objectives		
	1981 estimate	*1981 actual*	*1982 estimate*
Hawkeye Insurance Services, Inc.	$260,000	$169,000	$ 217,000
Central Hawkeye Life Insurance Company	137,000	171,000	480,000
Hawkeye Investment Management, Inc.	26,000	33,000	1,000
Hawkeye Farm Management	13,000	13,000	19,000
Iowa Higher Education Loan Program	80,000	145,000	196,000
Credit Card Center (service fees only)	34,000	47,000	187,000
Hawkeye Mortgage Company	16,000	(68,000)	87,000
STFIT	0	180,000	360,000
	$566,000	$690,000	$1,547,000

strategies.[3] Grand strategies, which are often called *master* or *business* strategies, are intended to provide basic direction for strategic actions. Thus, they
are seen as the basis of coordinated and sustained efforts directed toward
achieving long-term business objectives.

As theoretically and conceptually attractive as the idea of grand strategies
has proved to be, two problems have limited use of this approach in practice.
First, decision makers often do not recognize the range of alternative grand
strategies available. Strategic managers tend to build incrementally from the
status quo. This often unnecessarily limits their search for ways to improve
corporate performance. Other executives have simply never considered the
options available as attractive grand strategies.

Second, strategic decision makers may generate lists of promising grand
strategies but lack a logical and systematic approach to selecting an alternative.
Few planning experts have attempted to proffer viable evaluative criteria
and selection tools.

The purpose of this section is therefore twofold: (1) to list, describe, and
discuss 12 business-level grand strategies that should be considered by strategic
planners and (2) to present approaches to the selection of an optimal grand
strategy from available alternatives.

Grand strategies indicate how long-range objectives will be achieved. Thus,
a grand strategy can be defined as a comprehensive general approach that
guides major actions. As an example, Strategy in Action 9–2 presents a form
of the grand strategy of Eastern Air Lines.

Any one of the 12 principal grand strategies could serve as the basis for
achieving major long-term objectives of a single business: concentration, market
development, product development, innovation, horizontal integration, vertical
integration, joint venture, concentric diversification, conglomerate diversification, retrenchment/turnaround, divestiture, and liquidation. When a company
is involved with multiple industries, businesses, product lines, or customer
groups—as many firms are—several grand strategies are usually combined.
However, for clarity, each of these grand strategies is described independently
in this section with examples to indicate some of their relative strengths
and weaknesses.

Concentration

The most common grand strategy is *concentration* on the current business.
The firm directs its resources to the profitable growth of a single product, in
a single market, and with a single technology. Some of America's largest

---

[3] Among recent such models or theories of strategic management are those of Pearce (1981), Steiner (1979), Higgins (1979), Ansoff (1979), King and Cleland (1978), and Steiner and Miner (1977), all listed in the bibliography to this chapter.

Strategy in Action 9–2
The 1984 Grand Strategy of Eastern Air Lines*

The past five years have been turbulent for the airline industry. Deregulation was quickly followed by a dramatic increase in oil prices; high inflation; skyrocketing interest rates; the most severe and prolonged recession since the Great Depression; the formation of new, low-cost airlines; and the PATCO strike, resulting in imposition of new government controls on operations. Under these circumstances, it should not be surprising that one trunk carrier has gone bankrupt and that others are in perilous financial condition.

During this period, Eastern's basic strategy has remained consistent:

A commitment to a modern, efficient fleet and support facilities, necessarily accompanied by some financial risk.

Growth through productivity.

Protection of job security to the maximum extent possible.

Protection of yields by selectively and carefully offering competitive prices in our markets.

Formation of a route structure which permits efficient development of our marketing strength at our primary traffic hubs.

Protection of our traditional major markets.

Development of new market opportunities.

A commitment to quality.

While Eastern's financial results have been unsatisfactory, the success of this strategy can be measured by Eastern's performance relative to that of other major carriers. In 1982, Eastern ranked first among the trunk carriers in operating margin; and, as measured by Merrill Lynch's "Passenger Profitability Index," Eastern ranks behind only Southwest and USAir.

Thus, our strategy will remain essentially intact. There will be changes in emphasis to reflect an improving external environment, our financial structure, and the employee productivity improvements we are anticipating. However, the basic direction remains unchanged.

---

* The details of a company's grand strategy are among its most closely guarded secrets. Since this statement of Eastern Air Line's grand strategy was *intended* for public consumption, it necessarily omitted the huge volumes of detailed analysis that preceded this extremely abbreviated and superficial overview.

and most successful companies have traditionally adopted the concentration approach. Examples include W. K. Kellogg and Gerber Foods, which are known for their product; Shaklee, which concentrates on geographic expansion; and Lincoln Electric, which bases its growth on technological advances.

The reasons for selecting a concentration grand strategy are easy to understand. Concentration is typically lowest in risk and in additional resources required. It is also based on the known competencies of the firm. On the negative side, for most companies concentration tends to result in steady but slow increases in growth and profitability and a narrow range of investment options. Further, because of their narrow base of competition, concentrated firms are especially susceptible to performance variations resulting from industry trends.

Concentration strategies succeed for so many businesses—including the vast majority of smaller firms—because of the advantages of business-level specialization. By concentrating on one product, in one market, and with one technology, a firm can gain competitive advantages over its more diversified competitors in production skill, marketing know-how, customer sensitivity, and reputation in the marketplace.

A grand strategy of concentration allows for a considerable range of action. Broadly speaking, the business can attempt to capture a larger market share by increasing present customers' rate of usage, by attracting competitors' customers, or by interesting nonusers in the product or service. In turn, each of these actions suggests a more specific set of alternatives. Some of these options are listed in the top section of Figure 9–1.

When strategic managers forecast that the combination of their current products and their markets will not provide the basis for achieving the company mission, they have two options that involve moderate cost and risk: market development and product development.

Market Development

Market development commonly ranks second only to concentration as the least costly and least risky of the 12 grand strategies. It consists of marketing present products, often with only cosmetic modifications, to customers in related market areas by adding different channels of distribution or by changing the content of advertising or the promotional media. Several specific approaches are listed under this heading in Figure 9–1. Thus, as suggested by the figure, businesses that open branch offices in new cities, states, or countries are practicing market development. Likewise, companies that switch from advertising in trade publications to newspapers or add jobbers to supplement their mail-order sales efforts are using a market development approach.

Figure 9–1
Specific options under the grand strategies of concentration, market development, and product development

Concentration (increasing use of present products in present markets):
1. Increasing present customers' rate of usage.
   a. Increasing the size of purchase.
   b. Increasing the rate of product obsolescence.
   c. Advertising other uses.
   d. Giving price incentives for increased use.
2. Attracting competitors' customers.
   a. Establishing sharper brand differentiation.
   b. Increasing promotional effort.
   c. Initiating price cuts.
3. Attracting nonusers to buy the product.
   a. Inducing trial use through sampling, price incentives, and so on.
   b. Pricing up or down.
   c. Advertising new uses.

Market development (selling present products in new markets):
1. Opening additional geographical markets.
   a. Regional expansion.
   b. National expansion.
   c. International expansion.
2. Attracting other market segments.
   a. Developing product versions to appeal to other segments.
   b. Entering other channels of distribution.
   c. Advertising in other media.

Product development (developing new products for present markets):
1. Developing new product features.
   a. Adapt (to other ideas, developments).
   b. Modify (change color, motion, sound, odor, form, shape).
   c. Magnify (stronger, longer, thicker, extra value).
   d. Minify (smaller, shorter, lighter).
   e. Substitute (other ingredients, process, power).
   f. Rearrange (other patterns, layout, sequence, components).
   g. Reverse (inside out).
   h. Combine (blend, alloy, assortment, ensemble; combine units, purposes, appeals, ideas).
2. Developing quality variations.
3. Developing additional models and sizes (product proliferation).

Source: Adapted from Philip Kotler, *Marketing Management: Analysis, Planning, and Control,* 5th ed., 1984, p. 58. Reprinted by permission of Prentice-Hall, Inc., Englewood Cliffs, N.J.

Product Development

Product development involves substantial modification of existing products or creation of new but related items that can be marketed to current customers through established channels. The product development strategy is often adopted either to prolong the life cycle of current products or to take advantage of favorable reputation and brand name. The idea is to attract satisfied customers to new products as a result of their positive experience with the company's initial offering. The bottom section of Figure 9–1 lists some of the many specific options available to businesses undertaking product development. Thus, a revised edition of a college textbook, a new car style, and a second formula of shampoo for oily hair each represents a product development strategy.

Strategy in Action 9–3 shows how Kohler Company was able to combine market and product development into an extremely effective grand strategy.

Innovation

In many industries it is increasingly risky not to innovate. Consumer as well as industrial markets have come to expect periodic changes and improvements in the products offered. As a result, some businesses find it profitable to base their grand strategy on *innovation*. They seek to reap the initially high profits associated with customer acceptance of a new or greatly improved product. Then, rather than face stiffening competition as the basis of profitability shifts from innovation to production or marketing competence, they move on to search for other original or novel ideas. The underlying philosophy of a grand strategy of innovation is creating a new product life cycle, thereby making any similar existing products obsolete. Thus, this approach differs from the

Strategy in Action 9–3
A Tub-and-Toilet Dynasty

In 1983, with the home-building industry in a long-running slump, profits in the plumbing fixtures business were swirling down the drain. For companies that made tubs, toilets, sinks, and showers, it seemed a time to retrench.

Not, however, for the privately held Kohler Company of Kohler, Wisconsin, creator of the Infinity Bath, the Super Spa, and other exotica for people who want their bathrooms to be fun as well as functional. Even though Kohler had to lay off 300 of its 6,000 workers because of slow sales of some products, the company was going ahead with its most ambitious capital spending program ever. In 1983 Kohler invested $50 million, more than 10 percent of its expected

Continued on Page 256

Strategy in Action 9–3 (*concluded*)

sales of $400 million. The plan included a big expansion of its factories in Brown-wood, Texas.

Unlike most American executives, who were often criticized for trying to boost short-run profits at the expense of long-range investment, Chairman Herbert Kohler could afford to disregard the short-term bottom line. His family and relatives owned or controlled 90 percent of the Kohler stock. While the typical U.S. company reinvested 60 percent of its earnings, Chairman Kohler claimed to put 90 percent of his profits back into the firm.

Kohler viewed a recession as a grand opportunity to increase his share of the kitchen and bathroom business. Because of the slump, he pointed out, some building materials cost less than they did in 1980, and thus the construction of new factories was comparatively inexpensive. During the recession in 1973–75, Kohler expanded its facilities enough to overtake American Standard as the largest manufacturer of luxury plumbing fixtures in the United States.

When Herbert Kohler became chairman in 1972, he decided that plumbing had not reached its potential. Said he, "I felt we could innovate with shapes and colors to change the whole function of the bathroom and make it something stimulating, possibly even social."

The company has since introduced the Infinity Bath, a kidney-shaped tub for two (price: $2,000), and the Super Spa, a giant whirlpool ($4,000) that can come with a built-in table for those who, for example, want to play poker as they soak. Kohler's masterpiece is the $12,500 Environment, a pleasure chamber that pampers bathers with "tropic rain, jungle steam, chinook winds, and Baja sun," all accompanied by soothing stereo music.

Though plumbing fixtures are rarely mentioned in the same breath with computers or robots, Kohler was convinced that the bathroom business had considerable growth potential. He expected to see the day when whirlpools were virtually standard in middle-class homes.

Source: "Rub-a-Dub-Dub," *Time,* July 26, 1982, p. 37.

product development strategy of extending an existing product's life cycle. The automobile industry provides many excellent examples. Ford Motor Company's 1981 introduction of the sporty, economical, two-seater EXP was an effort to interest a segment of American drivers who traditionally bought foreign-made sports cars in trying a Ford product. This was an innovation strategy because a new life cycle had been started for Ford. At the same time, Ford modified the Fairmont to make it lighter and more fuel efficient. This was a product development strategy since the Fairmont life cycle was extended.

While most growth-oriented firms appreciate the need to be innovative occasionally, a few companies use it as their fundamental way of relating to their markets. An outstanding example is Polaroid, which heavily promotes each of its new cameras until competitors are able to match their technological innovation. By this time, Polaroid is normally prepared to introduce a dramatically new or improved product. For example, in short succession consumers were introduced to the Swinger, the SX-70, the One Step, and the Sun Camera 660.

Few innovative ideas prove profitable because research, development, and premarketing costs incurred in converting a promising idea into a profitable product are extremely high. A study by the management research department of Booz Allen & Hamilton Inc. provides some understanding of the risks. As shown in Figure 9–2, Booz Allen & Hamilton Inc. studied 51 companies and found that less than 2 percent of the innovative projects initially considered eventually reached the marketplace. Specifically, out of every 58 new product ideas, only 12 pass an initial screening test that finds them compatible with the company's mission and long-term objectives. Only seven of these remain after an evaluation of their product potential, and only three survive actual attempts to develop the product. Two of these still appear to have profit potential after test marketing; but, on the average, only one will be commercially successful. In fact, other studies show this success rate to be overly optimistic. For example, the results of one research project disclosed failure rates for commercial products to be as high as 89 percent.[4]

Horizontal Integration

When the long-term strategy of a firm is based on growth through the acquisition of one or more similar businesses operating at the same stage of the production-marketing chain, its grand strategy is called *horizontal integration.* Such acquisitions provide access to new markets for the acquiring firm and eliminate competitors. For example, Warner-Lambert Pharmaceutical Company's acquisition of Parke Davis reduced competition in the ethical drugs field for Chilcott Laboratories, a company Warner-Lambert had previously acquired. A second example is the long-range acquisition pattern of White Consolidated Industries, which expanded in the refrigerator and freezer market through a grand strategy of horizontal integration. In 1967 it acquired the Franklin Appliance Division of Studebaker, in 1978 it bought the Kelvinator Appliance Division of American Motors, in 1971 it acquired the Refrigerator Products Division of Bendix Westinghouse Automotive Air Brake, and finally in 1979 it bought Frigidaire Appliance from General Motors. For yet another example of a successful horizontal integration grand strategy, read the case of the

---

[4] Burt Schorr, "Many New Products Fizzle, Despite Careful Planning, Publicity," *The Wall Street Journal,* April 5, 1961.

Figure 9–2
Decay of new product ideas (51 companies)

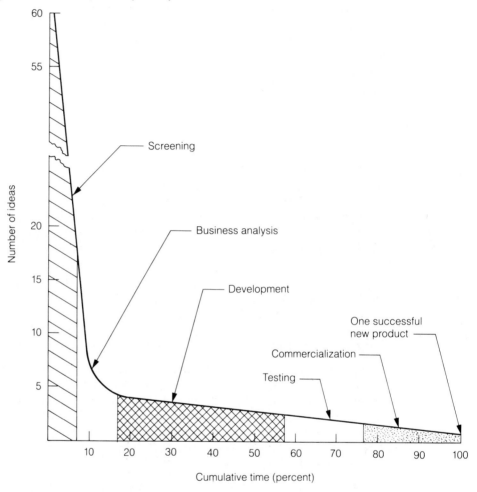

Santa Fe and Southern Pacific railroads in Strategy in Action 9–4. Thus, the combinations of two textile producers, two shirt manufacturers, or two clothing store chains would be classified as horizontal integrations.

Vertical Integration

When the grand strategy of a firm involves the acquisition of businesses that either supply the firm with inputs (such as raw materials) or serve as a customer for the firm's outputs (such as warehousers for finished products), *vertical integration* is involved. For example, if a shirt manufacturer acquires a textile producer—by purchasing its common stock, buying its assets, or through an exchange of ownership interests—the strategy is a vertical integration. In this case it is a *backward* vertical integration since the business acquired operates at an earlier stage of the production/marketing process. If the shirt manufacturer had merged with a clothing store, it would have been an example of *forward* vertical integration—the acquisition of a business nearer to the ultimate consumer.

Strategy in Action 9–4
Merging to Build a New Empire

In 1983 the Santa Fe and Southern Pacific railroads joined forces to form the third largest railroad in the United States, with 26,000 miles of track. Due to the $6.3 billion merger, only the Burlington Northern railroad (28,900 miles) and CSX (26,400) were bigger. The combined Santa Fe–Southern Pacific network stretched from Chicago in the North to New Orleans in the South to Portland in the West.

The new company was to be not just a railroad, but a business empire. Chicago-based Santa Fe Industries (1982 revenues: $3.16 billion) has gas wells, coal and uranium mines, and a forest-products division. The company was one of the largest U.S. producers of heavy crude oil. San Francisco–based Southern Pacific (1982 revenues: $3.1 billion) operated petroleum pipelines and leased executive aircraft, truck fleets, computers, mining machinery, and communications equipment. With huge holdings of farm land, timberland, and urban real estate, Southern Pacific was the largest private landlord in California.

[Southern Pacific] also owned the nation's only operational coal-slurry pipeline, which ran 273 miles between Arizona and Nevada. The pipeline allowed coal that has been mixed with water to be transported swiftly and cheaply.

Santa Fe and Southern Pacific saw their union as the best way to compete with two other big Western railroads that were built up through mergers: Burlington Northern and Union Pacific. Santa Fe and Southern Pacific intended to become more efficient by abandoning duplicate routes and pooling equipment. The combined 57,000-member work force of the two railroads would shrink but through attrition rather than layoffs.

Source: "Merging to Build New Empires," *Time,* October 10, 1983, p. 50.

Figure 9–3
Vertical and horizontal integrations

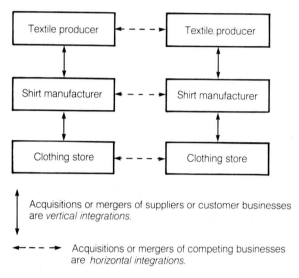

Acquisitions or mergers of suppliers or customer businesses are *vertical integrations.*

Acquisitions or mergers of competing businesses are *horizontal integrations.*

Figure 9–3 depicts both horizontal and vertical integration. The principal attractions of a horizontal integration grand strategy are readily apparent. The acquiring firm is able to greatly expand its operations, thereby achieving greater market share, improving economies of scale, and increasing efficiency of capital usage. Additionally, these benefits are achieved with only moderately increased risk, since the success of the expansion is principally dependent on proven abilities.

The reasons for choosing a vertical integration grand strategy are more varied and sometimes less obvious. The main reason for backward integration is the desire to increase the dependability of supply or quality of raw materials or production inputs. The concern is particularly great when the number of suppliers is small and the number of competitors is large. In this situation, the vertically integrating firm can better control its costs and thereby improve the profit margin of the expanded production/marketing system. Forward integration is a preferred grand strategy if the advantages of stable production are particularly high. A business can increase the predictability of demand for its output through forward integration, that is, through ownership of the next stage of its production/marketing chain.

Some increased risks are associated with both types of integration grand strategies. For horizontally integrated firms, the risks stem from the increased commitment to one type of business. For vertically integrated firms, the risks result from expansion of the company into areas requiring strategic managers

Figure 9–4
Typical joint ventures in the oil pipeline industry

Pipeline company (assets in $ millions)	Co-owners	Percent held by each
Colonial Pipeline Co. ($480.2)	Amoco	14.3
	Atlantic Richfield	1.6
	Cities Service	14.0
	Continental	7.5
	Phillips	7.1
	Texaco	14.3
	Gulf	16.8
	Sohio	9.0
	Mobil	11.5
	Union Oil	4.0
Olympic Pipeline Co. ($30.7)	Shell	43.5
	Mobil	29.5
	Texaco	27.0
West Texas Gulf Pipeline Co. ($19.8)	Gulf	57.7
	Cities Service	11.4
	Sun	12.6
	Union Oil	9.0
	Sohio	9.2
Texas–New Mexico Pipeline Co. ($30.5)	Texaco	45.0
	Atlantic Richfield	35.0
	Cities Service	10.0
	Getty	10.0

Source: Testimony of Walter Adams in *Horizontal Integration of the Energy Industry,* hearings before the Subcommittee on Energy of the Joint Economic Committee, 94th Congress, 1st sess. (1975), p. 112.

to broaden the base of their competencies and assume additional responsibilities.

Joint Venture

Occasionally two or more capable companies lack a necessary component for success in a particular competitive environment. For example, no single petroleum firm controlled sufficient resources to construct the Alaskan pipeline. Nor was any single firm capable of processing and marketing the volume of oil that would flow through the pipeline. The solution was a set of *joint ventures.* As shown in Figure 9–4, these cooperative arrangements could provide both the necessary funds to build the pipeline and the processing and marketing capacity to profitably handle the oil flow.

Strategy in Action 9–5
Moscow Woos Westerners for Joint Ventures

The Soviet government today set guidelines for joint business ventures between Soviet and Western firms, in an all-out bid to engage Western capital, technology, and management in the revision of the Soviet Union's socialist economy.

The rules leave no doubt that the partnerships will be dominated by Soviet firms, however. The partnerships should have "not less than" 51 percent Soviet ownership, a Soviet chairman of the board and general director, and "mainly" Soviet personnel, according to the Council of Ministers resolution released today by the official news agency, Tass.

The firms will be based in the Soviet Union, and Soviet and Western employees will be subject to Soviet employment regulations, with some exceptions possible for foreign workers.

The publication of the rules climaxes several months of Kremlin efforts to attract Western companies.

Since the concept of joint Soviet and Western enterprises first surfaced publicly here last spring, exploratory talks have been held with leading officials and business executives from at least a dozen Western countries, including the Netherlands, Britain, Finland, the United States, and Japan.

The aim of the efforts, today's announcement said, is to boost industrial output, "to attract into the national economy advanced foreign technology, managerial expertise, additional material and financial resources, [and] to develop the country's export base and reduce irrational imports."

Foreign shareholders are guaranteed the right to transfer hard currency earnings out of the Soviet Union.

Moscow has sweetened its courtship of Western companies with inducements. According to the new rules, the ventures will be tax free for the first two years and thereafter will be taxed at the after-deduction rate of 30 percent, considered modest by Western standards.

Despite the Soviet drive, Western diplomats and business executives based in Moscow who are skeptical about the chances for Soviet–Western joint ventures criticized today's release.

While the rules confirm Soviet interest in attracting Western business, Westerners in Moscow said they fail to demonstrate chances of reasonable profitability.

In addition, Western business executives balk at the stipulations placing employees under Soviet employment rules, many of which are unpublished. "It seems to take away the right of Western companies to hire and fire," one U.S.

Continued on Page 263

Strategy in Action 9–5 (*concluded*)

business executive in Moscow said. "That really undermines a Western business-man's means of exercising quality control."

The rules also prohibit joint ventures from direct marketing in the Soviet Union; instead, they must sell through a go-between—a Soviet foreign trade organization.

One big attraction is the vast warehouse of Soviet raw materials. The Soviet Union has several times the forest land of neighboring Finland, for example, but produces approximately the same amount of paper. In fact, paper pulp, along with machine building, chemical, light, and food production, are the key areas Moscow has pinpointed for joint ventures.

Source: Gary Lee, "Moscow Woos Westerners for Joint Ventures," *Washington Post*, January 27, 1987.

The particular form of joint venture discussed above is joint ownership.[5] In recent years it has become increasingly appealing for domestic firms to join foreign businesses through this form. For example, Bethlehem Steel acquired an interest in a Brazilian mining venture to secure a raw material source. The stimulus for this joint ownership venture was grand strategy, but such is not always the case. Certain countries virtually mandate that foreign companies entering their markets do so on a joint ownership basis. India and Mexico are good examples. The rationale of these countries is that joint ventures minimize the threat of foreign domination and enhance the skills, employment, growth, and profits of local businesses.

One final note: Strategic managers in the typical firm rarely seek joint ventures. This approach admittedly presents new opportunities with risks that can be shared. On the other hand, joint ventures often limit partner discretion, control, and profit potential while demanding managerial attention and other resources that might otherwise be directed toward the mainstream activities of the firm. Nevertheless, increasing nationalism in many foreign markets may require greater consideration of the joint venture approach if a firm intends to diversify internationally. These points are made vividly in Strategy in Action 9–5.

Concentric Diversification

Grand strategies involving diversification represent distinctive departures from a firm's existing base of operations, typically the acquisition or internal generation (spin-off) of a separate business with synergistic possibilities coun-

---

[5] Other forms of joint ventures (such as leasing, contract manufacturing, and management contracting) offer valuable support strategies. However, because they are seldom employed as grand strategies, they are not included in the categorization.

terbalancing the two businesses' strengths and weaknesses. For example, Head Ski initially sought to diversify into summer sporting goods and clothing to offset the seasonality of its snow business. However, diversifications are occasionally undertaken as unrelated investments because of their otherwise minimal resource demands and high profit potential.

Regardless of the approach taken, the motivations of the acquiring firms are the same:

> Increase the firm's stock value. Often in the past, mergers have led to increases in the stock price and/or price-earnings ratio.
>
> Increase the growth rate of the firm.
>
> Make an investment that represents better use of funds than plowing them into internal growth.
>
> Improve the stability of earnings and sales by acquiring firms whose earnings and sales complement the firm's peaks and valleys.
>
> Balance or fill out the product line.
>
> Diversify the product line when the life cycle of current products has peaked.
>
> Acquire a needed resource quickly; for example, high-quality technology or highly innovative management.
>
> Tax reasons, purchasing a firm with tax losses that will offset current or future earnings.
>
> Increase efficiency and profitability, especially if there is synergy between the two companies.[6]

When diversification involves the addition of a business related to the firm in terms of technology, markets, or products, it is a *concentric diversification*. With this type of grand strategy, the new businesses selected possess a high degree of compatability with the current businesses. The ideal concentric diversification occurs when the combined company profits increase strengths and opportunities, as well as decrease weaknesses and exposure to risk. Thus, the acquiring company searches for new businesses with products, markets, distribution channels, technologies, and resource requirements that are familiar but not identical, synergistic but not wholly interdependent.

Conglomerate Diversification

Occasionally a firm, particularly a very large one, plans to acquire a business because it represents the most promising investment opportunity available. This type of grand strategy is commonly known as *conglomerate diversification*. The principal and often sole concern of the acquiring firm is the profit pattern

---

[6]William F. Glueck, *Business Policy and Strategic Management* (New York: McGraw-Hill, 1980), p. 213.

of the venture. There is little concern given to creating product/market synergy with existing businesses, unlike the approach taken in concentric diversification. Financial synergy is what is sought by conglomerate diversifiers such as ITT, Textron, American Brands, Litton, U.S. Industries, Fuqua, and I.C. Industries. For example, they may seek a balance in their portfolios between current businesses with cyclical sales and acquired businesses with counter-cyclical sales, between high-cash/low-opportunity and low-cash/high-opportunity businesses, or between debt-free and highly leveraged businesses.

The principal difference between the two types of diversification is that concentric acquisitions emphasize some commonality in markets, products, or technology, whereas conglomerate acquisitions are based principally on profit considerations.

Retrenchment/Turnaround

For any of a large number of reasons a business can find itself with declining profits. Economic recessions, production inefficiencies, and innovative break-throughs by competitors are only three causes. In many cases strategic managers believe the firm can survive and eventually recover if a concerted effort is made over a period of a few years to fortify basic distinctive competencies. This type of grand strategy is known as *retrenchment*. It is typically accomplished in one of two ways, employed singly or in combination:

1. *Cost reduction.* Examples include decreasing the work force through employee attrition, leasing rather than purchasing equipment, extending the life of machinery, and eliminating elaborate promotional activities.
2. *Asset reduction.* Examples include the sale of land, buildings, and equipment not essential to the basic activity of the business, and elimination of "perks" like the company airplane and executive cars.

If these initial approaches fail to achieve the required reductions, more drastic action may be necessary. It is sometimes essential to lay off employees, drop items from a production line, and even eliminate low-margin customers.

Since the underlying purpose of retrenchment is to reverse current negative trends, the method is often referred to as a *turnaround* strategy. Interestingly, the turnaround most commonly associated with this approach is in management positions. In a study of 58 large firms, researchers Schendel, Patton, and Riggs found that turnaround was almost always associated with changes in top management.[7] Bringing in new managers was believed to introduce needed new perspectives of the firm's situation, to raise employee morale,

---

[7] Dan G. Schendel, G. Richard Patton, and James Riggs, "Corporate Turnaround Strategies: A Study of Profit Decline and Recovery," *Journal of General Management* 3 (1976), pp. 3–11.

and to facilitate drastic actions, such as deep budgetary cuts in established programs.

Divestiture

A *divestiture strategy* involves the sale of a business or a major business component. When retrenchment fails to accomplish the desired turnaround, strategic managers often decide to sell the business. However, because the intent is to find a buyer willing to pay a premium above the value of fixed assets for a going concern, the term *marketing for sale* is more appropriate. Prospective buyers must be convinced that because of their skills and resources, or the synergy with their existing businesses, they will be able to profit from the acquisition.

The reasons for divestiture vary. Often they arise because of partial mismatches between the acquired business and the parent corporation. Some of the mismatched parts cannot be integrated into the corporation's mainstream and thus must be spun off. A second reason is corporation financial needs. Sometimes the cash flow or financial stability of the corporation as a whole can be greatly improved if businesses with high market value can be sacrificed. A third, less frequent reason for divestiture is government antitrust action when a corporation is believed to monopolize or unfairly dominate a particular market.

Although examples of grand strategies of divestiture are numerous, an outstanding example in the last decade is Chrysler Corporation, which in quick succession divested itself of several major businesses to protect its mission as a domestic automobile manufacturer. Among major Chrysler sales were its Airtempt air-conditioning business to Fedders and its automotive subsidiaries in France, Spain, and England to Peugeot–Citroen. These divestitures yielded Chrysler a total of almost $500 million in cash, notes, and stock and, thus, in the relatively short term, improved its financial stability. Other corporations that have recently pursued this type of grand strategy include Esmark, which divested Swift and Company, and White Motors, which divested White Farm.

An example of the value of divestiture is shown in Strategy in Action 9–6. As discussed, Gulf & Western used the proceeds of divestitures together with savings from selective retrenchments to create tax write-offs and reduce the firm's huge level of long-term debt.

Liquidation

When the grand strategy is that of *liquidation,* the business is typically sold in parts, only occasionally as a whole, but for its tangible asset value and not as a going concern. In selecting liquidation, owners and strategic managers

Strategy in Action 9–6
Gulf & Western Slims Down

Charles Bluhdorn was one of the earliest and flashiest conglomerateurs, a master of the unfriendly takeover. Starting with a small auto-parts company in 1958, he assembled an incredible array of disparate businesses into Gulf & Western Industries (1982 sales: $5.3 billion). Bluhdorn eventually bought some 100 companies large and small, ranging from Paramount Pictures to publisher Simon & Schuster to New York City's Madison Square Garden. In one six-year period, he brought 80 firms into what became jokingly known as "Engulf and Devour." Bluhdorn died in February 1983, at 56, after a heart attack, and his successors were in no mood to keep up that pace. They contracted Gulf & Western almost as fast as Bluhdorn had expanded it.

In 1983, a new management team headed by Vice Chairman and Chief Executive Martin Davis, 56, announced a major streamlining program to rid the company of low-profit operations. Among the cast-offs: Arlington Park race track near Chicago and Roosevelt Raceway in New York, manufacturer E. W. Bliss, and Sega's video-game unit. The moves saved the company about $470 million in tax write-offs, but produced a loss of $215 million in the first year.

The divestitures were just the latest ordered by Davis, who went to Gulf & Western from Paramount in 1969 and took over immediately after Bluhdorn's death. Davis had earlier moved to sell off $650 million of company-owned stock in 30 companies, leaving the conglomerate with some $150 million in such holdings. The money was used to bring down the company's mountain of debt to $1.2 billion. Davis then also sold Gulf & Western's 21.4 percent stake in Brunswick, the sports equipment manufacturer, for $97 million. Davis likewise chopped away at the company's work force, reducing it by about 10,000 to 47,000.

Pointless mixing of dissimilar firms seemed finished at Gulf & Western. Said Shearson/American Express analyst Scott Merlis: "Few of their businesses were related to their other businesses." Instead, the company now seemed determined to focus sharply on a few areas: consumer products (apparel, Kayser-Roth; home furnishings, Simmons), entertainment (Paramount), and financial services (Associates Corp.).

Gulf & Western was only one of several companies to follow the newly fashionable divestiture route. Such firms as Beatrice Foods, Quaker Oats, and General Electric all sold off major holdings during 1982–1983.

Source: "The Big Sell-Off," *Time,* August 29, 1983, p. 45.

of a business are admitting failure and recognize that this action is likely to result in great hardships to themselves and their employees. For these reasons liquidation is usually seen as the least attractive of all grand strategies. However, as a long-term strategy it minimizes the loss to all stakeholders of the firm. Usually faced with bankruptcy, the liquidating business tries to develop a planned and orderly system that will result in the greatest possible return and cash conversion as the business slowly relinquishes its market share.

Planned liquidation can be worthwhile. For example, the Columbia Corporation, a $130 million diversified firm, liquidated its assets for more cash per share than the market value of its stock.

Selection of Long-Term Objectives and Grand Strategy Sets

At first glance the strategic management model, which provides the framework for study throughout this book, seems to suggest that strategic choice decision making leads to the *sequential* selections of long-term objectives and grand strategy. In fact, however, strategic choice is the *simultaneous* selection of long-range objectives and grand strategy. Figure 9–5 depicts the actual process. When strategic planners study their opportunities, they try to determine which are most likely to result in achieving various long-range objectives. Almost simultaneously they try to forecast whether an available grand strategy can take advantage of preferred opportunities so that the tentative objectives can be met. In essence, then, three distinct but highly interdependent choices are being made at one time. Usually several triads or sets of possible decisions are considered.

A simplified example of this process is shown in Figure 9–6. In this example the business has determined that six strategic choice options are available. These options stem from three different interactive opportunities (e.g., West Coast markets) that present little competition. Because each of these interactive opportunities can be approached through different grand strategies—in options 1 and 2 they are horizontal integration and market development—each offers the potential for achieving long-range objectives to varying degrees. Thus, a business can rarely make a strategic choice only on the basis of its preferred opportunities, long-range objectives, or grand strategy. Instead, the three elements must be considered simultaneously because only in combination do they constitute a strategic choice.

In an actual decision situation the strategic choice would be complicated by a wider variety of interactive opportunities, feasible company objectives, promising grand strategy options, and evaluative criteria. Nevertheless, Figure 9–6 does partially reflect the nature and complexity of the process by which long-term objectives and grand strategy are selected.

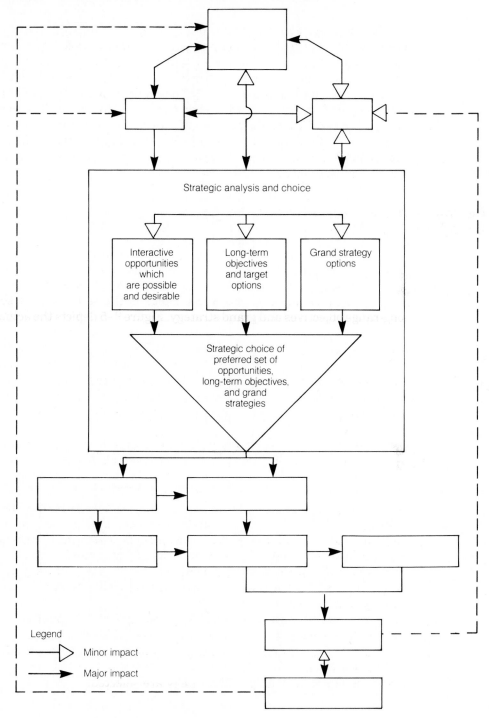

Strategic analysis and choice

Interactive
opportunities
which
are possible
and desirable

Long-term
objectives
and target
options

Grand strategy
options

Strategic choice of
preferred set of
opportunities,
long-term objectives,
and grand
strategies

Legend

Minor impact

Major impact

Figure 9-6
A profile of strategic choice options

	Six strategic choice options					
	1	2	3	4	5	6
Interactive opportunities	West Coast markets present little competition		Current markets sensitive to price competition		Current industry product lines after too narrow a range of markets	
Appropriate long-range objectives (limited sample):						
Average 5-year ROI	15%	19%	13%	17%	23%	15%
Company sales by year 5	+50%	+40%	+20%	+0%	+35%	+25%
Risk of negative profit	.30	.25	.10	.15	.20	.05
Grand strategies	Horizontal integration	Market development	Concentration	Selective retrenchment	Product development	Concentration

In the next chapter, the strategic choice process will be fully explained. However, knowledge of long-term objectives and grand strategies is essential to understanding that process. Thus, the topics were presented here first, even though a company's specific selections of long-term objectives and grand strategies are actually outputs based on choice, as the strategic management process model shows.

Sequence of Objectives and Strategy Selection

The selection of long-term objectives and grand strategies involves simultaneous rather than sequential decisions. While it is true that objectives are needed so that the company's direction and progress are not determined by random forces, it is equally true that objectives are valuable only if strategies can be implemented, making achievement of objectives realistic. In fact, the selection of long-term objectives and grand strategies is so interdependent that until the 1970s most business consultants and academicians did not stress the need to distinguish between them. Most popular business literature and practicing executives still combine long-term objectives and grand strategies under the heading of company strategy.

However, the distinction has merit. Objectives indicate what strategic managers *want* but provide few insights as to *how* this will be achieved. Conversely, strategies indicate what type of *actions* will be taken but do not define what *ends* will be pursued or what criteria will serve as constraints in refining the strategic plan.

The latter view of objectives as constraints on strategy formulation rather than as ends toward which strategies are directed is stressed by several prominent management experts.[8] They argue that strategic decisions are designed (1) to satisfy the minimum requirements of different company groups, for example, the production department's need for more inventory capacity, or the marketing department's need to increase the sales force and (2) to create synergistic profit potential given these constraints.

Does it matter whether strategic decisions are made to achieve objectives or to satisfy constraints? No, because constraints are objectives themselves. The constraint of increased inventory capacity is a desire (an objective), not a certainty. Likewise, the constraint of a larger sales force does not assure that it will be achieved given such factors as other company priorities, labor market conditions, and the firm's profit performance.

---

[8] See, for example, P. F. Drucker, *The Practice of Management* (New York: Harper & Row, 1954); R. M. Cyert, and J. G. March, *A Behavioral Theory of the Firm* (Englewood Cliffs, N.J.: Prentice-Hall, 1963); H. A. Simon, "On the Concept of Organizational Goals," *Administrative Science Quarterly* 9 (1964), pp. 1–22; and M. D. Richards, *Organizational Goal Structures* (St. Paul, Minn.: West Publishing, 1978).

Summary

Before learning how strategic decisions are made, it was important to understand the two principal components of any strategic choice, namely, long-term objectives and grand strategy. Such understanding was the purpose of the chapter.

Long-term objectives were defined as the results a business seeks to achieve over a specified period of time, typically five years. Seven common long-term objectives were discussed: profitability, productivity, competitive position, employee development, employee relations, technological leadership, and public responsibility. These, or any other long-term objectives, should be acceptable, flexible, measurable over time, motivating, suitable, understandable, and achievable.

Grand strategies were defined as comprehensive approaches guiding major actions designed to achieve long-term business objectives. Twelve specific grand strategy options were discussed. They included concentration, market development, product development, innovation, horizontal integration, vertical integration, joint ventures, concentric diversification, conglomerate diversification, retrenchment/turnaround, divestiture, and liquidation.

Questions for Discussion

1. Think of the business community nearest to your college or university. Identify businesses you believe are using each of the 12 grand strategies.
2. Try to identify businesses in your community that appear to rely principally on 1 of the 12 grand strategies. What kind of information did you use to classify the firms?
3. Write a long-term objective for your school of business that exhibits the seven qualities of long-term objectives described in this chapter.
4. Distinguish between the following pairs of grand strategies:
   a. Horizontal and vertical integration.
   b. Conglomerate and concentric diversification.
   c. Product development and innovation.
5. Rank each of the 12 grand strategy options on the following three scales:

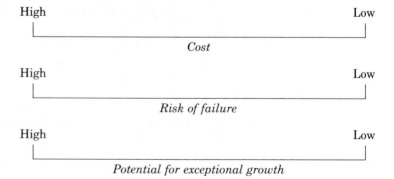

High   Low

Cost

High   Low

Risk of failure

High   Low

Potential for exceptional growth

6. Identify companies that use one of the eight specific options shown in Figure 9–1 under the grand strategies of concentration, market development, and product development.

Bibliography

Ansoff, H. I. "Strategies for Diversification." *Harvard Business Review,* September–October 1957, pp. 113–24.

————. *Corporate Strategy.* New York: McGraw-Hill, 1965.

————. *Strategic Management.* New York: John Wiley & Sons, 1979.

Cyert, R. M., and J. G. March. *A Behavioral Theory of the Firm.* Englewood Cliffs, N.J.: Prentice-Hall, 1963.

Drucker, P. F. *The Practice of Management.* New York: Harper & Row, 1954.

Glueck, W. F. *Business Policy and Strategic Management.* New York: McGraw-Hill, 1980.

Higgins, J. M. *Organizational Policy and Strategic Management.* Hinsdale, Ill.: Dryden Press, 1979.

King, R., and D. I. Cleland. *Strategic Planning and Policy.* New York: Van Nostrand Reinhold, 1978.

Kotler, P. *Marketing Management.* Englewood Cliffs, N.J.: Prentice-Hall, 1972.

Luck, D. J., and A. E. Prell. *Market Strategy.* New York: Appleton-Century-Crofts, 1968.

Osborn, A. F. *Applied Imagination.* 3rd rev. ed. New York: Charles Scribner's Sons, 1968.

Pearce, J. A., II. "An Executive-Level Perspective on the Strategic Management Process." *California Management Review,* Summer 1981, pp. 39–48.

————. "Selecting among Alternative Grand Strategies." *California Management Review,* Spring 1982.

Richards, M. D. *Organizational Goal Structures.* St. Paul, Minn.: West Publishing, 1978.

Schendel, Dan G.; G. R. Patton; and J. Riggs. "Corporate Turnaround Strategies: A Study of Profit Decline and Recovery." *Journal of General Management* 3 (1976), pp. 3–11.

Schorr, B. "Many New Products Fizzle, Despite Careful Planning, Publicity." *The Wall Street Journal,* April 5, 1961.

Simon, H. A. "On the Concept of Organizational Goals." *Administrative Science Quarterly,* 1964, pp. 1–22.

Steiner, G. A. *Strategic Planning.* New York: Free Press, 1979.

Steiner, G. A., and J. B. Miner. *Management Policy and Strategy.* New York: Macmillan, 1977.

Chapter 9 Cohesion Case Illustration

Long-Term Objectives and Grand Strategies at Holiday Inns, Inc.

Long-term objectives at Holiday Inns, Inc., exist at both the corporate and business levels. Selected examples of long-term objectives are provided below:

Corporate Long-Term Objectives:

Increase corporatewide return on equity to 17.5 percent by 1984.

Achieve and maintain a debt-to-invested-capital ratio that does not exceed a 40–50 percent range.

Improve the corporatewide after-tax margin to a minimum of 7 percent by 1984.

Ensure a corporationwide sales growth that will maintain hotel group contribution at less than 60 percent of sales by 1984.

Business Group Long-Term Objectives:

Increase the number of rooms in the HI system by 70,000 between 1982 and 1987. *(Hotel group)*

Improve hotel operating margins to 20 percent by 1984. *(Hotel group)*

Triple the number of company-owned properties in multiuser locations by 1987. *(Hotel group)*

Increase the cash flow generated by Delta for corporatewide use from $25 million in 1980 to $60 million in 1985. *(Transportation group)*

Increase the ROI from gaming operations to 15 percent by 1987. *(Casino group)*

Increase the average daily customer count at Perkins restaurants to 1,000 people per day by 1987. *(Restaurant group)*

These objectives provide examples of the strategic focus that long-term objectives can provide the firm. Strategic direction is further clarified through grand strategies.

Twelve fundamental grand strategies were discussed in Chapter 9. Each grand strategy is illustrated below as it might apply to a particular business group:

Concentration.   The *hotel group* might consider that continued emphasis on expansion of selected company-owned and franchised Holiday Inn properties has sufficient potential to achieve long-term objectives. This would call for a concentration on growth via the group's current approach with emphasis on maintaining and improving operating advantages and effectiveness.

Market Development.   The *hotel group* might determine that domestic growth potential is decreasing. If so, it might pursue a strategy that emphasizes major international expansion of the Holiday Inns network.

Product Development.   *Perkins* might determine that inadequate menu selection is one reason for its mediocre performance. A product development strategy would therefore pursue growth via systematic development and expansion of menu items.

Innovation.   The *transportation group* might consider pursuing growth via the systematic development of a revolutionary new ship design for shipping operations. This innovation-based strategy would be one option (probably a remote one) for the transportation group.

Horizontal Integration.   One way for the *gaming group* to grow rapidly would be to acquire casinos in key markets where the group currently competes or desires to compete.

Vertical Integration.   Vertical integration can be either *forward* or *backward*. For example, *Delta Steamships* might see growth via route expansion as fairly limited. As a result it might seek manufacturing capacity for LASH containers *(backward integration)* to serve its needs and those of other shippers. Another alternative is involvement in warehousing or brokering *(forward integration)* as a basis for shipping-related growth.

Joint Ventures.   The *hotel group* may project faster growth in the high-priced and budget-priced lodging segments than in the broad middle segment. It may seek joint ventures with chains in one or both of these segments to get a foothold and a possible expansion base.

Retrenchment.   Profits of the *transportation group* declined for several years in the late 1970s. A retrenchment strategy cutting out unprofitable routes, unnecessary overhead, and level of terminal services was a possible grand strategy for this group.

Divestiture. The *restaurant group* may determine that the best way to achieve long-term ROI objectives is to sell several subpar restaurant locations. Selling these as going concerns would represent a divestiture strategy if it represented the group's key orientation.

Liquidation. The *hotel group* acquired over 30 businesses supplying its institutional products needs in the 1960s. Most of these businesses solely supplied Holiday Inns' institutional and printing needs. The hotel group might choose to sell the equipment used by some of these businesses if sale of the business as a going concern is not realistic. This would be a liquidation strategy.

Concentric Diversification. The best way to view this grand strategy at Holiday Inns, Inc., is to look at selected decisions made at Holiday Inns when it was predominantly a hotel chain. Holiday Inns' expansion into the freestanding restaurant business and the casino-gaming business is a concentric diversification strategy in relation to Holiday Inns, Inc.'s dominant core business.

Conglomerate Diversification. From the same perspective, Holiday Inns, Inc.'s acquisition of Trailways and Delta Steamship represents a conglomerate diversification strategy in that these businesses were essentially unrelated to Holiday Inns' core businesses.

These examples illustrate each grand strategy concept. As you can see, each grand strategy is a possible alternative for at least one of Holiday Inns, Inc.'s businesses.

10

Strategic Analysis and Choice

The previous chapter described basic characteristics of major strategic alternatives that a firm might consider. Several questions remain. How does a company identify alternative strategies? What are some of the diagnostic tools used to identify and evaluate realistic alternative strategies in multibusiness companies? What factors influence the ultimate choice of strategy?

This chapter will examine possible answers to these questions. Techniques used to aid strategic choice at the corporate and business levels will be explored. Managerial, political, and behavioral factors affecting the choice of strategy will also be discussed.

The search for alternative strategies is both incremental and creative in that strategists begin by considering alternatives they are familiar with and think will work. These are usually incremental alterations of past strategies. Systematic comparison of external and internal factors is often used to search for alternative strategies. Creativity can be important in this internal/external comparison. The search for multiple alternatives depends on systematic comparison of the strengths, weaknesses, risks, and trade-offs of each alternative. Several alternatives are generated and systematically evaluated in a comparative framework. The quality of the ultimate choice is thereby logically enhanced. Evaluation of alternative strategies is much the same whether new alternatives or the old strategy is considered. The focus is the future. Both old and new strategies must be subjected to the same systematic evaluation if a logical choice is to be made.

Figure 10–1
The process of strategic analysis

	Corporate-level strategy	*Business-level strategy*
Time	Analysis of the overall company *portfolio* of businesses in terms of relative business unit strength *matched* with relative industry attractiveness and stage of development.	Analysis of the *match* between the business's current strategic position (company profile) and the major strategic opportunities and threats (environmental analysis) that exist or will exist in the planning time period.
	Identification of probable corporate performance if the current business unit portfolio is maintained with respective strategies.	Examining the probable results of pursuing the current strategy in light of the new business–environment match.
	Comparison of this projected corporate performance with tentative corporate objectives to identify major performance gaps.	Comparison of these results with tentative business objectives to identify major performance gaps and strategic concerns.
	Identification of alternative portfolios (including different strategy combinations at the business unit level) to close performance gaps.	Identification of alternative strategies to close performance gaps and confront (or avoid) strategic concerns.
	Evaluation of the alternatives and strategic choice.	Evaluation of the alternatives and strategic choice.

The process of strategic analysis and choice involves five incremental phases. Figure 10–1 identifies these phases at the business and corporate levels. Because strategic choice is a judgmental/analytical process meant to ascertain the future impact of one or more strategies on corporate (and/or business unit) performance, the answers to three basic questions are sought:

1. How effective has the existing strategy been?
2. How effective will that strategy be in the future?
3. What will be the effectiveness of selected alternative strategies (or changes in the existing strategy) in the future?

Strategic Analysis at the Corporate Level

A fundamental method of corporate strategic analysis in diversified, multi-industry companies is the business portfolio approach. General Electric, for example, has over 40 strategic business units (SBUs).[1] Thus, General Electric must decide how this portfolio of businesses should be managed to achieve corporate objectives. A corporate strategy is sought that sets the basic "strategic

---

[1] General Electric combined selected businesses or operations, regardless of organizational level, into SBUs for planning purposes.

An SBU is generally created when the following requirements are met by the component:

1. It has a unique business mission.
2. It has an identifiable set of competitors.
3. It is a viable competitor.
4. The SBU strategic manager can make or implement a strategic decision relatively independent of other SBUs.
5. Crucial operating decisions can be made within the SBU.

thrust" for each business unit in a manner consistent with the resource capabilities of the overall company.

The *portfolio approach,* with analysis of corporate-level strategy distinct from business-level strategy, is adaptable to multiproduct market firms in which each product/market is managed as a separate business or profit center and the firm is not dominated by one product/market. The approach involves examining each business as a separate entity and as a contributor to the corporation's total *portfolio* of businesses. In dominant product/market companies and single product/market firms, corporate strategy considerations are not separate and distinct from business-level considerations.

In a broad sense, corporate strategy is concerned with generation and allocation of corporate resources. The firm's portfolio of businesses are, to varying degrees, the generators and recipients of these resources. The portfolio approach provides a simple, visual way of identifying and evaluating alternative strategies for the generation and allocation of corporate resources.

The BCG Growth/Share Matrix

One of the most widely used portfolio approaches to corporate strategic analysis has been the growth/share matrix pioneered by the Boston Consulting Group (BCG) and illustrated in Figure 10–2. This matrix facilitates corporate strategic analysis of likely "generators" and optimum "users" of corporate resources. Strategy in Action 10–1 provides a description of the use of the BCG matrix at Mead Corporation.

To use the BCG matrix, each of the company's businesses is plotted according to market growth rate (percentage growth in sales) and relative competitive position (market share). Market growth rate is the projected rate of sales growth for the market to be served by a particular business. It is usually measured as the percentage increase in a market's sales or unit volume over the two most recent years. Market growth rate provides an indicator of the relative attractiveness of the markets served by each of the businesses in the corporation's portfolio of businesses. Relative competitive position is usually expressed as the ratio of a business's market share divided by the market share of the largest competitor in that market. Relative competitive position thus provides a basis for comparing the relative strengths of different businesses in the business portfolio in terms of the "strength" of their position in each business's respective market.

Businesses are plotted on the matrix once their market growth rate and relative competitive positions have been computed. Figure 10–2 represents the BCG matrix for a company with nine businesses. Each circle represents a business unit. The size of the circle represents the proportion of corporate revenue generated by that business unit. This provides visualization of the current importance of each business as a revenue generator.

Market growth rate is frequently separated into "high" and "low" areas by an arbitrary 10 percent growth line. Relative competitive position is usually

Figure 10–2
BCG's growth/share matrix

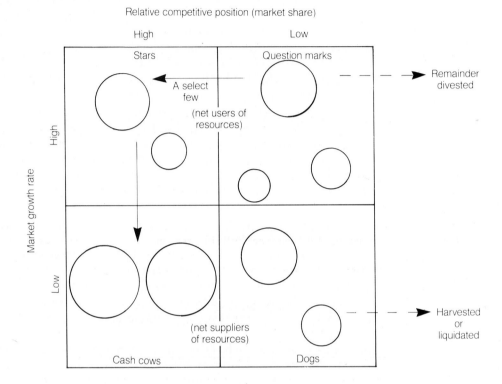

divided at a relative market share between 1.0 and 1.5, so that a "high" position signifies market leadership. Once plotted, businesses in the BCG matrix will be in one of four cells with differing implications for their role in an overall corporate-level strategy.

High-Growth/High Competitive Position.   The *stars,* as the BCG matrix labeled them, are businesses in rapidly growing markets with large market shares. Stars represent the best long-run opportunities (growth and profitability) in the firm's portfolio. These businesses require substantial investment to maintain (and expand) their dominant position in a growing market. This investment requirement is often in excess of what can be generated internally. Therefore, these businesses are short-term, priority consumers of corporate resources within the overall business portfolio.

Low-Growth/High Competitive Position.   *Cash cows* are high-market-share businesses in maturing, low-growth markets or industries. Because of their strong position and minimal reinvestment requirements for growth, these

Strategy in Action 10–1
Portfolio Management at Mead Corporation

Mead Corporation, under the direction of Chairman and CEO J. W. McSwiney, was one of the pioneers in the use of a portfolio approach in the strategic management of its numerous forest-products-related businesses. The following is excerpted from a presentation by J. W. McSwiney, President Warren L. Batts, and Vice Chairman William W. Wommack to Paper and Forest Products Analysts at the Princeton Club in New York about Mead's early experience using portfolio planning:

> As the first step toward achieving Mead's corporate goals, Mr. McSwiney assigned Bill Wommack full-time responsibility for developing a new strategic philosophy, a planning system, and then a strategy for each of Mead's businesses. The strategic concept he developed was straightforward and very effective:

> Obtain market leadership in markets we serve.

> If market leadership is not possible, redeploy our assets to markets where leadership potential exists.

> This concept can be translated into a matrix as follows:

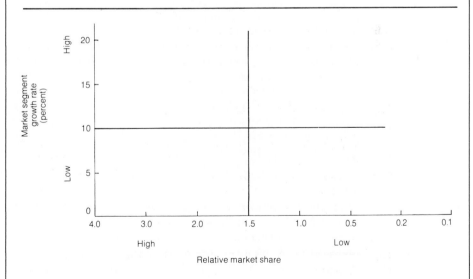

Continued on Page 282

Strategy in Action 10–1 (*continued*)

> We consider a high-growth market to be one that is growing by at least 10 percent in real terms. To us, relative market share is what counts. We consider a leadership position exists when a business has a market share that is at least 1.5 times the share of its next largest competitor, as shown by the vertical line at 1.5 in the figure above.
>
> Starting with the upper right-hand quadrant:
>
> For a business in a high-growth market with a low market share, we assess our chances for leadership, and either grow our share aggressively or get out.
>
> In a high-growth market with a high market share, we grow our share as rapidly as we can and invest to become the most cost-effective producer.
>
> In a low-growth market with a high market share, we maintain our market share and cost effectiveness. We also generate cash for the balance of the company.
>
> In a low-growth market with low market share, we operate to generate cash— we have generally found this means we get out.
>
> When we classified our businesses on this matrix, we found many were competing in low-growth segments with low market share. We decided that within five years we should eliminate those low-growth and low-market-share businesses and allocate capital to the remaining businesses so that they could attain greater market share and grow larger.
>
> Our first step was to dispose of 15 businesses where it was not practical to become a leader. They were essentially the low-growth, low-market-share businesses. This step generated $80 million in cash, plus it saved $25 million we would have had to invest if we'd kept them. Especially important, these actions immediately improved our mix of businesses and the total return from our assets.
>
> Second, we had to change the way our managers managed; plus we all had to operate in a more highly focused manner. We started with formal in-house training programs for some 300 Mead managers. [Our strategy] would not be carried out unless key managers truly understood the new . . . philosophy . . . and how to use the underlying analytical techniques. But even when managers understood what we were trying to do, some were unable to accept the discipline required. We had to reorganize several businesses and change a number of managers. Five of our six operating group vice presidents were changed, as well as 19 of our 24 division presidents. Fortunately, the talent to effect these changes was largely in-house.
>
> Finally, we put increased emphasis on managing our assets. We consider return on net assets the true measure of operating performance, so we tied each general manager's compensation to a balance between his business unit's earnings and its net assets.

Continued on Page 283

Strategy in Action 10–1 (*concluded*)

We categorized and managed our businesses from a strategic point of view as follows:

Poor businesses.

Those businesses which had good strategies in place.

Those businesses which needed a change in strategy.

Examining these categories demonstrates how we improved our results by:

Shifting assets.

Improving performance.

Carefully investing.

Category	Asset mix		Return on net assets	
	Year 1	Year 5	Year 1	Year 5
Poor businesses	13.2%	2.1%	2.4%	4.2%
No change	38.5	53.4	8.8	9.6
Change	48.3	44.5	2.8	11.8
Total corporate	100.0%	100.0%	4.7%	10.4%

In year 1 our sales totaled $1.1 billion. Four years later sales totaled $1.6 billion. This was a 9 percent compound growth rate, even though we had disposed of businesses having sales of $180 million. It is worth noting that sales of our Forest Products category increased at a 15 percent rate, so that percentage of the total rose to 56 percent.

Pretax earnings during this period increased from about $39 million to $167 million, or a 34 percent compound growth rate. Again, earnings in our Forest Products category increased sixfold.

We continually review our businesses, and we will reclassify a business and change its strategy when it's prudent to do so.

I believe we now have the fundamentals for long-term success firmly in place—both in the physical sense of good businesses serving growing markets, and in the management sense of realistic objectives, sound strategies—and the internal discipline to carry them out.

Source: Mead executive management presentation to Paper and Forest Product Analysts at the Princeton Club, New York, February 8, 1977. Reprinted with permission.

businesses often generate cash in excess of their needs. Therefore, these businesses are selectively "milked" as a source of corporate resources for deployment elsewhere (to stars and question marks). Cash cows are yesterday's stars and remain the current foundation of their corporate portfolios. They provide the cash to pay corporate overhead and dividends and also provide debt capacity. They are managed to maintain their strong market share while efficiently generating excess resources for corporatewide use.

Low-Growth/Low Competitive Position. The BCG matrix calls businesses with low market share and low market growth the *dogs* in the firm's portfolio. These businesses are in saturated, mature markets with intense competition and low profit margins. Because of their weak position, these businesses are managed for short-term cash flow (through ruthless cost cutting, for example) to supplement corporate-level resource needs. According to the original BCG prescription, they are eventually divested or liquidated once the short-term harvesting is maximized.

Recent research has questioned the notion that all *dogs* should be destined for divestiture/liquidation.[2] The thrust of this research suggests that *well-managed dogs* turn out to be positive, highly reliable resource generators (although still far less resource rich than cows). The well-managed dogs, according to these studies, combine a narrow business focus, emphasis on high product quality and moderate prices, strenuous cost cutting and cost control, and limited advertising. While suggesting that well-managed dogs can be a useful component of a business portfolio, these studies warn that ineffective dogs should still be considered prime candidates for harvesting, divestiture, or liquidation.

High-Growth/Low Competitive Position. *Question mark* businesses have considerable appeal because of their high growth rate yet present questionable profit potential because of low market share. Question mark businesses are known as cash guzzlers because their cash needs are high as a result of rapid growth, while their cash generation is low due to a small market share. Because market growth rate is high, a favorable market share (competitive position) should be easier to obtain than with the dogs in the portfolio. At the corporate level the concern is identifying the question marks that would most benefit from extra corporate resources resulting in increased market share and movement into the star group. When this long-run shift in a business's position from question mark to star is unlikely, the BCG matrix suggests divesting the business to reposition the resources more effectively in the remaining portfolio.

---

[2] Carlyn Y. Woo and Arnold C. Cooper, "Strategies of Effective Low-Market-Share Businesses," *Harvard Business Review,* November–December 1982, pp. 106–13; Donald Hambrick and Ian MacMillan, "Dogs," *Boardroom Reports,* October 15, 1981, pp. 5–6.

The BCG matrix was a valuable initial development in the portfolio approach to corporate-level strategy evaluation. The goal of the BCG approach is to determine the corporate strategy that best provides a balanced portfolio of business units. BCG's ideal, balanced portfolio would have the largest sales in cash cows and stars, with only a few question marks and very few dogs (the latter with favorable cash flow).

The BCG matrix makes two major contributions to corporate strategic choice: the assignment of a specific role or mission for each business unit and the integration of multiple business units into a total corporate strategy. By focusing simultaneously on comparative growth/share positions, the underlying premise of corporate strategy becomes exploitation of competitive advantage.

While the BCG matrix is an important visual tool with which to analyze corporate (business portfolio) strategy, strategists must recognize six limitations:

1. Clearly defining a *market* is often difficult. As a result, accurately measuring *share* and *growth rate* can be a problem. This, in turn, creates the potential for distortion or manipulation.

2. Dividing the matrix into four cells based on a *high/low* classification scheme is somewhat simplistic. It does not recognize the markets with *average* growth rates or the businesses with *average* market shares.

3. The relationship between market share and profitability underlying the BCG matrix—the *experience curve* effect—varies across industries and market segments. In some industries a large market share creates major advantages in unit costs; in others it does not. Furthermore, some companies with low market share can generate superior profitability and cash flow with careful strategies based on differentiation, innovation, or market segmentation. Mercedes-Benz and Polaroid are two examples.

4. The BCG matrix is not particularly helpful in comparing relative investment opportunities across different business units in the corporate portfolio. For example, is every star better than a cash cow? How should one question mark be compared to another in terms of whether it should be built into a star or divested?[3]

5. Strategic evaluation of a set of businesses requires examination of more than relative market shares and market growth. The attractiveness of an industry may increase based on technological, seasonal, competitive, or other considerations as much as on growth rate. Likewise, the value of a business within a corporate portfolio is often linked to considerations other than market share.[4]

---

[3] Derek F. Abell and John S. Hammond, *Strategic Market Planning* (Englewood Cliffs, N.J.: Prentice-Hall, 1979), p. 212.

[4] For an interesting elaboration of this point, see Walter E. Ketchell III, "Oh Where Oh Where Has My Little Dog Gone? Or My Cash Cow? Or My Star?" *Fortune*, November 2, 1981, pp. 148–52.

6. The four colorful classifications in the BCG matrix somewhat oversimplify the types of businesses in a corporate portfolio. Likewise, the simple strategic missions recommended by the BCG matrix often don't reflect the diversity of options available, as shown earlier in discussing dogs.

Before leaving the BCG matrix, the use of labels associated with this matrix deserves further comment. A recent survey of numerous executives in large firms using portfolio-planning techniques found widespread dislike of the *dog, question mark, cash cow,* and *star* terminology. Typical executive comments were as follows:

> To the extent that a division manager was to see a chart and see the word "dog" written next to his division, it's bound to create motivational problems. It's much easier to say that your mission is to reduce investment and you will be paid for achieving that objective and not for maximizing sales growth than to say you are a cash cow or a dog.
>
> We try to avoid the use of words such as cash cow or dog like the plague. If you call a business a dog, it'll respond like one. It's one thing to know that you are an ugly duckling—much worse to be told explicitly that you are.[5]

While criticism was widespread regarding BCG labels, there was strong support for use of more meaningful labels associated with positions in the BCG matrix or the GE planning grid (see Figure 10–3). Typical comments were as follows:

> In our company, the business unit labels are made explicit. In fact, the business unit managers are the ones who recommend what the strategy for their businesses should be. If we did not use explicit strategy labels, such as "build," "hold," and "harvest," the room for confusion over exactly what a business unit's strategy is would be very high. At the same time, it is important to remember that a business that's harvest today might need to have a build strategy tomorrow.
>
> Our business units know their strategies in terms such as "grow," "maintain," and "shrink." Only "withdraw" is not made explicit. Making strategy explicit helps in implementation; for example, it ensures that harvest managers won't ask for resources. . . . We don't label managers, but only their businesses; we keep moving people around since the idea is to develop well-rounded managers.[6]

This study suggests a preference for such strategy labels as *build, hold, harvest,* and *withdraw* rather than *star, cash cow, question mark,* and *dog* in the strategic planning activities of major multibusiness firms. The reasons are apparently threefold:

1. Some of the BCG terms are seen as negative and unnecessarily graphic.
2. The BCG terms are somewhat "static," while "build/hold/harvest" are more dynamic and action oriented.

---

[5] Anil K. Gupta and V. Govindarajan, "Build, Hold, Harvest: Converting Strategic Intentions into Reality," *Journal of Business Strategy,* March 1984, pp. 34–47.

[6] Ibid., p. 40.

Figure 10–3
General Electric's nine-cell planning grid

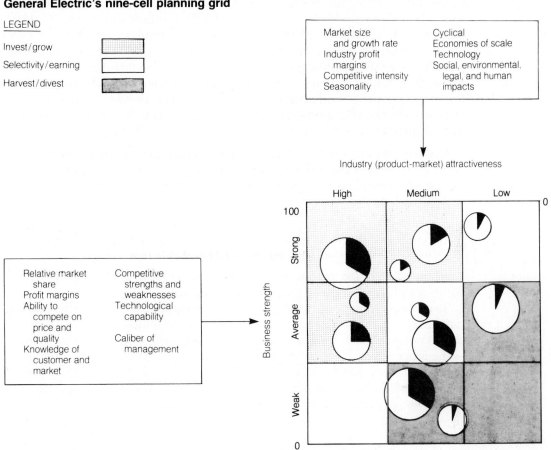

3. Terms like "dog/star/cash cow" have meaning only within a BCG context, while "build/hold/harvest" have universal validity and clarity of strategic intent even without a portfolio planning approach.

One executive's comment perhaps best illustrates the value of the preferred set of strategy labels:

> We have [generally] shied away from using any portfolio model. Yet we recognize that different businesses may need to have different strategic missions. In fact, our strategy documents require business unit managers to indicate explicitly the strategies for their units in terms such as "build," "hold," "harvest," "withdraw," and "explore."[7]

---

[7] Ibid., p. 35.

The GE Nine-Cell Planning Grid[8]

General Electric popularized an adaptation of the BCG approach (Figure 10–3) that attempts to overcome some of the matrix limitations mentioned above. First, the GE grid uses multiple factors to assess industry attractiveness and business strength, rather than the single measures (market share and market growth, respectively) employed in the BCG matrix. Second, GE expanded the matrix from four cells to nine—replacing the high/low axes with high/medium/low axes to make finer distinction between business portfolio positions.

To use the GE planning grid, each of the company's business units is rated on multiple sets of strategic factors within each axis of the grid:

Business strength factors: Market share, profit margin, ability to compete, customer and market knowledge, competitive position, technology, and management caliber are the factors contributing to business strength.

Industry attractiveness factors: Market growth, size and industry profitability, competition, seasonality and cyclical qualities, economies of scale, technology, and social/environmental/legal/human factors are identified as enhancing industry attractiveness.

A business's position within the planning grid is then calculated by "subjectively" quantifying the two dimensions of the grid.

To measure industry attractiveness, the strategist first selects those factors contributing to this aspect. The procedure then involves assigning each industry attractiveness factor a weight that reflects its perceived importance relative to the other attractiveness factors. Favorable to unfavorable future conditions for those factors are forecast and rated based on some scale (a 0- to-1 scale is illustrated below). A weighted composite score is then obtained for a business's overall industry attractiveness as show below.

Industry attractiveness factor	Weight	Rating*	Score
Market size	20	0.5	10.0
Project market growth	35	1.0	35.0
Technological requirements	15	0.5	7.5
Concentration (a few large competitors)	30	0	0
Political and regulatory factors	Must be nonrestrictive	—	—
Total	100		52.5

* High = 1.0; Medium = 0.5; Low = 0.0.

---

[8] Label terminology in the GE planning grid is more consistent with executives' preferences. The discussion of the GE labels is cross-referenced to BCG terminology to show the overlap between the two sets of labels.

To assess business strength, a similar procedure is followed in selecting factors, assigning weights to them, and then rating the business on these dimensions, as illustrated below.

Business strength factor	Weight	Rating*	Score
Relative market share	20	0.5	10
Production			
Capacity	10	1.0	10
Efficiency	10	1.0	10
Location	20	0	—
Technological capability	20	0.5	10
Marketing			
Sales organization	15	1.0	15
Promotion advantage	5	0	—
	100		55

* High = 1.0; Medium = 0.5; Low = 0.0.

These examples illustrate how one business within a corporate portfolio might be assessed using the GE planning grid. It is important to remember that what should be included or excluded as a factor, as well as how it should be rated and weighted, is primarily a matter of managerial judgment; and usually several managers are involved during the planning process. The result of such ratings is a high, medium, or low classification in terms of both the projected strength of the business and the projected attractiveness of the industry, as shown in Figure 10–3.

Three basic strategic approaches are suggested for any business in the corporate portfolio depending on its location within the grid: (1) invest to grow, (2) invest selectively and manage for earnings, or (3) harvest or divest for resources. The resource allocation decisions remain quite similar to those in the BCG approach. Businesses classified as *invest to grow* would be treated like the *stars* in the BCG matrix. These businesses would be accorded resources to pursue growth-oriented strategies. Strategy in Action 10–2 describes Kodak's search for new "star" businesses and allocation of resources to them as a way to examine new strategic thrusts. Businesses classified in the *harvest/divest* category would be managed like the *dogs* in the BCG matrix. They would follow strategies that provided net resources for use in other business units. Businesses classified in the *selectivity/earnings* category would either be managed as *cash cows* (providing maximum earnings for corporatewide use) or as *question marks* (selectivity chosen for investment or divestment).

While the strategic recommendations generated by the GE planning grid are similar to those from the BCG matrix, the GE nine-cell grid improves on the BCG matrix in three fundamental ways. First, as research discussed earlier pointed out, the terminology associated with the GE grid is preferable because it is less offensive and more universally understood. Second, the multiple measures associated with each dimension of the GE grid tap more factors relevant to business strength and market attractiveness than simply market share and market growth. This provides (or even forces) broader assessment during the planning process; considerations of strategic importance both in strategy formulation *and* in strategy implementation are brought to light.

Strategy in Action 10–2
Strategic Analysis at Kodak

By 1986, Kodak management decided to break its monolithic management into small groups that could help the company grow by entering new markets like electronics and biotechnology. For years, Kodak had relied on its high market share in its photographic equipment business. But with the "amateur film market," the main market served by Kodak, growing at only 6 percent versus a historical 10–15 percent and profits plunging by 51 percent to $565 million, Kodak had to look for new business to compliment its "cash cow."

Thanks largely to its overreliance on the photographic equipment business, Kodak had neglected to enter such markets as instant photography, 35-mm cameras, and VCRs even though they were natural extensions of Kodak's basic photography business. By 1986, 85 percent of Kodak's sales were related to its photographic equipment business.

The company has divided management in order to explore new ventures that range from cattle feed nutrients to medical equipment to electronic publishing, all of which relate to Kodak's expertise in pictures, graphics, or chemicals. Kodak is counting on its reputation for quality and its distribution strength to help propel the company into some of these new markets.

One of the key markets Kodak plans to enter is electronic imaging—systems that manipulate graphics and photographs the way computers manipulate text. The company has unveiled a $500,000 system that locates stored microfilm and scans it so that a computer can read it. Similar initiatives are under way to enter the medical markets with diagnostic equipment linked to Kodak's basic scientific skills.

All of Kodak's initiatives are part of an ongoing process of strategic analysis whereby company managers are trying to experimentally find Kodak's niches for the 1990s in ways that take advantage of its fundamental strengths of the past.

Source: Based on "Kodak Is Trying to Break Out of Its Shell," *Business Week,* June 10, 1985.

Finally, the nine-cell format obviously allows finer distinction between portfolio positions (most notably for "average" businesses) than does the four-cell BCG format.

The portfolio approach is useful for examining alternative corporate-level strategies in multi-industry companies. Portfolio planning offers three potential benefits. First, it aids in generating good strategies by promoting competitive analysis at the business level and substantive, comparative discussion across the company's business units, resulting in a strategy that capitalizes on the benefits of corporate diversity. Second, it promotes selective resource allocation trade-offs by providing a visualization of the corporatewide strategic issues and a standardized, "neutral" basis for resource negotiation. Thus, power struggles within the company can be more objectively focused and channeled. Third, some users feel portfolio approaches help in implementation of corporate strategy because increased focus and objectivity enhance commitment.[9]

Its visual appeal notwithstanding, the portfolio approach is useful in evaluation because it allows a thorough and comparative analysis of market share, market growth, industry attractiveness, competitive position, and/or product/market evolution of each business unit. This portfolio evaluation must be conducted routinely and repeatedly. In this way, the effectiveness of resource generation and allocation decisions in achieving corporate objectives can be monitored, updated, and altered.

Once portfolio strategies have been identified, business strategies must be determined. Portfolio approaches help clarify and determine broad strategic intent. But this is not enough. Basic decisions involving allocation of corporate resources and the general manner in which a business unit will be managed (invest to grow, for example) do not complete the process of strategic analysis and choice. Each business unit must examine and select a specific grand strategy to guide its pursuit of long-term objectives.

Grand Strategy Selection at the Business Level

Once business units in a multi-industry firm have been identified in terms of invest, hold, or harvest, each business unit must identify and evaluate its grand strategy options. If a unit has been identified as a resource generator within the corporate portfolio strategy, for example, several alternative grand strategies are available for fulfilling this role.

What factors should a single business consider in selecting its grand strategy? What is the relative attractiveness of each of the 12 grand strategy options discussed in Chapter 9 for a single business? Three approaches to answering these questions are the focus of this section.

---

[9] A discussion of the uses and limits of portfolio planning, including coverage of companies and industries in terms of portfolio usage, is found in P. Haspelslagh's "Portfolio Planning: Uses and Limits," *Harvard Business Review* 60, no. 2 (1982), pp. 58–73.

SWOT Analysis

SWOT is an acronym for the internal *S*trengths and *W*eaknesses of a business and environmental *O*pportunities and *T*hreats facing that business. SWOT analysis is a systematic identification of these factors and the strategy that reflects the best match between them. It is based on the logic that an effective strategy maximizes a business's strengths and opportunities but at the same time minimizes its weaknesses and threats. This simple assumption, if accurately applied, has powerful implications for successfully choosing and designing an effective strategy.

Environmental/industry analysis (Chapters 4 through 7) provides the information to identify key opportunities and threats in the firm's environment. These can be defined as follows:

Opportunities.   An *opportunity* is *a major favorable situation in the firm's environment.* Key trends represent one source of opportunity. Identification of a previously overlooked market segment, changes in competitive or regulatory circumstances, technological changes, and improved buyer or supplier relationships could represent opportunities for the firm.

Threats.   A *threat* is *a major unfavorable situation in the firm's environment.* It is a key impediment to the firm's current and/or desired future position. The entrance of a new competitor, slow market growth, increased bargaining power of key buyers or suppliers, major technological change, and changing regulations could represent major threats to a firm's future success.

Consumer acceptance of home computers was a major opportunity for IBM. Deregulation of the airline industry was a major opportunity for regional carriers (such as USAir) to serve routes that were previously closed to additional service. Some traditional carriers (such as Eastern) saw deregulation as a major threat and credit deregulation with a rapid decline in profitability in high-traffic routes. So opportunity for one firm can be a strategic threat to another. And the same factor can be seen as both a potential opportunity and a potential threat. For example, as the baby boom generation moves into the prime earning years, a major opportunity is arising for financial service firms, such as Merrill Lynch.[10] However, this group wants convenient financial services, which is a major threat to Merrill Lynch's established broker network.

Understanding the key opportunities and threats facing a firm helps managers identify realistic options from which to choose an appropriate strategy. Such understanding clarifies the most effective niche for the firm.

The second fundamental focus in SWOT analysis is identifying key *strengths*

---

[10] "Merrill Lynch's Dilemma," *Business Week,* January 6, 1984, p. 60.

and *weaknesses* based on examination of the company profile (Chapter 8). Strengths and weaknesses can be defined as follows:

Strengths. A *strength* is *a resource, skill, or other advantage* relative to competitors and the needs of markets a firm serves or anticipates serving. A strength is *a distinctive competence* that gives the firm a comparative advantage in the marketplace. Financial resources, image, market leadership, and buyer/supplier relations are examples.

Weaknesses. A *weakness* is *a limitation or deficiency in resources, skills, and capabilities* that seriously impedes effective performance. Facilities, financial resources, management capabilities, marketing skills, and brand image could be sources of weaknesses.

Sheer size and level of customer acceptance proved to be key strengths around which IBM built its successful strategy in the personal computer market. Braniff's limited financial capacity was a weakness that management did not sufficiently acknowledge, leading to an unsuccessful route expansion strategy and eventual bankruptcy after deregulation. Relative financial capacity was a weakness recognized by Piedmont Airlines, which charted a selective route expansion strategy that has been quite successful in a deregulated airline industry.

Understanding the key strengths and weaknesses of the firm further aids in narrowing the choice of alternatives and selecting a strategy. Distinct competence and critical weakness are identified in relation to key determinants of success for different market segments; this provides a useful framework for making the best strategic choice.

SWOT analysis can be used in at least three ways in strategic choice decisions. The most common application provides a logical framework guiding systematic discussions of the business's situation, alternative strategies, and, ultimately, the choice of strategy. What one manager sees as an opportunity, another may see as a potential threat. Likewise, a strength to one manager may be a weakness from another perspective. Different assessments may reflect underlying power considerations within the organization, as well as differing factual perspectives. The key point is that systematic SWOT analysis ranges across all aspects of a firm's situation. As a result, it provides a dynamic and useful framework for choosing a strategy.

A second application of SWOT analysis is illustrated in Figure 10–4. Key external opportunities and threats are systematically compared to internal strengths and weaknesses in a structured approach. The objective is identification of one of four distinct patterns in the match between the firm's internal and external situations. These patterns are represented by the four cells in Figure 10–4. Cell 1 is the most favorable situation; the firm faces several environmental opportunities and has numerous strengths that encourage pursuit of such opportunities. This condition suggests growth-oriented strategies

Figure 10–4
SWOT analysis diagram

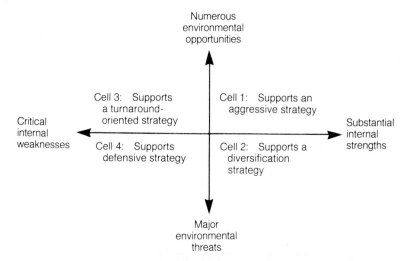

to exploit the favorable match. IBM's intensive market development strategy in the personal computer market was the result of a favorable match between strengths in reputation and resources and the opportunity for impressive market growth. Cell 4 is the least favorable situation, with the firm facing major environmental threats from a position of relative weakness. This condition clearly calls for strategies that reduce or redirect involvement in the products/ markets examined using SWOT analysis. Chrysler Corporation's successful turnaround from the verge of bankruptcy in the early 1980s is an example of such a successful strategy developed from a SWOT analysis that revealed mainly environmental threats and internal weaknesses.

In Cell 2, a firm with key strengths faces an unfavorable environment. In this situation, strategies would use current strengths to build long-term opportunities in other products/markets. Greyhound, possessing many strengths in intercity bus transportation, still faces an environment predominated by fundamental, long-term threats, such as airline competition and labor costs. The result was product development into nonpassenger (freight) services, followed by diversification into other businesses (e.g., financial services). A business in Cell 3 faces impressive market opportunity but is constrained by several internal weaknesses. Businesses in this predicament are like the question marks in the BCG matrix. The focus of strategy for such firms is eliminating internal weaknesses to more effectively pursue market opportunity. Apple's redirection of its "Lisa" technology to multiple products was an attempt to reformulate the company's technology-based strategy across several new product offerings in the microcomputer industry.

A major challenge in using SWOT analysis lies in identifying the position the business is actually in. A business that faces major opportunities may likewise face some key threats in its environment. It may have numerous internal weaknesses but also have one or two major strengths relative to key competitors. Fortunately, the value of SWOT analysis does not rest solely on careful placement of a firm in one particular cell. Rather, it lets the strategist visualize the overall position of the firm in terms of the product/market conditions for which a strategy is being considered. Does the SWOT analysis suggest that the firm is dealing from a position of major strength? Or must the firm overcome numerous weaknesses in the match of external and internal conditions? In answering these questions, SWOT analysis helps resolve one fundamental concern in selecting a strategy: *What will be the principal purpose of the grand strategy?* Is it to take advantage of a strong position or to overcome a weak one?[11] SWOT analysis provides a means of answering this fundamental question. And this answer is input to one dimension in a second, more specific tool for selecting grand strategies: the *grand strategy selection matrix.*

Grand Strategy Selection Matrix

A second valuable guide to the selection of a promising grand strategy is the matrix shown in Figure 10–5.[12] The basic idea underlying the matrix is that two variables are of central concern in the selection process: (1) the principal purpose of the grand strategy and (2) the choice of an internal or external emphasis for growth and/or profitability.

In the 1950s and 1960s, planners were advised to follow certain rules or prescriptions in their choice of strategies. Most experts now agree that strategy selection is better guided by the unique set of conditions that exist for the planning period and by company strengths and weaknesses. It is valuable to note, however, that even early approaches to strategy selection were based on matching a concern for internal versus external growth with a principal desire to either overcome weakness or maximize strength.

The same concerns led to the development of the grand strategy selection matrix. A firm in Quadrant I often views itself as overly committed to a particular business with limited growth opportunities or involving high risks because the company has "all its eggs in one basket." One reasonable solution

[11] A recent broad-based empirical study [L. G. Hrebiniak and C. Snow, "Top-Management Agreement and Organizational Performance," *Human Relations* 35, no. 12 (1982), pp. 1139–58], offers strong support that using SWOT analysis in this manner contributes to effective strategic choice. Examining 247 top-level managers in 88 organizations *and* eliminating the effects of other variables (types of planning, prior performance, industry), this study found strong, positive relationships between top management's agreement on the firm's strengths and weaknesses in relation to its environmental context and the measure of organizational performance—return on assets—used in the study. In other words, a comprehensive SWOT analysis, agreed upon by top management, provided one key input in the selection of an appropriate, effective strategy for the firm.

[12] John A. Pearce II, "Selecting among Alternative Grand Strategies," *California Management Review* 30, no. 2 (Spring 1982), pp. 23–31.

Figure 10–5
Grand strategy selection matrix

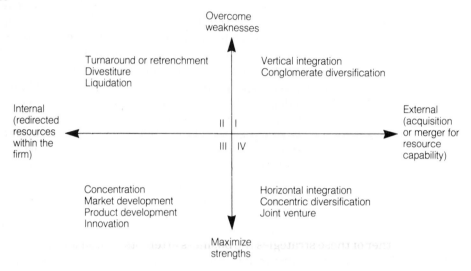

Source: John A. Pearce II, "Selecting among Alternative Grand Strategies," *California Management Review* 30, no. 2 (Spring 1982), p. 29.

is *vertical integration,* which enables the firm to reduce risk by reducing uncertainty either about inputs or about access to customers. Alternatively, a firm may choose *conglomerate diversification,* which provides a profitable alternative for investment without diverting management attention from the original business. However, the external orientation to overcoming weaknesses usually results in the most costly grand strategies. The decision to acquire a second business demands both large initial time investments and sizable financial resources. Thus, strategic managers considering these approaches must guard against exchanging one set of weaknesses for another.

A more conservative approach to overcoming weakness is found in Quadrant II. Firms often choose to redirect resources from one business activity to another within the company. While this approach does not reduce the company's commitment to its basic mission, it does reward success and enables further development of proven competitive advantages. The least disruptive of the Quadrant II strategies is *retrenchment,* the pruning of a current business's activities. If weaknesses arose from inefficiencies, retrenchment can actually serve as a *turnaround* strategy, meaning the business gains new strength by streamlining its operations and eliminating waste. However, when the weaknesses are a major obstruction to success in the industry, and when the costs of overcoming the weaknesses are unaffordable or are not justified by a cost-benefit analysis, then eliminating the business must be considered. Strategy in Action 10–3 illustrates a systematic divestiture and refocus strategy at Honeywell. *Divestiture* offers the best possibility for recouping the company's investment, but even *liquidation* can be an attractive option when the alternatives are an unwarranted drain on organizational resources or bankruptcy.

A common business adage states that a company should build from strength. The premise is that growth and survival depend on an ability to capture a market share that is large enough for essential economies of scale. If a firm believes profitability will derive from this approach and prefers an internal emphasis for maximizing strengths, four alternative grand strategies hold considerable promise. As shown in Quadrant III, the most common approach is *concentration* on the business, that is, market penetration. The business that selects this strategy is strongly committed to its current products and markets. It will strive to solidify its position by reinvesting resources to fortify its strength.

Two alternative approaches are *market* and *product development*. With either of these strategies the business attempts to broaden its operations. Market development is chosen if strategic managers feel that existing products would be well received by new customer groups. Product development is preferred when existing customers are believed to have an interest in products related to the firm's current lines. This approach may also be based on special technological or other competitive advantages. A final alternative for Quadrant III firms is *innovation*. When the business's strengths are in creative product design or unique production technologies, sales can be stimulated by accelerating perceived obsolescence. This is the principle underlying an innovative grand strategy.

Maximizing a business's strength by aggressively expanding its basis of operations usually requires an external emphasis in selecting a grand strategy. Preferred options here are shown in Quadrant IV. *Horizontal integration* is attractive because it enables a firm to quickly increase output capability. The skills of the original business's managers are often critical in converting new facilities into profitable contributors to the parent company; this expands a fundamental competitive advantage of the firm—management.

Concentric diversification is a good second choice for similar reasons. Because the original and newly acquired businesses are related, the distinctive competencies of the diversifying firm are likely to facilitate a smooth, synergistic, and profitable expansion.

The final option for increasing resource capability through external emphasis is a *joint venture*. This alternative allows a business to extend its strengths into competitive arenas that it would be hesitant to enter alone. A partner's production, technological, financial, or marketing capabilities can significantly reduce financial investment and increase the probability of success to the point that formidable ventures become attractive growth alternatives.

Strategy in Action 10–3
Honeywell Creates a New Strategy

One of the "BUNCH" is leaving the mainframe computer business. After a phased withdrawal that started three years ago, Honeywell, one of the makers in the group of mainframe manufacturers commonly known as the BUNCH (Burroughs, Univac, NCR, Control Data, Honeywell), is leaving to concentrate on factory automation, where its century-old expertise gives the company a chance for leadership.

Honeywell started in the computer business in 1955, through a joint venture with Raytheon, and decided to compete directly with IBM. Believing size to be critical, it bought GE's computer operation in 1970 and Xerox's computer business in 1976 when both decided to get out of the business. But by 1986, IBM controlled 71 percent of the mainframe computer business versus 3 percent for Honeywell.

Honeywell will concentrate on its strengths. The company has a growing $1.9-billion-a-year aerospace and defense business making torpedoes and navigational equipment. It has a $2.8 billion controls business where the company is the leader in both heat and air-conditioning controls for buildings and process controls for industry.

The company wants to concentrate on factory automation as its next growth vector. The company is pursuing the opportunity through logical development of its core control business, not through merger. Honeywell is focusing on the "brain" end of automation, as opposed to the "muscle" end (robots and machine tools). The brain end involves sensors, programmable controllers, software, and minicomputers—all conveniently similar to its control business competencies. The brain segment is worth $10 billion in sales annually and is growing at 15 percent annually.

Source: Based on "Strategic Withdrawal," *Forbes,* February 10, 1986.

Model of Grand Strategy Clusters

A third guide to selecting a promising grand strategy involves Thompson and Strickland's modifications of the BCG growth share portfolio matrix.[13] As shown in Figure 10–6, a business's situation is defined in terms of the growth rate of the general market and the company's competitive position in that market. When these factors are considered simultaneously, a business

---

[13] Arthur A. Thompson, Jr., and A. J. Strickland III, *Strategic Management: Concepts and Cases,* 3rd ed. (Plano, Tex.: Business Publications, 1984), p. 99. The BCG matrix was discussed earlier in this chapter.

Figure 10–6
Model of grand strategy clusters

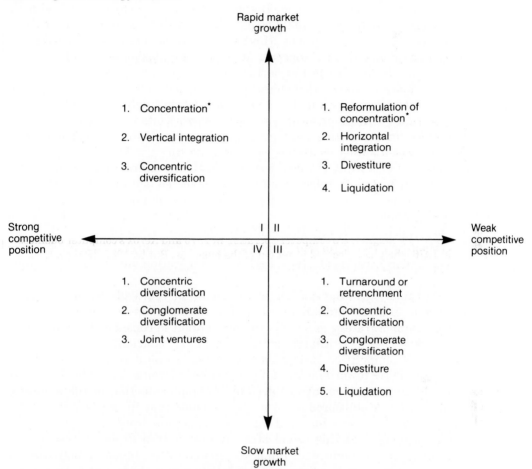

The grand strategy of innovation was omitted from this model. Apparently the authors felt that the notion of market growth was incompatible with the assumptions underlying the innovation approach.

Grand strategies are listed in probable order of attractiveness.

* In this model the grand strategy of concentration was meant to encompass market development and product development.

Source: Adapted from Arthur A. Thompson, Jr., and A. J. Strickland III, *Strategic Management: Concepts and Cases,* 4th ed. (Plano, Tex.: Business Publications, 1987).

can be broadly categorized in one of four quadrants: (I) strong competitive position in a rapidly growing market, (II) weak position in a rapidly growing market, (III) weak position in a slow-growth market, or (IV) strong position in a slow-growth market. Each of these quadrants suggests a set of promising possibilities for selection of a grand strategy.

Firms in Quadrant I are in an excellent strategic position. One obvious grand strategy for such firms is continued concentration on their current business as it is presently defined. Because consumers seem satisfied with the firm's current strategy, it would be dangerous to shift notably from the established competitive advantages. However, if the business has resources that exceed the demands of a concentration strategy, it should consider vertical integration. Either forward or backward integration helps a business protect its profit margins and market share by ensuring better access to either consumers or material inputs. Finally, a Quadrant I firm might be wise to consider concentric diversification to diminish the risks associated with a narrow product or service line; with this strategy, heavy investment in the company's basic area of proven ability continues.

Firms in Quadrant II must seriously evaluate maintaining their present approach to the marketplace. If a firm has competed long enough to accurately assess the merits of its current grand strategy, it must determine (1) the reasons its approach is ineffectual and (2) whether the company has the capability to compete effectively. Depending on the answers to these questions, the firm should choose one of four grand strategy options: formulation or reformulation of a concentration strategy, horizontal integration, divestiture, or liquidation.

In a rapidly growing market, even a small or relatively weak business is often able to find a profitable niche. Thus, formulation or reformulation of a concentration strategy is usually the first option to consider. However, if the firm lacks either a critical competitive element or sufficient economies of scale to achieve competitive cost efficiencies, then a grand strategy that directs company efforts toward horizontal integration is often a desirable alternative. A final pair of options involve deciding to stop competing in the market or product area. A multiproduct firm may conclude that the goals of its mission are most likely to be achieved if this one business is dropped through divestiture. Not only does this grand strategy eliminate a drain on resources, it may also provide additional funds to promote other business activities. As an option of last resort, a firm may decide to liquidate the business. In practical terms this means that the business cannot be sold as a going concern and is at best worth only the value of its tangible assets. The decision to liquidate is an undeniable admission of failure by a firm's strategic management and is thus often delayed—to the further detriment of the company.

Strategic managers tend to resist divestiture because it is likely to jeopardize their control of the firm and perhaps even their jobs. By the time the desirability of divestiture is acknowledged, the business has often deteriorated to the point of failing to attract potential buyers as a business. The consequences of such delays are financially disastrous for the owners of the firm, because the value of a going concern is many times greater than simple asset value.

Strategic managers who have a business in the position of Quadrant III and feel that continued slow market growth and a relatively weak competitive position are going to continue will usually attempt to decrease their resource commitment to that business. Minimal withdrawal is accomplished through retrenchment; this strategy has the side benefits of making resources available for other investments and of motivating employees to increase their operating efficiency. An alternative strategy is to divert resources for expansion through investment in other businesses. This approach typically involves either concentric or conglomerate diversification, because the firm usually wants to enter more promising arenas of competition than forms of integration or development would allow. The final options for Quadrant III businesses are divestiture, if an optimistic buyer can be found, and liquidation.

Quadrant IV businesses (strong competitive position in a slow-growth market) have a basis of strength from which to diversify into more promising growth areas. These businesses have characteristically high cash flow levels and limited internal growth needs. Thus, they are in an excellent position for concentric diversification into ventures that utilize their proven business acumen. A second choice is conglomerate diversification, which spreads investment risk and does not divert managerial attention from the present business. The final option is joint ventures, which are especially attractive to multinational firms. Through joint ventures a domestic business can gain competitive advantages in promising new fields while exposing itself to limited risks. Strategy in Action 10–4 describes Anheuser-Busch's approach to strategy analysis and choice under Quadrant IV circumstances.

Behavioral Considerations Affecting Strategic Choice

Strategic choice is a decision. At both the corporate and the business levels, this decision determines the future strategy of the firm.

After alternative strategies are examined, strategic choice is made. This is a decision to adopt one of the alternatives scrutinized. If the examination identified a clearly superior strategy, or if the current strategy will clearly meet future company objectives, then the decision is relatively simple. Such clarity is the exception, however, making the decision judgmental and difficult. Strategic decision makers, after comprehensive strategy examination, are often confronted with several viable alternatives rather than the luxury of a clearcut, obvious choice. Under these circumstances, several factors influence the strategic choice decision. Some of the more important are:

1. Role of past strategy.
2. Degree of the firm's external dependence.
3. Attitudes toward risk.
4. Internal political considerations and the CEO.
5. Timing.
6. Competitive reaction.

Strategy in Action 10–4
Anheuser-Busch's Choice of Strategy for the 1980s

In 1985 Anheuser-Busch completed a $2 billion, five-year expansion program that will increase its capacity 40 percent and add significantly to its 29 percent share of the beer market.

The St. Louis brewer is evaluating three options for its growth in the 1990s:

1. Diversification.
2. Overseas expansion.
3. A combination of both.

To evaluate and ultimately choose its strategy, Anheuser-Busch is using what its managers call learning probes—miniventures or experiments relative to each alternative strategy.

Anheuser-Busch's first learning probe was into the soft drink business. From the start, the test was the subject of considerable second-guessing. "Would Coke and Pepsi enter the beer industry from scratch and go up against Anheuser-Busch and Miller?" asks a skeptical rival brewer. "I think the answer would be no."

Anheuser-Busch's answer, after two years of testing, was no. "We learned it's a competitive jungle out there," says August Busch III, chairman, "Just like us and Miller in the brewing industry."

Root 66 beer and its sugar-free version—sold in five cities since 1980—have a respectable market share, but competitors contend it was achieved mostly through cents-off discounts offered to consumers. Chelsea, a citrus beverage that could have had the snob appeal and profit margin of Perrier, was hooted off the market by nurses and others who objected to the alcoholic content (0.4 percent) and beer-like appearance of the "not-so-soft drink."

Beer distributors were used for the soft drink test and also for a look at the snack business, where Anheuser-Busch is selling its new Eagle line in bars. One sign of success: distribution is being widened to 54 cities from a handful.

The third learning probe, less prominent than snacks or soda but more encouraging to several followers of Anheuser-Busch, is the company's development of Sesame Place educational parks in conjunction with Children's Television Workshop, producers of "Sesame Street."

The other alternative strategy, which requires even less capital and could pay off sooner than the others, is overseas expansion of the brewing business.

Continued on Page 303

Strategy in Action 10–4 (*concluded*)

International sales account for less than 1 percent of Anheuser-Busch's beer volume.

Company officials, reluctant to disclose much about the prospects for their learning probes, acknowledged that "beer earnings and share growth may slow as we approach our long-term 40 percent market share goal." The brewer is planning for that day by "getting our feet wet in new business areas, not massive diversification efforts."

Role of Past Strategy

A review of past strategy is the point at which the process of strategic choice begins. As such, past strategy exerts considerable influence on the final strategic choice.

Current strategists are often the architects of past strategies. Because they have invested substantial time, resources, and interest in these strategies, the strategists would logically be more comfortable with a choice that closely parallels past strategy or represents only incremental alterations.

This familiarity and commitment to past strategy permeate the organization. Thus, lower-level management reinforces the top manager's inclination toward continuity with past strategy during the choice process. In one study, during the planning process, lower-level managers suggested strategic choices that were consistent with current strategy and likely to be accepted while withholding suggestions with less probability of approval.[14]

Research by Henry Mintzberg suggests that the past strategy strongly influences current strategic choice.[15] The older and more successful a strategy has been, the harder it is to replace. Similarly, a strategy, once initiated, is very difficult to change because organizational momentum keeps it going.

Mintzberg's work and research by Barry Staw found that even as the strategy begins to fail due to changing conditions, strategists often increase their commitment to the past strategy.[16] Firms may thus replace key executives when performance has been inadequate for an extended period because replacing

---

[14] Eugene Carter, "The Behavioral Theory of the Firm and Top-Level Corporate Decisions," *Administrative Science Quarterly* 16, no. 4 (1971), pp. 413–28.

[15] Henry Mintzberg, "Research on Strategy Making," *Proceedings of the Academy of Management,* Minneapolis, 1972.

[16] Barry M. Staw, "Knee-Deep in the Big Muddy: A Study of Escalating Commitment to a Chosen Course of Action," *Organizational Behavior and Human Performance,* June 1976, pp. 27–44; Mintzberg, "Research on Strategy."

top executives lessens the influence of unsuccessful past strategy on future strategic choice.

Degree of the Firm's External Dependence

A comprehensive strategy is meant to effectively guide a firm's performance in the larger external environment. Owners, suppliers, customers, government, competitors, and unions are a few of the elements in a firm's external environment, as elaborated on in Chapters 4 through 7. A major constraint on strategic choice is the power of environmental elements in supporting this decision. If a firm is highly dependent on one or more environmental factors, its strategic alternatives and ultimate choice must accommodate this dependence. The greater a firm's external dependence, the lower its range and flexibility in strategic choice.

Two examples highlight the influence of external dependence on strategic choice. For many years Whirlpool sold most of its major appliance output to one customer, Sears. With its massive retail coverage and access to alternate suppliers, Sears was a major external dependence for Whirlpool. Whirlpool's strategic alternatives and ultimate choice of strategy were limited and strongly influenced by Sears' demands. Whirlpool's grand strategy and important related decisions in areas such as research and development, pricing, distribution, and product design were carefully narrowed and chosen with the firm's critical dependence on Sears in mind. Chrysler Corporation's dependence on federal loan guarantees and financial concessions by labor considerably limited the strategic choices available in the early 1980s. The decision of Chrysler's Lee Iaccoca to pay off several federal obligations before they were due was partially meant to increase Chrysler's flexibility by reducing one restrictive external dependence.

These examples show that a firm's flexibility in strategic choice is lessened when environmental dependence increases. If external dependence is critical, firms may include representatives of the external factor (government, union, supplier, bank) in the strategic choice process. In 1980, Chrysler, for example, took the unprecedented action of including Leonard Woodcock, president of the United Auto Workers, on its board of directors.

Attitudes toward Risk

Attitudes toward risk exert considerable influence on strategic choice. These attitudes may vary from eager risk taking to strong aversion to risk, and they influence the range of available strategic choices. Where attitudes favor risk, the range and diversity of strategic choices expand. High-risk strategies are acceptable and desirable. Where management is risk averse, the diversity of choices is limited, and risky alternatives are eliminated before strategic choices are made. Risk-oriented managers prefer offensive, opportunistic strategies. Risk-averse managers prefer defensive, safe strategies. Past strategy

Figure 10–7
Managerial risk propensity and strategic choices

Risk averse		*Risk prone*
Decrease choices	⟷	Expand choices
Defensive strategies	⟷	Offensive strategies
Stability	⟷	Growth
Incremental	⟷	Innovation
Minimize company weaknesses	⟷	Maximize company strengths
Strong ties to past strategy	⟷	Fewer ties to past strategy
Stable industry	⟷	Volatile industry
Maturing product/market evolution	⟷	Early product/market evolution

is quite influential in the strategic choices made by risk-averse managers, but it is less of a factor for risk-oriented managers. Figure 10–7 illustrates the relationship between attitudes toward risk and strategic choice.

Industry volatility influences managerial propensity toward risk. In highly volatile industries, top managers must absorb and operate with greater amounts of risk than their counterparts in stable industries. Therefore, managers in volatile industries consider a broader, more diverse range of strategies in the strategic choice process.

Product/market evolution is another determinant of managerial risk propensity. If a firm is in the early stages of product/market evolution, it must operate with considerably greater risk than a firm later in the product/market evolution cycle.

In making a strategic choice, risk-oriented managers lean toward opportunistic strategies with higher payoffs. They are drawn to offensive strategies based on innovation, company strengths, and operating potential. Risk-averse managers lean toward safe, conservative strategies with reasonable, highly probable returns. The latter are drawn to defensive strategies to minimize a firm's weaknesses and external threats, as well as the uncertainty associated with innovation-based strategies.

A recent study examined the relationship between the willingness of strategic business unit (SBU) managers to take risks and SBU performance. The study found a link between risk taking and strategic choice. Looking first at SBUs assigned build or star strategic missions within a corporate portfolio, researchers found that the general managers of higher-performing SBUs had *greater willingness to take risks* than did their counterparts in lower-performing build or star SBUs. Looking next at SBUs assigned harvest strategies, successful units had general managers *less willing to take risks* than general managers in lower-performing harvest SBUs.[17]

This study supports the idea that managers make different decisions depending on their willingness to take risks. Perhaps most important, the study suggests that being either risk prone or risk averse is not inherently good or bad. Rather, SBU performance is more effective when the risk orientation of the general manager is consistent with the SBU's strategic mission (build or harvest). While this is only one study and not a final determination of the influence of risk orientation on strategic choice, it helps illustrate the importance of risk orientation on the process of making and implementing strategic decisions.

Internal Political Considerations

Power/political factors influence strategic choice. The existence and use of power to further individual or group interests is common in organizational life. An early study by Ross Stagner found that strategic decisions in business organizations were frequently settled by power rather than by analytical maximization procedures.[18]

A major source of power in most organizations is the chief executive officer (CEO). In smaller enterprises, the CEO is consistently the dominant force in strategic choice, and this is also often true in large firms, particularly those with a strong or dominant CEO. When the CEO begins to favor a particular choice, it is often unanimously selected.

Cyert and March identified another power source that influences strategic choice, particularly in larger firms.[19] They called this the *coalition* phenomenon. In large organizations, subunits and individuals (particularly key managers) have reason to support some alternatives and oppose others. Mutual interest often draws certain groups together in coalitions to enhance their position on major strategic issues. These coalitions, particularly the more powerful ones (often called *dominant coalitions*), exert considerable influence in the strategic choice process. Numerous studies confirm the use of power and coalitions on a frequent basis in strategic decision making. Interestingly, one study found that managers occasionally try to hide the fact that they prefer judgmental/political bargaining over systematic analysis and that when politics was a factor, it slowed decision-making.[20]

---

[17] Gupta and Govindarajan, "Build, Hold, Harvest."

[18] Ross Stagner, "Corporate Decision Making," *Journal of Applied Psychology* 53, no. 1 (1969), pp. 1–13.

[19] Richard M. Cyert and James G. March, *A Behavorial Theory of the Firm* (Englewood Cliffs, N.J.: Prentice-Hall, 1963).

[20] See, for example, H. Mintzberg, D. Raisinghani, and Andre Theoret, "The Structure of Unstructured Decision Process," *Administrative Science Quarterly*, June 1976, pp. 246–75; and William Guth, "Toward a Social System Theory of Corporate Strategy," *Journal of Business*, July 1976, pp. 374–88.

Figure 10–8
Political activities in phases of strategic decision making

Phases of strategic decision making	Focus of political action	Examples of political activity
Identification and diagnosis of strategic issues	Control of: Issues to be discussed Cause-and-effect relationships to be examined	Control of agenda Interpretation of past events and future trends
Narrowing the alternative strategies for serious consideration	Control of alternatives	Mobilization Coalition formation Resource commitment for information search
Examining and choosing the strategy	Control of choice	Selective advocacy of criteria Search and representation of information to justify choice
Initiating implementation of the strategy	Interaction between winners and losers	Winners attempt to "sell" or co-opt losers Losers attempt to thwart decisions and trigger fresh strategic issues
Designing procedures for evaluation of results	Representing oneself as successful	Selective advocacy of criteria

Source: Adapted from Liam Fahey and V. K. Naroyanan, "The Politics of Strategic Decision Making," in *The Strategic Management Handbook*, ed. Kenneth J. Albert (New York: McGraw-Hill, 1983), p. 21-20.

Figure 10–8 illustrates the focus of political activity across phases of strategic decision making. It illustrates how the *content* of strategic decisions and the *processes* of arriving at such decisions are politically intertwined. Each phase in the process of strategic choice presents a real opportunity for political action intended to influence the outcome. The challenge to strategists is in recognizing and managing this political influence. If such processes are not carefully overseen, various managers can bias the content of strategic decisions in the direction of their own interests.[21] For example, selecting the criteria used to compare alternative strategies or collecting and appraising information regarding these criteria may be particularly susceptible to political influence. This must be recognized and, where critical, "managed" to avoid dysfunctional political bias. Reliance on different sources for obtaining *and* appraising information might be effective in this context.

Rather than simply being denoted as "bad" or inefficient, organizational politics must be viewed as an inevitable dimension of organizational decision making that must be accommodated in strategic management. Some authors argue that politics are a key ingredient in the "glue" that holds an organization together. Formal and informal negotiating and bargaining between individuals, subunits, and coalitions are indispensable mechanisms for organizational

---

[21] Liam Fahey and V. K. Naroyanan, "The Politics of Strategic Decision Making," in *The Strategic Management Handbook*, ed. Kenneth J. Albert (New York: McGraw-Hill, 1983), p. 21-18.

coordination.[22] Recognizing and accommodating this in choosing future strategy will result in greater commitment and more realistic strategy. The costs are likely to be increased time spent on decision making and incremental (as opposed to drastic) change.

Timing Considerations

The time element can have considerable influence on strategic choice. Consider the case of Mech-Tran, a small manufacturer of fiberglass piping that found itself in financial difficulty. At the same time it was seeking a loan guarantee through the Small Business Administration (SBA), it was approached by KOCH Industries (a Kansas City–based supplier of oil field supplies) with a merger offer. The offer involved 100 percent sale of Mech-Tran stock and a two-week response deadline, while the SBA loan procedure could take three months. Obviously, management's strategic decision was heavily influenced by external time constraints, which limited analysis and evaluation. Research by Peter Wright indicates that under such a time constraint, managers put greater weight on negative than on positive information and prefer defensive strategies.[23] The Mech-Tran owners decided to accept the KOCH offer rather than risk losing the opportunity and subsequently being turned down by the SBA. Thus, faced with time constraints, management opted for a defensive strategy consistent with Wright's findings.

There is another side to the time issue—the timing of a strategic decision. A good strategy may be disastrous if it is undertaken at the wrong time. Winnebago was the darling of Wall Street in 1970, with its stock rising from $3 to $44 per share in one year. Winnebago's 1972 strategic choice, focusing on increasing its large, centralized production facility, was a continuation of the strategy that had successfully differentiated Winnebago in the recreational vehicle industry. The 1973 Arab oil embargo with subsequent rises in gasoline prices and overall transportation costs had dismal effects on Winnebago. The strategy was good, but the timing proved disastrous. On the other hand, IBM's decision to hold off entering the rapidly growing personal computer market until 1982 appeared to be perfectly timed. Welcomed by Apple with a full-page advertisement in *The Wall Street Journal*, IBM assumed the market share lead by early 1983.

A final aspect of the time dimension involves the lead time required for alternative choices and the time horizon management is contemplating. Management's primary attention may be on the short or long run, depending on current circumstances. Logically, strategic choice will be strongly influenced by the match between management's current time horizon and the lead time

---

[22] Ibid.

[23] Peter Wright, "The Harrassed Decision Maker," *Journal of Applied Psychology* 59, no. 5 (1974), pp. 555–61.

(or payoff time) associated with different choices. As a move toward vertical integration, Du Pont went heavily into debt to acquire Conoco in a 1982 bidding war. By 1983, the worldwide oil glut meant that Du Pont could have bought raw materials on more favorable terms in the open market. This short-term perspective was not of great concern to Du Pont management, however, because the acquisition was part of a strategy to stabilize Du Pont's long-term position as a producer of numerous petroleum-based products.

Competitive Reaction

In weighing strategic choices, top management frequently incorporates perceptions of likely competitor reactions to different options. For example, if management chooses an aggressive strategy that directly challenges a key competitor, that competitor can be expected to mount an aggressive counterstrategy. Management of the initiating firm must consider such reactions, the capacity of the competitor to react, and the probable impact on the chosen strategy's success.

The beer industry provides a good illustration. In the early 1970s, Anheuser-Busch dominated the industry. Miller Brewing Company, recently acquired by Philip Morris, was a weak and declining competitor. Miller's management, contemplating alternative strategies, made the decision to adopt an expensive, advertising-oriented strategy. While this strategy challenged the big three (Anheuser-Busch, Pabst, and Schlitz) head-on, Miller anticipated that the reaction of the other brewers would be delayed due to Miller's current declining status in the industry. Miller proved correct and was able to reverse its trend in market share before Anheuser-Busch countered with an equally intense advertising strategy.

Miller's management took another approach in their next major strategic decision. In the mid-1970s they introduced (and heavily advertised) a low-calorie beer—Miller Lite. Other industry members had introduced such products without much success. Miller chose a strategy that did not directly challenge key competitors and, Miller anticipated, would not elicit immediate and strong counterattacks. This choice proved highly successful, because Miller was able to establish a dominant share of the low-calorie market before major competitors decided to react. In both cases, Miller's expectation of competitor reaction was a key determinant of strategic choice.

Contingency Approach to Strategic Choice

Ultimate strategic choices often depend on various assumptions about future conditions. The success of the strategy chosen is contingent, to varying degrees, on future conditions. And changes in the industry and environment may differ from forecasts and assumptions.

For example, Winnebago's strategy of centralized, economy-of-scale production and extensive inventories of large recreational vehicles (RVs) was contingent on a continued supply of plentiful, inexpensive gasoline for future customer use. With the Arab oil embargo, this contingency changed dramatically. Winnebago was left with extensive inventories of large RVs and high-break-even–oriented production facilities for large RVs. As a result, Winnebago was still trying to recover a decade later.

To improve their ability to cope in similar circumstances, an increasing number of firms have adopted a contingency approach to strategic choice. The critical assumptions on which success of the chosen strategy depends are identified. Conditions that may turn out to be different from the basic forecast or assumptions for these critical contingencies are identified, particularly negative ones.[24] A downturn in the economy, a labor strike, an increase in the prime rate, a technological breakthrough, or a shortage of critical material are examples of such contingencies. Once these scenarios are identified, managers develop alternative, contingency strategies for the firm. Such contingency strategies can be short and/or long term and are appropriate at the corporate-, business-, and/or functional levels. Firms using this contingency approach often identify trigger points to alert management that a contingency strategy should be considered. The trigger points are specific deviations in key forecasts of industry or environmental conditions (like the supply and price of gasoline) and are set to alert management to the need to consider the alternative strategy and allow sufficient lead time for implementation of the contingency response.

Summary

This chapter has presented and examined several considerations in strategic analysis and choice. The form of strategic analysis and choice varies considerably according to the stage of development of the firm, and the focus differs at the corporate and business levels.

For multi-industry and multiproduct/market firms, strategic analysis begins at the corporate level. Different strategies are examined in terms of generating and allocating corporate resources. The portfolio approach is one method of strategy examination at the corporate level. Portfolio matrixes and stage of product/market evolution are conceptual tools guiding the portfolio approach.

Strategic analysis and choice do not end with corporate-level strategy. Alternative business-level strategies must be examined within the context of each business unit in multi-industry firms, much as strategy is evaluated in single-product/service firms. Three approaches that facilitate grand strategy selection at the business level were discussed.

---

[24] Positive as well as negative alternatives should be considered. If circumstances are unusually positive, the firm may not be in a position to exploit the favorable circumstances. However, most firms are primarily concerned with negative deviation in key contingencies.

Strategic analysis often limits alternatives to several viable choices. Strategic choice seldom involves the luxury of making an obvious choice. Nonetheless, a choice must be made. Several factors influence strategic choice, such as propensity for risk, past strategy, and coalitions, which are outside the realm of purely analytical consideration. Some firms attempt a contingency approach to strategic choice by incorporating the flexibility to alter a chosen strategy if underlying assumptions change.

Choosing corporate- and business-level strategies is not the end of the strategic management process. Functional strategies must be identified and implemented to initiate and control daily business activities in a manner consistent with business strategy, as must organizational systems and processes to implement and control the strategy. The next section of this book examines the implementation phase of the strategic management process.

Questions for Discussion

1. How does strategic analysis at the corporate level differ from strategic analysis at the business level? How are they related?
2. Why would multi-industry companies find the portfolio approach to strategy evaluation useful?
3. Explain the role of SWOT analysis as a tool facilitating strategic choice at the business level. How is it similar/dissimilar to the grand strategy selection matrix and the model of grand strategy clusters?
4. What role does politics play in the development and evaluation of alternative strategies? Please explain.
5. Explain and illustrate the role of three behavioral considerations in strategy examination and choice.

Bibliography

Abell, Derek F. "Strategic Windows." *Journal of Marketing,* July 1978, pp. 21–26.

Buzzell, Robert D.; T. G. Bradley; and Ralph Sultan. "Market Share: A Key to Profitability." *Harvard Business Review,* January–February 1975, pp. 97–106.

Christensen, H. K.; A. C. Cooper; and C. A. DeKluyver. "The 'Dog' Business: A Reexamination." *Proceedings of the Academy of Management,* 1981 pp. 26–30.

Gupta, Anil K., and V. Govindarajan. "Build, Hold, Harvest: Converting Strategic Intentions into Reality." *Journal of Business Strategy,* March 1984, pp. 34–47.

_____. "Business Unit Strategy, Managerial Characteristics, and Business Unit Effectiveness at Strategy Implementation." *Academy of Management Journal* 27, no. 1 (1984), pp. 27–36.

Guth, William. "Toward a Social System Theory of Corporate Strategy." *Journal of Business,* July 1976, pp. 374–88.

Hambrick, D. C.; I. C. MacMillan; and D. L. Day. "Strategic Attributes and Performance in the MCG Matrix—A PIMS–Based Analysis of Industrial-Product Businesses." *Academy of Management Journal* 25, no. 3 (1982), pp. 510–31.

Haspeslagh, P. "Portfolio Planning: Uses and Limits." *Harvard Business Review,* January–February 1982, p. 58.

Hax, Arnoldo C., and Nicolas S. Majluf. "The Use of the Growth-Share Matrix in Strategic Planning." *Interfaces* 13, no. 1 (1983), pp. 8–21.

_____. "The Use of the Industry Attractiveness–Business Strength Matrix in Strategic Planning." *Interfaces* 13, no. 2 (1983), pp. 54–71.

Hedley, Barry. "Strategy and the Business Portfolio." *Long-Range Planning,* February 1977, pp. 8–15.

Hofer, Charles W. "Toward a Contingency Theory of Business Strategy." *Academy of Management Journal,* December 1975, pp. 784–810.

Hofer, Charles, and Dan Schendel. *Strategy Formulation: Analytical Concepts.* St. Paul, Minn.: West Publishing, 1978.

Macmillan, I. *Strategy Formulation: Political Concepts.* St. Paul, Minn.: West Publishing, 1978.

Mintzberg, Henry. "Research on Strategy Making." *Proceedings of the Academy of Management,* 1972, pp. 218–22.

_____. "Strategy Making in Three Modes." *California Management Review,* Winter 1973, pp. 44–53.

Mintzberg, Henry; D. Raisinghani; and Andre Theoret. "The Structure of Unstructured Decision Process." *Administrative Science Quarterly,* June 1976, pp. 246–75.

Murray, E., Jr. "Strategic Choice as a Negotiated Outcome." *Management Science* 24, no. 9 (1978), pp. 960–72.

Pearce, John A., II. "Selecting among Alternative Grand Strategies." *California Management Review* 30, no. 2 (1982), pp. 23–31.

Schoeffler, Sidney; Robert Buzzell; and Donald Heany. "Impact of Strategic Planning on Profit Performance." *Harvard Business Review,* March–April 1974, pp. 137–45.

Stagner, Ross. "Corporate Decision Making." *Journal of Applied Psychology,* February 1969, pp. 1–13.

Staw, Barry M. "Knee-Deep in the Big Muddy: A Study of Escalating Commitment to a Chosen Course of Action." *Organizational Behavior and Human Performance,* June 1976, pp. 27–44.

"Wanted: A Manager to Fit Each Strategy." *Business Week,* February 25, 1980, p. 166.

Chapter 10 Cohesion Case Illustration

Strategic Analysis and Choice at Holiday Inns, Inc.

Before evaluating alternatives and choosing a strategy for the 1990s at Holiday Inns, Inc., take a few minutes to review what has been done in the cohesion case sections up to this point. First, the company mission was examined. An essential issue that surfaced was whether Holiday Inns is in the travel business, hospitality business, or some broader combination of the two. Holiday Inns' executives have traditionally used the travel definition, although the mission must be readdressed as you evaluate and choose a strategy. Second, consecutive sections have examined the present and projected environment of Holiday Inns and analyzed the internal strengths and weaknesses of Holiday Inns at the corporate and business-group levels. Comparing these external and internal analyses is a key basis for generating, evaluating, and choosing corporate- and business-level strategies. Finally, different possible grand strategies for each business group were examined. Now, realistic alternative strategies for Holiday Inns must be identified, evaluated, and the strategies chosen that will guide Holiday Inns through the 1990s.

How is strategy analyzed and chosen at Holiday Inns? To begin, the distinction between corporate- and business-level strategy must be recognized. With both levels applicable at Holiday Inns, this illustration will concentrate initial identification at the business level. In other words, alternative grand strategies for each of Holiday Inns' business units will be identified. Subsequent evaluation and choice of business-level strategies will follow evaluation and choice of corporate-level strategy.

For each business group at Holiday Inns, what are the most appropriate grand strategy options? Exhibit 1 provides an answer. It places each business in its appropriate cell on the grand strategy selection matrix, which was discussed in this chapter (Figure 10–5). This helps identify the more appropriate grand strategies for each Holiday Inns business. At Trailways, for example, the key grand strategies to be evaluated are turnaround/retrenchment or divestiture (Quadrant II). In the restaurant group, Quadrants III and IV must be evaluated because there are attractive possibilities in both areas. Thus, it is important to look at market development or joint venture and concentration or horizontal integration.

How is the business placed in an appropriate quadrant? This cohesion case section will illustrate the placement of two of Holiday Inns' businesses and leave to you the assignment of fitting the other businesses in the two matrix dimensions.

Exhibit 1
Grand strategy selection matrix for Holiday Inns, Inc.

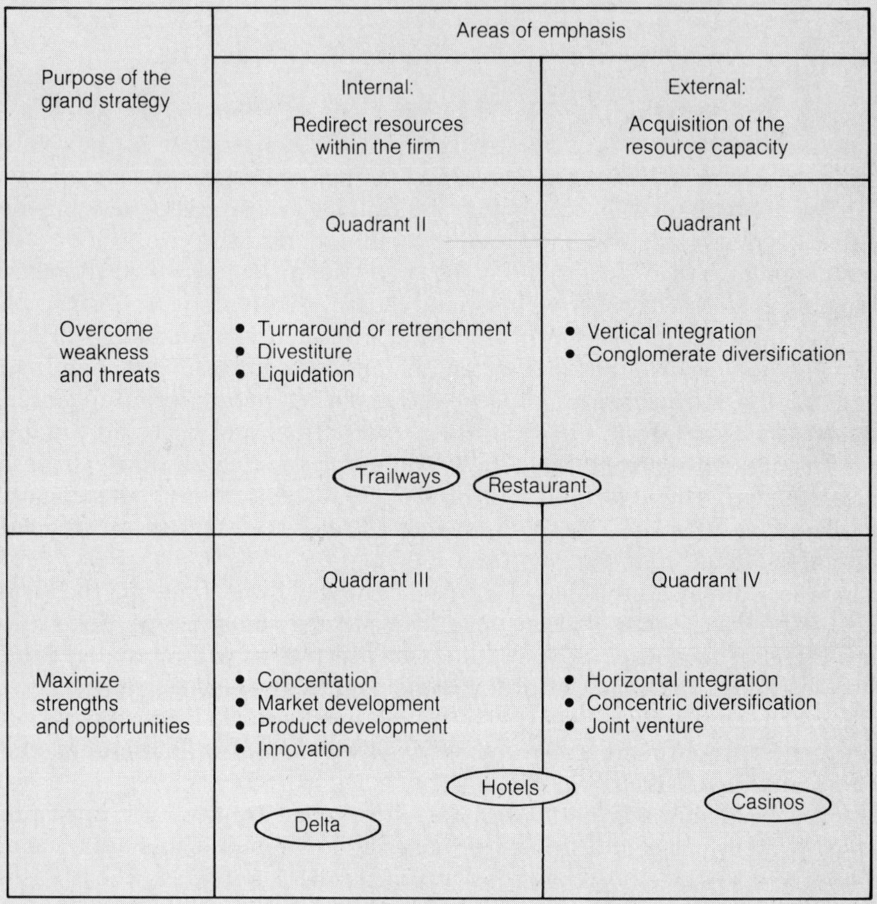

Purpose of the grand strategy	Areas of emphasis	
	Internal: Redirect resources within the firm	External: Acquisition of the resource capacity
Overcome weakness and threats	**Quadrant II** • Turnaround or retrenchment • Divestiture • Liquidation _Trailways_	**Quadrant I** • Vertical integration • Conglomerate diversification _Restaurant_
Maximize strengths and opportunities	**Quadrant III** • Concentration • Market development • Product development • Innovation _Hotels_ _Delta_	**Quadrant IV** • Horizontal integration • Concentric diversification • Joint venture _Casinos_

Trailways. Trailways faced numerous environmental threats—heavy competition, rising energy costs, lack of subsidies for terminals, and significant internal weaknesses (price/cost squeeze, aging terminals, inferior image). The primary focus of its ultimate strategy will necessarily have to overcome these weaknesses and threats. To pursue its ultimate strategy, Trailways will depend on and emphasize internal operating capabilities—it already has buses, terminals, and so on—rather than develop operating capacity through external acquisitions. Combining these two assessments, Trailways logically fits in Quadrant II of the grand strategy selection matrix.

Exhibit 2
Grand strategy options at each of Holiday Inns' businesses

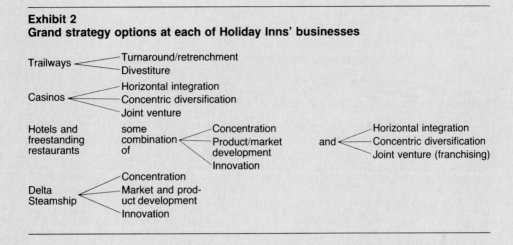

Restaurant Group.   The restaurant group faces key environmental opportunities (eating-out, age, and single-household trends) yet a mixture of threats (growing competition and industry leaders—Shoneys, etc.). Perkins has some internal strengths (franchising expertise, synergy with the core hotel business, Perkins' northern U.S. position) yet a conspicuous weakness—its poor track record. Group executives would surely argue that the purpose of its grand strategy is to maximize strengths and opportunities. The area of emphasis for anticipated growth is both internal and external. They would argue that the company is positioned to carry out company-owned growth (internal emphasis) and external operating capacity through franchising and possible acquisition of additional chains. CEO Mike Rose's comments suggest great concern about lack of success and inability to confront powerful competitors successfully. This suggests the Perkins operation may well be a Quadrant II candidate.

Other Groups.   It should now be possible to surmise why the other Holiday Inns businesses were placed as shown in Exhibit 1. These decisions can be briefly summarized. The hotel group has attractive strengths and environmental opportunities, while it (like restaurants) must emphasize both company-owned (internal) and franchise (external) growth. Delta Steamship has limited but important opportunities (growing Third World markets) and strengths (major U.S.–flag carrier) while depending primarily on internal resource capability. The casinos group, while facing impressive opportunities, must look outside for operational capabilities in the near future, thus its placement in Quadrant IV.

   This analysis suggests that the key grand strategy options for each of Holiday Inns' businesses are as shown in Exhibit 2.

Exhibit 3
Hotel group

Strategy alternatives	Strategy analysis
Pursue rapid growth through domestic and international expansion while seeking to become increasingly price competitive with quality budget chains. (Market development and joint venture franchising)	Hotels are HI's core business, the major profit contributor, and its greatest distinctive competencies. Rapid growth can only be achieved by taking on the lower-priced competitors because available locations are limited. But with markets maturing, and either increased financing or dependence on franchisees required, this alternative is risky.
Selective growth with company-owned movement into multiuser properties (resorts, airports, downtown) and gradual franchise expansion while maintaining the traditional upper-medium focus in price with high-quality service. (Concentration and joint venture franchising)	Consistent with changing travel patterns and shorter vacations for business and family travelers. Allows company-owned positioning in the more lucrative markets. Maintains favorable profit margins and positive cash generator role for corporate activity. Risks continual threat from quality budget chains, especially for the broad franchise base.

Exhibit 4
Transportation group

Strategy alternatives	Strategy analysis

Trailways:
  Stabilize market share and profitability through a combination of price competition, improved image, elimination of inefficient routes and equipment, more efficient terminals, and linking with motel network.
    (Retrenchment/turnaround)
Divestiture of the Trailways bus operation.
    (Divestiture)
	Transportation market is quite competitive, with Greyhound as well as the deregulated airline industry. Could increase ridership, but lowering prices in face of rising energy costs would threaten profit margins. Questionable whether Trailways' ridership is compatible with HI guest profile.

	Possibly extreme and even detrimental because the bus operation has contributed at a steadily growing rate of approximately 23 percent of corporate revenue since 1974. However, profitability has steadily declined, and the bus operation is not compatible with all other groups in terms of customer profile. Managerial and financial resources might be better used elsewhere.

Delta Steamship:
  Steady growth in new LASH cargo services seeking to exploit and expand market share in South American routes.
    (Concentration/market development)
	Delta has competitive start with LASH technology and a strong South American/West African route structure. Ships provide useful tax shelter and government subsidies against foreign competition. Cargo emphasis, however, is getting way outside.

Divestiture of Delta Steamship. (Typical strategy consideration that would be introduced at the corporate level)	Drastic improvement in sales and profits in 1978 makes Delta quite marketable. Steamship cargo and passenger services are increasingly removed from HI's core competencies, suggesting divestiture. But, as of now, an increasingly profitable unit to harvest until the right buyer appears.

Exhibit 5
Restaurant group

Strategy alternatives	Strategy analysis
Rapid expansion into freestanding restaurant business through additional acquisition as well as geographic expansion with Perkins franchises. (Market development, joint venture franchising, and horizontal integration)	A growing primary market, but strong competition nationwide. Organizational capacity of HI to absorb and manage rapid acquisition of additional regional chains is doubtful. Risk of a market shakeout with heavy level of competition is a real possibility.
Concentration and steady growth via the Perkins chain above. (Concentration and joint venture franchising)	Perkins provides an established, competitive base and competent management to guide its stable growth, backed as necessary by corporate resources. Allows HI to evaluate this new operating area before making additional acquisition or resource commitments.

Exhibit 6
Casino group

Strategy alternatives	Strategy analysis

Casinos:
  Rapid expansion into the four major U.S. areas for legalized gambling via direct investment and particularly joint ventures or acquisition.
 	
    (Horizontal integration, joint ventures)
	A rapidly expanding market that offers exceptional profit potential. A logical extension of HI's lodging and restaurant expertise, particularly when matched with another firm's gaming expertise. Limited U.S. areas having legalized gambling, so should move rapidly to secure a foothold in each area. Offers a natural international spin-off and ultimate lessening of corporate dependence on roadside travel accommodations and franchisees.

Stabilize with current endeavors into gaming and only gradually commit further resources. (Joint venture holding pattern)	Lets HI make sure gaming is an area it should be in before committing sizable resources. However, with limited areas available, could fall behind competition or newcomers (like Ramada Inns) in establishing a foothold.

Several specific grand strategy alternatives could be generated for subsequent analysis. To illustrate the discussion in Chapter 10, a limited range of strategy alternatives for subsequent analysis and choice will be presented.

Exhibits 3 through 6 show a limited range of alternative strategies within each of Holiday Inns' business groups. This set of alternative business strategies will then be used to generate a limited range of alternative corporate-level strategies. Each alternative will provide a brief analysis, which both illustrates the analysis of strategy and gives a basis for strategic choice.

When the analysis of each business group's alternative strategies is complete,

Exhibit 7
Business portfolio matrix for Holiday Inns

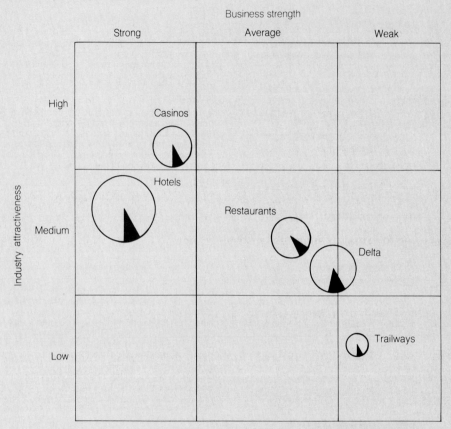

a choice must be made. To ensure consistent business-level choices, this choice must be made at the corporate level and finalized at each business level.

The critical issue at the corporate level for Holiday Inns, Inc., returns to its overall mission. Which of the following does it see as its mission?

1. Diversified firm in travel- and transportation-related industries.
2. Diversified firm in the travel-related industry.
3. Diversified firm in the hospitality industry.

Clearly, Holiday Inns' current business portfolio would align itself with the first mission statement. However, Holiday Inns has traditionally perceived itself within mission statement 2. Its corporatewide expertise and distinctive competence are strongest relative to statement 3. So, to choose a strategy, Holiday Inns, Inc., must also clarify its overall mission.

To illustrate corporate-level strategic choice, we have placed HI businesses in a business portfolio matrix in Exhibit 7. This matrix gives several insights into corporate-level strategy evaluation and choice.

HI's strongest position is in the hospitality-related area, with hotels providing stable growth and strong cash flow, while casinos also represent key areas for corporate growth.

Perkins restaurants are questionable, with a moderately attractive industry but continued weakness in historical performance.

Bus operation is the weakest portfolio member, with Trailways of questionable long-term value to the firm.

Delta provides a steadily profitable business, though without the potential of the hospitality group and clearly unrelated to that group.

The portfolio matrix suggests two basic corporate strategy choices for Holiday Inns, Inc.:

1. Stabilize and improve the current business portfolio.
2. Extend the success of the hotel business (concentration, product and market development), with major growth emphasis (particularly) in casinos.

The choice is related to the need for clarification of the company mission mentioned earlier, so that two points must be dealt with: the mission must be clarified and the corporate strategy chosen. This will set the parameters for business-level strategic choices. Holiday Inns' decision for the 1990s can be summarized as follows:

Company mission and corporate strategy: "Our strategy for the coming decade will be to grow consistently from our leadership base in *the hospitality industry,* seeking major positions in the closely related fields of hotels and casino gaming."

Business group strategies (refer to the earlier discussion):

Hotel group—option 2, product development with aggressive franchise growth and entry into new lodging segments.

Trailways—option 2, divestiture with a $15 million loss.

Delta—combination of options 1 and 2, continued cargo service expansion until profitable divestiture can be made.

Restaurants—option 2, turnaround or possible divestiture of Perkins.

Casinos—option 1, rapid growth into four major regions.

And the long-term objectives associated with the corporate strategy might be as follows:

"The primary goal of HI management is to maximize the value of HI stock to its shareholders."

Dividend payout of 25 to 30 percent of normalized earnings.

Maintain a debt/capital ratio under 50 percent.

Return on equity to exceed 17 percent annually.

Develop a favorable climate for the company in the communities in which it conducts its business through corporate philanthrophy, with an annual goal of $1.5 million in donations.

STRATEGIC MANAGEMENT MODEL

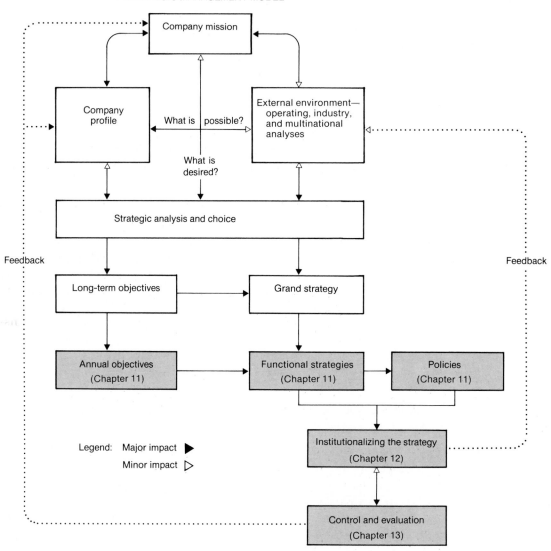

PART THREE

Strategy Implementation

The last part of this book examines what is often called the action phase of the strategic management process: implementation of the chosen strategy. Up to this point, three major phases have been covered: strategy formulation, analysis of alternative strategies, and strategic choice. While these phases are important, they alone cannot ensure success. The strategy must be translated into concrete action, and that action must be carefully implemented. Otherwise, accomplishment is left to chance. The three chapters in this section discuss key aspects of the implementation phase of strategic management.

Implementation is successfully initiated in three interrelated stages:

1. Identification of measurable, mutually determined *annual objectives*.
2. Development of specific *functional strategies*.
3. Development and communication of concise *policies* to guide decisions.

Annual objectives guide implementation by converting long-term objectives into specific, short-term ends. Functional strategies translate grand strategy at the business level into current action plans for subunits of the company. Policies provide specific guidelines for operating managers and their subordinates in executing strategies. Chapter 11 examines how to maximize the use of annual objectives, operating strategies, and policies to operationalize a strategy.

A new strategy must be institutionalized—must permeate the very day-to-day life of the company—to be effectively implemented. In Chapter 12, three organizational elements providing fundamental, long-term means of institutionalizing the company's strategy are discussed:

1. *Structure* of the organization.
2. *Leadership* of the CEO and key managers.
3. The fit between the strategy and the company's *culture*.

Strategy is implemented in a changing environment. Thus, execution must be controlled and evaluated if the strategy is to be successfully implemented and adjusted to changing conditions. The control and evaluation process must include at least three fundamental dimensions:

1. *Establish strategic controls* that "steer" strategy execution.
2. *Operations control systems* that monitor performance, evaluate deviations, and initiate corrective action.
3. *Reward systems* that motivate control and evaluation.

Chapter 13 examines each dimension of the control and evaluation process.

11

Operationalizing the Strategy: Annual Objectives, Functional Strategies, and Business Policies

Even after the grand strategies are determined and long-term objectives tentatively set, the strategic management process is far from complete. The tasks of operationalizing, institutionalizing, and controlling the strategy still remain. These tasks signal a critical new phase in the strategic management process: translating strategic thought into strategic action. Shifting from formulation to implementation gives rise to three interrelated concerns:

1. Identification of measurable, mutually determined annual objectives.
2. Development of specific functional strategies.
3. Communication of concise policies to guide decisions.

Annual objectives translate long-range aspirations into this year's budget. If annual objectives are well developed, they provide clarity, which is a powerful, motivating facilitator of effective strategy implementation. This chapter looks at how to develop annual objectives that maximize implementation-related payoffs.

Functional strategies translate grand strategy at the business level into action plans for subunits of the company. Operating managers assist in developing these strategies, which, in turn, helps clarify what the managers' units are expected to do in implementing the grand strategy. This chapter examines the value and characteristics of functional strategies and the key areas in an organization for which operating strategies enhance implementation of the grand strategy.

Policies are specific guides for operating managers and their subordinates. Policies, often misunderstood and misused, can provide a powerful tool for strategy implementation if they are clearly linked to operating strategies and long-term objectives. This chapter explains how to use policies in the implementation and control of a company's strategies.

Annual Objectives

Chapter 9 dealt with the importance of long-term objectives as benchmarks for corporate and business strategies. Such measures as market share, ROI, return on equity (ROE), stock price, and new market penetration provide guidance in assessing the ultimate effectiveness of a chosen strategy. While such objectives clarify the long-range purpose of a grand strategy and the basis for judging its success, they are less useful in guiding the operating strategies and immediate actions necessary to implement a grand strategy.

A critical step in successful implementation of grand strategy is the identification and communication of annual operating objectives that relate logically to the strategy's long-term objectives.[1] Accomplishment of these annual objectives adds up to successful execution of the business's overall long-term plan. A comprehensive set of annual objectives also provides a specific basis for monitoring and controlling organizational performance. Such objectives can aid in the development of "trigger points" that alert top management to variations in key performance areas that might have serious ramifications for the ultimate success of a strategy.

Qualities of Effective Annual Objectives

Annual objectives are specific, measurable statements of what an organization subunit is expected to achieve in contributing to the accomplishment of the business's grand strategy. Although this seems rather obvious, problems in strategy implementation often stem from poorly conceived or stated annual objectives. To maximize these objectives' contribution, certain basic qualities must be incorporated in developing and communicating them.

Linkage to Long-Term Objectives.   An annual objective must be clearly linked to one or more long-term objectives of the business's grand strategy. However, to accomplish this, it is essential to understand how the two types of objectives differ. Four basic dimensions distinguish annual and long-term objectives:

---

[1] An *annual* time frame is the most popular short-term planning horizon in most firms. Short-term objectives, particularly for a key project, program, or activity, may involve a shorter time horizon (e.g., a three- or six-month horizon). The discussion in this section accommodates such shorter horizons.

1. *Time frame.* Long-term objectives are focused usually five years or more into the future. Annual objectives are more immediate, usually involving one year.

2. *Focus.* Long-term objectives focus on the future position of the firm in its competitive environment. Annual objectives identify specific accomplishments for the company, functional areas, or other subunits over the next year.

3. *Specificity.* Long-term objectives are broadly stated. Annual objectives are very specific and directly linked to the company, a functional area, or other subunit.

4. *Measurement.* While both long-term and annual objectives are quantifiable, long-term objectives are measured in broad, relative terms; for example, 20 percent market share. Annual objectives are stated in absolute terms, such as a 15 percent increase in sales in the next year.

Annual objectives add breadth and specificity in identifying *what* must be accomplished in order to achieve the long-term objective. For example, the long-term objective "to obtain 20 percent market share in five years" clarifies where the business wants to be. But achieving that objective can be greatly enhanced if a series of specific annual objectives identify what must be accomplished each year to achieve that objective. If market share is now 10 percent, then one likely annual objective would be "to achieve a minimum 2 percent increase in relative market share in the next year."

Specific annual objectives should provide targets for performance of operating areas if the long-term objective is to be achieved. "Open two regional distribution centers in the Southeast in 1990" might be one annual objective that marketing and production managers agree is essential in achieving a 20 percent market share in five years. "Conclude arrangements for a $10 million line of credit at 1 percent above prime in 1989" might be the annual objective of financial managers to support the operation of new distribution centers and the additional purchases necessary to increase output in reaching the long-term objective.

The link between short-term and long-term objectives should resemble cascades through the business from basic long-term objectives to numerous specific annual objectives in key operating areas. Thus, long-term objectives are segmented and reduced to short-term (annual) objectives. The cascading effect has the added advantage of providing a clear reference for vertical communication and negotiation, which may be necessary to ensure integrated objectives and plans at the operating level.[2]

---

[2] Lawrence G. Hrebiniak and William F. Joyce, *Implementing Strategy* (New York: Macmillan, 1984), p. 110.

Figure 11–1
Logistic priorities in a manufacturing firm

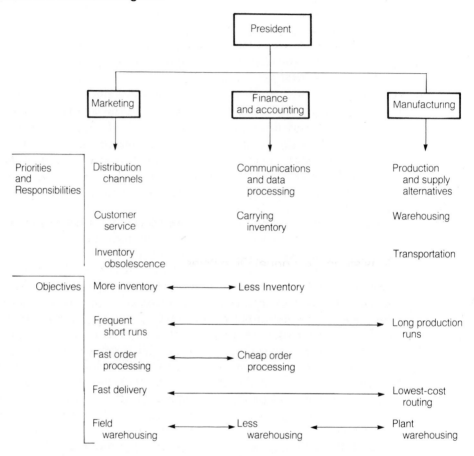

Source: Adapted from John F. Stolle, "How to Manage Physical Distribution," *Harvard Business Review*, July–August 1967, p. 95.

Integrated and Coordinated Objectives.   Implementation of grand strategies requires objectives that are *integrated and coordinated*. However, subunit managers (e.g., vice president of finance, vice president of marketing, vice president of production) may not consider such a "superordinate" purpose in setting annual objectives. Consider the example in Figure 11–1. As can be seen, priorities of the marketing function can easily conflict with those of manufacturing or finance/accounting. For example, manufacturing might logically prefer long production runs and plant warehousing to maximize efficiency. On the other hand, marketing might be better served by frequent, short production runs and field warehousing to maximize customer convenience. Other functional conflicts are evident in Figure 11–1. Without concerted effort to integrate and coordinate annual objectives, these natural conflicts can contribute to the failure of long-term objectives (and the grand strategy), even though the separate annual objectives are well designed.

Successful implementation of strategy depends on coordination and integration of operating units. This is encouraged through the development of short-term (annual) objectives. Expressed another way, annual objectives provide a focal point for raising and resolving conflicts between organizational subunits that might otherwise impede strategic performance.

Managers should be involved at key points in the planning process so that annual objectives are integrated and coordinated. These managers are brought together to discuss important data, assumptions, and performance requirements. This promotes discussion of key interdependencies and a clearer, possibly negotiated determination of annual objectives in key performance areas. Particularly if major strategic change is involved, participation is essential both to establish the relationship of short-term operating activities and long-term strategy *and* to integrate and coordinate operating plans and programs.

Consistency in Annual Objectives

Experience indicates that managers in the same organization will have different ways of developing objectives. For example, managers in different functions, departments, or other subunits will often emphasize different criteria. Due to this lack of consistency, units may not be comparable, commitment to objectives may differ, and the interdependence of units may be dysfunctional. For example, if the marketing area of the firm in Figure 11–1 had very clear, specific objectives regarding delivery time to customers while the manufacturing area's objectives in this regard were ill defined, conflict might be frequent and counterproductive to the strategic success of the firm.

Annual objectives are more consistent when each objective clearly states *what* is to be accomplished, *when* it will be done, and *how* accomplishment will be *measured*. Objectives can then be used to monitor both the effectiveness of an operating unit and, collectively, progress toward the business's long-term objectives. Figure 11–2 illustrates several effective and ineffective annual objectives. If objectives are measurable and state what is to be done and when it will be achieved in a clear, understandable manner, misunderstanding is less likely to occur among the interdependent operating managers who must implement the grand strategy.

Measurable.   *Measurability* cannot be overemphasized as a key quality of annual objectives. Unfortunately, some key results are easier to measure than others. *Line* units (e.g., production) may easily be assessed by clear, quantifiable measures, while criteria for certain *staff* areas (e.g., personnel) are more difficult to measure. However, successful implementation requires setting measurable

Figure 11–2
Operationalizing measurable annual objectives

Examples of deficient annual objectives	*Examples of annual objectives with measurable criteria for performance*
To improve morale in the divisions (plant, department, etc.).	To reduce turnover (absenteeism, number of rejects, etc.) among sales managers by 10 percent by January 1, 1989. *Assumption:* Morale is related to measurable outcomes (i.e., high and low morale are associated with different results).
To improve support of the sales effort.	To reduce the time lapse between order date and delivery by 8 percent (two days) by June 1, 1989. To reduce the cost of goods produced by 6 percent to support a product price decrease of 2 percent by December 1, 1989. To increase the rate of before- or on-schedule delivery by 5 percent by June 1, 1989.
To develop a terminal version of the SAP computer program.	To develop a terminal version of SAP capable of processing *X* bits of information in time *Y* at cost not to exceed *Z* per 1,000 bits by December 1, 1989. *Assumption:* There is virtually an infinite number of "terminal" or operational versions. Greater detail or specificity defines the objective more precisely.
To enhance or improve the training effort.	To increase the number of individuals capable of performing *X* operation in manufacturing by 20 percent by April 15, 1989. To increase the number of functional heads capable of assuming general management responsibility at the division level by 10 percent by July 15, 1989. To provide sales training to *X* number of individuals, resulting in an average increase in sales of 4 percent within six months after the training session.
To improve the business's image.	To conduct a public opinion poll using random samples in the five largest U.S. metropolitan markets and determine average scores on 10 dimensions of corporate responsibility by May 15, 1989. To increase our score on those 10 items by an average of 7.5 percent by May 1, 1990.

Source: Adapted from Laurence G. Hrebiniak and William F. Joyce, *Implementing Strategy* (New York: Macmillan, 1984), p. 116.

annual objectives in these difficult areas, as well. This is usually accomplished by initially focusing on *measurable activity,* followed by the identification of acceptable, measurable *outcomes.*

Other qualities of good objectives discussed in Chapter 9—acceptable, flexible, suitable, motivating, understandable, and achievable—also apply to annual objectives. While these will not be discussed here, the reader should review the earlier discussion to appreciate the qualities common to all objectives.

Figure 11–3
A case of misplaced priorities

CITIBANK

Citibank (New York State), N.A.
P.O. Box 227
Cheektowaga, New York 14225

January 18, 1988

Dear Silver Card Customer:

Several months ago we at Citibank began issuing The Silver Card to Goodyear customers.

The Silver Card revolving loan plan was established and offered by Citibank to provide a more effective nationwide tire and auto service credit card for customers of Goodyear's retail outlets.

As a national credit card, The Silver Card will offer you far more convenience than previously available. Our objective is to make The Silver Card the best credit card available anywhere.

Providing The Silver Card to over a million customers was an ambitious and complex effort and it resulted in account processing problems for some account holders. We understand how frustrating these types of problems can be for you. We are working around the clock to assure that any problems will be corrected promptly.

In the meantime, we trust that you will continue to patronize your Goodyear retail outlet as they will render you the finest products and service available anywhere.

We apologize for any inconvenience we may have caused you and we thank you for your patience and understanding.

Sincerely,

CITIBANK

Source: Mailed to the author, a Goodyear credit customer.

Priorities. Another critical quality of annual objectives involves the need to prioritize short-term objectives. Due to timing considerations and relative impact on strategic success, annual objectives often have *relative* priorities.

Timing considerations often necessitate initiating or completing one activity before another is started. Figure 11–3 shows how this became a problem for Citibank in implementing a program designed to expand its credit card base as part of an ambitious market development strategy in the financial services industry. Citibank's objective for establishing the accounting procedures needed to support the marketing program was not given sufficient priority.

While all annual objectives are important, some deserve additional attention because of their particular impact on the success of a strategy. If such priorities are not discussed and indicated, conflicting assumptions about the relative importance of annual objectives might inhibit progress toward strategic effectiveness.[3] Facing the real possibility of bankruptcy in 1983, Eastern Air Lines formulated a retrenchment strategy with several important annual objectives in labor relations, routes, fleet, and financial condition. But its highest priority involved maintaining the integrity of selected debt-related measures that would satisfy key creditors who could otherwise move to force bankruptcy.

Priorities are usually established in one of several ways. A simple *ranking* may be based on discussion and negotiation during the planning process. However, this does not necessarily communicate the *real* difference in the importance of objectives, so terms such as *primary, top, or secondary* may be used to indicate priority. Some businesses assign weights (for example, 0–100 percent) to establish and communicate the relative priority of each objective. Whatever the method, recognizing the priorities of annual objectives is an important dimension in implementing the strategy.

Benefits of Annual Objectives

Systematic development of annual objectives provides a tangible, meaningful focus through which managers can translate long-term objectives and grand strategies into specific action. Annual objectives give operating managers and personnel a better understanding of their role in the business's mission. This *clarity of purpose* can be a major force in effectively mobilizing the "people assets" of a business.[4] Strategy in Action 11–1 illustrates how specific annual objectives help focus a declining NBA.

A second benefit involves the process required to derive annual objectives. If these objectives have been developed through the participation of managers responsible for their accomplishment, they provide an "objective" basis for addressing and accommodating conflicting political concerns that might interfere with strategic effectiveness. Effective annual objectives become the essential link between strategic intentions and operating reality.

Well-developed annual objectives provide another major benefit: *a basis for strategic control*. The question of controlling strategy will be examined in greater detail in Chapter 13; but it is important to recognize here the simple yet powerful benefit of annual objectives in developing budgets, schedules, trigger points, and other mechanisms for controlling strategy implementation.

Annual objectives can provide motivational payoffs in strategy implementa-

---

[3] Ibid., p. 119.

[4] One recent book that supports this point is Thomas J. Peters and R. H. Waterman, Jr., *In Search of Excellence* (New York: Harper & Row, 1982). Extensive literature on one of the best-known management techniques, management by objectives (MBO), supports the value of objective setting in achieving desired performance. For a useful discussion of MBO, see Karl Albrecht, *Successful Management by Objectives* (Englewood Cliffs, N.J.: Prentice-Hall, 1978).

Strategy in Action 11–1
Annual Objectives and Functional Strategies at the National Basketball Association

By the mid-1980s, a safe bet around sport circles was that the NBA would not survive to the 1990s. Sixteen of 23 teams were losing money, TV ratings were dropping, and buyers for "for sale" franchises were nowhere to be found. In 1987, Commissioner David J. Stern identified three annual objectives and five functional strategies to turn the situation around.

Annual Objective for the NBA. Commissioner Stern set three objectives for 1988:

1. Gross league revenues will be $325 million.
2. All 23 teams will generate a profit.
3. The NBA's TV ratings will increase by 10 percent.

Functional Strategies for the NBA. Stern used five functional strategies designed to accomplish these objectives:

1. *Stop overspending for players.* Selected NBA teams had courted bankruptcy by overspending for players. The new salary strategy sets a salary pool beyond which a team cannot (normally) spend. The figure is arrived at by totaling NBA revenues, multiplying by 53 percent, and apportioning that amount equally among the 23 teams.
2. *Recruit businesspersons to buy sagging franchises.* Commissioner Stern personally took charge of targeting and recruiting successful businesspeople to acquire sagging NBA franchises. He felt such owners would understand, appreciate, and restore financial sanity to these problem franchises.
3. *Reduce overexposure on TV.* In 1984, over 200 NBA games were televised nationally on cable and network TV. This avalanche of available games depressed NBA ratings, which reduced advertising rates and league revenue. Commissioner Stern reduced the number of televised games to 55 regular season games and 20 playoff games. This strategy improved audience size and raised ratings, which, in turn, increased TV revenues.
4. *Institute a league MIS system.* The NBA developed an MIS system that offers each team an item-by-item revenue-and-expense comparison with other teams and NBA averages.
5. *Institute an antidrug program.* The NBA took the forefront among professional sports in fighting the drug problem. It developed a comprehensive drug program for its athletes, which allowed the NBA to generate sizable goodwill toward the league.

Source: Based on "Basketball: Business Is Booming," *Business Week*, October 28, 1986.

tion. If objectives clarify personal and group roles in a business's strategies and are also measurable, realistic, and challenging, they can be powerful motivators of managerial performance—particularly when they are linked to the business's reward structure.

While annual objectives provide a powerful tool in operationalizing business strategy, they aren't sufficient in themselves. Functional strategies, the *means* to accomplish these objectives, must be clearly identified to encourage successful implementation.

Developing Functional Strategies

A *functional strategy* is the short-term game plan for a key functional area *within* a company. Such strategies clarify grand strategy by providing more specific details about how key functional areas are to be managed in the near future.

Functional strategies must be developed in the key areas of marketing, finance, production/operations, R&D, and personnel. They must be consistent with long-term objectives and grand strategy. Functional strategies help in implementation of grand strategy by organizing and activating specific subunits of the company (marketing, finance, production, etc.) to pursue the business strategy in daily activities. In a sense, functional strategies translate thought (grand strategy) into action designed to accomplish specific annual objectives. For every major subunit of a company, functional strategies identify and coordinate actions that support the grand strategy and improve the likelihood of accomplishing annual objectives. Strategy in Action 11–1 illustrates key functional strategies used to implement the NBA's turnaround in the late 1980s.

Figure 11–4 illustrates the important role of functional strategies in implementing corporate and business strategy. The corporate strategy defined General Cinema Corporation's general posture in the broad economy. The business strategy outlined the competitive posture of its operations within the domestic movie exhibition industry. But to increase the likelihood that these strategies will be successful, more specific guidelines are needed for the business's operating components. Thus, functional strategies clarify the business strategy, giving specific, short-term guidance to operating managers. The example in Figure 11–4 shows possible functional strategies in the functional areas of operations, marketing, and finance. Additional functional strategies are necessary, most notably in the personnel area.

Differences between Business and Functional Strategies

To better understand the role of functional strategies within the strategic management process, they must be differentiated from grand strategies. Three basic characteristics differentiate functional and grand strategies:

Figure 11-4
Role of functional strategies at General Cinema Corporation

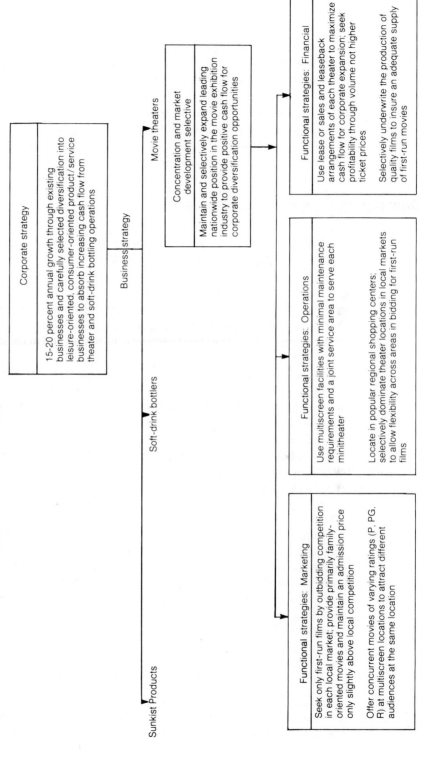

1. Time horizon covered.
2. Specificity.
3. Participation in the development.

Time Horizon.   The time horizon of a functional strategy is usually comparatively short. Functional strategies identify and coordinate short-term actions,
usually undertaken in a year or less. Sears, for example, might implement a
marketing strategy of increasing price discounts and sales bonuses in its appliance division to reduce excess appliance inventory over the next year. This
functional strategy would be designed to achieve a short-range (annual) objective that ultimately contributes to the goal of Sears' grand strategy in its
retail division over the next five years.

This shorter time horizon is critical to successfully implementing a grand
strategy for two reasons. First, it focuses functional managers' attention on
what needs to be done *now* to make the grand strategy work. Second, the
shorter time horizon allows functional managers to recognize current conditions
and adjust to changing conditions in developing functional strategies.

Specificity.   A functional strategy is more specific than a grand strategy.
Functional strategies guide functional actions taken in key parts of the company
to implement grand strategy. The grand strategy provides general direction.
Functional strategies give specific guidance to managers responsible for accomplishing annual objectives. Such strategies are meant to ensure that managers
know *how* to meet annual objectives. It is not enough to identify a general
grand strategy at the business level. There must also be strategies outlining
what should be done in each functional area if the annual (and ultimately
long-term) objectives of the company are to be achieved. Specific functional
strategies improve the willingness (and ability) of operating managers to implement strategic decisions, particularly when those decisions represent major
changes in the current strategy of the firm.

Figure 11–4 illustrates the difference in specificity of grand and operating
strategies. General Cinema's grand strategy for its movie theater division
gives broad direction on how the division should pursue a concentration and
selective market development strategy. Two functional strategies illustrated
in the marketing area give specific direction to managers on what types of
movies (first-run, primarily family-oriented, P, PG, R) and what pricing strategy (competitive in the local area) should be followed.

Specificity in functional strategies contributes to successful implementation
for several reasons. First, it adds substance, completeness, and meaning to
what a specific subunit of the business must do. The existence of numerous
functional strategies helps ensure that managers know what needs to be done

and can focus on accomplishing results.[5] Second, specific functional strategies clarify for top management how functional managers intend to accomplish the grand strategy. This increases top management's confidence in and sense of control over the grand strategy. Third, specific functional strategies facilitate coordination between operating units *within* the company by clarifying areas of interdependence and potential conflict.

Participants.   Different people participate in strategy development at the functional and business levels. Business strategy is the responsibility of the general manager of a business unit. Development of functional strategy is typically delegated by the business-level manager to principal subordinates charged with running the operating areas of the business. The business manager must establish long-term objectives and a strategy that corporate management feels contributes to corporate-level goals. Key operating managers similarly establish annual objectives and operating strategies that help accomplish business objectives and strategies. Just as business strategies and objectives are approved through negotiation between corporate managers and business managers, the business manager typically ratifies the annual objectives and functional strategies developed by operating managers.[6]

The involvement of operating managers in developing functional strategies contributes to successful implementation because understanding of what needs to be done to achieve annual objectives is thereby improved. And perhaps most critical, active involvement increases commitment to the strategies developed.

It is difficult to generalize about the development of strategies across functional areas. For example, key variables in marketing, finance, and production are different. Furthermore, within each functional area, the importance of key variables varies across business situations. Thus, in the next several sections, we will not exhaustively treat each functional area but will attempt to indicate the key decision variables that should receive attention in the functional strategies of typical areas.

Functional Strategies in the Marketing Area

The role of the marketing function is to profitably bring about the sale of products/services in target markets for the purpose of achieving the business's

---

[5] While a company typically has one grand strategy, it should have a functional strategy for each major subunit and several operating strategies within the subunit. For example, a business may specify distinct pricing, promotion, and distribution strategies as well as an overall strategy to guide marketing operations.

[6] A. A. Thompson, Jr., and A. J. Strickland III, *Strategy Formulation and Implementation*, 2nd ed. (Plano, Tex.: Business Publications, 1983), p. 77.

Figure 11–5
Functional strategies in marketing

Key functional strategies	Typical questions that should be answered by the functional strategy
Product (or service)	Which products do we emphasize?
	Which products/services contribute most to profitability?
	What is the product/service image we seek to project?
	What consumer needs does the product/service seek to meet?
	What changes should be influencing our customer orientation?
Price	Are we primarily competing on price?
	Can we offer discounts or other pricing modifications?
	Are pricing policies standard nationally or is there regional control?
	What price segments are we targeting (high, medium, low, etc.)?
	What is the gross profit margin?
	Do we emphasize cost/demand or competition-oriented pricing?
Place	What level of market coverage is necessary?
	Are there priority geographic areas?
	What channels of distribution are key?
	What are the channel objectives, structure, and management?
	Should the marketing managers change their degree of reliance on distributors, sales reps, and direct selling?
	What sales organization do we want?
	Is the sales force organized around territory, market, or product?
Promotion	What are key promotion priorities and approaches?
	Which advertising/communication priorities and approaches are linked to different products, markets, and territories?
	Which media would be most consistent with the total marketing strategy?

goals. Functional strategies in the marketing area should guide this endeavor in a manner consistent with the grand strategy and other functional strategies. Effective marketing strategies guide marketing managers in determining who will sell what, where, when, to whom, in what quantity, and how. Marketing strategies must therefore entail four components: product, price, place, and promotion. Figure 11–5 illustrates the types of questions that operating strategies must address in terms of these four components. Strategy in Action 11–2 shows how marketing strategies were used to implement a new business strategy at K mart.

Strategy in Action 11–2
K mart Operationalizes a New Business Strategy

Not long ago, employees in K mart discount department stores began shuffling shelves, replacing racks, moving whole departments, and blazing new aisles. When they finished, the stores had a new look, and K mart Corp., the world's second-largest retailer, had started on a new merchandising tack.

The trouble is that K mart can no longer rely entirely on its old strategy of growth through building new stores. Since the first K mart opened in 1962, offering everything from baby oil to motor oil at cut-rate prices, the stores have proliferated, turning the former S. S. Kresge Company from a so-so five-and-dime chain into the biggest retailer next to Sears Roebuck & Co.

Now, with stores in nearly all the 300 top metropolitan areas in the country, some of which are saturated, K mart's growth through expansion is increasingly limited. The answer is to try for more volume, and more profitable volume per store, from the cost-conscious consumers attracted by K mart's low prices. K mart can't risk losing its discount appeal, but at the same time it must move more and higher-quality goods. To achieve this new business strategy, K mart is relying heavily on a sophisticated operating strategy in merchandising. The standard K mart—a cavernous building of plain design filled with racks, bins, and metal shelves—has been changed here to emphasize the merchandise at least as much as the price tags and signs. Displays of clothing and other goods are being altered to stimulate impulse buying. In addition, higher-quality goods are being offered.

K mart's heavy advertising consistently has attracted customers, especially cost-conscious middle- and upper-income customers. "But too often we fail to merchandise all of the items that customers would buy from us after we get them into the store," said K mart's CEO. "We simply aren't getting enough of their spendable dollars."

Although the changes in K marts seem subtle, they're designed to create an atmosphere conducive to free spending. In women's apparel, rows and rows of long piperacks have been replaced by multilevel, circular, and honeycomb racks that allow customers to see whole garments. Higher-quality, more fashionable soft goods hang on the new racks. Delicatessen and snack counters have moved to a wall from their front-and-center position. Now, jewelry greets shoppers inside the entrances. "We wanted to get the popcorn out from in front of the door," said a K mart vice president. The jewelry includes higher-quality pieces and more brand-name items. Sales of women's wear and jewelry have increased in the redesigned stores, K mart managers say.

Source: "Mass Appeal," *Forbes,* May 5, 1986.

A functional strategy for the *product component* of the marketing function should clearly identify the customer needs the firm seeks to meet with its product and/or service. An effective functional strategy for this component should guide marketing managers in decisions regarding features, product lines, packaging, accessories, warranty, quality, and new product development. This strategy should provide a comprehensive statement of the product/service concept and the target market(s) the firm is seeking to serve. This, in turn, fosters consistency and continuity in the daily activity of the marketing area.

A product or service is not much good to a customer if it is not available when and where it is wanted. So, the functional strategy for the *place component* identifies where, when, and by whom the product/services are to be offered for sale. The primary concern here is the channel(s) of distribution—the combination of marketing institutions through which the products/services flow to the final user. This component of marketing strategy guides decisions regarding channels (for example, single versus multiple channels) to ensure consistency with the total marketing effort.

The *promotion component* of marketing strategy defines how the firm will communicate with the target market. Functional strategy for the promotion component should provide marketing managers with basic guides for the use and mix of advertising, personal selling, sales promotion, and media selection. It must be consistent with other marketing strategy components and, due to cost requirements, closely integrated with financial strategy.

Functional strategy regarding the *price component* is perhaps the single most important consideration in marketing. It directly influences demand and supply, profitability, consumer perception, and regulatory response. The approach to pricing strategy may be cost oriented, market oriented, or competition (industry) oriented. With a cost-oriented approach, pricing decisions center on total cost and usually involve an acceptable markup or target price ranges. Pricing is based on consumer demand (e.g., gasoline pricing in a deregulated oil industry) when the approach is market oriented. With the third approach, pricing decisions center around those of the firm's competitors. The discount pricing that occurred in the U.S. automobile industry in the 1980s, with several domestic and foreign producers usually following Chrysler's discount pricing initiatives, is an example of competitor-based pricing. While one approach (e.g., market demand) may predominate in a firm's pricing strategy, the strategy is always influenced to some degree by the other orientations.

Functional Strategies in Finance/Accounting

While most operating strategies guide implementation in the immediate future, the time frame for financial functional strategies varies because strategies in this area direct the use of financial resources in support of the business strategy, long-term goals, and annual objectives. Financial operating strategies with longer time perspectives guide financial managers in long-term capital

Figure 11–6
Functional strategies in finance

Key functional strategies	Typical questions that should be answered by the functional strategy
Capital acquisition	What is an acceptable cost of capital?
	What is the desired proportion of short- and long-term debt; preferred and common equity?
	What balance is between internal and external funding?
	What risk and ownership restrictions are appropriate?
	What level and forms of leasing should be used in providing assets?
Capital allocation	What are the priorities for capital allocation projects?
	On what basis is final selection of projects to be made?
	What level of capital allocation can be made by operating managers without higher approval?
Dividend and working capital management	What portion of earnings should be paid out as dividends?
	How important is dividend stability?
	Are things other than cash appropriate as dividends?
	What are the cash flow requirements; minimum and maximum cash balances?
	How liberal/conservative should credit policies be?
	What limits, payment terms, and collection procedures are necessary?
	What payment timing and procedure should be followed?

investment, use of debt financing, dividend allocation, and the firm's leveraging posture. Operating strategies designed to manage working capital and short-term assets have a more immediate focus. Figure 11–6 highlights some key questions financial strategies must answer for successful implementation.

Long-term financial strategies usually guide capital acquisition in the sense that priorities change infrequently over time. The desired level of debt versus equity versus internal long-term financing of business activities is a common issue in capital acquisition strategy. For example, Delta Airlines has a long-standing operating strategy that seeks to minimize the level of debt in proportion to equity and internal funding of capital needs. General Cinema Corporation has a long-standing strategy of long-term leasing to expand its theater and soft-drink bottling facilities. The debt-to-equity ratios for these two firms are approximately 0.50 to 2.0, respectively. Both have similar records of steady profitable growth over the last 20 years and represent two different yet equally effective operating strategies for capital acquisition.

Another financial strategy of major importance is capital allocation. Growth-oriented grand strategies generally require numerous major investments in facilities, projects, acquisitions, and/or people. These investments cannot generally be made immediately, nor are they desired to be. Rather, a capital allocation strategy sets priorities and timing for these investments. This also helps manage conflicting priorities among operating managers competing for capital resources.

Retrenchment or stability often require a financial strategy that focuses on the reallocation of existing capital resources. This could necessitate pruning product lines, production facilities, or personnel to be reallocated elsewhere in the firm. The overlapping careers and aspirations of key operating managers clearly create an emotional setting. Even with retrenchment (perhaps even more so!), a clear operating strategy that delineates capital allocation priorities is important for effective implementation in a politically charged organizational setting.

Capital allocation strategy frequently includes one additional dimension— level of capital expenditure delegated to operating managers. If a business is pursuing rapid growth, flexibility in making capital expenditures at the operating level may enable timely responses to an evolving market. On the other hand, capital expenditures may be carefully controlled if retrenchment is the strategy.

Dividend management is an integral part of a firm's internal financing. Because dividends are paid on earnings, lower dividends increase the internal funds available for growth, and internal financing reduces the need for external, often debt, financing. However, stability of earnings and dividends often makes a positive contribution to the market price of a firm's stock. Therefore, a strategy guiding dividend management must support the business's posture toward equity markets.

Working capital is critical to the daily operation of the firm, and capital requirements are directly influenced by seasonal and cyclical fluctuations, firm size, and the pattern of receipts and disbursements. The working capital component of financial strategy is built on an accurate projection of cash flow and must provide cash management guidelines for conserving and rebuilding the cash balances required for daily operation.

Functional Strategies in Research and Development

With the increasing rate of technological change in most competitive industries, research and development (R&D) has assumed a key functional role in many organizations. In the technology-intense computer and pharmaceutical industries, for example, firms typically spend between 4 and 6 percent of their sales dollars on R&D. In other industries, such as the hotel/motel and construction industries, R&D spending is less than 1 percent of sales. Thus, R&D may be a vital function—a key instrument of business strategy—although in stable, less innovative industries, R&D is less critical as a functional strategy than is marketing or finance.

Figure 11–7 illustrates the types of questions addressed by an R&D operating

Figure 11–7
Functional strategies in R&D

R&D decision area	*Typical questions that should be answered by the functional strategy*
Basic research versus commercial development	To what extent should innovation and break-through research be emphasized? In relation to the emphasis on product development, refinement, and modification?
	What new projects are necessary to support growth?
Time horizon	Is the emphasis short term or long term?
	Which orientation best supports the business strategy? marketing and production strategy?
Organizational fit	Should R&D be done in-house or contracted out?
	Should it be centralized or decentralized?
	What should be the relationship between the R&D unit(s) and product managers? marketing managers? production managers?
Basic R&D posture	Should the firm maintain an offensive posture, seeking to lead innovation and development in the industry?
	Should the firm adapt a defensive posture, responding quickly to competitors' developments?

strategy. First, R&D strategy should clarify whether basic research or product development research will be emphasized. Several major oil companies now have solar energy subsidiaries with R&D strategy emphasis on basic research, while smaller competitors emphasize product development research.

Directly related to the choice of emphasis between basic research and product development is the time orientation for these efforts mandated by R&D strategy. Should efforts be focused on the near or the long term? The solar subsidiaries of the major oil companies have long-term perspectives, while their smaller competitors appear to be focusing on the immediate future. These orientations are consistent with each business's strategy if the major oil companies want to ensure their long-term position in the energy field, while the smaller companies want to establish a competitive niche in the growing solar industry.

R&D strategy should also guide organization of the R&D function. For example, should R&D efforts be conducted solely within the firm or should portions of the work be contracted outside? A closely related issue is whether R&D should be a centralized or decentralized function.

The basic R&D posture of the firm influences each of these decisions because strategy in this area can be offensive, defensive, or a combination of these. If the R&D strategy is offensive, technological innovation and new product development are emphasized as the basis for the firm's future success, as is true for small, high-technology firms. However, this orientation entails high risk (and high payoff) and demands considerable technological skill, forecasting expertise, and the ability to quickly transform basic innovations into commercial products.

A defensive R&D strategy emphasizes product modification and the ability to copy or acquire new technology to maintain a firm's position in the industry. American Motors (AMC) is a good example. Faced with the massive R&D budgets of General Motors, Ford, and foreign competitors, AMC has placed R&D emphasis on bolstering the product life cycle of its prime products (particularly Jeeps) and acquiring small-car technology through a partnership arrangement with Renault of France.

A combination of offensive and defensive R&D strategy is often used by large companies with some degree of technological leadership. GE in the electrical industry, IBM in the computer industry, and Du Pont in the chemical industry all have defensive R&D strategies for currently available products *and* emphasis on an offensive R&D posture in basic, long-term research.

Functional Strategies in Production/Operations

Production/operations management (POM) is the core function in the business firm. POM is the process of converting inputs (raw material, supplies, people, and machines) into value-enhanced output. This function is most easily associated with manufacturing firms. However, it applies equally to all other types of businesses (including service and retail firms, for example).

Functional strategies in POM must guide decisions regarding: (1) the basic nature of the firm's POM system, seeking an optimum balance between investment input and production/operations output and (2) location, facilities design, and process planning on a short-term basis. Figure 11–8 illustrates these concerns by highlighting key decision areas in which the POM strategies should provide guidance.

The facilities and equipment component of POM strategy involves decisions regarding plant location, size, equipment replacement, and facilities utilization that should be consistent with grand strategy and other operating strategies. In the mobile home industry, for example, Winnebago's plant and equipment strategy entailed one large, centralized production center (in Iowa) located near its raw materials with modernized equipment and a highly integrated production process. Fleetwood, Inc., a California-based competitor, opted for dispersed, decentralized production facilities located near markets. Fleetwood emphasizes maximum equipment life and less integrated, labor-intensive production processes. Both are leaders in the mobile home industry.

The purchasing function is another area that should be addressed in the POM strategy. From a cost perspective, are a few suppliers an advantage or risky because of overdependence? What criteria (for example, payment requirements) should be used in selecting vendors? How should purchases be made in terms of volume and delivery requirements to support operations? If such questions are critical to the success of a grand strategy, functional strategy guidelines improve implementation.

Functional strategies for the planning and control component of POM provide guidelines for ongoing production operations. They are meant to encourage

Figure 11–8
Functional strategies in POM

Key operating strategies	Typical questions that should be answered by the functional strategy
Facilities and equipment	How centralized should the facilities be? (One big facility or several small facilities?)
	How integrated should the separate processes be?
	To what extent will further mechanization or automation be pursued?
	Should size and capacity be oriented toward peak or normal operating levels?
Purchasing	How many sources are needed?
	How do we select suppliers and manage relationships over time?
	What level of forward buying (hedging) is appropriate?
Operations planning and control	Should work be scheduled to order or to stock?
	What level of inventory is appropriate?
	How should inventory be used (FIFO/LIFO), controlled, and replenished?
	What are the key foci for control efforts (quality, labor cost, downtime, product usage, other)?
	Should maintenance efforts be preventive or breakdown oriented?
	What emphasis should be placed on job specialization? plant safety? use of standards?

efficient organization of production/operations resources to match long-range, overall demand. Often this component dictates whether production/operations will be demand oriented, inventory oriented, or subcontracting oriented. If demand is cyclical or seasonal, then POM strategy must ensure that production/operations processes are efficiently geared to this pattern. A bathing suit manufacturer would prefer inventories to be at their highest in the early spring, for example, not the early fall. If demand is less cyclical, a firm might emphasize producing to inventory, wanting a steady level of production and inventories. When demand fluctuations are less predictable, many firms subcontract to handle sudden increases in demand while avoiding idle capacity and excess capital investment. Thus, a POM strategy should aid in such decisions as:

What is the appropriate inventory level? Purchasing procedure? Level of quality control?

What is the trade-off in emphasizing cost versus quality in production/operations? What level of productivity is critical?

How far ahead should we schedule production? Guarantee delivery? Hire personnel?

What criteria should be followed in adding or deleting equipment, facilities, shifts, and people?

Figure 11–9
Operations management concerns associated with different elements of a strategy

Possible elements of strategy	*Concomitant conditions that may affect or place demands on the operations function*
1. Compete as low-cost provider of goods or services	Broadens market. Requires longer production runs and fewer product changes. Requires special-purpose equipment and facilities.
2. Compete as high-quality provider	Often possible to obtain more profit per unit, and perhaps more total profit from a smaller volume of sales. Requires more quality-assurance effort and higher operating cost. Requires more precise equipment, which is more expensive. Requires highly skilled workers, necessitating higher wages and greater training efforts.
3. Stress customer service	Requires broader development of servicepeople and service parts and equipment. Requires rapid response to customer needs or changes in customer tastes, rapid and accurate information system, careful coordination. Requires a higher inventory investment.
4. Provide rapid and frequent introduction of new products	Requires versatile equipment and people. Has higher research and development costs. Has high retraining costs and high tooling and changeover in manufacturing. Provides lower volumes for each product and fewer opportunities for improvements due to the learning curve.
5. Strive for absolute growth	Requires accepting some projects or products with lower marginal value, which reduces ROI. Diverts talents to areas of weakness instead of concentrating on strengths.
6. Seek vertical integration	Enables company to control more of the process. May not have economies of scale at some stages of process. May require high capital investment as well as technology and skills beyond those currently available within the organization.
7. Maintain reserve capacity for flexibility	Provides ability to meet peak demands and quickly implement some contingency plans if forecasts are too low. Requires capital investment in idle capacity. Provides capability to grow during the lead time normally required for expansion.
8. Consolidate processing (centralize)	Can result in economies of scale. Can locate near one major customer or supplier. Vulnerability: one strike, fire, or flood can halt the entire operation.
9. Disperse processing of service (decentralize)	Can be near several market territories. Requires more complex coordination network: perhaps expensive data transmission and duplication of some personnel and equipment at each location. If each location produces one product in the line, then other products still must be transported to be available at all locations. If each location specializes in a type of component for all products, the company is vulnerable to strike, fire, flood, etc. If each location provides total product line, then economies of scale may not be realized.
10. Stress the use of mechanization, automation, robots	Requires high capital investment. Reduces flexibility. May affect labor relations. Makes maintenance more crucial.

Figure 11–9 (*concluded*)
Operations management concerns associated with different elements in a strategy

Possible elements of strategy	Concomitant conditions that may affect or place demands on the operations function
11. Stress stability of employment	Serves the security needs of employees and may develop employee loyalty. Helps to attract and retain highly skilled employees. May require revisions of make-or-buy decisions, use of idle time, inventory, and subcontractors as demand fluctuates.

Source: From *Production and Operations Management: Manufacturing and Nonmanufacturing*, 2nd ed., by J. Dilworth. Copyright © 1983 by Random House, Inc. Reprinted by permission of the publisher.

POM operating strategies must be coordinated with marketing strategy if the firm is to succeed. Careful integration with financial strategy components (such as capital budgeting and investment decisions) and the personnel function are also necessary. Figure 11–9 helps illustrate the importance of such coordination by showing the different POM concerns that arise when different marketing/financial/personnel strategies are required as elements of the grand strategy.

Functional Strategies in Personnel

The strategic importance of functional strategies in the personnel area has become more widely accepted in recent years. Personnel management aids in accomplishing grand strategy by ensuring the development of managerial talent, the presence of systems to manage compensation and regulatory concerns, and the development of competent, well-motivated employees. Functional strategies in personnel should guide the effective utilization of human resources to achieve both the annual objectives of the firm and the satisfaction and development of employees. These strategies involve the following areas:

Employee recruitment, selection, and orientation.

Career development and counseling, performance evaluation, and training and development.

Compensation.

Labor/union relations and Equal Employment Opportunity Commission (EEOC) requirements.

Discipline, control, and evaluation.

Operating strategy for recruitment, selection, and orientation guides personnel management decisions for attracting and retaining motivated, productive employees. This involves such questions as: What are the key human resource needs to support a chosen strategy? How do we recruit for these needs? How sophisticated should the selection process be? How should new employees be introduced to the organization? The recruitment, selection, and orientation component of personnel strategy should provide basic parameters for answering these questions.

The development and training component should guide personnel actions taken to meet future human resource needs of the grand strategy. Merrill Lynch, a major brokerage firm, has a long-term corporate strategy of becoming a diversified financial service institution. In addition to handling stock transactions, Merrill Lynch is actively moving into such areas as investment banking, consumer credit, and venture capital. In support of these far-reaching, long-term objectives, Merrill Lynch has incorporated extensive early-career training and ongoing career development programs to meet its expanding need for personnel with multiple competencies.

Functional strategies in the personnel area are needed to guide decisions regarding compensation, labor relations, EEOC requirements, discipline, and control to enhance the productivity and motivation of the work force. Involved are such concerns as: What are the standards for promotion? How should payment, incentive plans, benefits, and seniority policies be interpreted? Should there be hiring preference? What are appropriate disciplinary steps? These are specific personnel decisions that operating managers frequently encounter. Functional strategies in the personnel area should guide such decisions in a way that is compatible with business strategy, strategies for other functional areas, and the achievement of annual objectives.

To summarize, functional strategies are important because they provide specifics on *how* each major subactivity contributes to the implementation of the grand strategy. This specificity, and the involvement of operating managers in its development, help ensure understanding of and commitment to the chosen strategy. Annual objectives, linked to both long-term objectives and functional strategies, reinforce this understanding and commitment by providing measurable targets that operating managers have agreed on. The next step in implementing a strategy involves the identification of *policies* that guide and control decisions by operating managers and their subordinates.

Developing and Communicating Concise Policies

Policies are directives designed to guide the thinking, decisions, and actions of managers and their subordinates in implementing an organization's strategy. Policies provide guidelines for establishing and controlling ongoing operations in a manner consistent with the firm's strategic objectives. Often referred to as "standard operating procedures," policies serve to increase managerial effectiveness by standardizing many routine decisions and controlling the discretion of managers and subordinates in implementing operational strategies. Logically, policies should be derived from functional strategies (and, in some instances, from corporate or business strategies) with the key purpose of aiding in strategy execution.[7] Strategy in Action 11–3 illustrates selected policies from several well-known companies.

The Purpose of Policies

Policies communicate specific guides to decisions. They are designed to control and reinforce the implementation of functional strategies and the grand strategy, and they fulfill this role in several ways:

1. *Policies establish indirect control over independent action* by making a clear statement about how things are *now* to be done. By limiting discretion, policies in effect control decisions and the conduct of activities without direct intervention by top management.

2. *Policies promote uniform handling of similar activities.* This facilitates coordination of work tasks and helps reduce friction arising from favoritism, discrimination, and disparate handling of common functions.

3. *Policies ensure quicker decisions* by standardizing answers to previously answered questions that would otherwise recur and be pushed up the management hierarchy again and again.

4. *Policies help institutionalize basic aspects of organization behavior.* This minimizes conflicting practices and establishes consistent patterns of action in terms of how organizational members attempt to make the strategy work.

5. *Policies reduce uncertainty in repetitive and day-to-day decision making,* thereby providing a necessary foundation for coordinated, efficient efforts.

6. *Policies can counteract resistance to or rejection of chosen strategies by organization members.* When major strategic change is undertaken, unambiguous operating policies help clarify what is expected and facilitate acceptance, particularly when operating managers participate in policy development.

7. *Policies offer a predetermined answer to routine problems,* giving managers more time to cope with nonroutine matters; dealing with ordinary and extraordinary problems is greatly expedited—the former by referring to established policy and the latter by drawing on a portion of the manager's time.

---

[7] The term *policy* has various definitions in management literature. Some authors and practitioners equate policy with strategy. Others do this inadvertently by using "policy" as a synonym for company mission, purpose, or culture. Still other authors and practitioners differentiate policy in terms of "levels" associated respectively with purpose, mission, and strategy. "Our policy is to make a positive contribution to the communities and societies we live in" and "our policy is not to diversify out of the hamburger business" are two examples of the breadth of what some call policies. This book defines *policy* much more narrowly as specific guides to managerial action and decisions in the implementation of strategy. This definition permits a sharper distinction between the formulation and implementation of functional strategies. And, of even greater importance, it focuses the tangible value of the policy concept where it can be most useful—as a key administrative tool to enhance effective implementation and execution of strategy.

Strategy in Action 11–3
Selected Policies that Aid Strategy Implementation

Wendy's has a *purchasing policy* to give local store managers the authority to buy fresh meat and produce locally rather than from regionally designated or company-owned sources.

(This policy supports Wendy's functional strategy of having fresh, unfrozen hamburgers daily.)

General Cinema has a *financial policy* that requires annual capital investment in movie theaters not to exceed annual depreciation.

(By keeping capital investment no greater than depreciation, this policy supports General Cinema's financial strategy of maximizing cash flow—in this case, all profit—to growth areas of the company. It also reinforces General Cinema's financial strategy of leasing as much as possible.)

Holiday Inns has a *personnel policy* that every new innkeeper attend Holiday Inns University's three-week innkeeper program within one year of being hired.

(This policy supports Holiday Inns' functional (POM) strategy of strict compliance with specific standards at every HI location by ensuring standardized training of every new innkeeper at every Holiday Inn whether company owned or franchised.)

IBM originally had a *marketing policy* not to give free IBM personal computers (PCs) to any person or organization.

(This policy attempted to support IBM's image strategy as a professional, high-value, service business and its effort to retain that image as it seeks to dominate the PC market.)

Crown, Cork and Seal Company has an *R&D policy* not to invest any financial or people resources in basic research.

(This policy supports Crown, Cork and Seal's functional strategy, which emphasizes customer service, not technical leadership.)

First National Bank of South Carolina has an *operating policy* that requires annual renewal of the financial statement of all personal borrowers.

(This policy supports First National's financial strategy, which seeks to maintain a loan/loss ratio below the industry norm.)

8. *Policies afford managers a mechanism for avoiding hasty and ill-conceived decisions in changing operations.* Prevailing policy can always be used as a reason for not yielding to emotion-based, expedient, or temporarily valid arguments for altering procedures and practices.[8]

Policies may be written and formal or unwritten and informal. The positive reasons for informal, unwritten policies are usually associated with some strategic need for competitive secrecy. Some unwritten policies, such as "promotion from within," are widely known (or expected) by employees and implicitly sanctioned by management. However, unwritten, informal policies may be contrary to the long-term success of a strategy. Still, managers and employees often like the latitude "granted" when policies are unwritten and informal. There are at least seven advantages to formal written policies:

1. Managers are required to think through the policy's meaning, content, and intended use.
2. The policy is explicit so misunderstandings are reduced.
3. Equitable and consistent treatment of problems is more likely.
4. Unalterable transmission of policies is ensured.
5. Authorization or sanction of the policy is more clearly communicated, which can be helpful in many cases.
6. A convenient and authoritative reference can be supplied to all concerned with the policy.
7. Indirect control and organizationwide coordination, key purposes of policies, are systematically enhanced.[9]

Policies can vary in their level of strategic significance. Some, such as travel reimbursement procedures, are really work rules that are not necessarily linked to the implementation of a specific strategy. At the other extreme, such organizationwide policies as Wendy's requirement that every location invest 1 percent of gross revenue in local advertising are virtually functional strategies.

Policies can be externally imposed or internally derived. Policies regarding EEOC practices are often developed in compliance with external (government) requirements. Likewise, policies regarding leasing or depreciation may be strongly influenced by current tax regulations.

Regardless of the origin, formality, and nature of the policy, the key point to bear in mind is the valuable role policies can play in strategy implementation.

---

[8] These eight points are adapted from related discussions by Richard H. Buskirk, *Business and Administrative Policy* (New York: John Wiley & Sons, 1971), pp. 145–55; Thompson and Strickland, *Strategy Formulation*, pp. 377–79; Milton J. Alexander, *Business Strategy and Policy* (Atlanta: University Publications, 1983), chap. 3.

[9] Adapted from Robert G. Murdick, R. Carl Moor, Richard H. Eckhouse, and Thomas W. Zimmerer, *Business Policy: A Framework for Analysis* (Columbus, Ohio: Grid, 1984), p. 65.

Carefully constructed policies enhance strategy implementation in several ways. Obviously, it is imperative to examine existing policies and ensure the existence of policies necessary to guide and control operating activities consistent with current business and functional strategies. Ensuring communication of specific policies will help overcome resistance to strategic change and foster greater organizational commitment for successful strategy implementation.

Summary

The first concern in the implementation of a grand strategy is to operationalize that strategy throughout the organization. This chapter discussed three important tools to accomplish this: annual objectives, functional strategies, and policies.

Annual objectives guide implementation by translating long-term objectives into current targets. Annual objectives are derived from long-term objectives, but they differ in time frame, focus, specificity, and measurement. For annual objectives to be effective in strategy implementation, they must be integrated and coordinated. They must also be consistent, measurable, and prioritized.

Functional strategies are a second important tool for effective implementation of a grand strategy. Functional strategies are derived from business strategy and provide specific, immediate direction to key functional areas within the business in terms of what must be done to implement the grand strategy.

Policies provide another means of directing and controlling decisions and actions at operating levels of the firm in a manner consistent with business and functional strategies. Effective policies channel actions, behavior, decisions, and practices to promote strategic accomplishment.

While annual objectives, functional strategies, and policies represent the start of implementation, much more remains. The strategy must be institutionalized—must permeate the basic foundation of the company. The next chapter examines the institutionalization phase of strategy implementation.

Questions for Discussion

1. Explain the phrase "translate thought into action." How does this relate to the relationship between grand strategy and operating strategy? between long-term and short-term objectives?
2. How do functional strategies differ from corporate and business strategies?
3. What key concerns must be addressed by functional strategies in marketing? finance? POM? personnel?
4. How do policies aid strategy implementation? Illustrate your answer.
5. Illustrate a policy, an objective, and an operating strategy in your personal career strategy.
6. Why are annual objectives needed when long-term objectives are already available? What function do they serve?

Bibliography

Albrecht, Karl. *Successful Management by Objectives.* Englewood Cliffs, N.J.: Prentice-Hall, 1978.

Alexander, Milton J. *Business Strategy and Policy.* Atlanta: University Publications, 1983, chap. 3.

Fox, Harold. "A Framework for Functional Coordination." *Atlanta Economic Review,* November–December 1973, pp. 10–11.

Friend, J. K. "The Dynamics of Policy Changes." *Long-Range Planning,* February 1977, pp. 40–47.

Helfert, E. A. *Techniques of Financial Analysis,* 4th ed. Homewood, Ill.: Richard D. Irwin, 1978.

Heskett, James L. "Logistics—Essential to Strategy." *Harvard Business Review,* November–December 1977, pp. 85–96.

Hobbs, John, and Donald Heany. "Coupling Strategy to Operating Plans." *Harvard Business Review,* May–June 1977, pp. 119–26.

Hofer, Charles. "Conceptual Scheme for the Implementation of Organizational Strategy." Boston: Intercollegiate Case Clearing House 9–378–737, 1977.

Hrebiniak, Lawrence G., and William F. Joyce. *Implementing Strategy.* New York: Macmillan, 1984.

Ingrasia, Paul. "McDonald's Seeks to Boost Dinner Sales to Offset Surge in Costs and Competition." *The Wall Street Journal,* October 16, 1978.

Kotler, Phillip. *Marketing Management: Analysis, Planning, and Control,* 3rd ed. Englewood Cliffs, N.J.: Prentice-Hall, 1976.

MacMillan, Ian C. "Strategy and Flexibility in the Smaller Business." *Long-Range Planning,* June 1975, pp. 62–63.

McCarthy, E. J., and William D. Perreault, Jr. *Basic Marketing,* 8th ed. Homewood, Ill.: Richard D. Irwin, 1984.

Murdick, Robert G.; R. Carl Moor; Richard H. Eckhouse; and Thomas W. Zimmerer. *Business Policy: A Framework for Analysis.* Columbus, Ohio: Grid, 1984.

Peters, Thomas J., and R. H. Waterman, Jr. *In Search of Excellence.* New York: Harper & Row, 1982.

Shapiro, Benson P. "Can Marketing and Manufacturing Coexist?" *Harvard Business Review,* September–October 1977, pp. 105–14.

Shirley, R. C.; M. H. Peters; and A. I. El-Ansary. *Strategy and Policy Formation: A Multifunctional Orientation,* 2nd ed. New York: John Wiley & Sons, 1981.

Stolle, John F. "How to Manage Physical Distribution." *Harvard Business Review,* July–August 1967, p. 95.

Tellier, Richard. *Operations Management: Fundamental Concepts and Methods.* New York: Harper & Row, 1978.

Vancil, Richard. "Strategy Formulation in Complex Organizations." *Sloan Management Review,* Winter 1976, pp. 2–5.

Weston, J. F., and E. F. Brigham. *Essentials of Managerial Finance,* 7th ed. Hinsdale, Ill.: Dryden Press, 1985.

Chapter 11 Cohesion Case Illustration

Functional Strategies at Holiday Inns, Inc.

The cohesion case in Chapter 10 dealt with strategy analysis and choice. It concluded with the identification of Holiday Inns' choice of corporate-level and business-level strategies. But choice of strategies is not the end of the strategic management process. The strategies must be implemented–translated into appropriate organizational action. The first step in implementation is making the strategy operational. This requires identification of annual objectives, functional strategies, and key policies.

Illustrating the process for each business group at Holiday Inns, Inc., would require extensive text. Instead, this section will isolate one business group—hotels—to identify annual objectives, operating strategies, and policies as discussed in this chapter. It should be kept in mind, however, that a similar effort would be required for each business group at Holiday Inns to effectively implement corporatewide and business-level strategies.

Exhibit 1 highlights key long-term objectives and the business-level strategy (concentration and market development) the hotel group seeks to pursue in its five-year plan.

Annual objectives, functional strategies, and policies must be linked to the grand strategy and long-term objectives in Exhibit 1 if the strategy is to be effectively implemented. Exhibit 2 briefly summarizes key annual objectives and the functional strategies used to implement the hotel group's strategy.

Exhibit 1
Long-term objectives and business-level strategy in the hotel group

Long-term objectives (five years)	*Business-level strategy*
Net addition of 70,000 new rooms by 1988	Maintain and expand HI's leadership position in the lodging industry by providing the largest number of high-quality, moderately priced, full-service lodging facilities worldwide with emphasis on selective, company-owned expansion into multiuser-oriented properties and steady expansion through franchising with continuous updating or elimination of older properties.
217,000 new and extensively renovated rooms in HI system by 1988	
95 percent of all HI-owned properties in multiuser areas	
50 new franchised properties per year	
17 percent return on investment	
40 percent debt-to-capitalization ratio	Maintain the leadership position as the number one brand preference among lodging customers.
Best price/value ratio in industry	

Exhibit 2
Operationalizing the hotel business strategy: Annual objectives and functional strategies

Annual objectives	*Functional strategies*
Maintain a 70 percent systemwide occupancy rate annually.	*Marketing.* Clearly identify the typical HI guest, provide superior price/value lodging services desired, and ensure customer awareness that these services exist.
Clear identification of customer profile and changes in same on an annual basis.	
Maintain 33 percent or greater customer preference for Holiday Inns next year.	*Marketing research.* Make sure HI knows clearly who its customers are, what they want, and when and where to provide it via a continuous $1.2 million annually budgeted consumer research program.
Lead the industry in the number of reservations each year.	
Prebook over one third of systemwide room-nights each year.	*Advertising.* Extensive magazine and TV advertising with largest industry budget and most recognized campaign—No Excuses—in the industry.
Average 50 new franchised properties per year for the next three years.	*Sales.* Offer the most advanced reservation system in the industry.
Have 50 percent or higher of new franchised units built by existing franchises in 1988.	*Franchising.* Maintain high level of franchise satisfaction and gradual expansion of franchise units systemwide.
Have every managerial or supervisory employee at both company-owned and franchised properties trained at HI University by 1988.	*Personnel.* Ensure highly skilled operating personnel for all hotel properties. To accomplish this, HI University offers one- to three-week courses for all new hotel managers, assistant managers, food and beverage managers, front office, sales, maintenance, and housekeeping supervisors, with mandatory attendance.
35 percent debt-to-capitalization ratio next year.	
17 percent operating margin (before taxes) each year.	
17 percent average return on equity each year.	
Ensure that every property failing two consecutive inspections is out of the HI system within one year.	*Financial.* Maintain a financially sound capital structure relative to industry averages by using 50 percent internal and/or equity financing of company-owned expansion. Maintain profitability and stable growth by improving operating margins and a steady return on equity. Call the $9\frac{5}{8}$ percent convertible subordinate debentures as soon as the stock price exceeds $22 per share.
	Operations. Ensure high-quality, standardized, superior-service lodging facilities throughout the HI network. Emphasize quality control, particularly at existing facilities, and update services offered systemwide to match changing customer profile and needs.
	Quality control. At least one unannounced quality control inspection at every property annually. Also, achieve 50 percent of all systemwide rooms being either new or substantially renovated every five years.
	Up-to-date services. Continuous improvement of services/facilities offered to match customer preferences. For example: HI-NET satellite communications network for multicity meetings and more king-sized beds for increasing number of single and business guests.

Annual objectives help clarify long-term objectives. For example, Holiday Inns' annual objective of at least 50 new franchised properties feeds directly into the five-year objective of 70,000 rooms in the system. With the average property consisting of approximately 225 rooms, 50 properties would add 11,250 rooms per year. The balance needed would be just under 14,000 (or 2,750 per year), well within the stated preferences for 80 percent franchisee and 20 percent company-owned hotels in the system. Five years at this rate would mean 56,250 franchised rooms.

Functional strategies guide managers while attempting to ensure synergy with the grand strategy. For example, Holiday Inns' quality control strategy of two unannounced visits annually with expulsion from the system if both are failed clarifies for quality control managers, property managers, and franchisees the implicit priorities of the grand strategy.

Finally, organizational policies help guide strategy implementation at Holiday Inns. For example, Holiday Inns has a systemwide policy that every new managerial or supervisory employee at a hotel property—innkeeper, restaurant manager, etc.—must attend Holiday Inns University's course (usually two or three weeks) for that position. This policy helps instill the "Holiday Inns way" and ensures that service standards related to the firm's leadership strategy are consistently implemented at the day-to-day operating level.

This section has highlighted annual objectives, functional strategies, and policies in the hotel group. Are other necessary areas that were not mentioned here useful in implementing the hotel group's strategy? Apply the vehicles for operationalizing grand strategies to each of Holiday Inns' other business units.

12

Institutionalizing the Strategy: Structure, Leadership, and Culture

Annual objectives, functional strategies, and specific policies provide important means of communicating what must be done to implement the overall strategy. By translating long-term intentions into short-term guides to action, they make the strategy operational. But the strategy must also be *institutionalized*— permeate the very day-to-day life of the company—if it is to be effectively implemented. Three organizational elements provide the fundamental, long-term means for institutionalizing the firm's strategy: (1) structure, (2) leadership, and (3) culture.

In the first part of this chapter, the focus will be on organizational structure, the formal reporting relationships and responsibilities within a company. In the second part, focus will shift to the leadership of top management in the accomplishment of strategic objectives. The final part of this chapter will focus on organizational culture—the shared values and beliefs of organization members.

The chapter has three major aims: (1) to present structural alternatives, their advantages and disadvantages, and their role in strategy implementation; (2) to discuss the key dimensions of leadership that are important in strategy implementation; and (3) to discuss the concept of organizational culture, explain how it influences organizational life, and examine ways to manage the strategy–culture relationship.

Structural Considerations

An organization is necessary if strategic purpose is to be accomplished. Thus, organizational structure is a major priority in implementing a carefully formulated strategy. If activities, responsibilities, and interrelationships are not organized in a manner that is consistent with the strategy chosen, the structure is left to evolve on its own. If structure and strategy are not coordinated, the result will probably be inefficiencies, misdirection, and fragmented efforts.

The need for structure becomes apparent as a business evolves. In a small firm where one person manages current operations and plans for the future, organizational structure is relatively simple. Owner-managers have no organizational problem until their hurried trips to the plant, late-night sessions assimilating financial information for their CPA, and pressed calls on potential customers are inadequate to meet the demands of a business's increasing volume. As the magnitude of business activity increases, the need to subdivide activities, assign responsibilities, and provide for the integration and coordination of the new organizational parts becomes imperative. Thus, how to structure the organization to effectively execute the business's strategy has become a major concern.

What is structure? A basically simple concept: the division of tasks for efficiency and clarity of purpose, and coordination between the interdependent parts of the organization to ensure organizational effectiveness. Structure balances the need for specialization with the need for integration. It provides a formal means of decentralizing *and* centralizing consistent with the organizational and control needs of the strategy.

Structure is not the only means for getting "organized" to implement the strategy. Reward systems, planning procedures, and information and budgetary systems are other examples that should be employed. In the day-to-day implementation of strategy, these elements operate *inter*dependently with the formal organizational structure to shape how things are done. These other means may also be important, but it is through structure that strategists attempt to balance internal efficiency and overall effectiveness within a broader environment.

What are the structural choices? Five basic types are currently used by most business firms:

1. Simple.
2. Functional.
3. Divisional.
4. Strategic business unit.
5. Matrix.

Diversity and size create unique structural needs for each firm, but these five structural choices involve basic underlying features common to most business organizations.

Strategy in Action 12–1
Ford Motor Company Organizes the Taurus Success

In the early 1980s, amidst a recession in the automobile business, Ford executives finally realized that fuel economy was not the only reason why consumers were buying import cars. They realized that Ford car quality was not comparable to Japanese products, and they set out to correct the problem. Company managers decided to take radical steps in planning, production, and labor relations in order to build a new, higher-quality car. Ford executives backed up this commitment by investing $3 billion on the development of the new cars and decided that the new models would replace the company's most stable line—Ford LTD and Mercury Marquis—which sold 273,000 units in 1985.

The first thing Ford did was change its traditional structure for building new cars. Instead of the sequential five-year process (in which each component works in isolation without communication between each component), Ford adopted a "Program Management" approach whereby representatives from each unit—planning, design, engineering, and manufacturing—worked together as a group and took final responsibility for the car.

The group first set out to determine which were the world's best-designed and -engineered automotive features. The group determined the 400 "best in class features," and then it determined how they were designed, assembled, and manufactured. And 80 percent of those features were incorporated in the Taurus.

In order to determine consumer preferences, Ford launched its largest series of market studies ever. Interviews at grocery stores, schools, car washes, self-service filling stations, focus groups, and other settings led to the identification of 1,401 suggested features. Ford incorporated over 700 of these "wants" in the Taurus and Sable cars.

Finally, Ford did something no one had done in the U.S. auto industry. It asked assembly line workers for their advice before the car was designed. Numerous suggestions were incorporated in the design. The Taurus team also signed long-term contracts with suppliers and invited them to participate in planning sessions as well.

The approach paid off. By 1987, Taurus had become the top U.S. automobile. Ford has 100,000-plus backlogs in orders. Elated dealers say that customers—some of whom haven't set foot in a domestic producer's showroom for years—are content to wait patiently for two months or more for a Taurus or Sable.

Source: Based on "Ford's Idea Machine," *Newsweek*, November 24, 1986; and "How Ford Hit the Bull's-Eye with Taurus," *Business Week*, June 30, 1986.

Figure 12–1
Simple and functional organizational structures

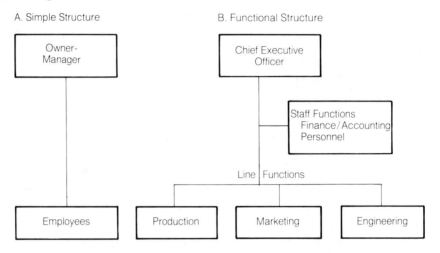

A. Simple Structure

```
┌──────────────┐
│   Owner-     │
│   Manager    │
└──────┬───────┘
       │
┌──────┴───────┐
│  Employees   │
└──────────────┘
```

B. Functional Structure

```
┌──────────────────┐
│ Chief Executive  │
│    Officer       │
└───────┬──────────┘
        │      ┌─────────────────────┐
        │      │ Staff Functions     │
        ├──────│ Finance/Accounting  │
        │      │ Personnel           │
        │      └─────────────────────┘
   Line │ Functions
   ┌────┴────┬──────────┬──────────┐
┌──────────┐┌──────────┐┌──────────┐
│Production││Marketing ││Engineering│
└──────────┘└──────────┘└──────────┘
```

Advantages	*Advantages*
1. Facilitates control of all the business's activities.	1. Efficiency through specialization.
2. Rapid decision making and ability to change with market signals.	2. Improved development of functional expertise.
3. Simple and informal motivation/reward/control systems.	3. Differentiates and delegates day-to-day operating decisions.
	4. Retains centralized control of strategic decisions.

Disadvantages	*Disadvantages*
1. Very demanding on the owner-manager.	1. Promotes narrow specialization and potential functional rivalry or conflict.
2. Increasingly inadequate as volume expands.	2. Difficulty in functional coordination and interfunctional decision making.
3. Does not facilitate development of future managers.	3. Staff-line conflict.
4. Tends to focus owner-manager on day-to-day matters and not on future strategy.	4. Limits internal development of general managers.

Structure is not an end in itself but rather a means to an end. It is a tool for managing the size and diversity of a business to enhance the success of its strategy. This section identifies structural options and examines the role of structure in strategy implementation.

Simple and Functional Organizational Structures

Figure 12–1 is a model of simple and functional organizational structures. In the smallest business enterprise, the simple structure prevails. All strategic and operating decisions are centralized in the owner-manager's domain. With the strategic concern primarily survival, and the likelihood that one bad decision could seriously threaten continued existence, this structure maximizes the owner's control. It also allows rapid response to product/market shifts and the ability to accommodate unique customer demands without coordination difficulties. Simple structures encourage employee involvement in more than one activity and are efficacious in businesses that serve a localized, simple product/market. This structure can be very demanding on the owner-manager and, as volume increases, can pressure the owner-manager to give increased attention to day-to-day concerns at the expense of time invested in strategic management activities.

Functional structure predominates in firms that concentrate on one or a few related products/markets. Functional structures group similar tasks and activities (usually production/operations, marketing, finance/accounting, research and development, personnel) as separate functional units within the organization. This specialization encourages greater efficiency and refinement of particular expertise and allows the firm to seek and foster distinct competencies in one or more functional areas. Expertise is critical to single-product/market companies and to firms that are vertically integrated. Strategy in Action 12–2 illustrates Crown, Cork and Seal's shift from a divisional structure to the centralized functional structure that was more consistent with its strategy. The functional structure allowed Crown, Cork and Seal to fine-tune its competitive advantage in understanding and responding to the technical needs of customers for hard-to-hold beverage containers. Strategy in Action 12–3 illustrates a similar move by Apple Computer Company.

The strategic challenge in the functional structure is effective coordination of the separate functional units. The narrow technical expertise sought through specialization can lead to limited perspectives and different priorities across different functional units. Specialists may not understand problems in other functional areas and may begin to see the firm's strategic issues primarily as "marketing" problems or "production" problems. This potential conflict makes the coordinating role of the chief executive critical if a strategy is to be effectively implemented using the functional structure. Integrating devices (such as project teams or planning committees) are frequently used in functionally organized businesses to enhance coordination and to facilitate understanding across functional areas.

Divisional Organizational Structure

When a firm diversifies its product/service lines, covers broad geographic areas, utilizes unrelated market channels, or begins to serve distinctly different customer groups, a functional structure rapidly becomes inadequate. For example, functional managers may wind up overseeing the production or marketing of numerous and different products or services. And coordination demands on top management are beyond the capacity of a functional structure. Some form of divisional structure is necessary to meet the coordination and decision-

Strategy in Action 12–2
From Divisional to Functional Structure at Crown, Cork and Seal

John Connelly became chief executive officer at Crown, Cork and Seal (CCS), a major company in the metal container industry, when CCS had fallen on hard times. In trying to compete on all fronts with much larger competitors like American Can and Continental Can, CCS had become overextended and was on the verge of bankruptcy. It had a product-oriented, divisional structure, similar to that of its larger competitors, which had been adopted to facilitate decentralized competition.

Connelly formulated a desperate retrenchment strategy to turn CCS around. The strategy focused CCS on the production of cans for hard-to-hold products, aerosol cans, and evolving international markets. The emphasis was to sell to large purchasers and provide extensive service in purchasers' canning operations. Thus, Connelly's strategy was to narrow CCS's scope to the most profitable product/market segments, build a service-related competitive advantage, and maintain tight fiscal control to overcome the imminent threat of bankruptcy.

Connelly quickly realized that the existing divisional structure was not consistent with the needs of the new strategy. Corporate-level overhead was both costly and unnecessary given the narrowed scope of CCS operations under the new strategy. To accommodate its narrow product/market scope and the need for tight fiscal control, Connelly reorganized CCS along functional lines, with three vice presidents—manufacturing, sales, and finance—reporting directly to him. This provided the centralized control needed for the retrenchment strategy and cut the managerial labor force by 24 percent. By making plant managers responsible for the profitability of their operations, he accommodated the strategy's need for tight control of geographically dispersed units within an efficient, streamlined functional structure.

CCS's strategy has been quite effective, with the company consistently leading the industry in return on equity, profitability, and return on investment. And the success of this strategy was clearly linked to an appropriate organizational structure and the strong, forceful leadership of John Connelly.

making requirements resulting from increased diversity and size. Such a structure is illustrated in Figure 12–2.

Days Inn's strategy to expand via new geographic markets in the 1970s required it to move from a functional structure to a divisional structure with three geographic divisions. Each division manager had major operating responsibility for company-owned properties in a particular geographic region of the United States. IBM has adopted a divisional organization based on different customer groups. For many years, Ford and General Motors adopted classic divisional structures organized by product groups.

A divisional structure allows corporate management to delegate authority for the strategic management of a distinct business entity. This can expedite critical decision making within each division in response to varied competitive environments, and it forces corporate management to concentrate on corporate-level strategic decisions. The semiautonomous divisions are usually given profit responsibility. The divisional structure thus seeks to facilitate accurate assessment of profit and loss.

Strategic Business Units

Some firms encounter difficulty in controlling their divisional operations as the diversity, size, and number of these units continues to increase. And corporate management may encounter difficulty in evaluating and controlling its numerous, often multi-industry divisions. Under these conditions, it may become necessary to add another layer of management to improve strategy implementation, promote synergy, and gain greater control over the diverse business interests. This can be accomplished by grouping various divisions (or parts of some divisions) in terms of common strategic elements. These groups,

Strategy in Action 12–3
Restructuring Apple Computer for the 1990s

Apple Computer, the pioneer of the personal computer industry, faced major challenges to its market position by the late 1980s from IBM and a host of others. Chairman John Sculley and the Apple management team adopted an aggressive strategy aimed at the business markets and centered on its MacIntosh line of computers.

To implement this strategy, Sculley and key Apple executives spent six weeks redesigning Apple's organizational structure. Below is the final memo from Sculley to all Apple employees and stockholders.

Continued on Page 364

Strategy in Action 12–3 (*continued*)

APPLE COMPUTER INTEROFFICE MEMO

Date: June 14, 1985
To: Board of directors
From: John Sculley
Subject: Company reorganization

The executive staff, key managers, and I have met almost daily over the past several weeks to develop a new organization. As you know, Apple has been a divisionalized company with several highly autonomous profit centers, which have acted almost like stand-alone companies:

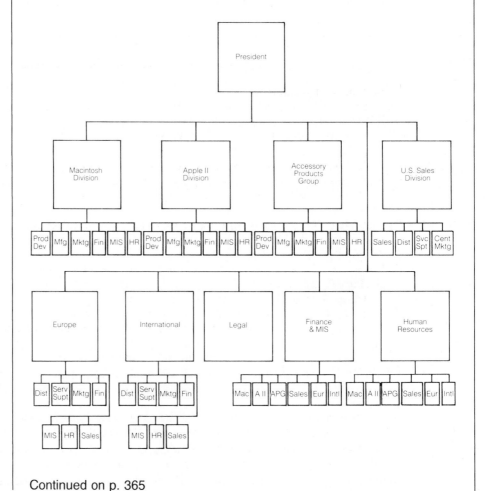

Continued on p. 365

Strategy in Action 12–3 (*concluded*)

I am pleased to announce a new structure, which is vastly simplified and organized around functions:

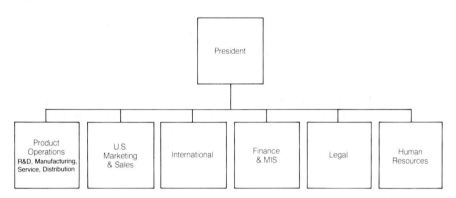

The new organization will reduce our break-even point. It should also simplify internal communication of company objectives and allow for greater consistency in their implementation.

We have selected leaders of each functional area who have had considerable experience in their specialty and in managing people.

In the process of moving to this new organization, we will reduce the number of jobs at Apple by 1,200. This is a painful and difficult decision. However, this streamlining will allow us to eliminate unnecessary job duplication in the divisional structure. (As shown in the organization chart, each division has had its own product development, manufacturing, finance, management information systems, and human resources staffs.)

The new organization should be more effective at providing products the marketplace wants and at providing them in a more timely manner. In addition to the greater effectiveness of the organization, it should also be more efficient—making us more profitable on lower sales than would have been the case with the former organization.

The reorganization will be costly in the short run. We take such a strong step only because it is clear that the new organization and management team will vastly improve Apple's probability for success as an industry leader.

Source: Apple Computer, Annual Report, 1985, p. 5.

commonly called strategic business units (SBUs), are usually structured based on the independent product/market segments served by the firm.

Figure 12–3 illustrates an SBU organizational structure. General Electric, faced with massive sales growth but little profit growth in the 1960s, was a pioneer in the SBU organization. GE restructured over 48 divisions into six

Figure 12–2
Divisional organization structure

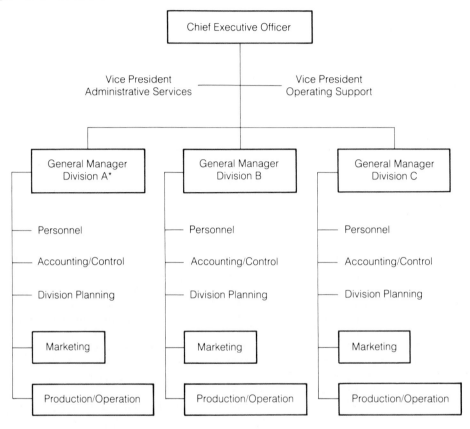

Advantages

1. Forces coordination and necessary authority down to the appropriate level for rapid response.
2. Places strategy development and implementation in closer proximity to the divisions' unique environment.
3. Frees chief executive officer for broader strategic decision making.
4. Sharply focuses accountability for performance.
5. Retains functional specialization within each division.
6. Good training ground for strategic managers.

Disadvantages

1. Fosters potentially dysfunctional competition for corporate-level resources.
2. Problem with the extent of authority given to division managers.
3. Potential for policy inconsistencies between divisions.
4. Problem of arriving at a method to distribute corporate overhead costs that is acceptable to different division managers with profit responsibility.

Figure 12–3
Strategic business unit organizational structure

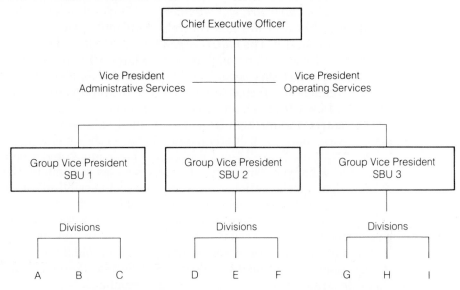

	Advantages		**Disadvantages**
1.	Improves coordination between divisions with similar strategic concerns and product/market environments.	1.	Places another layer of management between the divisions and corporate management.
2.	Tightens the strategic management and control of large, diverse business enterprises.	2.	Dysfunctional competition for corporate resources may increase.
3.	Facilitates distinct and in-depth business planning at the corporate and business levels.	3.	The role of the group vice president can be difficult to define.
4.	Channels accountability to distinct business units.	4.	Difficulty in defining the degree of autonomy for the group vice presidents and division managers.

(sector) SBUs. For example, three separate divisions making food preparation appliances were merged into a single SBU serving the housewares market.[1] General Foods, after originally defining SBUs along product lines (which served overlapping markets), restructured along menu lines. SBUs for breakfast foods, beverages, main meals, desserts, and pet foods allowed General Foods to target specific markets.[2]

---

[1] William K. Hall, "SBUs: Hot, New Topic in the Management of Diversification," *Business Horizons,* February 1978, p. 19.

[2] Ibid.

Matrix Organization

In large companies, increased diversity leads to numerous product and project efforts, *all with major strategic significance.* The result is a need for an organizational form that provides and controls skills and resources where and when they are most useful. The *matrix organization,* pioneered by firms like defense contractors, construction companies, and large CPA firms, has increasingly been used to meet this need. The list of companies now using some form of matrix organization includes Citicorp, Digital Equipment, General Electric, Shell Oil, Dow Chemical, and Texas Instruments.

The matrix organization provides for dual channels of authority, performance responsibility, evaluation, and control, as shown in Figure 12–4. Essentially, subordinates are assigned to both a basic functional area and a project or product manager. The matrix form is included to combine the advantages of functional specialization and product/project specialization. In theory, the matrix is a conflict resolution system through which strategic and operating priorities are negotiated, power is shared, and resources are allocated internally on a "strongest case for what is best overall for the unit" basis.[3]

The matrix structure increases the number of middle managers exercising general management responsibilities and broadens their exposure to organizationwide strategic concerns. Thus, it can accommodate a varied and changing project, product/market, or technology focus and can increase the efficient use of functional specialists who otherwise might be idle.

Citicorp used the matrix organization to implement an international expansion strategy focusing on both geographically different financial service requirements and at the same time targeting the multinational corporation market segment. The change was designed to increase the priority given to large, international organizations. The strategy ultimately gave Citicorp a better understanding of the worldwide financial needs and activities of multinational corporations than even the chief financial officers of these corporations had. Matrix structure was a strategic tool that allowed Citicorp to gain a competitive advantage with this important segment.[4]

While the matrix structure is easy to design, it is difficult to implement. Dual chains of command challenge fundamental organizational orientations. Negotiating shared responsibilities, use of resources, and priorities can create misunderstanding or confusion among subordinates. Strategy in Action 12–4 illustrates the varied reactions in Shell Oil's move to a matrix structure.

To overcome the deficiencies that might be associated with a permanent matrix structure, some firms are using a "temporary" or "flexible" *overlay structure* to accomplish a particular strategic task. This approach, used recently

---

[3] Arthur A. Thompson, Jr., and A. J. Strickland III, *Strategy Formulation and Implementation* (Plano, Tex.: Business Publications, 1983), p. 335.

[4] Paul J. Stonich, *Implementing Strategy* (Cambridge, Mass.: Ballinger, 1982), p. 60.

Figure 12–4
Matrix organizational structure

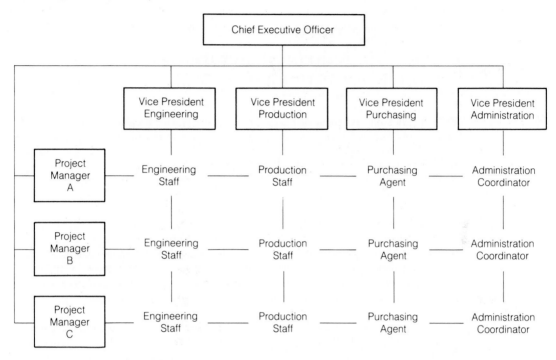

Advantages	Disadvantages
1. Accommodates a wide variety of project-oriented business activity.	1. Dual accountability can create confusion and contradictory policies.
2. Good training ground for strategic managers.	2. Necessitates tremendous horizontal and vertical coordination.
3. Maximizes efficient use of functional managers.	
4. Fosters creativity and multiple sources of diversity.	
5. Broader middle-management exposure to strategic issues for the business.	

by firms like General Motors, IBM, and Texas Instruments, is meant to take *temporary* advantage of a matrix-type team while preserving the shape and spirit of the underlying divisional structure.[5] Thus, the basic idea of the matrix structure, to *simplify and amplify the focus of resources on a narrow but strategically important product, project, or market,* appears to be an important structural alternative within large, diverse organizations.

---

[5] Robert H. Waterman, Jr., T. J. Peters, and J. R. Phillips, "Structure Is Not Organization," *Business Horizons,* June 1980, p. 20.

Strategy in Action 12–4
Shell Oil: Matrix Structure to Implement Strategy

Fifteen miles off the coast of Louisiana, a giant platform called Cognac rattles and shakes under the ceaseless activity. Hard-hatted roughnecks are spudding a new well, sending drilling bits twisting 1,200 feet through the choppy waters to reach rich reservoirs of crude oil beneath the Gulf of Mexico's floor. Meanwhile, 60 other wells drilled from the massive midsea factory shoot crude through a ganglion of pipe to onshore refineries. Everything about the Cognac field is imposing. It represents a capital investment of about $800 million, and every 24 hours it gushes out an awesome return: 16,000 barrels of oil worth $576,000 at current prices. Cognac, a mere blip on the Shell balance sheets, is a microcosmic example of the stupefying risks and rewards of the modern oil business. Shell, which analysts consider one of the best-run companies in the industry, employs a strategy different from that of competitors. Shell's corporate strategy focuses almost exclusively on the development of energy resources and petrochemicals.

Managing by Matrix.   To make and implement the far-reaching decisions this strategy requires, Shell management relies on a matrix system to structure its organization. Like most large corporations, Shell has managers who report to general managers who report to vice presidents. But it also has a network of interlevel, interdivisional teams that try to coordinate the activities of everyone from petroleum engineers to public relations specialists. As a result, more employees participate in decision making and understand the reasons for policies before they are dictated. And in theory, at least, the system helps guard against redundant activities. Instead of maintaining separate research projects for exploration and production, oil products, and chemicals, Shell has a single research division that serves the entire company.

The matrix can be exasperating at times. "We meet ourselves to death," complains Ken Spauling, manager of chemical-products plans. But it reinforces Shell's policy of delegating responsibility to "the level of maximum knowledge." J. B. Henderson, the president of Shell Chemical Co., for instance, doesn't decide whether or not to buy a certain cargo of crude oil for his facilities. "I can't make the decision intelligently," he says. "Someone in the buying department can."

Source: "Inside the Shell Oil Company," *Newsweek,* June 15, 1981, pp. 72–77. Condensed from *Newsweek.*

The Role of Structure: Linking Structure to Strategy

Which structure is best? Considerable research has been done on this question, and the collective answer is that it depends on the strategy of the firm. The structural design ties together key activities and resources of the firm. Therefore, it must be closely aligned with the needs/demands of the firm's strategy.

Alfred Chandler provided a landmark study in understanding the choice of structure as a function of strategy.[6] Chandler studied 70 large corporations over an extended time period and found a common strategy–structure sequence:

1. Choice of a new strategy.
2. Emergence of administrative problems; decline in performance.
3. A shift to an organizational structure more in line with the strategy's needs.
4. Improved profitability and strategy execution.

General Electric's recent history supports Chandler's thesis. Operating with a simple divisional structure in the late 1950s, GE embarked on a broad diversification strategy. In the 1960s, GE experienced impressive sales growth. However, GE also experienced administrative difficulties in trying to control and improve the corresponding lack of increase in profitability. In the early 1970s, GE executives redesigned its organizational structure to accommodate the administrative needs of strategy (ultimately choosing the strategic business unit structure), subsequently improving profitability of and control over the diversification strategy.

Chandler's research and the GE example allow us to make four important observations. First, all forms of organizational structure are not equally effective in implementing a strategy. Second, structures seem to have a life of their own, particularly in larger organizations. As a result, the need for immediate and radical changes in structure is not immediately perceived. Once the need is perceived, lagging performance may be necessary before politically sensitive structure is changed or organizational power redistributed. Third, sheer growth can make restructuring necessary. Finally, as firms diversify into numerous related or unrelated products and markets, structural change appears to be essential if the firm is to perform effectively.

Research on corporate stages of development provides further understanding of the structure–strategy relationship.[7] After studying numerous business firms, these researchers concluded that companies move through several stages

---

[6] Alfred D. Chandler, *Strategy and Structure* (Cambridge, Mass.: MIT Press, 1962).

[7] Several authors have dealt with stages of development. Some of the more frequently cited include J. T. Cannon, *Business Strategy and Policy* (New York: Harcourt Brace Jovanovich, 1968), pp. 525–28; Malcomb Salter, "Stages of Corporate Development," *Journal of Business Policy* 1, no. 1 (1970), pp. 23–37; Bruce Scott, "Stages of Corporate Development—Parts I and II," mimeographed (Boston: Harvard Business School, 1970); and Donald H. Thain, "Stages of Corporate Development," *Business Quarterly*, Winter 1969, pp. 33–45.

Figure 12–5
Corporate stages of development

Stage	Characteristics of the firm	Typical structure
I	Simple, small business. Offering one product/service or one line of products/services to a small, distinct local or regionalized market.	Simple to functional
II	Singular or closely related line of products/services but to a larger and sometimes more diverse market (geography, channels, or customers).	Functional to divisional
III	Expanded but related lines of products/services to diverse, large markets.	Divisional to matrix
IV	Diverse, unrelated lines of products/services to large, diverse markets.	Divisional to SBUs

as size and diversity increase. Figure 12–5 is a synthesis of these stage-of-development theories. The figure shows that a firm moves through each stage, size, diversity, and competitive environment change.

To compete effectively at different stages requires, among other things, different structures. Again, the choice of structure appears contingent on the strategy of the firm in terms of size, diversity of the products/services offered, and markets served. Two firms in the metal container industry help illustrate this point. Continental Can, the industry leader, employs a divisional structure. This is used to implement a diversification strategy intended to serve virtually every user of metal containers, as well as to compete in unrelated markets like forest products. Crown, Cork and Seal, the industry's fourth largest company, employs a modified functional structure to serve a limited domestic and international market of users with specialized container needs. Both firms are successful. Both derive their greatest revenues from the same industry. But each employs a different organizational structure because their strategies (narrow versus broad product/market scope) are different.

The choice of structure must be determined by the firm's strategy. And the structure must segment key activities and/or strategic operating units to improve efficiency through specialization, response to a competitive environment, and freedom to act. At the same time, the structure must effectively integrate and coordinate these activities and units to accommodate interdependence of activities and overall control. The choice of structure reflects strategy in terms of the firm's (1) size, (2) product/service diversity, (3) competitive environment and volatility, (4) internal political considerations, and (5) information/coordination needs for each component.

Even a change in strategy, with its accompanying alteration of administrative needs, does not lead to an immediate change in structure. The research of Chandler and others suggests that commitment to a structure lingers even when it's become inappropriate for a current strategy.[8] Whether this is due

---

[8] Chandler, *Strategy and Structure;* and J. R. Galbraith and D. A. Nathanson, *Strategy Implementation: The Role of Structure and Process* (St. Paul, Minn.: West Publishing, 1978).

Strategy in Action 12–5
Leadership Practices at Intel Corporation

Andrew Grove, founder and president of Intel Corporation, has made a conscious effort to foster informality in the management and decision-making practices of the highly successful microelectronics company he started in 1968. Visible examples of informality are many: no reserved parking, no executive dining rooms, no corporate jets (*everyone* flies coach), and rather than offices every manager from the chairman of the board and president on down operates out of a maze of cubicles separated by 5-foot-high sound-proofed partitions. A journalist, puzzled by this, once asked Andrew Grove if his company's emphasis on visible signs of egalitarianism was just so much affectation. Grove replied that it was not affectation but a matter of survival and offered the following explanation:

> In traditional industries where the chain of command is precisely defined, a person making a certain kind of decision is a person occupying a particular position on an organization chart. As the saying goes, authority (to make decisions) goes with responsibility (position in the management hierarchy). In businesses that deal mostly with information and know-how, however, a manager has to cope with a new phenomenon. Here a rapid divergence develops between power based on position and power based on knowledge. The divergence occurs because the base of knowledge that constitutes the foundation of the business changes rapidly.
>
> What do I mean? When someone graduates from college with a technical education, at that time and for the next several years that person will be very up-to-date in the technology of the time. Hence, he possesses a good deal of knowledge-based power in the organization that hires him. If he does well, he will be promoted, and as the years pass his position power will grow. At the same time, his intimate familiarity with current technology will fade. Put another way, even if today's veteran manager was once an outstanding engineer, he is not now the technical expert he once was. At high-technology firms, we managers get a little more obsolete every day.
>
> So a business like ours has to employ a management process unlike that used in more conventional industries. If we had people at the top making all the decisions, then these decisions would be made by those unfamiliar with the technology of the day. In general, the faster the change in the know-how on which a business depends, the greater the divergence between knowledge and position power is likely to be.
>
> Since our business depends on what it knows to survive, we mix "knowledge-power people" with "position-power people" daily, so that together they make the decisions that will affect us for years to come. We

Continued on Page 374

Strategy in Action 12–5 (*concluded*)

at Intel frequently ask junior members of the organization to participate jointly in a decision-making meeting with senior managers. This only works if everybody at the meeting voices opinions and beliefs as equals, forgetting or ignoring status differentials. And it is much easier to achieve this if the organization doesn't separate its senior and junior people with limousines, plush offices, and private dining rooms. Status symbols do not promote the flow of ideas, facts, and points of view. So while our egalitarian environment may appear to be a matter of style, it is really a matter of necessity, a matter of long-term survival.

This idea of mixing knowledge-based and position-based power underlines the quality circle movement and the participative management concept. The real benefit of the quality circle movement, the participative management concept, and our informality at work is not cosmetic, nor is it really to make people feel better (although that is not a bad consequence, either). It is to team up people with hands-on knowledge with those in positions of power to create the best solutions in the interest of both.

Source: "Breaking the Chains of Command," *Newsweek,* October 3, 1983, p. 23. Condensed from *Newsweek.* Copyright 1983, by Newsweek, Inc. All rights reserved. Reprinted by permission.

to inertia, organizational politics, or a realistic assessment of the relative costs of immediate structural change, historical evidence suggests that the existing structure will be maintained and not radically redesigned until a strategy's profitability is increasingly disproportionate with increasing sales.[9]

Organizational Leadership

While organizational structure provides the overall framework for strategy implementation, it is not in itself sufficient to ensure successful execution. Within the organizational structure, individuals, groups, and units are the mechanisms of organizational action. And the effectiveness of their actions is a major determinant of successful implementation. In this context, two basic factors encourage or discourage effective action—leadership and culture.[10] This section examines the leadership dimension as a key element in strategy implementation. In the next section, the importance of organizational culture in effectively executing strategy will be illustrated and discussed.

---

[9] C. W. Hofer, E. A. Murray, Jr., R. Charan, and R. A. Pitts, *Strategic Management* (St. Paul, Minn.: West Publishing, 1984), p. 20.

[10] Leadership and organizational culture are interdependent phenomena. Each aspect of leadership ultimately helps shape organizational culture. Conversely, the prevailing organizational culture can profoundly influence a leader's effectiveness. The richness of this interdependence will become apparent. The topics are addressed in separate sections because it is important to develop an appreciation of the role of each in strategy implementation. Strategy in Action 12–5 gives a vivid illustration of the interdependence of leadership, cultural, and structural considerations in strategy implementation.

Leadership, while seemingly vague and esoteric, is an essential element in effective strategy implementation. And two leadership issues are of fundamental importance here: (1) the role of the chief executive officer (CEO) and (2) the assignment of key managers.

Role of the CEO

The chief executive officer is the catalyst in strategic management. This individual is most closely identified with and ultimately accountable for a strategy's success. In most firms, particularly larger ones, CEOs spend up to 80 percent of their time developing and guiding strategy.

The nature of the CEO's role is both *symbolic* and *substantive* in strategy implementation. First, the CEO is a symbol of the new strategy. This individual's actions and the perceived seriousness of his or her commitment to a chosen strategy, particularly if the strategy represents a major change, exert a significant influence on the intensity of subordinate managers' commitment to implementation. Lee Iaccoca's highly visible role in the early 1980s as spokesperson for the "New Chrysler Corporation" on television, in Chrysler factories and offices, and before securities analysts was intended to provide a strong symbol that Chrysler's desperate turnaround strategy could work.

Second, the firm's mission, strategy, and key long-term objectives are strongly influenced by the personal goals and values of its CEO. To the extent that the CEO invests time and personal values in the chosen strategy, he or she represents an important source for clarification, guidance, and adjustment during implementation.

Major changes in strategy are often preceded or quickly followed by a change in CEO. The timing suggests that different strategies require different CEOs if they are to succeed. The resignation of L. M. Clymer as CEO at Holiday Inns clearly illustrates this point. Holiday Inns' executive group was convinced that casinos provide a key growth area for the company. Clymer chose to resign because his personal values and perception of what Holiday Inns should be were not consistent with this change. Research has concluded that a successful turnaround strategy "will require almost without exception either a change in top management or a substantial change in the behavior of the existing management team."[11] Clearly, successful strategy implementation is directly linked to the unique characteristics, orientation, and actions of the CEO.

Assignment of Key Managers

A major concern of top management in implementing a strategy, particularly if it involves a major change, is that the right managers are in the right

---

[11] Charles W. Hofer, "Turnaround Strategies," *Journal of Business Strategy* 1, no. 1 (1980), p. 25.

positions for the new strategy. Of all the tools for ensuring successful implementation, this is the one CEOs mention first. Confidence in the individuals occupying pivotal managerial positions is directly and positively correlated with top-management expectations that a strategy can be successfully executed.

This confidence is based on the answers to two fundamental questions:

1. Who holds the current leadership positions that are especially critical to strategy execution?

2. Do they have the right characteristics to ensure that the strategy will be effectively implemented?[12]

What characteristics are most important in this context? It would be impossible to specify this precisely, but probable characteristics include: (1) ability and education, (2) previous track record and experience, and (3) personality and temperament.[13] These, combined with gut feeling and top managers' confidence in the individual, provide the basis for this key decision.

Recently, numerous attempts have been made to match "preferred" managerial characteristics with different grand strategies.[14] These efforts are meant to capsulize, for example, the behavioral characteristics appropriate for a manager responsible for implementing an "invest to grow" strategy in contrast to those for a manager implementing a "harvest" strategy. Despite widespread theoretical discussion of this idea, two recent studies covering a broad sample of companies did not find a single firm that matched managerial characteristics to strategic mission in a formal manner. However, they did find several firms addressing such considerations in an informal, intuitive manner.[15] The following comment summarizes these findings:

> Despite the near unanimity of belief that, for effective implementation, different strategies require different skills . . . many corporate executives avoid too rigid an approach to matching managerial characteristics and strategy [for three reasons]: (1) exposure to and experience at managing different kinds of strategies and businesses is viewed as an essential component of managerial development; (2) too rigid a differentiation is viewed as much more likely to result in some managers being typecast as "good builders" and some others as "good harvesters," thereby creating motivational problems for the latter; and (3) a "perfect match" between managerial characteristics and strategy is viewed as more likely to

---

[12] William F. Glueck, *Business Policy and Strategic Management* (New York: McGraw-Hill, 1980), pp. 306–7.

[13] Ibid., p. 307.

[14] See, for example, J. G. Wisseman, H. W. Van der Pol, and H. M. Messer, "Strategic Management Archetypes," *Strategic Management Journal* 1, no. 1 (1980), pp. 37–45; William F. Glueck and Lawrence R. Jauch, *Strategic Management and Business Policy* (New York: McGraw-Hill, 1984), p. 365; Boris Yavitz and William H. Newman, *Strategy in Action* (New York: Free Press, 1982), p. 167; and "Wanted, a Manager to Fit Each Strategy," *Business Week*, February 25, 1980, p. 166.

[15] Anil K. Gupta and V. Govindarajan, "Build, Hold, Harvest: Converting Strategic Intentions into Reality," *Journal of Business Strategy*, Winter 1984, p. 41; Peter Lorange, "The Human Resource Dimension in the Strategic Planning Process," mimeographed (Cambridge, Mass.: Sloan School, MIT, 1983), p. 13.

result in overcommitment [or] self-fulfilling prophecies (a harvester becoming *only* a harvester) as compared with a situation where there was some mismatch.[16]

One practical consideration in making key managerial assignments when implementing strategy is whether to emphasize current (or promotable) executives or bring in new personnel. This is obviously a difficult, sensitive, and strategic issue. Figure 12–6 highlights major advantages and disadvantages associated with either alternative.

While key advantages and disadvantages can be clearly outlined, actual assignment varies with the situation and the decision maker. Two fundamental aspects of the strategic situation strongly influence the managerial assignment decision: (1) the changes required to implement the new strategy and (2) the effectiveness of past organizational performance. Figure 12–7 and the following discussion illustrate how these aspects might affect managerial assignments.

Turnover Situation. A company's performance has been ineffective for several years. The new strategy and the organizational requirements necessary to implement it represent major changes from the "way things have been done in the past." In this situation, the advantages of bringing in outside managers can be maximized. Because the experience necessary to implement the new strategy is unavailable or ineffective internally, outsiders are sought. Current executives may react defensively when faced with major changes, while outsiders generally undertake a new assignment with a positive commitment to the new direction and are not encumbered by internal commitments to people. Widespread changes will also be taken more seriously by employees if outsiders are brought in who possess skills that match the changes and supplement well-known inadequacies in current management.

Chrysler Corporation's situation in the early 1980s is a case in point. Following several years of ineffective, declining performance, Chrysler's board went outside the organization to recruit a new CEO (Lee Iaccoca) who was capable of redirecting Chrysler into a small-car-oriented strategy. Iacocca eventually brought in outsiders to fill over 80 percent of Chrysler's top-management positions because they had the new skills and commitment necessary to quickly and decisively implement Chrysler's new strategy.

Selective Blend. A different emphasis in key managerial assignments is needed when a company's new strategy requires major changes but the need for change is not based on poor performance. The company has been an effective performer with its previous strategy, yet changing market, competitive, technological, or other environmental factors necessitate a change in the company's strategic posture. IBM's move into the personal computer industry is a good illustration.

---

[16] Gupta and Govindarajan, "Build, Hold, Harvest," p. 41.

Figure 12–6
Key considerations in managerial assignments to implement strategy

	Advantages	Disadvantages
Using existing executives to implement a new strategy	Already know key people, practices, and conditions Personal qualities better known and understood by associates Have established relationships with peers, subordinates, suppliers, buyers, etc. Symbolizes organizational commitment to individual careers	Less adaptable to major strategic changes because of knowledge, attitudes, and values Past commitments may hamper hard decisions required in executing a new strategy Less ability to become inspired and credibly convey the need for change
Bringing in outsiders to implement a new strategy	Outsider may already believe in and have "lived" the new strategy. Outsider is unemcumbered by internal commitments to people. Outsider comes to the new assignment with heightened commitment and enthusiasm. Bringing in an outsider can send powerful signals throughout the organization that change is expected.	Often costly, both in terms of compensation and "learning-to-work-together" time Candidates suitable in all respects (i.e., exact experience) may not be available, leading to compromise choices Uncertainty in selecting the right person The "morale" costs when an outsider takes a job several insiders wanted "What to do with poor ol' Fred" problem

Source: Adapted from Boris Yavitz and William H. Newman, *Strategy in Action* (New York: Free Press, 1982), chap. 10; and Paul J. Stonich, *Implementing Strategy* (Cambridge, Mass.: Ballinger, 1982), chap. 4.

The advantages and disadvantages associated with either source of managerial talent are applicable in this situation. Using existing executives rewards past effectiveness and takes advantage of the knowledge of "people practices" and relationships necessary to integrate changes into a previously successful system. It also reinforces the company's commitment to individual careers

Figure 12–7
Four managerial assignment situations

		Effective	Ineffective
Changes required to implement the new strategy	**Many**	**Selective blend** *Current executives* via promotion and transfer where skills match new roles; otherwise, seek skills and experience via *outsiders*	**Turnover** *Outsiders* should be a high priority to provide new skills, motivation, and enthusiasm.
	Few	**Stability** *Current executives* and internal promotions should be a major emphasis in order to reward, retain, and develop managerial talent.	**Reorientation** *Outsiders* are important to replace weaknesses and "communication seriousness." *Current executives* should be a priority where possible via promotion, transfer, or role clarification.

Assessment of past organizational performance

and facilitates executive development. On the other hand, the outsider brings all the advantages described in Figure 12–6, especially skill and experience in one or more of the key change areas. But there is a critical difference— the past performance of this company. Thus, the advantage of the outsider as a "change agent" is much less important than his or her value as a provider of the key skills needed to *supplement* current management talent. Emphasis in this situation is a selective blend using current or promotable executives while objectively incorporating outsiders to provide needed knowledge and skill that is not available internally. Strategy in Action 12–6 illustrates the planned change of managers at successful McGraw-Hill to successfully institutionalize a very different strategic direction.

IBM's move into personal computers required major changes in the firm's past, highly successful market development strategy. IBM needed to sell and service a small computer primarily for numerous individual and small-business users. This was quite different than what was needed to lease or sell expensive computer systems and office equipment to large public and private organizations. IBM used existing talent to implement this small-computer strategy. Use of outsiders was primarily related to the development of direct retail outlets, a sales approach not used with past IBM products but critical to ensure IBM's long-term, profitable access to a broad, fragmented, and individualized market. So, IBM sought to selectively blend its "inside/outside" emphasis

Strategy in Action 12–6
Changing Management and Approach at McGraw-Hill

It seems like McGraw-Hill set out to prove that even in healthy organizations, change is often necessary. Even though the company had grown by a compounded rate of 17 percent, CEO Joseph Dionne set out to reorganize and refocus the company for the 1990s with the help of Harvard Business School professor Micheal Porter.

A central concern was to shift the assessment of management from quarterly results to a long-term vision. Dionne felt that with the company's old organization and style, the company was stifling the development of new products and that it would soon slow the company's growth. So, Dionne and Porter conceived of McGraw-Hill as a confederation of 19 market focus groups instead of a company organized around separate book, magazine, and statistical services divisions.

Each of the 19 market groups follows a specific industry like construction, transportation, and health care. Instead of gathering information for a single publication, the data goes into a giant database, which in turn can be drawn on by all to produce new products like specialty print publications or on-line services for personal computers.

While the virtual reconfiguration of McGraw-Hill's organization and the way it does business is exciting, it has thrown the company into turmoil. A host of managers have left the company, particularly managers from the publications divisions bitter at what they believe is mismanagement of the publications sector in order to make room for the payoff of electronics. Also hit with desertions is the econometrics forecasting group, Data Resources, which the company bought in 1979. Twenty percent of DR's executives have left since the reorganization was announced.

While the turnover and turmoil is difficult, top management at McGraw-Hill feels that most of these executives had grown with one media and that they were neither prepared nor receptive to the new technologies in information. They perceive the act of precipitating this turmoil as a proactive, astute decision that lets the company shape its destiny rather than waiting for the sales and earning declines that would have caused the same result—but with McGraw-Hill on the reacting, catch-up end of the equation.

The 19 market focus groups will have independence to chart their own course and make their own deals. The company is expecting revenues to exceed $1.5 billion in 1990 and reach $2.5 billion by 1995. Many remaining executives are unsure how much electronics can do for McGraw-Hill's big profit centers—magazines and books. Only time will tell whether these radical changes in the status quo will be effective.

Source: Adapted from "Marketing Is the Message at McGraw-Hill," *Fortune*, February 17, 1986, p. 27.

in new managerial assignments consistent with the key advantages of each approach.

Stability.   A stability situation is generally attractive in managing executive assignments. The company's past performance has been effective, and implementation requires only minor deviation from "the ways things were done in the past." The advantages associated with using current and promotable existing executives are maximized. These executives are familiar with people, practices, and the ways to get things done. They have established relationships with suppliers, buyers, peers, and subordinates. Past performance indicates that the managers have achieved assigned results. This is recognized through assignment to new responsibilities associated with the new strategy. In this situation, junior-level managers can be developed because an effective performance environment exists within which they will observe and acquire managerial and technical skills. The risk in this situation is that there are fewer opportunities to advance talented personnel who contributed to past effectiveness because change was minor and retaining the current executive teams was emphasized.

Wendy's hamburger chain was a firm facing this situation in the early 1980s. The firm had quite effectively carved a profitable niche in the fast-food industry. Its new strategy for the 1980s sought to emphasize three things: market penetration, product development, and diversification via Sister's Chicken 'n Biscuits. While this was an aggressive new strategy, the changes required were relatively minor: market penetration necessitated a slight shift in Wendy's franchising approach; product development efforts were well underway; and the Sister's chicken implementation plan would be modeled exactly after the Wendy's approach in the hamburger segment. Wendy's assignment of managerial positions emphasized the use of current management. The Sister's venture was seen as an ideal way to open up career opportunities for talented operating personnel. By 1984, 30 of the 37 members of Wendy's executive committee (its "top-management team") were new, but only 2 of the 30 new members came from outside the Wendy's organization.

Reorientation.   Some companies face a situation in which the fundamental changes required to implement a new strategy are minor—the basic strategy appears appropriate—yet past performance has been ineffective. With IBM at the top of the personal computer market in early 1984, the former leader, Apple, was in just such a situation. Its new strategy was an attempt to refocus on its formerly successful product development strategy by making key (yet relative few) organizational changes. For example, Steven Jobs (Apple's co-founder) sought to reinvigorate R&D efforts by personal involvement. Key managerial assignments in marketing and finance were filled from outside the company to systematically reorient Apple's competitive posture against IBM. Apple added a new CEO from outside the organization to oversee this effort. At the same time, Apple sought to transfer and clarify the roles of several current managers, particularly younger managers with product development skills, to aid in reinvigorating Apple's technological reputation.

Apple is an example of a company with a sound strategy but ineffective implementation. A key issue in this context is whether the ineffectiveness can be linked to inadequate skills or capabilities of the management team. If such inadequacies are found, outsiders could play a key role in reorienting or refocusing organizational efforts toward an otherwise sound strategy.

Organizational Culture[17]

Organizational culture is the set of important assumptions (often unstated) that members of an organization share in common. Every organization has its own culture. Organizational culture is similar to an individual's personality—an intangible yet ever-present theme that provides meaning, direction, and the basis for action. Much as personality influences the behavior of an individual, shared assumptions (beliefs and values) among members of an organization set a pattern for activities, opinions, and actions within that firm. The purpose of the next several sections is to help you first gain an understanding of the concept of culture, then ways to identify a company's culture, and finally an analytical framework for managing the strategy–culture relationship.

Important Assumptions.   We have just defined culture as that set of important assumptions that organization members share. The *important* assumptions are sufficiently central to the life of the organization so as to have a major impact on it. Members of an organization hold two principal types of assumptions in common: beliefs and values.

Beliefs include basic assumptions about the world and how it actually works. They derive from personal experience and are reinforced by it. Individuals also rely to some degree on the judgment and expertise of others they trust or can identify with to help them decide what to believe or not to believe. Examples of beliefs include "Money is the most powerful motivator" or "Most people follow the leader."

Values are basic assumptions about which ideals are desirable or worth striving for. They derive from personal experience and identification with those who have had an important influence on one's personal development since early childhood. Values represent preferences for ultimate end-states, such as striving for success or avoiding debt at all costs.

It is important to note that these definitions do not refer to what people *say* are their beliefs and values but rather to the beliefs and values they *actually hold, whether consciously or otherwise.* To illustrate, an important

---

[17] This section draws heavily on the outstanding work by Vijay Sathe of the Harvard Business School. The primary reference in compiling this work is Vijay Sathe, *Culture and Related Corporate Realities* (Homewood, Ill.: Richard D. Irwin, 1985).

professional assumption for a lawyer is client confidentiality. This value is taken for granted, and a lawyer may become conscious of it only if it is challenged or violated. For example, a client might question the lawyer about it, or a fellow lawyer might violate it, either of which would draw attention to this important value. Even after drawing attention to it, this value remains present and potent. It is usually hard to change, as are other beliefs and values that the individual actually holds, consciously (openly) or otherwise.

With this clarification of culture as assumptions involving personal beliefs and values, the meaning of *shared* in the definition of culture can be made more explicit.

Shared Assumptions: Internalized Beliefs and Values that Organizational Members Hold in Common.   A member of an organization can simply be aware of the organization's beliefs and values without sharing them in a personally significant way. Values and beliefs have more personal meaning if an individual complies with the set of values as a guide to appropriate behavior in the organization. The individual becomes fundamentally committed to the organization's beliefs and values when he or she internalizes them, that is, when the person comes to hold them as personal beliefs and values. In this case, the corresponding behavior is *intrinsically rewarding* for the individual—the person derives personal satisfaction from what he or she does in the organization because it is congruent with corresponding personal beliefs and values. *The assumptions become shared assumptions through the process of internalization by individual members of an organization.* And these shared, internalized beliefs and values shape the content and strength of an organization's culture.

Content of Culture.   The content of an organization's culture ultimately derives from three sources. First, the influence of the business environment in general, and the industry in particular, is an important determinant of shared assumptions. For example, companies in industries characterized by rapid technological change, such as computers and electronics companies, normally have cultures that strongly value innovation. Second, founders, leaders, and organizational employees bring a pattern of assumptions with them when they join the organization. These assumptions often depend on these individuals' own experiences in the culture of the national, regional, ethnic, religious, occupational, and professional communities from which they came. Third, the actual experience people in the organization have had in working out solutions for coping with the basic problems the organization encounters molds shared assumptions. For example, two companies may each value cooperation and internal competition, but one company may emphasize cooperation more in decision making and resource allocation, while internal competition may predominate in the other. J. C. Penney is a good example of the former, while PepsiCo is a good example of the latter. The cultures of these two companies consequently have quite different content, even though some of their basic assumptions about cooperation and internal competition are the same.

Taken together, these three principle sources suggest that the content of culture derives from a combination of prior assumptions and new learning experiences. Several important implications follow from this understanding of culture's content. First, culture is subject to development and change due to the learning going on in the organization as it copes with its problems of external adaptation and internal integration. Second, because existing basic assumptions do not change readily, changing culture is normally incremental and evolutionary rather than radical and revolutionary. In other words, culture is fairly resistant to major change, especially in the short run. Third, because its roots are in the cultures of the wider communities from which the people in the organization come, the content of an organization's culture is apt to be a variation on the beliefs and values associated with these "associated" cultures.

Not all cultures produce equally powerful effects. Some cultures are stronger than others.

Strength of Culture.   The strength of a culture influences the intensity by which organizational members comply with it as they go about their day-to-day activities. The three specific features of culture that determine its strength are *thickness, extent of sharing,* and *clarity of ordering.*

The number of important shared assumptions varies from one organization to another. *Thick* cultures have many; *thin* cultures have few. Cultures with many layers of important shared beliefs and values generally have a stronger influence on behavior. IBM, for example, has a thick culture made up of numerous shared beliefs and values, including respect for the individual, encouragement of constructive rebellion, and doing what is right. Thinner cultures have fewer shared assumptions and thus have a weaker influence on organizational life.

Second, some important assumptions are more widely shared than others. Few are completely shared in the sense that every member of the organization has internalized them. Cultures with more widely shared beliefs and values have a more pervasive impact because more people are guided by them. At IBM, most of the cultural assumptions are very widely shared.

Finally, in some organizational cultures the shared beliefs and values are clearly ordered. Their relative importance and their relation to each other are fairly unambiguous. In less ordered cultures, relative priorities and interrelationships are not so clear. Cultures whose shared assumptions are clearly ordered have a more pronounced effect on behavior because members of the organization are sure of which values should prevail in cases of conflicting interests.

Whereas its content determines in *what direction* a culture will influence organizational behavior, the *intensity* of its effect on behavior depends on a culture's strength. The stronger cultures are thicker, more widely shared, and more clearly ordered; consequently, they have a more profound influence on organizational behavior. Strong cultures are also more resistant to change, which can represent a major asset or liability depending on the culture's compatibility with the needs of the organization's chosen strategy. We will examine this issue in greater detail after first describing how to "decipher" or read a culture.

Deciphering a Culture.   Reading a culture is an interpretive, subjective activity. One cannot decipher a culture simply by relying on what people say about it. Other evidence, both historical and current, must be taken into account to infer what the culture is. There are no exact answers, and two observers may come up with somewhat different descriptions of the same culture. The validity of deciphering a culture must be judged by the utility of the insights the diagnosis provides.

The framework presented in Figure 12–8 provides a systematic method to help decipher or infer an organization's culture. Each important shared assumption creating an organization's culture may be inferred from one or more shared things, shared sayings, shared doings, and shared feelings. People examining a culture may come up with a somewhat different list of "shared" things, doings, sayings, and feelings. The important point is to distill from these various cultural manifestations a much more concise set of important shared beliefs and values.

Figure 12–9 provides a useful illustration of this approach to deciphering or reading the culture at Cummins Engine Company. Sixteen "manifestations" of culture are distilled into five important, shared assumptions that help Cummins managers understand and read their culture. The most subjective and tricky part in the process of deciphering a culture is in distilling the content of culture from its many manifestations. To do it well, those attempting to read a culture must empathize with the people in question and try to understand them in their own terms, rather than in the observer's terms.

How Culture Influences Organizational Life

Culture is a strength that can also be a weakness. It is a strength because culture eases and economizes communications, facilitates organizational decision making and control, and may generate higher levels of cooperation and commitment in the organization. The result is efficiency in that these activities are accomplished with a lower expenditure of resources (such as time and money) than would otherwise be possible. The stronger the culture, the greater its efficiency.

Culture becomes a weakness when important shared beliefs and values interfere with the needs of the business, its strategy, and the people working on the company's behalf. To the extent that the content of a company's culture

Figure 12–8
Framework for deciphering culture

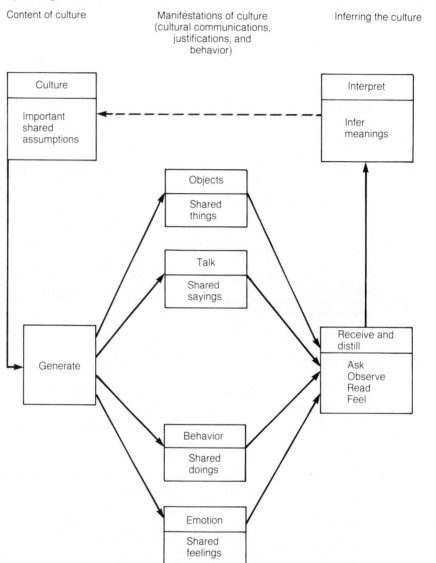

Content of culture

Manifestations of culture
(cultural communications,
justifications, and
behavior)

Inferring the culture

Culture

Important shared assumptions

Interpret

Infer meanings

Objects

Shared things

Talk

Shared sayings

Generate

Receive and distill

Ask
Observe
Read
Feel

Behavior

Shared doings

Emotion

Shared feelings

Source: Vijay Sathe, *Culture and Related Corporate Realities* (Homewood, Ill.: Richard D. Irwin, 1985), p. 17.

Figure 12–9
Inferring important shared assumptions from shared things, shared sayings, shared doings, and shared feelings for managers at Cummins Engine Company

Manifestations of the culture at Cummins	*Inferred culture at Cummins*

Shared things

ST1.   Shirt sleeves.
ST2.   One-company town.
ST3.   Open offices.
ST4.   No parking privileges.

Shared sayings

SS1.   Belief in travel, "get out there" to understand the customer.
SS2.   "Systems won't work" to meet customer needs.
SS3.   "Top management will tell us" what to do.

Shared doings

SD1.   Lots of meetings.
SD2.   Close direction from the top.
SD3.   Personal relationships and communications.
SD4.   Rallying to a crisis to meet the needs of the customer.
SD5.   Expediting behavior to achieve highly responsive service.
SD6.   Close relationships with union.

Shared feelings

SF1.   The company is good to me.
SF2.   We don't need to worry about what to do in a crisis.
SF3.   We take pride in shipping faster to the customer than our competition does.

Important shared assumptions

1. Provide highly responsive, high-quality customer service (SS1, SS2, SD4, SD5, SF3).
2. Get things done well and quickly ("expediting") (SD1, SD4, SD5, SF3).
3. Operate informally without systems (ST1, ST3, SS2, SD3, SD6).
4. Top management will tell us what to do if there is a problem (SS3, SD2, SF2).
5. See the company as part of the family (ST2, ST4, SD6, SF1).

Source: Adapted from Vijay Sathe, *Culture and Related Corporate Realities* (Homewood, Ill.: Richard D. Irwin, 1985), p. 18.

leads its people to think and act in inappropriate ways, culture's efficiency will not help achieve effective results. This condition is usually a significant weakness because it is hard to change a culture's content.

To take a closer look at how culture influences organizational life, we need to examine five basic processes that lie at the heart of any organization—cooperation, decision making, control, communication, and commitment.

Cooperation.   True cooperation cannot ultimately be legislated. Management can resort to carefully worded employment contracts, spell out detailed expectations, and devise clever incentive schemes to reward just the right behavior. However, even well-thought-out formal procedures can never anticipate all contingencies. When something unforeseen occurs, the organization is at the mercy of the employee's willingness to act in the spirit of cooperation,

which involves intent, goodwill, and mutual trust. The degree of true cooperation is influenced by the shared assumptions in this area. The example in
Figure 12–9 suggests that shared beliefs and values of informality and family
spirit generated high levels of true cooperation at Cummins Engine Company.

Decision Making.   Culture affects the decision-making process because
shared beliefs and values give organizational members a consistent set of
basic assumptions and preferences. This leads to a more efficient decision-
making process because fewer disagreements arise over which premises should
prevail.

As pointed out earlier, however, efficiency does not imply effectiveness. If
the shared beliefs and values are not in keeping with the needs of the business,
its strategy, and its members, dysfunctional consequences will result. In Figure
12–9's Cummins example, the reliance on the people at the top in crisis situations ("Top management will tell us what to do if there is a problem") was
efficient but no longer effective in the complex, multiplant environment that
Cummins' top management faced. This assumption had to be changed, and
Cummins' CEO eventually succeeded in changing it.

Control.   The essence of control is the ability to take action to achieve planned
results. The basis for action is provided by two different control mechanisms:
formal procedures and clans.

Formal procedures rely on adjusting rules, procedures, guidelines, budgets,
and directives. The *clan mechanism* relies on shared beliefs and values. In
effect, shared beliefs and values constitute an organizational "compass" that
members rely on to choose appropriate courses of action. Clan control derives
from culture.

A strong culture facilitates the control process by enhancing clan control.
Clan control is highly efficient; but again, efficiency and effectiveness should
not be confused. Apple Computer, for instance, heavily used clan control in
the 1970s. People responded to the rapid growth of the 1970s and the unexpected downturn in the early 1980s with "automatic pilot" responses. There
was no reliance on special incentives to motivate and very little use of new
systems, procedures, or directives. However, the clan method of control had
become inefficient because of growth and expansion. Apple's CEO John Sculley
attempted to change the Apple culture to place more value on using systems
to do the routine work without giving up Apple's valued "go for growth" beliefs.

Communication.   The major reasons people miscommunicate daily in organizational and everyday life include the technical problem of distortion between
the point where a communication starts out and the point where it is received.
A good example is the familiar parlor game in which a sentence that one
person speaks at the start of a human chain comes out distorted at the other
end. A second and more important hurdle in communication concerns difficul-

ties in interpretation. Even two-person, face-to-face communication, where the technical problem is minimal, is fraught with the danger of each person misunderstanding the other's meaning. More complex are the communication problems of one organization member trying to communicate with someone located in a different unit or of the corporate senior executive trying to communicate with the entire work force.

Culture reduces these dangers of miscommunication in two ways. First, there is no need to communicate in matters for which shared assumptions already exist; certain things go without saying. Second, shared assumptions provide guidelines and cues to help interpret messages that are received. Thus a strong culture encourages efficient and effective communication. And the advantage of this efficiency and effectiveness should not be underestimated; communications are the lifeblood of organizations.

Culture's content affects the content of communication. Some organizations' cultures value open communication: "Bad news is bad, but withholding it is worse." Other cultures do not value open communication. In these cultures, withholding relevant information that has not been specifically requested, secrecy, and outright distortion may prevail.

Commitment.   A person feels committed to an organization when he or she identifies with it and experiences some emotional attachment to it. A variety of incentives—salary, prestige, and personal sense of worth—tie the individual to the organization. Strong cultures foster strong identification and feelings through multiple beliefs and values that the individual can share with others.

In making decisions and taking actions, committed employees automatically evaluate the impact of alternatives on the organization. Committed people will put out the extra effort needed to get the organization out of a bind. For instance, at Cummins Engine Company the shared value of highly responsive customer service (see Figure 12–9) led the people to "move mountains" to meet intermittent and unexpected surges in product demand, without being given special incentives to do so. People had so thoroughly bought into the values of high-quality customer service and expediting behavior that these had become more than strategic objectives or operational directives. They were taken-for-granted assumptions for the people at Cummins.

Summary.   Culture has a pervasive influence on organizational life, but people working in an organization do not ordinarily recognize this because the basic assumptions and preferences guiding thought and action tend to operate at a preconscious level and remain outside their realm of awareness. Some of culture's manifestations—the shared words, actions, doings, and feelings indicated in Figures 12–8 and 12–9—may be apparent, but the underlying beliefs and values are frequently unstated and not always obvious. Their subtle quality is easily taken for granted. Like the fish who do not realize how much they depend on water, those who are most affected by culture often overlook its basic impact on cooperation, decision making, control, communication, and commitment.

The strength of culture determines its efficiency. However, the content of culture determines its effectiveness because content determines the direction in which culture influences organizational behavior. If the content of the culture guides organizational thinking and action in ways that are out of keeping with the needs of the business and its strategy, culture becomes ineffective, regardless of its efficiency. So, a key challenge facing strategic managers is to carefully manage the strategy–culture relationship to effectively implement the business's strategy.

The Strategy–Culture Connection

Culture gives employees a sense of how to behave, what they should do, and where to place priorities in getting the job done. Culture helps employees *fill in the gaps* between what is formally decreed and what actually takes place. As such, culture is of critical importance in the implementation of strategy.

A company's culture can be a major strength when it is consistent with strategy and thus can be a powerful driving force in implementation. The following examples at IBM and Delta Airlines illustrate how a supportive culture enhances employee efforts in implementing strategy:

> Delta Airlines has emphasized a market development strategy with a focus on customer service that requires a high degree of teamwork. Employees have become very receptive to substituting in other jobs to keep planes flying, baggage moving, and reservations confirmed. A simple story told in a recent book illustrates the degree to which these values are [inculcated] at Delta: A woman inadvertently missed out on a "Super Saver" ticket because the family had moved and, owing to a technicality, the ticket price was no longer valid. She called to complain. Delta's president intervened personally and, being there at the time, met her at the gate to give her the new ticket.[18]
>
> IBM's strategy in business machines has had as its basic premise offering unparalleled service to customers. A customer's explanation of his decision to choose IBM in a major computer system purchase for a hospital illustrates how values reinforcing this strategy permeate IBM employees: "Many of the others were ahead of IBM in technological wizardry. And heaven knows their software is easier to use. But IBM alone took the trouble to get to know us. They interviewed extensively up and down the line. They talked our language, no mumbo jumbo on computer innards. Their price was fully 25 percent higher. But they provided unparalleled guarantees of reliability and service. They even went so far as to arrange a backup connection with a local steel company in case our system

---

[18] Thomas J. Peters and Robert H. Waterman, Jr., *In Search of Excellence* (New York: Harper & Row, 1982), p. xxi.

crashed. Their presentations were to the point. Everything about them smacked of assurance and success. Our decision, even with severe budget pressure, was really easy.[19]

At both IBM and Delta Airlines, the beliefs and values (*culture*) that drive employee behavior are fully consistent with the "service-driven" strategies of the companies.

The opposite can occur. A culture can prevent a company from meeting competitive threats or adapting to changing economic or social environments that a new strategy is designed to overcome. One widely cited example is AT&T. AT&T adopted a marketing-oriented strategy for the 1980s to replace its service- and public-utility-oriented strategy. This new strategy was chosen in response to antitrust pressures, the Federal Communications Commission's decision to allow other companies to sell products in AT&T's once-captive markets, and the unregulated competition in the emerging telecommunications industry. AT&T has now labored for several years to behave like a marketing company, but with marginal success. Efforts to serve different market segments in different ways have run afoul of the strong values, beliefs, and norms managers have imbibed since the turn of the century—that it is important to furnish telephone service to everybody, and that you do so by not discriminating too much among different kinds of customers.[20] The solution seems obvious: change the culture. Changing the orientation of approximately 1 million employees is not easy.

A similar experience in the oil industry was reported in *Business Week:*

Five years ago the chief executives of two major oil companies determined that they would have to diversify out of oil because their current business could not support long-term growth and faced serious political threats. Not only did they announce their new long-range strategies to employees and the public, but they established elaborate plans to implement them. Each of the CEOs was unable to implement his strategy, not because it was theoretically wrong or bad, but because neither had understood that his company's culture was so entrenched in the traditions and values of doing business as oilmen that employees resisted (and sabotaged) the radical changes that the CEOs tried to impose. Oil operations require long-term investments for long-term rewards; but the new businesses needed short-term views and an emphasis on current returns. Successes had come from hitting it big in wildcatting, but the new success was to be based on such abstractions as market share or numbers growth—all seemingly nebulous concepts to them.[21]

After several years of pursuing diversification strategies, both companies are firmly back in the oil business, and the two CEOs have been replaced. *Business Week* analysts attributed each strategy's failure to the idea that

---

[19] Ibid., p. xx.

[20] "The Corporate Culture Vultures," *Fortune*, October 17, 1983, p. 66.

[21] "Corporate Culture," *Business Week*, October 27, 1980, p. 148.

"implementing them violated employees' basic beliefs about their roles in the company and the traditions that underlie the companies' cultures."[22]

These examples help demonstrate the important role of culture in institutionalizing a company's strategy. As a consequence, managing culture to successfully implement a strategy is critical. The issue is simple to state yet exceedingly difficult to effect. The critical issue that must be managed is whether the "fit" between the shared assumptions comprising an organization's culture is consistent with the implementation requirements of the chosen strategy.

Managing the Strategy–Culture Relationship

Managers have a difficult time thinking through the relationship between culture and the critical factors on which strategy depends. They quickly recognize, however, that key components of the company—structure, staff, systems, people, style—influence the way key managerial tasks are executed and critical management relationships are formed. And strategy implementation is largely concerned with adjustments in these components to accommodate the perceived needs of the new strategy. So, managing the strategy–culture relationship requires sensitivity to the interaction between the changes necessary to implement strategy and the compatibility or "fit" between those changes and the organization's culture. Figure 12–10 provides a simple but useful framework for managing the strategy–culture relationship by identifying four basic situations a company might face.

Link to Mission.   A company in cell 1 faces implementing a new strategy that requires several changes in structure, systems, managerial assignments, operating procedures, or other fundamental aspects of the organization. At the same time, most of the changes are potentially compatible with the existing organizational culture. Companies in this situation are usually those with a tradition of effective performance that are either seeking to take advantage of a major opportunity or attempting to redirect major product/market operations consistent with core, proven capabilities. Such companies are in a very promising position: they can pursue a strategy requiring major changes but still benefit from the power of cultural reinforcement.

Companies seeking to manage a strategy–culture relationship in this context need to emphasize four basic considerations. First, *key changes must be visibly linked to the basic company mission.* The mission provides a broad official foundation for the organizational culture. Therefore, top executives should use every internal and external forum available to reinforce the message that the changes are inextricably linked to the fundamental company mission. Second, *emphasis should be placed on using existing personnel* where possible to fill positions created in implementing the strategy. Existing personnel carry

---

[22] Ibid., p. 148.

Figure 12–10
Managing the strategy–culture relationship

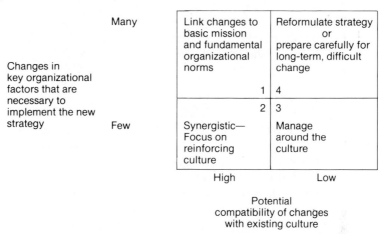

with them the shared values and norms that help ensure cultural compatibility as major changes are implemented. Third, *care must be taken if adjustments are needed in the reward system.* These should be consistent with currently rewarded behavior. If, for example, a new product/market thrust requires significant changes in the way sales are made and therefore in incentive compensation, common themes (e.g., incentive-oriented) must be emphasized. In this way, current and future approaches are related and the changes are justified (encourage development of less familiar markets). Fourth, *key attention should be paid to changes that are least compatible with current culture* so that current norms are not disrupted. For example, a company may choose to subcontract an important step in a production process because the process would be incompatible with current culture.

IBM's strategy in entering the personal computer market is an illustration. The strategy required numerous organizational changes to serve a radically different market. To maintain maximum compatibility with its existing culture, IBM went to considerable public and internal effort to link its new PCs with the corporation's long-standing mission. The message relating the PC to IBM's tradition of top-quality service appeared almost daily on television and in magazines. Internally, every IBM manager was given a PC. The corporation also emphasized the use of IBM personnel where feasible to fill new positions. But because production requirements were not compatible with current operations, IBM subcontracted virtually all manufacturing for the PC.

Maximize Synergy. A company in cell 2 is in the enviable position of needing only a few organizational changes to implement a new strategy; and those changes are potentially quite compatible with the current culture. A company in this position should emphasize two broad themes: (1) *take advantage of this situation to reinforce and solidify the company's culture* and (2) *use this time of relative stability to remove organizational roadblocks to the desired culture.* Holiday Inns' move into casino gambling required few major organizational changes for the parent company. Casinos were seen as resort locations requiring lodging, dining, and gambling/entertainment services. Holiday Inns had only to incorporate gambling/entertainment expertise into its management team, which otherwise had the complete capability to manage the lodging and dining requirements of casino (or any other) resort locations. This single, major change was successfully inculcated in part by selling it internally as completely compatible with Holiday Inns' mission to provide high-quality accommodations for business and leisure travelers. The resignation of then CEO Roy Clymer removed one final organization roadblock, legitimizing a culture that prided itself on quality service to the middle- to upper-income business traveler rather than one that placed its highest priority on family-oriented service. The latter value was fast disappearing from the Holiday Inns' culture, with the encouragement of most of Holiday Inns' top management, but was not yet fully sanctioned because of personal beliefs shared by Clymer. His voluntary departure helped solidify the new values top management wanted.

Manage around the Culture. A company in cell 3 must make a few major organizational changes to implement its new strategy. At the same time, these changes are potentially inconsistent with current organizational culture. The critical question for this firm is whether these changes can be made with a reasonable chance for success.

Consider, for example, a multibillion-dollar industry leader facing several major threats to its record of outstanding growth and profitability. To meet these threats, considerable effort is made to design a new organizational structure around major markets. After formally assessing the "cultural risks" of such a change, the proposal is rejected as too radical and too inconsistent with the company's functional culture. A positive alternative is available. Planning and coordination personnel can be increased to *manage around the culture* in implementing the strategy.[23] This can be an important means of implementation if a company faces changing a factor (like structure) that is inextricably linked to the organization's culture.

Several alternatives can facilitate managing around culture: create a separate company or division; use task forces, teams, or program coordinators; subcontract; bring in an outsider; or sell out. These are a few of the alternatives available, but the key idea is to create an alternative method of achieving the change desired without directly confronting the incompatible cultural

---

[23] Howard Schwartz and Stanley M. Davis, "Matching Corporate Culture and Business Strategy," *Organizational Dynamics,* Summer 1981, p. 43.

norms. As cultural resistance diminishes, the change may be absorbed into the organization.

Rich's is a highly successful, quality-oriented department store serving higher-income customers in several southeastern locations. With Sears and K mart experiencing rapid growth in mid- to lower-priced merchandise in the 1970s, Rich's decided to serve this market as well. Finding such merchandise inconsistent with the successful values and norms (a quality-merchandise, customer-service-oriented culture) of its traditional business, Rich's created a separate business called Richway to tap this growth area in retailing. Rich's found it necessary and appropriate to create an entire new store network to *manage around its culture*. Both businesses have since flourished, based in part on radically different cultures.

Reformulate.   A company in cell 4 faces the most difficult challenge in managing the strategy–culture relationship. The company must make numerous organizational changes to implement its new strategy. But the number and nature of the changes are incompatible with the current, usually entrenched, values and norms. AT&T, discussed earlier in this chapter, illustrates the substantial dilemma faced by a firm in this situation. Like AT&T, the company in this situation faces the awesome challenge of changing its culture—a complex, expensive, often long-term proposition. It is a challenge numerous organizational culture consultants say borders on an impossibility.[24] Strategy in Action 12–7 describes the decade-long experience at PepsiCo that was necessary to change its culture.

When faced with massive change and cultural resistance, a company should first examine whether strategy reformulation is appropriate. Is it really necessary to change many of the fundamental organizational factors? Can the changes be made with any real expectation that they will be acceptable and successful? If the answer to these questions is no, the business should seriously reconsider and reformulate its strategic plan. In other words, the strategy that the firm can realistically implement must be more consistent with established organizational norms and practices. Merrill Lynch & Co. provides a recent example of a firm that faced this dilemma. Seeking to remain number one in the newly deregulated financial services industry, Merrill Lynch chose to pursue a new, product development strategy in its brokerage business. The success of this strategy depends on Merrill Lynch's traditional, service-oriented brokerage network becoming sales and marketing oriented in order to sell a broader range of investment products to a more diverse customer base. Initial efforts to implement this strategy generated substantial resistance from Merrill Lynch's highly successful brokerage network. The strategy is fundamentally inconsistent with long-standing cultural norms at Merrill Lynch that emphasize personalized service and very close broker–client relationships.

---

[24] "Corporate Culture Vultures," p. 72.

Strategy in Action 12–7
The Pepsi Challenge: Creating an Aggressive Culture to Match an Aggressive Strategy

For decades, Coke's unchallenged position in the cola market was so complete that the brand name Coke became synonymous with cola drinks. It attained this distinction under Robert W. Woodruff, who served as chief executive for 32 years and was still chairman of the company's finance committee at age 90. Woodruff had an "almost messianic drive to get Coca-Cola [distributed] all over the world," according to Harvey Z. Yazijian, coauthor of *The Cola Wars*. So successful was Coke in accomplishing this under Woodruff and later J. Paul Austin that Coca-Cola became known as "America's second State Department." Its trademark became a symbol of American life itself.

"A real problem in the past," said Yazijian, "was that they had a lot of deadwood" among employees. Nevertheless, Coke's marketing and advertising were extremely effective in expanding consumption of the product. But the lack of serious competition and the company's relative isolation in its hometown of Atlanta allowed it to become "fat, dumb, and happy," according to one consultant. Coke executives are known to be extremely loyal to the company and circumspect to the point of secrecy in their dealings with the outside world.

In the mid-1950s, Pepsi, once a sleepy, New York–based bottler with a lame slogan, "Twice as much for a nickel too," began to develop into a serious threat under the leadership of Chairman Alfred N. Steele. The movement gathered momentum, and by the early 1970s, the company had become a ferocious competitor under chairman Donald M. Kendall and President Andrall E. Pearson, a former director of [the consulting firm] McKinsey & Co. The culture that these two executives were determined to create was based on the goal of becoming the number one marketer of soft drinks.

Severe pressure was put on managers to show continual improvement in market share, product volume, and profits. "Careers ride on 10ths of a market share point," offered John Sculley, a Pepsi vice president. This atmosphere pervades the company's nonbeverage units as well. "Everyone knows that if the results aren't there, you had better have your resume up-to-date," says a former snack-food manager.

To keep everyone on their toes, a "creative tension" is continually nurtured among departments at Pepsi, says another former executive. The staff is kept lean, and managers are moved to new jobs constantly, which results in people

Continued on Page 397

Strategy in Action 12–7 (*concluded*)

working long hours and engaging in political maneuvering "just to keep their jobs from being reorganized out from under them," says a headhunter.

Kendall himself sets a constant example. He once resorted to using a snowmobile to get to work in a blizzard, demonstrating the ingenuity and dedication to work he expects from his staff. This type of pressure has pushed many managers out. But a recent company survey shows that others thrive under such conditions. "Most of our guys are having fun," Pearson insists. They are the kind of people, elaborates Sculley, who "would rather be in the marines than in the army."

Like marines, Pepsi executives are expected to be physically fit as well as mentally alert: Pepsi employs four physical fitness instructors at its headquarters, and a former executive says it is an unwritten rule that to get ahead in the company, a manager must stay in shape. The company encourages one-on-one sports as well as interdepartmental competition in such games as soccer and basketball. In company team contests or business dealings, says Sculley, "the more competitive it becomes, the more we enjoy it." In such a culture, less competitive managers are deliberately weeded out. Even suppliers notice a difference today. "They are smart, sharp negotiators who take advantage of all opportunities," says one.

While Pepsi steadily gained market share in the 1970s, Coke was reluctant to admit that a threat existed, Yazijian says. Pepsi now has bested Coke in the domestic take-home market, and it is mounting a challenge overseas. At the moment, the odds are in favor of Coke, which sells one third of the world's soft drinks and has had Western Europe locked up for years. But Pepsi has been making inroads: Besides monopolizing the Soviet market, it has dominated the Arab Middle East ever since Coke was ousted in 1967, when it granted a bottling franchise in Israel. Still, Coke showed that it was not giving up. It cornered a potentially vast new market—China.

With Pepsi gaining domestic market share faster than Coke—in the last five years it has gained 7.5 percent to Coke's 5 percent—observers believe that Coke will turn more to foreign sales or food sales for growth. Roberto C. Goizueta, Coke's chairman, will not reveal Coke's strategy. But one tactic the company has already used is hiring away some of Pepsi's "tigers." Coke has lured Donald Breen, Jr., who played a major role in developing the "Pepsi Challenge"—the consumer taste test—as well as five other marketing and sales executives associated with Pepsi. Pepsi won its court battle to prevent Breen from revealing confidential information over the next 12 months.

The company's current culture may be unlikely to build loyalty. Pepsi may well have to examine the dangers of cultivating ruthlessness in its managers, say former executives.

Only time can tell if these comments are accurate or simply "sour grapes." Regardless, Pepsi has clearly sought to ensure consistency in every aspect of changing its culture from a passive to an aggressive one over the last 20 years.

Source: Based on the article "Corporate Culture: The Hard-to-Change Values that Spell Success or Failure," *Business Week*, October 27, 1980, p. 54.

Following the 1984 resignation of Merrill Lynch's CEO, numerous analysts reported serious reconsideration of this product development strategy toward one more consistent with traditional values and norms inculcated in the broker-age network.

For many businesses facing this dilemma, reformulation is not in the long-term interests of the firm. Oftentimes, as illustrated earlier in Strategy in Action 12–6 about McGraw-Hill, major external changes necessitate a new strategy that requires difficult changes in the fundamental culture of the organization. In the situation where the culture must be changed, several basic managerial actions—both symbolic and substantive—should be consid-ered as the bases for cultural change. Five types of basic managerial actions that will aid in the difficult process of changing organizational culture are discussed below.

Chief Executive's Role.   The CEO has to visibly lead the organization in *each* fundamental change. This is a symbolic role in communicating the need for change and recognizing initial successes; and it is a substantive role in making hard decisions. The top-management team must create the pressure for change and set an example that unequivocally demonstrates the serious-ness of the new direction.

Who Is Hired and Promoted.   One key way to begin the process of changing values and norms is to bring in new people who share the desired values. Likewise, indoctrination of new personnel into the company is a key time for clarifying and inculcating desired values. Companies can also remove employ-ees who strongly resist or blunt efforts to revamp the old culture. In extreme cases, this can mean changing top management.

Change the Reward Structure.   A powerful way of changing values and behavior is to link the reward structure and the desired change. This can be done individually and with subunits of the organization. Compensation is the most obvious reward, but resource allocation, perks, and other visible "rewards" help positively reinforce desired change.

Clarify Desired Behavior.   Unless managers are fully aware of the behavior required to get things done in the new culture, they will not change how they approach tasks and relationships. So, planning teams and other educa-tional vehicles must clarify what the "new rules" are and how the new behavior will enhance development and advancement in the company.[25]

Foster Consistency between Desired Changes and Rewards.   One ele-ment appears certain in changing culture: employees cannot be fooled. They

---

[25] Schwartz and Davis, "Matching Corporate Culture," p. 44.

understand the "real" priorities in the company. At the first inconsistency they will become confused, then reluctant to change, and eventually intransigent. So, consistency between what is said to be important and what is rewarded as such is critical in cultural change. Indeed, consistency in every aspect of a culture is essential to its success, as PepsiCo's transformation into an archrival of Coke shows in Strategy in Action 12–7.

Changing an organizational culture takes time. Strategy in Action 12–6 describes efforts at McGraw-Hill that have been under way since 1985. Executives who have succeeded in fundamentally transforming a culture estimate that the process requires from 6 to 15 years.[26] So, in trying to change underlying organizational factors, strategists must recognize that reshaping "the way things are done" in a company is often an incremental process. Small opportunities should be sought for making a change or initiating an action that visibly reinforces the spirit and direction of the new culture. Top management should continually try (and urge their subordinates to try, as well) to gradually build and nurture the company's shared psychological and attitudinal commitment to the new strategy so that the fit between shared employee values and the new strategic mission continually improves.

Summary

This chapter examined the idea that a key aspect of implementing strategy is the need to *institutionalize* that strategy so that it permeates daily decisions and actions in a manner consistent with long-term strategic success. Three fundamental elements must be managed to "fit" the strategy if that strategy is to be effectively institutionalized: organizational *structure, leadership,* and *culture.*

Five fundamental organizational structures were examined, and the advantages and disadvantages of each were identified. Institutionalizing the strategy requires a good strategy–structure fit. This chapter dealt with how this need is often overlooked until performance becomes inadequate and examined conditions under which alternative structures would be more appropriate.

Organizational leadership is essential to effective strategy implementation. The CEO plays a critical role in this regard. Assignment of key managers, particularly within the top-management team, is an important aspect of organizational leadership. The question of promoting insiders versus hiring outsiders is often a central leadership issue in strategy implementation. This chapter provided a situational approach to making this decision in a manner that best institutionalizes the new strategy.

In recent years, organizational culture has been recognized as a pervasive force influencing organizational life. Culture is described as the shared beliefs and values of organizational members, and it may be a major asset or liability

---

[26] "Corporate Culture Vultures," p. 70.

when implementing strategy. An approach to managing the strategy–culture fit was discussed in this chapter. We identified four fundamentally different strategy–culture situations based on the changes necessary to implement the strategy and the "fit" of these changes with the company's culture. Recommendations for managing the strategy–culture fit vary across the four situations.

Questions for Discussion

1. What key structural considerations must be incorporated into strategy implementation? Why does structural change often lag a change in strategy?
2. Which structure is most appropriate for successful strategy implementation? Explain how stage of development affects your answer.
3. Why is leadership an important element in strategy implementation? Find an example in a major business periodical of the CEO's key role in strategy implementation.
4. Under what conditions would it be more appropriate to fill a key management position with someone from outside the company when a qualified insider is available?
5. What is organizational culture? Why is it important? Explain two different situations a firm might face in managing the strategy–culture relationship.

Bibliography

"Corporate Culture." *Business Week,* October 27, 1980, pp. 148–60.

"Corporate Culture Vultures." *Fortune,* October 17, 1983, pp. 66–73.

Deal, Terrence E., and Allan A. Kennedy. *Corporate Cultures.* Reading, Mass.: Addison-Wesley Publishing, 1982.

Fenton, Noel J. "Managing the Adolescent Company." *Management Review,* December 1976, pp. 12–19.

Galbraith, Jay R., and Daniel A. Nathanson. *Strategy Implementation: The Role of Structure and Process.* 2nd ed. St. Paul, Minn.: West Publishing, 1978.

Hrebiniak, Lawrence G., and William F. Joyce. *Implementing Strategy.* New York: Macmillan, 1984.

Leontiades, Milton. *Strategies for Diversification and Change.* Boston: Little, Brown, 1980, chaps. 2, 3, 6.

————. "Choosing the Right Manager to Fit the Strategy." *Journal of Business Strategy,* Fall 1982, pp. 58–69.

Miles, R. E., and C. C. Snow. *Organizational Strategy, Structure, and Process.* New York: McGraw-Hill, 1978.

Peters, Thomas J. "Beyond the Matrix Organization." *Business Horizons,* October 1979, pp. 15–27.

Peters, Thomas J., and Robert Waterman. *In Search of Excellence.* New York: Harper & Row, 1982.

Sathe, Vijay. *Culture and Related Corporate Realities.* Homewood, Ill.: Richard D. Irwin, 1985.

Stonich, Paul J. *Implementing Strategy.* Cambridge, Mass.: Ballinger, 1982.

Tichy, N. M.; C. J. Fombrun; and M. A. Devanna. "Strategic Human Resource Management." *Sloan Management Review,* Winter 1982, p. 47.

"Wanted: A Manager to Fit Each Strategy." *Business Week,* Febuary 25, 1980, p. 166.

Yavitz, Boris, and William H. Newman. *Strategy in Action.* New York: Free Press, 1982.

Chapter 12 Cohesion Case Illustration

Institutionalizing the Strategy at Holiday Inns, Inc.

Holidays Inns has emphasized three key elements to institutionalize its strategy for the 1990s: organizational structure, selection and assignment of key managers, and organizational culture.

Organizational Structure.   Exhibit 1 provides an abbreviated look at the organizational structure of Holiday Inns, Inc. As you can see, Holiday Inns has a divisional structure with four rather autonomous business groups. This clearly reflects the needs of its corporate diversification strategy by providing each business group with its own functional support and broad decision-making capability. Second, the formerly separate products group has been reorganized within the hotel group. This clearly reflects the strategy of retrenchment and divestiture within the products group limiting it primarily to a service role for the hotel group's furnishing and equipment needs. Finally, Delta Steamship and Perkins restaurants have been organized as fully independent and autonomous units. This distinguishes Delta and Perkins from the hospitality businesses and facilitates rapid divestiture should Holiday Inns find the right opportunity to do so (which it did with Delta in 1983 and with Perkins in 1986).

Assignment of Key Managers.   Several key managerial assignments reflect a deliberate choice at the corporate level to effectively implement Holiday Inns' diversification strategy. Holiday Inns' three nonhotel divisions have as their presidents the former CEOs at Harrah's, Perkins, and Delta, respectively. Instead of putting a Holiday Inns-trained executive in charge, corporate management deliberately chose to maintain autonomy and leadership to meet the unique needs of these new groups. Finally, reflecting a corporate portfolio strategy that emphasizes casinos as a key growth area, gaming is the only business group other than hotels to have representation on the board of directors and of the corporate management level.

Mike Rose (CEO) and Roy Winegardner (chairman of the board) were initially successful franchisees before becoming involved with Holiday Inns' top-management team. Thus, they understand franchisees—an attribute critical to the franchise-dominated hotel and restaurant businesses. They also (particularly Rose) had less of a tie to Holiday Inns' previous family-oriented hotel philosophy and widespread, transportation-related diversification. This made

Exhibit 1
Organizational structure at Holiday Corporation

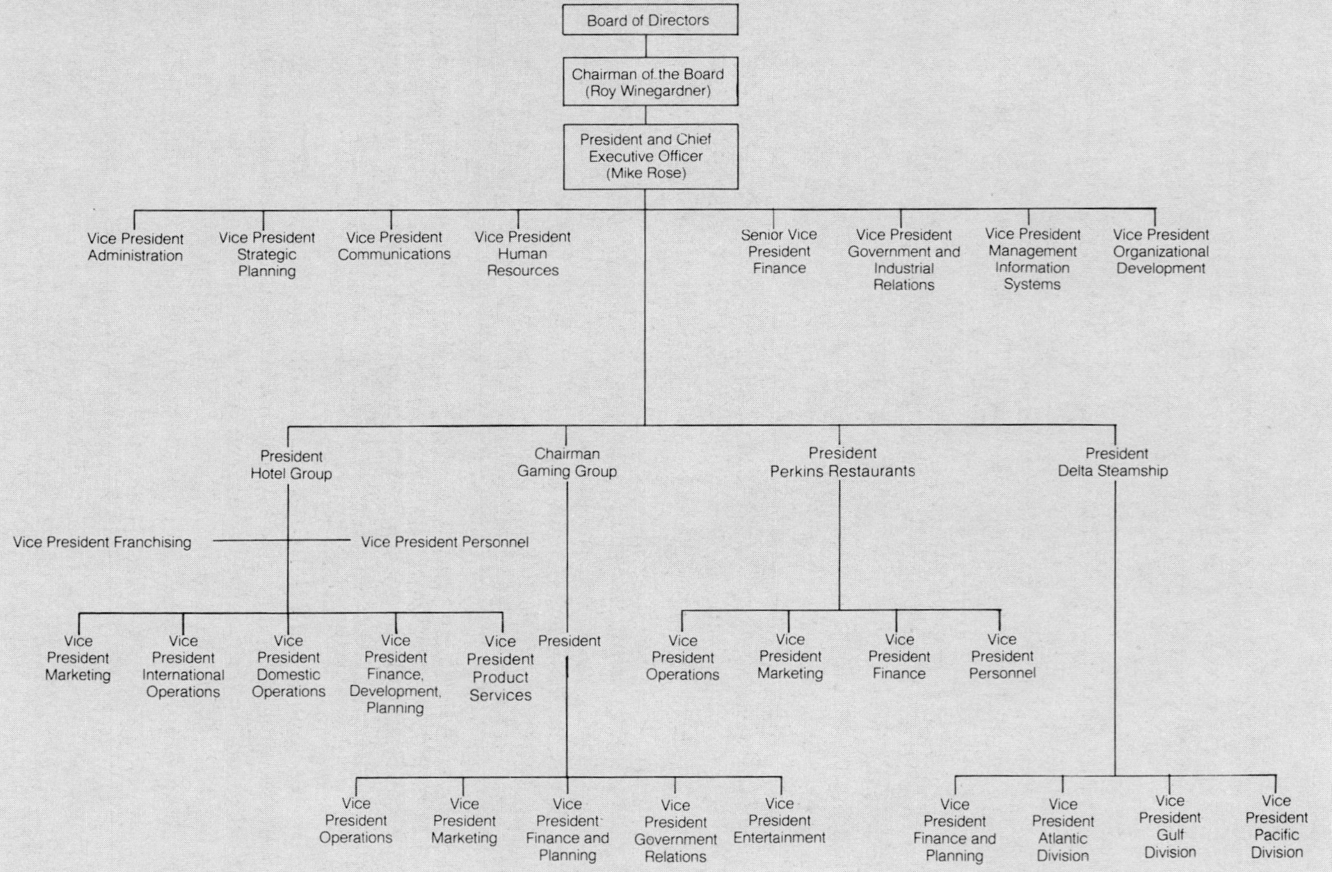

them more objective and effective in addressing and implementing the casino decision and several major divestitures (product group and transportation businesses).

Two additions to the board reflect Holiday Inns' institutionalization of its hospitality strategy. Donald Smith, senior vice president with PepsiCo and president of its Food Service Division, brings well-respected food-service experience to Holiday Inns' top-management team. Smith was credited with turning Burger King into a viable competitor with McDonald's in fast foods. James Farley, chairman and CEO of Booz Allen & Hamilton (a worldwide consulting firm), reflects a serious commitment to systematic strategic planning for Holiday Inns' future.

Organizational Culture. The structural and key managerial changes reflect a steady shift from an entrepreneurial to a professionally managed company. Refocusing on being a *hospitality* company in two industries—hotels and gaming—has been presented as the "new Holiday Corporation." The common threat for each operation is a strong service orientation that encourages and rewards superior individual performance. The "new" Holiday Inns sees its people assets as key to its service success, as reflected by its corporate philosophy and statements by Roy Winegardner, shown below:

Corporate Philosophy Statement:
We are a forward-looking innovative industry leader with clearly defined goals, producing superior products/services and consistently high return for our shareholders.

We will maintain integrity in both our internal and external relationsips, fostering respect for the individual and open two-way communications.

We will promote a climate of enthusiasm, teamwork, and challenge, which attracts, motivates, and retains superior personnel and rewards superior performance.

Our employees give us our greatest competitive advantage. We employ and develop high-quality people because they are the key to our continued leadership and growth.

Strategic Control: Guiding and Evaluating the Strategy

A strategy is selected and implemented over time so as to effectively position and guide a firm within an often rapidly changing environment. Strategies are forward looking, designed to be accomplished several years into the future, and based on management assumptions about numerous events that have not yet occurred.

How should managers undertake controlling a strategy? Traditional approaches to control seek to compare actual results against a standard. The work is done, the manager evaluates the work, and uses the evaluation as input to control future efforts. While this approach has its place, it is inappropriate as a means to control a strategy. Waiting until a strategy has been fully executed often involves five or more years, during which many changes occur that have major ramifications for the ultimate success of the strategy. Consequently, customary control concepts and approaches must be adjusted or replaced in favor of strategic controls that recognize the unique control needs of long-term strategies.

Strategic control is concerned with tracking the strategy as it is being implemented, detecting problems or changes in underlying premises, and making necessary adjustments. In contrast to post-action control, strategic control is concerned with controlling and guiding efforts on behalf of the strategy as action is taking place and while the end result is still several years into the future. Managers responsible for a strategy and its success are typically concerned with two sets of questions:

1. Are we moving in the proper direction? Are key things falling into place? Are our assumptions about major trends and changes correct? Are the critical things we need to do being done? Do we need to adjust or abort this strategy?

2. How are we performing? Are we meeting objectives and schedules? How are costs, revenues, and cash flows matching projections? Do we need to make operational changes?

Strategic controls, augmented by certain operational controls, are designed to answer these questions.

This chapter describes strategic controls and explains how to set them up. It then explains key operational control systems necessary to support strategic control. Reward systems are also explained in this chapter because they play a key role in directing strategy implementation and motivating strategic control. Finally, this chapter explains fundamental considerations in the evaluation of strategy once its implementation is complete.

Establishing Strategic Controls

Control of strategy can be characterized as a form of "steering control."[1] Ordinarily, a significant time span occurs between initial implementation of a strategy and achievement of its intended results. During that time, numerous projects are undertaken, investments are made, and actions are undertaken to implement the new strategy. Also during that time, both the environmental situation and the firm's internal situation are developing and evolving. Strategic controls are necessary to steer the firm through these events. They must provide the basis for correcting the actions and directions of the firm in implementing its strategy as developments and changes in its environmental and internal situations take place.

Prudential Insurance Company provides a useful example of the proactive, steering nature of strategic control. Several years ago, Prudential committed to a long-term market development strategy wherein it would seek to attain the top position in the life insurance industry by differentiating its level of service from other competitors in the industry. Prudential decided to establish regional home offices, thus achieving a differential service advantage. Exercising strategic control, Prudential managers used the experience at the first regional offices to reproject overall expenses and income associated with this strategy. In fact, the predicted expenses were so high that the location and original schedule for converting other regions had to be modified. Conversion of corporate headquarters was sharply revised on the basis of other early feedback. Thus the steering control (or strategic control) exercised by Prudential managers significantly altered the strategy long before the total plan

---

[1] B. Yavitz and W. H. Newman, *Strategy in Action* (New York: Free Press, 1982), p. 207.

was in place. In this case, major objectives remained in place while changes were made in the strategy; in other cases, strategic controls may initiate changes in objectives as well.

The four basic types of strategic control are:

1. Premise control.
2. Implementation control
3. Strategic survelliance.
4. Special alert control.

The nature of these four strategic controls is summarized in Figure 13–1.

Premise Control

Every strategy is based on assumed or predicted conditions. These assumptions or predictions are planning premises; a firm's strategy is designed around these predicted conditions. *Premise control is designed to check systematically and continuously whether or not the premises set during the planning and implementation process are still valid.* If a vital premise is no longer valid, then the strategy may have to be changed. The sooner an invalid premise can be recognized and revised, the better the chances that an acceptable shift in the strategy can be devised.

What Premises Should Be Monitored?   Premises are primarily concerned with two types of factors: environmental and industry. They are described below.

Environmental Factors.   A company has little or no control over environmental factors, but these factors exercise considerable influence over the success of the strategy. Inflation, technology, interest rates, regulation, and demographic/social changes are examples of such factors. Strategies are usually based on key premises about these factors.

Industry Factors.   These factors affect the performance of companies in a given industry. They differ among industries, and a company should be aware of the factors that influence success in its particular industry. Competitors, suppliers, substitutes, and barriers to entry are a few such factors about which strategic assumptions are made.

Premises, some major and some minor, are often made about numerous environmental and industry variables. To attempt to track every premise may be unnecessarily expensive and time-consuming. Therefore, managers must select those premises and variables that (*a*) are likely to change and (*b*) would have a major impact on the company and its strategy if they did.

Figure 13–1
Four types of strategic control

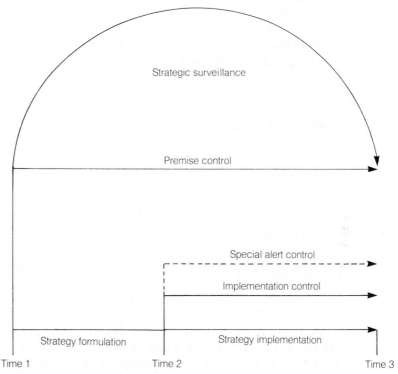

Source: Adapted from G. Schreyogg and H. Steinmann, "Strategic Control: A New Perspective,"
Academy of Management Review 12, no. 1 (1987), p. 96.

How Are Premise Controls Enacted?   The key premises should be identified during the planning process. The premises should be recorded, and responsibility for monitoring them should be assigned to the persons or departments who are qualified sources of information. For example, the sales force may be a valuable source for monitoring the expected price policy of major competitors, while the finance department might monitor interest rate trends. All premises should not require the same amount of effort; and, again, emphasis should be placed on key success premises so as to avoid information overload. Premises should be updated (new predictions) based on updated information. Finally, key areas within the company or key aspects of the strategy that the predicted changes may significantly impact should be preidentified so that adjustments necessitated by a revised premise can be determined and initiated. For example, senior marketing executives should be alerted about changes in competitors' pricing policies in order to determine if revised pricing, product repositioning, or other strategy adjustments are necessary.

Implementation Control

The action phase of strategic management is located in the series of steps, programs, investments, and moves undertaken over a period of time to implement the strategy. Special programs are undertaken. Functional areas initiate several strategy-related activities. Key people are added or reassigned. Resources are mobilized. In other words, managers convert broad strategic plans into concrete actions and results for specific units and individuals as they go about implementing strategy. And these actions take place incrementally over an extended period of time designed ultimately to enact the planned strategy and achieve long-term objectives.

Strategic control can be undertaken within this context. We refer to this type of strategic control as implementation control. *Implementation control is designed to assess whether the overall strategy should be changed in light of unfolding events and results associated with incremental steps and actions that implement the overall strategy.* The earlier example of Prudential Insurance Company updating cost and revenue projections based on early experiences with regional home offices is an illustration of an implementation control. The two basic types of implementation control are: (1) monitoring strategic thrusts (new or key strategic programs) and (2) milestone reviews.

Monitoring Strategic Thrusts. Implementing broad strategies often involves undertaking several new strategic projects—specific narrow undertakings that represent part of what needs to be done if the overall strategy is to be accomplished. These projects or thrusts provide a source of information from which managers can obtain feedback that helps determine whether the overall strategy is progressing as planned and whether it needs to be adjusted or changed.

While strategic thrusts seem a readily apparent type of control, using them as control sources is not always easy to do. Early experience may be difficult to interpret. Clearly identifying and measuring early steps and promptly evaluating the overall strategy in light of this early, isolated experience can be difficult.

Two approaches are useful in enacting implementation controls focused on monitoring strategic thrusts. One way is to agree early in the planning process on which thrusts, or phases of those thrusts, are *critical factors in the success of the strategy or of that thrust.* Managers responsible for these implementation controls single these out from other activities and observe them frequently.

The second approach for monitoring strategic thrusts is to use stop/go assessments linked to a series of meaningful thresholds (time, costs, research and development, success, etc.) associated with particular thrusts. Days Inns' nationwide market development strategy in the early 1980s included a strategic thrust of regional development via company-owned inns in the Rocky Mountain area. Time problems in meeting development targets led company executives to reconsider the overall strategy, ultimately deciding to totally change it and sell the company.

Milestone Reviews.   Managers often attempt to identify critical milestones that will occur over the time period the strategy is being implemented. These milestones may be critical events, major resource allocations, or simply the passage of a certain amount of time. In each case, *a milestone review usually involves a full-scale reassessment of the strategy and the advisability of continuing or refocusing the direction of the company.*

A useful example of strategic implementation control based on milestone review can be found in Boeing's product development strategy to enter the supersonic transport (SST) airplane market. Competition from the joint British/French Concord effort was intense. Boeing had invested millions of dollars and years of scarce engineering talent through phase I of its SST venture. The market was believed large, but the next phase represented a billion-dollar decision for Boeing. This phase was established as a milestone review by Boeing management. Cost estimates were greatly increased; relatively few passengers and predictions of rising fuel costs raised estimated operating costs; the Concord had massive government subsidy, while Boeing did not. All factors led Boeing management to withdraw, in spite of high sunk costs, pride, and patriotism. Only an objective, full-scale strategy reassessment could have led to such a decision.[2]

In this example, a major resource allocation decision point provided the appropriate point for a milestone review. Milestone reviews might also occur concurrent with the timing of a new major step in the strategy's implementation or when a key uncertainty is resolved. Sometimes managers may even set an arbitrary time period, say, two years, as a milestone review point. Whatever the basis for selecting the milestone point, the critical purpose of a milestone review is to undertake a thorough review of the firm's strategy so as to control the company's future.

Strategic Surveillance

By their nature, premise control and implementation control are focused control. The third type of strategic control, *strategic surveillance, is designed to monitor a broad range of events inside and outside the company that are likely to threaten the course of the firm's strategy.*[3] The basic idea behind strategic surveillance is that some form of general monitoring of multiple

---

[2] Ibid.

[3] G. Scheyogg and H. Steinmann, "Strategie Control: A New Perspective," *Academy of Management Review* 12, no. 1 (1987), p. 101.

information sources should be encouraged, with the specific intent being the opportunity to uncover important yet unanticipated information.

Strategic surveillance must be kept unfocused as much as possible and should be designed as a loose "environmental-scanning" activity. Trade magazines, *The Wall Street Journal,* trade conferences, conversations, and intended and unintended observations are all sources of strategic surveillance. While strategic surveillance is loose, its important purpose is to provide an ongoing, broad-based vigilance in all daily operations so as to uncover information that may prove relevant to the firm's strategy.

Special Alert Control

Another type of strategic control, really a subset of the other three, is special alert control. *A special alert control is the need to thoroughly, and often rapidly, reconsider the firm's basic strategy based on a sudden, unexpected event.* A political coup in the Middle East, an outside firm suddenly acquiring a leading competitor, an unexpected product difficulty like Tylenol's experience with poisoned capsules—all of these represent sudden changes that can drastically alter the company's strategy.

Such an occurrence should trigger an immediate and intense reassessment of the company's strategy and its current strategic situation. Many firms have developed crisis teams to handle initial response and coordination when faced with unforeseen occurrences that may have an immediate effect on the firm's strategy. Increasingly, companies are developing contingency plans along with crisis teams to respond to such circumstances as are illustrated in Strategy in Action 13–1.

Table 13–1 summarizes the major characteristics of the four types of strategic control. While each type of strategic control is different, they share a common purpose: to assess whether the strategic direction should be altered in light of unfolding events. Unlike operational controls, strategic controls are designed to continuously and proactively question the basic direction of the strategy.

Operations controls are concerned with providing action control. Strategic controls are concerned with "steering" the company's future direction. Both are needed to manage the strategic process effectively. The next section examines key types of operations control systems used to aid the strategic management process.

Operational Control Systems

Strategic controls are useful to top management in monitoring and steering the basic strategic direction of the company. But operating managers also need control methods appropriate to their level of strategy implementation. The primary concern at the operating level is allocation and use of the company's resources.

Strategy in Action 13–1
Examples of Strategic Controls

Premise Control at Citicorp

Citicorp has been pursuing an aggressive product development strategy intended to achieve earnings growth of 15 percent annually while becoming an institution capable of supplying clients with any kind of financial service anywhere in the world. A major problem Citicorp faces in achieving this earnings growth is its exposure because of earlier, extensive loans to troubled Third World countries. Citicorp remains sensitive to the wide variety of predictions about impending Third World defaults.

Citicorp established a basic planning *premise* that 10 percent of its Third World loans will default annually over the next five years. Yet it maintains active *premise control* by having each of its international branches monitor daily announcements from key governments and from inside contacts. When the premise is challenged, management attempts to adjust Citicorp's posture. For example, when Peru's president, Alan Garcia, stated that his country would not pay interest on its debt as scheduled, Citicorp raised its default charge to 20 percent of its $100 million Peruvian exposure.

Implementation Control at Days Inns

Pioneering the budget segment of the lodging industry, Days Inns' strategy placed primary emphasis on company-owned facilities as it insisted on maintaining roughly a 3-to-1 company-owned/franchise ratio. This ratio ensured total control over standards, rates, and so forth by the parent company.

As other firms moved into the budget segment, Days Inns saw the need to expand rapidly throughout the United States, and it decided to reverse its conservative franchise posture. This reversal would rapidly accelerate its ability to open new locations. Longtime executives, concerned about potential loss of control over local standards, instituted *implementation controls* requiring both regular franchise evaluation and annual milestone reviews. Two years into the program, executives were convinced a high franchise/company ratio was manageable, and they accelerated the growth of franchising by doubling the franchise sales department.

Continued on Page 412

Strategy in Action 13–1 (*concluded*)

Strategic Surveillance at IBM

In the early years of its attempt to make and sell computers (versus its staple typewriters and adding machines), IBM's strategy was targeted toward the scientific and research markets in government, universities, and industry. Its early experience was poor as these organizations appeared to have little money buying IBM's large, expensive mainframe computer. Yet no other organization or setting had a need for the volume computing capacity—at least that was IBM management's assumption.

Fortunately for IBM, one sales executive's reading included the *Librarian,* a trade magazine among librarians at the time. He noticed one article about the number of transactions handled in large libraries and the need for automated solutions.

This led to a suggestion to investigate libraries as a market for IBM's early mainframes. Executives also found libraries to be relatively flush with funds because of recent, generous funding from the New Carnegie Foundation. This market proved to be the basis for IBM's early success (some say its real survival) in the mainframe computer business. And the discovery of this early, important niche has been attributed to an IBM manager's regular readings—a form of strategic surveillance—which was the only source for information critical to IBM's ability to steer its mainframe computer strategy in a successful direction.

Special Alert Control at United Airlines

The sudden impact of an airplane crash could be devastating to a major airline. Few companies have made more elaborate preparations than United Airlines. Its executive vice president, James M. Guyette, heads a crisis team permanently prepared to respond. Members carry beepers and are always on call. If United's Chicago headquarters receives word that a plane has crashed, for example, they can be in a "war room" within an hour to direct the response.

Beds are set up nearby so participants can catch a few winks; while they sleep, alternates take their places. Members of this squad have been carefully screened through simulated crisis drills. "The point is to weed out those who don't hold up well under stress," says Guyette. Although the team was established to handle flight disasters, it has since assumed an expanded role. Earlier this year, the process was activated when American Airlines, Inc., launched a fare war. And, according to Gulette, "We're brainstorming about how we would be affected by everything from a competitor who had a serious problem to a crisis involving a hijacking or taking a United employee hostage."

Sources: Adapted from "Citicorp: What the New Boss Is up To," *Fortune,* February 17, 1986, p. 40; conversations with selected Days Inns executives; Peter Drucker, *Innovation and Entrepreneurship* (New York: Harper & Row, 1986); and "How Companies Prepare for the Worst," *Business Week,* December 23, 1985, p. 74.

Table 13–1
Summary characteristics of the four types of strategic control

Basic characteristics	Types of strategic control			
	Premise control	*Implementation control*	*Strategic surveillance*	*Special alerts*
Objects of control	Planning premises and projections	Key strategic thrusts and milestones	Potential threats and opportunities related to the strategy	Occurrence of recognizable but unlikely events
Degree of focusing	High	High	Low	High
Data acquisition				
Formalization	Medium	High	Low	High
Centralization	Low	Medium	Low	High
Use with:				
Environmental factors	Yes	Seldom	Yes	Yes
Industry factors	Yes	Seldom	Yes	Yes
Strategy-specific factors	No	Yes	Seldom	Yes
Company-specific factors	No	Yes	Seldom	Seldom

Source: Adapted from G. Scheyogg and H. Steinmann, "Strategic Control: A New Perspective," *Academy of Management Review* 12, no. 1 (1987), pp. 91–103.

Operational control systems guide, monitor, and evaluate progress in meeting annual objectives. While strategic controls attempt to steer the company over an extended time period (usually five years or more), operational controls provide post-action evaluation and control over short time periods—usually from one month to one year. To be effective, operational control systems must take four steps common to all post-action controls:

1. Set standards of performance.
2. Measure actual performance.
3. Identify deviations from standards.
4. Initiate corrective action or adjustment.

Three types of operational control systems are *budgets, schedules,* and *key success factors.* The nature and use of these three operational control systems are described in the next several sections.

Budgeting Systems

The budgetary process was the forerunner of strategic planning. Capital budgeting in particular provided the means for strategic resource allocations. With the growing use of strategic management, such allocations are now based on strategic assessment and priorities, not solely on capital budgeting.[4] Yet capital and expenditure budgeting, as well as sales budgeting, remain important control mechanisms in strategy implementation.

A budget is simply a resource allocation plan that helps managers coordinate operations and facilitates managerial control of performance. Budgets themselves do not control anything. Rather, they set standards against which action can be measured. They also provide a basis for negotiating short-term resource requirements to implement strategy at the operating level.

Most firms employ a budgeting system, not a singular budget, in controlling strategy implementation. Figure 13–2 represents a typical budgeting system for a manufacturing business. A budgeting system incorporates a series of different budgets fitting the organization's unique characteristics. Because organizations differ, so do their budgets. Yet most firms include three general types of budgets—revenue, capital, and expenditure—in their budgetary control system.

Revenue Budgets.   Most firms employ some form of revenue budget to monitor their sales projections (or expectations), because this reflects a key objective of the chosen strategy. The revenue budget provides important information for the daily management of financial resources and key feedback as to whether the strategy is working. For evaluative purposes, the revenue budget may be derived from revenue forecasts arrived at in the planning process, or it may be linked to past revenue patterns. For example, most hotel/motel operators emphasize daily revenue compared to revenue for the same day in the previous year as a monitor of sales effectiveness.

A revenue budget is particularly important as a tool for control of strategy implementation. Revenue budgets provide an early warning system about the effectiveness of the firm's strategy. And if the deviation is considerably below or above expectations, this budgetary tool should initiate managerial action to reevaluate and possibly adjust the firm's operational or strategic posture.

Capital Budgets.   Capital budgets outline specific expenditures for plant, equipment, machinery, inventories, and other capital items needed during the budget period.

To support their strategies, many firms require capital investment or divestiture. A firm committed to a strong growth strategy may need additional capacity or facilities to support increased sales. On the other hand, a firm intent on retrenchment may have to divest major parts of its current operations to generate additional resources. In both cases, the firm is concerned with management of significant financial resources, probably over an extended time period.

---

[4] Peter Lorange, *Corporate Planning* (Englewood Cliffs, N.J.: Prentice-Hall, 1980), p. 155.

Figure 13–2
A typical budgeting system for controlling strategy implementation

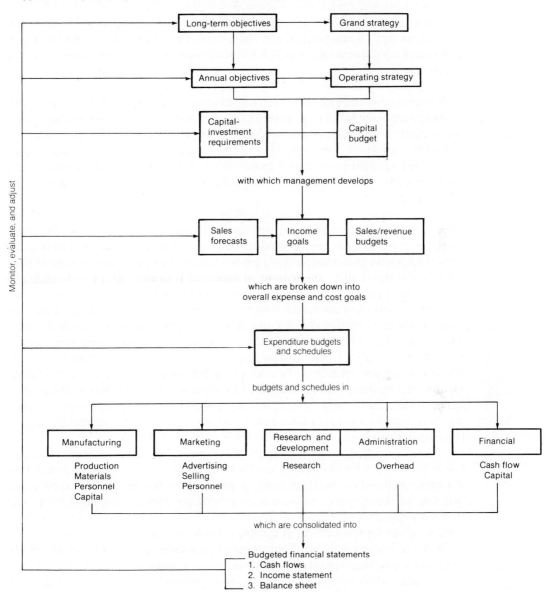

For effective control, a capital budget that carefully plans the acquisition and expenditure of funds, as well as the timing, is essential.

Two additional budgets are often developed to control the use of capital resources. A *cash budget* forecasts receipts and disbursements of cash—cash flow—during the budget period. And a *balance sheet budget* is usually developed to forecast the status of assets, liabilities, and net worth at the end of the budget period.

Expenditure Budgets.   Numerous expense/cost budgets will be necessary for budgetary control in implementation of strategy in various operating units of the firm. An expenditure budget for each functional unit and for subfunctional activities can guide and control unit/individual execution of strategy, thus increasing the likelihood of profitable performance. For example, a firm might have an expenditure budget for the marketing department and another for advertising activities.

In such budgets, dollar variables will be the predominant measure, although nondollar measures of physical activity levels may occasionally be used as a supplement.[5] For example, a production budget might include standards for expenditures as well as standards for output level or productivity. These nondollar variables might also include targets or milestones that provide evidence of necessary progress in particular strategic programs.

An expenditure or operating budget is meant to provide concrete standards against which operational costs and activities can be measured and, if necessary, adjusted to maintain effective strategy execution. The expenditure budget is perhaps the most common budgetary tool in strategy implementation. If its standards are soundly linked to strategic objectives, then it can provide an effective communication link between top management and operating managers about what is necessary for a strategy to succeed. It provides another warning system alerting management to problems in the implementation of the firm's strategy.

The budgeting system (see Figure 13–2) provides an integrated picture of the firm's operation as a whole. The effect on overall performance of a production decision to alter the level of work-in-process inventories or of a marketing decision to change sales organization procedures can be traced through the entire budget system. Thus, coordinating these decisions becomes an important consideration for the control of strategy implementation.

Figure 13–2 provides an illustration of how budgets can be coordinated to aid in coordinating operations. In this chart, production, raw material purchases, and direct labor requirements are coordinated with anticipated sales. In more comprehensive systems, other budgets may be included: manufacturing expense, inventories, building services, advertising, maintenance, cash flow, administrative overhead, and so on, as suggested earlier in this section.

---

[5] Ibid., p. 158.

Scheduling

Timing is often a key factor in the success of a strategy. Scheduling is simply a planning tool for allocating the use of a time-constrained resource or arranging the sequence of interdependent activities. The success of strategy implementation is quite dependent on both. So scheduling offers a mechanism with which to plan for, monitor, and control these dependencies. For example, a firm committed to a vertical integration strategy must carefully absorb expanded operations into its existing core. Such expansion, whether involving forward or backward integration, will require numerous changes in the operational practices of some of the firm's organizational units. A good illustration of this is Coors Brewery, which recently made the decision to integrate backward by producing its own beer cans. A comprehensive, two-year schedule of actions and targets for incorporating manufacture of beer cans and bottles into the product chain contributed to the success of this strategy. Major changes in purchasing, production scheduling, machinery, and production systems were but a few of the critical operating areas that Coors' scheduling efforts were meant to accommodate and control.

Key Success Factors

One useful way to effect operational control is to focus on "key success factors." Key success factors identify performance areas that must receive continuous management attention. These are the factors that are of greatest importance in implementing the company's strategies. Examples of key success factors focused on internal performance include: (1) improved productivity, (2) high employee morale, (3) improved product/service quality, (4) increased earnings per share, (5) growth in market share, and (6) completion of new facilities. Strategy in Action 13–2 illustrates the key success factors monitored by Chrysler management to control its turnaround strategy in the 1980s.

Each key success factor must have measurable performance indicators. Management of 1-2-3 from Lotus, for example, identified product quality, customer service, employee morale, and competition as the four key determinants of the success of their strategy to rapidly expend Lotus's software offerings. They identified three measures to monitor and control each key success factor as follows:

For product quality:
Performance data versus specifications.
Percentage of product returns.
Number of customer complaints.

For customer service:
Delivery cycle in days.
Percentage of orders shipped complete.
Field service delays.

Strategy in Action 13–2
Strategic Success Factors in Chrysler's Turnaround Strategy

When Lee Iacocca came to Chrysler in 1979, the Michigan State Fairgrounds were jammed with thousands of unsold, unwanted, rusting Chryslers, Dodges, and Plymouths. Foreign operations were leeching the lifeblood out of the company. And worst of all, cars were coming off the assembly line with loose doors, chipped paint, and crooked moldings.

According to Iacocca, the Chrysler experience highlighted four painful realities:

The quality of our products had declined.

Work practices had shortchanged productivity.

The government had become an enemy instead of an ally.

Foreign countries that the United States had defeated in war and rebuilt in peace were beating this country in its own markets.

Chrysler was faced with a choice. The company could go under—the suggestion of not a few—or efforts could be made to save the company, and with it, according to Iacocca, "the American way of doing business—with honesty, pride, ingenuity, and good old-fashioned hard work."

In charting Chrysler's turnaround strategy, Iacocca identified six key success factors essential to a successful turnaround. Chrysler executives used these six factors as the basis for their operational control of the turnaround strategy. Careful, systematic attention was given to monitoring progress on each factor as a key indicator of desired execution of the turnaround strategy.

1. Reduce *wage and salary expenses* by half the 1980 level. (Chrysler ultimately reduced its work force from 160,000 to 80,000 and received over $1.2 billion in wage and benefit sacrifices.)

2. Reduce *fixed cost* by over $4 billion. (Chrysler closed 20 plants and modernized the remaining 40 with state-of-the-art robot and computer technology.)

3. Reduce the *number of different parts* by one third. (Chrylser reduced the number of parts from 75,000 to 40,000, shaking $1 billion out of inventory in the process.)

4. Improve its *weak balance sheet*. (Chrysler retired its U.S. bank debt by converting $1.3 billion into preferred stock, and some preferred into common stock.)

Continued on Page 419

Strategy in Action 13–2 (*concluded*)

5. Improve the *quality of its components* and finished products. (Chrysler reduced warranty costs by 25 percent in 1982; it reduced scheduled maintenance costs to a level $20 to $200 below that of the competition.)

6. Implement a $6 billion *product improvement program*. (Chrysler has a lead in front-wheel-drive technology; it has the best fuel economy in the industry; it offers the industry's most extensive 50,000-mile warranty.)

Source: Based on Lee A. Iacocca, "The Rescue and Resuscitation of Chrysler," *Journal of Business Strategy* 4, no. 3 (1983), pp. 67–69.

For employee morale:
Trends in employee attitude survey.
Absenteeism versus plan.
Employee turnover trends.

For competition:
Number of firms competing directly.
Number of new products introduced.
Percentage of bids awarded versus standard.

Key success factors succinctly communicate the critical elements for which operational managers must be responsible in making the strategy successful. Because their achievement requires the successful performance of several key individuals, these factors can be a foundation for teamwork among managers in meeting the company's strategic objectives.

Budgeting, scheduling, and monitoring *key success factors* are important means to control the implementation of strategy at the operational level of the company. Common to each operational control system is the need to establish measurable standards and to monitor performance against these standards. The next section examines how to accomplish this important role.

Using Operational Control Systems: Monitoring Performance and Evaluating Deviations

Operating control systems require the establishment of performance standards. In addition, progress must be monitored and deviations from standards evaluated as the strategy is implemented. Timely information must be obtained so that deviations can be identified, the underlying cause determined, and actions taken to correct *or* exploit them.

Figure 13–3 illustrates a simplified report on the current status of key performance indicators linked to the firm's strategy. These performance indicators represent progress after two years of a five-year plan intended to differentiate the firm as a customer-service-oriented provider of high-quality products.

Figure 13-3
Monitoring and evaluating performance deviations

Key success factors	Objective, assumption or budget	Forecast performance at this time	Current performance	Current deviation	Analysis
Cost control: Ratio of indirect overhead to direct field and labor costs	10%	15%	12%	+3 (ahead)	Are we moving too fast or is there more unnecessary overhead than originally thought?
Gross profit	39%	40%	40%	0%	
Customer service: Installation cycle in days	2.5 days	3.2 days	2.7 days	+0.5 (ahead)	Can this progress be maintained?
Ratio of service to sales personnel	3.2	2.7	2.1	−0.6 (behind)	Why are we behind here? How can we maintain the installation cycle progress?
Product quality: Percentage of products returned	1.0%	2.0%	2.1%	−0.1% (behind)	Why are we behind here? Ramifications for other operations?
Product performance versus specification	100%	92%	80%	−12% (behind)	
Marketing: Sales per employee monthly	$12,500	$11,500	$12,100	+$600 (ahead)	Good progress. Is it creating any problems to support?
Expansion of product line	6	3	5	+2 products (ahead)	Are the products ready? Are the perfect standards met?
Employee morale in service area: Absenteeism rate	2.5%	3.0%	3.0%	(on target)	
Turnover rate	5%	10%	15%	−8% (behind)	Looks like a problem! Why are we so far behind?
Competition: New product introductions (average number)	6	3	6	−3 (behind)	Did we underestimate timing? Implications for our basic assumptions?

Management's concern is comparing *progress to date* with *expected progress* at this point in the plan. Of particular interest is the *current deviation* because it provides a basis for examining *suggested actions* (usually from subordinate managers) and for finalizing decisions on any necessary changes or adjustments in the company's operations.

In Figure 13–3, the company appears to be maintaining control of its cost structure. Indeed, it is ahead of schedule on reducing overhead. The company is well ahead of its delivery cycle target, while slightly below its service/sales personnel ratio objective. Product returns look OK, although product performance against specification is below standard. Sales per employee and expansion of the product line are ahead of schedule. Absenteeism in the service area is meeting projections, but turnover is higher than planned. Competitors appear to be introducing products more rapidly than expected.

After deviations and the underlying reasons for them are identified, the implications of these deviations for the ultimate success of the strategy must be seriously considered. For example, the rapid product line expansion indicated in Figure 13–3 may be in response to competitors' increased rate of product expansion. At the same time, product performance is still low and, while the installation cycle is slightly above standard (improving customer service), the ratio of service to sales personnel is below its target. Contributing to this substandard ratio (and perhaps reflecting a lack of organizational commitment to customer service) is the exceptionally high turnover in customer service personnel. The rapid reduction in indirect overhead costs might mean that administrative integration of customer service and product development requirements has been reduced too quickly.

As a result of this information, operations managers face several options. The deviations observed may be attributed primarily to internal factors or discrepancies. In this case, priorities can be scaled up or down. For example, greater emphasis might be placed on retaining customer service personnel while de-emphasizing overhead reduction and new product development. On the other hand, the management team could decide to continue as planned in the face of increasing competition and decide to accept or gradually improve the customer service situation. Another possibility is reformulating the strategy or a component of the strategy in the face of rapidly increasing competition. For example, the firm might decide to shift emphasis toward more standardized or lower-priced products to overcome customer service problems and take advantage of an apparently ambitious sales force.

This interpretation of Figure 13–3 is but one of many possible explanations. The important point is the critical need to monitor progress against standards and give serious, in-depth attention to both the reasons underlying observed deviations and the most appropriate responses to them.

Evaluations such as this are appropriate for organizational subunits, product groups, and operating units in a firm. Budgets, schedules, and other operating control systems with performance targets and standards linked to the strategic plan deserve this type of attention in detecting and evaluating deviations. The time frame is more compressed—usually quarterly or even monthly during the budgeted year. The operating manager typically reviews year-to-date progress against budgeted figures. After deviations are evaluated, slight adjustments may be necessary to keep progress, expenditures, or other factors in line with programmed needs of the strategy. In the unusual event that deviations are extreme—usually because of unforeseen changes—management is alerted to the possible need for revising the budget, reconsidering certain functional plans related to budgeted expenditures, or examining the units and effectiveness of the managers responsible.

An acceptable level of deviation should be allowed before action is taken; if not, the control process will become an administrative overload. Standards should not be regarded as absolute because the estimates used to formulate them are typically based on historical data, which, by definition, are "after the fact." Furthermore, absolute standards (keep equipment busy 100 percent of the time, or meet 100 percent of quota) are often used with no provision for variability. Standards are also often derived from averages, which, by definition, ignore variability. These difficulties suggest the need for defining acceptable *ranges* of deviation in budgetary figures or key indicators of strategic success. This approach helps in avoiding administrative difficulties, recognizing measurement variability, delegating more realistic authority to operating managers in making short-term decisions, and hopefully improves motivation.

Some companies use trigger points for clarification of standards, particularly in monitoring key success factors. A *trigger point* is a level of deviation of a key indicator or figure (such as a competitor's actions or a critical cost category) that management identifies in the planning process as representing either a major threat or an unusual opportunity. When that point is "hit," management is immediately alerted ("triggered") to consider necessary adjustments in the firm's strategy. Some companies take this idea a major step forward and develop one or more *contingency plans* to be implemented once predetermined trigger points are reached. These contingency plans redirect priorities and actions rapidly so that valuable reaction time is not "wasted" on administrative assessment and deliberation of the extreme deviation.

Correcting deviations in performance brings the entire management task into focus. Managers can correct performance by changing measures. Perhaps deviations can be resolved by changing plans. Management can eliminate poor performance by changing how things are done, by hiring new people, by retraining present workers, by changing job assignments, and so on. Correcting deviations from plans, therefore, can involve all of the functions, tasks, and responsibilities of operations managers. Operational control systems are intended to provide essential feedback so that company managers can make the necessary decisions and adjustments to implement the current strategy.

Reward Systems: Motivating Execution and Control

Execution and control of strategy ultimately depend on individual organizational members, particularly key managers. And motivating and rewarding good performance by individuals and organizational units are key ingredients in effective strategy implementation. While positive reinforcements are given primary emphasis, sanctions or negative reinforcements are important tools for controlling and adjusting poor performance. Motivating and controlling individual efforts, particularly those of managerial personnel, in execution of strategy is accomplished through a firm's reward–sanction mechanisms—compensation, raises, bonuses, stock options, incentives, benefits, promotions, demotions, recognition, praise, criticism, more (or less) responsibility, group norms, performance appraisal, tension, and fear. These mechanisms are positive and negative, short run and long run.

Control mechanisms align personal and subunit actions and objectives with the objectives and needs of the firm's strategy. This is not easy, and reward–sanction structures controlling strategy execution vary greatly across different firms. For example, Harold Geneen, former CEO of ITT, purportedly used an interesting combination of money (compensation and incentives), tension (strict accountability for results), and fear to control individual managers' efforts toward strategy implementation. According to one author:

> Geneen provides his managers with enough incentives to make them tolerate the system. Salaries all the way through ITT are higher than average—Geneen reckons 10 percent higher—so that few people can leave without taking a drop. As one employee put it: "We're all paid just a bit more than we think we're worth." At the very top, where the demands are greatest, the salaries and stock options are sufficient to compensate for the rigors. As someone said, "He's got them by their limousines."
>
> Having bound his men to him with chains of gold, Geneen can induce the tension that drives the machine. "The key to the system," one of his men explained, "is the profit forecast. Once the forecast has been gone over, revised, and agreed on, the managing director has a personal commitment to Geneen to carry it out. That's how he produces the tension on which the success depends." The tension goes through the company, inducing ambition, perhaps exhilaration, but always with some sense of fear: what happens if the target is missed?[6]

BIC Pen Company takes a different approach. Its reward structure involves incentive systems, wide latitude for operating managers, and clearly specified objectives to motivate and control individual initiative. All employees are invited to participate in a stock purchase plan whereby up to 10 percent of their salary can be used to purchase stock at a 10 percent discount from the market price. Functional managers are given wide rein in operational decisions

---

[6] Anthony Sampson, *The Sovereign State of ITT* (New York: Steig & Day, 1973), p. 132.

while being held strictly accountable for results. The director of manufacturing, for example, is free to spend up to $500,000 for a cost-saving machine, as long as profit margin objectives are maintained. Commenting on his approach to rewarding executives, BIC's president, Robert Adler, said:

> We have a unique bonus system, which I'm sure the Harvard Business School would think is crazy. Each year I take a percentage of profits before tax and give 40 percent to sales, 40 percent to manufacturing, and 20 percent to the treasurer to be divided up among executives in each area. Each department head keeps some for himself and gives the rest away. We never want bonuses to be thought of as salaries because they would lose their effect. So we change the bonus day each year so that it always comes as a pleasant surprise, something to look forward to.[7]

These two examples highlight several generalizations about the use of rewards and sanctions to control individuals, particularly managers, in strategy execution. Financial incentives are important reward mechanisms. They are particularly useful in controlling performance when they are directly linked to specific activities and results. Intrinsic, nonfinancial rewards, such as flexibility and autonomy in the job and visible control over performance, are important managerial motivators. And negative sanctions, such as withholding financial and intrinsic rewards or the tensions emanating from possible consequences of substandard performance, are necessary ingredients in directing and controlling managers' efforts.

The time horizon on which rewards are based is a major consideration in linking rewards and sanctions to strategically important activities and results. Numerous authors and business leaders have expressed concern with incentive systems based on short-term (typically annual) performance. They fear short-term reward structures can result in actions and decisions that undermine the long-term position of a firm. A marketing director who is rewarded based on the cost effectiveness and sales generated by the marketing staff might place significantly greater emphasis on established distribution channels than on "inefficient" nurturing and development of channels that the firm has not previously used. A reward system based on maximizing current profitability can potentially shortchange the future in terms of current investments (time, people, and money) from which the primary return will be in the future.[8] If the firm's grand strategy is growth through, among other means, horizontal integration of current products into new channels and markets, the reward structure could be directing the manager's efforts in a way that penalizes the ultimate success of the strategy. And the marketing director, having per-

---

[7] C. R. Christensen, K. R. Andrews, and J. L. Bower, *Business Policy: Text and Cases* (Homewood, Ill.: Richard D. Irwin, 1978), p. 318.

[8] W. R. King and D. I. Cleland, *Strategic Planning and Policy* (New York: Van Nostrand Reinhold, 1978), p. 364.

formed notably within the current reward structure, may have moved on to other responsibilities before the shortcomings emerge.

Short-term executive incentive schemes typically focus on last year's (or last quarter's) profits. This exclusive concentration on the bottom line has four weaknesses in terms of promoting a new strategy:[9]

1. It is backward looking. Reported results reflect past events and, to some extent, past strategy.

2. The focus is short term, even though many of the recorded transactions have effects over longer periods.

3. Strategic gains or losses are not considered due to, among other things, basic accounting methods.

4. Investment of time and money in future strategy can have a negative impact. Since such outlays and efforts are usually intermingled with other expenses, a manager can improve his or her bonus by *not* preparing for the future.

While there are clear dangers in incentive systems that encourage decidedly short-run thinking and neglect the longer term, there is real danger in hastily condemning short-term measures. Arguing that managers must be concerned with long-run performance is easy; it also may be too easy to make the mistake of concluding that short-term concerns are not important or that they are necessarily counterproductive to the strategic needs of the organization. Such a simplistic and quick conclusion can be dangerous. In an effectively implemented strategy, short-term objectives or aims support, and are critical to, the achievement of long-term strategic goals. The real problem is not the short- versus long-term concerns of management; it is the lack of integration of and consistency between long- and short-term plans and objectives in the control system that is vital to the successful implementation of strategy.[10] The critical ingredients for the achievement of this consistency are appropriate rewards and incentives.

To integrate long- and short-term concerns, reward systems must be based on the assessment and control of both the short-run and long-run (strategic) contributions of key managers. An effective reward system should provide payoffs that control and evaluate the creation of *potential* future performances as well as last year's results. Figure 13–4 illustrates a management reward system tied to a five-year cycle of strategy implementation. Review and evaluation in a specific year include *both* an assessment of performance during that year *and* an evaluation of progress toward the five-year strategic objectives. The annual objectives and incentives in each year can reflect adjustments

---

[9] Yavitz and Newman, *Strategy in Action*, pp. 204–9.

[10] Lawrence G. Hrebiniak and William F. Joyce, *Implementing Strategy* (New York: Macmillan, 1984), pp. 204–9.

Figure 13–4
Annual incentive system with long-term perspective

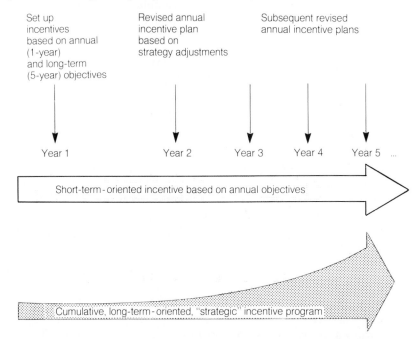

necessary for successful implementation of the strategy. This helps integrate short- and long-term considerations in strategy implementation by linking adjustments necessary in supporting revised, long-term considerations to next year's reward structure. The second component in the management reward system in Figure 13–4 is an incentive based on cumulative progress toward strategic objectives. It is shown as increasing in size or amount over time, which reinforces a long-term, strategic perspective. Incentives such as stock options, deferred bonuses, or cumulative compensation indexed to future performance indicators are ways this reward component could be structured. The key ingredient is an incentive system linked to longer-term progress toward strategic goals. This approach reinforces the interdependence of performance over the five-year period rather than the importance of any one year.

These incentive priorities (long-term versus short-term) should vary depending on the basic nature of the strategy. Figure 13–5 provides the results of a recent study illustrating this point. Comparing the importance of 11 criteria used in determining bonuses for SBU managers, the researchers found that long-term criteria were more important determinants of bonuses in SBUs with "build-oriented" strategies than in SBUs with "harvest-oriented" strategies. Short-term criteria were important in both types of SBUs, although these criteria were much more important than long-term criteria for determin-

Figure 13–5
Perceived importance of various performance dimensions in determination of SBU general manager's incentive bonus

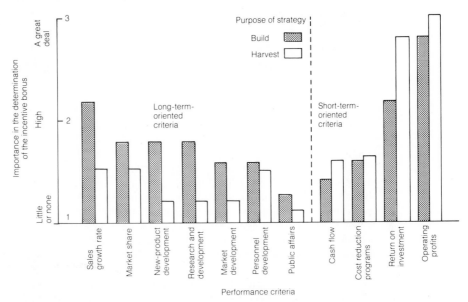

Source: Anil K. Gupta and V. Govindarajan, "Build, Hold, Harvest: Converting Strategic Intentions into Reality," *Journal of Business Strategy*, Winter 1984, p. 43.

ing incentive structures in harvest-oriented SBUs. Strategy in Action 13–3 illustrates how top executives at two multibusiness companies that participated in this research link reward structures for their SBUs to each SBU's basic strategy.

Another refinement suggested in constructing incentive systems that reward long-term (strategic) as well as short-term thinking is the use of *strategic budgets*.[11] In this approach, strategic budgets are employed simultaneously with operating budgets, but the objectives and plans associated with each budget vary a great deal. The focus of the operating budget is control and evaluation of business as usual. The strategic budget specifies resources (and targets) for key programs or activities linked to major initiatives that are integral to the long-term strategy. Concerned that executive incentive plans can and should give more explicit weight to strategic activities, proponents of a strategic budget approach suggest three basic steps:[12]

---

[11] Peter Lorange, *Implementation of Strategic Planning* (Englewood Cliffs, N.J.: Prentice-Hall, 1982); and "Strategic Control: Some Issues in Making It Operationally More Useful," in *Latest Advances in Strategic Management,* ed. R. Lamb Warren (Englewood Cliffs, N.J.: Prentice-Hall, 1986).

[12] Yavitz and Newman, *Strategy in Action,* p. 179.

Strategy in Action 13–3
Linking Incentive Compensation to Strategy in Large Multibusiness Firms

Recent research suggests large firms are moving away from uniform (usually "bottom-line") profit criteria to determine incentives in favor of multiple criteria linked in some way to business unit strategy. Below are reports from two multibusiness firms:

At a $5 billion producer of specialty chemicals and metal alloys, the strategic plan for each business is prepared before the annual budgeting process. The objective of the annual budgeting process, however, is not just to prepare an operating budget but also what executives in this firm refer to as a *strategic budget*. The latter "budget" lists specific strategic actions that the business unit manager would, in line with the long-range strategic plan, need to undertake during the coming year. Examples of items in such a strategic budget are: "increase market share from x percent to y percent," "prepare a strategic plan to reposition product P by such and such date," "find a buyer for subunit A," and so on. Managers are required to submit progress reports on a quarterly basis on accomplishments vis-à-vis this strategic budget. On a yearly basis, these accomplishments are evaluated for the purposes of determining the second half of a manager's incentive bonus. The link between the strategic mission and the incentive system then becomes a straightforward task—one part of the bonus is linked to certain items in the annual operating budget, and the other part to certain other items in the annual strategic budget.

At a $5 billion producer of electronics components and equipment, 25 percent of every SBU manager's bonus is based on corporate performance ("we want them to take a broader, corporatewide perspective") and the remaining 75 percent is split equally between the SBU's bottom-line and nonfinancial objectives. A group vice president detailed how this incentive system operates: "I have three units. I essentially get the same data on each. But in the nonfinancial objectives— more so than in the financial ones—I try to evaluate the three units against their strategic missions. For instance, for [business with a build strategy], I look for acquisitions planned, progress on capital projects, market share, and so forth. For my other two units [with maintain and harvest strategies], I focus on pricing, elimination of low-margin items, cost control, and the line. It is in these nonfinancial objectives where you can differentiate the performance criteria by strategy."

In firms that appear to have made the maximum progress toward matching the incentive system to strategy, the bonus is usually split into two parts: one

Continued on Page 429

Strategy in Action 13–3 (*concluded*)

based on financial figures—such as earnings, return on investment, and cash flow—and the other based on the manager's accomplishments with regard to certain "strategic milestones" derived from the long-range strategic plan.

Source: Adapted from Anil K. Gupta and V. Govindarajan, "Build, Hold, Harvest: Converting Strategic Intentions into Reality," *Journal of Business Strategy,* Winter 1984, pp. 39–47.

1. Measure progress toward strategic targets separately from results of established operations.
2. Determine incentive awards separately for established operations and for progress toward strategic targets.
3. Devise a long-term, stock option equivalent to encourage revisions of strategy and entrepreneurial risk taking.

Common to each of these reward and sanction approaches is growing recognition of the need for a two-tiered incentive system linked to short-run and long-term considerations. The relative emphasis in terms of reward linkages should be determined by the focus of the strategy. For businesses with growth-oriented strategies, for example, incentive systems weighted toward long-term payoffs are more appropriate. Strategy in Action 13–4 illustrates a clear emphasis on this type of executive reward system among *INC* magazine's top 100 growth firms. Each incentive emphasizes long-term value based on either stock appreciation, length of the option, or a combination of both. While this emphasis is appropriate, short-term operating objectives deserve attention so that short-term performance is geared toward long-term objectives. For businesses pursuing more immediate strategic goals, the incentive emphasis should shift accordingly. In harvest business units of large firms, for example, greater emphasis on short-term, easily quantified performance indicators appears to be the basis for reward systems designed to evaluate strategic results.

Summary

Two fundamental perspectives—strategic and operational control—provide the basis for designing strategy control systems. Strategic controls are intended to steer the company toward its long-term strategic direction. Premise controls, implementation controls, strategic surveillance, and special alerts are four types of strategic control. Each is designed to meet top management's need to track the strategy as it is being implemented, detect underlying problems, and make necessary adjustments. These strategic controls are linked to the environmental assumptions and key operating requirements necessary for successful strategy implementation.

Strategy in Action 13–4
Linking Bonus Compensation to Strategy: What the *INC* 100 Fastest-Growing Companies Grant

Type of long-term compensation	Definition	Number of INC 100 companies	
Investment:			
Incentive stock option	Right to purchase company stock at a set price over period not to exceed 10 years; price must equal 100 percent of fair market value at grant with optionee limited to $100,000 (plus unused carryovers) per year in aggregate exercise cost, must be exercised in order of grant; capital gains at sale if acquired shares held at least one year after exercise and two years after grant.	New plan Continuing plan Total	29 54 83
Nonqualified stock options	Rights to purchase company stock at a set price over a stated period, often years; typically, price is 100 percent of market value at grant, but can be less. Gain at exercise is taxable income.	New plan Continuing plan Total	2 55 57
Stock purchases	Short-term rights to purchase company stock, typically at a discount from market value and/or with financing assistance from the company. Shares may be subject to transfer restrictions.	New plan Continuing plan Total	2 7 9
Noninvestment:			
Stock appreciation rights	Right to receive in stock and/or cash appreciation the gain in market value of specified number of shares since grant, typically granted in conjunction with stock options.	New plan Continuing plan Total	1 8 9
Stock grants (restricted stock)	Grants of stock, typically subject to transfer restrictions and risk of forfeiture until earned by continued employment with the company.	New plan Continuing plan Total	— 1 1

Source: "Beyond the Paycheck: Compensating for Growth," *INC,* September 1983, p. 110.

Operational control systems identify the performance standards associated with allocation and use of the company's financial, physical, and human resources in pursuit of the strategy. Budgets, schedules, and key success factors are the primary means of operational control.

Operational control systems require systematic evaluation of performance against predetermined standards or targets. A critical concern here is identification and evaluation of performance deviations, with careful attention paid to determining the underlying reasons and strategic implications for observed deviations before management reacts. Some companies use trigger points and contingency plans in this process.

The reward system is a key ingredient in motivating managers to emphasize execution and control in steering the business toward strategic success. Companies should emphasize incentive systems that ensure adequate attention to strategic thrusts. This usually requires a concerted effort to emphasize long-term performance indicators rather than solely emphasizing short-term measures of performance. Short- and long-term performance considerations must be integrated to ensure performance consistent with the company's strategy and to provide a basis for monitoring future short-run performance against objectives incrementally linked to long-term strategic outcomes.

Questions for Discussion

1. Distinguish strategic control from operating control. Give an example of each.
2. Select a business that has a strategy you are familiar with. Identify what you think are its key premises. Then select the key indicators you would use to monitor each premise.
3. Explain the differences between implementation controls, strategic surveillance, and special alerts. Give example of each.
4. Why are budgets, schedules, and key success factors essential to operations control and evaluation?
5. What are key considerations in monitoring deviations from performance standards?
6. How would you vary an incentive system for a growth-oriented versus a harvest-oriented business?
7. Why do strategists prefer reward systems similar to that shown in Figure 13–4? What are the advantages and disadvantages of such a system?

Bibliography

Bales, Carter. "Strategic Control: The President's Paradox." *Business Horizons,* August 1977, pp. 17–28.

Bower, Joseph. "Planning and Control." *Journal of General Management* 1, no. 3 (1974), pp. 20–31.

Camillus, J. C. "Six Approaches to Preventive Management Control." *Financial Executive,* December 1980, pp. 28–31.

Christopher, W. "Achievement Reporting—Controlling Performance against Objectives." *Long-Range Planning,* October 1977, pp. 14–24.

Diffenbach, J. "Finding the Right Strategic Combination." *Journal of Business Strategy,* Fall 1981, pp. 47–58.

Hobbs, John, and Donald Heany. "Coupling Strategy to Operating Plans." *Harvard Business Review,* May–June 1977, pp. 119–26.

Horovits, J. N. "Strategic Control: A New Task for Top Management." *Long-Range Planning,* June 1979, pp. 2–7.

Lenz, R. T. "Determinants of Organizational Performance: An Interdisciplinary Review." *Strategic Management Journal* 2 (1981), pp. 131–54.

Lorange, P., and D. Murphy. "Considerations in Implementing Strategic Control." *Journal of Business Strategy* 4 (1984), pp. 27–35.

Merchant, Kenneth A. "The Control Function of Management." *Sloan Management Review* 23, no. 4 (1982), pp. 43–55.

Newman, W. H. *Constructive Control: Design and Use of Control Systems.* Englewood Cliffs, N.J.: Prentice-Hall, 1975.

Rappaport, Alfred. "Executive Incentives versus Corporate Growth." *Harvard Business Review,* July–August 1978, pp. 81–88.

Rockart, J. F. "Chief Executives Define Their Own Data Needs." *Harvard Business Review,* March–April 1979, pp. 85–94.

Schreyögg, G., and H. Steinmann. "Strategic Control: A New Perspective." *Academy of Management Review* 12, no. 1 (1987), pp. 91–103.

Yavitz, B., and W. H. Newman. *Strategy in Action.* New York: Free Press, 1982, chap. 12.

Chapter 13 Cohesion Case Illustration

Guiding and Evaluating the Strategy at Holiday Inns, Inc.

Holiday Inns' corporate strategy sought to focus the company's growth in the two business sectors of hotels and casino gaming while seeking to divest businesses that were not directly tied to this new hospitality focus. That meant divesting Trailways, Delta, and eventually Perkins.

The business strategy of the hotel group centered on both product and market development, the intent being to expand the company's participation in all segments of the evolving lodging industry in a profitable, leadership fashion. The business strategy of the gaming group focused on market development, seeking to ensure a leadership position for the company's Harrah's operation in each of the four U.S. markets for legalized gambling as well as in any newly legalized markets.

Several controls used by Holiday Inns executives to guide and evaluate these two business-level strategies will be illustrated below.

Strategic Control

Premise Control

The company's renewed focus on hotels centered on accelerated, steady expansion of the number of franchised Holiday Inns properties in domestic and international urban markets. This decision to initially emphasize continued Holiday Inns expansion rather than immediate expansion into other types of lodging chains (budget, high-priced, etc.) was based on the company's market research-derived premise that for the next five years or more, the mid-priced segment of the lodging industry would remain the place where 75–80 cents out of every lodging dollar would be spent. At the same time, management was preparing the company for expansion (via newly named chains) into various segments of the lodging industry when the demand became more convincing. So they carefully monitored this premise on which the initial lodging strategy was predicated; if they detected a change in the size of the mid-priced segment as well as acceleration in the growth of one or more of these other segments (which they considered a strong possibility at some future date), Holiday Inns' top management would alter the initial strategy to the extent of implementing aggressive development of new chains (or brands) designed to compete in these faster-growing segments.

By 1985, this premise control had led Holiday Corporation (the corporate name was changed to reflect the company's emphasis on several lodging chains—or *brands,* as they called them) to move by acquisition or internal development into five different lodging segments. They were as follows:

Holiday Inn Hotels—the current leader in the full-service, mid-priced market segment.

Holiday Inn Crowne Plaza Hotels—hotels that offer extra amenities and personalized services in selected urban areas.

Embassy Suites Hotels—the world's largest all-suite hotel system, offering spacious suite accommodations and extra services. Established via acquisition.

Hampton Inn Hotels—a limited-service hotel chain providing streamlined facilities without restaurants in the rapidly growing budget segment. Internally developed with heavy franchising emphasis.

The Residence Inn Hotel—a recently acquired, unique system of residential-style, all-suite properties designed for guests staying five days or longer.

Implementation Control

One of the key strategic thrusts of Holiday Corporation's strategy of maintaining and expanding its leadership position in the lodging industry has been to intensify the level of franchising associated with its lodging chains. By so doing, the company felt it would be in a position to more rapidly and aggressively move into attractive or growing locations since the requirement for capital in a very capital-intensive business would be supplied by the franchisee, not the Holiday Corporation. Therefore, the company could invest its capital in the means necessary to sell and manage each lodging network rather than in the land and buildings necessary to secure each new site.

In 1985, two years into the plan, corporate management monitoring the success of this thrust concluded that while it was working, its impact on return on stockholder equity could be accelerated. The original thrust had the gradual effect, as the number of franchises relative to company-owned properties increased, of improving ROE by replacing operating income generated by ownership of properties with higher-return income from franchise fees and assessments requiring less capital investment. But managers monitoring the implementation of this key strategic thrust concluded that its impact could be accelerated by doing two things:

1. The company could begin to sell off selected lodging properties to interested investors and retain a management contract with them to operate the property as a Holiday Inn Hotel. Interested, passive investors

(such as pension funds or insurance companies) got an attractive yet secure investment with reasonably guaranteed returns—the historical track record of the facility gave clear evidence of its income-producing capability. And the Holiday Corporation was able to sell an asset for many times its book value, keep control of the location and continue to derive income via management fees, and use that additional, sizable revenue ($87 million in operating income and $328 million in cash flow in 1985 alone) to support expansion of its several lodging and gaming businesses.

2. The company could increase its leverage of the company's still-extensive asset base to increase the capital available to support corporatewide growth.

They therefore changed its conservative debt/invested capital ratio policy from a required ratio of 30–40 percent to a ratio of 45–60 percent.

Implementation control, focused on one strategic thrust having to do with increasing ROE and market presence via increased franchising, led Holiday Corporation to adjust two other thrusts—debt policy and management services—so as to fine-tune the direction of the company's chosen strategy.

Strategic Surveillance

An interesting example of Holiday Corporation's benefit from the use of strategic surveillance occurred with regard to its attempt to develop a satellite communications network, HI-NET, as a state-of-the-art offering linking its lodging facilities—particularly those catering to convention business—to provide teleconferencing, in-room entertainment, and other as yet unforeseen benefits. Top executives viewed being first with this technology (in the lodging and gaming industries) and at the forefront of this technology as essential competitive advantages for its future as a market leader. Consistent with this assumption, several executives regularly read satellite communications information, attended trade shows, and otherwise strategically surveyed events in this area.

This surveillance led two Holiday Inns executives to become aware of an emerging company, Communications Satellite Corporation, which was very much at the technological forefront of satellite and microwave communications. Subsequent investigation led to a long-term joint venture between the two firms to develop the HI-NET communications satellite network into the world's largest privately owned satellite communication system. Partly as a result of strategic surveillance by several Holiday Corporation executives, the firm was able to speed up the development of its HI-NET system and was more likely to ensure its use of the field's latest technology.

Special Alert Control

Holiday Corporation's gaming business, Harrah's, was committed to a strategy of rapid market development so as to maintain and expand its leadership position in the U.S. gaming industry. Building from its dominant position in Nevada markets, Harrah's moved quickly in an effort to become a dominant force in the newly legalized Atlantic City market. It developed its own Harrah's property and bought a 50 percent interest in another property owned by Donald Trump, the Trump Casino Hotel, so as to be able to further dominate the Atlantic City market should it continue its explosive early expansion.

At the same time, Harrah's executives carefully monitored two indicators of the future direction of the Atlantic City market—supply of gaming floor space (to include the number of tables and slot machines) and number of Atlantic City visitors—on a monthly basis. Uncertain about the stability of the Atlantic City gaming environment, these factors were monitored so as to alert Harrah's management about changing market fundamentals that would seriously erode potential profitability in the new gaming market. By 1986, the growth in market demand had not kept pace with supply additions of 12.5 percent and 12.8 percent in the two previous years, thus alerting Harrah's management to reevaluate their degree of emphasis on this market as a realistic source for continued rapid growth in profitability and market share. This in turn led to a slight change in strategy, with Holiday Corporation deciding to sell its 50 percent interest in the Trump Casino in Atlantic City, to finalize a 15,000-square-foot expansion of its Harrah's Marina in Atlantic City, and to initiate construction of a hotel/casino in Laughlin, Nevada, which is a new, rapidly growing gaming market.

Operations Control

Each of the hotel businesses and the Harrah's casino gaming business use several types of operational control to monitor and evaluate the implementation of their strategies on a year-to-year basis. We will briefly describe two operational control systems within the hotel group that serve this purpose: expenditure budgeting and quality control.

Expenditure Budgeting System

The Holiday Inn chain has adopted an expenditure budgeting system, which it calls *operations management systems (OMS),* to control the profitability of each Holiday Inn. The purpose of this system is to monitor and control profitability at individual inn locations by providing weekly budgets for the use of hotel resources that reflect the cyclical nature of occupancy patterns throughout the year. This OMS budgeting system provides the local managers, called innkeepers, with projected staff scheduling needs, energy control (based on weather forecasts), departmental (inn, restaurant, and lounge) expenditures, and usage, inventory control, and quality assurance needs for each week throughout the year to help control profitability yet attempt to ensure the full-service level of quality portrayed in Holiday Inns' mission and promotion. The weekly budgets are updated monthly, and innkeepers report they are very helpful in making the day-to-day management decisions necessary to keep profitability in line.

Quality Control

The Holiday Inns chain puts major emphasis on its efforts to maintain and control the quality of its 1,800 plus locations. It is essential that continued, careful efforts be made to ensure that each facility offers standardized, high-quality accommodation and service. At the heart of the system used to do this is a staff of 30 full-time inspectors, who travel over 1.5 million miles each year and perform approximately 5,000 unannounced, biannual inspections of properties in the Holiday Inns system. Many properties are actually inspected three times a year through this program, where the inspector makes a 24-hour, unannounced inspection of up to 1,100 different items ranging from the quality of a mattress to the greeting from a waiter to the cleanliness of bar utensils. Hotel properties failing two inspections in a row are removed from the system. Chairman Mike Rose proudly reported in 1986 that "To reinforce our commitment to continually improving product quality, we eliminated from our Holiday Inn system 59 hotels that did not meet our standards or our customers' expectations of quality for Holiday Inn Hotels last year."

Reward Systems at Holiday Corporation

A basic, corporatewide objective at Holiday Inns is to achieve an annual return on stockholders' equity of between 18 and 20 percent over the planning period. This objective represents the basic objective pursued by each business unit's strategy. Top management at the Holiday Corporation implements several reward systems designed to encourage executive and employee performance in this direction. Selected programs are as follows:

Employee Savings Plan

The company instituted in 1985 a program whereby all employees could contribute up to 16 percent of their earnings on a pre-tax basis, which would be matched by the company and used to purchase Holiday Corporation common stock in the employee's name. The company's matching contribution would vest (become fully controlled by an employee leaving the company) in eight years.

This plan has two effects consistent with the company's hospitality businesses and their dependence on personalized attention by individual employees to project the proper full-service image. First, it links every employee's financial savings program at least partially to the successful operation—profitability and sales growth—of each lodging or gaming property. And the company's matching contribution has the effect of leveraging the employees' potential benefits if they provide good service (and the stock does well). Second, it ties employees motivated by this program to the company for at least eight years—enough time to identify and keep highly productive employees while resulting in no cost to the company if some employees, hopefully those that don't measure up, leave before eight years.

Executive Stock Programs

The company has two plans under which executives and key employees are awarded shares of stock or stock options in the company's common stock. One program awards shares of common stock subject to forfeiture restrictions ranging from two to six years, which restrictions are in turn linked to the time horizons associated with key strategic programs the recipients are responsible for implementing. A second stock option program grants key management personnel the option to purchase the company's stock at a price equal to its market value at the date of the grant. Obviously, both programs link key executives' financial rewards to improved stock performance. Furthermore, each program takes effect over time, which further links reward to long-term, strategic success.

Long-Term Performance Plans

Holiday Corporation also has a long-term performance plan under which contingent awards of cash and shares of common stock are granted to key executives. Awards are paid only if the company's financial performance *over a four-year period* meets or exceeds standards determined by the Executive Compensation Committee of Holiday Corporation's board of directors. This program focuses rewards on the long-term performance of the company and the strategies executives develop.

All of these reward systems are clearly designed to link the actions of employees and key executives with the company's long-term objectives.

Epilogue

A Summary of Key Decisions Made by Holiday Inn Executives in Positioning the Company for the 1990s

Become a Narrowly Focused, "Hospitality" Company

The first key decision made by top management at Holiday Inns, Inc., was to redefine the company from being a broadly diversified, transportation-related company to a much more narrowly focused, hospitality company. The following comments made by key Holiday Inns executives serve to explain this fundamental corporate change. Roy Winegardner, commenting to *Business Week:*

> We are in the process of reshaping Holiday Inns into a different company. Holiday Inns is actually a hospitality company—a concept that will limit its scope to lodging, entertainment, and food. . . . In the future, the company will get into as few businesses as possible, and only those that have good growth, high returns, and are synergistic with our main business—hotels.

Mike Rose, to the New York Society of Security Analysts:

> We concluded that we simply could not provide the right kind of management to the wide variety of businesses we were in at the time, so we set about divesting ourselves of those that did not fit with our hospitality strategy.

Divest Businesses in the Transportation Group, the Products Group, and the Perkins Restaurant Chain

Between 1979 and 1986, Holiday Inns, Inc.'s top management systematically sold off virtually all businesses not directly involved with either its hotel group or its gaming group. In each case, they sold going concerns and waited for the right opportunity to sell so as to minimize their losses associated with getting out of the business.

Trailways was sold in 1979; Delta Steamship was sold in 1985; and the Perkins chain was sold in 1986. Selected products group businesses were sold as opportunities arose throughout this time period. The products group became essentially the procurement device for the hotel group and also provided facilities-planning services to the entire lodging system.

Shift to a Product Development Strategy within the Hotel Group

Holiday Inns' key decision looking to the 1990s was to focus solely on lodging and gaming. The essence of the initial strategy was to encourage steady growth in the Holiday Inn Hotel chain and rapid growth of the Harrah's hotel/casino business. Early comments by Chairman Mike Rose were as follows. Speaking to New York security analysts in the early 1980s:

> The key to our long-term direction is the fact that our hotel business will be our core business for the future. . . . The mission of the hotel group is to grow Holiday Inns' leadership position in the broad, midscale segments of the lodging industry, to grow our consumer recognition as the preferred brand in the lodging industry. . . . While we think the percentage growth of demand will be highest in the high-price or image segment, in absolute terms demand for rooms in the moderate-price segment will grow three times faster than in either the high-price or low-price segments.

By the late 1980s, the strategy shifted from a major emphasis solely on Holiday Inns as the hotel focus to the development of several different lodging chains, each targeted at a specific segment of the maturing lodging industry. Each chain, including Holiday Inns, was now referred to as one of the company's hotel *brands* or *products*. Seemingly, to lessen the emphasis on, and identity solely with, Holiday Inns, the company reorganized itself as Holiday Corporation. The following remarks made by Mike Rose in 1986 reflect this significant shift in strategy:

> Under our new name, Holiday Corporation, 1986 was a year of great accomplishment for our company. Holiday Corporation is now a multiple-brand hospitality company specializing in hotels and hotel/casinos. We intend to concentrate on the hotel and hotel/casino businesses, developing profitable market segments within those businesses where we either enjoy leading positions or see our way clear to establishing a leading position. In January, we acquired a 50 percent interest in the Residence Inn system, which enjoys a leadership position in the extended-stay market. Our other new hotel brands, Embassy Suites and Hampton Inn, are experiencing exceptional growth. And our core Holiday Inn brand as well our Holiday Inn Crowne Plaza brand are enjoying exceptional growth. We have designed distinctive hotel products that meet the specific needs of well-defined customer segments. All of our brands are intended to be leaders in their segments, which allows them to use sophisticated marketing techniques to increase market share despite intense competition.

Decrease Capital Intensity and Increase Leverage

In the early 1980s, management was committed to a conservative debt policy and a continuation of its standing policy of maintaining a 4-to-1 franchise/company-owned ratio in ownership of hotel facilities. Note the following comment by Mike Rose to security analysts in 1982:

> We can see significant opportunities for unit growth in our hotel business, both domestically and abroad. Our intent is to develop through a combination of franchisee growth and parent company investment. We expect to maintain the current relationship of four franchise units for each parent unit into the 1990s. . . . We intend to remain conservative in our debt policy, keeping a debt/invested capital ratio between 30 and 40 percent, which maintains excellent extra borrowing capacity.

By the late 1980s, perhaps in an effort to more easily increase ROE while at the same time speeding up the growth of each new brand in the face of greatly intensified competition, Holiday Corporation had significantly changed its posture toward company-owned properties and leverage. This can be seen in the following remarks made by Mike Rose in 1986:

> Our plan calls for accelerated disposition of assets as we reduce the capital intensity of our businesses. Operating income generated by ownership of properties will be replaced in part by high-return management and franchise income. . . . After thorough study, we raised the company's target for its debt/invested capital ratio to 45–60 percent. This higher leverage is supported by the value of the company's assets and strong cash flow. . . . We want to own fewer properties while significantly increasing the number of franchised properties and properties where we have long-term management contracts. . . . This allows us to expand our market positions using limited amounts of the company's capital.

Guide to Strategic Management Case Analysis

The Case Method

Case analysis is a proven educational method that is especially effective in a strategic management course. The case method complements and enhances the text material and your professor's lectures by focusing attention on what a firm has done or should do in an actual business situation. Use of the case method in the strategic management course offers you an opportunity to develop and refine analytical skills. It can also provide exciting experience by allowing you to assume the role of the key decision maker for the organizations you will study.

When assuming the role of the general manager of the organization being studied, you will need to consider all aspects of the business. In addition to drawing on your knowledge of marketing, finance, management, production, and economics, you will be applying the strategic management concepts taught in this course.

The cases in this book are accounts of real business situations involving a variety of firms in a variety of industries. To make these opportunities as realistic as possible, the cases include a variety of quantitative and qualitative information in both the presentation of the situation and the exhibits. As the key decision maker, you will need to determine which information is important, given the circumstances described in the case. Keep in mind that the

This guide was developed by John A. Pearce II, Richard B. Robinson, Jr., and William R. Bayer.

results of analyzing one firm will not necessarily be appropriate for another since every firm is faced with a different set of circumstances.

Preparing for Case Discussion

The case method requires an approach to class preparation that differs from the typical lecture course. In the typical lecture course, you can still benefit from each class session even if you did not prepare, by listening carefully to the professor's lecture. This approach will not work in a course using the case method. For such a case course, proper preparation is essential.

Suggestions for Effective Preparation

1. *Allow adequate time in preparing a case.* Many of the cases in this text involve complex issues that are often not apparent without careful reading and purposeful reflection on the information in the cases.

2. *Read each case twice.* Because many of these cases involve complex decision making, you should read each case at least twice. Your first reading should give you an overview of the firm's unique circumstances and the issues confronting the firm. Your second reading allows you to concentrate on what you feel are the most critical issues and to understand what information in the case is most important. Make limited notes identifying key points during your first reading. During your second reading, you can add details to your original notes and revise them as necessary.

3. *Focus on the key strategic issue in each case.* Each time you read a case you should concentrate on identifying the key issue. In some of the cases, the key issue will be identified by the case writer in the introduction. In other cases, you might not grasp the key strategic issue until you have read the case several times. (Remember that not every piece of information in a case is equally important.)

4. *Do not overlook exhibits.* The exhibits in these cases should be considered an integral part of the information for the case. They are not just "window dressing." In fact, for many cases you will need to analyze financial statements, evaluate organizational charts, and understand the firm's products, all of which are presented in the form of exhibits.

5. *Adopt the appropriate time frame.* It is critical that you assume the appropriate time frame for each case you read. If the case ends in 1985, that year should become the present for you as you work on that case. Making a decision for a case that ends in 1985 by using data you could not have had until 1986 defeats the purpose of the case method. For the same reason, although it is recommended that you do outside reading on each firm and industry, you should not read material written after the case ended unless your professor instructs you to do so.

6. *Draw on all of your knowledge of business.* As the key decision maker for the organization being studied, you will need to consider all aspects of the business and industry. Do not confine yourself to strategic management concepts presented in this course. You will need to determine if the key strategic issue revolves around a theory you have learned in a functional area, such as marketing, production, finance, or economics, or in the strategic management course.

Participating in Class

Because the strategic management course uses the case method, the success and value of the course depend on class discussion. The success and value of the class discussion, in turn, rely on the roles both you and your professor perform. Following are aspects of your role and your professor's, which, if kept in mind, will enhance the value and excitement of this course.

The Student as Active Learner

The case method requires your active participation. This means your role is no longer one of sitting and listening.

1. *Attend class regularly.* Not only is your grade likely to depend on your involvement in class discussions, but the benefit you derive from this course is directly related to your involvement in and understanding of the discussions.
2. *Be prepared for class.* The need for adequate preparation has already been discussed. You will benefit more from the discussions, will understand and participate in the exchange of ideas, and will avoid the embarrassment of being called on when not prepared. By all means, bring your book to class. Not only is there a good chance you will need to refer to a specific exhibit or passage from the case, you may need to refresh your memory of the case (particularly if you made notes in the margins while reading).
3. *Participate in the discussion.* Attending class and being prepared are not enough; you need to express your views in class. You can participate in a number of ways: by addressing a question asked by your professor, by disagreeing with your professor or your classmates (by all means, be tactful), by building on an idea expressed by a classmate, or by simply asking a relevant question.
4. *Participate wisely.* Although you do not want to be one of those students who never raises his or her hand, you should also be sensitive to the fact that others in your class will want to express themselves. You have probably already had experience with a student who attempts to dominate each class discussion. A student who invariably tries to dominate the class discussion breeds resentment.

5. *Keep a broad perspective.* By definition, the strategic management course deals with the issues facing general managers or business owners. As already mentioned, you need to consider all aspects of the business, not just one particular functional area.

6. *Pay attention to the topic being discussed.* Focus your attention on the topic being discussed. When a new topic is introduced, do not attempt to immediately introduce another topic for discussion. Do not feel you have to have something to say on every topic covered.

Your Professor as Discussion Leader

Your professor is a discussion leader. As such, he or she will attempt to stimulate the class as a whole to share insights, observations, and thoughts about the case. Your professor will not necessarily respond to every comment you or your classmates make. Part of the value of the case method is to get you and your classmates to assume this role as the course progresses.

The professor in a strategic management case course performs several roles:

1. *Maintaining focus.* Because multiple complex issues need to be explored, your professor may want to maintain the focus of the class discussion on one issue at a time. He or she may ask you to hold your comment on another issue until a previous issue is exhausted. Do not interpret this response to mean your point is unimportant; your professor is simply indi. iting there will be a more appropriate time to pursue that particular comment.

2. *Getting students involved.* Do not be surprised if your professor asks for input from volunteers and nonvolunteers alike. The value of the class discussion increases as more people share their comments.

3. *Facilitating comprehension of strategic management concepts.* Some professors prefer to lecture on strategic management concepts on a "need-to-know" basis. In this scenario, a lecture on a particular topic will be followed by an assignment to work on a case that deals with that particular topic. Other professors will have the class work through a case or two before lecturing on a topic to give the class a feel for the value of the topic being covered and for the type of information needed to work on cases. Still other professors prefer to cover all of the theory in the beginning of the course, thereby allowing uninterrupted case discussion in the remaining weeks of the term. All three of these approaches are valid.

4. *Playing devil's advocate.* At times your professor may appear to be contradicting many of the comments or observations being made. At other times your professor may adopt a position that does not immediately make sense, given the circumstances of the case. At other times your professor may seem to be equivocating. These are all examples of how your professor might be playing devil's advocate.

Sometimes the professor's goal is to expose alternative viewpoints. Sometimes he or she may be testing your resolve on a particular point. Be prepared to support your position with evidence from the case.

Assignments

Written Assignments

Written analyses are a critical part of any strategic management course. In fact, professors typically put more weight on written analyses than on exams or quizzes. Each professor has a preferred format for these written analyses, but a number of general guidelines will prove helpful to you in your written assignments.

1. *Analyze.* Avoid merely repeating the facts presented in the case. Analyze the issues involved in the case and build logically toward your recommendations.
2. *Use headings or labels.* Using headings or labels throughout your written analysis will help your reader follow your analysis and recommendations. For example, when you are analyzing the weaknesses of the firm in the case, include the heading Weaknesses. Note the headings in the sample case analysis that follows.
3. *Discuss alternatives.* Follow the proper strategic management sequence by (1) identifying alternatives, (2) evaluating each alternative, and (3) recommending the alternative you feel is best.
4. *Use topic sentences.* You can help your reader more easily evaluate your analysis by putting the topic sentence first in each paragraph and following with statements directly supporting the topic sentence.
5. *Be specific in your recommendations.* Develop specific recommendations logically and be sure your recommendations are well defended by your analysis. Avoid using generalizations, clichés, and ambiguous statements. Remember that any number of answers are possible, and so your professor is most concerned about how your reasoning led to your recommendations and how well you develop and support your ideas.
6. *Do not overlook implementation.* Many good analyses receive poor evaluations because they do not include a discussion of implementation. Your analysis will be much stronger when you discuss how your recommendation can be implemented. Include some of the specific actions needed to achieve the objectives you are proposing.
7. *Specifically state your assumptions.* Cases, like all real business situations, involve incomplete information. Therefore, it is important that you clearly state any assumptions you make in your analysis. Do not assume your professor will be able to fill in the missing points.

Oral Presentations

Your professor is also quite likely to ask you and your classmates to make oral presentations on a particular case. Oral presentations are usually done by groups of students. In these groups, each member will typically be responsible for one aspect of the overall case. Keep the following suggestions in mind when you are faced with an oral presentation:

1. *Use your own words.* Avoid memorizing a presentation. The best approach is to prepare an outline of the key points you want to cover. Do not be afraid to have the outline in front of you during your presentation, but do not just read the outline.

2. *Rehearse your presentation.* Do not assume you can simply read the outline you have prepared or that the right words will come to you when you are in front of the class making your presentation. Take the time to practice your speech, and be sure to rehearse the entire presentation with your group.

3. *Use visual aids.* The adage "a picture is worth a thousand words" contains quite a bit of truth. The people in your audience will more quickly and thoroughly understand your key points—and will retain them longer—if you can use visual aids. Think of ways you and your team members can use the blackboard in the classroom; a graph, chart, or exhibit on a large posterboard; or, if you will have a number of these visual aids, a flip chart.

4. *Be prepared to handle questions.* You will probably be asked questions by your classmates. If questions are asked during your presentation, try to address those that require clarification. Tactfully postpone more elaborate questions until you have completed the formal phase of your presentation. During your rehearsal, try to anticipate the types of questions that you might be asked.

Working as a Team Member

Many professors assign students to groups or teams for analyzing cases. This adds more realism to the course since most strategic decisions in business are addressed by a group of key managers. If you are a member of a group assigned to analyze a case, keep in mind that your performance is tied to the performance of the other group members, and vice versa. The following are some suggestions to help you be an effective team member:

1. *Be sure the division of labor is equitable.* It is not always easy to decide how the workload can be divided equitably since it is not always obvious how much work needs to be done. Try breaking the case down into the distinct parts that need to be analyzed to determine if having a different person assume responsibility for each part is equitable. All team members should read and analyze the entire case, but different team members can be assigned primary responsibility for each major

aspect of the analysis. Each team member with primary responsibility for a major aspect of the analysis will also be the logical choice to write that portion of the written analysis or to present it orally in class.

2. *Communicate with other team members.* This is particularly important if you encounter problems with your portion of the analysis. Since, by definition, the team members are dependent on each other, it is critical that you communicate openly and honestly with each other. It is therefore essential that your team members discuss problems, such as some members not doing their fair share of work or members insisting that their point of view dominate the team's report.

3. *Work as a team.* Since a group's output should reflect a combined effort, the whole group should be involved in each part of the analysis, even if different individuals assume primary responsibility for different parts of the analysis. Avoid having the marketing major do the marketing portion of the analysis, the production major handle the production issues, and so forth. This will both hamper the group's aggregate analysis and do all of the team members a disservice by not giving each member exposure to decision making involving the other functional areas. The strategic management course provides an opportunity to look at all aspects of the business situation, to develop the ability to see the big picture, and to integrate the various functional areas.

4. *Plan and structure team meetings.* When working with a group on case analysis, it is impossible to achieve the team's goals and objectives without meeting outside of class. As soon as the team is formed, establish mutually convenient times for regular meetings, and be sure to keep this time available each week. Be punctual in going to the meetings, and manage the meetings so they end at a predetermined time. Plan several shorter meetings, as opposed to one longer session right before the case is due. (This, by the way, is another way realism is introduced in the strategic management course. Planning and managing your time is essential in business, and working with others to achieve a common set of goals is a critical part of life in the business world.)

Summary

The strategic management course is your opportunity to assume the role of a key decision maker in a business organization. The case method is an excellent way to add excitement and realism to the course. To get the most out of the course and the case method, you need to be an active participant in the entire process.

The case method offers you the opportunity to develop your analytical skills and to understand the interrelationships of the various functional areas of business; it also enables you to develop valuable skills in time management, group problem solving, creativity, organization of thoughts and ideas, and human interaction. All of these skills will prove immensely valuable when you enter the job market and begin your career.

Sample Case

Pennsylvania Movie Theatres, Inc.

The Corporate Perspective

1 Pennsylvania Movie Theatres, Inc. (PMT), was an organization of largely autonomous and previously independent theatres located throughout Pennsylvania. Seven years ago, 28 manager-owners of privately held operations exchanged their theatre ownership for PMT stock and the right to continue as theatre managers with the newly formed corporation. At their first annual meeting, the managers voted to select a five-member board of directors from their ranks to coordinate theatre operations and to oversee all corporate activities. Further, they determined that one new director would be elected each year to fill a scheduled vacancy. Each director would serve in a part-time capacity for a four-year term at $3,000 per year.

2 The PMT managers believed that as a corporation they would have better opportunities and capabilities than were available to them when they owned their theatres separately. Because of their system of cooperative exchange, they would be able to minimize film rental and advertising costs. They could also offer better opportunities for advancement to their assistant managers. Additionally, the corporate form enabled the managers to provide support to weaker member theatres because of their collective managerial experience and collective financial strength. Taking a long-term perspective, the managers believed that this consolidation arrangement would result in a more profitable operation for all theatres.

3 The PMT managers wished to offer their communities a safe, inexpensive, and pleasurable leisure-time activity. By satisfying these and other societal needs, they believed they could achieve their basic corporate objectives of survival and profitability. Among other pertinent societal needs, the managers saw the desire for:

1. A safe, inexpensive form of entertainment.
2. A wholesome, imaginative, and stimulating children's diversion.
3. A forum for social debate.
4. An opportunity for family activity.
5. A source for employment of local labor forces.
6. An escape from demanding realities.
7. An opportunity for educational and cultural enhancement.

4 Because of their concern for satisfying these needs, the managers chose their films carefully, attempting to offer high-quality movies at the peak of their popularity. They were also concerned with appealing to an audience that included people of all ages and descriptions. The managers saw the corporation as a group of family theatres, so they wanted to ensure that, with few exceptions, a family unit could attend any show at a PMT theatre without totally sacrificing the enjoyment of any single member. Since their incorporation, PMT theatres had, therefore, restricted their film offerings

This case was prepared by John A. Pearce II of George Mason University.

primarily to those movies rated G (general audience), PG (parental guidance suggested), and R (restricted to persons over 18). With rare exceptions, X-rated, but never hard-core pornographic, films had been shown.

5   The managers also wanted to ensure that the family could enjoy a movie in pleasant surroundings. They attempted to maintain a future-oriented perspective in supervising the daily operations of the theatres as well as in selecting films to be shown. Theatre facilities were periodically renovated, and employees were well trained. All of these efforts were expended in order to provide the most comfortable of theatre experiences and to ensure continued audience patronage.

6   PMT gauged its corporate performance in a number of different ways, among which were ticket sales by type, show time, and movie rating; quarterly revenues; and quarterly profits. Last year, PMT's seventh in operation, the net profits of the PMT theatres dropped almost 7 percent from the year before, even though during the same period, the theatre industry at large had reached all-time-high profit levels. Two years ago, the return on investment achieved by PMT had been 11.7 percent, while the industry average was 11.3 percent. Last year, the return on investment for PMT was down to 10.1 percent, while the industry average climbed to 11.8 percent. The industry average return on investment for the past five years was 10.9 percent.

7   In reviewing the performance of individual films shown during the past year, the PMT directors found that the few X-rated films they had offered far and away resulted in the greatest profit per film, followed by those rated R. They also noted that on dates when their competitors had shown pornographic-type films, they had appeared to outdraw PMT theatres. Further, since adult ticket sales were the most profitable, the loss of these customers probably represented an associated loss in net income.

An Alternative

8   A major film distributor recently approached the PMT directors with an offer to supply them with a selection of good-quality X-rated and pornographic-type films for the minimum contract period of 12 months. If ordered, these films would constitute approximately one third of the movies shown at any single theatre during the year, with the remaining two thirds being supplied by the corporation's present distributor.

9   While a revised movie offering would not require any major technological changes for PMT (for example, the present projection screens and sound system would be adequate), it would have a potentially strong psychological impact on both the PMT employees and their audiences.

10   Thus, the directors realized that a large and varied set of factors needed to be taken into consideration prior to any contractual commitment to the second distributor.

11   One such factor was the possible consequence of a bill, currently before the Pennsylvania state legislature, that would ban the showing of pornographic films within the state. Although the bill was being hotly debated, it was given only a 10 percent chance of being passed. The directors were also watching the upcoming gubernatorial election in the state with particular interest. One of the declared candidates was running as a morality candidate, and a major plank in his platform was the banning of all X-rated films in Pennsylvania theatres. While he was given only a 5 percent chance of being elected, the news media had given great attention to the morality issues raised by this candidate, as they had to the pending legislation.

12   On the other hand, the directors perceived a widespread belief among the general population that sexual explicitness in any medium had some value. They also sensed growing support for the individual's right to decide what did or did not possess redeeming social value.

13   Another factor the directors considered was that as the nation's affluence increases, so do its leisure time and its demand for leisure-time activities, such as movie theatre entertainment. They were uncertain, however, about the effects that current economic conditions would have on their operations. They expected an economic recession but were unsure whether the accompanying period of tight money would bring more people to the theatre in lieu of more expensive forms of entertainment or, alternatively, whether all entertainment businesses would suffer.

14   Another consideration affecting the directors' decision was the fact that the majority of PMT theatres were located in small- to medium-sized towns with an average population of 23,569 people. All of the theatres were in downtown business districts, and all theatre fronts opened onto main shopping streets. In nearly every case, however, the PMT theatres had a competitor within two city blocks. These facts concerned the directors since they believed trends toward liberalism were relatively slow to develop in small towns and any failure on their part would be to the immediate advantage of their competitors.

15   The possible impact on price policies and theatre hours was also considered. The average price for an adult movie ticket at a PMT theatre in the past year was $3.68, while the average price for PMT competitors was estimated at $3.83. Should the second contract be approved, PMT estimated that its average could rise to $3.77, reflecting the corporation's ability to increase its rates for the X-rated movie audiences.

16   Although show hours varied slightly among PMT theatres, the pattern for weekdays includes a matinee at 2 P.M. and two evening shows at 7:30 P.M. and 9:30 P.M. On weekends, a late-afternoon performance at 5:30 P.M. was added. On Saturdays, the matinee was often reserved for the showing of children's films, which were scheduled by the individual managers especially for this purpose. Although these films contributed no profit to the corporation—because of their low ticket prices—the managers felt this policy developed goodwill between the theatre and the community. No change in the theatre hours was anticipated by the directors in the event the second supplier contract was signed.

17   In addition to price policies (selective rate increases needed) and modifications in theatre hours (no changes required), the directors considered the possible effects of showing X-rated films on other facets of the theatres' operations, for example, media advertising and in-theatre promotion.

18   PMT theatres advertised through the radio and newspaper media. Whether or not the new contract with the supplier of the X-rated films was signed, these two media would continue to be used, with the expectation that neither costs nor potential audiences would change significantly.

19   Concession stand operations were not expected to be affected, since on previous occasions when X-rated movies were shown, managers did not notice any changes in concession volume or item preference. The directors believed the concession stand would continue to yield approximately 93 cents (gross) per customer regardless of the movie being shown.

20   PMT's distribution channels should be unaffected in the event that a contract with the second film supplier was approved. No additional distribution costs were expected,

therefore, but some inventory control changes would be necessary. The main change would be that the two brands of film would need to be kept separate in the film depository, which would be possible through the initiation of a second numerical filing system. The PMT managers recognized the difficulties commonly associated with such a new system but felt the required adjustments could be quickly overcome.

21   No attempt had yet been made to determine how nonmanagerial PMT employees would feel about an increase in the number of X-rated films being shown in their theatres. Of central concern was the impact the change might have on the employees' interest in union membership. To management's knowledge, no attempt had ever been made by its employees to bring in a union. The directors attributed this desired situation to its employee relations effort and to the high turnover rate among its teenage employees. To date, there had been only one incident, involving a 55-year-old female street booth ticket clerk who objected to "dirty films," to indicate the employees might react negatively to any increase in X-rated offerings.

Consolidated Projections

22   After conducting the broad-based assessment of the impact that offering X-rated and pornographic films might have on PMT's profits, the directors reached the following projection for three years from now, assuming the second contract was signed:

Likelihood of reaching or exceeding industry average	30%
Likelihood of equaling their own performance of last year	30
Likelihood of a 10 percent decrease in the PMT return on investment from the previous year	20
Likelihood of a 20 percent (or greater) decrease in the PMT return on investment from the previous year	20

23   Overall, the directors foresaw an opportunity to increase business by attracting a new segment of moviegoers. Additionally, the prospective new supplier argued that regular adult PMT customers would attend the theatre more often. Thus, the directors believed a revised film offering would enable them to better meet the interests of an enlarged segment of the population and, in return, these customers would help ensure PMT's long-term survival.

24   Should they contract with the second supplier, the directors planned to monitor the corporate performance carefully. Among their targets would be the following:

1. Adult ticket sales per movie for all but X-rated films should remain stable or increase slightly.
2. Children's ticket sales should remain stable or increase slightly.
3. Adult ticket sales per movie on X-rated films should exceed adult ticket sales per movie for films of any other rating.
4. Quarterly profits, adjusted for seasonal variations, should reflect an upward trend.

In the event any of these targets were not being met, it would signal a need to reassess the wisdom of the revised film offering.

25   Although the PMT directors had the responsibility of proposing corporate strategy, the success of the strategy rested on the commitment of the managers in carrying it out. The question arose for the directors as to the extent to which the managers would give the films of the second supplier a real chance. Although, or since, a manager's bonus reflected the degree of profit of his theatre, he may be reluctant to fully implement a new strategy regardless of the directors' judgment. A recent straw vote of managers to the question "Do you favor an increased offering of X-rated and pornographic-type films?" showed 12 in favor, 5 against, and 11 undecided.

26   It appeared that the results of the straw vote somewhat paralleled the performance of the voting managers' theatres. Managers who were experiencing increasing revenues tended to vote against the second supplier, those with relatively level sales seemed to be undecided, while those with decreasing or typically low sales favored the proposal. Such voting tendencies might have been a reflection of the managers' bonus system. Each manager-owner received an annual bonus equal to 60 percent of the pretax net income of their individual theatre and a $\frac{1}{28}$ share of a pool composed of 25 percent of the pretax net income of all theatres.

27   In two months, the annual stockholders' meeting would take place. The managers all anticipated that the main order of business would be a discussion of the directors' proposal regarding a contract with the second distributor.

Sample Case Analysis

Pennsylvania Movie Theatres, Inc.

Pennsylvania Movie Theatres, Inc. (PMT), was formed in 1978 when 28 independent motion picture houses scattered throughout Pennsylvania joined together primarily to obtain economic efficiencies garnered through mutual cooperation and control. A five-member board of directors (costing the corporation $15,000 a year) will be proposing to its members in two months the regular showing of quality X-rated or pornographic films in numbers far in excess of their current practice. The board believed the exhibition of this type film in this quantity would

> increase business by attracting a new segment of moviegoers. Additionally, . . . regular adult PMT customers would attend the theatre more often. Thus, the directors believed a revised film offering would enable them to better meet the interests of an enlarged segment of the population and, in return, these customers would help ensure PMT's long-term survival [23].[1]

Taken in these terms, the board will be proposing a major policy change that will be of strategic importance to the chain should the results of the decision be either a success or a failure. The following is an analysis of the situation facing motion picture exhibitors in general and, more specifically, of PMT as an exhibitor in the state of Pennsylvania, with a recommended plan of action given the described circumstances.

History and Background Information

A motion picture exhibitor is just one of many entities competing for the public's time and dollars. Inexpensive mass entertainment has always been part of the American scene—tent and wandering minstrel shows first entertained the masses, followed by vaudeville shows mounted in any number of theatre chains strung across the country. By the early 1920s, the motion picture had become the country's major form of mass entertainment, and this form dominated until the early 1950s. Today this industry is in a state of decline as its overall growth rate is less than the population's, and it exhibits many of the other characteristics of an industry in decline—many motion picture studios have either gone out of business (Republic, Monogram, PRC), merged (United Artists/MGM, Universal/International), or become part of a larger conglomerate (Paramount Studios, Warner Brothers, Columbia Pictures). Fewer and fewer films are being produced solely for theatre distribution each year; and in-theatre motion picture viewing is being substituted by videocassette recorder (VCR) and broadcast and cable television viewing. Although under these conditions of overall decline "success" is only comparative and may entail a holding action until the organization can switch

---

This analysis has been prepared by Professor Joseph Wolfe of the University of Tulsa for class demonstration purposes and does not constitute the only analyses, observations, and conclusions that could be drawn from the case.

[1] The bracketed numbers refer to the numbered paragraphs in the case.

its resources and capabilities to more profitable and growth-oriented markets or industries, survival depends on the building of efficient market access, strong customer loyalty, a strong theatre image, simplified inventory controls, efficient operations, streamlined management control, and the elimination of excess labor or a change from labor-intensive to capital-intensive operations. The key functional area in this situation should be that of finance, and the business's strategic focus must be placed on financial strength and maximum investment recovery. It is not clear whether PMT realizes the strategic requirements of its situation. The chain was created to reduce expenses in film rentals and advertising, and PMT managers wished to provide career opportunities for their assistant managers [2]. PMT also wished to help its weaker theatres with collective financial strength, but it is not explained how this was to be realized. Additionally, it is not known to what degree PMT has (1) made its theatres more accessible to the public, (2) caused its present customers to be more loyal to *PMT* than to its inevitable competitor [14] only two blocks away, (3) created a strong and readily identifiable image in the marketplace, (4) simplified and made more rational the booking of films for 28 theatres rather than just 1, (5) made its operations more automated and capital intensive, and (6) put into place management controls, which yield valuable operational and strategic information.

Not only does PMT face difficulties due to the declining nature of its industry, the chain faces the problems of survival in a state or geographic area that is experiencing low or negative growth in addition to a general population that is moving toward those age categories least likely to attend a motion picture theatre. As shown in Exhibit 1, America's population is growing the fastest in the 40- to 49-year-old category, followed by the 30 to 39 and 65-and-over age groups. Over the past 10 years, the state of Pennsylvania's population grew only .06 percent, and its population for the next decade is expected to fall 1.0 percent. While this decrease is not as great as that for other "rustbelt" states, such as New York, this nation's growth states and cities are far from Pennsylvania and are therefore inaccessible to PMT as it is currently structured. It must also be assumed that the small towns in which PMT has its theatres are losing their populations at a greater rate than for the state of Pennsylvania in general, as these small towns offer the fewest economic opportunities for their younger citizens.

A Porter competitive forces-type analysis (refer to Chapter 5) highlights the formidable problems facing PMT's board of directors. Although a number of barriers to entry exist, these barriers provide little solace at this time since most firms are attempting to leave rather than enter the industry. Economies of scale, however, do not appear to exist, and the products (the theatre itself and the films it shows) are basically nondifferentiated; although a theatre's structure is somewhat unique, its capital requirements are low and the technology to run a theatre is easily obtained. On the supply side of the Porter model, the theatre owner's potential attendance figures are largely controlled by the quantity, quality, and diversity of new and old films available for showing. Additionally, as a buying/renting group of theatres, PMT is in a relatively weak bargaining position as it represents the interests of small theatres with consequently low rental revenue yields per screening. The threat of substitutes also plays an important factor in this industry. As already stated, numerous substitutes for motion picture theatre viewing exist. On a broader level, however, the public in general can pursue any number of different diversions—both active (jogging, sailing, gardening, reading, games of chance) and passive (record listening, sporting event attendance, television viewing).

Exhibit 1
Selected demographic data

Population age mix changes, 1980–1990[*]

Under age 20	+ 2.1%
Age 20–29	− 4.3
Age 30–39	+28.5
Age 40–49	+37.4
Age 50–64	− 2.0
Age 65 and over	+19.6

Geographic population shifts, 1970–1990[†]

Pennsylvania, 1970–80 (+71,000)	+ .06%
Pennsylvania, 1980–90	− 1.0
New York, 1980–90	− 6.2
Oklahoma, 1980–90	+15.8
Texas, 1980–90	+23.0
Nevada, 1980–90	+59.6

Interpretations:

1. Population growth will be the greatest in the 40–49 age class and impressive in the 30–39 and over-65 age groups. These groups are the least likely to attend a motion picture theatre.

2. Pennsylvania's population is basically flat or falling during the case's time period, and this trend can be expected to continue in the future. America's population growth lies in states other than in the Northeast.

[*] U.S. Department of Commerce, "Note on the U.S. Lodging Industry," *Casebook,* 1982, p. 865.

[†] U.S. Bureau of Census, 1982.

The most important factors shaping the nature of competition in the motion picture theatre industry, however, are those factors encouraging a high degree of rivalry between those already in the industry. Exhibit 2 summarizes those factors. PMT faces a motion picture theatre of its same type and size in almost every small town; the industry's growth is not only slow but also negative; it is very difficult to physically differentiate one theatre from another or to make its offerings unique if the house classifies itself as a first-run theatre [4]; a customer can easily attend one theatre over another, given they are only two blocks away from each other; fixed costs are relatively high if a mortgage exists on the building and/or its property; the product is perishable (a customer missing from the theatre is gone forever for that particular film in a PMT theatre); and exit barriers are high since few other businesses can use the configuration typically employed by a motion picture theatre.

Although PMT has not created a formal mission statement, such a statement can be derived from its belief in the societal needs fulfilled by motion picture viewing [3]. A switch to a greater emphasis on X-rated films would appear to violate the following desirable ends in its derived mission statement—an opportunity for family activity and an opportunity for educational and cultural enhancement. Alternatively, the change in programming, if successful, would enhance PMT's desires to be a forum for social

Exhibit 2
Factors causing intense rivalry among an industry's participants

1. Numerous, equally sized companies.
2. Slow industry growth.
3. Low differentiation and switching costs.
4. High fixed costs; product is perishable.
5. Capacity increases in large increments.
6. Exit barriers are high.
7. Rivals are diverse in their strategies, origins/histories, and personalities.

debate, provide an escape from demanding realities, and be a source for the employment of the local labor force. More problematical for PMT is its desire to provide a safe, inexpensive form of entertainment, as many consider pornography to be mentally and spiritually unsafe for the viewer and physically unsafe for those who may be subjected to the passions and mental states incited by the subject matter. The provision of a wholesome, imaginative, and stimulating children's diversion may or may not be impugned since the films would be shown only during evening screenings, although children could be exposed to PMT's X-rated advertisements, marquee displays, and lobby posterboards.

Of greater import concerning the use of X-rated films, however, is the impact of their use on the screening times allowed for regular fare, given the board's assumption that additional screening times (and hence no additional labor costs) would not be created. Exhibit 3 shows that PMT's current product mix exhibits 5 G-rated films, 25 PG-rated films, and 20 R-rated films. One could immediately question how family-oriented a theatre chain could be when approximately 38 percent of its films are of the R-rated *(Scarface, Rambo, Terminator)* variety, but PMT's future mix would employ 17 R-rated films while sacrificing 15 films acceptable to larger audiences. Additionally, even though PMT's new distributor promises a supply of high-quality pornographic

Exhibit 3
Change in product mix per theatre with X-rated films

Rating	Estimated current mix		Estimated future mix	
	Percent	Number	Percent	Number
G	10.0%	5	6.7%	3
PG	49.0	25	33.7	18
R	38.0	20	26.3	14
X	3.0	2	33.3	17*
Total	100.0%	52†	100.0%	52

* Assumes all X-rated films will be supplied by the new distributor.

† Assumes PMT theatres operate all year and are single screened; also assumes a number of films will run for more than one week, but many children's matinee films only show on Saturday. Although almost 100 new films are produced each year for the American market, at least one third of them will receive little commercial exposure, while only about 20 percent of "Hollywood's" output receives an extended run.

Exhibit 4
PMT versus industry ROI performance

	1984	*1985*	*Average*	*Change*
PMT	11.7%	10.1%	10.9%	−13.8%
Industry*	11.3	11.8	11.6	+ 4.4

* Five-year industry average ROI was 10.9 percent; 1985's results were an 8.3 percent improvement over the five-year historical average.

films, the quality of these films, although suitable to a certain type of clientele, may not be superior to the intrinsic quality of the general-interest films they would have to replace.

As part of their preparation for PMT's annual stockholders' meeting, the directors generated ROI likelihood estimates associated with the chain exhibiting X-rated films for three years. By their X-rated decision, the board is attempting to reverse the negative long-term trend shown in Exhibit 4. PMT's current ROI has fallen 13.8 percent from 1984 to 1985. Its average two-year performance and its most recent year's performance are both below and counter to the industry's ROI performance. This negative trend would not be reversed by their X-rated film decision, based on the expected value of the events anticipated both by the board and by the set of alternative optimistic and pessimistic scenarios presented in Exhibit 5. Additionally, the results they anticipate will only occur after two years of ROI experiences that will be inferior to the results they have historically obtained.

Exhibit 5
Alternate ROI likelihood estimates after three years*

Estimate category	*ROI*	*Board estimate*	*Optimistic estimate*	*Pessimistic estimate*
Likelihood of reaching or exceeding industry average	11.8%	30.0%	50.0%	10.0%
Likelihood of equaling own performance of last year	10.1	30.0	35.0	15.0
Likelihood of a 10 percent decrease in PMT ROI from the previous year	9.1	20.0	10.0	60.0
Likelihood of a 20 percent (or greater) decrease in PMT ROI from the previous year	8.1	20.0	5.0	15.0
Estimated ROI		10.0%	10.8%	9.4%

* ROI used in all calculations, although PMT desires an increase in *profits;* open-ended points beyond extremities were not calculated (i.e., exceeding industry average of 11.8 percent or a greater than 20 percent decrease in ROI).

Interpretation: PMT's ROI projection after three years of X-rated films is 10 percent, which is not an improvement over its current return of 10.1 percent; comparatively optimistic estimates (which probably cannot be obtained due to the falling trend experienced by PMT for the past two years) produce an ROI of only 10.8 percent, which is not a significant improvement given the three years needed to obtain it; comparatively pessimistic estimates produce an ROI of 9.4 percent, which is a decline of 7.2 percent from 1985's results (the decline from 1984 to 1985 was 13.8 percent).

Problem Statement

It would appear at first glance that PMT's problem or decision in this case is one of determining if the showing of X-rated films is advisable given the risks and opportunities incurred by this decision. In a larger sense, however, the use of X-rated films is only a decision element within PMT's basic desire to change the strategic direction of its theatre chain in the name of greater profits [2] and long-term survival [23]. PMT could follow a number of routes toward the accomplishment of these ends; and the showing of X-rated films, with the directors' belief that this type of film would "increase business by attracting a new segment of moviegoers," [23] is merely the implementation of a grand strategy of either product development or concentric diversification, depending on how markets and products are defined. As the implementation of a grand strategy of product development, PMT is attempting to sell a new concentration of products (X-rated films) to a new market (the adult, usually male, customer). As the implementation of a grand strategy of concentric diversification, the exhibition of X-rated films represents a distinctive departure from PMT's existing operations base (a significant divergence from its family theatre orientation) for both customer type and product while simultaneously obtaining synergies through the use of the same projection technology.

Exhibit 6 lists 12 grand strategies outlined in Chapter 9. The problem in this case is to pick which grand strategy, given PMT's resource and resource acquisition position, is the strategy most likely to accomplish the profit and survival criteria PMT has established for itself. Once the grand strategy has been chosen, the board must then outline the components of the grand strategy so that it can be implemented in a timely and correct fashion. In the final analysis, the showing of X-rated films may or may not be included as part of this grand strategy.

Alternative Choices

The "correct" strategy for any organization is a function of the salient characteristics of the organization's internal and external environments. A grand strategy cluster analysis, which considers these factors, will therefore be employed to prioritize the alternative grand strategies that could be used by PMT (refer to Chapter 9).

As shown in Exhibit 7, grand strategy cluster analysis requires the classification of PMT's (1) markets as experiencing rapid or slow growth and (2) relative strength of competitive position. Based on our previous analysis, PMT's markets are growing slowly or are actually shrinking in size. It cannot be determined precisely from the case whether PMT's individual theatres are strong or weak in their specific geographic areas, but it is assumed PMT as a corporation does not face a comparably sized chain and therefore possesses a relatively strong competitive position. On this basis, PMT finds itself in cell IV, which indicates the employment of the grand strategies of concentric diversification, conglomerate diversification, and joint ventures, in order of their level of decreasing attractiveness.

Concentric Diversification

In a general sense, this grand strategy involves a distinctive departure "from a firm's existing base of operations, typically the acquisition or internal generation of a separate business with synergistic possibilities counterbalancing the two businesses' strengths

Exhibit 6
Grand strategies

1. Concentration
2. Market development
3. Product development
4. Innovation
5. Horizontal integration
6. Vertical integration
7. Joint venture
8. Concentric diversification
9. Conglomerate diversification
10. Retrenchment/turnaround
11. Divestiture
12. Liquidation

Exhibit 7
Model of grand strategy clusters

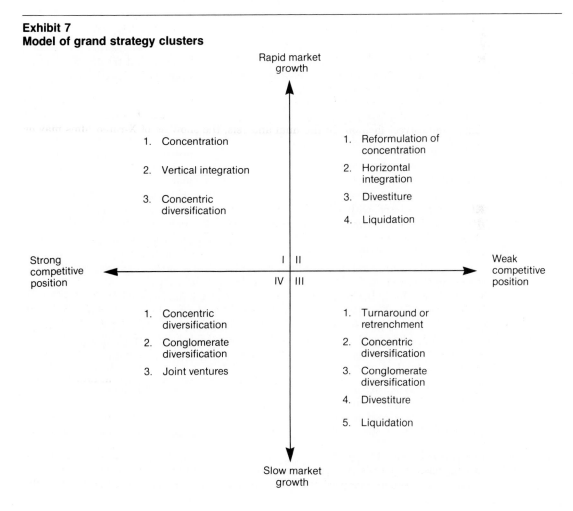

Exhibit 8
Disadvantages (or down-side risks) associated with the decision to exhibit X-rated films

1. The innovation is easily copied—any advantage gained from the decision to exhibit X-rated films would be temporary, as it could be easily duplicated by other theatre chains if the innovation is successful, and therefore is of little long-term value. The innovation does not generate customer loyalty or a preferable supplier relationship, as it is assumed other distributors of "quality" X-rated films exist. Additionally, the contract period is only for a 12-month period, and all ROI projections are based on a continuous supply of quality pornographic films for a 36-month period.
2. Many of the planning premises employed by the board are not viable, or the factors that would make them viable are not completely under the control of the theatre chain.
3. No clear mandate for X-rated films has come from the chain, as its individual members appear to be voting their pocketbooks (or bottom-line profits)—the degree of enthusiasm for implementing the decision is variable and could produce mixed results.
4. Given the long-term negative repercussions should the innovation be unacceptable to the public, the weighted-ROI results are not substantial enough to warrant the risk involved—the expected monetary value of the investment is not positive enough to risk the likelihood of failure.

---

and weaknesses."[2] For PMT this strategy could take the specific form of (1) a greater offering of X-rated films (a distinct move away from a family orientation and toward the cultivation of a male audience), (2) the showcasing or special treatment of other types of films (classics, recent rereleases, and documentaries), or (3) the expansion of similar theatres in larger towns or cities.

Alternative 1—Concentric Diversification via X-Rated Films. Although the PMT board of directors appears to favor this alternative, many negative features are associated with the decision. Based on the board's estimates, the ROI generated by the decision is not an improvement in the performance already being obtained by the chain. Additionally, all their estimates have not considered competitive reactions by other motion picture theatres. Exhibit 8 outlines the substantial downside or negative elements associated with the decision—the innovation is easily copied if successful but could easily backfire if it failed; many of the planning premises employed by the board are not viable, or the factors that would make them viable are not completely under the control of the board (see Exhibit 9); no clear mandate for X-rated films has cᵢ me from the chain, and the board has recognized [25] that the "success of the strategy rested on the commitment of the managers in carrying it out."

On the pro side of the debate, the showing of X-rated films would at least temporarily allow ticket prices to be increased, additional concession stand revenues would be generated, and no new media costs would be involved. From the board's point of view, they would be showing that they are able to make decisions and are doing something to reverse the chain's downward slide in profitability and rate of return.

Alternative 2—Concentric Diversification via Showcased Films. This alternative would entail the scheduling of special films, or series of films built around themes ("Great Actors, Great Faces," a Cary Grant commemorative, "The World's Greatest Adventure Films"), or films appealing to special audiences (films of social conscience,

---

[2] John A. Pearce II and Richard B. Robinson, Jr., *Strategic Management*, 3rd ed. (Homewood, Ill.: Richard D. Irwin, 1988).

Exhibit 9
Derived planning premises

1. Adult ticket sales per movie for all but X-rated films should remain stable or increase slightly (current average ticket for last year was $3.68).
2. Children's ticket sales should remain stable or increase slightly.
3. Adult ticket sales per movie on X-rated films should exceed adult ticket sales per movie for films of any other rating. (X-rated ticket prices would have to average $3.96 per adult if overall average ticket sold is to climb to its estimated $3.77. See Appendix for calculations.)
4. Quarterly profits, adjusted for seasonal variations, should reflect an upward trend.

past and near-present elaborate musical fantasies, those great silent comedians). The advantages of this alternative are product differentiation and lowered costs. These special films could be scheduled on a theatre's off-night, or at specific times for senior citizens, or for social clubs with unique interests in conjunction with a meal (as in a dinner theatre operation). Rather than merely displaying the normal fare created by Hollywood, the theatre itself could create its own distinctive personality by the films it selects to supplement the regular diet being fed to the masses. Film rental costs would be very low or nonexistent as many of the films are in the public domain, and ticket prices could be sold at a premium because of the showing's unusual nature or could be sold in blocks, thereby guaranteeing revenues for each series. The disadvantages of this alternative are increased planning and creativity. Under this alternative, PMT would have to do more than just "throw something on the screen," and it would also have to understand the entertainment needs of each town in which it operates a theatre. It would also have to obtain the (part-time) services of a film historian to compile the film series, introduce each film to the audience, or prepare a descriptive catalog for each series.

Alternative 3—Concentric Diversification via Selective Geographic Relocation. This alternative would entail the establishment of theatres in towns (1) with greater populations or larger disposable incomes, (2) where direct competition does not exist, or (3) where the direct competition is weak. Under option 1 above, PMT would be dealing with larger potential audiences or audiences with more money to spend and thus the ability either to afford motion picture entertainment or to pay a higher price for the entertainment they purchase. Under option 2, PMT would obtain a monopolistic position within its market area. Under option 3, PMT would not have a monopolistic position but would have a comparative advantage over its rival. Taken in total, these options would take PMT's operations out of areas that are not conducive to economic well-being while placing itself in areas or situations that are potentially more profitable. The disadvantages of alternative 3 are the costs of relocation or the building of a new theatre if an older one is not available for renovation, the need to become established as a viable entertainment entity in the new community, and the probable capital loss on the sale of the old theatre being vacated.

Solution Choice

Depending on the time frame allowed by the PMT board of directors, the organization should implement alternatives 2 or 3. If the board wishes to engage in an effort that would cost very little to implement and would cost very little if it failed, PMT should choose alternative 2. No capital costs are involved; excess capacity probably already exists within its theatres, so few paying customers would be pushed aside for the special showings; and a different type of clientele with outstanding public relations value would be created. If the board takes a longer-term point of view, it should implement alternative 3—after thoroughly researching the competitive position facing each of its theatres and the competitive situation existing in alternative towns and cities in Pennsylvania. Based on the voting pattern on the X-rated film issue, 12 theatres appear to be experiencing decreasing or low sales, while 11 theatres appear to be experiencing level ticket sales. Accordingly, theatre owners in this group are candidates for relocation decisions. Under no circumstances should PMT exhibit X-rated films as a strategy of concentric diversification. Any advantage obtained by this move would be temporary, and the long-term consequences of failure are too high.

In addition to the implementation of either alternatives 2 or 3 and depending on the time horizon for action chosen by PMT, the board should seek to obtain the advantages of cooperation mainly in the areas of financial control and reporting, capital expenditures, and the sharing of management expertise, since these are the strategic imperatives of an organization operating in the decline stage of its industry's life cycle. At this time, it appears PMT is only a nominally organized confederation rather than an integrated organization, and the board has yet to deal with those basic issues of industrial decline.

Appendix: Calculations for New Average X-Rated Ticket Price

Current condition:

Film category	Proportion of total	Ticket price	Weighted component
G, PG, and R	.97	$3.68	$3.57
X	.03	3.68	3.68
Totals	1.00	$3.68	$3.68

Proposed condition:

Film category	Proportion of total	Ticket price	Weighted component
G, PG, and R	.67	$3.68	$2.45
X	.33	3.96	1.32
Totals	1.00	$3.77	$3.77

Assumptions:

1. Attendance roughly approximates the product mix.
2. Prices for G, PG, and R films will remain stable.

Interpretations:

1. PMT believes the use of X-rated films will enable it to increase its overall ticket prices by 7.6 percent.
2. PMT's forecasted average ticket price is 3.2 percent above what its competition is currently obtaining.
3. PMT must be assuming the competition will not exhibit X-rated films, or the competition will not cut prices in an attempt to hold customers attracted to the X-rated films shown by PMT.

PART FOUR

Cases

SECTION

Strategy Formulation

Case 1

Wendy's (A): Beating the Odds

1   In just 11 years, Wendy's International grew from one store to over 1,800 company-owned and franchised outlets. Between 1974 and 1979, Wendy's growth was explosive with sales, including company-owned and franchised units, growing 4,200 percent ($24 million to $1 billion). In the same period, revenues from company-owned store sales and from franchise royalties grew 726 percent ($38 million to $274 million). Net income increased 2,091 percent in this period from $1.1 million to $23 million. Earnings per share made substantial gains from $.12 in 1974 to $1.54 in 1979, a 1,283 percent rise. Wendy's grew to a position of being the third-largest fast-food hamburger restaurant chain in the United States, ranking behind Burger King and McDonald's, the leading U.S. hamburger chain.

2   Wendy's entry and amazing growth in the hamburger segment of the fast-food industry shocked the industry and forced competitors within it to realize that their market positions are potentially vulnerable. Wendy's flourished in the face of adversities plaguing the industry. Throughout the 1970s, experts said the fast-food industry was rapidly maturing. Analysts for *The Wall Street Journal* and *Business Week*, citing a "competitively saturated fast-food hamburger industry," predicted in the early 1970s that the

This case was prepared by Richard Robinson of the University of South Carolina. Copyright © by Richard Robinson, 1986.

Wendy's venture would not succeed. As they saw it, market saturation, rising commodity prices, fuel costs, and labor costs were already plaguing the fast-food industry.

3   Clearly unconcerned about such commentary, R. David Thomas pushed Wendy's relentlessly. It opened an average of one restaurant every two days through 1979 and became the first hamburger chain to top $1 billion in sales in its first 10 years.

History

4   R. David Thomas had an idea. He knew Americans love hamburgers. If he could develop a hamburger better than those currently offered, he believed he could use it to establish a leadership position in the competitive fast-food hamburger market.

5   In November 1969, Thomas, an experienced restaurant operator and Kentucky Fried Chicken franchisee, began to put his idea into reality when he opened Wendy's first unit in downtown Columbus, Ohio. A year later, in November 1970, Wendy's opened its second unit in Columbus, this one with a drive-through pickup window. In August 1972, Wendy's sold L. S. Hartzog the franchise for the Indianapolis, Indiana, market, kicking off Wendy's rapid expansion into the chain hamburger business. Later the same year, Wendy's Management Institute was formed to develop management skills in managers, supervisors, area directors, and franchise owners. After five years, company revenues exceeded $13 million with net income in excess of $1 million. Sales for both company-owned and franchised units topped $24 million for the same period. In June 1975, the 100th Wendy's opened in Louisville, Kentucky. Three months later, Wendy's went public. December 1976 saw Wendy's 500th open in Toronto, Canada. In 1977, Wendy's went national with its first network television commercial, making it the first restaurant chain with less than 1,000 units to mount a national advertising campaign. Eleven months later, Wendy's broke yet another record by opening its 1,000th restaurant in Springfield, Tennessee, within 100 months of opening the first Wendy's in Columbus. In 1979, Wendy's signed franchise agreements for eight European countries and Japan and opened the first European restaurant, company-owned, in Munich, West Germany. Also 1979 saw test marketing of a limited breakfast menu, a children's menu, and salad bars.

Wendy's Developmental Concept: The Last 10 Years

The Menu

6   Wendy's management team believes that its limited menu has been a key factor contributing to Wendy's success. The idea was to concentrate on doing only a few things, but to do them better than anyone else. As a result, the aim was to provide the customer with a Cadillac hamburger that could be custom-made to meet individual preferences.

7   The basic menu item was the quarter-pound hamburger made of only fresh, 100 percent beef hamburger meat converted into patties daily. This kept Wendy's out of head-on competition with McDonald's and Burger King's $1/10$ pound hamburger. If people desired a bigger hamburger, they could order a double (two patties on a bun) or a

triple (three patties on a bun). Besides having just one basic menu item, the hamburger, Wendy's also decided to differentiate itself by changing their hamburger's design. Instead of the traditional round patty found in competing fast-food outlets, Wendy's patty was square and sized so its edges would stick out over the edge of the round bun. The unique design alleviated the frequent complaint by most people that they were eating a breadburger. Other menu decisions included the following:

1. To offer different condiments to the customers—cheese, tomato, catsup, onion, lettuce, mustard, mayonnaise, and relish.
2. To provide a unique dairy product, the frosty—a cross between chocolate and vanilla flavors that borders between soft ice cream and a thick milk shake.
3. To serve a product that was unique in the fast-food market—chili.
4. To sell french fries because the public expected a hamburger outlet to offer them.

Facilities

8   Under Thomas's direction, the exterior style and interior decor of all Wendy's restaurants conformed to company specifications. The typical outlet was a freestanding one-story brick building constructed on a 25,000-square-foot site that provided parking for 35 to 45 cars (see Exhibits 1 and 2). There were some downtown storefront-type restaurants, which generally adhered to the standard red, yellow, and white decor and design. Most of the freestanding restaurants contained 2,100 square feet, had a cooking area, dining room capacity for 92 persons, and a pickup window for drive-in service (see Exhibit 3). The interior decor featured table tops printed with reproductions of 19th century advertising, Tiffany-styled lamps, bentwood chairs, colorful beads, and carpeting.

9   Generally, the strategy was to build a functionally modern building that would reflect the old-fashioned theme. Another plus for their building design was its flexibility. With only minor changes, they could sell almost any type of food in the building. It would also be possible to change from the Gay 90s theme to any other theme in just a matter of days.

10   The most unique feature in their building design was the addition of the pickup window, and Wendy's was the first major restaurant chain to successfully implement the use of one. Here, Wendy's was able to gain an advantage because their units could be smaller and at the same time handle the larger amount of business volume generated by using the pickup window. The logic for implementing the use of the pickup window was that people in their cars don't fill up tables or take up a parking space. The result showed that on a square-foot basis, Wendy's units did more business than any other chain.

11   The building design also contributed to what Michael J. Esposito, an investments analyst for Oppenheimer & Company, has called the most impressive part of the company's operation: the delivery system. In a report recommending Wendy's as an investment, Esposito wrote:

> In our judgment, the transaction time (time elapsed from when order is placed
> to its delivery to the customer) is the lowest in the industry, generally averaging
> about one minute. Utilizing a grill system where a constant flow of hamburgers

Exhibit 1
Typical freestanding building design

is cooked at a relatively low temperature, a worker takes the hamburger off the grill, places it on a bun, adds the condiments ordered by the customer, assembles and wraps the sandwich. Another crew member supplies chili, french fries, beverage, and a frosty dessert, and another reviews the order and releases it to the customer.

The Marketing Strategy

12   In their book, *The Chain-Restaurant Industry,* Earl Sasser and Daryl Wycoff stated:

> The Wendy's strategy was described by one analyst as "selling better hamburgers than McDonald's or Burger King at a cheaper price per ounce." As he commented, it takes no more labor to prepare a large hamburger at a higher price.

13   To support the higher-priced hamburger, Wendy's marketing strategy has been to stress the freshness and quality of their product. The objective of this strategy is to target Wendy's for the world's fastest-growing market segment. By offering a freshly ground, made-to-order hamburger as well as stylish, comfortable decor, Wendy's was aiming squarely at a key segment of the population: young adults with a taste for

Exhibit 2
Wendy's typical site 1—typical lot layout for freestanding unit

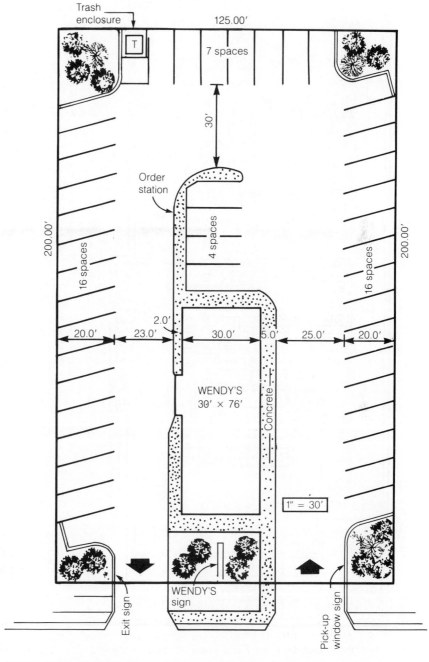

Lot area, 25,000 square feet; building, 2,310 square feet; parking spaces, 43.

Exhibit 3
Restaurant interior layout

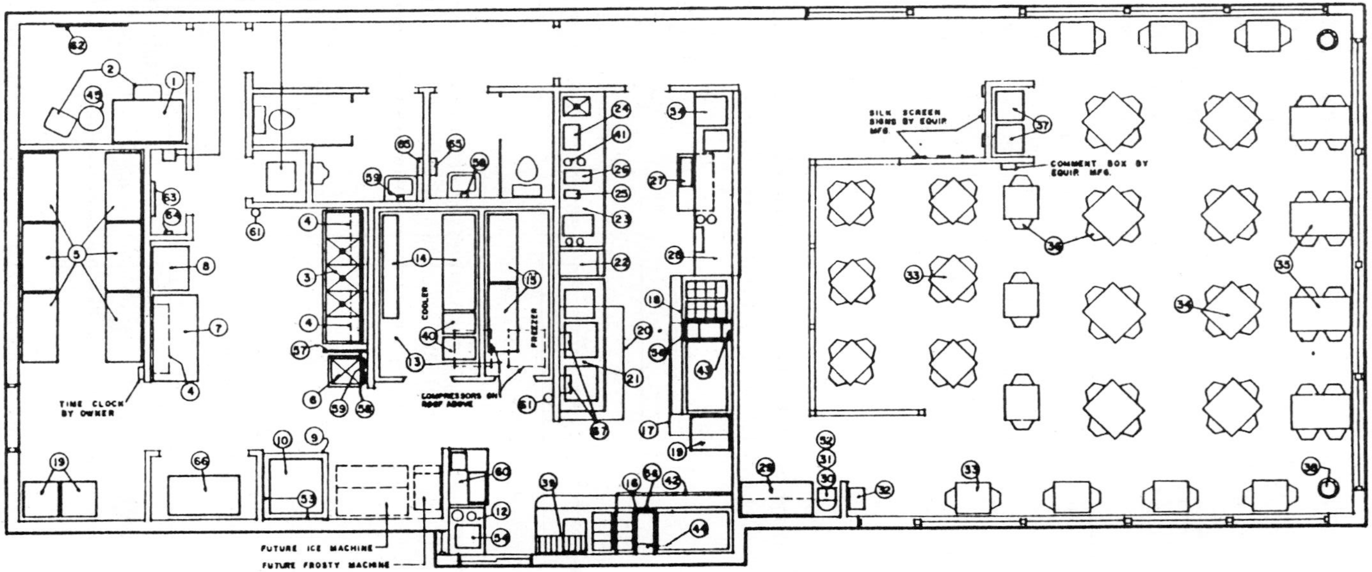

Key:
1. Desk.
2. Chair.
3. Sink unit.
4. Wall shelving.
5. Wall shelving.
6. Sink unit.
7. Work table.
8. Hamburger patty-making machine.
9. Exhaust canopy system.
10. Range top.
11. Open number.
12. Cashier counter assembly.
13. Walk-in cooler/freezer.
14. Wire shelving.
15. Frozen french fry storage platform.
16. Custom cooks counter assembly.
17. Exhaust canopy system.

18. Custom cook.
19. Bun rack.
20. Exhaust canopy system.
21. Custom fry station assembly.
22. Frosty machine.
23. Rear counter assembly.
24. Coffee maker.
25. Tea machine.
26. Hot chocolate machine.
27. Ice and drink machine.
28. Front counter assembly.
29. Condiment station.
30. High chair.
31. Booster chairs.
32. Water fountain.
33. Pedestal tables.
34. Pedestal tables.

35. Pedestal tables.
36. Side chairs.
37. Waste containers.
38. Costumers.
39. Condiment holder.
40. Meat racks.
41. Marshmallow holder.
42. Exhaust canopy system (fire protection).
43. Custom paper holder.
44. Custom paper holder.
45. Floor safe.
46. Litter receptacle.
47. Tiffany-style light fixtures.
48. Carpet.
49. Wall covering.
50. Beads.

51. Installation package.
52. Booster chair hanger.
53. Stainless wall panel.
54. Cash registers.
55. Open number.
56. Bun cabinet.
57. Stainless partition.
58. Towel dispenser.
59. Soap dispenser.
60. Ice and drink machine.
61. Fire extinguishers.
62. Coat hook bar.
63. Broom holder.
64. Hose holder.
65. Hand dryers.
66. Syrup tank rack.
67. French fry computers.

better food. With the post–World War II babies reaching their 20s and 30s, those young adults have been expanding faster than any other age group. As a result, it is thought that Wendy's success is coming not so much at the expense of the other burger chains but from having selected a special niche in the otherwise crowded market. Most agree that Wendy's basically expanded the market, and statistics from customer surveys bear out the claim. Fully 82 percent of all Wendy's business comes from customers over 25, an unusually old market for any fast-food chain. By contrast, McDonald's generated 35 percent of its revenues from youngsters under 19.

14   Wendy's advertising efforts have emphasized nationwide television advertising to attract this young adult market. Since 1974, Wendy's "Hot 'n' Juicy" advertising theme has been central to this effort. In the late 1970s, with its position established, Wendy's national advertising started focusing on new market segments like dinner after 4 P.M. after family meals on weekends. Apparently feeling the Hot 'n' Juicy theme had served its purpose, Wendy's adopted a new advertising theme: "There Ain't No Reason to Go Anyplace Else."[1] This theme has sparked considerable attention, particularly a negative reaction to the word *ain't* and the phrase's double negative.

Franchising

15   In 1972, Wendy's management made the decision to become a national chain as quickly as possible, which meant growing through franchising. The franchises were awarded on an area basis rather than single-store franchises. As a result, Wendy's 10 largest franchise owners operated a total of 406 restaurants by 1979. The franchise agreements were among the most straightforward in the restaurant industry and are deliberately designed to establish a fair business relationship. They specify the number of units to be opened within a certain time frame, the area to be developed, a technical assistance fee, and a royalty of 4 percent of gross sales. They also stipulate that 4 percent of gross sales be spent for local and national advertising. Wendy's operated no commissaries and sold no food, fixtures, or supplies to franchise owners.

16   To support their growing network of franchised restaurants, Wendy's franchise operations department maintained a staff of 50 franchise area supervisors who are the company's operations advisers to the franchise owners. They are charged with ensuring that Wendy's quality standards are met throughout the entire franchise network.

17   Wendy's also provided the following services to their franchisees:

1. Site approval procedures for locations.
2. On-site inspection and evaluation by a staff representative.
3. Counseling in business planning.
4. Drawings and specifications for buildings.
5. Training for franchisees at Wendy's headquarters.
6. Advice on supplies from suppliers selected by Wendy's and assistance in establishing quality-control standards and procedures for supplies.
7. Staff representatives to help in the opening of each restaurant.

---

[1] An article in *The Wall Street Journal* (July 8, 1980, p. 29) offered another explanation: "Wendy's ads showed diners biting into its hot and juicy hamburgers and then mopping juice from their chins. But some people thought the image projected by the ads was hot and greasy. Many franchises quit advertising, in effect voting no confidence in the company's marketing plan."

8. Assistance in planning opening promotion and continuing advertising, public relations, and promotion.

9. Operations manual with information necessary to operate a Wendy's restaurant.

10. Research and development in production and methods of operations.

11. Information on policies, developments, and activities by means of bulletins, brochures, reports, and visits of Wendy's representatives.

12. Paper-goods standards.

13. National and regional meetings.

18 The criteria used by Wendy's for franchisee selection is basically simple but strictly adhered to. They look for good proven business ability. The applicant must demonstrate that he or she is interested in making profits and does not mind getting involved. Wendy's did not make their profits by selling goods and services to their franchisees. Their income came from the restaurants' sales volume. Therefore, the franchisee must be able to build sales.

19 Wendy's operates company-owned restaurants in 26 markets around the following cities:

Columbus, Ohio	33	Indianapolis, Indiana	15
Cincinnati, Ohio	20	Dallas/Ft. Worth, Texas	26
Dayton, Ohio	26	Houston, Texas	25
Toledo, Ohio	12	Oklahoma City, Oklahoma	12
Atlanta, Georgia	35	Tulsa, Oklahoma	12
Tampa, Sarasota,		Memphis, Tennessee	13
St. Petersburg,		Louisville, Kentucky	14
Clearwater, Florida	22	Syracuse, New York	10
Jacksonville, Florida	15	Harrisburg, Pennsylvania	22
Daytona Beach, Florida	4	Philadelphia, Pennsylvania	20
Detroit, Michigan	20	Virginia Beach, Virginia	15
Portland, Oregon	10	Charleston, West Virginia	14
Reno, Nevada	6	Parkersburg, West Virginia	20
Greensboro, North Carolina	10	Munich, West Germany	2

Other than Detroit, no franchises exist in these markets.

20 At the end of 1979, there were 1,385 franchised restaurants operated by 161 franchise owners in 47 states and 3 foreign countries.

21 In a report to the Securities and Exchange Commission, Wendy's discussed the current state of its franchise program and described the franchise owners' relationship with the company:

Although franchised areas exist in all states except three, areas of some states remain unfranchised. In addition, most franchise owners have the right to build more units in their franchised areas than had been constructed at December 31, 1979. At that date, no franchise owner had more than 88 stores in operation. Several franchise owners operate restaurants in more than one state.

The rights and franchise offered by the company are contained in two basic documents. A franchise owner first executes a development agreement. This document gives the franchise owner the exclusive right to select proposed sites on which to construct Wendy's Old Fashioned Hamburgers restaurants within a certain geographic area (the franchised area), requires the submission of sites to the company for its acceptance, and, upon acceptance of a proposed site by the company, provides for the execution of a unit franchise agreement with the company to enable the franchise owner to construct, own, and operate a Wendy's Old Fashioned Hamburgers restaurant upon the site. The development agreement provides for the construction and opening of a fixed number of restaurants within the franchised area in accordance with a development or performance schedule. Both the number of restaurants and the development and performance schedules are agreed upon by the franchise owner and the company prior to the execution of the development agreement. The development agreement also grants a right of first refusal to the franchise owner with respect to the construction of any additional restaurants in the franchised area beyond the initially agreed-to number.

The development agreement requires that the franchise owner pay the company a technical assistance fee. The technical assistance fee required by newly executed development agreement is currently $15,000 for each franchise restaurant which the franchise owner has agreed to construct. Under earlier forms of the development agreement or franchise agreements, this fee was either $5,000, $7,500, or $10,000. However, approximately 12 existing franchise owners have the right under certain circumstances to receive additional franchise areas on the basis of the earlier $10,000 fee.

The technical assistance fee is used to defray the cost to the company of providing to its franchise owners site selection assistance; standard construction plans, specifications, and layouts; company review of specific restaurant site plans; initial training in the company's restaurant systems; and such bulletins, brochures, and reports as are from time to time published regarding the company's plans, policies, research, and other business activities.

22 From time to time, the company has reacquired franchised operations. A summary of these acquisitions is presented in Exhibit 4. In 1979, the company adopted a rather aggressive approach to franchise acquisition. Of 145 new company-owned operations in 1979 (representing a 50 percent increase during the year), 84 were acquired from franchisees. This major shift to company-owned restaurant growth away from franchised growth reflects the concern for systemwide control of quality as well as the increasing competition for available locations. Exhibit 5 illustrates the emphasis on company-owned growth since 1974. Granting large territorial franchises rather than single-outlet franchises was similarly practiced by Burger King in its formative stages. At Burger King, this led to franchise empires that were bigger than parent-company operations. Wendy's emphasis on company-owned growth may well be intended to avoid the problem that led to Burger King's decline in the late 1960s.

Finances

23 Wendy's revenues (see Exhibit 6) increased steadily between 1975 and 1980. Net income dropped in 1979 compared to 1978, but Thomas explains:

> During 1979, we were informed by the U.S. Department of Labor that a review of company labor practices for a three-year period indicated that certain company

Exhibit 4

	Acquisition date	Company acquired	Restaurants in operation	Location	Accounting treatment	Common shares issued/ purchase price
1.	7/31/76	Wendy's Management, Inc., and subsidiaries	40	Atlanta, Georgia Indianapolis, Indiana Louisville, Kentucky Jacksonville, Florida	Purchase	733,195
2.	10/1/77	Wendy's Old Fashioned Hamburgers of New York, Inc.	5	Syracuse, New York	Purchase	Immaterial
3.	6/30/78	Wendy's of West Virginia, Inc.	33	West Virginia Eastern Kentucky Southeast Ohio	Pooling	535,000
4.	9/30/78	Springfield Management Company, Inc., and Dakota Land Corp.	6	Springfield, Ohio Richmond, Indiana	Pooling	39,294
5.	5/26/59	1620 South Atlantic, Inc. Forsyth, Inc. RR&WW, Inc. Reaves & Reaves Restaurants, Inc.	14	Greensboro, North Carolina Winston-Salem, North Carolina Daytona Beach, Florida	Pooling	268,900
6.	5/30/79	Wendcorp of Nevada, Inc. Wendcorp of Portland, Inc.	16	Reno, Nevada Portland, Oregon	Pooling	245,815
7.	8/31/79	Susquehanna Food Services, Inc.	40	Southeastern Pennsylvania and northern Delaware	Pooling	508,861
8.	11/30/79	Wendy's of Virginia, Inc.	14	Southeastern Virginia	Purchase	$5,520,000

Exhibit 5
Growth in company-operated restaurants

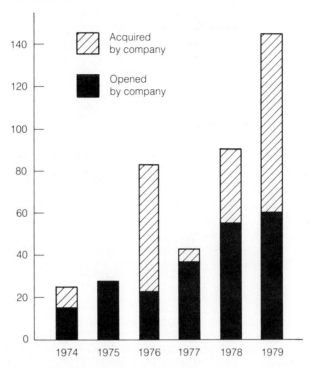

policies had not been uniformly adhered to, and, as a result, the company was not in full compliance with the Fair Labor Standards Act.

Based on this review and the company's own investigation, we have determined that $3,800,000 should be accrued and charged against 1979 pretax income. Had this charge not been made, 1979 net income would have been $25,096,000, an increase of 8 percent over the $23,215,000 originally reported a year earlier. We believe company labor practices now comply with both company policy and the act, and, in addition, future compliance will not materially affect net income in 1980 and ensuing years.

24   Whether the cost of labor compliance was the only cause of the abrupt slowdown in Wendy's steady increase in revenue and profit is questionable. Several factors suggest that Wendy's, after a decade of rapid growth, was reaching the limits of its current capabilities.

25   The heart of Wendy's success has been its streamlined, limited menu with primary emphasis on a quality hamburger. Since 1977, beef prices have soared, as shown in Exhibit 7. And while Wendy's has responded with tighter controls and a series of price increases just under 15 percent for 1979 alone (see Exhibit 8), this has still contributed to a decline in profitability.

Exhibit 6

WENDY'S INTERNATIONAL, INCORPORATED
Consolidated Statement of Income
For the Years Ended December 31, 1975–1979

	1979	1978	1977	1976	1975
Revenue:					
Retail operations	$237,753,097	$198,529,130	$130,667,377	$71,336,626	$35,340,665
Royalties	30,564,613	23,396,211	11,810,277	4,655,432	1,567,008
Technical assistance fees	2,822,500	3,540,000	2,510,000	1,560,000	622,500
Other, principally interest	2,903,261	2,685,909	1,802,691	965,521	246,901
Total revenues	274,043,471	228,151,250	146,790,345	78,517,579	37,777,074
Costs and expenses:					
Cost of sales	146,346,806	113,812,874	72,482,010	40,509,285	19,629,179
Company restaurant operating costs	51,193,050	43,289,285	28,088,460	14,348,150	7,292,391
Department of labor compliance review	3,800,000				
Salaries, travel, and associated expenses of franchise personnel	4,187,399	3,148,532	1,936,877	1,156,493	622,879
General and administrative expenses	15,741,592	13,292,845	8,191,394	4,137,226	2,581,166
Depreciation and amortization of property and equipment	7,355,818	5,444,092	3,767,259	2,240,215	799,876
Interest	4,357,973	3,771,878	3,215,432	2,583,876	995,410
Total expenses	232,982,638	182,759,506	117,681,432	64,975,245	31,920,901
Income before income taxes	41,060,833	45,391,744	29,108,913	13,542,334	5,856,173
Income taxes:					
Federal:					
Current	15,583,700	18,324,600	12,052,200	5,784,600	2,926,700
Deferred	1,303,200	1,020,800	323,700	(19,600)	(501,900)
	16,886,900	19,345,400	12,375,900	5,765,000	2,424,800
State and local taxes	1,077,500	1,559,700	1,296,200	694,400	298,800
Total income taxes	17,964,400	20,905,100	13,672,100	6,459,400	2,723,600
Net income	$ 23,096,433	$ 24,486,644	$ 15,436,813	$ 7,082,934	$ 3,132,373
Net income per share	$1.54	$1.63	$1.04	$.57	$.29
Weighted average number of common shares outstanding	14,970,526	15,017,708	14,855,503	12,525,294	10,645,694
Dividends per common share	$.40	$.14	$.125	$.004	$.001

Source: Wendy's International, Form 10-K, 1979.

Exhibit 7
Yearly average meat price per pound for company-owned stores

1969	$.59	1975	$ .69
1970	.62	1976	.72
1971	.64	1977	.72
1972	.67	1978	1.02
1973	.90	1979	1.29
1974	.74		

Exhibit 8
Percentage price increases for hamburgers

1/1/77	0.6%	10/22/78	0.15%
3/1/77	0.3	10/29/78	0.10
12/10/77	6.0	12/17/78	3.40
3/19/78	3.0	1/14/79	3.06
4/16/78	2.5	2/25/79	3.60
5/21/78	1.8	4/8/79	0.10
7/23/78	1.2	4/15/79	0.03
10/1/78	1.7	12/16/79	4.45

Exhibit 9
Average sales per restaurant

	1979		1978	
	Amount	Percent change*	Amount	Percent change*
Company	$624,000	(2.9)%	$642,900	14.3%
Franchise	618,800	(12.4)	706,000	11.7
Systemwide	620,000	(10.0)	688,800	13.0

* Percent increase (or decrease) over the same figure for the previous year.

26   Further evidence suggests that Wendy's may have been reaching a plateau in its historical pattern of growth. The average sales per restaurant, which climbed steadily from $230,000 in 1970 to $688,800 in 1978, declined significantly in 1979 at both company-owned and franchised restaurants, as shown in Exhibit 9. The impact on the parent company was felt in every revenue category, as shown in Exhibit 10. Wendy's continued to experience increased retail revenue (company-owned stores) and royalties (from franchises based on a percent of sales) but at a drastically slower rate. And for the first time, Wendy's experienced a decrease in technical assistance (franchise) fees.

Exhibit 10
Changes in revenue from 1978 to 1979

| | 1979 | | 1978 | |
	Amount*	Percent†	Amount	Percent
Retail operations	$39,224,000	19.8%	$67,862,000	51.9%
Royalties	7,168,000	30.6	11,586,000	98.1
Technical assistance fees	(718,000)	(20.3)	1,030,000	41.0
Other, principally interest	(217,000)	(8.1)	883,000	49.0

* Absolute dollar increase (or decrease) over the previous year.
† Percent increase (or decrease) over the previous year.

27   Other evidence of a slowdown in Wendy's growth can be seen in the rate of new store openings. For the first time in its history, Wendy's experienced a decline in the rate of new store openings, as shown in Exhibit 11.

28   While revenue and profitability growth slowed in 1979, Thomas was confident this was only temporary. Feeling strongly that Wendy's was in a good position to finance continued growth, Thomas offered the following observation:

> While construction money is more difficult to obtain than in the last few years, lines of credit already arranged guarantee financing of 1980 company plans to open 60 or more restaurants. We also anticipate exploring avenues of long-term debt to finance our growth beyond 1980. We believe that with $25 million of long-term debt, exclusive of capitalized lease obligations, and over $100 million in shareholders' equity, we have substantial untapped borrowing power.

Exhibit 12 summarizes Wendy's balance sheet for 1978 and 1979.

Wendy's Future

29   Addressing Wendy's stockholders in early 1980, R. David Thomas offered the following assessment of Wendy's first 10 years:

> We are proud to be marking the 10th anniversary of Wendy's International, Inc. Just 10 years ago, in November 1969, we opened the first Wendy's Old Fashioned Hamburgers restaurant in downtown Columbus, Ohio. Now, after a decade of explosive growth, there are Wendy's quick-service restaurants in 49 of the 50 states and in Canada, Puerto Rico, Germany, and Switzerland.
>
> At year-end 1979, there were 1,818 Wendy's restaurants in operation, 411 more than at the close of 1978. Of the 433 company-operated restaurants, 84 were acquired from franchise owners during 1979. It was a year of progress for our international expansion program as we opened our first restaurants in Europe and entered into agreements for development of Japan, France, Belgium, Luxembourg, the Netherlands, Switzerland, Spain, Germany, and the United Kingdom.
>
> During 1979, the company established a research and development department, which is testing a number of potential menu items. The salad bar, which was

Exhibit 11
New restaurant openings: 1979 versus 1978

	Company*		Franchise		Systemwide	
	1979	1978	1979	1978	1979	1978
Open at beginning of year	348	271	1,059	634	1,407	905
Opened during the year	71	77	340	425	411	502
Purchased from franchise owners	14	—	(14)	—	—	—
Total open at end of year	433	348	1,385	1,059	1,818	1,407
Average open during year	381	309	1,235	828	1,616	1,137

* Restaurants acquired from franchise owners in poolings of interest have been included since date of opening.

Exhibit 12

WENDY'S INTERNATIONAL, INCORPORATED
Consolidated Balance Sheets
For the Years Ended December 31, 1978, and 1979

	1979	1978
Assets		
Current assets:		
Cash	$ 2,285,180	$ 1,021,957
Short-term investments, at cost, which approximates market, including accrued interest	12,656,352	27,664,531
Accounts receivable	4,902,746	3,248,789
Inventories and other	2,581,528	1,855,313
Total current assets	22,425,806	33,790,590
Property and equipment, at cost Schedule 5:		
Land	30,916,049	23,906,365
Buildings	40,784,581	30,049,552
Leasehold improvements	16,581,947	8,954,392
Restaurant equipment	34,052,952	24,461,860
Other equipment	9,722,666	8,413,363
Construction in progress	1,751,788	2,027,570
Capitalized leases	21,865,829	18,246,427
Total property and equipment before depreciation	155,675,812	116,059,529
Less: Accumulated depreciation and amortization	(20,961,702)	(13,543,473)
Total property and equipment	134,714,110	102,516,056
Cost in excess of net assets acquired, less amortization of $699,410 and $481,162, respectively	8,408,788	5,207,942
Other assets	7,152,131	2,377,648
Total cost over net assets and other assets	15,560,919	7,585,590
Total assets	$172,700,835	$143,892,236

Exhibit 12 *(concluded)*

	1979	1978
Liabilities and Shareholders' Equity		
Current liabilities:		
Accounts payable, trade	$ 10,174,980	$ 11,666,272
Federal, state, and local income taxes		7,839,586
Accrued expenses:		
Administrative fee		664,770
Salaries and wages	2,368,244	1,970,977
Interest	433,540	369,603
Taxes	1,932,192	1,498,521
Department of Labor compliance review	3,800,000	
Other	1,576,851	739,588
Current portion, term debt, and		
capitalized lease obligations	3,891,247	2,781,671
Total current liabilities	24,177,054	27,530,988
Term debt, net of current portion	25,097,688	15,308,276
Capital lease obligations, net of		
current portion	18,707,838	15,130,617
	43,805,526	30,438,893
Deferred technical assistance fees	1,995,000	2,117,500
Deferred federal income taxes	2,027,604	664,300
Shareholders' equity:		
Common stock, $.10 stated value;		
authorized: 40,000,000 shares; issued and		
outstanding: 14,882,614 and 14,861,877		
shares, respectively	1,488,261	1,486,188
Capital in excess of stated value	34,113,173	33,962,916
Retained earnings	65,094,217	47,691,451
Total shareholders' equity	100,695,651	83,140,555
Total liabilities and shareholders' equity	$172,700,835	$143,892,236

Source: Wendy's International, Form 10-K, 1979.

tested in our Columbus, Ohio, market, had been introduced into 171 restaurants by year-end.

In 1979, our industry was faced with major challenges, such as inflation and energy problems. Higher labor costs and rising beef prices affected Wendy's profitability and depressed profits for our entire industry. The minimum wage, which affects 90 percent of our employees, increased in January 1979 and January 1980. Ground beef prices increased to an average of $1.29 per pound in 1979, 79 percent higher than the 1977 average price. During 1979, we minimized our retail price increases, with the goal of increasing our market share. This strategy, coupled with more aggressive marketing, helped rebuild customer traffic in the latter part of the year. Although holding back on price increases affected our margins, we believe it was appropriate and that margins benefited by our cost efficiencies, especially in purchasing and distribution.

During 1979, we remained flexible and open to changing customer needs and attitudes, and we continued to take the steps necessary to achieve and support future growth and profitability as we—

> Tested and implemented a highly successful salad bar concept.
>
> Tested a breakfast concept and other menu items.
>
> Began development of the European and Japanese markets.
>
> Initiated a new marketing program designed to increase dinner and weekend business.
>
> Prepared to open another 250 to 300 Wendy's restaurants systemwide in 1980.

30   And, setting the tone for Wendy's in the 1980s, Thomas said:

> We are aware, as we enter our second decade, that we have achieved a unique position in a highly competitive industry. It was no less difficult and competitive 10 years ago than it is today, we believe, than it will be 10 years from now. We intend to build further on our achievement of being recognized as a chain of high-quality, quick-service restaurants. We will continue to produce fresh, appealing, high-quality food; price it competitively; and serve it in a clean, attractive setting with employees who are carefully selected, well trained, and responsive to our customers.

31   Similar to the way they questioned R. David Thomas's venture into the hamburger jungle in 1970, several business writers once again began to question Wendy's future. Illustrative of this is the following article, which appeared in *The Wall Street Journal:*

> Wendy's International, Inc., is making changes it once considered unthinkable.
>
> Wendy's faced the choice confronting many companies when the initial burst of entrepreneurial brilliance dims: Should it stick with the original concept and be content with a niche in a bigger market, or should it change and attempt to keep growing? Wendy's chose to revamp its operations. It is adding salad bars, chicken and fish sandwiches, and a children's meal to its menu, adopting a new advertising strategy, and considering whether to alter the appearance of its restaurants.
>
> Some observers predict Wendy's will regret the quick changes. "This is a company that was able to convince a certain segment of the country it had a different taste in hamburgers," says Carl De Biase, an analyst with Sanford C. Bernstein & Co. in New York. "They've achieved their mandate, and anything they do now is just going to screw up the concept."
>
> But Robert Barney, Wendy's president and chief executive officer, says the company is "in some very difficult times right now." Among the problems: discontented franchise holders and the likelihood that beef prices will rise sharply again in the second half. Barney says Wendy's doesn't even "have the luxury of waiting to see" how each change works before moving to the next one.
>
> This spring, shortly after the changes began, Thomas resigned as chief executive, saying he wanted more time for public relations work and community affairs. Thomas, who is 47 years old and will continue as chairman, had been closely identified with the old ad campaign and with company resistance to broadening the menu.
>
> The company has been doing a little better so far this year, and franchisees say they're much more optimistic. The menu changes, they say, were long overdue.

"It had been suggested to everyone in the company," says Raymond Schoenbaum, who operates 33 Wendy's outlets in Alabama and Georgia. "But the mentality wouldn't allow menu diversification before. It had to be forced on them."

Barney concedes that prior to last year "we never did a lot of planning." But that has been remedied, he says, partly with a "research and development department" that will examine new menu prospects.

Not everyone believes that tinkering with the menu will bring back customers and profits. Edward H. Schmitt, president of McDonald's, predicts an image problem for Wendy's and maintains that the company will lose the labor advantage it held over other fast-food outlets. He adds that McDonald's tried and abandoned salad bars. "It's practically a no-profit item," he says, "and it's a high-waste item."

Some franchisees complain that the new children's meal, called Fun Feast, will draw the company into a can't-win competition with McDonald's and Burger King for the children's market, which Wendy's has avoided so far. "Every survey we have says we shouldn't go after that market," a franchisee reports. "Our chairs aren't designed for kids to climb on, and our carpet isn't designed for kids to spill ketchup on."

But Barney insists that Fun Feast isn't intended to attract children. He says Wendy's is trying to remove the adults' reason for not coming to the restaurant. "Where we tested it," he says, "we didn't sell so many of them but we did see an increase in adult traffic."

Wendy's may evolve from a sandwich shop into a more generalized quick-service restaurant that doesn't compete as directly with McDonald's and Burger King. "We're going to be between" McDonald's and quick-service steakhouses, says Schoenbaum, the Georgia and Alabama franchise holder.

To this end, Schoenbaum says, Wendy's will reduce the abundance of plastic fixtures in its restaurants and perhaps cut down on the amount of glass. He says the glass makes Wendy's a pleasant, brightly lit lunch spot but doesn't create a good atmosphere for dinner.

Wendy's officials confirm that they are considering altering the appearance of their restaurants, but they aren't specific. And as for whom Wendy's competes with, Barney says: "We're in competition with anywhere food is served, including the home."[2]

---

[2] "Its Vigor Lost, Wendy's Seeks a New Niche," *The Wall Street Journal,* July 8, 1980, p. 29.

Case 2

Wendy's (B): Managing a Maturing Organization

1   Wendy's opened its first store in 1969; by 1983, it had 2,460 stores. Early on, the company made the decision to be a large national chain, rather than a small regional one, and to grow as rapidly as possible. Wendy's early mission adhered to a limited menu, resisting product additions to protect the restaurants' assembly-line delivery system.

2   In the late 1970s, Wendy's was a typical emerging young company with entrepreneurial leadership and entrepreneurial management. Everything went fine until beef prices soared in 1978. Wendy's limited menu (mainly hamburgers) made the company extremely vulnerable when the price of beef rose.

3   At this time, Wendy's created its research and development department and quickly began testing new products: the salad bar, a chicken sandwich, and breakfast. R&D was playing catch-up.

4   Recognizing that the customers who supported Wendy's early growth might not be the same people who could maintain its growth rate into the future, Wendy's sought to identify new growth opportunities while simultaneously beginning the process of transforming itself from an entrepreneurial company to a professionally managed business.

5   Focusing on a long-term growth strategy of continued U.S. penetration, international growth, and concentric diversification into the chicken segment, Wendy's management team plans to have 4,000 Wendy's restaurants by 1990. This case examines Wendy's strategic initiatives during the period between 1979 and 1983.

Product/Market Development

6   Committed to the idea that a restaurant was better off doing a few things well rather than many things poorly, Wendy's founder, R. David Thomas, originally limited Wendy's menu to hamburgers, chili, french fries, soft drinks, and a frosty dessert. But in 1979, the soaring price of beef, together with a decline in traffic, lowered profits for the first time since the company was organized.

7   Wendy's did not have a research and development department until 1978. The department quickly began to test new products, and, one year later, Wendy's became the first fast-food chain to introduce a salad bar. Accounting for 7 to 8 percent of the typical Wendy's sales within a year, the salad bar lessened the company's dependence on beef and appealed to people in new market segments. It was credited with boosting the female customer base from 10 percent to 50 percent of the total. Explaining this success, Thomas said, "Women, weight-conscious people, and customers with smaller appetites are finding the salad bar an attractive and welcome addition to their neighborhood Wendy's."

This case was prepared by Richard Robinson and Patricia McDougall, both of the University of South Carolina. Copyright © by Richard Robinson and Patricia McDougall, 1986.

8   The chicken sandwich was another R&D-derived response to high beef prices. "The filet of chicken breast sandwich supports our high-quality image," remarked Mr. Thomas, "and provides another opportunity for our existing customers to eat in our restaurants." The chicken sandwich averages about 6 percent of sales in the typical Wendy's.

9   Commenting on Wendy's future product development focus, Joseph Madigan, executive vice president and chief financial officer, offered the following in early 1981:

> Quality has always been the rule for Wendy's products. During 1980, we took several steps which will enable us to continue as the quality leader in the industry and which we are confident will ensure our future growth.
>
> Our research and development department, now over two years old, has helped develop quality products that will keep us growing in the future.
>
> The department develops new products within these guidelines:
>
> 1. Any product additions must reinforce our quality image.
> 2. They must be profitable.
> 3. They must expand a market base.
> 4. They must increase frequency of visits.
> 5. They must merge easily into our system of operations.
> 6. They must help reduce vulnerability to beef prices.

10   Commenting further on product/market developments, Mr. Madigan offered the following summary of a perspective quite different than the founding Wendy's philosophy:

> Another new product we are introducing is a children's menu item. The Wendy's Kids' Fun Pak gives us the child-size portion we've needed and gives parents the reason they've wanted to make Wendy's their lunch or dinner choice.
>
> Each of the new menu items expands our customer base by appealing to more market segments than was possible with our original menu. At the same time, each new item gives us the chance to increase the frequency of visits of our existing customer base.
>
> We are now testing several different breakfast menus and combinations of items. Our aim is to build that part of the day, but we will not move beyond the test stage until we have the product we are sure is the best in the business. Research and development will continue to play an important role in our future as we develop the products that satisfy our customers and meet the needs of our business.
>
> We are constantly aware of the changing environment in which we do business. To keep pace with these changes, we continually evaluate our products, our restaurants, and other key elements of our business. In 1980, we built a restaurant in which we are testing several variations on the basic Wendy's style and appearance. This restaurant is providing us with valuable insights, and what we are learning is being incorporated into the plans for our future restaurants.

11   With the salad bar, chicken sandwich, and Wendy's Kids' Fun Pak representing approximately 18 percent of company store sales, taco salad was introduced in 1982 with the company's first national market support for a new menu item.

12   Taco salad is marketed as a complete meal of less than 400 calories. It has several virtues for Wendy's. It is preferred by women, thereby helping to further expand the

chain's traditional male-oriented customer base. Taco salad is a low-cost item as most of its ingredients are already available at Wendy's restaurants. This helps to hold down the introduction cost to a mere $45 per store. Sales of taco salad will also help reduce the amount of chili that must be thrown away at the end of each day.

13 As a focal point in reaching Wendy's stated goal of increasing average sales per restaurant to $1 million a year within five years,[1] product testing and development has become a high priority in the 1980s. Recipes, procedures, and kitchen equipment are tested in the company's new research and development laboratory.

14 The core of the strategic role of R&D in achieving the objectives of higher unit sales and better margins is not just menu diversification but developing new products that increase both incremental sales and profitability. Each new product is designed to accomplish a specific sales-building task. For example, one product might be designed to target a specific demographic group or a particular consumer trend, such as the shift toward dinner, while another product might be aimed at boosting volume in a specific day part. In a presentation to security analysts, president and CEO Ronald Fay outlined Wendy's R&D program to build sales into four sharply defined objectives— "higher check averages, more frequent visits, increased party size, and a far broader customer base."

15 After moving cautiously during the 1981–82 recession, Wendy's introduced four major product changes in 1983: the bacon cheeseburger; improved french fries; an upgraded "Garden Spot" salad bar with eight additional food items; and its hot stuffed baked potatoes. In what appears to be Wendy's most significant new product since the salad bar, the baked potatoes were offered plain or with a choice of five toppings: cheese, broccoli and cheese, bacon and cheese, chili and cheese, and sour cream and chives. The company expects to serve about 225 million baked potatoes annually, thus further lessening Wendy's dependence on beef and providing another alternative to consumers who prefer lighter meals. Spot checks of franchisees following the introduction revealed that many units have experienced average weekly sales gains in excess of 10 percent since the baked potatoes' introduction.

16 Fay touts the plain potato as 99 percent fat free and a good source of vitamin C. He points to its versatility as "something better for Wendy's kind of people." Barney added his expectation that "the baked potato should have as much impact as the salad bar had on the fast-service food industry."

17 Products introduced by Wendy's since 1978 now produce between 25 and 30 percent of total store sales, reducing burger sales in the typical Wendy's from 60 percent to 40 percent of total store revenue within the past four or five years. The company is testing gourmet hamburgers, chicken club sandwiches, BLTs, and dessert items and is expanding its test of the fish sandwich and dinner items.

18 Breakfast will soon be offered at all company-operated and most franchised Wendy's. The chain is trying to crack the breakfast market by attacking McDonald's lack of variety.[2] The breakfast features four made-to-order omelets, French toast, a scrambled egg platter, and an egg sandwich with a choice of toppings. Part of the slowness in moving into breakfast is due to concern over maintaining consistent quality—for example, how to make a good omelet in 30 seconds.

---

[1] The $1 million average sales goal represents a 40 percent increase from its 1982 base.

[2] In 1982, McDonald's generated $780 million (10 percent of its total revenue) from breakfast sales. That translates into approximately $120,000 annually at the typical McDonald's location.

19   Wendy's officials seem more enthusiastic about the potential of dinner items. Dinner entrees such as chicken parmesan, country beef and gravy, and chopped beef with mushroom sauce are being tested. "Our biggest obstacle is getting people to think of us as a fast-service restaurant that offers a superior dining experience," stated William Welter, senior vice president for marketing. Company officials concede there is a lot of new ground to break in attracting the dinner crowd but point to success in a recent promotional program featuring Sunday as a family day.

20   McDonald's also appears eager to cultivate a dinner business. Like Wendy's, McDonald's is finding it difficult to persuade the customer who was in earlier for a quick lunch to come back for the evening meal. McDonald's may be further handicapped by its close association with the "sandbox" set. McDonald's president and CEO, Fred Turner, insists, "we want to move toward the adult user." He cites McNuggets, just 310 calories for six pieces, as a move to appeal to adults and speculates on the possibility that modified table service at the dinner meal time may be helpful.

21   Wendy's expenditures for R&D in 1983 were almost five times greater than in 1980 as menu management became a top priority. While new products can create excitement, incremental sales, and better profits, Wendy's officials recognize that the menu cannot be expanded indefinitely. The company is prepared to offer some items on a seasonal basis, offer products with a strong regional appeal only in certain areas, and replace some products on the menu.

22   Besides meeting the criteria of higher check averages, more frequent visits, increased party size, and a broader customer base, new products must also fit smoothly into Wendy's assembly-line delivery system. Fay emphasizes the commitment to superior speed and service and places preserving the integrity of the delivery system as paramount as the company strives toward its $1 million per unit sales goal.

Financial

23   Wendy's revenues result primarily from sales by company-operated restaurants (see Exhibit 1). Royalties and technical assistance fees from franchisees make up the other major sources of revenue. The franchise agreement requires that the franchise owner pay a royalty equivalent to 4 percent of sales. It also calls for a technical assistance fee to defray such costs as site-selection assistance, specifications and layouts, initial training, and so on. Currently, the fee is $15,000 for each franchise restaurant the

---

Exhibit 1
Changes in revenues from 1978 to 1982

	1982	1981	1980	1979	1978
Revenues					
Retail operations	92.2%	91.4%	89.0%	86.8%	87.0%
Royalties	6.9	7.9	10.2	11.2	10.3
Technical assistance fee	.3	.3	.4	1.0	1.5
Other	.6	.4	.4	1.0	1.2
	100.0%	100.0%	100.0%	100.0%	100.0%

franchise owner has agreed to construct. This compares to McDonald's $12,500 franchise fee and 3 percent royalty and Burger King's $40,000 franchise fee and 3.5 percent royalty.

24   With the exception of the buns sold by New Bakery Company of Ohio, Inc., Wendy's does not sell fixtures, food, or supplies to the franchise owners. The New Bakery Company of Ohio, Inc., a wholly owned subsidiary of Wendy's, supplies buns for 450 company-operated restaurants and for 478 franchise restaurants. It was acquired in 1981.

25   Royalty income from franchised restaurants increased 9 percent in both 1982 and 1981. However, royalties as a percent of total revenue declined in both years, largely as a result of the company's acquisition of 161 formerly franchised restaurants.

26   Total revenues increased 24 percent in 1982 (compared to 1981) to $608 million (see Exhibit 2). After the 1979 dip, net income continued on its upward growth track into 1982, up 20 percent from 1981, on top of a 22 percent increase in 1981, and a 30 percent increase in 1980 (see Exhibit 3). Net income's five-year growth rate was 23 percent per year since 1977.

27   Earnings per share increased 12 percent in 1982 to $1.13 (see Exhibit 4). The five-year data reflect 3-for-2 stock splits in both 1981 and 1982. The debt-to-equity ratio declined to 39 percent at the end of 1982 from 49 percent (see Exhibit 5), reflecting increased borrowing capacity available to the company. In addition, $25 million in unused contractual lines of credit were available to the company at the end of 1982.

28   Of the $70.6 million in 1982 capital expenditures, $38.9 million was for new domestic Wendy's restaurants, $12.3 million for new Sisters and international restaurants, and $19.4 million principally for costs associated with the image enhancement program, restaurant refurbishings, and computerized registers (see Exhibit 6).

Exhibit 2
Revenue ($ millions): Five-year compounded annual growth, 33 percent

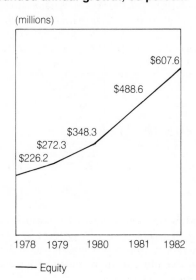

(millions)

$607.6
$488.6
$348.3
$272.3
$226.2

1978   1979   1980   1981   1982

— Equity

Exhibit 3
Net income ($ millions): Five-year compounded annual growth, 23 percent

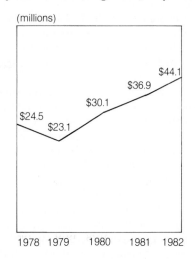

Exhibit 4
Earnings per share (dollars): Five-year compounded annual growth, 20 percent

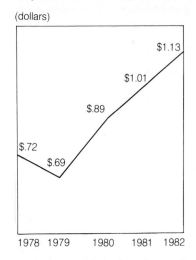

29   For Wendy's company-operated restaurants, profit margins at the store level improved to 18.1 percent from 16.7 percent in 1981 and 17.5 percent in 1980. In Wendy's 1982 annual report, this improvement was attributed to lower overall food costs (primarily beef—see Exhibit 7), more efficient product usage and reduction of food waste, and a reduction in couponing.

Exhibit 5
Debt to equity ($ millions)

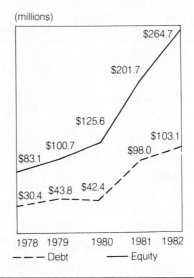

(millions)

$264.7

$201.7

$125.6

$100.7 $103.1

$83.1 $98.0

$30.4 $43.8 $42.4

1978 1979   1980   1981 1982
– – – Debt   —— Equity

Exhibit 6
Capital expenditures ($ millions)

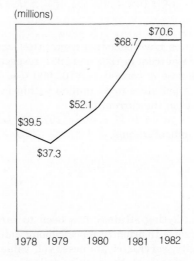

(millions)

$70.6

$68.7

$52.1

$39.5

$37.3

1978 1979   1980   1981 1982

Exhibit 7
Yearly average beef price per pound for company-owned stores

1977	$ .72	1980	$1.23
1978	1.02	1981	1.14
1979	1.29	1982	1.11

Exhibit 8
Average sales per restaurant (in thousands of dollars)

	1982	Percent change	1981	Percent change	1980	Percent change	1979	Percent change	1978	Percent change
Company	$706	1%	$702	6%	$665	7%	$624	(3)%	$643	14%
Franchise	701	6	662	8	615	(1)	619	(12)	706	12
Systemwide	703	4	674	7	627	1	620	(10)	689	13

Exhibit 9
Selected financial data (percent)

	1982	1981	1980	1979	1978
Return on average equity	19.50%	22.00%	26.60%	25.10%	34.20%
Return on average assets	14.00	15.20	18.20	18.60	22.30
Current ratio	.80	.58	.55	.93	1.23
Ratio of debt to equity	39.00	49.00	34.00	44.00	37.00
Ratio of debt to total capitalization	28.00	33.00	25.00	30.00	27.00

30   Retail prices have benefited from price increases. Average price increases were 3 percent and 8 percent in 1982 and 1981, respectively. Average 1982 sales per restaurant systemwide rose 4 percent to $703,000 (see Exhibit 8). Wendy's goal of increasing annual sales per store to $1 million within five years will require a sales increase of 40 percent from the current base.

31   Exhibits 9 through 11 contain 1978–82 selected financial ratios, balance sheets, and statements of income.

Operations

32   Wendy's marketing strategy has been to target the high-quality end of the quick-service market with primary appeal among young and middle-age adults, and its philosophy of quality, service, cleanliness, and value was aimed at this key segment of the population. With post–World War II babies reaching their 30s, these young adults have been expanding faster than any other age group. Wendy's success has come not so much at the expense of the other burger chains but has tended to expand the market.

33   Other demographic trends, such as the increase in working women, greater frequency of eating out, and the heightened interest in nutrition and health have all had a favorable impact.

34   A "new image" exterior design is in keeping with Wendy's market niche. Moving further away from the brightly colored, plastic fast-food atmosphere, restaurants with the new upgraded image feature copper-colored roof panels and decorative awnings and lighting. Interior changes emphasize quality and comfort.

35   To expand at sites that may not accommodate a full-sized restaurant, the company has built and is testing 11 more compact and less costly to build units and is also testing a drive-through-only restaurant.

36   Advertising spending has been increased. Franchise owners, in addition to spending 3 percent of their gross receipts for local advertising and promotions, have increased their contribution to Wendy's national advertising program (WNAP) from 1 percent to 1.5 percent of gross sales (see Exhibit 12). The total amount spent on advertising and promotions in 1983 came to about $75 million. While other competitors have

---

Exhibit 10

WENDY'S INTERNATIONAL, INCORPORATED, AND SUBSIDIARIES
Consolidated Balance Sheet
For the Years Ended December 31, 1978–1983
(in thousands of dollars)

	1983	1982	1981	1980	1979	1978
Assets						
Current assets:						
Cash	$ 8,177	$ 8,098	$ 9,210	$ 5,876	$ 2,285	$ 1,022
Short-term investments, at cost which						
approximates market	24,257	30,410	12,877	7,012	12,656	27,665
Notes receivable	8,781	2,026	2,713	186	—	—
Accounts receivable	1,990	7,180	7,841	5,328	4,903	3,249
Inventories and other	14,481	8,581	5,967	6,305	2,582	1,855
Total current assets	57,686	56,295	38,608	24,707	22,426	33,791
Property and equipment, at cost:						
Land	75,420	66,349	54,121	40,410	30,916	23,906
Buildings	126,246	103,765	82,212	56,920	40,785	30,050
Leasehold improvements	67,337	57,699	45,881	21,787	16,582	8,954
Restaurant equipment	113,597	92,735	75,317	48,853	34,053	24,462
Other equipment	29,367	22,495	19,016	10,808	9,723	8,413
Construction in progress	2,445	1,540	1,300	2,895	1,752	2,028
Capitalized leases	52,281	50,301	51,975	22,286	21,866	18,246
Total property and equipment before						
depreciation	466,693	394,884	329,822	203,960	155,676	116,060
Less: Accumulated depreciation and						
amortization	(88,782)	(67,442)	(48,814)	(29,725)	(20,962)	(13,543)
	377,911	327,442	281,008	174,235	134,714	102,516
Other assets:						
Unexpended construction funds	539	5,973	7,067	—	—	—
Cost in excess of net assets acquired, net	20,325	18,631	19,408	8,648	8,409	5,208
Investment in and advances to equity						
subsidiaries	27,553	23,931	14,410	—	—	—
Other	22,699	23,686	15,728	11,278	7,152	2,378
Total cost over net assets and other						
assets	71,116	72,221	56,613	19,926	15,561	7,586
Total assets	$506,713	$455,958	$376,229	$218,868	$172,701	$143,892

Exhibit 10 *(concluded)*

	1983	1982	1981	1980	1979	1978
Liabilities and Shareholders' Equity						
Current liabilities:						
Accounts payable, trade	$ 41,739	$ 30,224	$ 36,899	$ 24,685	$ 10,175	11,666
Federal, state, and local income taxes	10,924	13,959	4,074	6,256	—	7,840
Accrued expenses:						
Salaries and wages	7,035	4,715	3,486	3,440	6,168	1,971
Taxes	9,883	8,032	6,228	3,100	1,932	1,499
Other	8,107	6,498	5,853	3,220	2,010	1,774
Current portion of long-term obligations	11,001	7,102	9,836	4,340	3,891	2,782
Total current liabilities	88,689	70,530	66,376	45,042	24,177	27,531
Long-term obligations, net of current portion:						
Term debt	42,514	59,913	52,242	22,458	25,098	15,308
Capitalized lease obligations	44,157	43,157	45,714	19,960	18,708	15,131
	86,671	103,070	97,956	42,418	43,806	30,439
Deferred technical assistance fees	1,270	1,105	1,433	1,644	1,995	2,118
Deferred income taxes	21,801	16,520	8,726	4,168	2,028	664
Shareholders' equity:						
Common stock, $.10 stated value						
Authorized: 60,000,000 and 40,000,000						
shares, respectively						
Issued and outstanding: 40,746,000 and						
38,322,000 shares, respectively	4,079	4,075	3,832	1,496	1,488	1,486
Capital in excess of stated value	107,727	107,345	78,550	34,875	34,113	33,963
Retained earnings	200,271	155,648	119,356	89,226	65,094	47,691
Translation adjustments	(3,795)	(2,335)				
Total shareholders' equity	308,282	264,733	201,738	125,596	100,696	83,141
Total liabilities and shareholders' equity	$506,713	$455,958	$376,229	$218,868	$172,701	$143,892

been increasing couponing, Wendy's has reduced it from the 1981 level of 3.1 percent of sales to a 1.3 percent level.

37   Advertising in the fast-food burger chain industry has become more fierce since Burger King launched its now famous and controversial comparative advertising campaign. The "Battle of the Burgers" claimed that the Whopper beat the Big Mac and Wendy's hamburger and also claimed that Burger King's hamburgers were flame broiled while McDonald's and Wendy's fried their hamburgers. Wendy's and McDonald's filed lawsuits leading to out-of-court settlements in which Burger King agreed to phase out the campaign.

38   In March 1983, Burger King introduced its "Project BIB" or "Broiling Is Better" campaign. This modified version of its earlier ads singles out McDonald's, but not Wendy's, by name. Burger King has posted an average 10 percent monthly sales gain since the campaign began. With pugnacious Burger King and with McDonald's $300 million ad budget, Wendy's has changed to harder-hitting campaigns than such previous campaigns as "Hot 'n' Juicy," and "Ain't No Reason to Go Anyplace Else."

39   Unlike Burger King's controversial comparative ad campaign, Wendy's has opted to make its point of supposed differences between itself and its two main rivals without

Exhibit 11

WENDY'S INTERNATIONAL, INCORPORATED, AND SUBSIDIARIES
Consolidated Statement of Revenue and Earnings
For the Years Ended December 31, 1978–1983
(in thousands of dollars)

	1983	1982	1981	1980	1979	1978
Revenue:						
Retail operations	$665,591	$560,516	$446,800	$310,067	$237,753	$ 198,529
Royalties	49,505	41,918	38,619	35,555	30,565	23,396
Technical assistance fees	*	1,856	1,223	1,406	2,823	3,540
Other	5,287	3,350	1,938	1,280	2,903	2,686
Total revenue	720,383	607,640	488,580	348,308	274,044	228,151
Costs and expenses:						
Cost of sales	371,176	315,473	257,735	187,968	146,347	113,813
Company restaurant operating costs	168,048	143,326	114,233	67,714	54,993	43,289
Direct expenses of franchise personnel	7,674	6,023	5,061	4,544	4,187	3,149
General and administrative expenses	42,318	31,686	24,521	19,831	15,742	13,293
Depreciation and amortization of property and equipment	24,892	20,906	15,308	9,782	7,356	5,444
Interest net	6,799	9,519	7,070	3,748	4,358	3,772
Total costs and expenses	620,907	526,933	423,928	293,587	232,983	182,760
Income before income taxes	99,476	80,707	64,652	54,721	41,061	45,391
Income taxes	44,756	36,605	27,800	24,625	17,964	20,905
Net income	54,720	44,102	36,852	30,096	23,097	24,486
Retained earnings—beginning of year	155,648	119,356	89,226	65,094	47,691	25,234
Cash dividends		(7,810)	(6,722)	(5,964)	(5,694)	(1,943)
Pooled Subchapter S corporations' reclassifications						(283)
Effect of conforming fiscal year end of pooled corporation						196
Retained earnings—end of year	$210,868	$155,648	$119,356	$ 89,226	$ 65,094	$ 47,690
Per share data:						
Net income per share	$1.00	$1.13	$1.01	$.89	$1.54	$1.63
Weighted average shares outstanding	54,701†	39,165	36,445	33,774	14,971	15,018
Dividends per share	$.20	$.20	$.19	$.18	$.38	$.13

* Reported as part of other Revenue.
† Reflects 4-for-3 stock split in 1984.

Exhibit 12
Advertising and promotion expenses

	1982	1981	1980
Company expenses	$25,201,000	$21,429,000	$12,778,000
WNAP	$16,000,000	$13,000,000	$11,000,000
Franchise	In addition to WNAP contributions, each franchise owner must spend 3 percent of gross receipts for local advertising and promotions.		

actually naming either Burger King or McDonald's, though the commercials make it clear who Wendy's targets are. They are referred to as "two famous hamburger places" or as "some hamburger places." The five 30-second spots proclaim in a humorous way that Wendy's, unlike some other chains, makes its burgers with fresh, not frozen, ground beef; that its burgers are served hot off the grill; and that customers don't have to step aside or park for special orders. The "Wendy's Kind of People" campaign was rumored to be in response to pressure from franchisees demanding a more aggressive marketing stance, but Wendy's executives denied the published report.

40   Kicking off 1984 was the nationally televised commercial with three elderly ladies shown standing at a Brand X hamburger counter. Pointing to the idea that Wendy's single hamburger has more beef "despite its modest name" than some bigger-named competitors, one elderly woman demands, "Where's the beef?" The commercial has prompted fan clubs for one of the actresses, inspired a taunt at high school basketball games, and spawned a complaint from the Michigan State Office of Services to the Aging that the commercial is demeaning to the elderly. Wendy's officials responded that the commercial is actually a positive portrayal of an elderly woman demanding her rights as a consumer.

41   Wendy's delivery system—its drive-in window and single order and pickup line—has been one of the most impressive segments of the company's operations. With its goal of 15 seconds to fill an order inside the restaurant and 25 seconds for the pickup window (from the time the order is given), speed of service is recognized as essential. For its basic snake-line system to work, order takers get customers' requests before they get to the cash register during peak lunch periods. Outside order takers and change takers even have been initiated near the pickup window (the pickup window accounts for over 40 percent of Wendy's sales).

42   The sight of a jammed-up line may cause potential customers to forgo eating at Wendy's. The company has already found it necessary in some instances to depart from its single-line concept and has launched multilines in downtown Manhattan, Chicago, and Columbus. But Chairman Barney has indicated a preference to opening new units if suburban single lines get jammed up, rather than changing to multilines in the suburban restaurants.

43   A variety of management programs have been initiated to improve restaurant efficiency. Since 1981, the ratio of management at all operating levels has increased. Management turnover has been reduced with a five-day workweek aimed at removing some of the work burden. A comanager, assistant manager, and, in busier restaurants, a trainee-manager, are being utilized. Trainees or assistants can now move up to

manager within a year and a half rather than waiting two or three years, as was the case previously. A computerized cash register data system was installed to increase managers' productivity, and over 300 restaurants were using the system by late 1982. The technology can eliminate as much as 20 hours of administrative work per month, thus freeing managers to devote more attention to customers and crew personnel.

Franchising

44   Two main thrusts appear to characterize Wendy's franchising emphasis for the 1980s: (1) enhanced operational control and support of domestic franchises and (2) expansion through international locations.

45   Commenting on domestic emphasis, Ronald Fay, president and chief operating officer, offered the following overview in early 1983:

> Over the last two years in units where franchisees have not kept up with development plans, such as Los Angeles, we have withdrawn development rights and involved new franchisees in those markets. We refranchised that area last year, and our present franchisees now are committed to add 20 new stores each year in L.A. for the next several years.
>
> Now we are laying the groundwork to further stimulate franchised growth—especially in high-density areas. Wendy's will begin to franchise individual units in certain markets to augment our area franchise approach of the past 13 years.[3] During the next three years, we may award several hundred such unit franchises.

46   In early 1980, Wendy's established a new regional structure for managing company-owned and franchise outlets. It increased the number of personnel in regional operating centers by 25 percent, with each of them supervising fewer restaurants than in the past, placing major emphasis on having more company personnel to assist the franchise organization in maintaining operational excellence. A key emphasis in this regard was to improve communications and cooperation between management and franchisees. Wendy's established a Franchise Advisory Council to provide a formal communication link between the company and the franchisees. It was comprised of key company personnel and franchisees selected on a regional basis by their peers. Touted to be the most important element in strengthening the company–franchisee relationship during 1980 was the introduction of Wendy's new senior management to the franchise system. Beginning in August 1980, Wendy's senior management group traveled to every region of the country and conducted a series of "town hall meetings" with its franchisees. This process has continued, according to Fay, because "the exchange of information and philosophy at such sessions contributes significantly to Wendy's future development."

47   When interest rates hit historical highs in 1981 and 1982, many potential franchisees could not find funds locally. To encourage franchise restaurant expansion and to generate additional royalty revenues, a financial assistance program was arranged for qualified franchise owners. Under the "Wenequity" program, franchise owners lease the land and building while owning their business. The company formed a wholly owned

---

[3] To foster its initial development, Wendy's pursued an area franchising strategy in which franchise contracts were awarded for cities and parts of states, with the average franchise owner operating nine restaurants. Area franchising strategy was instrumental in Wendy's achieving its record growth.

Exhibit 13

	1980–1983 growth rate	Mid-1983	1982	1981	1980
Company	41%	860 (35%)	827 (34%)	748 (34%)	506 (25%)
Franchised	4½%	1,600 (65%)	1,603 (66%)	1,481 (66%)	1,528 (75%)
Total		2,460	2,430	2,229	2,034

subsidiary to purchase newly constructed stores and lease them back to franchisees. Wendy's packaged the restaurants in groups of 20 or more and marketed them to investors, primarily insurance companies. The finance subsidiaries received 25 percent of their capital from Wendy's and 75 percent from privately placed debt, with the rent paid by the franchisees being more than adequate to service the debt. By early 1983, the Wenequity program had helped franchisees build 87 stores. Currently, the program is winding down.

48   To accelerate the growth of the Wendy's system through the development of minority markets and to provide opportunities for minorities through franchise ownership, the company established a minority franchise program. Since its inception in 1979, 12 restaurants have opened under the program.

49   In 1981, Wendy's acquired 161 franchise restaurants in Denver, Phoenix, Seattle, suburban Atlanta, Chicago, Milwaukee, and Lakeland, Florida. The company has withdrawn development rights and involved new franchisees in markets where franchisees have not kept up with development plans. Combined with the 81 company stores opened in 1981, the percent of company-owned stores increased from 25 percent at the end of 1980 to 34 percent in 1981.

50   The expansion of company-operated stores has also accelerated. Sixty-six stores were added in 1982, with about 80 to be added in 1983. Plans for the following two years are to increase company operations to about 100 additions per year. The growth rate of company-owned stores from 1980 to 1983 has been 41 percent, contrasted with the growth rate in franchised stores of 4.5 percent (see Exhibit 13).

51   Wendy's has identified 200 markets as underrepresented. For example, in Wendy's hometown of Columbus, there are 48 Wendy's, while Chicago has only 41 in operation; Philadelphia, only 29; and Houston, only 18. The population in Columbus numbers only 37,000 people per Wendy's restaurant. In contrast, in Chicago there are 140,000 people per unit; in Los Angeles, 221,000; and in New York, 370,000 people per unit. In Los Angeles, where company analysts feel that the market can support four times the number of Wendy's there now, the area has already been refranchised as noted earlier.

52   In a stated effort to stimulate growth, especially in high-density areas, the company announced a unit franchise strategy to augment its area franchise approach of the past 13 years. This concept (unit franchise strategy) enables individuals who could not develop a multiunit franchise to join the Wendy's family, Ronald Fay explained. "Additionally, single-unit franchising gives Wendy's the opportunity to develop each market to its maximum potential."

53   The major shift to company-owned restaurants and unit franchising, away from large-area franchising, reflects the concern for systemwide control of quality. This

move may well be intended to avoid the problem that led to Burger King's decline in the late 1960s—franchise empires were bigger than parent-company operations.[4]

International

54   Wendy's established an international division in 1979, and, by 1983, there were 125 Wendy's operating outside the United States. Franchised restaurants numbered 100: 70 in Canada, 15 in Japan, 8 in Puerto Rico, 3 each in Switzerland and Australia, and 1 in Malaysia. In addition, there are 14 company operations in Germany, 6 in Spain, and 5 in the United Kingdom. Openings were slated for the first Wendy's in Italy, Hong Kong, Singapore, and Mexico. Company development is expected to focus on the United Kingdom, Spain, and Germany, with franchisees being most active in Japan.

55   Of the fast-food hamburger chains, McDonald's is the best established internationally, with approximately 1,500 units in 32 countries. Those units are heavily concentrated in Canada (335), Japan (212), Australia (107), and various parts of Europe. McDonald's is expected to accelerate its development of the international market, where it has been adding 150 units a year. Burger King presently has 224 overseas units in 18 countries, 58 of which were added in 1982. The company is expected to begin rapid international expansion in 1986.

56   With concern that the American fast-food market may be approaching the saturation point, some fast-food chains have turned to overseas markets to meet growth goals. *Nation's Restaurant News* reports the market potential in western Europe is enticing because fast food currently represents less than 3 percent of all meals consumed away from home. Further reinforcing the contention that this market is still largely untapped, European per-capita spending on fast food is only $3.50 a year, compared to approximately $150 for each American in 1982.

57   However, there are numerous pitfalls and high risks to overseas expansion. Investment in land, buildings, and equipment for a new McDonald's in Germany is at least $1 million, compared with less than $750,000 at home. Labor may run 40 percent of revenues in that same West German store, while labor consumes only about 20 to 25 percent of the typical domestic unit's revenue. These higher fixed and variable costs result in lower per-unit profit margins overseas. While 1981 operating profits at U.S. McDonald's units were 17.5 percent, European McDonald's units ranged between only 7 to 9 percent.

58   With the recognition that international development is both a slow and costly undertaking, Wendy's officials project that it takes about 26 trips to establish the first store in each country. Aside from the language problems, there is distribution to set up, finding products that meet specifications, and construction site approval, among others.

59   Wendy's international activity has accelerated, with 22 restaurants opened in 1982 and 32 openings scheduled for 1983. Citing the need to increase penetration, Wendy's officials have indicated that the major thrust of international operations will be on the franchise side. International management has been strengthened through the creation of a European zone office in London and a Far East zone office in Honolulu. From these bases, senior Wendy's personnel will support the worldwide franchises and company operation in such staff functions as quality assurance, construction, marketing, and purchasing.

---

[4] In 1981, over 80 percent of the Burger King restaurants were franchise operations.

60   Second only to Canada in number of restaurants, Japan has become a primary market for Wendy's. In developing this market, Wendy's associated itself with the Daiei Group, Japan's largest retailer (annual sales of $4 billion). This allowed Wendy's to take advantage of profitable opportunities while limiting development costs and currency risks to acceptable levels. Plans in 1983 were to add 12 more restaurants to the 15 already operating there. Of those 15, only 8 were in operation prior to 1982. A training center was established in 1982 in Japan, as well as in England and Germany, to develop local managers and crew people.

61   Besides Japan, Wendy's is making inroads on other continents. In Madrid, the company advertised on commercial television for the first time outside of North America. The Australian licensees opened the first three Australian Wendy's in Melbourne in 1982. The company is especially excited about the potential of the Australian market since the lifestyle there is so similar to that in the United States.

62   In 1982, company operations in Spain and the United Kingdom were profitable at the store level. Industry analysts project profitability of overseas operations in late 1985 or early 1986.

63   Reflecting on the international sphere as Wendy's future arena for franchising (and licensing) growth, Edward Lifmann, international director, offered the following:

> We've developed the flexibility necessary to be successful overseas in the face of differing eating habits and tastes. Eating times vary, so we've changed our hours. Living and shopping habits vary from the American style of suburban development, so we're mainly basing in-line units in urban centers. New product sizes and offerings have been developed to meet local tastes and dietary needs.

Competitors

64   In 1983, Wendy's laid claim to approximately 5 percent of the fast-food industry's total sales of $38 billion, accounted for 9.4 percent of the $18 billion hamburger segment, and claimed the position of the third-largest hamburger chain behind direct competitors, McDonald's and Burger King (see Exhibit 14).[5]

65   Having originally left the adult market to Wendy's, Burger King is now going after it with a vengeance. Burger King has oriented its advertising to adults and is appealing to health-conscious consumers with its salad bar. Its newest menu entree is a salad sandwich in pita bread.

66   Burger King recently developed the Whopper Express, a tiny outlet in the Wall Street area of New York City, where the customer can walk in, be served, and walk out again in 2½ minutes. With a slimmed-down menu, this unit is about one third the size of a normal Burger King and is designed to penetrate high-volume urban areas where rent costs would normally make it impossible to locate.

67   Although McDonald's has been injured by the battle of the burgers campaign and has had problems with the perception of its burgers' quality, the company holds a staggering 42 percent of the hamburger market share. As an early entrant into the industry, McDonald's has premium site locations and mammoth size. With 6,000 domestic units and about 1,500 overseas units, McDonald's is more than twice the size of

---

[5] With Hardee's 1982 acquisition of 380 Burger Chef restaurants, Hardee's moved slightly above Wendy's in sales and number of units.

Exhibit 14
How the three hamburger giants slice the market (estimated 1983 sales—$ billions)

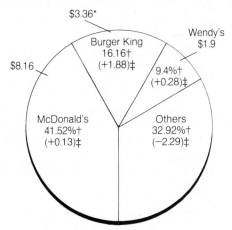

Note: Fiscal years ended December 1983 for McDonald's and Wendy's; May 1984 for Burger King.
* Market share.
† Percent of market.
‡ Percentage-point change in market share since 1981.
Source: "The Fast-Food War: Big Mac under Attack," *Business Week,* January 30, 1984, p. 46.

Pillsbury's Burger King and triple that of Wendy's. Its return on equity is more than 20 percent, and its growth is expected to center on international focus. McDonald's is also said to be testing smaller, limited-menu stores (McSnacks) and looking at such previously neglected markets as schools, parks, and military installations.

68   After failing with the McChicken and McRib Sandwich, McDonald's introduced Chicken McNuggets, which accounted for 12 percent of sales by 1983, and it is reviewing a low-calorie Big Mac, a McFeast sandwich, a Mexican product, caramel rolls, and biscuits. McDonald's has not been definitive on the major challenges: developing new products, getting dinner business, and advertising.

69   With the average American household spending nearly one in three food dollars away from home, nearly twice the proportion of two decades ago, ethnic and upscale outlets are trying to lure more of the fast-food industry's $38 billion in sales by pecking away at the hamburger customer base.[6] Mexican food sales increased 21 percent in 1983 to become a $1.6 billion market. Barbecue has gained popularity as modern cooking machines have made it possible to mass produce this food.

70   With customers' interest in anything fresh perceived as healthy, gourmet pizza with fresh ingredients is gaining customer attention. Fresh pasta with a variety of sauces is another Italian entree grabbing customers. Small bakeries with croissants, quiche, muffins, and so forth may be making a comeback. Chicken chains are also doing well, and Japanese food may be ready to take off.

_____
[6] U.S. Bureau of Labor Statistics' Consumer Expenditure Surveys indicate that in 1980–81, 33 percent of the food budget was spent on food away from home. In 1960–61, it was 17 percent.

Exhibit 15
The baby boom matures (age distribution of the U.S. population)

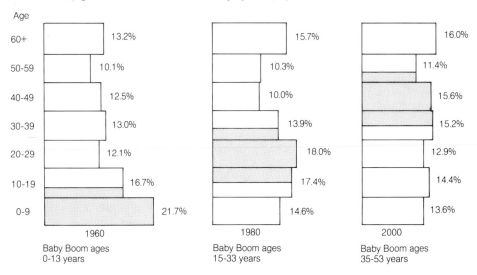

Age	1960	1980	2000
60+	13.2%	15.7%	16.0%
50-59	10.1%	10.3%	11.4%
40-49	12.5%	10.0%	15.6%
30-39	13.0%	13.9%	15.2%
20-29	12.1%	18.0%	12.9%
10-19	16.7%	17.4%	14.4%
0-9	21.7%	14.6%	13.6%
	Baby Boom ages 0-13 years	Baby Boom ages 15-33 years	Baby Boom ages 35-53 years

71   With the fast-food customer becoming more sophisticated, numerous restaurants are positioning themselves one step above typical fast-food outlets and one step below the typical full-service restaurant. For example, Atlanta-based D'Lites, which specializes in light fast food, offers a typical fast-food meal at half the calories of other outlets (498 calories versus 1,066 calories). Gourmet hamburgers, costing from $3 to $5, are also doing well.

72   Some of the fast-food restaurants have recently expanded menus and upgraded decor, such as A&W's new "Good Food." The A&W outlet serves a broad menu with such dishes as shrimp tempura, pasta with a variety of sauces, and hamburgers and hotdogs with a "dress-your-own" bar, but they serve the food very fast and use disposables.

73   Wendy's former director of franchising, Graydon Webb, has founded the upscale fast-food restaurant G. D. Ritzy's, which serves extravagant peanut butter and jelly sandwiches, spicy chili, hotdogs, hamburgers, and gourmet ice cream, among other fast-food items.

74   Fast-food prices have generally risen more quickly over the past few years than have table-service restaurant menu prices, and the price differential has narrowed, although the sit-down restaurants are still more expensive.

75   As the baby boom generation (see Exhibit 15) who fueled fast-food's growth in the 1970s are moving into their more sedate 30s, the baby boomers are beginning to trade up to medium-priced, full-service restaurants because, with their maturing tastes in food, they perceive greater value for their food dollars.

Sisters' Development

76   Scoffing at reports that the fast-food burger industry may be oversaturated, Wendy's officials portray the company's recent move into the chicken restaurant industry as an avenue in which to apply the principles that built its success to other segments of the industry and as an opportunity for further growth.

77   Before investing in hamburgers, Wendy's founder made his first million in chicken. R. David Thomas, who named his 65-foot houseboat *The Colonel* after Colonel Harland Sanders, Kentucky Fried Chicken's founder, was admittedly strongly influenced by the "Chicken King." At the age of 32, Thomas obtained an interest in four nearly bankrupt Kentucky Fried Chicken carryouts in Columbus, Ohio. For $65, Thomas was promised 45 percent of the Columbus franchise if he could turn the carryouts around, pay off a $200,000 deficit, and make a profit. The restaurants began to prosper, and four more Columbus locations were added. In 1968, Thomas sold the restaurants back to the parent company for $1.5 million.

78   After selling his interest in the Columbus Kentucky Fried Chicken franchise, Thomas became regional operations director for the parent company. In working and traveling with Colonel Sanders, he had the opportunity to observe and to learn from Sanders' mistakes.

79   A decade later, when CEO Robert Barney thought there was a void in the chicken industry that could be filled by an upscale restaurant serving quality food, Barney and Thomas asked James Near, an experienced restaurateur and former Wendy's franchisee, to develop this concept. With the conviction that the same principles which built its success could be applied to other segments of the industry, Wendy's initially owned 20 percent of Sisters International and, in 1981, exercised its option to purchase the remaining 80 percent.

80   In a Wendy's press release announcing the nationwide expansion of Sisters, Near, president and chief operating officer of Sisters International, Inc., indicated that Wendy's corporate muscle would greatly enhance Sisters' growth. He said, "We can take advantage of Wendy's financial strength as well as their extensive knowledge of the marketplace. Additionally, we have a ready-made franchising network of successful operators who know what quality is."

81   As the first major diversification by Wendy's, company officials are excited about the future prospects of Sisters. Near predicts that Sisters will "continue the tradition of quality, service, and value which is Wendy's hallmark." The Sisters' concept, to combine the self-service of the quick-food industry with the full menu and warmth of comfortable dining facilities of the traditional family restaurant, is designed to appeal specifically to the maturing, value-conscious consumer.

82   Principal in this target group are the baby boomers, who are producing, although belatedly, a baby boom echo. Exhibit 16 gives comparative age data between 1970 and 1980. By 1990, 45 percent of all Americans will be between 20 and 49 years of age, compared with 32 percent in 1960.

83   As one of the best-performing categories in 1983, chicken chains saw growth of 19.7 percent in the previous year to become a $4 billion segment of the fast-food industry (see Exhibit 17). U.S. per-capita consumption of chicken grew at more than twice the rate for hamburgers during the last decade.

84   With its country classic decor, the Sisters chicken and biscuits building (see Exhibit 18) is styled as a turn-of-the-century home, framed with a picket fence and flower beds. The interior design is accented with antique china, collector glassware, and gaslight-style lighting projecting a warm country feeling. The restaurant design also includes carryout and drive-through service.

85   Sisters has a breakfast menu as well as a lunch and dinner menu. Breakfast includes fresh buttermilk biscuits with pork sausage, ham, beef steak, and scrambled eggs.

Exhibit 16
Age structure of the resident population of the United States: April 1, 1980, and April 1, 1970

| | Population | | Percent distribution | | Population change, 1970–1980 | |
Age	April 1, 1980	April 1, 1970	April 1, 1980	April 1, 1970	Number	Percent
All ages	226,504,825	203,235,298	100.0%	100.0%	23,269,527	11.4%
Under 5 years	16,344,407	17,162,836	7.2	8.4	−818,429	−4.8
5–9 years	16,697,134	19,969,056	7.4	9.8	−3,271,922	−16.4
10–14 years	18,240,919	20,804,063	8.1	10.2	−2,563,144	−12.3
15–19 years	21,161,667	19,083,971	9.3	9.4	2,077,696	10.9
20–24 years	21,312,557	16,382,893	9.4	8.1	4,929,664	30.1
25–34 years	37,075,629	24,922,511	16.4	12.3	12,153,118	48.8
35–44 years	25,631,247	23,101,173	11.3	11.4	2,530,074	11.0
45–54 years	22,797,367	23,234,790	10.1	11.4	−437,423	−1.9
55–64 years	21,699,765	18,601,669	9.6	9.2	3,098,096	16.7
65–74 years	15,577,586	12,442,573	6.9	6.1	3,135,013	25.2
75–84 years	7,726,826	6,121,627	3.4	3.0	1,605,199	26.2
85 years and over	2,239,721	1,408,136	1.0	0.7	831,585	59.1
Median age	30.0	28.0	(x)	(x)	(x)	(x)

Source: U.S. Census, 1980 and 1970.

Exhibit 17
Fast-food industry total sales—$38 billion

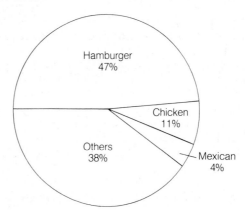

The lunch and dinner menu features fresh (never frozen) spicy or mild fried chicken, buttermilk biscuits, creamed chicken (an innovative way to control food cost), cole slaw, baked beans, fried potato wedges, Sisters' spicy rice, corn on the cob, and strawberry shortcake. Salad bars, dessert bars, and baked potato bars are being added. Dining room customers receive their meals on plates rather than the traditional chicken boxes of most chains.

Exhibit 18

86   According to industry analysts, new Sisters units are producing $850,000 in annual revenue per location on an average $500,000 capital investment (see Exhibit 19). This compares with average sales of $468,000 per store for Kentucky Fried Chicken's 837 company stores and average sales of $355,000 per store for Kentucky's 3,641 franchised stores. Church's 1,137 company-owned stores averaged $413,100, and Church's reported a $378,860 per-store average for its 242 licensed stores. The average cost of a new Church's restaurant was $350,000 in 1983.

Exhibit 19
1982 comparison of a typical Wendy's and Sisters restaurant

	Building size	Seating	Needed capitalization	Revenue per store	Sales-to-investment ratio	Margins
Sisters	2,100 sq. ft.	84	$500,000	$850,000	1.70	10–11% *
Wendy's	2,100 sq. ft.	92	$613,000	$703,000	1.15	15%

* Estimated.

---

87   Franchising will follow the same path that led to Wendy's rapid growth. Franchises will be awarded by counties or metropolitan areas to enable the franchise owner to have a number of restaurants and build an organization. All current Wendy's franchise owners will be considered first for their existing territories, with some Wendy's company markets to be available to new prospective franchisers for Sisters. Contracts have been signed with 45 franchise groups and call for the opening of 470 franchised Sisters by 1988.

88   By late 1983, 42 Sisters were operating in 15 markets. Between 150 and 250 restaurants are expected to be operating at the end of 1985. Enthusiastic over the initial success, Barney hopes "to make Sisters the Wendy's of the chicken restaurant industry by making chicken special again." Wendy's competitors are watching with interest. Burger King is hinting that it may try its hand at a new chain. McDonald's, which is expected to accumulate an excess cash flow of $1 billion between 1984 and 1990, is thought to be considering acquiring something in the food-service area.

Management Reorganization

89   For the first 11 years of its history, Wendy's was guided by an entrepreneurial spirit that gave the company the fastest growth record in the history of the food-service industry. This accelerated growth from one restaurant into a franchised worldwide system employing approximately 29,000 people demanded a restructuring of management. With sales of over $1 billion a year, and with continued growth in sales and earnings becoming increasingly difficult to achieve, the consensus that a shift in philosophy from an entrepreneurial to a more professionally managed firm was necessary had become evident by the late 1970s. At the end of 1982, Wendy's management had changed substantially, with only 7 of its present 37 officers having been officers in 1979.

90   With the pressure of soaring beef prices, inflation, and recession, founder and former Chairman R. David Thomas, who presently serves as senior chairman of the board, took the first step in April 1980 when he recommended to the board that President Robert L. Barney be named chief executive officer. Mr. Barney, who has since been named chairman of the board in addition to being chief executive officer, implemented the remainder of the management reorganization plan.

91   Rounding out Wendy's top management team is President Ronald Fay, a former franchisee with 32 years of experience in the industry at all levels of restaurant operations and management. Wendy's top executive trio has combined restaurant industry experience of more than 90 years.

92   The marketing department was reorganized under the direction of Darrough Diamond. Bringing more than 15 years of marketing experience to his new position as senior vice president of marketing, Mr. Diamond consolidated Wendy's field marketing programs into a regional marketing concept. He grouped company-owned and franchise restaurants into regions by geographic location and market penetration, with field marketing supervisors assigned to coordinate national and local marketing programs in each region. In addition, Dancer Sample was named Wendy's new national advertising agency.

93   A new regional structure was also instituted for the company operations and franchising department. The department was given more personnel, with each supervising fewer restaurants than in the past. In response to an emphasis in 1980 on improving communications and cooperation between company management and franchisees, the Franchise Advisory Council was created (see the discussion of the council in the earlier section on franchising).

94   In addition to revamping marketing and operations, a senior management group was formed to provide improved direction and control for achieving the company's goals and objectives and implementing management's strategies for future growth.

95   The 1981 acquisition of 161 franchises forced the company to again increase its operations management staff, in keeping with the company's strategy of increasing the ratio of supervisory personnel to number of stores. Along with the enlarged marketing effort, this pushed 1981 company restaurant operating costs to 25.6 percent of retail sales, compared with 21.8 percent in 1980 and 23.1 percent in 1979. The rise continued in 1982, escalating to 26 percent of sales.

96   Although now a more professionally managed company, the entrepreneurial spirit is still alive at Wendy's.

Case 3

Federal Express: Is There Any "Zip" Left in ZapMail?

Introduction

1   As the annual stockholders' meeting for Federal Express Corporation was approaching on September 29, 1986, increasing interest focused on Chief Executive Officer Fred Smith's future plans to improve the profit performance of ZapMail and the company as a whole.

Background

History

2   The birth of Federal Express Corporation in 1973 marked a virtual revolution in the air cargo industry. Initially conceived by company founder Fred Smith in an economics paper written while he was an undergraduate at Yale, the idea of an all-freight airline for small, time-sensitive packages ran counter to all the proven caveats of an established air freight industry. Smith proved to be a better predictor of market need than his professor, however. His economics paper received a C−, yet Federal Express is now a Fortune 500 company earning multimillion-dollar profits annually.

3   Prior to Federal's market entry, the traditional air freight industry consisted of "freight forwarders," firms who sent packages as cargo on regular passenger airlines. Fred Smith contended that these companies were not in a position to provide adequate service to an ever-expanding, technologically based economy.

4   The forwarders were restrained from providing rapid delivery by passenger airline schedules designed to meet the needs of travelers. Passenger flights ran primarily during the daytime, with planes grounded at night. Able to move cargo for only 12 hours each day, it was virtually impossible for the forwarders to guarantee overnight delivery of packages. Passenger flight schedules also limited forwarders in the number of cities they could service. Above all, the freight forwarded provided airport-to-airport service only. Costs and inconvenience associated with transporting a package to and from the airport were left to the shipper and cosigner.

5   Given the seemingly obvious shortcomings of the existing air freight industry, Smith conceived the idea of an all-freight airline combined with a pickup and delivery service. Packages would be picked up from shippers, flown to a central location during the night, sorted, and flown to their destination for delivery the next day. This "hub-and-spokes" concept was tailored specifically for shippers of priority materials for whom speed of delivery is more important than cost. As Smith himself observed in later years:

This case was written by Professor Per V. Jenster, McIntire School of Commerce, University of Virginia, with the assistance of Deborah Chevion, Joanne Gardner, and Deborah Rinehart. Copyright © Per V. Jenster, 1986.

America was spreading out technologically. . . . The efficacy of our society is to be smarter, not to work harder . . . that's what we (Federal Express) are all about—reacting to the needs of today's society, which wants things done fast, or I should say faster.

6   Upon returning from Vietnam in 1972, only six years after receiving the mediocre economics grade, Fred Smith began to put his air express idea into action and became the founding father of Federal Express Corporation: "A whole new airline for packages only."

7   The nature of the Federal Express concept required a tremendous capital outlay before Smith and his fledgling company could even begin operations. In addition to the normal start-up costs facing any entrepreneur, Smith needed to purchase entire fleets of airplanes and delivery vehicles, lease airport hangars and runway space, and finance the building of an air terminal. Never one to be daunted by seemingly insurmountable obstacles, however, Smith addressed these astronomical cash outflow requirements by embarking upon the largest venture capital campaign in American business history. Between 1972 and 1974, Smith managed to raise a staggering $40 million in equity capital as well as $50 million in loans.

8   In its first two years of operation, Federal Express lost an average of $1 million each month. The effects of the 1973–74 fuel crisis and recession were felt strongly by the new company. Even as daily package counts increased, the company failed to gain ground in overcoming the immense start-up costs.

9   Undeterred, Fred Smith retained confidence in the soundness of the people and ideas behind Federal Express. The company finally broke even and realized its first profits in July 1975. That same year overall revenues surpassed $1 million per week, and package counts averaged 11,500 daily. Since 1975 Federal's revenues have more than doubled every two years.

10   The company, as of 1984, owned approximately 60 percent of the small-package and -document delivery market, in spite of several new firms that joined the market in the late 70s and early 80s. While these newcomers were struggling to merely establish themselves in the new industry, Federal was moving light-years ahead in terms of technology, service, and organization.

Industry and Competitors

11   Federal Express competed in the small-package/document market of the $6 billion air cargo industry. This market had been the fastest-growing sector of the industry over the past six years, with 20 percent annual growth rates. The two major factors defining the express market were package size and delivery time constraints.

Trends 1973–1982

12   After Federal Express's entry and cultivation of the new, express-mail market, many other courier companies saw the potential for increasing their market share of the air freight industry. Two new entrants were Emery Air Freight and Purolator. Competition in the new industry became heated. The race was on to establish networks and to gain market share. Many of these networks were based on the hub-and-spokes

concept originally innovated by Federal Express. Expansions included huge asset acquisition of planes, trucks, and distribution centers.

Trends 1982–1985

13   The three-year period following the industry expansion was characterized by increasing competition for market share, which translated into fierce price wars. United Parcel Service, the largest privately owned U.S. package transporter, lowered the industry price floor for its Second-Day Air service in 1982. This price decrease forced Federal Express to emphasize its own two-day option, Standard Air, at a lower price.

14   The continuing competition brought new innovations into the industry. In 1984, Federal Express introduced its Overnight Letter, proffering a 10:30 A.M., next-day delivery service. Purolator responded to Federal Express's move by offering the Puroletter, while Emery offered the Urgent Letter and Urgent Pouch. In 1985, UPS introduced Next-Day Air Letter. As the 1985 price war continued, Federal Express's revenue per package declined by 8.7 percent, while Emery suffered a decrease of 26 percent per package. These shrinking margins placed a greater emphasis on cost cutting and control.

Trends 1986

15   The industry began to look toward international expansion as the U.S. market appeared to become saturated. By 1986, Federal Express had achieved 95 percent coverage, while UPS offered service to every address in the 48 continental states, Hawaii, and Puerto Rico. Additional pressures arose from the decline of U.S. industrial production, shrinking the demand by domestic business for overnight express.

16   This decline motivated the courier companies to look beyond the domestic market, focusing on ever-expanding international trade. As business itself became more global in nature, demand for improved document transportation offered new opportunities for overnight express carriers overseas.

Fred Smith

17   The dramatic success of Federal Express Corporation can, without question, be attributed to aggressive, expertly designed marketing, management, and expansion strategies. It is equally indisputable that the main impetus for these strategies is Chairman Frederick W. Smith.

18   Remarkable ingenuity and foresight allowed Fred Smith to establish an industry-leading enterprise and, indeed, an entire industry in a remarkably short period of time. Organizationally speaking, the structure and corporate personality of Federal Express emanate entirely from its brash, outspoken founder. Smith's eclectic background (comprised of, among other things, an Ivy League education followed by two tours of duty in Vietnam) combined with his aggressive entrepreneurial spirit have given Federal Express and its employees a sense of commitment to excellence that has been the cornerstone of the firm's success.

19   Following Federal's emergence as one of the most profitable new ventures of the 1970s, Smith, himself, emerged as a symbol of glamour and entrepreneurial achievement

in the corporate world. At its outset, the Federal Express concept was considered to be reckless, yet Smith's ingenuity and stubborn devotion to his brainchild convinced investors, and eventually the world, of the soundness of his air freight innovation.

20   Throughout Federal's history, Smith has dominated the planning function. He has set goals and policy for all aspects of the company's operations and has been the guiding force in the evolution of Federal's corporate image. Robert Sigafoos characterized Smith most effectively in the following manner in his book, *Absolutely Positively Overnight!*:

> Smith fits nicely into that special category of skillful, opportunistic, egotistical, strong-willed "one-man shows" heading successful ventures into contemporary corporate America. . . . Fred Smith possesses the desire for power and achievement found in all great corporate leaders.

21   Simply put, Fred Smith is Federal Express. His dominance was strongly felt throughout the development and introductory stages of the company's newest service, ZapMail.

ZapMail

The Opportunity

22   With the emergence of the high-tech boom in the early 1980s, it became apparent that telecommunications technology was destined to make its mark on the document transfer industry. Fred Smith saw an opportunity, even a necessity, for Federal Express to enter the market, and, with his customary drive and charisma, he committed a major portion of the company's resources to the development of ZapMail, an electronic mail facsimile transmission system.

23   The ZapMail system, catering to those times "when overnight just isn't enough," was developed as a combination of the courier service with a facsimile transmission network. The network was already an integral part of Federal's internal operations which enabled the company to track packages, couriers, and customer orders. ZapMail, in essence, expanded the use of the network from the transfer of information *about* customers' documents to the transfer of those documents themselves. The addition of facsimile technology to the network enabled Federal to use telephone lines (or satellites) to transmit an actual photographic image of a document from a transmitting to a receiving terminal.

The Concept

24   Conceptually, the ZapMail system was relatively simple to understand. Federal placed at least one facsimile machine in each of its 318 Business Service Centers located throughout the United States. Accommodating the needs of the customer, a Federal courier would pick up the customer's document and take it to the nearest Business Service Center. The document would then be transmitted by ground line and/or satellite to another machine in a Federal Express office near the destination (see Exhibit 1). A courier at that office would then deliver the transmitted copy to the addressee, hopefully not more than two hours later. Upon introduction in July 1984, the new system had a few problems, but Federal was committed to providing complete customer

Exhibit 1
Ground line reliance

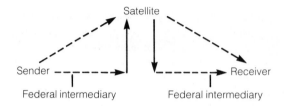

satisfaction with ZapMail. Customers whose documents were not delivered within two hours were generally given refunds.

25   ZapMail service initially cost $35 for up to 10 pages, with an additional charge of $1 for each page thereafter. The money-back guarantee on two-hour delivery applied only to documents of 10 pages or less. Because of the speed limitations of facsimile technology, Federal had to add an hour to delivery time for each additional 10-page increment after the initial one. The installation of high-speed transmission lines by AT&T, though, enabled Federal to cut transmission time down to five seconds per page. Further technical improvements were to be expected after Federal launched satellites, further cutting transmission time and also limiting dependence on AT&T, a potential competitor in electronic data transfer. The price of ZapMail service was projected to decrease with increased sales volume and technical improvements. Amortization of the substantial system start-up costs would also result in lower prices. Soon after its introduction, ZapMail service was expanded in response to consumer demand to include the rental and installation of receiving terminals in customers' offices. "Zap-Mailers" rented for $525 per month plus $.25 per page and a $10 delivery cost.

The Strategy

26   Federal Express was criticized for its use of facsimile machines rather than a computer-based system. Critics argued that facsimile machines were slow transmitters and produced low-quality images. They also believed that since computers were destined to dominate the electronic data transfer market in the future, it was frivolous to implement a facsimile system in the present.

27   Due to the proliferation of computers in business offices, industry analysts estimated that the market for computer mailboxes would grow to more than $1 billion by 1990. Federal Express, however, was "wagering [that] the personal computer won't conquer offices as fast as some competitors think." The fact that neither sender nor receiver need own or operate a computer made facsimile transmission a very appealing short-term alternative for businesses.

28   As Fred Smith put it, ZapMail was based in "a medium which lends itself to the way people [now] work, with paper." Federal's strategy was to utilize proven facsimile technology in the present while developing computer technology for introduction in the future, when the systems were more refined and the market more accepting. It was hoped that the eventual introduction of a complete Federal Express data transfer network would benefit from the early establishment of customer loyalty to the ZapMail service.

The Market's Response

29 The market did look promising. In 1984, 500,000 ZapMail terminals were installed, with an additional 250,000 installations expected by the end of 1985. As of March 1985, 100,500 units had already been installed. The ZapMail concept was, apparently, right in line with the changing needs of business. There was a very real demand for two-hour document transmission. George M. Stamps, president of GMS Consulting, Westport, Connecticut, predicted, "Shipments will soar and prices will drop by one third in the red-hot facsimile market this year [1985]." Although ZapMail was still a long way from breaking even, Stamps thought the service would succeed.

30 Federal Express, too, predicted enormous growth in the electronic mail/facsimile market and set investment projections at $1.2 billion for ZapMail. Satellite transmission would eventually supplant groundlines, and reliance on outside suppliers of telecommunications services (such as AT&T) would be reduced. Federal would use and install its own satellites, leading to a decrease in operating costs and steady improvement in bottom-line profits for ZapMail.

The Industry and Competitors

31 Facsimile machine production was regulated by the Consultative Committee for International Telephone and Telegraph (CCITT) for intercompany compatibility. By 1986, four categories of facsimile machines had been established. Group 1 standards (set in 1974) produced a machine that would send a document in six minutes per page. By 1976, group 2 machines could send documents in half the time. Group 3's improvements not only cut the sending time down to one minute but included better quality of reproduction. The group 4 standards had been set to produce machines that can send documents in one to five seconds per page. While these fourth-generation machines existed, they were not widely available.

Trends

32 The major change in the facsimile industry during the preceding 12 years had been improvement in machine efficiency, while prices dropped in 1986 to half the original 1974 prices. The four major advantages of facsimile transfer included:

> No special training required.
> No typing time involved. The facsimile machine would transfer an image of the actual document.
> Handles graphics, including signature reproductions.
> Can operate unattended.

33 Although these advantages and the price decreases might have indicated opportunities to improve document transfer for many businesses, the 500,000 facsimile machines installed as of 1984 represented only a fraction of the 25 million potential business users. Many of these machines were bought outright from original manufacturers, such as Xerox, Sharp Electronics Corporation, Harris/3M, and Teleautograph. Not only did Federal Express have to contend with these purchases, but both Western Union and MCI Communications Corporation offered facsimile services—EasyLink and MCI Mail, respectively.

Exhibit 2
Long-distance courier comparison chart

	Area served	Weight limits	Overnight costs	Delivery time	Refunds
Airborne Freight	U.S. and 31 other	None	1 lb.—$14 2 lbs.—$25	Noon	Yes
DHL	U.S. and 12 other	70 lbs./box 210 lbs./bill	5 ozs.—$14 25 lbs.—$25	Varies	No
Emery Worldwide	Most of North America	None	8 ozs.—$14 2 lbs.—$23	10:30 A.M.	No
Federal Express	98% U.S. coverage and 81 other	None	½ lb.—$14	10:30 A.M.	Yes
Purolator	All of U.S.	125 lbs.	2 lbs.—$13.75	11:59 A.M.	No
UPS	Any address in U.S. and P.R.	70 lbs.	1 lb.—$11.50 2 lbs.—$12.50	Varies	No
U.S. Postal Service	All of U.S.	70 lbs.	2 lbs.—$10.75	3:00 P.M.	Yes

Exhibit 3
Segment information (in thousands of dollars)

	Express delivery	ZapMail	Corporate	Total
1986				
Revenues	$2,573,229	$ 32,981	$ 0	$2,606,210
Operating income	406,800	−131,880	−62,779	212,141
Identifiable assets	1,887,107	170,351	218,904	2,276,362
Depreciation	191,574	18,860	1,970	212,404
Capital expenditure	529,867	134,345	10,559	674,771
1985				
Revenues	$2,015,920	$ 14,741	$ 0	$2,030,661
Operating income	308,183	−121,894	−49,566	136,723
Identifiable assets	1,668,029	185,945	45,532	1,899,506
Depreciation	158,203	12,281	1,849	172,333
Capital expenditure	496,223	70,410	4,421	571,054

The Problem

34   Unfortunately, this improvement in profits did not materialize on schedule (see Exhibits 2 through 4). ZapMail continued to lose money due to several factors. Customers balked at the original $35 charge for 10 pages and were only partially appeased when the company exercised a $10 price cut. Technical bugs increased customer resistance. Messages were garbled, and machines often broke down due to overloaded groundlines, an integral part of the data transmission.

35   Leasing fees, coupled with the inability to handle the volume produced by NEC's (Japanese manufacturer of the ZapMail hardware) high-speed machines, resulted in

Exhibit 4

FEDERAL EXPRESS
Consolidated Income Statement
(in thousands of dollars)

	1986	1985	1984
Revenue	$2,606,210	$2,030,661	$1,436,305
Operating expenses:			
Salaries	1,162,920	907,186	622,675
Equipment and facilities rental	214,372	146,389	87,572
Depreciation	212,404	172,333	111,956
Fuel	149,688	133,473	93,520
Maintenance and repairs	125,087	90,992	59,482
Other	529,598	443,565	295,892
Operating income	212,141	136,723	165,208
Other income:			
Interest capitalized	6,808	9,736	11,851
Interest income	10,908	9,209	13,166
Gain on disposition of aircraft	11,877	8,499	2,463
Other expenses:			
Interest expense	65,505	72,329	36,350
Net other	12,024	8,460	4,078
Pretax income	164,205	83,378	152,260
Taxes	32,366	7,301	36,830
Net income	$ 131,839	$ 76,077	$ 115,430
EPS	2.64	1.61	2.52

frequently faulty transmissions. Though rapid development of satellite capability could solve many of the problems stemming from overused groundlines, these prospects were dampened by the *Challenger* space shuttle disaster in January 1986. Until NASA resumed the shuttle project (scheduled for 1988 at the earliest), there would be no means of launching commercial satellites.

36   Not to be defeated, Federal announced on March 20, 1986, a moratorium on new ZapMail installations "until the bugs were worked out." Despite hard-nosed efforts by management, costs continued to escalate. "The bugs" were proving quite expensive to repair. Federal was facing new competitors in its base business (overnight delivery) as well. It was becoming apparent that a substantial reinvestment of earnings in the overnight carrier business would be necessary in the near future.

37   Competition for market share was fierce, demanding ever-increasing attention to cost and innovation. While Federal had shown overall profit gain of 42 percent to $131.8 million in the year ended May 31, 1986, ZapMail had lost $132 million on revenue of only $33 million (see Exhibits 5 through 8).

38   Strategically, ZapMail seemed to make sense. It would surely take time for a whole new communications system to catch on, and Smith did not like the idea of doing away with ZapMail, which had, for all practical purposes, been his brainchild. He pointed to the birth of telephone technology as evidence that communication networks don't spring up "overnight." As with the telephone, consumers needed time to realize

Exhibit 5

FEDERAL EXPRESS
Consolidated Balance Sheet
(in thousands of dollars)

	1986	1985
Assets		
Current assets:		
Cash	$ 185,036	$ 12,189
Net receivables	347,010	292,797
Spare parts	49,342	56,537
Tax refund	0	42,858
Prepaids	31,902	18,763
Total current assets	613,290	423,144
Property and equipment:		
Flight	$ 841,410	$ 774,114
Ground support	418,053	341,108
Computer	391,146	297,509
Other P&E	551,992	380,285
	2,202,601	1,793,016
Less: Depreciation	650,756	446,993
Net P&E	1,551,845	1,346,023
Other assets	111,227	130,339
Total assets	$2,276,362	$1,899,506
Liabilities and Shareholders' Equity		
Current liabilities:		
Current long-term debt	$ 72,979	$ 44,730
Accounts payable	184,534	127,721
Accruals	174,397	144,427
Total current liabilities	$ 431,910	$ 316,878
Long-term debt	561,716	607,508
Deferred taxes	189,513	159,810
Other commitments	1,509	3,043
Total liabilities	$1,184,648	$1,087,239
Stockholders' equity:		
Common stock	$ 5,081	$ 4,703
Paid-in capital	530,618	340,753
Retained earnings	598,215	466,811
Less: Deferred compensation	42,200	0
Total equity	$1,091,714	$ 812,267
Total liabilities and equity	$2,276,362	$1,899,506

Exhibit 6
Federal Express revenues ($ millions)

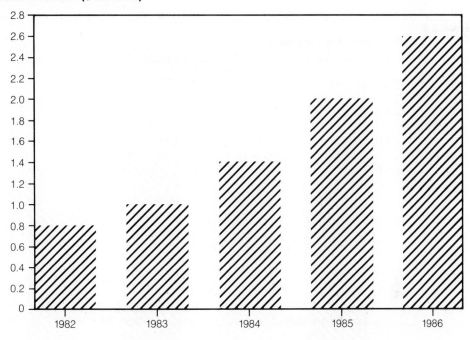

Exhibit 7
Federal Express net income ($ millions)

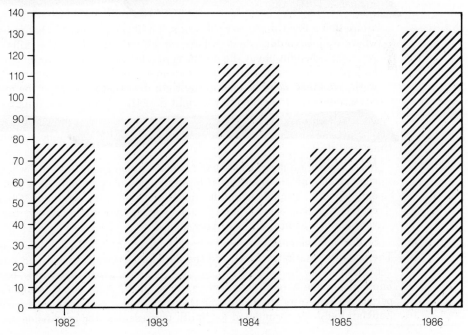

Exhibit 8
Federal Express operating income ($ millions)

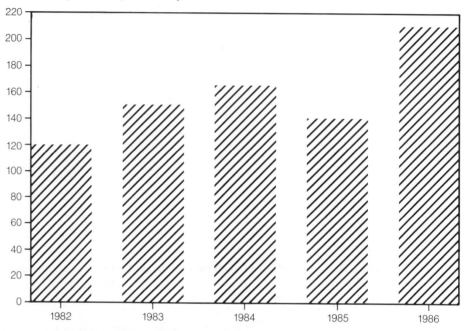

that the benefits of ZapMail are so essential to modern business that everyone must subscribe, thus making the network a success. Smith reasoned:

> We've had a few things over the years, small things mostly, that we've cut loose where we just couldn't do it—where we felt we didn't have the skills or where we hadn't thought about the business problem in sufficient detail. . . . But as to ZapMail, as best I can tell at the moment, there's no question it is going to work. We know we're headed in the right direction in terms of the market. The basic numbers are headed in the right direction. It's now just a matter of when.

39   But financial problems persisted, and the question became, "Aren't we risking our stronghold in overnight mail? Can judgment be that easy?" Publicly, Smith had argued that:

> Most innovation doesn't look like it makes much financial sense when you're right in the middle of battle—it looks like you never should have done it. It's only when it's been done and it's out there that everybody says, "Oh, but of course, that was easy." Then the money starts flowing in and you become a very big deal, and it all looks very logical.

40   Senior management wondered what lay ahead for ZapMail and for Federal Express. The potential market existed, and the ZapMail service seemed to be a sound concept, yet sales revenue had been disappointing. Something was very wrong, but what? Could ZapMail become a profitable service? If so, how? And, if not, could Fred Smith be persuaded to see its shortcomings? Decisions and a plan for the immediate future of ZapMail had to be formulated for Smith to present to the stockholders.

Case 4

New Coke: Coca-Cola's Response to the Pepsi Challenge

The Announcement of the New Taste—
April 23, 1985

Shortly before 11 A.M. the doors of the Vivian Beaumont Theater at Lincoln Center opened to 200 newspaper, magazine, and TV reporters. The stage was aglow with red. Three huge screens, each solid red and inscribed with the company logo, rose behind the podium and a table draped in red. The lights were low; the music began. "We are. We will always be. Coca-Cola. All-American history." As the patriotic song filled the theater, slides of Americana flashed on the center screen—families and kids, Eisenhower and JFK, the Grand Canyon and wheat fields, the Beatles and Bruce Springsteen, cowboys, athletes, the Statue of Liberty—and, interspersed throughout, old commercials for Coke. No political candidate would have gotten away with such patrioteering without howls of protest, and the members of the press weren't seduced by the hype.[1]

1   Chairman Goizueta came to the podium and boasted, "The best has been made even better. Some may choose to call this the boldest single marketing move in the history of the packaged goods business. We simply call it the surest move ever made because the taste of Coke was shaped by the taste of the consumer."

2   New Coke was launched. The American people reacted immediately and violently. After three months of vigorous, unrelenting protest, stunned and humbled Coca-Cola executives called a second press conference to tell the American people that Coke was sorry. The corporate giant announced that it would reissue the original Coca-Cola formula as Coke Classic and asked the forgiveness of the American people.

3   How could a $7 billion corporation with a sterling track record commit such a blunder? How could this giant international company so totally misread consumers' feelings? How dare it tamper with an American institution? Or, did Coca-Cola orchestrate the entire affair as a huge publicity stunt to get millions of dollars of free advertising for its new Coke and boost the sales of the old one?

Industry Analysis

4   The soft drink industry is dominated by two main competitors, The Coca-Cola Company and Pepsi-Cola. Both depend on a network of bottling companies to distribute their bottled soft drinks. Coca-Cola uses its own network of wholesalers for its fountain syrup distribution, while Pepsi distributes its fountain syrup through its bottlers.

5   A principal concern of the industry is long-term growth potential and how this growth is affected by changing population demographics, per-capita saturation, and

---

This case was prepared by Patricia P. McDougall of Georgia State University, and Manfred Heubner, Jon Morris, and Patricia A. Timms. Copyright © Patricia P. McDougall.

[1] Thomas Oliver, *The Real Coke, The Real Story* (New York: Random House, 1986), p. 131.

Exhibit 1
Growth in per capita consumption of soft drinks, 1965–1990

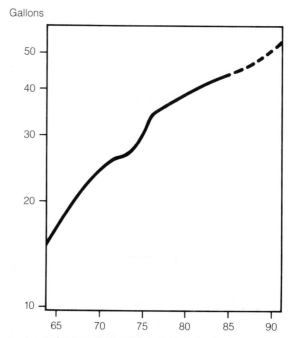

Gallons

Sources: NSDA Sales Survey; Beverage Marketing Corporation; and
The Boston Consulting Group.

changing consumer preferences. Changes in these variables have caused changes in
the channels of distribution that are likely to change the cost structure of the industry.

Industry Growth

6   Growth in the soft drink industry can be increased by consumption per individual
and by population growth. Total consumption in the industry over the last two decades
has risen by a 6½ percent compound annual growth rate. Since the population of the
United States is growing at only about 2 percent a year, the strongest potential for
growth in the U.S. industry is through per-capita growth. As reflected in Exhibit 1,
per-capita growth has risen steadily from about 16.2 gallons per year in 1965 to where
Americans now each drink over 40 gallons of soft drinks per year.

7   Industry analysts view the aging population and the approach of the point of saturation in per-capita consumption as the two main issues influencing the prospects for
future growth. Some analysts have argued that these factors may even reverse the
industry's historical growth rate.

8   The 15-to-24 and 25-to-34-year-old age groups have been the heaviest pop drinkers.
Exhibit 2 graphs the age composition trends of the U.S. population. These heavy-

Exhibit 2
Projected age composition of U.S. population

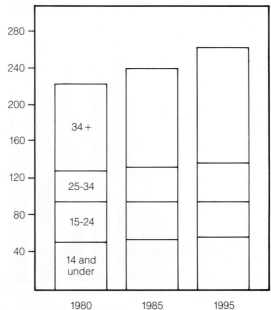

Population (millions)

Source: Predicasts Composite Forecasts.

consumption groups are becoming a smaller percentage of the total population, while older groups, which have historically consumed fewer soft drinks, will grow rapidly. The real question is whether the present younger-age, heavy-consumption groups will retain their consumption patterns as they get older.

9   Optimistic analysts cite industry data such as Exhibit 3, which shows soft drink consumption for three sample periods. While the chart does show that older people drink less than younger people at any given time period, people are increasing their consumption even as they age. For example, today's 50-to-59 age group consumed more in 1980 than when they were 40 to 49 years old (in 1970), and more than 10 years earlier when they were 30 to 39 years old (in 1960).

10   Perhaps the more critical issue is the fear that the market may be approaching the point of saturation in per-capita consumption. Just how many gallons of soft drinks can Americans drink per year? A tapering off of the growth rate in per-capita consumption appears to have already started. From 1965 to 1971, the annual growth rate was 6.9 percent, but the following 1971–77 period shows a drop to 5.4 percent, and another drop to 3.7 percent for the 1977–83 period. While still positive, these growth rates are slower than those to which the industry has become accustomed.

11   Changing consumer perferences are expected to influence the sources of growth as consumers switch to healthier products. Exhibit 4 shows that growth in the industry has come from growth in the low-calorie or diet segment. This trend is expected to

Exhibit 3
Soft drink per capita by age group (8-ounce servings)

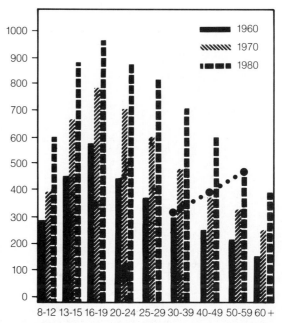

Source: Coca-Cola U.S.A. (*Beverage Digest,* August 17, 1984).

continue, and by 1990 this segment is expected to account for about 40 percent of total soft drink consumption.

Changing Channels of Distribution

12   More convenient availability has increased soft drink sales as the beverages have become available in more and more outlets. On the bottled side, the most important channel is supermarkets, which accounted for 46 percent of 1984 sales. Convenience stores accounted for 20 percent, other retail outlets accounted for 17 percent, and vending accounted for 17 percent. But one has to remember the importance of the fountain side of the business as well. Fountain sales represent 33 percent of total industry sales.

Bottler Structure

13   The bottling side of the business has undergone radical changes from the small plant in every town to the big consolidated production centers of today (see Exhibit 5). This consolidation means bigger plants with lower production costs that can compete more aggressively in the marketplace. Substantial scale economies exist, as both labor

Exhibit 4
Growth of diet versus naturally sweetened soft drinks

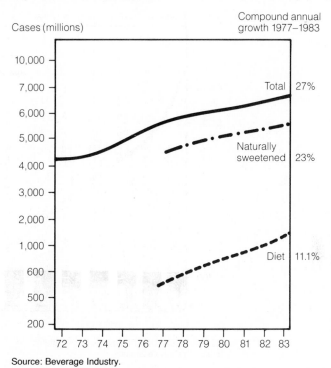

Source: Beverage Industry.

and factory expenses decrease as size increases. All this translates into lower cost per case, as seen in Exhibit 6. This cost savings has helped offset the increase in cost due to the proliferation in brands.

Product Introductions

14   Starting in the 1980s there has been a barrage of new products or product reformulation changes. There have been few entrants into the sugared cola category, as most product introductions have principally occurred in such segments as diet colas, lemon-lime, and juice-containing drinks.

Competitors

15   The two major competitors—Coke and Pepsi—controlled 68 percent of the market in 1985. Most significant of the smaller competitors were Dr Pepper, 7UP, and Royal Crown.

16   As reflected in Exhibits 7 and 8, Coke and Pepsi dominate the top soft drink brands. A comparison of the top 10 brands for 1984 (Exhibit 7) and 1985 (Exhibit 8) offers many insights into the nature of competition in the soft drink industry. While Coke ranked as number one in 1984, the division of Coke sales between new Coke and

Exhibit 5
Consolidation of U.S. soft drink production facilities

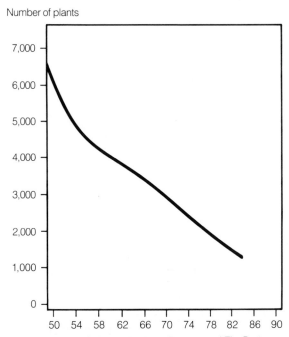

Number of plants

Sources: NSDA; U.S. County Business Patterns; and The Boston
Consulting Group estimates.

Coke Classic allowed Pepsi to capture the number one spot in 1985, although Pepsi's market share fell from 18.1 percent in 1984 to 17.6 percent in 1985. The 1985 combined market share of new Coke and Coke Classic was 23.3 percent. While Coke occupied only two of the top five spots in 1984, the introduction of new Coke allowed the company to seize three of the top five spots in 1985. The phenomenal growth rates of Diet Coke and Diet Pepsi should also be noted.

17   Although marketing very similar products, the two giants of the industry differ significantly in their strengths and weaknesses. Coke's major strengths and weaknesses are detailed first, followed by Pepsi's strengths and weaknesses.

18   Coke's strengths:

1. Coca-Cola has a strong lead in the international arena, with about 60 percent of its profits derived from overseas soft drink operations. Pepsi, its nearest competitor, is far behind in international sales.

2. Decentralized management allows Coke to make quick decisions in the domestic and international markets. Coke's domestic operations are divided into bottling and fountain. Bottling is divided into five selling areas, with all responsibility at the area level.

3. Coke has a well-diversified product line and is the top seller in most of the flavor segments—brand Coca-Cola, Coca-Cola Classic, Diet Coke, Sprite, Caffeine-

Exhibit 6
Impact of historically increasing plant size on average soft drink bottling costs

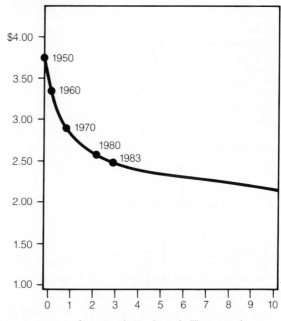

Cost/case (constant 1984$)

Average plant volume (million cases)

Source: The Boston Consulting Group.

Exhibit 7
Top 10 soft drink brands for 1984

Brand	1984 market share (percent)	1984 brand growth (percent)
1. Coke	24.8%	+3.3%
2. Pepsi	18.1	+5.0
3. Diet Coke	6.9	+60.0
4. 7UP	5.3	+1.0
5. Dr Pepper	4.7	+8.0
6. Sprite	3.3	+27.0
7. Diet Pepsi	3.1	+31.0
8. Mountain Dew	2.8	+3.5
9. Royal Crown	2.2	−5.0
10. Tab	2.1	−24.0
Top 10	73.3	+8.0
Other brands	26.7	+1.0

Source: *Beverage World,* March 1985, p. 44.

Exhibit 8
Top 10 soft drink brands for 1985

Brand	1985 market share (percent)	1985 brand growth (percent)
1. Pepsi	17.6%	+5.1%
2. Coca-Cola Classic	17.3	−25.0
3. Diet Coke	8.0	+26.0
4. Coke	6.0	—
5. Dr Pepper	4.7	+9.0
6. 7UP	4.6	−7.0
7. Diet Pepsi	3.6	+25.0
8. Sprite	3.4	+10.3
9. Mountain Dew	2.6	+2.2
10. Royal Crown	2.1	+4.0
Top 10	69.9	+6.0
Other brands	30.1	+4.3

Source: *Beverage World,* March 1986, p. 47.

Free Diet Coke, and Minute Maid. These products allow the Coca-Cola system to better segment the market and better position itself in the different segments.

4. Coke is the number one supplier of syrup for fountain sales. Coke is especially strong in sales to fast-food restaurants. Its network of wholesalers is considered top notch.

19 Coke's weaknesses:

1. Much of the original bottler's contract, which was developed in the early 1900s, is still in effect today. Because the contract fixes the price of syrup, Coke has no control over the price. Despite some amendments, this contract still represents an obstacle to the company.

2. Many small bottlers, lacking the economies of scale to compete in today's marketplace, still exist in the system.

3. The extensive product line could be considered a weakness as well as a strength, as more products and more fragmentation result in a higher cost of production, inventory, and distribution. In addition, cannibalizing existing products has become an important factor.

20 Pepsi's strengths:

1. Pepsi-Cola has strong, concentrated bottlers, which, because of their large size, have good economies of scale and are thus low-cost producers.

2. Pepsi has more flexibility in its pricing policies since the company is not hampered by a fixed-price contract with its bottlers.

3. The lack of diversity in its product line helps control production costs, and advertising can be more focused. Only recently, with the introduction of Slice, did Pepsi enter the flavored category.

    4. By acquiring Pizza Hut, Kentucky Fried Chicken, and Taco Bell, Pepsi has become the largest fast-food restaurant chain in America. Ownership of these outlets secures distribution for its fountain syrup.

    5. Advertising has been the most effective in the industry. The use of superstars like Michael Jackson has heightened the Pepsi image and has resulted in a strong position in the youth segment of the market.

21   Pepsi's weaknesses:

    1. Pepsi lacks substantial diversification into the international market. Most of its revenues come from domestic operations.

    2. With only about 30 percent of its total revenue coming from soft drinks, management's attention may be diverted from this important aspect of the business.

    3. Pepsi's weakness in the fountain side of the business is evident, with only a 20 percent share of the market. Pepsi lacks Coke's huge network for distribution and is trying to secure distribution by buying fast-food restaurant chains.

    4. Pepsi's diversification into fast-food chains has made its existing syrup customers very unhappy. Wendy's recently switched to Coke because it viewed Pepsi as a competitor, not a supplier.

The Coca-Cola Company

22   As related by Thomas Oliver in *The Real Coke, The Real Story,* an Atlanta pharmacist registered a trademark for "French Wine Cola—Ideal Nerve and Tonic Stimulant" in 1885. The name for the brew was appropriate as it is said to have contained cocaine, along with wine and a few other ingredients. After about a year, the formula was changed, and the name was changed to Coca-Cola because it was thought that the two Cs, written in the Spencerian script that was popular at the time, would look good in advertising. Coke was sold by traveling salesmen as a cure for hangovers and headaches.

23   Asa Candler bought the rights to Coca-Cola in 1889 and expanded the business by selling syrup to wholesalers, who in turn sold to drugstores. The syrup was mixed with carbonated water and served at soda fountains.

24   Later that year, two Tennessee businessmen purchased for $1 the right to bottle throughout nearly all of the United States. Feeling that drugstore fountain sales would predominate, Candler wanted no part of the expensive bottling operation. The two men promptly sold regional bottling rights to other businessmen in the South and, later, in the rest of the country. By 1930, there were approximately 1,000 independent bottlers.

25   Ernest Woodruff purchased The Coca-Cola Company in 1919 for $25 million. Woodruff was president of what was later to be known as the Trust Company of Georgia, the bank whose vault still guards the secret recipe for Coke. The formula was so secret that no more than three people at any time ever know the proper mixture of its ingredients.

26   By the 1920s, the company was embroiled in legal battles against imitators and was facing bankruptcy. Profits were falling, sugar prices were rapidly increasing, and, because of the contract, syrup was sold to bottlers at the fixed cost set in 1899. Robert

Woodruff, Ernest's son, was brought in as president in 1923 to restore morale and profits.

27   When Woodruff took control, Coke was sold in the United States, Canada, Cuba, and Puerto Rico but was otherwise unknown around the world. Woodruff outlined a plan to test Coke in Europe, and when the board refused to grant approval, he proceeded in secrecy to establish a foreign sales department. Within three years the foreign department showed a profit.

28   During World War II, Coke became a morale booster to the overseas troops. Initially the drink was shipped from a base in Iceland, but this became impractical as demand increased. In 1943, General Dwight Eisenhower requested that the War Department establish 10 bottling plants in North Africa and Italy. The War Department supplied the machinery and personnel, usually soldiers who had worked for Coca-Cola prior to the war. At the end of the war, there were 64 worldwide plants, which had been built at government expense. These were incorporated without cost into the company. By 1985, Coke was distributed to 155 countries and consumed more than 303 million times a day. Coke is as much a symbol of the United States as is the Statue of Liberty. It is so strongly identified with the United States that when an ambassador is expelled for political reasons, Coke is sometimes soon exiled as well.

Management

Past Players

29   **Robert Woodruff—"The Boss."**   Robert Woodruff, known as "The Boss," became president of The Coca-Cola Company in 1923. In 1954, he "officially retired," but many felt he effectively controlled the company until his death in 1985. At the time of the announcement of the new Coke formula, it was speculated that management had waited for Woodruff's death to make the change. In fact, he endorsed the change.

30   **J. Paul Austin—Chairman of the Board, 1970–1981.**   Lingering a year beyond his expected retirement in 1980, he created an Office of the Chairman, whose vice chairmen essentially operated the company on a day-to-day basis.

31   **J. Lucian Smith—President and COO of the Coca-Cola Company, 1976–1980.**   He was against the annual price cap on syrup. Disputes with bottlers over the escalating syrup costs pitted him against Austin and Keough.

Present Players

32   **Roberto C. Goizueta—Chairman and CEO of The Coca-Cola Company.**   Goizueta joined Coca-Cola in 1961 after fleeing Cuba when Castro came to power. A chemist by training, Goizueta did not come up through the traditional marketing route.

33   **Donald R. Keough—President and COO of The Coca-Cola Company.**   Keough was president of Coca-Cola USA, the domestic soft drink arm of The Coca-Cola Company, when the FTC challenged Coke in 1971 as well as in the late 1970s during con-

frontations with bottlers. He and Goizueta were considered the prime contenders as Austin's replacement.

34   **Brian Dyson—President of Coca-Cola USA.**   In 1978, Dyson was lured by Keough from his native Argentina, where he worked for the international sector, to head up Coca-Cola USA. Dyson led the company's involvement in the refranchising efforts. He argued effectively that the success of The Coca-Cola Company depended on the success of its bottlers.

35   **Sergio Zyman—Senior Vice President of Marketing for Coca-Cola USA.** Mexican-born Zyman defected from Pepsi-Cola in 1979. He has been vice president of bottler operations, director of fountain sales, and Keough's executive assistant. In September 1983, Zyman was selected to head Project Kansas—an experiment to explore the possibility of a reformulation of Coke.

36   **Roy Stout—Director of Marketing Research.**   In 1979, Stout was given the first of several new colas to test. As early as 1976, Stout had compiled a top-secret report, which showed leadership over Pepsi as no longer a given. Research by Stout's department forced management to consider that decline in market share might be related to taste. Stout was an active participant in Project Kansas.

The Beginnings of Trouble

37   In spite of an outwardly healthy image, behind-the-scenes troubles in the 1970s began to distract Coke executives from their primary mission. Beginning with the 1971 salvo fired by the FTC, charging that the bottlers' contract restricted competition, to the fight with bottlers over the price of syrup, a dispute which eventually resulted in the chairman and the company president not speaking with each other, many say Coke executives just lost sight of the heart of the matter—selling Coke. Critics charge that Coke's personnel decisions began to reflect the good old boys' regime. Keough has been quoted as saying that compensation was awarded "not on performance, but perfect attendance."

38   Coke executives seemed to forget more and more that Coke was not a private company but a public company responsible to its shareholders. Profits fell to a compound annual rate of only 7 percent between 1978 and 1981, and net income for 1980 increased a mere one-half percent.

Walls Down

39   In 1971, the FTC challenged Coke, charging that the bottlers' contracts granting territorial exclusivity violated antitrust laws by restricting competition. If the government prevailed, anyone could invade a bottler's territory. This concept was known as "walls down" at Coke headquarters. This would make a bottler's future uncertain, thus reducing the value of the franchise, with anarchy predicted to result. The bottler's contract granted each bottler an exclusive right *in perpetuity* to bottle Coke in his area, and, with the exception of soda fountains, no one else could sell Coke in that market, and the company could not refuse to sell them syrup.

40   An administrative law judge ruled in October 1975 that the bottlers' territorial exclusivity was not a violation of federal trade regulations, but two and a half years later the ruling was reversed, and the FTC reinstituted the complaint. By 1978, little else was discussed at company headquarters. Long-range planning was prevented; the system Coke knew might not exist. Keough later complained that after he assumed office in 1974, the first 50 meetings he attended were legal briefings on the FTC battle. Admitting that he had made a mistake, Keough said, "I should have hired a roomful of lawyers and told them to deal with it, and we could have gotten on with the business."

41   It was not until 1980 that the complaint was ruled in favor of Coca-Cola. The years of turmoil had caused the company to lose sight of its main objective.

Escalating Syrup Costs

42   Dating back to 1899, the original bottlers' contract set syrup at a fixed price. In 1921, the contract was modified to fix the price of syrup at the 1921 current price, subject to quarterly adjustments based on the price of sugar. Only the rising cost of sugar could be passed on to the bottler. This agreement worked well for 50 years until the 70s, when the spiraling costs of the other syrup ingredients made it barely possible for the company to make a profit on Coke. So, once again, Coke found itself in conflict with the bottlers over modifying the contract.

43   Even within the company there was disagreement as to how the contract should be amended. Lucian Smith, the president and COO at the time, advocated a totally flexible price that would reflect future inflation, while others felt some accommodation to the bottlers was necessary and favored an annual cap on how much the company could raise the price of syrup.

44   As to be expected, the bottlers put up a fierce resistance to any amendment. Keough described the fight as like trying to talk someone out of a birthright, as "Every bottler on his dying bed calls his son to his side and, speaking his last words, says, "Don't you ever let them mess with that contract.""

45   In the end Keough went around Smith and convinced Austin and Woodruff to favor an annual cap. The board of directors agreed soon after. As a result, Smith and Austin's relationship became so strained that the two highest-ranking executives of the company didn't even speak to each other. Because of Smith's preoccupation with the syrup amendment at the expense of day-to-day business, Austin reduced Smith's power by creating an Office of the Chairman, in which seven executive vice presidents in essence assumed Smith's duties as COO. A slighted Smith resigned a year later.

Changes in Bottling Franchise Ownerships

46   One of Dyson's first goals as the new head of Coca-Cola USA in 1978 was to alter the company's laissez-faire attitude toward changes in bottling franchise ownerships. It had always been company policy not to get involved with franchise transfers. If a bottler decided to sell, Coca-Cola could not stop him from transferring the contract to a new owner, who had all rights in perpetuity. Thus, the company had no real control over who was selling its products or how well the products were being sold. Dyson argued effectively that The Coca-Cola Company should involve itself in franchise ownership since the owner's performance determined the company's performance.

47   So, in 1979, the Washington, D.C., franchise was purchased by the managers of the franchise through a leveraged buyout structured by Keough and Dyson. Dyson's strategy was that each time a franchise came up for sale, Coca-Cola would either find a friendly buyer or purchase and later resell it. This would allow Coke to organize regional companies into larger distributorships that made more sense geographically.

The Pepsi Challenge

48   While Coca-Cola was absorbed in legal and internal battles, Pepsi had its eye on sales. In the 1960s, Pepsi made a major change in its advertising strategy: it stopped talking about the product and started talking about the user. The 1963 "Pepsi Generation" advertising campaign captured the imagination of the baby boomers. It enhanced the image of Pepsi-Cola and anyone who chose to drink it.

49   Pepsi took the lead in 1975 supermarket sales and has led in every year since, except 1976. Supermarket sales are regarded as the freedom-of-choice segment, since in other segments the customer often has limited choice—he can buy only the brand that is offered.

50   Supermarket sales represent about a third of Coke's total market, with fountain sales and vending sales making up the other two thirds. Since contracts with major fountain clients, such as McDonald's, are based on Coke's status as the number one cola, Coke felt it imperative to lead in all categories; otherwise, fountain clients might switch to Pepsi.

51   The Pepsi Challenge shook The Coca-Cola Company to its foundation. It all started in 1975, when Larry Smith was sent to Dallas to crack the market in Coke's heartland, the South. Pepsi was number three in Dallas, lagging behind Coke and the home brew, Dr Pepper. Smith could not even entice a major grocery chain with an offer to finance a Pepsi promotion. Pepsi would pay the chain money and sell it Pepsi at a discount in exchange for newspaper ad promotion and prominent in-store displays. The chain was not interested. It didn't need Pepsi.

52   Coke had a 35 share, Dr Pepper had 25, and Pepsi had 6. The nationwide Pepsi Generation theme wasn't working in Texas. Convinced that people were drinking Coke for its name, not its taste, Smith requested a custom-made advertising campaign for his market. Alan Pottasch, the advertising mastermind of the Pepsi-Cola Company, was opposed to local campaigns because they were always product oriented and would interfere with his carefully built emphasis on the user rather than the beverage. If it succeeded in one area, bottlers in other areas would hear of it and want it for their territories, and a campaign that works in one place might not in another.

53   Putting his job on the line, Smith hired the in-house advertising agency of the Southland Corporation's 7-Eleven convenience store chain to help him come up with a campaign. Field tests to determine how people felt about Pepsi gave consumers a choice between two unmarked colas and asked them which tasted better. Pepsi was chosen by most of the people. A couple hundred taste tests gave a slim advantage to Pepsi, 52 to 48. In comparative advertising, a valid test that demonstrates a preference, however slim the margin, gives a company the legal right to claim superiority.

54   Pepsi ran its Dallas TV commercial showing loyal Coke drinkers selecting Pepsi as the better-tasting drink of the two unmarked colas. Coke tried to disprove the claim but found when they ran their own test that it wasn't false. Coke had never tested its soda against any competitive product. Coke's counteradvertising was unsuc-

Courtesy The Coca-Cola Company.

cessful; in fact, it played into Pepsi's hands, mentioning Pepsi in an ad for the first time. Pepsi's share quickly went from 6 to 14. The Challenge extended to Houston, moved to Los Angeles, and by 1983 was spread across the country. Only Atlanta, Coke's headquarters, was spared the insult of the Challenge.

55   Both Coke and Pepsi now agree that Coke's sales were not significantly hurt by the Challenge. Pepsi's sales did increase, but the increased share came from the shares of other soft drink producers, as the beverage industry developed more and more into a two-horse race.

56   Wounded pride led to an obsession with Coke's image as number one. What concerned Coke the most was the loss in share in the food store segment of the business. Even when Coke outspent Pepsi in advertising, Pepsi still maintained its share leadership in supermarket sales (see Exhibit 9 for a comparison of Coke and Pepsi shares in food stores). Pepsi used its lead in supermarket sales to claim superiority over Coke.

57   These two giants do not fight for market share for the fun of it. One point of overall market share represents $250 million in sales at the wholesale level. So, one can easily see why Coca-Cola management was concerned about Coke's poor share performance in the supermarket segment.

Exhibit 9
Share of sugar colas (total food stores)

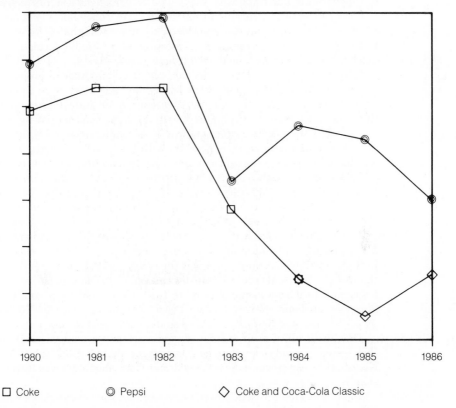

| | 1980 | 1981 | 1982 | 1983 | 1984 | 1985 | 1986 |

□ Coke   ◎ Pepsi   ◇ Coke and Coca-Cola Classic

Coke's Market Research and Project Kansas

58   In the mid-1950s, Coke was outselling Pepsi by a 2-to-1 margin; however, this wide margin was gradually narrowed by Pepsi long before the introduction of new Coke. As early as 1976, Coke's marketing department compiled a top-secret report that showed leadership over Pepsi was no longer a given. The report was largely ignored by executives.

59   A later report claimed that in 1972, 18 percent of soft drink users were exclusive Coke drinkers and a mere 4 percent drank only Pepsi, while 10 years later the tally was 12 percent to 11 percent in Coke's favor. One suggested reason for Coke's tenuous lead was Coke's greater availability. Even if someone wanted Pepsi, in some places he or she might find only Coke.

60   Stout developed a complicated formula to measure the effect of advertising on sales. The results of the formula indicated that despite the fact that Coke spent far more on advertising than Pepsi, Coke's advertising programs were not effective enough. Pepsi, on the other hand, had very effective ad campaigns, most notably the Pepsi

Generation and the Michael Jackson spots. Coke had earlier turned down Michael Jackson as a candidate for its advertising because he was considered too flashy and his appearance didn't jibe with the company's image as the all-American boy.

61 Pepsi's relentless attacks had narrowed Coke's once large lead down to a mere 4.9 percent. Even more disturbing to Coke executives was that Coke was actually trailing in the grocery store segment by 1.7 percent. Coke finally decided that the loss in its market share basically boiled down to one factor—taste.

62 In September 1983, Zyman became manager of a special project, Project Kansas, so named after a newspaper article by William Allen White in the Emporia (Kansas) *Gazette:* "Cola-Cola is the sublimated essence of all that America stands for. A decent thing, honestly made, universally distributed, and conscientiously improved with the years." Perhaps because of his newness to headquarters or because of his foreign background, Zyman had little problem with the idea of changing the formula, and he was quick to accuse reluctant managers of an inability to act with the times.

63 Coke had previously begun to investigate the public's willingness to accept a different Coke, conducting 1,000 interviews in 10 major markets to test the public's response. Two key findings were: (1) exclusive Pepsi drinkers would be interested in a new Coke and (2) many people didn't think Coke should be tampered with.

64 A year after Project Kansas was born, the technical department finally felt it had developed the right formula, and Coke initiated blind taste tests between the new formula and Pepsi. According to *Beverage Digest,* Coke conducted 190,000 tests among the 13-to-59-year-old group. The tests centered on two key questions: (1) how consumers responded to a new formula in taste tests versus old Coke and (2) how new Coke faired versus Pepsi. New Coke beat Pepsi 47 to 43 percent, with 10 percent expressing no preference, and new Coke outscored old Coke 55 to 45 percent.

65 Throughout all of their studies, researchers never made it clear to the consumers they tested that old Coke could be taken off the shelves if the new Coke was introduced. No actual research was done as to whether Coke should merely introduce a line extension.

66 Top-management reaction to the new formula was mixed. Some wanted to introduce a second Coke. Others pointed out that Coke's product line was already unwieldly, and bottlers would not be happy about adding yet another. Concern over the fountain business raised questions as to which Coke companies like McDonald's would choose. If McDonald's chose the new taste over old Coke, executives felt it would damage the flagship brand. The obsession with being number one in all phases ruled out the idea of a second cola since two Cokes would most likely split Coke's market share, allowing Pepsi to become the number one soft drink, an intolerable possibility for Coke.

67 Finally, Coke's market share decline (refer back to Exhibit 9) and Stout's taste tests, which continued to show new Coke winning out over old Coke and Pepsi by staggering margins, forced Keough to ignore his gut reaction against toying with America's heritage. Keough, Chairman Goizueta, Director of Corporate Marketing Herbert, and Dyson met and agreed to give Coke a new taste.

68 How to handle the introduction of new Coke was carefully considered. Since Coke's corporate culture wouldn't let the company admit in any way that Pepsi was superior, the introduction couldn't say that in taste tests new Coke beat Pepsi, because someone may then ask how old Coke did versus Pepsi. By not being more candid about taste, taste became the focal issue as the public judged new Coke against old Coke.

Reaction to the Announcement and the Return of Old Coke

Pepsi Declares a Holiday

69 Pepsi placed full-page ads of Pepsi President Roger Enrico's congratulatory letter to Pepsi bottlers in the nation's major newspapers the same day as the Coke press conference. The letter read in part:

> It gives me great pleasure to offer each of you my heartiest congratulations. After 17 years of going at it eyeball to eyeball, the other guy just blinked. Coca-Cola is withdrawing their product from the marketplace, and is reformulating brand Coke to be more like Pepsi. . . . Maybe they finally realized what most of us have known for years: Pepsi tastes better than Coke . . . we have earned a holiday. We're going to declare a holiday on Friday. Enjoy!

Public Reaction

70 Public reaction to the introduction of new Coke was swift and, for the most part, very negative. To many consumers, changing Coke's formula was like rewriting the Constitution. Many Americans, especially those who lived in the South, saw Coke as

Courtesy The Coca-Cola Company.

an institution and a link to a simpler past. In short, these mainstream middle Americans felt betrayed by an old friend. Many frenzied consumers rushed to grocery stores and bought huge supplies of the soon-to-be-scarce old Coke. Some people spent hundreds of dollars stockpiling old Coke.

71   Newspapers all over the country ran negative articles about the new product, adding more fuel to the fire. By the middle of May, over 5,000 calls per day were being received by Coke's consumer affairs department. Coke answered over 40,000 letters in the spring of 1985. The vast majority of the calls and letters were negative. Most people were more upset with the fact that the taste had been changed rather than the new taste per se. By the end of spring, Coke came to the painful realization that it had vastly underestimated the sentimental feelings millions of consumers had for Coke.

Bottler's Reaction

72   Initially, most of Coke's bottlers supported the introduction of new Coke. Even the southern bottlers were at least convinced of long-term gains. However, the short-term effects were not viewed with optimism. As one Coke bottler put it, "Getting from here to there could be a little rough."

73   Some Coke bottlers reported immediate acceptance by their customers. Most of these bottlers were located in the northeastern part of the country. In these markets, the introduction of new Coke actually increased the bottlers' market shares. However, in order to gain wide acceptance, new Coke was going to have to be welcomed by consumers in the South, as the South represented Coke's high-per-capita markets.

74   Those bottlers who feared negative short-term effects saw their fears realized when the full force of public resentment hit. Frank Barron, whose territory in Georgia led the world in per-capita sales of Coke, saw his volume "go to hell in a handbasket" by mid-June. His experience was hardly unique. On July 3rd, several large bottlers met with Brian Dyson, president of Coca-Cola USA, to tell him that they had to come back with the old Coke. But the later reintroduction of Coke Classic did not offer the bottlers a panacea. A July 29, 1985, *Leisure Beverage Insider* article stated that the extension of brand Coke with Coke Classic meant an 18 percent increase in costs due to packaging, warehouse space, production capability, truck space, ingredients, labels, crowns, point-of-purchase materials, and labor. Despite this rather gloomy out-look, virtually all of Coke's bottlers hailed the reintroduction of the old Coke.

Fountain Sales

75   McDonald's is Coke's number one customer, selling Coke as its only cola product. At Coke's request, McDonald's was the first major customer to run a promotion for Coke. McDonald's use of Coca-Cola-brand-identified cups in the promotion marked the first time McDonald's had ever used a supplier's package. The purpose behind the promotion was to get a quick trial run for the new formula. McDonald's, with over 7,200 restaurants in the United States, was an obvious choice. It was never disclosed how much Coke paid for the promotion, but it seems likely that the cost was not small.

76   McDonald's stayed with the new Coke for about a year, but in May 1986 it decided to go back to the old formula. The decision was made quietly as McDonald's issued a

simple statement saying that its marketing research results indicated that Coke Classic was the choice of the majority of its customers, and, based on that finding, McDonald's had no choice but to change. The option of carrying two colas was never considered. McDonald's felt it would be too confusing and expensive to carry both Coke and Coke Classic.

77   The key issue for food-service restaurants was the limited number of fountain heads. Most dispensing units have only four heads; thus, if a restaurant were to offer Coke Classic and new Coke, two of the four heads would be for a sugared cola product. This would likely mean dropping one flavored offering, such as an orange or a root beer. In essence, restaurants were forced to choose one brand of Coke over the other. At least in the fountain segment, the reintroduction of the old formula cannibalized new Coke's sales.

Wall Street

78   The introduction of new Coke and the subsequent introduction of Coke Classic barely caused a twitter in Coke's stock price. Despite its proclamations of victory, Pepsi's stock price showed no sudden upward or downward movement that could be traced to either of the two announcements.

79   Asked to summarize what happened in the soft drink industry in 1985 and to make predictions for 1986, three top analysts offered the following thoughts in a 1986 issue of *Beverage World:*

> *Emmanuel Goldman of Montgomery Securities:* New Coke can't just be yanked from the shelf. Some consumers actually liked it.

> *Martin Romm of Boston Corporation:* (1) Given the current numbers, Coke seems to be showing resonably good results with the two brands together. The sum of the parts is greater than the whole. (2) Pepsi-Cola has definitely benefited from the current situation. In a sense, the new and the old versions of Coke are competing with one another. (3) Consumers have embraced the Pepsi brand while rejecting new Coke.

> *Allan Kaplan of Merrill Lynch:* (1) Coke took a chance. What it refers to right now as its fighting brand (new Coke) is going to go head to head with Pepsi for the new generation of soft drink consumers who like sweeter drinks. The new Coke is as sweet, if not slightly sweeter, than Pepsi. (2) Coke feels it has retained the people who liked the old Coke with Coca-Cola Classic. It will use the new Coke to attack the new generation. New Coke will be around for a while.

Two Cokes

80   When the return of old Coke as Coke Classic was announced at a news conference on July 11, 1985, the scene of this conference was entirely different. Goizueta told those present:

> Today, we have two messages to deliver to the American consumer. First, to those of you who are drinking Coca-Cola with its great new taste, our thanks. . . . But there is a second group of consumers to whom we want to speak today, and our message to this group is simple: we have heard you.

Courtesy The Coca-Cola Company.

81   In the months following the decision to sell new Coke and Coke Classic, the company's marketing strategy shifted emphasis from specific brands to categories—the megabrand strategy was developed. All drinks with the name *Coke* were grouped together—Coke, Coke Classic, Cherry Coke, Diet Coke, Caffeine-Free Coke, Caffeine-Free Diet Coke, and later, Diet Cherry Coke—thus providing a new way to read the numbers.

82   By the end of 1985, Pepsi had become the number one soft drink, but Coke Classic was gaining rapidly. The switch of McDonald's and Hardee's back to Coke Classic presented a crippling blow to new Coke's projections of success. The following year, *Beverage World* reported that Coke Classic returned to its number one spot, Pepsi followed in second place, and sales for new Coke stabilized as the new Coke finished the year ranked as number 9, with 2.3 percent of the overall market.

83   Commenting on Coca-Cola's decision to change the formula, Keough said, "Some critics will say Coca-Cola made a marketing mistake. Some cynics will say that we planned the whole thing. The truth is, we are not that dumb and we are not that smart."

Case 5

PepsiCo and the Cola War

Introduction

1   In the late 1800s, soda fountains flourished in drugstores and ice cream parlours across the nation. Friends met there to socialize and to take breaks from work. At the time, sodas were made to order and came in a variety of flavors. On occasion, inventive "soda jerks" experimented with new flavor combinations. It was from such an experiment that Caleb D. Bradham invented Pepsi-Cola in his New Burn, North Carolina, pharmacy. By the time Pepsi-Cola was invented, cola beverages were already popular worldwide. As early as the 1880s, fountain operators had begun to experiment with Peruvian coca leaf and African kola nut extracts.

2   Bradham began marketing Pepsi-Cola in 1903 and a year later purchased a factory to manufacture and bottle his invention. By 1904, bottled soft drink sales were rapidly overtaking fountain sales, and Bradham's bottling plant enabled him to compete in the growing market. Soon he developed a network of franchise bottlers in the states around North Carolina. By the end of 1909, there were 250 Pepsi-Cola bottlers with operations in at least 24 states. In all, Bradham franchised more than 300 Pepsi-Cola bottlers, and, under his leadership, Pepsi-Cola got off to an excellent start.

3   Although the company got off to an excellent start, there was a time when it was struggling to survive. Pepsi enjoyed handsome profits until 1917, when the United States entered World War I. During the war, price controls on key ingredients (such as sugar) made production possible, but when the war ended, so did price controls. By May of 1920, the price of sugar had quadrupled from $.055 to $.225 per pound. The rapid increase in sugar prices was disastrous for the industry, which sold soft drinks to customers for a nickel a bottle at the time. Price increases led to inevitable reductions in volume, cash flow, and profits. Although Bradham tried to raise working capital and to reorganize the company, these efforts failed. With bankruptcy fast approaching, in 1923 the company's assets were sold for $30,000.

4   Pepsi-Cola's new owner, Roy Megargel, shared Bradham's dream of distributing Pepsi nationally. He led the company through two reorganizations and ultimately to a second bankruptcy in 1931, following the stock market crash.

5   Charles G. Guth, president of Loft, Inc., was the next person to play a prominent role in the life of the company. Loft and its subsidiaries owned and operated approximately 250 candy stores, most with soda fountains. In May of 1931, Guth noted that his company had used an average of 31,584 gallons of Coca-Cola syrup yearly for three years. He believed that this high-volume usage of Coca-Cola syrup should have enabled his company to become a Coca-Cola wholesaler, but The Coca-Cola Company refused to give him a jobber's discount. Thus, Guth responded by switching to Pepsi. However, Pepsi had already filed a petition for bankruptcy, so Guth met with Roy

Copyright © 1986 by Neil H. Snyder. All rights reserved. This case was prepared by Neil H. Snyder, DeAnn Chappell, Lorraine Norian, Brian Pauleen, Kellen Smith, and Marie Smith of the University of Virginia McIntire School of Commerce. It is designed to be used as a basis for discussion rather than to illustrate either effective or ineffective handling of an administrative situation.

Megargel to develop the "Pepsi-Cola Company." On August 10, 1931, Pepsi was back in business.

6   Guth's first priority for the new company was to improve Pepsi-Cola's taste. Upon accomplishing this objective, he replaced Coca-Cola in his soda fountains with Pepsi-Cola, but Guth's customers were not entirely pleased with his decision. Fountain sales decreased by one third, and the number of Pepsi-Cola bottlers declined as well. Coca-Cola was by far the most popular soft drink, and it was especially strong in the enormous New York market. This fact motivated and encouraged Pepsi's new leaders to initiate a change. In 1933, Guth introduced a very simple idea that turned Pepsi's net losses into millions of dollars of net earnings. He decided to sell twice as much Pepsi-Cola for a nickel as the other brands offered. One loyal Pepsi customer had this to say about the move:

> Guth had long been aware that to induce the New York public to purchase his relatively little-known Pepsi-Cola, rather than another cola then far better known, he must offer some sort of sales inducement. . . . Then, late in 1933, with the 12-ounce bottle for $.10 making no progress, he suddenly decided to offer that same 12-ounce bottle for $.05. . . . It was a revolutionary idea . . . no other cola had ever tried it![1]

7   Walter S. Mack was the next president and CEO of Loft. He recognized the importance of advertising in gaining wide acceptance of a new product competing against a well-established industry giant, so he hired professional marketers to promote Pepsi. Things really started moving when the advertising agency created the following extremely successful radio jingle—the first jingle aired in U.S. advertising history:

> Pepsi-Cola hits the spot
> Twelve full ounces, that's a lot
> Twice as much for a nickel, too
> Pepsi-Cola is the drink for you.[2]

8   The jingle was so popular, in fact, that it was recorded in 55 languages. Additionally, more than 1 million copies were released for play in juke boxes, and "Pepsi-Cola Hits the Spot" was even played in Carnegie Hall.

9   By 1939, the Loft board of directors had lost its interest in candy. Thus, the company was reorganized, and the candy division was eliminated. Loft was now in a position to devote its full attention to Pepsi-Cola, and on June 30, 1941, Loft, Incorporated changed its name to the Pepsi-Cola Company.

10   Al Steele, a man who had been a vice president at Coca-Cola, became Pepsi's next president. Having failed to fulfill his ambitions at Coca-Cola, Steele was determined to make Pepsi the number-one-selling soft drink. As the years passed, competition intensified, and Pepsi began chipping away at Coke's dominant market position. By the early 1960s, Pepsi was ready to engage Coke in the international arena. An aggressive foreign expansion effort was led by Donald Kendall, the next and current Pepsi

---

[1] Martin W. Milward, *Twelve Full Ounces,* 1962.

[2] *The Pepsi-Cola Story* (Purchase, N.Y.: PepsiCo, Inc., 1985).

chief executive, who increased the number of overseas bottlers from 70 in 1957 to 278 in 1962. Throughout Europe, Pepsi became Coke's major cola rival.

Key Executives

11   The chairman of the board and chief executive officer of PepsiCo, Inc., Don Kendall, was born March 16, 1921, in the Dungeness Valley of Washington State. He excelled in athletics—track, boxing, and football—during high school, and he earned a football scholarship to Western Kentucky State University. After three semesters in school, he dropped out and enlisted in the navy, where he rose to the rank of lieutenant. He left the navy in 1947 to work for Pepsi and began his meteoric rise.

12   Kendall's first job with the company was on a bottling line in New Rochelle, New York. Later, he took over a truck route and soon became a syrup salesman. Kendall distinguished himself in sales, and his impressive record earned him a promotion to the national sales office in New York. Three years later, at age 35, he became vice president of marketing, and at age 39 he became president of Pepsi's overseas operations.

13   In 1959, Kendall represented Pepsi at the American National Exhibition in Moscow, and he prevailed upon an acquaintance of his, Vice President Richard M. Nixon, to invite Soviet Premier Nikita Kruschev to visit the Pepsi display. Kruschev enjoyed the product, and Pepsi eventually became the first U.S. company to manufacture a consumer product in the Soviet Union. In 1963, Kendall was named president and chief executive officer of Pepsi-Cola Company, and in 1971 he became chairman of the board and CEO of PepsiCo, Inc.

14   In addition to his work with PepsiCo, Kendall has served as the chairman of various associations. Among these are the U.S.–U.S.S.R. Trade and Economic Council, the American Ballet Theatre Foundation, and the U.S. Chamber of Commerce.

15   Roger Enrico became president and chief executive officer of the Pepsi-Cola USA division of PepsiCo in 1983. He was born and raised in Chisolm, Minnesota, where at the age of 13 he began his career in the soft drink business with a small independent bottler. After graduating from Babson College, he went to work for General Mills in the employee relations department. Fifteen months later, he joined the navy and served for four years.

16   Enrico's career with PepsiCo has taken him through a variety of positions. He has been the vice president/South Latin America for PepsiCo International, president of Frito-Lay/Japan, and senior vice president of sales and marketing for Pepsi-Cola Bottling Group. During his term as president of Pepsi-Cola USA, Enrico has been very active in Pepsi's quest to catch Coke and take the leadership position in the soft drink industry. In 1984, he decided to use NutraSweet® exclusively in Pepsi's diet line. Pepsi was the first soft drink company to make this move, but Coke followed the lead very quickly. Additionally, he introduced two major new products to the Pepsi line—Slice and Diet Slice.

17   Senior Vice President of Sales Ronald W. Tidmore is responsible for the sale of all Pepsi's soft drinks. He leads a dedicated and hard-working group that made Pepsi the recipient of the 1984 award for the U.S. company with the best sales force. The

field of competitors for this award included such companies as Coca-Cola, Nabisco Brands, and Beatrice Foods.

The Pepsi Salespeople

18   Dealing directly with bottlers, Pepsi salesmen are responsible for more than just selling the product. They are the company's front line in motivating the bottlers to excel. Additionally, they work with each bottler to develop specific marketing programs and to evaluate the success of these programs. The sales management team is involved in selling, too. Tidmore, for example, personally visits bottlers to sell Pepsi's programs and strategies. Also, Pepsi's local sales managers serve as consultants to the firm's bottlers. Pepsi bottlers invest as much as $20 million in their operations, so they expect the company's salespeople to take initiative to assist them and to know the ins and the outs of the bottling business. According to Tidmore, "Our approach is 'ready, aim, fire.' It's important to make things happen; if you're doing something wrong, you can always change course."

The Competition

19   When Pepsi-Cola was introduced to the market, Coca-Cola was well established, and Coke customers were extremely loyal to the product. Thus, from the beginning Pepsi fought hard for market share, and it experienced difficulty in penetrating most markets. The New York area was an especially difficult market for Pepsi to crack, but it was a vital area because of its size and because every competitor understood from the beginning that market share was the name of the game. At the time, New York had the highest per-capita rate of consumption of soft drinks in the country.

20   To attract customers in New York, in 1933 Pepsi introduced a new concept—it offered 12 ounces of cola for the 6-ounce price. The idea was very attractive and very successful. By 1938, Coke had no doubts about Pepsi's potential threat, and it began to take defensive measures to protect its market position. For example, Coke sued Pepsi over trademark violations concerning Pepsi's use of the word *cola* in its name. A series of legal battles resulted in a stalemate, and Pepsi continued to use *cola* in its name. In 1939, Pepsi introduced an advertising campaign that included the jingle "Pepsi-Cola Hits the Spot." This jingle was so effective that it ran until 1950.

21   During World War II, Coca-Cola got unexpected help entering the international market. Coke's brand loyalty was so strong among GIs that the U.S. government funded the construction of Coca-Cola bottling plants throughout the world. After the war, The Coca-Cola Company was so far in front of its competitors in developing the international market that it would take firms like Pepsi almost 30 years to begin to catch up. Today, Coke is still the dominant influence in the international soft drink industry.

22   In 1961, Pepsi introduced a theme for its product that became the foundation for its current advertising strategy. Pepsi people, we were told, were of all ages, but they had two things in common. They were young at heart, and they lived life to the fullest. This strategy became more and more popular as the Depression and World War II–era children matured and had children of their own—the baby boom generation. Growing old and losing the vitality associated with being young was difficult for the former group to accept, and the latter group represented such a large portion of the population that they began to set the pace for the rest of the nation.

23 Pepsi's 1961 campaign offered the following theme: "Now It's Pepsi—For Those Who Think Young." Coke responded with its theme, "Things Go Better with Coke." As the baby boom generation matured, Pepsi launched its "Pepsi Generation" campaign and began associating its product with sports stars, the modern-day woman, and the man on the move. Adventure and excitement were what Pepsi people wanted. As the nation moved from euphoria to reality with the onset of the Vietnam War and concern about the destruction of planet Earth, Pepsi offered Pepsi people hope with this theme: "You've Got a Lot to Live, Pepsi's Got a Lot to Give." At about the same time, Coke began the "It's the Real Thing" campaign and redesigned its logo.

24 Establishing brand loyalty has always been the objective of Pepsi's advertising, but in the 1970s and 1980s it pursued it with a vengeance. In 1977, Pepsi introduced the "Pepsi Challenge" by asking consumers to choose the cola they liked best (Pepsi or Coke) using blind taste tests. Pepsi's results showed that consumers preferred Pepsi, so Coke conducted its own taste tests. Coke's tests showed that consumers preferred Coke. In 1980, Pepsi used the slogan "Catch that Pepsi Spirit." In 1981, "Pepsi's Got Your Taste for Life" became its theme.

25 When it became obvious that advertising alone would not win the cola war, Coke and Pepsi began to slash prices. These price cuts not only reduced profit margins for Coke and Pepsi, but they affected secondary competitors (such as 7UP and Dr Pepper) even more. To survive, secondary soft drink manufacturers were forced to expand the battle to increase market share.

26 In an attempt to capitalize on the health craze sweeping the United States, 7UP emphasized the purity of its product with the slogan "Crisp and Clean, No Caffeine. Never Had It, Never Will!" Both Pepsi and Coke retaliated by introducing caffeine-free colas of their own. Then, in 1983, Coca-Cola began a comparative advertising campaign pitting Sprite against 7UP. In 1985, Pepsi introduced its own lemon-lime soft drink, Slice.

27 Pepsi's most recent attempt to improve consumer allegiance involves associating its product with successful singers, such as Michael Jackson, Lionel Richie, and Tina Turner. This marketing strategy has helped PepsiCo establish Pepsi-Cola as "The Choice of a New Generation."

Production and Distribution

28 Although PepsiCo owns a few bottling companies, most of its bottlers are independent. The company provides its syrup to bottlers, who are responsible for producing soft drinks and distributing them to retailers.

Marketing

29 Brand loyalty in the soft drink industry is not a thing of the past, but manufacturers can no longer depend on a large, stable base of die-hard consumers to support their products. Consumers used to be "true to their soft drink" no matter what. But now, because of fierce competition for market share, the soft drink industry is oversegmented, and the products differ so slightly that consumers are confused. The soft drink today

Exhibit 1

A. *Market shares of soft-drink sales for Pepsi and Coke (in supermarkets), January 1986*

	Percent
Pepsi	19.3
Coke	18.2
New Coke	3.5
Classic Coke	14.7

B. *Soft-drink manufacturers, all brands (market share in percent)*

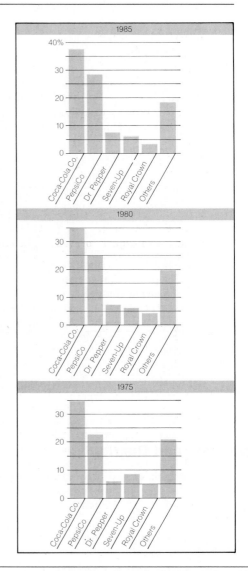

Source: Data from A. C. Nielsen.

Source: Data from John C. Maxwell, Jr., at Furman Saks Mager Dietz & Birney. Used with permission.

is perceived by many consumers more as a commodity than a soda. This situation creates enormous problems for PepsiCo, Coca-Cola, and the other competitors in the industry who continually seek to differentiate their products.

30   Pricing has also contributed to the decline in brand loyalty. Price competition is now the norm in the industry, and more than 50 percent of soft drink purchases are made on impulse. Due to low prices in general, frequent promotions by distributors, and the impulse nature of the purchasing decision, many consumers today buy the soft drink with the lowest price.

31   The standardization of production and distribution methods used by competitors contributes to the lack of differentiation in the industry as well. The cycle begins when the syrup is formulated; it progresses as the syrup is shipped to bottlers for conversion into soft drinks; and it ends with the delivery of the product to retailers. Rather than establishing their own independent systems, smaller producers of soft drinks (like Dr Pepper) contract with Pepsi-Cola or Coca-Cola distributors to bottle, store, and distribute their products. Thus, product differentiation based upon production and distribution methods is virtually nonexistent.

32   Advertising and promotion are the most important tools used by soft drink manufacturers to distinguish their products. Competitors in the industry rely upon endorsements by famous people and reminder advertising to create and reinforce the image they want their products to have. Emotional appeals and identification tactics are used to increase brand loyalty. Slogan and ad theme changes reflect Pepsi's, and Coke's, desire to adjust to even slight shifts in consumer demographics, attitudes, values, likes, and dislikes. Since advertising costs are so high, they are monitored closely, and promotions by local bottlers are encouraged and subsidized by the manufacturer.

Market Share

33   Market share is the crucial measure of a soft-drink company's success in the cola war because it translates into sales revenue and profit. Pepsi's market share has been increasing steadily, and the gap between Pepsi and Coke has been reduced. Exhibit 1 shows soft drink market share data for the years 1975, 1980, and 1985.

34   The market share calculation includes sales of soft drinks in three categories: grocery store sales, fountain sales, and vending machine sales. In 1984, Pepsi led Coke by almost 2 percentage points in grocery store sales. Coke led in fountain and vending sales. However, grocery store sales are the first to reflect changes in consumer preferences, because retailers try to stock their shelves with the best-selling products all the time. Fountain and vending sales, on the other hand, are influenced by long-term contracts that are negotiated periodically.

Finances

35   PepsiCo, Inc., is a diversified company with holdings in the soft drink, snack food, and restaurant industries. Among its soft drink products are Pepsi, Slice, Diet Pepsi, Pepsi Free, and Mountain Dew. PepsiCo owns Frito-Lay, the leader in salty snacks, which manufactures Fritos corn chips, Lay's potato chips, Chee-tos, and other products. The company's restaurants include Pizza Hut and Taco Bell. Exhibit 2 shows the company's net sales and operating profits by industry. Exhibit 3 shows selected financial data for the firm for the years 1981 through 1985.

Exhibit 2
PepsiCo today: Three major businesses ($ in millions)

	1985		1984		1983	
Net sales:						
Soft drinks	$3,128.5	39%	$2,908.4	39%	$2,940.4	43%
Snack foods	2,847.1	35	2,709.2	36	2,430.1	35
Restaurants	2,081.1	26	1,833.5	25	1,529.4	22
Total	$8,056.7	100%	$7,451.1	100%	$6,899.9	100%
Operating profits:						
Soft drinks	$ 263.9	31%	$ 246.4	30	$ 126.2	20%
Snack foods	401.0	47	393.9	48	347.7	55
Restaurants	194.0	22	175.2	22	154.3	25
Total	$ 858.9	100%	$ 815.5	100%	$ 628.2	100%

The Biggest Marketing Blunder Ever or a Wise Gamble?

36   In April 1985, The Coca-Cola Company announced that it was dropping its flagship brand, Coca-Cola, and replacing it with a new and improved soft drink called "New Coke." According to Coke's management and the results of extensive taste tests conducted throughout the United States, the new formula was preferred to the original Coke. It was sweeter and had a lighter taste than the old formula (a taste similar to Pepsi).

37   Faithful consumers of "old" Coke were outraged. Peter Behr suggested that Coke "badly misjudged the depth of brand loyalty they had spent years and bundles of advertising dollars creating. And they also overlooked the stubborn streak in many consumers who don't like being told what's good for them."

38   Within two days of the announcement, Pepsi produced and began airing a commercial depicting a confused teenaged girl questioning Coke's reformulation. She took her first sip of Pepsi and commented, "Mmm, now I know why." Pepsi also declared a company holiday (see Exhibit 4), and it advertised in newspapers across the nation that Pepsi had "The Taste Too Good to Change." Next, they introduced a series of hard-hitting commercials emphasizing consumer anger among die-hard Coke loyalists. Within a month, Pepsi-Cola sales had jumped 14 percent from the previous year.

39   In August 1985, Coke reintroduced "old" Coke as Coca-Cola Classic after it had been off the market for 10 weeks. What at first appeared to be a debacle may have turned out to be the very best thing that could have happened to Coke. In 1985, its revenue increased 10 percent, but because of high advertising costs its operating income from soft drinks "remained flat at $880 million."

40   However, it got a good return on its advertising investment. According to *Advertising Age,* Coca-Cola led all other advertisers in consumer recall, with a record-setting 7 percent for 1985. Pepsi was a distant second with a 3 percent recall rate. Ted Lannan, a research analyst with SRI Research, said, "Coca-Cola had a great recall number.

Exhibit 3

PEPSICO INC. AND SUBSIDIARIES
Selected Financial Data
(dollars in thousands except per share amounts, unaudited)

	1985	1984	1983	1982	1981
Summary of Operations					
Net sales	$ 8,056,662	7,451,106	6,899,884	6,492,380	6,025,261
Cost of sales and operating expenses	7,319,600	6,738,432	6,359,372	5,881,603	5,454,352
Net interest expense	98,996	118,982	121,618	114,409	111,893
	7,418,596	6,857,414	6,480,990	5,996,012	5,566,245
Income from continuing operations before unusual credits (charges) and income taxes	638,066	593,692	418,894	496,368	459,016
Unusual credits (charges)	25,900[a]	(156,000)[b]	—	(79,400)[d]	—
Income from continuing operations before income taxes	663,966	437,692	418,894	416,968	459,016
Federal and foreign income taxes	243,885	162,677	140,602	213,467	190,146
Income from continuing operations . . . . $	420,081	275,015	278,292	203,501	268,870
Income per share from continuing operations . . . . . $	4.51[a]	2.90[b]	2.95	2.18[d]	2.92
Average shares and equivalents outstanding . . . . . #	93,567	95,827	95,480	94,904	93,060
Cash dividends declared . . . . $	161,160	156,185	151,358	147,127	129,944
Per share . . . . $	1.755	1.665	1.620	1.580	1.420
Year-End Position					
Total assets . . . . $	5,861,160	4,876,404	4,421,079	4,005,390	3,883,057
Long-term debt [e] . . . . $	1,162,668	669,641	799,765	843,901	804,597
Shareholders' equity . . . . $	1,837,682	1,853,376	1,794,158	1,650,465	1,556,264
Per share . . . . $	20.95	19.74	19.18	17.68	16.99
Shares outstanding . . . . #	87,706	93,908	93,561	93,374	91,605
Statistics and Ratios					
Return on average shareholders' equity [f] . . . . %	22.0	18.5	16.2	17.6	18.3
Return on revenues [f] . . . . %	5.0	4.5	4.0	4.4	4.5
Long-term debt [e] to total capital employed [g] . . . . %	26.6	18.7	23.6	28.3	27.0
Total debt to total capital employed [g] . . . . %	34.5	26.5	31.7	34.6	40.7
Employees . . . . #	150,000	150,000	154,000	133,000	120,000
Shareholders . . . . #	72,000	62,000	60,000	48,000	49,000

[a] The unusual credit in 1985 related to an adjustment of the reserve for the refranchising of several company-owned foreign bottling operations ($14,900 after-tax or $ 16 per share).

[b] The unusual charge in 1984 related to the refranchising of several company-owned foreign bottling operations ($62,000 after-tax or $ 65 per share).

[c] In 1982 PepsiCo adopted the Statement of Financial Accounting Standards (SFAS) No. 52 on foreign currency translation. Prior year results have not been restated for SFAS 52.

[d] The unusual charge in 1982 related to a reduction in net assets of foreign bottling operations ($ 83 per share). The charge was without tax benefit.

[e] Long-term debt includes capital lease obligations.

[f] The return on average shareholders' equity and return on revenues are calculated using income from continuing operations before unusual credits (charges) and after income taxes.

[g] Total capital employed is total debt, shareholders' equity, deferred income taxes and other liabilities and deferred credits.

Seven percent in any one month is great, but to average that number over the course of a year is phenomenal."

41   After the schock of the announcement about dropping the original Coke wore off, Coca-Cola's image took off. According to Emanuel Goldman of Montgomery Securities in San Francisco, "They [Coke] are going to come out of this thing smelling like a rose. Coke Classic's image is up in the sky. People aren't taking Classic for granted. It's something they love and adore."

Exhibit 4

```
PEPSICO
ANDERSON HILL ROAD               Western Union Mailgram
PURCHASE, N.Y.      10577
```

1-0100200112011 04/22/85 ICS NY79621   NVFA
00966 MLTN VA 04/22/85

ROGER B FLINT — SLS MGR
PCBC OF CENTRAL VIRGINIA
PO BOX 5106
CHARLOTTESVILL VA 22905

APRIL 22, 1985

TO: ALL PEPSI-COLA BOTTLERS AND PEPSI-COLA COMPANY PERSONNEL

IT GIVES ME GREAT PLEASURE TO OFFER EACH OF YOU MY HEARTIEST
CONGRATULATIONS.

AFTER EIGHTY SEVEN YEARS OF GOING AT IT EYEBALL TO EYEBALL, THE
OTHER GUY JUST BLINKED. COCA-COLA IS WITHDRAWING THEIR PRODUCT
FROM THE MARKETPLACE, AND IS REFORMULATING BRAND COKE TO "BE
MORE LIKE PEPSI." TOO BAD RIPLEY'S NOT STILL AROUND... HE COULD HAVE
A FIELD DAY WITH THIS ONE.

THERE'S NO QUESTION THE LONG TERM MARKET SUCCESS OF PEPSI HAS
FORCED THIS MOVE.

EVERYONE KNOWS WHEN SOMETHING IS RIGHT, IT DOESN'T NEED CHANGING.

MAYBE THEY FINALLY REALIZED WHAT MOST OF US HAVE KNOWN FOR
YEARS... PEPSI TASTES BETTER THAN COKE.

WELL, PEOPLE IN TROUBLE TEND TO DO DESPERATE THINGS... AND WE'LL
HAVE TO KEEP OUR EYE ON THEM... BUT, FOR NOW, I SAY VICTORY IS SWEET
AND WE'VE EARNED A CELEBRATION. WE'RE GOING TO DECLARE A HOLIDAY
ON FRIDAY. ENJOY!

BEST REGARDS,

ROGER

20:34 EST

MGMCOMP

TO REPLY BY MAILGRAM MESSAGE, SEE REVERSE SIDE FOR WESTERN UNION'S TOLL-FREE PHONE NUMBERS

42 According to *Beverage World,* Pepsi ended 1985 with a 17.6 percent market share; Coke Classic came in with a 17.3 percent share; and new Coke garnered 6 percent. That made new Coke a better seller than either 7UP or Dr Pepper in 1985. And, at $350 million of annual sales per point of market share, the executives at Coke may think Pepsi claimed victory too early in the game. On the other hand, McDonald's Corporation, Coke's biggest fast-food customer, announced that it was returning to the Classic Coke, and many others believe that new Coke's future success is not guaranteed.

43   Whether Coke executives planned these events or not is subject to debate. They claim they did not and that they "are not that smart and not that stupid." Nonetheless, they took the biggest gamble in the history of business by risking their goodwill and the loyalty of their customers. It could have backfired, but it did not.

Antitrust Issues in the Soft Drink Industry

44   On January 24, 1986, PepsiCo agreed to buy most of the 7UP Company from Philip Morris Companies for $380 million, and on February 20, 1986, Coca-Cola announced that it would purchase Dr Pepper for $470 million. The two mergers would have given Pepsi a 35 percent share and Coke a 46 percent share of the total soft drink market. Together they would have controlled more than 80 percent of the market, thus raising serious questions about violations of antitrust laws. But the Royal Crown Cola Company, maker of RC Cola, filed suit in federal court on June 19, 1986, to prevent the mergers. On June 24, 1986, Philip Morris stated that it would not sell 7UP to Pepsi, but Coke said that it planned to continue with its purchase of Dr Pepper. However, there is widespread speculation that Coke's offer to buy Dr Pepper was only a ploy designed to upset the Pepsi/7UP merger by raising questions in the Federal Trade Commission about antitrust violations.

Case 6

Comdial Corporation

1   March 1986 was a critical month for Comdial Corporation of Charlottesville, Virginia, a $100 million manufacturer of telecommunications equipment. Ted B. Westfall, chairman and chief executive officer of Comdial, was faced with the problem of guiding the firm in a volatile market with intense competition.[1] Capacity utilization was down to 40 percent, and the firm had been forced to lay off 900 of its 2,200 employees over the past year. After two years of substantial losses, Comdial was burdened with a debt-to-equity ratio of over 130 percent.

2   A team of independent analysts had identified four possible alternatives for seeing the company through this trying period of industry shakeout. One option was to carve out a high-quality, high-service marketing niche, emphasizing the firm's proven reliability and customer service along with a "Made in America" pitch to a growing market of small-business customers.

3   A second and more drastic alternative was to liquidate domestic manufacturing operations and move their production to the Far East to take advantage of lower labor costs. The firm could then continue to market to the more price-sensitive residential market as well. This course, though radical, would allow the company to achieve lower manufacturing costs while continuing to capitalize on its superior knowledge and technological expertise.

4   A third option was to go after the large, business system market. The high margins and massive scale of operations in this arena were quite attractive.

5   The final alternative involved reshaping Comdial's mission, broadening the firm's operations to include the manufacture of other specialized plastic products. Such a shift would help utilize excess capacity while enabling the firm to scale back its communications production toward its more successful product lines. All four options appeared risky but feasible. What would it take to pilot Comdial back down the road to sustained growth and profitability?

Company History

6   Comdial was formed in 1977 as a telephone equipment concern. Its first goal was to reduce the cost of push-button telephone set dialers while improving their functions. By 1982 the company completed development of a state-of-the-art dialer and was preparing to build a plant to complete telephone sets and to develop distribution channels for them. At the same time, General Dynamics announced that it would leave the telephone business and sell off its divisions that were producing such equipment. Comdial took advantage of this opportunity by buying the two divisions—Stromberg–

This case was prepared by Professor Per V. Jenster with assistance from S. Barnes, C. Bierly, K. Gothie, M. Park, and L. Wilt of the McIntire School of Commerce, University of Virginia. © Copyright 1987 Per V. Jenster.

[1] Mr. Westfall had served as chairman of the board since September 1981 and chief executive officer of the company since December 1981. He was previously a consultant to ITT from 1975 until September 1982 and served as executive vice president and director of ITT from 1964 to 1974.

Carlson Telephone Set Division, located in Charlottesville, Virginia, and American Telecommunications Corporation (ATC) in Upland, California. Stromberg–Carlson manufactured high-quality standard telephone sets and key systems and provided a large telephone refurbishment service. ATC was a leading manufacturer of character and decorator telephone sets.

7   In February of 1982, Comdial acquired R&G Communications, a large telephone refurbishing company. In June of that year, the company acquired a telephone retail chain in order to develop expertise in operating its own distribution channel. In late August, the firm acquired an 80 percent interest in Scott Technology Corporation, a development-stage company researching a device that automatically allowed small telephone systems to select the cheapest long-distance carrier. The company made a major overseas commitment in January 1984 to invest in HPF, the second-largest telephone producer in France. Another overseas interest was the development of a credit card verification terminal in conjunction with British Telecom. Comdial also negotiated at that time for highly automated factory facilities in South Wales.

8   By the beginning of 1982, Comdial reached the position of fourth-largest domestic manufacturer of telephone sets. However, the strong position of the firm changed dramatically in late 1982 after AT&T announced that it would reorganize its retail distribution of telephone equipment. Sales by Comdial to Bell Phone Centers dropped from $53 million in 1982 to $13 million a year later. Since these sales produced the highest margins, the effect on earnings was substantial.

9   The new Bell regional companies were legally forbidden to market new telephone equipment in 1983. The restriction was lifted after the January 1, 1984, divestiture of AT&T, and this was seen as a major opportunity for Comdial, as it hoped to supply the seven regional Bell operating companies (RBOCs) with telephone equipment. However, the retail telephone market was severely affected by heavy overstocking, primarily with imported products. Sales to the RBOCs dwindled as the regional companies failed to gain a strong position as distributors in the home phone market. As a consequence, during 1984 Comdial closed down its ATC operations in El Monte, California, and its manufacturing facilities in Upland, California, and put these properties up for sale. In addition, Comdial reduced its retail operations, American Phone Centers, from 19 stores to 11 stores in accordance with a change in primary focus from residential sales to small-business sales. As a further response to its challenging economic position, Comdial sold its overseas interest in HPF as well as its interest in the project with British Telecom.

Industry and Competition

10   The telecommunications industry, including telephone manufacturing, had experienced a dramatic increase in competition, changing distribution channels, and rapid technological innovation. The number of long-distance carriers and manufacturers of telephone systems had increased dramatically, spurring differentiation strategies based on cost, quality, and services offered.

11   The telephone manufacturing industry of 1985 could be broken down into three basic markets: (1) standard telephones, used by households and small businesses, (2) telephone systems for small businesses, and (3) large network systems ranging from a few hundred lines to more than 100,000 lines. International Telephone and Telegraph

(ITT) had emerged as the leader in the network systems market but also made significant sales to the household and small-business markets.

12   Comdial faced strong competition from two other domestic manufacturers as well, GTE and AT&T. AT&T marketed network systems to Bell Telephone companies, various long-distance carriers, and private businesses. AT&T was also established in the highly competitive and price-sensitive standard telephone business but was shifting its concentration to multifunctional home telecommunications systems. The Canadian Northern Telecom was also a rival in the systems market.

13   In addition, Comdial was facing increased Far Eastern competition in the standard telephone business, which was having an adverse effect on revenues because of reduced prices and volume. These low-cost products from the Far East were introduced in 1983 and quickly gained market share. Although the quality of these products was initially very poor, it had since been upgraded to meet or surpass that of domestic products while remaining significantly cheaper. Traditional products sold through supply distributors had been largely displaced by imports. Furthermore, domestic manufacturers had shifted much of their production overseas to take advantage of the cheaper labor. ITT imported from a Spanish subsidiary; AT&T had shifted manufacturing operations to Singapore; and GTE was purchasing products made in the Far East.

14   Rapid changes in technology and the pressure of increased competition, resulting in price wars and intensive cost-cutting efforts, had produced a shakeout in the industry—the profitable suppliers were becoming entrenched, while the nonprofitable ones were disappearing.

Operations

15   Comdial currently operated with 1,300 employees in a 500,000-square-foot facility in Charlottesville, Virginia. Only 40 percent of capacity was being utilized with production of 25,000–30,000 phones per week, down from 60,000–70,000 phones per week in 1983. Of the phones being produced, 12,500 were push-button models.

16   In 1985, the company had opened a new plant in the Shenandoah Valley. In order to utilize its excess capacity, Comdial was subcontracting for the Electrolux Corporation; basically, Comdial molded plastic for them. This was viewed as a possibly continuing trend, with several other subcontracting proposals on the drawing board.

17   The corporation manufactured its telephone terminal equipment by fabricating metal parts, molding plastics using injection machines, and automatically sequencing and inserting semiconductors onto printed wiring boards. Final assembly and testing was performed on mechanized conveyor lines. These processes required machinery costing more than $100,000.

18   Like the machinery, raw materials also came from many suppliers. These materials included raw plastic powder, ABS plastic, steel, aluminum, and nylon. Transformers, wiring boards, receivers, microphones, capacitors, diodes, and other hardware were typically purchased from suppliers, as it would have been too costly for Comdial to manufacture them. Upon arrival, all materials were thoroughly inspected by specification engineers to ensure top quality. The company had not experienced any significant production problems or delays due to shortages of materials or components.

19   All materials inventories were stored in the Charlottesville facility, with levels kept as low as possible. A 30-day supply of raw materials and a 2-day work-in-process

inventory were maintained. Finished goods were shipped as soon as they were completed.

Products

20 Comdial manufactured a full line of single- and multiline telephones. Beginning in 1985, it began supplying a variety of business systems, ranging from 2 central office trunks (a circuit between two exchanges) with 4 telephones to 20 central office trunks with 80 telephones.

21 Comdial's single-line telephones included the standard desk, wall, and rotary models and a standard desk telephone with a message-waiting flash and a flash for access to PBX features. A PBX (private branch exchange) is a switching exchange located on a site and used by that site. Also included was the "Maxplus" line of desk and wall phones with such features as speakerphone, message waiting, and the "Voice Express." The latter was a full-featured autodialer/speakerphone, which could be used as a single-line telephone or with an IA2 key system (a telephone system which could be programmed to automatically dial selected numbers—features normally included line pick-up, hold, recall, and intercom).

22 Comdial's multiline telephones included both the standard 6-, 10-, 20-, and 30-button phones used behind IA2 key systems, with a variety of new features and a new line of 6- and 10-button phones for use with the IA2 key systems and with features such as TAP (transfer access phone) and speakerphone.

23 Comdial's business systems included the "Maxplus II," a two-trunk system using central office or PBX power, which provided all the features of an IA2 key system except intercom. "Maxplus III" was a three-trunk and one-intercom system with all the functions of the standard IA2 system. One of the most popular was the "Executech Key System," which ranged in size from 3 central office trunks and 8 phones to 14 trunks and 32 phones. The standard system was alreayd full featured, with speakerphone as the only option. Comdial produced 200 of these systems a week. "Westars" was a hybrid key/PBX system that featured a least-cost routing and message accounting system at a competitive price, and "Tracs" was a least-cost routing and message accounting system designed to be added to already-existing key systems and PBXs.

Markets

24 Comdial marketed to both the residential and small-business areas. It sold most of its products through independent distributors, who sold to interconnects (sellers to final users who installed systems), and through independent telephone companies for lease or resale to end-users. The company also sold smaller quantities directly to the government and to manufacturers of PBX equipment. Comdial distributed residential telephone products primarily through the RBOCs, with which it acquired contracts in 1984. The company had wide distribution for its business systems through 10 of the major distributors of telecommunications equipment. In addition, Comdial had its own retail operation, American Phone Centers.

25 Comdial's sales were made monthly through short-term purchase orders issued by customers. The company also had long-term supply contracts with some of the RBOCs, although these contracts were nonexclusive.

26   Comdial was the only American manufacturer of single-line systems, which were used in both residential and business products. In the past, the company's business product line had been limited primarily to the standard single-line telephones and multiline telephone terminals for use with the key service units. The trend recently, however, had been away from plain old telephones (POTs) to more sophisticated, high-tech products. The company had also shifted its primary focus to the small-business product lines because of the deluge of cheaper foreign-made systems in the residential market.

27   Comdial's current marketing strategy was to focus on innovation, developing phones with more features in order to compete more effectively. The emphasis was on quality and customer service rather than price. By using a push–pull strategy emphasizing its quality product, competitive pricing, custom features, and prompt delivery, Comdial hoped to increase distribution channels and customer loyalty.

28   By March 1986, Comdial held 20 to 25 percent of the market for traditional phone products and about 10 percent of the key system market. There was great opportunity for growth in the telecommunications industry, especially with key system products. Figures from Dataquest Inc. (1986) indicated industry spending would increase more than 28 percent between 1985 and 1987, and over 38 percent of total sales would be attributed to key systems, PBX, and automatic call distributors.

Labor

29   In 1985, Comdial reduced the number of its employees from approximately 2,200 to 1,300, with most of the cuts coming from the manufacturing area. With these cuts, manufacturing employees currently outnumbered indirect or support personnel by a ratio of 3.5 to 1.

30   Wages for Comdial varied according to the task performed. On average, assembly workers were paid $5.65 per hour, with product specialists earning $9 per hour. Since these wages were relatively low for the Charlottesville area, an incentive plan was in effect. If a worker produced 124 percent of a set quota, he/she was paid 125 percent of the base salary. The employees viewed the quota as very achievable, with 90 percent of them exceeding the standard. The wages in the Shenandoah facility were, on average, $1 less per hour than at the Charlottesville facility. As a result, the most labor-intensive operations were performed at the Shenandoah site. While it could generally be said that Comdial operated with one shift, the capital-intensive machines operated with three shifts to gain fuller, more efficient usage.

31   Labor at Comdial was nonunionized, with the last major attempt to organize a union occurring five years ago. At that time, the workers voted the union down by a margin of 5 to 1. Based on the employees' actions, Comdial believed that its employee relations were generally satisfactory, and the company had experienced no work stoppages.

Financial Position

32   Comdial Corporation had suffered substantial operating losses since the divestiture of AT&T and the subsequent loss of sales to the Bell System. In 1982, the Bell System, Comdial's largest distributor, accounted for nearly one third of the company's sales.

Exhibit 1

COMDIAL CORPORATION
Selected Consolidated Statements of Operations Data
For the Year Ended December 31
(in thousands, except per share data)

	1981	1982	1983	1984	1985
Net sales	$ 6,669	$56,909	$141,860	$118,705	$ 85,196
Cost of sales	5,211	39,298	105,473	116,911	84,999
Gross profit	1,458	17,611	36,387	1,794	197
Marketing, administrative, and general expenses	3,175	10,644	22,151	23,446	17,372
Engineering, research and development	710	2,330	7,421	6,918	3,268
Earnings (loss)*	(4,035)	(665)	1,147	(39,423)	(30,500)
Earnings (loss) per share*	(0.69)	(0.08)	(0.07)	(2.53)	(1.76)
Weighted average shares outstanding	5,840	8,746	15,635	15,569	17,278

* Before extraordinary credit.

Selected Consolidated Balance Sheet Data
For the Year Ended December 31
(in thousands)

	1981	1982	1983	1984	1985
Working capital	$3,882	$30,246	$ 36,087	$ 41,141	$ (8,281)
Total assets	7,829	76,512	134,934	112,157	77,118
Short-term borrowings	350	359	36,200	8,768*	43,905*
Long-term debt	490	27,259	1,979	45,426	1,788
Stockholders' equity	3,100	29,589	79,135	43,097	20,074

* Includes current maturities on long-term debt.

Comdial sustained operating losses of approximately $39.5 million in 1984 and a further net loss of $30.5 million in 1985, as seen in Exhibits 1 and 2.

33   Cost-cutting efforts in 1985 were successful in decreasing the inventories from $43,025,000 on December 31, 1984, to $37,946,000 on September 27, 1985. However, the company's current ratio declined from a high of 3.1 on March 29, 1985, to a low of 0.98 at the end of the third quarter, and the quick ratio dropped to 0.35 from 1.07. Profitability continued to decline in 1985, and stockholders' equity had dropped from $79 million at 1984 year-end to $36.4 million at the close of the third quarter 1985. Comdial had managed to reduce its long-term debt from $49.4 million on December 31, 1984, to under $7 million after three quarters in 1985.

The Decision

34   As management examined the alternatives before them, Comdial faced an uncertain future. It had once been a growing and profitable company with subsidiaries around the world, but now it has been stripped of all but its strongholds in Virginia, and it

Exhibit 2

COMDIAL CORPORATION AND SUBSIDIARIES
Consolidated Statements of Operations

	Year Ended December 31		
(In Thousands Except Per Share Amounts)	1985	1984	1983
NET SALES:	$ 85,196	$ 118,705	$ 141,860
COST AND EXPENSES:			
Cost of sales	84,999	116,911	105,473
Engineering, research and development	3,268	6,918	7,421
Marketing, administrative and general	17,372	23,446	22,151
Minority interest in subsidiary	—	—	(98)
	105,639	147,275	134,947
EARNINGS (LOSS) FROM OPERATIONS	(20,443)	(28,570)	6,913
OTHER INCOME (EXPENSE)			
Equity in loss from Semiconductor operations	(2,429)	(4,682)	(4,384)
Equity in loss from European operations	—	(455)	(733)
Gain on disposal of European operations	4,537	—	—
Loss on disposal of Upland facility	(3,601)	—	—
Interest expense	(7,761)	(6,066)	(1,144)
Other income (expense)	(803)	350	2,541
EARNINGS (LOSS) BEFORE INCOME TAXES AND EXTRAORDINARY CREDIT	(30,500)	(39,423)	3,193
INCOME TAXES	—	—	2,046
EARNINGS (LOSS) BEFORE EXTRAORDINARY CREDIT	(30,500)	(39,423)	1,147
EXTRAORDINARY CREDIT - BENEFIT FROM TAX LOSS CARRYFORWARD	—	—	1,615
NET EARNINGS (LOSS)	$ (30,500)	$ (39,423)	$ 2,762
NET EARNINGS (LOSS) PER COMMON SHARE AND COMMON EQUIVALENT SHARES (1983)			
BEFORE EXTRAORDINARY ITEM	$ (1.76)	$ (2.53)	$ .07
EXTRAORDINARY ITEM	—	—	.11
	$ (1.76)	$ (2.53)	$ 0.18
WEIGHTED AVERAGE COMMON SHARES OUTSTANDING AND COMMON EQUIVALENT SHARES (1983)	17,278	15,569	15,635

See notes to consolidated financial statements.

Exhibit 2 *(concluded)*

COMDIAL CORPORATION AND SUBSIDIARIES
Consolidated Balance Sheets

ASSETS	December 31	
(In Thousands Except Par Value)	1985	1984
CURRENT ASSETS:		
Cash and short term investments	$ 3,758	$ 968
Accounts receivable (less allowance for		
doubtful accounts: 1985-$2,172; 1984-$2,806).	11,715	17,509
Inventories	30,112	42,682
Prepaid expenses and other current assets	1,002	2,746
TOTAL CURRENT ASSETS	46,587	63,905
INVESTMENT AND ADVANCES - SUBSIDIARIES	—	7,029
PROPERTY, PLANT AND EQUIPMENT - NET	25,481	30,563
ASSETS HELD FOR DISPOSITION	1,199	9,800
OTHER ASSETS	3,851	860
	$ 77,118	$ 112,157

LIABILITIES AND STOCKHOLDERS' EQUITY	December 31	
(In Thousands Except Par Value)	1985	1984
CURRENT LIABILITIES:		
Accounts payable	$ 4,613	$ 5,020
Accrued payroll and related expenses	1,897	1,765
Plant close-down accrual	—	1,592
Other accrued liabilities	4,244	5,313
Income taxes payable	209	306
Current maturities on long-term debt	43,905	8,768
TOTAL CURRENT LIABILITIES	54,868	22,764
LONG-TERM DEBT	1,788	45,426
MINORITY INTEREST AND OTHER		
LONG-TERM LIABILITIES	388	870
STOCKHOLDERS' EQUITY:		
Common stock $0.01 par value and paid-in capital:		
Authorized 25,000 shares; issued 17,975		
and 15,979 shares, respectively	98,331	91,249
Other	(1,397)	(1,792)
Accumulated deficit	(76,860)	(46,360)
TOTAL STOCKHOLDERS' EQUITY	20,074	43,097
	$ 77,118	$ 112,157

See notes to consolidated financial statements.

was carrying a heavy debt load into an uncertain, competitive environment. Should Comdial concentrate on a high-quality, high-service strategy and rely on "Made in America" patriotism to carry the company into a successful niche in the small-business market? Management knew that the firm would still have to produce its basic "plain old telephones." Often distributors demanded access to both POTs and to more complex systems when carrying a line for a manufacturer. But a niche strategy would depend on a large-scale movement toward that hybrid market. Otherwise, the firm would continue to flounder under low margins and unused capacity. But could Comdial, with its strained financial resources, really hope to establish itself, or would specialization prove fatal?

35   Moving operations overseas seemed to be an even riskier alternative. Though a lower-cost structure promised long-run price competitiveness, the firm would undoubtedly sustain additional losses in trying to move out of its domestic manufacturing operations. The Shenandoah plant could continue to serve the firm as corporate headquarters, a quality control and maintenance facility, and a place of storage for needed inventory; but, if production was to be moved to the Far East, the 500,000-square-foot Charlottesville facility would have to be disposed of, and how strong would the market be in an area that hosted only two other major manufacturing facilities? Further, could Comdial really hope to compete in the highly elastic, basic home phone market? In addition, how could creditors and stockholders be convinced to back such a major move when the company was already in a precarious situation?

36   Similarly, Westfall wondered how stockholders would react to an announcement of a new emphasis on subcontracting and, consequently, of a redefined company mission. After Comdial's stock price had dropped from a high of $33 per share to as low as $2.25 in just three years, would the stockholders' faith in management be sufficient to support a shift into various new areas of production? The move did seem to have real potential. Comdial had well-respected expertise in specialized plastic molding, and the venture with Electrolux had certainly proved successful. Further work in subcontracting would allow the company to put its equipment to use in a more profitable area, but could the firm afford to commit the resources necessary to attract sufficient interest? Did management have the ability to lead the firm into this new area?

37   The final alternative—entry into the higher-margin, big-business market—seemed very attractive from a financial standpoint. Though the firm had little experience in that area, it was an arena that had certain synergies with the markets the company was already in. Given the size of potential projects, a few major clients could significantly boost the firm's utilization of key resources. That market was a heavily competitive one, however, and it was currently dominated by much larger companies, such as Harris and ITT. Could Comdial find a niche among such industry giants?

38   The choice facing Comdial was not an easy one. Each option seemed full of danger, but failure to act could also prove fatal. The firm could not continue to sustain losses. Whatever it did, management knew that it would have to have the support of stockholders and creditors. The decision was a critical one. The survival of Comdial depended upon mapping out a successful direction for the future.

Case 7

EADCOR, A.G. (1985)

Our firm seems to be facing two crucial questions as we approach the late 1980s, and the answers to both will be instrumental in guiding our future posture in Africa. First, how can we as a private development bank (PDB) most effectively position ourselves to participate in the long-term economic changes in the equatorial region of Africa? Second, we're concerned about how we can best monitor and guide our lending, investment, and service activities from our headquarters here in Basle.

If your analyses reveal other equally important issues which I should pursue with our board of directors, I will naturally appreciate your assessment and suggestions!

1   With these general remarks, Rudolph Garner, president of EADCOR (Equatorial African Development Corporation), opened his first meeting with a consultant whom he hoped would be able to assist with any needed revisions to EADCOR's evolving strategy.

2   The private development banking industry was comprised of various institutions which could develop and promote, finance, and provide supportive services to bankable projects in various parts of the world. Funding syndication, project management, market research, and employee training were among the services provided by the PDBs.

Corporate Background

3   EADCOR was founded in the early 1970s by the Richland family, and other equity investments soon followed from major multinational corporations (MNCs) headquartered in Europe and the United States. The Richlands' wealth had been accumulated from international trading, manufacturing, and natural resource development, including mining in South Africa. Each of the several investors felt a substantial responsibility to aid in the economic development of equatorial Africa, but they also recognized that significant profits might eventually be earned by firms which knew the most effective ways to participate in such economic changes.

4   The investments of a few hundred thousand Swiss francs (one SF at the time = $.50 U.S.) from each MNC were relatively small in relation to their corporate size, but the combined resources thus available to EADCOR gave it the base for potentially significant participation in dozens of projects simultaneously. As a matter of practice, EADCOR sought to maintain less than a controlling equity interest in its projects in order both to stimulate local entrepreneurial initiatives and to simplify compliance with various countries' regulatory requirements.

5   The goals of EADCOR were known to be viewed somewhat differently by various constituents, but the executives felt that job creation, export enhancement, profitability,

Copyright © 1985. This case was prepared by Dr. John H. Grant as a basis for analysis and class discussion rather than to illustrate either effective or ineffective handling of a managerial situation; its preparation was made possible with the cooperation of IMEDE, Lausanne, Switzerland, and a firm which prefers to remain anonymous.

and public image were the prime criteria. Each project, however, could be seen as offering a potentially different mix of such payoffs.

6   During its initial years of operation, EADCOR's portfolio reflected a conservative investment philosophy and earned a steady stream of interest income, mostly from the United States and Europe. More recently, however, investments and loans to more than 30 projects across several countries in the equatorial region of Africa had resulted in some encouraging growth situations, but losses had been incurred on 6 projects. With total assets of SF76 million and revenue of SF8 million, the firm earned aftertax profit of SF800,000 in 1981.

7   EADCOR's initial image as being a "South African operation" because of close association with the Richland family had slowly faded, so the credibility of its involvement with Black African nations was beginning to improve.

8   The appropriate management processes and investment mix remained unclear, however, in part because of the differing perspectives between the branch offices in Zimbabwe and Swaziland and the headquarters in Switzerland.

Contrasting Business Contexts

9   The senior executives of EADCOR had been recruited from earlier careers in international business, with particular emphasis in banking. While they were familiar with the dynamic operating environments in equatorial Africa, they were also comfortable with the sophisticated banking environments in Zurich, London, and New York. The corporate offices were located in a modern, though not elegant, building in Basle's central business district, and the firm leased an apartment in a nearby hotel for use by visiting executives from out of town.

10   Various small businesses in Malawi, Kenya, and Swaziland faced numerous operating difficulties arising from erratic sources of material, changing government regulations, frequently untrained labor forces, and limited sources of equity capital. Attempts to coordinate the operating goals and results were often hampered by poor communications systems between the individual businesses, the regional office, and corporate headquarters.

11   Because some of the local managers had more political savvy than they had economic skills or concerns, they often misinterpreted the financial risks they were taking and the informational needs expected by the executives in Basle. Similar difficulties, of course, faced the managers of many competing intermediary institutions as they sought to provide similar services in developing countries.

"Intermediary" Institutions

12   The PDBs were but one of several types of organizations which provided competing and complementary services between the suppliers and users of financial capital. Intergovernmental organizations like the World Bank Group and the Arab Development Funds were instrumental in major projects. Various countries' banks and parastatal development finance institutions were focused toward specific geopolitical areas. On the other hand, foreign-based MNCs and private consulting firms tended to specialize

by tasks or industries. The PDBs thus were often seen as hybrid organizations which could provide both financial and managerial services to either established or newly developed firms.

13   Several PDBs operated in developing regions of the world (e.g., Latin America, Asia, and Africa). Operating with names like SIFIDA, FRIDA, ADELA, and PICA, such PDBs ranged in size from that of EADCOR to others seven times as large. The economic performance of these firms was very difficult to judge, however, because of the varying project relationships, timing of profit recognition, and methods of accounting.

14   Different intermediary institutions developed reputations and skills at various levels and degrees of efficiency. Performance could vary along dimensions such as responsiveness to local needs, capacity to attract foreign investment, management development, and skill in project identification and implementation. The various intermediaries could thus develop differential comparative advantages in various project settings.

15   One rather aggregate dimension along which the intermediaries differed was the extent of project participant interaction. For example, the World Bank Group and consultants tended to pursue a high degree of interaction with other supporting agencies, but most local banks and PDBs pursued little collaboration with related organizations.

16   The extent of assistance needed from development banking institutions tended to vary by a country's level of economic development. In the least developed countries, the investment opportunities (or "absorptive capacity") tended to be quite limited, but as development progressed, the need for supportive financial institutions increased. However, beyond a certain stage of sophistication, countries' markets for capital and services were so efficient that development banks became much less important. As different economic and political trends moved through sub-Saharan Africa, the demand for PDBs' services varied substantially.

Trends Affecting Equatorial Africa

17   While loans to businesses in sub-Saharan African countries had increased sixfold to a level of almost SF14 billion during the decade ending in 1980, the total private investment remained at slightly less than SF2 billion. At the same time, 75 percent of the latter funds were concentrated in Nigeria and the Ivory Coast. Such increases in funding could not realistically be expected to continue, however, because declining oil prices would cause some of the OPEC countries to become net users rather than investors or lenders of funds. In addition, slow economic growth in most OECD countries was leading those governments to reduce their overseas developmental assistance (ODA).

18   Within many of the equatorial African countries themselves, the general economic conditions were deteriorating, so equity investments often appeared less attractive. GNP per-capita growth had declined, export volume fell in absolute terms, and agricultural productivity was weak except for crops like rice. In some countries, loans had to be "rescheduled," so the banks developed even more conservative attitudes toward the region. The net effect of these trends was an increasing need for the types of intermediary services which PDBs could provide at a time when the potential suppliers had fewer resources or less economic incentive to participate in the development of such economies.

EADCOR's Operations

19   The diverse activities of the corporation remained highly centralized in the office of Rudolph Garner. Although some efforts had been made to delegate certain decisions, the vice president, Henry Reed, the various employees, consultants, and project managers continued to seek "Rudy's" input or agreement to many decisions. (Exhibit 1 presents the firm's organization chart.)

20   Between 1976 and 1982, EADCOR's project investments had become spread across more countries (see Exhibit 2), and commitments had increased in agricultural and industrial sectors at the expense of handicrafts (see Exhibit 3 for more detail). The processes for selecting projects varied substantially, with some being proposed by EADCOR's stockholders, others being recommended by the field offices, and still others arising from direct contacts with the corporate office by institutions and entrepreneurs in various countries.

21   The system for planning and control in use at EADCOR placed rather heavy reliance on financial forecasts and subsequent comparisons. Data for budgeting projections typically came from the field office, the existing or proposed project manager, and the corporate headquarters. The bases for differing projections from various sources

Exhibit 1

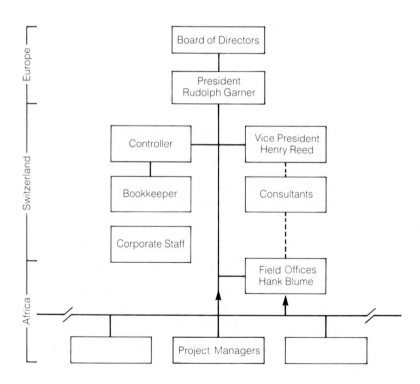

Exhibit 2

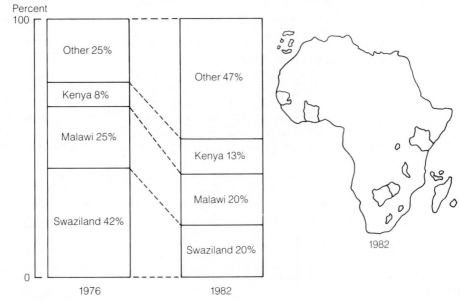

Source: EADCOR's project files.

were often not well documented, so the headquarters staff often made the final decisions regarding the project estimates, participation levels, and the like.

22   Recent experiences with the procedures revealed that the budgets sometimes were not fully consistent with the strategic plans for the projects. Further, budgetary changes for ongoing projects were often changed without there having been a thorough review of the related assumptions and controllable factors causing the changes. As Hank Blume explained, "These rather loose procedures reflect the fact that project managers' competencies are sometimes overestimated, government policies often change with virtually no notice, and expected materials are occasionally in very short supply." Coordination difficulty across the 30 existing projects was also seen as being particularly difficult because managers at different levels viewed the risks and potential payoffs much differently. For example, some project managers were willing to assume a "quick gamble with other people's money," while others were seeking to "save the economy of their village."

23   In Basle, the senior executives wanted to be able to demonstrate some genuine short-term progress toward their various goals so the stockholders would consider larger investments, but they simultaneously realized that the long-term employment and developmental objectives would be difficult to achieve.

24   While there were persistent problems with certain aspects of EADCOR's operations, Garner and Reed felt that substantial progress had been made in recent years, and

Exhibit 3

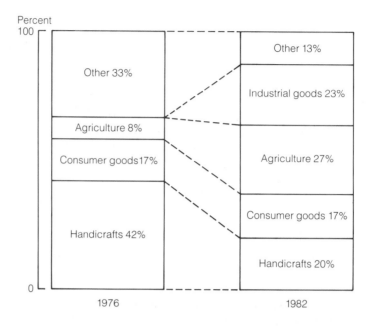

they were anxious that future changes build on past accomplishments rather than destroy them.

Future Directions

25   "Given the situation in which we find ourselves," commented Henry Reed, "it seems that we must incorporate several elements into our strategy, but the number of possible alternatives appears to be unlimited. This chart [see Exhibit 4] summarizes some of our thinking, but the weighting and timing of our efforts clearly must be added. Perhaps an entirely different approach would be even better."

26   EADCOR's executives realized that changes in their range of services could affect both their relative competency level as well as the risks they would be assuming. In addition, efforts to establish effective interaction with other agencies required substantial administrative effort, and such relationships often became specialized with regard to particular countries or types of business opportunities.

27   As various strategic alternatives and implementation systems were being considered, the possible economic consequences also had to be assessed. While the vast majority of EADCOR's income had always been in the form of interest, other PDBs had substantial portions of their revenues from service fees, operating income, and capital gains. Implicit in such results were differences in the depth, scope, and duration of involvement by the PDBs in particular projects.

28   "EADCOR must do more than just provide money," Garner observed as his meeting with the consultants drew to a close. "The countries need more than money if they are to develop. On the other hand, we've had more experience with complex financing

Exhibit 4

Elements	Alternative strategies	
	"Interaction" strategy	*"Wide-service" strategy*
Credibility (or reputation)		
Interaction with related organizations		
Technical competence in project management		
Size of bank		
Specialized services capability		
Acceptability in Africa		

than with the general management of projects. We have no advantage as consultants or teachers! Whatever you recommend, I'll want your advice about how to make it work, because we can all see that our present approach will be even less adequate in the future if we hope to grow."

Case 8

Sit 'n Pick Essential Products, Inc.

1   Ray Campbell sat back and admired his work. After months of redesigning he finally had the Sit 'n Pick to his satisfaction. The combination stool and pail looked good and was sturdy enough to hold a 300-pound person. The production problems were resolved. Now it was really up to his sister Carolyn to market his invention.

2   Ray had studied drafting in college before being persuaded to quit and go to work for his uncle in a family business. When embezzlement by the uncle caused the business to fail, Ray began working for Plastic Formers Company as the production plant manager. He frequently designed and constructed the plastic molds used in the company's production processes.

3   A dentist asked Ray to design a dome that could be used by dentists for protection when they were working with dangerous chemicals. Water accessibility and ventilation inside the dome were required. Ray designed a product that he demonstrated at a National Dental Association meeting. The product was instantly successful and was very profitable for the dentist, but Ray's salary at Plastic Formers did not change. He vowed to design a product that he could patent; something essential.

4   When Plastic Formers became erratic in paying him, Ray quit, bought a farm, and went to work as a quality control manager for a major electronics company. It was the farm that provided the impetus to develop Sit 'n Pick.

5   Ray's wife was plagued by a bad back and had difficulty picking the vegetables in their large garden on the farm. She asked Ray to build a bucket she could sit on. The result, after a number of modifications, was Ray's useful product that could be patented—Sit 'n Pick. (See Exhibit 1.)

6   The product is manufactured in a rotational mold. Four pounds of hot polyethelene are poured into the mold, which is then rotated to coat the inside. When the polyethelene is cooled, the mold is removed. One mold produces four Sit 'n Picks every 20 minutes.

7   Because the plastic is hard, Ray's wife suggested a pad be added to the seat. The center reinforcing bar acts as a built-in handle. Most people who saw it suggested that the only thing missing was a handle. Ray decided to add a label that identified the handle and also provided an address for the company.

HANDLE
Essential Products, Inc.
P.O. Box 519
Newell, North Carolina
28126

Source: A Case Research Association case. This case was prepared by Linda E. Swayne as a basis for class discussion rather than to illustrate either effective or ineffective handling of an administrative situation.

Exhibit 1
Sit'n Pick in use

8   Ray's sister, Carolyn Ward, was willing to take on the task of marketing Sit 'n Pick. She had experience in sales, first as a real estate agent and then with a producer of custom business magazines, where she was responsible for selling advertising space.

9   Now that the product was ready, Ray and Carolyn were trying to decide on a price. Ray spent his own money to incorporate, obtain the patent, and develop the product. (See Table 1.)

10   Ray wanted to manufacture Sit 'n Picks in his garage workshop, but it appeared that he would have to pay $5,500 yearly in insurance. A local manufacturer had the capability of producing Sit 'n Picks. Using one mold, the cost per unit would be $7.65. By purchasing additional molds at a cost of $1,000 each, the cost could be reduced to the amounts shown in Table 2.

11   Each Sit 'n Pick was made of 4 pounds of plastic at a cost of 60 cents per pound. Quantity discounts for the plastic were at such high levels that Ray didn't ever think

Table 1
Start-up costs

Incorporation fees and taxes	$ 552
Patent fees	650
Injection mold (additional molds $1,000 each)	1,621
Die to stamp pads (seat cushion)	80
Jigsaw to cut out pail piece	125
R&D	5,382
Prototype production	400
Total	$8,810

Table 2
Cost of producing

Number of molds	Per-unit cost
1	$7.65
7	6.25
10	5.00
12	4.16

they would buy enough to qualify. Therefore the minimum raw material cost was $1.60 per unit.

12   At lower levels of production, the machine retooling charge and labor were relatively high per unit, resulting in the $7.65 cost. If sales were good, Ray planned to buy more molds.

13   Other costs would be incurred in completing the product (see Table 3).

14   The seat pad was being cut out of polyurethane foam that was firm and tear resistant. If the density of the pad was reduced by 1 pound, the seat would be a little softer and slightly cheaper. The pad costs $.49 in material, $.011 in shipping to Charlotte, and $.05 tooling charge (actual charge, $15 per set-up), for a total of $.551.

15   The cost for glue, boxes, and instruction sheets would also fall if larger orders were placed. Costs were based on an initial production run of 250 units.

16   Other operating costs that were incurred include a warehousing charge, telephone, and product liability insurance (see Table 4).

17   Ray and Carolyn were very concerned about product liability. Ray designed the Sit 'n Pick to hold a 300-pound person in hot weather with the sun directly hitting it. The insurance company recommended the instruction sheet (disclaimer statement), which indicated Sit 'n Pick was not to be used by those weighing more than 300 pounds, and it was not to be used as a step stool. Actually the Sit 'n Pick was a

Table 3
Sit 'n Pick manufacturing costs

Unit to be picked up at plant	$7.65
Seat pad	.551
Glue to attach pad to seat	.20
Label to identify handle, manufacturer	.075
Mailing label	.02
Box for shipping	.67
Tape to close box	.03
Instruction sheet (includes disclaimers)	.126
Labor (pack, prepare; 100/hour)	.05
Transportation	.09
Actual product cost, ready to ship	$9.462

Table 4
Operating costs per month

Warehouse	$200
Telephone	65
Insurance	17.5
Office supplies	10
Total	$292.5

pretty handy stool as long as all weight was kept on the stool portion. Any shift of weight to the pail portion, because of its design, would cause the climber to fall. (See Exhibit 2.)

18   After figuring cost information, Ray and Carolyn had to determine the price they thought consumers would be willing to pay. A skimming strategy had definite appeal since Ray was interested in recouping his investment as quickly as possible. However, a plastic stool was selling for $3.79 at a typical discount store, and plastic buckets could be purchased for as little as 88 cents. A stool and bucket could cost $4.67, which is significantly *less* than Ray's production costs for a Sit 'n Pick. How much more would customers be willing to pay for the novel combination of a stool and bucket?

19   A critical decision in determining price was the target market. Will Sit 'n Pick be purchased by serious home gardeners and DIYs (do-it-yourselfers) for their own use, or will it be purchased as a gift? The individual buying the product for his or her own use would likely compare the cost of purchasing a stool plus a pail against the cost of Sit 'n Pick. A gift item, on the other hand, is more subject to specific price points—the customer is looking for a $10 gift, a $20 gift, or a $25 gift. The target market selected directly affects distribution and promotion decisions that had to be made.

20   Ray was certain that patent infringement could be easily avoided by simple modifications to his idea. He estimated that Essential Products would only have one season without direct competition. Mass producers of plastic products (such as Rubbermaid) would have significantly better marketing opportunities. The company needed to move quickly to get the product to the marketplace. Carolyn knew that if they sold through retailers, they would be able to speed up distribution. There were over 7,000 farm/ garden supply stores in 1982 and many more garden supply departments in discount and department stores (Table 5). A variety of merchant wholesalers, agents, brokers, commission merchants, and manufacturers' representatives were available to service the retailers.

21   If Essential Products were to use a channel of distribution rather than direct marketing, more decisions had to be made. Transportation charges, quantity discounts, cash discounts, functional or trade discounts, and promotional allowances had to be computed in the analysis to determine the price for Sit 'n Pick.

22   Postage and handling fees would be an additional cost to final consumers who purchased directly from Essential Products. This is a common practice in direct marketing, and customer resistance was not expected to the typical $2 postage and handling fee. However, transportation charges to channel members would vary considerably with the distance shipped. If they used delivered pricing (FOB destination), they had to

Exhibit 2
Sit 'n Pick instability

consider a single-zone or multiple-zone pricing policy. An individual Sit 'n Pick weighed 6 pounds, and a four-pack box weighed 27 pounds. The shipping charges from Newell, North Carolina, are illustrated in Exhibit 3 and Table 6.

23   In thinking about offering a quantity discount, Carolyn knew several questions had to be answered:

1. What would be the minimum quantity required before the discount would be applied?
2. How many quantity categories should be established for additional discounts on larger purchases?
3. What is the maximum quantity to qualify for additional discounts (maximum discount allowed)?
4. What should be the amount of discount for each category?

24   In the nursery/garden supply industry, quantity discounts are typically offered and vary from 8 percent to 15 percent for wholesalers and 33 percent to 50 percent for retailers. Wholesalers and retailers demand the larger discounts from smaller, lesser-known manufacturers.

Table 5
Retail farm/garden supply stores by size (1985)

Annual store sales	Number of retail stores	Total sales (in $ millions)
Less than $50,000	1,029	$ 27,557
$50,000 to less than $100,000	931	66,305
$100,000 to less than $250,000	2,076	343,804
$250,000 to less than $500,000	1,593	565,501
$500,000 to less than $1 million	1,083	739,839
Over $1 million	605	989,013
Total	7,317	$2,732,019

Source: *Statistical Abstract*.

Exhibit 3
Shipping charge zones from Newell, North Carolina

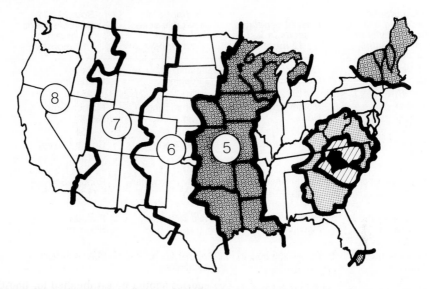

25   Cash discounts of 2/10, net 30 are commonplace in the nursery/garden supply industry. Carolyn thought Essential Products would probably have to match that discount.

26   Rather than using a longer distribution channel, Carolyn favored direct marketing
to consumers, either by direct mail or by the shopping section of *Southern Living* or
similar magazines.

27   According to Simmons Market Research Bureau, in 1984, 4 percent of the adult
population purchased gardening-related products by mail or phone. *Southern Living*
readers have a slightly higher usage of mail or phone. Six percent of *Southern Living*
readers have purchased gardening products by mail or phone over the last 12 months.

Table 6
Shipping charges for zones (1985)

Zone	6 pound		27 pound	
	Parcel post	Private carrier	Parcel post	Private carrier
1	$1.58	$1.57	$ 2.45	$ 3.30
2	1.74	1.57	2.92	3.30
3	2.04	1.89	3.85	4.54
4	2.50	2.30	5.18	5.83
5	3.18	2.59	7.20	7.08
6	3.92	2.98	9.38	8.82
7	4.74	3.39	11.60	10.64
8	6.49	3.82	16.99	12.56

Exhibit 4
Magazine readers' gardening activities (1985)

	Did outdoor gardening as a leisure activity in last 12 months	Bought vegetable seeds in last 12 months	Bought $10+ vegetable seeds in last 12 months	Bought $20+ vegetable seeds in last 12 months	Bought $20+ vegetable garden fertilizer in last 12 months
1.	Organic Gardening 187	Organic Gardening 137	Organic Gardening 210	Organic Gardening 251	Organic Gardening 166
2.	Sunset 171	Mother Earth News 109	Country Living 149	Mother Earth News 158	Popular Science 115
3.	Mother Earth News 154	Field & Stream 107	Mother Earth News 130	Country Living 139	Popular Mechanics 110
4.	Country Living 138	Sports Afield 103	Family Handyman 130	Popular Science 125	Country Living 110
5.	Popular Mechanics 128	Popular Mechanics 102	Field & Stream 118	Popular Mechanics 119	Family Handyman 105
6.	Better Homes & Gardens 125	Family Handyman 102	Popular Mechanics 111	Field & Stream 108	Mother Earth News 105
7.	Family Handyman 123	Mechanix Illustrated 102	Better Homes & Gardens 107	Family Handyman 101	Field & Stream 104
8.	Popular Science 119	Popular Science 102	Popular Science 106	Better Homes & Gardens 96	Better Homes & Gardens 95
9.	Outdoor Life 118	Outdoor Life 101	Sports Afield 105	Mechanix Illustrated 84	House Beautiful 95
10.	Field & Stream 118	Country Living 99	Outdoor Life 104	Southern Living 80	Sunset 99
11.	Southern Living 118	Better Homes & Gardens 97	Mechanix Illustrated 97	Sports Afield 76	Southern Living 88
12.	House Beautiful 116	Sunset 91	House Beautiful 82	House Beautiful 72	Sports Afield 88
13.	Mechanix Illustrated 112	Southern Living 88	Southern Living 75	Outdoor Life 62	Mechanix Illustrated 85
14.	Sports Afield 101	House Beautiful 77	Sunset 50	Sunset 11	Outdoor Life 81

Index of 100 =
Composition of   32.6%   46.3%   14.9%   5.6%   6.7%
Source: EMRB study, 1984.

Bought flower seeds in last 12 months	Bought $10+ flower seeds in last 12 months	Bought $20+ flower seeds in last 12 months	Bought trees, plants, seeds by mail in last 12 months
Organic Gardening 120	Country Living 167	Country Living 215	Organic Gardening 336
Sports Afield 108	Organic Gardening 162	Organic Gardening 155	Mother Earth News 314
Country Living 106	Better Homes & Gardens 122	Popular Science 147	Country Living 257
Popular Science 106	Popular Mechanics 122	Popular Mechanics 146	Popular Mechanics 189
Better Homes & Gardens 106	Popular Science 119	Family Handyman 140	Family Handyman 175
Mother Earth News 105	Family Handyman 117	Mother Earth News 133	Southern Living 149
Popular Mechanics 102	Mother Earth News 109	Mechanix Illustrated 124	Better Homes & Gardens 148
Field & Stream 101	Mechanix Illustrated 108	Better Homes & Gardens 115	Mechanix Illustrated 124
Sunset 100	House Beautiful 95	Field & Stream 104	House Beautiful 121
Outdoor Life 99	Field & Stream 95	House Beautiful 101	Outdoor Life 114
Family Handyman 95	Sports Afield 91	Sports Afield 101	Popular Science 110
House Beautiful 93	Southern Living 83	Southern Living 95	Sports Afield 109
Mechanix Illustrated 91	Outdoor Life 74	Outdoor Life 91	Field & Stream 100
Southern Living 90	Sunset 54	Sunset 43	Sunset 56
43.4%	8.6%	3.8%	4.0%

Table 7
Magazine circulation and cost comparisons for gardening-oriented publications (1985)

Magazine	Circulation	Cost of classified (one-half page, black and white)	Cost of display (one-third page, four color)
Better Homes & Gardens	8,058,839	$5,604.2	$35,221
Country Living	1,183,916	2,180	14,290
Family Handyman	1,204,148	1,305	8,950
House Beautiful	867,736	1,190	12,940
Mother Earth News	857,010	1,190	6,760
Organic Gardening	1,378,628	1,620	N.A.
Outdoor Life	1,514,660	1,500	12,210
Popular Science	1,803,994	2,205	13,675
Southern Living	2,253,569	1,700	15,920
Sunset	1,387,855	1,103.5	N.A.

Note: N.A. indicates not available.
Source: *Consumer Magazine and Agri-Media Rates and Data,* July 27, 1985.

28   Total adult subscribers were 2,253,000 in 1985; however, 6,488,000 adults were reached by the publication, which is food and gardening oriented for the South. *Southern Living* charged $1,700 for a 2¼-by-2-inch ad inserted one time. Camera-ready copy was required.

29   Recently information was received from another publication, *Organic Gardening,* which seemed like a better, less expensive alternative to *Southern Living.* Circulation and costs for selected magazines indicate that *Organic Gardening* could be a good choice (see Exhibit 4 and Table 7).

30   Carolyn felt that a national list of adults with gardening interests could be purchased from one of the many mail list suppliers for about $40 per thousand. The direct mail piece could be very simple and inexpensive or very "slick" (with color photos and special offers) at a higher price. The price that was determined for the product would affect the kind of direct mail piece that should be developed.

31   Everything seemed to revolve around the price for Sit 'n Pick. Carolyn favored a direct marketing strategy using classified sections of magazines and direct mail. She thought those customers would be willing to pay $19.95 for a Sit 'n Pick. Ray preferred using a longer channel of distribution (W–R–C) because Essential Products would sell in quantity to a few buyers, and Ray could use the cash flow to begin other products. Many issues had to be resolved, and quickly, if the product was going to be available for the spring start of the gardening season.

Strategy Implementation

Case 10

The Simons Lumber Company

Introduction

1   "I guess we are in a predicament that many of our competitors would envy," said Stephen Simons. "Our company's reputation is among the best in the industry, we make a respectable profit in both good and bad economic times, and we know our business, but it is very difficult to enlarge our niche without running into competition from a national wholesaler or manufacturer."

2   Simons had spent the past 16 years of his life in this company, although in the past 4 years he spent only 50 percent of his time at the business, having started an unrelated venture in 1982. Now, as this new venture was taking more of his time, Simons was trying to decide the best course of action for the lumber business. Whereas his father had focused on managing the "top line" of the income statement, Stephen Simons had focused primarily on the "bottom line." Stephen Simons now wondered whether his emphasis had been carried too far and if it was time for a change in focus. Should he try to plot a course of planned expansion or should he be content to continue dominating the niche the company now occupies? Given the difficulty of obtaining market information on a narrow product line in a limited geographic area, Simons is not even sure that his firm is dominating its selected niche. He thought his company

Exhibit 1

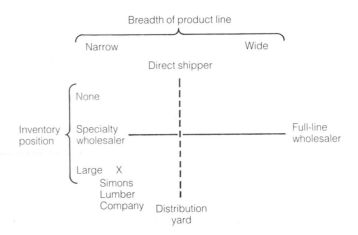

still had the largest market share in its products, but he suspected that position may be eroding.

The Wholesale Lumber Industry

3   Wholesale lumber companies provide the linking pin between the lumber producer and retailer or end-user of the lumber. These wholesale companies are generally small, family-owned businesses, although the past 20 years have seen the rise of larger national or regional wholesalers. Even the larger wholesalers tend to be privately owned, and currently only one lumber wholesaler's stock is traded publicly.

4   There are at least two dimensions on which lumber wholesalers may differ (Exhibit 1). The first dimension is the breadth of product line handled. Full-line wholesalers carry the entire spectrum of lumber and building products. Studs, plywood, and dimension lumber for building are major product lines for these firms. These products are often regarded as commodities, and the profit margin per unit may be extremely small; but the market for these products is large, and they tend to sell in large blocks. Given the financial resources and exposure in this type of business, full-line wholesalers tend to be larger than average in size.

5   As opposed to the full-line wholesaler, the specialty wholesaler has an extremely narrow product line, often only one or two products. Specialty wholesalers are generally found where there is a high degree of product or market knowledge required. Sales volumes are usually smaller for a specialty wholesaler, but markups are generally higher.

6   A second dimension that distinguishes wholesalers is their inventories. Direct shippers are wholesalers that seldom take physical possession of the products they sell. Their function is to obtain and order from a customer, place it with a mill for production, and the mill then ships it directly to the wholesaler's customer. A distribution yard wholesaler, however, maintains a physical inventory of the product line, in the geographic market where business is conducted. Because of the financial risk and require-

ments of maintaining a physical inventory, profit margins are generally considerably higher for a distribution yard wholesaler.

7   Some wholesalers (primarily distribution yards) add additional value to their products by remanufacturing or altering the size, shape, finish, and so on of certain products. It is much easier to enter the wholesale business as a direct shipper than as a distribution yard, because the requirements for entry are limited to mill and customer contacts, as well as credit line for working capital. Many wholesale lumber businesses are started by a sales representative leaving an established firm to start his own direct-shipper company. Often, if the new venture is successful, the new wholesaler will then add distribution yard facilities to his company.

8   In actual practice, the distinctions between direct shippers and distribution yards should be considered a continuum since many companies may have both direct and distribution yard sales. The 1982 Census of the Wholesale Trade showed 1,317 lumber wholesalers without a yard (direct shippers) and 1,950 wholesalers with a yard (distribution yards).

9   The North American Wholesale Lumber Association reported that a survey of its members for 1983 showed that average sales per distribution yard were approximately $6.5 million, a 26 percent increase over the previous year. The average sales of the membership companies (both direct and distribution yards) were approximately $21 million in 1983.

10   The industry still depends heavily on person-to-person contact for developing relationships between customers and suppliers. Wholesalers maintain lists of active, inactive, and potential customers, which are then used by their sales representatives to solicit orders. While face-to-face contact was once the most prevalent method of soliciting business, telephone contact is now far more prevalent given the cost of travel. One wholesale trade association survey estimated the average lumber wholesaler's telephone expense during 1983 was $84,000. Obviously, the telephone expense is dependent on the intensity of the firm's marketing area and its geographic trading area.

11   Inasmuch as lumber is an undifferentiated product, suppliers in this industry compete heavily on price and service (product expertise, advantageous delivery schedules, etc.). Those products which are regarded as commodities, such as 2x4s and plywood, are exceedingly price sensitive, and most customers have little loyalty to a particular manufacturer or wholesaler. Specialty items are somewhat more differentiated, and a customer may be dependent on a wholesaler for highly technical information. Brand or supplier loyalty is somewhat greater in this class of product.

12   The major market for lumber in the United States is the housing industry, and the wholesale lumber industry shares many characteristics with it. First, housing demand is highly interest rate sensitive. Generally, when mortgage rates increase, the demand for new housing falls. Thus, given the swings in interest rates, both the housing and lumber markets are highly cyclical.

New housing units started 1977–1984 (in thousands)

1978	1979	1980	1981	1982	1983	1984
2,036	1,760	1,313	1,100	1,072	1,712	1,753

13   While demand for lumber may be cyclical, there have been certain changes in the industry in the past 10 years that have affected competition. With energy costs increasing through the 1970s and freight carriers deregulated in the 1980s, the cost of transportation became a significant portion of the lumber cost. Many wholesalers, especially those dealing in price-sensitive commodity items, found it necessary to add a traffic manager to their staffs in order to remain competitive. Increased transportation costs also led wholesalers to focus on species of lumber that were geographically closer to the consuming market. In the last 20 years, the amount of lumber from the Pacific Northwest that shipped to markets east of the Rockies declined dramatically, while southern pine and eastern Canadian woods increased their market share in the eastern half of the United States.

Company History

14   In 1894 Robert Simons joined with partner Bernard Taylor to open a lumberyard in downtown Baltimore. With a small inventory and two delivery wagons, the two men soon prospered. After 15 years of successful operation, Simons bought out Taylor to establish Robert Simons & Sons. The company followed a typical growth path for a lumberyard; that is, serving a wider and larger range of customers. Individual consumers, building contractors, and, later, industrial accounts were sought. As the company entered the 1920s, its customer base was centered around the building contractor and industrial trade. This period of prosperity led to profitable years at the company, but Simons' son, who was now president, followed the same conservative financial methods as his father. Thus, the Great Depression was a serious, but not catastrophic, event for the company.

15   By World War II, the company entered its fastest growth period, supplying material for the war effort. Its largest single customer was the federal government, with large contractors and shipbuilders making up the balance. As the war ended, the nation's attention turned to home building. The pent-up demand during the Depression and the war years produced a huge surge in building, and, by this time, the company had evolved into a large, full-line retailer, carrying the inventory of plywood, studs, roofing materials, etc., as well as a wholesale supplier of timbers to other retail lumber companies within a 50-mile radius.

16   As the 1950s ended, the third Simons to manage the company was facing increasing competitive pressure from much larger retail lumber companies. Sales volume was at a record high for the company, but profits were down due to margins eroding under competitive price cutting. Since Simons was well known and respected by the lumber retailers (he had just completed a three-year term as president of their national trade association), he decided to eliminate the high-volume, high-exposure retail business and concentrate on wholesaling or supplying the needs of his former competitors. A year after the switch was made, annual sales had dropped 70 percent, with profits down 10 percent.

17   The business continued basically unchanged through the 1960s until 1969, when the fourth Simons joined the company as a salesman. The difference between the two generations was apparent by the approach each took to the company. The elder Simons focused on sales and customer relations, even though many of the sales were not very profitable. The younger Simons concentrated on smaller, high-profit segments of the market. Profits, not total sales, was the emphasis of the young Simons. At that time, the company's customer base was approximately 40 percent retail yards and 60 percent large contractors and industrials. Throughout the early 1970s, the company focused on developing the higher-margin retail lumber customer and de-emphasizing the contractor business, where sales were always subject to competitive bidding. The geographic trading area was expanded to a 200-mile radius of Baltimore. Products were added that were more architectural and less industrial in nature.

Organization/Management

18   The company is currently managed by the fourth generation of the Simons family, Stephen Simons. Simons had spent his entire adult life in the business, with the exception of the period he was away working toward a graduate degree. The small size of the company prevented even a functional organization, since each employee had to be able to do several jobs, which might have been unrelated. The office was located in suburban Baltimore, and at this location were the president, the two inside salespeople, and a secretary. Simons handled all of the purchasing and financial duties as well as those sales calls which required engineering or technical information. Karen Welsh and Jane Watson, the two salespeople, handled the more routine orders and inquiries as well as shipping details. Mrs. Welsh and Mrs. Watson had both started with the company as secretaries approximately six years ago. As they became increasingly familiar with the company's customers and products, they began to assume increasing sales responsibilities. The secretary/bookkeeper took care of general office work and the operation of the company's minicomputer.

19   The yard and sawmill were located on an eight-acre site in an industrial section of Baltimore. Over the years, the market value of this property had increased dramatically, and Simons wondered whether it was still economically feasible to operate a lumber company from this site. The property consisted of the building where the millwork machines were housed and another small storage building where some of the finished lumber was stored. Most of lumber was stored outside, and the lack of inside storage had limited the types of products which the company could consider carrying in its inventory.

20   The yard foreman and six workers were employed at this location. Joe David, the yard foreman, had been employed by the company for 10 years, having taken over from a predecessor who had been there for 40 years. David was given a great deal of discretion in the operation of the yard. Unless there was a special requirement, David scheduled all production as well as maintained the elderly and specialized sawmill machines. He was generally responsible for the hiring, management, and discipline of six subordinate employees.

21   The company enjoyed a high degree of loyalty from most of its employees. The office salespeople and the yard foreman received annual bonuses based on the company's profit, and, in good years, these bonuses were in the range of 25 percent of base salary. Unlike a large number of its competitors, the company did not lay off its yard employees during the slow winter months, and Simons believed this steady employment policy helped maintain the workers' loyalty. The company also contributed a certain amount to a qualified profit-sharing trust for the employees' retirement.

Corporate Philosophy

22   In its long history, the company had gone through several expansions/contractions, yet its objective had always been to focus on high-profit and fairly small types of markets, where its flexibility and ability to provide specialized service allowed it to compete successfully. Simons' philosophy had been to avoid marketing wars with major wholesalers and manufacturers and to compete in those market segments which appeared too small or unattractive to its bigger competitors. When Simons Lumber shifted from a retailer to a wholesaler in the late 1950s, the company adopted a policy of not competing with its customers. This policy, which had earned it a high degree of customer loyalty, had also had its costs. On a number of occasions, Simons had lost orders to other wholesalers who bid the job direct to the contractor (thus eliminating the retailer). During the 1960s, Stephen Simons had considered buying a treating plant, which chemically preserved the lumber. Simons correctly believed that this field was a high-growth area but did not follow through with the acquisition because it would have meant competing with one of the company's largest customers at the time. As it turned out, this customer was later lost, and Simons regretted not having entered the treating business.

23   In terms of financial philosophy, Simons had always followed a conservative path. For the past several years, the company had carried no long-term debt, and generally has retained almost all of its current earnings each year.

24   Through its philosophy of operating in sheltered niches, as well as its highly conservative financial posture, Simons Lumber had always generated a profit and seldom, if ever, incurred a loss.

Product Line

25   The company marketed three main types of products: timbers, laminated beams, and roof decking. As of 1984, timbers, laminated beams, and decking accounted for 50 percent, 35 percent, and 15 percent of total sales, respectively. These products were used on expensive single-family construction as well as commercial buildings. The timbers were generally used for structural purposes, such as exposed beam ceilings. Simons bought this material from lumber mills in the Pacific Northwest and often remilled the lumber to the customers' specifications. Although the timbers carried a high profit margin, they also had high handling and manufacturing costs associated with them. Demand for this product had been fairly stable over the past 10 years and had shown very little growth.

26   The laminated beams were used in applications very similar to that of the solid-sawn timbers, but the laminated beams (or glulams) offered significantly greater strength than a solid-sawn timber and had greater dimensional stability and aging characteristics. These advantages had a price, however, in that a laminated beam was about 50 percent more expensive than a comparable piece of solid-sawn timber. Generally speaking, glulams were used in more contemporary types of architecture, whereas solid-sawn timbers were seen in more rustic or traditional structures. The market for laminated beams had grown steadily over the past five years, even with the entry of new competitors.

27   Roof decking was a product that was generally applied over exposed beams to form the ceiling of the structure. After the decking was nailed down, insulation and roofing shingles were applied to complete the roof of the structure. Decking was produced in a variety of sizes and grades, but Simons carried only the premium grades since the appearance of the ceiling was so critical in these applications.

Marketing Promotion

28   The marketing effort of Simons Lumber Company was concentrated in the Middle Atlantic area of the United States. Because lumber had a fairly high weight-to-value ratio, freight costs made it difficult for the company to be competitive much more than 250 miles from its distribution yard. The company's primary customers were retail lumber dealers. While chain retailers bought from the company, approximately 80 percent of the company's sales were to independently owned retail lumber dealers. When a builder needed a timber-type product, he generally contacted the lumber retailer who was supplying the other construction lumber on the job. This retailer then asked for quotations from suppliers like Simons.

29   Up until the 1960s, the geographic scope of the business was limited enough that personal sales calls were the main thrust of the company's marketing effort. As the geographic area expanded, customers were seen personally on a less frequent basis and increasing emphasis was placed on telephone sales. The bulk of the telephone contacts consisted mainly of order taking; that is, quoting price and availability to customers. Technical or large jobs were handled either by Stephen Simons or the senior salesperson. Simons was worried that too much of the telephone contact was coming in from the customers, rather than being initiated by his sales personnel. While he had sent the two sales people to several telemarketing seminars sponsored by the telephone company, outgoing calls generally increased for a time and then subsided.

30   Advertising the company and its products had been frustrated by the lack of an effective medium for this effort. Until very recently, there was no publication for the wholesale trade that focused on the company's geographic area. The use of a national publication was judged too costly to be effective. For these reasons, the company had relied on exhibiting at the one annual trade show that was located in the Middle Atlantic market as well as using direct mail. The direct-mail efforts, undertaken on a somewhat sporadic basis, had generally been successful in temporarily increasing the sales of existing products, but Simons realized that these efforts must be more consistent and regular if they were to have a major and long-lasting effect. At the current time, Simons had initiated a program of a direct mailing to retail lumber dealers on a once-a-month level of frequency. Additionally, the two salespeople had been assigned a number of accounts, which they were to contact and solicit on a regular basis.

A Look at Competitors

31   While competition was keen in the wholesale lumber industry, the niches in which the Simons Company operated were somewhat protected. The company did, however, face different competitors in each of its product lines.

32 Over the past 15 years, the number of competitors in the timber portion of the business had declined. Major competitors in New York and Washington failed in the last housing recession. While some benefit accrued to the company from the failings of its competitors, direct shippers and new products prevented this occurrence from being a major windfall. The increasing popularity of treated yellow pine timbers had resulted in the loss of market share in certain very small timber sizes. Likewise, a large national wholesaler had started to carry a small inventory of popular-size timbers that cost significantly less than Simons'. While the quality of the competitor's timber was so much lower that they could not be used for exposed applications, the competitor's cost advantage had resulted in the loss of a certain amount of business where the appearance of the lumber was not important. Finally, packaged home kits which featured exposed beams had also increased competition for Simons since some homebuyers opted for a packaged home, which did not contain Simons beams, rather than a custom-built home, which Simons might have been able to supply.

33 In the laminated sector of the market, the company had competed with several of the largest wholesalers in the country who operated in the Baltimore area over the past 15 years only to see these wholesalers exit the market in disarray. While laminated beams carried a high profit margin, this product normally sold in fairly small quantities (compared to the commodity products these wholesalers were used to) and required a substantial amount of technical expertise and advice. The most successful competitor, Rogers Supply, was another small (but larger than Simons) wholesaler located approximately 60 miles away. Like Simons, this wholesaler supplied a quality product and technical information; but, unlike Simons, Rogers distributed the product to anyone, retailer or builder. While Rogers' distribution technique angered retailers who may have been eliminated from a sale, these retailers often continued to buy from Rogers if the price was advantageous.

34 Competition in the decking market depended on the size and grade of decking being considered. Of the three products that Simons handled, decking had less value added than any of the other products and was considered by some to be almost a commodity product. For this reason, profit margins were about half of what Simons received on its other two product classes.

35 Two-inch-thick decking constituted the majority of decking sales in the Simons' market area, and this product was carried by a number of small and large competitors. Especially in the lower grades, competition was fierce, and price alone often determined which supplier got the order. Simons concentrated on the premium appearance grade of decking, which highly complimented the timbers and beams that it sold. The competition was somewhat less rigorous than in the lower grades, and profit margins were better, although total sales volume was smaller.

36 A smaller portion of the total decking market was 3-inch-thick decking, which was used on very large residential jobs as well as commercial construction. Simons was one of the few wholesalers in the area to stock this product, and when small quantities were needed or the material was needed rapidly, Simons had little competition. On larger jobs (a truckload or more) when the material was not needed immediately, Simons faced competition from direct-shipment wholesalers and from the lumber manufacturers themselves. Whereas a sale from inventory carried a markup of 15 to 20 percent, a direct sale often carried a markup of 5 percent or less, depending on the order size. Simons often quoted the larger jobs on a direct-shipment basis, but the main focus had been on the smaller orders where little competitive pressure exists.

Financial Information

37   The stock of the company was owned by Stephen Simons (33 percent) and his father (67 percent). While the elder Simons had not been active in the company since his retirement 13 years ago, he controlled the majority of the stock and still came to the office every day. Any major changes in the company's operations had to meet with his approval.

38   Stephen Simons had found it difficult to assess the company's performance relative to its competitors. Since most of its competitors were closely held, there were few financial comparisons available, and much of the data published in secondary sources were based on companies that are very different in size, geographical scope, and product specialization. During the late 1970s, the industry trade association collected information from member companies and published averages that Simons found very useful. These reports showed that, compared to industry averages, Simons Lumber had lower total sales per employee, a lower growth rate, and among the highest gross margin per employee and the highest return on sales. Simons found this data very useful, but the reports were discontinued in 1982 because so few wholesalers were willing to release sensitive financial information.

39   The company had always followed a conservative financial policy. Suppliers had always valued their relationship with the company, since it had discounted every invoice since its founding. At the present time, the conservative financial posture had become dysfunctional. The company, like other closely held firms, had seldom paid a dividend. Until 1975, earnings were small enough that this did not pose a problem. However, the past 10 years had seen a large increase in the level of earnings without a corresponding increase in cash usage. Now, the IRS was suggesting that the amount of cash retained was unreasonable and wanted the company to pay a sizable dividend.

40   Income statements and balance sheets for the past five years are presented in Exhibits 2 and 3. Several facts should be noted about the financial statements:

1. Starting in 1984, purchase discounts were netted against the company's purchases, rather than presented separately.
2. The pension expense represents payments to employees who retired prior to the inception of the current pension plan.
3. Federal and state taxes are not a constant percentage of profits due to various credits and adjustments.
4. Inventory values are calculated on a LIFO basis.
5. The life insurance figure is the cash surrender value of policies on the officers.

Future Outlook

41   The future of the Simons Lumber Company is highly dependent on the choices made in the next year. Given the fairly stable nature of the company's products and personnel, Simons is reasonably confident that the company can continue to earn a satisfactory profit over the next five years with minimal supervision on his part. On the other hand, expansion would dictate many major changes in personnel and the way the company currently operates.

Exhibit 2

	1981	1982	1983	1984	1985
Assets					
Current assets:					
Cash	$ 148,213	$ 250,524	$ 599,944	$ 695,267	$ 418,391
Marketable securities	423,102	401,362	135,645	180,006	1,048,743
Accounts receivable/trade	154,242	220,227	146,880	161,234	189,082
Accounts receivable/other	14,366	23,741	94,688	95,638	100,825
Inventory	529,948	582,436	427,128	515,288	505,727
Life insurance	120,777	141,824	166,546	296,334	313,962
Total current assets	1,390,648	1,620,112	1,570,831	1,943,767	2,567,731
Fixed assets (net):					
Land	158,460	158,460	85,500	85,500	85,500
Buildings	0	0	0	0	0
Machinery and equipment	54,857	61,617	47,150	37,797	36,072
Transportation	70,999	64,192	12,067	7,148	0
Office fixtures	17,301	13,384	16,944	4,830	6,264
Total fixed assets	301,617	297,652	161,662	135,274	127,836
Total assets	$1,692,265	$1,917,765	$1,732,492	$2,079,041	$2,704,566
Liabilities and Stockholders' Equity					
Current liabilities:					
Accounts payable—trade	$ 300,711	$ 359,026	$ 15,861	$ 28,624	$ 284,939
Accrued salaries	52,060	33,964	0	121,410	220,362
Federal and state taxes payable	11,353	(276)	42,839	27,090	26,344
Accrued profit-sharing pay	34,200	34,200	11,400	57,000	45,600
Total current liabilities:	398,324	426,915	70,101	234,124	577,245
Stockholders' equity:					
Preferred stock (2,394 shares 7% cumulative—$100)	239,400	239,400	239,400	239,400	239,400
Common stock (978 shares outstanding)	185,820	185,820	185,820	185,820	185,820
Retained earnings	868,722	1,065,630	1,237,172	1,419,697	1,702,102
Total stockholders' equity . .	1,293,942	1,490,850	1,662,392	1,844,917	2,127,322
Total liabilities and stockholders' equity	$1,692,265	$1,917,765	$1,732,492	$2,079,041	$2,704,566

Exhibit 3

	1981	1982	1983	1984	1985
Sales	$2,441,559	$2,478,704	$2,115,194	$2,808,037	$3,124,242
Cost of goods sold	1,576,373	1,614,939	1,241,359	1,734,360	1,998,253
Gross profit	865,186	863,765	873,835	1,073,677	1,125,989
Yard expenses:					
Payroll and payroll taxes . .	175,750	176,700	176,493	185,820	193,840
Maintenance	38,243	25,095	18,445	20,340	51,619
Delivery expenses	8,370	11,558	12,470	2,544	4,590
Gas and oil	14,343	19,492	16,205	16,958	16,931
Electricity	6,998	6,205	6,283	8,402	9,893
Depreciation	30,997	50,287	31,445	26,408	22,813
Total yard	274,700	289,338	261,341	260,471	299,687
Administrative expenses:					
Payroll and payroll taxes . .	198,489	218,198	218,717	267,803	267,030
Group insurance	19,521	22,215	26,963	22,048	16,942
Office rent	10,501	12,369	13,994	15,650	16,255
Office supplies	16,781	11,290	15,324	13,631	21,307
Advertising	3,350	3,002	1,395	1,132	1,845
Insurance	38,663	40,157	38,293	33,953	24,229
Professional expenses . . .	3,040	3,059	8,797	5,206	10,606
Local taxes	7,877	8,170	8,512	8,989	10,784
Travel and entertainment . .	23,839	16,199	10,456	2,504	1,628
Dues and subscriptions . . .	7,230	5,974	6,625	5,273	5,666
Contributions	276	243	190	8,398	846
Pension expense	70,161	78,181	83,706	87,231	90,223
Profit-sharing expense . . .	34,200	34,200	11,400	57,000	45,600
Interest expense	5,200	5,210	5,341	5,105	0
Telephone	15,130	17,961	20,281	21,709	22,637
Bad debts	1,102	10,406	950	561	1,353
Miscellaneous expense . . .	4,342	0	0	0	0
Total administrative . . .	459,701	486,833	470,942	556,193	536,950
Operating profit	130,785	87,594	141,552	257,013	289,353
Other income:					
Interest income	65,092	83,249	67,097	80,186	99,058
Rental income	25,080	23,370	18,240	1,520	0
Purchase discounts	29,826	31,160	26,828	0	0
Miscellaneous	2,784	5,159	(2,831)	5,360	3,612
Total other income	122,782	142,937	109,334	87,066	102,670
Net profits before taxes	253,566	230,531	250,886	344,079	392,023
Federal and state taxes	39,900	42,231	51,602	44,916	47,500
Net profits after taxes	$ 213,666	$ 188,300	$ 199,283	$ 299,163	$ 344,523

Organizational chart

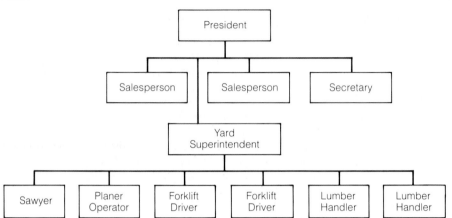

Case 11

Citicorp: British National Life Assurance

1   Ira Rimerman, group executive, Consumer Services Group, International, Citicorp, was in his third-floor office at Citicorp's headquarters in New York City on January 16, 1986, when he received notice from the board of Citicorp that his MEP (major expenditure proposal) to acquire the British National Life Assurance Company, Ltd. (BNLA), in England had been approved. For a total investment of $33.3 million, Citicorp was now in the life underwriting business.[1]

2   Although pleased with the board's approval, there were several issues on Mr. Rimerman's mind as he thought back over the last few months when his staff analyzed and developed suggestions for a business strategy for BNLA, including key policies, tactics, and organizational changes.

Citicorp's History

3   Citicorp's corporate history spanned 175 years, from its early inception as a small commercial bank in New York City in 1812 through its growth into one of the world's largest financial services intermediaries. A recurring historical theme seemed to be the firm's ability to correctly identify the developing trends in the marketplace and to devise appropriate strategies for taking advantage of them.

4   The firm first emerged as a significant bank in the latter part of the 19th century by responding successfully to the transition of the United States from an agricultural to an industrial economy. Since the mid-1960s, the firm had transcended the corporate treasurer and the metropolitan New Yorker as its sole funding sources and found ways to attract the more than $1.5 trillion consumer savings market in the United States.

5   During the 1960s and 1970s, Citicorp completed two separate but integral strategic efforts that revolutionized the company and influenced the whole financial services industry. First, in 1967, the firm formed a bank holding company, which permitted it to broaden its geographic and product bases. Second, in the early 1970s, it redefined its business from a U.S. commercial bank with branches abroad to a global financial services enterprise with the United States as its home base. By 1980, the firm had further broadened its scope by defining its business as that of providing services and information to solve financial needs. Exhibits 1 and 2 provide a summary of the firm's financial profile.

Citicorp's Strategy

6   The firm's strategic plan called for three separate kinds of world-class banks, all of which could leverage off an unrivaled global network. By the mid-1980s, the Investment

---

This case was prepared by Professors John M. Gwin, Per V. Jenster, and William K. Carter of the University of Virginia.

[1] All financial information related to BNLA has been changed for proprietary reasons.

Exhibit 1
Citicorp and subsidiaries—revenues earned and rates of return achieved

	Revenues ($ billions)	ROA (percent)	ROE (percent)
1981	$4.0	.46%	13%
1982	5.1	.59	16
1983	5.8	.67	16
1984	6.6	.62	15
1985	8.5	.62	15

ROE = (Net income − Preferred dividends)/Average common equity.
ROA = Net income/Average total assets.
Source: 1985 Annual Report of Citicorp.

Exhibit 2

CITICORP AND SUBSIDIARIES
Consolidated Balance Sheet
For the Year Ending December 31
(in billions of dollars)

	1985	1984
Assets		
Cash, deposits with banks, and securities	$ 40	$ 31
Commercial loans	$ 58	$ 59
Consumer loans	55	43
Lease financing	3	2
Allowance for credit losses	1	1
Net	115	103
Premises and other assets	18	17
Total	$173	$151
Liabilities		
Deposits	$105	$ 90
Borrowings and other liabilities	42	39
Long-term debt	16	13
Capital notes and redeemable preferred	2	2
	165	144
Stockholders' Equity		
Preferred stock	1	1
Common stock	1	1
Additional paid-in capital	1	1
Retained earnings	5	4
	8	7
Total	$173	$151

Source: 1985 Annual Report of Citicorp.

Exhibit 2 (concluded)

CITICORP AND SUBSIDIARIES
Consolidated Income Statement
(in billions of dollars, except per-share amounts)

	1985	1984	1983
Interest revenue	$19.5	$18.2	$15.2
Less: Interest expense	14.0	13.9	11.2
Provision for credit losses	1.3	.6	.5
Net	4.2	3.7	3.5
Other revenues	3.0	2.3	1.8
	7.2	6.0	5.3
Operating expenses	5.5	4.5	3.7
Income before income taxes	1.7	1.5	1.6
Income taxes	.7	.6	.7
Net income	$ 1	$ .9	$ .9
Earnings per share:			
Common and equivalent	$ 7.12	$ 6.45	$ 6.48
Fully diluted	7.11	6.36	6.15

Source: 1985 Annual Report of Citicorp.

CITIBANK AND SUBSIDIARIES
Consolidated Balance Sheet
(in billions of dollars)

	1985	1984
Assets		
Cash, deposits with banks, and securities	$ 40	$ 28
Loans and lease financing, net	75	69
Premises and other assets	16	15
Total	$131	$112
Liabilities		
Deposits	$ 92	$ 78
Borrowings and other liabilities	29	26
Long-term debt	3	2
Stockholders' Equity		
Capital stock	1	1
Additional paid-in capital	1	1
Retained earnings	5	4
Total	$131	$112

Source: 1985 Annual Report of Citicorp.

Bank, also known as the Capital Markets Group, enabled the firm to fully intermediate the capital flows of the world, with over $6 billion in transactions in the swap market. The Institutional Bank was the principal supplier of financial service mechanisms to corporations and governments worldwide. Finally, the Individual Bank served the individual consumer on a worldwide basis.

7   Walter B. Wriston, former chairman of Citibank/Citicorp, explained the firm's strategy:

> Over time, it seemed to us, the institution without access to the consumer would slowly become an institution without adequate funding. In addition, consumer-led economic recoveries are becoming more the rule than the exception, and we looked for ways to participate. For all of these reasons, you have often heard about this consumer transition and the identification of the consumer as a key to our strategy in the middle 70s. It was usually described as risky, but there are also risks in doing nothing.[2]

8   The holding company structure was used to overcome the geographic constraints of the domestic businesses. It also allowed for a few acquisitions and for the creation of de novo units to build a global network which, among other things, featured a unique competitive franchise for bank cards within the Individual Bank. Wriston also remarked:

> It costs about $150 per year to service an individual through a branch system. That number plummets to $20 if we use the credit card as our primary delivery vehicle. In short, through fees and merchant discounts, the card as a stand-alone product is a profitable endeavor. By the 1990s, it may well become the core delivery mechanism when augmented by automatic teller machines and home banking. . . . We envision a world of 35 million Citicorp customers producing earnings of $30 per customer. . . . We had big plans for this group when it started, and we can now see a time by which it will become a billion-dollar business.

9   The 1980s also dictated a new philosophy, which differed from traditional bank practice and from the media's bias for focusing on size as a measure of success. Commercial asset growth on the books of Citicorp was discouraged. In fact, management stretched its imagination to take assets off the firm's books, not to put them on. In 1983, more than $2 billion in loans generated in the United States by the Institutional Bank were sold to others by the Investment Bank. That number was expected to reach $20 billion by 1989. Wriston further explained:

> Our stockholders benefit, since we keep part of the spread while someone else keeps the assets (and the risk). But in order to make this a viable business, you must have both the asset-generating capability and the distribution capability nationwide and worldwide.

10   The worldwide orientation was further encouraged as cross-border lending started to slow down. Citicorp predicted that individual countries would be forced to develop

---

[2] *The Citi of Tomorrow: Today,* Walter B. Wriston's address to the Bank and Financial Analysts Association, New York, March 7, 1984.

their own indigenous capital markets. Thus, there was an opportunity to develop a "multidomestic" strategy which would enable Citicorp to offer full financial services in 60 to 80 countries before 1990.

The Five *I*s

11 In the early 1980s, Citicorp added two more "*I*s" to the strategic thrust, which had initially included development of the Investment Bank, the Individual Bank, and the Institutional Bank. The two embryonic "*I*s" were the Information and Insurance businesses. According to Wriston:

> We want to be in the information business simply because we are in the information business. Information about money has become almost as important as money itself. As bankers, we are familiar with the time value of money. As investors, we must think of the time value of information. The central core of any decision-making process is information. The fact that you know something relevant before, or more clearly than, your competitors may lead you to act sooner, to your advantage. Herein lies the problem: determining what is relevant. Hence, the packaging of information and its distribution will be critical. . . . We eventually intend to become a main competitor, as a preeminent distributor of financial database services worldwide. This is only possible with a truly global system, one through which information is distributed with electrons rather than the mail.[3]

12 The rationale for entering the insurance business was simple: insurance services accounted for fully 40 percent of all financial services in 1985. Citicorp would therefore not be a truly effective financial services enterprise without offering these products. Insurance was also a natural adjunct to the consumer business, considering the outmoded and expensive agency method of distribution that dominated the industry. Moreover, the firm was already a major factor in credit insurance. For example, one third of its second-mortgage customers bought credit life insurance.

13 The Banking Holding Company Act of 1956, and specifically Regulation Y, Section 4(c)-8 for the Board of Governors of the Federal Reserve System, prohibited banks from engaging in life insurance underwriting (with certain exceptions). Thus, the firm's insurance strategy was primarily aimed at an overseas expansion. This expansion was made possible by the Federal Reserve Board's ruling, requested by Citicorp, which enabled the firm to establish a fully competitive insurance operation in the United Kingdom. The board concluded:

> The general activity of underwriting life insurance in the United Kingdom can be considered usual in connection with banking or other financial operations in the United Kingdom.

14 This shift in the board's attitude enabled Citicorp to consider expansion into insurance, to identify the United Kingdom as a potential country in which to do so, and ultimately to pursue BNLA for acquisition.

15 Citicorp's goals for the five *I*s as of 1986 can be summarized as follows:

---

[3] Consistent with these plans, Citicorp acquired Quotron, a firm specializing in informational databases.

1. *Institutional.*
   a. Trim work force from 20,000 to 17,000.
   b. Pull back from middle markets overseas.
   c. Push investment banking products more.
   d. Clean up loan portfolio, reduce write-offs.
2. *Investment.*
   a. Build credible corporate finance group, especially in mergers and acquisitions.
   b. Hold on to investment banking talent.
   c. Wire 90 trading rooms around the globe.
   d. Improve coordination between London, Tokyo, and New York.
3. *Individual.*
   a. Continue to grow fast in retail banking.
   b. Make all acquired S&Ls profitable.
   c. Push international consumer business.
4. *Information.*
   a. Leave Quotron alone to calm customers.
   b. Develop new products.
5. *Insurance.*
   a. Push for easing limits on banks.
   b. Grow overseas.
   c. Cross-sell more insurance products through customer base.[4]

16 The 1985 sector performance is displayed in Exhibit 3.

Citicorp's Structure and Objectives

17 The Investment Bank, the Institutional Bank, and the Individual Bank were each organized into a sector and headed by a sector executive. Activities related to insurance and information were under the auspices of group executives within the three sectors, until such time as they justified the creation of their own sectors.

18 Each of the three sectors were composed of several groups, divisions, and business families, headed by a group executive, with business managers reporting to him or her. The organization of the Individual Bank, which is of particular interest in this case, was somewhat different from the other banks. As dictated in John S. Reed's (chairman of Citicorp since 1985) memorandum of March 9, 1976 (internally known as the "Memo from the Beach"), the business manager was responsible for the day-to-day operation, whereas a division executive's responsibility was strategic in nature.

19 This meant that a branch manager in, say, Hong Kong, would report to an area manager, then a country manager, a division manager, a group executive, a vice chairman or sector executive, and then the chairman. In effect, the flat structure placed only three layers of management between the most junior branch manager and the Policy Committee (30 senior executives) of Citicorp.

20 In January 1986, Reed issued a set of guidelines developed by the Policy Committee, which included Citicorp's objectives for the next 10 years (Exhibit 4) and its values (Exhibit 5). Exhibit 6 (A and B) displays the organizational structure of the Individual Bank and Consumer Services Group International.

---

[4] Source: Citicorp and *Business Week*, December 8, 1986.

Exhibit 3

CITICORP AND SUBSIDIARIES
Sector Performance
(in millions of dollars)

	1985	1984	Percent change
Individual Bank			
Net revenue	$4,120	$3,107	33
Operating expenses	3,614	2,735	32
Other income and expense	102	(12)	N.A.
Income before taxes	608	360	69
Net income	$ 340	$ 222	53
ROA	.61%	.51%	
ROE	15.3 %	12.7 %	
Institutional Bank			
Net revenue	$2,168	$2,068	5
Operating expenses	1,500	1,275	18
Income before taxes	668	793	(16)
Net income	$ 392	$ 454	(14)
ROA	.54%	.64%	
ROE	13.6 %	15.9 %	
Investment Bank			
Net revenue	$1,589	$1,241	28
Operating expenses	803	587	37
Income before taxes	786	654	20
Net income	$ 425	$ 343	24
ROA	1.34%	1.33%	
ROE	33.5 %	33.2 %	
Unallocated			
(Certain corporate-level items which are not allocated among sectors)			
Revenue	$ 28	$ (79)	N.A.
Operating expenses	148	116	28
Additional provision for credit losses	226	68	132
Income before taxes	(346)	(263)	(32)
Net income	(159)	(129)	(23)

N.A. = Not available.

The International Opportunity

21   In the 1985 Annual Report, the board stated:

> We recognize that, ultimately, our success will be directly attributable to our
> ability to offer our consumers worldwide preeminent service for each of their
> relationships with us. Our view is that by pursuing service excellence across all

Exhibit 4
Citicorp objectives—January 29, 1986

Citicorp's objective is to continue to build the world's leading financial services organization by creating value for our stockholders, customers, staff members, and the communities where we live and work. Creation of value is dependent on building an internal environment based on integrity, innovation, teamwork, and a commitment to unquestioned financial strength.

Value for the shareholder

12 percent to 18 percent compound growth in earnings per share.
Improving return on equity to 17/18 percent (maintaining the internal hurdle at 20 percent).
A strong balance sheet, including a 10 percent capital position and a AA+ credit rating.
Performance profile (earnings, market position, returns) improving within the top 30 companies in the world.
Improving market position for our businesses, defined by explicit market share reporting.
Well-diversified geographic and business earnings, assets, and liabilities.

Value for our customer

Maintain and build our two customer sets, institutional and individual, through customer service excellence, professionalism, product innovation, and the energy of our response to customer needs. Regularly monitor progress through external and internal surveys.

Value for our staff

Maintain an open, challenging, rewarding, and healthy working environment characterized by excellence and fairness in dealing with our employees. Business unit management is responsible for maintaining this working environment, and will support and adhere to the People Management beliefs outlined in the attached statement. [See Exhibit 5.] We will regularly monitor such support and adherence with specific, measurable goals.

Value for the communities in which we operate

Management of each business unit and/or geographic location is part of the community within which we operate and has an obligation:
To contribute to community values.
To participate in appropriate ways.
To work to change the legal and regulatory environment to enhance our "opportunity space."
To deal with our communities in an open, straightforward manner.

---

of our efforts, we enhance our standing with our customers and thereby the likelihood that they will choose us for a growing share of their financial needs.[5]

22   Internationally, Citicorp expanded its presence in a number of markets during 1985 while maintaining returns well in excess of corporate standards. In that year, Citicorp completed significant acquisitions in Italy (Banca Centro Sud), Belgium (Banque Sud Belge), and Chile (Corporacion Financiera Atlas) as well as consumer businesses in Colombia, Guam, and India.

23   Richard S. Braddock, sector executive of the Individual Bank and director of Citicorp and Citibank, explained:

We view our opportunities in the international marketplace as substantial, not only because our share tends to be relatively small in most places, but also because we have the opportunity to apply lessons learned from market to market and to expand attractive and proven product packages.[6]

---

[5] Citicorp 1985 Annual Report, p. 11.

[6] Ibid.

Exhibit 5
Excellence in people management: What we believe

The basics

While people management is a part of our business, there are certain nonnegotiable assumptions we make about how we will deal with the people who make up Citicorp. These basics must take precedence in everything we do.
Respect for individuals.
Treating people with dignity, openness, honesty, and fairness.

Citicorp values

In addition to our other specific Citicorp values (innovation, integrity, and service excellence), we have a set of values related to people management. These are things we feel strongly about, and which are driven by the needs of our business.
Meritocracy—emphasizing excellence of performance, professionalism, and effectiveness as the determining factors for selection, retention, rewards, and advancement. Recognizing good performance wherever and whenever it occurs. Appropriately exiting consistent nonperformers.
Independent initiative—promoting personal freedom to act and allowing people to succeed and to learn from failure.
Listening—creating an environment where we really hear what people say. Working together so that people throughout the organization have an impact.
Development—consciously building experience and talent of our people with the goal of professional growth. Creating a balance between developmental experiences and current contribution.

Working style

Our working styles will vary in different business situations and environments. The following describe the ways in which we approach people management, each applied as appropriate to individual business conditions.
Teamwork—building effective business-driven partnerships within the organization. Achieving a balance between cooperation and entrepreneurial spirit.
Integration—helping new people and new businesses to effectively and appropriately become part of the Citicorp culture.

The Consumer Service Group, International (CSGI)

24   The Consumer Service Group, International, within the Individual Bank, was organized in separate divisions: the Asia–Pacific division had its headquarters in Tokyo; Europe–Middle East–Africa (EMEA) division, in London; the Western division, in Rio de Janeiro; Payment Products Division (Diners Club), in Chicago; and Systems Division, in New York. The group employed 26,000 people in 69 businesses, located in 39 countries.

25   John Liu, senior human resource officer, Consumer Services Group, International, summarized how Citicorp's culture was reflected by the group:

> We want to be part of the largest low-cost provider of financial service in the world. As such we don't focus only on banks, such as Chase Manhattan. Rather, we look also at Sears, AMEX, and others who provide financial services. This is the stretch we hold in front of us.
>
> In order to help achieve this, we have to find new ways of doing things. Taking insurance as an example, Citicorp practices its decentralized operational mode, sometimes referred to as the "thousand flowers" approach.
>
> In insurance, to use a metaphor, we want to have a thousand flowers bloom. Over time, we'll put the flowers together in a bouquet, and if we don't like the shape of it, we'll take this or that flower away. However, today we just started our picking, and that is why you'll find insurance activities in the Institutional

Exhibit 6

A. Individual Bank

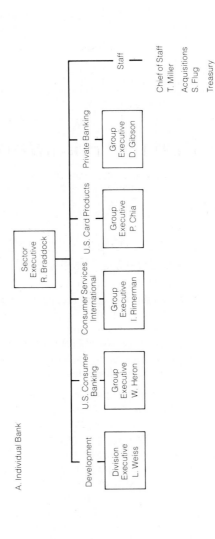

B. Consumer Services Group-International

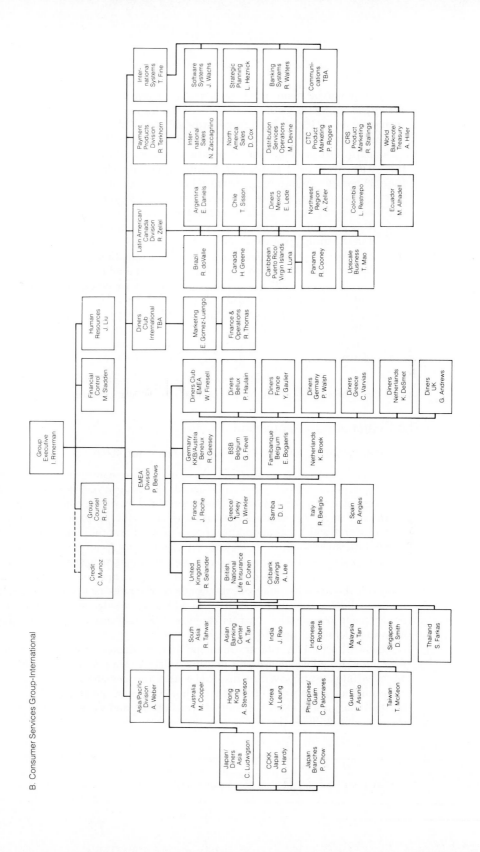

Bank (commercial insurance), the Investment Bank (brokerage insurance activities), and with us in the Individual Bank (life underwriting, mortgage insurance, etc.). It's all emerging slowly out of our philosophy, and the BNLA acquisition is the first major life underwriting acquisition we have ever had.

As part of this stretch, the corporation applies certain hurdle rates to guide this vision. We have a stated hurdle rate, internally, such as an ROE of no less than 20 percent. Additionally, we also have an ROA hurdle rate of 90 basis points. In our group, we use our own internal hurdle rates as a way of managing our businesses. One such hurdle rate which comes to mind is to target a ratio of 1.5 between consumer net revenue and delivery expenses.

Within the group, we want to more than double our earnings over the next five years. We want to do this partly through acquisitions, of which we must have done at least 10 over the past three years and added more than 6,000 people. Although we still will make acquisitions, we clearly must slow down and develop these new businesses.

The acquisitions have not been hostile and for the most part have been either "hospitalized" or unprofitable businesses. This has given us certain advantages, but also created challenges when it comes to integrating a new business into our organization.[7]

26   The unique culture and reward system of CSGI is reflected in Exhibit 7, which summarizes the results of an organizational survey of its senior managers.

The Search for an Acquisition

27   Liu further explained how the BNLA acquisition came about:

About three years ago, we started a drive to get into insurance and encouraged our people in the United Kingdom, Australia, Germany, and Belgium to start to look into insurance. As you know, there are three ways you can get into a new business: You can (a) acquire, (b) start a de novo unit, or (c) do a joint venture.

In England, which was one of the largest and most profitable markets (relatively) for life insurance, we initially identified Excelsior Life Assurance[8] as a possibility in early 1984. As an insurance company of substantial size in the United Kingdom, the acquisition would immediately bring us into this market on a large scale. However, the more we analyzed the numbers, the more concerned we got. This was a significant investment, and we had little knowledge about life insurance. So when our joint venture partner (a large U.S. insurance company) withdrew, we reconsidered our options.

Then Citicorp's U.K. country manager and the European division manager of the United Kingdom sponsored (identified) BNLA as a potential candidate for our move into life underwriting insurance. After the identification of the candidate, an acquisition team was put together. The team consisted of people from across our U.K. businesses as well as outside consultants and were all selected for their specific skills as they related to this opportunity.

---

[7] Interview with John Liu.

[8] The name has been changed to protect confidentiality.

Exhibit 7
Summary of organizational surveys conducted by the case writers[*]

	Low degree/extent				High degree/extent		
	1	2	3	4	5	6	7

1. Loyalty
2. Promotion from within
3. Extent managers are free to take independent actions
4. Degree to which goals are venturesome
5. Degree of accountability for individual managers
6. Encouragement of risk taking
7. Goals used as context
8. Lateral communications
9. Clear measures to judge managerial performance
10. Organization successful in developing talent from within
11. Extent to which conflicts are discussed openly
12. Encouragement to innovate
13. Clarity of goals
14. Overall communication
15. Opportunities for individual growth and development
16a. Formality of planning
16b. Completeness of planning
17. Clarity of organizational roles
18. Performance demands
19. Departmental understanding of goals
20a. Innovativeness in decision making
20b. Timeliness in decision making

Citicorp ----- BNLA ———

[*] Questionnaires were completed by managers and outside observers. Items of the questionnaire are summarized and labeled because of proprietary reasons; values indicate average scores.

Exhibit 7 (*concluded*)

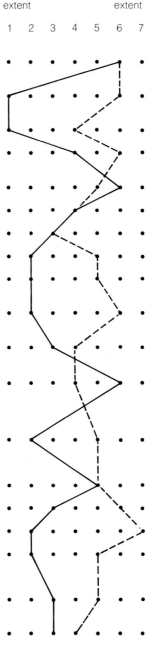

	Low degree/extent				High degree/extent		
	1	2	3	4	5	6	7

21. Fit between compensation and performance
22. Encouragement of constructive criticism
23. Downward communication
24. Support received to carry out job responsibilities
25. Clear expectations
26. Degree of cooperation
27. Degree of coordination
28. Extent of clear plans
29. Matching of managerial talents and jobs
30. Organization's ability to cope with urgent matters
31. Extent to which middle managers' jobs are defined in qualitative terms
32. Extent to which superiors depend on own judgment versus quantitative performance data when evaluating subordinates
33. Extent to which managers obtain feedback from performance data versus getting it from superior
34. Extent of promotion from within
35. Use of merit pay
36. Use of stocks to award performance
37. Extent to which superior's judgment determines subordinates' raises versus company policies
38. Use of status symbols and perquisites as rewards
39. Extent to which above are distributed according to strict company policies

One of the important issues for us is now to decide how to integrate the business—should we fully integrate, keep it at an arm's-length distance, or somewhere in between, and how should we do it. With this decision also comes the question of what type of person to put into the driver's seat.

The United Kingdom

28   The U.K. economy is the sixth largest in the world and is in transition, as is the U.S. economy, from an industrial to a service orientation. By 1985, the United Kingdom had the lowest level of legal/regulatory control for domestic and international financial activity of any developed country. However, U.K. regulation of life insurance underwriting, particularly with regard to reserves, was among the most stringent in the world. The government was considered politically stable, and the conservatives in power were committed to controlling inflation and government spending to provide a platform for economic growth. Even though 12 percent of the work force was unemployed, there was little social unrest.

29   The United Kingdom was expected to remain self-sufficient in oil for the remainder of the century. Inflation was expected to be controlled in the 5–7 percent range, and there were expected to be no major changes in either the political system or the regulatory environment. Expected growth figures for U.K. GNP for 1986 and 1987 were 1.5 percent and 2.6 percent, respectively. Inflation was expected to be around 5 percent for the same two periods.

The U.K. Life Assurance Market

30   The U.K. life assurance market was considered large and growing. Growth in new premiums went from $1.9 billion in 1980 to $4.7 billion in 1983. During the same period, average growth of premium income rose from $7.8 billion to $13.2 billion, and total sums insured grew an average of 17 percent to $295 billion. There were 289 licensed underwriters in the United Kingdom. The relative size of the top 12 companies is presented in Exhibit 8.

31   Analyses showed that life assurance in the United Kingdom was seen as both a protection instrument and a consumer investment. The policies accumulate cash value and also yield dividends to policyholders. There were basically three types of underwriters in the marketplace: industrial, orthodox, and linked life.

32   The industrial companies offered small-value policies, which were targeted at the lower socioeconomic groups. The premiums were collected in person, usually monthly, by employed agents, who did little actual "selling." The policies carried high administrative overheads and were, therefore, relatively poor values for the consumer. This sector of the market was dominated by Prudential, which wrote 65 percent of the new policies issued each year. This type of insurance had a vast customer base, with over 70 million policies in existence. At the same time, this type of policy had a declining market share, and smaller companies were retrenching because of overhead inefficiencies.

33   The orthodox life companies offered larger-value policies, which catered to the more affluent customer. This type of policy was distributed through "independent" professionals who usually had some other relationship with the customer. These independent agents could be insurance brokers, solicitors (attorneys), accountants, banks, or estate agents. It was fairly common in the United Kingdom for all of these groups to offer

Exhibit 8
Major players in the life market (worldwide premium income)

			Premium income				
	Classification	Ranking	$ MM value	Percent of total	Percent increase on 1982/1981	Percent increase on 1981/1980	Size of life fund, end 1982 ($ billions)
0 Prudential	Stock	1	$ 1,656	13%	12%	16%	$ 9.4
0 Legal and General	Stock	2	775	6	15	10	6.6
0 Standard Life	Mutual	3	630	5	13	20	6.3
0 Norwich Union	Mutual	4	565	4	19	13	3.8
0 Hambro Life	Stock	5	464	4	20	32	2.1
0 Commercial Union	Stock	6	444	4	12	15	3.8
0 Eagle Star	Stock/Sub	7	414	3	21	28	2.2
0 Abbey Life	Stock/Sub	8	353	3	8	63	1.4
0 Sun Life	Stock	9	328	3	2	25	2.1
0 Scottish Amicable	Mutual	10	319	3	24	38	2.5
0 G.R.E.	Stock	11	318	3	14	27	2.8
0 Pearl	Stock	12	311	2	8	10	1.9
Subtotal			6,577	53	13	21	44.9 (56%)
0 Others	13/48		4,924	40	15	21	
0 Balance			823	7	5	15	36.1 (44%)
			$12,324	100%	15%	21%	$81.0

Note: $1.20 = £1.

insurance as a part of their service portfolio to their clients. These independent agents typically offered policies from three to six different underwriters. The firms which offered orthodox policies had traditionally not "marketed" to their consumer base for fear of offending the professional intermediary. There were different "classes" of agents who covered specific market segments.

34   The linked life policy was relatively new and was introduced in the 1960s as an alternative to the orthodox life policy. It targeted the same consumer as the orthodox policy but was sold normally by a commission-paid, self-employed sales force, much like insurance representatives in the United States. Policyholders of linked life insurance did not "participate" in the profits of the underwriter through dividends, but their investments were placed in a number of funds (similar to mutual funds) managed by the underwriter. Thus, the linked life policyholder took investment risk/return, and the underwriter provided a death guarantee. The range of products offered by the three types of underwriters is depicted in Exhibit 9.

35   Trends in the U.K. market indicated that the role of single-premium life assurance was expanding. This type policy was one in which a single payment was made to the underwriter at the beginning of the policy life, and no further premiums were due. Before the creation of the single-premium policy, most life policy premiums were paid yearly over the life of the policy. Logically, there was no single-premium industrial underwriting, given the socioeconomic status of most policyholders. The target for the single-premium policies was the "banked homeowner"—a person who had a relationship with a bank and owned his or her home.

Exhibit 9
Product range

	Nonprofit/ participating	Relative importance (low/high)	Industrial	Traditional	Linked
Protection					
Whole life	NP	L	—	✓	—
	P	L	✓	✓	✓
Term	NP	H	✓	✓	✓
Permanent health	NP	M	—	✓	—
Savings					
Endowment	NP	L	—	✓	—
	P	H	✓	✓	✓
Pensions	NP	L	—	✓	—
	P	H	✓	✓	✓
Annuities	NP	M	—	✓	✓
Single-premium bonds	P	H	—	✓	✓
Group schemes					
Pension (can include term and PH insurance)	N/A	H	—	✓	✓

36   In addition to the expansion of the single-premium policy, there had been a decline in share of the industrial policy from 13 percent of total insurance in 1980 to 6 percent in 1983. The growth sectors of the market were linked life and personal pensions (which were similar to the individual retirement account in the United States).

37   Premium income had generally become increasingly volatile, because single-premium income had grown from 12 percent of total premium income in 1980 to 22 percent in 1983. Since 1968, the growth segments for premium income were linked life, personal pensions, and mortgage endowment. In 1983, the government introduced "Mortgage Interest Relief at Source" (MIRAS), which caused mortgage repayments on insurance-linked mortgages to appear more competitive than conventional mortgages, and thus causing an increase in the mortgage endowment business. In March of 1984, the British government abolished Life Assurance Premium Relief (LAPR).

38   In their attempt to expand their share of the market, traditional companies had begun moving into the linked life segment. Major growth was expected in pension-related policies as the most efficient (from a tax perspective) savings medium. Allied Dunbar and Guardian Royal Exchange exemplified a movement to "full financial services."

39   For the future, the desire of the government to increase the "portability" of pensions could open a major new market. At this time, personal pensions were sold only by life assurance companies (by law). The removal of this restriction was under consideration and would bring new banks into the market. There was some concern that the government policy of "fiscal neutrality" between savings mediums could cause further amendment to tax laws, but this was not expected in the short term.

40   In the future marketplace, it would be possible for banks to exploit their customer bases and "sell" insurance, instead of being passive providers. Building societies (very similar to U.S. savings and loan institutions, and responsible for writing most home mortgages in the United Kingdom) did not currently have legislative permission to

Exhibit 10
Intermediaries' view of key market segments

	Currently important	Likely to increase in importance
Self-employed	90	65
People on medium incomes	82	46
Owners/directors of small companies	80	57
People on high incomes	79	53
Young couples	78	57
Middle-aged couples	72	43
Women	68	51
People with free capital	66	39
Retired couples	46	38

function as insurance brokers, as did the banks. It was expected that the societies would request that power in 1986–87, which would bring more new players to the market. There would be an increase in the pensions business to reach the large self-employed group in the United Kingdom. Exhibit 10 offers a view of the current and future importance of key segments in the U.K. market.

41   In summary, the U.K. life underwriting market was the seventh largest in the world and was growing. Life assurance in the United Kingdom filled a dual role for the consumer—protection and savings/investment. The market was led by large and well-established players, but there were major market opportunities for other well-managed companies. The market was differentiated by distribution methods, and the long-term profit stream generated by most firms led to high investor confidence and high share prices. U.K. premium income in 1982 totaled $28 billion, of which $12 billion was in life assurance underwriting. The market was predominantly U.K.–owned, as were the major players, though a company did not necessarily need to be a general insurance firm to compete successfully in either market. Each market involved different legislative bases, different distribution channels, and different skills. U.K. firms were significant in world markets, particularly nonlife, where they received over 50 percent of the premium income.

The U.K. Financial Services Market

42   There were five major categories of financial services in the United Kingdom: transaction accounts, savings, shelter (home) financing, lending, and protection. Exhibit 11 is a chart of the major players and other entrants in these markets. The total savings market had grown from $124 billion in 1980 to $193.6 billion in 1983. The relative share figures for the major institutions in the savings market are shown in Exhibit 12. Shelter finance had grown from $62.8 billion to $108.8 billion in the same period. A synopsis of the growth and change in the unsecured loan market is shown in Exhibit 13.

43   Banks were leading the expansion into the related areas of mortgage financing, estate agency (trust), stockbrokering, and life assurance underwriting. Building societ-

Exhibit 11
Elements of the market

Service category	Major players	Other entrants
Transaction accounts	Clearing banks	—
Savings	Building societies; life assurance companies	Banks
Shelter finance	Building society	Banks; finance houses
Lending	Banks	Finance houses; in-store credit
Protection	Life assurance companies; general insurance companies	—

Exhibit 12
Market movements—Savings

	"50 percent of deposits with insurance companies"	
	1980 (percent)	1983 (percent)
Insurance funds	45%	50%
Building society	28	28
Banks	13	7½
National savings	7	7
Shares, etc.	7	7½
Total market	$124 billion	$193.6 billion

Compound growth 16 percent per annum (RPI 8.3 percent compound).
Insurance funds ($97 million at end 1983) are not accessible.

Note: $1.20 = £1 for all years.

ies now offered checkbook access to savings and ATM networks. Legislation intended to equalize competitive roles in the market had been passed. Technological advancements were expected at this point but were not yet in place. The market would continue to change rapidly due to continuing deregulation and increasing technological sophistication. Traditional barriers were falling, and banks were leading the way into other sectors of the economy to satisfy consumer demand. Insurance was an integral part of the market and was supported by past and present government and fiscal policy.

Citicorp in the United Kingdom

44　The Consumer Services Group (U.K.) was dominated by Citibank Savings, a mature business operating in four specific markets:

> *Finance house:* indirect financing for autos and home improvement.
>
> *Mortgage banking:* consumer mortgages through association with insurance firm partners.

Exhibit 13
Market movements—Unsecured loans

	"Not participating as a principal—but providing cover to repay"	
	1980 (percent)	1983 (percent)
Finance houses	34%	29%
Bank loans	29	37
Bank credit cards	18	21
In-store cards	11	9
Other	8	4
Total market	$7.1 billion	$13.2 billion

Compound growth = 23 percent.
   An estimated 30 percent of bank and finance house loans are covered by life/disability insurance to cover repayments.
   New developments from 1982 on larger loans give bullet repayments covered by endowment insurance.
   Statistics exclude "loan backs" from long-term savings under an insurance policy.

Retail cards: private label card operation for London's High Street retailers, as well as the European Banking Centre, traveller's checks, and Diners Club.

Consumer banking: cross-selling a portfolio of products to consumers, such as personal loans, checking (transaction) accounts, mortgages, and insurance.

45   Citibank Savings had 39 branches in the United Kingdom, 19 of which were recognized as direct branches within the consumer bank.

U.K. Life Assurance Consumers

46   U.K. life assurance consumers were underinsured relative to those of other developed nations. The total life coverage as a percent of yearly average wage as compared for seven industrialized nations was:

United Kingdom	88%
France	147
Sweden	148
Australia	178
United States	183
Canada	184
Japan	325

47   The product was seen by U.K. consumers as intangible and offering no present benefit. The contracts were viewed as a "mass of small print" and were inflexible once purchased. The purchase pattern was characterized as infrequent and having a

Exhibit 14
U.K. consumer behavior

	Holding (percent)	Recent purchase (percent)*	Future purchase (percent)†
Key product groups			
Endowment mortgage	9%	17%	9%
Mortgage protection	16	24	16
Protection cover	35	42	19
Endowment cover	42	63	39
Total (including multipurchase)	74%	100%	57%

* Purchased in the last 12 months.
† Expected purchase in the next 12 months.

Exhibit 15
Consumer "types"

	Medium	Purchase	Timing	Knowledge	Mind set
Thinking young couple	Broker direct to company	Buys	Regular	Sophisticated	Protection
Young family man	Agent salesman	Sold	Spasmodic	Low—trusting	Protection/ savings
Middle-age man	Any	Sold	Spasmodic	Low—wants known company	Protection/ savings
Self-employed	Salesman broker	Sold	Spasmodic	Learns quickly; decision maker	Savings
Late arrivals	Direct (coupon response)	Indirectly sold	Once	Low	Protection (burial policy)

high unit cost, and the consumer had a "low knowledge base" about the product. The benefits perceived were "peace of mind," a response to issues of social responsibility, and investment/tax avoidance. Seventy-four percent of U.K. households had life coverage, which included 45 percent of all adults (predominantly men). A chart of U.K. consumer behavior regarding purchase by product type is presented as Exhibit 14. The major reasons for purchase were "protection" and "house purchase." In general, no major alternatives were considered, and the decision to buy insurance coverage was a joint one in the family. The amount of coverage was generally based on affordability rather than need, and shopping among companies was minimal. Exhibit 15 characterizes the major segments of the market; required company attributes from the consumers' view are shown in Exhibit 16.

48   The life assurance market was not as mature as its size might indicate. Most consumers were underinsured, and over half the adult population had no coverage at all. There was a key role to be played for protection products (distinct from investment products). Linked life companies concentrated on "investment policies," and the benefits

Exhibit 16
Required company attributes—What to look for in a company (excluding industrial)

	Spontaneous (percent)	Prompted (percent)
Well-known	33%	60%
Good reputation	27	51
Good investment performance	23	30
Good salespeople	15	56
Long established	8	43

to the policyholder were neither fixed nor guaranteed by the company but were invested in a separate range of funds (at the risk/return of the consumer). In this sense, linked life firms worked very much like mutual fund companies in the United States. Their sources of income were profits from insurance underwriting, a 5 percent bid/offer differential on investments in the funds, and a ¾ percent fund management fee. The products were sold through a direct sales force, which was normally paid only by commission.

49   In the U.K. market, 15 percent of adults had a linked life policy (33 percent of adults with life assurance coverage). The policies were most popular in the under-55 age range and in London and the southeast of England.

The History of British National Life Assurance

50   British National Life Assurance was a spin-off company from the British National Insurance Society. It was created in 1982 by Sir William Baltimore[9] as a subsidiary of EXCO Corporation[10] (a large U.S. company) when EXCO Corporation had decided to diversify into financial services. British National Insurance remained a property and casualty life underwriter, while BNLA became the life underwriting business of EXCO Corporation. The managing director of the new firm was Ernest Smith,[11] a true English gentleman and skilled manager. The sales director was Frank Jones,[12] a charismatic and skilled salesman with considerable experience in the insurance business.

51   EXCO Corporation took very little interest in the performance of BNLA and allowed Mr. Smith and Mr. Jones to manage the company as they saw fit. In essence, Mr. Jones controlled sales and marketing, and Mr. Smith controlled public relations and administration.

52   In the interim, Sir William Baltimore retired from EXCO Corporation. He subsequently became director of insurance development (on a consulting basis) for Citicorp's Consumer Services Group, International, EMEA Division, headquartered in London.

---

[9] The name has been changed to protect confidentiality.

[10] The name has been changed to protect confidentiality.

[11] The name has been changed to protect confidentiality.

[12] The name has been changed to protect confidentiality.

Exhibit 17
BNLA organization chart

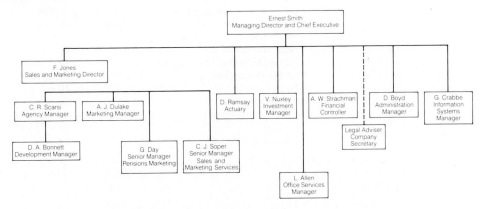

53   The consumers' view of the Citicorp/BNLA merger was that it offered wider financial services as a result, and a bank-owned insurance company was seen positively. Negative reaction to the fact that it was American owned could be foreseen.

54   In January of 1986, BNLA employed 392 people, 101 at its headquarters and 250 comprising the sales force from 22 branches. Each branch had a branch manager and an administrative assistant. An organizational chart and staff analysis are provided in Exhibits 17 and 18.

55   There were 47,600 policyholders and $305 million dollars in life insurance in force. However, BNLA policy lapses and salesperson turnover were twice the industry average. The commission-only sales force was the major distribution method for BNLA products, and its productivity was some 75 percent below average. The sales force was inappropriately trained, and the commission structure resulted in low pay relative to the competition.

56   BNLA spent considerable sums of money training a sales force that was paid poorly relative to industry averages. Mr. Jones subscribed to the philosophy that a high-quality product would essentially sell itself and that, therefore, high commissions were unnecessary. His view was that sales goals would be achieved, in the long run, as a result of high training levels and high-quality products. This became known in the organization as "Frank's Philosophy." This philosophy also constrained promotional activities to direct selling only. The marketing department was therefore mostly engaged in arranging flashy conventions and gimmicks for the sales force.

57   Communication between top management and the organization was generally considered poor or nonexisting. Bad news, such as the lack of profits, the low sales force performance, and information about the negative cash flows was never passed along to the management team. Although annual budgets were compiled, their content was never shared with departments. Conversely, no formal system existed for monthly reporting on departmental activities.

58   Smith believed that financial reporting should be kept to a minimum, although all required disclosures were always filed on time. The financial officer had a small minicomputer at his disposal. Moreover, the firm had taken steps to automate the office environment at its headquarters by establishing a word processing pool.

Exhibit 18
British National Life staff analysis

Department	January 1986
Actuarial	5
Administration	21
Operations and office services	10
Data processing	21
Finance	16
Investment	3
Personnel and training	—
Legal	1
Marketing	13
Sales	9
Credit insurance (from November 1986)	—
Managing director	2
Branch managers	22
Branch administrators	19
Subtotal	142
Salaried sales force	N.A.
Total	142
Sales associates	250

N.A. = Not applicable.

59   Toward the end of 1984, EXCO Corporation decided that it was not going to make a go of BNLA (or of financial services generally) and put the company up for sale. The company knew that it was "on the block," and employee morale took a nose dive. This enhanced the "rudderless" sense of the company, as performance became even less an issue and "Frank's Philosophy" became the guiding force in the firm. A culture–reward system profile of BNLA is shown in Exhibit 7.

BNLA Product/Market Posture

60   At the time of the Citicorp acquisition, BNLA was a linked life firm which offered six basic products to the market:

1. *Plan-for-Life*—a highly flexible policy offered the consumer control over the content of his or her plan. The consumer decided what proportion of the premium to devote to savings or protection, and this could be changed as needs and circumstances warranted.

2. *Plan-for-Capital*—a regular savings plan with high investment content and minimum life coverage. It was ideal for someone who wanted to save dynamically for 8 to 10 years. The proceeds were free from basic-rate income tax (the "off-the-top" rate in the United Kingdom), from personal capital gains tax, and, after 10 years, from higher-rate tax as well. This product was quite similar to

the individual retirement account in its tax treatment. It differed in its small insurance cover.

3. *Plan-for-Investment*—a lump-sum plan to invest in the company's different funds. The capital invested was allocated a set number of units, depending on the current value of the fund. At any time, the plan had a value equivalent to the bid (sell) value of the price of units multiplied by the number of units held. This fund was very similar to the mutual funds offered through brokerage houses in the United States, except there were certain tax advantages not offered in U.S. mutual funds.

4. *Plan-for-Retirement*—a retirement annuity policy which was suitable for the self-employed and those who had no private pension scheme—a unit-linked investment approach but with outstanding tax advantages. This plan was similar to the Keogh plans in the United States but was free of investment limits.

5. *Plan-for-Executive*—an individual pension plan suitable for senior members of a trading company (brokerage house) who wished to add to their retirement benefits. This was a very specialized policy and was, once again, similar to the IRA, except that both the executive and his or her employer could contribute.

6. *Plan-for-Pension Preservation*—a specialized plan conforming to legislation passed in 1970, which allowed the transfer of vested pension funds from a previous employer into this plan without tax penalties.

61   In addition to these plans, a brokerage provided access to general insurance, such as motor, house contents (homeowners), and building insurance (United Kingdom insurance companies are not permitted to act as insurance brokers). The BNLA product line was generally complete and well rounded and fulfilled the all-around needs of the consumer, from protection and investment to retirement planning.

BNLA—A Financial Perspective

62   Accounting standards in the United States required earnings on a life insurance policy to be recognized evenly over the years of premium payments. U.K. life insurance regulations, in contrast, required maintenance of prudent reserves that resulted in a new life assurance company generating losses or very low profits during its early years. The function of the regulations was to severely restrict dividend payments and thereby protect policyholders. U.S. accounting was significantly less conservative; when the balance sheet of a U.K. life firm was recast to comply with U.S. accounting, the reported equity generally increased considerably.

63   Citicorp's customary financial goals and targets were designed for traditional banking businesses and did not lend themselves to evaluating an investment in a life insurance company. For that reason, Citicorp measured BNLA performance against a hurdle rate of 20 percent ROE on BNLA's recorded equity. Based on Citicorp's projections at the time of the acquisition, BNLA was expected to produce negative ROEs in 1985 and 1986 (see Exhibit 18) and to achieve the 20 percent hurdle rate for the first time in 1991. To comply with U.S. accounting, BNLA's recorded equity at the time of the acquisition was adjusted as follows (in millions; please note that all BNLA financial data have been changed for proprietary reasons):

Book values of assets	$77.1	
Book amount of liabilities	66.9	
Book value of equity	$10.2	
Adjustments to comply with U.S. accounting:		
Write-downs of assets	−3.5	
	$ 6.7	
Reduction of reserves	+6.5	
Adjusted equity	$13.2	
Portion acquired	100%	
Purchased equity	$13.2	
Purchase price	13.7	$13.7
Goodwill	$ 0.5	
Additional capital infusion		19.6
Total investment*		$33.3

*Investment was made in pounds sterling and was fully hedged via the forward market.

64   Exhibit 19 presents summary financial data on BNLA, including forecasts. For 1985, production of new life policies was 40 percent below forecast. Operating expenses were 50 percent higher than forecast and about 50 percent higher than the industry norms for a firm at this stage of development. This is fairly consistent with expense levels of previous years.

The Acquisition

65   During the time when Citicorp U.K. was actively seeking an insurance company to acquire, Bob Selander was the new country manager of Citicorp's U.K. business. The acquisition of an insurance company was a part of the strategic plan he inherited from his predecessor. Sir William Baltimore had previously developed a list of potential acquisitions for consideration.

66   The first possibility which came to light was Excelsior Life Assurance—one of the largest life assurance firms in the United Kingdom. Sir William Baltimore had been a director of Excelsior Life Assurance and knew its inner workings very well. Upon his recommendations and with the joint venture participation of another life assurance firm, an acquisition plan was put together. Late in the process, the joint venture partner withdrew from the deal, and Citicorp decided that Excelsior Life Assurance was too large to acquire alone. The search was reopened.

67   After considering several moderately sized firms, it was decided that the goodwill portion of the purchase price for a moderately sized firm would never allow such an acquisition to make Citicorp's internal hurdle rates. The search was moved to smaller firms. From a list of 12 life assurance firms, BNLA emerged as the most desirable candidate. Exhibits 19 and 20 discuss Citicorp's rationale for the acquisition. Not only was BNLA of a size that permitted the acquisition to be managed, but there was fairly little to be paid for the goodwill of the company. In short, the price was right, and the potential was there. Negotiations with EXCO Corporation and with Ernest Smith continued for some time, and, finally, the purchase price was agreed upon. Citicorp had its U.K. life assurance company.

Exhibit 19
BNLA operating forecast, including required synergies—Restated according to U.S. accounting principles (in millions of dollars)

	1985	1986	1987	1988	1989
Premiums, net	$19.9	$47.0	$74.5	$109.9	$153.1
Reinsurance	0	2.7	8.5	12.5	15.0
Investment income	3.2	8.4	12.9	19.8	30.4
Total revenues	$23.1	$58.1	$95.9	$142.2	$198.5
Benefits paid	$ 3.1	$ 4.2	$ 7.2	$ 13.3	$ 34.1
Increase in reserves	12.0	40.5	66.4	96.4	119.3
Commissions	2.9	6.7	11.6	17.2	23.4
Operating expenses	5.5	7.8	7.4	9.1	12.5
Total expenses	$23.5	$59.2	$92.6	$136.0	$189.3
Income before taxes*	$ (0.4)	$ (1.1)	$ 3.3	$ 6.2	$ 9.2
Income taxes	0	0	0.8	2.8	4.3
Net income	$ (0.4)	$ (1.1)	$ 2.5	$ 3.4	$ 4.9
ROE:					
On BNLA equity	(7%)	(5%)	7%	9%	12%
By Citicorp formulas	(30%)	(40%)	6%	11%	16%

* Reconciled with BNLA's stand-alone forecast, under U.K. accounting principles, as follows:

	1985	1986	1987	1988	1989
U.K. pretax income, without synergies	$(0.7)	$(3.9)	$(2.4)	$(0.6)	$ 1.5
Adjustment for U.S. accounting rules		(0.1)	(0.1)	(0.1)	(0.1)
Impact of synergies		1.1	4.0	4.9	5.6
Impact of capital infusion	0.3	1.8	1.8	2.0	2.2
Income before taxes, as reported above	$(0.4)	$(1.1)	$ 3.3	$ 6.2	$ 9.2

BNLA forecast balance sheets, including required synergies—Restated according to U.S. accounting principles (in millions of dollars, as of December 31 of each year)

	1985	1986	1987	1988	1989
Securities	$91	$126	$177	$257	$363
Reinsurance receivable	0	1	7	13	15
Other assets	4	8	21	38	59
Total assets	$95	$135	$205	$308	$436
Insurance reserves	$62	$103	$169	$266	$385
Other liabilities	1	1	3	6	10
Common stock	32	32	32	32	32
Retained earnings	0	(1)	1	4	10
Total	$95	$137	$205	$308	$437

Exhibit 19 *(concluded)*

BNLA historical blance sheets—According to U.K. accounting principles (in millions, as of December 31 of each year; all balances restated at an exchange rate of 1 pound sterling = $1.4)

	1984	1983
Securities	$56	$38
Other assets	4	1
Total assets	$60	$39
Insurance reserves	$56	$31
Other liabilities	1	5
Capital	3	3
Total	$60	$39

BNLA historical income statements—According to U.K. accounting principles (in millions; all balances restated at an exchange rate of 1 pound sterling = $1.4)

	1984	1983
Premiums, net	$31	$ 5
Investment income	4	3
Total revenues	$35	$ 8
Benefits paid	$ 3	$ 3
Increase in reserves	25	7
Commissions	1	1
Operating expenses	9	1
Total expenses	$38	$12
Income before taxes	$ (3)	$ (4)
Income taxes	0	0
Net income	$ (3)	$ (4)

Note: Caution should be exercised in comparing BNLA financial data with that of Citicorp, or even with that of other U.K. life assurance companies. This is because, first, there were some significant differences between traditional banking businesses and a U.K. life insurance operation, especially in rules governing the accounting recognition of earnings and in U.K. tax and regulatory requirements. Second, these differences were exaggerated in the case of a relatively new, rapidly growing U.K. life assurance company, where the reported amount of equity may have been as large as 60 percent of reported assets because of the conservatism inherent in regulatory requirements. Third, it was also difficult to make meaningful financial comparisons among different U.K. life companies. An immature firm had a financial picture bearing little resemblance to that of an older, established competitor, which may have reported equity as low as 2 percent of total assets.

Source: Citicorp MEP; the data have been altered for proprietary reasons.

Exhibit 20

Memorandum

To: Group Executive

From: Divisional Executive

Re: U.K. Insurance Acquisition MEP

Date: 14th August 1985

As you know, in 1981 Citibank submitted an application to the Fed seeking permission to expand its line of insurance activities in the United Kingdom to write whole life in addition to its traditional base of credit life. This action was felt appropriate given that in the United Kingdom expanded insurance activities are considered a normal part of the banking sector, with most large U.K. banks engaged in such activities through wholly owned insurance subsidiaries. Therefore, for Citibank to enjoy equal footing with the competition, approval would be necessary since these activities are not otherwise permitted under Citibank's U.S. charter.

Upon receiving permission from the Fed in early 84, we were then confronted with the business decision of how best to tackle this new opportunity. A team from within Citibank Savings was formed to evaluate the marketplace and make a recommendation on how to proceed. In this effort they were assisted by a senior insurance consultant from the United Kingdom who had a prior relationship with Citibank. A broad range of companies were evaluated as possible acquisition candidates, and several points became clear. A direct sales force (versus mass solicitation) was considered key as well as the company's ownership structure (i.e., if publicly owned, how could a takeover be affected).

Considerations of size became important because additional Fed approval would be required for any takeover. A unique opportunity confronted us to acquire a major U.K. insurer, PQ Life Assurance, but the cost of such an acquisition was put at a figure several hundred million dollars higher than the desired size of investment.* This acquisition, which would have been a joint venture, was approved internally within Citibank, but closure with our proposed partners failed.

We then shifted our thinking back to internal de novo growth and in so doing have reevaluated several smaller acquisition candidates which had surfaced previously. Acquiring a smaller company may be regarded as "accelerated de novo," and we are actively pursuing the acquisition of British National Life Assurance Company at a cost of $13.7MM (goodwill of $0.5MM), with a further capital increase of $19.6MM bringing the total investment to $33.3MM. If we were to pursue the internal de novo growth route we would also require additional capital of about $19.6MM, as our current capitalization of $3MM supports the credit life business only. These capital levels are prescribed by the U.K. insurance regulatory bodies in order to meet minimum solvency margins.

---

* Note: All numbers in this document have been changed for proprietary reasons.

Exhibit 20 (continued)

The following analysis compares forecasted earnings through acquisition versus internal growth. On a cumulative basis through 1990, the acquisition route produces over $17MM in incremental earnings.

It is important to note that there is a lag in profitability in an emerging life assurance business due to the slow buildup of premium income (net of commissions), which in the earlier years is not sufficient to cover the fixed costs of the distribution system. The difference in profitability between the two alternatives below is simply a reflection of this curve, and, once a steady state is achieved, both propositions would yield the same results.

PCE $MM	De novo	Acquisition	B/(W)
1985	$ (.5)	$(1.3)	$ (.6)
1986	(1.3)	(2.9)	(1.6)
1987	(3.6)	.4	4.0
1988	(3.5)	1.3	4.8
1989	(2.5)	2.5	5.0
1990	(1.3)	4.9	6.2
	$(12.7)	$ 4.9	$17.8

This MEP assumes no tax credit against the operating losses in 1985 and 1986. In 1987, the first full year of profitability, the loss carryforward is absorbed. In any event, no current U.K. taxes will likely be payable at least until 1990, and the tax expense is therefore all U.S. deferred.

Your approval of the attached MEP is recommended.

CITIBANK
Interoffice Communication

To:	Office:	Kensington	Subject:	British National
	Person:	Divisional Executive		Life Acquisition
From:	Office:	Hammersmith	Reference:	AAA/dcb
	Person:	U.K. Country Business Managers	Date:	13th August 1985

Attached is an MEP convering the proposed acquisition of 100 percent of British National Life Assurance Company Limited (BNL) for a price not to exceed U.S.$13.7MM. We have also included a $19.6MM capital injection in this MEP, as

Exhibit 20 *(continued)*

we anticipate this being the incremental requirement under U.K. statutory provisions prior to adequate earnings levels being achieved. Injection of this capital will also improve the companies' earnings performance, allowing earlier consolidation for tax purposes.

Rationale

Life insurance continues to be viewed as a key element to our Individual Bank strategy in the United Kingdom. Consumers view life insurance not only as protection but also as a tax-planning and investment opportunity. Fifty percent of total U.K. consumer savings are invested in insurance-company-managed funds. In order to meet the full financial needs of the U.K. consumer, we must offer life-insurance-related services. In order to do so, we filed in 1981 and received U.S. Federal Reserve Board approval in 1984 to sell and underwrite life insurance through our U.K. subsidiaries. To date these have been involved only in the credit-life-related areas complementary to our Citibank Savings lending activities.

We have been pursuing a full-service life insurance sales and underwriting firm to broaden our presence in the U.K. consumer market. Due to extremely high premiums, the acquisition of a large company giving us an immediate and substantial presence has been eliminated as an option. Instead, we have decided to develop our existing insurance operations and look at BNL as an opportunity to accelerate our de novo expansion. BNL gives us an existing infrastructure, including systems, investment management, and a direct sales force; a reasonably capable management team; and an appropriate product line. Utilizing BNL and our existing customer base, we anticipate substantial sales/revenue synergies, which could not otherwise be realized by a de novo development in less than two years.

Based on our projections, a de novo development of a direct-sales insurance business involving the hiring of management, systems and product development, and branch/sales force recruitment and training would require 18 to 24 months and U.S.$3.5MM in expenses before any sales occur. Cumulative, after-tax losses through 1990 on a start-up would be U.S.$12.7MM. This compares with the BNL acquisition cumulative profits of U.S.$4.9MM through 1990.

The success of the acquisition is dependent on our providing BNL with sales prospects from our existing U.K. customer portfolio. This will enhance sales force performance by increasing new policy sales per salesperson by 50 percent in 1986 and up to 100 percent in 1990. The resultant sales per salesperson in 1990 are expected to be at the level currently achieved by mature direct-sales forces in the life insurance industry.

Company background

The origins of BNL date back to 1920, but true development started with the relaunch of the company as a direct-selling, unit-linking life company in January 1983, and today it has 34M policyholders with $218MM insurance in force. 1984 premiums were $4.2MM generated through a direct sales force of 247 operating out of 22 branch offices. Its premium income in 1984 was $17.2MM single and $3.2MM regular.

Exhibit 20 *(concluded)*

A wholly owned subsidiary of XYZ Corporation [this company's identity is altered to protect confidentiality], the firm is now being sold as part of XYZ's efforts to refocus on its nonfinancial business activities.

Financial expectations

BNL presently loses approximately $3.1MM pre-tax due to start-up expenses and the higher costs in the growth phase of a life insurance company. With our purchase of BNL, the company will be able to offer insurance to the 1MM consumers with whom we have an established relationship in the United Kingdom. We expect this to nearly double sales and lead to a fifth-year achievement of our corporate hurdle rates. Cumulative losses prior to breakeven in year three will amount to U.S.$4MM. Of the $1.3MM premium, goodwill is anticipated to be $.5MM, after allowing for a $.8MM adjustment to revalue policyholder liabilities.

Regulatory and other considerations

Any agreement will be subject to U.K./U.S. regulatory approvals where we do not anticipate any objections to the acquisition, given the small size and our existing permissions.

The purchase will be subject to our audit and acceptance of:

BNL's operating system, controls, and procedures.
A review of contracts, leases, and other documentation.
Personnel, legal, and regulatory compliance.
A review of their investment portfolio.
The financial statements and tax returns (Peat Marwick will handle)
Current policyholder portfolio (we will retain an outside actuarial consultant for valuation purposes).

Additionally, we will require management continuity and will negotiate employment contracts with several key managers to ensure continuity after our acquisition.

The companies' headquarters are approximately one-hour's drive from our Hammersmith offices, so I envision no management complications due to location.

The company will initially be managed independently from our other Individual Bank activities, focusing on the necessary adjustments to ensure Citicorp standards are met. The building of sales momentum is the next priority, with further synergies to be explored at a later date. Given the apparent strength of the BNL management team, minimal personnel moves into BNL are anticipated. The existing managing director will report to me, and I will retain the insurance expertise currently on my staff.

I recommend your approval.

Case 12

Sunset Flowers of New Zealand, Ltd.

1   After 18 months of residing in the United States, John Robertson, a New Zealander, glances frequently at a map of the United States on his wall, wondering when he will get the time and resources to travel into the various metropolitan areas of the central, southern, and eastern states. Though such travel, he believes he can gain an improved appreciation of the characteristics of the markets for fresh cut flowers, an item that he began importing into the United States from New Zealand during his summer "vacation" from school.

2   In August 1981, John and his family left New Zealand for Seattle so that he could study for his M.B.A. degree at the University of Washington. A month earlier, he had resigned from his job and leased their house and small farm. John, age 29, had a degree in business from Massey University in New Zealand and was a chartered accountant. The Robertsons looked forward to both the learning and living experience in the United States. On completion of the degree, they intended to return to New Zealand, where John would seek employment in a senior management position with a company involved in exporting.

3   New Zealand is a country the size of Oregon, with a population of 3 million. The relatively small size of its population base coupled with its distance from world markets presents a barrier to its ability to establish an industrial base competitive with those of the leading world industrial nations. Therefore New Zealand is highly dependent on world trade, importing fuel and manufactured products, and gaining most of its overseas exchange through the exports of agricultural produce. Its FOB exports average around 22 percent of gross domestic product, compared with the U.S. figure of 8 percent. In order to hold its place in the world economy, New Zealand lobbies hard to remove the restrictions imposed on imported agricultural products by the EEC, Japan, and the United States. Alongside this campaign, efforts are being made to diversify into horticultural products like fresh flowers and fruit.

Exposure to Exporting and Cut Flower Production— New Zealand Experiences

4   Immediately prior to leaving New Zealand, John had been employed for almost four years as the financial manager of a company involved in growing, wholesaling, and exporting live ornamental trees and shrubs. The company used agents to sell its product on world markets, including two based in the United States, one in Japan, and one in Europe. The agents were paid retainers and typically provided services for several export companies. The experience gained from working for this company provided John with a background in the procedures necessary for exporting and an insight into the problems that exporters face when trying to compete in foreign markets, where control over representation is hindered by distance and knowledge of business procedures.

Source: Harry R. Knudson, Graduate School of Business Administration, University of Washington, Seattle, WA 98195. © Harry R. Knudson, 1985.

5   It was while working for this company that John was introduced to cut flower products. First, the Robertsons raised finance sufficient to allow them to purchase a farm. The farm contained land suitable for the cultivation of horticultural crops. One of the undertakings that John gave the banks that financed them was that he would establish horticultural crops on the land that would bring in export income to apply towards mortgage payments. Second, the Robertsons became acquainted with some neighbors, the Pratts, who were first-class horticulturalists. They had planted seven acres of a new variety of a Leucadendron plant that yielded a 2-foot stem with a red leaflike flower. They were excited about the stem's potential for export as a cut flower.

6   John and Gary Pratt met regularly to establish the costings on and productivity of the Leucadendron. Having established these factors, they remained uncertain of the product's export potential. Both agreed that it should market extremely well. John decided to invest in it in a small way and planted an acre. During this period, the first year's yields were being exported through an established export company whose principal line of business involved exporting fresh fruit and vegetables. The company had a large market share of this business, and had assumed a significant share of the exports of New Zealand cut flowers. The New Zealand cut flower export industry was small (total FOB exports in 1979 being NZ$1 million)[1] and, with the exception of a trade in orchids, immature. Export companies provided the many part-time cut flower growers with the marketing infrastructure that they themselves were unable to put together.

7   As the harvesting season progressed, the returns paid to Gary by the exporter declined, until they reached a point that production levels of 10,000 stems or fewer became only marginally economical. Gary and John met with the export company to discuss the trends. The company explained that price was a function of volume, and that the lower prices were a result of the increased volumes being placed on the world markets. Export market returns were substantiated by documentation.

8   Gary and John were not convinced by the explanation. However, they knew little about world markets for fresh cut flowers and could only speculate as to the reasons for the price movements. As there were no other established flower export houses to turn to, the only way to research the matter seemed to be to do so themselves. As John was going to be in the United States for M.B.A. studies, an opportunity presented itself for him to carry out some research, at least in the United States.

Introduction to the U.S. Fresh Cut Flower Market (September 1981 to March 1982)

9   When the Robertsons arrived in Seattle in September 1981, the harvesting season for the Leucadendron was nearing an end. It was due to begin again in March 1982. John found that because of his workload in the M.B.A. program and the need to get "acclimatized," he could not devote time to conduct any research on the structure of the U.S. fresh cut flower market. Thus at the end of the winter quarter of 1982, when he picked up a sample carton of Leucadendron flowers consigned by Gary to him at Sea-Tac Airport, his ideas on how to approach the market were not defined. He took the flowers home and on inspection found that they had kept well in transit and that their quality was good.

---

[1] NZ$1.00 = US$0.75 (June 1982).

Table 1
Estimates of Leucadendron cut flower yields*

	1981	1982	1983	1984
Gary Pratt	10,000	80,000	200,000	420,000
All other growers	10,000	80,000	800,000	1,870,000
Total stems yielded	20,000	160,000	1,000,000	2,290,000

* Yields assume *new* plantings of Leucadendrons as follows:

1980:   4,000 plants, 2 acres.
1981: 24,000 plants, 12 acres.
1982: 132,000 plants, 66 acres.
1983: 50,000 plants, 25 acres.

10   In the six days remaining before school began again, John felt that he should concentrate his efforts on gaining and assembling information concerning the production and shipping costs associated with the product, production forecasts, import procedures, the basic structure of the U.S. cut flower industry, and market reaction to the Leucadendron.

Production and Shipping Costs

11   John recalled that the grower required NZ$0.30 per stem to break even at volumes around 10,000 stems per year, and that harvesting and packing costs amounted to NZ$0.12 per stem. By calling Air New Zealand in Los Angeles, he was told that the "commodity rate" for fresh cut flowers from Auckland to Los Angeles (or San Francisco) varied according to quantity. John decided that their rate of NZ$2.00 per kilo, which he calculated to be NZ$0.11 per stem, was appropriate for his costings. These production, packing, and shipping costs totaled NZ$0.53, which on conversion came to US$0.40.

Production Forecasts

12   The yields from the Leucadendron plant showed impressive growth. In its first year of production, five flower stems could be cut from it. In the second year, this would increase to 10, in the third to 25, and in the following years up to 30 annually. The productive life of the plant was unknown but was estimated conservatively at seven years. In 1981, plants were only grown in New Zealand, where this particular hybrid had been developed. Rumors had circulated in New Zealand about the export potential of this new flower, and extensive plantings were being made. It was possible to envisage yields available for export similar to those in Table 1.

13   John based his estimates of plantings on his memories of the trends that were appearing before he left New Zealand. No industry survey existed. His knowledge of trends was aided by the nature of the business in which he previously worked—one that was involved in the propagation of plants for sale, including Leucadendron plants to the cut flower growers.

Import Procedures

14   When picking up the samples from the airport, John had been told by airline officials that he would have to engage the services of a customs broker if he was going to undertake imports of invoice value greater than $250. Presuming such brokers to be the experts on procedures required to import, he called to make an appointment with one. The broker was most helpful. John was told that imported cut flowers were required to be inspected by USDA on arrival. Once given clearance, duty was assessed at the rate of 8 percent on FOB value. The broker would arrange for these clearances through USDA and U.S. Customs. The broker charges a fee for such services, which is fixed for shipments regardless of size but which will vary among brokers. The broker with whom the meeting was held charged $50 per shipment. Should the client wish, the broker would arrange for any freight forwarding required.

The Basic Structure of the U.S. Cut Flower Industry

15   Little time was available to research the industry structure. Before showing the sample Leucadendrons to anyone in the industry, however, John wished to understand a little about the marketing infrastructure. Whereas he wanted industry reaction to the qualities of the flower, he also wanted their reaction to a price. He allocated a little time to research in the business school library. The *Business Periodicals Index* directed him to an article in *Fortune* magazine (May 18, 1982, pp. 68–75) titled "Billions in Blossoms." This helped give an impression of the size, competitiveness and sophistication of the industry. He could find no material that disclosed the general markups adopted in the industry by wholesalers and retailers. With such knowledge, he felt he could have observed similar flowers in retail florist shops, asked for prices, and then calculated back to get an idea of the price that a wholesaler might pay from a grower or distributor. Concerned over his limited knowledge of market prices and structure, he called several retail florist shops to observe prices. Unfortunately, he saw no flowers that remotely resembled the Leucadendron.

Market Reaction to the Leucadendron

16   Because of their ability to purchase large shipments of product, the wholesale florists were considered by John to be the sector of the industry that he should approach. Through such approaches, he wanted to find out

Reactions to its color and form.

Reactions to its four-week vase life.

Response to price.

Quantities they could move at a given price.

17   Before proceeding, John called Gary to get up-to-date information on export marketing strategies being adopted by other exporters in the 1982 Leucadendron season. Gary advised that there were considerable quantities of flowers ready, but that few markets for them were being found. A few were being sold in the United States, giving growers poor returns, similar to the previous year. The outlook for this product from a grower's perspective was now grim. Because of the urgency expressed by Gary,

John decided it was important to close some sales in addition to recording market reaction. For a 27-inch stem length, he decided to seek $0.95 per stem from a wholesaler. This gave more than adequate returns, and he felt that he had about $0.20 per stem to negotiate down if this seemed necessary. His calculations were worked out as follows:

Production, packing, and shipping costs	$0.40
Duty, 8 percent on FOB invoice value	0.05
Broker, assume 500 stems per shipment	0.10
Allowance for grower profit	0.10
Allowance for distributor's return	0.10
Additional profits, negotiable if necessary	0.20
Price to be sought from wholesaler	$0.95

18   Having never had sales experience, and not knowing how wholesale florists conduct business, John was apprehensive when he arrived for an appointment with a Seattle wholesale florist. The buyer's reaction to the samples was promising. He had never seen the product before, was impressed by its color and qualities, and soon had called other members of the firm to view it. The wholesaler was prepared to pay $0.90 for a 27-inch stem if given exclusive rights to distribute in Washington State. John indicated that he would not sell to others in the area for the next month if the wholesaler ordered weekly quantities of 1,000 or more stems. The wholesaler placed an order with him for 2,500 stems, delivery in a week, and payment a week following this.

Issues of Business, Organizational, and Marketing Policy (April 1982 to June 1982)

19   While John was pleased with the reactions from the wholesaler, he was aware that he had made the approach with insufficient preparation. Had he underpriced the product? Was the credit of the firm sound? Are "exclusive rights" typically given in this industry, and should he have conceded them? Was the reaction one that is normal when a new product is shown to a market, and will repeat orders be placed? In addition to these market-related issues, there were administrative and organizational issues to consider. What should be his role in the marketing chain? Should he act as an agent taking a commission, or buy from Gary and resell the product? What form of organization should he establish?

20   With the spring quarter beginning, time was again to become a major constraint on his activities. The demand for the product by the Seattle wholesaler slowed after the second order. The firm's buyer, however, had begun purchasing on his own account and was having John land them in Los Angeles, where he said he was selling them in the flower market. The arrangement suited John. After sales of 10,000 stems, however, orders mysteriously ceased. A check bounced. Most of the account was settled over the next six months.

21   These trading experiences occurred in the first seven weeks of the spring quarter. John told Gary that at the end of this quarter he wanted some more sample product delivered to him so that he could promote in markets outside Seattle. He also asked to be posted a copy of a market research publication that included research on the U.S. flower market, research funded by the New Zealand Export–Import Corporation. John had decided to take time in the summer recess to more professionally investigate the market. He also wanted to form an organization with the ability to trade successfully in the U.S. flower markets should his investigations suggest that the Leucadendron had potential.

22   From this brief exposure to conducting business in the United States, John had begun to appreciate the differences in the business customs between his homeland and the United States. The experience of negotiating the collection of an overdue debt had highlighted his lack of familiarity with credit and collection procedures. He felt that the inclusion of a U.S. businessperson in any organization he set up would overcome this weakness. He also felt it was important to involve the supplier in any such organization. A stable source of high-quality product seemed to be a condition of success in a market in fresh flowers. The distance between producer and distributor in this case seemed to reinforce the need for such involvement. At the end of the spring quarter, John decided to sound out his ideas with his landlord, Earl Sandquist, an experienced businessman. His proposal was to set up a company in Washington State having three equal shareholders—Gary Pratt, Earl Sandquist, and himself. This company would research the potential of the market for Leucadendrons and proceed to import and market them should such efforts seem warranted. The proposal was accepted, and "Sunset Flowers of New Zealand, Ltd.," was formed.

Introducing Sunset Flowers to the Trade (July 1982 to December 1982)

23   Armed with a market research report on the U.S. flower industry, newly printed business cards and promotional sheets, and eight flower cartons of Leucadendrons (1,200 stems), John accompanied Earl on one of his regular business trips to San Francisco. The plan was to visit the San Francisco flower market, learn more about the operation of the industry, meet wholesalers, promote the product, and find a market for it. John reflected on this venture.

> When I think back to those three days, I am amused. We achieved a lot, yet knew so little. I walked from wholesaler to wholesaler in the market, giving away samples and business cards. I could claim to be a grower from New Zealand, and at times this would get a very attentive ear. I met some most helpful wholesalers. It is amazing what you can learn from such casual conversations. They will recommend someone in Boston, New York, etc. to sell to. The most difficult times I experienced were when they asked about other flowers. I was lost. After visiting the market, I would return to the hotel room and write up records on potential customers. Earl and I would then spend time calling wholesalers throughout the country. Before doing so, we would decide who should make the call—for some situations, we felt that my New Zealand accent caught the attention best. In others Earl would speak as the president of the U.S. office. The Society of American Florists helped direct us to wholesalers, as did the Yellow Pages. By the time we returned to Seattle, we had located many of the best wholesalers in the United States. We followed up these efforts by sending letters and sample product throughout the United States.

Table 2
Cut flower export/handling and marketing activities

Physical handling of product	Possible ownership changes	Factors affecting marketability
Production	Grower	Ability to meet market requirements
Harvesting		Timing; grading; quality control; packaging
Packing	Export house	
Customs/agricultural clearance in country of export	Sunset Flowers of New Zealand (FOB NZ)	Pricing
International airfreighting		Distribution capabilities of importer
Customs/agricultural clearance in country of import	Sunset Flowers of New Zealand (CIF NZ)	Product promotion
Shipment distribution	Distributor	
Unpacking and processing	Wholesaler	Availability of market feedback
Arranging for final sale	Retailer	Use of market feedback
	End-consumer	

24   The time taken between sampling product to a wholesaler and then getting an order was at least three weeks. The wholesaler would want to test the product and get retailer reaction before committing orders. The delay was much longer than expected, and to the impatient grower in New Zealand, was interpreted as a further sign of weakness of demand. John flew to Los Angeles to promote in the flower market there. His samples this time included two other New Zealand cut foliage products, becoming available in 1983. In Los Angeles he tried also to promote directly to the most exclusive retailers. In Beverly Hills he got an enthusiastic reception. He collected a few weekly orders for carton lots. The idea of distributing directly to retailers had not previously seemed possible, as most retailers wanted only a few stems at a time, not the 150 in a carton lot. His retail contacts also provided him with information on how florists planned to present the Leucadendron to the end-consumer. Because they seemed popular for arrangements in hotels, he decided to fly back to Seattle via Las Vegas.

25   Reaction by florists who catered for the hotels and casinos in Las Vegas was not as enthusiastic as he expected. There were few major retailers, and they preferred to talk about their depressed trade due to the slow hotel business rather than new flower introduction. The samples suffered from the heat, and their wilted appearance did them no justice.

26   Four weeks after the first trip to San Francisco, and in debt to shareholders for $3,000 (which had been spent on stationary, travel, and accommodation), Sunset Flowers began to see the results of its efforts. John began calling wholesalers weekly to take orders for product to be delivered to them the following week. He would call Gary weekly to relay the order details. Gary would harvest the flowers and fly them in bulk to either San Francisco or Los Angeles. On arrival, John would instruct his import broker to clear them, break up the shipment, and consign them by air or truck to various wholesalers. Sunset Flowers bought the flowers from Gary and resold them to the wholesalers. Table 2 provides a chart of activities involved in handling and promoting this imported cut flower product.

27   Between the middle of July and the end of September 1982, Sunset Flowers had sales of Leucadendrons totaling $37,000, for approximately 50,000 stems. The end of September marked the end of the harvesting season for the year. Sunset Flowers had a customer list of 80 accounts, 30 of which could be termed active on a regular basis. The product was regarded by the trade as being high priced, and compared with a more common flower like a rose or carnation, its sales were low. Wholesalers expressed the view that they would turn over a lot more volume if its price were lower. To achieve the volumes so far, the price for a 27-inch stem had been dropped to $0.85 per stem, West Coast price.

28   Sunset Flowers learned that the market for fresh cut flowers is characterized by periods of peak demand. The trade spoke of Valentine's, Mother's, Thanksgiving, Christmas, and Memorial days as being the highest sales periods. Sunset Flowers had noticed some dampening in the demand for the Leucadendron as the season progressed. Total quantities sold continued to increase over time, however, as the new markets were penetrated. The cause of the dampening in demand was unclear. A suvery of retail reaction to a sample package of product in Chicago had been conducted by a prominent wholesaler. It indicated that most retailers like the Leucadendron. Given time for more market exposure, client use, and movement down in price, Sunset Flowers anticipated that greater volumes would be sold in 1983. Because of its red coloring, the Valentine's Day market was seen to be an important one to service. Gary was asked to try to have production available for this market.

29   In 1982, Sunset Flowers had been responsible for distributing most of the Leucadendron Safari Sunset sold in the United States. The company had begun to make a name for itself not only in the U.S. market as "the company from New Zealand" but also in New Zealand as the company that managed to sell Leucadendrons. Its promotional efforts were known to the Leucadendron flower growers.

30   As it marketed the Leucadendron, wholesalers persistently asked what else Sunset Flowers had available. They particularly wanted to know whether the company had supplies of cymbidium orchids, which New Zealand and Australia supply to the U.S. market from August to November, a supply that meets demand in the U.S. production "off-season." It soon became apparent that unless Sunset Flowers got involved in servicing the market with cymbidium orchids, its credibility in the market as a distributor from "down under" would be at stake. By August, Sunset Flowers had begun to market other flower varieties. At the end of 1982, $30,000 of orchid sales and $9,000 of sales of flower sources from Australia had been made, in addition to Leucadendrons.

Problems of Product Quality and Timing
(July 1982 to February 1983)

31   Sunset Flowers was positioned as a middleman in the channel of distribution. As such, it was expected to look after and appreciate the problems of both the supplier and the customer of its product. When problems arose in the supply of the product, the business of its customer was affected. When market conditions changed, the business of the supplier was affected. As the operation developed, it became clear that the way to reduce the occurrence of problems was for Sunset Flowers to get to know buyers *and* their markets, and suppliers *and* their products, extremely well. It seemed that an ongoing business relationship might even require more than this, perhaps best described as a degree of trust among all parties.

32   As Sunset Flowers developed its business, its ability to cope with problems without upsetting its supplier and customer relationships was tested.

Quality of Supplies

33   Although Leucadendron supplies from Gary Pratt were always received in good order, supplies of product from other growers were not. Sunset Flowers did not have systems set up to enable it to inspect all products at port of entry. If below-standard product was sent, customers would receive it. Sunset Flowers needed responsible suppliers to succeed.

Timing of Supplies

34   Sunset Flowers was learning the importance of having supplies of the correct color of flower delivered to the customer in time for the major flower days. Because of a poor summer in New Zealand in 1983, the Leucadendron had not been ready for Valentine's Day. Four weeks prior to Valentine's Day, however, Sunset Flowers had been led to believe by a supplier that flowers would be ready. Accordingly, the company had advertised this fact to the trade and spent $2,000 printing a colored promotional pamphlet. This was a costly error, both in terms of customer relations and dollars expended.

Quarantine Problems

35   Three shipments in a row of product from Australia had to be fumigated at the port of entry. Sunset Flowers took the advice of its Australian supplier, who maintained that the treatment would not affect the quality of the flowers. Two shipments were distributed. Customer complaints revealed that the longevity of the flower had suffered.

36   The position of Sunset Flowers in the marketplace could not be taken for granted. These errors had damaged its credibility.

Managing the Day-to-Day Operations

37   In its first three months of operations, the business was conducted by John from his home in Seattle. As turnover increased, he found that he spent much of his time on the telephone. His wife, Ann, typed correspondence, most of which was promotion oriented, and followed up introductory telephone calls to potential wholesale clients. The need soon arose to have access to both a telephone answering and telex service, the latter to better relay orders to New Zealand. Then came the need for filing space. In October, Sunset Flowers set up an office in a motel room in Everett. While the location required John to travel some distance to operate the business, it was attractive for other reasons. Most important, it located John close to Earl's office and therefore allowed the two to communicate regularly. Second, Earl owned the property and offered the room at no charge.

38   Sunset Flowers painted, carpeted, and furnished its new office. As telex sendings and receipts increased, it became more economical for the company to purchase its own machine rather than use a telex service. A station wagon was bought for the company's use. The decisions to make these investments followed a review of the company's cash flow and the ability of Sunset Flowers to develop into a viable company in 1983.

39   While running the business and working toward his M.B.A. kept John busy, he found that the two interests were able to be worked together remarkably well. He treated each as an exercise in learning that complemented the other. His office provided a first-class environment to conduct his studies in, and he selected course work for his remaining M.B.A. requirements that would help the "Sunset Group" develop. For instance, he researched the potential of the U.S. markets for certain fresh fruits from New Zealand in order to ascertain whether this was a market that a U.S.–based company with a New Zealand supply orientation and a U.S. market orientation could serve well.

Company Finances

40   From its inception, Sunset Flowers had relied on funds provided by shareholders and credit arrangements with its suppliers as its only sources of finance. To finance the initial company expenditure, most of which consisted of travel on the West Coast, Earl and John each used their personal finances. Such expenditure was recorded as shareholder advances to the company, and later capitalized. The cut flower growers in New Zealand had agreed to allow six weeks of credit on their accounts. Payment was made to New Zealand by check. Because of the length of time that checks took to clear through the international banking system, the banking system provided a further "extension of credit" of up to 10 days.

41   The time taken to collect receivables from wholesalers varied. Although Sunset Flowers set out with a policy of payment within two weeks, it soon became apparent that such terms would not be acceptable to most customers in the trade. Collection times varied between two weeks and two months.

42   Table 3 outlines the income statements and balance sheets for the period ending December 31, 1982 and 1983. In its first year of operations, the company struggled to break even. Shareholders were not reimbursed for their time. All setup costs were written off when incurred.

Defining Corporate Objectives and Structure

43   In August 1982, the venture was discussed in Seattle by Earl, John, and Alan Frampton, John's father-in-law. Alan was about to retire from his position as dean of the Agricultural and Horticultural Science Faculty at Massey University in New Zealand. He was interested in the concept of Sunset Flowers and seemed an ideal person to help coordinate the functions of the company in New Zealand. It was agreed that he should become a fourth shareholder in the company. Table 4 lists the overall objectives of the company that were established at the meeting. It was felt that the group should investigate the possibility of entering the market for other products, and that the company should be structured in such a way to allow this. The structure derived is illustrated in Table 5.

44   In December 1982, Sunset Holdings, Ltd. was registered in New Zealand. While its main purpose was to serve as a nontrading holding company, it could be used to trade when taxation or legal matters indicated that an advantage to the group would

Table 3
Sunset Flowers of New Zealand, Ltd.—Balance sheet as of December 31*

	1981	*1983*
Current assets:		
Accounts receivable	$ 9,099	$19,582
Less prov. for bad debts	500	3,500
Total	8,589	16,082
Current bank account		1,071
Short-term bank deposit	1,679	10,104
Total assets	10,278	27,257
Current liabilities (less):		
Creditors	3,682	6,862
Shareholder advances	4,947	3,255
Total	8,629	10,117
Working capital	1,629	17,140
Fixed assets:		
Vehicle and telex machine	2,245	2,245
Less: prov. for depreciation		1,123
Total		1,122
Net assets	$ 3,894	$18,262
Shareholders' funds:		
Issues and paid-up capital	$ 500	$10,000
Retained earnings 1983	3,394	3,394
Add profits 1983		4,868
		8,262
Total shareholders' funds	$ 3,894	$18,262

* All amounts are in U.S. dollars.

accrue if transactions were recorded in New Zealand instead of the United States. With the exception of Sunset Flowers of New Zealand, Ltd., no subsidiary companies had been formed.

45   Whenever John read the "Definition of Objectives for the Group" (Table 4), he never failed to be inspired. They indicated that challenging times lay ahead. As he went about his day-to-day tasks, however, he wondered whether they incorporated achievable goals. He had a family to support, and his savings were becoming depleted as he neared the end of the M.B.A. program. He felt that he should continue with the venture only if it could generate him a salary of $30,000 in the 12 months following graduation.

46   As he considered his career, he turned over in his mind and discussed with Ann and Earl some of the issues that seemed relevant when considering the prospects of the venture.

> *Strengths.* Experience in the U.S. cut flower marketplace. A track record leading to a dominant market share in Leucadendrons. A customer list of U.S. cut flower wholesalers. An office with basic equipment to run an import operation from.

> *Weaknesses.* A trading history in a few products only. A necessity to rely on supplier responsibility for quality product. Uncertain sources of additional product.

Opportunities. Location in a national market large by world standards. Potential to tap the significant production increases of horticultural products forecasted from New Zealand (Exhibit 1).

Threats. Potential competition from New Zealand exporters with capital behind them. Potential barriers from quarantine requirements. Trade barriers. Exchange rate movements.

Table 4
Definition of objectives for the group

Company purposes

The main purpose is to establish a marketing company in the United States to distribute and to market products derived principally (but not exclusively) from the agricultural and horticultural industries of New Zealand (and Australia).

The Company needs to be a successful commercial enterprise in the United States and not dependent on any particular product or market so that it can provide a sound, permanent, import/export service for New Zealand (and Australian) producers.

The Company will engage in related and complementary activities capable of supporting its main purpose and that contribute to its effectiveness and efficiency.

The Company needs to be able to provide attractive rewards to all who participate from production to final sale.

Objectives

1. *Profit*—The main objective of the Company is to maintain profitable operations. Profitability is essential if the other objectives of the Company are to be met. Profit must be sufficient to:
    (a) Pay a 25 percent return on invested capital.
    (b) Provide investment capital for the development of the Company.
2. *Sales growth*—A high sales growth will be sought. In 1984, sales of $1 million are targeted.
3. *Market share*—The Company seeks to become the dominant exporter to the United States of the products it handles from New Zealand (and Australia).
4. *Risk diversification*—The Company will develop a diversified product range within each trade in which it does business. Areas of trade under consideration include:
    (a) Fresh cut flowers.
    (b) Live ornamental and fruit plants.
    (c) Fresh fruit, including strawberries, blueberries, kiwi fruit, and feijoas.
    (d) Woolen products, including knitwear and sheepskins.
    (e) Market research services to exporters interested in the U.S. market.
5. *Innovation*
    (a) Market innovation—The Company will use innovative promotional techniques to reach end-users and seek to differentiate markets by the use of brands.
    (b) Product innovation—The Company will seek to acquire rights to market new products from New Zealand, will suggest new products for trial, and will seek to export to New Zealand and Australia products from the United States.

Table 4 *(concluded)*

Company growth strategy

1. The Company will seek to grow by forward and backward integration consistent with its marketing goals.
2. The Company will grow through diversification.

Company portfolio plan

The Company will maintain a balanced product portfolio, seeking in 1983 to establish a "cash cow" in order to aid its development.

Company structure and shareholding

A holding company will be established in New Zealand, to own the majority of the shares in U.S.–based subsidiary companies. Shareholders of the holding company will consist of Alan Frampton, Earl Sandquist, and John Robertson, each owning one third of the shares.

Table 5
Proposed corporate structure of the Sunset Group

The Sunset Group

Alan Frampton—33.3%	John Robertson—33.3%		Earl Sandquist—33.3%

Sunset Holdings, Ltd.

Gary Pratt—25%	Sunset Flowers of New Zealand, Ltd.	75%	Registered in U.S.A.
"Fruit Grower"—25%	Sunset Produce of New Zealand, Ltd.	75%	Registered in U.S.A.
Unknown—25%	Sunset Market Research, Ltd.	75%	Registered in U.S.A.

Exhibit 1
Potential growth in horticultural export values to 1990

$million
FOB
(1982$)

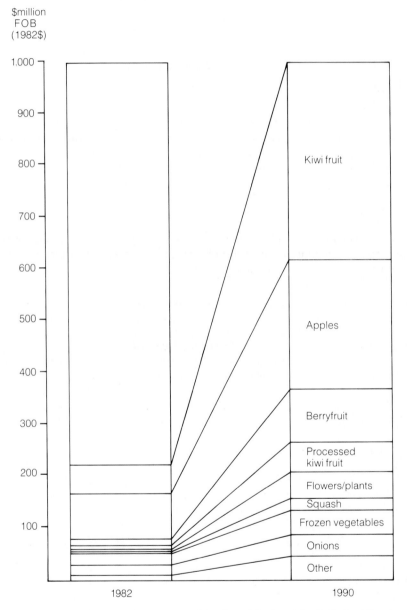

Source: Horticultural Export Development Committee, *A Review of the Horticultural Export Industry* (Wellington, New Zealand: Agpress/Printcraft, 1982).

Case 13

Merrill Lynch & Co. (B)

Introduction

1   Until 1940, Merrill Lynch was a mid-sized brokerage firm whose most noteworthy achievement was surviving the Depression. At that time, however, cofounder Charles E. Merrill became convinced that brokerage houses, which had catered to the elite, had ignored a huge potential market. Merrill thus renamed his stockbrokers "account executives" and built a vast system of retail branches to sell Wall Street to Main Street. The firm used its retail distribution muscle to leverage itself into the leadership position in institutional brokering, trading, and investment banking.

2   Merrill Lynch remained the leading brokerage firm on Wall Street through the 1970s. During that period, the firm evolved from a product-oriented partnership to a financial market-oriented, diversified services corporation. It also dealt successfully with extensive deregulation of the financial services industry in the late 1970s and early 1980s.

3   The Merrill Lynch of 1984 emerged as a publicly owned, financial conglomerate with a market orientation targeted to four principal groups of customers: individuals, corporations, institutions, and governments.

An Industry of Dynamic Change

4   The development of the financial services industry was determined by a line of important deregulation milestones: the Federal Reserve Board's removal of interest rate ceilings on banks' large certificates of deposit in 1970; the Securities and Exchange Commission's 1975 dictum to stop the fixing of brokerage commissions; the creation of six-month market rate certificates of deposit for banks and thrifts in 1978; and landmark legislation in 1980 and 1982 that cleared the way for interest-bearing checking accounts nationwide and the removal of the remaining interest rate ceilings on bank accounts. These deregulation milestones combined with product innovation, government economic policy, rapid inflation, and historically high interest rates to produce a turbulent industry environment.

5   With market positions no longer set by regulation and with savers free to choose from a selection of investments, the financial services industry rapidly took on the characteristics of an industry shaped by market forces.

6   The first such characteristic was consolidation of resources, with companies trying to achieve economies of scale. Two methods used to achieve these economies were (1) merging with similar institutions (see Exhibit 1) and (2) developing new services suited to distribution through existing facilities. A striking example of consolidation was the 1981 acquisition of Dean Witter Reynolds by Sears Roebuck & Co., which combined with Sears's Allstate and Coldwell Banker subsidiaries to make Sears a retail financial supermarket. The creative development of Universal Life insurance by E. F. Hutton

---

This case was prepared by Frank L. Winfrey of the University of Wisconsin at Parkside and John A. Pearce II of George Mason University. Copyright © 1985 by John A. Pearce II.

Exhibit 1
Mergers involving Wall Street firms, 1981–1982

Acquired company	Acquiring company	Date	Price ($ millions)
Bache	Prudential	June 1981	376
Shearson Loeb Rhoades	American Express	June 1981	1,038
Salomon Brothers	Phibro	October 1981	554
Dean Witter Reynolds	Sears, Roebuck	December 1981	607
Foster and Marshall	Shearson/AmEx	March 1982	75
Loewi	Kemper	May 1982	64
Robinson-Humphrey	Shearson/AmEx	June 1982	77

Source: "The Morning After at Phibro-Salomon," *Fortune*, January 10, 1983, p. 76.

Life in 1980 was an example of a new service suited to distribution through existing facilities, since the offices of E. F. Hutton stockbrokers performed the function.

7   Specialization through the unbundling of services was a second new characteristic of the industry. For example, discount brokers emerged after the "unfixing" of brokerage commissions in 1975. Discounters offered a no-frills transaction service without advice, or a broad product line, to their customers. By forgoing research services, discount brokers routinely underpriced their full-service competitors, such as Merrill Lynch, by as much as 70 percent of the normal commission. In 1983, discount firms accounted for about 15 percent of the share volume generated by individual investors.

8   A third characteristic was a profit squeeze in the financial services industry. Heightened competition exerted strong pressure on profit margins, which led to an increased emphasis on each company's productivity. An example of the pressure on profit margins was the trimming of staff research positions among merged firms. Typically, when firms with research staffs merged, the new organization promptly cut back the equivalent of one staff, thus reducing costs and improving profit margins.

9   The consulting firm McKinsey and Company reported that the financial services companies most likely to survive the 1980s would be either relatively large firms (assets in excess of $1.5 billion) with plenty of excess capital or relatively small firms (assets of less than $800 million), which would be able to move quickly into specialized markets.

10   On May 1, 1975, the Securities and Exchange Commission "unfixed" commission rates on stocks. Over the following nine years, the average commission paid by institutional customers declined by about 40 percent, which meant that firms in the industry had to attempt to extract maximum revenues from other parts of the business. The source of these revenues became the retail operations, which focused on the individual investors. The fervor to expand and to obtain retail business flourished in what became a highly competitive environment.

11   While the industry exhibited an increasing concentration of capital through merger activity, the capital devoted to the securities industry actually declined as many firms diversified to other interests, such as real estate, insurance, oil and gas investments, and employee relocation services.

12   Survival for the major brokerage firms in the new environment seemed to require firms to be all things to all people. The traditional mandate to the brokers to sell stocks was supplanted by a new priority to capture assets. The idea was to get as

Exhibit 2
How Merrill Lynch ranks against its rivals (as of December 31, 1982)

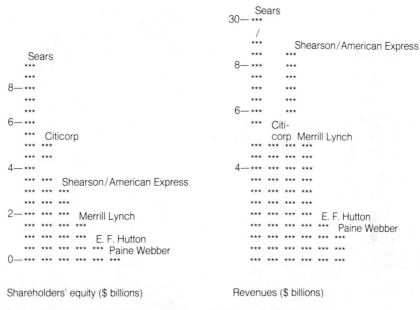

Shareholders' equity ($ billions)   Revenues ($ billions)

Source: "Merrill Lynch's Big Dilemma," *Business Week,* January 16, 1984, p. 62.

much of the clients' funds as possible: the risk money, the savings money, the sheltered income, and the insurance premiums. Revenues from such nonequity products grew from about 15 percent to about 50 percent of firms' retail income from 1975 to 1984.

13   The retail broker was naturally the one elected to market the new products, and the broker was expected to introduce new products to existing and prospective clients. The strategy was intended to work to the advantage of the brokers, whose income would not be exclusively tied to the Dow, given their involvement with a satchel of diversified products.

14   The trouble was that the product proliferation created too many products for the broker to understand expertly. To exacerbate the problem, there was an ever-widening array of options, commodities, financial futures, tax shelters, financial planning, life insurance, annuities, cash management accounts, and money market funds. Virtually every large brokerage house needed its own expensive and elaborate support system to help the increasingly less authoritative brokers.

The New Face of the Competition

15   Merrill Lynch had long been the largest firm in the brokerage business in terms of assets, revenues, and range of activities. The financial services industry transitions that occurred from 1975 through 1984 rapidly changed its preeminent position, making the firm one of the new pack (see Exhibits 2 and 3). The new entities Merrill Lynch faced matched its financial strength and scope of activity.

Exhibit 3
The score on the Big Five (as of September 30, 1981, $ millions)

	Shearson/ American Express	Citicorp	Merrill Lynch	Prudential- Bache	Sears/ Dean Witter
What they get:					
Revenues	$ 7,000	17,300	3,800	13,200	2,770
Net income	510	420	200	N.A.	630
What they've got:					
Assets	23,700	121,700	15,700	67,500	32,700
What they do:					
Securities brokerage	**		**	**	**
Securities trading	**	**	**	**	**
Cash management services			**		**
Investment management	**	**	**	**	**
Commodities brokerage	**		**	**	**
Corporate underwriting					
United States	**		**	**	**
International	**	**	**	**	**
Commercial banking					
United States		**			
International	**	**	**		
Savings and loan operations					**
Small-loan offices		**			**
Credit cards, charge cards	**	**			**
Traveler's checks	**	**			
Foreign exchange trading	**	**	**	**	**
Leasing	**	**	**	**	**
Data processing services	**	**	**	**	**
Property and casualty insurance	**			**	**
Life insurance, health insurance	**		**	**	**
Mortgage insurance					**
Mortgage banking	**	**	**		**
Real estate development				**	**
Commercial real estate brokerage			**		**
Residential real estate brokerage			**		**
Executive relocation services			**		**

N.A. = Not available.

Source: "The Fight for Financial Turf," *Fortune,* December 28, 1981, p. 57.

Sears Roebuck & Co.

16   In late 1981, Sears became a major force in the financial services industry. The giant retailer augmented its presence in insurance and consumer credit by acquiring Dean Witter Reynolds Organization Incorporated, the nation's fifth-largest investment firm, and Coldwell Banker and Company, the nation's largest real estate broker. These two firms added to Sears's already impressive stable of existing financial services— Allstate property, casualty, and life insurance; mortgage life insurance; 87 Allstate Savings and Loan Association branches in California (with $3 billion in assets); interest-bearing credit for some 25 million active users of Sears credit cards; automobile and boat installment loans; and commercial realty and store leasing.

17   The company's 831 retail stores, 2,388 catalog outlets, 1,950 stand-alone Allstate Insurance sales offices, 348 Dean Witter offices, 87 savings and loan branches in California, and several hundred real estate locations clearly offered the Sears organization enormous competitive potential on a distributional basis.

18   Sears's in-house database on consumer credit, by far the biggest of its kind, became the nucleus for a carefully targeted selling of home loans or financial products to prequalified Sears customers. The database, data processing, and telecommunications capabilities of the company were also upgraded to provide a convenient nationwide electronic payment system capable of providing complete financial transaction services.

BankAmerica Corporation

19   BankAmerica Corporation skirted the Glass–Steagall and Bank Holding Company Acts, which barred banks from markets and products that included mutual funds, insurance and securities underwriting, and brokerage services, when it purchased Charles Schwab and Company, the country's largest discount brokerage firm. Because Schwab served only as an executor of orders and neither bought stock for its own account nor underwrote stock issues, BankAmerica was able to conform to the letter of the law. In acquiring Schwab, BankAmerica obtained a highly automated brokerage firm plus some 220,000 investors for its customer base. Beyond that, the acquisition offered a way for Bank of America, the nation's second-largest bank, to provide brokerage service to its 4 million customers.

20   In early 1984, Bank of America announced it would rent branch space to Capital Holdings Group of Louisville, Kentucky. Capital was an insurance holding company that planned to sell automobile, homeowner, and life insurance from the branch locations. A Bank of America spokesperson said the arrangement was designed to give the bank a head start in the race of commercial banks to expand into other financial services, such as the insurance business.

Shearson/American Express

21   American Express's acquisition of Shearson Loeb Rhoades linked the number one company in one financial field with the number two company in another financial field. American Express was a unique financial house whose 113-year history had revolved around money transfers, travel services, card services, insurance, and international banking. Shearson was a brokerage house which had been developed through

Exhibit 4
Segments of the financial services retail market as determined by Shearson/American Express

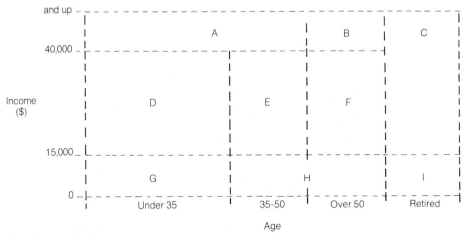

Key to the classification of investors:
   A—Up and comers.
   B—Affluent established.
   C—Affluent retired.
   D—Successful beginners.
   E—Mainstream family.
   F—Conservative core.
   G—Young survivors.*
   H—Older survivors.*
   I—Retired survivors.*
*Denotes incomes below targeted levels.
Source: "Fire in the Belly at American Express," *Fortune,* November 28, 1983, p. 92.

a series of acquisitions of old-line brokerages. The merger created an entity that could offer a plethora of financial services packages from the combination of the American Express credit card operations with 11 million cardholders, Shearson's money market fund and securities operations, Shearson's mortgage banking operations, Warner/Amex Cable and Satellite Communications subsidiaries, American Express Fireman's Fund insurance, and American Express International Banking Corporation. Additionally, shortly after the merger, Shearson/American Express acquired the Boston Company, an investment management firm; Balcor, a packager of real estate investments; four regional securities brokerage firms; the Trade Development Bank of Geneva (one of Switzerland's five largest banks), an overseas banking firm catering to the owners of "flight capital" and other very wealthy individuals; and Investors Diversified Services of Minneapolis, a company that specialized in selling life insurance, annuities, and mutual funds to individuals, particularly middle Americans. The Shearson/American Express strategy was to use the company's various sales forces to promote products manufactured by Shearson—Fireman's Fund, the International group, and the Travel Related Services group—to targeted individuals (see Exhibit 4).

22   Shearson/American Express made a distinct effort to change the image of its sales force to adapt to the new competitive environment. The firm renamed its 4,500 stockbrokers "financial consultants" and outfitted each of them with a private office.

23   In April 1984, Shearson/American Express agreed to acquire Lehman Brothers Kuhn Loeb Incorporated. The purchase was an expedient way for Shearson to strengthen two of its weakest lines—investment banking and trading, particularly in fixed-income and equity securities. The company was renamed Shearson Lehman/American Express.

Citicorp

24   Citibank expanded its activities into the retail securities industry when it began to offer discount brokerage services at its 275 New York City branches. Some 600 of the nation's more than 14,500 banks offered discount brokerage services by early 1984. The Citibank discount brokerage accounts were handled by Q&R Clearing Corporation, a unit of Quick and Reilly Incorporated, the New York discount brokerage concern. Although Citibank had been offering such services as a part of its "personal asset account," Citibank's entrance into the brokerage business represented an expansion of financial service activity by Citicorp, Citibank's parent.

25   As part of Citicorp's effort to develop a nationwide presence in the financial services industry, the company purchased savings and loan associations in California, Illinois, and Florida and developed industrial banks, which offered commercial banking services (except checking accounts and trust services) in some 22 states.

26   Citicorp, the nation's largest bank holding company, pushed the state of New York unsuccessfully for changes in state banking laws to allow it to sell insurance. However, Citicorp did achieve a position in the travel and entertainment segment of the financial services industry with its acquisition of the Diners Club credit card operations. In late 1983, Citicorp purchased a maximum allowable 29.9 percent share of the London stockbrokerage firm Vickers da Costa (Holdings) PLC and approximately 75 percent of Vickers's overseas operations, which included branches in Hong Kong, Singapore, Tokyo, and New York.

27   These services, combined with its traditional banking services, strongly positioned Citicorp as major entrant in the financial services industry of the 1980s.

E. F. Hutton

28   In its 1982 annual survey of the 1,000 leading U.S. companies, *Forbes* magazine ranked E. F. Hutton first in the brokerage group in return on equity, first in return on capital, and first in per-share earnings growth. According to Lipper Analytical Associates, E. F. Hutton had the highest production per retail account executive in the industry. Besides its retail brokerage operations, Hutton was also active in tax-sheltered investments, life insurance, annuities, investment management programs, and Hutton Credit company, which specialized in commercial paper. Still, E. F. Hutton chose to be viewed as one of the last basic securities business specialists. This was an image that Hutton management hoped would attract investors who felt stifled in the larger, less entrepreneurial financial supermarkets.

29   E. F. Hutton was the first brokerage firm to enable its clients to electronically access their account information via personal computer or videotex. This "Huttonline" service allowed Hutton customers to tap into the CompuServe Network and retrieve any of their account information. The system also provided a broker–client electronic mail link so that each could leave messages to the other in the system. This helped to leverage both the customers' time and the brokers' time. The electronic system was seen as a major new way to hold down expenses and generate revenues.

Prudential/Bache

30   After the acquisition of Bache Halsey Stuart Shields by Prudential in 1981, the firm was renamed Prudential-Bache and reorganized into eight major operating groups structured around its various sales forces and lines of business. The firm offered more than 70 different investment products, including stocks, options, bonds, commodities, tax-favored investments, and insurance. A group of mutual funds was offered by the company through the investment management of Prudential, which represented a transfer of fund management resulting in a considerable savings to Prudential-Bache. The combination also produced several new investment products in areas such as real estate, options, and oil and gas investments, which were sold by both Prudential-Bache account executives and Prudential insurance agents licensed by the National Association of Securities Dealers.

31   Prudential, working through its Prudential Bank and Trust Company in Hapeville, Georgia, announced it would offer a credit card with a line of credit through one of the existing major credit card networks.

Merrill Lynch

32   The 1983 earnings for Merrill Lynch rose more than 50 percent over the historically high levels of 1982 and 1981. However, this earnings pattern was threatened by competitive challenges resulting from the deregulated industry.

33   One of the essentials for competing in the new environment was a strong capital position. In 1973, Merrill Lynch's total stockholder equity was less than half a billion dollars, but by 1984, the company was above $2 billion. Merrill Lynch also continued to improve its return on equity in 1982 and 1983, though it lagged the industry average on this measure. Overall, it appeared that Merrill Lynch had the financial strength to compete on multiple fronts in the financial services industry (see case appendixes).

34   Despite environmental transitions and increasingly direct competition from Sears Roebuck & Co., Shearson/American Express, Prudential-Bache, Citicorp, and other formidable companies, Merrill Lynch moved deftly to innovate services and to defend and expand its markets. By 1984, it, too, had formed a state-chartered bank. Merrill Lynch formed the bank in New Jersey through a legal loophole in the federal definition of a bank by simply not offering a demand deposit service. The purpose of this new bank unit was to take consumer deposits, move into consumer lending, and offer unsecured lines of credit attached to VISA cards.

35   Merrill Lynch identified 38 products that affluent households purchased from 20 different financial service vendors, such as lawyers, accountants, banks, finance companies, and real estate brokers. It then began packaging those services, creating total financial-care products, such as the cash management account (CMA).

36   The success of the cash management account service was a star example of product innovation. The service went from 4,000 customers in 1978 to over 1 million customers in 1983. The significance of the product was magnified because it brought to Merrill Lynch a great many high-quality customers who had not previously done business with the firm.

37   Although Merrill Lynch's greatest strength was its retail system of 431 branch offices with 8,763 brokers, it had become a handicap as well. Because of its broad range of customer services, its compensation methods, and its full-service brokerage house culture, Merrill Lynch's approach remained very expensive at a time when discount brokering and other low-cost methods were gaining legitimacy and market share.

38   To counter the problem, Merrill Lynch began to convert its account executives into financial advisers. These advisers were seen as the hub of a network of salaried professionals and assistants specializing in insurance, lending, and tax matters. This new structure served a twofold purpose: (1) to upgrade, modernize, and reduce the labor intensiveness of internal communications and (2) to allow the company to gain control of the marketing and delivery function from its account executives. Customer communications and control of the client relationship were seen as a means for Merrill Lynch to gain the primary share of the profit derivable from a given product or service, thus permitting increased profitability for the firm.

The Potential for a Brokers' Mutiny

39   Merrill Lynch account executives shared four concerns with their counterparts in competing firms pertaining to the reorientation of the brokerage business.

40   An information overload developed as companies introduced new products and services. Brokers were expected to acquire a familiarity with the new products and new services in addition to their daily routine of 8 to 12 hours of selling, prospecting, environmental scanning, and transaction-related paperwork.

41   Many brokers maintained that their best clients resisted one-stop financial shopping, preferring instead to use specialists. Successful brokers did not want to dilute their image as brokers with their wealthy investor clients.

42   The new products and new services did not offer much, if any, return to the individual brokers. The commissions on selling insurance or annuities relative to selling equities did not warrant the effort and, thus, represented a significant opportunity cost to an individual broker. Some of the new services, such as cash management accounts, did not even offer commissions while requiring account executive time.

43   The increased pressure by management to sell the new products and new services made many brokers uneasy. Many felt that some of the new products ill-served certain investors. Those brokers recognized that the key to their long-run success rested in serving their clients well, not by pushing their firm's new products or services.

The Merrill Lynch Cash Management Account Financial Service

44   The cash management account (CMA) financial service combined a brokerage account with other major financial services to simplify and organize most day-to-day money transaction activities of participants. The CMA account was made available to investors who placed $20,000 or more in any combination of securities and cash in a Merrill Lynch brokerage account.

45   Idle cash in the securities account was invested automatically in shares of one of three no-load CMA money market funds (the CMA Money Fund, the CMA Government Securities Fund, or the CMA Tax-Exempt Fund), or the generated cash was deposited

in an insured savings account. Dividends earned from any of the money funds were reinvested in the CMA account daily, and the interest on the savings account was compounded daily and credited monthly.

46   The CMA service provided investors with imprinted checks that could be used like bank checks to gain access to the assets in the account (both cash and securities). Additionally, a special VISA debit card issued through Bank One of Columbus provided the means to access a CMA account.

47   The program was set up so that a CMA account provided a line of credit backed by the assets in a hierarchy of cost of the asset, cash, money market funds, and then margin-loan (borrowing) power. These assets were accessible through either a VISA transaction or a CMA check.

48   The CMA program provided comprehensive monthly statements listing all transactions in the account chronologically. All securities transactions, money market fund earnings, interest on savings, and VISA and checking transactions were provided separately by category.

49   The innovative Merrill Lynch CMA account worried bankers and competing brokerage firms. The combination of a money fund with a debit card backed by a line of credit based on a customer's securities and funds on deposit proved to be an extremely popular product. Industry sources estimated that at least 6 million investors were prospective customers for these types of accounts, and it was reported that 1,000 new CMA accounts were being opened each day at Merrill Lynch. This phenomenal success prompted bankers and the other brokerage houses to start programs similar to the Merrill Lynch CMA account service.

50   Bache announced a similar product, the Bache Command Account, with an added feature of automatic insurance coverage on the account holder through its parent, Prudential Insurance Company of America.

51   Shearson/American Express introduced a financial management account (FMA), which required a $25,000 cash or securities minimum. Shearson's FMA provided an American Express Gold Card to its participants, and its monthly statement also provided a summary of net worth for the current month and on a year-to-date basis for the customer.

52   Dean Witter's so-called Triple-A program allowed customers to draw on their investment accounts using checks or debit cards, with any idle funds automatically swept into high-yield money market funds.

53   Citibank offered a "personal asset account" encompassing the same combination of money funds, credit, and range of banking and investment services as its competitors.

54   Paine Webber had only some 35,000 clients with its version of the CMA, the "Resource Management Account," in early 1984, but the average balance in its customers' accounts was nearly twice the $70,000 to $80,000 average in the Merrill Lynch accounts.

55   The CMA account marked a change in fundamental focus for Merrill Lynch as the firm made an effort to increase its large-volume retail business and reduce its exposure to low-profit customers. The president of Merrill Lynch's Individual Services unit announced that the firm no longer desired to seek small accounts for its account executives. Such accounts were to be handled in the future by a clerk operating in a client services department at each branch. This move was designed to cut the cost of servicing individuals.

56   In some parts of the country, as many as 25 percent of the Merrill Lynch stockbrokers switched to competitor firms every year due to the increased pressure from the firm

to be more productive. In response to this turnover problem, Merrill Lynch began to use litigation to prevent its brokers from walking away with clients or, at least, to force them to pay back the $16,000 to $18,000 cost of their training. It was a particularly active litigant because it was trying to change the dynamics of the relationship among the firm, the broker, and the customers. It wanted its customers to think of themselves as Merrill Lynch customers rather than as clients of a particular account executive. This was a large part of the rationale for the initiation of the CMA service—to develop customers who would stay with Merrill Lynch even if their broker account executive moved to another brokerage firm.

Additional New Products

57   Sophisticated investors were chased by a pride of brokerage house felines in the 1980s: CATS, LIONS, and TIGERS. These were acronyms for a successful variety of zero-coupon Treasury certificates Merrill Lynch and other firms packaged for individual retirement accounts (IRAs). Merrill Lynch also introduced a new stock fund tied to the performance of the Standard & Poor's 500 Stock Index, which proved to be very successful.

58   In late 1983, Merrill Lynch expanded its consumer lending activities by the introduction of its equity access account, a type of second mortgage which also proved to be very successful.

59   Merrill Lynch introduced the capital builder account (CBA) in early 1984. The product was quickly dubbed the "Son of CMA," as it was basically a lower-priced and streamlined version of the CMA targeted at the more modest investor, requiring a minimum investment of only $5,000, but it required customers to pay for each service above an allotted number of transactions.

Merrill Lynch Research

60   To provide professional, accurate, and timely research to its customers, Merrill Lynch assembled the largest research staff in the investment business. Merrill Lynch employed 94 equities analysts, who covered 1,200 domestic firms, 200 foreign firms, and over 40 industries. Along with this vast breadth of coverage, the research staff was consistently rated as having the best analysts of the major brokerage firms.

61   Most of the men and women of Merrill Lynch's research division were finance trained M.B.A.s with operating experience from the industries they were assigned to cover. Merrill Lynch managed to attract and retain such talented analysts through a combination of factors: Merrill Lynch's prestigious research reputation, an attractive pay scale, extensive staff resources, and the computer-based opinion retrieval system (the QRQ system).

62   The Merrill Lynch QRQ system was an expanded equity database which contained the detailed financial projections developed by the research analysts. This information was made available electronically to all branch offices at each account executive's desk. The data base contained current-year, next-year, and quarterly estimates of earnings; current and projected dividend rates; and the analysts' assessments of rates of growth in dividends and earnings projected five years into the future.

63 Besides providing fundamental equity analyses, Merrill Lynch's research effort employed 12 technical analysts, who studied market data and produced technical market analyses, investment strategy advice, and fixed-income and government securities analyses.

The MRP Program (A Personnel Development Program)

64 The Merrill Lynch Management Readiness Program (MRP) was designed to respond to the need to identify talented employees and to prepare them for management positions. The first step in the program involved a selection process in which several levels of management participated in choosing candidates for the program.

65 The second step, the participant's seminar and program kickoff, was a highly interactive event. The employees studied themselves and the organization and began action planning. Each participant left the seminar with established career goals and a development plan detailing skill and knowledge areas necessary to achieve the goals. The participant's managers were given tools to help them and their subordinates define development goals and activities for the six-month program.

66 High-level managers served as mentors and were given development activities with four assigned protégés. They met monthly with the protégés and used whatever information and instructional approach they preferred.

67 In the final phase of the MRP, participants wrote a profile, or self-statement, that documented their goals and skills. The profiles were then presented to a wide range of high-level managers throughout the company to acquaint them with the potential management candidates. In its first two years of operation, more than 83 employees experienced some type of positive job change, such as a promotion or special assignment.

The Perspective of Merrill Lynch's Management

68 In addresses to the Los Angeles Society of Securities Analysts and to the Twin Cities Society of Securities Analysts, Roger E. Birk, then president of Merrill Lynch, and Donald T. Regan, then chairman and chief executive officer of Merrill Lynch, outlined management's view of the firm's strengths and basic corporate objectives.

69 The two senior officers listed six major strengths:

1. Merrill Lynch's leadership in diverse market areas.
2. The firm's top credit ratings and financial strength.
3. A strong sales force backed by sophisticated staff and equipment.
4. Merrill Lynch's ability and willingness to adapt to new customer needs and attempts to provide better services.
5. The leadership, vision, and experience of the senior management group (which was relatively young and thus well positioned to offer long-term continuity).
6. Merrill Lynch's strong but flexible management by objectives (MBO) planning system.

70 The president and chairman listed three basic objectives for the company: (1) to improve profitability on a long-term sustainable basis; (2) to soften the cyclicality of earnings—both within their established operating areas and through the addition of new services; and (3) to make each cyclical peak higher than the preceding peak.

Future Directions

71   In 1984, Merrill Lynch was attempting to automate the delivery of its investment information. The firm bought a sizable interest in the cable television Financial News Network and had experimented with a two-way cable system that provided Merrill Lynch research through the Dow Jones News/Retrieval® System.

72   To expand its business information and business communications interests, Merrill Lynch announced that it planned to build a satellite communications center and office park on a 350-acre site on New York's Staten Island in conjunction with the Port Authority of New York and New Jersey.

73   In March 1984, Merrill Lynch announced a joint venture with International Business Machines Corporation (IBM) for the delivery of stock-quote and financial data to IBM desktop computers. The plan called for marketing the service to brokerage firms, banks, thrift institutions, real estate firms, and insurance companies. Merrill Lynch saw the financial information services business as a means to cut its costs and generate revenue from existing operations, such as its research and support units.

74   These attempts by Merrill Lynch to position itself as a technology leader in financial services were interpreted by analysts as strategies designed to reverse its recently eroding stature as the dominant force in the industry.

Appendix A

MERRILL LYNCH & CO.
Statements of Consolidated Earnings
Years Ended December 30, 1983, December 31, 1982, and December 25, 1981
(in thousands of dollars except per share amounts)

	1983 *(52 weeks)*	*1982* *(53 weeks)*	*1981* *(52 weeks)*
Revenues:			
Commissions	$1,523,291	$1,132,898	$ 928,645
Interest	1,792,478	1,943,980	1,835,471
Principal transactions	675,527	656,212	427,879
Investment banking	746,638	595,515	359,881
Real estate	392,035	245,051	167,759
Insurance	116,371	116,471	116,313
Other	440,566	336,074	202,234
Total revenues	5,686,906	5,026,201	4,038,182

Appendix A *(concluded)*

Expenses:			
Compensation and benefits	2,266,278	1,732,483	1,295,255
Interest	1,432,555	1,607,915	1,511,103
Occupancy and equipment rental	325,349	243,836	168,556
Communications	230,331	188,725	151,471
Advertising and market development	229,537	155,818	138,772
Brokerage, clearing, and exchange fees	143,824	121,645	93,578
Office supplies and postage	106,309	88,930	75,746
Insurance policyholder benefits	49,887	27,865	28,135
Other	356,514	303,739	242,151
Nonrecurring charges	153,500	—	—
Total expenses	5,294,084	4,470,956	3,704,767
Earnings before Income taxes	392,822	555,245	333,415
Income taxes	162,659	246,414	130,541
Net earnings	$ 230,163	$ 308,831	$ 202,874
Earnings per share:			
Primary	$ 2.68	$ 3.79	$ 2.57
Fully diluted	$ 2.59	$ 3.74	$ 2.57

Appendix B

MERRILL LYNCH & CO.
Consolidated Balance Sheets
December 30, 1983, and December 31, 1982
(in thousands of dollars, except per share amounts)

	1983	1982
Assets		
Cash and securities on deposit:		
Cash	$ 223,353	$ 311,939
Interest earning deposits	577,302	584,229
Cash segregated and securities on deposit for regulatory purposes	358,179	363,661
Total cash and securities on deposit	1,158,834	1,259,829
Receivables:		
Brokers and dealers	600,137	734,015
Securities borrowed	876,703	464,665
Customers (less reserve for doubtful accounts of $73,920 in 1983 and $79,304 in 1982)	6,061,184	4,777,978
Loans (less reserve for doubtful accounts of $16,925 in 1983 and $11,250 in 1982)	887,732	615,397
Resale agreements	5,975,094	4,361,346
Other	1,298,755	967,811
Total receivables	15,699,604	11,921,212
Securities inventory, at market value:		
Money market instruments	2,192,726	1,545,781
Governments and agencies	2,450,424	2,058,036
Corporates	1,320,529	963,401
Municipals	864,404	804,264
Total securities inventory	6,828,083	5,371,482

Appendix B *(concluded)*

	1983	*1982*
Other assets:		
Investment securities	462,373	624,749
Property, leasehold improvements, and equipment (less accumulated depreciation and amortization of $180,722 in 1983 and $155,755 in 1982)	615,699	443,738
Equity advances for residential properties	372,957	412,363
Deferred insurance policy acquisition costs	99,269	87,953
Other	902,264	575,913
Total other assets	2,452,562	2,144,716
Total assets	$26,139,084	$20,697,239

Liabilities and Stockholders' Equity

	1983	*1982*
Liabilities:		
Short-term borrowings:		
Bank loans	$ 1,033,777	$ 501,738
Commercial paper	4,890,164	2,684,387
Repurchase agreements	7,609,198	6,237,890
Demand and time deposits	869,814	1,004,933
Securities loaned	593,386	800,601
Total short-term borrowings	14,996,339	11,229,549
Long-term borrowings:	1,264,096	756,869
Total borrowings	16,260,435	11,986,418
Commitments for securities sold but not yet purchased, at market value:		
Governments and agencies	1,408,248	641,994
Corporates	536,934	585,572
Municipals	52,418	50,421
Total commitments for securities sold	1,997,600	1,277,987
Other liabilities:		
Brokers and dealers	394,777	541,576
Customers	3,168,070	3,123,700
Drafts	514,953	397,277
Insurance liabilities	129,537	84,937
Income taxes	143,275	295,594
Compensation and benefits	560,107	468,840
Other	1,082,311	1,088,028
Total other liabilities	5,993,030	5,999,952
Stockholders' equity:		
Common stock, par value $1.33⅓ per share; 200,000,000 shares authorized in 1983 and 1982; 89,970,834 shares issued in 1983, and 78,559,846 shares issued in 1982	119,960	104,746
Paid-in capital	419,551	112,191
Accumulated translation adjustment	(7,355)	(4,280)
Retained earnings	1,390,683	1,226,757
Total stockholders' equity	1,922,839	1,439,414
Less:		
Treasury stock, at cost; 442,089 shares in 1983 and 515,022 shares in 1982	9.314	6.532
Unamortized expense of restricted stock grants	25.506	—
Total	1,888,019	1,432,882
Total liabilities and stockholders' equity	$26,139,084	$20,697,239

Appendix C

MERRILL LYNCH & CO.
Five-Year Financial Summary
Year Ended Last Friday in December, 1979–1983
(in thousands of dollars except per share amounts)

	1983 (52 weeks)		1982 (53 weeks)		1981 (52 weeks)		1980 (52 weeks)		1979 (52 weeks)	
Revenues:										
Commissions:										
Listed securities	$ 852,920	15.0%	$ 650,385	12.9%	$ 554,512	13.7%	$ 630,876	20.9%	$ 421,887	20.6%
Options	166,712	2.9	167,487	3.3	125,564	3.1	141,960	4.7	80,023	3.9
Commodities	187,572	3.3	168,730	3.4	156,107	3.9	159,616	5.3	103,501	5.0
Over-the-counter securities	106,352	1.9	53,993	1.1	61,066	1.5	57,415	1.9	29,386	1.4
Mutual funds	126,730	2.2	46,595	.9	24,494	.6	22,309	.7	7,061	.4
Money market instruments	83,005	1.5	45,708	.9	6,902	.2	—	—	—	—
Total commissions	1,523,291	26.8	1,132,898	22.5	928,645	23.0	1,012,176	33.5	641,858	31.3
Interest:										
Margin loans	462,127	8.1	450,566	9.0	619,401	15.3	447,182	14.8	340,475	16.6
Securities owned and deposits	905,679	15.9	856,988	17.0	676,778	16.8	433,694	14.3	296,097	14.4
Resale agreements	424,672	7.5	636,426	12.7	539,292	13.3	249,999	8.3	178,177	8.7
Total interest	1,792,478	31.5	1,943,980	38.7	1,835,471	45.4	1,130,875	37.4	814,749	39.7
Principal transactions:										
Money market instruments	18,079	.3	23,163	.5	15,103	.4	12,263	.4	4,868	.2
Governments and agencies	45,710	.8	143,434	2.8	60,687	1.5	22,472	.7	17,387	.9
Corporates	399,430	7.0	289,308	5.8	223,285	5.5	210,205	7.0	174,136	8.5
Municipals	212,308	3.8	200,307	4.0	128,804	3.2	55,950	1.9	35,233	1.7
Total principal transactions	675,527	11.9	656,212	13.1	427,879	10.6	300,890	10.0	231,624	11.3
Investment banking:										
Underwriting and advisory fees	247,743	4.3	206,934	4.1	147,051	3.6	106,410	3.5	79,006	3.9
Selling concessions	498,895	8.8	388,581	7.7	212,830	5.3	172,768	5.7	83,647	4.1
Total investment banking	746,638	13.1	595,515	11.8	359,881	8.9	279,178	9.2	162,653	8.0
Real estate:										
Brokerage	272,980	4.8	160,397	3.2	100,555	2.5	39,940	1.3	8,586	.4
Relocation Fees	64,951	1.1	56,863	1.1	45,209	1.1	28,729	1.0	28,758	1.4
Other	54,104	1.0	27,791	.6	21,995	.6	17,698	.6	15,679	.8
Total real estate	392,035	6.9	245,051	4.9	167,759	4.2	86,367	2.9	53,023	2.6

Insurance:										
Life	60,895	1.1	55,992	1.1	52,514	1.3	47,325	1.6	42,780	2.1
Annuities	46,975	.8	52,616	1.0	37,352	.9	13,426	.4	6,561	.3
Mortgage guaranty	—		—		20,251	.5	23,237	.8	20,867	1.0
Other	8,501	.1	7,863	.2	6,196	.2	6,507	.2	6,800	.3
Total insurance	116,371	2.0	116,471	2.3	116,313	2.9	90,495	3.0	77,008	3.7
Other	440,566	7.8	336,074	6.7	202,234	5.0	122,492	4.0	71,081	3.4
Total revenues	5,686,906	100.0	5,026,201	100.0	4,038,182	100.0	3,022,473	100.0	2,051,996	100.0
Expenses:										
Compensation and benefits	2,266,278	39.8	1,732,483	34.5	1,295,255	32.1	1,079,283	35.7	736,728	35.9
Interest	1,432,555	25.2	1,607,915	32.0	1,511,103	37.4	879,002	29.1	638,498	31.1
Occupancy and equipment rental	325,349	5.7	243,836	4.8	168,556	4.2	123,817	4.1	100,671	4.9
Communications	230,331	4.1	188,725	3.8	151,471	3.7	113,610	3.8	90,025	4.4
Advertising and market development	229,537	4.0	155,818	3.1	138,772	3.4	101,185	3.3	60,006	2.9
Brokerage, clearing, and exchange fees	143,824	2.5	121,645	2.4	93,578	2.3	83,028	2.7	57,060	2.8
Office supplies and postage	106,309	1.9	88,930	1.8	75,746	1.9	53,752	1.8	40,014	2.0
Insurance policyholder benefits	49,887	.9	27,865	.6	28,135	.7	24,087	.8	19,554	1.0
Other	356,514	6.3	303,739	6.0	242,151	6.0	203,180	6.7	116,721	5.6
Nonrecurring charges	153,500	2.7	—		—		—		—	
Total expenses	5,294,084	93.1	4,470,956	89.0	3,704,767	91.7	2,660,944	88.0	1,859,277	90.6
Earnings before income taxes	392,822	6.9	555,245	11.0	333,415	8.3	361,529	12.0	192,719	9.4
Income taxes	162,659	2.9	246,414	4.9	130,541	3.3	160,460	5.3	75,773	3.7
Net earnings	$ 230,163	4.0%	$ 308,831	6.1%	$ 202,874	5.0%	$ 201,069	6.7%	$ 116,946	5.7%
Earnings per share:										
Primary	$ 2.68		$ 3.79		$ 2.57		$ 2.72		$ 1.60	
Fully diluted	$ 2.69		$ 3.74		$ 2.57		$ 2.71		$ 1.60	
Average shares used in computing earnings per share:										
Primary	86,410,000		82,744,000		80,920,000		74,088,000		72,892,000	
Fully diluted	92,178,000		84,478,000		80,950,000		74,354,000		72,892,000	

Per share and share amounts have been restated to reflect the two-for-one common stock split that was distributed in June 1983.

Appendix D

MERRILL LYNCH & CO.
Statements of Changes in Consolidated Financial Position
Years Ended December 30, 1983, December 31, 1982, and December 25, 1981
(in thousands of dollars)

	1983	1982	1981
Source of funds:			
Net earnings	$ 230,163	$ 308,831	$ 202,874
Cash dividends	(66,284)	(52,232)	(45,480)
Earnings retained	163,879	257,599	157,394
Non-cash charges:			
Nonrecurring charges	153,500	—	—
Other	237,652	168,465	161,513
Increase (decrease) in:			
Commitments for securities sold but not yet purchased	719,613	46,362	443,480
Brokers and dealers payable	(146,799)	258,360	(80,742)
Customers payable	44,370	648,272	161,510
Drafts payable	117,676	(253,163)	340,526
Income taxes	(152,319)	143,873	(114,814)
Compensation and benefits	91,267	195,092	46,237
Other liabilities	(5,717)	203,028	269,326
Other, net	(349,580)	(149,359)	(165,254)
Funds provided before financings	873,542	1,518,529	1,219,176
Increase (decrease) in financings:			
Short-term:			
Bank loans	532,039	(495,259)	(351,332)
Commercial paper	2,205,777	836,966	753,966
Repurchase agreements	1,371,308	324,605	2,765,822
Demand and time deposits	(135,119)	300,253	(37,159)
Securities loaned	(207,215)	259,323	(93,175)
	3,766,790	1,225,888	3,038,122
Long-term:			
Senior debt	623,910	102,733	134,701
Subordinated debt	(116,683)	152,395	—
Issuance of common stock	97,850	—	—
Sale of common stock under employee stock plans and conversion of convertible subordinated debentures, net of treasury stock and restricted stock grants	196,436	15,443	44,468
	801,513	270,571	179,169
Funds provided from financings	4,568,303	1,496,459	3,217,291
Total funds provided to increase assets	$5,441,845	$3,014,988	$4,436,467
Increase (decrease) in assets:			
Cash and securities on deposit	$ (100,995)	$ 247,052	$ (239,262)
Brokers and dealers receivable	(133,878)	395,838	(188,207)
Securities borrowed	412,038	235,157	93,287
Customers receivable	1,283,206	102,575	(95,562)
Loans receivable	272,335	269,679	(35,541)
Resale agreements	1,613,748	(66,980)	2,081,264
Securities inventory	1,456,601	1,158,716	2,155,794
Other, net	638,790	672,951	664,694
Increase in assets	$5,441,845	$3,014,988	$4,436,467

Case 14

Sharpco, Inc. (1985)

1   In 1972, James Sharplin and two brothers decided to open a welding and steel fabrication shop in Monroe, Louisiana. The Sharplins formed a corporation, Sharpco, Inc., bought a parcel of land at the eastern edge of Monroe, and built a small shop building. Most of the initial equity investment was in the form of welding machines, tools, and other items contributed by the three owners. James worked full time at Sharpco while his brothers pursued other interests. The company was profitable from the first year. Sales grew steadily, and the shop was expanded several times during the 1970s. In the early 1980s, James exchanged his interest in some commercial property the Sharplins owned for his brothers' shares of Sharpco stock.

2   Sharpco is engaged in four distinct business areas—all related to heavy equipment, especially crawler tractors (often called "bulldozers" or "caterpillars"). First, the company makes and sells a number of welded steel items for heavy equipment. Second, Sharpco markets new and used crawler tractor parts. Third, James and his workers provide repair service for heavy-equipment owners. Finally, Sharpco does high-strength repair welding for heavy equipment. Each of these business areas will be discussed further under the heading "Operations."

3   In January 1985, the business was moved to a new 30,000-square-foot facility in what had become a rapidly expanding commercial and industrial area along Interstate Highway 20. Among the more than 20 firms on highway I-20 near Sharpco are heavy-equipment dealers representing Deere and Company (makers of John Deere equipment), Case Power and Equipment Company, and Fiat-Allis, Inc. (successor to Allis Chalmers, Inc.). Dealers for the other two major brands of heavy construction equipment, International Harvester and Caterpillar, are located about three miles away. Exhibit 1 shows the location of the new Sharpco plant. Table 1 provides geographic and demographic data relevant to Sharpco's main trade area.

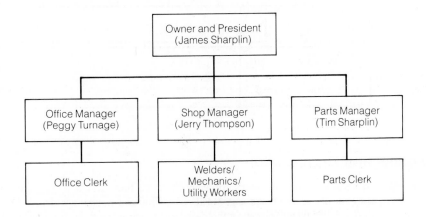

This case was prepared by Arthur Sharplin of McNeese University.

673

Exhibit 1
Sharpco's location

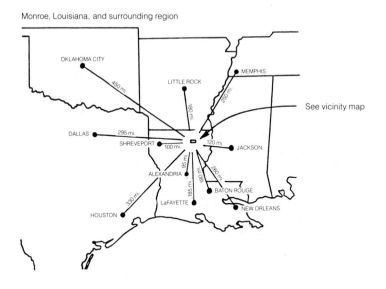

Monroe, Louisiana, and surrounding region

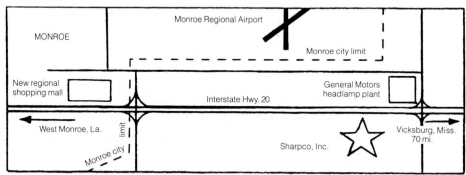

Sharpco vicinity

Personnel and Organization

4   In recent years, the work force at Sharpco has varied from as many as 30 down to
its 1985 level of 11. As a general rule, Sharpco keeps a cadre of experienced workers
and fills in with temporary welders and mechanics during busy periods. The company
has no formal organization chart. However, the diagram shown on p. 673 was drawn
by James Sharplin to represent the organization as it existed in 1985.

Table 1
Geographic and demographic data

	Monroe	Ouachita Parish (county)	Northeast Louisiana (16 parishes)	Louisiana (entire state)	United States
Population, July 1982 (thousands)	57	141	434	4,373	230,000
Per-capita income, 1981	$6,973	$7,486	$5,897	$8,113	$8,917
Change in population 1980–82 (percent change for entire period)	−0.9%	1.2%	1.4%	4.0%	2.8%
Change in *real* per-capita income, 1979–81 (percent change for entire period)	−5.1%	−3.1%	−2.9%	1.0%	−0.4%
Value of agricultural production, 1982 ($ millions)	N.A.	$14	$48	$1,407	$158,700
Personal income, 1982 ($ millions)	N.A.	$1,380	$16,010	$44,000	$2,578,600
Work force employed in manufacturing, 1982 (percent)	N.A.	18.1%	14.9%	14.6%	20.0%
Work force employed in construction, 1982 (percent)	N.A.	8.6%	5.7%	9.6%	5.8%
Work force employed in farming, 1982 (percent)	N.A.	1.2%	6.6%	3.2%	2.0%
Approximate land area, 1982 (thousands of acres)	N.A.	401	6,519	28,494	2,264,960
Proportion of land area in farms, 1982 (percent)	N.A.	23.4%	40.7%	31.3%	46.0%

N.A. = Not available.

5   The lines of authority at Sharpco are not rigidly followed. James routinely bypasses each of his direct subordinates and deals directly with workers. "The managers all work as a team," says James. "Any one of us can make a major or minor decision— or write a $10,000 check." Everyone in the organization is expected to pitch in wherever there is a need for extra help and to accept direction from whoever knows most about the particular job being done. The insert on p. 676 provides brief comments made by James Sharplin concerning each of the key employees.

6   There is no formal performance appraisal at Sharpco and no written compensation policy. Sharpco furnishes medical insurance for James, Jerry, and Tim (Peggy is covered under her husband's policy furnished by his employer). The company also pays about one half the cost of insurance for each worker. The managers are paid on a salary basis. Hourly paid workers make from $6 to $9 an hour, about average for the area. Every year, James says, he ranks the employees in order of what he considers to be their contribution to the company. Then he adjusts the pay of any whose pay seems inequitable. Practically all hiring and firing is done by James personally, although Jerry Thompson has authority to terminate any of his workers.

Operations

7   Exhibit 2 shows a typical crawler tractor, with the main relevant parts labeled. Practically all of Sharpco's mechanical repair work and most of the parts sales are related to tractor undercarriages, final drives, and steering clutches. The undercarriage is

James Sharplin discusses Sharpco's key people

Jerry is 30 years old. He is my mother's grandnephew. Jerry is dedicated to Sharpco. He has a great deal of ability to get the job done. He is a good welder and the best mechanic we have. The men respect him, and that helps make him a good manager. Customers like him; they ask for him. They know they can depend on what he says. During the move, when we were all running just to keep up, Jerry sold two excavator buckets. He worked right through a weekend, even though he had the flu, to get the buckets built. He has a good memory, too. He can usually tell a customer if we have a part without even checking the computer. Jerry's main recreation is hunting. I try to make sure he has some time off during hunting season. When I decided to furnish him a company pickup, I made sure it was something he has always wanted but never felt that he could afford—a four-wheel-drive "mud hog."

Peggy is in her 40s. She has taken a number of college courses. Although Peggy does not have a degree, she knows much more than most college graduates. She is as dedicated as any employee I have. She is the most cost-conscious person in the whole organization, including me. After just a year of working with computers, she knows more about them than the computer "expert" who sold us the machine. Somehow, Peggy and the computer were an instant match. Peggy is a highly religious lady. I think this accounts in some degree for her diligence, and I know I can trust her with anything I have. There has never been the slightest need for me to check up on her. Everyone here respects her, and her presence helps keep foul language and rowdy behavior at a minimum. Peggy is usually miles ahead of me with any information I need—like sales statistics. She put the used parts on the computer without any guidance. And the information was in a form she knew I could use. If things move too fast, she just works nights and Saturdays. She does all the advertising better than any ad agency could. She comes up with the ideas, does the copy, and just runs it by me for approval. Peggy is a perfectionist.

Tim is 25 years old. He is my nephew. Tim is strictly work, family, church, and school. He attends Northeast Louisiana University part-time, studying business. Tim has a good number of outside obligations, including school. But whenever I need him he is here. He asked me if he should let his school wait while we get over the move and get things back on an even keel. I told him that he might take one course instead of two, only if he thought it best, but I felt he should continue his education without a break. He works hard—wants to do things right. He grew up on a farm, where he often had neither the time nor the equipment to do quality work. Tim is learning fast. In the long term I think he will be one of our most important people. In fact, he is now. He had to come almost from ground zero—learning welding, learning crawler tractors, learning fabrication. He has done remarkably well in the two years since he came to work here.

Exhibit 2
A typical crawler tractor

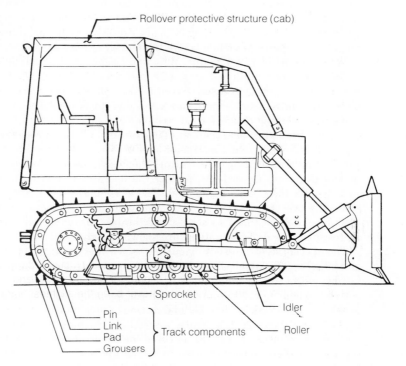

that part of the tractor nearest the ground, including the heavy steel tracks, along with rollers, sprockets, and structural members designed to pull the tracks and keep them in alignment. The final drive is a large, closed gear box, which transmits power to the track. In Exhibit 2 the final drive is hidden from view behind the sprocket. The steering clutches are located above the final drives. They allow either the left or right final drive to be disengaged so that the brake can be applied on the respective side, causing the tractor to turn.

8   The tracks and related components cannot be insulated from the sand, dirt, and gravel in which a tractor usually operates. Consequently, all of the moving surfaces wear away steadily, especially those which are in contact with one another. The track chain is similar to a large bicycle chain. As the track is pulled by the sprocket around the idler and rollers, the pins wear mainly on just one side. Each pin fits into a bushing, which also wears in the direction of the stress. A typical undercarriage will require major repair after 3,000 hours of use and overhaul after 1,500 additional hours. Major repair consists of removing the tracks and turning each pin and the respective bushing half around so that the least-worn surfaces are in contact. To do this, a portable hydraulic press is used to press out one of the pins. This may require

200 tons of force. Then the tracks, weighing as much as 3,000 pounds each, are moved to the track press, where the remaining pins are pressed out, along with the respective bushings. All parts are then inspected and the tracks reassembled, with the pins and bushings in their new positions. While the track is off, all undercarriage components are inspected for cracks, leaking oil seals, excessive wear, and other defects. Of course, any needed repairs are made before the tractor is reassembled.

9   When major overhaul is due, pins and bushings are replaced, idlers and rollers exchanged or reconditioned, and new sprockets installed. With about every second major overhaul, worn grousers have to be cut off and new ones welded onto the track pads. The entire track chain may also have to be replaced. Less frequently, final drives and steering clutches require repair.

10   Among the items Sharpco manufactures are roll-over protective structures (cabs), such as that shown on the tractor in Exhibit 2. Many of Sharpco's customers are involved in land clearing. The tractors they use must have heavy steel screens welded or bolted around the cabs to protect the operator from tree limbs. Sharpco makes and installs those screens as well. The cabs and screens are made from ordinary steel. However, most of the items the company makes involve the use of high-strength steel, about three times as strong and hard as ordinary steel (and more than twice as costly). Several of these items are shown in Exhibit 3.

11   The special steel is used for cutting edges and strength members on the blades and buckets. This steel is purchased from major steel distributors and stocked in 8-foot-by-20-foot sheets, ranging in thickness from three eighths of 1 to 2 inches. A portable acetylene cutting torch, which runs on a small track, is used to cut the steel to shape. Pieces which are to become cutting or digging edges are clamped in a vertical position and the edge beveled at a steep angle using the same kind of automatic torch. Curved pieces of mild steel (used for noncritical parts of digging buckets) and the steel pins and bushings used to attach the buckets to hydraulic excavators and backhoes are furnished by a local machine shop.

12   After the parts of a digging bucket or land-clearing blade are cut and shaped, they are welded together just enough to hold them. Then they are carefully inspected prior to final welding. To ensure against failure, Sharpco workers weld all critical points manually, allowing components to cool between layers of weld material. This process requires special high-strength electrodes (welding rods). Less critical welds can be made with semiautomatic machines, which are much faster and easier to operate than manual ones and which use large rolls of wire instead of individual welding electrodes.

13   Sharpco digging buckets range in size from small standard buckets weighing only 300 pounds to trapezoidal buckets weighing over a ton and measuring 17 feet across. A trapezoidal bucket is designed to dig a complete drainage canal as the hydraulic excavator or backhoe to which it is attached slowly drives along the intended canal path, scooping out as much as three feet of new ditch with each stroke and laying the dirt aside. Sharpco land-clearing blades and rakes weigh up to 8 tons. The largest Sharpco vee blade has two serrated cutting edges, each 20 feet long. Pushed by the largest production model tractor made by Caterpillar or Fiat-Allis, one of these blades clears a swath 16 feet wide through timber up to 30 inches in diameter.

14   Blades and buckets require replacement of cutting edges and other wearing surfaces after extended use. Each item is designed so that the worn parts can be cut loose and new ones installed through a procedure similar to the original manufacture.

Exhibit 3
Items Sharpco makes using high-strength steel

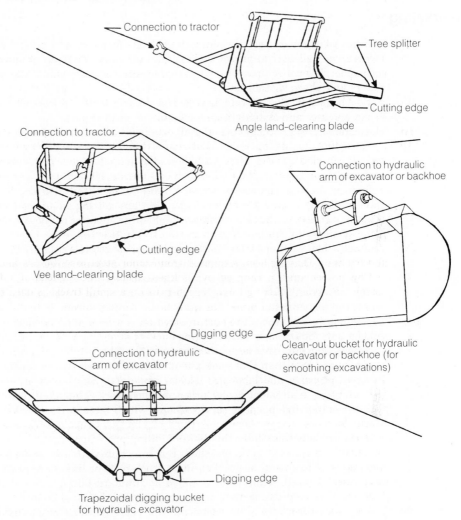

Connection to tractor

Tree splitter

Cutting edge

Angle land–clearing blade

Connection to tractor

Cutting edge

Vee land–clearing blade

Connection to hydraulic
arm of excavator or backhoe

Digging edge

Clean-out bucket for hydraulic
excavator or backhoe (for
smoothing excavations)

Connection to hydraulic
arm of excavator

Digging edge

Trapezoidal digging bucket
for hydraulic excavator

Source: Drawn by Joy Kight.

15   All of the items Sharpco reconditions or manufactures are painted at the Sharpco plant. Rollers and small parts are simply dipped into a paint vat. Larger items are spray painted. In addition, practically all of the equipment that comes in to be repaired is covered with dirt and mud. Cleaning is accomplished in the wash area, using a special high-pressure washer. Construction machinery and components to be repaired are usually brought to the Sharpco plant on customer trucks, although Sharpco does keep several trucks of varying sizes to make pickups and deliveries when necessary. The layout of the new Sharpco facility is shown in Exhibit 4.

Marketing

16   Sharpco's customers include contractors, large farmers, and other heavy-equipment owners, as well as equipment dealers who purchase Sharpco products and services for resale. Several equipment dealers employ Sharpco to repair tracks and recondition rollers and idlers for them.

17   Sharpco subscribes to a computerized used-parts dealer network whereby subscribers exchange price and availability information on needed parts. As a result, the company ships an increasing number of parts, especially used ones, to dealers around the country.

18   Although the customer list totals more than 1,000, 100 contractors accounted for two thirds of Sharpco's 1984 cash flow. For example, one land-clearing contractor, with just four tractors, was billed $86,000 during 1984. Eighty percent of Sharpco's 1984 sales were to customers within a 100-mile radius of Monroe. "That is changing rapidly, though," said Peggy Turnage. "We are getting inquiries from all over the country because of the dealer network." For the months of August, September, and October 1984, 90 equipment owners, mostly contractors, were billed $342,742 out of Sharpco's total sales of $416,557. Shown this list of customers, James Sharplin identified 57 of them as having been regular customers for at least three years.

19   Sharpco's overall pricing policy, as expressed by James Sharplin, is "whatever the traffic will bear." For new tractor parts, he says, this is normally about 80 or 85 percent of dealer retail price. For used parts, it ranges from 25 to 60 percent of retail, depending upon whether the part in question is a frequently needed one or one which seldom fails. Sharpco prices its digging buckets at or above dealer list prices. According to James Sharplin, this is justified because the Sharpco buckets have a significantly lower failure rate than those equipment dealers furnish. When repair jobs are priced in advance, parts and labor are usually combined. Sharpco tries to stay just below usual original equipment dealer prices on such work. This often results in the loss of jobs to smaller independent service shops, which often price well below what major tractor dealers charge. About one third of Sharpco's repair work is done on a time-and-materials basis. Under this kind of billing procedure, customers usually bargain on major components to be installed. But minor items (such as bolts, steel plate for welding reinforcement, and replacement track pads or links) are priced at 90 percent of suggested retail, while labor is billed at standard billing rates, currently $26 per hour (local new tractor dealers charge an average of $28 an hour).

20   Prices are also used to keep Sharpco concentrated in its main businesses. When a customer insists that the company repair a transmission or engine, for example, the price for that work is intentionally elevated. Price changes are also used to control the overall level of work activity. When spurts in demand occur, hourly rates and markups on materials are increased, both for time-and-materials work and for work which is priced in advance. When demand slackens, workers are laid off until the crew is down to the 10- or 12-person cadre of experienced workers. Only then are prices and markups sacrificed to sustain sales volume.

21   The primary means of promotion is direct mail. A typical mail-out is illustrated in Exhibit 5. Currently the mailings are sent to all customers once a month. James has made plans, however, to program the company's computer to segment the mailing

Exhibit 4
Sharpco plant layout

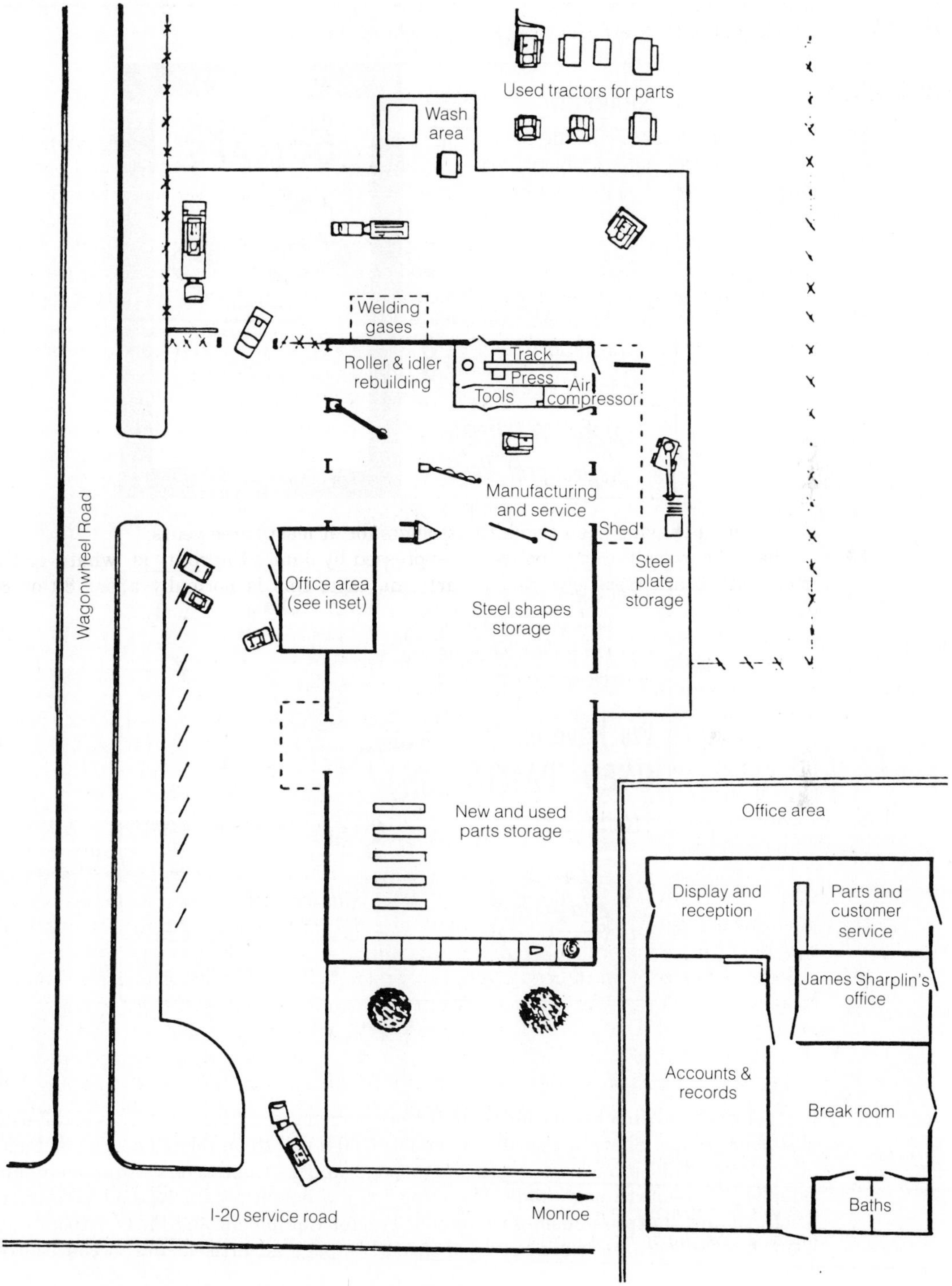

Used tractors for parts

Wash area

Welding gases

Roller & idler rebuilding

Track

Press

Tools

Air compressor

Manufacturing and service

Shed

Steel plate storage

Office area (see inset)

Steel shapes storage

Wagonwheel Road

New and used parts storage

I-20 service road

Monroe

Office area

Display and reception

Parts and customer service

James Sharplin's office

Accounts & records

Break room

Baths

Exhibit 5

Outside

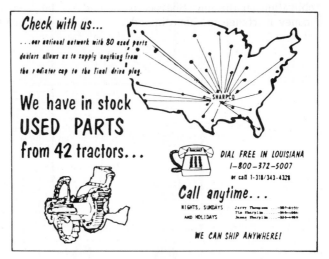

Inside

list along several dimensions and to mail more personalized advertisements to differing customer groups. Sharpco also spends about $700 a month on telephone Yellow Pages advertising. This provides for one-fourth page under "Contractors' Equipment and Supplies," one-fourth page under "Welding," and a business-card-type advertisement briefly listing Sharpco's businesses under "Tractor Equipment and Parts." About once a quarter, Sharpco inserts a series of three two-page advertisements in consecutive issues of *The Contractor's Hotline,* a national weekly newspaper offering heavy equipment and parts for sale to about 5,000 equipment owners and dealers. These advertisements cost about $1,400 for each three-week sequence. James, Jerry Thompson, and Tim Sharplin make infrequent sales calls within about 50 miles of Monroe.

Finance and Accounting

22   Summaries of Sharpco's recent financial statements are provided in the case appendix. The short-term borrowings shown on the 1984 balance sheet are represented by 180-day notes held by a small bank in Delhi, Louisiana, the Sharplin family's hometown. These notes are secured by mortgages on Sharpco's inventories and the Sharpco plant. As they mature, accrued interest is paid and principal refinanced as needed. James has signed continuing guarantee agreements with regard to all present and future Sharpco debt at the bank.

23   The bank has agreed to convert the short-term debt to a single 5-year loan, with 15-year amortization and interest established annually at the bank's prime rate, normally about 1½ percent above New York prime. In addition to the five-year loan, the bank has agreed that it will provide Sharpco a $150,000 credit line for any needed additional working capital.

24   The long-term debt on the 1984 balance sheet includes a $200,000 purchase-money obligation on the new Sharpco plant and the land on which it sits. The purchase-money mortgage is subordinated to the bank debt mentioned above. Sharpco's old plant with related long-term debt attached was given in part payment to the developer who built the new plant. By prior agreement with the developer, James Sharplin designed the office area and mechanical features (piping and electrical systems, cranes, etc.) of the new plant and constructed them using Sharpco workers and several subcontractors. This effort was financed with short-term bank borrowing. Upon completion, the new Sharpco facility was appraised at $760,000.

25   In early 1984, Peggy Turnage computerized the company's accounting records. The computer in use is a Dynabyte featuring 20 megabytes of hard-disk storage, a 16-bit microprocessor, and three interactive terminals. The two extra terminals are located in James Sharplin's office and on the customer service counter. The new parts inventory of about 1,500 items is carried on a first-in, first-out basis. When a used tractor is purchased for parts, the cost of the tractor, plus all labor required to disassemble it, is added to used-parts inventory. When a used part is sold, the entire selling price of the part is subtracted from the inventory line item representing the tractor from which it came. A subsidiary file is kept for each tractor, indicating which parts have been sold. So anyone inquiring at one of the terminals can easily determine which used parts are available for sale. James Sharplin has been advised that the accounting procedure he is following significantly understates the used-parts inventory. Despite a recommendation from the company's CPA, he has not authorized changing the procedure.

26   Sharpco's steel inventory is taken at the end of each year and priced at current costs. The steel consists of plates (rectangular flat pieces, four or more feet in both width and length) and shapes (long, straight pieces of various cross-sectional configurations—e.g., rounds, angles, beams, and channels). No plate or shape is included in inventory if any part of it has been used. In addition, a large quantity of steel, all

entirely usable but of slow-selling shapes and sizes, is not counted because it has been declared "obsolete." As a result of these practices, the steel inventory is shown on company books at perhaps one half its current market value. In addition, Sharpco owns many land-clearing blades, digging buckets, and tractor parts which were "traded in" or abandoned by customers but for which no actual credit was given. Many of these items were later restored to usable condition during slack periods. Total value of these, as estimated by James Sharplin, is $15,000.

27   A job record is prepared for each customer order requiring shop work. One copy is kept in the office and another in a rack in the shop. Each worker is responsible for entering time worked on respective jobs. Parts and other materials issued to jobs are recorded on the office copies of job records. When a job is finished, the shop copy of the job record is brought to the office, and an invoice is completed.

28   Several years ago Peggy Turnage compared the time applied to customer jobs to the total time for which employees were paid. She found that fully one third of employee time was unaccounted for. After telling of that experience, she said, "As soon as I can get the right computer program, I will set up a control system to charge every hour for which we pay employees to a customer job or to cleanup and maintenance."

Interview with James Sharplin

29   The following are excerpts from an interview conducted on February 5, 1985.

30   **Q:** James, what do you think is your most important business area?

31   **A:** Well, I'd say used tractor parts are going to be our biggest money maker in the long run. When you can buy a D7E [a mid-size Caterpillar tractor] for $10,000, sell $25,000 worth of parts off it, and still have two thirds of it left, that's got to be a good situation. More and more people are looking at saving that 10 or 15 percent, or whatever it is. They don't really care if the part is used or not as long as it is not hurt. The major tractor dealers have done a really good job, but their prices have just continued to climb. We're able to offer the customer a good part at 50 or 60 percent off dealer list. Customers are looking for that. They also know they can depend on us to install the parts we sell and to stand behind them. There is no question, also, that we are better at providing parts and undercarriage service for the whole list of crawler tractors—John Deeres, Caterpillars, Cases—than the average dealer is for just one brand of tractor.

32   **Q:** What do you think are the major attributes that you or Sharpco has that will allow you to be successful—just in a general way?

33   **A:** We know a great deal more about any undercarriage than dealers do. Of course, dealers have to know the whole tractor, and we limit our mechanic work to the undercarriage. The various undercarriages are quite similar, of course, and we've just had a world of experience in that particular area. Also, there's not a better high-quality welding shop, especially for construction equipment, in North Louisiana. We know that business. We're good at it.

34   **Q:** What do you think about your crew right now, James? How does it stack up?

35   **A:** On the whole, they're the best group of workers for this type of business in the Monroe area. We have to pick and choose the jobs that we put individual

workers on, but we put them on the jobs they're best at doing. Gene Lowe, for instance, is probably the best layout man and general welder that we've got. We use him just for that. But look at Jerry Hodges, who is our fastest welder. We'll let him weld the project out after Gene has cut out the pieces and tacked them together. Charlie LaBorde is real good with customers. So we like to send him out on field jobs, where he'll be in direct contact with the customer. Rodney Gee is another excellent man. He's a kind of handyman. He takes care of our tractor-trailer rig like it was his own. He's a good welder and a good mechanic. He just generally has a great attitude about anything Sharpco wants him to do.

36   **Q:** What about the production things you do—the track press, for example, and the roller and idler shop?

37   **A:** We run our track press operation quite differently from the way dealers do. We arranged the track press in a room by itself with all the necessary equipment— the turntable, all the tooling. We have it where one man can run the whole operation. It's a two-man job at most dealers. We've kept real good account of the number of hours it takes to do a job, and we've steadily improved on that. The track press operator we have now, Juan Hernandez, has run the press for six years. He's by far the best I've ever seen. About a year ago, Juan hurt his back, and Jerry Thompson and I filled in for him until he recovered enough to work again. He had major surgery. For at least a month or a month and a half after he came back we wouldn't let him lift anything. Just having him here during that time was a great help because he knew so much about how to set up the machine. We rebuild idlers by building up [with an automatic welder] the wear surfaces and replacing the seals—and they are as good as new. We do not weld on the rollers, though, like some dealers do. To get "new" quality, we replace the worn outer shells of rollers and reuse the shafts, bushings, and collars if they are not hurt. This costs more, and we lose some sales when customers just look at price. But I can't think of a single failure on one of our reshelled rollers.

38   **Q:** Why is the crew so small right now, James?

39   **A:** I prefer to keep it small and work just a bit of overtime in order to keep a good steady crew over a long period of time. Besides that, it's so much easier to manage 10 people compared to 20 people. I know all these people. I know their problems. I know what makes them tick. I know what will motivate them. When I had 20 or 30 people, I couldn't say that.

40   **Q:** What are your long-term plans now for Sharpco, James?

41   **A:** Just to continue doing what we're good at and to keep our eyes open for any area where we can do a good job and make money. Grow if it will; but the big thing is to stay profitable and get it to where we can take just a little more time off.

42   **Q:** Do you mean where *you* can take a little more time off?

43   **A:** No. I mean the key people—Peggy, Jerry, Tim—and myself, of course.

44   **Q:** What problems concern you most?

45   **A:** Well, the problem is always the same: How to keep expenses down and jack up revenue. I do not ignore human costs, but I have to focus mainly on dollars.

There seems to be a conspiracy out there to keep us from making money. Besides, if we are profitable enough, I can handle most of the other problems that crop up. One thing I'm going to do, as soon as we get over the move, is to spend most of my time for two or three months with the computer and the accounting system, just getting on top of the numbers. I want to know where the sales and profits are coming from—geographically, of course, but also what kinds of customers, what parts and services. I want to know where the costs are, too. We already know a lot of that. I just need to study it and set up the reporting system a little better. I also want to figure out the best ways to promote sales of parts, especially used ones, and digging buckets. The farm economy is down, and land clearing is about dead. But there is always some construction work going on, and people are tending to fix their old equipment rather than buy new stuff. We are broadening our market area, too.

46   **Q:** James, how do you feel about your customers? Just tell me what your feelings are.

47   **A:** Quite often, in dealing with them in the past from the place we had built over the years and which was, at best, just adequate for the job, I felt a little inferior. From the instant we moved into our new place, I have felt better. For one thing, I'm not apologetic about a price, not timid at all about giving a man a price quick. I offered no apology yesterday when Charles Brooks said, "You're killing me." I sense a new attitude on the part of customers. They seem to be more favorable toward us.

48   **Q:** The question I was asking, James, had more to do with whether you develop any kind of personal relationship with your customers.

49   **A:** Absolutely, with every one that I possibly can. Any way we can get interaction, joking or talking about common interests, we do. These things help me to remember the customer, of course. But it also gives us something to talk about and ask about the next time we see them. We've developed relationships with people that go back to when we first went in business. Take the Costello brothers. We're able to deal with them and do a great deal of business. Certainly, we give them prices, but I think the work—most of it, anyway—would be ours regardless of the price. We know not to get ridiculous, and they trust that we won't. Other customers, like Tom Fussel, have just become real close friends over the years. Tom came by here last week and said, "I'm gonna send you a picture of Sharpco when you first went in business. You had three blades in your only building. You didn't even have a door in the back. The shop was so small those three blades completely filled it." He said, "From there to here, you've come a long way—and during that time all the dealers seem to have gone downhill." And he just looked at me and said, "I wonder why that is?"

Appendix: Financial Summaries

SHARPCO, INC. **Balance Sheets**				
	1981	*1982*	*1983*	*1984*
Assets				
Current assets:				
Cash	$ 49,420	$ 8,760	$ 10,205	$ 8,108
Accounts receivable	58,791	56,887	148,531	114,320
Reserve for bad debts	(9,974)	(19,702)	(22,311)	(20,659)
Notes receivable, stockholder	49,427	61,604	79,221	87,637
Inventory	177,322	95,308	144,499	315,108
Total current assets	$324,986	$202,857	$360,145	$504,514
Fixed assets:				
Building and improvements	120,766	120,766	188,668	294,491
Machinery and equipment	141,897	141,897	113,444	113,444
Office furniture and equipment	15,856	15,856	13,464	27,943
Vehicles	54,431	62,556	104,021	95,896
Total	332,950	341,075	419,597	531,774
Less: Accumulated depreciation	163,271	197,074	194,408	138,219
Net depreciated assets	169,679	144,001	225,189	393,555
Land	34,010	47,770	55,530	95,000
Total fixed assets	$203,689	$191,771	$280,719	$488,555
Other assets:				
Utility deposits	500	500	950	1,180
Total assets	$529,175	$395,128	$641,814	$994,249
Liabilities and Stockholders' Equity				
Current liabilities:				
Accounts payable	$ 28,458	$ 5,839	$ 48,487	$ 23,124
Accrued expenses	19,819	12,587	13,860	12,602
Withheld and accrued taxes	6,171	5,391	1,467	1,252
Accrued payroll	—	—	—	1,163
Accrued income taxes (overpayment)	11,636	(4,533)	(318)	6,430
Notes payable	171,600	81,281	185,872	268,505
Deposit from customers	9,000	—	—	—
Total current liabilities	$246,684	$100,565	$249,368	$313,076
Long-term liabilities:				
Notes payable	21,293	8,094	59,390	259,009
Stockholders' equity:				
Common stock	33,582	33,582	33,582	33,582
Less: Treasury stock	(11,316)	(11,316)	(11,316)	(11,316)
Retained earnings	238,932	264,203	310,790	399,898
Total stockholders' equity	$261,198	$286,469	$ 33,056	$422,164
Total liabilities and stockholders' equity	$529,175	$395,128	$641,814	$994,249

SHARPCO, INC.
Income Statements

	1981	1982	1983	1984
Revenue:				
Welding shop	$278,101	$ 297,547	$ 219,137	$ 268,366
Undercarriage shop	289,344	568,378	642,610	577,298
Direct parts sales	145,304	144,971	197,098	312,915
Steel	82,115	53,460	42,188	44,924
Miscellaneous	10,819	9,048	8,194	17,447
Total revenue	$805,683	$1,073,404	$1,109,227	$1,220,950
Direct costs:				
Materials	327,829	565,993	559,097	570,100
Labor	80,117	100,499	112,259	118,684
Subcontractors	5,548	11,339	16,846	13,756
Freight	5,813	5,422	6,757	8,007
Other direct costs	238	77	50	560
Total direct costs	$419,545	$ 683,330	$ 695,009	$ 711,107
Gross profit	386,138	390,074	414,218	509,843
Indirect costs	318,779	359,336	361,599	408,125
Profit before taxes	67,359	30,738	52,619	101,718
Income taxes	11,636	5,467	6,032	12,610
Net profit	$ 55,723	$ 25,271	$ 46,587	$ 89,108

Inventories, December 31, 1984

Steel	$ 34,685
New parts	162,995
Used parts	100,152
Supplies	548
Finished goods	12,120
Work in process	4,608
Total	$315,108

Sales by month (unadjusted)

	1981	1982	1983	1984
January	$55,974	$ 73,463	$ 60,666	$ 51,492
February	67,743	91,547	82,996	74,689
March	78,002	111,144	69,295	41,780
April	73,360	79,510	52,365	70,196
May	85,944	126,957	45,374	151,595
June	32,936	77,153	94,390	142,620
July	65,898	108,988	137,806	142,505
August	69,470	138,695	138,878	116,862
September	66,891	95,743	87,621	183,710
October	77,054	83,119	149,283	115,987
November	76,967	56,725	105,716	49,168
December	51,325	24,812	76,682	64,228

Case 15

Arthur D. Little, Inc., and the Toxic Alert (A and B)

We who are associated with Arthur D. Little, Inc., are indeed fortunate in that, in the course of serving our personal, professional, and corporate interests, we serve society as well. Our central function, that of bridging the gap between the development of new knowledge and its practical application by business and government, has never been more important. We do this by developing new products and processes based on emerging technologies, like genetic engineering or artificial intelligence, and other consulting assignments; we also transfer know-how to developing economies through the ADL Management Education Institute programs. In pursuing our professional work for our clients, the relationship of our activities to the societies in which we operate is a matter of daily, overriding concern.

John Magee, President, 1984

1   Arthur D. Little, Inc. (ADL), an internationally known consulting firm, was founded in Boston in 1886 and moved to neighboring Cambridge in 1917, a year after MIT made the same move. The company thus became the first research-oriented commercial organization in a city which later would be home to hundreds of high-tech firms. By 1984 ADL employed over 2,600 people and had offices in 14 countries. Sales volume for 1984 exceeded $200 million.

2   More than 1,400 ADL employees worked in the extensive network of laboratories and office buildings at Acorn Park, the company's 40-acre headquarters campus in North Cambridge. The research, engineering, and management consulting services offered by ADL involved disciplines ranging from strategic management to hazardous waste management to forensic economics. Thirty-seven corporate vice presidents served as "professional services officers" in charge of various technical specialties. Twenty-nine more vice presidents and senior vice presidents oversaw geographic offices or administrative functions. Ten independently organized "complementary business units," each with its own president and staff, offered a wide range of services such as systems management, opinion research, and property valuation. Five of these units were headquartered at Acorn Park; two more were located in nearby Lowell.

3   Arthur D. Little had experienced consistent growth in revenues for the past decade, from $81 million in sales in 1975 to $213 million in 1984. Net income had grown from $3.1 million in 1975 to $6.1 million in 1983 but fell to $3.6 million in 1984. Disappointing results in three of the complementary business units accounted for the drop, according to the 1984 annual report. (See Exhibit 1 for a 10-year summary of the firm's financial highlights. Tables 1 and 2 summarize 1984 financial results.)

4   Until 1969, ADL was wholly owned by the Memorial Drive Trust, a deferred compensation profit-sharing plan whose beneficiaries were past and present employees of the firm. Thirty percent of ADL's stock was sold to the public in 1969, but two thirds

---

This case was prepared by John A. Seeger, associate professor of management at Bentley College, Waltham, Massachusetts, to serve as a basis for class discussion. It was presented at the annual meeting of the Case Research Association, 1985. Permission to republish should be obtained from CRA and the author. Copyright © 1986 by John A. Seeger.

Exhibit 1
Ten-year summary of financial highlights (dollars and shares in thousands, except per share data)

(dollars and shares in thousands, except per-share data)		1984	1983	1982	1981	1980	1979	1978	1977	1976	1975
Operating results for the year	New contracts, net*	$174,420	$158,268	$132,972	$144,755	$136,911	$116,063	$129,963	$ 96,566	$ 75,777	$ 67,353
	Index	259	235	197	215	203	172	193	143	113	100
	Professional service income, net*	$161,097	$147,580	$141,174	$137,119	$127,463	$116,099	$ 99,098	$ 87,585	$ 70,908	$ 64,621
	Index	249	228	218	212	197	180	153	136	110	100
	Royalties and venture income	$ 1,421	$ 1,619	$ 1,344	$ 3,104	$ 3,434	$ 2,340	$ 1,772	$ 3,113	$ 2,038	$ 1,595
	Index	89	102	84	195	215	147	111	195	128	100
	Revenues	$213,363	$192,478	$181,398	$175,600	$163,215	$141,036	$120,879	$106,619	$ 86,221	$ 80,827
	Index	264	238	224	217	202	174	150	132	107	100
	Salaries, wages and other employment costs	$112,999	$102,598	$ 97,483	$ 94,298	$ 86,900	$ 79,922	$ 67,419	$ 60,189	$ 49,753	$ 45,016
	Index	251	228	217	209	193	178	150	134	111	100
	Income from operations	$ 9,063	$ 10,724	$ 11,086	$ 12,651	$ 10,826	$ 11,080	$ 10,344	$ 11,082	$ 6,529	$ 6,080
	Index	149	176	182	208	178	182	170	182	107	100
	Income before taxes on income	$ 7,456	$ 11,088	$ 10,496	$ 12,800	$ 10,975	$ 10,984	$ 10,545	$ 10,834	$ 6,971	$ 6,257
	Index	119	177	168	205	175	176	169	173	111	100
	Net income	$ 3,611	$ 6,070	$ 5,510	$ 6,740	$ 5,793	$ 5,777	$ 5,300	$ 5,578	$ 3,574	$ 3,142
	Index	115	193	175	215	184	184	169	178	114	100
	Cash flow from operations	$ 8,728	$ 10,988	$ 9,976	$ 10,257	$ 8,832	$ 8,388	$ 7,460	$ 7,226	$ 4,628	$ 4,217
	Index	207	261	237	243	209	199	177	171	110	100
	Revenues per share	$ 84.47	$ 76.57	$ 72.17	$ 69.86	$ 64.93	$ 56.11	$ 48.09	$ 42.42	$ 34.30	$ 31.91
	Income before taxes on income per share	$ 2.95	$ 4.41	$ 4.18	$ 5.09	$ 4.37	$ 4.37	$ 4.20	$ 4.31	$ 2.77	$ 2.47
	Earnings per share	$ 1.43	$ 2.41	$ 2.19	$ 2.68	$ 2.30	$ 2.30	$ 2.11	$ 2.22	$ 1.42	$ 1.24
	Dividends declared per share	$ .70	$ .70	$ .70	$ .60	$ .50	$ .48½	$ .44	$ .37	$ .23	$ .17
Financial position at year end	Cash and cash equivalents	$ 10,301	$ 14,337	$ 8,380	$ 14,554	$ 12,550	$ 11,841	$ 12,912	$ 17,622	$ 11,945	$ 4,993
	Index	206	287	168	291	251	237	259	353	239	100
	Accounts receivable and unbilled services	$ 56,209	$ 49,707	$ 45,414	$ 38,487	$ 36,823	$ 31,328	$ 27,633	$ 24,589	$ 20,448	$ 22,744
	Index	247	219	200	169	162	138	121	108	90	100
	Working capital	$ 27,761	$ 28,001	$ 24,906	$ 24,226	$ 24,353	$ 21,677	$ 19,521	$ 22,888	$ 19,077	$ 17,237
	Index	161	162	144	141	141	126	113	133	111	100
	Total assets	$107,520	$102,575	$ 91,442	$ 87,142	$ 79,333	$ 71,321	$ 65,860	$ 60,119	$ 49,904	$ 37,784
	Index	285	271	242	231	210	189	174	159	132	100
	Long-term debt and capital lease obligations^b	$ 3,617	$ 3,488	$ 3,830	$ 4,212	$ 4,624	$ 4,972	$ 5,212	$ 6,952	$ 7,944	$ 1,220
	Index	296	286	314	345	379	408	427	570	651	100
	Stockholders' equity	$ 61,197	$ 58,865	$ 54,555	$ 50,805	$ 45,573	$ 41,037	$ 36,479	$ 32,291	$ 27,634	$ 24,647
	Stockholders' equity per share	$ 24.16	$ 23.42	$ 21.70	$ 20.21	$ 18.13	$ 16.33	$ 14.51	$ 12.85	$ 10.99	$ 9.81
Other data	Return on average stockholders' equity	6.0%	10.7%	10.5%	14.0%	13.4%	14.9%	15.4%	18.6%	13.7%	13.4%
	Net income as percent of revenue	1.7%	3.2%	3.0%	3.8%	3.6%	4.1%	4.4%	5.2%	4.1%	3.9%
	Average number of shares outstanding	2,526	2,514	2,514	2,514	2,514	2,514	2,514	2,514	2,514	2,534
	Number of employees at year end	2,606	2,424	2,330	2,340	2,394	2,529	2,308	2,078	1,821	1,798
	Index	145	135	130	130	133	141	128	116	101	100

of that had been reacquired by individual employees or by the Employee Investment Plan. In 1985 about 10 percent of ADL's stock was held by the public, while 78 percent was controlled by the trustees of the trust and the plan. The company had contributed to these plans (and charged to operations) about $9 million in each of the past three years.

Consulting Operations

5   ADL dealt with an average of 1,000 clients and undertook about 4,000 to 5,000 individual assignments annually, according to Senior Vice President and General Manager of Professional Operations Alfred E. Wechsler. Some three quarters of ADL's clients were repeat customers.

6   New projects and activities at ADL went through a formal acceptance procedure, usually beginning with a prospective client contacting a professional staff member, who would draft a proposal for the work. The proposal was submitted to a 10-member management group composed of 5 permanent members of the senior staff and 5 junior

Table 1

ARTHUR D. LITTLE, INC.
Consolidated Balance Sheets at December 31
(dollar amounts in thousands)

	1984	*1983*	*1982*
Assets			
Cash and cash equivalents	$ 10,301	$ 14,337	$ 8,380
Receivables and unbilled services	56,209	49,707	45,414
Prepaid and other current assets	3,957	4,179	4,169
Total current assets	70,467	68,223	57,963
Land	2,301	2,241	2,241
Buildings and leasehold improvements	33,002	30,591	29,428
Equipment, furniture, and fixtures	31,447	27,498	23,369
Less: Accumulated depreciation	(33,840)	(28,834)	(24,442)
Total net fixed assets	32,910	31,496	30,596
Investments and other assets	4,143	2,856	2,883
Total assets	$107,520	$102,575	$ 91,442
Liabilities and Equity			
Accounts payable	$ 4,145	$ 6,446	$ 4,304
Accrued expenses	24,850	19,835	16,350
Accrued income taxes	3,398	4,471	2,860
Advance payments from clients	10,313	9,470	9,543
Total current liabilities	42,706	40,222	33,057
Long-term debt	1,487	1,199	1,394
Capital lease obligations	2,130	2,289	2,436
Total liabilities	46,323	43,710	33,057
Common stock and paid-in capital	4,908	4,427	4,427
Retained earnings	56,289	54,438	50,128
Total stockholders' equity	61,197	58,865	54,555
Total liabilities and equity	$107,520	$102,575	$ 91,442

Table 2

ARTHUR D. LITTLE, INC.
Consolidated Income Statements for Years Ended December 31
(dollar amounts in thousands)

	1984	*1983*	*1982*
Revenues	$213,363	$192,478	$181,398
Employment costs	112,999	102,598	97,483
Other operating expenses	40,456	35,877	33,949
Client reimbursable costs	50,845	43,279	38,880
	204,300	181,754	170,312
Income from operations	9,063	10,724	11,086
Income from short-term investments	884	1,038	1,902
Other income (charges)	(2,491)	(674)	(2,492)
Income before taxes	7,456	11,088	10,496
Provision for income taxes	3,845	5,018	4,986
Net income	$ 3,611	$ 6,070	$ 5,510

ADL professionals who rotated every three months. The management group met every morning to evaluate all potential assignments according to a four-question formula.

7   The four questions, said Wechsler, were:

Is the work something that ADL would be happy to do?

Will the work create a conflict of interest with other work ADL is doing?

Can the client pay the bill?

Does ADL have the staff on hand to do the job?

8   Upon acceptance of the project, a budget was established and an ADL professional was given the task of assembling a team to do the job, drawing from whatever disciplines were needed. The team leader did not have to get approval from department managers for the use of their people.

9   A 10-year graph in ADL's 1983 annual report showed billings to U.S. federal government–sponsored projects ranging between $25 million and $27 million per year from 1979 to 1983, while U.S. state and local government revenues were $10 million to $13 million per year. No similar graph was included in the 1984 annual report, but tabulated results showed federal billings rose by $3.2 million in 1984, while state and local government business dropped by $3 million.

Company Policies

10   The founder of ADL, Dr. Arthur Dehon Little, was deeply committed to the idea that science and technology were the keys to progress. He felt that positive thinking and a "can do" attitude could successfully apply new ideas to the problems of industry and government. In 1921, the 35th anniversary of ADL's founding, Dr. Little found a symbolic representation of his credo and a lasting beacon for his firm: he decided not only that it *should* be possible to make a "silk purse from a sow's ear," but that his people *would* do it. Starting with 1,000 ears, his staff boiled up a gelatinous goo, spun a thread from it, and produced a purse, which is now on display at the Smithsonian Institution.

11   The same sense of irreverence for dogma was shown again 56 years later, when the firm set out to debunk another platitude of impossibility, the old cliche "It went over like a lead balloon." Anthony Baldo, writing in the *Cambridge Chronicle,* reported, "for ADL staffers, this provided a weighty challenge. . . . In fact, three very differently designed lead balloons were created. Curiously, the winning entry was so buoyant that it tore away from where it was tied. 'It was last seen going over the Atlantic,' said Alma Triner, ADL's vice president for public relations."

12   ADL attempted to provide its staff with an intellectual climate to encourage free thinking as well as bottom-line results, wrote Baldo. Staff members were not required to work on a specific quota of projects. Staff members set their own goals. Nobody was required to work on a project found personally objectionable. No dress code existed, and personnel were free to decorate their offices any way they liked. "I think we have a lot of respect for each other as individuals," the *Chronicle* quoted ADL President John F. Magee. "We have a respect for individual tastes and idiosyncrasies."

13   "Humor, too, has a place within ADL's corporate structure," continued the *Chronicle.* "It starts at the top with the firm's chairman of the board, Robert K. Mueller, who has written a book called *Behind the Boardroom Door.* While the book is about corporate

rivalries and politics, Mueller, according to an ADL release, mostly concludes that 'too few businessmen, and hardly any directors, have the ability to laugh at themselves.' "

14   At the corporate level, a set of governing policies reinforced the firm's fundamental regard for people and the communities within which it operated. For example, ADL supported the "Sullivan Principles"[1] and conducted evaluations of the equal rights provisions of those principles for corporations maintaining offices in South Africa. As a corporate policy, ADL donated 2.5 percent of its pretax income to projects and institutions "designed to improve the quality of life in our communities throughout the world." Corporate policy also prohibited development work on weapons systems.

15   Additionally, company-paid staff time was contributed to a variety of public interest programs, and staff members were encouraged to contribute their own personal time to education, social programs, and political service. Senior Vice President D. Reid Weedon, Jr., was a prime example of the kind of community involvement found in the ADL staff; he served as a life member of the MIT Corporation, a life trustee of the Boston Museum of Science, and board chairman of the Winchester Hospital.

16   The company also carefully preserved its links with the university community. In 1984, the presidents of MIT, Smith College, and the Woods Hole Oceanographic Institution—Paul E. Gray, Jill Ker Conway, and Paul M. Frye—were members of the Arthur D. Little board of directors. So was C. Roland Christensen, university professor at Harvard University and one of the country's leading authorities in the field of business policy.

17   In the spring of 1984, Arthur D. Little, Inc., was justifiably proud of its standing as a socially involved and concerned pillar of the community.

18   By the spring of 1985, however, some residents of Cambridge, Arlington, and Belmont were referring to Arthur D. Little and its officers as arrogant, hypocritical, lying, avaricious outlaws—unwelcome intruders in the community and threats to the safety and security of all. The president's letter to the stockholders in the annual report published in March 1985 noted,

> Over the years we have taken considerable pride in the manner in which our pursuit of our professional and corporate objectives serves the interest of society as well.
>
> Ironically, during the past year the company has been plagued by activist community opposition to certain research that we consider of vital importance to the defense of the United States, its military personnel, and civilian population against chemical warfare agents. The purpose of the research, performed in a safe, secure laboratory built in our Cambridge, Massachusetts, headquarters, is to develop better protective materials and methods of detecting and detoxifying chemical agents. This work is important, and the chemicals are handled in a manner that assures the safety of our staff and our neighbors. It is worth noting that, although safety is the expressed concern, opponents of our research for the U.S. Department of Defense appear to be unconcerned about nondefense-related research with substances of comparable hazard. I am saddened, however,

---

[1] In 1978, the Reverend Leon Sullivan proposed a list of voluntary guidelines which have become the accepted standard of ethical and moral behavior for American employers in South Africa. These principles seek improvement in the economic, educational, and social life of South African workers, through full integration, equal benefits, fair and equal pay at the workplace, and through employee assistance outside of work as well.

by the strain in the fine relations we have enjoyed with Cambridge since the early days of this century.

The Toxic Alert

19   Chief among ADL's critics was a loosely knit community organization called the North Cambridge Toxic Alert Coalition (later shortened to Toxic Alert). Key members of the organization as of August 1985 are described in the lined insert below. Charlie Rose, a professional organizer and one of Toxic Alert's founders, described the conditions which led to its formation:

> People in North Cambridge already had a strong feeling they were being dumped on. For years, W. R. Grace and the Dewey and Almy chemical company had left chemical wastes standing in ponds. They often spilled naphthalene and left whole neighborhoods smelling like mothballs; that frightened people, and when the managers denied spilling anything it made people mad. The old city dump caught fire occasionally. The subway construction over the past five years threatened a lot of changes. There was a growing awareness. John O'Connor and I had seen the changes. We had scoped out an organizing plan for W. R. Grace a year earlier.

Key members of the Toxic Alert

Ed Cyr—age 28; native of North Cambridge; studied economics at University of Massachusetts, now studying planning at University of Massachusetts at Boston; former organizer for Cambridge Economic Opportunity Commission and North Cambridge Planning Team; executive director, Cambridge Committee of Elders.

John O'Connor—age 31; professional organizer; coordinator of the National Campaign against Toxic Hazards, an umbrella organization with affiliates in 28 states; travels and speaks extensively, concentrating in 1985 on the superfund law; studied sociology and journalism at Clark University.

Charlie Rose—age 27; New England codirector of the Clean Water Action Project; professional organizer, beginning in 1977 as a Volunteer in Service to America (VISTA); the only Toxic Alert worker not resident in Cambridge.

Sharon Moran—age 27; three-year resident; involved with Toxic Alert from its founding; B.A. in chemistry, Boston University; paralegal worker with an environmental law firm.

Wendy Baruch—pretzel salesperson at public events, known near Fenway Park for her singing pretzel call; teaches home construction skills; with Dan Grossman, led the ADL balloon release project and was interviewed on "20/20" and other programs; major interest: waste cleanup at W. R. Grace.

Hillary Frank—on leave from studies at Harvard University; employed by CWAP, on loan to Toxic Alert; ran first canvas for TA; keeps member records, does the telephone and mail work to encourage meeting attendance and committee work.

Dan Grossman—age 27; MIT Ph.D. candidate, political science; Cambridge resident since 1977; Toxic Alert representative to the health care task force of the Massachusetts legislature.

Michael Kanter—owner/manager of Cambridge Natural Foods store; 12 years in Cambridge; B.A. in history, University of Buffalo.

Steve Schnapp—age 39; eight-year resident; professional organizer on Boston's North Shore; studied organization at Boston University; chairperson, Cambridge Peace Commission.

Richard Durling-Shyduroff—director, Cambridge Institute of the Arts and Sciences; provided sound systems and space for membership meetings and fund-raising events in his headquarters building.

Then the discovery that ADL was testing nerve gas came as the last straw. Things crystallized. We sat down and planned it. There were already good people in the neighborhood. We brought in skilled, professional, paid organizers beginning in the summer of 1984.

20   As New England codirector of the Clean Water Action Project, Charlie Rose had resources available. CWAP employed door-to-door canvassers who spent half their time soliciting funds (on commission). Their remaining time was spent studying and applying community skills in Rose's "Organizing School." "Canvassers should get people involved," said Rose. "It's not enough just to let people pitch money into the hat." One CWAP canvasser, Hillary Frank, became a mainstay of the Toxic Alert.

21   Toxic Alert operated through meetings of subcommittees, a steering committee, the membership at large, and meetings planned as media events for the whole population. The group had a volunteer treasurer but no other officers. There were no elections; anyone with the initiative to find the steering committee meetings could attend. Members of the steering committee took turns chairing the larger membership meetings, which might see 25 to 40 attendees.

22   Originally the steering committee was made up of representatives of other neighborhood organizations, who generally listened to and agreed with the ideas of the professional organizers. By August of 1985 many of its members were local residents who took initiative and carried out programs without the organizers' involvement.

23   Between meetings, organizers and volunteers knocked on doors and made telephone calls, sought business support, wrote and distributed newsletters and publicity flyers, met with government officials, and maintained liaison with the press.

24   Ed Cyr, another Toxic Alert founder and a professional organizer, reported spending one hour per week at the *Cambridge TAB* and two hours at the *Cambridge Chronicle* (both weekly newspapers). "The *Boston Globe* never did catch on with the story," Cyr said. "It was really a television-type story." Cyr succeeded in bringing ABC's "20/20" to one communitywide meeting. "It's not hard to get coverage when you have a sexy issue," he said. "You just find an assignment editor four days ahead of the event, and then visit with them every day." Contacts with local radio and television stations were handled by Charlie Rose.

A Chronology of Controversy

25   Before a partisan audience and a battery of cameras at a community meeting sponsored by the Toxic Alert in March of 1985, Reid Weedon reviewed the events of the previous two years.

26   In January of 1983, he said, Arthur D. Little informed the Cambridge police and fire departments that work in a planned new laboratory facility "would involve highly toxic materials of particular interest to the Department of Defense." Specific information on chemical names, structures, and toxicities was not requested by the city officials, Weedon said. In a series of meetings, Cambridge police and fire officials reviewed the design. Several modifications were made at their suggestion.

27   Construction proceeded with an investment of approximately $800,000. In September of 1983 the building was ready for operation, and ADL again met with Cambridge fire and police officials, this time with instructions on handling public safety in the event of fire or intrusion into the facility.

28   In the event of fire, the laboratory should be allowed to burn to the ground. In the event of unauthorized entry into the laboratory, police should surround it and allow nobody to leave, but under no circumstances should they attempt to enter it themselves. The laboratory, it was explained, was engaged in testing highly toxic materials, including Department of Defense "surety agents." ADL technical people would respond to any alarm; nobody should enter without their assessment of the hazards involved. Furthermore, it was requested in the interest of security that the city authorities make no public announcements that would call attention to the laboratory.

> **TA:** See there? "Surety agents," they call them. That's nerve gas and blister agents—the most deadly stuff ever invented for killing people. And ADL wanted the city authorities to lie about it for them.[2]

> **ADL:** We didn't want or ask anyone to lie about anything. It was in the best interests of the public and our employees not to advertise that we had chemical warfare materials here. It was in the interest of maximizing safety.

29   Cambridge officials, under reciprocal public safety agreements with neighboring towns, asked ADL to inform the authorities in Arlington and Belmont. After touring the laboratory, the town manager of Arlington informed ADL that he could not, in good conscience, comply with the request for confidentiality; he would raise the issue at the next meeting of the selectmen, October 17.

30   "On that same day," wrote Sheldon Krimsky later, "ADL issued a news release announcing the opening of a high-security laboratory for the testing and analysis of toxic materials. The news release was skillfully written and avoided any mention that the facility would be handling chemical warfare agents or that the research undertaken there would be defense related."[3]

> **ADL:** There was nothing secret about the work. We sent memos to literally hundreds of staff members, because we were concerned about staff reaction. We held a reception for the lab's dedication; that's what the press release was for. It just never occurred to us that this would be a safety concern to the community. We made the assumption, perhaps naively, that since it *was* safe, people would recognize that.

31   A *Boston Globe* story on the Arlington selectmen's meeting was noticed by Nancy Cyr in Cambridge; her calls to Cambridge city hall resulted in the issue's appearance on the City Council agenda that same night. The council asked the city's commissioner of health and hospitals, Dr. Melvin Chalfen, to inspect the new laboratory. He did so on October 19.

32   The council also asked for a hearing with Arthur D. Little's officers, who appeared on October 24. They reported that the Levins Laboratory (it was named to honor Dr. Philip L. Levins, the senior ADL officer who had advocated the facility's construction, who had died in a swimming accident before its completion) was the safest conceivable facility for its purpose, and that its purpose was in the public interest. ADL's contracts

---

[2] Throughout this case, inserts like this are used to interject points of view of the Toxic Alert (TA) or Arthur D. Little managers (ADL).

[3] Sheldon Krimsky, "Local Control of Research Involving Chemical Warfare Agents," in *Science and Technology in a Democracy: Who Should Govern?* ed. Malcolm L. Goggin (Knoxville: University of Tennessee Press, 1986).

with the Department of Defense dealt with detecting chemical nerve agents, with neutralizing them, and with developing improved protective clothing.

> **TA:** All very well, but it doesn't explain why we should welcome nerve gas in one of the most densely populated cities in the country. Put the laboratory in the desert or on some military post where it can be properly guarded, and those arguments make sense. Not here.

> **ADL:** The words *nerve gas* have a frightening connotation. They show a deliberate attempt to misdescribe the situation. We don't receive gas. We don't store gas. We use these agents in liquid form, in minute quantities. It's not easy to disperse these materials. Even when it's used on the battlefield, this material isn't a gas, by and large. It's an aerosol. This talk about "gas" is designed purely to heighten people's anxieties.

33   The Cambridge City Council had faced a similar issue before. In 1976 a substantial public debate erupted over the dangers and propriety of genetic research, in which DNA molecules might be modified to create new life forms—in the worst-case scenario to create an "Andromeda strain" of lethal bacteria. After a great deal of political gesturing and scientific consideration, Cambridge became the first city in the country to regulate genetic research. Its new ordinance, based on federal guidelines developed by the National Institute of Health, became a model for other cities facing the same problem.

34   Following its meeting with Arthur D. Little management, the Cambridge City Council called for creation of a Scientific Advisory Committee "to advise the City Council and the commissioner of health and hospitals on issues of public health and safety related to the environmental hazards of ADL's research with chemical warfare agents." Arthur D. Little had already received its first consignment of nerve agents and begun testing.

35   In the fall of 1983 and winter of 1984 several individual city councillors attempted to stop the ADL work or to gain a moratorium while the Scientific Advisory Committee (SAC) was organized and deliberating. ADL officials responded that the terms of their contracts with the Department of Defense imposed a schedule which could not be interrupted. ADL offered a 30-day moratorium on initiation of new contracts and offered to cooperate with any committee, but would not interrupt work already begun. Finally, on March 13, 1984, Dr. Chalfen issued an emergency order barring the testing of five specified nerve and blister agents until the SAC rendered its report.

> **ADL:** A moratorium would have removed any incentive for the council to appoint the committee or for the committee to act. Dr. Chalfen had previously told us he considered the laboratory to be safe. He issued his order under pressure from the city council, not on the basis of his professional judgment.

36   On March 16, Arthur D. Little went to court, claiming that no city action could legally infringe on Department of Defense work, since federal regulation (in this case, by DOD) took precedence over regulation by local authorities. Superior court Judge Robert Hallisey granted an injunction to restrain the city from enforcing the commissioner's order. Tests continued at the Levins Laboratory.

37   On April 12, 1984, the Scientific Advisory Committee held its first meeting. Dr. Sheldon Krimsky, a former member of the panel which had drawn up the city's regulations on DNA research, served as chairman. The names, occupations, and institutional affiliations of the SAC members are shown in the lined insert on the following page.

Membership of the Cambridge Scientific Advisory Committee

Sheldon Krimsky (chair)—associate professor of urban and environmental policy, Tufts University; Ph.D. in philosophy of science.

Ann Hochberg (vice chair)—fisheries specialist, New England Fishery Management Council; B.A. in biology, M.S. in oceanography.

Frederick Centanni, Jr.—Cambridge resident; business element manager, EG&G Wakefield.

Edmund Crouch—research fellow in energy and the environment, Harvard University; Ph.D. in high-energy physics.

Edward Cyr—Cambridge resident; executive director, Cambridge Committee of Elders.

Lou DiBerardinis—industrial hygienist, Department of Environmental Health and Safety, Harvard; B.S. in chemical engineering, M.S. in industrial hygiene.

Joseph Fantasia—Cambridge resident and restaurant owner, active in Chamber of Commerce affairs; Cornell University.

Paul Fennelly—Arlington resident; group scientist and manager, Environmental Measurements Department, GCA Technology Division, GCA Corporation; Ph.D. in physical chemistry.

Richard Goldstein, M.D.—Department of Microbiology and Molecular Genetics, Harvard Medical School; Ph.D. in biology.

Jack Martinelli—Cambridge resident and Volkswagen mechanic; Ph.D. in chemistry; former student of Judith Harris.

Henry Mautner—chairman, Department of Biochemistry and Pharmacology, Tufts University School of Medicine; Ph.D. in medicinal chemistry.

John O'Connor—Cambridge resident; coordinator, National Campaign against Toxic Hazards.

David Ozonoff, M.D.—chief, Environmental Health Section, Boston University School of Medicine; former president, Massachusetts Public Health Association.

Placido John Paula—radiation technologist, Office of Environmental Health and Safety, Harvard University.

John J. Malone—Belmont resident; director, Belmont Department of Public Health; member, Governor's Hazardous Waste Council.

Ralph Wolfe—Cambridge resident; technical coordinator, Skidmore, Owings & Merrill; M.Arch. degree; son of a chemist.

---

38   In May, the city's legal department attempted to end the temporary restraining order on the basis of a technical consulting report. The court ruled for ADL and continued the preliminary injunction barring enforcement of the city's health regulation. Cambridge retained a prominent Boston law firm, Palmer and Dodge, to continue the case.

39   For the next five months, the Scientific Advisory Committee worked to define and resolve the complex issues of technology and values which underlay the risk and benefit arguments of ADL and the city. Subcommittees were set up to investigate the physical and chemical properties of nerve agents, the various scenarios which could result from releases at ADL, and comparable risks presented by other chemicals in general use. Exhibit 2 shows one of many graphic representations presented in the SAC report. It is a "ground zero" map of the ADL area, showing the "zone of lethality" for the plume of gas emanating from a postulated half-liter spill of the agent "VX," with a southwesterly wind.

40   In September 1984, the committee issued its final report. The risks involved in transporting and processing chemical warfare agents in densely populated areas were not justified, the SAC concluded. Even though the risk might be very small, as ADL contended, the consequences if an accident did occur were such that the ADL work should not continue. The SAC found no discernible benefit to the city from the work's

Exhibit 2
"Ground zero" map of ADL area

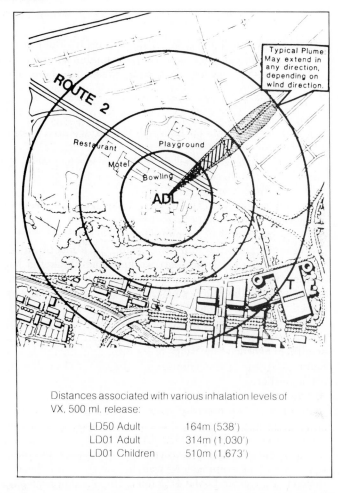

Distances associated with various inhalation levels of
VX, 500 ml. release:

LD50 Adult	164m (538')
LD01 Adult	314m (1,030')
LD01 Children	510m (1,673')

location in Cambridge; a majority of members saw no benefit in the work regardless
of its location.

    ADL: That report is incompetent. It was not written by a group of scientists.
To call that a "Scientific" Advisory Committee was absurd! The representation
on that committee of anyone who knew anything about risk analysis and these
materials was essentially nil. There were some scientists, but what kind? There
was one man, from MIT, who had direct working experience with this kind of
issue. But he was the only one, and he quit the Committee—in disgust.[4]

---

[4] Members of the Scientific Advisory Committee expressed substantial surprise at this comment by a high
ADL official. They reported that the chairman of MIT's Department of Nutrition and Food Sciences, Dr. Gerald
N. Wogan, had contributed greatly to the subcommittee on toxicity before international commitments forced
his resignation from the SAC for lack of time. When asked for clarification, Dr. Wogan commented, "In disgust?
That certainly is not the case."

41   Judge Hallisey called a meeting to hear attorneys' arguments on the federal "supremacy" issue. He would rule separately on the reasonableness of Cambridge's action, if the local regulation were found to be valid. Pending those decisions, the court continued its restraining order against Dr. Chalfen's regulation. The testing continued.

> **TA:** And it's *still* going on. ADL still says it's their own job to decide whether it's safe enough, and nobody else's opinion counts for beans. They'll appeal this forever, and the courts will always give them another restraining order. We thought the SAC decision would *decide* something. Are we going to stand for this?

42   Impatient residents of the North Cambridge area were already concerned over another environmental issue—the location and disposal of chemical wastes on a 17-acre W. R. Grace site scheduled for industrial development. This was fertile ground for dissent, and the "nerve gas" issue was both threatening and compelling. SAC members Ed Cyr, John O'Connor, and Ralph Wolfe decided to organize, and O'Connor asked Charlie Rose for help. The North Cambridge Toxic Alert Coalition took shape with a community meeting in October 1984.

43   "We were surprised at the turnout," Ed Cyr said later. "It showed again the basic law of organizing: the number of bodies at a meeting depends on the hours of dirty work done before." Toxic Alert workers had blanketed North Cambridge with three different flyers, had knocked on doors and rung telephones to build grass roots communications. "After the October meeting, it was like a tidal wave," Cyr continued. "People signed up. We had 40 or 45 people helping plan the next steps."

44   Loudly, NCTAC challenged both W. R. Grace and Arthur D. Little to appear at a public meeting on November 29, 1984. W. R. Grace countered by holding a series of small neighborhood meetings of its own, announcing it would not attend the NCTAC affair. ADL made no comment on the NCTAC challenge and was not expected to attend either.

45   "We saw no benefit in appearing at a meeting where we had no idea of the agenda, the structure, the process," said ADL's John Magee later. "There was no assurance of an opportunity to do anything but be pilloried."

46   Television crews did attend the November meeting, and so did the managers of the W. R. Grace division concerned with the real estate development. Patently obvious to viewers of the evening news was the empty chair labeled "Arthur D. Little." Speakers included Ed Cyr and John O'Connor, Dr. Sheldon Krimsky, Cambridge City Manager Robert Healy, a city councillor, and two technical consultants on environmental pollution. At the close of the meeting an angry Ed Cyr called for the city to retaliate against the absent Arthur D. Little by freezing building permits, refusing permission to park on public land, or shutting off water and sewer connections until the firm agreed to talk. The following day at 3 P.M., he announced, the Toxic Alert would meet on the highway outside ADL to release a cloud of black balloons, demonstrating how the wind could carry particles from Acorn Park to the neighboring blocks of densely packed two- and three-family houses. Television crews were invited to the demonstration; an ABC News "20/20" crew working on the story filmed the launching the next day. Cameras in pursuit, the Toxic Alert balloon people then strode into the Arthur D. Little reception area, demanding a meeting with President John Magee. The negotiation process for defining a forum for public debate began.

> **TA:** So we win a round. But we still don't have Weedon and Magee out where people can see them. People have to hear ADL's arguments firsthand, to recognize how blind these guys are. They're still testing nerve gas next door. We have to get them out in the open.

47   Four days after the NCTAC meeting, on December 3, 1984, the Bhopal tragedy in India made poison gas a common topic and a more credible threat. ABC Television, which had filmed the Cambridge meeting without a specific production schedule, aired the ADL segment on "20/20" the following week. Toxic Alert members continued to organize.

48   On December 14, 1984, superior court Judge Robert Hallisey ruled in favor of the city of Cambridge on the "supremacy" question, establishing the right of the local government to regulate activities on DOD work at Arthur D. Little. ADL requested reconsideration of the issue. On January 14, Judge Hallisey issued a supplemental decision reconfirming his stand. Still to be heard were arguments over whether Cambridge's actions were reasonable. In the meantime, the testing continued.

49   Negotiations also continued between Toxic Alert leaders and ADL management about the timing and format of a public meeting in which each side could present its views. On several occasions, steering committee members visited ADL to demand that a date be set. After each meeting, local TV crews with minicameras were waiting to interview participants, often for the live 5:30 news. Finally, March 7 was selected.

50   At the end of January 1985, 61,000 residents in North Cambridge, Arlington, and Belmont received by first-class mail a package of materials including a three-page letter from ADL President John Magee, a four-page specification on the Levins Laboratory, and a four-page reproduction of a *Cambridge Chronicle* story describing Arthur D. Little's history, strengths, and virtues. The first lined insert below contains excerpts from this letter and enclosures.

> **TA:** Will you look at this! We've been trying to smoke him out and here he comes, all by himself! Comparing nerve gas to water, for God's sake! Valuing our good opinion! So sorry they had to turn down this work before! And so very, very safe! That lab has enough nerve gas on hand to kill 300,000 people, but we should all have confidence because it's so very safe. This letter is a Christmas present from Magee to the Toxic Alert!

51   Reaction to ADL's communication was not limited to NCTAC activists. Weekly newspapers in all three affected communities took note of the mailing, and their readers responded with a barrage of letters to the editors, printed in mid-February. Three of these letters are excerpted in the inserts found on the next page. Following them are segments of a *Cambridge Chronicle* editoral of March 14.

52   "Public reaction was either moderately supportive or 'ho-hum'," said John Magee later. There are a lot of people in those communities and very few letters in the newspapers. A substantial number of people called or wrote in support, and of course those people don't write to the papers. When you look at the demonstrations and think of the numbers of people involved—why, I've almost gotten to know them on a first-name basis, because it's always the same small group."

53   On February 26, 1985, superior court Judge Hallisey ruled that the Cambridge regulation prohibiting chemical warfare agent work was valid and enforceable under the law. In an addendum to the decision, called "remarkable" by both parties and

---

Excerpts from John Magee's letter of January 28, 1985

Dear Neighbor,

You probably have heard about some research being conducted in one of our analytical chemistry laboratories on highly toxic substances, referred to in the press as "nerve gases." . . . Although as liquids these agents are no more volatile than water, we realize the term *nerve gas* causes reasonable people to wonder whether the existence of such substances in the neighborhood should be cause for concern.

Because we value your good opinion and the friendship of our community, I would like to share with you the reasons we consider this research so important and why we are doing it here in Cambridge rather than in some isolated area. . . . We believe something must be done to reduce the threat of uncontrolled toxic chemicals in the environment. . . . Before our Levins Laboratory was constructed, we had to turn down community requests, including one from the Commonwealth of Massachusetts, for work involving dioxins and other contaminants. We did not like having to refuse to help our home state.

The research . . . is for defensive and protective purposes only . . . to develop better methods of detecting minute quantities . . . and safer, more effective means of destroying them on a large scale. We also are working to develop better protection, including clothing, for people who might be exposed to these substances.

We are doing the work here in Cambridge because this kind of chemical analysis cannot be performed in isolation. . . . Moving the laboratory to a remote location would mean moving much of our technical work out of Cambridge. This we do not want to do. . . . We have a record as good citizens of the community and a major investment here.

We invested nearly a million dollars . . . worked closely with the Cambridge city manager and the relevant public safety officials. . . . The result, experts concur, is a laboratory that advances the state of the art for the safe handling of hazardous substances.

If you have any comments or questions . . . I would appreciate your sending those to: Mr. D. Reid Weedon, Jr., senior vice president. We are interested in your views.

Sincerely,

/s/   John F. Magee, President and Chief Executive Officer

Excerpts from letters to the editors, *Cambridge Chronicle* and *Arlington Advocate*, March 7 and 21, 1985 (ellipses omitted)

Do you know what "the arrogance of power" is? It's a large corporation deciding to do something extremely dangerous to others and using its money and influence to steamroll over the local opposition. It's writing a patronizing letter to the locals afterward, saying, essentially, "If you only knew the facts you'd understand," as if we're too ignorant or misguided to realize what's really in our best interest. It's writing us a letter and saying, at the end, that if we have a reply, we should send it to someone else. Who is D. Reid Weedon, Jr., and why do I care whether he reads my reply to your letter?

Anyone who would build a lab for testing nerve gas in one of the most heavily populated urban areas in the United States is clearly beyond the reach of rational protest.

As ADL's neighbors we cannot accept this risk. Magee never wanted to know whether his neighbors feel safe. He never wanted us to know the lab exists. His new-found concern is insulting and absurd.

This is one resident who doesn't give a hoot about how many safety precautions they've taken. That just proves how lethal the stuff is. Testing those chemicals in our highly populated area is damn poor policy from a company that I've come to expect good judgment from.

Excerpts from a *Cambridge Chronicle* editorial, March 14, 1985 (ellipses omitted)

There are times when it is prudent to recognize that most lead balloons do not, in fact, fly. Now is the proper time for the Arthur D. Little Company to recognize that the best way to remain [a] "good neighbor" is to give up its quixotic battle against the city's ban on nerve agent testing.

ADL has handled the nerve agent issue with rather surprising stupidity, first attempting to stonewall its residential neighbors and city hall, then, belatedly, attempting to patch things up with a deceptively reassuring mass mailing (which included, for the record, a reprint from the *Chronicle*. It is not likely the firm will ask for reprint permission on this editorial.)

ADL has not come up with any particularly convincing arguments on its own behalf. Above all, company officials have stressed that the facilities where the nerve agents are stored and tested are "state-of-the-art" safe.

The one fact which inevitably weakens any defense of ADL's position is that what's at issue here is a substance to which exposure can mean instant death, pure and simple. The city's ban is not an effort to restrict research, and it is not yet another attempt to overregulate business. Instead, the ban is the proper execution of the city's responsibility to its people.

---

the press, the judge expressed reservations about his decision, thinking it unfair but unavoidable under the law. The next day he removed the restraining order which prevented the regulation's enforcement. The testing stopped.

54   In preparation for the March 7 public meeting, Toxic Alert wrote to the directors of ADL, inviting them to attend the meeting in order to inform themselves, independently of management, on the issues and the potential impact on the company's good name. The letter also appealed for formation of a board-level committee on social responsiveness. It noted that ADL's relationships with its neighbors had always been so positive that board inputs to management had not been necessary. Now the inputs were needed, the letter said, but "it seems unlikely such a committee would be organized at Mr. Magee's own request, given his level of commitment to continued testing." One director responded to the Toxic Alert letter; none attended the March 7 meeting.

55   "Some directors asked my advice—what would management prefer they do about the invitation," John Magee recalled. "My reaction was, 'Do what you please.' In their view, it wouldn't have been appropriate to attend as board members."

March 1985: The Public Forum

56   Television crews, reporters, and some 300 citizens attended the March 7 meeting in the auditorium of the Fitzgerald School in Cambridge. Moderator Anthony Cortese gave a brief chronology of events, noting that testing operations were now stopped due to the recent court decision, and outlined the rules of the program: each side would have 30 minutes, 45 minutes would be allowed for questions from the floor, and each side would have 5 minutes for summarizing. Cortese introduced D. Reid Weedon, Jr., John Magee, ADL Vice President for Chemical and Food Sciences Judith Harris, and Safety Officer R. Scott Stricoff. Weedon presented the ADL case.

The Arthur D. Little Position

57   Arthur D. Little, he said, had two concerns—one with the hazards of their work and another with the hazards of banning research. Safety for ADL staff and the community

had always been uppermost in their minds, in all their work on pesticide wastes, PCBs, dioxin, and chemical warfare agents such as nerve gas, "or, really, nerve agents, since they're not gasses." All authorities who had seen the Levins Laboratory had praised it as representing the state of the art in safety. Indeed, ADL was now doing design work for the U.S. Centers for Disease Control. Weedon quoted expert authorities to vouch for the lab's safety and noted the health and hospitals commissioner had delayed five months between inspecting the lab and issuing his regulation—hardly the behavior of someone concerned about public health perils.

58   Weedon described the precautions taken in transporting nerve agents under armed escort and showed the audience a gray steel cannister, called a "pig," which had withstood drops from an army helicopter onto concrete without damage to the flame-sealed glass vials packed inside it. A pig could carry five 20-milliliter (ml) vials of liquid. On arrival at the laboratory, each vial was opened and its contents transferred to 1-ml vials. Since most experiments required less than 1 milliliter, any risk of spilling was minimized by working with the smaller standard quantity.

59   Near the end of the SAC deliberations, ADL had announced it would limit its inventory to a maximum of 40 milliliters of any of the three most hazardous nerve agent concentrates: Sarin (GB), Soman (GD), and VX. Additionally, the combined inventory of all three would not exceed 100 milliliters, although larger quantities of Mustard (HD) and Lewisite (L), up to a combined inventory of 500 milliliters, might be on hand at one time. Weedon referred to ADL's self-imposed limit of $\frac{1}{10}$ of a liter as a primary safeguard against the kind of accidental spills postulated in the SAC report.

60   Further, said Weedon, ADL used mostly dilute concentrations and would never leave a spill to evaporate. Household bleach was an effective decontaminating agent. The SAC report scenario showing a "puff" of gas, as from an explosion, could not happen because the agents decomposed in temperatures over 500 degrees. Besides, the injury and fatality counts deemed possible by the SAC assumed none of the injured received medical treatment—again, an assumption without credibility. Any accidents in any of the 14 laboratories doing this kind of work in America had resulted in injuries successfully treated; no testing-related fatalities had ever been reported. The assumptions used in the SAC report, Weedon said, were totally unrealistic. It was not fair to postulate impossible risks.

61   Weedon went on to describe the need for knowledge about chemical warfare agents, which were in current use in the Iran–Iraq war and might pose a threat to American military forces at any time. There was need, too, for research using these agents for medical applications. Hodgkin's disease had been found by an Army lab to respond to a nerve agent, and Alzheimer's disease was thought to be a prospective target. But if there could be no research, he said, there might be no cures.

62   "We're often asked, 'Why locate chemical warfare work in Cambridge?'" Weedon said. "The appropriate answer is, 'Because it is safe, and Arthur D. Little is here.' Usually the larger part of the work in an assignment does not use toxic materials and therefore is done outside the toxic materials laboratory. The next question is, 'Why not locate just the toxic materials laboratory elsewhere?' We do not have, nor do we expect, sufficient volume of work on chemical warfare agents to justify full-time staff in such a laboratory.

63   "Furthermore, a separate location would require medical personnel whenever people were in the laboratory, full-time guard service, and immediate-response technical and maintenance support services. All of these services are in place at our Acorn Park

facility, and duplication, while possible, would price us out of the competition," Weedon said.

64   He went on to enumerate a list of toxic chemicals, many similar to the nerve agents, which were widely used in medical schools and were available from lab supply houses with no regulation at all. "A typical hardware store or garden center will have on its shelves a quantity equivalent to more than 100 lethal doses of the pesticide Malathion in concentrated form, in totally unventilated spaces. This pesticide acts on the human nervous system by exactly the same biochemical mechanisms as do the DOD chemicals GD, GB, and VX. . . . True, ounce for ounce, Malathion is less toxic than the chemical warfare agents. But because use and storage of Malathion is totally uncontrolled and the available quantities are so large, I submit that the risk of exposure to this nerve agent is much greater than the risk of exposure to similar chemicals safely stored within the Levins Laboratory."

65   Weedon concluded the ADL presentation with an appeal for the city to establish standards and regulations for *all* toxic agents, rather than banning a certain class of them based on their purpose as weapons of war. Arthur D. Little, he volunteered, stood ready to use its substantial talents to help the city in this effort.

66   "Arthur D. Little has been a part of Cambridge since the early days of this century," Weedon concluded. "We love this city. We're proud of it. The city we love is a world-class city, which provides an environment that encourages and supports scientific talent in a spirit of research and investigation. We trust you also wish, as we do, to protect that very special environment that is Cambridge."

The Toxic Alert Presentation

67   Five speakers shared the presentation and summary of the Toxic Alert position. The moderator introduced Ed Cyr, Sharon Moran, John O'Connor, and Steve Schnapp, all of the Toxic Alert, and David Ozonoff, M.D., a Cambridge resident and SAC member. Steve Schnapp began the presentation.

68   Responding to ADL's many assurances of safety, Schnapp said, "It seems to me we've heard this kind of corporate reassurance before." As the house lights dimmed and a slide of a bushy-whiskered sea captain appeared on the screen, Schnapp continued:

> Captain Edward J. Smith said, "I cannot conceive of any kind of vital disaster happening to this vessel. Modern shipbuilding has gone beyond that." On April 12, 1912, Captain Smith's ship, the Titanic, struck an iceberg and sank with a loss of 1,500 lives. *John Magee says there is no credible danger in nerve gas testing at ADL. The risk is vanishingly small.*

69   The captain's picture changed to a slide showing a newsboy hawking papers with the headline "Titanic Lost!" and then to a handful of capsules. Schnapp continued,

> "We have firmly established the safety, dosage, and usefulness of Kevidon," said Frank Gettman, the president of William S. Merrill Company in 1960. "There is still no positive proof of a causal relationship between the use of thalidomide during pregnancy and malfunctions in the newborn." But in 1962 the drug was pulled off the market. More than 8,000 children suffered grave birth defects. *John Magee says, "There are more risks in the kitchens of Cambridge than in the laboratories of Arthur D. Little."*

70   The slide switched to a view of Niagara Falls.

"When you come right down to it," said an ad of Hooker Chemical Company in the 1940s, "you would be hard pressed to find any group of people who care as much about the environmental well-being of Niagara Falls as the people at Hooker." In 1979, 239 families were evacuated from the Love Canal neighborhood. *Arthur D. Little cares just as much for Cambridge.*

71   The slide showed a refugee family leaving Love Canal and then the ominous cooling towers of a nuclear power plant.

"Do you think I'd work here if it was dangerous?" said William Metzger, a Three Mile Island employee, shortly before the catastrophic near-meltdown of March 29, 1979. *"If this lab weren't safe," said Alma Triner, vice president for public relations at Arthur D. Little, "I wouldn't be working here."*

72   The slide changed again, to show a chemical plant and then a *Newsweek* photograph of the Bhopal disaster.

"A factory is not a small stone that can be shifted elsewhere," State Labor Minister Tarasingh Viyogi told the provincial assembly of Madhya Pradesh in India. "There is no danger to Bhopal, nor will there be." *Arthur D. Little, working with compounds 50 to 100 times more toxic than methyl isocyanate, is just as certain of their safety.*

73   "All of those assurances came from highly trained, competent people who most probably believed what they were saying," Schnapp said. "Will Cambridge be next on the 11 o'clock news?"

74   Sharon Moran told of attending the first Cambridge City Council meeting on the topic, in October of 1983. She described how Mr. Weedon "spent 10 minutes telling the council there wasn't any nerve gas at ADL. There were chemical surety agents, he said. It came out later these were liquids, which would explode into a shower of tiny droplets called an aerosol when a chemical warfare shell detonated. *That* was nerve gas, and ADL didn't have any. Later the SAC received a letter saying ADL would vaporize the liquid agents. Tonight again they say they don't."

75   Moran told of hearing "evasive answers" on what agents were at the laboratory and what tests and end results were expected. "What can you believe?" she asked. "What disturbs me is that, in spite of all their professional expertise, they couldn't—or maybe they didn't want to—be clear and coherent and forthcoming about what substances they were using. Confusing us with technical jargon is too often the trick of the arrogant scientist—not the kind of behavior I expect from a company with a commitment to be a good neighbor, as ADL has told us they have.

76   "Left out of tonight's presentation," said Moran, "was information about the agents themselves. They were invented with one purpose: killing people. One 100th of a drop of agent VX will kill you, if it touches your skin or if you inhale it. These chemicals affect the nervous system, causing all bodily processes to go haywire. The victim sweats intensely, and vomits and defecates uncontrollably. Finally, the person becomes completely paralyzed and unable to take a breath; death follows by asphyxiation. Nerve agents are awesomely lethal, compared to compounds like Malathion. That is why I find it disturbing when Mr. Magee minimizes their danger by telling us that greater danger exists in the average kitchen.

77   "Also disturbing," said Moran, "was ADL's discounting of the SAC's findings. This was a group of professionals, not a bunch of radicals, and they found that an accidental release *could* happen. It is not impossible. Further, however small the risk, it was unacceptable in so densely populated an area. The only group that likes the idea of ADL's work is ADL. This kind of work should be done in remote military installations." Morgan concluded, "Commercial companies have too much at stake to be the sole judges of whether their work is acceptable."

78   David Ozonoff introduced himself as a physician with a bias in favor of public health. "The issue here," he said, "is not freedom of inquiry as Mr. Weedon would have the audience believe. The testing of nerve gas has about the same relationship to science as pornography has to photojournalism. Nor is the issue about trading one risk for another. There is a perfect way to have no risk at all from nerve gas in the city of Cambridge, and that is not to do this work in the city. Nor is the issue about regulation; Cambridge can and should regulate ADL, because otherwise they would be regulated only by the Department of Defense—reputed to be the worst polluter in the country.

79   "In fact," Ozonoff said, "everybody knows what the issue is about: it's the Willie Sutton principle. You may remember that, when somebody asked the late bank robber Willie Sutton why he robbed banks, he said, 'Because that's where the money is.' EPA money has dried up, and consultants are turning to where the money is—the Department of Defense."

80   Ozonoff concluded, "This controversy is about risk and the notion of what is acceptable. Some risks are unacceptable even though their numeric measurements are very, very small; examples are the presence of dangerous chemicals in drinking water, asbestos in schools, and cyanide in Tylenol capsules. The Levins Laboratory risks are also very small, but they are real, and they have been judged unacceptable by everyone in the community except ADL."

81   Ed Cyr took the platform next to argue that this was not a question for scientists or managers to answer. "This is too important to be left to experts, businessmen, or scientists because they are unable to deal with being wrong, and that makes them dangerous," Cyr said. "Informed citizens," he went on, "have a basic right to full information about all the risks they are exposed to. More importantly, they have a right to decide for themselves what risks they will take.

82   "I will not fall into the scientists' trap of trying to prove how an accident could happen," Cyr said. "Instead, I look at why I am afraid in this case the stage has been set for one." Claiming that public officials and businesses normally keep accidents secret until they get out of hand, Cyr said, "We must judge the people who would run the facility as well as the facility itself. ADL planned the lab in secret, with no public consideration in siting, design trade-offs, or security considerations. ADL went to great lengths to make sure we were *not* informed until contracts were in hand; they asked our police and firefighters to lie for them.

83   "It would be good if I could tell you that, when the story broke, ADL saw the folly in their approach and came clean. At least then we would know they were capable of admitting a mistake. But no. At every meeting, ADL has downplayed the danger and played us for fools. They paint themselves as victims, even after 16 weeks of hearings at the SAC. No Cambridge project has ever been looked at as thoroughly as this one.

84   "Can you trust ADL to safely manage this lab, when they worked so very hard to avoid telling you about it in the first place? . . . Can you trust a company that regularly,

in forum after forum, compares these incredibly deadly chemicals to *water?* to *backyard pesticides?* and to things that are commonly found in your *kitchen?*

85   "Do *you* believe the Department of Defense intends to kill a million Russians with 2 gallons of Liquid Plumber?"

Discussion and Summaries

86   John O'Connor summarized for the Toxic Alert, calling the ADL public relations campaign a "snow job" to cover the main reason for ADL's involvement—to make money. "The community has the right to say no to nerve gas testing," he said, demanding that ADL drop its appeal, renounce nerve gas forever, and move present stocks out of Cambridge. "The one person with power to do that is Mr. Magee," O'Connor continued. "We are angry, frightened—and also on the move to ensure that not one dime of taxpayer money will be used to support a corporation that is chemically trespassing on our city. If need be, we will take to the streets like the founders of our country, to demand that our rights as citizens to be free from toxic hazards be recognized."

87   Mr. Magee summarized for Arthur D. Little, voicing appreciation for the audience's courtesy. He held up a quarter-teaspoon to demonstrate how small the quantity involved at any one time was, and how hard it would be to make that quantity reach beyond ADL's property. He quoted a recent visitor as saying the facility was "superb." Cambridge officials had been kept informed from the beginning, he said, adding, "We've continued to stay in touch with the city, and *not once* have city officials, even yet, expressed concern to us about the safety of our laboratory!"

88   "That's not true," said a voice from the back of the hall.

89   "That is true," Magee replied.

90   "I was in the laboratory, and I told Mr. Weedon at the time I examined it that I wasn't impressed with. . . ."

91   Magee interrupted, "Who are you?"

92   "My name is Tom Danehy, and I'm a city councillor, and I live in Cambridge, not in Wellesley."

93   "I must admit I was speaking specifically of the fire, police, and public health officials," said Magee.

94   "Those aren't the ones we elect," Danehy concluded.

95   Magee resumed his talk with an attack on what he called the bias of Dr. Ozonoff. Magee said Ozonoff, as director of a group called the Committee for Responsible Genetics, had taken a position against *any* defensive research on chemical or biological warfare agents. "That political stand has nothing to do with neighborhood safety," Magee said, "and we shouldn't let that point of view be imposed on the community under the disguise of a concern for neighborhood safety." He urged all who were "really concerned with safety" to join with ADL to help the city develop comprehensive regulations for all toxic substances, wherever they were used.

96   As the crowd left the auditorium, members of the Toxic Alert took an "exit poll," asking whether nerve gas work should be done in Cambridge. Four people said it should; 127 said no. Recognizing the possible bias in the population, the poll takers also asked whether respondents were members of Toxic Alert or employees of ADL. Seven were ADL workers, while 39 were Toxic Alert members.

TA: See that? Seven employees here, but only four votes for the testing. Do you suppose three sevenths of ADL's own people are on our side? Think what we could do with that!

ADL: We got a stronger reaction from staff members to raising the price of tuna sandwiches in the cafeteria than to this issue.

Spring and Summer 1985: The Debate Continues

97   Commenting in the *Cambridge Chronicle* on the impact of the interruption in testing, laboratory manager Dr. Judith Harris said that ADL was currently committed to several DOD contracts and had "several million dollars" in proposed contracts under consideration. "If we are forced to close down for some time, I think there's going to be a serious problem," she said, noting that if the ban on research held, ADL would have to subcontract its work to another of the nation's 14 high-security laboratories. "We'd have to send this to some other downtown area," she said, noting that most of the other labs were in densely populated areas like Birmingham, Alabama, or Columbus, Ohio.

98   In the weeks after the public forum, the *Cambridge Chronicle* took a strong editorial stand against nerve agent testing, and other local groups also took public positions on the issue. In a March 20 letter to ADL, the presidents of the Cambridge, Arlington, and Belmont Leagues of Women Voters supported the ban on testing. Alma Triner, ADL's vice president for public relations, told the *Chronicle* that the leagues' position was "very disappointing" to the company, which had contributed funds to league projects in the past. The league "has lost credibility in the eyes of ADL" as a result of its stand, Triner said.

99   While gaining local support, however, the movement lost ground in the courts. On March 12, ADL asked the state appeals court for a stay of Judge Hallisey's order; three days later Judge John Greaney complied, reinstating the injunction against enforcing Dr. Chalfen's regulation. Cambridge attorneys at once asked State Supreme Judicial Court Justice Paul Liacos to remove the case from the Appeals Court and hear it directly at the Supreme Court level, short-cutting one step of the appeals process. The case was heard by the Supreme Judicial Court on April 4, but no immediate finding was expected. Although no formal announcements were made, it was assumed by Toxic Alert members that testing had resumed in the Levins Laboratory.

100   On March 30, 1985, the new Boston subway station next door to ADL was opened. Toxic Alert members took advantage of the large crowds to picket with the message that the entire station was inside the "zone of lethality." On April 5, a group called the Boston Committee for No Business as Usual held a "twitch-in" rally in front of ADL's offices. On April 12, at the annual meeting of Arthur D. Little stockholders, pickets walked the sidewalks in front of the Harvard Club in Boston, passing out leaflets questioning the ability of management to view the situation objectively.

ADL: The "twitch-in" was a demonstration by about six people who called them-selves the "Revolutionary Communist Youth Brigade" and operate out of an office at MIT. The *Globe* covered the annual meeting but didn't do a story because the demonstration was a nonevent involving the usual 8 to 10 people.

101   On April 19, State Representative Thomas Gallagher introduced a bill which would ban the testing of chemical warfare agents within a mile of any home, business, or public road. For the next two months the scope of possible regulations was debated in the Joint Legislative Committee on Health Care, whose chairman toured the ADL laboratory and said he was much impressed. On June 12, ADL's Dr. William Augerson testified to the committee on the need for regulating *all* highly toxic chemicals, not just those designed as weapons. He named 16 "relatively common chemicals" whose toxicity, he said, equaled that of the agents prohibited in Cambridge. The list included strychnine, parathion, phosgene, arsine, and methyl isocyanate. A special task force was eventually set up by the legislature, to report back in the fall. At the same time, Cambridge's Scientific Advisory Committee continued to work on drafting an ordinance to control toxic substances in general.

102   On May 28, 1985, the Army's undersecretary of research and development, Amaretta Hoeber, met with ADL and Toxic Alert representatives in the offices of Senator Edward Kennedy to reiterate the nation's needs for this research and the Army's confidence in its safe conduct at Acorn Park. On June 3, the Cambridge City Council okayed a referendum question for the November ballot, asking voter opinion on the ADL testing work.

103   As the summer passed, both sides awaited the ruling of the Supreme Judicial Court. The Supreme Court of the United States would be the next legal step if the Massachusetts loser decided to appeal further. Toxic Alert members wondered about their own next steps, and expected Arthur D. Little again to avoid complying with the health and hospitals regulation. How, they pondered, could they most effectively raise the cost of ADL to the point where testing would be abandoned? In the meantime, testing continued at the Levins Laboratory.

104   Publisher Russel Pergament of the *Cambridge Tab* summarized the situation on July 23:

> The story is simple. ADL says they don't plan to manufacture these deadly nerve gases, a thimbleful of which can kill thousands. No sir. They plan to study ways of making these gases inert. That reminds me of the guy who was arrested for stealing hubcaps. When the police collared him, he said, "But, officer, I wasn't stealing them, I was putting them back on." And so it is with ADL, who have double talked, double dealed, and deceived the city's health department since day one about their plans here. They never played straight with the city, and so they rate no special considerations, especially in view of the great danger their work puts local families in.

> **ADL:** Quoting a Russ Pergament editorial from *The Tab* as a voice of local opinion is like quoting *The National Enquirer* as an authority on national mores.

August 1985: The Supreme Court Decision

105   It was August 1, 1985, and John Magee had just learned of the Massachusetts Supreme Court decision upholding Cambridge's right to ban the nerve agent work at Arthur D. Little.

106   "Of course, we'll abide by Commissioner Chalfen's order not to work with the material," John Magee said. "Then we'll have to see the court order and talk with our clients about what to do from here. It's not clear ADL has standing to carry the case

further. If the proper basis is the supremacy of federal regulation, then it might have to be appealed by a federal agency.

107   "Maybe this will make life simple for us. I can tell the staff I'm sorry, but we fought as good a fight as we could and we lost. So, I'm sorry, but we're out of that business.

108   "No, I wouldn't *like* to be out of the business—not particularly. But I'm not a strong advocate of being *in* the business. Contrary to what a lot of people think, it's not my baby. There are a number of people, though, who do feel we should be in the business— Judy Harris, Bill Augerson, Art Schwope. They're professionals. They feel that this is important work, and I feel that one of my jobs is to facilitate their doing work that they can do and want to do and work that's important. We have never backed away from work that met those tests just because it was unpopular with some constituency.

109   "But, if you're out of it, you're out of it."

110   John Magee was unaware of the Pergament column and did not recall the local editorials. "Those things have no impact, really," he said. "Oh, we receive the papers, and of course we have a clipping service. And we recognize they have an impact on other people. But do they cause us to stop and ask ourselves whether we're doing the right thing? No."

111   Most ADL people, Magee said, believed the company's standing in the community had not been damaged by the controversy. "There may be some circles where our standing is diminished," he said, "and that may be true with some of our staff as well. But in other circles we've received sympathy—where people say, 'They got to you, just like they've gotten to Harvard or MIT or Polaroid in the past.' Still other circles have expressed substantial admiration for our willingness to stand up and fight."

112   Magee speculated on how he and his managers formed their impressions of the people arrayed against them. "When it becomes difficult to engage these people in a discussion of the technical issues," he said, "then you begin to consider the question, are there other issues that are driving them? We look for what brings them together. We know Ozonoff and Krimsky are very active in antimilitary political activity.

113   "Ozonoff has been quoted as making some outlandish statements concerning the level of risk involved. The idea that one drop of this stuff could kill 10,000 people or whatever . . . that we have enough to kill . . . I don't know. . . . Anybody who is a serious student of the risks involved with toxic materials and dispersal issues *has* to see that as not being a factual estimate. It assumes people line up to get precisely the right dose. So there's got to be some kind of motivation here, to put out that kind of number. It's not put out as a factual analysis.

114   "We don't use gas at all. *We're* not the ones who are using misnomers or clouding the issue with semantics." Reminded that ADL's contracts included work on detection of gas, which seemed to imply the presence of gas, Magee paused. "I don't think we're generating any aerosols," he said. "I'd have to check."

115   Had the testing been pursued up to now as a matter of principle? "Well, there are principles and principles," said Magee. "If the principle is one of essential ethics, then you press it. But if it's a matter of being allowed to do something we think we ought to be allowed to do, then there is a practical limit to how far you want to press it, because there are alternatives. For example, if this is saying to us that Cambridge is no longer a healthy community for an organization like ours, then we have options. We have to address the issue of principle in that context."

116   The company decided against further appeal of the legal issues. On September 4, the local press reported, an Army Technical Escort Unit removed the remaining chemical materials from the Levins Laboratory. In the November municipal elections, a nonbinding referendum question found 3,459 voters favoring the right of ADL to work with chemical warefare agents; 18,952 voted against the research.

Arthur D. Little, Inc., and the Toxic Alert (B)

117   Arthur D. Little's annual report for the year 1985 listed gross revenues of $233 million, with after-tax income of $6 million and earnings of $2.35 per share. U.S. government revenues for 1985 totaled $32.7 million, a gain of $2.1 million from the previous year's figure. Under the heading, "Our relationship with society," the annual report said,

> All of us who are associated with Arthur D. Little, Inc., take considerable pride in the fact that, in pursuing our own professional and corporate objectives, we serve society as well. Our basic business function fills some essential social and economic needs.
>
> > We bridge the gap between theory and practice by applying the findings of fundamental research to the practical needs of industry and governments.
> >
> > Because we work for both industry and government and understand the problems and objectives of both, we are able to bridge potentially counterproductive or adversarial gaps between the two sectors and facilitate cooperation toward common goals.

118   The report made no mention of the nerve agent controversy. At the annual meeting of the stockholders, on April 11, 1986, John Magee was asked to comment.

119   "The first impact," he said, "was the distraction. And the work is suspended, of course, but the people are still on the staff; there are some expenses there. The facility is not in full use now, but in the longer term it will be useful.

120   "We learned from the experience. We presumed too much on our long-term relationship with the city and its politics; it was more fragile than we expected. Cambridge showed a great lack of understanding about the nature of research. A city with such a volatile political climate may not be an appropriate host to a company such as ours."

121   At the board of directors meeting on April 11, John Magee was elected chairman, replacing the retiring Robert Mueller. He now serves as both president and chairman.

Case 16

Pizza Delights, Inc.: The St. George Street Restaurant

1. Earnest Outbanks, manager of the St. George Street Pizza Delights in Roebuck, South Carolina, hung up the phone after a two-hour conversation with Leonard Lloyd, owner of three Pizza Delights in Greer, South Carolina. It was 11 P.M. on the night of April 5, 1986, and soon it would be time to close. It occurred to Outbanks as he glanced around the restaurant he had successfully managed for five years that both he and Lloyd were on the verge of a major decision, the outcome of which was certain to shape the rest of their careers. He tried to concentrate on the job at hand, but his thoughts kept returning to Lloyd's proposal.

2. Outbanks' career in the pizza business had started some 10 years earlier, in 1976, when he became a cook for Pizza Delights during high school. Lloyd's involvement began in 1981, when he bought his first Pizza Delights restaurant in Greer, South Carolina. By 1986, at the tender age of 25, Outbanks had become well established as the manager of the St. George Street Pizza Delights in Roebuck, a small community approximately five miles to the southeast of Spartanburg, South Carolina. Lloyd, on the other hand, had by 1986 established a chain of three successful Pizza Delights franchise restaurants throughout the rural Greer area, which was approximately 20 miles from Spartanburg.

3. Since Outbanks had taken over the company-owned restaurant on St. George Street in 1981, he had managed to change a sluggish, break-even operation into the second most profitable Pizza Delights in the greater Spartanburg area (see Exhibit 1 for income statements for 1983–85). His achievements had not escaped the attention of many fellow businesspeople in the fast-growing communities which surrounded the restaurant. Leonard Lloyd had learned of Outbanks' achievements too, as he was always on the lookout for a way to enter the more lucrative Spartanburg market.

4. Lloyd had contacted Outbanks on several occasions during the spring of 1986 in hopes of persuading Outbanks to join him in buying the restaurant from Pizza Delights. Although Lloyd's idea sounded quite attractive to Outbanks, who had had visions of owning his own franchise for several years, he was reluctant to give an answer right away. Outbanks' career with Pizza Delights had been quite successful, and he believed that his future with the firm was bright. However, he knew that Lloyd could not be kept waiting forever and was determined to make a decision in the near future.

5. The remainder of this case will describe the history, environment, and operations of the Pizza Delights Corporation, the restaurants on St. George Street and in Greer, as well as Lloyd's franchising plans for Outbanks' restaurant.

Pizza Delights, Inc.: Company Background and Structure

6. The Pizza Delights chain was established in the greater Omaha, Nebraska, area in the late 1960s. The restaurants offered the customer a limited range of Italian dishes

---

This case was prepared by Jay Horne, Christine Perkins, Kim Goates, Peter Asp, and Ken Sarris under the direction of Dr. James J. Chrisman, University of South Carolina, and associate editor, *Case Research Journal*. This case was prepared for classroom discussion and was not intended to illustrate either effective or ineffective handling of administrative situations.

Exhibit 1

A. Pizza Delights: The St. George Street location income statements, 1983–1985

	1985	*1984*	*1983*
Gross food sales	$557,278	$478,603	$422,375
Less: Allowances	7,869	7,547	7,038
Sales promotions	34,394	32,982	31,651
Net food sales	515,015	438,074	383,686
Plus: Vending machines	1,734	2,103	1,923
Game machine	1,582	1,661	1,843
Total revenue	518,331	441,838	387,452
Cost of goods sold	144,406	133,225	117,486
Gross profit	373,925	308,613	269,966
Operating costs:			
Management salary	54,373		
Crew labor	56,445	111,391	108,476
Other labor	12,979		
National advertising	7,544		5,637
Co-op advertising	12,652	22,880	7,629
Local advertising	9,001		8,538
Operating costs	12,795		13,330
Utilities cost	19,531		16,343
Maintenance	9,749	40,464	9,019
Uniforms	349		1,113
Other	2,474		2,110
Premiums	5	1,110	210
Operating profit	176,028	132,778	97,981
Plus: TJTC credit	4,435	0	0
Less: Fixed costs	47,467*	33,985*	35,647
Total profit	$132,996	$ 98,793	$ 62,334

* See fixed cost schedule.

B. Fixed cost schedule for 1984–1985 income statements

	1985	*1984*
Fixed costs	$47,466	$33,985
TJTC expense	161	54
Bank charges	570	615
Personal property tax	221	254
Real estate taxes	3,939	3,939
Licenses and fees	269	289
Equipment depreciation	10,149	7,774
Leasehold amortization	2,618	2,768
Building rental	17,417	15,813
Contingent lease rent	8,442	502
Insurance	2,441	1,909
Abandonment and property	1,236	65
Goodwill amortization	3	0

including pizza, spaghetti, and cavatini. The restaurants proved to be very successful. They offered something the public wanted—a high-quality pizza with a high level of personal service. The original restaurants enjoyed immediate success, since it was one of the first chains in the area to offer strictly pizza and other Italian dishes.

7   Due to its early successes, Pizza Delights was an attractive acquisition candidate. It caught the attention of a large food manufacturing corporation, which purchased the company as well as the rights to its secret recipes in the late 1970s. With the corporation's financial backing, Pizza Delights restaurants began to spring up all over the United States at an even faster rate than before. Throughout this period of national expansion, the high degree of quality and service that were Pizza Delights' trademark were maintained.

8   Since 1983, Pizza Delights had introduced several new products, which were "big sellers." These products included a small pan pizza (1983), the double-decker pizza (1984), and the Italian turnover pizza (1985). All of these products required a great deal of refrigerator space for storage. However, according to restaurant managers, Pizza Delights had not provided the additional freezer capacity needed to store these items.

9   Additionally, as Pizza Delights was owned by a large food corporation, all the supplies used at company-owned restaurants had to be obtained from the parent company. These items included everything from straws and napkins to pizza dough and pepperoni. If an emergency situation occurred, such as a shortage of green peppers, the restaurants were allowed to make purchases from outside suppliers as long as these purchases, in total, did not exceed 1 percent of yearly sales for the individual restaurant. However, this practice was not generally encouraged by the corporation.

10   Franchised restaurants had more flexibility in this respect. To ensure standardization, certain items, such as printed napkins and pizza ingredients, still had to be purchased from the parent corporation. However, other items (such as pizza cutters) could be purchased from outside sources. This was important for possible cost reductions as purchasing solely from the corporation tended to inflate costs. For example, ladles to dip pizza sauce currently cost $8 when purchased from the corporation. Outside suppliers offered this item for a lower price, sometimes as much as 10 to 20 percent less than charged by the corporation.

11   In 1986, the headquarters of Pizza Delights remained in Omaha. The chain had grown to nearly 1,500 restaurants. Management planned to open 100 to 200 new restaurants per year over the next decade. To accommodate this growth, six regional offices, located in the population centers of the United States, had been added since the 1970s. These regions were subdivided into areas, which were further subdivided into districts (see Exhibit 2). Each region, area, and district had a full-time staff of managers, accountants, inspectors, and other personnel to ensure that each individual restaurant fulfilled its duties to the corporation.

12   This hierarchical maze created some problems for the individual restaurants, however. For example, any purchase exceeding $500 had to be approved by the area supervisor, the district manager, and the regional vice president before the restaurant manager could proceed with the investment. This situation sometimes created a time lag of several months between requests and implementation. As a result, many of the restaurant managers had given up trying to solve certain problems and, instead, merely tolerated them.

Exhibit 2
The Pizza Delights hierarchy

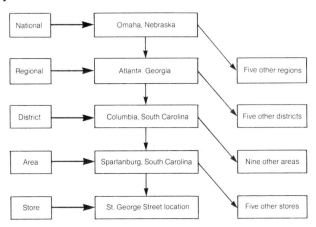

History of the St. George Street Restaurant

13 The St. George Street Pizza Delights was built in 1974 primarily to serve customers in Roebuck, a small community five miles southeast of Spartanburg, South Carolina. It also served commuters who traveled on Interstate 85, a major traffic artery into Spartanburg.

14 The restaurant was modestly successful from the start, showing low to moderate profits during its first few years. As the populations of Roebuck, Spartanburg, and the surrounding areas grew, so initially did the restaurant's profits. With this population growth, however, came increased competition (and lower profits) as other fast-food chains began to appear along a strip of St. George Street for several miles. By 1981, when Outbanks became manager, there were a total of three direct pizza competitors within one mile of the restaurant, not to mention the numerous other fast-food competitors which did business in the area.

15 Outbanks had inherited a restaurant which had many problems. First of all, the crew at the restaurant had been described by the district manager as probably the "most lazy and inhospitable bunch he had ever met." Second, food costs at the restaurant had been astronomical. Cheese costs in particular were extremely high. High food costs were partially attributable to the fact that many of the employees were either taking home free pizzas or giving them away to their friends. In addition, the cooks were not preparing the pizzas according to Pizza Delights standards. None of the ingredients were weighed, which often resulted in more ingredients being used on the individual pizzas than were needed.

16 As a result of the increased competition as well as the inefficiencies in operations, the restaurant's net profits before taxes had dipped to their lowest level since 1975 ($42,680) when Outbanks assumed control in 1981. Outbanks attempted to alter these problems by replacing most of his staff and training the new employees himself. He also began to implement new policies to improve the efficiency of operations. Due to

Exhibit 3
Colleges and universities in Spartanburg County: Enrollments

Institution	Enrollment
University of South Carolina— Spartanburg	2,778
Spartanburg Technical College	1,813
Converse College	1,078
Spartanburg Methodist College	1,067
Wofford	1,034
Rutledge College—Spartanburg	447

Source: *South Carolina Statistical Abstract, 1984.*

his extensive experience in the pizza business, as well as his ability to deal effectively with high school– and college-age employees, most of the more obvious problems had been solved, and the restaurant's profits rose steadily under his stewardship.

The Greater Spartanburg Environment

17   Located in northern South Carolina, Spartanburg was a city of approximately 45,000 persons. Situated in an agricultural region that produced crops such as cotton, peaches, melons, and feed crops, the city was the seat of Spartanburg County and was part of the tri-county region (Spartanburg, Greenville, and Pickens counties) that made up the Greenville–Spartanburg SMA (standard metropolitan area). Spartanburg boasted a variety of employment opportunities for its residents in manufacturing industries, such as textiles, metals, rubber, paper, chemicals, clothing, and plumbing supplies. In addition, it was the site for several colleges and universities (see Exhibit 3). Unfortunately, the area had not shared equally in the growth experienced in other parts of South Carolina and the South Atlantic region (Delaware, District of Columbia, Florida, Georgia, Maryland, North Carolina, South Carolina, Virginia, and West Virginia) in recent years.

18   For example, the populations of the surrounding SMA and county were growing at a rate exceeding the average for the United States. However, between 1978 and 1984 this growth rate had not kept pace with the population growth experienced in the rest of South Carolina or in the South Atlantic region. In fact, the population in the city of Spartanburg had actually declined (see Exhibit 4).

19   Despite lackluster population growth, the Spartanburg area was relatively prosperous in comparison to the rest of South Carolina. Even so, the effective buying incomes of area inhabitants lagged both the total United States and the South Atlantic region. To make matters worse, Spartanburg was falling further behind national and regional averages and had recently lost some of its advantage over the rest of South Carolina (see Exhibit 5).

Exhibit 4
1978 and 1984 Population statistics for Spartanburg, Spartanburg County, the Greenville–Spartanburg SMA, South Carolina, the South Atlantic region, and the United States (population and households in thousands)

Year	Total population	Percent of U.S.	Total households	Percent of U.S.	Median Age	Percent of population by age group				
						0–17	18–24	25–34	35–49	≥50
			Spartanburg							
1978	46.9	.02%	16.7	.02%	31.2	26.8%	14.2%	14.6%	16.3%	28.1%
1984	44.9	.02	17.4	.02	32.2	24.5	13.3	17.0	16.0	29.2
Percent change	−6.2%		+4.2%							
			Spartanburg County							
1978	196.7	.09	67.8	.09	30.6	28.0	12.6	16.7	17.2	25.5
1984	213.5	.09	78.3	.09	32.1	26.6	11.1	17.2	19.6	25.5
Percent change	+8.5%		+15.5%							
			Greenville–Spartanburg SMA							
1978	541.4	.25	184.5	.24	29.8	27.9	13.9	17.1	17.1	24.0
1984	605.0	.25	222.1	.26	31.3	26.2	12.6	17.8	19.5	23.9
Percent change	+11.7%		+20.4%							
			South Carolina							
1978	2,934.8	1.3	933.8	1.2	27.7	31.2	14.5	15.9	16.0	22.5
1984	3,353.4	1.4	1,172.0	1.4	29.8	28.2	13.3	17.6	18.1	22.7
Percent change	+14.3%		+25.5%							
			*South Atlantic Region**							
1978	34,981.7	15.9	12,186.8	15.9	30.3	28.2	13.4	15.7	16.3	26.4
1984	39,904.5	16.8	14,612.2	16.8	32.3	25.4	12.1	17.2	18.5	26.8
Percent change	+14.1%		+19.9%							
			United States							
1978	219,768.5	100	76,904.7	100	30.1	28.8	13.2	15.7	16.4	26.0
1984	238,274.7	100	86,926.6	100	31.7	26.3	12.2	17.4	18.3	25.9
Percent change	+8.4%		+13.0%							

* Includes Delaware, District of Columbia, Florida, Georgia, Maryland, North Carolina, South Carolina, Virginia, and West Virginia.
Source: "Survey of Buying Power," *Sales and Marketing Management,* 1979 and 1985.

20   The outlook for retailing, particularly eating-and-drinking establishments, was not exceedingly bright either. Sales did increase for retailers between 1978 and 1984 in Spartanburg and the surrounding area. And as Exhibit 6 shows, this growth rate compared favorably overall to that experienced on average in the United States. Unfortunately, Exhibit 6 also shows that the rate of growth in retailing for the Greenville–Spartanburg SMA did not compare favorably to average growth rates in South Carolina and the South Atlantic states. Additionally, contrary to trends in South Carolina, the South Atlantic states, and the United States in general, eating-and-drinking establishments' share of total retail sales in the Greenville–Spartanburg SMA had declined

Exhibit 5
Effective buying incomes in 1978 and 1984: Spartanburg, Spartanburg County, the Greenville–Spartanburg SMA, South Carolina, the South Atlantic region, and the United States

	Total EBI ($000s)	Per capita EBI	Average household EBI	Median household EBI
Spartanburg				
1978	$ 308,625	$ 6,580	$18,481	$14,721
1984	410,214	9,136	23,576	18,782
Percent change	+32.9%	+38.8%	+27.6%	+27.6%
Spartanburg County				
1978	1,127,798	5,734	16,634	14,702
1984	1,943,381	9,102	24,820	21,828
Percent change	+72.3%	+58.7%	+49.2%	+48.5%
Greenville–Spartanburg SMA				
1978	3,203,011	5,916	17,360	15,349
1984	5,434,481	8,983	24,469	21,540
Percent change	+69.7%	+51.8%	+41.0%	+40.3%
South Carolina				
1978	15,425,876	5,256	16,519	14,047
1984	28,550,182	8,514	24,360	20,969
Percent change	+85.1%	+62.0%	+47.5%	+49.3%
South Atlantic region				
1978	212,961,331	6,088	17,475	14,681
1984	408,218,168	10,230	27,937	23,576
Percent change	+91.7%	+68.0%	+59.9%	+60.6%
United States				
1978	1,439,815,449	6,552	18,722	16,231
1984	2,576,533,480	10,813	29,640	25,496
Percent change	+78.9%	+65.0%	+58.3%	+57.1%

Source: "Survey of Buying Power," *Sales and Marketing Management,* 1979 and 1985.

substantially in the 1980s. The outlook for eating-and-drinking places in the city was the least favorable. Eating-and-drinking-place sales had increased only 5 percent since 1978, while they had increased 73 percent on average in the United States and had more than doubled in the rest of South Carolina during the same period. There were greater opportunities outside the city, though, as the migration to the suburbs provided increased demand for restaurants in these locations.

Competition in the Spartanburg Area

21   The pizza industry had rapidly expanded in the 1980s. With this trend came increased competition for the St. George Street Pizza Delights from nationally owned pizza chains

Exhibit 6
Total retail and eating-and-drinking-place sales in 1978 and 1984: Spartanburg, Spartanburg County, the Greenville–Spartanburg SMA, South Carolina, the South Atlantic region, and the United States

	Total retail sales	Sales per capita	Eating-and-drinking places		
			Total sales	Sales per capita	Percent of total retail
Spartanburg					
1978	$ 417,207	$ 8896*	$ 41,507	$885*	9.9%
1984	526,485	11,725*	43,625	972*	8.3
Percent change	+26.2%	+31.8%	+5.1%	+9.8%	
Spartanburg County					
1978	635,084	3,229	58,911	299	9.3
1984	1,015,451	4,756	79,688	373	7.8
Percent change	+59.9%	+47.3%	+35.3%	+24.7%	
Greenville–Spartanburg SMA					
1978	1,911,506	3,531	175,057	323	9.2
1984	3,117,321	5,153	257,667	426	8.3
Percent change	+63.1%	+45.9%	+47.2%	+31.9%	
South Carolina					
1978	9,243,104	3,149	670,142	228	7.3
1984	15,484,516	4,618	1,343,043	401	8.7
Percent change	+67.5%	+46.6%	+100.4%	+75.9%	
South Atlantic region					
1978	129,343,686	3,697	11,434,037	327	8.8
1984	220,144,917	5,517	19,950,436	500	9.1
Percent change	+70.2%	+49.2%	+74.5%	+52.9%	
United States					
1978	817,461,457	3,720	71,602,628	326	8.8
1984	1,296,659,715	5,442	124,035,013	564	9.6
Percent change	+58.6%	+46.3%	+73.2%	+73.0%	

* Retail sales per capita for the city are higher than for the county, SMA, state, region, and nation due to the large number of noncity resident sales.
Source: "Survey of Buying Power," *Sales and Marketing Management,* 1979 and 1985.

and even from companies producing frozen pizzas sold in grocery stores. In addition to being in fierce competition with 17 local and nationally owned pizza places, the St. George Street restaurant competed with a total of 170 restaurants of other types and with several other Pizza Delights restaurants in the greater Spartanburg area. One of these Pizza Delights restaurants was within a few miles of the St. George Street operation. Exhibits 7 through 9 provide average common size income statements, balance sheets, and financial ratios, respectively, for traditional and fast-food restaurants with less than $1 million in sales for 1985. Exhibit 10 provides a map with the locations of competitors in the St. George Street area. Pizza Delight's major pizza competitors are described below. Exhibit 11 summarizes the product, service, and pricing strategies of these competitors.

Exhibit 7
Average common size income statements for traditional and fast-food restaurants in the United States with less than $1 million in sales for 1985

	Traditional* (n = 481)	Fast-foods† (n = 301)
Sales	100.0%	100.0%
Cost of goods sold . . .	43.8	39.3
Gross profit	56.2	60.7
Operating expenses . .	52.6	55.0
Other expenses	1.6	2.7
Net profit before taxes	2.1%	3.0%

* Includes restaurants selling prepared foods and drinks for consumption on the premises. Caterers and industrial and institutional food service establishments are also included (SIC 5812).

† Includes franchise operations (SIC 5812).

Source: Robert Morris Associates, *1986 Annual Statement Studies.*

Exhibit 8
Average common size balance sheets for traditional and fast-food restaurants in the United States with less than $1 million in sales for 1985

	Traditional* (n = 481)	Fast foods† (n = 301)
Assets		
Cash and equivalents	12.1%	14.9%
Trade receivables (net)	4.3	1.9
Inventory	7.6	4.8
All other current assets	2.6	2.6
Total current assets	26.6	24.2%
Fixed assets (net)	56.3	53.0
Intangibles (net)	4.5	6.2
All other noncurrent assets	12.6	16.6
Total assets	100.0%	100.0%
Liabilities and owners' equity		
Current liabilities	40.0%	38.6%
Long-term debt	32.8	35.6
All other noncurrent liabilities	2.9	2.1
Total liabilities	75.7	76.3
Owners' equity (net worth)	24.3	23.7
Total liabilities and owners' equity	100.0%	100.0%

* Includes restaurants selling prepared foods and drinks for consumption on the premises. Caterers and industrial and institutional food service establishments are also included (SIC 5812).

† Includes franchise operations (SIC 5812).

Source: Robert Morris Associates, *1986 Annual Statement Studies.*

Exhibit 9
Financial ratios for traditional and fast-food restaurants in the United States with less than $1 million in sales for 1985

	Traditional restaurants*			Fast-food restaurants†		
	Upper quartile	Median	Lower quartile	Upper quartile	Median	Lower quartile
Ratios						
Current	1.3	0.7	0.3	1.2	0.6	0.3
Quick	0.8	0.4	0.2	0.9	0.4	0.1
Sales/receivables	INF	451.0	74.9	INF	INF	507.1
Cost of sales/inventory	46.1	27.4	16.1	59.6	42.7	28.2
Sales/working capital	51.0	−38.5	−12.1	56.2	−31.4	−11.8
Times interest earned	4.9	2.0	0.4	5.9	2.5	1.0
Cash flow/current portion of long-term debt	4.5	1.6	0.7	5.4	2.4	1.2
Debt/equity ratio	1.0	3.2	−26.2	1.2	3.8	−14.5
Asset turnover	5.2	3.5	2.2	5.1	3.3	2.4
Return on equity (percent)	62.1%	23.1%	4.6%	81.6%	36.7%	15.9%
Return on assets (percent)	17.1%	5.3%	−3.1%	20.0%	9.6%	1.0%

Note: INF = Infinite.

* Includes restaurants selling prepared foods and drinks for consumption on the premises. Caterers and industrial and institutional food service establishments are also included (SIC 5812); 481 establishments studied.

† Includes franchise operations (SIC 5812); 301 establishments studied.

Source: Robert Morris Associates, *1986 Annual Statement Studies.*

Domino's

22   Domino's, Inc., was the leading competitor for delivery pizza. The company's strategy was to offer its customers fast delivery service (usually less than 30 minutes) for a medium-priced pizza. Domino's sold only pizza; the firm did not include other Italian dishes on its menu. Domino's pizza was of reputedly low to medium quality, however.

Little Caesar's

23   This was a chain restaurant located in Perkins Plaza off White Rock Road and St. George Street. Little Caesar's catered to the take-out customer; it did not make deliveries or provide facilities for eat-in dining. Its pizza was of medium quality and was medium priced. The chain also offered customers special Greek and Italian salads, sandwiches, and sliced pizza. To get volume, Little Caesar's frequently placed two-for-one coupons in local newspapers.

Pizza Factory

24   Located in the nearby Stephenson Plaza, this national chain restaurant provided take-out services as well as eat-in dining facilities for customers. Its customer service was low, however, as the restaurant had no waitresses. Pizza Factory offered customers a

Exhibit 10
Locations of the St. George Street Pizza Delights and its competitors

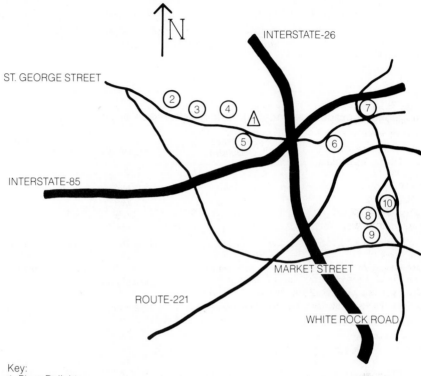

Key:
1. Pizza Delights
2. St. George Cinema and Video Arcade
3. Stephenson Plaza (Pizza Factory)
4. Domino's
5. St. George Plaza (Schiano's)
6. Showbiz Pizza
7. Perkins Plaza (Little Caesar's)
8. Pizza Hut
9. Competing Pizza Delights
10. Pizza Inn

low-priced, medium-quality pizza as well as a variety of sandwiches, a salad bar, and alcoholic beverages.

Showbiz Pizza

25 Showbiz Pizza was a national chain restaurant catering to small children. Its dining room decor included dancing bears, games, and other attractions for children. Showbiz offered customers a medium-quality pizza at a medium to high price.

Pizza Hut

26   Pizza Hut was the largest and most important competitor of Pizza Delights. Its strategy was to be a full-line pizza competitor, offering a medium- to high-priced product with correspondingly high levels of service and product quality. The company had been quite successful in introducing new pizza products, which it advertised heavily.

Exhibit 11
Comparisons of product, service, and pricing strategies of pizza competitors

	Pizza Delights	Domino's	Little Caesar's	Pizza Factory
Services				
Eat-in	Yes	No	No	Yes
Take-out	Yes	Yes	Yes	Yes
Delivery	No	Yes	No	No
Buffet	No	No	No	No
Luncheon menu	Yes	No	No	Yes
Salad bar	Yes	No	No	Yes
Service level	High	High (delivery only)	Low	Low
Products (dinner only)				
Quality	Medium/high	Low/medium	Medium	Medium
Number of pizzas on menu	6	2	6	6
Types of pizzas	2	1	1	1
Sizes	3	2	3	3
Slices	No	No	Yes	No
Meat/fish toppings	6	4	6	9
Vegetable toppings	6	7	7	10
Italian dishes	Spaghetti	No	No	No
Sandwiches (Number × Sizes)	4	0	3 × 2	4
Salads (excluding bar)	No	No	3 × 3	No
Alcoholic beverages	Beer	No	No	Beer
Other beverages	Soft drinks, tea, milk, coffee	Coke	Soft drinks	Soft drinks, tea
Prices				
Medium cheese pizza	$ 7.45	$ 6.02	$ 6.78	$ 6.70
Medium 5–7 toppings (#)	10.00 (6)	—	10.29 (5)	9.55 (6)
Medium 8–11 toppings (#)	10.80 (9)	11.12 (9)	—	11.25 (11)
Large cheese pizza	9.85	8.17	9.28	8.00
Large 5–7 toppings (#)	12.70 (6)	—	13.52 (5)	10.95 (6)
Large 8–11 toppings (#)	13.55 (9)	15.42 (9)	—	13.25 (11)
Toppings—medium/large	.85/.95	1.02/1.45	.77/.96	.85/.95
Italian dishes	1.99–3.39	—	—	—
Sandwiches	2.89	—	2.25–2.69	2.49
Salads	2.49	—	1.20–4.69	2.59
Alcohol (glass)	.95	—	—	.75
Other beverages	.50–.75	.65	.48–.87	.55–.75

Exhibit 11 (*concluded*)

	Showbiz	*Pizza Hut*	*Pizza Inn*	*Schiano's*
Services				
Eat-in	Yes	Yes	Yes	Yes
Take-out	No	Yes	Yes	Yes
Delivery	No	No	Yes	No
Buffet	No	No	Yes	No
Luncheon menu	Yes	Yes	Yes	No
Salad bar	No	Yes	Yes	No
Service level	High	High	High	High
Products				
Quality	Medium	Medium/high	Low/medium	High
Number of pizzas on menu	5	10	12	6
Types of pizzas	1	3	2	2
Sizes	3	3	4	3
Slices	No	No	No	No
Meat/fish toppings	4	7	6	5
Vegetable toppings	6	8	7	6
Italian dishes	No	Spaghetti	Spaghetti, lasagna	Parmigiana, calzone, lasagna
Sandwiches (Number × Sizes)	5	3 × 2	4	6 × 2
Salads (excluding bar)	1	No	1	2
Alcoholic beverages	Beer	Beer	Beer, wine	Beer, wine
Other beverages	Soft drinks, tea, milk, coffee	Soft drinks, tea, milk, coffee	Soft drinks, tea, milk, coffee	Soft drinks
Prices				
Medium cheese pizza	$ 8.09	$ 7.05–7.25	$ 5.80–7.80	$ 4.95–6.45
Medium 5–7 toppings (#)	10.99 (6)	9.80 (6)	9.35–9.75 (7)	9.20–10.70 (6)
Medium 8–11 toppings (#)	—	10.60 (9)	10.20–10.70 (9)	10.20–11.70 (8)
Large cheese pizza	9.99	9.45–9.65	9.00–9.50	7.20–8.70
Large 5–7 toppings (#)	12.99 (6)	12.50 (6)	11.85–12.35 (7)	12.20–13.70 (6)
Large 8–11 toppings (#)	—	13.35 (9)	12.80–13.40 (9)	13.20–14.70 (8)
Toppings—medium/large	.90/1.00	.90/1.00	.85/.95	.85/1.00
Italian dishes	—	2.09–4.49	1.89–3.89	3.29–6.95
Sandwiches	1.39–2.59	2.79–3.79	.79–2.59	2.15–4.55
Salads	2.29	2.79	1.99	1.79–3.49
Alcohol (glass)	.99	1.00	1.00	.95–1.60
Other beverages	.50–.79	.50–.80	.45–.80	.65

27   Although Pizza Hut did not operate a restaurant on St. George Street, its White Rock Road location was only a few miles to the east of the St. George Pizza Delights. It had been more successful than the other Pizza Delights restaurant located nearby. Moreover, the growing population in the area had caused the Pizza Hut Corporation to consider building a new restaurant on St. George Street. Such a move would have a direct impact on Pizza Delights because 30 to 35 percent of its customers were from the Roebuck area. However, after conducting a market survey, Pizza Hut decided not to build a new restaurant in Roebuck in 1986, although this possibility was still under consideration for the future.

Pizza Inn

28   Besides Pizza Hut, Pizza Inn was Pizza Delights' most formidable competitor. Pizza Inn offered customers a variety of services including eat-in dining, take-outs, home delivery (started in early 1986), a salad bar, a luncheon buffet during the weekdays, and a dinner buffet every Tuesday. Its pizza was low to medium priced, with corresponding levels of quality.

Schiano's

29   Schiano's was an example of the expanding pizza competition in the St. George Street area. This restaurant was, in 1986, under construction directly across the street from Outbanks' restaurant. Schiano's was planning to offer a dining room with extensive service in the new St. George plaza. This chain restaurant offered a high-quality, high-priced "New York"–style pizza.

Grocery Stores

30   The grocery stores in the area stocked a diverse line of pizzas and pizza products, including microwave pizzas, store-made pizzas, and national brands of frozen pizzas. For the do-it-yourself customers, grocers also offered prepackaged pizza ingredients, such as instant pizza crust, sauces, grated pizza cheese, sliced pepperoni, and so on. These take-home products were generally of lower quality than the pizzas served in restaurants. They were, however, also much lower in price (prices generally ranged from 79 cents to $4).

Delivery

31   One trend in the fast-food industry, especially for pizza, had been to increase speed and efficiency. This trend was responsible for the opening of several delivery pizza stores in the greater Spartanburg area, such as Domino's. In an attempt to penetrate this market for delivered pizza, Pizza Delights had opened a delivery store in August 1984 in Arcadia, South Carolina, just outside of the Spartanburg city limits. This store only produced pizzas that were to be delivered. The delivery area included only those areas within a 10-mile radius of the store, excluding approximately 30 percent of the Spartanburg–Roebuck area. Since there was only one Pizza Delights delivery location, many problems had developed. In order to save transportation and delivery costs, the Arcadia store held orders until a large number of pizzas could be delivered to one area. This practice helped lower costs, but it hurt customer relations since delivery time sometimes exceeded one hour, and pizzas were frequently delivered cold. According to market research, approximately 75 percent of the customers were dissatisfied with the current delivery service offered by the Arcadia Pizza Delights.

Products and Markets of the St. George Street Restaurant

32   The St. George Street restaurant did not have a specific target market, according to Earnest Outbanks. All types of individuals frequented the restaurant. In addition to regular customers, which composed 58 percent of the customer base, this store was convenient to shoppers of the two nearby plazas, commuters, and theater-goers. Almost 50 percent of the St. George Street restaurant's customers drove between three and five miles to the restaurant. Market research suggested that customers of the St. George Street restaurant frequented this restaurant fairly often, usually on a monthly basis.

33   Although pizza was the primary product, other menu items (such as sandwiches, spaghetti, and a salad bar) were available to offer diversity to the customer. Exhibit 12 lists the menu items and prices for the St. George Street restaurant. Exhibit 13 provides a per-item breakdown of food and beverage sales and costs for 1984–85. Studies indicated that the quality of the pizza was the most important reason customers visited the St. George Street location, with service being high on their list as well.

Sales Fluctuations

34   Over any 12-month period, sales at the St. George Street restaurant were lowest in January, February, and March. Sales in these months accounted for only 13 percent of yearly revenues. April through June sales accounted for 24 percent of yearly sales, while 31 percent of annual sales occurred between October and December. The highest sales period was between July and September, where 32 percent of annual sales were realized. September, which accounted for 18 percent of annual sales alone, was typically the best month for the restaurant. The high sales levels in September were due to Roebuck High School's weekly football games. After the games spectators and students often meet for an evening snack at Pizza Delights.

35   Sales fluctuations also occurred during the week (see Exhibit 14). Monday was the slowest day, accounting for 8.5 percent of weekly sales. Friday's sales were the highest (23.4 percent).

36   Lunch sales were always low. The best day for lunchtime sales was Friday, but even on this day lunch sales averaged only 3.3 percent of weekly revenues. The slowest day for lunch was Tuesday, which accounted for a mere 1.8 percent of weekly sales. When the Italian turnover pizza was introduced as a strictly lunchtime item, the Pizza Delights Corporation felt that sales for lunch would increase. However, this situation did not occur at the St. George Street location; sales simply shifted from the small pan pizzas to the Italian turnovers.

Advertising and Sales Promotion

37   Pizza Delight's advertising could be divided into three types: national, co-op, and local ads. National advertising was done countrywide, targeting mass markets to familiarize people with the Pizza Delights name as well as its products. Co-op advertising was done on a district-by-district basis and included mention for the individual restaurants and products. Both types of ads were financed by the restaurants on a percentage-of-

Exhibit 12
The St. George Street location—menu items and prices

	Small	*Medium*	*Large**
Pizza			
Double decker (3 varieties)	$8.00	$10.80	$13.55
Pan pizzas			
Cheese	5.05	7.45	9.85
Delight (6 toppings)	7.30	10.00	12.70
Super Delight (9 toppings)	8.00	10.80	13.55
Additional toppings	.75	.85	.95
(pepperoni, ham, pork, beef, Italian sausage, mushroom, onion, green pepper, black olive, jalapeno pepper, anchovy, extra cheese)			

	Small	*Regular*
Spaghetti		
Meat sauce	$1.99	$ 3.19
Meatballs	2.39	3.39
Salad bar		
As a meal		2.49
With a meal		1.99
Children under 12		.99
Sandwiches		
4 varieties		2.89
Drinks		

Soft drinks

Pitcher	2.25	Coffee	.50	Beer	
Large	.75	Milk	.55	Glass	.95
Medium	.70	Ice Tea	.65	Pitcher	3.95
Small	.65				

Luncheon specials: Monday–Friday

	Pizza only	*Pizza/salad bar (one trip)*
Italian turnover†		
Cheese	$2.49	$3.88
Sausage	2.49	3.88
Small pan pizza		
Pepperoni	1.79	3.18
Supreme (6 toppings)	2.19	3.58

* Small pizzas serve one–two people; medium, three–four people; large, five–six people.

† Guaranteed to be ready in 10 minutes or your lunch is free.

sales basis. This arrangement applied to company-owned and franchised restaurants. Neither company-owned nor franchised restaurants had any input into these decisions and basically just implemented whatever campaign the corporation recommended.

38   Local ads were paid for by the individual restaurants and placed in local papers. Franchise owners had greater discretion than managers of company-owned restaurants concerning the types and amounts of local promotions used. The St. George Street restaurant's advertising expenses amounted to over $29,000 in 1985. As shown in

Exhibit 13
The St. George Street location—gross profit by product line

	1985	1984
Pizza		
Eat-in pizza	$204,886	$168,174
Carry-out pizza	215,806	181,774
Net pizza	420,692	349,948
Plus: Pizza allowances	5,772	4,806
Coupon sales	31,213	30,241
Total promotion/advertising sales	36,985	35,047
Gross pizza sales	457,677	384,995
Cost of pizza dough	20,530	17,793
Cost of toppings	38,066	30,666
Cost of cheese	47,944	41,698
Cost of paper—pizza	6,580	5,663
Freight	99	1,157
Total pizza cost	113,219	96,977
Gross profit on pizza	$344,458	$288,018
Beer		
Sales	$ 13,747	$ 13,236
Costs	4,453	4,004
Gross profit on beer	$ 9,294	$ 9,232
Drinks		
Sales	$ 39,599	$ 33,200
Costs	8,162	6,584
Gross profit on soft drinks	$ 31,437	$ 26,616
Other		
Salad sales	$ 26,295	$ 27,012
Pasta sales	9,069	9,873
Sandwich sales	5,615	4,805
Other promotion/advertising revenue	5,278	5,482
Total other sales	46,257	47,172
Cost of other sales	18,572	20,649
Gross profit on other sales	$ 27,685	$ 26,523

Exhibit 1, this represented a substantial increase over advertising expenses for 1983 and 1984.

39   All national and co-op advertising for the St. George Street location was coordinated by an advertising firm in Washington, D.C. A sample announcement of a new national promotional campaign for the Italian turnover is provided in Exhibit 15. The main component of the co-op advertising for the greater Spartanburg area restaurants was a monthly four-color, free-standing insert in the city newspaper. This ad usually was accompanied by coupons for selected items, allowing customers a 15 to 20 percent discount off regular prices. The bulk of the greater Spartanburg area co-op advertising was done in the fall, when sales tended to be the highest.

Exhibit 14
Daily sales breakdowns

	Lunch		Dinner	
	Dollars	*Percent*	*Dollars*	*Percent*
Monday	$198	1.9%	$ 692	6.6%
Tuesday	186	1.8	716	6.8
Wednesday	191	1.8	874	8.3
Thursday	260	2.5	1,390	13.3
Friday	350	3.3	2,105	20.0
Saturday	308	2.9	1,761	16.8
Sunday	205	1.9	1,277	12.1
Average sales per week		$10,513		

Exhibit 15
Promotional announcement to Spartanburg Pizza Delights

HOT NEWS FROM YOUR FRIENDS AT BEAUMONT GREEN ADVERTISING

To: Pizza Delights managers and employees/Spartanburg

Date: February 26, 1986

Subject: Advertising for the Italian turnover

Background

Many of you will recall the tremendous success that the introduction of the small pan pizza had on our business in 1983. In 1986, the opportunity to stimulate both trial and frequency at lunch lies mainly in the area of menu expansion. Therefore, the Italian turnover has been developed. This new product will increase your sales and profits at lunch. You have all shown your operational strength with the double-decker pizza introduced in 1984. Let's make the Italian turnover the success story of 1986!

Television

Starting March 14, 1986, and running through May 1, 1986, three new TV commercials focusing on the Italian turnover will be run.

Radio promotions

A radio promotion has been developed and implemented. This promotion is provided free of charge in exchange for Italian turnovers for give-aways. Details of the promotion are provided below.

WASQ–FM will encourage listeners to be the X number caller that spotted the WASQ logo on one of the Italian turnover outdoor billboards. Winner receives two Italian turnovers and two medium soft drinks. There to be three give-aways per day, Monday thru Friday, for a total of 60 give-aways.

Outdoor

There will be #18 outdoor boards strategically placed in the area. The message will be "Turn over a New Lunch with the Italian Turnover," which is the main print advertising theme for the introduction of the Italian turnover. These boards will be posted from March 26, 1986, to May 10, 1986.

40   The St. George Street location also did a variety of sales promotions. If a child read five books in one month, he or she would receive a free small pan pizza. The restaurant also did birthday parties and allowed participants the opportunity to create their own pizzas in the kitchen. Two other promotions which the St. George Street restaurant ran in the past were "family night" and "football night." Family night was a dinner promotion in which a family could buy a large pizza and a pitcher of soft drinks for $9.95. This was a companywide promotional effort which was discontinued because of low response on a national level. However, this promotion was a huge success at the St. George Street restaurant. The football promotion involved taking small pan pizzas to the Roebuck High School game and selling them with a soft drink for 99 cents. This promotion was also discontinued because the district office felt that it would ruin Pizza Delight's high-quality/high-service image. Despite the district office's concerns, the football night promotion received tremendous consumer response, usually producing sales of around $800 per game.

Internal Operations

Order Processing

41   As shown in the work flow diagram of the St. George Street restaurant provided in Exhibit 16, when an order was punched into the computer terminals located at the waitress station and the cash register, it was printed out on a printer located over the cook's make table and at the waitress station. If the order was for a pan pizza, the cook had to walk 20 feet to the walk-in cooler and get a dough shell. If the order was for a double-decker pizza, the dough was rolled out on the table at that time. The pizza, whether it was regular, double decker, or pan, was then made on the table and placed in the oven.

42   Next, the ticket was placed on an order stand at the end of the make table, where an employee in charge would place it on a ticket holder. When sales volume was extremely high (for example, on the weekends), the movement of the ticket led to problems and lost pizzas.

43   After the pizza was cooked, it was given to the customer at the cash register, where payment was also received in the case of to-go orders. For in-store orders, the waitress would take it and the ticket out to the customer.

Operating Concerns

44   Outbanks realized that there were several major problems at his restaurant that needed to be corrected. All of these problems troubled him, but none had yet been solved.

45   Most of Outbanks' concerns stemmed from the physical facilities at the restaurant itself. Cooler space at the restaurant was inadequate. Frequent opening and closing of the cooler kept items from staying cold. This led to several problems in trying to maintain high-quality products. For example, customers consistently complained that the beer was too warm, perhaps explaining why beer sales had not increased like other items had. Keeping beer cold was not the only concern. According to Outbanks,

Exhibit 16

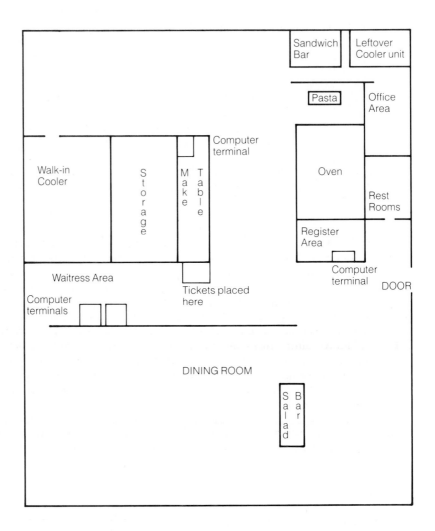

because pizza ingredients and other foods were not kept cold enough, inventory spoilage was very high ($175–$200 per month) and was increasing. To make matters worse, each Friday and Saturday when sales reached their weekly peak, employees had to shuffle other items around in the walk-in freezer to make room for the dough shells. This situation often caused older stock to be used last, leading to an even larger amount of spoilage.

46   Outbanks had spoken to the district manager about purchasing a new walk-in cooler for the restaurant but had no idea how long it would take for the Pizza Delights hierarchy to approve the purchase. The new walk-in cooler was estimated to cost approximately $11,000.

47   Outbanks' restaurant had several other capacity problems which needed to be corrected. In 1986, the restaurant used a conveyor-type oven in its operations. The oven was only two years old and was in good repair. It had two conveyors. The upper conveyor was kept in operation at all times; the lower conveyor was used only during peak periods. Both conveyors were 10 feet long. Up to four uncooked pizzas could be loaded on the first 2 feet of each conveyor. The oven itself was 6 six feet long and could accommodate up to 12 pizzas at a time, 6 per conveyor. The last 2 feet of the conveyors were used to allow the pizzas to cool off before serving. The conveyor oven allowed a more uniform-quality pizza than the traditional oven. However, for preparing other items (such as spaghetti or hot sandwiches), the traditional oven had an advantage over the conveyor oven.

48   Another limitation was that the speed of the conveyors which passed through the oven could not be adjusted up or down. As a result, the pizzas and other products could not be cooked any faster than the conveyor allowed. Although cooking time for the conveyor-type oven was faster (eight minutes for cooking and one minute for cooling) than traditional pizza ovens under normal circumstances, it limited the number of products which could be produced on an extremely busy night. With traditional ovens, on the other hand, it was possible to "stack" cook the pizzas. This procedure, while lowering the quality of the final product (e.g., burnt pizzas) and sometimes creating confusion among the workers, did allow many more pizzas to be cooked during the course of an evening. Outbanks had considered purchasing another conveyor oven at an installed price of $12,500 but had not discussed this idea with the area supervisor or with Leonard Lloyd. By contrast, a traditional oven would cost $8,200 installed.

49   Limited dining room and parking capacity also constrained sales. The dining room consisted of 22 tables, which could seat 88 customers. During peak sales nights, customers were forced to form a line out the door while waiting for an empty seat. Furthermore, the parking lot had only 30 spaces, which created havoc on Friday and Saturday nights as take-out customers tried to rush in and out, while families and friends slowly ushered their way into the line for dining in. Due to the limited parking, employees were required to park in a dirt field behind the restaurant. Outbanks estimated paving the field would allow 15 extra parking spaces for customers at a cost of $8,000.

Employees

50   Outbanks' staff included two assistant managers, Pete Gorman and Betty Franks. Gorman, a 36-year-old ex-high school teacher, had been an assistant manager at another Pizza Delights for several years prior to joining Outbanks' staff. He was considered a stringent, rule-oriented manager, who was trying to do everything in his power to gain a head-manager position. Franks was a recent graduate of Clemson University. She had brought many innovative ideas to the restaurant, including the idea to weigh out the cheese instead of using cheese cups as had been done previously. Outbanks had not totally accepted this idea, but since he knew of a manager in another location who had cut his cheese costs by 10 percent using this technique, he decided it was worth a second look. The assistant managers were responsible for supervising the restaurant when Outbanks was not working and for helping him with other managerial chores, such as purchasing, inventory, scheduling, and so on. Both assistant managers were required to work a minimum of 55 hours per week. Assistant managers were

paid $5.80 per hour for the first 55 hours worked and time-and-one-half for any additional hours after that.

51   In addition to Outbanks, Gorman, and Franks, the St. George Street restaurant employed 17 hourly workers, including 6 waitresses, 7 cooks, 2 dishwashers, and two "employees in charge" (EICs). The majority of these employees worked on a part-time basis. All employees were evaluated every six months, and they automatically received a 10-cent raise regardless of performance.

52   The waitresses were paid on an hourly basis, below the minimum wage. Nonetheless, with tips included, their overall wage usually amounted to well above the hourly minimum wage of $3.35. The waitress was responsible for seating customers, taking orders, and presenting the product to the customer. Since waitresses were continuously in contact with the consumer, they played a vital role in providing the excellent service that Pizza Delights was famous for.

53   The cooks were hired at, or slightly above, the minimum wage. Their duties included doing the prep work, cooking the food, and ensuring the cleanliness of the facility. They also played a vital role in the business by ensuring that the food prepared was of the highest quality possible.

54   The dishwashers were usually hired at minimum wage and were usually promoted to cook after a few months. Besides washing dishes, their duties included keeping the dining room and other work areas as clean as possible.

55   The EICs were those cooks or waitresses that, through experience and expertise, had shown that they could handle additional responsibilities. Paid in excess of $4 per hour, they were responsible for the supervision of the cooking processes and the daily bookkeeping. They were, thus, instrumental in ensuring product quality.

56   Commenting on his employees, Earnest Outbanks once said, "The St. George Street Pizza Delights is a quality restaurant because everyone from me to the dishwashers works as a team to provide the best product, with the best service to our customers." This was in stark contrast to the way the restaurant had been operated prior to Outbanks assuming the manager's position in 1981. Despite the improvements made in this area, Outbanks also realized that, in general, employee commitment was low due to the fact that the cooks and waitresses were generally young college or high school students who often had conflicting responsibilities, such as school or another job.

Labor Costs

57   By company policy, all labor costs were computed daily. Pizza Delights had established a labor grid, which stipulated how many employees were needed each hour the restaurant was open based on normal per-hour sales. One labor grid was used during lunch hours (11 A.M. to 4 P.M.), and another was used for dinner hours (4 P.M. to closing). These grids are provided in Exhibit 17. Outbanks also used the average break times of employees to compute his daily labor costs. At the end of the day, the actual number of hours were compared to the suggested labor grid hours. Any variances had to be explained to the district manager.

58   The number of employees needed per sales dollar was higher during lunch hours because of the lower per-item price of lunchtime products and because of the extra

Exhibit 17
Projected labor schedule—lunch and dinner

Lunch		Dinner	
Projected sales per hour	Projected labor needs (number of workers)	Projected sales per hour	Projected labor needs (number of workers)
$ 0– 41	2	$ 0– 95	2
42– 61	3	96–143	3
62– 87	4	144–190	4
88–119	5	191–211	5
120–156	6	212–255	6
157–180	8	256–295	8
181–202	9	296–338	9
203–245	10	339–379	10
246–298	11	380–423	11
299–342	12	424–461	12
343–387	13	462–507	13
388–450	14	508–547	14
451–519	15	548–589	15
520–614	16	590–631	16
615–695	17	632–673	17

Notes to labor schedule:
Average total hours of breaktime per week:

Monday	Tuesday	Wednesday	Thursday	Friday	Saturday	Sunday
2.6	2.6	2.9	3.5	4.6	4.2	1.9

Average hourly pay scale per position:

Assistant managers	$5.80
Employees in charge	$4.10
Cook	$3.45
Waitresses	$2.30 plus tips
Dishwasher	$3.35

demands in providing a 10-minute guarantee for serving the small pan and Italian turnover pizzas.

59   Since the introduction of the Italian turnover pizza, Pizza Delights required that a minimum of 10 employees be present during the guaranteed hours of 11 A.M. to 1:30 P.M., Monday thru Friday, in order to better promote the new product. No minimum was specified for the weekends, however. Before it was introduced, the St. George Street restaurant was operated quite efficiently with a total of 28 employee-hours between 8 A.M. and 4 P.M. on Monday, Tuesday, Wednesday, Saturday, and Sunday; 33 total employee-hours on Thursday; and 38 total employee-hours on Friday. These hours had increased to almost 55 hours per day on average during the weekdays, due to Pizza Delight's new policy after the Italian turnover pizza was introduced. Since Outbanks had not realized any additional profits from the Italian turnover, he wondered if he could operate the restaurant as profitably as he did before it was introduced.

Lloyd's Greer Area Pizza Delights
Franchise Operations

60   With a population of approximately 10,000 persons in 1985, Greer, South Carolina, could be categorized as a typical small southern town. The inhabitants of this small community were very family oriented. The town was custom made for a restaurant providing a high level of customer service, as Lloyd's original Pizza Delights franchise did.

61   Eating out was not very common in Greer in the early 1970s, partly because there were only two places in town to eat (a diner and a truck stop) and partly because the residents generally preferred to eat at home. However, in the mid-1970s the attitudes of the population began to change as several fast-food restaurants were opened. Grabbing a hamburger or some chicken after church or after a Little League game became fashionable and convenient.

62   Lloyd's Pizza Delights restaurant was the last fast-food restaurant built in the community, although it was company owned during the first three years of operations. Recognizing the potential of the restaurant, Lloyd, an area businessman, purchased the franchise from Pizza Delights in 1981 for $375,000 plus $1.2 million for the right to use the company's brand name.

63   In his first year of operation Lloyd succeeded in increasing the seating capacity at the restaurant from 65 to 150 people. He felt that the demand for pizza in the Greer area could easily accommodate a dining area of that size. Sales revenues increased 7 percent that year. However, the restaurant did not operate at full capacity.

64   In 1982, disenchanted by the slow growth in sales, Lloyd decided to offer customers more specials and new dining options. Two-for-one coupons were placed in the local newspapers on a regular basis. Taking advantage of his two ovens and massive dining area, Lloyd also began to offer a lunch buffet during the weekdays to attract students from a nearby community college. Sales revenues increased by 10 percent almost overnight, and many customers began inquiring about the possibility of a Sunday buffet. Lloyd's decision to extend the buffet to Sundays allowed him to capture a significant share of the after-church market, increasing sales during a time of the week when sales had traditionally been low.

65   The first Greer franchise restaurant was very successful, with sales increasing by about one third since 1982. The only direct pizza competitor for the Greer restaurant was Papa Joe's. This restaurant offered relatively little service and relied almost entirely on take-out business.

66   Due to his success at the Greer location, Lloyd had purchased the franchises to two additional Pizza Delights restaurants in two small rural communities, both approximately 5 to 10 miles outside of Greer, in 1983 and 1984. Both of these restaurants followed the same strategy as the Greer restaurant, and both were profitable. Lloyd had been able to retain the managers who had previously worked for the Pizza Delights Corporation by giving them a minority ownership position in these restaurants.

Lloyd's Plan

67   Although Lloyd had not worked out all the details of how the St. George Street restaurant should be operated, he had made some initial inquiries at the Pizza Delights' district office in Columbia, South Carolina, to determine if purchasing the restaurant would be feasible. The district office quoted Lloyd a price of $725,000 for the physical facilities

plus an annual payment of 12 percent of the restaurant's net profits before taxes. The Pizza Delights brand name was valued at over $1 million. However, Lloyd knew he would not have to pay this fee since he had already purchased the brand rights for the Greer restaurants.

68   Lloyd hoped that many of the same strategies he had used at the Greer restaurants would be feasible at the St. George Street location. He wanted to offer a buffet-style dinner or lunch to customers at least once or twice a week. He also wanted to try to offer more in the way of coupon and promotional gimmicks to attract more customers and balance out sales. Outbanks had wanted to attempt such a move for several years but had been constrained by the corporation's policies. Franchising would at least partially solve this problem.

69   All these policies had been quite successful in Greer, and Lloyd saw no reason why these successes would not be transferable to the Roebuck/Spartanburg area despite the differences between the two locales. In addition, Lloyd toyed with the idea of setting up a delivery service at the St. George Street location. Spartanburg was a college town, and Lloyd expected that such a service would be welcomed by students in the area. If a delivery operation was started, it would require two half-time employees (paid at the minimum wage) plus the purchase of two used cars for approximately $5,000 apiece. Gas, maintenance, depreciation, and other related operating expenses associated with the vehicle were estimated at 20 cents per mile.

70   Lloyd felt that these proven strategies, combined with new ideas and Outbanks' managerial abilities, would ensure success for the St. George Street location.

Franchise Ownership and Financing Arrangements

71   Lloyd was prepared to invest $250,000 in the St. George Street restaurant and planned to borrow the rest of the needed capital from one of the financial institutions in the area. In 1986 the prime rate for commercial borrowing was 7.5 percent. However, Lloyd realized that he would probably be required to pay a premium of at least 1.5–2.5 percent over prime.

72   After talking with a Spartanburg banker, Lloyd learned that he would need a minimum of 25 percent equity to back the franchise and would be required to give the bank a first mortgage on the restaurant, as well as pledge all his personal assets as security. The loan itself would probably be a term loan amortized over 15 years, with a balloon payment after 3 to 5 years. Lloyd figured that payments for a straight 15-year amortized loan of $500,000 at 10 percent interest would amount to $5,373 per month or almost $65,000 per year.

73   The Spartanburg banker also informed Lloyd that franchise loans were not frequently approved by her bank, citing an example of another Pizza Delights franchise in Greenwood, South Carolina, that was recently denied a loan. Exhibits 18 and 19 provide the income statement and balance sheet for the Greenwood Pizza Delights franchise.

74   Lloyd was not particularly worried by the banker's pessimism, however, as the types of loans sought differed (the Greenwood franchise wanted capital for equipment purchases and for building a new restaurant), the local area environments differed (Greenwood was a rural community more like Greer than Spartanburg in terms of population and area demographics), and the financial performance of the St. George Street restaurant was stronger. Lloyd also had a successful track record in business and had never experienced problems obtaining financing in the past; he saw no reason why it would be different this time around.

Exhibit 18
1985 Income statement for the Greenwood Pizza Delights

Sales		$638,284
Food in	$322,928	
Food out	239,260	
Food delivery	14,064	
Food subtotal	576,252	
Beverages in	61,612	
Beverages delivery	120	
Beverages subtotal	61,732	
Premiums	300	
Cost of goods sold:		
Food cost	167,600	
Beverage cost	16,800	
Premiums	0	184,400
Gross profit		453,884
Operating expenses:		
Advertising	22,000	
Auto and delivery expenses	600	
Payroll	198,325	
Repairs	19,403	
Utilities and telephone	30,504	
Operating supplies	10,320	
Other operating expenses	22,408	303,560
Operating profit		150,324
Administrative expenses:		
Royalty fee	19,000	
Insurance	12,450	
Interest	7,770	
Depreciation	27,250	
Rent	42,000	
Taxes and licenses	4,000	
Other administrative expenses	18,610	131,080
Net profit before taxes		$ 19,244

75   Although all the details had not been discussed, as part of the proposed franchising plan, Outbanks was expecting to receive a one-quarter to one-third interest in the store, plus his normal salary, for services rendered. Outbanks also expected to have complete control over the day-to-day operations of the restaurant. In respect to strategy and policy matters, Outbanks believed that both he and Lloyd would have an equal voice. Such an arrangement, Outbanks felt, was similar to the deal Lloyd had made with the managers at his franchise restaurants in Greer.

76   Outbanks also expected to be required to cosign the note and pledge his personal assets as collateral. His financial commitment to the franchise would be considerably less than Lloyd's, though, as Outbanks had only around $25,000 to $30,000 to invest.

Earnest's Dilemma

77   After turning over the pros and cons of current operations in his mind, Outbanks still was not sure whether he should join Lloyd in the franchising venture or stay with the company and try to progress up the corporate ladder. Outbanks did understand

Exhibit 19
1985 Balance sheet for the Greenwood Pizza Delights

Assets

Cash in bank	−$ 14,200	
Cash on hand	1,000	
Investments	2,700	
Accounts receivable	1,500	
Inventory	7,500	
Total current assets	− 1,500	
Automobiles	17,500	
Less: Depreciation	− 9,500	
Net automobiles	8,000	
Equipment	150,000	
Less: Depreciation	− 70,000	
Net equipment	80,000	
Leasehold improvements	10,200	
Less: Depreciation	− 3,000	
Net leasehold	7,200	
Total fixed assets	95,200	
Deposits	220	
Insurance reserve fund	1,700	
Prepaid insurance	3,000	
Prepaid rent	4,200	
Franchise fees	17,000	
Total other noncurrent assets	26,120	
		$119,820

Liabilities

Accounts payable	$ 650	
Other current liabilities	13,300	
Total current liabilities	13,950	
Long-term liabilities	50,000	63,950

Equity

		$ 55,870
Liabilities and equity		$119,820

that his restaurant was currently making hefty profits (Exhibit 1), profits that he was not sharing in. He also understood that he was responsible for most of the restaurant's current successes. Moreover, he admired Lloyd for his success with the Greer Pizza Delights franchises. Nonetheless, Outbanks wondered if Lloyd's plans, which had worked so well in Greer, would achieve comparable levels of success in the St. George Street restaurant. He also knew that Pizza Delights was growing rapidly and that there might soon be an area supervisor position open for a young, energetic manager with a proven track record.

78   Personal problems also caused Outbanks to wonder whether he would continue to have the time, money, and motivation to devote to such a venture. A major dispute with his now-estranged wife had greatly taxed Outbanks' mental and physical endurance. This dispute, which Outbanks expected to end in divorce, was also likely to deplete his financial resources once it had been settled.

79   Despite all the problems Outbanks had to contend with, as he began to prepare for closing time he knew it was time to fish or cut bait. He resolved that he would give Lloyd his decision before the end of the following week.

Case 17

The Wal-Mart Corporation

1   One of the world's least likely billionaires resides in the small town of Bentonville, Arkansas. Although Samuel Walton reached the customary retirement age of 65 in 1983, he is still up before dawn every day. In an old Chevrolet that has been described as a rolling junkyard, he drives himself to work—the headquarters of the corporation that he created. When he is not meeting with his executives, Walton is flying around in the company plane, visiting his more than 600 discount stores in 19 states.

2   Over the past 15 years the Wal-Mart Corporation has compiled an extraordinary record of growth and financial performance. Its record is all the more remarkable because the discount retailing industry is relatively mature. See Exhibit 1 for a comparison of Wal-Mart's performance with that of several of its competitors and potential competitors.

Beginnings

3   Sam Walton's success was not achieved overnight. In fact, Wal-Mart went public only in 1970, at which time Walton owned what amounted to a modest chain of 27 stores. All were located in small towns and cities in Arkansas and the immediately adjoining states. By that time, Walton had almost 20 years of experience with discount stores in his chosen market niche, and he had developed most of the essential elements in his business strategy.

4   Samuel C. Walton, the son of a banker who later entered the farm mortgage business, was born on March 29, 1918. There was a younger brother, James L. "Bud" Walton, now a senior vice president and one of the directors of Wal-Mart. Sam Walton graduated from the University of Missouri in 1940 with a degree in economics. He then worked for two years with J. C. Penney as a management trainee. There, he was exposed to Penney's philosophy of building loyalty in both customers and employees. While waiting for induction into the wartime military, he met his future wife, Helen Robson. The Waltons have four children.

5   After three years in the military, Sam Walton started out on his own in 1945 by buying the franchise of a 10,000-square-foot Ben Franklin store in Newport, Arkansas. Ben Franklin was a chain of conventional dime stores modeled on the concept originally introduced by the legendary F. W. Woolworth. The following year, brother Bud joined Sam in Newport to "learn the business." One year later, Bud opened his own Ben Franklin store in Versailles, Missouri. When Sam lost the lease to his store building in Newport in 1950, he relocated in Bentonville and opened Walton's 5 & 10. In 1952, he opened his second store, a Ben Franklin franchise in Fayetteville, Arkansas. By 1959, the Waltons operated nine Ben Franklin stores in small towns in Arkansas, Kansas, Oklahoma, and Missouri.

6   In 1962, their first large discount store opened in Rogers, Arkansas, under the name of Wal-Mart's Discount City. In five years, their chain had grown to 13 Wal-

Source: Prepared by Benjamin Harrison, Georgia State University. Copyright © 1985. Used by permission.

Exhibit 1
Comparative figures for selected discount chain retailers

	1979	1980	1981	1982	5-year growth (percent)
Earnings growth, year to year					
Wal-Mart	40.1	35.2	48.7	49.4	41.0%
Ames Department Stores	31.5	5.2	14.7	25.3	19.0
K mart	41.0	.8	−15.7	19.1	N.M.*
SCOA	49.8	−7.6	14.2	12.5	21.0
Zayre	22.1	5.3	22.8	59.3	24.0
	1978	**1979**	**1980**	**1981**	**1982**
Return on equity					
Wal-Mart	25.9	28.1	26.2	28.9	30.0%
Ames Department Stores	19.7	21.9	21.3	20.7	17.2
K mart	19.0	17.4	11.4	9.2	10.3
SCOA	28.2	33.6	25.0	23.6	22.5
Zayre	10.1	11.4	10.7	11.7	12.8
Return on assets					
Wal-Mart	11.0	10.5	10.3	10.8	11.5
Ames Department Stores	7.6	7.2	7.5	7.9	7.7
K mart	8.3	6.8	4.4	3.4	3.7
SCOA	9.1	11.1	8.7	8.9	8.7
Zayre	3.3	3.4	3.3	3.6	4.5
Operating income, percent of sales					
Wal-Mart	6.7	7.2	7.4	7.7	8.2
Ames Department Stores	6.5	4.6	4.5	4.9	4.6
K mart	7.5	7.0	5.6	4.4	5.3
SCOA	6.9	7.2	6.7	6.8	6.8
Zayre	4.7	4.9	5.0	5.2	5.8
Net income, percent of sales					
Wal-Mart	3.3	3.3	3.5	3.4	3.7
Ames Department Stores	3.0	2.8	2.8	2.8	3.1
K mart	2.9	2.8	1.8	1.3	1.5
SCOA	2.6	3.5	3.0	3.0	3.1
Zayre	1.0	1.1	1.1	1.2	1.6

* Not meaningful.
Source: Standard & Poor's, *Industry Survey,* 1984.

Mart stores, plus 7 Ben Franklin stores. Net profits had grown to $393,000 on sales of $9 million.

7   The discount store represented a new type of retail institution that several other firms were experimenting with at about the same time. The general concept was to offer a broad range of merchandise in a large, open store at lower prices and with less atmosphere and less service than was usual in the traditional department store. At first, the Wal-Mart stores and other discount stores were aimed at the price-conscious shopper, who was assumed to be more concerned with price and convenience than

with product quality or service. But in more recent years the discount stores have broadened their appeal, and many of the chains have attempted to modify their approach to satisfy the needs of a wider range of customers.

The Record of Growth

8   By 1970, Sam Walton was prepared to start thinking Big, very Big. But because his stores were located in the "boondocks," suppliers were unwilling to service his needs as efficiently as he desired. Walton decided that the company needed to build its own warehouse distribution center. When he approached the banks for a $5 million loan, however, his request was rejected because the bankers could not accept his projections for Wal-Mart's growth. Walton's five-year plan called for a 150 percent annual rate of growth, with a gross of $230 million at the end of five years. See Exhibit 2 to appreciate how well Walton met his objective.

9   Not having been able to obtain the funds he needed from the banks, Walton sold 30,000 shares of common stock for a total of $3.1 million in the over-the-counter market. One thousand dollars of Wal-Mart's stock in 1970 would be worth some $2.5 million in less than 15 years. With the proceeds obtained from the first stock sale, Wal-Mart constructed its corporate headquarters and the first distribution center in Bentonville and accelerated the construction of new stores. Two years later, its shares began trading on the New York Stock Exchange, and Wal-Mart turned to the equity markets on five subsequent occasions, raising a total of $123 million. A second and larger distribution center was built in Bentonville in 1974. Meanwhile, Wal-Mart expanded beyond the original "magic circle" of four states with stores in Louisiana, Texas, Tennessee, Kentucky, and Mississippi.

10   Something of a milestone was reached in 1977 when *Forbes* magazine ranked Wal-Mart number one among discount, variety, and department stores for the preceding five years in regard to return on equity, return on assets, sales growth, and earnings growth. If anything, Wal-Mart has increased that lead, as will be apparent from an examination of the data presented in Exhibit 1. In 1984, *Forbes* again ranked Wal-Mart the best managed of the nation's retail chains.

11   In that same year, Wal-Mart began acquiring already existing stores with the purchase of 16 Mohr-Value stores, expanding operations into Illinois. By the late 1970s, most of the other discount chains also began buying up existing stores in order to maintain their rates of growth. Very high interest rates and escalating construction costs made new construction relatively more expensive, and the less efficient of the smaller chains could not keep up with the increasing price competition that developed in most markets. Wal-Mart, however, continued to concentrate its stores in small towns, most of which could not support more than one large discount store.

12   More acquisitions followed. In 1978, Wal-Mart acquired the Hutcheson Shoe Company of Fort Smith, Arkansas, as a fully owned but separately operated division. Two years later, 162 leased jewelry departments, formerly licensed by Hatfield Distributors, were acquired. In 1981, Wal-Mart purchased the relatively large chain of 106 Kuhn's Big-K stores for $7.5 million in preferred stock. This move expanded Wal-Mart's presence in Kentucky, Tennessee, and Alabama and marked its entry into South Carolina and Georgia. Wal-Mart purchased the Big-K stores primarily to obtain their locations and has kept 92 of them, selling off those whose locations conflicted with existing

Exhibit 2

WAL-MART STORES, INC., AND SUBSIDIARIES
Ten-Year Financial Summary
(dollar amounts in thousands except per-share data)

	1983	1982	1981	1980	1979	1978	1977	1976	1975	1974
Earnings:										
Net sales	$3,376,252	$2,444,997	$1,643,199	$1,248,176	$900,298	$678,456	$478,807	$340,331	$236,209	$167,561
Licensed department rentals and other income, net	22,435	17,650	12,063	10,092	9,615	7,767	5,393	3,803	2,478	1,805
Cost of sales	2,458,235	1,787,496	1,207,802	919,305	661,062	503,825	352,669	251,473	176,591	123,339
Operating, selling, and general and administrative expenses	677,029	495,010	331,524	251,616	182,365	134,718	95,488	66,427	46,618	32,206
Interest costs:										
Debt	20,297	16,053	6,608	4,438	3,119	2,068	1,680	1,758	1,800	1,099
Capital leases	18,570	15,351	10,849	8,621	6,595	4,765	3,506	2,419	2,157	1,234
Taxes on income	100,416	65,943	43,597	33,137	27,325	19,656	14,818	10,925	5,526	5,534
Net income	124,140	82,794	55,682	41,151	29,447	21,191	16,039	11,132	5,995†	5,954
Per share of common stock:										
Net income										
Primary*	1.82	1.25	.86	.87	.48	.37	.29	.20	.11†	.11
Fully diluted*	1.82	1.25	.86	.67	.48	.35	.27	.19	.11†	.11
Dividends*	.18	.13	.10	.075	.055	.04	.021	.016	.013	.007
Stores in operation at the end of the period	551	491	330	276	229	195	153	125	104	78
Financial position:										
Current assets	$ 720,537	$ 589,161	$ 345,204	$ 266,617	$191,860	$150,986	$ 99,493	$ 76,070	$ 55,860	$ 45,254
Net property, plant, equipment, and capital leases	457,509	333,026	245,942	190,562	131,403	100,550	68,134	48,744	43,409	30,677
Total assets	1,187,448	937,513	592,345	457,879	324,666	251,865	168,201	125,347	99,473	76,126
Current liabilities	347,318	339,961	177,601	170,221	98,868	74,891	43,289	33,953	27,076	18,748
Long-term debt	106,465	104,581	30,184	24,862	25,965	21,489	19,158	17,531	11,132	10,578
Long-term obligations under capital leases	222,610	154,196	134,896	97,212	72,357	59,003	41,190	26,534	25,069	16,410
Preferred stock with mandatory redemption provisions	6,861	7,438								
Common stockholders' equity	488,109	323,942	248,309	164,844	127,476	96,482	64,417	47,195	36,050	30,207
Financial ratios:										
Current ratio	2.1	1.7	1.9	1.6	1.9	2.0	2.3	2.2	2.0	2.4
Inventories/working capital	1.5	2.0	1.7	2.4	1.9	1.8	1.6	1.5	1.8	1.6
Return on assets†	13.2	14.0	12.2	12.7	11.7	12.6	12.8	11.2	7.9	12.6
Return on stockholders' equity‡	38.3	33.3	33.8	32.3	30.5	32.9	34.0	30.9	19.8	24.4

* All per-share data prior to 1983 have been adjusted to reflect the 100 percent stock dividend paid July 9, 1982, to holders of Wal-Mart common stock.
† The company adopted the LIFO method of costing inventories in 1975, which resulted in a reduction in net income of $2,347,000 (?)
‡ On beginning-of-year balances.
Source: Annual Report.

Wal-Mart stores. Wal-Mart is proud of having quickly integrated the Big-K employees into its operations. According to the 1982 annual report, the application of Wal-Mart's management style in the new stores resulted in "dramatic increases in productivity." In the same year, Wal-Mart purchased a photo processing plant in Terrell, Texas. The most recent major acquisition came in 1983 with the purchase of 32 Woolco stores over 10 states.

13   By the middle of 1984, there were 676 stores in 19 states, and annual sales for the fiscal year ending January 31, 1985, were expected to pass $6 billion. That would put Wal-Mart within striking distance of F. W. Woolworth and Montgomery Ward. Three distribution centers had been built in Bentonville, and others had been built in Searcy, Arkansas; Palestine, Texas; and Cullman, Alabama. Plans for 1984 called for more than 100 new stores to be opened and for the construction of another distribution center in Mount Pleasant, Iowa. In addition, Wal-Mart leases a warehouse in Grand Prairie, Texas, which processes all imports, most of which are from the Orient.

14   A few of the newer stores are near or actually in urban markets. It is not yet clear how well they will perform in a more competitive environment, but at least Wal-Mart should be able to capitalize on its well-honed operational efficiencies, which will be discussed later. In 1983, Wal-Mart also opened its first Sam's Wholesale Club, in Midwest City, Oklahoma. This was a cash-and-carry operation, open to members only and aimed at owners of small businesses. Three more such warehouses were due to be opened in 1984.

Strategy and Operations

15   Sam Walton has always considered himself to be a Christian businessman and to be committed to good human relations. Certainly, outside observers are generally impressed by the high morale within the company, and the company claims that turnover is well below industry averages. One rather typical press account characterized Wal-Mart as the chain that "discounts everything but people." All employees, for example, are called "associates." As stated in the 1983 annual report:

> All associates shall be considered equal in importance to the company's successful operation; every customer shall be treated fairly and courteously; each goal set by the company shall be predicated on its responsibility to offer the highest quality merchandise at the lowest possible price, and no short-term strategy shall be pursued unless it enhances the long-term strength and profitability of the company.

16   The most distinctive aspect of Wal-Mart's strategy has always been its commitment to small-town and rural markets, which have been largely overlooked by the other discount chains. The first discount stores were in towns with populations between 5,000 and 25,000 and which were not within convenient commuting distance of urban markets. Jack Shewmaker, the chief operating officer, has observed that the gasoline crisis of the 1970s substantially assisted Wal-Mart insofar as shoppers were less willing to drive long distances to reach the larger markets. In terms of growth, Wal-Mart's original market area in Arkansas and in contiguous states was especially favorable because much of it had been so depressed economically and had expanded disproportionately after 1960. Just how well Wal-Mart was supported by its small markets did not become fully apparent until the period of recession and intensified price competition that so greatly reduced the earnings of most of Wal-Mart's more traditional competitors in the early 1980s.

17   Small towns offered substantial operational advantages. Land, construction expenses, wages, and taxes were usually lower. Few, if any, of these towns had seen discount stores before, so there was no established local competition. And the markets were too small to comfortably support a second discount store, which created a very effective barrier to entry for any potential competitors. Wal-Mart has kept its stores rather closely clustered, gradually expanding its operations out from northwestern Arkansas. With the stores close together an area can be saturated. Advertising is also more effective, and considerable savings can be realized on transportation charges.

18   In order to reserve its capital for operations and to maintain a comfortable level of liquidity, Wal-Mart has always leased most of its property. Currently, most of the warehouses and 95 percent of the stores are leased. Some stores have been leased from commercial developers, in which case Wal-Mart always attempts to secure a long-term lease with a fixed rent, although there may be a provision to contribute a share of the store's profits. A number of stores are occupied under a scale–leaseback provision; Wal-Mart builds the store to its specifications and at a site of its choice and then sells it to local interests from whom it leases it back. Other stores and several of the warehouses are leased from local government entities who financed the construction through revenue bonds.

19   In spite of its identification with the small-town market, Wal-Mart's average store size as measured by area and sales is comparable to that of the other discount chains. In 1982, its average sales figure of $6.2 million was behind that of K mart at $7.1 million. Sears, as a general-purpose department store, averaged much higher sales, $22.6 million. Wal-Mart's store size in terms of area is currently about 50,000 square feet, although some are as small as 30,000 square feet and as large as 80,000 square feet. More importantly, Wal-Mart has achieved an enviable record of productivity in terms of sales per square foot of floor space. The 1983 figure of $145 per square foot was about 20 percent higher than the industry average.

20   The mixture of goods that Wal-Mart carries is comparable to that of most of the other discount chains. In its isolated rural markets Wal-Mart has always made a special effort to satisfy the needs of its customers as fully as possible in order to provide true one-stop shopping. All stores, even the smallest, have the same 36 departments. Like the other discounters, Wal-Mart functions on a cash-and-carry basis, although charge cards and bank cards are accepted. An unconditional money-back guarantee is in effect in order to build customer confidence. The breakdown of sales by category of goods in 1982 was as follows:

Type of good	Percent of sales
Soft goods	30%
Hard goods	27
Sporting goods, toys	11
Stationery, candy	11
Health, beauty aids	9
Gifts, records, electronics	4
Footware	3
Jewelry	3
Pharmaceuticals	2

21   The sales figures for footware, jewelry, and pharmaceuticals are combined for licensed and owned departments. In the case of licensed departments, the rentals are included. These departments were originally leased because Wal-Mart did not feel fully qualified to operate them, but gradually the company has been buying them out.

22   What sets Wal-Mart's product line somewhat apart is that Wal-Mart has always carried a high proportion of national name goods, which convey an image of quality and which can be sold at premium prices. The official policy has been to sell brand name goods at prices equal to or lower than the prices charged by any local competitors for the same goods. Store managers check the prices competitors are charging every week, and they are expected to cut their own prices if they are not the lowest in town. In some departments Wal-Mart sells private label goods for the extremely price-conscious shopper, though such goods are purchased only if they offer exceptional value and if quality is ensured.

23   Advertising expense has averaged less than 2 percent of sales. It is fairly evenly distributed among the media of radio, TV, newspapers, and circulars and is concentrated in the local markets. Local advertising is much cheaper than national advertising, and Wal-Mart can realize some economies in advertising because most of its small markets are contiguous.

24   Purchasing is highly concentrated at the corporate headquarters and is usually direct from the manufacturer. The hotels of Bentonville are heavily booked by salespersons calling on Wal-Mart's buyers. Wal-Mart buys no more than 2½ percent of its goods from any one supplier in order to keep its options open. The company's buyers make half-a-dozen buying trips annually to the Orient, where they seek out goods with high labor content that can be imported at significant savings for their customers.

25   At Wal-Mart, efficiency starts at the top. All offices are very plain, and general administrative expenses are only 2 percent of sales. But the greatest efficiency that Wal-Mart has realized is in distribution. As noted earlier, the company has built a chain of distribution centers. In 1983, they handled 83 percent of all goods purchased, a very high proportion, with the remainder being shipped directly to the stores by the manufacturers. As recently as 1975, Wal-Mart warehoused only 60 percent of its goods. To move goods from the distribution centers to the stores, Wal-Mart runs its own trucking operation. The distribution centers and the stores have been spaced so that no store is more than six hours by road from a distribution center. Most of the stores are grouped rather closely together, so trucks can easily visit more than one store on a trip. The trucks themselves run carefully planned routes and whenever possible return to the distribution centers with inbound goods. They run empty only about 25 percent of the time. All in all, Wal-Mart spends only about 2 percent of sales for distribution, compared with an industry average of almost twice that.

Personnel

26   Sam Walton has certainly prospered under the free enterprise system, and many of the associates have their own incentives to contribute as effectively as possible to Wal-Mart's success. As with any retail chain, the store managers are the most critical employees aside from top management. Their salaries, which averaged $50,000 in 1983, are based on store profits. In return, managers have great discretion in ordering stock and planning displays. Experience has shown that shoppers in small rural markets

often have unpredictable tastes, which may differ sharply from those of their neighbors a few miles away.

27   Performance, however, is closely tracked. Every month each store receives its sales results for the month and a printout showing how it ranked in relation to all other stores. Expenses are tracked for everything from taxes and rent to phone service and paper clips. Store managers are expected to go over their report line by line with their district managers. Wal-Mart's buyers could hardly be put on commission, but star performers are singled out for commendation by a "buyer of the month" program.

28   Lower-level employees are likewise encouraged to show initiative and contribute their ideas. One of the most successful such programs has been the VPI (volume-producing item) program, whereby the managers of departments within stores are given a free rein to promote and price particular products. The sales of departments in different stores are tracked carefully and are ranked against each other. The department managers themselves are eligible for bonuses.

29   Another very successful program, involving all the associates, has been to combat shrinkage. Employees whose suggestions reduce shrinkage are rewarded with half of the savings over the average loss for the previous three years. Over a period of five years, shrinkage fell from 2.2 percent, about average for the industry, to 1.3 percent.

30   All associates are eligible to join a stock purchase plan in which stock may be purchased through payroll deductions. About one third of the associates have elected to do so. Although Wal-Mart has always considered that its employee relations are good, there was an attempt to organize employees in 1977. Management successfully argued that a union would be contrary to the best interests of both management and the employees themselves.

31   Wal-Mart believes unabashedly in promoting itself among its associates, customers, and neighbors. Several recent slogans have been "Our people make the difference," "PEP" (people, enthusiasm, productivity), and "You ain't seen nothin' yet." Store managers are encouraged to stage their own local promotions. A favorite device is the "Western Day," when associates dress in Western garb and the store is appropriately decorated. One manager even arranged to have a team of paratroopers descend into his parking lot in order to draw a crowd for his opening. Wal-Mart also strives to build good community relations wherever it locates. Associates are encouraged to participate in civic activities, and the company sometimes supports local activities directly. In 1982, the Wal-Mart Foundation awarded 335 scholarships of $1,000 each in each community where a Wal-Mart store had been operating for a year or more.

32   Top management at Wal-Mart believes in staying close to the business. Sam Walton and Jack Shewmaker, the chief operating officer, attempt to visit each store at least twice a year in order to assist managers in dealing with local problems and to gather ideas for improving the organization. They credit most of their successful ideas to store managers and other employees.

Organizational Structure

33   Wal-Mart's stock is closely held. Walton Enterprises, a holding company comprised of Sam Walton and his children, owns 42 percent of the approximately 70 million shares of Wal-Mart stock. At the current (1984) market value of about $35, that holding is worth $1 billion. Institutional investors hold another 30 percent of Wal-Mart; employees, 8 percent; and all others, 13 percent.

34   Notwithstanding Wal-Mart's reliance on its store managers and good employee relations, the company is highly centralized, reflecting the firm's long-standing commitment
to cost control and efficiency. In 1984 Sam Walton held the titles of chief executive
officer and chairman of the board. According to all reports, he remains very much
involved in the business, coming to work daily and traveling constantly to visit stores.
In fact, he is so involved that some observers have expressed concern that the company
may experience difficulty when he is no longer at the helm. He does not seem to be
preparing a successor, although one of his sons, S. Robson Walton, is vice chairman,
secretary, and general counsel.

35   The other principal officers are David Glass, the chief financial officer, and Jack
Shewmaker, who has been president and chief operating officer since 1978. Shewmaker,
the son of a retail merchant, was born in 1939 in a small town not far from Bentonville.
He studied to be an engineer at the Georgia Institute of Technology until being forced
to drop out because of illness. Later he worked for the Outboard Marine Corporation
and Kroger. In 1970, Shewmaker joined Wal-Mart as a district manager in charge of
store openings. Shewmaker is very much a "Theory Y" manager who believes that
the role of management should be to provide an environment in which people should
be encouraged to do the best that they are capable of doing. He explains that his
greatest thrill is to take someone he has confidence in, give them an opportunity,
teach them some of the things that he knows, and watch them achieve things.

36   There are three regional vice presidents who work for corporate headquarters. Below
each of them are three or four district managers, each of whom, in turn, oversees 10
to 12 stores. The managers have primary responsibility for their department heads
and other employees. Information on operations from all levels is relayed to headquarters by a highly sophisticated management information system. Terminals at each
store are used to wire merchandise requests to headquarters, where the central computers are linked directly to over 200 vendors. Individual stores keep very close track of
their inventories with a system of point-of-sale terminals.

Financial Performance

37   Wal-Mart's remarkable performance had not gone unnoticed. As the company noted
in its annual report for 1983, *Dun's Business Month* rated Wal-Mart one of the five
best-managed companies in the United States. In 1984, the *Fortune* survey of the
Service 500 revealed that Wal-Mart's total return to investors (appreciation of stock
plus reinvested dividends) over the period 1973–83 was 47.76 percent, higher than
that of any other retailer of any type except for Service Merchandise, a much smaller
chain of catalog stores based in Nashville, Tennessee.

38   Exhibit 2 shows selected financial data for Wal-Mart for the past 10 years. Exhibit
1 shows financial ratios of Wal-Mart in comparison with those of several other discount
chains. K mart is often considered Wal-Mart's principal competitor, though K mart
stores are usually in larger towns and cities. But if Wal-Mart is to fulfill its ambitious
plans for growth, it will eventually have to compete head to head with K mart. K
mart is currently making enormous investments in upgrading the image and appearance
of its stores.

39   SCOA Industries is a smaller chain (1984 revenues: $1.3 billion) based in Columbus,
Ohio, and it is concentrated outside of Wal-Mart's area. It is included here because

its figures are second only to Wal-Mart's among the discount chains. SCOA is also an interesting case because it is an old established firm, the former Shoe Corporation of America, which has successfully restructured and renamed itself to move out of a declining industry.

40　Zayre is more comparable to Wal-Mart in terms of scale (1983 revenues: $2.1 billion), and its ratios are more representative of the discount retail industry as a whole. Finally, Ames Department Stores is the largest (1983 revenues: $647 million) of several other chains of discount and variety stores that have specialized in rural markets. These chains have been quite successful, and recent reports indicate that as they expand their market areas they are beginning to compete with each other and with Wal-Mart.

Prospects for the Future

41　Sam Walton shows no signs of being ready to retire or to scale back his expectations for future growth. His most recent five-year projection, released in 1983, calls for growth in sales and profits of 30 to 35 percent a year. Discount retailing as a whole is expected to show a growth of 10 to 13 percent a year for the remainder of the decade.

42　Like the other discount retailers, Wal-Mart will confront changes in the competitive environment. There are new players, especially in the larger markets, such as catalog showrooms, home centers, specialty stores, and off-price retailers. Each of them offers different combinations of merchandise, price ranges, services, and convenience. At the same time, Wal-Mart is facing competition in some of its small-town markets, some of which are not as small as they once were.

43　The demographic and economic trends are not especially favorable to Wal-Mart. The general rate of population increase has slowed to 1 percent annually, where it is expected to remain at least until the 1990s. Nor can most of Wal-Mart's rural market areas expect to continue the sort of economic expansion that they experienced in the earlier decades. With more two-earner families and an older, more productive work force, there will be an increasing proportion of upscale spenders in the general population. But many of the upscale shoppers will have less time in which to spend larger incomes, which should benefit the larger, one-stop stores if they can carry the proper mix of products and services.

44　Most of the retail chains seem to have discovered what Sam Walton realized at least 20 years ago: that rapid growth is no substitute for the maintenance of favorable margins. The largest chains, including K mart, Penney's, and Sears, have committed themselves to major campaigns to move their merchandise and their physical plants upscale in a search for higher margins. In 1982 and 1983, they also made major efforts to streamline operations and cut costs. The particular challenge to Wal-Mart will be to retain the loyalty of its traditional shoppers while gaining enough new business to meet its expansion goals.

45　Although Wal-Mart appears at least as well equipped as any of its competitors to meet the challenges of the 1980s, no one in such a competitive industry can afford to be complacent. One source of concern to some observers has been that Sam Walton does not appear to be training a successor. He remains so involved with the day-to-day affairs of the company that it is difficult to imagine it without him. Notwithstanding the highly rationalized nature of Wal-Mart's operations, Walton's personal charisma has always been considered a major factor in Wal-Mart's success.

46   As Shewmaker has commented about Walton: "With the money he is reported to have, you would have figured he would disappear to a South Sea island. But he is totally committed to the company."

47   It has also been argued that Wal-Mart cannot continue to grow as it has without venturing outside of its traditional small-town markets. The company's planners seem to agree. As we have noted, Wal-Mart has tentatively ventured into several suburban markets, with results that are not yet clear. In addition, it has opened two new types of stores, the discount warehouses and a single drugstore. Another basic option is a policy of geographical expansion, which Wal-Mart will probably continue to pursue. It will soon be apparent whether or not Wal-Mart has again confounded the skeptics.

C

Strategic Control and Evaluation

Case 18

Manville Corporation (1987)

Perhaps no other mineral is so woven into the fabric of American life as is asbestos. Impervious to heat and fibrous—it is the only mineral that can be woven into cloth—asbestos is spun into fireproof clothing and theater curtains, as well as into such household items as noncombustible drapes, rugs, pot holders, and ironing-board covers. Mixed into slurry, asbestos is sprayed onto girders and walls to provide new buildings with fireproof insulation. It is used in floor tiles, roofing felts, and in most plasterboards and wallboards. Asbestos is also an ingredient of plaster and stucco and of many paints and putties. This "mineral of a thousand uses" (an obsolete nickname—the present count stands at around 3,000 uses) is probably present in some form or other in every home, school, office building, and factory in this country. Used in brake linings and clutch facings, in mufflers and gaskets, in sealants and caulking, and extensively used in ships, asbestos is also a component of every modern vehicle, including space-ships.

1   This was written by columnist Bruce Porter in 1973, just as the dangers of breathing asbestos dust were becoming widely recognized by those outside the asbestos industry. From about the turn of the century, Johns–Manville Corporation (renamed Manville Corporation in 1981) had been the world's leading asbestos company, involved in mining and sale of the raw fibers as well as development, manufacture, and marketing of

---

Source: Arthur Sharplin, McNeese University.

intermediate and finished asbestos products. This distinction made Manville the target of a trickle of asbestos health lawsuits in the 1920s and early 30s which would become a flood by the 1980s.

2   Late on the evening of August 25, 1982, the Manville board of directors, after a briefing on bankruptcy reorganization and upon the recommendation of three senior outside directors who had been studying the issue, voted to file a petition for protection from creditors under Chapter 11 of the U.S. Bankruptcy Code. The petition had already been prepared and was filed the next day. It would be more than four years before a plan to emerge from court protection would be offered for approval by creditors and stockholders.

Company Background

3   Until the 70s, Manville was a successful company by the usual standards. Incorporated in 1901, the company had seen consistent growth in sales and profits. Dividends had been paid every year except for the war years of 1915–16 and the depths of the Depression in 1933–34. The company had been one of the Dow Jones Industrial 30 for many years.

4   In the decades before 1970, Manville's sales had grown somewhat slower than the gross national product. But the company had benefited from relatively low fixed costs, due to a largely depleted and depreciated capital base and the total absence of long-term debt in the capital structure. With low operating and financial leverage, the firm had been able to adapt to sales downturns in 1957, 1960, 1967, and 1970 and still earn profits in each of those years. By 1970, Manville had nearly $800 million in book value net worth, garnered almost entirely from the mining, manufacture, and sale of asbestos products, for which it held a dominant market position.

5   During the 1960s, a number of the senior officials who had been with the company since the 1930s died or retired. Compared just to the 1966 board of directors, the 1970 board had a majority of new members. In 1970, departing from a tradition of promoting from within, the board of directors installed an outsider, psychologist Richard Goodwin, as president. Goodwin immediately set about changing the company's image. He arranged to move the corporate headquarters from its old Madison Avenue brick building to Denver, purchasing the 10,000-acre Ken Caryl ranch and planning a luxurious "world headquarters," the first phase of which was to cost $60 million.

6   Goodwin led the company through more than 20 small acquisitions—in lighting systems, golf carts, irrigation sprinklers, and other products. In the process, Manville's long-term debt went from zero to $196 million, and fixed costs increased several fold. A short, steep recession in 1975 cut Manville's profits in half, back to 1970 levels. U.S. asbestos sales had begun a rapid decline, which was to accelerate and total more than 50 percent in just five years. And Manville was suffering reverses in its fight against asbestos tort lawsuits (discussed below).

7   In what *Fortune* magazine called "The Shootout at the J–M Corral," Goodwin was removed in September 1976 and John A. McKinney—Manville's legal/public affairs chief, who had joined the company before 1950—took over as chief executive. McKinney divested many of the Goodwin acquisitions and turned his attention to what he called "aggressive defense" of the asbestos lawsuits and the search for a "substantial acquisition." He also made plans for a $200 million expansion in the company's fiberglass operations. In his 1977 "President's Review," McKinney wrote, "We do not expect asbestos fiber to dominate J–M earnings to the extent it has in the past." (In 1976,

asbestos fiber alone—not including manufactured asbestos products—provided about half of Manville's operating profit, though it constituted only about one eighth of sales.)

8   After Ideal Basic Industries, a major producer of potash and portland cement, spurned a Manville buyout initiative, the company began a takeover battle (with Texas Eastern Corporation) for Olinkraft Corporation, a wood products company concentrated in paperboard and paper. Olinkraft's main assets were about 600,000 acres of prime southern timberland and several paper mills.

9   Manville won the battle and closed the deal in the last half of 1978. The purchase price was $595 million, half paid in cash and half represented by a new issue of preferred stock. That price was 2.24 times Olinkraft's book value and over twice its recent market value. While the Olinkraft merger was being negotiated, Manville common stock declined in value to $22, a total drop of over $225 million. Olinkraft's shares rose to approximate the purchase price of $65 a share. In conformity with "purchase method accounting," Olinkraft's assets were placed on Manville's books at the purchase price, creating over $300 million in new net worth.

10   Manville's sales and common stock earnings reached peaks of $2.92 billion and $144 million (expressed in constant 1981 dollars), respectively, in 1978. But both would fall steadily afterward, to $1.64 billion and a $101 million *loss* in 1982.

11   In 1981, management reorganized the company, separating the asbestos operations into incorporated divisions. Also, the executives surrendered their stock options for "special incentive units," which were soon to become valueless, and signed "special termination agreements," providing for large severance settlements after any "change in control" of the company. The company also reaffirmed its commitment to indemnify its executives and directors against the asbestos lawsuits.

12   Although Manville was able to defer the asbestos health costs (they totaled only $12 million in 1981) and extract more than $100 million in cash flows from the Olinkraft assets, the situation in early 1982 was worsening. Company debt had been downgraded. Coopers and Lybrand, the company's accounting firm, had qualified its opinion on Manville's financial reports. Manville's insurance carriers had stopped paying asbestos settlements and providing defense against the asbestos lawsuits. At the same time, the number and size of the asbestos health judgments were skyrocketing (although the large awards were all stayed by appeals). Suits frequently named Manville officials in their personal capacities. And, after 1980, many juries awarded punitive damages, sometimes over $1 million per claimant, in addition to compensatory damages.

13   The five highest-paid executives of Manville in 1982 had all been with the company since at least 1952. The 1982 board of directors had the same membership as the 1976 board and was mostly unchanged since the 1960s. One of the five long-tenured executives left just before the Chapter 11 filing, and others would leave afterward, generally with severance pay and pensions. For example, on August 1, 1986, John A. McKinney retired with $1.3 million in severance pay and retirement pay exceeding $300,000 per year. His salary had increased from $408,750 to $638,005 per year while Manville was in Chapter 11.

14   Financial summaries are shown in Exhibit 1 (1978 until August 26, 1986) and Exhibit 2 (after August 26, 1986) of Appendix A.

The Asbestos Tort Lawsuits

15   Beginning in the 1920s a steadily increasing number of lawsuits were filed on behalf of Manville employees who had fallen ill or died from breathing asbestos dust (made up of microscopic fibers released as the product is mined or otherwise handled—or

through normal deterioration as asbestos-containing buildings and machines vibrate and as asbestos tiles, roof coverings, brake linings, water pipes, and so forth are eroded or abraded). By 1982 there was litigation pending against the company on behalf of over 16,000 persons, who generally claimed that their injuries (mostly asbestosis—see inset) had resulted from Manville's suppression and manipulation of research and publicity about asbestos dangers. An average of 425 cases were being filed each month in the first half of 1982, and the company's projections were for over 32,000 new cases by the year 2001. Appendix B provides a chronology of selected events related to the asbestos lawsuits.

Asbestos diseases

Ingested asbestos causes mechanical injury to moving tissue, especially the lungs. The microscopic fibers are impervious to body fluids and oxygen and are almost impossible to filter out of air. The constant motion of the lungs causes tissue to be penetrated and cut by the fibers. This leads to progressive and irreversible scarring, thickening, and calcification of the lungs and their linings, a condition called asbestosis. A rare and always fatal cancer, mesothelioma, is strongly connected with asbestos exposure, as are increased incidence and severity of many other respiratory ailments. The first outward symptoms of asbestos disease typically appear 10 to 30 years after exposure begins. But early damage is easily detectable by X rays, and some cancers and respiratory deficiencies show up after only a year or two.

The Bankruptcy Reorganization

16   Manville Corporation and its 20 main subsidiaries filed petitions for reorganization under Chapter 11 of the U.S. Bankruptcy Code on August 26, 1982 (Appendix C provides a description of bankruptcy reorganization). The company would later cite management's stated desire to "obtain prompt and equitable payment" of all allowed claims and to "create and preserve values to the extent possible" for the equity holders as reasons for the filings. Manville's two Canadian divisions, which owned the world's largest asbestos mine and some asbestos manufacturing facilities, emerged from reorganization in 1983, and Manville sold the common stock of those divisions to a group headed by the divisions' managers. Under the sale agreement, Manville will continue to share the profits of these divisions. Also, the Forest Products Division emerged from reorganization in 1984, paying all its creditors essentially the full value of their claims. That division remained a subsidiary of Manville Corporation.

17   On May 23, 1986, Manville submitted its "Second Amended and Restated Plan of Reorganization" for the remaining divisions. The plan had the support of the legal representative the court had appointed to represent future asbestos victims and each of the claimant committees except the one representing equity holders. Ballots were mailed to unsecured creditors (including asbestos claimants) and equity holders in September 1986, and confirmation hearings were scheduled to begin in December that year. Appendix D summarizes the Manville reorganization plan.

18   Based on a liquidation analysis performed by Morgan Stanley and Company, Manville estimated that liquidation would provide 47 to 69 percent recovery for asbestos claims (including property damage claims) and unsecured creditor claims. Manville estimated that execution of the plan would provide 99 to 100 percent recovery for these claims.

Appendix A: Financial Summaries

Exhibit 1
Financial summaries, before August 26, 1982

MANVILLE CORPORATION
Income Statements
(in millions of dollars)*

	1982 (6 months)	1981	1980	1979	1978
Sales	$949	$2,186	$2,267	$2,276	$1,649
Cost of sales	784	1,731	1,771	1,747	1,190
Selling, general, and administrative expenses	143	271	263	239	193
R&D and engineering expenses	16	34	35	31	33
Operating income	6	151	197	259	232
Other income, net	1	35	26	21	28
Interest expense	35	73	65	62	22
Income before income taxes	(28)	112	157	218	238
Income taxes	2	53	77	103	116
Net income	(25)	60	81	115	122
Dividends on preferred stock	12	25	25	24	0
Net income for common stock	$ (37	$ 35	$ 55	$ 91	$ 122

* Totals may not check, due to rounding.

MANVILLE CORPORATION
Statement of Revenues and Income from Operations by Business Segment
(in millions of dollars)*

	1981	1980	1979	1978	1977	1976
Revenues:						
Fiberglass products	$ 625	$ 610	$ 573	$ 514	$ 407	$ 358
Forest products	555	508	497	0	0	0
Nonfiberglass insulation	258	279	268	231	195	159
Roofing products	209	250	273	254	204	171
Pipe products and systems	199	220	305	303	274	218
Asbestos fiber	138	159	168	157	161	155
Industrial and special products	320	341	309	291	301	309
Corporate revenues, net	12	9	11	20	12	(22)
Intersegment sales	(95)	(84)	(106)	(94)	(74)	(56)
Total	$2,221	$2,292	$2,297	$1,677	$1,480	$1,291
Income from operations:						
Fiberglass products	$ 90	$ 91	$ 96	$ 107	$ 82	$ 60
Forest products	39	37	50	0	0	0
Nonfiberglass insulation	20	27	27	35	28	18
Roofing products	(17)	9	14	23	14	8
Pipe products and systems	0	(5)	18	26	24	(3)
Asbestos fiber	37	35	56	55	60	60
Industrial and special products	50	55	43	36	25	19
Corporate expense, net	(23)	(38)	(23)	(23)	(24)	(49)
Eliminations and adjustments	3	11	(2)	1	3	2
Total	$ 198	$ 223	$ 280	$ 260	$ 212	$ 116

* Totals may not check, due to rounding.

Exhibit 1 *(concluded)*

MANVILLE CORPORATION
Balance Sheets
(in millions of dollars)*

	June 30, 1982	December 31			
		1981	*1980*	*1979*	*1978*
Assets					
Cash	$ 10	$ 14	$ 20	$ 19	$ 28
Marketable securities	17	12	12	10	38
Accounts and notes receivable	348	327	350	362	328
Inventories	182	211	217	229	219
Prepaid expenses	19	19	20	31	32
Total current assets	576	583	619	650	645
Property, plant, and equipment:					
Land and land improvements		119	118	114	99
Buildings		363	357	352	321
Machinery and equipment		1,202	1,204	1,161	1,043
Total PPE		1,685	1,679	1,627	1,462
Less: Accumulated depreciation and depletion		(525)	(484)	(430)	(374)
		1,160	1,195	1,197	1,088
Timber and timberland, net		406	407	368	372
	1,523	1,566	1,602	1,565	1,460
Other assets	148	149	117	110	113
Total assets	$2,247	$2,298	$2,338	$2,324	$2,217
Liabilities					
Short-term debt	$	$ 29	$ 22	$ 32	$ 23
Accounts payable	191	120	126	143	114
Employee compensation and benefits		77	80	54	45
Income taxes		30	22	51	84
Other liabilities	149	58	61	50	63
Total current liabilities	340	316	310	329	329
Long-term debt	499	508	519	532	543
Other noncurrent liabilities	93	86	75	73	60
Deferred income taxes	186	185	211	195	150
Total liabilities	1,116	1,095	1,116	1,129	1,083
Stockholders' equity					
Preferred	301	301	300	299	299
Common	60	59	58	208	197
Capital in excess of par	178	174	164	0	0
Retained earnings	642	695	705	692	643
Cumulative currency translation adjustment	(47)	(22)	0	0	0
Less: Cost of treasury stock	(3)	(3)	(4)	(4)	(6)
Total stockholders' equity	1,131	1,203	1,222	1,196	1,134
Total liabilities and stockholders' equity	$2,247	$2,298	$2,338	$2,324	$2,217

* Totals may not check, due to rounding.

Exhibit 2
Financial summaries, after August 26, 1982

MANVILLE CORPORATION
Income Statements
(in millions of dollars)*

	1985	1984	1983	1982
Sales	$1,880	$1,814	$1,729	$1,772
Other income, net	62	59	61	34
	1,942	1,873	1,791	1,806
Cost of sales	1,473	1,400	1,370	1,391
Selling, general and administrative expenses	246	238	224	222
R&D and engineering expenses	35	36	35	28
Operating income	188	200	161	163
Gain on disposition of assets	151	0	(3)	110
Asbestos health costs	52	26	20	16
Interest expense	23	21	26	52
Chapter 11 costs	9	17	18	2
Income from continued operations	(47)	135	100	(56)
Income taxes	(1)	58	40	35
Net income from continued operations	45	77	60	88
Net income from discontinued operations	0	0	7	10
Net income	$ 45	$ 77	$ 67	$ 98

* Totals may not check, due to rounding.

MANVILLE CORPORATION
Statement of Revenues and Income from Operations by Business Segment
(in millions of dollars)*

	1985	1984	1983	1982
Revenues:				
Fiberglass products	$ 803	$ 781	$ 718	$ 609
Forest products	459	451	415	436
Specialty products	674	645	683	829
Corporate revenues, net	43	38	36	15
Intersegment sales	(37)	(42)	(61)	(82)
Total	$1,942	$1,873	$1,791	$1,806
Income from operations:				
Fiberglass products	$ 106	$ 115	$ 97	$ 75
Forest products	43	63	52	48
Specialty products	33	28	19	51
Corporate expense, net	(1)	(6)	(6)	(18)
Eliminations and adjustments	7	0	0	7
Total	$ 188	$ 200	$ 161	$ 164

* Totals may not check, due to rounding.

Exhibit 2 *(concluded)*

MANVILLE CORPORATION
Balance Sheets
(in millions of dollars)*

	December 31			
	1985	1984	1983	1982
Assets				
Cash	$ 7	$ 9	$ 19	$ 11
Marketable securities, at cost	314	276	240	206
Accounts and notes receivable	314	285	277	310
Inventories	153	164	141	152
Prepaid expenses	29	17	22	17
Total current assets	817	752	700	696
Property, plant, and equipment:				
Land and land improvements	95	96	97	108
Buildings	299	308	303	332
Machinery and equipment	1,160	1,121	1,036	1,090
Less: Accumulated depreciation and depletion	538	513	472	547
	1,017	1,013	984	983
Timber and timberland, net	385	392	395	402
	1,402	1,405	1,379	1,385
Other assets	174	182	174	154
Total assets	$2,393	$2,339	$2,253	$2,236
Liabilities				
Short-term debt	$ 26	$ 20	$ 94	$ 12
Accounts payable	84	102	65	86
Accrued employee compensation and benefits	94	81	14	63
Income taxes	12	18	9	32
Other accrued liabilities	69	35	26	29
Total current liabilities	286	256	209	221
Long-term debt	92	84	713	736
Liabilities subject to Chapter 11 proceedings	578	574	5	12
Other noncurrent liabilities	115	67	61	60
Deferred income taxes	144	162	136	140
Total liabilities	1,214	1,142	1,122	1,170
Stockholders' equity				
Preferred stock	301	301	301	301
Common stock	60	60	60	60
Capital in excess of par	178	178	178	178
Retained earnings	667	713	635	568
Cumulative current translation adjustment	(26)	(53)	(41)	(39)
Cost of treasury stock	(2)	(2)	(2)	(2)
Total stockholders' equity	878	896	831	765
Total liabilities and stockholders' equity	$2,393	$2,339	$2,253	$2,236

* Totals may not check, due to rounding.

Appendix B: Selected Events Concerning Asbestos and Health

19 *1898.* Manville founder and inventor of uses for asbestos, Henry Ward Johns, dies of "dust phthisis pneumonitis," later known as asbestosis.

20 *1929.* Manville defending early lawsuits for asbestos deaths. The company claims employees assumed the risks of employment, knew or should have known the dangers, and were contributorily negligent. Legal documents in these cases bear signatures of senior Manville officials who would remain with the company until the 1960s.

21 *1930.* Dr. A. J. Lanza, of Metropolitan Life Insurance Company (Manville's insurer), begins a four-year study on the "Effects of Inhalation of Asbestos Dust upon the Lungs of Asbestos Workers."

22 *1933.* Based on interim results of his study, Dr. Lanza suggests Manville engage an outside consultant to do dust counts at company plants. A decision is made to train an insider to do this rather than bring in someone from outside the company.

23 *1934.* Asbestosis considered for classification as a disease for workmen's compensation purposes. Manville's chief attorney writes to the company:

> In particular we have urged that asbestosis should not at the present time be included in the list of compensation diseases, for the reason that it is only within a comparatively recent time that asbestosis has been recognized by the medical and scientific professions as a disease—in fact, one of our principal defenses in actions against the company on the common law theory of negligence has been that the scientific and medical knowledge has been insufficient until a very recent period to place on the owners of plants or factories the burden or duty of taking special precautions against the possible onset of the disease in their employees.

24 After reviewing a draft of Dr. Lanza's report (above, 1930), Manville Vice President and Corporate Secretary Vandiver Brown writes Dr. Lanza, requesting changes. His letter states, "All we ask is that all of the favorable aspects of the survey be included and that none of the unfavorable be unintentionally pictured in darker terms than the circumstances justify. I feel confident that we can depend upon you and Dr. McConnel to give us this 'break.'"

25 *1935.* Brown writes another industry executive, Sumner Simpson, "I quite agree that our interests are best served by having asbestosis receive the minimum of publicity." He is commenting on Simpson's response to a letter by Anne Rossiter (editor of the industry journal *Asbestos*) in which she has written, "You may recall that we have written you on several occasions concerning the publishing of information, or discussion of, asbestosis. . . . Always you have requested that, for obvious reasons, we publish nothing and, naturally, your wishes have been respected."

26 *1936.* Messrs. Brown and Simpson convince nine other asbestos companies to provide a total of $417 per month for the industry's own three-year study of the effects of

asbestos dust on guinea pigs and rabbits by Dr. LeRoy U. Gardner. Simpson writes Gardner, "We could determine from time to time after the findings were made, whether we wish any publication or not." In a separate letter, Brown states, "The manuscript of your study will be submitted to us for approval prior to publication." Gardner will tell the companies of "significant changes in guinea pigs' lungs within a period of one year" and "fibrosis" produced by long fibers and "chronic inflammation" caused by short fibers. He will make several requests for additional funding but will die in 1946 without reporting final results.

27   *1940.* Lawsuits have increased in number through the 1930s, but Manville continues to successfully defend or settle them, using the same defenses as in the 1920s but adding a statute-of-limitations defense, made possible by the long latency period of asbestos diseases. The companies continue to be able to prevent significant publicity about asbestos and health. The war will bring spiraling sales and profits, as thousands of tons of asbestos is used in building war machines, mainly ships—resulting in exposure of tens of thousands of shipyard workers and seamen, thousands of whom will die of asbestos diseases decades later.

28   *1947.* A study by the Industrial Hygiene Foundation of America finds that from 3 to 20 percent of asbestos plant workers already have asbestosis, and a Manville plant employing 300 is producing "5 or 6 cases annually that the physician believes show early changes due to asbestos."

29   *1950.* Dr. Kenneth W. Smith, Manville chief physician, has given superiors his report that of 708 workers he studied, only 4 were free of asbestos disease. Concerning the more serious cases, he has written, "The fibrosis of this disease is irreversible and permanent so that eventually compensation will be paid to each of these men, but as long as the man is not disabled it is felt that he should not be told of his condition so that he can live and work in peace and the company can benefit from his many years of experience."

30   *1952.* John A. McKinney, Fred L. Pundsack, Chester E. Shepperly, Monroe Harris, and Chester J. Sulewski, who will be Manville's top five officers as it prepares to seek bankruptcy court protection in 1982, have all joined the company in various capacities.

31   *1953.* Dr. Smith tries to convince senior Manville managers to authorize caution labeling for asbestos. In a 1976 deposition he will characterize their responses: "We recognize the potential hazard that you mentioned, the suggested use of a caution label. We will discuss it among ourselves and make a decision." Asked why he was overruled, Smith will say, "Application of a caution label identifying a product as hazardous would cut out sales."

32   *1956.* The board of governors of the Asbestos Textile Institute (made up of Manville and other asbestos companies) meet to discuss the increasing publicity about asbestos and cancer, and agree that "every effort should be made to disassociate this relationship until such a time that there is sufficient and authoritative information to substantiate such to be a fact."

33   *1957.*   The Asbestos Textile Institute rejects a proposal by the Industrial Health Foundation that asbestos companies fund a study on asbestos and cancer. Institute minutes report, "There is a feeling among certain members that such an investigation would stir up a hornet's nest and put the whole industry under suspicion."

34   *1959.*   An increasing number of articles connecting asbestos with various diseases have appeared in scholarly medical journals over the last few years.

35   *1963.*   Dr. I. J. Selikoff, of Mt. Sinai Medical Center in New York, reads a report of his study of asbestos workers before the American Medical Association meeting. Like the earlier research, the Selikoff study implicates asbestos ingestion as the causal factor in many thousands of deaths and injuries. Selikoff will soon estimate that at least 100,000 more Americans will die of asbestos diseases this century. The study and the articles, news stories, and academic papers which follow will focus public attention on the asbestos and health issue. An estimated 100 articles on asbestos-related diseases will appear in 1964 alone.

36   *1964.*   For the first time, Manville agrees to place caution labels on asbestos products. The labels say, "Inhalation of asbestos in excessive quantities over long periods of time may be harmful," and suggests that users avoid breathing the dust and wear masks if "adequate ventilation control is not possible." The consistent position of Manville managers regarding their failure to warn users earlier will be restated in 1986:

> During the periods of alleged injurious exposure, medical and scientific authorities, government officials, and companies supplying products containing asbestos fiber believed that the dust levels for asbestos recommended by the U.S. Public Health Service did not constitute a hazard to the health of workers handling asbestos-containing insulation products. *Accordingly, the company has maintained that there was no basis for product warnings or special hazard controls until the 1964 publication of results of scientific studies linking pulmonary disease in asbestos insulation workers with asbestos exposure.* [emphasis added]

37   *1970.*   The senior managers and directors from the 1930s have retired, most within the last few years. Compared to the 1966 board of directors, the 1970 board has a majority of new members. The five managers who joined the company in the late 1940s and early 1950s and who will lead Manville into Chapter 11 reorganization are in senior positions now—McKinney and Pundsack are vice presidents. However, outsider Richard Goodwin is installed as president.

38   *1973.*   Manville and other asbestos companies lose their last appeal in the case of Clarence Borel, who died of mesothelioma and asbestosis before the decision. In reviewing the case, the U.S. Court of Appeals writes what many considered a scorching indictment of Manville and the other defendants. The court concludes, "By the mid-1930s the hazard of asbestos as a pneumoconiotic dust was universally accepted. . . . Indeed the evidence tended to establish that the defendants gave no instructions or warnings at all. . . . The unpalatable facts are that in the 20s and 30s the hazards of working with asbestos were recognized." Concerning the caution labels, which came after Borel's exposure, the decision states, "None of the so-called cautions intimated the gravity of the risk: the danger of a fatal illness caused by asbestosis and mesothelioma or other cancers. . . . The admonition that a worker should 'avoid breathing the dust' is black humor: there was no way for insulation workers to avoid breathing asbestos dust."

39   ***1976.*** Psychologist Richard Goodwin is asked to resign as president, and lawyer/public affairs specialist John A. McKinney takes over. McKinney will shortly be elevated to chairman of the board, and Fred Pundsack will become president. Asbestos use is dropping rapidly, and Goodwin has increased long-term debt from zero to $196 million by buying companies in other fields. But asbestos is still so profitable that the fiber alone—not including manufactured asbestos products—produces 51 percent of Manville's operating profit while constituting only about 12 percent of sales.

40   ***1977.*** A mass of papers from asbestos company files, variously called the "Sumner Simpson Papers" and the "Raybestos–Manhattan Correspondence," is accidentally discovered by plaintiff attorneys and presented in a New Jersey asbestos lawsuit. The papers include the letters from the 1930s mentioned earlier. In admitting the new evidence in another trial, a South Carolina judge will soon write, "The Raybestos–Manhattan correspondence reveals written evidence that Raybestos–Manhattan and Johns–Manville exercised an editorial prerogative over the publication of the first study of the asbestos industry, which they sponsored in 1935. It further reflects a conscious effort by the industry to downplay, or arguably suppress, the dissemination of information to employees and the public for fear of the promotion of lawsuits."

41   ***1978.*** The stream of asbestos lawsuits has become a flood. Armed with the Raybestos–Manhattan correspondence, asbestos victims are seeking huge amounts, often including punitive damages. The Manville executives choose not to mention the lawsuits in the 1977 annual report, but the Securities and Exchange Commission report on Form 10-K reveals that there are now 623 asbestos lawsuits for amounts totaling at least $2.79 billion. This year alone, the number of suits will double. Many court decisions are going against Manville, although the company is able to delay paying in most cases by appealing decisions, requesting new trials, and other legal tactics.

42   ***1979.*** Asbestos use declines another 35 percent this year alone. This is compounded by a recession in construction, which will last through 1982. Manville's sales and earnings, buoyed by the Olinkraft acquisition to $2.92 billion and $144 million, respectively, start a steady decline, which will lead to sales of only $1.64 billion in 1982 and a $100 million annual-rate loss for the first half of that year (these figures are in constant 1981 dollars).

43   ***1981.*** No significant changes in senior managers or directors have occurred since 1976. The directors decide to reorganize the company, segregating the asbestos-related elements into separately incorporated divisions. Special termination agreements, commonly called "golden parachutes," are approved for all the top executives. Actual asbestos health costs have never been a significant expense and this year total only $12 million, less than .5 percent of sales. But Manville is now losing many cases—and, shown the Raybestos–Manhattan correspondence and other new evidence, juries fre-

quently award hundreds of thousands of dollars in punitive damages. Manville's insurers are refusing to pay, or even to provide defense against, the asbestos lawsuits. Many of the recent lawsuits name the directors and officers personally—but the recently restated corporate bylaws promise that the company will indemnify them.

44   *1982.*   Manville continues to forestall payments to asbestos claimants—through repeated appeals and other legal tactics. But the company's operations are increasingly unprofitable, and major losses are reported for both the first and second quarters. The asbestos judgments increase in number and magnitude. A consulting firm hired by Manville reports that 40,000 additional lawsuits will cost the company $1.9 billion by the year 2001. Upon the recommendation of McKinney and three outside directors, the board of directors approves the Chapter 11 filing on the evening of August 25, and the necessary papers are filed in the U.S. Bankruptcy Court for the Southern District of New York the next day. All the asbestos lawsuits and all efforts to collect previously won judgments are stopped. Within a few days the company is awash in cash, as accounts receivable flow in and $615 million in debt is stayed. An estimated 2,000 of the 16,500 present asbestos claimants will die during the years Manville is negotiating its reorganization plan, and, with few exceptions, none of the 16,500 will be paid. In support of Manville's decision to reorganize under bankruptcy law, First Boston Corporation and Morgan Stanley and Company prepare secret reports estimating the "going concern value" of the company's assets at slightly above their $1.8 billion liquidation value.

Appendix C: How Chapter 11 Works

45   Chapter 11 of the U.S. Bankruptcy Code is based upon the assumption that a business is worth more as a going concern than in liquidation. If this is true, stockholders and creditors may get more out of a troubled company by allowing it to continue operating than by shutting it down. Additional benefits of keeping the company operating are that employees keep their jobs and the community keeps the tax base and economic and social activity related to the firm.

46   To assure maintenance of the company's value and equitable distribution of claims on that value, a U.S. bankruptcy judge assumes oversight of any firm which desires to "reorganize" under Chapter 11. Insolvency is not a prerequisite. A committee of unsecured creditors and one made up of stockholders is appointed to assist management and the court in arriving at an equitable plan. Other committees or advocates may be established to represent interests which diverge from those of shareholders and unsecured creditors.

47   In negotiations with the committees, company executives prepare a formal reorganization plan and submit it to creditor and stockholder groups for approval. One hundred eighty days is allowed for this, but the period is routinely extended. If all impaired classes of claimants approve the plan, the court may confirm it and place it into effect. "Impaired" claimants are those whose legal, equitable, or contractual rights are modified by the plan, except by curing defaults and reinstating maturity or providing for cash payment. The plan may also be confirmed if the judge holds that it treats nonapproving impaired classes equally with respect to other classes of equal rank and that allowed claims of nonapproving classes will be fully satisfied under the plan before more junior classes receive any distribution at all.

48   While the plan is being negotiated, approved, and confirmed, all prefiling claims are stayed. Executory contracts may be unilaterally cancelled by the debtor, and mortgaged assets may be abandoned to mortgagees. Management operates the company in the "ordinary course of business" and is protected against direct control or removal by stockholders. Major assets, including whole divisions, may be divested with court approval.

49   Ideally, the plan will provide that the value of the going concern which emerges from reorganization will be allocated first to the administrative costs of the proceeding and then to the claimant classes in order of their "absolute priority in liquidation." This suggests that prefiling claims on the debtor estate will be satisfied in this sequence: (1) secured debt (up to the value of respective collateral as of the filing date), (2) unsecured debt, and (3) equity claims in order of preference (e.g., preferred, then common). However, plans commonly depart from this "fair and equitable" standard in order to get the support of junior claimant classes. Also, the "value" claimants receive may be in the form of cash, securities, or other real or personal property.

50   Provision is made to pay postfiling claims as they come due. To ensure that the reorganized firm is viable, prefiling claims not provided for in the plan are discharged.

Appendix D: Selected Provisions of the Manville Plan

51   Class 1 claims (unpaid administrative expenses totaling about $26 million—most administrative costs were paid as accrued) will be paid in full upon consummation.

52   Class 2 claims (secured debts) will be reinstated, with interest, and $13.4 million in arrearages will be paid in cash.

53   Class 3 claims (over $80 billion in property damage claims—due to the need to remove asbestos from existing buildings—most of which were filed after 1982) will be paid as they are "liquidated" from the PD trust (set up to pay the property damage claims). The PD trust will be initially funded with $125 million in cash and any insurance proceeds in excess of the $615 million committed to fund the trust for asbestos health claims (the trust). Any future funding for the PD trust will come from the excess of that needed by the trust to pay asbestos health claims.

54   Class 4 claims (existing asbestos health claims, totaling over $30.5 billion, and claims for contribution and indemnity by Manville's asbestos company codefendants) will be paid from the trust as they are liquidated and approved by the "Claims Resolution Facility," to be controlled by a panel of trustees approved by the bankruptcy court (none of the initial trustees has been affiliated with Manville Corporation). The trust will also be responsible for defending asbestos lawsuits brought against it, Manville, past and present Manville executives and directors, and certain insurance companies. Future asbestos health claims are not classified, but they will also be paid from the trust as liquidated. The trust will be funded with the following assets:

     1. All rights under settlement agreements Manville has or will execute with its insurers by the consummation date (30 days after an order of the bankruptcy court confirming the plan becomes final and unappealable). Manville reported the "face value" of these agreements to be $505 million as of May 23, 1986. Payment of the agreed amounts by the settling insurers is contingent upon a number of conditions, among them approval of the agreements by the bankruptcy

court (none had been approved when Manville filed its plan) and a final and unappealable court order barring future asbestos claims against the insurers.

2. $150 million in cash and accounts receivable.

3. A $50 million unsecured Manville Corporation note, promising payment with interest in two equal installments in the third and fourth years after the consummation date.

4. A Manville Corporation unsecured bond requiring payments of $75 million a year, without interest, from the 4th through the 25th year after the consummation date, subject to deferral after the 13th year if the trust is adequately funded in accordance with specified standards.

5. A Manville Corporation unsecured bond requiring payment of $75 million in each of the 26th and 27th years after the consummation date, subject to deferral if the trust is adequately funded in accordance with specified standards.

6. Certain interest on amounts set aside to fund the trust if consummation occurs later than July 1987.

7. If needed by the trust in accordance with specified standards and starting in the fifth year after consummation, up to 20 percent of Manville's profits and 20 percent of proceeds from the federal government (Manville claims government should pay part of the asbestos costs mainly because many of the claims resulted from work on navy ships).

8. One half of Manville's common stock at consummation. For four years after consummation the trust must vote this stock for management's nominees for directorships unless Manville allows certain events to occur which might prejudice the trust. With certain exceptions, this stock cannot be transferred by the trust for five years after consummation. The company has the right of first refusal on any sale of common stock by the trust which would result in the buyer holding more than 15 percent of Manville's outstanding common stock.

9. New convertible preferred stock, which would give the trust 80 percent of the firm's common equity if converted on the consummation date (convertibility is restricted).

55   Class 5 claims (about $20 million in miscellaneous claims on behalf of employees, users of defective roofing and siding products, and so forth) will be paid in full as liquidated, requiring payment of about $1 million in cash upon consummation.

56   Class 6 claims (unsecured claims not to exceed $472.5 million and not included in other classes) will be paid as follows:

1. Paid in cash if under $10,000—or if holder is willing to reduce claim to $10,000.

2. Paid pro rata share of $247.5 million less amounts paid in compliance with item 1, just above.

3. Issued "Class 6 note" for remaining principal amount of claim. Class 6 notes will be four-and-one-half-year, unsecured obligations of Manville Corporation drawing 12 percent interest and requiring biannual payments after consummation of at least $33.75 million each. They may be redeemed by Manville at any time and may be accelerated under certain conditions.

4. Paid cash for certain interest and investment income, which will accrue if consummation does not occur by July 1, 1987.

5. Issued "Class 6 interest debentures," Series B preference stock, common stock, and common stock warrants for interest accrued from August 26, 1982 (the date of Manville's Chapter 11 petition), to the consummation date.

57   Class 7 claimants (preferred stockholders) will receive for each preferred share a share of new Series B preference stock, which will pay cumulative dividends of $2.70 per share beginning six years after consummation (if certain conditions are met) and about 1.94 shares of common stock.

58   Class 8 claimants (common stockholders) will receive their pro rata share of 8.3 percent of common shares outstanding at consummation, subject to further dilution down to about 3 percent.

59   Class 9 claimants (certain purchasers of Manville common stock who have sued the company and certain of its officers and directors in federal court) will receive payment to the extent of certain insurance proceeds.

60   Among the "conditions precedent" to consummation of the plan are final and unappealable court orders establishing the following:

1. Any future asbestos health claims against Manville, the settling insurers, or the Canadian subsidiaries which were divested in 1983 are prohibited.
2. Allowed Class 6 claims (unsecured claims not elsewhere classified) will never exceed $472.5 million.
3. No punitive damages will be allowed for Class 3 or Class 4 claims (asbestos property damage and asbestos health claims) except for previously issued final judgments respecting liquidated asbestos health claims.
4. All transfers of property to the trusts by Manville are "legal, valid, and effective transfers," vest "good title to such property free and clear of all encumbrances, debts, obligations, liabilities, and claims other than asbestos claims as contemplated by the plan," are not "fraudulent," and "do not, except as contemplated by the plan, subject the trusts to any liability."
5. Certain agreements with the settling insurers are approved.

61   After consummation of the plan Manville's 15-person board of directors will consist of 8 preconsummation directors and 7 new directors. Two of the new directors will be chosen from persons suggested by representatives of the asbestos health claimants, three from a list of candidates approved by Manville and representatives of the asbestos health claimants, one from a list approved by Manville and the Unsecured Creditors' Committee, and another selected by the board of directors in consultation with claimant committees.

62   The eight preconsummation directors include six outside directors. The years they joined the Manville board are as follows: three in 1969, one in 1972, one in 1976, and the last in 1982. The outside director who joined in 1982 did so when his firm was hired as Manville's Chapter 11 law firm. The two inside directors are Manville's senior inside lawyer, G. Earl Parker, and the president, W. Thomas Stephens. The chairman of the board will be George C. Dillon, who has been a director of Manville since 1969.

63   The new directors include the chief executive of a regional discount store chain, the chief financial officer of a national department store chain, a professor of finance, a management consultant, a lawyer, and a financial consultant.

Case 19

Union Carbide of India, Ltd.

1   December 2, 1984, began as a typical day in the central Indian city of Bhopal. Shoppers moved about the bustling, open-air market. Here and there a customer haggled with a merchant. Beasts of burden, donkeys and oxen, pulled carts or carried ungainly bundles through the partly paved streets. Children played in the dirt. In the shadow of a Union Carbide pesticide plant, tens of thousands of India's poorest citizens milled about the shantytown they called home. A few miles away, wealthy Indians lived in opulence rivaling that of the first-class districts of London or Paris. Inside the plant, several hundred Indian workers and managers went about their duties, maintaining and operating the systems that produced the mildly toxic pesticide, Sevin. Most of the plant was shut down for maintenance, and it was operating at far below capacity.

2   At about 11 P.M. one of the operators noticed that the pressure in a methyl isocyanate (MIC) storate tank read 10 pounds per square inch—four times normal. The operator was not concerned, thinking that the tank might have been pressurized with nitrogen by the previous shift. Around midnight several of the workers noticed that their eyes had begun to water and sting, a signal experience had taught them indicated an MIC leak. The leak, a small but continuous drip, was soon spotted. The operators were still not alarmed because minor leaks at the plant were quite common. It was time for tea, and most of the crew retired to the company canteen, resolving to correct the problem afterward.

3   By the time the workers returned it was too late. The MIC tank pressure gauge was pegged. The leak had grown much larger, and the entire area of the MIC tanks was enveloped in the choking fumes. The workers tried spraying water on the leak to break down the MIC. They sounded the alarm siren and summoned the fire brigade. As the futility of their efforts became apparent, many of the workers panicked and ran upwind, some scaling the chain-link and barbed-wire fence in their frantic race for survival.

4   By 1 A.M. only a supervisor remained in the area. He stayed upwind, donning his oxygen-breathing apparatus every few minutes to check the various gauges and sensors. Pressure in the MIC tank had forced open a relief valve, and the untreated MIC vapor could be seen escaping from an atmospheric vent line 120 feet in the air.

5   The cloud of deadly white gas was carried by a southeasternly wind toward the Jai Prakash Nagar shanties. The cold temperature of the December night caused the MIC to settle toward the ground (in the daytime, or in the summer, convection currents probably would have raised and diluted the MIC).

6   As the gaseous tentacles reached into the huts there was panic and confusion. Many of the weak and elderly died where they lay. Some who made it into the streets were blinded. "It was like breathing fire," one survivor said. As word of the gas leak spread, many of Bhopal's affluent were able to flee in their cars. But most of the poor were left behind. When the gas reached the railroad station, supervisors who were not immediately disabled sent out word along the tracks, and incoming trains

Source: Arthur Sharplin, McNeese University. The research assistance of Aseem Shukla is gratefully acknowledged. Copyright © A. Sharplin, 1986.

were diverted. This diversion cut off a possible means of escape but may have saved hundreds of lives. Because the whole station was quickly enveloped in gas, arriving trains would have been death traps for passengers and crews.

7   Of Bhopal's total population of about 1 million, an estimated 500,000 fled that night, most on foot. The surrounding towns were woefully unprepared to accept the gasping and dying mass of people. Thousands waited outside hospitals for medical care. There was no certainty about how to treat the gas victims, and general-purpose medical supplies were in hopelessly short supply. Inside the hospitals and out, screams and sobs filled the air. Food supplies were quickly exhausted. People were even afraid to drink the water, not knowing if it was contaminated.

8   During the second day, relief measures were better organized. Several hundred doctors and nurses from nearby hospitals were summoned to help medical personnel in Bhopal. Just disposing of the dead was a major problem. Mass cremation was necessary. Islamic victims, whose faith allows burial rather than cremation, were piled several deep in hurriedly dug graves. Bloated carcasses of cattle and dogs littered the city. There was fear of a cholera epidemic. Bhopal's mayor said, "I can say that I have seen chemical warfare. Everything so quiet. Goats, cats, whole families—father, mother, children—all lying silent and still. And every structure totally intact. I hope never again to see it."

9   By the third day, the city had begun to move toward stability, if not normalcy. The Union Carbide plant had been closed and locked. A decision was made to consume the 30 tons of MIC that remained by using it to make pesticide. Most of the 2,000 dead bodies had been disposed of, however inappropriately. The more than 100,000 injured were being treated as rapidly as the limited medical facilities would allow, although many people simply sat in silence, blinded and maimed by an enemy they had never known well enough to fear. For them, doctors predict an increased risk of sterility, kidney and liver infections, tuberculosis, vision problems, and brain damage. The potential for birth defects and other long-term effects is not clear. However, months after the incident newspapers reported a high incidence of stillbirths and congenital deformities among the population that was affected by the gas.

Company Background

10   The Ever-Ready Company, Ltd. (of Great Britain), began manufacturing flashlight batteries in Calcutta in 1926. The division was incorporated as the Ever-Ready Company (India), Ltd., in 1934 and became a subsidiary of Union Carbide Corporation of New York. The name of the Indian company was changed to National Carbide Company (India), Ltd., in 1949 and to Union Carbide (India), Ltd. (UCIL), in 1959. The 1926 capacity of 40 million dry-cell batteries per year was expanded to 767 million by the 1960s. In 1959, a factory was set up in India to manufacture the flashlights themselves.

11   By the 1980s, UCIL was involved in five product areas: batteries, carbon and metals, plastics, marine products, and agricultural chemicals. Table 1 provides production statistics for UCIL products. The company eventually operated 15 plants at eight locations, including the headquarters operation in Calcutta. Union Carbide's petrochemical complex, established in Bombay in 1966, was India's first.

12   The marine products operation of UCIL was begun in 1971 with two shrimping ships. The business is completely export oriented and employs 15 deep-sea trawlers. Processing facilities are located off the east and west coasts of India. The trawlers now harvest deep-sea lobsters in addition to shrimp.

Table 1
Production statistics

Class of goods	1983 Capacity	Production levels					
		1983	1982	1981	1980	1979	1978
Batteries (millions of pieces)	792	510.4	512.2	411.3	458.8	460.3	430.3
Flashlight cases (millions of pieces)	7.5	6.7	6.7	7.4	6.9	6.4	5.7
Arc carbons (millions of pieces)	9.0	7.5	7.0	7.0	6.7	6.2	6.1
Industrial carbon electrodes and shapes (millions of pieces)	2.5	0.5	0.5	0.5	0.3	0.5	0.2
Photoengravers' plates/strips for printing (tonnes)*	1,200	412.0	478.0	431.0	399.0	469.0	506.0
Stellite castings, head facings, and tube rods (tonnes)	150	17.5	12.7	16.4	14.5	15.8	18.2
Electrolytic manganese dioxide (tonnes)	4,500	3,335	3,085	3,000	2,803	2,605	2,700
Chemicals (tonnes)	13,600	7,349	6,331	6,865	7,550	8,511	8,069
Polyethylene (tonnes)	20,000	18,144	17,290	19,928	19,198	16,324	12,059
MIC-based pesticides (tonnes)	5,000	1,647	2,308	2,704	1,542	1,496	367
Marine products (tonnes)	5,500	424	649	642	601	648	731

* One tonne = 1,000 kilograms = 2,214 pounds. One British long ton = 2,240 pounds. One U.S. ton = 2,000 pounds.

Source: The Stock Exchange Foundation, Bombay, India, *The Stock Exchange Official Directory* 17, no. 29 (July 18, 1983).

13   In 1979, UCIL initiated a letter of intent to manufacture dry-cell batteries in Nepal. A 77.5 percent owned subsidiary was set up in Nepal in 1982, and construction of an Rs. 18 million plant was begun.

14   The agricultural products division of UCIL was started in 1966 with only an office in Bombay. Agreement was reached with the Indian government in 1969 to set up a pesticide plant at Bhopal. Land was rented to UCIL for about $40 per acre per year. The initial investment was small, only $1 million, and the process was simple. Concentrated Sevin powder was imported from the United States, diluted with nontoxic powder, packaged, and sold. Under the technology-transfer provisions of its agreement with UCIL, Union Carbide Corporation (U.S.A.) was obliged to share its more advanced technologies with UCIL. Eventually the investment at Bhopal grew to exeeed $25 million, and the constituents of Sevin were made there. Another Union Carbide insecticide, called Temik, was made in small quantities at Bhopal.

Exhibit 1
The Foreign Exchange Regulation Act

The act was originally enacted as a temporary measure in 1947, and it was made permanent in 1957. It was revised and redrafted in 1973. It covers various aspects of foreign exchange transactions, including money changing, buying or selling foreign exchange in India or abroad, having an account in a bank outside India, and remitting money abroad.

The purpose of the act is to restrict outflow of foreign exchange and to conserve hard-currency holdings in India. One requirement of the act is that any company in which the nonresident interest is more than 40 percent "shall not carry on in India or establish in India any branch or office without the special permission of the Reserve Bank of India." But the Reserve Bank of India has authority to exempt a company from the provisions of the act. The 40 percent requirement was changed to 49 percent by Rajiv Gandhi's government.

High-technology companies are frequently exempted from the equity-ownership provisions of the act. Other companies that have operated in India for many years are sometimes exempted if they agree not to expand their Indian operations.

Policies in India regarding nationalization of foreign-owned companies have varied. A number of major oil companies have been nationalized. For example, Indian Oil Corporation, Bharat Petroleum, and Hindustan Petroleum used to be, respectively, Burmah Shell, Mobil, and Stanvae (Standard Vacuum Oil Company, an Esso unit). More typically, a multinational company is asked to reduce its holdings to 49 percent or less by offering shares to the Indian public and Indian financial institutions. Multinationals that have diluted equity to meet the 49 percent requirement include CIBA–GEIGY, Parke-Davis, Bayer (aspirin), Lever Brothers (which operates as Hindustan Lever in India), Lipton, and Brooke-Bond.

---

15   The assets of UCIL grew from Rs. 558 million in 1974 to Rs. 1,234 million in 1983 (the conversion rate stayed near 9 rupees to the dollar during this period, moving to about 12 as the dollar strengthened worldwide during 1984 and 1985; see Table 3). The *Economic Times* of India ranked UCIL number 21 in terms of sales among Indian companies. Union Carbide Corporation (U.S.A.) owned 50.9 percent of UCIL's stock, and Indian citizens and companies owned the remainder. When Indira Gandhi was voted out of office in 1977, the Janata (Peoples') Party strengthened the Foreign Exchange Regulation Act (FERA) (see Exhibit 1). As a result, IBM and Coca-Cola pulled out of India; IBM's business in India was taken over by ICIM (International Computers Indian Manufacturers), a domestic firm. Another similar firm was set up to perform the maintenance services for the existing IBM computers.

16   Since 1967 the chairman of the board of UCIL has been an Indian, and foreign membership on the 11-member board of directors has been limited to four. One expert on Indian industry affairs said, "Though the foreigners on the board are down to four from six in previous years, they continue to hold sway over the affairs of the company." Major capital expenditures by UCIL were required to be approved by Union Carbide Corporation. Also, the Bhopal plant submitted monthly reports to U.S. corporate headquarters detailing operations and safety procedures. And inspections of the plant were carried out from time to time by Union Carbide technical specialists.

Operations at Bhopal

17   On the surface, the UCIL insecticide factory is a typical process plant. A wide diversity of storage tanks, hoppers, and reactors are connected by pipes. There are many pumps and valves and a number of tall vent lines and ducts. Ponds and pits are used for waste treatment, and several railway spur lines run through the plant. Figure 1 is a

Figure 1
The UCIL pesticide factory at Bhopal

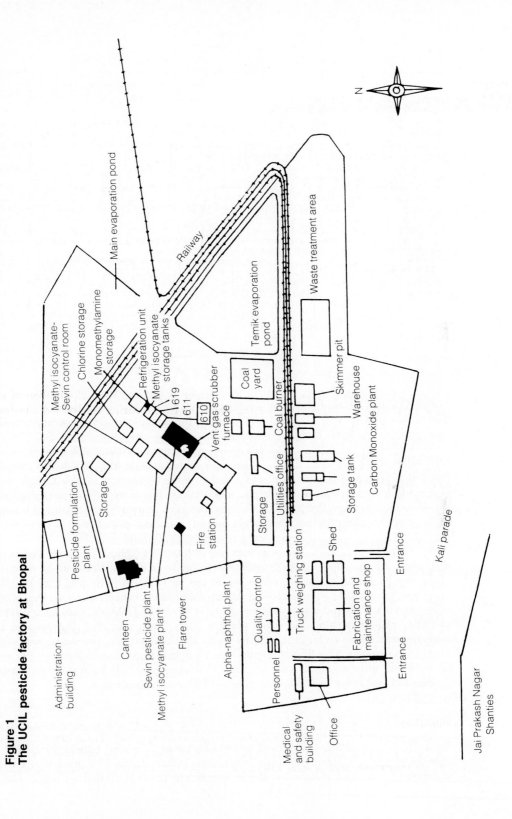

Figure 2
The methyl isocyanate manufacturing process

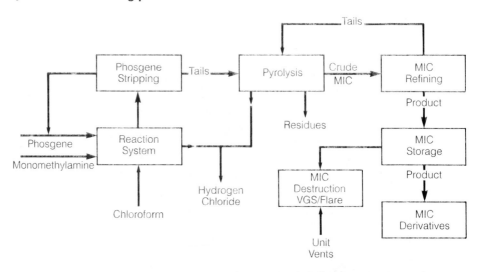

diagram of the factory. Figure 2 is a schematic of just the MIC manufacturing process. The pesticide plant was designed and supplied by Union Carbide Corporation, which sent engineers to India to supervise construction.

18   Sevin is made through a controlled chemical reaction involving alpha-naphthol and MIC. Alpha-naphthol is a brownish granular material, and MIC is a highly reactive liquid that boils and becomes a gas at usual daytime temperatures. When plans were first made to begin production of alpha-naphthol at Bhopal in 1971, a pilot plant was set up to manufacture the product. Because the pilot plant was successful, a full-size alpha-naphthol plant (in fact, the world's largest) was constructed and placed in operation in 1977.

19   In the meantime, work had begun on the ill-fated MIC plant. But even before the MIC plant was completed in 1979, problems began to crop up with the alpha-naphthol plant, resulting in a shutdown for modifications in 1978. In February 1980 the MIC plant was placed into service. The alpha-naphthol plant continued in various stages of shutdown and partial operation through 1984. Mr. V. P. Gokhale, managing director of UCIL, called the alpha-naphthol plant a "very large mistake." But he said the company was forced to build it in order to retain the operating license issued by the Indian government. The Bhopal factory was designed to produce 5,000 tons per year of Sevin but never operated near capacity; UCIL has generally been the third largest producer of pesticides in India, sometimes slipping to number four.

Finance

20   Tables 2, 3, 4, and 5 and Figure 3 provide financial facts and figures for UCIL. As mentioned earlier, Union Carbide Corporation (U.S.A.) holds 50.9 percent of UCIL's common shares. The remainder of the shares are publicly traded on major Indian

Table 2
Summary of income statements (for years ended December 25)

	1984 Rs. lakhs*	1983 Rs. lakhs	1982 Rs. lakhs
Income:			
Sales (excluding value of products used internally—Rs. 57,65.80 lakhs; previous year—Rs. 53,92.51 lakhs)	222,89.77[†]	210,19.60	206,38.14
Other sources	1,32.40	1,96.06	2,83.28
Total	224,22.17	212,15.66	209,21.42
Expenditure:			
Materials consumed	99,16.01	91,59.84	95,46.63
Excise duty	34,03.09	28,58.85	28,65.04
Operating expenses	65,97.52	66,68.39	60,98.25
Depreciation	5,01.12	4,75.79	4,16.14
Interest	4,73.15	5,75.29	5,26.61
Total	208,90.89	197.38.16	194,52.67
Profit before taxation	15,31.28	14,77.50	14,68.75
Provision for taxation	7,10.00	5,45.20	5,02.00
Profit after taxation	8,21.28	9,32.30	9,66.75
Transfer to investment allowance reserve	1,05.00	75.00	1,90.00
Subtotal	7,16.28	8,57.30	7,76.75
Transfer from development rebate reserve	13.08	9.38	1.22
Balance brought forward from previous year	1,07.92	0.00	26.30
Available for appropriation	8,37.28	8,66.68	8,04.27
Appropriations:			
Debenture stock redemption reserve	1,00.00	70.00	90.00
Unclaimed dividends paid	0.01	0.01	0.03
Interim dividend (@ R. 0.50 per share)	1,62.92	0.00	
Proposed dividend (subject to taxation)	0.00	4,88.75	4,88.75
General reserve	0.00	2,00.00	2,25.49
Balance carried forward to balance sheet	5,74.35	1,07.92	0.00

* 1 lakh = 100,000.

† Placement of commas in numbers differs from American practice.

stock exchanges. Most of these shares are held by about 24,000 individuals. However, a number of institutional investors own substantial blocks. The Indian government does not own any UCIL stock directly, although the Life Insurance Corporation of India, the country's largest insuror and owner of many UCIL shares, is owned by the Indian government. During the months before the Bhopal disaster, UCIL's common shares hovered around Rs. 30, but dropped to a low of Rs. 15.8 on December 11, recovering only slightly in succeeding weeks.

21   In 1974, the U.S. Export-Import Bank, in cooperation with First National Citibank of New York, agreed to grant loans of $2.5 million to buy equipment for the MIC project. Also, the Industrial Credit and Investment Corporation of India (ICICI) authorized a Rs. 21.5 million loan, part of which was drawn in 1980. Finally, long-term loans were provided by several Indian financial institutions and insurance companies. Some of these loans were guaranteed by the State Bank of India.

Table 3
Wholesale price levels in the United States and India and dollar-to-rupee conversion rates,
1974–1984

Year	U.S. producer price index*	India wholesale price index†	Conversion rate‡
1974	161.1	169.2	8.111
1975	175.1	175.8	8.914
1976	183.6	172.4	8.985
1977	195.8	185.4	8.703
1978	197.1	185.0	8.189
1979	215.8	206.5	8.108
1980	244.5	248.1	7.872
1981	269.8	278.4	8.728
1982	280.7	285.3	9.492
1983	285.2	398.5	10.129
1984	291.1	334.0	11.402
1985			11.930§

* Wholesale price index before 1978. Arithmetic average of January–December monthly figures. Base year, 1967 (January–December).

† Arithmetic average of April–March monthly figures. Base year, 1970 (April 1970–March 1971).

‡ Arithmetic average of monthly figures (rupees per dollar).

§ October 7, 1985, only.

22   Profits of several million dollars from the Bhopal facility were originally predicted for 1984. Several factors kept these expectations from being realized. First, an economic recession made farmers more cost conscious and caused them to search for less expensive alternatives to Sevin. Second, a large number of small-scale producers were able to undersell the company, partly because they were exempt from excise and sales taxes. Seventeen of these firms bought MIC from UCIL and used it to make products virtually identical to Sevin and Temik. Finally, a new generation of low-cost pesticides was becoming available. With sales collapsing, the Bhopal plant became a money loser in 1981. By late 1984, the profit estimate for that year had been adjusted downward to a $4 million *loss* based on 1,000 tons of output, one fifth of capacity.

23   To forestall what may have seemed inevitable economic failure, extensive cost-cutting efforts were carried out. The staff at the MIC plant was cut from 12 operators on a shift to 6. The maintenance team was reduced in size. In a number of instances, faulty safety devices remained unrepaired for weeks. Because a refrigeration unit, designed to keep the MIC cool, continued to malfunction, it was shut down. Though instrumentation technology advanced at Union Carbide's other pesticide plants, the innovations were only partly adopted at Bhopal.

24   The UCIL directors disclaim fault for the incident. The "Report of the Directors," included in UCIL's 1984 annual report, states:

> At no time had any significant fault been found with the working or safety precautions taken by your company. Your company had taken all safety precautions to avoid any accident in the plant, which had been operated all along with trained and qualified operators.

Table 4
Summary of balance sheets (as of December 25)

	1984 Rs. lakhs*		1983 Rs. lakhs		1982 Rs. lakhs	
Funds employed						
Fixed assets:						
Goodwill at cost	30.00		30.00		30.00	
Fixed assets	44,18.59†		41,07.55		40,51.60	
Capital expenditure in progress . . .	2,23.36	46,71.95	5,50.51	46,88.06	4,43.86	45,25.46
Investments		1,37.48		92.37		96.52
Current assets:						
Stores and spares at cost	7,32.53		6,86.16		6,40.67	
Stocks	32,63.68		30,05.56		31,32.50	
Sundry debtors	16,27.25		23,93.25		30,00.83	
Cash and bank balances	5,38.88		4,23.79		5,22.05	
Loans and advances	12,23.91		8,87.32		7,87.21	
Interest accrued on investments . . .	0.03		0.25		0.25	
Subtotal	73,86.28		73,96.33		80,83.51	
Less: Current liabilities	20,53.60		21,34.92		23,36.49	
Less: Provisions	6,10.68		10,07.14		10,71.12	
Subtotal	26,64.28		31,42.06		34,07.61	
Net current assets		47,22.00		42,54.27		46,75.90
Total		95,31.43		90,34.70		92,97.88
Financed by						
Share capital and reserves:						
Share capital—issued and subscribed	32,58.30		32,58.30		32,58.30	
Reserves and surplus	35,97.32	68,55.62	29,38.97	61,97.27	24,95.43	57,53.73
Loan capital:						
Secured loans	13,53.56		14,33.75		22,32.15	
Unsecured loans	13,22.25	26,75.81	14,03.68	28,37.43	13,12.00	35,44.15
Total		95,31.43		90,34.70		92,97.88

* 1 lakh = 100,000.

† Placement of commas in numbers differs from American practice.

Personnel

25 Until 1982, a cadre of American managers and technicians worked at the Bhopal plant. The Americans were licensed by the Indian government for fixed periods of time. While in India they were expected to train Indian replacements. From 1982 onward, no American worked at Bhopal. Although major decisions, such as approval of the annual budget, were cleared with Union Carbide (U.S.A.), day-to-day details such as staffing and maintenance were left to the Indian officials.

26   In general, the engineers at the Bhopal plant were among India's elite. Most new engineers were recruited from the prestigious Indian Institutes of Technology and were paid wages comparable with the best offered in Indian industry. Successful applicants for engineering jobs with UCIL were given two years of training before being certified for unsupervised duty.

Table 5
Summary of common stock issues

| Year | Paid-up common stock | | Remarks |
	Number of shares	Total amount (Rs. 000)	
1959–1960	2,800,000	28,000	800,000 right shares issued, premium Rs. 2.50 per share, proportion 2:5.
1964	3,640,000	36,400	840,000 right shares issued, premium of Rs. 4 per share, proportion 3:10.
1965	4,095,000	40,950	455,000 bonus shares issued, proportion 1:8.
1968	8,190,000	81,900	2,047,500 right shares issued at par, proportion 1:2; 2,047,500 bonus shares issued, proportion 1:2.
1970	12,285,000	122,850	4,095,000 bonus shares issued, proportion 1:2.
1974	18,427,500	184,275	6,142,500 bonus shares issued, proportion 1:2.
1978	21,722,000	217,220	3,294,500 shares issued, premium Rs. 6 per share, to resident Indian shareholders, the company's employees, and financial institutions.
1980	32,583,000	325,830	10,861,000 bonus shares issued, proportion 1:2.

27   Until the late 1970s only first-class science graduates or persons with diplomas in engineering were employed as operators at Bhopal. New employees were given six months of theoretical instruction followed by on-the-job training. As cost-cutting efforts proceeded in the 1980s, standards were lowered significantly. Some operators with only a high school diploma were employed, and training was much less rigorous than before. In addition, the number of operators on a shift was reduced by about half, and many supervisory positions were eliminated.

28   The Indian managers developed strong ties with the local political establishment. A former police chief became the plant's security contractor, and a local political party boss got the job as company lawyer. *Newsweek* reported that a luxurious guest house was maintained, and lavish parties were thrown there for local dignitaries.

29   In general, wages at the Bhopal plant were well above those available in domestic firms. A janitor, for example, earned Rs. 1,000 per month, compared to less than Rs. 500 elsewhere. Still, as prospects continued downward after 1981, a number of senior managers and the best among the plant's junior executives began to abandon ship. The total work force at the plant dropped from a high of about 1,500 to 950. This reduction was accomplished through voluntary departures rather than layoffs. An Indian familiar with operations at Bhopal said, "The really competent and well-trained employees, especially managers and supervisors, got sick of the falling standards and indifferent management, and many of them quit despite high salaries at UCIL. Replacements were made on an ad hoc basis. Even guys from the consumer products division, who only knew how to make batteries, were drafted to run the pesticide plant."

Marketing

30   The population of India is over 700 million persons, although its land area is only about one third that of the United States. Three fourths of India's people depend on agriculture for a livelihood. Fewer than one third of the population are literate. Modern

Figure 3
UCIL financial charts

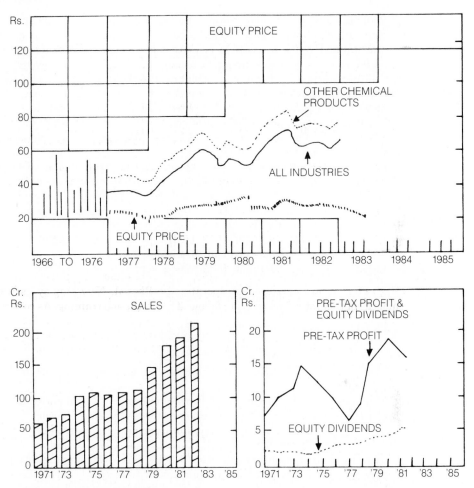

Note: 1 crore = 10 million rupees.

communications and transportation facilities connect the major cities, but the hundreds of villages are largely untouched by 20th-century technology. English tends to be at least a second language for most Indian professionals but not for ordinary Indians. There are 16 officially recognized languages in the country. The national language is Hindi, which is dominant in 5 of India's 22 states. The working classes speak hundreds of dialects, often unintelligible to citizens just miles away.

31   India's farmers offer at best a challenging target market. They generally eke out a living from small tracts of land. Most have little more than subsistence incomes and are reluctant to invest what they have in such modern innovations as pesticides. They are generally ignorant of the right methods of application and, given their linguistic

diversity and technological isolation, are quite hard to educate. To advertise its products, UCIL has used billboards and wall posters as well as newspaper and radio advertisements.

32   Radio is the most widely used advertising medium in India. The state-owned radio system includes broadcasts in local languages. Companies can buy advertising time on the stations, but it is costly to produce commercials in so many dialects. Much of the state-sponsored programming, especially in rural areas, is devoted to promoting agriculture and instructing farmers about new techniques. Often the narrators mention products such as Sevin and Temik by name.

33   Movies provide another popular promotional tool. Most small towns have one or more cinema houses, and rural people often travel to town to watch the shows. Advertisements appear before and after main features and are usually produced in regional languages (though not in local dialects).

34   Until recently, television was available only in the cities. During 1984, a government program spread TV relay stations at the rate of more than one each day, with the result that 80 percent of the population was within the range of a television transmitter by the end of the year. Still, few rural citizens had access to television receivers.

35   Pesticide sales are highly dependent on agricultural activity from year to year. In years of drought, like 1980 and 1982, UCIL's pesticide sales suffered severe setbacks. In 1981, abundant rains helped spur pesticide sales.

36   Figure 4 is a map of India. India has a very extensive network of railways; the total track mileage is second only to the Soviet Union. The road and highway system crisscrosses the areas in between the railway lines. The railway system was especially significant to UCIL's pesticide operation because Bhopal lies near the junction of the main east–west and north–south tracks in India. Bhopal is also just south of the vast Indo–Gangetic plain, the richest farming area in India. An Indian familiar with the agricultural economy remarked, "Overall, physical distribution of pesticides is not too monumental a task. Getting farmers to use them and teaching them how are the real problems."

37   The marketing division for agricultural products was headquartered in Hyderabad. Under the headquarters were eight branch offices scattered all over the country. Sales were made through a network of distributors, wholesalers, and retailers. Sales representatives from the branch offices booked orders from the distributors and wholesalers. Retailers got their requirements from wholesalers, who, in turn, were supplied by distributors. The distributors got their stocks from the branch offices. The branch office "godowns" (warehouses) were supplied directly from the Bhopal plant. The retailers' margin was 15 percent. Wholesalers and distributors each received about 5 percent. Most of the retailers were family or individually owned, although some of UCIL's pesticides were sold through government agricultural sales offices.

Events of 1985

38   In early 1985, the government of India canceled the operating license of the Bhopal plant, clearing the way for the plant's dismantlement. The likelihood that this would happen provoked a Bhopal political leader to remark, "We've lost 2,000 lives, now must we lose 2,000 jobs?"

39   Manslaughter and other charges were filed against UCIL executives. Union Carbide Corporation Chairman Warren Anderson had been briefly detained by Indian officials

Figure 4
Map of India

when he went to India shortly after the incident. Still, both companies continued for months to enjoy good relations with the Indian government. This may have been true in part because many leading Indian citizens and institutions have a financial interest in UCIL. And, except for the Bhopal incident, Union Carbide had an excellent safety record in India.

40   Warren Anderson said, "The name of the game is not to nail me to the wall but to provide for the victims of the disaster." He said he expected to be mainly concerned with the incident for the rest of his working life. Union Carbide Corporation offered to help provide funding for a hospital to treat the Bhopal victims. The company also contributed $1 million to a victims' relief fund. UCIL offered to built a new plant, one that would use nontoxic inputs, on the Bhopal site. One proposal was for a nonhazardous "formulation plant" to be constructed by UCIL and operated by the state government. Alternatively, UCIL suggested a battery factory to be owned and operated by the company. Both ideas were turned down in a letter dated May 15, 1985.

41   Within months after the incident, Union Carbide (U.S.A.) faced lawsuits in amounts far exceeding the company's net worth. That company's stock dropped from its mid-50s trading range to the low 30s. A dozen or more American attorneys signed up thousands of Bhopal victims and relatives of victims and filed suits in America purporting to represent them. The attorney general of India was authorized to sue Union Carbide in an American court. He stated that compensation had to be in accordance with American standards. A Minneapolis law firm that specializes in product liability cases was retained to represent India.

42   By March 1985 the streets of Bhopal were bustling again. There were cars, cattle, and crowds of people. But everywhere there were reminders of the disaster. Many people wore dark glasses and covered their faces with shrouds to protect their injured eyes from the sunlight or to keep others from seeing their blindness. At the city's main police station, women and children continued to seek help. Vegetables shriveled by the poison gas were putting forth green shoots here and there. Occasionally, someone still fell sick from eating fish contaminated by MIC.

43   In the modernistic masonry-and-glass headquarters in Danbury, Connecticut, Union Carbide officials could look out on the beautiful Connecticut countryside and consider how best to manage the company's public affairs and how to grapple with the needs in India. Half a world away, in philosophical as well as physical distance, the poor of Jai Prakash Nagar, then poorer than ever, peered out from their shanties onto dusty streets and undoubtedly pondered quite different questions: From where would tomorrow's food come? How long would the pain inside and the dimming of vision last? And, just as important, what source of wealth would replace the pesticide plant? And how long would it be before its effects were felt?

44   In late June 1985, a lawsuit consolidating about 100 claims was filed in the United States by famed attorney F. Lee Bailey and his associates. The Indian government continued to press its lawsuit and to engage in out-of-court negotiations with Union Carbide. As the lawsuits in America moved forward, the legal issues involved became clearer:

1. Should the cases be tried in U.S. courts or in Indian courts? Both legal systems are based on English common law, but punitive damages are almost unheard of in Indian courts, and compensatory damage awards are much lower than in America.

2. Should settlements be based on American standards simply because Union Carbide, the 51 percent parent of UCIL, is an American company, or on the much lower standards in India?

3. Who is responsible for the incident—Union Carbide, the Indian managers at Bhopal, the mostly Indian board of directors of UCIL, or the Indian government?

4. Which victims should be represented by the Indian government and which by the U.S. attorneys who went to India after the incident and signed up clients?

5. Did Union Carbide fail to properly warn the Indian managers at UCIL of the dangers posed by MIC?

6. Did Union Carbide fail to ensure that appropriate safety equipment was installed at the Bhopal facility?

45   Negotiations between Union Carbide and Asoke K. Sen, the Indian law minister, seemed to have broken down in June 1985. Union Carbide had made a $230 million

offer, with payment to be spread over 20 years. Mr. Sen said the offer was worth only $100 million in current terms and continued, "Union Carbide's offer is based on a total lack of appreciation of the magnitude of the problem, so is hardly worth consideration." He said that doctors have treated 200,000 Indians injured by the gas leak and that the government is having to build 15,000 housing units and a 100-bed hospital to care for the most seriously ill.

46   On the other hand, a Union Carbide spokesperson said that $100 million could "pay the heirs of each dead person 100 years annual income . . . and the seriously injured 20 years annual income," leaving funds left over. The U.S. district judge under whom the Indian court cases were consolidated requested that Union Carbide pay $5 million in emergency aid, but that was rejected by the Indian officials. Mr. Sen said that India had already spent several times more than that on relief and that $5 million would not serve a critical need. A $268 million "five-year master plan" of economic development was announced by Indian officials in August 1985, but funding had not been approved. The plan called for redevelopment near the plant and in the city of Bhopal, including building 5,000 houses, 12 hospitals, an electric trolley transportation system, and a number of "work sheds" to employ and train the unskilled and semiskilled among the gas victims.

47   As Union Carbide (U.S.A.) struggled to recover from the disaster and restore its favorable public image, four events thrust the company back to the forefront of national and international news coverage. In June 1985, hundreds of persons were poisoned by California watermelons grown on soil to which the Union Carbide pesticide Temik had been applied (improperly applied, according to the company). In August, a leak of the chemical intermediate aldecarb oxime at the company's Institute, West Virginia, plant, the only U.S. facility to make MIC, sent 135 people to hospitals. A few days later another accidental discharge of chemicals at a Union Carbide plant just miles from the Institute facility caused a public health scare. Finally, GAF Corporation increased its holdings of Union Carbide stock and announced an effort to gain control of the corporation. Union Carbide managers rushed to erect takeover barriers and took actions to make the company less desirable as a merger candidate. Union Carbide Corporation (U.S.A.) was reorganized into two separately incorporated divisions, one for chemicals and plastics and one for other products. As part of the reorganization, the company wrote down various assets by nearly $1 billion (almost none of this was related to UCIL) and made plans to spend $500 million of surplus in the employee retirement fund "for general corporate purposes."

48   Even though West Virginia Governor Arch Moore publicly criticized Union Carbide's handling of the aldecarb oxime leak and CEO Warren Anderson admitted that the company had waited too long to warn residents, Union Carbide stock moved above $50 a share for the first time since the Bhopal incident.

49   A number of UCIL employees and gas victims interviewed nearly a year after the incident generally agreed that "Union Carbide" (no distinction was made between the U.S. parent and its Indian subsidiary) and the government were to blame, that proper safety measures could have prevented the disaster, that the plant should be dismantled, and that the victims should receive economic and medical help as well as compensation for their injuries. A visitor to the area at about that time wrote,

> I saw the notorious UCIL plant from a distance. There are no plans to reopen
> it. Most of the workers have found other jobs. Bhopal looks normal on the surface,

but a claims court right opposite the railway station with a big crowd of widows and dependents who had come to take their claims was a grim reminder.

Also got some first-hand accounts. Most of the railway personnel are coughing and wheezing even now. There are lots of people whose lungs have been permanently damaged (the corrosive nature of the gas has caused fibrosis, i.e., formation of scar tissue, so lung volume has reduced).

50   As the end of 1985 approached, there were few indications of progress toward settling the lawsuits. None of the victims had been compensated. UCIL was essentially out of the pesticide business, although the company's other divisions, especially those involving batteries and flashlights, remained profitable. UCIL's common stock traded near 30 rupees (Rs. 30), where it had been before the disaster, and Union Carbide Corporation common stock was still trading above $50.

Case 20

Goodyear Tire & Rubber Company (South Africa)

Overview

1 In 1985 and 1986, Goodyear Tire & Rubber Company faced its most trying years in South Africa since starting operations there in 1916. Civil unrest, resulting from a system of apartheid, added to the depressed economic conditions of the country to create a troubled business environment. These problems were coupled with growing calls from social activists and political pressures in the United States for companies to divest their holdings in South Africa. Goodyear executives voiced opposition to divestiture, arguing that it would harden white segregationist attitudes and harm the workers it was supposed to help.

Background and Outlook: Goodyear Tire & Rubber Company

2 The Goodyear Tire & Rubber Company was incorporated in Ohio on August 29, 1898, and went on to become the world's largest tire and rubber company. By 1986, it controlled one third of the U.S. tire business and one fifth of the world market. The company produced tires and transportation products, which included new tires, retreads, wheels, rims, automotive belts and hoses, molded parts and foam cushioning, industrial rubber, and chemical and plastic products. Other Goodyear businesses provided defense systems, military aviation systems, agricultural products, and automotive accessories and repair services through 2,000 retail stores.

3 In the 1970s and 1980s the company faced competition from two major firms, Michelin of France and Bridgestone of Japan. To battle that competition the company spent $3.2 billion to upgrade plant and equipment around the world, $2 billion of it tied directly to radial tires. By 1985, Goodyear controlled 20 percent of the world tire market, ahead of Michelin (13 percent) and Bridgestone (8 percent).

4 In 1984, Goodyear had earnings of $411 million on sales of $10.2 billion, a record year for the company, but the value of the stock fell from $36.87 in December 1982 to $24 in November 1984. (See Appendix A; also see Exhibit 1 for data on gross revenues, operational profit margin, return on equity, net income, earnings per share, and share prices from 1975 to 1985.)

5 Goodyear's position in the tire business was stronger than ever in 1986, and the company was hoping to use cash from its tire business to finance its expansion into aerospace, oil, and gas. One of the biggest reasons for this newfound strength was Goodyear's highly sophisticated production methods. Some of its plants were considered at least 50 percent more efficient than major competitors' old passenger-tire plants. Goodyear had by far the largest single share of the U.S. market for tires of all types— almost 30 percent of the industry's total capacity. Firestone was a distant second with 14 percent, followed by Gencorp with 11 percent, and Goodrich and Uniroyal

---

This case was prepared by John A. Pearce II of George Mason University and Julio O. DeCastro of the University of South Carolina. Copyright © 1986 by John A. Pearce II.

Exhibit 1
Goodyear financial statistics

Year	Gross revenues ($ millions)	Operating profit margin (%)	Return on equity (%)	Net income ($ millions)	Working capital ($ millions)	Senior capital ($ millions)	Shares (000s)	Earnings per share ($)	Dividends per share ($)	Dividend payments (%)	Price range	Price/earnings	Average yield (%)
1975	$ 5,452.5	7.4%	8.9%	$161.6	$ 987	$ 880.1	71,645	$2.24	$1.10	49%	23⅛–12¾	8.0	6.1%
1976	5,791.5	6.3	6.6	122.0	1,077	930.2	71,775	1.69	1.10	67	25¼–20¼	13.5	4.8
1977	6,628.0	8.1	10.4	205.8	1,240	1,125.8	71,466	2.85	1.20	42	23⅞–16¾	7.1	5.9
1978	7,489.1	7.9	10.7	226.1	1,496	1,418.4	71,535	3.12	1.30	42	18½–15⅜	5.4	7.7
1979	8,238.7	5.0	6.8	146.2	1,534	1,462.1	71,681	2.02	1.30	64	18⅞–11⅞	7.6	8.5
1980	8,444.0	6.2	9.0	206.7[a]	1,477	1,240.6	71,761	2.85[a]	1.30	46	18⅜–10¾	5.1	8.9
1981	9,152.9	2.2	10.3	243.9	1,527	1,157.8	72,071	3.36	1.30	39	20¼–15⅞	5.4	7.2
1982	8,688.7	8.1	10.8	247.6	1,576	1,174.1	74,142	3.35	1.40	42	36⅞–17⅞	8.2	5.1
1983	9,735.8	7.4	10.1	270.4[b]	1,388	665.2	105,425	2.71[b]	1.40	52	36⅜–27	11.7	4.4
1984	10,240.8	7.5	13.0	411.0	1,342	656.8	106,493	3.87	1.50	39	31½–23	7.0	5.5
1985[c]	9,585.1	5.8	12.0	412.4	950	997.5	108,110	3.84	1.60	42	31¼–25⅛	7.3	4.9

[a] Before $24 million (33 cents a share) credit in 1981 and $17.2 million (24 cents a share) credit in 1982.

[b] Before $35.1 million (35 cents per share), extraordinary credit in 1983.

[c] Financial statistics for the year 1985 reflect changes in reporting that caused dollar figures to artificially appear depressed.

Adapted from Standard & Poor's Corporation records, 1985.

Exhibit 2

THE GOODYEAR TIRE & RUBBER COMPANY AND SUBSIDIARIES
Consolidated Statement of Income
(dollars in millions, except per share)

	Year Ended December 31,		
	1985	1984	1983
Net Sales	$9,585.1	$9,628.5	$9,031.6
Other Income	118.2	85.5	61.4
	9,703.3	9,714.0	9,093.0
Cost and Expenses:			
Cost of goods sold	7,635.1	7,581.9	7,073.5
Selling, administrative and general expense	1,469.6	1,357.7	1,316.1
Interest and amortization of debt discount and expense	105.2	117.3	108.6
Plant closures and sale of facilities	(2.4)	(9.8)	73.8
Foreign currency exchange	32.7	45.8	55.6
Minority interest in net income of foreign subsidiaries	6.6	6.4	6.4
	9,246.8	9,099.3	8,634.0
Income from continuing operations before income taxes and extraordinary item	456.5	614.7	459.0
United States and foreign taxes on income	155.2	253.8	226.5
Income from continuing operations before extraordinary item	301.3	360.9	232.5
Discontinued operations	111.1	50.1	37.9
Income before extraordinary item	412.4	411.0	270.4
Extraordinary item—gain on long term debt retired	—	—	35.1
Net Income	$ 412.4	$ 411.0	$ 305.5
Per Share of Common Stock:			
Income from continuing operations before extraordinary item	$2.81	$3.40	$2.33
Discontinued operations	1.03	.47	.38
Extraordinary item—gain on long term debt retired	—	—	.35
Net Income	$3.84	$3.87	$3.06

with 10 percent each. Exhibit 2 gives Goodyear's consolidated income statements for the years 1983 to 1985.

6   Goodyear executives hinted at a sales goal of $15 billion by 1989, and Chairman Robert E. Mercer also sought to boost return on sales to 5.0 percent, up from 3.1 percent in 1983, and to increase return on equity to 15 percent, up from 10.1 percent in 1983. He reportedly believed those goals could not be attained as long as the company was tilted toward the cyclical and slow-growth tire business.

7   As a result, in the early 1980s, the company began to diversify into industries that promoted faster growth and higher profit margins. Though Goodyear wanted to keep growing market share in the tire business, Chairman Mercer said that he would like tires to constitute only one half of total corporate sales. For this reason, Goodyear acquired Celeron Corporation in 1983, which was involved in natural gas production and transmission. The other half would be evenly divided between Celeron and the aerospace division. While analysts of the industry seemed to concur that Goodyear was doing the wise thing by diversifying, they were not sure the company had the expertise to run its new businesses.

8   The aerospace subsidiary of Goodyear was an impressive performer. The division had sales of $617 million in 1985, representing an increase of 85 percent over the previous year, and had matched or surpassed the industry average of 15 percent return on equity for each of the past four years. However, because the company was heavily dependent on military sales (70 percent of 1985 sales) it was difficult to predict the future growth of the company. The president of the division, Robert Clark, hoped for a minimum of 10 percent growth annually throughout the second half of the 1980s.

9   The corporate officers had even higher expectations. They hoped that the aerospace division would contribute 25 percent of Goodyear sales by 1990, which would require a 43 percent growth rate in the last four years of the decade. Thus, the possibility of one or more related acquisitions to boost the size of the operation was frequently rumored.

10   Celeron earnings declined from 1981 to 1985 after their 1981 peak of $108 million on sales of $901 million. The drops were attributed to a natural gas glut and the sale of a small electric utility subsidiary. After the company became a Goodyear subsidiary in 1985, Goodyear refused to disclose earnings, but Celeron sales in 1984 were known to have dropped to $762 million. The short-term prospects of beneficial changes in the price of natural gas were slim for 1986; however, the long-term prospects of the division looked brighter—partly because of the expected profits from its $750 million pipeline, which would carry 300,000 barrels of crude oil daily from southern California to west Texas. The pipeline was expected to be finished by 1987.

Civil Unrest in South Africa

11   The white population of South Africa traced its ancestry back to 1652. A group of Dutch settlers headed by Jan Van Riebeeck landed near the Cape of Good Hope. This white group of Dutch heritage did not consider themselves colonialists: they called themselves Africaners (Africans) and believed that South Africa was their country.

12   In political power since 1948, the governing Nationalist party tried to maintain the power and privileges in the hands of the Africaners through the policy of "Grand Apartheid." With this policy they intended to keep the Republic of South Africa as a white nation by dividing black South Africans among 10 "independent countries." In this way, whites could send the blacks not needed for low-level labor jobs to a "homeland."

Given the freedom of these independent countries, blacks were thought to be less likely to cause problems in white South Africa.

13   The government pursued this strategy in four ways: forced resettlement, influx control, financial deprivation of the homelands, and denationalization. Forced resettlement meant the forcible transportation of blacks to the homelands. Once in the homelands, the influx control laws prevented blacks from going back to white South Africa. A passbook system was used to implement the influx laws. Only blacks with a passbook could cross the checkpoints and go into the white cities. The government introduced denationalization by stripping 7.8 million black South Africans of their citizenship when it declared 4 of the 10 homelands as financially "independent" states.

14   In 1960, Grand Apartheid faced its first big test. A major black protest organized by the militant African National Congress (ANC) against the passbook system resulted in the deaths of 67 blacks and the wounding of 186 others in what would become known as the Sharpeville massacre. The massacre and the ensuing economic turmoil led to the imposition of rigid exchange controls in 1961 to prevent the outflow of capital. These exchange controls prevented any foreign company from removing capital assets from South Africa without the authorization of the South African minister of finance. The controls, which were abolished in 1983, were pegged to an artificial "financial rand," which forced a company that wanted to divest from its South African holdings to forfeit as much as 30 percent of its capital.

15   In 1976, police assaulted unarmed demonstrators in the homeland of Soweto, resulting in 600 deaths and 6,000 arrests. To defuse tension, the government issued an initiative to allow independent black labor organizations. This was followed in the early 1980s by a climate of repression, in which union leaders were often imprisoned for weeks or months without trial.

16   By 1984, the African National Congress was South Africa's largest and most influential black organization; its influence was due to the fact that it was recognized by the United Nations and was thoroughly entrenched in the black townships. The ANC espoused the overthrowing of the government and the nationalization of industry. It had been underground since 1960, when it was banned after the Sharpeville massacre.

17   The ANC was involved in a military struggle against the South African government, but its forces numbered only 8,000. Linked to guerilla warfare that diminished after March 1984, when Swaziland and Mozambique pledged to cooperate in the elimination of ANC bases, its minimal activities consisted principally of attacks on key South African and commercial military installations.

18   The South African government had the most advanced military force in all of Africa. The South African Defense Force could mobilize 250,000 men, had advanced combat equipment, and was thought by some observers to possess nuclear weapons. It was widely believed that the South African Army could contain any domestic military struggle—at least for a short period of time. The power of the South African military was exemplified by its 108 combat aircraft, one light bomber squadron, two fighter squadrons with Mirage III EZ and eight III DZ aircraft, three Daphne class submarines, and two destroyers with two wasp ASN helicopters.

19   The year 1985 was one of the most violent in South African history. Violence in the black townships produced 700 deaths and countless numbers of detainees. The country was declared to be in a state of emergency in July by President P. W. Botha.

20   The most revered leader of the black movement, Nelson Mandela, who had been in prison for treason since the Sharpeville massacre in 1962 (and to whom the government made numerous unaccepted clemency offers under the condition that he agree

to renounce revolutionary methods to overthrow the government), was ailing and, in October 1985, was hospitalized. Observers agreed that his death would have triggered an explosion of violence unlike any seen before in South Africa and, in turn, more government repression.

21 In August 1985, highly placed South African officials hinted that the government was ready to introduce dramatic social and economic reforms. However, President P. W. Botha failed to live up to the expectations. He announced only that his government would consider (1) extending national citizenship to the 24 million blacks; (2) improving, but not abolishing, the influx laws; and (3) negotiating with unspecified black leaders. No timetable for these changes was offered.

22 The Botha announcements were regarded as disappointing by all but strong government supporters. They were seen as too unspecific, too mild, and generally unresponsive to the country's pressing economic and social problems. Consequently, immediately following the announcements, U.S. federal and state governments moved to adopt tougher positions on the issue of investment in South Africa.

23 On September 9, 1985, President Reagan, prodded by growing concerns in the U.S. Senate over the South African situation, imposed a number of sanctions on the South African government. His white House executive order included a ban on U.S. bank loans to the South African government, a prohibition of computer sales and nuclear technology to South Africa's security agencies, and a ban on the sale of South African gold Krugerrands in the United States, all subject to approval by U.S. trading partners.

24 In an unprecedented move, a group of leading South African businessmen headed by Gavin W. H. Relly, chairman of the board of Anglo American Corporation, flew to Luzaka, Zambia, on September 13, 1985, to begin talks with Oliver Tambo, president-in-exile of the ANC. This marked the first time that the business community had bypassed the government in an effort to resolve issues of special concern to the black population.

25 In mid-1986, the civil unrest and the struggle between the government of Mr. Botha and the opposing forces continued. The economic situation in South Africa was deteriorating with no relief in sight, and another new force was coming into play. The black unions boasted a growing membership of 700,000 workers, thereby constituting half of the organized labor. Even though a strike called in October 1985 by the National Union of Mineworkers had collapsed after three days, the growing power of the South African black unions was expected to pressure the South African government for social action.

26 Nothing had come of the September 13, 1985, meeting between a group of South Africa's leading businessmen and the leadership of the ANC. The ANC leadership reiterated its position regarding nationalization of industry and armed struggle. But the decision by the businessmen to bypass the government and to talk directly with the rebels merited attention because it opened the door to possible solutions to the problems of South Africa.

The Economic Climate in South Africa

27 According to the Investor Responsibility Research Center, a Washington organization backed by business, 13 U.S. companies (including General Foods, Pan American World Airways, and PepsiCo) left south Africa in 1985. However, the South African holdings of those companies were a very small percent of the total foreign investment in the

Exhibit 3
U.S. companies disinvesting South African holdings

Apple Computer—citing "political reasons," suspended all operations in August, with October 1 closedown date.

BBDO International—sold 75 percent ownership in South African agency to local directors in August.

Blue Bell—sold a jeans manufacturing plant on December 31, 1984.

City Investing—financial services group sold as part of corporate liquidation program.

Coca-Cola—sold a majority interest in its bottling operation; control will be transferred over two years.

Ford Motor—merged automobile operation into Anglo American Corporation's Signa Motors Corporation in February, reducing stake to 40 percent and surrendering management.

General Foods—sold 20 percent stake in Cerebos affiliate.

Helena Rubinstein—closed cosmetics sales operation in June.

International Harvester—sold truck operation in August.

Oak Industries—sold electronic components plant in April.

Pan American World Airways—closed operations in April.

PepsiCo—sold both South African bottling plants in January.

Perkin-Elmer—sold manufacturing instruments and electrical components, as well as sales office, to former employees in February.

Phibro-Salomon—closed Johannesburg office in August.

Singer—sold marketing and distribution operations in April.

Smith International—sold affiliate in May as part of shift from mining and minerals to petroleum products.

Tidwell Industries—sold its home-building subsidiary to a local construction company in July.

West Point-Pepperell—sold a minority in a textile company in June.

Source: *Business Week*, September 23, 1985, p. 106.

country. A complete list of all U.S. companies that had left the country by October 1985 is given in Exhibit 3.

28   Other companies, including Ford Motor and Coca-Cola, were trying to reduce their stakes in South Africa. On January 30, 1985, Ford announced that it was merging its South African Auto Business with Amcar, a subsidiary of Anglo American Corporation, one of South Africa's biggest corporations. Ford retained 42 percent of the new company. Pursuing a similar strategy, Coca-Cola sold its controlling interest in Amalgamated Beverage Industries to South African Breweries for $36.6 million, retaining a 30 percent share.

29   The economic conditions in South Africa reached a low point in 1985. The rand, South Africa's official currency, lost 50 percent of its value from January to August and had an additional 35 percent plunge in September through October. Inflation was running at 16 percent, and the GNP, which had been stagnant since 1980, was forecast to fall 25 percent in 1985. It was estimated that just to maintain the current unemployment rate—which had averaged 13 percent from 1980 to 1985—the country's economy would need to grow at a 5 percent rate annually. Interest rates in South Africa in late 1985 were 20 percent, with black unemployment at 30 percent. (Refer to Appendix B for information on economic and social conditions in South Africa.)

30   The average after-tax return on investment of the 300 American companies with direct investments in South Africa fell from 30 percent in 1980 to 7 percent in 1983 and to 5 percent in 1985.

31   In August 1985, after international banks refused to roll over about half of South Africa's $12 billion short-term debt, the country declared a moratorium on repaying

the debt. Furthermore, to protect itself from the outflow of capital, it reimposed the exchange controls that it had lifted in 1983.

The Disinvestment Issue and South Africa

32   The proponents of disinvestment wanted changes in the corporate policies of U.S. firms with operations in South Africa. Change options included adherence to the Sullivan principles, social development expenditures, and total withdrawal. Institutions engaged in disinvestment included universities, churches, unions, and state governments.

33   In October 1985, laws in 11 U.S. cities and 9 states required public funds to divest some or all of their stock in companies with operations in South Africa. Additional disinvestment bills were introduced in 19 states in 1985, including New York and California, which had a combined continued investment of $26 billion in corporate securities.

34   Some states, like Connecticut, instituted provisions that linked disinvestment decisions to compliance with the Sullivan principles. The Connecticut law required that the state divest from its holdings in any company with failing Sullivan grades. Also, in November 1985, the U.S. Congress considered legislation sponsored by U.S. Representative Stephen Solars of New York and U.S. Representative William Gray III of Pennsylvania, which prohibited new investments in South Africa and required all companies operating in South Africa to adhere to principles similar to Sullivan's.

35   Banks, fund managers, and companies with state contracts were also touched by the disinvestment calls. Major New York banks saw large depositors withdrawing their funds. Fund managers, such as Kemper International Fund, were asked by clients to sell the stock of companies operating in South Africa in their portfolios. New York City had a proposal under review by which companies with operations in South Africa would be penalized when bidding for city contracts.

Goodyear's Social Responsiveness in South Africa

36   Goodyear began selling tires in South Africa in 1916. In 1946, a subsidiary, Goodyear Tire & Rubber Company (South Africa), constructed a tire plant at Uitenhage, South Africa. Throughout its 50-year history in South Africa, Goodyear had perceived itself as a positive force in the nation's racial struggle.

37   Goodyear was one of the original 12 charter subscribers of the Sullivan principles. The Reverend Leon H. Sullivan, a director of General Motors Corporation, developed a series of principles in 1977, to which companies operating in South Africa would voluntarily abide in an effort to reduce racial discrimination in South African employment. At first, 12 companies endorsed the principles; but, by 1982, 146 of the 400 American companies with subsidiaries in South Africa had signed the pact. Compliance to the principles was monitored by the consulting firm of Arthur D. Little. In 1986, the principles were especially important because investment recommendations on companies operating in South Africa had been tied to good Sullivan grades by a number of universities, pension funds, and state and local governments (see Exhibit 4 for more detailed information on the Sullivan principles).

38   Goodyear claimed it had a history of eliminating discrimination that predated the Sullivan principles, and it cited as an example its institutionalization of an equal-

Exhibit 4
The Sullivan principles

The six Sullivan principles call for companies to:	The signatories promise periodic reports on their progress in implementing these principles. According to Arthur D. Little, Inc. (the signatory companies' monitoring agency), the sixth report, published in November 1982, found:	The monitoring organization graded as follows:
1. Desegregate all eating, comfort, and work facilities.	*Principle 1:* All but one of the reporting units state all facilities are desegregated.	32: Making good progress (category I)
2. Implement equal and fair employment practices for all employees and acknowledge the right of black workers to form their own unions.	*Principle 2:* All but one have common medical, pension, and insurance plans for all races.	38: Making progress (category II) 37: Need to become more active (category III)
3. Ensure equal pay for all employees doing equal or comparable work for the same period of time.	*Principle 3:* Black employees are receiving higher average pay increases than whites, though the average percent increase is less than the previous year.	
4. Initiate and develop training programs to prepare substantial numbers of blacks and other nonwhites for supervisory, administrative, clerical, and technical jobs.	*Principle 4:* The proportion of blacks participating in training programs for sales positions has continued to increase.	
5. Increase the number of blacks and other nonwhites in managerial and supervisory positions.	*Principle 5:* The proportion of blacks in supervisory positions has dropped, indicating a lack of progress in this area in weaker economic times.	
6. Improve the quality of employees' lives outside the work environment (e.g., housing, schooling, recreation and health facilities); provide for the right of black migrant workers to a normal family life; and assist the development of black and other nonwhite-owned and -operated businesses.	*Principle 6:* Contributions for community development have doubled since last year, amounting to about $11 million.	

In December 1984, Reverend Sullivan revised his code. The new code included a provision that requires U.S. companies to take public, political action against apartheid.

Adapted from "Shomer, South Africa: Beyond Fair Employment," *Harvard Business Review,* May–June 1983, pp. 145–50.

pay-for-equal-job program before the Reverend Sullivan promoted his voluntary non-segregation code in 1977. However, Goodyear admitted that it only desegregated the company cafeteria and locker rooms as a result of preliminary discussions of the code.

39   After reviewing the progress in 1982, Reverend Sullivan concluded that the signatory companies were meeting their objective of improving the quality of life for black workers, but he stated that further advances ought to be made in the training and placement of black managers, the development of black-owned enterprises, and the upgrading of black educational and health services. Statistics showed that only 6 percent of the 1,450 managerial-level vacancies throughout South Africa in 1981 and 1982 were filled by blacks. Arthur D. Little found that the main black advancement was from unskilled to semiskilled or skilled production positions, with a decline in administrative and clerical jobs.

40   Goodyear was one of the few companies to have been awarded top grades for its South African employment policies from Arthur D. Little since the inception of the Sullivan principles. In contrast, Firestone South African Operations, which was 25 percent owned by Firestone, had never passed the Sullivan test. Exhibit 5 gives a list of the Sullivan signatories with their rating for 1983.

41   By 1985, Goodyear had a 1.1 million-square-foot plant in South Africa, with an investment of $100 million dollars and an employee work force of 2,500 workers (64 percent black), making the company one of the top 10 American employers in South Africa (see Exhibit 6). In late 1985, the company completed a $20 million plant expansion that enabled it to produce radial truck tires, thereby further demonstrating its commitment to South Africa.

42   The company had spent $6 million on nonwhite education in South Africa by 1986. Part of this investment was made out of self-interest. Goodyear realized that greater prosperity for South Africa's 23 million blacks, coupled with political stability, could mean greater sales in South Africa in the long run. Chairman Mercer said that they would not be making tires there if they thought of South Africa as having a market of only 4.5 million whites. A 1986 estimate was that blacks owned 430,000 of the 3 million cars operated in South Africa.

43   Capsulizing the corporate viewpoint, Jacques Sardas, Goodyear International president, said, "Because South Africa has always been profitable, the company has never considered leaving. Our presence there is good for our shareholders as well as South Africans—all of them."

Goodyear's Dilemma

44   By 1986, the company operated plants in 29 countries, and Goodyear's overseas operations were having problems in countries with high inflation and government price controls, thereby prohibiting the company from passing on increases in the price of raw materials. This caused a reduction in international profits, with foreign operating income falling 35 percent to $191 million from 1983 to 1985. Dividends from foreign operations decreased from $85 million in 1982 to $67.6 million in 1983 to $44 million in 1984. The company's net foreign assets exceeded $1.1 billion in 1985, after deducting minority shareholders' equity.

45   Traditionally, Goodyear's profit margins in South Africa had been among the best the corporation achieved in any country but contributed less than 1 percent of Goodyear's

Exhibit 5
List of Sullivan signatories as of October 1983

Rating categories

I.   Making good progress
II. Making progress
III. Needs to become more active
     IIIA. Low point rating on principles 4–6
     IIIB. Has not met basic requirements of principles 1–3
IV. Endorsors (companies with few employees or little equity)
     IVA. No employees
     IVB. Fewer than 10 employees
     IVC. Less than 19 percent equity in South African operation
V.   New signatories
VI. Nonreporting signatories

Alphabetical list of signatories

AFIA Worldwide Insurance	IIIA
Abbott Laboratories	II
American Cyanamid Company	I, VI
American Express Company	IVB
American Home Products Corporation	V
American Hospital Supply Corporation	II
American International Group, Inc.	IIIB
Armco, Inc.	II, IVB
Ashland Oil, Inc.	IIIA, IVA, VI
Borden, Inc.	I
Borg-Warner Corporation	II
Bristol-Myers Company	II
Burroughs Corporation	I
Butterick Company, Inc.	IIIA
CBS, Inc.	IIIA
CIGNA Corporation	II
CPC International, Inc.	II, IVA
Caltex Petroleum Corporation	I
Carnation Company	IIIB
Carrier Corporation	V
J. I. Case Corporation	IIIA, IVA
Caterpillar Tractor Company	II
Celanese Corporation	IIIA
The Chase Manhattan Corporation	II
Chicago Bridge and Iron Company	V
Citicorp	I, IVC
The Coca-Cola Company	I, II
Colgate-Palmolive Company	I
Control Data Corporation	I
Cooper Industries, Inc.	II
Cummins Engine Company, Inc.	IVB
D'Arcy MacManus & Masius Worldwide, Inc.	IIIB

Alphabetical list of signatories

Dart & Kraft, Inc.	VI
Deere & Company	II, IVA
Del Monte Corporation	II
Deloitte Haskins & Sells	IVC
Dominion Textile, Inc.	VI
Donaldson Company, Inc.	IIIA
The Dow Chemical Company	IV, IVB
E. I. DuPont de Nemours and Company	II
The East Asiatic Company, Ltd.	VI
Eastman Kodak Company	I
Englehard Corporation	VI
Exxon Corporation	I
FMC Corporation	VI
Federal-Mogul Corporation	IIIA
Ferro Corporation	IIIA
The Firestone Tire & Rubber Company	IIIB, IVA
John Fluke Manufacturing Company, Inc.	IIIA
Fluor Corporation	II
Ford Motor Company	I
Franklin Electric Company, Inc.	VI
General Electric Company	II, VI
General Motors Corporation	I
The Gillette Company	I
Goodyear Tire & Rubber Company	II
W. R. Grace and Company	IIIA
Walter E. Heller International Corporation	IVC
Heublein, Inc.	II
Hewlett-Packard Company	II
Honeywell, Inc.	II
Hoover Company	IIIA
Hyster Company	II
International Business Machines Corporation	I
International Harvester Company	IIIA, IVB
International Minerals and Chemicals Corporation	IIIA
International Telephone and Telegraph Corporation	I, IVC, VI
The Interpublic Group of Companies, Inc.	VI
Johnson Controls, Inc.	VI
Johnson and Johnson	I
Joy Manufacturing Company	VI
Kellogg Company	II
Eli Lilly and Company	I, II, IVA
Marriott Corporation	IIIA
Marsh and McLennan Companies	VI
Masonite Corporation	IIIB
McGraw-Hill, Inc.	I

Exhibit 5 *(concluded)*

Alphabetical list of signatories		*Alphabetical list of signatories*	
Measurex Corporation	VI	Rexnord, Inc.	IIIA
Merck & Company, Inc.	I, II	Richardson-Vicks, Inc.	IIIA
Mine Safety Appliances Company	IIIB	Rohm and Haas Company	IIIA, IVB
Minnesota Mining and Manufacturing Company	I	Schering-Plough Corporation	II
Mobile Oil Corporation	I	Sentry Insurance—A Mutural Company	IIIA
Monsanto Company	I	Smith Kline Beckman Corporation	II, V
Motorola, Inc.	IIIA	Sperry Corporation	I
NCNB Corporation	IVB	Squibb Corporation	IIIA
NCR Corporation	IIIA	The Standard Oil Company (Ohio)	II, IIIA
Nabisco Brands, Inc.	II	The Stanley Works	II
Nalco Chemical Company	IIIB	Sterling Drug, Inc.	IIIA
Norton Company	II, IIIA, IVB	Tampax, Inc.	I
Norton Simon, Inc.	IVA	J. Walter Thompson Company	VI
Olin Corporation	IIIA, IIIB, VI	Time, Inc.	IVB
Oshkosh Truck Corporation	IVA	The Trane Company	IIIB
Otis Elevator Company	II	Union Carbide Corporation	I, II, IVB
The Parker Pen Company	II	The Upjohn Company	II, IIIA
Pfizer, Inc.	I, II	Warner Communications, Inc.	I, IIIA
Phelps Dodge Corporation	IIIA, VI	Warner-Lambert Company	II, IIIA
Phillips Petroleum Company	II	Westinghouse Electric Corporation	I
Reader's Digest Association, Inc.	IIIA, IVA	Wilbur-Ellis Company	IIIA
		Xerox Corporation	I

Source: Leape, Baskins, and Underhill, *Business in the Shadow of Apartheid* (Lexington, Mass.: Lexington Books, 1985).

Exhibit 6
The 12 largest U.S. employers in South Africa

Company	*Number of workers*
Coca-Cola	4,800
Ford Motor	4,600
General Motors	4,000
Mobil	3,300
USG*	2,600
Goodyear	2,600
Caltex Petroleum	2,200
Allegheny International	2,000
IBM	1,900
General Electric	850
Dresser Industries	800
Xerox	800

* Formerly U.S. Gypsum.
Source: *Business Week,* February 11, 1985, p. 38.

annual corporate profits overall. The company admitted that the South African operations dipped into red ink in 1985 for the first time in its history, though it would not disclose specific figures.

46   If Goodyear were to leave its South African operations it would face the possibility of a government-mandated buyout, with the payment made in bonds denominated in deteriorating rands and stretched over a long period of time. Alternatively, Goodyear could take the best price offered from a South African or European competitor. A divestiture would, in effect, lock Goodyear out of the South African tire market that it helped develop, because the same protectionist trade barriers that helped make South Africa such a good business proposition for business already in place would prevent it from having any kind of operations there once it had ceased domestic operations.

47   In 1986, only 3 percent of Goodyear's 107 million outstanding shares were held by universities, pension funds, or financial institutions—the groups that might be inclined to follow calls for divestment by social activists interested in promoting black causes. Such occasional but mounting calls accused Goodyear of supporting apartheid because it paid South African taxes and sold tires to the country's police and military. However, if U.S. stockholders had been disinvesting up to mid-1986, it had been so gradual as to leave share prices unaffected.

48   Goodyear had a history of not giving in to political and economic pressures in the foreign countries in which it did business. The company did not want to set a negative precedent by leaving its South African operations. Douglas Hill, Goodyear International's executive vice president, told *Fortune* magazine that "leaving South Africa would send a message to other countries that Goodyear is a company that folds its tents when things get hot."

49   In the face of social unrest, national economic declines, uncertain business forecasts, and multifaceted political pressures, Goodyear had not publicly declared its stand on the disinvestment question by mid-1986. Surely, its strategic options were being thoroughly considered.

Appendix A: The Goodyear Tire & Rubber Company and Subsidiaries—Comparison with Prior Years

(Dollars in millions, except per share)	1985	1984	1983	1982
Net Sales	$9,585.1	$9,628.5	$9,031.6	$8,780.4
Income from continuing operations before extraordinary items and cumulative effect of accounting change	301.3	360.9	232.5	260.5
Discontinued operations	111.1	50.1	37.9	52.1
Extraordinary items:				
Gain on long term debt retired	—	—	35.1	17.2
Tax benefit of loss carryovers	—	—	—	—
Cumulative effect on prior years of accounting change for capital leases	—	—	—	—
Net Income	412.4	411.0	305.5	329.8
Net Income per dollar of sales	4.3¢	4.3¢	3.4¢	3.8¢
Depreciation and depletion	$ 300.5	$ 292.3	$ 280.3	$ 250.3
Capital Expenditures	1,667.6	610.9	478.7	391.4
Properties and Plants—Net	4,025.0	3,036.7	2,819.2	2,718.2
Total Assets	$6,953.5	$6,194.3	$5,985.5	$5,885.9
Long Term Debt and Capital Leases	997.5	656.8	665.2	1,174.5
Shareholders' Equity	3,507.4	3,171.3	3,016.2	2,777.2
Per Share of Common Stock:				
Income from continuing operations before extraordinary items and cumulative effect of accounting change	$ 2.81	$ 3.40	$ 2.33	$ 2.64
Discontinued operations	1.03	.47	.38	.52
Extraordinary items:				
Gain on long term debt retired	—	—	.35	.18
Tax benefit of loss carryovers	—	—	—	—
Cumulative effect on prior years of accounting change for capital leases	—	—	—	—
Net Income*	3.84	3.87	3.06	3.34
Dividends**	1.60	1.50	1.40	1.40
Book Value—on shares outstanding at December 31	32.44	29.78	28.61	28.09
Price Range:				
High	31-1/4	31-1/2	36-3/8	36-7/8
Low	25-1/8	23	27	17-7/8
Employees:				
Average during the year	134,115	133,271	128,760	131,665
Total compensation for the year	$2,709.8	$2,623.2	$2,459.1	$2,388.1
Shareholders of record***	72,582	75,619	76,014	83,915
Common Shares:				
Outstanding at December 31	108,110,085	106,492,709	105,425,079	98,866,612
Average outstanding	107,369,517	106,138,171	99,907,522	98,794,352

* Based on average shares outstanding—see note on Net Income Per Share.
** Dividends are the historical dividends paid by The Goodyear Tire & Rubber Company.
*** Includes shareholders of record of Celeron for periods prior to the merger.
The method of accounting for foreign currency translation was changed in 1981 (SFAS No. 52).
The method of accounting for capitalizing interest was adopted in 1979 (SFAS No. 34).
Financial information for 1976–1982 has been restated to include Celeron on a pooling of interests basis—see note on Business Combination.
Financial information for 1976–1984 has been restated to reflect the discontinued operations of the Celeron group—see note on Discontinued Operations.

1981	1980	1979	1978	1977	1976
$9,267.8	$8,541.7	$8,300.6	$7,500.0	$6,633.6	$5,796.2
257.2	219.0	159.8	227.9	206.5	124.9
94.8	69.4	42.0	25.2	22.5	22.0
—	—	—	—	—	—
16.4	24.0	—	—	—	—
—	—	—	—	—	(3.5)
368.4	312.4	201.8	253.1	229.0	143.4
4.0¢	3.7¢	2.4¢	3.4¢	3.5¢	2.5¢
$ 241.4	$ 234.4	$ 229.6	$ 215.1	$ 204.7	$ 195.6
377.2	291.4	378.9	423.3	298.5	243.7
2,632.7	2,558.5	2,462.4	2,280.1	2,075.3	1,968.1
$5,972.9	$6,024.2	$5,838.1	$5,565.2	$4,934.9	$4,642.7
1,245.4	1,337.3	1,531.8	1,469.0	1,168.2	1,050.0
2,647.1	2,647.5	2,400.1	2,303.3	2,126.3	2,000.0
$ 2.64	$ 2.28	$ 1.69	$ 2.46	$ 2.26	$ 1.37
.97	.72	.44	.27	.25	.24
—	—	—	—	—	—
.17	.25	—	—	—	—
—	—	—	—	—	(.03)
3.78	3.25	2.13	2.73	2.51	1.58
1.30	1.30	1.30	1.30	1.20	1.10
27.27	27.45	25.55	24.60	23.50	22.07
20-1/4	18-3/8	18-7/8	18-1/2	23-7/8	25-1/4
15-7/8	10-3/4	11-7/8	15-3/8	16-3/4	20-1/8
138,487	144,860	154,374	154,291	153,033	151,386
$2,428.1	$2,263.1	$2,242.5	$1,979.8	$1,767.2	$1,491.0
93,731	98,421	96,169	92,547	86,952	86,073
97,056,843	96,435,863	93,944,690	93,613,834	90,468,273	90,637,740
97,375,348	96,253,559	94,642,857	92,557,520	91,283,675	91,025,235

Appendix B: South Africa

Area

Including homelands (larger than all Atlantic Coast seaboard of the United States)—   472,359 square miles

Namibia—Southwest Africa—   317,827 square miles

	Number of persons	Percent
Population		
African	20,084,319	72%
White	4,453,273	16
Mixed	2,554,273	9
Asian	794,369	3
Total	27,886,234	100%
1948–1976		
Forced removals of blacks from white areas to black areas	2,108,000	
Labor force		
African	7,537,000	
White	1,970,000	
Mixed	1,023,000	
Asian	272,000	
Total	10,802,000	
Average wage differentials, white to black		
Manufacturing	4 to 1	
Mining	6 to 1	
Employees of U.S. corporations		
Black (African, Asian, mixed)	70,000 (estimated)	
White	30,000 (estimated)	
Government		

Republic of South Africa established in 1961 on basis of voting rights for national parliament restricted to whites. Four states and 10 reserves or homelands.

Blacks offered vote in homelands and resident townships located on white land. Four homelands declared independent.

Source: Adapted from "Southern Africa Perspectives," *South Africa Fact Sheet* (New York: Africa Fund), undated.

Case 21

Payless Cashways, Inc.: 1981 to 1985

1   In 1982, Payless Cashways (PC) was widely regarded as the retailer to watch in the rapidly growing market for home improvement products; and, by 1983, it was among the top 50 firms, in terms of price/earnings ratio, traded on the New York Stock Exchange. But suddenly, in 1984, PC's earnings and share prices dropped, leaving investors and competitors to wonder whether this "Cinderella story" had come to an end.

Payless Cashway's Early Years: 1930–1981[1]

2   PC began as a single family-owned lumberyard in Pocahontas, Iowa, in 1930. By 1950, the firm had grown to six stores (five in Iowa and one in Arizona); and, in 1969, it became a publicly held corporation comprised of 16 stores scattered over a wide geographic area.

3   In 1981, PC considered itself a mass merchandiser catering to the do-it-yourself (DIY) market, including farmers, ranchers, and suburban and rural homeowners. Contractor business, which accounted for only 5 percent of sales, was not actively solicited; that is, home building contractors were welcome but given no special privileges. PC believed its one-price and cash-and-carry policies for all customers distinguished it from many competitors.[2] Growth and profitability, summarized in Exhibit 1, have been remarkable in recent years, especially in relation to most competitors.

4   Each PC retail store carried approximately 13,000 SKUs (stock keeping units, i.e., items) in 1981 and was designed as a one-stop shopping center that sold virtually all the tools and materials needed to build, maintain, remodel, and decorate a home, ranch, or farm. Exhibit 2 shows the product mix.

5   For pricing purposes, merchandise was divided into five groups: (1) basic, (2) sell-up, (3) add-on, (4) decorative, and (5) seasonal and sundry items. Basic items were tightly controlled at the corporate level; every effort was made to keep them in stock and to price them competitively. Higher margins were realized on sell-up, add-on, and decorative merchandise. David Stanley, PC's president, once remarked, "You can't buy a commodity from us without passing high-margin goods on the way out."[3]

6   Merchandise was approximately 85 percent uniform across stores in 1981; the remaining 15 percent reflected adjustments for differences in local building codes and regional customer preferences. Although top management pushed hard toward increased centralization in all functional areas, especially purchasing, merchandising, and advertising,

---

This case was prepared by E. K. Valentin of Weber State College, Ogden, Utah, as a basis for class discussion. Distributed by the Case Center, Case Research Association, and Institute for Strategic Management, University of Tennessee. All rights reserved to the author and the Case Research Association. Permission to use the case should be obtained from the Case Center, Case Research Association.

[1] Anyone not familiar with building materials retailing should read the appendix before proceeding further.

[2] The term *competitor* denotes any firm in the home improvement retailing sector, even firms whose geographic markets do not coincide with PC's at this time. As prosperous chains expand, major collisions seem virtually inevitable. In Houston, Texas, for example, eight chains added 27 new stores between 1977 and 1981.

[3] *American Building Supplies*, April 1982, p. 6.

Exhibit 1
PC performance summary

	1977	1978	1979	1980*	1981
Revenue ($000)	183.5	248.3	316.1	303.0	479.1
Cost of sales ($000)	124.6	169.7	217.9	272.9	335.6
Interest expense ($000)	1.6	2.8	4.8	7.7	8.2
Net income ($000)	8.9	11.9	14.4	10.9	16.6
Working capital ($000)	29.5	37.8	49.5	57.4	63.4
Current ratio	2.41%	2.38%	2.17%	2.71%	2.81%
Earnings per share ($)	.78	1.03	1.25	.95	1.43
Number of stores	52	60	68	78	86

* Note: PC changed its inventory accounting method in fiscal 1980 from FIFO to LIFO.
Sources: Respective annual reports.

Exhibit 2
Product mix percentages

	1972	1976	1977	1978	1979	1980	1981
Wood products	42%	32%	31%	30%	29%	28%	27%
Manufactured products	21	24	24	23	21	22	21
Metal products	16	16	15	15	15	14	13
Plumbing and electrical	7	10	11	12	14	16	17
Paint and sundries	5	5	5	5	6	6	7
Hardware	3	4	4	4	5	5	5
Tools, lawn and garden	3	5	6	7	7	6	7
Floor coverings	3	4	4	3	3	3	3
Total	100%	100%	100%	100%	100%	100%	100%

Sources: Respective annual reports.

the extent to which it was actually achieved is not very clear. Conversations with PC's vendors and former employees have revealed that some store managers resisted centralization because they believed local control over such functions was vital. Corporate staffs, they maintained, were unfamiliar with local preferences and market conditions and, therefore, could not be effective. Nevertheless, staff functions, it seems, were beefed up substantially in 1981.

7   Slightly less than 20 percent of all merchandise sold in 1981 passed through the company's redistribution warehouses, which enabled the firm to make volume purchases at significantly lower prices on some items. To defray warehouse operating expenses, stores were charged 6.5 percent above cost for warehouse merchandise. Exhibit 3 is a list of warehouse locations and sizes.

8   Most stores were quite similar. Few, if any, were located in prime retail areas, such as open malls; nevertheless, accessibility generally was good. Before 1981, it was PC's policy to locate on rail sidings; but later, PC seemed willing to exchange rail access for improved proximity to other retailers, sometimes competitors. In 1981,

Exhibit 3
Warehouse locations and sizes

Location	Size (square feet)	
	1980	1981
Ankeny, Iowa	45,000	90,000
Indianapolis, Indiana	37,500	97,000
Kansas City, Missouri	30,000	48,000
Tulsa, Oklahoma	37,500	37,500
Carrollton, Texas	44,000	44,000
Houston, Texas	37,500	65,500
Albuquerque, New Mexico	15,000	20,000
Denver, Colorado	18,000	18,000
Sacramento, California	20,000	40,000
Total	284,500	460,000

Source: SEC form 10-K, November 1981.

only 20 percent of the stores produced significantly more or less than $6 million in annual sales. Exhibit 4 provides a listing of stores in operation or under construction, locations, sizes, and opening dates. All stores opened or scheduled to be opened from 1979 through 1982 were built by PC rather than acquired.

9   Exhibit 5 depicts PC's 1981 organizational structure, with ages shown in parentheses. David Stanley joined PC in 1980 and was previously employed by Piper, Jaffray and Hopwood, Inc., a regional investment broker, where he was executive vice president. John Breedlove joined PC in 1981 and was previously senior vice president of marketing and purchasing with West Building Materials. Dale Pond, who held the title of vice president and director of marketing with Bernstein Rein (consultants), also came in 1981. Other officers had been with PC for more than five years.

Further Developments: 1982–1985

10   Financial and other pertinent data for recent years are given in Exhibit 6. Other significant occurrences are outlined below.

1982 Highlights

11   During the fiscal year ending in November, new stores were opened in the following cities:

City	Number of stores	City	Number of stores
Houston, Texas	1	Denton, Texas	1
Irving, Texas	1	Dallas/Ft. Worth, Texas	3
Decatur, Illinois	1	Quincy, Illinois	1
Springfield, Illinois	1	Cedar Rapids, Iowa	1
Davenport, Iowa	1	Kansas City, Missouri	1

Exhibit 4
Store locations, sizes, and opening dates

City or town	Metropolitan area	State	Opened	Remodeled	Store square feet	Other square feet	Acres
Phoenix (north)	Phoenix	Arizona	1980	—	22,000	67,100	6
Phoenix	Phoenix	Arizona	1970	1978	22,000	59,500	7
Tempe	Phoenix	Arizona	1956	1974	17,300	26,700	3
Tucson	Tucson	Arizona	1947	1973	11,400	31,000	4
Tucson	Tucson	Arizona	1973	—	28,100	40,700	5
Bakersfield	Bakersfield	California	1977	—	20,000	51,000	6
Fresno	Fresno	California	1977	—	20,000	53,000	7
Modesto	Modesto	California	1977	—	20,000	52,000	6
Roseville	Sacramento	California	1978	—	20,000	52,000	5
Sacramento	Sacramento	California	1977	—	28,700	47,100	7
Colorado Springs	Colorado Springs	Colorado	1973	1978	25,400	50,500	6
Aurora	Denver	Colorado	1978	—	29,000	52,000	6
Denver	Denver	Colorado	1968	1975	16,600	57,000	7
Sheridan	Denver	Colorado	1972	1977	21,700	44,800	9
Westminster	Denver	Colorado	1978	—	20,000	48,000	5
Atlantic	Omaha	Iowa	1961	1970	14,800	42,100	7
Cedar Rapids	Cedar Rapids	Iowa	1982	—	24,000	54,800	7
Davenport	Davenport	Iowa	1949	1977	25,500	47,700	7
Davenport	Davenport	Iowa	1982	—	24,000	50,400	6
Des Moines	Des Moines	Iowa	1972	1978	25,800	67,400	10
Des Moines (southeast)	Des Moines	Iowa	1978	—	20,000	51,000	10
Early	Early	Iowa	1931	1977	11,600	41,300	4
Ft. Dodge	Ft. Dodge	Iowa	1981	—	24,000	60,100	6
Iowa Falls	Iowa Falls	Iowa	1947	1971	12,600	7,000	7
Iowa City	Iowa City	Iowa	1975	—	20,000	46,700	7
Manchester	Manchester	Iowa	1955	1978	16,300	48,700	7
Pocahontas	Pocahontas	Iowa	1930	1977	12,600	35,700	5
Sioux City	Sioux City	Iowa	1949	1979	26,900	83,600	7
Waterloo	Waterloo	Iowa	1980	—	22,000	50,000	7
Bloomington	Bloomington	Illinois	1981	—	24,000	55,800	7
Champaign	Champaign	Illinois	1981	—	24,000	54,800	9
Silvis	Davenport	Illinois	1953	1977	23,400	39,400	8
Decatur	Decatur	Illinois	1982	—	24,000	54,800	8
Quincy	Quincy	Illinois	1982	—	24,000	52,800	7
Springfield	Springfield	Illinois	1982	—	24,000	54,800	7
Greenwood	Indianapolis	Indiana	1979	—	26,000	61,000	6
Indianapolis (east)	Indianapolis	Indiana	1979	—	26,000	50,000	7
Indianapolis (west)	Indianapolis	Indiana	1979	—	26,000	52,000	7
Kokomo	Kokomo	Indiana	1980	—	22,000	52,000	6
Lafayette	Lafayette	Indiana	1980	—	22,000	48,000	6
Muncie	Muncie	Indiana	1980	—	20,000	54,000	8
Fort Wayne (north)	N. Fort Wayne	Indiana	1980	—	22,000	47,000	10
Fort Wayne (south)	S. Fort Wayne	Indiana	1980	—	22,000	52,000	7
Terre Haute	Terre Haute	Indiana	1981	—	24,000	53,900	7
Elwood	Elwood	Kansas	1973	1978	27,000	48,600	8
Kansas City	Kansas City	Kansas	1973	1977	24,700	44,300	10
Lenexa	Lenexa	Kansas	1978	—	26,000	52,000	6
Topeka	Topeka	Kansas	1970	1979	26,700	51,700	9
Wichita (south)	Wichita	Kansas	1981	—	24,000	54,800	8
Wichita	Wichita	Kansas	1978	—	20,000	52,000	6

Exhibit 4 *(concluded)*

City or town	Metropolitan area	State	Opened	Remodeled	Store square feet	Other square feet	Acres
Austin	Austin	Minnesota	1951	1975	15,100	39,400	5
St. Paul (south)	Minneapolis–St. Paul	Minnesota	1968	1973	19,100	58,900	8
Worthington	Worthington	Minnesota	1958	1977	12,600	36,400	8
Kansas City (east)	Kansas City	Missouri	1977	—	20,000	54,000	6
Kansas City (north)	Kansas City	Missouri	1973	1977	26,200	45,700	5
Kansas City (south)	Kansas City	Missouri	1973	1977	24,800	48,400	7
Raytown	Kansas City	Missouri	1982	—	24,000	52,150	6
Springfield	Springfield	Missouri	1976	—	20,000	57,200	15
Bellevue	Omaha	Nebraska	1981	—	24,000	54,800	9
Omaha	Omaha	Nebraska	1968	1977	29,200	58,300	13
Albuquerque	Albuquerque	New Mexico	1962	1977	28,200	50,700	8
Albuquerque	Albuquerque	New Mexico	1973	—	30,700	33,200	5
Santa Fe	Santa Fe	New Mexico	1973	1977	26,300	47,200	5
Edmond	Oklahoma City	Oklahoma	1977	—	20,000	56,000	6
Olkahoma City	Oklahoma City	Oklahoma	1977	1979	25,000	52,000	7
Oklahoma City (south)	Oklahoma City	Oklahoma	1981	—	24,000	48,700	5
Tulsa	Tulsa	Oklahoma	1976	—	21,000	51,600	5
Tulsa (west)	Tulsa	Oklahoma	1978	—	20,000	50,000	7
Eugene	Eugene	Oregon	1973	1977	21,300	61,200	8
Salem	Salem	Oregon	1978	—	20,000	46,500	6
Abilene	Abilene	Texas	1971	1975	21,500	52,600	8
Austin (north)	Austin	Texas	1980	—	22,000	46,000	7
Austin (south)	Austin	Texas	1980	—	22,000	46,000	6
Addison	Dallas/Fort Worth	Texas	1971	1975	22,300	65,100	7
Arlington	Dallas/Fort Worth	Texas	1973	1977	28,000	48,800	5
Colleyville	Dallas/Fort Worth	Texas	1982	—	24,000	59,400	6
Denton	Dallas/Fort Worth	Texas	1982	—	24,000	53,800	6
Duncanville	Dallas/Fort Worth	Texas	1971	1975	15,600	49,300	8
Fort Worth	Dallas/Fort Worth	Texas	1973	1978	23,000	43,660	7
Garland	Dallas/Fort Worth	Texas	1971	1975	15,600	52,100	7
Irving	Dallas/Fort Worth	Texas	1982	—	24,000	52,800	6
Lewisville	Dallas/Fort Worth	Texas	1982	—	24,000	53,600	6
Mesquite	Dallas/Fort Worth	Texas	1971	1975	27,600	58,400	7
North Fort Worth	Dallas/Fort Worth	Texas	1973	1979	26,800	66,500	7
Plano	Dallas/Fort Worth	Texas	1982	—	24,000	53,000	7
Stafford	Dallas/Fort Worth	Texas	1979	—	26,000	51,600	5
White Settlement	Dallas/Fort Worth	Texas	1982	—	24,000	52,650	6
El Paso	El Paso	Texas	1970	1979	19,400	49,700	8
Houston (east)	Houston	Texas	1979	—	26,000	44,000	7
Houston	Houston	Texas	1981	—	26,000	46,000	6
Houston (north)	Houston	Texas	1979	—	26,000	52,000	6
Houston (southeast)	Houston	Texas	1979	—	26,000	47,500	5
Humble	Houston	Texas	1979	—	26,000	42,000	6
Lubbock	Lubbock	Texas	1977	—	20,000	48,000	7
Sherman	Sherman	Texas	1980	—	20,000	58,000	6
Texarkana	Texarkana	Texas	1976	—	20,000	63,000	9
Tyler	Tyler	Texas	1973	1979	23,000	54,200	10
Waco	Waco	Texas	1975	1979	24,200	58,600	10

Source: SEC Form 10-K, November 1981.

Exhibit 5
1981 Organization

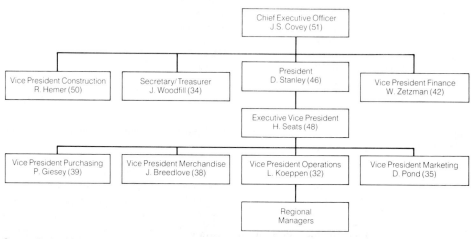

Source: Derived from SEC Form 10-K, November 1981.

Additionally, the company purchased an existing store in Indianapolis, Indiana, and two in Colorado Springs, Colorado. The company sold 1.1 million shares of common stock and sold and leased-back 12 stores to finance capital expenditures and to provide working capital.

12   David Stanley was elected chief executive officer, but J. Stanley Covey stayed on as chairman of the board. Richard Hemer was elected senior vice president, construction; Bruce Hokanson was promoted to the new position of regional executive for the Kansas City and Denver districts; and Brad Talley was hired as director of the MIS department.

13   Stanley summarized 1982 by noting that "Our company's marketing and expansion philosophies of concentrating in major metropolitan areas with high density of population and housing continue in force. . . . In 1983, we will open 10 new stores. . . . Eight of the 10 new stores will have a retail sales area of approximately 31,000 square feet, an increase from the 24,000-square-foot sales area we have constructed for several years." He also noted that in December of 1982 (one month after the end of the 1982 fiscal year) PC purchased the seven-store Lumberjack chain, which operated six stores and distribution centers in Sacramento and Stockton, California. Moreover, 770,000 common shares were sold, mainly to finance the Lumberjack acquisition.

1983 Highlights

14   In addition to the Lumberjack acquisition (for $26.3 million) and the acquisition of a single store in Salina, Kansas, PC opened new stores in the following market areas:

Market area	Number of stores
Dallas/Ft. Worth, Texas	1
Evansville, Indiana	1
Phoenix, Arizona	1
Houston, Texas	3
Columbus, Ohio	3
Fresno, California	1

The average new store cost approximately $2.4 million and was stocked with inventory valued at over $1 million.

15   Stanley's 1983 report to stockholders suggested that

> Improved marketing and merchandising programs, enhanced training and educational activities, strategically sound acquisitions, and increased experience at all levels of management have contributed to this year's record growth. Our important market share and financial gains are a result of our company's fundamental strength and vitality. . . . With a strong balance sheet and a strengthened and experienced management team firmly in place, the company initiated an accelerated growth plan consistent with our strategy of market dominance.

16   Results from a three-market study revealed tradesmen, defined as persons earning at least 1 percent of their annual income from home improvement work, comprised 17 percent of the customer mix and accounted for 32 percent of total store visits.[4] The 1984 advertising program, it was announced, would focus increasingly on promoting projects rather than products. Other research, involving 30,000 interviews, provided PC with demographic and motivational profiles of the customer, insights into shopping patterns, and a better understanding of PC's price, quality, value, assortment, and service images in relation to competitors.

17   The cost of this research was partially defrayed by offering key manufacturers the opportunity to purchase an integrated advertising package that would feature their products on television, radio, the front page of a tabloid, and store signs. This program was completely sold out for 1983 and contributed nearly $3 million. The usual promotional incentives offered by manufacturers (e.g., cooperative advertising allowances) were not adversely affected by PC's package and were used as additional sources of advertising funds.

18   Tom Stanton was promoted to regional executive; Jean Warren was elected assistant treasurer; Fred Olsen was elected vice president, human resources; and Stephen Lightstone replaced Wayne Zetzman as chief financial officer.

---

[4] Tradesmen should not be confused with building contractors.

Exhibit 6
Summary data for 1982–1985 (in millions of dollars)

PAYLESS CASHWAYS, INC.
Performance Summary: 1982–1985
(except for earnings per share and sales per square foot)

	1982	1983	1984	1985
Revenue	$603.2	$864.9	$1,175.6	$1,389.7
Cost of sales	420.9	593.8	812.8	954.2
Interest expense	7.4	6.0	12.1	17.7
Depreciation and amortization	7.8	11.1	17.0	25.2
Income before taxes	43.6	64.7	67.3	68.0
Net income after taxes	23.1	34.6	37.1	38.1
Earnings per share*	.96	1.29	1.15	1.12
Assets	263.2	368.7	553.8	605.8
Working capital	91.1	101.0	139.2	125.3
Inventories	111.9	165.8	247.9	233.6
Current assets	144.1	182.3	260.7	260.2
Equity	143.7	205.2	257.2	332.9
Number of stores	100	118	157	169
Sales per square foot	293	305	347	337

* Adjusted to neutralize the effect of a two-for-one stock split in May 1983.

PAYLESS CASHWAYS, INC.
Changes in Financial Position
(in millions of dollars)

	1982	1983	1984	1985
Cash from operations	$33.6	$ 11.1	$28.4	$ 92.9
Sale of common stock	23.4	30.0		43.0
Sale and lease-back of stores	17.3			
Net change in long-term debt	(4.2)	13.2	75.4	(41.6)
Cash dividends	(2.4)	(3.2)	(9.5)	(5.5)
Other		.1	(.1)	3.5
Cash from financing	34.1	40.1	65.8	(.6)
Investment of capital	39.6	78.3	99.7	77.7
Change in cash and securities	28.1	(27.1)	(5.5)	14.6

Sources: Respective annual reports.

1984 Highlights

19　In the 1984 annual report, PC labeled itself a full-line building materials specialty retailer serving the home improvement and maintenance needs of the serious do-it-yourselfer and tradesman. PC added 19 stores by completing three acquisitions: Prime Home Improvement Centers, Inc. (14 stores for 2,998,000 shares and $1 million in cash), headquartered in Denver, Colorado; Wood Brothers Lumber of Tucson, Arizona (2 stores for $8.7 million); and Sommerville Lumber and Supply Company, Inc. (3 stores for 2,350,000 shares), based in Boston, Massachusetts. In addition, 21 newly constructed retail facilities were opened, and plans to open 15 more stores in 1985 were announced. The new stores are located in:

Store location	Number of stores	Store location	Number of stores
Cincinnati, Ohio	4	Springfield, Ohio	1
Milford, Ohio	1	Lima, Ohio	1
Findlay, Ohio	1	Visalia, California	1
Mesa, Arizona	1	Tucson, Arizona	1
Denver, Colorado	1	College Station, Texas	1
Dallas, Texas	1	Houston, Texas	1
Longview, Texas	1	Boston, Massachusetts	1
Joplin, Missouri	1	Columbia, Missouri	1
Des Moines, Iowa	1	Indianapolis, Indiana	1

20   Yet, "[F]or all the growth in numbers of retail facilities and sales," noted David Stanley, "our earnings can only be described as disappointing. . . . A project-oriented advertising emphasis early in the year proved incompatible with the high interest rates and adverse spring weather conditions. . . . In midyear, we returned to a more conventional advertising program with greater emphasis on specific products and price promotion." The Houston, Texas, market was particularly hard hit by unfavorable circumstances; and it appeared to the CEO that implementation of PC's operating policies and systems in the acquired Lumberjack stores had a detrimental impact on performance.

21   When asked by *Barron's* about increasing competition from warehouse stores, Mr. Stanley confessed to being impressed with Home Depot's accomplishments but maintained that PC's problems were of a nonrecurrent nature and had little, if anything, to do with competitive influx. "We're tilted more toward the professional than Home Depot," he said, "and we're the everyday low pricer. Home Depot's pricing leans toward things like sales and selective price cutting."[5]

22   John P. Herron, who had held senior positions with J. C. Penney, joined PC in September as executive vice president. Also, at year's end, PC's database system, designed to provide sales, gross margin, and perpetual inventory information by SKU item, neared completion. Five regional merchandising managers and five regional advertising managers were installed to provide a better feel for the "pulse" of the marketplace and to enhance PC's ability to respond to changing and localized preferences. In October, PC began to issue its own credit card ($1,000 and $5,000 limits, respectively, for consumers and tradesmen) in an attempt to promote customer loyalty and increase the size of the average sale.

23   Although the 1984 annual report portrays the firm as one with a firm grip on the future, despite some disappointments, it notes that, according to some observers, the industry seems to be shifting toward sameness, characterized by product and price parity. Accordingly, Mr. Stanley raised the question: "What will set PC apart from the rest?"

24   Similar questions were raised on Wall Street. For instance, a Kidder, Peabody & Company report observed that in June 1983, Payless Cashways was among the 50

---

[5] *Barron's*, January 14, 1985, p. 22.

highest P/E stocks on the New York Stock Exchange.[6] But the earnings decline in 1984 seriously undermined investor confidence, causing common share prices to drop from over 25 near the start of the fiscal year to 13½ near the end. "A number of observers," the report noted, "believe that the decline . . . was primarily a function of competitive factors and that these factors will continue well into the future. . . . Conversely, a controversial but less negative interpretation suggests that the decline in earnings resulted from a confluence of negative factors that are . . . unlikely to reoccur. . . . The difference is critical since the former interpretation suggests that Payless will no longer be the captain of its own destiny, with future growth to be determined by factors outside the company's control." David Stanley concluded in early 1985 that "This company is growing up. Practices that worked as a smaller company will not support our future. . . . We recognize that a number of major changes are occurring in our industry. We are alert to these changes and are addressing them vigorously."

1985 Highlights

25   Newly constructed retail facilities, financed largely via a 2.3 million-share common stock issue that generated $43 million, were opened during the year in the following cities:

City	Number of stores	City	Number of stores
Dayton, Ohio	1	Lubbock, Texas	1
Evansville, Indiana	1	Oklahoma City, Oklahoma	1
Houston, Texas	4	Omaha, Nebraska	1
Louisville, Kentucky	4	Tulsa, Oklahoma	1

26   In addition, four Handy Dan stores in the Kansas City, Missouri, market were acquired; and six stores were closed—two in the Denver, Colorado, area; one in Pocahontas and one in Early, Iowa; one in Tucson, Arizona; and one in St. Paul, Minnesota. The St. Paul store was closed because the inefficiency of operating one store in a large market became evident; the others, according to David Stanley, were closed due to overlapping sales territories resulting from various acquisitions. Also, the distribution center in Tulsa, Oklahoma, was closed during the year. Plans for 1986 include opening 12 additional retail facilities and closing 1 store in Tempe and 1 in Tucson, Arizona. United Building Centers agreed to purchase five PC stores located in Iowa Falls, Atlantic, and Manchester, Iowa, and in Worthington and Austin, Minnesota. Stores open during the entire fiscal year averaged $8.8 million in sales, or $337 per square foot. Nevertheless, earnings per share decreased by three cents to $1.12.

27   In addition to serving as president and CEO, David Stanley was elected chairman of the board; John P. Fischer was elected vice president, western region; and Harlon

---

[6] Kidder, Peabody & Company, *Purchase Recommendation,* March 13, 1985.

Exhibit 7
Executive officers, 1985

Name	Age	Position(s) held	Date elected
D. Stanley	50	President	April 1980
		Chief executive officer	May 1982
		Chairman of the board	April 1985
R. E. Hemer	54	Senior vice president	June 1982
		Director	April 1984
L. L. Koeppen	36	Vice president, operations	July 1981
J. H. Breedlove	42	Vice president, merchandising	December 1981
D. C. Pond	39	Vice president, marketing	September 1981
S. A. Lightstone	40	Vice president, finance	November 1983
S. M. Stanton	37	Vice president, planning	April 1984
L. J. French	38	General counsel and secretary	August 1984
M. H. Didier	45	Vice president, facility development	June 1982
J. F. Woodfill	38	Vice president, treasurer	April 1984
D. O'Halloran	37	Vice president, controller	April 1984
B. J. Talley	40	Vice president, MIS	October 1985
S. K. Boyd	34	Vice president, stores	June 1984
R. L. Weverka	43	Vice president, south	October 1981
B. E. Hokanson	36	Vice president, midwest	June 1984
K. R. Maynard	36	Vice president, east region	August 1985
J. P. Fischer	45	Vice president, west	February 1985
M. Cohen	63	Chairman, Summerville Lumber	March 1984
H. Cohen	55	President, Summerville Lumber	March 1984
		Director	October 1984

Source: SEC Form 10-K, November 1984.

Seats resigned as executive vice president. At year's end, the firm's officers consisted of the individuals listed in Exhibit 7. Exhibit 8 is a listing of stores and distribution centers in operation at the end of 1985.

28 Dramatic profitability improvement was not expected in 1986; yet, Mr. Stanley expected increased productivity from lower employee turnover and enhanced benefits, as well as from the new management information system. "This company is positioning itself not merely to withstand the current retail climate," he stated in early 1986, "but to prosper in spite of it."

Appendix: A Note on Home Improvement Retailing

29 The home improvement retailing sector consists of lumberyards, building materials centers, home centers, hardware stores, the likes of Sears and K mart and other discount stores, warehouse outlets, and specialty stores that focus on paint and glass, wall coverings, plumbing and electrical supplies, and other items. Unfortunately, no clear-cut classification system exists; labels usually are self-applied. *Home Center Magazine's* *1984 Profile of the Home Center Market: Summary Report,* for example, states that to qualify as a home center, a store must carry hardware, lumber and/or plywood,

---

Exhibit 8
Operating facilities, 1985

Retail stores

Arizona (10)	Kansas (9)	Nevada (2)
California (14)	Kentucky (3)	New Mexico (3)
Colorado (17)	Massachusetts (3)	Ohio (12)
Illinois (6)	Minnesota (2)	Oklahoma (7)
Indiana (14)	Missouri (9)	Oregon (2)
Iowa (13)	Nebraska (3)	Texas (40)

Redistribution centers

Phoenix, Arizona
Sacramento, California
Indianapolis, Indiana
Kansas City, Missouri
Lake Dallas, Texas
Ankeny, Iowa
Houston, Texas
Denver, Colorado

Source: 1985 annual report.

---

interior wall paneling and/or mouldings.[7] Additionally, it must carry several, though not all, related items, such as tools, floor coverings, electrical and/or plumbing products, lawn and garden products, and automotive supplies. *National Home Center News* distinguishes among home centers, hardware stores, discounters, specialty stores, including paint stores, and Sears.[8] The most pertinent SIC categories are Lumber and Other Building Materials Dealers (521), Paint, Glass, and Wallpaper Stores (523), and Hardware Stores (525).

30   *Barron's* suggested PC is positioned somewhere between a lumber yard and a hardware store, which is also where *Barron's* places the three other major home improvement retailers who amassed over $1 billion in sales in 1984; namely, Lowe's, W. R. Grace's home center division, and Evans Products Company.[9] Yet none of these or other competitors have quite the same customer or product mix; and none matched PC's steady growth and profit performance over the decade prior to 1984. Goldman Sachs' research report notes that, in view of the diversity among chains, comparisons are difficult.[10] The report notes, for instance, that PC's sales-per-square-foot figures seem overstated because lumber sales are included in the calculations even though virtually no lumber is displayed in the retail area of the typical PC store. Furthermore, when the yard area is considered, it can be argued that most PC stores approach the size of the average warehouse store. The newer stores, for instance, contain over 30,000 square

---

[7] *1984 Profile of the Home Center Market: Summary Report, Home Center Magazine*, p. 2.

[8] *National Home Center News*, July 15, 1985, pp. 19–20.

[9] *Barron's*, July 14, 1985, p. 22.

[10] Joseph H. Ellis and Amy P. Gassman, *Investment Research Report: Payless Cashways, Inc.* (New York: Goldman Sachs, November 22, 1983).

feet of retail selling space; 30,000 square feet of warehouse space; and 16,000–20,000 square feet of covered outside storage, and are located on six to seven acres with parking for 175 cars.

31   Although classification schemes are far from uniform, some useful distinctions can be made. First, lumber and building materials retailers can be categorized as contractor or consumer oriented. Contractor yards often started out by serving professional contractors and showed little interest in serving consumers until the do-it-yourself (DIY) movement caught on in the 1970s. Since DIY sales generally produce higher gross margins and are much less cyclical than contractor sales, many old-time lumberyards were given quick "face lifts" to make them more appealing to consumers. Typically, larger and brighter signs were installed, interiors were redecorated, floor space was expanded, merchandise assortments were augmented, and the power of advertising was discovered. Some yards were rebuilt from the ground up with substantially larger display areas; and new stores were built with the DIY segment in mind.

32   But while trying to attract consumers, such yards also tried to retain their building contractor clientele and generally expected much (though sometimes less than 50 percent) of their sales volume to come from the latter segment. Contractors usually are contacted periodically by an outside sales force, buy on account, are quoted lower prices than consumers, are served from a special contractor desk, and often have a special entrance. Outlets of this type usually are located in industrial rather than prime retailing areas.

33   Physically, consumer-oriented lumberyards closely resemble contractor yards, except that they cater almost exclusively to the DIY trade. Professionals may be treated no differently than consumers, and no outside sales force is maintained.

34   The label *home center* is usually applied to merchants that sell little, if anything, to contractors, often are located in or near open malls or other store clusters, and, in addition to building materials, often sell lawn furniture, housewares, sporting goods, automotive supplies, and lawn and garden items. Over the past decade or two, such stores have grown more rapidly than other types of building materials retailers. Large hardware stores tend to be small home centers.

35   Warehouse stores, which typically utilize stores abandoned by other retailers, are no-frills operations that contain up to 100,000 square feet of retail floor space and carry approximately 25,000 to 30,000 SKU, are rapidly gaining popularity. Announcements of warehouse openings appear regularly in the trade press. Home Depot, Inc., founded in 1978 by three very astute former executives with other home improvement chains, is the innovator. Imitators and would-be imitators, to date, include Home Club, Mr. How, Home Pro (Home Centers of America), Houseworks (W. R. Grace), and Bowater Home Centers (founded by a British conglomerate). PC opened one such store (55,000 square feet of retail space) in a former Dallas dance hall.

36   During its brief existence, Home Depot (HD) has grown to 31 stores (including stores in Atlanta, Dallas, and Phoenix) and sales and profits, respectively, near $425 million and $15 million in 1984.[11] However, security analysts warn that, in view of the requisite financial commitments and expertise, the warehouse format can be as disastrous as it has been spectacularly successful for HD. As if to punctuate these warnings, Bowater sold its two stores (located in Dallas) to HD in 1983.

---

[11] *Barron's*, January 14, 1985, pp. 22–45.

Exhibit 9
Number of firms and number of stores

	1976	1978	1980	1982	1984
Number of firms	10,572	9,857	8,896	8,783	9,488
Number of stores	25,232	25,584	26,599	26,297	25,012

Source: Home Center Research Bureau, *1984 Profile of the Home Center Market: Summary Report,* 1984.

Exhibit 10
Modernization and housing expenditures (in billions of dollars)

Year	DIY modernization	Professional modernization	Total modernization	New housing
1974	$11.3	$13.9	$25.2	$40.6
1975	14.4	15.3	29.7	34.4
1976	16.4	16.8	33.2	47.3
1977	18.8	18.8	37.6	65.7
1978	21.1	21.0	42.1	75.8
1979	24.2	23.2	47.4	78.6
1980	26.5	24.9	51.4	63.1
1981	27.7	25.6	53.3	61.9

Source: *Building Supply News,* May 1982. This publication is now called *Building Supply & Home Centers.*

37   Among HD's success factors is a top-management team that seldom misses spending some time of each day on the retail floor, paying wages far above the norm, and stressing service along with low prices and quality merchandise. One survey indicated that HD is the preferred overall DIY retailer in its markets. Selection, variety, and price were the main perceived advantages. However, various competitors were generally preferred for several high-margin lines, including paint, plumbing and electrical items, tools, and hardware.

38   Despite the growth of chains, independents sold approximately 65 to 70 percent of all building materials in 1983; and only four chains have market shares greater than 1 percent. In contrast, five general-merchandise discount chains account for approximately 50 percent of that sector's sales.

39   Nevertheless, several prosperous chains are steadily increasing market shares. PC, for instance, grew from 78 stores in 1980 to 169 by the end of 1985. But, unlike many competitors, PC grew mostly by building new stores, making no acquisitions during David Stanley's tenure until 1983. Some large diversified firms (e.g., Lone Star Industries) have gotten out of building materials retailing entirely; and others (e.g., Boise Cascade and Weyerhaeuser) are in the process of leaving or scaling back. Stores operated by these chains were often acquired rather than built by them and, when divested, are usually sold in large blocks to other large building materials chains (see Exhibit 9).

Exhibit 11
Residential upkeep expenditures (in billions of dollars)

Year	Amount	Year	Amount
1971	$16.2	1978	$37.5
1972	17.5	1979	42.2
1973	18.5	1980	46.3
1974	21.1	1981	46.4
1975	25.2	1982	45.3
1976	29.0	1983	49.3
1977	31.3		

Source: U.S. Department of Commerce, *Residential Altera-tions and Repairs,* Series C50-84-Q1.

40   On the demand side, the surge in DIY activity has been attributed to favorable demographic, economic, and psychological factors. Among other things, the 25-to-44 age group grew very rapidly; new housing became very expensive; labor costs skyrocketed; and American values increasingly embraced independence and self-help.

41   *Building Supply & Home Centers* magazine estimated that, in 1984, America's homeowners would spend $57.4 billion for the modernization and repair of their homes and expected this figure to reach $73 billion by 1990.[12] DIY expenditures equaled payments to professional contractors for the first time in 1970; in 1984, approximately $36.2 billion, or 63 percent, is expected to come from the DIY segment. Exhibits 10 and 11 provide additional information.

---

[12] *Building Supply & Home Centers,* October 1984, p. 62.

Case 22

A. H. Robins and the Dalkon Shield

1   Founded in 1866, A. H. Robins is a diversified, multinational company with base operations in Richmond, Virginia. Robins is primarily a manufacturer and marketer of two types of pharmaceuticals: those marketed directly to the consumer and those dispensed solely through the medical profession (commonly known as ethical pharmaceuticals). However, Robins is more than a pharmaceutical company. Pet care products, health and beauty aids, and perfumes are among the many products manufactured by the company under brand names which include Robitussin® cough syrup, Sergeant's® pet care products, Chap Stick® lip balm, and Caron® perfumes.[1]

2   In 1866, Albert Hartley Robins opened a tiny apothecary shop for the purpose of providing to the medical profession research-formulated, clinically proven, and ethically promoted pharmaceuticals. Over a century later, the Robins' philosophy remains unchanged. After three generations of operation, Robins is still led by members of the Robins family. Currently, the company has almost 6,000 full-time employees. Making employees feel like family has long been recognized as important to the overall success of the company. The ability to "converse as decision makers and to be treated as first class" causes Robins' employees to take great pride in their company and to demonstrate a very high degree of loyalty to the firm. As an example of this concern for the views of employees, one Robins' salesman said that "his advice often carries greater weight than that of the firm's market research department."[2]

3   This sense of family extends beyond work, too. The company sponsors activities that include a company softball team and company trips, and it offers employees little things that tend to make a big difference, such as free coffee and birthday holidays. Claiborne Robins believes that "his greatest assets are the people that work for him." According to the *Richmond Times-Dispatch,* "When a person is employed by A. H. Robins, it's almost for life. Only on rare occasions do people not reach retirement with this company."

The Intrauterine Device Environment[3]

4   The market for birth control devices in the 1970s was very volatile. Before the inception of intrauterine devices (IUDs), several artificial methods of birth control were available to consumers. Included in this group were the diaphragm, the condom, and the pill. Each of these methods offered women significantly better birth control protection than

---

[1] Trademarks of A. H. Robins.

[2] Quotations in this section were provided by *Product Management,* October 1972; A. H. Robins, *75th Anniversary Book;* and the *Richmond Times-Dispatch,* June 23, 1985.

[3] Quotations in this section were provided by Dr. Thomsen's testimony before the Committee on Government Operations, House of Representatives, June 13, 1973; and the SAF-T-COIL information pamphlet.

afforded by natural measures. However, the diaphragm and the condom lacked what women seemed to want most from birth control devices—spontaneity. Thus, the pill was viewed by consumers as the ultimate form of contraception. Unquestioned, because it solved the perennial problem of birth control, the pill enjoyed a prosperous existence. The pill was convenient and safe, and it offered exceptional birth control protection.

5   The discovery of the pill's harmful side effects caused many women to lose confidence in oral contraceptives. The realization of problems like an increased risk of heart disease, dramatic mood swings, and excessive weight gain gave rise to a national concern over the safety of the pill. This concern was the focus of the Gaylord Nelson hearings of the early 1970s. These hearings publicly exposed the harmful side effects of oral contraceptives. "It is estimated . . . that within six months of the Gaylord Nelson hearings . . . up to 1 million women went off the birth control pills."

6   Since the pill was no longer viewed as the ultimate answer to birth control, women returned to traditional methods of contraception. However, they refused to sacrifice convenience and almost foolproof protection. What could have been better than a device—not a "dangerous" drug—that offered the same protection as the pill, at a comparable price, and with more convenience? The stage was set for the introduction of the IUD. Previously, IUDs had been used only on a small scale in various Planned Parenthood clinics. It was not until the harmful side effects of the pill were made public that IUDs were viewed as commercially viable.

7   An IUD is a "small, flexible piece of sterile plastic, which is inserted into the uterus by the physician to prevent pregnancies." The minute the device is inserted it is effective. "Once an IUD has been inserted, it entails no further costs, no daily protective procedures. It works only inside the uterus—without effects on your body, blood, or brain; it doesn't cause you to gain weight, or have headaches or mood changes. And it provides the user with a most satisfying method of contraception."

8   Because of the simplicity of the device, manufacturing costs are low, and profits can be high. When volume is sufficient, an IUD can be manufactured, sterilized, and packaged for 35 to 40 cents, and it can be sold for $3.00 to $3.50. Due to the size and profit potential of the birth control market, the manufacturers of IUDs were well positioned to reap a bountiful harvest, but competition was tough. The secret to success was timing, and the winners would be the first in the market. Firms competing in the market realized that "unlike most consumer products, new drugs and delivery devices must first gain acceptance among a small group of specialists. If the specialists accept this, their patients will too." Therefore, the marketing effort was directed at physicians, knowing that they would refer the device to their patients.

The Dalkon Shield[4]

9   Dr. Hugh Davis, an assistant professor of medicine at Johns Hopkins University and an expert in birth control, was instrumental in developing the Dalkon Shield. Dr. Davis conducted research on patients using the shield, and he reported a pregnancy rate of 1.1 percent (comparable with the pill). The competitive advantage the Dalkon Shield had over other IUDs was the "larger surface area designed for maximum coverage and maximum contraceptive effect." The potential of the Dalkon Shield was great,

---

[4] Quotations in this section provided by Dr. Thomsen's testimony and the *Richmond Times-Dispatch*, June 23, 1985.

and drawing from its already established reputation and distribution channels in the pharmaceutical industry, the IUD seemed to be a logical addition to Robins' product offerings.

10   On June 12, 1970, A. H. Robins paid $750,000, a royalty of 10 percent of future net sales, plus consulting fees to acquire the Dalkon Shield. At the time of purchase, Robins had no expertise in the area of birth control. Although it did hire consultants, Robins had neither an obstetrician nor a gynecologist on its staff. It assigned assembly of the shield to the corporate division of the company that manufactures Chap Stick lip balm. Before buying the product, however, Robins' medical director, Frederick A. Clark, Jr., reviewed statistical tests performed by Dr. Davis on the shield. These tests showed that in 832 insertions, 26 women became pregnant. Dr. Davis' tests, however, were done on the original shield, not the one ultimately sold by Robins. The major difference between the original shield and the one sold by Robins was the addition of a multifilament tail.

11   When it went to the market, Robins was excited about its product. "Possibly no other IUD has received the benefit of such ecstatic claims by its developer, its manufacturer, and the admiring multitude." Robins used promotional methods that were designed especially for acceptance of the shield within the medical profession. Foremost among these promotions was a text written by Dr. Davis, *Intrauterine Devices for Contraception—The IUD*. The appendix of his book lists complications reported with the use of 10 major brand IUDs. The shield was presented in a very good light, with only a 5.4 percent complication rate. The complication rate of the competition ranged from 16.9 percent to 55.7 percent.

Difficulties Emerge

12   A. H. Robins began selling the Dalkon Shield on January 1, 1971. On June 22, 1971, when a doctor reported that his shield-wearing daughter suffered a septic spontaneous abortion (miscarriage caused by infection), the company was particularly concerned about the safety aspects of the shield. The main concern was the shield's unique multifilament tail, which has since been accused of actually drawing infection from the vagina into the normally sterile uterus. Ironically, the product that was thought to be the ultimate form of birth control turned sour (36 alleged deaths and 13,000 alleged injuries), and it had a devasting effect on A. H. Robins.

Difficulties with Research[5]

13   Although the text written by Dr. Davis had been accepted by the medical profession as a major textbook on IUDs, the problems with IUDs raised many concerns, and the text was referred to as a "thinly disguised promotion of the shield." Examination revealed that Robins possessed data from five formal studies based on the experience of about 4,000 shield users. Three of these five studies were performed by people with financial interests in the shield. The foremost of these studies was done by Dr. Davis. He claimed a pregnancy rate of 1.1 percent, an expulsion rate of 2.3 percent,

---

[5] Most of the information in this section was taken from Dr. Thomsen's testimony, May 30–31, 1973, and June 1, 12–13, 1973.

a medical removal rate of 2.0 percent, and a total complication rate of 5.4 percent. However, another study conducted over an 18-month period and dated October 25, 1972, showed a 4.3 percent pregnancy rate.

14   In an interview broadcast on "60 Minutes," Paul Rheingold, a New York attorney who has represented 40 Dalkon Shield users, said that "This IUD got on the market with no animal tests, and with whatever minimal clinical . . . or testing on human subjects . . . the company wanted to do, which turned out to be practically nothing."

Financial Implications[6]

15   Approximately 4.5 million Dalkon Shields were sold by Robins, producing an estimated profit of $500,000. "The product generated total revenues to the company of $13.7 million in four and a half years. But, during the first six months of 1985, Robins paid out $61.2 million in Dalkon-related expenses." By June 30, 1985, Robins and Aetna Life and Casualty Company (Robins' insurance company) had paid $378.3 million to settle 9,230 Dalkon Shield cases. This exhausted all but $50 million of Robins' product liability insurance. Legal fees and other costs related to the shield have totaled $107.3 million. Robins' portion of the total Dalkon claims has been $198.1 million. Robins announced an anticipated minimum cost to handle future Dalkon expenses of $685 million, excluding punitive damages.

16   Exhibits 1 through 11 present financial information on the company contained in its 1984 annual report.

Bankruptcy[7]

17   On August 21, 1985, A. H. Robins filed for bankruptcy under Chapter 11 of the Federal Bankruptcy Code. "When it filed its request for reorganization on August 21, Robins listed $2.26 in assets for each $1 in debts and talked publicly about the strengths of the company when items related to the Dalkon Shield birth control device were excluded."

18   Robins noted that it had a profit of $35.3 million from net sales of $331.1 million in the first six months of 1985. What the sales and profits did not show was the extent to which Robins was having to dip into its retained earnings to pay Dalkon-related bills. "Dalkon payments had taken away only 1.7 cents for each $1 in Robins sales from 1974 through 1983, but then jumped to 12.3 cents in 1984. And when it jumped to 18.5 cents in the first six months of this year (1985), there wasn't enough left from sales to meet other expenses."

19   "The petition in bankurptcy court stops the flow of Dalkon payments. A perceived advantage for Robins in seeking the Chapter 11 route is that the company's reorganization plan would likely stretch out Dalkon payments so that a cashflow problem wouldn't recur." "The action was taken [in bankruptcy court] in an effort to ensure the economic vitality of the company, which is, of course, critical to our ability to pay legitimate claims to present and future plaintiffs."

---

[6] Information for this section was taken from the *Richmond Times-Dispatch,* August 22 and 25, 1985.

[7] Questions in this section were provided in the *Richmond Times-Dispatch* between August and September 1985, and selected October 1985 issues of *The Wall Street Journal.*

Exhibit 1
Net sales ($ millions)

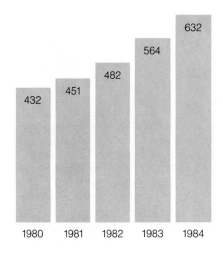

Exhibit 2
Net earnings or loss ($ millions)

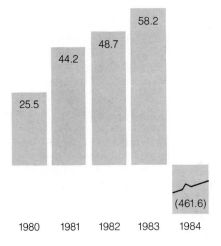

20   A. H. Robins' petition in bankruptcy court has been at the center of a heated debate. Those in support of the company have argued that "A. H. Robins' move into bankruptcy court could ensure that there is money for all who are suing the company instead of letting 'the first wolves who tear at the carcass' get it all." On the other hand, Aaron M. Levine, a lawyer for women filing against Robins, believes that "This is a company that's saying, "We'll pay our suppliers, and we'll pay for TV ads, and we'll pay for

Exhibit 3
Earnings or losses per share ($)

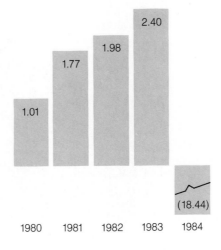

Exhibit 4
Dividends per share ($)

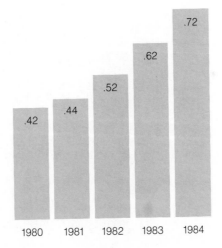

the syrup for the Robitussin, and we'll pay our workers, but as far as this one particular group of creditors is concerned—the women we have maimed—we won't pay."

21   Levine pointed to Robins' own estimates that it has $466 million in assets and only $216.5 million owed to creditors. "Certainly this is far from the usual type of debtor who files a bankruptcy court petition." According to Levine's motion, Robins' petition was instituted not to benefit a corporation in distress, as the laws are intended,

Exhibit 5
Worldwide R&D expenditures ($ millions)

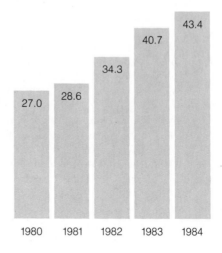

Exhibit 6
Capital additions ($ millions)

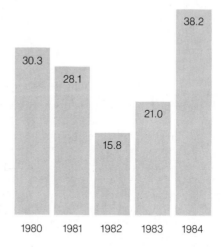

"but to enable the petitioner to escape the jurisdiction of another court when the day of reckoning for their alleged acts of misconduct was at hand." The National Woman's Health Network, for instance, said at a news conference that the company is financially healthy but is trying to duck its responsibility to women who have filed lawsuits. On the other hand, Roscoe E. Puckett, Jr., a spokesman for Robins, contends that "The best hope for all concerned is for A. H. Robins to remain financially healthy. To do that, we had to stop the financial hemorrhaging that threatened to destroy the company to the detriment of everyone, including the legitimate Dalkon Shield claimants." "Other factors include our desire to ensure that all persons to whom the company has an obligation are treated fairly, to preserve the assets of the company and maintain its current operations."

22   To supplement Dalkon expenses and to alleviate the tight cash flow position that Robins has experienced recently, it requested a $35 million credit limit "to meet $25 million of cash needs of its U.S. operations, $2 million in letters of credit for foreign suppliers, and $8 million of credit for its foreign units." This credit limit was the subject of heated debate among the Internal Revenue Service, the attorneys for more than 10,000 women who have filed suit against Robins, and various Robins' creditors. "The IRS contends that Robins owes about $61 million in corporate income taxes from as far back as 1978. Arguing on behalf of the agency, Assistant U.S. Attorney S. David Schiller told the judge that Robins had failed to prove that it needs the entire $35 million of credit or that it couldn't get the loans elsewhere under more favorable terms." The credit line requested by Robins was ultimately approved by a federal court judge. "Under the agreement, Robins will receive $23 million from Manufacturers Hanover Trust Company, New York, and $12 million from the Bank of Virginia. The arrangement, which was opposed vigorously by the Internal Revenue Service and others with claims pending against Robins, assigns the two banks priority for payments among all Robins creditors."

23   "In approving the credit agreement, Judge Robert R. Merhige, Jr., acknowledged that some of the terms 'could be questioned.' But he said he felt compelled to 'give way to the business judgment' of the company's managers. He also expressed concern that denying the request might harm the company's prospects for obtaining credit."

The Future

24   In October (1984), the company filed in Federal District Court in Richmond a motion seeking a class action to resolve all punitive damage claims arising from Dalkon Shield litigation. The goal is a single trial for the purpose of determining if A. H. Robins should, in fact, be liable for punitive damages and, if so, the amount of those damages in respect to all present and future Dalkon Shield claimants. It is our view that this is the only fair means of settling this issue. In addition to the class action, the court has been requested to establish a voluntary opt-in proceeding to dispose of claims for compensatory damages on a facilitated basis. Such a proceeding would allow those plaintiffs who so desire to advance their claims with a minimum of delay and expense.[8]

25   Additionally, the company initiated an advertising campaign for the purpose of persuading women using the shield to have them removed at the company's expense. As of the publication date of the company's 1984 annual report, "More than 18,250 inquiries [had] been received. . . . The company [had] paid for 777 examinations and 4,437 removals."

---

[8] A. H. Robins, *Annual Report,* 1984.

Exhibit 7

A. H. ROBINS COMPANY, INCORPORATED, AND SUBSIDIARIES
Selected Financial Data
(dollars in thousands except per share and ratio data)

	1984	1983	1982	1981
(Dollars in thousands except per share and ratio data)				
Operations				
Net sales	**$631,891**	$563,510	$482,324	$450,854
Cost of sales	**237,508**	220,628	195,008	190,759
Marketing, administrative and general	**222,939**	196,495	168,963	157,852
Research and development	**43,352**	40,686	34,279	28,572
Total operating costs and expenses	**503,799**	457,809	398,250	377,183
Operating earnings	**128,092**	105,701	84,074	73,671
Interest income	**7,560**	8,350	8,085	8,437
Interest expense	**(3,240)**	(5,441)	(10,308)	(3,564)
Litigation settlement income	**1,205**	2,256	3,135	3,379
Reserve for Dalkon Shield claims	**(615,000)**			
Litigation expenses and settlements	**(77,950)**	(18,745)	(7,091)	(3,318)
Provision for losses on disposition of businesses				
Other, net	**(13,190)**	(144)	(3,740)	(4,997)
Earnings (loss) before income taxes	**(572,523)**	91,977	74,155	73,608
Provision for income taxes (benefits)	**(110,910)**	33,756	25,462	29,380
Net earnings (loss)	**$(461,613)**	$ 58,221	$ 48,693	$ 44,228
Per Share Data				
Earnings (loss) per share	**$(18.44)**	$2.40	$1.98	$1.77
Dividends per share	**.72**	.62	.52	.44
Stockholders' equity (deficit) per share	**(5.23)**	14.69	13.29	12.52
Weighted average number of shares outstanding	**25,037**	24,295	24,552	25,015
Balance Sheet Data				
Cash and cash equivalents	**$ 91,627**	$133,381	$ 79,986	$ 89,024
Working capital	**122,344**	229,525	200,810	177,259
Current ratio	**1.7 to 1**	3.2 to 1	4.0 to 1	3.1 to 1
Property, plant and equipment, net	**$135,685**	$107,651	$ 98,079	$ 96,457
Depreciation and amortization	**16,310**	10,253	10,384	10,096
Total assets	**648,129**	509,663	439,983	443,942
Long-term obligations, exclusive of Dalkon Shield reserve	**25,330**	48,322	51,040	48,232
Stockholder's equity (deficit)	**(127,851)**	355,837	321,085	310,201

Amounts for 1983 and prior years have been reclassified to conform to 1984 presentation.

See Note 12 of Notes to Consolidated Financial Statements for information on litigation.

† Results preceded adoption of Statement of Financial Accounting Standards No. 52 which revised the method of translating foreign currency.

* Results were computed on a FIFO basis.

Exhibit 7 (*concluded*)

1980[†]	1979[†*]	1978[†*]	1977[†*]	1976[†*]	1975[†*]	1974[†*]
$432,328	$386,425	$357,070	$306,713	$284,925	$241,060	$210,713
187,496	157,895	146,636	122,374	108,519	89,304	71,233
160,477	139,782	131,195	114,490	101,568	85,378	77,128
27,033	20,522	18,951	16,107	12,729	10,690	9,568
375,006	318,199	296,782	252,971	222,816	185,372	157,929
57,322	68,226	60,288	53,742	62,109	55,688	52,784
5,614	5,767	3,469	2,033	2,355	1,726	2,465
(4,741)	(4,194)	(3,469)	(2,106)	(1,719)	(1,189)	(1,134)
3,590	28,934					
(4,616)	(6,005)	(9,560)	(3,331)	(1,146)	(5,065)	
(9,129)						
(4,112)	(13,539)	901	(2,675)	(2,710)	(2,518)	(1,209)
43,928	79,189	51,629	47,663	58,889	48,642	52,906
18,458	34,443	21,713	20,862	27,534	23,095	25,989
$ 25,470	$ 44,746	$ 29,916	$ 26,801	$ 31,355	$ 25,547	$ 26,917
$1.01	$1.71	$1.15	$1.03	$1.20	$ .98	$1.03
.42	.40	.34	.32	.30	.27	.26
11.16	10.52	9.20	8.39	7.69	6.79	6.04
25,314	26,107	26,127	26,127	26,127	26,127	26,126
$ 49,705	$ 69,381	$ 72,058	$ 43,611	$ 50,769	$ 41,763	$ 29,228
146,258	153,411	156,632	128,838	126,904	100,387	89,459
3.0 to 1	2.9 to 1	3.7 to 1	3.5 to 1	4.1 to 1	3.5 to 1	4.5 to 1
$ 80,511	$ 59,994	$ 55,350	$ 49,751	$ 39,066	$ 34,640	$30,418
10,950	8,806	8,427	6,837	6,076	5,007	4,322
390,570	379,597	326,073	287,045	262,668	223,544	190,263
35,346	26,518	27,809	16,718	20,412	6,740	5,620
280,394	272,673	240,275	219,242	200,802	177,275	157,695

Exhibit 8

A. H. ROBINS COMPANY, INCORPORATED AND SUBSIDIARIES
Consolidated Statements of Operations
(dollars in thousands except per share data)

Year Ended December 31	1984	1983*	1982*
Net Sales	$631,891	$563,510	$482,324
Cost of sales	237,508	220,628	195,008
Marketing, administrative and general	222,939	196,495	168,963
Research and development	43,352	40,686	34,279
Total operating costs and expenses	503,799	457,809	398,250
Operating Earnings	128,092	105,701	84,074
Interest income	7,560	8,350	8,085
Interest expense	(3,240)	(5,441)	(10,308)
Litigation settlement income	1,205	2,256	3,135
Reserve for Dalkon Shield claims	(615,000)		
Litigation expenses and settlements	(77,950)	(18,745)	(7,091)
Other, net	(13,190)	(144)	(3,740)
Earnings (Loss) Before Income Taxes	(572,523)	91,977	74,155
Provision for income taxes (benefits)	(110,910)	33,756	25,462
Net Earnings (Loss)	$(461,613)	$ 58,221	$ 48,693
Earnings (Loss) per Common Share	$(18.44)	$2.40	$1.98
Average number of shares outstanding	25,037	24,295	24,552

*Reclassified to conform to 1984 presentation.
The Notes to Consolidated Financial Statements are an integral part of these statements.

Exhibit 9

A. H. ROBINS COMPANY, INCORPORATED AND SUBSIDIARIES
Consolidated Statements of Stockholders' Equity (Deficit)
(dollars in thousands except per share data)

	Common Stock ($1 Par Value)	Additional Paid-In Capital	Retained Earnings (Deficit)	Cumulative Translation Adjustments	Treasury Stock (At Cost)	Total
Balance—January 1, 1982...........	$26,127	$700	$295,851	84	$(12,561)	$310,201
Net earnings.........................			48,693			48,693
Cash dividends—$.52 per share			(12,696)			(12,696)
Translation adjustment for 1982				(16,559)		(16,559)
Purchase of treasury stock—644,000 shares..					(8,844)	(8,844)
Issued for stock options—24,550 shares..	24	266				290
Balance—December 31, 1982	26,151	966	331,848	(16,475)	(21,405)	321,085
Net earnings.........................			58,221			58,221
Cash dividends—$.62 per share			(14,997)			(14,997)
Translation adjustment for 1983				(9,250)		(9,250)
Issued for stock options—61,900 shares..	62	716				778
Balance—December 31, 1983	26,213	1,682	375,072	(25,725)	(21,405)	355,837
Net loss			(461,613)			(461,613)
Cash dividends—$.72 per share			(17,936)			(17,936)
Translation adjustment for 1984				(10,051)		(10,051)
Purchase of treasury stock— 1,040,404 shares....................					(17,070)	(17,070)
Issued for stock options—20,300 shares..	21	201				222
Shares reissued with acquisition— 1,243,707 shares.....................		9,427			13,333	22,760
Balance—December 31, 1984	$26,234	$11,310	$(104,477)	$(35,776)	$(25,142)	$(127,851)

The Notes to Consolidated Financial Statements are an integral part of these statements.

Exhibit 10

A. H. ROBINS COMPANY, INCORPORATED AND SUBSIDIARIES
Consolidated Balance Sheets
(dollars in thousands)

December 31	1984	1983	1982
ASSETS			
Current Assets			
Cash	$ 1,792	$ 1,534	$ 5,792
Certificates of deposit and time deposits	13,426	57,700	14,349
Marketable securities	76,409	74,147	59,845
Accounts and notes receivable—net of allowance for doubtful accounts of $2,613 (1983—$2,560, 1982—$2,473)	111,313	112,260	107,790
Inventories	84,611	82,714	72,219
Prepaid expenses	5,643	6,674	5,136
Deferred tax benefits	15,800		3,537
Total current assets	308,994	335,029	268,668
Property, Plant and Equipment			
Land	6,313	6,552	6,940
Buildings and leasehold improvements	106,165	89,374	75,933
Machinery and equipment	90,260	70,169	68,453
	202,738	166,095	151,326
Less accumulated depreciation	67,053	58,444	53,247
	135,685	107,651	98,079
Intangible and Other Assets			
Intangibles—net of accumulated amortization	82,502	50,201	53,140
Note receivable, less current maturity			8,044
Deferred tax benefits	106,700		
Other assets	14,248	16,782	12,052
	203,450	66,983	73,236
	$648,129	$509,663	$439,983

Exhibit 10 (concluded)

LIABILITIES AND STOCKHOLDERS' EQUITY (DEFICIT)

Current Liabilities

Notes payable	$ 16,129	$ 7,116	$ 5,419
Long-term debt payable within one year	21,600	3,225	1,325
Current portion of reserve for Dalkon Shield claims	51,000		
Accounts payable	23,855	23,989	20,807
Income taxes payable	11,850	28,589	12,269
Accrued liabilities:			
Dalkon Shield costs	22,653	11,094	2,134
Other	39,563	31,491	25,904
Total current liabilities	186,650	105,504	67,858
Long-Term Debt	11,400	33,000	36,225
Reserve for Dalkon Shield Claims, Less Current Portion	564,000		
Other Liabilities	13,930	12,270	14,022
Deferred Income Taxes		3,052	793

Stockholders' Equity (Deficit)

Preferred stock, $1 par—authorized 10,000,000 shares, none issued			
Common stock, $1 par—authorized 40,000,000 shares	26,234	26,213	26,151
Additional paid-in capital	11,310	1,682	966
Retained earnings (deficit)	(104,477)	375,072	331,848
Cumulative translation adjustments	(35,776)	(25,725)	(16,475)
	(102,709)	377,242	342,490
Less common stock in treasury, at cost—1,793,347 shares			
(1983—1,996,650 shares, 1982—1,996,650 shares)	25,142	21,405	21,405
	(127,851)	355,837	321,085
	$648,129	$509,663	$439,983

The Notes to Consolidated Financial Statements are an integral part of these statements.

Exhibit 11

A. H. ROBINS COMPANY, INCORPORATED AND SUBSIDIARIES
Consolidated Statements of Changes in Financial Position
(dollars in thousands)

Year Ended December 31	1984	1983*	1982*
Cash Provided by Operations			
Net earnings (loss)	$(461,613)	$58,221	$ 48,693
Non-cash expenses			
Depreciation and amortization	16,310	10,253	10,384
Deferred tax benefit, reserve for Dalkon Shield claims	(125,933)		
Reserve for Dalkon Shield claims	615,000		
Other, net	6,140	2,477	3,201
	49,904	70,951	62,278
Operating Requirements, (Increase) Decrease			
Accounts and notes receivable	1,686	(7,212)	(18,172)
Inventories	125	(10,424)	(4,647)
Accounts payable, income taxes payable and accrued liabilities	(147)	36,279	(13,936)
Other, net	2,955	4,910	5,477
	4,619	23,553	(31,278)
Investments			
Capital additions	(38,155)	(20,955)	(15,815)
Acquisitions	(51,809)	(5,700)	(2,035)
	(89,964)	(26,655)	(17,850)
Cash flow from operations	(35,441)	67,849	13,150
Cash Provided by (Utilized in) Financial Activities			
Notes payable and long-term debt	5,933	543	(648)
Purchase of treasury shares	(17,070)		(8,844)
Issuance of treasury shares for acquisition	22,760		
	11,623	543	(9,492)
Less Cash Dividends Paid	17,936	14,997	12,696
Net increase (decrease) in cash and cash equivalents	$(41,754)	$53,395	$(9,038)

*Reclassified to conform to 1984 presentation.

The Notes to Consolidated Financial Statements are an integral part of these statements.

Exhibit 11 *(continued)*

1. Significant Accounting Policies

Consolidation

The consolidated financial statements include the accounts of A. H. Robins Company, Incorporated and all majority-owned subsidiaries. Accounts of subsidiaries outside the U. S. and Canada are included on the basis of a fiscal year beginning December 1 (or date of acquisition) and ending November 30. All significant intercompany accounts and transactions have been eliminated.

Inventories

Inventories are valued at the lower of cost or market. The cost for substantially all domestic inventories is determined on the last-in, first-out (LIFO) method while cost for foreign inventories is based on the first-in, first-out (FIFO) method.

Property, Plant and Equipment

Property, plant and equipment are recorded at cost and are depreciated over their estimated useful lives. Depreciation for all companies is computed on the straight line method for assets acquired after 1979. Depreciation on assets acquired in 1979 and prior years is computed on the declining balance method for domestic companies and on the straight line method for foreign companies.

Intangible Assets

Excess of cost over net assets of subsidiaries acquired after October 31, 1970 is being amortized over a period of 40 years or less. Excess cost of $17,357,000 relating to companies acquired prior to that date is not being amortized. Expenditures for development of patents are charged to expense as incurred. Patents purchased and trademarks are being amortized over their determinable lives.

Income Taxes

The Company provides for deferred income taxes on items of income or expense reported for tax purposes in different years than for financial purposes. The investment tax credit is included in earnings in the year the credit arises as a reduction of any provision for income taxes.

The Company files a consolidated Federal income tax return with its domestic subsidiaries. Income taxes, if any, are provided for on earnings of foreign subsidiaries remitted or to be remitted. No provision is made for income taxes on undistributed earnings of foreign subsidiaries reinvested in the companies.

Retirement Plans

The Company and certain of its subsidiaries have retirement plans for their employees. Costs of the plans are funded when accrued except for the plans of certain foreign subsidiaries. Unfunded prior service costs are provided for over periods not exceeding 40 years. Certain medical and life insurance benefits are provided for qualifying retired employees. The annual costs for these programs are not material and are expensed when paid.

Earnings (Loss) Per Share

Earnings (loss) per share are based on the weighted average number of common shares and common share equivalents outstanding during each year.

2. Acquisitions and Divestitures

On January 5, 1984, the Company acquired all of the outstanding stock of Quinton Instrument Company, Inc. for which the Company issued 1,243,707 shares of its common stock valued for accounting purposes at $18.30 per share and paid $20.1 million in cash. The total acquisition cost was $42.9 million, which consisted of the assigned value of the above-mentioned shares, the cash paid and acquisition expenses. The Company accounted for the acquisition as a purchase and accordingly has included Quinton's results of operations in its financial statements beginning January 5, 1984. On an unaudited pro forma basis, assuming the acquisition had occurred on January 1, 1983, the Company's net sales, net earnings and earnings per share would have been $587,328,000, $56,992,000 and $2.23, respectively. The pro forma amounts reflect estimated adjustments for goodwill amortization, depreciation and interest expense. Goodwill of $27,118,000 is being amortized on a straight line basis over a period of 40 years.

On April 2, 1984, the Company acquired substantially all of the assets associated with radio stations WRQK-FM and WPET-AM in Greensboro, North Carolina. The acquisition price was $7.6 million.

In December 1984, the Company acquired all of the outstanding stock of Lode B. V., an established ergometer manufacturer located in the Netherlands. Lode B. V., an addition to the Company's Medical Instruments Division, has been accounted for by the purchase method and did not result in a significant impact on 1984 financial results.

In March 1983, the Company acquired substantially all of the assets of Scientific Protein Laboratories, a company primarily engaged in the manufacture of animal-derived pharmaceutical products.

Also in March 1983, the Company sold its Quencher cosmetics line at an after-tax gain of $801,000.

In November 1982, the Company acquired the assets of U. S. Clinical Products, Incorporated, located in Richardson, Texas. U. S. Clinical Products engages primarily in the manufacturing and marketing of tamper-resistant seals used in hospitals on intravenous containers after the manufacturer's closure has been removed.

Exhibit 11 (*continued*)

3. Foreign Operations

At December 31, 1984, undistributed earnings of foreign subsidiaries totaled approximately $70,981,000 including amounts accumulated at dates of acquisition. Of this amount, $14,600,000 might be subject to net additional Federal income taxes if distributed currently. No provision has been made for income taxes on these undistributed earnings.

Foreign currency exchange losses included in earnings amounted to $1,187,000 in 1984 (1983—$938,000, 1982—$2,436,000). Net foreign assets included in the consolidated financial statements at December 31, 1984 were $75,098,000 (1983—$93,011,000, 1982—$101,271,000).

4. Inventories

| | (Dollars in thousands) | | |
	1984	1983	1982
Finished products	**$41,814**	$43,462	$38,467
Work in process	**18,425**	16,186	8,221
Raw materials and supplies	**24,372**	23,066	25,531
	$84,611	$82,714	$72,219

Substantially all domestic inventories were valued on the last-in, first-out (LIFO) method while most foreign inventories were valued on the first-in, first-out (FIFO) method. Approximately 68% of inventories was valued under LIFO in 1984 (1983—70%, 1982—65%) and the remainder under FIFO. Current cost (FIFO method) of inventories exceeded the LIFO values by $3,281,000 in 1984; $4,424,000 in 1983; and $3,546,000 in 1982.

5. Long-Term Debt

Long-term debt, net of amounts payable within one year, is summarized as follows:

| | (Dollars in thousands) | | |
	1984	1983	1982
8¾% promissory note due annually to 1988		$19,700	$21,025
Bonds, interest rate 55% of prime, due annually from 1984 to 1991 . . .	**11,400**	13,300	15,200
	$11,400	$33,000	$36,225

Annual maturities of long-term debt for the next five years are: 1985—$21,600,000; 1986—$1,900,000; 1987—$1,900,000; 1988—$1,900,000; and 1989—$1,900,000.

The 8¾% promissory note was redeemed at par subsequent to year end and therefore has been reclassified as long-term debt payable within one year.

Interest incurred during 1984 of $2,500,000 was capitalized and included in property, plant and equipment. No interest was capitalized in 1983 or 1982.

6. Lines of Credit

At December 31, 1984, unused lines of credit which do not support commercial paper or similar borrowing arrangements and may be withdrawn at the banks' option amounted to $12 million with domestic banks. Aggregate compensating balances were not material.

7. Stock Options

The Company has stock option plans for officers and certain key employees. The qualified stock option plan of 1973 as amended in 1982 was terminated on January 31, 1983 except as to outstanding options. A new incentive stock option plan was approved by the stockholders on April 26, 1983 under which 1,000,000 shares of common stock were made available for the granting of options. The plans are administered by a committee, subject to certain limitations expressly set forth in the plan, with authority to select participants, determine the number of shares to be allotted to a participant, set the option price, and fix the term of each option.

Transactions of the qualified and nonstatutory stock option plans are summarized below:

| | Shares Available for Option | Options Outstanding | |
		Shares	Price per Share
Balance—Dec. 31, 1981 . .	1,355,300	241,350	$10.19 to $11.38
Exercised		(24,550)	10.19 to 11.38
Canceled and expired . . .	4,150	(4,150)	10.19
Balance—Dec. 31, 1982 . .	1,359,450	212,650	10.19 to 11.38
Terminated—1973 Plan . .	(602,450)		
Exercised		(61,900)	10.19 to 11.38
1983 Plan	1,000,000		
Balance—Dec. 31, 1983 . .	1,757,000	150,750	10.19 to 11.38
Granted	(488,500)	488,500	13.69
Exercised		(20,300)	10.19 to 13.69
Canceled and expired . . .	13,700	(13,700)	11.38
Balance—Dec. 31, 1984 . .	1,282,000	605,250	10.19 to 13.69

The options are exercisable at any time until their expiration dates, which are in 1986 (136,550 shares) and 1994 (468,700 shares).

Exhibit 11 *(continued)*

8. Provision for Income Taxes

The provision for income taxes includes:

	(Dollars in thousands)		
	1984	1983	1982
Currently payable:			
Domestic	**$ (4,061)**	$13,563	$ 1,572
State	**1,580**	2,745	3,639
Foreign.	**9,234**	10,947	11,859
	$ 6,753	$27,255	$17,070
Deferred:			
Domestic	**$(110,009)**	$ 5,917	$ 8,238
State	**(8,648)**	270	292
Foreign.	**994**	314	(138)
	$(117,663)	$ 6,501	$ 8,392
Total provision	**$(110,910)**	$33,756	$25,462
Earnings (loss) before income taxes consist of:			
Domestic	**$(590,925)**	$71,613	$52,974
Foreign.	**18,402**	20,364	21,181
	$(572,523)	$91,977	$74,155

Note 12 in the Notes to Consolidated Financial Statements discusses a minimum reserve established by the Company in 1984 for pending and future claims related to the Dalkon Shield. These claims are deductible for tax purposes as incurred by the Company. It is the Company's belief that the currently recognized claims will be fully deductible against its future taxable income. However, generally accepted accounting principles limit the recognition of future tax benefits to those amounts assured beyond any reasonable doubt. Accordingly, the Company has recognized for financial statement purposes only those benefits arising from the carryback of product liability expenses against income tax expenses previously recognized by the Company. At December 31, 1984, the Company had, for financial statement purposes only, unrecognized loss carryforward deductions in the amount of $138,132,000 and unrecognized foreign and investment tax credits carryforward of $86,939,000.

Should the realization of product liability claims produce a taxable loss in a future period, the Company is permitted under provisions of the U. S. Internal Revenue Code to carry such loss back as a deduction against previous taxable income for a period up to 10 years. Such loss may also be used to reduce future taxable income for a period up to 15 years.

In 1984, the Company realized net tax benefits of $5,206,000, primarily in the form of investment tax credit and depreciation, from its investment in tax benefit leases under the "safe harbor" leasing provisions enacted in 1981 and 1982. These benefits reduced the 1984 provision for domestic taxes currently payable and increased the provision for deferred taxes. As current tax benefits are realized, the Company has reduced its purchase cost of the leases and established a deferred tax liability for the leases' future taxable income. Interest income is accrued on the unrecovered purchase cost. The excess of the purchase cost and accrued interest over the cumulative

tax savings expected is amortized on an interest method during the years temporary excess tax savings are produced. The interest accrued and investment amortized during the lease terms have no material effect on earnings. At December 31, 1984, the balance of unrecovered investment and accrued interest was $1,071,000.

Deferred income taxes result from tax leases and from income and expense items reported for financial accounting and tax purposes in different periods. The source of these differences and the tax effect of each is shown below:

	(Dollars in thousands)		
	1984	1983	1982
Reserve for Dalkon Shield claims.	**$(125,933)**		
Discounted portion of install-ment note receivable	**574**	$1,106	$1,520
Tax depreciation in excess of books . . .	**2,134**	1,480	1,096
Other	**356**	988	585
Tax benefit from tax leases	**$ 5,206**	2,927	5,191
	$(117,663)	$6,501	$8,392

Reconciliation of the effective tax rate and the Federal statutory rate is as follows:

	Percent of Pretax Income (Loss)		
	1984	1983	1982
Statutory Federal tax rate.	**(46.0)%**	46.0%	46.0%
Product liability claims in excess of amounts carried back.	**15.2**		
Foreign, investment and other tax credits not recognized after loss carryback	**11.1**		
Federal tax on foreign earnings	**1.4**	(1.1)	(3.1)
State taxes on income, net of Federal tax benefit.	**(1.3)**	2.8	3.6
Investment and other tax credits		(2.1)	(2.8)
Foreign earnings taxed at higher (lower) effective tax rate.	**.1**		.3
Puerto Rican earnings exempt from tax . .	**(1.1)**	(6.7)	(9.0)
Tax exempt interest.	**(.1)**	(.3)	(1.2)
All other, net	**1.3**	(1.9)	.5
	(19.4)%	36.7%	34.3%

A wholly owned subsidiary in Puerto Rico operates under partial income tax exemptions granted for periods through 1999. The estimated tax saving from the Puerto Rican operation was $6,200,000 in 1984 (1983—$6,200,000, 1982—$6,700,000). Puerto Rican withholding taxes are provided on those earnings expected to be repatriated prior to expiration of the exemptions.

During 1983, the Internal Revenue Service completed its examination of the Company's tax returns for the years 1978 through 1980 and proposed a deficiency of income taxes of approximately $6,400,000. The Company is contesting the proposed deficiency which arises from a proposed reallocation of income from the Company's Puerto Rico subsidiary. It is likely that a similar deficiency will be proposed for the years 1981 and 1982.

Exhibit 11 *(continued)*

Management believes that any additional income taxes that may result from the proposed deficiency, and from the probable proposed deficiency related to the same issues for the years 1981 and 1982, should not have a material adverse effect on the consolidated financial position of the Company.

9. Business Segment Information

Information about operations in different business segments and in various geographic areas of the world is included on page 32 of this report and incorporated herein by reference.

10. Retirement Plan

The Company and certain of its subsidiaries have retirement plans covering substantially all of their employees. The total retirement expense for 1984 was $6,908,000 (1983—$6,246,000, 1984—$5,435,000). The actuarial present value of accumulated plan benefits, assuming a weighted average rate of return of 8% in 1984 (1983—8%, 1982—6.5%), and plan net assets available for benefits of domestic defined benefit plans as of January 1, 1984, 1983 and 1982 are as follows:

| | (Dollars in thousands) | | |
	1984	1983	1982
Actuarial present value of accumulated plan benefits:			
Vested	**$40,895**	$35,601	$30,925
Nonvested..................	**3,472**	3,250	4,351
	$44,367	$38,851	$35,276
Net assets available for benefits.....	**$55,621**	$47,287	$36,017

Assets available for benefits and the actuarial present value of accumulated benefits have not been determined for several minor foreign pension plans which are not required to report such information to government agencies.

Other liabilities include $6,635,000 of accrued pensions and severance benefits in foreign subsidiaries (1983—$7,063,000, 1982—$7,100,000).

11. Commitments

Rentals of space, vehicles and office and data processing equipment under operating leases amounted to $6,718,000 in 1984 (1983—$6,428,000, 1982—$5,843,000).

Minimum future rental commitments under all noncancelable operating leases at December 31, 1984 with remaining terms of more than one year are as follows:

	(Dollars in thousands)
1985	$2,515
1986	1,804
1987	1,634
1988	1,265
1989	822
Later years	1,853
Total minimum future rentals.............................	$9,893

The Company has agreed to repurchase, at the option of the shareholder until such time as the securities are registered, the shares of the Company issued to the former Quinton Instrument Company, Inc. shareholders. Upon tender of the shares, the Company will repurchase the shares at the current market price. At December 31, 1984, there were 1,017,103 shares subject to this agreement.

As of December 31, 1984, the Company had outstanding commitments of $8 million for the construction of plant, office and research and development facilities.

12. Litigation

Dalkon Shield—In June 1970, the Company acquired the rights to the Dalkon Shield, an intrauterine contraceptive device. Approximately 2.8 million devices were sold in the U.S. through June 1974. Approximately 1.7 million of the devices were sold abroad.

Numerous cases and claims alleging injuries claimed to be associated with use of the device have been filed against the Company in the U.S. ("Claims"). Only a few claims have been filed in foreign jurisdictions. The alleged injuries fall under the following general groups: perforation of the uterus or cervix, infection of the female reproductive system, pregnancy, ectopic pregnancy, spontaneous abortion which may be accompanied by sepsis, death, sterility, fetal abnormality and premature delivery, painful insertion and removal, and miscellaneous injuries. In addition to compensatory damages, most cases also seek punitive damages.

As of December 31, 1984, there were approximately 3,800 Claims pending against the Company in Federal and state courts in the U.S. The Company expects that a substantial number of new Claims will be filed against the Company in the future.

Through December 31, 1984, the Company had disposed of approximately 8,300 Claims. In disposing of these Claims, the Company and its insurer have paid out approximately $314.6 million. Prior to 1981, substantially all disposition costs (including legal expenses, but excluding punitive damages) were charged to applicable products liability insurance carried by the Company. The Company incurred costs in excess of insurance in the following amounts: 1981—$3.3 million; 1982—$7.1 million; 1983—$18.7 million; and 1984—$78.0 million (exclusive of the reserve described below).

Of the Claims disposed of prior to December 31, 1984, 50 were tried to conclusion. Of that number, 27 resulted in verdicts for compensatory damages in favor of plaintiffs and 23 in verdicts in favor of the Company. Seven of the plaintiff verdicts (involving compensatory awards aggregating approximately $5 million) and one verdict in favor of the Company are the subject of pending appeals. Eight of the plaintiff verdicts also

Exhibit 11 (*continued*)

included awards of punitive damages in an aggregate amount of $17,227,000. Six of these punitive awards aggregating $8,827,000 have been paid; two are the subject of appeals. Punitive damage awards are not covered by insurance and are payable by the Company.

The Company is unable to assess its potential exposure to additional punitive damage awards. It has recently filed a motion in the United States District Court for the Eastern District of Virginia seeking certification of a class of present and prospective claimants in both Federal and state courts for the purpose of determining and finally resolving in a single proceeding whether the Company should be liable for punitive damages by reason of the Dalkon Shield and, if so, the aggregate amount of additional punitive damages that should be awarded.

The Company had product liability insurance covering compensatory awards with respect to the Dalkon Shield for pertinent periods prior to March 1978. In October 1984, the Company settled its suit, commenced in 1979, against its insurer concerning coverage of Dalkon Shield liability. From existing coverage and some additional coverage resulting from the settlement of this suit the Company had at December 31, 1984, approximately $70 million of insurance coverage that it expects to be able to use.

In anticipation of the conclusion of the insurance coverage suit, the Company commissioned a study, the purpose of which was to provide management of the Company with data to establish a loss reserve for the future costs in compensatory damages and legal expenses of the disposition of pending and future Claims. The study estimated the amount of this future disposition cost based on the following: (1) an estimate of total injuries based on an epidemiological analysis of published literature regarding the Dalkon Shield and other IUDs; (2) a statistical analysis of all Claims filed during the period 1981 through 1983 which constitute 51% of all Claims filed since the inception of the litigation through December 31, 1983; and (3) a statistical analysis of disposition timing and costs of all Claims filed during the period January 1, 1979 through December 31, 1983 and disposed of prior to October 1, 1984. The information on claims filed and disposition timing and costs was extracted from a database which contains information on Claims filed through December 31, 1983. The study utilized information from the periods discussed above, which was believed to be more representative of future experience, rather than the entire litigation period which would have produced a materially higher estimate of disposition cost.

Based on the study's estimate of disposition cost and a review of 1984 fourth-quarter settlement cost data, management established a reserve, net of insurance, of $615 million against 1984 earnings in the accompanying consolidated financial statements. Management believes this represents a reasonable estimate of a minimum reserve for compensatory damages and legal expenses for pending and future Claims. The reserve does not provide for any punitive damages or damages from Dalkon Shield litigation abroad since there is no substantive basis to quantify such exposures. In taking into account 1984 fourth quarter settlement cost data, management excluded the cost of a single group settlement which management believes is reasonable to assume is not representative of the expected future disposition of Claims. If the excluded settlement cost had been factored as an increasing trend into projected future cost of disposition of Claims, the reserve would have been increased by a material amount.

Based on the study's projected schedule of disposition of pending and future Claims, the payout of the reserve will take place over many years. The Company has reduced its 1984 provision for income taxes by $125.9 million, representing the expected minimum tax benefit to be realized by loss carrybacks to 1983 and prior years, plus reductions in deferred taxes expected to turn around in the tax loss carryforward period. The net effect of the reserve, less estimated tax benefits, is $489.1 million or $19.53 per share.

Continuing uncertainties associated with the litigation preclude a determination of the ultimate cost of the Dalkon Shield litigation to the Company. There has been a significant increase in the number of new Claims filed per month and additional pressure on and a resulting increase in some settlement values which, if continued, would result in a greater Claim disposition cost than the amount estimated by the study. Whether this represents a long term trend or is, as management believes is reasonable to assume, the temporary result of publicity associated with several Dalkon Shield related events in 1984 and 1985 causing a temporary acceleration in the rate of filing of Claims with a subsequent leveling to those shown in the study will only be determined by future experience.

In addition to these uncertainties, there are other factors which could affect, either favorably or unfavorably, the ultimate outcome of the Dalkon Shield litigation and the resulting financial impact on the Company. Among them are:

- The Dalkon Shield removal campaign initiated on October 29, 1984
- The types of injuries alleged in future Claims
- The effect of the passage of time, including the effect of statutes of limitations
- The level of litigation activity relating to devices sold abroad
- The method of disposition of Claims
- The class action intended to resolve the question of punitive damages.

Exhibit 11 (concluded)

Accordingly, the reserve may not necessarily be the amount of the loss ultimately experienced by the Company. It is not likely, however, that the ultimate loss will be less than the amount reserved. Further, the exposure of the Company for additional compensatory and punitive damages awards over and above this reserve, although not presently determinable, may be significant and further materially adversely affect the future consolidated financial condition and results of operations of the Company.

Other—In December 1982, the United States District Court for the Southern District of New York determined that the suit filed in 1977 by Kalman and Anita Ross, stockholders of the Company, should be certified as a class action for damages on behalf of persons who purchased the Company's Common Stock during the period March 8, 1971 through June 28, 1974. In addition to the Company, certain of its present and former officers and directors are defendants. This suit alleges dissemination of false and misleading information and failure to disclose other information concerning the Dalkon Shield. After completion of discovery, an agreement was reached under which the Company will pay $6.9 million in settlement of this class action. This agreement is subject to final judicial approval. The action against the individual defendants will be dismissed, subject to final judicial approval. A provision for this settlement has been recorded in 1984 and included in Other, Net.

In March 1980, Zoecon Corporation filed a civil action against the Company and Miller-Morton Company, a subsidiary since merged into the Company, alleging unfair competition (a claim since abandoned) and patent infringement in connection with the marketing of the Sergeant's Sentry V flea and tick collar. The Company counterclaimed alleging patent invalidity on the part of Zoecon Corporation. The case has now been disposed of by way of a settlement having no material financial impact on the Company.

Case 23

Tylenol's Capsule Crisis: Part I

1   On February 8, 1986, a 23-year-old woman in Yonkers, New York, died from a cyanide-contaminated Tylenol capsule. In 1982, when seven people in Chicago died after ingesting similarly tainted Tylenol capsules, the company Johnson & Johnson (J&J), recalled 31 million bottles and spent about $100 million on marketing and repackaging. The first move of the chairman, Jim Burke, was to stop the manufacture and sale of the over-the-counter (OTC) capsule, much like he did in 1982. The frustrating nightmare for Tylenol executives—seemingly random poisonous tampering with a few capsules of the company's best-known product—had returned. They faced a strategic crisis! How to respond? What to do with a $525 million-sales-per-year product? And when to do it?

Background—Johnson & Johnson

2   J&J was incorporated in New Jersey in 1887 by Robert Wood Johnson and his two brothers with $100,000 of capital and 14 employees. During his tenure, he established the company as a leader in the health care industry by such moves as introducing revolutionary surgical dressings and establishing a bacteriological laboratory. Over the years, the company experienced a rapid growth through internal development by introducing new products, by acquiring established companies, and by international expansion. The company's 1985 earnings were $613.7 million on revenue of $6.42 billion.

3   J&J manufactures and sells a broad range of products in health care and other fields all over the world. The company's products are divided into four industry segments as follows:

4   **Consumer.** This segment consists of products that are marketed to the general public and distributed both through wholesalers and directly to independent and chain retail outlets. It includes toiletries and hygienic products, baby care items, first aid products, and nonprescription drugs.

5   **Professional.** This segment consists of ligatures and sutures, mechanical wound closure products, diagnostic products, dental products, medical equipment and devices, surgical dressings, surgical instruments, and related items used principally by the professional fields, including hospitals, physicians, dentists, diagnostic laboratories, and clinics. These products are marketed principally through surgical supply and other dealers.

This case was prepared as a basis for class discussion by Yaakov Weber of the University of Kentucky. Copyright © 1987 by Yaakov Weber.

Exhibit 1
Sales and operating profit by business segment (in millions of dollars)

Segment	1981		1980	
	Sales	Operating profit	Sales	Operating profit
Consumer	$2,362.8	$338.4	$2,124.7	$263.7
Professional	1,734.4	177.9	1,540.5	191.5
Pharmaceutical	1,118.6	314.7	1,008.1	228.2
Industrial	243.7	32.9	303.4	29.5
Total	$5,399.0	$837.7	$4,837.4	$712.9

6   **Pharmaceutical.**   This segment consists principally of prescription drugs, including contraceptives and therapeutics, and veterinary products. These products are distributed both directly and through wholesalers for use by health care professionals and the general public.

7   **Industrial.**   These products are converted or consumed by industrial users and, in general, not available to or used by the general public. This segment consists of textile products, collagen sausage casings, and fine chemicals. Sales are directly to users and through a variety of industrial trade channels.

8   Sales and operating profit for the four industry segments are presented in Exhibit 1. Balance sheet and income statements appear in appendixes provided with Case 24. Exhibit 2 shows several financial ratios comparing J&J and its major competitors.

9   The international business began with the establishment of an affiliate in Canada in 1919 and one in Great Britain in 1924. Their international business is conducted by subsidiaries manufacturing many of J&J's products in about 50 countries and selling in most countries of the world. The principal products marketed and the methods of distribution used by J&J's international subsidiaries vary across countries and cultures. About 40 percent of J&J's sales and more than half of its after-tax earnings came from overseas. Exhibit 3 shows the foreign sales of J&J and its major competitors.

10   J&J views research and development (R&D) as a key strength supporting its domestic and international business. Major research facilities are located not only in the United States but also in Belgium, Brazil, Canada, Switzerland, the United Kingdom, and West Germany. Exhibit 4 shows the costs of worldwide research activities relating to the development of new products, the improvement of existing products, the technical support of products, and compliance with governmental regulations for the protection of the consumer. These costs are charged directly against income in the year incurred. Exhibit 5 compares J&J's R&D expenditure with its major competitors'.

11   J&J was the last of the large, public companies to nominate outsiders for its board of directors, relenting in 1978 only under pressure from the New York Stock Exchange. The stock exchange required J&J to accept two outsiders, enough to dominate a three-

Exhibit 2
Financial ratios of major drug companies (corporatewide—includes all products)

Company (OTC analgesic product)	1980				1981				1982				1983				1984			
	EPS*	ROI†	NI‡	D/C§	EPS	ROI	NI	D/C	EPS	ROI	NI	D/C	EPS	ROI	NI	D/C	EPS	ROI	NI	D/C
Johnson & Johnson (Tylenol)	2.17	12.9%	$400	3.0%	2.51	13.1%	$468	3.4%	2.79	13.0%	$523	4.8%	2.57	11.3%	$489	6.01%	2.75	11.4%	$515	6.8%
Bristol-Myers (Bufferin and Excedrin)	2.04	13.1	271	7.5	2.29	13.0	306	6.0	2.59	13.3	349	6.1	3.00	14.2	408	4.7	3.45	15.1	472	4.4
American Home Products (Anacin and Anacin 3)	2.84	20.0	446	0.2	3.18	20.1	497	0	3.59	20.7	560	0	4.00	21.2	627	1.9	4.26	21.4	656	1.9
Sterling Drug (Bayer Aspirin)	2.04	10.2	123	5.5	2.15	10.3	130	5.0	2.17	10.2	132	7.2	2.24	9.8	137	8.1	2.39	9.9	145	7.4

* EPS = Earnings per share.

† ROI = Return on investment (percent).

‡ NI = Net income (millions of dollars).

§ D/C = Debt/capital ratio (percent).

Exhibit 3
Foreign sales of major drug companies

Company (OTC analgesic product)	1981		1982		1983		1984	
	Foreign sales ($ millions)	Percent of total sales	Foreign sales ($ millions)	Percent of total sales	Foreign sales ($ millions)	Percent of total sales	Foreign sales ($ millions)	Percent of total sales
Johnson & Johnson (Tylenol)	$2,373	44%	$2,457	43%	$2,389	40%	$2,389	39%
Bristol-Myers (Bufferin and Excedrin)	1,257	36	1,223	34	1,175	30	1,264	30
American Home Products (Anacin and Anacin 3)	1,387	34	1,412	31	1,360	28	1,050	23
Sterling Drug (Bayer Aspirin)	828	44	769	41	703	37	699	38

Exhibit 4
Research expenditure by Johnson & Johnson ($000)

Year	Expenses*
1984	$421,200
1983	405,100
1982	363,200
1981	282,900
1980	232,800
1979	192,688
1978	163,617

* These expenses are charged directly to income in the year in which they were incurred.

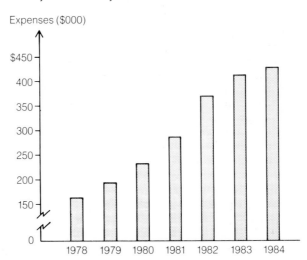

Exhibit 5
Corporatewide R&D expenditure of major drug companies (in millions of dollars)

Company (analgesic product)	1981 Amount spent	1981 Percent of sales	1982 Amount spent	1982 Percent of sales	1983 Amount spent	1983 Percent of sales	1984 Amount spent	1984 Percent of sales
Johnson & Johnson (Tylenol)	$282	5%	$363	6%	$405	7%	$421	7%
Bristol-Myers (Bufferin and Excedrin)	144	4	161	4	185	5	212	5
American Home Products (Anacin and Anacin 3)	115	3	137	3	161	3	N.R.	N.R.
Sterling Drug (Bayer Aspirin)	67	4	70	4	81	4	88	5

member audit committee. But J&J has since brought 7 outsiders onto the board to join 10 insiders.

12   J&J articulates its business principles in a document called *Our Credo*—a code of corporate behavior that has a mystical but nonetheless palpable influence on the company. Chairman Jim Burke commented after the first Tylenol crisis: "All of us at McNeil Consumer Products and J&J truly believe that the guidance of the Credo played the most important role in our decision making." The Credo is a legacy of "the General," Robert Wood Johnson, the son of one of the founding Johnson brothers. He was the man who, during his long rule from 1938 to 1963, shaped the company's philosophy and culture. First given to employees in 1947, the guiding principles of the credo have been renewed over the years, in part through Credo challenge meetings. The beginning of a series of Credo challenge meetings was in 1975, with an invitation for 24 officers from the United States and overseas to challenge the Credo. They debated for hours before changing even a paragraph in the document. The final result, which was prominently displayed in every manager's office, is shown in Exhibit 6. It commands that the company serve customers first, employees second, the communities in which it operates third, and finally its stockholders. J&J has sometimes sacrificed earnings in what it perceived to be the best interests of the customers. For example, when sun worshipers discovered that Johnson's Baby Oil is an excellent tanning agent, J&J played along with an advertising campaign aimed at teenagers: "Turn on a tan, baby." As evidence began to accumulate that overexposure to the sun promotes skin cancer, J&J voluntarily killed the campaign in 1969, at an estimated cost of about 15 percent of baby oil sales.

13   J&J put a great emphasis on its decentralized organizational structure. The 1981 annual report revealed the main reasons for having decentralized units, which:

> share a commitment to meeting the special needs of a well-defined customer. In doing so, they create a wide variety of innovative ways to successfully run their businesses.
>
> We feel that the secret to liberating that productivity is decentralization— granting each company sufficient autonomy to conduct its business without

Exhibit 6

Our Credo

We believe our first responsibility is to the doctors, nurses and patients,
to mothers and all others who use our products and services.
In meeting their needs everything we do must be of high quality.
We must constantly strive to reduce our costs
in order to maintain reasonable prices.
Customers' orders must be serviced promptly and accurately.
Our suppliers and distributors must have an opportunity
to make a fair profit.

We are responsible to our employees,
the men and women who work with us throughout the world.
Everyone must be considered as an individual.
We must respect their dignity and recognize their merit.
They must have a sense of security in their jobs.
Compensation must be fair and adequate,
and working conditions clean, orderly and safe.
Employees must feel free to make suggestions and complaints.
There must be equal opportunity for employment, development
and advancement for those qualified.
We must provide competent management,
and their actions must be just and ethical.

We are responsible to the communities in which we live and work
and to the world community as well.
We must be good citizens — support good works and charities
and bear our fair share of taxes.
We must encourage civic improvements and better health and education.
We must maintain in good order
the property we are privileged to use,
protecting the environment and natural resources.

Our final responsibility is to our stockholders.
Business must make a sound profit.
We must experiment with new ideas.
Research must be carried on, innovative programs developed
and mistakes paid for.
New equipment must be purchased, new facilities provided
and new products launched.
Reserves must be created to provide for adverse times.
When we operate according to these principles,
the stockholders should realize a fair return.

Johnson & Johnson

unnecessary constraints. In short, we believe decentralization equals creativy equals productivity.

14   To accomplish this purpose, a new company was created whenever a new product or market handled by any unit was deemed important enough to warrant a separate dedicated effort. This was the case with McNeil Consumer Products Company, which was created in 1976 to focus exclusively on the consumer product opportunity for Tylenol products in the OTC analgesic business. McNeil Pharmaceutical, then, was able to concentrate on prescription products, including Tylenol with codeine.

Background—Tylenol (before the first crisis in September 1982)

15   On January 15, 1959, J&J acquired McNeil Laboratories, Inc., manufacturer of pharmaceutical products (including Tylenol), in exchange for 622,008 common shares ($32 million in 1959). Through the 1960s, McNeil carefully promoted Tylenol among doctors and pharmacists as an alternative pain reliever for people who suffer stomach upset and other side effects from aspirin. The drug—which is an acetaminophin-based, or nonaspirin, analgesic—found consumer favor because it is less irritating to the stomach than aspirin.

16   In 1974, J&J acquired StimTech, a fledgling health care company built around a new product. The product, an electronic pain-killing device, was intended as a substitute for analgesic drugs—including J&J's Tylenol. StimTech was founded in 1971 to market a transcutaneous electronic nerve stimulator (TENS). The unit, coinvented by Hagfors in the 1960s, blocks pain sensations electronically by stimulating nerve fibers in the patient's skin.

17   TENS is claimed effective against headaches, arthritis, and back pain, without any of the side effects of drugs used to treat the same infirmities. But while J&J's aggressive marketing made Tylenol the number one OTC drug in the United States, StimTech foundered. The three founders charged J&J with quashing StimTech as a potential competitor. A U.S. district judge in Minneapolis has upheld a jury's finding that J&J bought the company to suppress development of its product. Judge Miles W. Lord, who presided over the trial in summer 1981, said the evidence "fully justifies" a verdict of fraud, antitrust violations, and breach of contract. J&J had to pay $170 million to the three entrepreneurs who started StimTech. George S. Frazza, J&J's general counsel, noted that about 10 other companies now market TENS equipment, including Medtronic, Minnesota Mining, and Dow-Corning, and that the company will continue to invest in it and promote it. He was also confident that J&J will win its appeal.

18   In early 1975, Bristol-Myers decided to challenge Tylenol with a cut-rate imitation called Datril. At first, McNeil showed some hesitancy about all-out combat. But by late 1975 McNeil cut Tylenol's price by one third and began to advertise Tylenol heavily. Tylenol's spectacular rise is shown in Figure 1. After the battle was over, the 12 products in the Tylenol line had taken an overwhelming 37 percent share of the $1.3 billion analgesic market (over $400 million), more than Bayer, Bufferin, and Anacin combined—the three best-selling headache cures until Tylenol came along. Datril has been all but annihilated. For an illustration of the analgesic market share of the major competitors, see Figure 2.

Figure 1
Sales of 12 products in Tylenol line

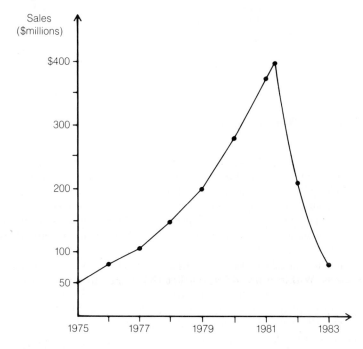

Figure 2
The OTC analgesic market, 1982

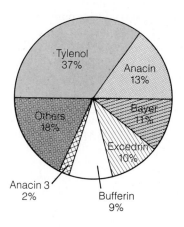

Exhibit 7
Changes in sales, stock price, and market share

	Per incident	Immediately post-incident
Tylenol sales	$480 million (12 months preceding incident)	$90 million (12 months following incident)
Stock price (per share)	$46 (day before incident)	$38 (one week later)
OTC market share	37% (day before incident)	7% (three weeks later)

19   While J&J was large and widely diversified, its Tylenol product line had a huge and direct impact on J&J. In late 1982, Tylenol contributed an estimated 7.4 percent of J&J's worldwide sales of $5.4 billion and 17 to 18 percent of its $467.6 million in net earnings in 1981. A rise of 25 percent in Tylenol-derived profits was estimated for 1982, compared to a corporatewide estimate of increased profits of around 16 percent. As the summer of 1982 drew to a close, McNeil executives were confident Tylenol would take over 50 percent of the market by 1986. J&J stock had risen in two years from a low of $20 to $46, reflecting in part the stock market's attraction to Tylenol's success. Within a few days, market share and stock prices would drop dramatically.

The First Crisis: 1982

20   On September 30, 1982, the Cook County (Chicago) Medical Examiner's Office reported that three people had been killed as the result of ingesting cyanide in Tylenol capsules. That morning, calls came from newspapers, TV, and radio stations as far away as Honolulu and Ireland. And, as the story started to break, even more calls began to pour in from pharmacies, doctors, hospitals, poison control centers, and hundreds of panicked consumers. Within a few days, Chicago's mayor, Jane Byrne, went on television urging her constituents to stop taking Tylenol.

21   Many retailers immediately removed the entire Tylenol line of tablets, capsules, and elixirs from their shelves. A senior vice president for marketing at Revco D.S., Inc., in Twinsburg, Ohio, said that buyers "are switching brands" and that the chain was getting "hundreds of phone calls" from people with Tylenol products not implicated in the scare. Tylenol's market share and J&J's stock price fell rapidly, as shown in Exhibit 7.

22   International sales were affected differently in each country. The governments of Guatemala and Puerto Rico banned sales of Tylenol, and the Venezuelan government ordered consumers to "break their bottles" of the painkiller. In the Philippines, where Tylenol capsules were introduced only three months earlier yet where Tylenol tablets had been available for some time, the government's health minister banned the sale of the capsules and ordered a recall. All post offices and customs sections in ports of entry were ordered to seize capsules brought into the country. In Canada, sales were

not banned, and Canada's Department of Health initiated industrywide discussions about ways to ensure that consumers could detect product tampering. In Europe, Tylenol was unaffected, primarily because it was not yet widely available.

First Reaction of J&J

23   Despite the commitment of J&J to decentralization, J&J Chairman James Burke elevated the management of the crisis to the corporate level. He personally took charge of the company's response and delegated responsibility for running the rest of the company to other members of J&J's executive committee. Burke's reason for doing this was "because the crisis was a major public health problem and a major threat to the company as a whole and to other products bearing the company's name." The crisis committee consisted of J&J Chairman James Burke, J&J President David Clare, Vice President of Public Relations Lawrence Foster, McNeil Consumer Products Chairman David Collins, General Counsel George Frazza, and executive committee member Arthur Quilty. This committee met twice daily.

24   Their first move was to immediately stop manufacturing and selling Tylenol capsules. Next they suspended all advertising for Tylenol and recalled 93,000 bottles scattered across Ohio. This was an expensive process—telegrams to doctors, hospitals, and distributors alone cost almost a half-million dollars. In a meeting with the FBI and the Food and Drug Administration (FDA), Burke advocated a recall of all Extra-Strength Tylenol capsules, but he was counseled against it. The FBI feared that this move would tell the murderer he could bring a major corporation to its knees, and the FDA feared it might cause more public anxiety. However, following the seventh victim and what appeared to be copycat strychnine poisoning with Tylenol capsules in California, the FDA agreed with Burke that he had to recall Tylenol capsules worldwide. This 31 million-bottle recall raised the expense of this incident to over $100 million.

25   While recognizing possible dangers in trying to manage the news media, J&J's crisis team decided to open its doors and to have a close relationship with the press. Burke and Foster felt the company could use the media to quickly get out maximum information to the public so as to both prevent a panic and gain credibility. For example, on the first day after the Chicago deaths, the crisis committee learned that cyanide was in fact used in the quality assurance facility next to the Tylenol manufacturing plant. The cyanide was used to test the purity of raw materials. Consistent with this "open" approach, the public relations department immediately released this information to the press. An obvious advantage from having close relationships with the media was that the company could get its most accurate and up-to-date information around the country (and the world) via reporters calling in for comments.

Making a Strategic Decision: 1982

26   Within weeks, consumer groups advocated immediate action and tamper-proof packaging for OTC drugs, but FDA Commissioner Arthur Hayes, Jr., argued that this was not possible. To quell consumer panic, the FDA and members of the OTC medicines

industry formed a committee to develop standards for tamper-resistant packages. The FDA's recommendation for a tamper-resistant regulation was rumored to go along with industry suggestions allowing marketers to select from among many different types of tamper-resistant packagings. It also was expected to recommend that the special packaging would be required on all new products after 90 days and that all old packaging must be off the shelves after 15 months. The proposal put the cost of the regulation at $20 million to $30 million annually, or about 1 cent per item. The FDA prepared a 30-second commercial that had Commissioner Arthur H. Hayes urging consumers to check medications carefully.

27   Most companies were awaiting word of the specifics of the FDA regulation before making public any marketing plans regarding permanent protective packaging or advertising. Several companies, including American Home Products and Norcliff-Thayer, were taking temporary steps to protect products, such as glued boxes and cellophane wrappings.

28   Despite the uncertainty surrounding final resolution of the packaging issue, Tylenol's competitors were not standing idly by. American Home Products had just introduced Anacin 3, a nonaspirin analgesic like Tylenol, and immediately benefited from the damage to Tylenol's reputation. AHP increased production at both of its Anacin 3 plants from two to three shifts on a round-the-clock basis. Bristol-Myers, producer of Excedrin, said that demand was up considerably. During the same time, Bristol-Myers reported that a poisoning incident occurred with Excedrin capsules in Colorado. This led Bristol-Myers to remove all Excedrin capsules from Colorado shelves, to urge consumers to switch to tablets, and to take out newspaper ads telling consumers how to exchange Excedrin capsules for tablets.

29   While the controversy over instituting tamper-proof containers swirled around it, J&J's crisis team sifted through its strategic options. Larry N. Feinberg, an analyst for Dean Witter Reynolds, Inc., said that it would take a great deal of time to reestablish the Tylenol brand and that "J&J may never be able to reestablish its credibility fully." Robert Benezra, an analyst for Alex, Brown & Sons, said that "destroying all Tylenol capsules wherever they can find them will be the only way they can effectively deal with the problem of consumer hesitancy." He contended that the company might eventually come up with a new brand name for the now-tainted capsules. Most analysts estimated that it would take J&J at least 18 months to repair the damage done to its product, based on the quick move of J&J to halt public distrust. Both analysts and retailers agreed that the company had earned its good reputation and deserves public support. Sumner H. Goldman, vice president of merchandising at Super Valu Stores, Inc., said that "They've done one of the best marketing jobs on Tylenol in the history of health and beauty aids marketing." But he too believed it would be a long road back for Tylenol.

30   David H. Talbot, a health care analyst with Drexel Burnham Lambert, estimated that Tylenol's initial recalls would cost $50 million after taxes—enough to hold its 1982 earnings rise to only 1 or 2 percent. Most of the recall costs were incurred in buying back Tylenol bottles from retailers and consumers and shipping them to disposal points. The cost of testing all the recalled capsules for the presence of poisons exceeded their value; therefore, all the withdrawn capsules were destroyed. The company estimated that costs would drop third-quarter earnings from 78 cents a share in 1981 to

51 cents in 1982. Security analysts projected a 70 percent drop in what normally would have been $100 million plus in sales for Tylenol's over-the-counter line of products in the fourth quarter. It was estimated that prescription sales of Tylenol with codeine, about $18 million a quarter, would not be affected. Some analysts said that the company would be lucky if Tylenol could make half of the sales that originally were expected for the next year (the precrisis estimate was half a billion dollars).

31   Joseph Chiesa, McNeil president, said that "There was a lot of noise out there, most of it associating Tylenol with death." One possible option was abandoning Tylenol and reintroducing the pain reliever under a new name. Another possibility was to switch to Tylenol tablets. There's a hidden danger, however, in the switch back to tablets: it may lead to a serious decline in the previously fast-growing revenues of the analgesics market as a whole. Michael LeConey, a health care analyst with Merrill Lynch, said that the more expensive extra-strength capsule format mass-marketed by Tylenol was a significant factor for the revenues per headache dosage: "The number of headaches certainly hasn't gone up by 15 to 20 percent a year, as the dollar growth in the market would indicate. A lot of this has been due simply to the upgraded capsule format." An extra-strength capsule in a jar of 100 cost about 5.5 cents, while an extra-strength tablet cost only 4.5 cents. Another alternative was simply to follow the FDA recommendation: keep Tylenol but use new packaging. The cost of the new packaging, which would give more protection than the minimum required by the FDA, would be about 2.4 cents per package.

32   James Burke called in Young & Rubicam, J&J's oldest advertising agency, to poll consumer attitudes about the Tylenol poisoning crisis. He said that one of the things which bothered him "was the extent to which J&J was becoming deeply involved in the affair. The public was learning that Tylenol was a J&J product, and the dilemma was how to protect the [J&J] name and not incite whoever did this to attack other J&J products." The results of the company surveys revealed that more than 47 percent of the American public were aware of the fact that J&J is the parent company behind Tylenol. Before the poisoning less than 1 percent of consumers knew this fact. Other results indicated that 94 percent of all Americans knew about the Tylenol tragedy; 90 percent knew that the problem involved only the capsule form; 93 percent thought that the problem could occur for any capsule, not just Tylenol; and 90 percent believed the maker was not to blame. According to a survey among Tylenol users, 87 percent said they realized the maker of Tylenol was not responsible for the deaths; 61 percent still were not likely to buy extra-strength capsules in the future; 50 percent felt that way about Tylenol tablets as well as capsules; and 35 percent of all Tylenol users threw away the product in their homes. A survey of individuals who were not regular Tylenol users showed that 80 percent had little interest in ever using the brand. Burke concluded that there was a strong residue of fear and anxiety. But crisis team member Joseph Chiesa said that "The problem with consumer research is that it reflects attitudes and not behavior. The best way to know what consumers are really going to do is put the product back on the shelves and let them vote with their hands."

The Decision

33   James Burke said that management looked at all options and was convinced, according to the surveys, that there was a core of loyal users who wanted the product in capsules as well as tablet form. The frequent Tylenol user was seen as much more inclined to

go back to the product than the infrequent user. Thus, the company decided to concentrate on bringing back the loyal customers first. Burke argued that reintroducing the product under another name could very well be misleading anyway. He noted that even if the brand lost half its business, which the company saw as the worst scenario, it would still be the leading analgesic in the marketplace. Therefore, J&J decided to rebuild the brand with a new Tylenol package in a triple-safety-sealed, tamper-resistant package. He declared that J&J had never been run for the short term and that he had no doubts about whether the brand would survive.

34   Still, the big question was how quickly—or whether—consumer confidence in Tylenol, and J&J, could be restored.

The Implementation

35   Timing was crucial. If J&J brought Tylenol back before the hysteria had subsided, the product might die on the shelves. If the company waited too long, the competition would gain an enormous lead.

36   To rebuild consumer confidence in Tylenol, J&J bought an estimated $1 million plus in TV time during a four-day period and ran a 60-second commercial at the same time on all three big networks. The commercials ran a total of 14 times from October 24 through October 27. In those spots, the medical director of McNeil Consumer Products Company, Dr. Thomas Gates, urged consumers "to continue to trust Tylenol." He reminded viewers of the 20 years of trust established by Tylenol and said that his company would do all it could to regain that trust. He noted that the company would be back on the market with capsules as soon as it developed tamper-resistant packaging and that, until then, viewers should take tablets. The commercials did not run in Chicago, where Tylenol products had not yet returned to the shelf; cut-ins were made locally, with spots for two other J&J products.

37   At the end of October, Burke mobilized 2,259 salespeople from all of J&J's domestic subsidiaries to persuade doctors and pharmacists to begin recommending Tylenol tablets to patients and customers. This was the same way Tylenol was marketed 22 years ago.

38   McNeil sued its insurers to recover at least $110 million in product recall and business interruption expenses incurred to remove its Extra-Strength Tylenol from the market (see Exhibit 8). The suit asked the court to decide whether there was coverage under the defendants' policies for costs associated with McNeil's production halt and nationwide recall of the capsules after some were laced with cyanide. McNeil's insurers were expected to vigorously oppose the suit.

39   J&J also took steps in the international market. Lawrence Freeman, president of J&J/Philippines, for example, appeared on prime-time TV to explain the difference between capsules, which are only 4 percent of all Tylenol sales, and tablets. Throughout Canada, J&J asked all pharmacists to place the product behind the dispensary counter to reassure the public that there was no possibility of tampering with the product. In Australia, the company continued with its original plans to go national by 1983, because Tylenol was sold in a locally made plastic blister pack, which J&J officials said was tamper proof.

40   In November 1982, in a closed-circuit press conference, carried live by satellite TV transmission to more than 1,000 media representatives in 30 cities, J&J introduced

Exhibit 8
Insurers sued by McNeil

Insurer	Coverage ($ millions)
North River	$19.9
Transit Casualty	0.5
Employers of Wausau	4.6
Aetna Casualty and Surety	12.5
American Centennial	5.0
Granite State	10.9
First State	5.0
Northbrook Excess and Surplus	9.0
Affiliated F. M.	50.0

the new packaging for Tylenol and its future plans. The new capsules were being offered with triple safety protection even though any one of the three closures would comply with government regulations, which had been issued a few days before the conference. The protection included (1) glued flaps on the outer box, (2) a tight plastic neck seal, and (3) an inner foil seal over the mouth of the bottle. In addition, a bright yellow warning label read: "Do not use if safety seals are broken."

41   The plans included the following steps:

1. Newspaper ads running one full week in November and again in December, offering consumers a $2.50 coupon for any Tylenol product to replace any product they may have discarded. The coupon could be received by calling a toll-free number.

2. Implementation of a "Continue to Trust Tylenol" ad campaign similar to the earlier commercials.

3. Complete distribution of newly packaged capsules by 1982 year-end.

4. Resumption of product-oriented advertising early in 1983.

5. Attempting to persuade Chicago's Mayor Byrne to lift the total ban on the sale of Tylenol products in that city.

6. Repackaging of many J&J consumer products, including toiletries, in tamper-resistant containers.

After the Crisis

42   The results of the steps taken by J&J were impressive. AdWatch, a monthly survey of consumer awareness of advertising, conducted a telephone survey from November 1 through November 27, 1982, asking consumers to name the medicine and drug

Exhibit 9
Percent of public awareness of advertising of leading brands in the medicine and drugs industry

| Brand | Month (1982) | | | | | |
	June	July	August	September	October	November
Tylenol	18.7%	17.5%	16.6%	19.8%	16.6%	25.7%
Anacin	6.2	6.8	10.6	8.8	8.5	5.5
Anacin 3*	—	—	—	—	—	3.4
Bayer	4.6	2.8	4.6	6.8	7.0	3.3

* Not in top three until November.

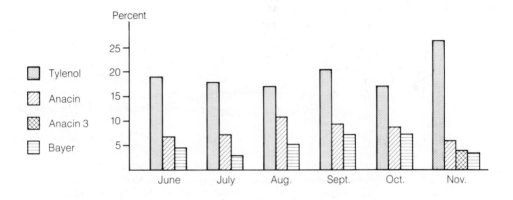

advertising that first came to mind. Tylenol was named by 25.7 percent, up from 16.6 percent in October (see Exhibit 9)—an increase of 9.1 percent, which was the largest of any advertiser mentioned by consumers in this survey. These results were due to the "trust us" TV spots, which were cited by 80 percent of those mentioning Tylenol ads.

43   By the fifth week after the tragedy, 59 percent of regular Tylenol users said they would either definitely or very likely buy Tylenol in the future, up from 40 percent in the first week after the poisoning. That figure rose to 77 percent when the regular users were asked whether they would buy Tylenol in a tamper-resistant container, a result attributed by Jim Burke to the growing confidence due, in part, to the TV commercials of October 24–27.

44   Despite increasingly competitive advertising and promotion by rivals, research indicated a dramatic rise in Tylenol market share, as shown in Figure 3. The research measured sales of a variety of products via retail scanner data in grocery outlets in Massachusetts, Indiana, Wisconsin, and Texas. The sample base represented less than 1 percent of the population, but its primary value was in indicating trends and changes

Figure 3
Analgesic dollar shares in four U.S. cities, before and after poisoning (food stores only)

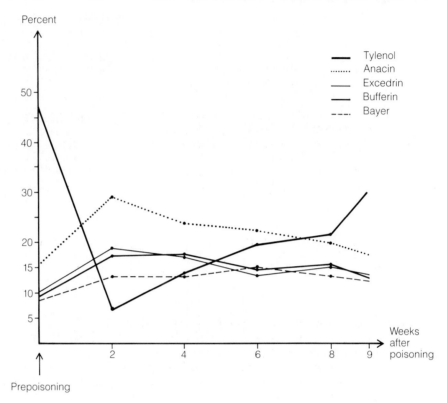

in market shares rather than absolute figures. Some 30 percent of purchases during week nine were with the $2.50 coupon McNeil ran in thousands of newspapers to help customers replace product they may have thrown away.

45   A year after the tragedy, Jim Burke referred to the fairness of the American public:

> A remarkable poll by the Roper organization taken three months after the tragedy showed 93 percent of the public felt J&J handled its responsibility either very well or fairly well. But the public also gave very high marks to the FDA, the law enforcement agencies, the drug industry in general, and the media! The public knew that all of these institutions were working—together—and in their interest! And what did our customers do? They gave us back our business. . . . Our latest Nielsen, taken in July–August [1983], shows Tylenol has regained over 90 percent of the business we enjoyed prior to the tragedies.

Figure 4
Estimated OTC analgesic markets, 1984 and 1985[*]

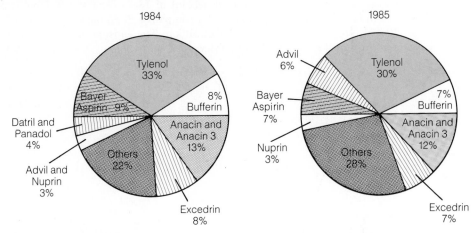

1984

Tylenol
33%

8%
Bufferin

Bayer
Aspirin 9%

Datril and
Panadol
4%

Anacin and
Anacin 3
13%

Others
22%

Advil and
Nuprin
3%

Excedrin
8%

1985

Advil
6%

Tylenol
30%

Bayer
Aspirin
7%

7%
Bufferin

Nuprin
3%

Anacin and
Anacin 3
12%

Others
28%

Excedrin
7%

*$1.8 billion 1985 market.

Source: Standard & Poor's Corporation.

46   In November 1983, Jim Burke received the Advertising Council's public service award. He spoke of the J&J credo and said that "If we do the other jobs properly, the stockholder will always be well served."

47   The drug industry, in general, recovered from the crisis. The total OTC drug volume amounted to about $6.5 billion in 1983, up 4.1 percent from 1982; the rise for 1984 was estimated at about 6 to 8 percent, and it was expected to expand by about 45 percent until the end of the decade. The modest growth in recent years reflected the growing number of elderly people in the population, the introduction of new proprietary drugs, the switching of prescription drugs to OTC status, and increased self-treatment to avoid the high cost of medical care.

48   In the spring of 1984, the FDA approved two new Ibuprofen products for OTC sale, which caused important changes in the $1.5 billion analgesic market and were expected to affect negatively such drugs as Bayer's Aspirin, Bristol-Myers' Bufferin and Excedrin, and Tylenol (see Figure 4). The drug, which is the first new major nonprescription painkiller introduced in nearly 30 years, relieves pain as well as reduces inflammation and fever. It has been available for more than 10 years on a prescription basis under the Motrin name, which is manufactured and marketed by the Upjohn Company. Now the Ibuprofen products, Advil and Nuprin, are being produced (under license from Upjohn) by American Home Products and Bristol-Myers, respectively.

49   In August 1985, U.S. District Judge Fred Lacey ruled that McNeil could not recover lost profits under the business interruption clause of its property insurance policy. He found that J&J's loss of profits following the Tylenol recall didn't fit the definition of loss set forth in the business interruption clause. Yet even with this unfavorable ruling, the beginning of 1986 saw J&J's top management satisfied with Tylenol's performance, which generated about 18 percent of J&J's earnings. Tylenol capsules alone accounted for about 6 percent of the company's 1985 earnings of $613.7 million, or $3.36 a share, on revenues of $6.42 billion. The capsule business represented about one third of the $525 million in Tylenol sales in 1985.

Case 24

Tylenol's Capsule Crisis: Part II

1   On February 8, 1986, Diane Elsroth, a 23-year-old New Yorker, died after taking a tainted Extra-Strength Tylenol capsule. This sent an all-too-familiar shudder through J&J. At the end of the first week, J&J shares traded in the New York Stock Exchange had fallen to $47.25 from $52.50 before the death and were expected by some analysts to fall in the second week to about $40 to $42.

2   The immediate move of J&J was to stop the manufacture and sale of Tylenol. The company asked retailers to remove from their shelves only the remaining 200,000 bottles that were in the lot containing the suspect capsule. The recall and cost of rebuilding Tylenol's market share was expected, according to Jim Burke, to cost the company $100 million to $150 million after taxes for 1986.

Information for Decision Making

3   There were several options available for J&J. The first was simply to abandon capsules for nonprescription drugs and to convince, if possible, capsule users to convert to the company's caplets (smooth-coated, capsule-shaped tablets developed in 1983). Since 1983, McNeil had aggressively promoted the caplets, which had grown to account for about 15 percent of Tylenol brand sales in 1985. Top company executives pulled out consumer surveys from three years ago that showed that 90 percent of capsule users would be willing to use caplets if given reason to try. But a telephone survey J&J conducted over the weekend of this second crisis found that only 59 percent of capsule users said they would be willing to use caplets or tablets if capsules weren't available. This alternative was expected to result in a $150 million pre-tax charge against first-quarter earnings. Analysts said the moves could expect to cost the company between 60 cents and 80 cents a share, reducing its previously anticipated per-share earnings for 1986 to about $3. See the appendixes for sales and operating profit figures, balance sheets, and income statements. Frank Young, the FDA commissioner, said that the agency "did not suggest, direct, or pressure J&J" into such action and "This is a matter of J&J's own business judgment."

4   Industry officials argue that tablets often have to be larger than capsules to contain the same amount of active medicine, and this may make some tablets harder to swallow. Drug company executives say that consumers clearly prefer the capsules, which are easier to swallow and less foul tasting. Moreover, Burke said that "Some consumers have the impression that [the capsules] work better."

5   Most drug makers resisted the idea of abandoning the capsules, and Burke said that if "we get out of the capsule business, others will get into it" and also that pulling the capsules would be a "victory for terrorism." The spokesperson for the industry trade group said that "For the entire industry to walk away from capsules now would be like throwing out the baby with the bath water."

This case was prepared as a basis for class discussion by Yaakov Weber of the University of Kentucky. Copyright © 1987 by Yaakov Weber.

6   Some people called on the manufacturers to switch to new tamper-resistant gelatin capsules, which already are being manufactured by two companies. Eli Lilly's Qualicaps division was working on such capsules, which involved placing an easily visible band of gelatin around the capsule to seal the cap to the capsule body. The spokesperson of this company argued that it will enable drug makers to seal capsules at regular production line speeds. But drug industry officials said that they were reluctant to adopt this option because it was a costly step and the new capsules were too susceptible to breakage, both during the manufacturing process and after the capsules leave the plant.

7   Another alternative for tamper-resistant capsules had been available since 1983 from the Capsugel unit of Warner-Lambert Company. The top half of this capsule slips down entirely over the bottom half and snaps or locks into place. The spokesperson said that even if someone can open the capsule, it would be extremely hard to do so without damaging it.

8   Each alternative had been received coolly by the drug makers. The basic concern was the reliability of these methods and the feeling that until the capsule-tampering technology improved, there was little they could do. As a spokesperson of one drug maker said, "Nothing is 100 percent tamper proof."

9   It was with similar opinions that J&J executives sought to plan their long-range responses to this latest crisis. Chairman Burke quickly convened virtually the same crisis team. On their agenda was whether to respond much the same way they did in 1982, to take more drastic steps and either drop the Tylenol name or terminate the use of capsules[1] in OTC medicine, or some other response.

---

[1] J&J had over $500 million invested in capsule-making/filling facilities in the United States alone.

Appendix A: Sales and Operating Profit by Business Segment (in millions of dollars)

Segment	1985		1984		1983		1982		1981		1980	
	Sales	Operating profit	Sales	Operating profit	Sales	Operating profit	Sales	Operating profit	Sales	Operating profit	Sales	Operating profit
Consumer	$2,774.5	$ 408.7	$2,600.7	$305.0	$2,530.7	$412.9	$2,477.0	$362.4	$2,362.8	$338.4	$2,124.7	$263.7
Professional	2,207.0	149.2	2,004.2	111.6	2,043.1	121.5	1,931.5	152.6	1,734.4	177.9	1,540.5	191.5
Pharmaceutical	1,439.8	461.1	1,295.7	427.0	1,175.8	345.6	1,118.6	314.7	1,008.1	288.5	8,688.0	228.2
Industrial*	—	—	223.9	38.9	223.3	21.1	233.8	23.9	293.7	32.9	303.4	29.5
Total	$6,421.3	$1,019.0	$6,124.5	$882.5	$5,972.9	$901.1	$5,760.9	$853.6	$5,399.0	$837.7	$4,837.4	$712.9

* In 1985, sales and earnings of industrial products have been merged with the remaining three segments.

Appendix B: Summary of Operations and Statistical Data, 1975–1985 (dollars in millions except per share figures)

	1985	1984	1983
Earnings data			
Sales to customers			
Domestic	$3,989.9	3,735.9	3,610.5
International	2,431.4	2,388.6	2,362.4
Total sales	6,421.3	6,124.5	5,972.9
Interest income	107.3	84.5	82.9
Royalties and miscellaneous	48.1	38.0	49.4
Total revenues	6,576.7	6,247.0	6,105.2
Cost of products sold	2,594.2	2,469.4	2,471.8
Selling, distribution and administrative expenses	2,516.0	2,488.4	2,352.9
Research expense	471.1	421.2	405.1
Interest expense	74.8	86.1	88.3
Interest expense capitalized	(28.9)	(35.0)	(36.9)
Other expenses including nonrecurring charges	50.3	61.8	99.9
Total costs and expenses	5,677.5	5,491.9	5,381.1
Earnings before provision for taxes on income	899.2	755.1	724.1
Provision for taxes on income	285.5	240.6	235.1
Earnings before extraordinary charge	613.7	514.5	489.0
Extraordinary charge (net of $50.0 taxes)	—	—	—
Net earnings	$ 613.7	514.5	489.0
Percent of sales to customers	9.6	8.4	8.2
Domestic net earnings	$ 376.6	305.6	281.8
International net earnings	$ 237.1	208.9	207.2
Per share of common stock	$ 3.36	2.75	2.57
Percent return on average stockholders' equity	19.5	17.3	16.8
Percent increase over previous year			
Sales to customers	4.8	2.5	3.7
Net earnings per share	22.2	7.0	2.0
Supplementary expense data (1)			
Cost of materials and services	$3,441.0	3,285.8	3,205.9
Total employment costs	1,941.1	1,935.8	1,920.8
Depreciation and amortization	250.5	226.3	209.8
Maintenance and repairs (2)	132.7	124.0	119.6
Total tax expense (3)	466.2	418.6	415.2
Total tax expense per share (3)	2.55	2.23	2.18
Supplementary balance sheet data			
Property, plant and equipment—net investment	$1,839.9	1,720.6	1,668.2
Additions to property, plant and equipment	366.3	366.0	401.3
Total assets	5,095.1	4,541.4	4,461.5
Long-term debt	185.3	224.8	195.6
Common stock information			
Dividends paid per share	$ 1.28	1.18	1.08
Stockholders' equity per share	$ 18.33	16.04	15.82
Average shares outstanding (millions)	182.9	187.4	190.5
Stockholders of record (thousands)	53.5	53.8	49.3
Employees (thousands)	74.9	74.2	77.4

(1) Excludes in 1982 an extraordinary charge of $100 million ($50 million after taxes or $.27 per share) associated with the withdrawal of Tylenol capsules.

(2) Also included in cost of materials and services category.

(3) Includes taxes on income, payroll, property, and other business taxes.

1982	1981	1980	1979	1978	1977	1976	1975
3,304.0	3,025.9	2,633.6	2,372.1	1,991.3	1,713.6	1,493.2	1,268.0
2,456.9	2,373.1	2,203.8	1,839.5	1,506.0	1,200.5	1,029.3	956.7
5,760.9	5,399.0	4,837.4	4,211.6	3,497.3	2,914.1	2,522.5	2,224.7
88.9	78.8	50.0	43.3	28.7	18.9	19.3	11.8
49.3	28.6	26.4	23.1	17.2	16.8	16.7	15.6
5,899.1	5,506.4	4,913.8	4,278.0	3,543.2	2,949.8	2,558.5	2,252.1
2,450.9	2,368.4	2,194.3	1,950.2	1,580.3	1,368.0	1,222.9	1,071.7
2,248.8	2,030.6	1,794.2	1,505.3	1,258.9	1,002.3	847.9	746.6
363.2	282.9	232.8	192.7	163.6	131.8	112.5	97.8
74.4	60.7	37.0	21.9	13.5	8.5	6.3	8.8
(46.3)	(43.5)	(32.7)	—	—	—	—	—
20.9	23.4	12.9	16.2	12.7	7.0	7.4	8.4
5,111.9	4,722.5	4,238.5	3,686.3	3,029.0	2,517.6	2,197.0	1,933.3
787.2	783.9	675.3	591.7	514.2	432.2	361.5	318.8
263.8	316.3	274.6	239.6	215.1	184.9	156.1	135.0
523.4	467.6	400.7	352.1	299.1	247.3	205.4	183.8
(50.0)	—	—	—	—	—	—	—
473.4	467.6	400.7	352.1	299.1	247.3	205.4	183.8
8.2	8.7	8.3	8.4	8.6	8.5	8.1	8.3
235.8	262.2	184.6	172.4	144.4	129.3	107.5	90.5
237.6	205.4	216.1	179.7	154.7	118.0	97.9	93.3
2.52	2.51	2.17	1.92	1.67	1.41	1.18	1.06
17.8	19.5	18.8	19.1	18.8	17.8	16.7	17.1
6.7	11.6	14.9	20.4	20.0	15.5	13.4	14.8
.4	15.7	12.8	15.2	18.2	19.8	11.0	13.6
3,078.1	2,843.4	2,532.4	2,200.1	1,803.0	1,494.5	1,294.4	1,151.0
1,821.7	1,693.6	1,535.2	1,337.4	1,101.6	892.0	785.1	682.9
176.2	152.4	138.7	121.2	103.1	86.5	77.5	68.6
123.6	126.2	116.1	118.2	102.0	89.1	74.8	61.9
436.3	477.0	425.3	373.2	323.0	274.9	231.1	203.7
2.32	2.56	2.30	2.04	1.80	1.57	1.32	1.17
1,577.9	1,335.6	1,161.9	947.8	788.2	652.4	568.5	528.3
470.2	388.5	364.0	273.3	228.5	171.7	119.2	136.0
4,209.6	3,820.4	3,342.5	2,874.0	2,382.4	2,019.8	1,730.7	1,537.1
142.2	91.7	70.1	69.5	52.1	37.1	26.7	39.4
.97	.85	.74	.67	.57	.47	.35	.28
14.80	13.51	12.24	10.82	9.47	8.43	7.45	6.61
188.0	186.4	184.8	183.3	179.4	175.2	174.6	173.7
43.0	38.2	35.6	35.6	31.9	31.2	31.1	31.0
79.7	77.1	74.3	71.8	67.0	60.5	57.9	53.8

Appendix C

JOHNSON & JOHNSON AND SUBSIDIARIES
Consolidated Balance Sheet
At December 29, 1985, and December 30, 1984
(dollars in millions)

	1985	1984
Assets		
Current assets		
Cash and cash items	$ 129.2	94.4
Marketable securities, at cost, which approximates market value	606.4	348.1
Accounts receivable, trade, less allowances $39.7 (1984, $32.0)	959.4	877.3
Inventories (Notes 1 and 3)	955.1	945.4
Prepaid expenses and other receivables	246.4	248.5
Total current assets	2,896.5	2,513.7
Marketable securities, non-current, at cost, which approximates		
market value	148.7	162.3
Property, plant and equipment, at cost (Note 1)		
Land and land improvements	170.6	157.1
Buildings and building equipment	1,210.6	1,103.9
Machinery and equipment	1,410.3	1,202.3
Construction in progress	151.6	156.0
	2,943.1	2,619.3
Less accumulated depreciation and amortization	1,103.2	898.7
	1,839.9	1,720.6
Other assets	210.0	144.8
Total assets	$5,095.1	4,541.4
Liabilities and Stockholders' Equity		
Current liabilities		
Loans and notes payable (Note 4)	$ 229.3	201.4
Accounts payable	401.4	301.6
Accrued liabilities	328.7	326.4
Taxes on income	65.3	87.1
Salaries, wages and commissions	95.1	80.2
Miscellaneous taxes	52.5	45.7
Total current liabilities	1,172.3	1,042.4
Long-term debt (Note 4)	185.3	224.8
Deferred taxes on income	121.3	91.7
Certificates of extra compensation (Note 10)	58.0	53.0
Deferred investment tax credits	40.2	42.2
Other liabilities	167.1	155.3
Stockholders' equity		
Preferred stock—without par value (authorized and unissued 2,000,000 shares)	—	—
Common stock—par value $1.00 per share (authorized 270,000,000 shares;		
issued 191,832,000 and 191,831,000 shares)	191.8	191.8
Additional capital	247.6	278.6
Cumulative currency translation adjustments (Note 6)	(291.9)	(366.4)
Retained earnings	3,499.6	3,119.1
	3,647.1	3,223.1
Less common stock held in treasury, at cost (8,980,000 and 8,986,000 shares)	296.2	291.1
Total stockholders' equity	3,350.9	2,932.0
Total liabilities and stockholders' equity	$5,095.1	4,541.4

See Notes to Consolidated Financial Statements

Appendix D

JOHNSON & JOHNSON AND SUBSIDIARIES
Consolidated Balance Sheet

At January 1, 1984 and January 2, 1983 (Dollars in Millions Except Per Share Figures)	1983	1982*
Assets		
Current assets		
Cash and cash items	$ 122.6	140.4
Marketable securities, at cost, which approximates market value	303.9	225.1
Accounts receivable, trade, less allowances $28.1 (1982, $24.8)	836.4	758.1
Inventories (Notes 1 and 6)	992.2	957.5
Prepaid expenses and other receivables	202.0	172.0
Total current assets	2,457.1	2,253.1
Marketable securities, non-current, at cost, which approximates market value	181.5	222.1
Property, plant and equipment, at cost (Note 1)		
Land and land improvements	149.9	142.2
Buildings and building equipment	1,050.0	924.7
Machinery and equipment	1,106.2	1,005.9
Construction in progress	163.6	238.6
	2,469.7	2,311.4
Less accumulated depreciation and amortization	801.5	733.5
	1,668.2	1,577.9
Other assets	154.7	156.5
Total assets	$4,461.5	4,209.6
Liabilities and Stockholders' Equity		
Current liabilities		
Loans and notes payable (Note 7)	$ 214.4	213.9
Accounts payable	311.2	312.1
Taxes on income	13.6	1.3
Salaries, wages and commissions	78.1	75.0
Miscellaneous taxes	47.7	53.6
Miscellaneous accrued liabilities	258.8	244.3
Total current liabilities	923.8	900.2
Long-term debt (Note 7)	195.6	142.2
Certificates of extra compensation (Note 11)	46.6	42.9
Deferred investment tax credits	41.0	35.3
Other liabilities and deferrals	223.1	279.8
Minority interests in international subsidiaries	4.9	9.7
Stockholders' equity		
Preferred stock—without par value (authorized and unissued 2,000,000 shares)	—	—
Common stock—par value $1.00 per share (authorized 270,000,000 shares; issued 191,562,000 and 189,361,000 shares)	191.6	189.4
Additional capital	272.1	234.5
Cumulative currency translation adjustments (Note 4)	(260.7)	(163.5)
Retained earnings	2,824.5	2,540.1
	3,027.5	2,800.5
Less common stock held in treasury, at cost (234,000 shares)	1.0	1.0
Total stockholders' equity	3,026.5	2,799.5
Total liabilities and stockholders' equity	$4,461.5	4,209.6

*Reclassified to conform to 1983 presentation.

See Notes to Consolidated Financial Statements.

Appendix E

JOHNSON & JOHNSON AND SUBSIDIARIES
Consolidated Balance Sheet

At January 3, 1982 and December 28, 1980 (Dollars in Millions Except Per Share Figures)	1981	1980
Assets		
Current assets		
Cash and cash items	$ 101.2	92.8
Marketable securities, at cost, which approximates market value	325.8	266.3
Accounts receivable, trade, less allowances $22.2	705.9	643.8
Inventories (Notes 1 and 5)	900.1	848.8
Prepaid expenses and other receivables	169.2	119.3
Total current assets	2,202.2	1,971.0
Marketable securities, non-current, at cost, which approximates market value	193.5	143.9
Property, plant and equipment, at cost (Note 1)		
Land and land improvements	123.9	110.6
Buildings and building equipment	772.9	659.7
Machinery and equipment	899.1	810.2
Construction in progress	217.7	196.0
	2,013.6	1,776.5
Less accumulated depreciation and amortization	678.0	614.6
	1,335.6	1,161.9
Other assets	89.1	65.7
Total assets	$3,820.4	3,342.5
Liabilities and Stockholders' Equity		
Current liabilities		
Loans and notes payable (Note 7)	$ 195.4	167.0
Accounts payable, trade	247.0	232.3
Miscellaneous accounts payable	50.0	51.2
Taxes on income	90.8	72.2
Salaries, wages and commissions	70.9	67.1
Miscellaneous taxes	50.2	52.9
Miscellaneous accrued liabilities	176.9	130.8
Total current liabilities	881.2	773.5
Long-term debt (Note 7)	91.7	70.1
Certificates of extra compensation (Note 11)	38.3	32.8
Deferred investment tax credits	30.1	23.7
Other liabilities and deferrals	239.6	163.8
Minority interests in international subsidiaries	11.6	9.5
Stockholders' equity (Note 9)		
Preferred stock—without par value (authorized and unissued 2,000,000 shares)	—	—
Common stock—par value $1.00 per share (authorized 270,000,000 shares; issued 187,297,023 and 185,647,266 shares)	187.3	185.6
Additional capital	178.2	144.3
Cumulative currency translation adjustments (Note 3)	(85.7)	—
Retained earnings	2,249.1	1,940.1
	2,528.9	2,270.0
Less common stock held in treasury, at cost (235,299 and 234,399 shares)	1.0	.9
Total stockholders' equity	2,527.9	2,269.1
Total liabilities and stockholders' equity	$3,820.4	3,342.5

See Notes to Consolidated Financial Statements.

Appendix F

Johnson & Johnson and Subsidiaries

Consolidated Balance Sheet at December 30, 1979 and December 31, 1978

(Dollars in Thousands Except Per Share Figures)

ASSETS	1979	1978
Current Assets		
Cash and certificates of deposit	$ 127,340	147,475
Marketable securities, at cost, which approximates market value	184,025	253,740
Accounts receivable, less allowances $19,763 (1978 $15,838)	596,421	468,997
Inventories (Notes 1 and 4)	745,434	601,322
Expenses applicable to future operations	64,950	29,945
Total current assets	1,718,170	1,501,479
Marketable Securities, Non-Current, at cost, which approximates market value	144,694	45,494
Property, Plant and Equipment, at cost, less accumulated depreciation and amortization $546,302 (1978 $479,929) (Notes 1 and 5)	947,783	788,240
Other Assets	63,307	47,156
Total assets	$2,873,954	2,382,369

LIABILITIES AND STOCKHOLDERS' EQUITY	1979	1978
Current Liabilities		
Loans and notes payable (Note 7)	$ 96,382	58,058
Accounts payable	237,112	192,218
Taxes on income	84,577	59,808
Other accrued liabilities	210,816	158,636
Total current liabilities	628,887	468,720
Long-Term Debt (Note 7)	69,549	52,125
Certificates of Extra Compensation (Note 10)	30,104	28,341
Deferred Investment Tax Credits	20,614	17,857
Other Liabilities and Deferrals	129,959	105,979
Minority Interests in International Subsidiaries	8,195	8,519
Stockholders' Equity		
Preferred Stock—without par value (authorized and unissued 2,000,000 shares)	—	—
Common Stock—par value $2.50 per share (authorized 70,000,000 shares; issued 61,290,424 and 59,931,524 shares) (Notes 2 and 8)	153,226	149,829
Additional capital	158,069	105,506
Retained earnings	1,676,298	1,446,441
	1,987,593	1,701,776
Less common stock held in treasury, at cost (78,333 and 78,433 shares)	947	948
Total stockholders' equity	1,986,646	1,700,828
Total liabilities and stockholders' equity	$2,873,954	2,382,369

See Notes to Consolidated Financial Statements.

Appendix G

JOHNSON & JOHNSON AND SUBSIDIARIES
Consolidated Balance Sheet
at January 2, 1977, and December 28, 1975
(dollars in thousands except per share figures)

ASSETS

	1976	1975*
Current Assets		
Cash and certificates of deposit	$ 47,509	38,300
Marketable securities, at cost which approximates market value	230,591	199,921
Accounts receivable, less allowances $11,182 (1975 $11,320)	315,179	288,465
Inventories (Notes 1 and 3)	456,170	396,940
Expenses applicable to future operations	17,883	21,281
Total current assets	1,067,332	944,907
Marketable Securities, Non-Current, at cost		
(market value at year-end 1976—$58,092; 1975—$29,536)	59,612	34,147
Property, Plant and Equipment, at cost less accumulated		
depreciation and amortization (Notes 1 and 4)	568,456	528,252
Other Assets	35,319	29,750
Total assets	$1,730,719	1,537,056

LIABILITIES AND STOCKHOLDERS' EQUITY

	1976	1975*
Current Liabilities		
Loans and notes payable (Note 6)	$ 26,290	27,575
Accounts payable	125,023	99,424
Taxes on income	56,304	29,927
Other accrued liabilities	94,223	109,698
Total current liabilities	301,840	266,624
Long-Term Debt (Note 6)	19,058	30,832
Capitalized Long-Term Lease Obligations	7,650	8,570
Certificates of Extra Compensation (Note 9)	29,001	28,579
Deferred Investment Tax Credit	13,793	11,654
Other Liabilities and Deferrals (Note 12)	51,292	35,078
Minority Interests in International Subsidiaries	6,146	4,882
Stockholders' Equity		
Preferred Stock—without par value (authorized and unissued 2,000,000 shares)	—	—
Common Stock—par value $2.50 per share		
(authorized 70,000,000 and 63,000,000 shares, issued 58,353,499		
and 58,136,616 shares, 1976 and 1975, respectively) (Note 7)	145,884	145,342
Additional capital	74,738	68,545
Retained earnings	1,082,548	938,181
	1,303,170	1,152,068
Less common stock held in treasury, at cost (101,883 shares)	1,231	1,231
Total stockholders' equity	1,301,939	1,150,837
Total liabilities and stockholders' equity	$1,730,719	1,537,056

Reclassified to conform to 1976 presentation. See Note 12.
See Notes to Consolidated Financial Statements.

Case 25

Tri-County Educational Foundation

1   The Tri-County Educational Foundation was founded by Marsha and Lee Tessa in 1974 as a nonprofit service organization. The purpose of the foundation was to research, design, develop, and disseminate art and science programs. Two years later the founders, with six other artists, scientists, and educators, had the foundation chartered in the state of Illinois.

2   Shortly after the charter was granted, the Tessa family donated over 1,200 acres of land in central Illinois to be used by the foundation. With the help of friends, the group constructed a geodesic dome on the property. This building became known as the Discovery Dome and served as the Tri-County Foundation's program center.

Funding and Growth

3   During its first years, the foundation was funded by donations and grants from the U.S. Department of Interior, Caterpillar Tractor, Interlake Steel, International Harvester, the Pullman Foundation, the Illinois Arts Council, and the National Endowment for the Arts. With this available money the foundation developed its first programs and increased its staff from two volunteers to three full-time and three part-time paid positions.

4   The full-time staff consisted of Lee Tessa, executive director; Marsha Tessa, program director; and John Bradley, program coordinator. These three, who were educators employed at a small liberal arts college in Illinois, were to fulfill their roles in the foundation during the summer months and on weekends when school was in session. The part-time employees were Cindy Rogers, secretary and bookkeeper, and Joe and Vince Arnold, both college students, who handle the maintenance jobs for the foundation.

5   The first programs were a film and a series of slide programs produced during the years 1974 to 1976. The programs were a collection of interviews with artists and scientists. These were used by the National Park Service, state parks, schools, colleges, and public television stations throughout the Midwest.

6   In 1976 the foundation developed an innovative program, Art in the Woods, which integrated art and science. It brought people of all ages and backgrounds together with highly skilled artists and scientists to learn in the 1,200-acre wooded classroom. This program became the basis from which new programs were developed during the following seven years.

7   At the December 1983 board of directors meeting, it was decided to expand the foundation's operations. Additional donors from the business sector were to be sought, as well as donors from the general public, to finance the proposed expansion. At the same time it was decided the board of directors would be increased from 6 to 12 members within the next 12 months. It was felt the foundation could then draw upon

This case was prepared by Professor Paul E. Arney of Bradley University and is intended to be used as a basis for class discussion. The name was changed to protect the confidentiality of the foundation. Presented and accepted by the refereed Midwest Case Writers Association Workshop, 1986. All rights reserved to the author and to the Midwest Case Writers Association.

the expertise of these board members, and it could also make the foundation more visible to the communities it served.

8   Tri-County started at once to expand its program and prepared to operate year-round programs. Professional artists and scientists were sent into schools and community centers to present workshops, hands-on demonstrations, lectures, and performances. Nature trails were developed on the foundation's land, and a minimuseum of art and science collections was assembled in the Discovery Dome.

October Board Meeting

9   The first meeting of the expanded board of directors was held in the latter part of October 1984. Among the new members were John Love, a retired vice president of an international manufacturing firm, and Bob Jetter, a business consultant. The meeting was called to order by William Scott, president of the board. After he introduced the new board members, Scott called upon Cindy Rogers for a financial report.

10   Cindy reported that although the annual fund-raising campaign had been successful, the costs of the new programs had drained the treasury. She further reported that there were insufficient funds to pay the salaries of the full-time staff for the next two months. She also recommended the cancellation of programs scheduled for November and December.

11   Lee Tessa, the executive director, explained that he and his wife, Marsha, were willing to forgo their two months' salaries as a donation to the foundation. John Bradley, program coordinator, offered his salary for the balance of the year as his contribution to the foundation. It was explained to the new board members that this was a normal situation and that every year the salaried personnel made this gesture when funds ran out.

12   John Love inquired as to how this could happen if a budget was being followed. He also wanted to know if the canceling of the programs for the rest of the year was also a normal situation.

13   Lee Tessa told the board that things were not quite as grave as Cindy had indicated. He explained that he expected to receive within the next two weeks a small grant, which would finance the scheduled programs for November and December. He then pointed out that during the first two weeks of January grants for 1985 would be rolling in.

14   Mrs. Rogers was asked to distribute to the board for its approval the proposed budget for 1985 (see Exhibit 1).

15   The original members of the board of directors indicated their willingness to approve the budget; however, Love and Jetter wanted additional information. Love asked if there was a detail of the expected expenses for the various programs. The detailed expenses were then distributed to the board.

16   Jetter questioned how the amount of contributions was determined. He was told that the expenses were computed first, and the expected revenues other than contributions were estimated. The difference between these two totals was the amount needed for a balanced budget and would be acquired from contributions. Both Love and Jetter claimed they understood, but they felt the system left a lot to be desired. Love told the board that most companies work the other way; that is, first they forecast the income and then they determine what expenses can be afforded.

Exhibit 1
Tri-County Foundation proposed budget for year ending December 31, 1985

Anticipated income

Fees:

School fees (art programs)	$ 1,000	
School fees (science programs)	1,500	
Student fees	5,000	
Concert fees	5,900	
Community program fees	6,000	
Total anticipated fees		$19,400

Grants:

Midwest Science Council	15,400		
N.E.A.	15,000		
Illinois Art Council	7,000		
Midwest Music Council	2,000		
Total grants		39,400	
In kind goods and services		8,000	
Public contributions		25,120	
Total anticipated income			$91,920

Anticipated expenses

Staff salaries:

Executive director	$14,000	
Program director	11,000	
Program coordinator	7,500	
Secretary/bookkeeper	9,000	
Maintenance	5,200	
Total staff salaries		$46,700

Professional fees:

Art exposure programs:			
Summer Art	8,500		
Art in Schools and Community	10,875	$19,375	
Science exposure programs:			
Summer Nature	1,500		
Science in Schools and Community	500	2,000	
Total professional fees			21,375

Art exposure programs:

Suzuski Symphony Concert	5,880		
Summer Art	7,700		
Art in Schools and Community	6,255		
Total art exposure programs		19,835	

Science exposure programs:

Teacher Field Training	140		
Summer Nature	590		
Science in Schools and Community	880		
Total science exposure programs		1,610	
General administrative expenses		2,400	
Total anticipated expenses			$91,920

17   Jetter took issue with the expense computation. He wanted to know why the salary expenses were not contributed to the various programs in order to have a true cost of each program.

18   Scott explained, "We are artists, scientists, and educators. We are not accountants."

19   Love fired back, "Jetter and I are not accountants either, but give us a month and

Exhibit 2
Tri-County Foundation art exposure programs for 1985

I. Suzuski Symphony Orchestra concert

On October 13 the Suzuski Symphony Orchestra will present a one-hour morning workshop for music teachers, students, parents, and others. The workshop will be held in conjunction with other workshops and lectures which focus on the theme of "The Potential of the Child." The Suzuski Orchestra will present a 90-minute evening concert. This special event is sponsored by the foundation to promote our country's national 1979 theme, "The Year of the Child." It is estimated that 800 children and 350 adults will attend. The price will be $10 for adults and $3 for children.

II. Artists in the schools and community centers

Professional artists present workshops, demonstrations, lectures, and performances in schools and community centers for students, teachers, parents, senior citizens, and interested community members. The artistic fields represented are dance, drama, pottery, weaving, painting, photography, drawing, sculpture, poetry, blacksmithing, music, and printmaking. Ten schools have indicated their desire for this program at a $100 fee. Forty community workshops have been booked at $150 each.

III. Summer art workshop

Professional working artists present 30 workshops at the Tri-County Foundation's 1,200-acre classroom. There will be two one-week sessions of intensive workshops. Artists share their knowledge and skills with students (maximum of 25 students per instructor). Estimated attendance is 500 students. Fee will be $10.

Exhibit 3
Tri-County Foundation science exposure programs for 1985

I. Teacher field science training program

Sixty elementary teachers will participate in four weeks of field science studies. The study program will focus on how to use science study areas that are accessible to most teachers in urban and rural areas. There are no proposed fees for this program.

II. Scientists in the schools

Professional scientists present lectures and workshops for students, teachers, and parents interested in geology, marine biology, botany, wildlife management, conservation, water fowl of Illinois, solar energy, field science, and others. Ten schools have contracted for this program. The fee will be $150.

III. Summer nature program

Schools provide transportation for students to the Tri-County Foundation for field science studies in habitats of central Illinois, fish and wildlife conservation, and identification of birds, insects, mammals, reptiles, and their relation and adaption to the environment. There is no fee for this program.

we will be willing to find the data you need for a workable budget. It will make possible a budget to control your expenses, whereby you won't have to depend upon the sacrifice of salaries in order to balance your checkbook every year."

20   After a brief discussion, it was decided that the budget be tabled until November, when the board would hold a special meeting.

21   Scott next asked Marsha Tessa for a report of programs for the following year. Marsha distributed the proposed program for 1985 (see Exhibits 2 and 3).

Exhibit 4
Time expenditure precentage of each salaried staff member according to program classification

	Art exposure programs	Science exposure programs	General administration
Executive director	60%	25%	15%
Program director	70	20	10
Program coordinator	50	30	20
Secretary	70	20	10
Bookkeeper	60	20	20
Maintenance	60	25	15

22   Jetter said he was impressed with this program but felt that the fees were unrealistic and could not be justified until after all costs, including salaries of the staff and the general administrative expenses, were distributed among the various programs. The board agreed and adjourned until the next month.

November Meeting

23   When the board reconvened in November, Jetter and Love presented three reports of data which they obtained from the staff and from a careful examination of material in the foundation's files.

24   Jetter started to explain the first (see Exhibit 4), which indicated the percentage of the time each staff member had allocated to each of the two major program types and to general administrative duties. He pointed out that there existed a difference among the staff members as to how much time each had spent performing the tasks in these three expense classifications. For example, the program director allocated 70 percent of her time to the art exposure programs, while the program coordinator spent only 50 percent of his time on these programs.

25   Several of the board members inquired as to why these differences occurred. Jetter explained that Marsha Tessa played a more active role in the art exposure program than did her husband or John Bradley. However, Bradley spent more time in general administrative work than had Mrs. Tessa, since his experience in commercial art qualified him to prepare advertising to promote the foundation.

26   John Love interrupted the discussion and commented, "The important point here is not the cause of the differences in the time allocation but rather the effect these differences have upon the proposed budget and upon the amount of the fees for the various programs."

27   William Scott agreed with Love and asked Bob Jetter to continue with his findings of time allocation by the staff members.

28   Jetter drew the board's attention to his second and third reports (see Exhibits 5 and 6), in which the time expenditures of the art exposure programs and the science exposure programs were each subdivided according to the specific programs.

29   It was explained to the board that these two reports simply indicate a breakdown of the first report. For example, of all the time each staff member spent on art exposure

Exhibit 5
Staff's total time on art exposure allocated by specific programs

Program	Percent of staff time
Suzuski Symphony Concert	10%
Summer Art Workshops	40
Artists in Schools and Community	50

Exhibit 6
Staff's total time on science exposure allocated by specific programs

Program	Percent of staff time
Teacher Field Science	10%
Summer Nature Program	25
Scientists in Schools and Community	65

programs, 10 percent was spent on the Suzuski Symphony Concert, 40 percent was spent on Summer Art Workshops, and 50 percent was spent on Artists in Schools and Community. The same idea applies to the third report.

30   After a brief discussion, the president of the board asked Jetter and Love to prepare a revised budget which would reflect this new information. John Bradley asked the two how they planned to price each of the programs. When asked if they could complete both of these assignments by the December meeting, the two replied they could. The November meeting was adjourned.

Competitive Industry Analysis

Case 26

Note on the Ambulance Industry

1   The typical ambulance firm is in the business of providing two categories of medical service. Most observable is the limited on-the-scene emergency aid given to stabilize the effects of accidents or sudden illness, and the subsequent movement of the victim to acute care facilities. While less noticeable, the more profitable facet of the industry involves scheduled transportation of convalescent patients to medical offices, nursing homes, or hospitals. Long dominated by locally owned one- to five-unit firms, the industry has been substantially influenced by competitive struggles rather than an uncompromising concern for the patient's welfare.

The Industry's Historical Posture

2   Until the early 1970s, ambulance enterprises, unlike other components in the health care industry, appeared to be free of most environmental constraints. Low barriers to entry allowed large numbers of aggressive competitors to battle for the available business and often allowed the least professional to succeed.

3   Characterizing the industry in 1972, insurance company research reported that

The research and written case note information were presented at a Case Research Symposium and were evaluated by the Case Research Association's Editorial Board. This case note was prepared by J. Kim DeDee of the University of Wisconsin at Oshkosh as a basis for class discussion. Distributed by the Case Research Association. All rights reserved to the author and the Case Research Association. Reprinted with permission.

less than 3 percent of the nation's ambulance attendants were qualified. Further investigations by the U.S. Public Health Service estimated that 60,000 needless deaths and 100,000 permanent disabilities occurred each year due to poorly trained and ill-equipped emergency personnel. One analyst connected with a 1972 congressional investigation commented:

> Accidents are the leading cause of death among Americans, and highway accidents make up by far the largest percentage of these deaths. Fully 15,000 of the 55,000 highway deaths each year could be avoided with proper emergency medical services at the scene of the accident and enroute to the hospital. . . . Experts in emergency medical care estimate that 30 percent of coronary-related deaths each year could be averted with proper emergency medical attention.

Also, according to a 1968 University of Michigan research effort:

> 20 percent of accident victims could have been saved by such simple procedures enroute to the hospital as keeping the throat open to permit breathing, or using intravenous fluids. . . . Less than half of the ambulance attendants in the country are trained in even the most rudimentary Red Cross first-aid procedures.

Industry Trends prior to 1970

4   With varying degrees of intensity, four significant factors had contributed most to the historical nature and structure of the ambulance industry: the personnel, the vehicles and equipment, the regulatory structure, and competitive rivalries.

5   **Personnel.**   The primary determinant of the industry's quality standards prior to 1970 was the selection, training, and compensation of personnel. Fledgling companies recruited inexperienced employees into a work environment emphasizing contiguous 24-hour shifts with sleep periods often interrupted by high-stress trauma calls. Employees were also responsible for the maintenance and repair of the equipment, vehicles, and housing facilities.

6   Organizationally, ambulance firms were usually divided into four areas along functional lines. The owner/manager divided his time among general business practices, competitive struggles, and representing the interest of the firm to local governmental offices. The dispatcher managed the normal billing routine, took incoming telephone messages, determined the status of the emergency necessity, and directed the closest unit to the site of the call. The driver was often promoted from within the organization but in many cases only needed a chauffeur's license and had little, if any, emergency experience. At the lowest level of the organization was the attendant, whose principal responsibility focused on the immediate care, comfort, and transportation of the victim. Legal entry-level qualifications normally did not require previous experience but probably included the 26-hour Red Cross standard first-aid course. Ironically, the dimensions of this training program did little to enhance the employee's competency level. Instead of being designed to aid in the safe movement of the patient, the Red Cross program only explained techniques of momentary and initial care. To that end, the course was deficient in such critical areas as emergency childbirth, back and neck injuries, extrication, and transportation.

7   Vehicles and Equipment.   A second major force affecting the industry was the acquisition of the firm's most substantial revenue-generating asset: the vehicle fleet. While numerous criteria would normally be expected to play a role in the vehicle selection decision, aesthetics coupled with myopic consumer demands proved paramount. Job order shops began to lengthen and customize luxury automobiles for ambulance use, but, in most cases, critical structural components such as braking, suspension, steering, cooling, and electrical systems remained unaltered. These vehicles were difficult to handle and subject to excessive component failures during adverse driving conditions. Confronted with the high fixed costs of these units, many firms elected to cut costs in equipment and supplies, narrowing their working inventory to a single back board; a few board splints, elastic bandages, and dressings; and an assortment of restraint devices for combative patients.

8   Regulatory Structure.   Contrary to the rest of the health care industry, the ambulance segment had not been subject to much federal, state, or local regulation. During the 1960s some states did begin to enact laws setting minimum licensing standards for vehicles and personnel; however, because of wording irregularities, a limited number of inspectors, and the piecemeal approach to most regulations, serious problems of quality control existed in large portions of the industry.

9   Competition.   Competition had an unusual impact on the industry. Consumers requesting emergency services rarely evaluated the final services. Frequently, the nonpayment rate on emergency service calls approached 60 percent (the rate for patient transfers was much lower). To counter the risk of revenue losses, management exercised a number of options including selective withholding of services, cash discounts for early payment, and collection agencies for overdue accounts.

10   In addition, pressures were applied by larger firms on local governments to supply partial subsidies covering the costs of indigent use of emergency services. Revenue for the transfer business often originated from federal (medicare), state (medicaid), and private insurance programs. Essentially, these third-party payers offered payments of between 70 and 100 percent for those with insurance coverage.

11   Competitive rivalry in some geographic locales was often so bitter that it involved call-jumping through the use of transistorized radio monitors, delaying responding to an emergency call until the firm's own unit became available, and sabotage of a rival's vehicles or equipment at the accident scene.

Recent Industry Developments

12   By 1985 the ambulance service industry had evolved through 15 years of unprecedented and turbulent change. The catalysts for the reversals in the prehospital, or emergency medical services (EMS) industry as it is now known, came from a number of sources. During the 1960s numerous organizations formed, focusing special attention on the growing morbidity of highway accidents. President Johnson's Committee on Highway Safety and the National Academy of Sciences provided key impetus in the passage of the Highway Safety Act of 1966. This law essentially allowed states the use of federal moneys to establish minimum performance standards for emergency medical processes and to improve their existing ambulance provision systems. Later, in 1967, the Department of Transportation published its "Emergency Medical Services" standards, which contained numerous provisions affecting the scope and breadth of emergency medical coverage.

13   A second major piece of legislation, the Emergency Medical Service Systems Act, was enacted in 1975. It was revised in 1976 to extend through 1980. This legislation provided additional federal money for the design and development of emergency medical systems and to support long-range planning at the state level. The Department of Health, Education, and Welfare, the Department of Transportation, and the National Highway Traffic and Safety Administration (DOT–NHTSA) further increased the involvement of the federal government in such areas as standard setting, prehospital critical care system development, and ambulance design criteria.

14   Realizing these federal funding initiatives were temporary, virtually all states began efforts to establish regional EMS programs. Under these programs clear identification of the individual components of each geographic system became necessary. Also, standardized guidelines and criteria were written as tools of implementation to these regional emergency care processes.

15   Typically, state EMS systems were divided into four functional elements: (1) system administration—long-range planning, operations, and evaluation of the total prehospital emergency care process; (2) manpower—routine position descriptions and revised training formats; (3) equipment—the vehicles and medical or extraction devices; and (4) communication—the geographic scope of emergency two-way radio traffic and the use of 911 telephone numbers.

16   The major thrust of the EMS system, however, centered on the increasingly complex network of components necessary to respond to patients in life-threatening situations. The sequence of events associated with a typical emergency medical routine were:

1. *Identification of emergency incident.* The person making the discovery assesses and defines the situation in which immediate aid is required.

2. *Access to EMS system.* A telephone call is placed to the appropriate agency, which then dispatches all necessary aid units (police, fire, extrication, or ambulance).

3. *Arrival of first response personnel.* Appropriate personnel arrive at scene and begin initial assessment and treatment of patient(s).

4. *Prehospital stabilization of patient.* Field personnel decide on the use of predetermined procedures for particular life-threatening conditions or make radio contact with a trained physician in a designated hospital. Vital information concerning the patient's condition is provided while the physician directs the application of appropriate medical treatment.

5. *Transport of patient.* Following stabilization, the patient's condition is continually monitored while being transported to hospital. Physician may order additional treatment while enroute via radio contact.

6. *Transfer of patient responsibility.* Vital information concerning the patient's condition is transmitted as the patient undergoes initial hospital examination and/or treatment.

17   In most cases individual state EMS agencies added further detail to qualifications the DOT–NHTSA specified for ambulance vehicles. Primary design criteria were established covering size, floor plans, ground clearance, emergency equipment, and electrical,

Exhibit 1
Cost classification of 1985 emergency vehicles

Vehicle	Price Range
Type I: Converted hearse (used mainly for patient transfers)	$38,000–$42,000
Type II: Van ambulance	25,000– 29,000
Type III: Heavy-duty cab/chassis; dual rear wheels	38,000– 40,000
Type IV: Chevrolet Suburban; 4-wheel drive	12,000– 17,000

Source: Collins Industries, Inc.

cooling, suspension, and braking systems. Normally recommended color schemes included orange accent stripes on a white background, with ample room for the blue Star of Life emblem, and the organization's logo and phone number. See Exhibits 1 and 2.

18   Many city and county agencies refined the governmental momentum through increased operating budgets covering EMS salaries, training, vehicles, equipment, and reimbursements to private firms. This, however, put the local EMS system in the vulnerable position of being heavily supported by tax dollars, while nearly all other health care services were paid for by individuals or third-party payers.

19   Organized medicine had also stimulated improvements in emergency medical care. The patriarch of health care, the American Medical Association, had moved increasingly toward advancing emergency medical skills, technologies, and research. Other groups, such as the American College of Surgeons and the Committee on Injuries of the American Academy of Orthopedic Surgeons, working in concert with concerned local physicians, designed numerous trauma care delivery training programs, instruction films and manuals, and skill-building workshops. By 1983 these organizations further standardized essential position descriptions and equipment criteria (see Exhibit 3).

20   Currently, the nationally recognized entry-level position for basic life support personnel is the emergency medical technican (EMT). Primary training topics emphasize airway obstruction, pulmonary or cardiac arrest, cardiopulmonary resuscitation, and bleeding control. Closely related subjects include shock treatment, splinting, poisoning, emergency childbirth, and general evaluation of anatomic subsystems.

21   While several variations exist in the ranks of emergency medical paraprofessionals, the highest level currently attainable is the paramedic. Requirements for certification and licensing specified by state law usually include up to two years of college-level training in advanced airway management, administration of intravenous fluids, cardiac monitoring and defibrillation, and administration of medications for resuscitation.

22   As increased revenues became more available after the passage of medicare and medicaid acts, the additional demands placed on personnel necessitated commensurate increases in compensation. Currently, in larger cities, salaries for entering employees approach $15,500 annually with top salary levels for EMTs exceeding $25,000 (see Exhibit 4). Probationary paramedics in municipalities can earn $20,700 with advancement potential exceeding $35,700.

23   A number of indirect factors also contributed to the evolution of EMS care. Physicians modified their practice patterns by eliminating house calls, compelling patients to go

Exhibit 2
Advanced life support (ALS) internal and external configurations

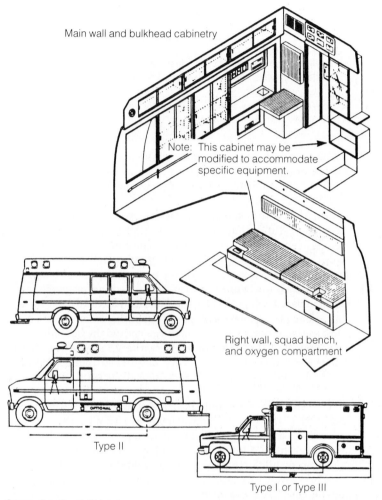

Main wall and bulkhead cabinetry

Note: This cabinet may be modified to accommodate specific equipment.

Right wall, squad bench, and oxygen compartment

Type II

Type I or Type III

Source: Frontline Vehicles, Inc.

directly to local hospitals, often through the use of emergency vehicles. To meet this challenge, many hospitals expanded their trauma center personnel and emergency facilities. As their experience with emergency care grew, hospitals came to view with alarm the lack of sophistication in the transportation arm of emergency care. Many hospital administrators responded with their own hospital-based ambulance systems, while others chose to cooperate more fully in training and developing existing providers.

24   Interestingly, this myriad of environmental factors proved advantageous to some firms. As the central objective of the industry changed from high-speed transport to more definitive at-the-scene treatment, the image of the paramedic began to parallel

Exhibit 3
Profile of equipment and supplies for basic and advanced life support systems

Item	Number	Unit price
Basic life support		
Ventilation/airway equipment:	1	
Suction apparatus		$ 396
Oxygen equipment		288
Airways		Variable*
Immobilization devices/splints:		
Traction	2	75
Extremity splints		120
Backboards	2	125
Dressings		Variable*
Pneumatic antishock garment	1	300
Radio:		
Two-way permanent	1	1,300
Two-way portable	1	900
Obstetrical kit	2	Variable*
Light equipment		75
Aluminum cot/mattress	1	850
Stretchers	3	200
Audio/lighting equipment	1	800
Miscellaneous		350
Advanced life support system		
Intravenous equipment		90
Airways/tubing/laryngoscope		130
Cardiac monitor/defibrillator	1	7,875
Drugs		Variable*
Mechanical cardiac compression unit	1	3,917

* Variable cost normally charged to the patient.
Source: American College of Surgeons, Dixie U.S.A., Inc., and casewriter's computations.

Exhibit 4
Average annual pay and labor costs, 1985

Provider	Emergency medical technician	Paramedic	Adminis-trator	Range of labor cost/ unit hour	Average labor cost/ unit hour
Private company	$12,754	$16,721	$29,277	$12.03–$35.03	$20.99
Separate municipal	15,248	19,709	24,913	11.01– 49.46	31.38
Hospital-based	13,999	19,381	28,091	17.19– 35.89	27.40
Fire department	18,818	25,528	35,725	10.30– 45.32	25.98
County-operated	14,261	18,664	27,730	11.05– 55.89	21.53
Overall average	14,520	18,540	29,516		
Change from 1984	−12.44%	−8.78%	+.08%		

Source: *Journal of Emergency Medical Services,* January 1985.

those of police and fire department personnel. Also, the increased stature of the industry's professional organizations precipitated additional skill enhancement workshops and seminars as well as more sophisticated, research-oriented publication journals. Finally, the growing investment in capital equipment and compensation erected significant barriers to market entry for marginal providers.

The Competitive Arena

25 The prehospital emergency care industry can normally be divided into four classes of providers, two not-for-profit and two for-profit. The not-for-profit sector consisted of municipal (police and fire department) service units and rural volunteer organizations; profit-oriented EMS firms included those operated by hospitals and small private providers. Cost structures differed widely among these industry participants.

26 **Municipal Services.**   Spurred by various federal programs and growing pressures from constituents, the commitment of local municipalities to upgrade the quality and availability of urban emergency services had shown some growth in recent years. Consequently, the scope of police and fire departments was broadened in some locales to include on-the-scene medical assistance and treatment. While the municipal EMS was increasingly paid for with tax revenues, patient transfer services were normally handled by a private ambulance service.

27 **Volunteer Organizations.**   The volunteer segment of the industry operating along with rural not-for-profit firefighting associations included those who periodically donated their time and first-aid skills to a particular geographic community. Fees collected supported training and equipment rather than compensation. Industry sources estimated that approximately 25 percent of the total EMS market was served by volunteer providers.

28 **Hospitals.**   Some hospitals, pressed financially by declining bed use and more competition, instituted ambulance businesses as feeder systems for their more definitive health care facilities. With the hospital name and logo prominently displayed on both the ambulance and the uniforms of EMS personnel, such services often become a powerful marketing tool in the community.

29 **Private Providers.**   The dominant force in the industry, however, continued to be the small profit-oriented enterprise. This segment was beset with high capital investments in vehicles, heavy insurance costs, and the need to keep personnel on duty for 24-hour time frames. While some firms did pursue the state of the art in equipment and training, many could be characterized as undermanaged and poorly motivated to provide state-of-the-art emergency care.

Future Industry Directions

30 Analysts believed that a number of important factors would affect the future shape and direction of the emergency medical industry:

1. The increasing costs and sophistication of medical technology would require continued assessment of labor, equipment, and all related performance variables.

2. As demands for quality grew, prior training and experience requirements would place added burdens on the small provider.

3. Private firms would find it increasingly difficult to maintain high operating standards and remain profitable, especially where local governments were interested in starting a municipal EMS.

4. Since municipal EMS programs were expensive, their perceived inefficiencies could come under more careful voter scrutiny in future economic downswings.

5. Pressures would escalate concerning technical malpractice. Providers, technicians, and equipment manufacturers would fall under closer legal observation.

6. Antitrust law complexities would have an increased effect on communities that promote both tax-based and private ambulance services.

7. With more competitive compensation schedules, the ambulance field should be able to attract more career-minded individuals.

8. There would be increased controversy over the amount of on-the-scene care as opposed to more immediate transport of the accident victim.

9. It would become increasingly important for EMS providers to work in closer proximity with health care planning agencies.

10. Comprehensive statewide and interstate EMS systems would be developed further.

11. EMS would become an even more integral process to the total health care delivery system. Competing ambulance firms may be integrated into this unified system, forcing cooperative rather than purely competitive postures.

12. With federal and state budgets in decline, the market could swing back toward heavier reliance on private EMS providers.

Case 27

The Tulip City Ambulance Company, Inc. (TCA)

1 In early February of 1985, Marshal (Mart) Berghorst, president and board chairman of Tulip City Ambulance, reviewed the recent activities of the firm to assure himself that they were appropriate at this time. He was particularly concerned whether or not these activities could improve the overall financial position of the company and contribute to his own long-term personal goals. The past five years were especially traumatic. Except for 1983, emergency medical service (EMS) volume, once the firm's mainstay, dropped steadily. Profits fluctuated widely. Fixed assets, which included the vehicle fleet, were almost fully depreciated, and the use of either specialty vehicle fell short of expectations. (Exhibits 1 through 6 contain income, balance sheet, and supplemental data for 1980 through fiscal year 1984.) During 1984, morale among the work force was consistently lower than at any time in the firm's 24-year history. Further compounding these dilemmas were unfavorable competitive and industry conditions, both locally and nationally.

2 Berghorst believed that the company had grown successfully during its first 20 years because of continued community acceptance of his service offerings, the spirit of cooperation that existed with Bellview General Hospital, and the absence of conflict with the city government. However, with so much turbulence beginning to show in the immediate environment, Berghorst again contemplated how the firm's direction might change. In light of these concerns a number of recurring questions surfaced in his mind. How should TCA alter its basic service mix: should the new direction be toward revitalizing emergency medical care and transport or toward the more lucrative routine transfers? What would be the most likely scenarios concerning the entry of either Bellview General Hospital or the city government into the ambulance market? If Tulip City remains in the EMS sector, what would be the personnel and equipment requirements necessary for an advanced life support (ALS) state rating? Since this firm has grown beyond the limits of one-man management, what role should Karl VerBeek play in the future? In the midst of his planning, Marshal had just been contacted by James Vanlaar, Tulip City's controversial competitor. This man offered, in conjunction with St. Luke's Hospital, to buy a 100 percent interest in the company, thus giving him almost total dominance in the regional metropolitan area.

3 Maintenance of Tulip City's growth pattern was particularly important to Berghorst. Although he was less than 50, he had on occasion considered leaving the firm, but only if it could stand on its own without his direct intervention. Now that his family had grown, and his wife was pressuring him to enjoy more leisure time, Mart felt a lesser need to increase his wealth. Instead, he wanted his ventures, including Tulip City, to be self-supportive with a favorable reputation within the community.

This case was prepared by J. Kim DeDee of the University of Wisconsin at Oshkosh and Richard C. Johanson of the University of Arkansas as the basis for class discussion rather than to illustrate either effective or ineffective handling of a managerial situation. Tulip City Ambulance is a disguised company name; however, all key relationships remain intact.

Distributed by the North American Case Research Association. All rights reserved to the authors and the North American Case Research Association. Permission to use the case should be obtained from the authors or the North American Case Research Association.

Exhibit 1
Competitive summary of normal-duty ambulance volume for years 1980–1984 (EMS and transfers only)

| | | | Daily calls and accounts receivable collection rates | | |
Year	Population*	TCA†	Rate (percent)	Van's	Total‡
1980	145,500	EMS 12.0	62%	.5	12.5
		T/F 12.5	86	1.0	13.5
1981	147,525	EMS 11.0	62	1.0	12.0
		T/F 13.5	86	1.2	14.7
1982	154,900	EMS 10.0	62	2.0	12.0
		T/F 14.5	87	2.0	16.5
1983	162,650	EMS 10.0	63	2.5	12.5
		T/F 14.5	87	2.5	17.5
1984	170,780	EMS 9.5	63	3.5	13.5
		T/F 15.0	87	2.0	18.0

* Manchester, 85 percent; Springdale, 15 percent.
† DeYoung calls included.
‡ Totals that don't agree reflect other competitors.
Source: Company records and casewriter's computations.

Exhibit 2
Summary of special vehicle use for years 1980–1984

Year	Neonatal unit calls	Price	Collect rate (percent)	Trauma unit calls	Price	Collect rate (percent)
1980	125	$218.75	85%	5	$249.00	88%
1981	265	227.50	85	12	257.10	87
1982	280	235.30	84	11	255.40	89
1983	300	249.75	83	13	277.80	86
1984	320	270.50	86	13	288.80	84

Note: Both special units were put into service at July 1, 1980.
Source: Company records.

TCA—Company History

4   In 1960, following his wife's troubled pregnancy, which required several emergency trips to the hospital, Mart concluded that neither of the two funeral homes nor the existing independent provider offered an acceptable degree of quality in emergency ambulance care. Soon after the baby was born, Mart solicited some friends who possessed high-speed driving skills and who enjoyed a periodic respite from home each week. Next, the 20-year-old entrepreneur combined a $500 savings with other family members' capitalization to place a down payment on a low-mileage Cadillac hearse. Additional

Exhibit 3
Tulip City Ambulance revenue and critical expense summary for years 1980–1984

	1980	*1981*	*1982*	*1983*	*1984*
Ambulance/EMS:					
Revenue					
Base rate	$ 60.00	$ 65.00	$ 65.00	$ 65.00	$ 65.00
Mileage rate	.50	.50	.60	.60	.65
Distance	8.00	8.00	8.00	9.00	10.00
Miscellaneous	12.00	11.50	12.50	13.00	13.50
Total	76.00	80.50	82.30	83.40	85.00
Expenses					
Fuel (9/m.p.g.)	.84	.84	.84	.95	1.05
Labor	12.00	12.60	13.20	14.00	14.60
Maintenance	310.00	335.00	350.00	370.00	390.00
Insurance	450.00	450.00	470.00	470.00	470.00
Ambulance/transfer:					
Revenue					
Base rate	60.00	60.00	65.00	65.00	65.00
Mileage rate	.75	.85	.90	1.00	1.00
Distance	17.00	17.00	17.00	18.00	18.50
Total	72.75	74.45	80.30	83.00	83.50
Expenses					
Fuel (12/m.p.g.)	1.35	1.35	1.35	1.43	1.43
Labor	18.00	18.90	19.80	21.00	21.90
Baby unit van:					
Revenue					
Base rate	125.00	130.00	130.00	135.00	140.00
Mileage rate	1.25	1.30	1.30	1.35	1.45
Distance	75.00	75.00	81.00	85.00	90.00
Total	218.75	227.50	235.30	249.75	270.50
Expenses					
Fuel (12/m.p.g.)	6.00	6.00	6.50	6.75	7.15
Labor	24.00	25.20	26.40	28.00	29.20
Maintenance	365.00	785.00	835.00	880.00	925.00
Insurance	350.00	725.00	730.00	740.00	750.00
Trauma unit:					
Revenue					
Base rate	150.00	150.00	150.00	150.00	150.00
Mileage rate	1.65	1.70	1.70	1.75	1.85
Distance	60.00	63.00	62.00	73.00	75.00
Total	249.00	257.10	255.40	277.75	288.95
Expenses					
Fuel (11/m.p.g.)	5.20	5.50	5.35	6.30	6.50
Labor	24.00	25.20	26.40	28.00	29.20
Maintenance	75.00	150.00	600.00	175.00	190.00
Insurance	275.00	550.00	560.00	560.00	600.00

Note: All maintenance and insurance amounts are annual expenses per unit, fuel at $.95/gallon, and distance in miles.

Exhibit 4

TULIP CITY AMBULANCE, INC.
Comparative Income Statements
For Periods Ending December 31

	1980	1981	1982	1983	1984
Operating income:					
EMS	$332,880	$323,207	$300,395	$304,410	$294,738
Transfers	331,922	366,852	424,988	439,278	441,924
Special units:					
Baby unit	13,672	30,143	32,942	37,462	43,280
Trauma unit	623	1,543	1,405	1,805	1,877
Total operating revenue	679,097	721,745	759,730	782,955	781,818
Operating expenses:					
Wages	194,236	203,948	213,730	258,370	269,694
Depreciation	51,350	51,350	36,350	42,850	16,600
Maintenance	4,190	4,935	5,555	6,350	9,200
Fuel	13,788	15,253	15,885	15,678	17,218
Uncollectible accounts:					
EMS	126,494	122,818	114,150	112,632	109,053
Transfer	46,469	51,360	55,248	57,106	57,450
Special units	1,015	2,218	2,404	2,847	3,387
Linen and supplies	1,348	1,482	1,556	1,635	1,715
Total operating expenses	438,890	453,364	444,878	497,468	484,317
Gross margin	240,207	268,381	314,852	285,487	297,502
Administrative expenses:					
Salaries	91,200	99,050	107,000	115,105	123,355
Payroll taxes	20,350	23,816	24,950	29,056	31,444
Employee benefits	52,716	56,055	59,335	69,093	72,714
Telephone	3,685	3,870	5,070	5,365	5,680
Utilities	5,460	6,000	6,550	6,870	7,220
Insurance	5,525	6,175	6,195	8,225	8,275
Advertising	0	800	900	1,000	1,100
Property taxes	9,300	9,300	12,100	12,100	12,100
Supplies	1,208	1,260	1,330	1,400	1,460
Postage	2,480	2,497	2,800	2,813	2,933
Miscellaneous	1,606	1,680	1,815	1,905	2,000
Professional services	3,000	3,300	3,565	3,750	3,930
Total administrative expenses	196,530	213,803	231,610	256,682	272,211
Income from operations	43,677	54,578	83,242	28,805	25,291
Nonoperating income/expenses:					
Interest expense	34,947	27,842	19,440	16,527	8,452
Income before taxes	8,370	26,736	63,802	12,278	16,839
Taxes	2,183	6,684	21,055	3,069	4,210
Income after taxes	$ 6,548	$ 20,052	$ 42,747	$ 9,208	$ 12,629

bank financing was obtained to convert the vehicle into ambulance service, build working capital, and provide initial rent on an abandoned gas station with a working hoist.

5   An important reason for the firm's early success came from the "gentlemen's agreement" negotiated with the Poindexter Funeral Home to handle its emergency nighttime calls. This allowed the funeral directors a full-night's sleep without any appreciable effect on profits.

Exhibit 5

TULIP CITY AMBULANCE, INC.
Comparative Balance Sheets
as of December 31

	1980	1981	1982	1983	1984
Assets					
Current assets:					
Cash	$ 2,500	$ 511	$ 2,232	$ 1,364	$ 1,536
Accounts receivable	84,187	90,356	92,777	81,517	82,364
Inventory	337	371	389	409	429
Prepaid insurance	6,175	6,195	8,225	8,275	8,690
Total current assets	93,199	97,433	103,623	91,565	93,019
Fixed assets:					
Land	75,000	75,000	75,000	75,000	75,000
Buildings	128,000	128,000	128,000	128,000	128,000
Less: Accumulated depreciation	(73,000)	(81,000)	(89,000)	(97,000)	(105,000)
Vehicles	208,275	208,275	208,275	234,275	234,275
Less: Accumulated depreciation	(97,100)	(138,350)	(164,600)	(197,350)	(203,850)
Equipment	20,000	20,000	20,000	23,000	23,000
Less: Accumulated depreciation	(8,500)	(10,500)	(12,500)	(14,500)	(16,500)
Furniture and fixtures net	4,000	3,900	3,800	3,700	3,600
Total fixed assets	256,675	205,325	168,975	155,125	138,525
Total assets	$349,874	$ 302,758	$ 272,598	$ 246,690	$ 231,544
Liabilities/equity					
Current liabilities:					
Current maturity of notes	$ 51,582	$ 39,272	$ 45,642	$ 21,409	$ 11,532
Accounts payable	310	425	390	450	680
Payroll taxes payable	13,320	14,140	14,968	17,429	18,342
Wages/salaries payable	4,391	4,662	4,935	5,746	6,047
Income taxes payable	546	1,671	5,263	767	1,052
Other	245	380	589	325	430
Total current liabilities	70,394	60,550	71,787	46,126	38,083
Noncurrent liabilities:					
Notes payable	131,139	91,867	46,223	43,768	32,236
Total liabilities	201,533	152,417	118,010	89,894	70,319
Owners' equity:					
Common stock ($10 par)	40,000	40,000	40,000	40,000	40,000
Paid-in capital	5,000	5,000	5,000	5,000	5,000
Retained earnings	103,341	105,341	109,588	111,796	116,225
Total equity	148,341	150,341	154,588	156,796	161,225
Total liabilities/equity	$349,874	$ 302,758	$ 272,598	$ 246,690	$ 231,544

6   Late in 1961, Mart left his mechanic's position at the local Ford dealership and accepted the presidency of the recently incorporated Tulip City Ambulance Company. His list of responsibilities covered the maintenance of the base, vehicle, and equipment. In addition, Berghorst surprised the industry with a promotion campaign he inaugurated that placed the firm's telephone stickers wherever there was a high probability of an emergency occurrence.

7   During the early growth years, Mrs. Berghorst began to handle all office and dispatching duties, while Mart concentrated more earnestly on the company's transfer services.

Exhibit 6
Summary of accountant's footnotes

1. TCA uses the accrual method of accounting for reporting and tax purposes.
2. Accounts receivable are stated at actual mounts minus an estimated sum for uncollectibles based upon past trends.
3. All fixed assets are stated at cost. Depreciation for tax and reporting requirements is computed with the straight-line method with minimum salvage values. The useful lives of the assets are: buildings, 15 years; furniture and fixtures, 15 years; vehicles, 4 years; and equipment, 10 years. Full depreciation of the fixed assets are: primary base, 1984; secondary base, 1989; vehicles (Chevrolet), 1986. All other assets are fully depreciated.
4. Repairs and maintenance are generally charged to operations as they occur. When an asset is sold or removed from service, its cost and related depreciation are omitted from the accounts, with the gain or loss being recognized at the time of removal.
5. The real estate mortgage is 9 percent on both items of property. The debt on the primary base will be released in December of 1985 and the debt on the secondary base in December of 1989.

By the end of 1962, both funeral homes elected to drop out of the ambulance business. They converted their vehicles into hearses and sold their emergency telephone numbers to Tulip City. This ploy doubled the firm's emergency volume to four daily calls and cut in half the number of competitors. The fledgling enterprise, however, faced even stiffer competition from the county's only other provider, the DeYoung Ambulance Company.

8   With over 4,000 independent and volunteer organizations in existence, Tyson DeYoung had been able to parlay a sizable inheritance and extensive debt financing into the third-largest ambulance company in the United States. He had reasoned that because most firms served relatively small local areas, economies of scale prevented them from realizing sufficient return on invested capital. By contrast, DeYoung had operations in Michigan, Illinois, and Indiana and planned to expand into Ohio and Kentucky. DeYoung ambulances were positioned at most regional sporting events, entertainment programs, and the Indianapolis Motor Speedway. This latter tactic exposed the firm's name and logo to almost 350,000 spectators who attended the various time trials, parades, and the Memorial Day race. Further recognition was also gained through national radio and regional television coverage of these events.

9   The DeYoung growth pattern in property and equipment remained consistent through the early 1970s. By 1976 he had committed a series of strategic errors, and the company's revenue and cash flow plummeted. Later that year Tyson DeYoung died of alcoholism, and his widow sold the one remaining vehicle and the accounts receivable to Tulip City for $5,000. No employees were retained.

10   For the rest of the decade, Tulip City held close to a monopoly position and, under the direction of Marshal Berghorst, accomplished the following results: opened and equipped a second base, doubling the firm's operating radius; acquired the assets of two bankrupt competitors; diversified into specialty emergency transport services (hospital to hospital) for premature infants and critically injured adults; vertically integrated into new ambulance construction; and introduced entry-level standards and development courses for all personnel.

The Operating Environment

11   Located between two interstate highways in Michigan's Lower Peninsula, Manchester and its border city, Springdale, have recently experienced sizable population growth patterns. Part of this 5 to 6 percent annual increase was attributed to the favorable economic climate of the region, the strong religious work ethic of its inhabitants, and the community's lower-than-average age and higher-than-average income levels. Another force behind this expansion was the continuing industrialization of the tri-county metropolitan area. Because Manchester/Springdale was within close proximity to the huge automotive complexities of eastern Michigan and had a large university, industry analysts considered it ideal for the location of low-technology manufacturing plants. Prior to 1980, TCA's only operational constraint came from Tyson DeYoung's competitive maneuverings. Since 1980, however, the firm has faced a growing number of threatening developments.

The Competition

12   Although it has gone through periods of refinement, the ambulance industry has always been intensely competitive. Tulip City has not only competed directly for consumer acceptance but also for referrals from medical personnel concerning transfers to and from hospitals, rest homes, and related institutions. In the last five years the company has fared well in this toughening environment, demonstrating fundamental user attitudes toward its services. Total ambulance requests in Manchester/Springdale exceeded industry norms to one daily call for each 6,600 people. This, however, reflected only partially on Tulip City's effectiveness. While the company held a clearly dominant position, its share of the market had shown an overall steady decline in the last half decade (see Exhibit 1).

13   The newest competitive threat to face Tulip City originated from a small group of missionaries organized "to provide a fully licensed and highly qualified Christian ambulance service to the people of Manchester and Springdale." Developed solely as a charitable venture, the firm relied primarily on contributions to cover its variable costs but in 14 months was able to increase its volume load to five calls a week.

14   Tulip City's most significant competitive threat came from the easily recognized Van's Ambulance Service. Since its inception in early 1980, this firm's principal objective, according to founder David Vanlaar, "was to obtain market position and respect using luxury emergency vehicles. This company was not created to produce short-term profits but to provide a viable growth-oriented activity for myself and those who follow my business philosophy."

15   In January of 1976 Vanlaar dropped out of college to enter the U.S. Army. While there, he worked as a heavy-equipment operator, lived frugally, and in four years was able to meet the initial payment requirements on one of the few remaining Cadillac ambulances to be produced. The firm obtained sufficient resources through loan agreements from Manchester's second-largest hospital (St. Luke's—370 beds) to penetrate substantially into Tulip City's market position. Rather than rely on personal selling, Vanlaar's primary marketing approach was the ornate vehicle, large Yellow Pages advertisements, and sales of a subscription service. The subscription service annually offered families one emergency or one transfer call at less than 35 percent of normal competitive rates. In addition, Vanlaar distributed bright green bumper stickers with the company name, logo, and phone number.

16   Vanlaar felt that regardless of situational complexities, requests for his ambulance were specific rather than general. Thus, to maintain corporate integrity, company policy stated that when the car was tied up on either a transfer or an emergency and a second call came in, the initial call would be completed under lights and siren status to avoid referring the later call to a competitor. Despite repeated complaints from medical personnel and patients' families, the policy was never altered.

17   Van's principal company strategy stressed minimizing response time to or from the trauma scene. Important to this process were the speeds attained by the high-performance vehicle. After a number of police warnings and newspaper editorials, Vanlaar was summoned with a reckless driving charge (92 MPH in a 25-MPH zone) and ordered to appear in court. In an effort to convince the jury and the general public of the validity of his methods, Vanlaar retained a Chicago-based law firm known for its truculence.

18   A motivated prosecution presented a force of expert witnesses that included a noted orthopedic surgeon, who stated, "In the past 13 years I have had occasion to be familiar with more than a few emergency cases. In no instance can I recall where speed in transportation of the injured patient materially affected the patient's outcome. . . . Actually, what is necessary is appropriate methodology adequately applied at the scene, which, I can state parenthetically, the Van's personnel are either unable or unwilling to provide, and then a reasonable speed, say, 10 miles an hour over posted limits, with allowed passage through red traffic lights. . . . This is required if our streets are to remain safe for all concerned." After two days of heated court debate, Vanlaar was acquitted of all charges.

19   After this legal victory, Vanlaar went on the offensive. To counter the growing conflict he knew was developing between his firm, the regional emergency medical industry, and the city police and fire department, he initiated a series of half-page newspaper advertisements. Each promotion began with the question "Did you know . . ." and included at least one of the following topics:

1. That firemen, professing to be first-aiders, have stood waiting by dying patients for professional medical help and not attempted any life-supporting techniques?

2. That police agencies have ordered ambulance attendants away from persons needing service because the attendants were not of their particular political choice? At least one such patient died.

3. That people in need have waited 45 minutes for ambulance service because they called a police or fire agency first?

4. That the county is going to use hundreds of thousands of dollars to accomplish what is already being done "tax free" because of a lack of cooperation with available resources?

20   The promotional campaign, which was intended to be politically conservative, included quotes related to "Progression without Taxation" and "Don't waste time calling a police or fire agency first; call us directly and immediately for your medical emergencies. The Vanlaar Ambulance Company—the state's most progressive service."

The Hospitals

21   In the late 1970s and early 1980s Manchester saw a significant trend toward the provision of fuller emergency medical services being offered by both hospitals. St. Luke's seized the opportunity to increase its emergency room volume with direct and continued support of the Van's Ambulance Company. In addition to financial assistance, St. Luke's on numerous occasions supplied materials, provided training, and shared news coverage of important events with David Vanlaar or his company. In August of 1983, Bellview General Hospital (450 beds), the city's largest and most centrally located facility, was acquired by a national chain noted for its innovative and aggressive management style. Following a year of extensive reorganization, Jackson Baker was offered and accepted the position of vice president of hospital projects and reported directly to the executive committee. After preparing in-depth analyses on a number of potential investments, Jackson decided to promote the idea of a hospital-based ambulance service, which he felt would better position the trauma center within the organization's overall strategic objectives. Bellview was profitable and in fairly sound financial condition but recently had experienced a reduced bed-use factor similar to the rest of the industry. To assure future growth patterns for the hospital, the following key points were stressed in his report.

22   A properly designed and maintained hospital-based ambulance service should:

1. Provide access to additional revenue sources from a relatively small investment base ($125,000).
2. Increase to 41–42 percent the number of patients being admitted through the trauma center.
3. Create a valuable marketing tool and generate goodwill in the community through exposure of the hospital name and logo and vehicles and uniforms.
4. Utilize more effectively the trauma center personnel.
5. Act as an effective feeder system to more definitive care, helping alleviate the unused capacity problem.
6. Countervail the market share gained by St. Luke's through their direct financial assistance of Van's Ambulance Service.
7. Allow complete emergency care for the patient from trauma scene to possible extended-care admission.
8. Provide the hospital complete control over the trauma unit and baby unit vehicles and crews and allow the hospital to absorb the 50 percent profits and cash flows now shared with the Tulip City Ambulance Company.

23   During September of 1984, the executive committee began deliberations on the proposal and instructed Mr. Baker to develop a management team, refine or modify certain objectives, and begin negotiations with principal resource suppliers. Discussions continued between Baker and the executive committee, and by early December a tentative arrangement was reached. The project was given secondary status to allow the hospital time to evaluate any improvements in the overall EMS system, especially as it pertained to the city government's entry into the arena. Although the potential advantages of the project appeared to outweigh its shortcomings, Baker estimated the hospital's entry into the ambulance market at less than 50/50. If the city government did proceed with their EMS proposal without any corresponding improvement in the for-profit sector, that probability dropped to zero.

Manchester's Response

24 The Manchester situation was much as other cities of its size. The alienation that continued to grow in the citywide EMS sector became a political issue. After the elections, Paul Wynski, the newly elected commissioner of Manchester's Primary Services Department, set out to pursue two principal objectives. First came the desire to put his office at the forefront of the city's growth pattern; and second, he wanted to personally establish some tangible evidence that would identify his potential for higher government offices.

25 As commissioner, Wynski was responsible for the total operations and performance of two separate groups, the City Protection Group (police) and the Fire Protection and Control Group. A simple breakdown of the $22 million budget indicated 76 percent covered salaries for 870 employees, while the remainder went to property, plant, and equipment. Included in this final category was the central administration building, 18 regional fire stations, 21 diesel pumpers, 7 ladder trucks, and a fleet of patrol cars.

26 To meet his intentions, Mr. Wynski contemplated a number of alternatives but settled on a municipal tax-based EMS rescue-and-transportation system. His initial strategy was to begin strictly as an advanced emergency care treatment-and-extraction service, with later expansion into patient transport. Paramedic training, beyond the emergency medical technician (EMT) rating that was held by many police and fire department personnel, was estimated to take one additional year. Another six months would be necessary to operationalize the total EMS process.

27 Wynski believed in change and innovation but was practical enough to realize that any major variation in his department would be a formidable task. To help win approval of his proposal from the city commission, he distributed the memo shown in Exhibit 7 to all of his colleagues.

28 Commissioner Wynski was pleasantly surprised at the outcome of the meeting. Most commissioners heartily agreed with the general intentions of the proposal and gave tacit approval to the design of his emergency medical paramedic system.

29 Enthusiastically returning to his office, Wynski promptly scheduled a meeting with his staff, intent on further development of the EMS model. To increase the profile of his ambulance system concept, the commissioner also called both television stations and the local paper to arrange detailed news releases. Later that year, as his plans took on a more defined focus, Commissioner Wynski commented: "There are notable differences in the design of a tax-supported EMS system with those in the for-profit sector. For example, our initial capital requirements will be high—approaching $300,000. Our operating and development costs, however, should decline rapidly in the next three years. There is an 85 percent probability that Manchester will have a government-sponsored EMS system by the middle of 1985 and, with computerized billing and collection procedures, be self-supported by early 1988."

The Tulip City Operations

30 By 1980, Tulip City and the reorganized DeYoung service had both achieved solid reputations in the private ambulance sector. Following the acquisition, the parent company and its subsidiary occupied two bases with garages at strategic points in Manchester and Springdale. The bases, both located in low-income areas, were extensively refurbished to provide living, office, and meeting space in addition to usual

---

Exhibit 7

Memorandum

To: All city commissioners
From: Paul L. Wynski, Commissioner of Primary Services
Re: Establishment of a class A emergency medical service system
Date: April 16, 1984

As a result of the growing unrest in the current independently operated emergency medical service (EMS) system, I would appreciate your opinions on the following project objectives.
 I plan to make a more formal presentation of these generalized goals at the commission meeting scheduled May 3, 1984.

Critical objectives

1. Establishment of a citywide advanced life support (ALS) emergency rescue-and-treatment system.
2. Expansion into emergency transport of trauma victims.
3. Development of billing and collection procedures encouraging the service to become self-supporting.

Rationale for the system

1. No qualified paramedics operate in Manchester.
2. Tulip City Ambulance—the city's largest provider—only offers basic life support (BLS).
3. Manchester may set a state-recognized precedent.
4. Alleviation of expanding turmoil in the current EMS system arising from the Van's Ambulance Company's operating style.

Future tactics include

1. Additional research focusing on property, plant, equipment, and personnel costs.
2. In-depth observation of municipal services currently operating in adjoining states.
3. Expert judgments detailing legal complexities and antitrust laws.

kitchen facilities. The Manchester locations of the two services shared the central administration office and a 2,600-square-foot garage that housed a majority of the vehicles and associated maintenance and repair equipment.

31   In January of 1975, as a move to show support for Springdale, Tulip City enlarged its base capacity there and built a similar but smaller garage (1,800 square feet). This structure covered the primary and backup vehicles and assorted rental wheelchairs, hospital beds, and ancillary devices.

32   All the buildings were either built or reconditioned by Berghorst and construction teams he assembled and, at the end of 1980, were in acceptable operating condition. Since 1980, however, after extensive usage and exposure, no major repairs or upgrading have been performed on any of the firm's property or facilities.

The Human Resources

33   Berghorst became president of Tulip City in 1962 and board chairman in 1965 (Exhibit 8). He was recognized by various industry associations as one of the most knowledgeable experts in ambulance company management. On occasion he had acted in this capacity

Exhibit 8
Organization chart, Tulip City Ambulance, Inc.

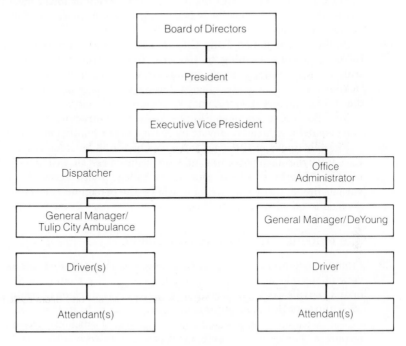

to consult with various EMS agencies and private concerns. Berghorst always exercised a dynamic and personal style of management in the running of the company. It was generally agreed, however, by the other managers that if Mart liked an idea it was implemented; if he didn't, it was dropped. He has distanced himself somewhat from the firm since 1980, when he became heavily involved with a car lot for expensive European automobiles and related foreign travel.

34   Karl VerBeek was hired into the position of executive vice president and general manager of Tulip City in July of 1974. He had previously been a sales manager with a large international pharmaceutical firm, a position he later gave up as too confining and without challenge to open a small delicatessen specializing in natural foods. Over the years he developed a close but sometimes strained friendship with Berghorst on both professional and social levels. His initial responsibilities at Tulip City were to build a more refined technical work force, establish financial stability, and put the firm into a more effective posture with the city's political infrastructure. Karl's manner of presenting ideas and his penchant for challenging work brought him immediate success. His 96-hour workweeks were reduced to 70 in 1983. This extra time afforded him the opportunity to continue a graduate degree in business (M.B.A.) and put more sophistication into the daily administration of Tulip City. In anticipation of a larger organization, VerBeek began strengthening the firm's control and planning systems, showing special emphasis on reducing uncollectible accounts and formalizing equipment purchase decisions. With an eye on eventual ownership of the firm, he has maintained his emergency medical qualifications and performed nearly every management task.

35   From time to time Karl received executive-level offers from Bellview General and his former employer. In recent months he has become a little more than irate at the CEO's autocratic style and his occasional override of lower-level decisions. VerBeek has made it known that he is beginning to weigh more carefully his personal costs for such a move.

36   Phillip Lasser joined Tulip City in 1976 as manager/driver of the newly acquired DeYoung service. Coming to the firm from a technical position in Bellview General's emergency department, he faced the effort of rebuilding the tarnished image of DeYoung as an exacting challenge. Lasser kept his team small but continued to stress the state of the art in emergency ambulance technology.

37   Mrs. Berghorst, while continuing her role as director, has long since left the office and dispatching duties to devote more time to her family and various social obligations.

38   The remainder of the work force was balanced between full- and part-time people. Except for the office personnel, all were licensed EMTs, with a few pursuing paramedic-level training at the local community college. With access to temporary help from various fire and police department EMTs, the personnel needs of the firm were usually deemed to be adequate.

The Marketing and Operations Culture

39   From the beginning Tulip City had been a market-oriented company retaining a wide view of its role in emergency health care. Rather than view itself as a provider of luxury convalescent transportation or as an overextension of trauma center technology, the Tulip City/DeYoung organization saw itself in the business of offering high-quality, cost-effective methods through the utilization of efficiently designed and maintained resources. The company further believed there were substantial differences in these three approaches. In the first, emphasis is placed strictly on the vehicle, avoiding almost all personal responsibility. In the next, the growing but limited understanding of the EMT may be stressed beyond its intended realm during critical time frames when the patient should be moved to more advanced knowledge and equipment. In the final method, a balance is reached between immediate care and stabilization of the patient with that of appropriately timed and prepared transport.

40   The total organization's philosophy normally began with the training and indoctrination of new members. Only those near completion of the 100-hour EMT course were considered for employment. Their skills and personalities were then evaluated by current team members during a two-week trial period. Once accepted, individuals were expected to cooperate fully with the team effort and to update their abilities through periodic seminars and training programs.

41   The Tulip City philosophy was further enhanced through the production and use of its ambulance fleet. Since 1970, the company had become almost totally integrated by producing all but one of its own heavy-duty emergency vehicles. Few firms in the industry could duplicate this achievement. To minimize production costs and allow for immediate recognition in the community, specialization played an important role in the construction of the company's two types of vehicles.

42   After extensive negotiations with a number of local dealers, Berghorst settled on the Ford F-250 Econoline and F-350 chassis (driver compartment and frame/wheels only) for the type II and type III units, respectively. Structurally, these trucks were purchased with the "ambulance preparation package," which, in addition to deluxe driving compartments, included extended-duty cooling, air conditioning, braking, suspension, and electrical systems. The first half of 1980 was a critical time in the upgrading of the company ambulance fleet with the purchase of three vans and two F-350 chassis.

43   Getting these vehicles ready for service was a temporary but central activity for Berghorst. The total process was characterized by expert craftsmanship, coordination of a host of detail work, and a deep sense of personal pride. Upon completion of each project, Berghorst often remarked, "These units are dependable, durable, good looking, and cost about 80 percent of the normal going price." Both styles of Tulip City emergency ambulances were made up of many individual parts, such as cabinetry, stainless steel support and hinge devices, leather work, vacuum and pressure lines, and a labyrinth of electronic circuitry.

44   The production process basically involved six stages. First, various pressure and vacuum lines were positioned alongside the electrical wiring harnesses and cables. Second, the fiberboard flooring was anchored, upon which a balance of right- and left-side cabinets were installed. Next, the linoleum, Formica®, and other veneers were cut, fitted, and bonded into position for all countertops, cabinetry, and floor surfaces. Fourth, the ventilation, internal lighting, support mechanisms, and switches were installed, as was the leather seating and padding devices. The fifth stage involved the securing of the scene lights, warning lights, and siren apparatuses. Finally, the car was driven to a custom detail shop, where the federally mandated accent strips and company name and logo were handpainted into place. The entire operation took about five weeks per unit to complete.

45   Toward the end of 1978 an awkward situation started to develop in the geographic area surrounding Manchester and Springdale. A number of peripheral hospitals found they could no longer cope with the increased severity of some trauma victims and the growing number of neonatal (premature) births.

46   At the culmination of much discussion and negotiation, Tulip City and Bellview General jointly agreed to build two vehicles capable of addressing these unique needs. The specifics of the program stated that Berghorst would design and build customized patient treatment chambers retrofitted on a type III/Modulance chassis for stable emergency transportation between the outlying hospital and Bellview General.

47   The value of the baby unit was its capacity to carry a neonatologist, registered nurse, inhalation therapist, and ancillary equipment to the smaller outlying hospital and return with the crew and one to four incubators. The patient(s) could then be stabilized by the team before and during transport to Bellview's recently expanded neonatal intensive care unit (NICU).

48   Slightly larger in size than the baby unit, but with a similar internal configuration, the trauma unit was intended mainly for emergency transfers of adults between hospitals. Staffed by an emergency room physician and a carefully selected and trained crew, the use of this unit has been very disappointing. Revenue, maintenance, and repairs of either vehicle are shared equally by both program partners (see Exhibit 2).

49   The normal maintenance routine of the fleet included periodic servicing (every 5,000 miles) of the engine and structural lubrication systems. Every 30,000 miles, the brakes, shock absorbers, batteries, and related components were upgraded or replaced, while at 100,000 miles the drive train (engine, transmission, etc.) and other major components were completely rebuilt. This final measure, which was supervised closely by Berghorst, was estimated to cost at least $5,200 and extend the life of the vehicle another 30,000 miles (see Exhibit 9).

Exhibit 9
Vehicle evaluation schedule as of December 31, 1984

Date in service	Vehicle	Unit cost ($000)	Annual mileage (000)	Evaluation
1/76	Van (3)	$13.9	5.0	Moderately poor condition. Life: 30,000 miles.
1/78	Cadillac (5)	12.5	2.0	Very poor condition. Life: 7,500 miles.
7/80*	Van	16.9	20.5	Good condition. Life: 8,000 miles.
7/80	Van	16.9	20.0	Good condition. Life: 10,000 miles.
7/80	Van	16.9	18.0	Good condition. Life: 19,000 miles.
7/80	Modulance baby unit	29.7	12.5	Good condition. Life: 44,000 miles.
7/80	Modulance trauma unit	26.3	3.0	Excellent condition. Life: 5 years.
1/83	Van†	26.3	14.0	Excellent condition. Life: 70,000 miles.

* All units purchased since 1980 are expected to be rebuilt or replaced at 100,000 miles.
† Chevrolet.
Source: Company records.

50   The remainder of the company's fleet consisted of three Ford vans, five Cadillacs, and a recently purchased Chevrolet high-top custom-built ambulance. Management rebuilt the Fords according to schedule and then considered them as backup vehicles.

51   By contrast, the 1975 Cadillacs were purchased in poor condition and, unlike the rest of the fleet, were never upgraded. They were used essentially for long-distance transfers. The Chevrolet was purchased rather impetuously by Berghorst during a convention; but, when confronted by his executive vice president on the decision, his response was "I got a deal that I couldn't pass up," and the matter was dropped.

52   Tulip City/DeYoung facilities and equipment were specifically designed to meet the expanding needs of Lincoln County and, in a growing number of cases, an even larger circle of operations. The two bases, radio network, skill level of the work force, and the complexity of the vehicle fleet have given the company much flexibility to respond quickly to ever-widening consumer demands.

53   Realizing that the consumer's purchase of ambulance service was difficult to segment into any workable classification scheme and that a note of urgency normally circumvented the unsought nature of the product offering, management utilized a variety of promotional techniques. Supplementing the prominent positioning of the company's name and logo on vehicles and uniforms was the widespread use of Yellow Pages advertisements. Since the first reaction of a person in need of an ambulance is to use the telephone or Yellow Pages, the company has tried to capitalize on the expected benefits from this medium.

54   In March of 1981, Tulip City introduced its first prime-time television commercial. Product awareness messages featuring the transfer, EMS, and specialty units reached approximately 300,000 people in the lower portion of the state. In addition to the

single-station TV commercials, other advertisements were aired on three local radio stations and published in the area newspaper.

55   Tulip City's promotional efforts in the early stages were decidedly transfer oriented. However, due to the increasing relationship between the EMS and the transfer business, the theme was later geared more specifically toward emergencies.

Finance and Accounting

56   Tulip City retained a local CPA firm to draw up financial statements for management decision-making and income tax purposes. The accounting documents conformed to generally accepted reporting requirements for companies classified in this industry. Earnings not retained were taxed as personal income at both the federal and state levels. Even with the growing complexity of the business, and the resultant financial documentation, no management/accountant discussions of consequence have taken place since 1979.

57   Management was not sure whether TCA's billing rates were set at premium levels. This was due mainly to the uncertainty over the pricing strategies of both competitors in the greater Manchester area. While it was relatively easy to obtain reliable estimates of what Van's was charging at any one point in time, his fluctuating pricing policy made industry guidelines all but impossible to establish. Moreover, it became increasingly evident that rates patients would accept varied according to the services performed and the image of the firm whithin the local community.

58   Payroll was distributed biweekly, with nonexempt personnel receiving 76 regular hours and 8 overtime hours within each of the 26 pay periods. To minimize morale and turnover problems, Berghorst advocated steady increases in pay levels (at something less than inflation) for the 12 full-time and various part-time EMTs. After the addition of the new vehicle in 1983, the number of EMTs was increased to 14.

59   The following schedule reflects supportive data for the calculation of total wages, salaries, and associated compensation expenses.

Wage/salary schedule

Position	1980	1981	1982	1983	1984
EMT/hourly	$ 6.00/hour	$ 6.30/hour	$ 6.60/hour	$ 7.00/hour	$ 7.30/hour
Part-time	29,500	30,975	32,520	34,146	35,860
Dispatcher	10,200	10,700	11,235	11,800	12,390
Office administrator	11,500	12,100	12,705	13,340	14,000
Office part-time	12,000	12,600	13,230	13,840	14,585
CEO	35,000	40,000	45,000	50,000	55,000
Excecutive vice president	22,500	23,650	24,883	26,075	27,380
Taxes	7.13%	7.86%	7.78%	7.78%	8.00%

60   Initial corporate policy was to finance expansion from retained earnings, although other methods of raising funds were used when generally needed. Through the first 15 years of the company, the small family of investors continued to increase their holdings until they reached current levels.

61   In recent years and for a variety of reasons, the firm often increased its debt load. Excessive short-term requirements were met through open lines of credit with the state's two largest banks. Each note was generally secured by corporate accounts receivable. Bank debt was also used to finance the vehicle fleet at prevailing interest rates, with security based on the ambulances and corporate property holdings.

62   Since 1978 the firm has purchased ambulances in four- or five-lot sizes, causing periodic strains to its interest and debt capacity. Also, since 1979, Berghorst has taken increased amounts of retained earnings to help finance his other business ventures.

The View of the Future

63   Karl VerBeek once again considered the growing myriad of problems facing the firm through 1985. He knew that TCA had to clarify its direction if it were to remain a leader in the industry. Revenue from EMS operations showed almost constant decline, price battles with Vanlaar were always a threat, and volume related to the transfer business appeared headed for a plateau.

64   Even the specialty vehicles raised new problems, not the least of which was how these units could be used and what would happen to total revenue if Bellview General went ahead with plans to incorporate their own ambulance service.

65   The city government's challenge to Tulip City was also increasing; not only were plans well under way to establish municipal-based emergency aid and treatment at the scene but, it was generally assumed, once this operation was in place a transport process for each victim would soon follow.

66   As the executive vice president glanced at the financial documents he had accumulated on his desk, his attention shifted to the meeting Mart had requested take place that afternoon.

67   In addition to the ambulance business, Mart Berghorst made frequent trips overseas to buy high-priced European automobiles. These were later converted to American pollution control standards and sold on his retail lot. Immediately after returning from one such trip, Berghorst called in his executive vice president for the following conversation:

> I am quite pleased with the way you have managed the operations of Tulip City and DeYoung over the past few years. I don't have your formal education, but I do have a nose for what is right or wrong concerning expenses and profits. This business seems to be doing as well as can be expected. We have talked in the past about setting up a more sophisticated planning process with budgets, objectives, goals, strategies, and a computer. I again gave your idea some thought while I was in Europe, but I still feel that this business is changing so rapidly and Vanlaar has thrown so much confusion into the local area with his severe price cutting and antagonistic operations that we can only plan a few days at a time. Your efforts to obtain cost data on different aspects of this business have been helpful, but that is as detailed as I want to go.
>
> It has been my policy on past occasions to buy vehicles or equipment when I thought the price was right. I've made some mistakes, especially with the Cadillacs and the high interest rates we paid on them and the Fords. We've gotten fairly good use out of the truck fleet, but the luxury cars were a complete waste of money, and I wish I had never bought them.

68   Berghorst's principal concern at this point in the discussion centered on the way his executive vice president had managed the business during periods of inflation, high interest rates, and general upheavals in the local economy. His primary reason for the meeting soon became evident.

Personally, Karl, I have struggled to reach a position in this business where I would have more time to spend on my other interests and with my family. I have been tempted to milk this venture dry and then walk away from it. Now, I feel it is only fair to let you know that, much to my surprise, David Vanlaar called me about six weeks ago with an initial offer to buy the company. While at first I thought he was joking, he went on to say that St. Luke's would support his intention by providing partial financing for the acquisition.

The CPA and I were to meet with Vanlaar, Dykema (administrator of St. Luke's), and some bank officials to discuss our records, books, and financial operations. No meeting ever took place, however, and I thought the matter was dropped. Then yesterday morning Vanlaar and Dykema called from the bank and gave me an offer, which I feel is much more (but I really don't know) than the firm is worth. Even though I seriously doubt that Vanlaar could handle an operation like this one, I also think I would be foolish not to accept the offer.

As I have mentioned to you before, Karl, I will sell this company to you as well. But you know our relationship with Bellview General is becoming strained, and it is up for grabs if they will bankroll you like St. Luke's is doing for Vanlaar.

69   Karl VerBeek left the meeting angry and resentful to call his wife and ponder the future.

Case 28

Note on the Deregulated Airline Industry

Focus

1   The U.S. airline industry can be segmented into three groups: major, national, and regional airlines. Major carriers are defined by the Civil Aeronautics Board (CAB) as those carriers with more than $1 billion in revenues annually. National carriers are airlines that have annual revenues of $75 million to $1 billion. Regional airlines are those with revenues less than $75 million annually.

2   In 1984, there were 11 major carriers in the United States, 16 national carriers, and over 260 regional or commuter airlines. Exhibit 1 presents a listing of major and national airlines.

3   Major airlines' operations can be broken down into international and national operations, but this industry note will deal only with national operations, since to include international factors would require the consideration of several additional complex issues, such as exchange rate, political risk, and foreign governments' regulations.

4   Furthermore, only the passenger travel activity of the three groups will be considered. Other services offered by the carriers, such as airmail or air cargo, will not be discussed for two reasons. First, these other activities are not main generators of revenue, and second, there are other airlines which specialize in some of those services, and they have their own unique characteristics. Including an analysis of nonpassenger travel would not help in accomplishing the main purpose of this industry note, namely, to identify the broad framework of critical factors that have impacted the airline industry since deregulation.

5   Finally, data for the years 1979–84 will be used to support the analysis, since these years reflect most, if not all, of the factors which affected the industry in its deregulation period.

Impact of Deregulation

The Pre-Deregulation Era

6   For 40 years, from 1938 until late 1978, all airline carriers were subject to CAB regulation, and four conditions characterized this pre-deregulation era:

1. Fares that were tightly controlled.
2. Competition that was restricted.
3. New service(s) that could be granted only if the carrier proved to the CAB that there was a public need.
4. Cost increases, such as in labor cost, that were passed by the carriers directly to the consumer.

This industry note was prepared by John A. Pearce II of George Mason University.

Exhibit 1
Carrier grouping in 1984

Major carriers*	
American Airlines	Republic Airlines
Continental Air Lines	Trans World Airlines
Delta Air Lines	United Airlines
Eastern Air Lines	USAir, Inc.
Northwest Airlines	Western Air Lines
Pan American World	
Airways	

National carriers	
Air California	Ozark Air Lines
Air Florida System	Pacific-Southwest
Alaska Airlines	Piedmont Aviation
Aloha Airlines	Southwest Airlines
Capitol International	Texas Air Corporation
Airways	Transamerica
Flying Tiger	Wien
Frontier Airlines	World Airways
Hawaiian Airlines	

* Braniff International was dropped from the list in 1983.

7   As a result of these conditions, competition among the various carriers concentrated on services and schedule convenience. Furthermore, competition between national and regional carriers was minimal because regional airlines were largely feeder airlines to the larger national carriers, who would then provide the link that carried passengers to their final destinations.

The Deregulation Era

8   The passage of the Airline Deregulation Act in October 1978 set in motion a complete transformation of the U.S. airline industry. Among other changes, this act removed almost all market entry barriers and fare control. Consequently, the industry became more susceptible to swings in the business cycle, leading the industry to a major shake-up, with various players and factors involved. The remainder of this industry note will provide detailed information regarding those players and factors. The discussion will be presented in a manner which highlights the considerations that were critical to the airline industry.

Political and Legal Factors

9   Before the Airline Deregulation Act, the U.S. airline industry was treated as other important public utilities—such as electric and telephone services. This meant total regulation of fares, of markets, and, consequently, of competition. However, the deregulation act enabled airlines not only to set their own fares but also allowed trunk

carriers to eliminate services to marginally profitable markets. As a result, the route systems of all carriers were substantially restructured, and a number of new carriers entered the market. Specifically, prior to deregulation, the 11 major airlines shown in Exhibit 1, plus Braniff International, served 679 locations. At the end of 1981, these same carriers served 692 locations, but these locations represented the deletion of 132 cities and the addition of 145 others.

10   A company-specific illustration of the rerouting that took place involved Pan American World Airways. Between September 1980 and September 1982, its airlines operations lost over $906.9 million. Pan Am's stock went as low as $2.50 in 1982, bringing the company's market value to only $180 million—approximately the price of two new 747 airplanes. Edward Acker, the chairman of Pan Am, attributed the situation to several reasons, one of which was the disorganized, unprofitable domestic route system. Therefore, one of the first things he did when he took over the chairmanship in late 1981 was to rearrange Pan Am's domestic network to work mainly as a feeder system for the company's international flights from New York, Miami, Los Angeles, and San Francisco. By the second quarter of 1983, the company was again generating profits. This example also illustrates how major and national airlines exited from many short-haul, lighter-density routes during the years from 1979 to 1983. The decreased competition of major airlines created some attractive growth potential for the various regional airlines, and, in response, several regional carriers not only added routes but also expanded former routes and acquired larger, longer-range aircraft. Some even arranged with major airlines to provide reciprocal traffic feed and to share facilities, such as reservation systems and ticketing. For instance, Dolphin Airlines, a two-year-old carrier, signed agreements with Ozark, Delta, Republic, Northwest, and American airlines that included joint and add-on fares. Specifically, American Airlines agreed to take a passenger into a Dolphin hub city, and Dolphin would carry that passenger anywhere on its Florida network for $19.

11   However, the U.S. government retained control over other important aspects of the airline industry. For instance, the Federal Aviation Administration (FAA) monitored the safety of the airplanes and controlled air traffic. This power was enhanced as a consequence of the illegal strike by members of the Professional Air Traffic Controllers Organization (PATCO) in August 1981. As a result of the subsequent firing of the strikers, the FAA was designated to hire and train new controllers and to allocate slots to airlines because of reduced traffic in airports.

12   To a lesser extent, government regulations affected the industry through a subsidy program. The government paid a number of carriers to provide services for communities too small to support profitable operations. From June 30, 1980, to June 30, 1982, the government paid a total subsidy of $181.6 million. Of this amount, approximately 37 percent went to major airlines; 47 percent, to the national airlines; and 16 percent, to the regional airlines. Overall, subsidization accounted for 1 percent of the total revenue of all certified airlines.

Economic Factors

13   Bad economic conditions hurt the airline industry in many ways. For example, looking upstream in the industry, aircraft purchases represented multimillion-dollar capital outlays—amounts beyond airlines' cash capabilities. Attempts to enter money markets

to borrow the necessary funds became extremely difficult and even unprofitable when interest rates were high. Delta Airlines can be a case study that reflects these problems. Until the end of 1981, Delta International was considered by many experts to be the world's most profitable airline. But due to various factors, one of which was the general state of the economy, Delta's profits shrank from $146.5 million in 1981 to $20.8 million in 1982. Then, in its 1983 fiscal year, Delta reported a loss of $86.7 million, its first loss in 36 years. The 1980–82 recession, combined with record-high interest rates, forced Delta to delay the delivery of its new Boeing 757s and 767s.

14   Delta was not the only airline hurt by the recession. Most major carriers, as well as nationals and regionals, experienced sharp reversals of their profit trends. For instance, TWA fell from a $25.6 million profit in 1982 to a $16.2 million loss in 1983, while Eastern's deficit grew from $3 million to $33.7 million during the same period. Only United and American airlines generated profits. United went from a $4.4 million loss to a $109.9 million profit. American Airlines enjoyed a jump from $466,000 to $34.4 million in profits, largely attributable to the selling of tax credits. An even worse pattern could be shown if the national and the approximately 260 regional airlines were included in the analysis. With few exceptions (for example, Southwest), the recession forced small carriers to remain in the red because of low traffic and high interest rates. This led to a total of $1.3 billion in operating loss in the years 1980–82 for all airlines combined, compared to an estimated profit of $200 million–$800 million in 1983.

15   When the U.S. economy started to improve, particularly in the second half of 1983, carriers began to realize some profits. For instance, the net income of Southwest Airlines for the first half of 1983 reached $13 million, up 30 percent over the same period in 1982. People Express showed a $4.2 million net profit in the second quarter of 1983, on top of a $3 million gain in the first quarter. Northwest Airlines, which had a net loss of $1.5 million in the last quarter of 1982, jumped to a $14.4 million net profit in the second quarter of 1983.

Price/Cost Structure

16   Profitability in the airline industry depended largely on a carrier's ability to control costs, particularly those for labor and fuel.

17   **1. Labor Cost.**   Employee wages and salaries were among the largest controllable expenses faced by the airlines, particularly the major ones. Wages grew steadily during the period of government regulation, but the carriers passed down most of their costs to consumers. After deregulation, however, the pass-through technique could not be used since passengers had the option of using cheaper competitors. In 1984, Air Line Pilots Association (ALPA) members earned about $69,000 a year for about 50 hours of flight per month, and mechanics earned an average of $30,000 a year, plus fringe benefits. In contrast, the new, small, nonunionized airlines could hire unemployed pilots to fly 70 hours a month for approximately $30,000 a year. In fact, labor cost represented 33 to 37 percent of the total operating costs of the major airlines in 1982. On the other hand, nonunionized national and regional carriers enjoyed a substantial advantage over the majors by keeping their labor costs in the 19–27 percent range (see Exhibit 2).

Exhibit 2
Labor costs as a share of total 1982 cost

Low-fare airlines

Muse Air	19%
People Express	20%
Southwest	27%

Major carriers

Continental	34%
Eastern	37%
Pan Am	34%
Republic	36%
TWA	35%
Western	34%

Source: Adapted with modifications from "Airlines in Turmoil," *Business Week,* October 10, 1983, p. 100.

18   This cost differential was perhaps the main reason that small airlines were able to offer and sustain low fares for a long period of time. The new airlines utilized their cost savings to promote their low-fare strategies. People Express, for example, succeeded in generating more than $2 million in profits during the first nine months of 1982, while Pan Am, Eastern, and TWA were all in the red. The key to People's success was a cost base which averaged 5.3 cents per seat-mile, compared to an 11-cent average for major airline competitors. This advantage enabled People Express to offer a one-way ticket to Florida for only $69, thus luring passengers from Eastern, Delta, and others.

19   Another successful small airline was Southwest, which gained market share by controlling its costs while charging rock-bottom fares. Cost control at Southwest did not stop at labor costs. Its ticketing procedures were simplified, with 55 percent of its tickets sold through its cash registers, 15–18 percent through its vending machines, and the remaining 25 percent through travel agents. In contrast, travel agents sold 60 percent of Delta's tickets and 50 percent of USAir's tickets, while charging a 10 percent commission. Such cost savings provided Southwest and other similar carriers an additional leverage against competition.

20   To compete with these nationals and regionals, larger carriers were pressed to cut labor costs, trim work rules, and increase workers' productivity. Republic Airlines,

which lost $214 million from 1979 through 1981, bargained successfully for $73 million in 1982 temporary pay cuts and wage deferrals. In early 1983, Republic received an additional 15 percent pay cut for nine months, which translated to about $100 million in savings.

21   The threat of Pan Am's bankruptcy enabled it to obtain a 10 percent wage cut from its employees, saving approximately $110 million in 1983. In return, employees received stock ownership and profit-sharing plans, which Pan Am's management counted on to boost employee morale as well as productivity. Pan Am also cut its work force by 5,000 workers down to a level of 25,000.

22   Western Airlines reached an agreement with its unionized labor in early 1983 to accept a 10 percent pay cut, which translated to a $50 million savings. In exchange, the airline gave its workers 25 percent of the company stock. Even the financially strong United succeeded in persuading its pilots not only to defer two wage increases but also to increase their flying time 15 percent. In return, the company provided a lifetime no-layoff guarantee.

23   These examples have one particular common and unique feature—almost all the concessions were made in a relatively friendly and cooperative atmosphere. However, other airlines (such as Continental Air Lines and, to a lesser extent, Eastern Airlines) took a confrontational approach. For example, despite an excellent route structure, strong marketing, and an efficient fleet, Eastern had serious liquidity problems resulting from high labor costs and an accelerated capital-spending program. As a result, Eastern's lenders disapproved the additional costs that would have been incurred from new contracts with IAM and the Transport Workers Union, which represented Eastern's flight attendants. The company then appealed to its workers, asking for a 15 percent pay cut to save $300 million through 1985. Eastern added that if the employees refused the proposed cut, the carrier would either go out of business—as happened to Braniff in 1982—or would face reorganization under Chapter 11 of the bankruptcy laws—as Continental had done only a few weeks prior. Pressures and threats from both sides made the disruption of Eastern's services imminent, influencing travel agents to avoid bookings on the airline. However, only hours before the planned strike was to have taken place, an agreement was reached. Basically, it called for wage cuts and the formation of a team of outside consultants who would study Eastern's books and records to see whether they supported the company's claims of near-insolvency.

24   Perhaps the most dramatic example of the confrontational approach was provided by Continental Airlines. In 1982, the company asked for $90 million in permanent pay cuts and work rule improvements from its pilots, and got them. Yet, Continental continued to lose money at a potentially disastrous rate. Five contributing factors were known:

1. Price wars that were ravaging the industry.
2. A weak economy and accompanying low traffic levels, particularly at Continental's main hub in Houston.
3. The competition from Continental's low-cost rivals, such as Muse Air, Southwest Airlines, and People Express. (Refer again to Exhibit 2.)
4. A poor marketing strategy.
5. Management instability.[1]

---

[1] "Airlines in Turmoil," *Business Week,* October 10, 1983, pp. 98, 102.

25   In combination, these factors led the company to report an $18 million loss in the second quarter of 1983, instead of an expected $10 million profit. Therefore, Continental asked its pilots and flight attendants to make up the difference. They declined. Consequently, on September 24, 1983, Continental asked for protection from its creditors under Chapter 11 of the Bankruptcy Code of 1978. An important aspect of this law was that it permitted the company to dismiss its union contracts. The financial impact was a 50 percent pay cut for pilots and flight attendants, shorter vacations, suspension of the pension plan, and tighter work rules designed to increase productivity. These cost savings enabled a redesign of Continental's marketing strategy. It offered a "price-slashed" fare of $99 between any two cities in the country. Continental claimed this fare would satisfy its cash needs if its planes could fill 40 percent of their seats. This meant the company had dropped its load factor from 65 to 40 percent, which enabled it to compete head to head against its low-cost rivals.

26   **2. Fuel Cost.**   Fuel costs were the second most important element, after labor expenses, in the cost structure of the airline industry. Fuel costs for a single airline were as high as 34 percent of operating expenses, as was the case with Pan Am. This high percentage resulted from two facts: (1) most jets used by major carriers were not fuel efficient and (2) fuel cost was itself very high. For example, in 1981, Pan Am's fuel cost was $1.15 per gallon. Fortunately, however, by the end of 1982, the glut of oil in world markets, record-high inventories, and reduced industry demand started fuel prices on a downward trend. In 1982, Pan Am's fuel costs had dropped to 95 cents per gallon. Exhibit 3 displays trends in fuel consumption and revenues and illustrates the downward trend of fuel consumption for the years 1975 through 1982.

27   In the area of fuel costs, regional carriers again enjoyed an important advantage over the major airlines. The cost of fuel per gallon was essentially the same for all airlines, but the use of fuel-efficient airplanes that seated from 8 to 50 passengers on economical runs of up to 250 miles proved to be a successful weapon in the small airlines' efforts for survival and market share.

28   The basic niche strategy used by regionals usually involved providing services between major cities and airports that were underused or ignored. For example, Atlantic Express realized that people from New York's Long Island found it extremely time-consuming to commute through New York's airports. Therefore, in January 1983, Atlantic inaugurated service from Republic Airport in Farmingdale to several major cities, including Boston, Syracuse, New York, and Albany. In March 1983, Atlantic Express's load factor—defined as the percentage of filled seats on a given flight—was only 10 percent. But by the end of July, its load factor reached 49 percent, its break-even point. For major carriers, a load factor of up to 60 percent was needed to break even because of higher fuel costs and less fuel-efficient planes.

29   Perhaps an even more striking case was that of Waring Air. In December 1982, the company received certification from the FAA to begin business as a scheduled carrier. By the end of 1983, with only four eight-seat planes, Waring had reached $770,000 in sales and a profit of $75,000. In most of its routes, only four passengers were required to reach the break-even point. However, no major airlines could obtain such results with their 90- to 150-seat aircraft.

30   In 1982, almost 20 million people flew with regionals whose aircrafts held fewer than 50 seats. In that same year, regional airlines served 817 airports in North America,

Exhibit 3
Fuel consumption versus traffic for major carriers (monthly)

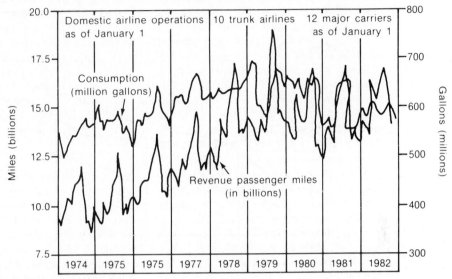

Source: Civil Aeronautics Board.

compared to only 766 in 1981. In fact, about 65 percent of all airports in the United States were being serviced exclusively by regional carriers.

31   In response to such challenges, many major and national airlines tried to minimize the effects of their cost disadvantage. To reduce fuel costs, most large carriers decided to upgrade their fleets. Delta and Eastern Airlines, for example, retooled their fleets by purchasing Boeing 757s, the most advanced and most fuel-efficient jetliners in the world. Other national carriers, such as Southwest, emphasized the flexible, smaller, fuel-efficient Boeing 737-200, which became the world's best-selling airplane in 1980 and 1981, with orders of 106 and 129 planes, respectively.

32   As a result of such conservation steps, total fuel consumption for major airlines declined 8 percent in 1982, following an increase of 5 percent in 1981 and far larger jumps in the two preceding years, as shown in Exhibit 3.

33   An issue related to fuel costs concerned what economists call the substitution effect. They argue that the consumer is only willing to pay a certain price for a certain good or service. Once the price exceeds that level, the consumer will attempt to substitute a less expensive product (for example, margarine for butter, vinyl for leather). The phenomenon also operated in the airlines industry. Since many airline passengers were tourists, there was a time/cost trade-off involved in their decision to choose air travel over other methods of transportation. As fuel costs rose, the travel-time savings offered by air travel were increasingly offset by the dollar savings offered by substitute transportation modes. This specific condition seriously affected Delta Airlines. From June 1982 until June 1983, many of Delta's traditional Florida passengers chose to drive instead of fly. Since Florida travelers constituted 25 percent of Delta's passengers,

Exhibit 4
Airline traffic statistics

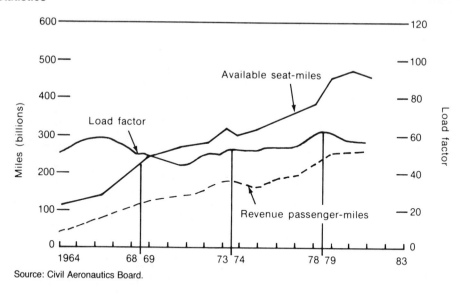

Source: Civil Aeronautics Board.

the airline faced a serious problem. As a counterstrategy, Delta discounted approximately 90 percent of its Florida tickets, resulting in a very substantial decline in its 1982–83 fiscal year profit margins.

Capacity Utilization

34   Idle capacity translates to lower income and eventually less profit or even loss. What made this issue especially complicated in the airline industry was that demand fluctuated around seasonal variations. For example, traffic evaporated as schools opened, while business travel was at its heaviest from October through May.

35   From 1979 to 1984, capacity in the airline industry, as measured by available seat-miles, rose faster than traffic demand. As seen in Exhibit 4, the industry experienced a fairly stable load factor, while available seat-miles were constantly increasing. As a result, the average certified carrier was losing money. In addition, the rising capacity had an important implication for the industry's future, namely, that even modest increases in rates might further depress demand.

36   A widely used measure of an airline's ability to market its capacity effectively was the ratio between the carrier's share of total revenue passenger-miles flown by its industry group and its share of domestic capacity—available seat-miles. A positive traffic/capacity relationship, meaning a greater share of traffic than capacity, indicated an above-average load factor and effective marketing of capacity. Exhibit 5 illustrates these relationships for the 11 major carriers in 1982. An important observation is that some of those carriers shown in Exhibit 5 had positive ratios and yet were losing money. The explanation was that it was not enough for airlines to utilize their available

Exhibit 5
Airline market shares

Airline	Share of total revenue passenger-miles	Share of total available seat-miles
American	14.9%	13.8%
Continental	13.3	14.4
Delta	14.1	14.4
Eastern	4.8	5.1
Northwest	4.0	4.0
Pan Am	4.4	4.4
Republic	4.4	5.0
TWA	9.3	8.9
United	19.9	19.1
USAir	3.1	3.1
Western	4.2	4.1

Source: Adapted with modification from Thomas Canning, "Air Transportation: Current Analysis," *Standard & Poor's Industry Survey,* October 1983, p. A60.

capacity. Rather, the prices they charged also had to be high enough to cover operating costs. In many cases, sufficient margins were not achieved as a consequence of high labor costs, high fuel costs, and fare wars.

37   Another measure that reflected the underutilization of airlines' capacities was the post-1978 decline in the share of domestic traffic transported by the U.S. major carriers. For instance, in June 1982, the major carriers accounted for 87 percent of the revenue passenger-miles for all CAB-certified airlines. Before deregulation, however, those carriers accounted for 95 percent of the revenue passenger-miles. This shift illustrates the success of national and regional carriers in obtaining larger market shares and also partially explains the occurrence of fare wars.

Demographics and Psychographics

38   During the late 1970s and early 1980s, the Sunbelt states of Florida, Texas, Arizona, and California experienced the nation's greatest population growth, enabling further penetration by carriers in these areas. In fact, between September 1978 and December 1981, the West and the South accounted for approximately 70 percent of the new stations added by both major and national airlines. This growth was more than twice that in the North Central and Northeast regions of the country during the same period. Houston, Orlando, Phoenix, Dallas/Fort Worth, and Las Vegas all showed substantial increases in the number of airlines and the number of flights serving their airports. Weekly departures from Orlando increased over 50 percent, while flights from Phoenix rose about 60 percent. Airlines that were either creating new hubs at those cities or connecting those cities to their existing hubs were United, American, Southwest, Pacific Southwest, Delta, and Dolphin Airlines.

39   A psychographic-related effect on the airline industry was the preference organizations had for holding their conferences in warm cities, particularly during fall and winter seasons. Such high-margin travel combined with normal business travel to account for 50 percent of all passenger-miles, prompting many airlines to undertake aggressive strategies designed to increase their direct sales to associations and corporate meeting planners. The rationale for these actions were twofold. First, airlines sought to eliminate their excess capacity. Second, they wished to reduce the commissions they paid to travel agents and meeting planners. Travel agents, who sold more than 65 percent of domestic air tickets, charged a 10 percent commission on each ticket they sold. When airlines could save this commission, they could be more flexible in offering discounts directly to associations and corporations. The potential importance of these actions is suggested by the statistics in 1982 that showed that U.S. organizations held about 10,000 conventions and 707,000 company meetings.

40   Finally, demographic and psychographic information, such as birth and death rates, styles of living, and educational patterns, were crucial to the planning process of all airlines. Exhibit 6 presents an example of how one such variable, disposable personal income, could be used to improve carrier predictions of industry growth trends.

An Industry Overview of Competitive Strategies

41   The passage of the Airline Deregulation Act resulted in a massive restructuring of the industry. Increased competition and greater fare flexibility were some of the goals as well as the end results of the act. After historically controlling about 95 percent of the passenger travel business, major airlines experienced sharp (8 percent) declines in passenger-miles with accompanying declines in revenues and profits. New entrants enjoyed certain cost advantages over the major, well-established carriers attributable to the use of nonunion labor forces with much lower wage scales, greater flexibility in work rules, and more fuel-efficient aircraft that were much less expensive to operate.

42   Regional carriers also skillfully executed some innovative and well-planned strategies. For example, many relied on older airports, which offered ease of access because of their centralized locations. Regional airlines also attempted to select routes that did not put them in head-to-head competition with larger airlines. In fact, as discussed earlier, some regionals established cooperative agreements with major and national carriers, such as working as feeders or by providing the last portions of trips for their passengers.

43   In many respects, the operating strategies of the national carriers were similar to those of the majors. Both emphasized hub areas where they had strong competitive positions as a basis for extending their operations to other profitable locations. Piedmont's grand strategy, for example, was to connect medium-sized cities in the Southeast with major cities in Florida, the Southwest, and the West. Piedmont's success with the strategy resulted in a fivefold growth in net income between 1979 and 1983.

44   In contrast, the main strategy of the major airlines following deregulation was the establishment of hub operations. This requires designing feeder routes to bring passengers to a central hub, where they could be transferred to other flights of the same carrier. Some airlines, United and Delta among them, established multiple hubs to capture or keep bigger shares of strategically located airports or cities.

45   With the major carriers, however, differences existed in the way they responded to deregulation and the new competitive environment. One clear contrast can be seen

Exhibit 6
Airline performance and disposable personal income

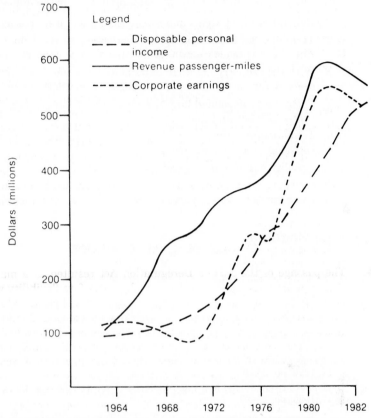

Source: Thomas Canning, "Air Transport: Current Analysis," *Standard & Poor's Industry Survey,* October 1983, p. A5.

in the experience of USAir and Braniff. USAir followed a conservative path by adding new stations gradually, by being very selective in its equipment purchases, and by stressing the suitability of its new planes to its primarily short-haul system. This well-planned growth raised the company's net income from $22 million in 1978 to $59.6 million in 1982.

46   In contrast, Braniff aggressively started 48 nonstop segments and entered 18 new cities in the United States after only two months of deregulation. As its financial position steadily deteriorated, Braniff took some desperate actions in 1981 and early 1982, trying to create turnaround momentum. Strategies included the sale of some of its fleet, the cancellation of new orders, the abandonment of unprofitable routes, and the restructuring of its debt with its creditors. Despite all of these actions, Braniff was forced to file for bankruptcy in May 1982. Following reorganization and after being acquired by Hyatt Corporation in Chicago, Braniff staged a downscaled comeback in early 1984.

Conclusion

47   As the first half-decade of the modern deregulated era drew to a close, several observations seemed relevant to strategic planning in the airline industry:

1. Demand was relatively and somewhat predictably seasonal.
2. Technological innovation offered increasing release from high fuel consumption.
   But new airplanes would require considerable capital expenditures.
3. With the industry life cycle in its maturity stage, the success of one airline
   seemed always to come at the expense of another.
4. Profitability depended largely on a carrier's ability to control costs, particularly
   those for labor and fuel.
5. Telecommunications technology increasingly threatened the industry as a
   substitute for business travel.
6. Mobility barriers were greatly diminished.
7. Low operating ratios, high contribution margins, and capital intensity all served
   as important, though partial, determinants of a carrier's profitability.

Recommended Reading

"Another Airline Price War Is in the Making." *Business Week,* October 3, 1983, pp. 46–47.

Dreyfack, Medeleine. "Airlines Battle for Survival." *Marketing & Media Decisions,* April 1983,
pp. 119–26.

Farrell, Kevin. "New Airlines Go Regional." *Venture,* July 1983, p. 73.

Fenwick, Thomas. "Airlines." *U.S. Industrial Outlook,* 1983, pp. 44:6–44:8.

Kozicharow, Eugene. "Carriers Press to Cut Labor Costs." *Aviation Week & Space Technology,*
August 29, 1983, pp. 29–31.

Ott, James. "Airlines Pursue Convention Market." *Aviation Week & Space Technology,* August
15, 1983, pp. 28–29.

"Regional Carriers Facing Multiple Challenges." *Aviation Week & Space Technology,* January
17, 1983, pp. 28–29.

Case 29

The Fall and Rise of Braniff

> We have our costs under control . . . and our economic picture will vastly improve from here on out. (H. L. Lawrence, February 29, 1980)
>
> Braniff is a financially sound company. Braniff isn't in financial trouble. Braniff isn't in a financial hole. (H. L. Lawrence, August 21, 1980)
>
> Braniff is on the right course and should do well. (H. L. Lawrence, December 31, 1980)

Problems of a Billion-Dollar Airline

1   Braniff International Chairman Harding L. Lawrence had a goal: to make Braniff a billion-dollar airline. When the deregulation of the airline industry first took effect in October 1978, Lawrence seized the opportunity to embark on an ambitious growth strategy. In just one year, Braniff expanded its passenger capacity by 37 percent to become the nation's sixth-largest airline. In that one year, 1979, Braniff was indeed the billion-dollar airline that Lawrence had envisioned. Revenues rose by 65 percent from the beginning of the expansion to a total of $1.35 billion by year-end.

2   The expansion included the addition of 20 domestic destinations as well as service to Europe, Asia, and the Pacific. Such large-scale expansion proved costly for Braniff. Its operating expenses rose 55 percent in 1979, as compared with an average industry rise of 21 percent. Furthermore, to service all of its new routes, Braniff borrowed heavily to acquire additional aircraft. Braniff's debt-to-equity ratio of 2.9 was one of the highest in the industry. Beginning with the third quarter of 1979, net losses were reported for four consecutive quarters.

3   Braniff had originally undertaken its expansion strategy to protect itself against its larger competitors, especially American Airlines. The management at Braniff anticipated that under deregulation its competitors would drastically reduce fares, a move that would drive smaller airlines out of business. Braniff felt that increased size would be its best means of survival if such fare wars occurred. However, much of the expansion was based on "second-choice" routes that no other carrier wanted, either because of low traffic or because a particular airline was already firmly entrenched on that particular route.

4   Braniff was not alone in facing financial strain. The entire airline industry encountered sharply rising fuel costs coupled with a general slowdown in airline traffic because of the onset of an economic recession. It was not surprising that the increased competition and the fare wars that Braniff had feared became a reality. But due to its expansion activities, Braniff was more exposed to these hardships than most other major carriers.

5   By late 1980, Braniff was in serious financial trouble. Owing to its failure to meet earnings requirements, planned stock offerings had to be canceled. The firm was also

This case was prepared by John A. Pearce II of George Mason University (School of Business Administration, Fairfax, Virginia 22030) and J. Kay Keels of the University of South Carolina. Copyright © 1985 by John A. Pearce II.

blocked from using its bank line of credit. In addition, some of the airline's creditors had placed it on a cash-only status. Braniff's shortage of cash was becoming desperate, and drastic measures were required to remedy the situation.

6 Braniff began by cutting capacity through the elimination of several of its less profitable routes. By October 1980, capacity had been slashed by nearly one third from a year earlier. The flashy Concorde service from Dallas to London and Paris, several of the Pacific flights, and a number of domestic flights were all gone.

7 One fund-raising tactic employed by Braniff was selling aircraft. During 1980 more than 20 jets were sold, including 15 727-200s to American Airlines and a 747 jumbo jet to an Argentine firm.

8 A second measure the company took to ease the cash shortage was to borrow from banks, insurance companies, and suppliers. To obtain these loans, Braniff was required to take the drastic step of offering its planes and equipment as collateral.

9 Although strapped for cash, Braniff was forced to engage in drastic fare cutting to remain competitive. In some domestic markets, the cuts exceeded 80 percent.

10 In the last quarter of 1980, Lawrence appealed to Braniff employees to help the company ease its financial problems. All employees were asked to accept a 10 percent pay cut. As a show of sincerity, Lawrence pledged to cut his own $300,000-per-year salary by 20 percent if the deal was accepted. This time the Lawrence confidence backfired. On the one hand, the chairman was assuring the press that Braniff's financial condition was solid, while on the other hand he was appealing to Braniff's employees because the firm's financial position was tenuous. The unions representing Braniff's employees cited Lawrence's duplicity as they rejected the pay cut plan, even though some employees had already been laid off as a result of worsening financial conditions.

11 Merger talks were begun with Eastern Air Lines late in 1980. Although a joint agreement might have helped to pull Braniff through its financial troubles, Eastern itself was experiencing cash problems that ultimately ended the merger talks.

12 Overall, Lawrence's turnaround measures were viewed as too little, too late. Under pressure from bankers and other lenders, Braniff's board solicited Lawrence's resignation on December 31, 1980.

13 On January 7, 1981, John J. Casey, formerly board vice chairman, was named president, chairman of the board, and chief executive officer of Braniff. Among other problems, Casey inherited a long-term debt that had grown to over $600 million. Braniff's lenders took an active role in designing a new course for the airline by selecting a group of assistants for Casey known for their financial expertise.

14 Under Casey's direction, Braniff's operations were streamlined to emphasize three major areas: marketing, to plan and sell the product; operations, to produce and maintain the product; and finance, to analyze expenses and report on revenues. Management's immediate objectives were to increase revenues and decrease expenses. Initial strategies to achieve these objectives included reassigning resources to areas that were most profitable, eliminating unprofitable operations, and selling additional aircraft.

15 Shortly after his election, Casey succeeded in rallying company employees to Braniff's cause. Effective March 1, 1981, all the airline's unions approved an employee salary program whereby all employees' pay, including that of top management, was cut by 10 percent. The pay cuts, deemed "voluntary contributions," were put into a special fund to help meet corporate cash requirements. Perhaps employees were convinced of Casey's commitment when he suspended his own $180,000 per year salary indefinitely.

16   A crisis arose simultaneously. Some $40 million in principal and interest on Braniff's long-term debt was due on March 1. Braniff sought a deferral until July 1, which its creditors reluctantly granted. The approval was contingent on two factors: (1) initiation of the employee salary program and (2) the company's development of a detailed operating plan for the remainder of the year.

17   To handle the debt restructuring, Casey brought in Howard P. Swanson as his top financial executive. Swanson was credited with having performed a similar task at Trans World Airlines.

18   Despite all these efforts, the question of Braniff's viability was raised by its auditors in the annual report issued at midyear 1981. Casey emphasized that the firm's continuation was at least partially dependent on the continued deferral of debt payments.

19   Surprisingly, the deferral was again granted. This time Casey's new man, Swanson, was credited with convincing the airline's lenders to forgive interest payments on debt outstanding until February 1982. The once-critical July 1 deadline passed, and Braniff was still operating.

Changes in Market Strategy

20   Just before the final quarter of 1981, Braniff moved to strengthen its management. Howard Putnam, president and chief executive officer of Southwest Airlines, was named president and chief operating officer of Braniff. The contrast between Southwest and Braniff was dramatic. For the previous six quarters, Southwest had posted the airline industry's highest margin of operating profit, while Braniff was the industry's biggest loser. Putnam's appointment was viewed as a positive sign. Observers felt that he would not have accepted the job had he not believed that a Braniff turnaround was possible.

21   Putnam first moved to completely revamp Braniff's fare structure. The new marketing strategy, called Texas Class, featured discounted single-class air service for a single price. The result was that the number of different fares charged by Braniff nationwide dropped from 582 to just 15. The fares were to be available every day for every seat on every Braniff flight. Putnam referred to the strategy as "getting back to basics." Braniff had been transformed from a conventional trunk airline into one that more nearly resembled a commuter airline. Under the system, the new fares undercut regular coach fares by an average of 45 percent. The success of the strategy depended on the success of the new fare system in generating additional passenger traffic. Braniff was relying on the convenience and simplicity of the new system to appeal to travel agents and the general public.

22   Braniff's fare strategy was revolutionary and risky. If it worked, Braniff would have effected a complete change in the structure of air travel prices. No longer would there be discounts and other fancy pricing tactics; just prices, some high and some low. However, one undesired effect of the Texas Class fare structure was retaliation by Braniff's competitors. American Airlines, Braniff's chief competitor, announced that it would immediately meet Braniff's fares on every competing route.

23   As a further attempt to make its resources more productive, Braniff scheduled its planes to fly more hours every day. For example, late-night and early-morning departures were added to existing routes. In addition to the employee pay cut, pilots agreed to fly 10 extra hours per month, half of them without pay. Layoffs continued to reduce

the size of Braniff's work force, and they were used as still another attempt to reduce costs.

24   As the February 1 deadline for debt payment approached, Braniff's only hope for survival was yet another extension. Braniff was broke, but it continued to operate. Although no major U.S. airline had ever failed, many observers questioned how much longer the carrier's creditors would support its operation because they held the liens on Braniff's planes. The 37 creditors—22 banks, 13 insurance companies, and 2 suppliers—had to be convinced one more time. Braniff sought an agreement to have its debt commitments extended to October 1, 1982, and again to be forgiven the $40 million in interest payments.

25   Braniff's competitors, especially its chief rival, American Airlines, would benefit directly from the company's bankruptcy. American had retaliated immediately in the fare wars, even though that meant substantial losses for it as well. However, American was large and strong enough to withstand such losses in the short term, and it knew Braniff was not. Furthermore, American had added several directly competing routes in an attempt to defeat Braniff's strategy. Now there was evidence that American was urging Braniff's creditors to withdraw their support.

26   The creditors had little incentive to let the troubled carrier fail. If Braniff was forced into bankruptcy, creditors would be left with their collateral—dozens of 727 jets—for which there was almost no market owing to the recession-induced U.S. travel

---

Table 1

BRANIFF INTERNATIONAL
Balance Sheet
(system data; amounts in thousands of dollars)

	March 31, 1982	Year of 1981	Year of 1980	Year of 1979
Assets				
Current assets:				
Cash and short-term investments	$ 29,213	$ 42,480	$ 13,626	$ 23,724
Notes and accounts receivable	141,342	150,923	176,670	136,664
Less: Allowance for uncollectible accounts	7,960	7,462	5,894	4,825
Spare parts, supplies, and other	40,825	47,333	48,925	49,895
Less: Allowance for obsolescence	4,896	4,790	4,673	4,737
Total current assets	198,524	228,484	228,654	200,722
Investments and special funds	1,670	1,706	1,702	1,792
Operating property and equipment:				
Flight equipment	757,916	733,232	863,325	952,553
Ground property, equipment, and other	152,771	154,089	165,501	155,705
Less: Allowance for depreciation	342,780	341,512	323,362	335,703
Owned property and equipment—net	567,907	585,809	705,464	772,556
Leased property under capital leases	111,212	114,670	151,100	152,757
Less: Accumulated depreciation	45,910	47,230	71,643	68,081
Capital leases property—net	65,302	67,440	79,457	84,676
Equipment purchase deposits	9,397	9,397	13,724	30,391
Owned and leased property and equipment—net	642,606	662,646	798,645	887,623
Nonoperating property and equipment, owned and leased—net	38,731	38,731	219	284
Other assets	15,447	14,236	17,950	45,648
Total assets	$ 896,978	$ 945,803	$1,047,170	$1,136,069

Table 1 *(concluded)*

	March 31, 1982	Year of 1981	Year of 1980	Year of 1979
Liabilities and Stockholders' Equity				
Current liabilities:				
Current maturities of debt and notes payable	\$ 78,329	\$ 77,806	\$ 35,718	\$ 16,319
Current obligations under capital leases	4,307	4,428	10,217	10,543
Air traffic liabilities	79,685	95,911	87,727	38,634
Other	198,088	194,948	187,737	196,736
Total current liabilities	361,409	373,093	321,399	262,232
Noncurrent liabilities:				
Long-term debt	395,118	401,731	444,602	480,311
Advances from associated companies				
Obligations under capital leases	70,430	71,782	79,473	86,918
Other	30,851	30,652	7,598	3,309
Total noncurrent liabilities	496,399	504,165	531,673	570,538
Deferred credits:				
Deferred income taxes	2,755	2,755	2,849	10,240
Deferred investment tax credits				
Other	48,170	33,776	1,292	4,087
Total deferred credits	50,925	36,531	4,141	14,327
Stockholders' equity:				
Preferred stock	121,483	119,330	110,000	80,000
Common stock	15	15	15	15
Subscribed and unissued				
Total capital stock	121,498	119,345	110,015	80,015
Additional capital invested	67,188	67,188	67,188	67,188
Total paid-in capital	188,686	186,533	177,203	147,203
Retained earnings:				
Retained earnings	−200,441	−154,519	12,754	141,769
Net unrealized loss noncurrent market equity security				
Total stockholders' equity	−11,755	32,014	189,957	288,972
Less: Treasury stock				
Stockholders' equity, net	−11,755	32,014	189,957	288,972
Total liabilities and stockholders' equity	\$ 896,978	\$ 945,803	\$1,047,170	\$1,136,069

slump. The alternative was for lenders to accept some equity and forgive some total long- and short-term private debt, which at this point had reached \$733.2 million.

27   Throughout this period Braniff continued its slimming and trimming tactics. Late in April 1982, the South American routes were leased to Eastern Air Lines in a \$30 million deal. Despite Braniff's precarious financial position, its officials were guardedly optimistic that the Eastern deal might lead the way toward generating sufficient revenues for survival. The exact extent of its financial recovery is suggested in Tables 1 and 2.

28   Two weeks later Braniff surprised the industry and some of its own executives. At midnight on May 12, 1982, it suspended all flying operations. The reason for the abrupt cessation of service was not immediately clear, but it was suggested that one of Braniff's lenders had called in its portion of the debt. The carrier was one step away from bankruptcy proceedings.

29   Even as the announcements halting flights and telling workers to stay home were made, Braniff directors were meeting to decide whether to file under Chapter 11 or

Table 2

BRANIFF INTERNATIONAL
Income Statement Data—Revenues, Expenses, and Income
(amounts in thousands of dollars)

	1981	1980	1979
Operating revenues			
Transport scheduled:			
Passenger, first class	$ 12,518	$ 40,334	$ 50,002
Passenger, coach	202,622	250,657	257,146
Total passenger revenues	215,140	290,991	307,148
Freight	9,306	13,032	17,580
Air express	603	182	230
Excess baggage	1,751	2,204	6,780
Total property revenues	11,660	15,418	24,590
Priority U.S. mail	4,629	5,909	1,509
Nonpriority U.S. mail	73	136	38
Foreign mail	129	142	95
Total mail revenue	4,831	6,187	1,642
Other	1,013	1,154	779
Total scheduled revenues	232,644	313,750	334,159
Transport nonscheduled:			
Charter, passenger	1,307	1,827	3,113
Charter, freight			
Total nonscheduled revenues	1,307	1,827	3,113
Total transport revenues	233,951	315,577	337,271
Transport-related:			
Subsidy			
Other transport-related	7,885	7,892	7,177
Total transport-related revenues	7,885	7,892	7,117
Total operating revenues	$241,836	$323,469	$344,448
Operating expenses			
Flying operations	$133,938	$146,720	$174,931
Maintenance	21,338	27,761	34,366
Passenger service	25,073	31,511	38,679
Aircraft and traffic servicing	48,065	58,009	63,852
Promotion and sales	39,896	50,789	44,690
General and administrative	12,869	15,974	10,479
Transport-related	4,415	5,156	4,195
Amortization of development and			
preoperating expenses, etc.	711	2,078	2,339
Depreciation, owned flight equipment	14,444	13,046	13,812
Depreciation, other than owned flight equipment	3,124	3,121	2,682
Amortization, capital leases	3,335	2,285	2,834
Total depreciation	21,614	20,530	21,667
Total operating expenses	$307,208	$356,450	$392,859
Operating profit or (loss)	$ (65,372)	$ (32,981)	$ (48,411)
Nonoperating Profit or (Loss)			
(Interest expense on debt)	(5,021)	(16,164)	(12,347)
(Interest expense on capital leases)	(1,669)	(1,933)	(2,559)
(Total interest expense)	(6,690)	(18,097)	(14,906)
Capitalized interest		(3,190)	2,344
Capital gains or (losses) operating property	5,269	741	1,775
Other income and (expenses), net	(9,295)	(19,526)	(811)
Nonoperating income and expenses, net	(10,716)	(40,072)	(9,977)

Table 2 *(concluded)*

	1981	1980	1979
Net income			
Net income or (loss) before income taxes	(76,088)	(73,053)	(58,388)
(Income taxes for the period)		(470)	(12,012)
Net income or (loss) after income taxes	(76,088)	(73,523)	(46,376)
Nonrecurring items:			
Income (loss) discontinued operations			
Extraordinary items income (loss)			
Accounting changes income (loss)			
Net income (loss) after nonrecurring items	(76,088)	(73,523)	(46,376)

Chapter 7 of federal bankruptcy proceedings. Under Chapter 11, the company would be protected from its creditors, while the court oversaw its reorganization plans. Chapter 7 would guide the liquidation of the company's assets.

30   A few hours later Howard Putnam declared that he had not taken the Braniff job in order to preside over its liquidation. Braniff was filing to reorganize under Chapter 11.

31   Bankruptcy experts were puzzled by the way that Braniff had proceeded. Normally a troubled firm files under Chapter 11 and continues to operate while being protected from creditors. But Braniff had first shut down its operations, then laid off its employees, and finally filed for reorganization. Despite the unorthodox procedure, Putnam insisted that the airline would resume operations either under its own name or under someone else's as a consequence of a merger. Putnam explained that the decision to cease operations was made because Braniff was simply out of cash. The next day, May 13, 1982, would have been a scheduled payday for Braniff employees, and Putnam indicated that the company could not have met its payroll.

32   Braniff was allowed 120 days to file its reorganization plan with the courts. Management quickly decided that its best hope lay in a joint venture. Throughout the remainder of 1982, Braniff engaged in merger talks with several airlines. As the filing deadline drew near, Braniff obtained an extension on its filing date. As a result, 1982 closed without a concrete decision.

The Hyatt Alternative

33   Through the first quarter of 1983, Braniff's fate remained in question. Putnam negotiated with 16 airlines concerning the utilization of the company's aircraft, equipment, facilities, and personnel. Only Pacific Southwest Airlines (PSA) presented a viable plan. Although major creditors and the bankruptcy court approved the pact, it was rejected by a U.S. appeals court, thereby terminating the Braniff–PSA talks.

34   With its last hope of a joint venture seemingly gone, Braniff's management turned its attention toward a reorganization plan that stopped just short of full liquidation. The plan was due to be submitted in federal bankruptcy court on April 4, 1983. Under the plan, the firm would divest itself of all assets related to flying and would form a small business that would provide ground service and contract maintenance for other carriers. Braniff officials continued to believe that a live company in any form was

better for creditors than a dead one. In Braniff's favor, the court deadline was postponed until April 18 because of a crowded court calendar.

35   In the meantime, Braniff began talks with Hyatt Corporation, the Chicago-based hotel chain. Hyatt offered an investment proposal in return for an interest-bearing note and a majority of the voting stock in the reorganized company. Under the Hyatt plan, Braniff would resume flight operations.

36   The talks with Hyatt encountered some major obstacles, most notably the disapproval of Howard Putnam, who considered the plan to be underfunded. Even after the original offer was raised considerably, Putnam still opposed it. As the April 18 deadline for filing reorganization plans drew near, no agreement had been reached. Braniff filed its original ground service proposal but with the stipulation that a revised plan could be filed to include resumption of flight operations. Clearly, the door was being left open for Hyatt to sweeten its offer. The talks continued.

37   Finally, in June 1983, Braniff and Hyatt agreed on a plan to put Braniff back in the air. Hyatt would ensure the new airline some $70 million in funding and in return receive 80 percent interest in the reorganized airline and more than $300 million in Braniff tax credits.

38   The agreement still faced numerous hurdles. First, there was an effort by American Airlines to squelch the deal. American knew that Hyatt was having trouble convincing Braniff's creditors to accept the Hyatt offer. American attempted to sway the creditors by offering to buy Braniff's remaining fleet, thus effectively halting any plan that would put Braniff in the air again. Second, the environment was less than ideal for a new entrant into an industry already plagued by overcapacity and revenue-draining fare wars. Third, the immediate problem was to get Braniff's major creditors to agree to the proposal. Many of them were skeptical and feared they might end up as two-time losers. Finally, the proposal required the approval of the bankruptcy court.

39   The major obstacle turned out to be the secured creditors' objections to the lease offer made to them by Hyatt. As holders of the liens on Braniff's planes, the creditors felt that they could realize a larger yield by selling the aircraft. For weeks, Hyatt's Jay Pritzker, a principal in the firm, mediated between Braniff's management and its creditors, trying to secure agreement from the lenders.

40   After much negotiation, an acceptable offer was tendered; the last major hurdle had been cleared. In September 1983, the Braniff reorganization plan was approved by a federal bankruptcy court, and the stage was finally set for Braniff to fly once again.

41   Hyatt's plan for Braniff was ambitious, but it held many advantages. From the beginning, the plan had the support of Braniff's unsecured creditors and its employees. Most of its unions granted positive cost advantages in wage contract renegotiations. These concessions alone gave Braniff the chance to operate as one of the lowest-cost carriers in the industry. In addition, many Braniff workers volunteered to work for free prior to the start-up date to get their jets back in the air. Some employees even came out of retirement to help with the restart.

42   Industry analysts believed that Hyatt's toughest job would be to put together a capable management team. Though none of the top management of the "old" Braniff remained, good management was a Hyatt trademark. It had consistently been rated as one of the best-managed chains in the lodging industry. Perhaps Hyatt could bring from outside the industry what the airline lacked.

43   Braniff also had to win over doubting and somewhat disgruntled travelers and travel agents. When the airline had abruptly shut down in 1982, many of its passengers had been left stranded, holding worthless tickets. Competing airlines were reluctant to honor Braniff tickets because they knew they would be unable to collect from Braniff. Additionally, because travel agents sell more than 60 percent of all airline tickets, their acceptance was crucial.

44   Hyatt's strategy was aimed at getting travelers and agents to try the "new" Braniff. Hyatt was confident that its service was good enough to keep customers once it had them. To attract customers, a joint promotional campaign with the March of Dimes was initiated whereby 5 percent savings on the ticket price would be donated to the March of Dimes. To build goodwill among travel agents, Braniff held elaborate receptions

in many cities that it served and gave agents free tickets as well. An additional aid to booking travelers came as part of a lawsuit settlement against Braniff's old rival, American Airlines. Braniff was awarded the right to placement in American's computerized reservations system.

45   The new Braniff that began flight operations on March 1, 1984, was a sleeker, slimmer edition of the former major carrier. There were no overseas flights and no first-class services. Instead, Braniff divided its passenger segments into business traveler and leisure traveler. Braniff was counting heavily on the business traveler and offered its "business cabin" area as a special attraction.

46   The new airline initially employed some 2,200 people to handle its flight schedule of 30 727 planes to 19 cities.

47   Despite the tenuous condition of an industry that had not fully recovered from recession, despite the many months of management failure and employee unrest, despite the doubts of creditors, despite the obstacles posed in trying to win over a skeptical public, and despite the stiff competition that Braniff faced on every one of its planned routes, the new Braniff proudly rolled down the runways once again.

Case 30

Air Canada

Introduction

1   In mid-1986, senior executives at Air Canada were confronted with two of the most dramatic events ever to hit both the federally owned airline and the industry: privatization and deregulation. Just as the top management was preparing its response to a federal government white paper, "Freedom to Move," containing proposals to radically change the regulatory environment, it was reported in the media that a memorandum signed by Transport Minister Donald Mazankowski contained a recommendation to sell up to 40 percent of the stock of Air Canada with the remainder to be sold at a future date. It was now up to Air Canada's managers to respond to the various issues it faced.

2   This case first sets out the changes in regulatory policy taking place in mid-1986. Next a brief history of the industry, together with a summary of the effects of regulatory reform in the United States and a summary of the changing attitudes of other carriers, provides perspective to the issues faced by the management of Air Canada.

Current Changes in Regulatory Policy

3   In February of 1984, Lloyd Axworthy, then Canada's minister of transport, announced plans to substantially liberalize and ultimately deregulate the Canadian airline industry. On May 10 of the same year, Axworthy introduced a "New Canadian Air Policy," which brought about a substantive change in the approach to regulation in the airline industry. Prior to May 10, regulatory policy encompassed the following:

Complete entry regulation for firms and routes.

Complete regulation of airfares.

Selective service quality regulation, including frequency of service, capacity, aircraft type, and intermediate stop requirements.

Regulation of conditions surrounding airfares.

Regulation of exit from markets.

Regulation of the geographic region in which a carrier might fly and the level and type of service it could provide.

The use of PCN (public convenience and necessity) criteria for entry and exit with the benefits of competition given little weight.

4   In this status quo policy, Air Canada was charged with maintaining a profitable operation and was subject to the same regulation as other carriers. In the May 10 policy, Canada was divided into two areas, north and south, with the "old" rules applying to the north and a wholesale change in the rules governing the south as follows:

This case was prepared by David W. Gillen, Wilfrid Laurier University, and Tae H. Oum and Michael W. Tretheway of the University of British Columbia. Copyright © 1986 by Mark C. Baetz and David W. Gillen.

Unlimited entry into round-trip charter market.

Freedom of exit from market when faced with new entry.

Consolidation of licenses and removal of the conditions of service on airline routes.

Freedom to reduce prices.

Price increases allowed up to the inflation rate of air input price index excluding labour.

PCN remained the basis for regulatory decision making.

Air Canada was restricted from engaging in competitive pricing and scheduling practices unless it was responding to similar actions by private carriers. Air Canada could also not receive funds from the government unless it met "acceptable financial tests."

5   The thrust of the May 10 policy was to introduce significant elements of competition into the airline industry but was not intended to be deregulation. Rather, it contained "made in Canada" provisions designed to allow adjustment and strategic planning among incumbent carriers. It soon became apparent that the policy was increasing service and competition, with greatest expansion in the industry at the regional and commuter levels. In fact, Air Canada and CP Air gave up a few routes to smaller airlines with whom they had interline agreements. Unlike the United States, few new carriers emerged, but the United States had undergone complete deregulation, and Canada was only liberalizing.

6   The May 10 changes in the regulatory structure were the first changes to policy despite the gradual liberalization of the industry begun in the mid- to late 1970s. In 1985, the federal minister of transport, Honourable Don Mazankowski, issued a white paper entitled "Freedom to Move," which essentially outlined the changes to transport policy the government was intent on making; specifically, to deregulate. In particular, the white paper suggested elimination of price and entry controls and a change in the basis of decision making by the regulators from PCN to an emphasis on "fit, willing, and able."

7   Air Canada faced significant changes in the political and economic environment in which it operated. However, the May 10, 1984, policy change said nothing about what *to do* with the crown carrier, only what the airline could not do. In particular, the 1978 Air Canada Act seemed to have established a relative ranking of objectives—the airline was, like private carriers, first to be profit oriented and was placed in the same position before regulation as other *private* carriers. The change in regulatory policy, in effect, removed any remaining basis for maintaining a crown air carrier; it seemed the natural course of events would lead to a wholly or partially privatized Air Canada.

Brief History

8   Air Canada (called Trans Canada Airlines until 1963) was created in 1932 to provide a transcontinental air network linking all regions of Canada and to provide service to areas private carriers would not. The crown carrier and the regulation of the industry went hand in hand. Air Canada was given preferred treatment, was treated differently before regulatory agencies (until 1977), and was the focal point with regard to regulatory decisions involving other carriers to ensure they complemented, not competed, with

the crown carrier. In essence, a crown carrier had been selected as the appropriate instrument to ensure national linkages and also a continuous and high level of service.

9   Since the mid-1970s, regulatory policy had been gradually liberalized. Restrictions on charter operations (both domestic and international) were reduced, and charter-class fares were permitted albeit with fences such as advanced booking, minimum stay, and cancellation conditions on scheduled flights. There was also a gradual easing and eventual elimination (in 1979) of all restrictions on CP Air's capacity on transcontinental routes, which increased the carrier's ability to compete with Air Canada. A significant event in this period was the passage of the New Air Canada Act, which placed Air Canada on an equal footing with other carriers under regulatory control. Furthermore, the act instructed the crown carrier to be market oriented and profit seeking.

10   In the past, the management of Air Canada believed regulatory reform had proceeded far enough and argued together with senior executives at CP Air and Pacific Western Airlines (PWA) for a "middle ground." Wardair wanted a more rapid move to deregulation, while the Canadian Transport Commission stated that an evolutionary not revolutionary change to greater reliance on market forces was needed. Even after the Air Transport Committee hearings held in 1982, the positions of the participants cited above had not changed.

11   It was not until 1984, when Lloyd Axworthy introduced reforms to the regulatory environment, that some changes in the position of managements took place. CP Air in particular responded to the new direction in regulatory policy by bringing in senior management from the United States (where the airline industry was deregulated in 1978) and becoming very aggressive with mergers to take over EPA (Eastern Provincial Airways) and Nordair. PWA similarly changed its management personnel and structure in the face of seemingly inevitable change. Air Canada was against the reform, and senior management voiced their opposition at every opportunity. This response led the minister of transport, who represented the equity shareholder, to tell them to stop and align themselves with government policy. The airline grudgingly capitulated.

Deregulation in the United States

12   Although the 1978 U.S. Airline Deregulation Act provided for a phased implementation of reform, the U.S. Civil Aeronautics Board, under the chairmanship of Dr. Alfred Kahn, effectively moved to complete deregulation immediately after its passage. Because entry was made totally free, the U.S. industry witnessed the emergence of new carriers within two to three years after its passage. Most of these could be characterized as low cost, nonunion, and without restrictive work rules. As these carriers entered markets, severe pressure was put on incumbent carriers.

13   Before an appearance of the new carriers (it takes a year or two to organize an airline from scratch), carriers which had been confined to specific city-pair markets began to branch out, entering other markets when they saw some synergy with current operations or lucrative profit potential. Several charter carriers, such as World and Capital, commenced scheduled services. Intrastate carriers crossed former regulatory boundaries. Local service carriers started to add transcontinental routes suited to their networks.

14   With deregulation, both incumbent and new-entrant carriers were faced with various strategic choices. In terms of pricing, incumbent carriers generally selected from one

of three alternatives: (1) capacity-controlled discount fares (i.e., "fences" around various discount fares so that price-insensitive passengers would not shift out of higher to lower fare classes); (2) peak and off-peak pricing (i.e., higher prices at peak times and lower prices at off-peak or low-load factor times); (3) predatory pricing to meet the competitive response of low-fare new-entrant carriers.

15   New-entrant carriers, who were mostly nonunionized with cost structures lower than the incumbent or major carriers, chose from one of four pricing categories: (1) less for less (i.e., low fare and no-frills service targeted at price-sensitive travellers), (2) more for less (i.e., full service at less than standard coach fares to steal market share), (3) more for more (i.e., higher fares but first-class service), or (4) same for same (i.e., same service as incumbents at same price but aggressive marketing and/or scheduling to steal market share). Studies on the U.S. experience found that the least successful choice was "more for less."

16   Both incumbent and entrant carriers were also faced with another set of strategic choices as follows: (1) wide-market full service (i.e., full service to many destinations and multiple hubs); (2) wide-market no-frills service; (3) focused-market full service (i.e., a geographic niche with a defensible hub city); and (4) focused-market no-frills service (usually combined with "less for less" pricing in high-density markets). Studies found that the two most successful strategies were wide-market full service and focused-market full service. The focused-market full-service strategy was successfully combined with a "more for more" pricing strategy to focus on the price-insensitive but service-sensitive traveller.

17   The main technical and analytical aspects of the impact of deregulation in the United States up to 1985 were as follows:

> U.S. load factors increased on average since deregulation. (They fell off with the recession but were still greater than those of previous recessions). As the local service carriers added long-stage and higher-density routes, their load factors rose toward those of the larger trunks.

> Former U.S. charger airlines became scheduled airlines.

> Freight decreased in importance for passenger carriers (from 9 percent to 6 percent of revenues). Specialized air express carriers, such as Federal Express, UPS, and Puralator, emerged.

> There appears to have been some synergy between regional/feeder and transcontinental routes. Similarly, there may have been synergy between transcontinental and international routes.

> The feed from third-level carriers became important to the trunk and local-service carriers. Nevertheless, no attempt was made to merge a third-level carrier into a large carrier. This suggests there must have been some cost saving in keeping the two types of services separate.

> Since deregulation, almost all air carriers adopted hub-and-spoke route networks. There were two types of hubs. The "complexing" type of hub coordinated batches of arrivals and departures to provide passengers with good service. Since resources could be idle for long periods, it was expensive to operate. A point-to-point hub operated at low cost on a continuous basis. It was suitable only for markets where service levels were not as important as price.

Annual productivity growth increased from 2.8 to 5.1 percent, thereby outperforming the U.S. business sector.

18   The number of employees in the U.S. airline industry, in December 1985, was 31,500 *greater* than in December 1978. However, there were significant structural changes within the industry, with the major carriers losing over 9,000 employees since 1978, the nationals gaining 15,000, and new entrants and commuter airliners gaining 25,000. The use of part-time labour increased. While more than 100 airlines were formed after deregulation, 36 carriers sought bankruptcy court protection, and 26 were bought by others.

19   Wage rates in the U.S. industry had increased at the rate of inflation since the early 1980s, and average compensation per employee increased every year since deregulation.

20   Aggregate operating profits recovered from the 1979–82 recession to establish two record highs in 1984 and 1985.

Alternative Policies with Respect to Air Canada

21   The move from a regulated environment to competition between firms represented a fundamental structural change. Management decisions were no longer insulated and inefficiency no longer protected by the artificial administrative rules characteristic of regulation.

22   The management of Air Canada faced a more difficult task than other carriers since it entered the competitive marketplace with the shackles of crown ownership and it was unclear what course the government would follow. Air Canada's major competitor had traditionally been CP Air, but this could change with deregulation. (The operating and financial statistics of Air Canada and CP Air for the past four years are contained in Tables 1 and 2). A set of alternative policies which the government could pursue is outlined below.

23   **Option I: Pre-May 10, 1984, Air Canada Policy.**   This is a status quo policy in which Air Canada is 100 percent federally owned. The carrier has reasonable access to public funds without achieving a rigorous private-sector investment test and is expected to establish and provide a service standard for all of Canada.

24   **Option II: Post-May 10, 1984, Air Canada Policy.**   The carrier must achieve a private-sector test for access to additional funds. The carrier is constrained somewhat in its ability to initiate competitive moves in domestic markets. Federal government ownership of 100 percent of Air Canada continues.

25   **Option III: Privatization without Breakup.**   Air Canada is sold to the private sector in entirety. There is no breakup of Air Canada, nor are any of its divisions or routes spun off.

26   There are three alternative ways to privatize Air Canada. The first of these is sale of Air Canada to the highest bidder. Under this alternative, Air Canada is most likely to be sold to a single entity (unlikely another airline). The new owner will exercise

Table 1
Air Canada financial data ($ millions)

	1980	*1981*	*1982*	*1983*	*1984*
Operating revenues:					
Passenger	$1,642.9	$1,857.0	$1,860.9	$1,844.5	$1,989.0
Cargo	219.1	255.3	264.6	269.7	298.5
Other	119.8	145.9	180.4	199.4	230.0
Total operating revenues	1,981.8	2,258.2	2,305.9	2,313.6	2,517.5
Operating expenses:					
Salaries, wages, and benefits	694.7	773.5	842.1	831.3	873.2*
Aircraft fuel	418.6	567.2	566.4	538.5	542.2
Depreciation, amortization, and obsolescence	130.2	131.1	152.7	144.4	164.7
Other (e.g., maintenance, administration, operation)	647.9	712.8	770.5	771.0	894.6
Total operating expenses	1,891.4	2,184.6	2,331.7	2,285.2	2,474.7
Net income (loss)	$ 57.0	$ 40.1	$ (32.6)	$ 3.8	$ 27.0
Total assets	$1,688.3	$1,869.9	$2,040.6	$2,190.6	$2,512.6
Long-term debt and capital leases (including current portion)	633.5	710.0	891.6	1,092.5	1,315.2
Shareholders' equity	501.2	528.2	482.3	486.1	513.1
Debt/equity	56%	57%	65%	69%	72%
Operating statistics:					
Revenue passenger-miles (RPM)† (millions)	15,176	14,351	13,590	12,728	13,905
Available seat-miles (ASM)‡ (millions)	22,521	22,008	21,524	19,588	20,396
Passenger load factor (percent)	67.4%	65.2%	63.1%	65.0%	68.2%
Yield per RPM (in cents)	10.8	12.9	13.7	14.4	14.3
Fleet size	122	122	113	115	108
Average number of employees	23,700	23,500	23,300	21,600	21,800

* Statistics Canada figures for 1984 are as follows:

1. Salaries and wages	=	769.5
2. Fuel and oil	=	541.5
3. Depreciation	=	151.9
4. Maintenance, operation, and administration	=	828.5
		2,291.5

† RPM = Number of passengers flown times length of flight.

‡ ASM = Total number of passenger seats available times the number of miles flown.

Source: Air Canada annual reports.

complete control over Air Canada, and by all rights the carrier should rapidly become a very effective competitor especially in a deregulated environment.

27   A second method for the sale of Air Canada would be a general sale or placement of stock. This, for example, is the method that was used for the sale of Pacific Western Airlines in late 1983. Under this scenario, the ownership of Air Canada is likely to be dispersed among a fairly large number of investors. In this case, there is no assurance that the new owners of Air Canada will exercise effective control over the carrier.

28   A third alternative for the privatization is to sell shares to the company's employees. Air Canada's management have previously recommended this option, at least in part. There is a precedent for this, given that several airlines in the United States (such as Eastern Air Lines and Pan American) have sold stock to their employees as a

Table 2
CP Air financial data ($ millions)

	1980	*1981*	*1982*	*1983*	*1984*
Operating revenues:					
Passenger	$ 521.7	$ 639.9	$ 642.5	$ 661.9	N/A*
Cargo	61.2	62.9	77.0	82.2	
Other	100.9	111.5	143.3	121.5	
Total operating revenues	683.8	814.3	862.8	865.6	932.9
Operating expenses:					
Flying	234.9	308.1	305.1	301.8	N/A[t]
Aircraft and servicing	92.3	106.3	119.8	118.2	N/A
Sales	115.9	136.9	163.3	171.6	N/A
Other	219.2	265.8	288.7	275.6	
Total operating expenses	662.3	817.1	876.9	867.2	879.9
Net income (loss)	$ 6.8	$ (17.5)	$ (34.7)	$ (13.1)	$ 17.2
Interest on long-term debt	$ (22.4)	$ (37.8)	$ (57.0)	$ (38.8)	$ (41.6)
Long-term debt	292.3	453.2	585.0	414.7	523.3
Debt/equity	86.4%	91.3%	95.8%	53.8%	N/A
Current assets	$ 147.0	$ 148.8	$ 105.0	$ 129.6	$ 248.1
Properties	484.0	670.0	818.4	738.0	859.8
Operating statistics:					
Revenue passenger-miles (millions)	5,797	5,992	5,531	5,735	10,233[‡]
Available seat-miles (millions)	8,265	8,727	8,446	8,196	14,614[‡]
Passenger load factor (percent)	70.1%	68.7%	65.5%	70.0%	70.0%
Yield per RPM (in cents)	9.0	10.7	11.8	11.5	N/A
Fleet size	30	32	31	31	31
Average number of employees	8,291	8,860	7,994	7,370	7,555

* N/A—information was not available.

[t] Statistics Canada figures (from CP annual reports) for 1984 are as follows:
  1. Salaries and wages = 253.5
  2. Fuel and oil = 215.3
  3. Depreciation = 55.9
  4. Management, operations, and administration = 355.2
  $\overline{879.9}$

[‡] Revenue passenger-miles and available seat-miles are expressed in kilometers in 1984.

means to provide productivity incentives and to achieve wage and work-rule concessions from labour. Some of the new upstart airlines in the United States also had employee stock ownership. People Express required a substantial ownership of its stock before one could become an employee of the airline.

29   **Option IV: Privatization with Breakup.**   Under this policy, there is a dismemberment of the carrier into one or more pieces. Each of the pieces in turn is sold to the private sector.

Methods of Breakup

30   There are a number of different ways in which Air Canada could be broken up. One potential breakup is to divide Air Canada into a domestic airline and an international airline. While this would significantly reduce the size of Air Canada in an absolute sense, it does little to reduce the dominance of Air Canada in domestic markets.

31   There is causal evidence suggesting that there are some synergies (or as economists would say, economies of scope) between domestic and international operations. For example, prior to U.S. deregulation, Pan American Airlines operated essentially no domestic routes within the United States (other than a few routes from the West Coast to Hawaii). One of Pan Am's first moves in the deregulated U.S. environment was to open several domestic routes. It was also successful in obtaining control of a domestic carrier, National Airlines. Pan Am, however, soon found that simply having a domestic route system did nothing to improve its overall position. It discovered that for a good synergy between domestic and international operations, the domestic operations must feed the international operations. As a result, from 1980 to 1986 the former National Airlines network has essentially disappeared. Pan Am has transferred the employees and the airplanes to different routes which better feed Pan Am's major international hubs in New York, Miami, Los Angeles, and San Francisco. By careful planning of schedules and routes, Pan Am was able to carry international passengers for a much longer trip length. The passenger could now travel on the domestic system to the international gateway and from there overseas.

32   A second alternative being considered was to have Air Canada broken into two or three pieces. Each of these smaller carriers would have a set of regional routes. Each of these regional carriers in turn would receive rights and the necessary equipment and personnel to operate in transcontinental markets. This would give each of the regional carriers an intelligent route structure in the sense that the regional carrier would be able to gather feed and take it on the long hauls. The two (or three) carriers would compete with each other and with CP Air and Wardair on transcontinental routes. Each of the new regional carriers would also be in competition with one or more of the existing regional carriers.

Air Canada as Dominant Player in the Industry

33   Air Canada's management faced the legacy of being a crown corporation and having been a favoured firm in the industry. As a result of this favoured status, other carriers and interested groups, such as the Consumer Association of Canada, expressed concern with respect to Air Canada's dominance of the market and the effect it would have on the performance of a deregulated airline industry. In 1986, Air Canada had a 60 percent share of the domestic Canadian market. This large market share was a concern if it represented a substantial number of markets in which the carrier was a monopoly. It could also be a concern if it indicated that Air Canada had deeper financial pockets than its competitors and thus was able to survive a long and protracted battle to achieve monopoly power.

34   Some observers of the Canadian airline industry suggested that Air Canada's dominance of the domestic market per se was no need for concern. Some claimed that the threat of entry into markets would force Air Canada to behave properly. Others, such as former Minister of Transport Lloyd Axworthy, suggested that Air Canada's relatively high cost structure would give it a disadvantage in markets. Axworthy claimed that potential competitors could quickly drive Air Canada out from a market due to its high fares.

35   From 1984 to 1986, CP Air and others moved more quickly than Air Canada to lower cost structures. In particular, CP Air was much more aggressive than Air Canada in reducing work forces and in asking labour for wage cutbacks and work rule concessions.

Simulation of Alternative Scenarios

36   Experts on airline cost-and-demand analysis performed simulations of each of the following scenarios:

1. *Pre–May 10 Air Canada policy:* Air Canada has reasonable access to public funds for its capital needs without going through a rigorous private-sector investment test.

2. *May 10 policy:* There is continued 100 percent public ownership with access to additional public funds only when the private sector's criterion is met. Air Canada is constrained in its ability to act competitively in domestic markets.

3. *Privatization without breakup:* It is assumed the new owners exercise control over the carrier.

4. *Privatization in two pieces:* Each piece has a regional network and transcontinental rights.

Results of Cost Simulations

37   The results of the simulations of alternative policies toward Air Canada are summarized in Table 3.

38   As compared to the pre–May 10 Air Canada policy, the May 10 Air Canada policy resulted in a cost efficiency improvement of 3.1 percent, a total saving of $108 million. This occurred principally through reducing the excess capital stock of Air Canada by applying a more rigid financial test for accessing public funds.

39   Privatization without breakup would result in Air Canada improving its cost efficiency by 10.6 percent. This in turn provides incentives for CP Air and the regionals to improve their cost efficiency by 1.3 percent and 1.6 percent, respectively, amounting to a total saving of $239 million. Air Canada's cost saving comes from a significant reduction in capital stock (25 percent), dropping 10 percent of its points (which increase average traffic density of its network by 10 percent), and reduction of labour input prices by 5 percent. Since Air Canada's labour input prices have served as an industry standard, the reduction of Air Canada's labour prices is likely to trigger other carriers' labour prices by the same factor.

40   Privatization in two pieces reduces Air Canada's total cost by only 7.2 percent because the two new carriers must separately serve some identical points on their transcontinental routes. This reduces benefits of density economies. Total cost saving of the industry would be about $169 million.

41   Privatization in three pieces would reduce Air Canada's cost by 7.8 percent and the industry's cost by 5.3 percent. Total saving would be about $181 million. Note there is very little difference in cost savings between a two- and three-way breakup.

42   In analyzing public policy toward Air Canada, two issues need to be considered: (1) whether to change its ownership (that is, privatization) and (2) whether to break it up to reduce its market dominance. The issue of policy toward Air Canada is inextricably intertwined with that of regulatory policy. Outcomes of regulatory reform depend critically on how Air Canada functions in Canadian markets. Similarly, outcomes of policy changes toward Air Canada depend on the regulatory environment.

43   If Air Canada were to be privatized, the sale price the government could realize would depend on whether a privatized Air Canada was free to roam in a protected regulated environment or had to face the discipline of a free market. In the free market case, Air Canada's sale price will depend on whether it can use its current market dominance to its advantage or be restrained or perhaps broken up.

Table 3
Cost simulation results for alternative Air Canada policies (regulatory policy fixed at the May 10, 1984, policy)

	Industry	*Air Canada*	*CP Air*	*Regionals*
(a) Pre–May 10 Air Canada policy (status quo):				
Output* (in millions)	4,443	2,680	1,236	527
Passenger	74.3%	76.2%	73.3%	66.4%
Freight	19.2%	21.2%	18.7%	10.6%
Charter	6.5%	2.6%	8.0%	23.0%
Capital cost ($ millions)	$445	$280	$110	$55
Total cost ($ millions)	$3,468	$2,069	$783	$616
(b) May 10 Air Canada policy:				
Changes:				
Capital stock†	Only Air Canada changes	10% reduction	No change	No change
Results:				
Total cost ($ millions)	$3,404	$2,004	$783	$616
Percent change	−1.8%	−3.1%	0%	0%
(c) Privatization without breakup:				
Changes:				
Output	No change	No change	No change	No change
Points served	Only Air Canada changes	10% reduction	No change	No change
Stage length‡	Only Air Canada changes	10% increase	No change	No change
Labour prices	5% reduction	5% reduction	5% reduction	5% reduction
Capital stock	Only Air Canada changes	25% reduction	No change	No change
Results:				
Total cost ($ millions)	$3,229	$1,850	$773	$606
Percent change	−6.9%	−10.6%	−1.3%	−1.6%
(d.1) Privatization in two pieces:				
Changes:				
Output	No change	50% each piece	No change	No change
Points	Only Air Canada changes	60% each piece	No change	No change
Stage length	No change	No change	No change	No change
Labour prices	5% reduction	5% reduction	5% reduction	5% reduction
Capital stock	Only Air Canada changes	37.5% of total	No change	No change
Results:				
Total cost ($ millions)	$3,299	$1,920	$773	$606
Percent change	−4.9%	−7.2%	−1.3%	−1.6%

Table 3 *(concluded)*

	Industry	Air Canada	CP Air	Regionals
(d.2) Privatization in three pieces:				
Changes:				
Output	No change	33.3% each piece	No change	No change
Points	Only Air Canada changes	46% each piece	No change	No change
Stage length	No change	No change	No change	No change
Labour prices	5% reduction	5% reduction	5% reduction	5% reduction
Capital stock	Only Air Canada changes	25% each piece	No change	No change
Results:				
Total cost ($ millions)	$3,287	$1,908	$773	$606
Percent change	−5.3%	−7.8%	−1.3%	−1.6%

* Output is expressed in terms of revenue tonne kilometers. It is measured in these units because passengers and cargo have been aggregated. To translate this measure into revenue passenger-miles, each passenger is assumed to weigh 200 pounds.

† Capital stock refers to the total dollar value of all capital employed, including aircraft, engines, buildings, properties, and inventory.

‡ Stage length refers to average distance flown between cities.

44   Privatization could take one of three forms:

1. *Sell on the open market to the highest bidder.* The price received would reflect expectations of changes in regulatory policy. The new shareholders could force efficiency improvements by the airline.

2. *General stock sale.* This would be an open market operation, which could disperse ownership widely among individuals and institutions. In contrast to number one, dispersed shareholders might not be able to force management to improve efficiency.

3. *Sale to employees.* This could represent a majority or minority interest. Efficiency gains would presumably be easier to obtain since labour would have an equity incentive.

There were various combinations of the above that could be considered. In addition, the government could hold minority or majority interests in the air carrier.

45   A privatized Air Canada, even in a liberalized policy environment, is likely to achieve some significant cost savings. These savings are conditional on the assumption that a privatized Air Canada will have no objective other than maximizing profits subject to the same regulatory constraints other carriers face. It is also assumed that Air Canada is no longer required to establish a level of service to be maintained everywhere in Canada. It will further be free to drop some points not as well suited to its fleet of jet aircraft. Finally, it will no longer be required to establish and maintain a high level of wages to be copied by all other Canadian air carriers.

46   Costs were simulated for this scenario and found to fall by 6.9 percent. The sources of these gains are reducing excess capital (it will no longer be required to set a high service standard in all markets), dropping some short-stage routes better suited to regional or third-level carriers, and a modest (5 percent) reduction in real wages.

47   Research on airline cost functions has demonstrated that Air Canada has no economies of firm size to exploit (there may be diseconomies) and has exhausted most economies of traffic density. This suggests that it is unlikely to add any new Canadian cities to its network. It also suggests that it would not attempt to increase density of service in existing markets. This would result in no net increase in Air Canada's traffic, although the dropping of some short-stage routes would increase its stage length. In other words, existing carriers should not fear Air Canada attempting to gobble up the 40 percent of domestic traffic it does not already have, since doing so would not give it any cost advantage. There is a qualification to this: Air Canada has presently achieved all available economies of traffic density, and costs may be relatively flat (that is, constant) even with increases in density; so while Air Canada would not lower costs by going after a greater share of its existing markets, it would not be faced with cost increases either.

48   Much of the cost savings predicted to come from privatization are attributable to removing Air Canada's requirement of maintaining the service standard for Canada. This requirement results in higher service levels than some markets warrant and maintenance of service on some short-stage-length routes. Eliminating Air Canada's use as a policy instrument, not privatization per se, results in savings.

Privatization with Breakup

49   In the simulation, Air Canada was broken up into one or two pieces, and each piece was sold to the private sector. Each consisted of a set of regional routes coupled with some transcontinental routes. The pieces were allowed to compete with each other, particularly in transcontinental markets.

50   The simulations indicated that a two-way breakup would result in cost savings of 4.9 percent, while a three-way breakup would result in cost savings of 5.3 percent. The reduction in excess capital was the major contributor to cost savings, as in the case of privatization without breakup.

51   Since there would be some duplication of points by the new carriers, traffic density (output per point) would fall 17 percent for a two-way breakup and 28 percent for a three-way breakup relative to a single large carrier. Returns to traffic density were roughly constant in this range, so there should be no cost advantage or disadvantage to this. Nevertheless, the smaller broken-up pieces of Air Canada could seek to improve their market shares. If both carriers were aggressive and successful, this could be at the expense of existing private carriers, such as CP Air.

52   There was some evidence that there is an S-curve effect of market share versus capacity offered. That is, up to a 50 percent market share, a carrier could add a given percentage to the number of seats it offered per week in a market and gain a *greater* increase in its market share. After a 50 percent market share, there are decreasing market share returns to capacity additions. This means that CP Air and others should have less to fear from a dominant (60 percent market share) Air Canada than from a set of smaller broken-up carriers. The latter are more apt to set off a capacity war.

Changes in Both Crown Carrier and Regulatory Policy

53   Impacts become increasingly speculative with both regulatory and crown carrier policy changes. There was a common thread, however. A privatization policy (with or without breakup), just like a move toward advanced liberalization or deregulation, involves

an increase in competitive behaviour in airline markets. Both policies combined would lead to more of the benefits of competition (such as reduced costs leading to lower fares leading to greater traffic) and more of the costs of competition (dropping jet service to small communities, greater profit variability, asking labour for wage or work rule concessions).

54   The main points of simultaneous changes in these policies were as follows:

Both privatization (with or without breakup) and regulatory reform lower costs.

If both occur at the same time, the speed at which markets adjust to new cost levels may be faster.

Cost reductions should be greater with deregulation and a breakup of Air Canada, particularly if part of Air Canada is transferred to existing carriers, allowing them to reap traffic density economies.

A privatized Air Canada may be more apt to drop short-stage routes under the freedoms of advanced liberalization or deregulation. This could result in even stronger (or at least faster) growth for small carriers than without privatization.

The pieces of a broken-up Air Canada could attempt to increase each of their market shares under greater regulatory freedom, possibly at the expense of existing carriers.

The pieces of a broken-up Air Canada, due to their stronger regional affiliations, may be less inclined to drop small regional points from their networks.

Impact on the Organization

55   In assessing the various scenarios described above, the senior management of Air Canada also had to consider the impacts on their own internal organization as well as that of its competitors, particularly CP Air.

56   Air Canada had significantly more employees than anyone else in the industry. They were not only tied to work rules established through union contracts of the past but also suffered from the politicization of changes to meet competition, due to their crown status. Their competition did not face this significant constraint in adjusting to the new market conditions. Indeed, CP Air had been successful in extracting work rule changes and wage concessions from their various labour groups. CP Air was reported to have had traditionally somewhat higher salaries for pilots and co-pilots, but Air Canada had significantly higher salaries for general management—about 50 percent higher.[1] In summary, on the labour front, Air Canada faced formidable problems. It had more employees, the unions were powerful and could politicize the process of negotiation, average wages were traditionally higher,[2] and thus, to remain competitive, greater concessions were needed.

57   In the short term, not only was the airline faced with a need to lower input costs but also to increase productivity. From the experience of U.S. airlines with deregulation, a significant change would have to occur in Air Canada's route network, specifically to move to a hub-and-spoke system, and this would mean dropping some cities and

---

[1] See *Statistics Canada Catalogue,* No. 51–206, 51–101.

[2] For example, from 1975 to 1981, average wages for Air Canada employees were approximately $4,000 greater than the next closest competitor, CP Air. In 1981, Air Canada paid an average salary of approximately $39,000.

perhaps adding others. As a crown corporation, it had been difficult to drop any city from its route structure because of the political consequences.

58   In the longer term, to maintain its status of 10th largest carrier in the world, Air Canada planned to purchase new aircraft, a decision which was probably the most important a carrier had to make. The type of aircraft selected was contingent upon the network structure as well as market size. Air Canada's fleet of DC-9 and Boeing 727 aircraft were ready to be replaced—representing a major capital outlay—and the type selected would determine the carrier's success in a given market setting. The key factors were to avoid the overcapacity of the past and have the flexibility to shift between markets. Air Canada was aiming to grow on its intercontinental routes.

59   A final compounding factor was the decision-making structure of Air Canada. As in many large corporations, there was a large bureaucracy. Any decision not only went through a number of layers but was also being decided by managers who had a "regulatory psychology." Both of these factors had to change if the airline was going to be competitive. CP Air had not only streamlined its management and vested decision-making power in fewer top managers but had also brought in a new president from the United States, where the industry had been deregulated for several years.

60   Some observers felt that Air Canada suffered the malaise of similar state-owned firms: inefficiency from overcapitalization, inefficient pricing principles, and managers who had long periods of tenure and who had little incentive to adopt the most efficient input combinations because they could not realize the gains from their efforts.

Privatization of Air Canada

61   In 1984, a Toronto-based group of Air Canada employees created the Air Canada Employee Ownership Committee. The committee surveyed Air Canada employees and found that about a quarter of the airline's employees were interested in purchasing stock. The group developed and presented to the federal government an employee buyout plan for up to 40 percent of the airline, but in early 1985 Prime Minister Mulroney stated publicly:

> Air Canada is not for sale. There may be some persuasive arguments in the case of Air Canada that some people can make in regard to the disposition of equity. I'll take a look at it. But Canada needs a national airline.[3]

62   Various observers of the prospects for privatizing Air Canada pointed out that one of the difficulties would be setting an appropriate price for an equity issue. The federal government would want to obtain a good return on its ever-increasing investment; for example, in the 1978 Air Canada Act, Ottawa assumed approximately $329 million of the airline debt in exchange for 329,000 shares. At the same time, an equity issue would have to be priced to overcome concerns that the airline was facing a possibly tougher environment with deregulation.

63   Another issue was the percentage of equity to be privatized. If Air Canada was partially privatized, it might suffer from the continuing "shackles of crown ownership," yet if only partially privatized, a continuing status as Canada's national airline might ensure preferential treatment in international bilateral airline agreements, thereby

---

[3] *Globe and Mail,* January 15, 1985, p. 1.

providing continued access to the more profitable overseas flights. (All international routes were negotiated on a bilateral basis.)

64   Another issue was the potential ownership of the airline. Given that Air Canada had acquired a good international reputation, there might be investor interest outside Canada. However, the federal government might not allow even a significant majority of Air Canada shares to be held outside Canada.

65   By mid-1986, the government had given no indication of its intentions on the privatization issue, only that the federal cabinet's privatization committee was studying a document related to the issue. The press noted in June 1986 that "Executives of Air Canada have been pushing the government to sell off at least part of the company for some time. The company needs an injection of cash to go ahead with future plans to revitalize its fleet."[4]

Position of Air Canada's Management

66   The issues of deregulation and privatization had been examined and discussed by various players (see appendix). It was now time for Air Canada's management to take a position. Should they push for both privatization and deregulation? If so, what would be the strategic and organizational consequences?

Appendix: Position of Key Stakeholders, 1981–1986

Air Canada

67   In 1981 both top managers of Air Canada, Claude Taylor and Pierre Jeannoit, responded to the Economic Council of Canada's call for deregulation by claiming competition was already fierce. Both argued that the recent introductions of discount fares and liberalized entry regulations gave the Canadian consumer most of the benefits of deregulation. Both stated a move away from government protection toward free competition would ruin the industry. It was not until 1984 and only after strong arguments from Lloyd Axworthy, then minister of transport, that Air Canada executives supported the moves to deregulation. The support was cautious and called for a plan of regular reviews. By 1986 both executives were calling for privatization so they could better meet competition from CP Air.

CP Air

68   Manning, a vice president of CP Air, concurred with Air Canada executives claiming that deregulation would create market chaos. CP generally wanted the industry regulations to remain intact but to have CP given greater freedom to compete equally with Air Canada. By 1984, CP recognized regulation had created inefficiencies and welcomed the changes introduced by Lloyd Axworthy. The company was being restructured for

---

[4] *Kitchener-Waterloo Record*, June 18, 1986, p. B7.

the forthcoming changes in the competitive environment, although there was concern about the market dominance of Air Canada and its favoured position as the crown-owned carrier.

Other Airlines

69 A major voice lobbying for regulatory changes was Max Ward of Wardair, a major charter airline. He continuously argued for greater freedom for Wardair in the domestic market.

70   Regional carriers, such as Eastern Provincial and Pacific Western, favoured moves to a more liberalized environment.

Government

71 Officials at both Transport Canada, the policymaking body, and the Air Transport Board of the Canadian Transport Commission sided with Air Canada and CP Air. They continuously frustrated all efforts to introduce greater competition, and it was only after Lloyd Axworthy circumvented their actions that any signs of competition and lower fares were introduced.

Other Groups

72 Labour unions lobbied heavily to stop any moves to deregulation or any freer competition. Labour has been the biggest gainer from regulation both in terms of higher wages and greater employment because of work rules.

73   Academics and the Consumers Association of Canada had always called for freer competition so that firms in the industry were subject to the rigours of the marketplace. Both groups argued such competition would provide a broader range of price–quality fare combinations.

Case 31

People Express

Overview

1   By taking advantage of an opportunity created by airline industry deregulation to use a strategy of low-cost, no-frills packages, People Express went from a small start-up to one of the 10 largest airlines in the United States in only six years. An associated key to this growth was the company's human resource program that made the employees part owners of the company in exchange for their agreement to perform multiple tasks for the airline. At the core of this program was a commitment from the company to build from within and to avoid acquisitions. But, in fact, by 1986, the company had reoriented its growth strategy and had embarked on a major acquisitions binge.

History of the Company

2   People Express (PE) started its operations in July 1980, when Chairman Donald Burr, then president and chief operating officer of Texas Air International, and eight other Texas Air executives, including Senior Vice President in Charge of Marketing Gerald Gitter and Chief Financial Officer Harold Paretti, left Texas Air to start their own airline in the hope of taking advantage of the recent deregulation of the industry.

3   The company started with three small Boeing 737s, which traveled from Newark to small northeastern cities, such as Buffalo, Columbus, and Norfolk. The company chose Newark as its main terminal because of some unique cost advantages. Located across the river and 10 minutes away from New York City, Newark was a terminal that major airlines had not considered, yet it was near enough to New York City that passengers would be willing to fly through there in order to save some money.

4   The timing of the start-up was perfect. Venture capitalists were high on the prospects of upstart airlines in a newly deregulated industry. With the backing of the San Francisco venture capital firm of Hambrecht and Quist and the investment bank Morgan Stanley, PE was able to raise more than $24 million in a public offering in 1981 of 3 million shares at $8.50 a share, providing the company with the necessary capital for a fast expansion program. The timing of the stock offering was linked to a glut in the used-aircraft market, specifically of the small 737s that PE needed. The company bought 17 737s from Lufthansa for $3.7 million each. All in excellent condition, these planes had an original cost of $17 million apiece. Consistent with their efficiency policies, PE changed the planes' interior layout by taking out the hot meals galleys and adding 28 seats, so that the planes flew with an industry high of 118 seats for 737s.

5   The most important characteristic of the airline was its low-fare, no-frills concept. PE usually entered new markets by charging approximately one third of what regular carriers charged, but PE offered no amenities. All extras, including baggage checking and meals, were available only at additional charges. This concept revolutionized the airline industry and was credited with making air travelers out of people who normally

This case was prepared by John A. Pearce II of George Mason University and Julio O. DeCastro of the University of South Carolina. Copyright © by John A. Pearce II.

Exhibit 1
Comparison of average cost per seat, per mile, for a sample of airlines, 1981

Airline	Cost per seat-mile
USAir	$0.1107
Piedmont	0.0928
Frontier	0.0866
TWA	0.0863
Pan American	0.0815
Eastern	0.0811
Muse Air	0.0710
People Express	0.0666

Source: *Fortune*, March 22, 1982.

would not have flown. Burr referred to PE as his "Trailways of the Airways" and stated as his major accomplishment the fact that the airline had helped make the airline seat a commodity.

6   The reason that PE was able to afford its rock-bottom fares was that the company had the lowest cost per passenger seat–mile in the industry. Exhibit 1 gives a comparison of cost per seat-mile for a "basket" of airlines for 1981. Although at that time PE's cost per seat-mile hovered around 6.66 cents, it went further down to 5.4 cents per seat-mile in mid-1984.

7   PE managed to keep its cost down by extracting tremendous productivity from employees and planes. Not only did PE's 737 jets have almost 30 percent more seats than similar planes from other airlines, the jets also flew between 10 to 11 hours a day, which was 3.5 more hours than the industry average. With the additional seats and flying hours, PE was able to more than double the planes' traditional productivity.

8   In addition to the increased plane productivity, PE was able to extract maximum productivity from its employees. The company had an average of 57 employees per aircraft, versus an industry average of 149. It should be noted, however, that this number was biased by the fact that PE used outside contractors to handle its aircraft maintenance, baggage handling, and telephone reservations. Nevertheless, PE proved that it could extract extremely high productivity from its employees because of the versatility of its human resource system. Since the company was not unionized, each employee could be expected to perform many tasks. This fact, coupled with the company's skill in recruiting and motivating employees to work long hours for lower pay, provided PE with a critical edge over its competitors.

Growth at People Express

9   With the expanded capability of the 17 737s bought from Lufthansa and another 47 727s bought from Braniff, Alitalia, and Delta at fire-sale prices, PE embarked on an accelerated growth program.

10   To an expanding list of major and minor northeastern cities on its schedule, PE added Florida in 1982, taking on Eastern Air Lines, the market leader. The challenge

to Eastern was immediately successful because it was not able to match PE's reduced prices due to the established firm's precarious financial situation.

11   Then, in 1983, PE entered into an agreement with Southwest Airlines, a Houston-based airline that had pioneered the low-fare, no-frills, and employee part-ownership concepts. Through this agreement, PE flew to Houston from Newark and thus linked its system with that of Southwest. Southwest was in charge of ground handling at Houston's Hobby Airport. This appeared to be the first step toward a national link of low-fare carriers. The arrangement was synergistic because Southwest needed planes at a time that PE was seeking use for some of its newly bought, used 727s. Part of the payment for the arrangement was in the form of a one-year renewable lease of the 727s to Southwest.

12   In 1984, with its newly acquired 727s, PE began longer-haul routes to major cities, such as Chicago, Minneapolis, and Detroit. PE next acquired four 747s and began flying to London, San Francisco, Los Angeles, and, for $99, nonstop from San Francisco to Brussels. By October 1985, PE was offering over 400 daily flights to 49 cities in the United States plus London and Brussels. An airline acquisition spree by PE included Frontier Airlines, based in Denver; Britt Airlines, which served 29 midwestern cities from its Chicago base; and an additional St. Louis hub. Provincetown Boston Airlines, which was one of the largest commuter airlines in the United States with over 500 daily flights, was also acquired in late 1985. By February 1986, Provincetown was also offering flights from its New England and Florida bases. In all, by June 1986, PE and its merged airlines had over 700 daily flights to 133 airports.

13   The financial strength of People Express, Inc., is shown in the financial statement provided in Exhibit 2.

Donald Burr

14   The prime mover behind the phenomenal growth of PE was its chairman, Donald Burr. In 1970, Burr left the presidency of Texas International Airlines with a group of co-workers to start PE. The cornerstone of the new airline would be the fact that every employee should be an owner and a manager. Burr believed that making employees coparticipants in the fortunes of the company would make them work harder.

15   PE was built with a very distinctive look at jobs. Instead of being tied to the same task, PE employees would be able to switch jobs regularly when the workers thought it more convenient. Burr expected managers (all of the airline employees were called managers) to accept lower base salaries in exchange for a piece of the company and a say in how and when they would do their jobs. Burr believed that this approach would give PE an edge in prices that would allow it to become the cost leader among airlines and thus offer the lowest fares.

16   Most of these concepts were not new. Houston-based Southwest Airlines, the success story of the airline industry in the late 1970s, pioneered the low-fare and employee ownership programs among airlines. Employees at Southwest owned 13 percent of the company's stock by June 1986, and the airline had enjoyed enormous success by promoting itself as a viable alternative to automobile and bus travel. Burr took the Southwest concept and pushed it further. Employees at PE owned approximately one third of the company's stock by January 1986. But what set the company apart from other airlines was the employee relations program. Burr credited the loose organization of the company for giving it enough flexibility to meet its growth challenges.

17 As a strong leader who allowed no dissention, Burr pushed the company's first two presidents, both of whom were members of the group that came to PE from Texas International, to resign, and he fired the managing officer, who had been the architect of the company's human resources policy. Further proof of his autocratic and centralized managing style was his unwillingness to allow other internal officers, even the company's president, to be on the board of the company.

The People Express Approach to Human Resource Relations

18 In order to build PE's human resources program, Burr and Managing Director Lori L. Dubose tried to build on the successful employee relations program at Southwest Airlines.

19 In order to join PE, every new employee was expected to buy and hold at least 100 shares of the airline, which the company offered at a 70 percent discount. They could borrow the money and pay with payroll deductions. In return, profit-sharing payments to the employees could be as high as 30 percent of their regular wages. PE also paid 100 percent of medical and dental expenses and provided every employee with a $50,000 life insurance policy.

Exhibit 2

PEOPLE EXPRESS
Consolidated Income Account
Years Ended December 31 ($000 omitted)

	1985	1984
Operating revenues	$ 977,864	$ 586,802
Operating expenses:		
Flying operations	95,380	50,352
Maintenance	121,481	72,144
Fuel and oil	272,623	178,635
Passenger service	62,064	30,568
Traffic, etc., service	161,111	96,990
Promotion and sales	158,070	74,304
General and administrative	34,719	31,192
Depreciation and amortization	48,967	32,453
Total operating expenses	$ 954,415	$ 566,638
Operating income	$ 23,449	$ 20,164
Other income, net	5,482	19,039
Total	28,931	39,203
Interest expense	60,549	37,303
Income taxes	4,081*	252
Net income	$ (27,537)	$ 1,648
Preferred dividends	$ 11,496	$ 5,313
Balance for common stock	(39,033)	(3,665)
Earnings for common stock	$ (1.60)†	$ (0.16)
Year-end shares:		
Cl. B Com.	1,928,484	1,928,484
Common	24,411,665	21,268,800

* Credit from income taxes.
† As reported on 24,400,000 (1984, 22,746,000) average shares.

Exhibit 2 *(concluded)*

PEOPLE EXPRESS
Consolidated Balance Sheet
As of December 31 ($000 omitted)

	1985	1984
Assets		
Cash	$ 88,352	$ 37,198
Accounts receivable	73,405	24,506
Parts	17,639	8,824
Prepayments, etc.	31,092	17,488
Total current assets	210,488	88,016
Property and equipment	725,440*	539,867
Excess acquisition cost	76,656	—
Other assets, etc.	53,115	10,426
Total assets	$1,065,669	$638,309
Liabilities		
Debt due	$ 19,957	$ 22,900
Accounts payable	128,403	65,319
Income taxes	44,253	—
Accruals	53,520	24,938
Air traffic liabilities	47,422	8,744
Total current liabilities	293,555	121,901
Long-term debt	478,726	288,655
Capital lease obligations	61,826	36,848
Deferred income	14,566	—
Other liabilities	6,333	—
Preferred stock ($0.01):		
Series A $2.64 cum. cv.	35	35
Series B $2.50 cum. cv.	14	—
Common stock ($0.01)	244	213
Cl. B common stock ($0.01)	19	—
Additional paid-in capital	291,957	230,771
Deficit	42,113	1,885
Deferred compensation	(24,340)	(25,194)
Notes receivable	(15,123)	(13,035)
Total liabilities	$1,065,699	$638,309
Net current assets	$ (83,067)	$ (33,885)

* Depreciation: 1985, $84,562,000; 1984, $46,401,000.

Source: *Moody's Transportation Manual,* 1986, p. 1439.

20　　The profit-sharing, stock ownership, and employee self-determination programs were ways of making up for the airline's low base salaries. PE pilots made $22,000 to $70,000 per year, while their counterparts at other airlines averaged $90,000 and could earn as much as $170,000.

21　　On the premise that every employee was a manager, Burr and his human relations personnel decided to design an organization with only three management levels. At PE there were 11 managing officers, 29 general managers, and 4,000 full-time flight managers, maintenance managers, and customer service managers. The employees were divided in groups of 20 with two team leaders and a team manager. The company hired independent firms to handle such tasks as telephone reservations and aircraft maintenance.

22   PE frequently "farmed out" blue-collar jobs, which were prone to unionization. Burr acknowledged that the company avoided unions because he believed that the company's competitive strategy depended on free individuals doing what they freely enjoyed. Further, he believed that a union in PE would be the ultimate humiliation for him and would force him to quit. However, in mid-1985, Burr dropped the antiunion rhetoric following his acquisition of Frontier Airlines, which employed five groups of unionized employees.

23   The human relations program at PE allowed the company to become the cost leader in the industry. While wages consumed 35 percent of revenues for the average airline, at PE wages accounted for only 20 percent.

Fares were also pared by the PE policy of charging passengers only for the services they wanted. Every extra service provided by the airline was charged extra to the customer. Soft drinks were 50 cents, and each suitcase checked was $3, while in other airlines customers paid the cost of food and baggage handling whether or not they used those services.

24   Even though PE's operating cost of 5.38 cents per passenger seat–mile in July 1984 was the lowest in the industry (Continental, 6.19 cents; American, 7.61 cents; United, 7.98 cents), since the fares of the airline were so cheap the company had to fill more seats (67.8 percent) than the industry average (59.9 percent) in order to break even.

25   PE's human relations system also caused troubles. Its pilots resented the company organization chart, which gave equal clout to pilots and flight attendants. At the time PE started in 1980, pilots at the airline did not mind the fact that they were earning far less than their counterparts in other airlines because the industry was in a downturn and there were few pilot jobs. But when the industry bounced back and higher-paying jobs at other airlines became available, PE's pilots started leaving in dozens. In the first four months of 1985, 65 of 1,100 pilots left the airline.

26   Another shortcoming of the human resources program was that the stock ownership and profit-sharing programs tied a significant portion of employee compensation to the fortunes of Wall Street. In late 1984, when PE reported a fourth-quarter $14.2 million operating loss, the company's stock lost more than 50 percent of its market value. With the plunge of the stock the profit-sharing payments stopped, which seemingly caused a fall in employee morale. With a low stock price, the lure of stock ownership for the employees also decreased.

The Acquisition Path at People Express

27   Chairman Burr had repeatedly stated that the airline's growth would come from within and that the airline would not buy other carriers. However, in October 1985, the airline reversed this strategy when it agreed to buy Frontier Airlines after a bidding war with Burr's former boss, Texas Air Chairman Frank Lorenzo. PE agreed to pay $24 a share or $300 million for the airline, which had lost $44.9 million in the two previous years. PE paid $37 million out of internal funds, with the remainder of its $87 million share to come from a securities offering. The other $213 million came from a fund that Frontier had built in order to help the employees take the company private.

28   Even though Frontier was a relatively small airline (42 planes, $303 million revenue for the first six months of 1985), the acquisition allowed PE to expand to the best

hub in the West, Denver, at which there was otherwise no room for new competitors because all of the airport gates were being used.

29   In order to get Frontier's unions to agree to the sale, Burr promised union leaders that he would keep Frontier operating independently, and he agreed to a group of concessions that included a job guarantee for at least four years for all Frontier employees. The unions in return agreed to honor major wage concessions made in the spring of 1985, as part of the effort to buy Frontier themselves.

30   A major ingredient of the Frontier acquisition was how the two companies would mix. Frontier had five unions and a rigid hierarchical and bureaucratic organization, while PE had a loose organization and no unions. Burr decided that only the routes and connections of the two airlines would be merged, and the rest of the airlines would be run independently. He hoped, however, that over time the fundamental ideas of PE would take root in Frontier. Experts on the airlines industry foresaw potential troubles, especially at negotiation time, when both airlines' employees would want the best of pay and benefits. These difficulties would be compounded by the fact that in order to get the unions to agree to the Frontier acquisition by PE, the airline granted Frontier employees major concessions, which PE employees did not have.

31   As soon as the deal had been completed, PE announced that it would cut fares to 100 cities served by Frontier and would immediately begin scheduling no-frills pricing for the airline.

32   By December 1985, PE claimed that the combination with Frontier was boosting the airline's traffic. The airline added two round trips to its five daily flights between Denver and Newark and was considering replacing some of the 727s on the route with 747s, which would seat 400 passengers.

33   In December 1985, the company announced that it would acquire Britt Airways, a Midwest commuter line, for an undisclosed amount of money. Britt Airways was based in Terre Haute, Indiana, and had hubs in Chicago and St. Louis. The company flew 46 small planes to 29 cities in the Midwest.

34   Britt Airways had followed a strategy similar to PE, buying secondhand planes and flying them to out-of-the-way destinations. In the years prior to 1985, the airline had expanded to become one of the biggest commuter airlines in the United States. According to a PE spokesperson, Britt had posted a net income of several million dollars a year using very conservative accounting policies.

35   In February 1986, PE agreed to lend Provincetown Boston Airlines (PBA) enough money to keep the airline flying while negotiating its acquisition. PBA primarily served areas in New England and Florida and had been in bankruptcy proceedings (Chapter 11) since March 1985. The airline was once one of the biggest commuter airlines in the United States, with more than 500 daily flights. However, by February 1986, that total had dropped to 300 daily flights, mainly because of two image-shattering events. In November 1984, the airline was temporarily grounded by the FAA because of safety violations, and a month later, one of the airline's planes crashed in Jacksonville, Florida, and 13 passengers were killed. By the time PE approached the airline, it had failed to meet its payroll for the first time. Although no specific figures were given, a PE executive estimated that its total investment would come to less than $10 million.

36   PE defended its acquisitions as necessary in light of an industrywide trend to build hub-and-spoke systems in which commuter carriers would feed passengers to the big

airlines. PE felt it imperative to get large enough to achieve additional economies of scale if it was to successfully confront its even larger competitors.

37   Another of PE's reasons for these acquisitions was that United, American, and Delta airlines had moved to build fleets and route systems that blanketed the country. PE officials considered that such actions hurt their airline since they allowed the major carriers to cross-subsidize; that is, to use the profits from the uncontested routes to subsidize the routes where they faced competition from low-cost carriers like PE, thereby enabling the majors to match PE's low-cost pricing.

38   Exhibit 3 presents a map with the locations served by the combination of PE, Frontier, PBA, and Britt.

The Problems of People Express

39   Even though PE's problems surfaced publicly in mid-1986, their roots could often be traced to the company's acquisition of 47 727 jets in 1984. While the smaller 737s that the company operated earlier were perfect for the short hauls and for the 65 percent loads that the company needed in order to break even, the 727s, with their 185 seats, were more expensive to operate on the short hauls, and their 65 percent of capacity level was more difficult to achieve.

40   In order to reach its targeted load levels, the company became an aggressive competitor in markets that were heavily contested by full-service airlines like Delta and Eastern, forsaking its strategy of concentrating on mid-sized cities that the company could easily penetrate. Exhibits 4, 5, and 6 provide PE data on its number of passengers, average capacity used, and net income for the years 1981–86.

41   The company was successful in some markets, such as in Florida where the financially weakened Eastern could not afford to drop its rates to compete with PE. But most major airlines fought back with a host of saving programs that matched or undercut PE's fares. An important reason why PE was not able to counter the moves by the other airlines was that its reservations system was only able to handle one peak and one off-peak rate, while the sophisticated computer services of Delta and American were able to offer a host of prices and selections that undercut PE for a specific number of seats or for tickets bought well in advance of their flight dates.

42   PE's computer and reservation problems also contributed to passenger discontent as a result of overbooking. Overbooking, the practice of reserving more seats than were available in the airplane, was common among airlines, but at PE it was carried to an extreme. By early 1985, it was common for media to report stories of passengers left stranded by "People Distress." The computer system of PE contributed to the problem because when a reservation was canceled on a flight that had been for a round-trip ticket, the computers were not able to cancel the return flight. Therefore, ticket agents nationwide were authorized to further overbook to compensate for "anticipated" vacancies.

43   Burr attributed the overbooking practice to the fact that the company was almost alone in not requiring a deposit on reservations, so it had a larger percentage of no-shows than any other airline. Insiders admitted that on some occasions the airline was overbooking by more than 100 percent, which meant that the airline accepted reservations for almost 400 passengers on a 185-seat flight.

44   It was a common practice for PE and its competitors to offer a free ticket plus a seat on the next departing plane to any passenger left stranded. The airline contended

Exhibit 3
Map of the combined routes of People Express, Frontier, PBA, and Britt Airways

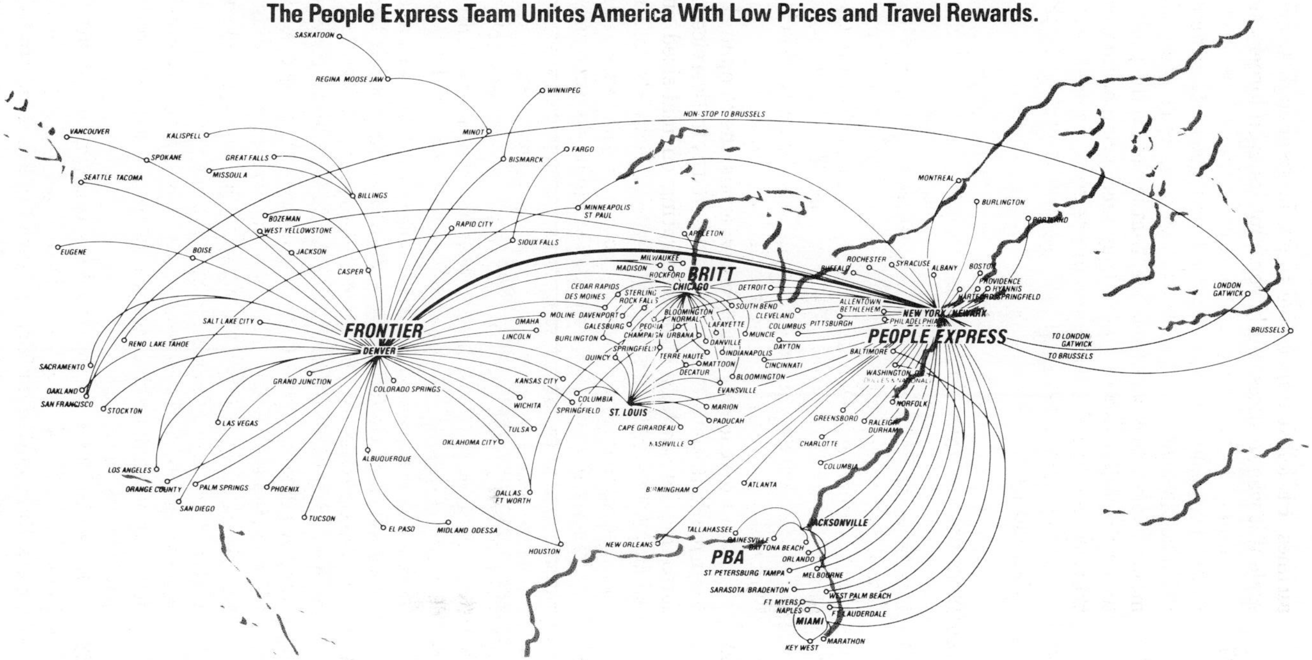

The People Express Team Unites America With Low Prices and Travel Rewards.

Exhibit 4
Graph of the number of passengers per year, 1981–1986

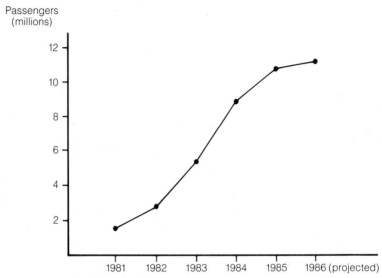

Source: *Time Magazine,* July 7, 1986.

Exhibit 5
Average percent of capacity used, 1981–1986

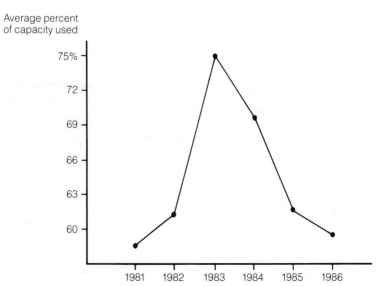

Source: *Time Magazine,* July 17, 1986.

Exhibit 6
Net income, 1981–1986

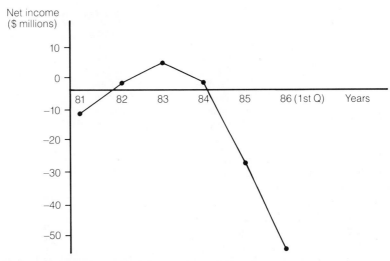

Source: *Time Magazine,* July 7, 1986.

that the expenses incurred by handling these tickets were minimal, although a practice had surfaced by which unscrupulous passengers were deliberately getting bumped from airplanes in order to collect free tickets.

45   The airline's image with travelers was also tarnished by its delay record, which, with 130 delays per 1,000 departures, was the worst performance by an airline in 1985. PE officials attributed the delays to the fact that the airline was operating out of the Newark airport, which sat in the middle of the most congested airspace in the world, the New York area. Inside sources also attributed the delays to the airline flight schedules. These schedules were so tight that if a delay occurred in the morning, the plane involved would continue to run late all day. By February 1985, the company attempted to correct the problem by increasing the average time the plane was on the ground from 20 minutes to 43 minutes. Still, from February to April 1985, 65 percent of the airline flights arrived late at their destinations.

46   There were also problems with the contracted services of maintenance and baggage handling. The company's maintenance contractor, Buttler International, was strained by the pace with which the airline was growing. One of the main causes was that instead of relying on one type of aircraft—like the 737s it had used exclusively before 1985—PE expanded to 737s, 727s, and 747s, which created a greater variety of maintenance problems. Since PE had purchased these aircraft second-hand from Alitalia, Braniff, and Delta, and since they all were built slightly differently, maintenance complexity increased. In order to fulfill its contract with PE, Buttler hired mechanics fresh out of school, who worked slower than veteran mechanics, thereby adding further to the delays.

47   The extra revenues collected for baggage handling did not improve the quality of the service. In fact, PE was losing 14,000 pieces of luggage a month, and stories

Exhibit 7
Passenger complaints filed at Transportation Department, January–March 1986

Airline	Passengers flow (in 100,000)	Complaints per 100,000 passengers
People Express	35.04	10.30
Pan American	33.15	4.86
Continental	41.43	4.22
TWA	42.24	3.88
Eastern	100.49	3.03
United	93.63	2.06
American	103.51	1.93
Northwest	31.77	1.57
Western	26.85	1.49
Delta	94.85	0.60

Source: *The Wall Street Journal*, May 19, 1986.

abounded of stolen luggage and of bags being opened and stripped of their contents. By April 1986, after the airline installed a sophisticated computer system for sorting and tracking bags, the monthly average of lost luggage went down to 7,000 bags, of which 98 percent were eventually returned.

48   The operational problems PE experienced resulted in a diminished public image, as shown in the comparison of passenger complaints between the major carriers presented in Exhibit 7. PE had by far the highest passenger complaint rate for the January–March period of 1986, more than double the rate of the closest competition. PE executives discounted these Department of Transportation figures by saying that some PE policies, such as in-flight ticketing and charges for checked baggage, were not used by other airlines and that these differences evoked some customer complaints.

49   The company's high-visibility human resources program was also suffering. In an expanding airline like PE, where everyone had to be available to do every job, few competencies were being developed in specific areas of airline operations. Further, after the company's stock lost 50 percent of its value in early 1986, a tremendous demoralizing effect rippled through the company, making clear how fragile PE's employee ownership program really was in the face of financial misfortune.

50   The acquisition of Frontier heightened PE's existing load problems and created new cash flow difficulties. After an attempt to transform Frontier into a carrier similar to PE backfired, PE officials returned Frontier to its full-service origins. Unfortunately, by that time too much image damage had been done, and Frontier's customers failed to accept the airline's professed recommitment to quality service. In part as a consequence, PE's combined airlines posted a $58 million first-quarter 1986 loss. Financial analysts were predicting a loss for the year of $120 million.

51   With problems mounting and with the possibility of a severe cash crunch in sight, PE announced a 10 percent price increase for all its flights in March 1986. The company followed with price increases in May and June, and the load factors fell from 56 percent in May to an all-time low of 45 percent in June. These figures were especially distressing

Exhibit 8
Prospectus for People Express Frequent Flyer Program

THE PEOPLE EXPRESS TEAM

AT LAST, A FREQUENT FLYER PROGRAM THAT REWARDS THE BUSINESS AS WELL AS THE BUSINESSPERSON.

Introducing the People Express Team Travel Reward—it asks the least and offers the most of any frequent flyer program.

As little as 20,000 miles gets you a free coach round trip, and car rental for a weekend, anywhere the People Express Team flies in the mainland U.S. and Canada (others often require up to 50,000 miles).

And because we fly to over 125 cities, it's the only frequent flyer program a frequent flyer needs.

What's more, thanks to our Corporate Bonus Program, your company earns miles—on top of the ones you accrue. To defray travel costs—as if our prices don't do that already. Use as sales incentives. Christmas bonuses. Or anything for that matter.

To get things off to a flying start, from now through June 5, fly 3 round trips or 6 individual flights (totaling at least 1,000 miles) and we'll give you a coach round trip. Free—just fly between Sept. 14 and Nov. 19.

For more information on Travel Reward and its Corporate Bonus Program, ask for an application at the Airport. Or on your next People Express, Frontier, Britt or PBA flight. Or write to: Travel Reward, PO Box 224908, Dallas, Texas 75222/4908.

Do it for yourself. And for the company.

PEOPLExpress
FLY SMART

FOR FIRST CLASS RESERVATIONS CALL: **1 (800) 344-4000.**
FOR RESERVATIONS CALL: **(212) 319-9494; (718) 204-5353; (516) 542-1120; (914) 328-0329.**
FOR **PICK UP & GO** RESERVATIONS CALL: **1 (800) 445-9494.** ©1986 PEOPLE EXPRESS AIRLINES

Source: *The Wall Street Journal,* May 1, 1986.

since these months were normally the year's busiest because of the added traffic from the nonbusiness core of PE's passengers.

52   With PE's long-term problems in attracting the business customer becoming more acute, the airline announced in May 1986 that all its planes would be refitted with first-class and business-class sections by November 1986, at a total cost of $7 million. The company officials made clear that the company would remain loyal to its low-fare customers by making dozens of low-price seats available on all flights. At the same time, the airline announced an immediately effective frequent flyer program, which would include all of the company's airlines. Exhibit 8 provides a copy of the public announcement of the frequent flyer program.

Corporate Disaster

53   On June 17, 1986, with the company's cash flow down to $50 million from $120 million, the airline analyst for Goldman, Sachs & Company issued a sell recommendation for PE stock. That same day, PE's stock fell one quarter to 7.5 on a volume of 485,000 shares. The following day, PE announced a 30 percent cut on its ticket prices to 52 cities, in an attempt to stop the fall of the stock.

54   The following Friday, the first day PE's lower fares were advertised, 3.3 million shares of the company's stock were traded, and the price fell to $6 per share. The following Monday, the free-fall continued, with 3.5 million shares traded and the stock closing at 5.5. On June 23, the airline issued a press release announcing that all or parts of the company might be sold.

55   On July 11, 1986, after rejecting an offer of Texas Air Corporation to buy the company for $9 a share or $235.8 million, PE reached a tentative agreement with United Airlines, which agreed to purchase Frontier for $146 million. But on September 16, 1986, after the deal with United fell through, Texas Air agreed to buy People Express, Inc., for $298 million in securities.

Case 32

Daimler–Benz: The Global Truck Industry

1   Dr. Gerhard Liener, Daimler–Benz's managing director for acquisitions and foreign operations, was analyzing the international strategy of the firm's truck group, headquartered in Stuttgart, West Germany. It was on January 29, 1986, and he wondered how long his company would be able to maintain its strength in the face of increased global competition posed by European and American truck companies, international joint ventures, and the lurking threat of Japanese export of large commercial vehicles.

History of Daimler–Benz

2   Daimler–Benz was the product of a merger between two German automobile manufactuers, Benz et Cie and Daimler Motoren Gesellschaft, in 1926. Karl Benz and Gottlieb Daimler, both pioneers in the automotive industry, set up their respective companies in 1883 and 1890. Both firms manufactured expensive cars as well as commercial vehicles and large engines for locomotives, ships, and zeppelins.

3   Shortly after the merger, Daimler–Benz began to grow rapidly. Production increased from 10,829 vehicles in 1927 to over 42,000 by 1938. Innovations in diesel power, success in racing, and a revival of the German economy all contributed to this growth. Unfortunately, this expansion was abruptly halted when most of the company's production facilities were destroyed in World War II. Daimler–Benz was quick to rebuild, however, and by 1950 production had exceeded the prewar high.

4   In the years that followed, Daimler–Benz saw even more phenomenal growth. Output increased from 104,000 units in 1956 to over 300,000 units by 1969. A commitment to quality was the trademark of this company, which produced a highly specialized line of commercial vehicles. Expansion and acquisitions internationally kept the supply of vehicles growing with the demand for them. By 1985, Daimler–Benz produced 541,039 cars (up 13.1 percent over 1984) and 220,213 commercial vehicles (up 4.4 percent from 1984), of which 65,407 (down 3.8 percent) were trucks over 6 tons. The total concern achieved 1985 revenues of DM51,900 million (up 19 percent), of which DM37,079 million came from cars and commercial vehicles. Daimler–Benz exported 53.6 percent of its production.

Daimler–Benz and the Truck Industry

5   Over the years, the commercial vehicle market had evolved into a complex and competitive arena. With an emphasis on quality and reliability, Daimler–Benz was the largest producer of diesel trucks in the world as well as Europe's largest commercial vehicle producer. Daimler–Benz had a long tradition of truck assembly overseas, which had been forced by "local content" rules (i.e., rules specifying that a certain part of the

This case was written by Dr. Per V. Jenster, McIntire School of Commerce, University of Virginia, Charlottesville, 22923; Dr. Alfred Kotzle, Institute for Planning and Organization, University of Tubingen, Tubingen, G-7400, West Germany; and Dr. Franz X. Bea, Institute for Planning and Organization, University of Tubingen, Tubingen, G-7400, West Germany.

value-added process must reside locally). For this and other reasons, Daimler–Benz over the years established truck and bus plants in Brazil and Argentina, as well as in Turkey, Spain, Yugoslavia, Indonesia, Saudi Arabia, Nigeria, and Hampton, Virginia. Additionally, there were 23 assembly plants worldwide in which Daimler–Benz had no ownership.

6   Daimler–Benz had increasingly realized the strategic importance of a global presence, and this had led it to pursue acquisition candidates in America, the world's largest market for commercial vehicles. This process resulted in the 1977 acquisition of Euclid (a heavy-equipment manufacturing subsidiary of White), which was divested in 1983; Freightliner, Inc., Oregon, 1981; and a 49 percent stake in Fabrica de Autotransportes Mexicana (FAMSA), Mexico, in 1985. Dr. Liener explained this effort to *Financial Times:* "We must think of our sons," suggesting that the long-term health and development of the truck group was at stake.

7   FAMSA employed 865 office and factory workers and had a production capacity of 15,000 commercial vehicles, although the expected 1986 sales would not exceed 4,000 vehicles due to the poor Mexican economy. When asked why Daimler–Benz chose Mexico for this operation, Mr. Hans-Jurgen Hinrichs, sales director of FAMSA, clarified that "The white spot on the map annoyed us." He suggested that "Daimler–Benz's policy of trying to be everywhere in the world, even when the prospects in the short term don't appear to be too great," would continue to pay dividends of the type the group collected when its patience and persistence in the Middle East was rewarded in the startling truck sales boom after the mid-1970s oil price rise. It was also acknowledged that there were still some gaps in Daimler–Benz's world coverage, but that it had been talking seriously to the Chinese about truck sales and assembly there.

Competition

8   The nature of the competitive environment had changed over the last 10 years. Daimler–Benz was now facing a three-pronged assault from Western Europe, Japan, and the United States in the international truck industry. Exhibit 1 presents the 1984 production of heavy-duty trucks by the major manufacturers.

9   The idea of international competition was actually much more complex than the Europe–United States–Japan triad might suggest, due to the fact that ownership interests often crossed national boundaries. For instance, many of America's largest truck producers were under European control. Renault had a large stake in Mack Trucks, which itself had many subsidiaries in foreign markets. The Swedish Volvo's recent purchase of White Motor Corporation and Daimler–Benz's 1981 purchase of Freightliner, Inc., gave these large European firms a very strong foothold in the U.S. market. Similarly, Iveco, a Fiat subsidiary, was increasing its presence in the United States as well.

10   In 1985, the first signs of Japanese interest in the European truck market had become apparent. Hino, Mitsubishi, Isuzu, Mazda, and Toyota all displayed commercial vehicles at the Brussels motor show at the beginning of the year. And while all except Hino had been making increasing inroads into Europe's light commercial vehicles, Hino's exhibits were in weight ranges up to 15 tons.

11   In the United States, Japanese truck producers were moving swiftly into market niches that the domestic manufacturers had abandoned, thinking they would be too expensive to supply with American vehicles. Significantly, the Japanese are being

Exhibit 1
Heavy trucks international production by major manufacturers, 1984

Manufacturer	Where produced	Units	Manufacturer	Where produced	Units
Daimler–Benz (66,000 units in 1983)	Germany	38,000	General Motors (13,000 units in 1983)	USA	18,000
	USA/Canada	20,000		Korea	1,000
	Brazil	6,000		Great Britain	500
	Argentina	1,000		Brazil	500
		65,000			20,000
IHC (Navistar) (23,000 units in 1983)	USA/Canada	35,000	Nissan (17,000 units in 1983)	Japan	19,000
	Australia	1,000			
		36,000	Fiat IVECO (19,000 units in 1983)	Italy	14,000
Volvo (30,000 units in 1983)	Sweden	26,000		Germany	3,000
	USA	10,000		France	750
		36,000		Argentina	1,000
Paccar (19,000 units in 1983)	USA/Canada	30,500		Brazil	250
	Mexico	1,000			19,000
	Great Britain	500	Isuzu (15,000 units in 1983)	Japan	17,000
		32,000	Renault RVI (20,000 units in 1983)	France	15,000
Mack (14,000 units in 1983)	USA/Canada	29,000		Spain	1,500
Mitsubishi (17,000 units in 1983)	Japan	22,000		Great Britain	500
					17,000
Saab–Scania (17,000 units in 1983)	Sweden	22,000	MAN (12,000 units in 1983)	Germany	11,000
Hino (15,000 units in 1983)	Japan	21,000		Austria	1,000
Ford (12,000 units in 1983)	USA	19,500			12,000
	Great Britain	1,000			
	Brazil	500			
		21,000			

aided and abetted in this process by the U.S. producers. For example, Nissan Diesel signed an agreement to supply a new generation of medium-weight trucks to International Harvester, now Navistar, and distribute them through Navistar's 850 dealers. At the same time, Nissan planned to sell through its own distribution company based in Texas.

12 General Motors, which held nearly 40 percent of the shares in Isuzu, decided to start selling Isuzu class 3 lightweight trucks through its own network of 250 dealers in 20 states. Ironically, GM seemed to be filling out gaps in its own range because it believed that Hino and Toyota would aggressively attack the diesel sectors (classes 3–8) in the States. For its U.S. venture, Hino had linked up with Mitsui, the major Japanese trading house, which had long been associated with Toyota but had also been selling trucks through its own distribution network. Between the two distribution networks, they saved more than 20 dealerships on sales in excess of 1,000 trucks per year, with an expected increase of 4,000 by 1990.

13   By the same token, General Motors and Ford each had many subsidiaries in Europe, especially in the United Kingdom, producing commercial vehicles that had large shares of their markets as well. Paccar, which manufactured Kenworth and Peterbilt trucks, had affiliates in Europe, Africa, and the Middle East. Navistar and Mack also sold a large number of their vehicles to foreign customers.

14   It was apparent from the large number of subsidiaries, acquisitions, joint ventures, and assembly plants located throughout the world that the European and U.S. truck manufacturers found it effective for several reasons to maintain a strong global presence, with production and assembly taking place in multiple locations. The Japanese produced and exported trucks at an increasing rate without relying on foreign manufacturing subsidiaries or joint ventures.

15   Export of commercial vehicles from Japan increased by nearly 40 percent from 1979 to 1980. More importantly, while North America was the largest market for these vehicles, sales to EEC countries increased by 34 percent that year, and sales to other European countries jumped a staggering 92 percent. "Led by the traditional Japanese powers, Toyota, Nissan, and others, this nation is making the true run at the world truck market."[1]

Freightliner, Inc.

16   On July 31, 1981, Daimler–Benz completed its acquisition of Freightliner Corporation, previously a subsidiary of Consolidated Freightways, Inc. (CFI). The $300 million transaction gave Daimler–Benz full ownership of Freightliner's four truck assembly plants (located in Portland, Oregon; Mt. Holly, North Carolina; Indianapolis, Indiana; and Burnaby, British Columbia, Canada) along with Freightliner's parts manufacturing plants in Portland, Oregon; Gastonia, North Carolina; and Fremont, California. Freightliner's two Vancouver financial subsidiaries, Freightliner of Canada, Ltd., and Freightliner Financial Services, Ltd., were also included in the deal.

17   Freightliner, headquartered in Portland, Oregon, manufactured and sold mainly heavy-duty trucks of the class 8 variety, signifying a gross weight of at least 33,000 pounds. The Freightliner acquisition gave Daimler–Benz an immediate 10 percent share of the class 8 truck market to add to its existing lines of class 6 and class 7 trucks, sold through Mercedes–Benz of North America. Freightliner had also been previously involved in sales of medium-duty trucks as a result of its truck-marketing ties with Volvo. As a result of the Daimler–Benz acquisition, however, this collaboration was terminated.

18   Freightliner was formed by Consolidated Freightway, Inc., in 1939 in order to design and build trucks more suitable to the long-haul traffic in the West, where the majority of CFI's driving was done. During the 1950s, Freightliner began to sell to other truckers as well, with sales to CFI gradually making up a smaller percentage of total revenue.

19   Freightliner's trucks were marketed by White Motor for over 20 years but were never distributed in the eastern United States. In 1977, Freightliner set up its own organization of 207 dealers after White Motor began to lose market share. In order to achieve increased sales, it was decided that improved eastern service was needed; and, to help accomplish this, a new plant was opened in Mt. Holly, North Carolina,

---

[1] *Financial Times,* November 29, 1985.

Table 1
U.S. market shares for class 8 trucks

Manufacturer	1980	Manufacturer	1985
IHC	20.4%	IHC (Navistar)	21.3%
Mack	19.5	Mack	19.1
Paccar	15.4	Paccar	16.3
GMC	14.4	**Freightliner**	**13.5**
Ford	12.0	Ford	11.6
Freightliner	**9.0**	GMC	9.0
White	9.0	White	8.2
Others	1.3	Others	0.7

in 1979. This was followed by the closing of the Chino, California, assembly plant in September 1980. The closing was blamed partly on the sharp decrease in demand for heavy-duty trucks experienced after the peak reached in 1979. This decrease in demand caused a sales drop of 36 percent early in 1980, which led to the dismissal of Freightliner's president, William Critzer.

20   Critzer's successor was Ronald Burbank, who had just been named chief operating officer of CFI. He continued on as president and chief executive officer after the acquisition by Daimler–Benz; and, aided by a rise in heavy-duty truck demand, an improved product range, and strong sales efforts, he was able to greatly expand sales, thus reaching full capacity in 1984. However, its inability to fully meet demand caused the U.S. market share to decline somewhat in 1984, whereas its Canadian share continued to increase.

21   The demand for heavy-duty trucks of 134,000 vehicles declined slightly in 1985 from 138,000 in 1984 (compared to 80,000 in 1983), whereas 145,000 medium-heavy vehicles were sold in both years. Despite the growing competition, Freightliner was able to sell 20,809 (against 20,526 in 1984) heavy-duty vehicles in North America, producing sales of $1.6 billion. This meant an improvement in Freightliner's U.S. market share from 12.8 percent to 13.5 percent, whereas the Canadian market share dropped to 12.3 percent from 13.2 percent. Table 1 provides an overview of the market share for the various U.S. competitors. Freightliner furthermore saw a 10 percent reduction in employees to 5,439 from 6,059 in 1984.

The Future of Daimler–Benz

22   Daimler–Benz had weathered the 1980–83 world recession that sent sales of most truck manufacturers plummeting, and sales at Daimler–Benz had even been relatively stable. Its expansion policy had been one of wise acquisitions and cautious movement into new markets. Its reputation for quality, value, and innovation had up until now been unequaled. The question for Dr. Liener was how to sustain the strategic position in a global industry where competition was increasing.

Case 33

Volvo Bus of North America

1   Jan-Olof Rabe, president and chief executive officer (CEO) of Volvo Bus Company of North America, sat alone in his second-floor office. Although it was only 6 o'clock, the December night had already dropped its curtain between the tree-lined Volvo complex and the Chesapeake, Virginia, environs. Rabe swung his chair around and stared into the darkness. Lights reflected off expensive white-and-blue china; coffee remaining in the cup had long been too cold to enjoy. In the distance flashing white lights signaled to aircraft the location of three Portsmouth radio towers. They reminded him of Sweden.

2   Thoughts of home broke his concentration. Within a few days he would return to Sweden to meet, yet again, with the corporate board. What would they finally decide? Would he soon return home permanently? He would like that.

3   He reflected on his foreign service. He had had five successful years as general manager of Volvo's Indonesian plant. Nine months ago Volvo management had given him a three-year charter to turn around the Volvo bus operation in North America. But, by October 1985, barely six months later, top executives seriously began to discuss the possibility of closure in the face of continued heavy losses.

4   Was closure the best alternative? The company had already invested considerable time and resources. Pulling out meant surrendering the North American bus market to German and American competitors. In only three years the environment had drastically changed. To reestablish itself, if Volvo were to exit now, would be even more costly in the future. Just what went wrong?

5   In many ways, Volvo Bus Company of North America paralleled the situation at General Electric's Video and Audio Division, producer of television receivers and VCRs, headquartered at nearby Portsmouth, Virginia. Both were divisions of multibusiness, multinational corporations, with plants and sales worldwide. Both, placing top priority on quality, employed advanced technology and asynchronous production lines in their production processes. Both unionized divisions geared their rates to a national rather than a local wage scale. Both firms had been battered by intense price competition, especially from foreign companies with U.S. plants. GE's Video Division had announced cessation of manufacturing operations nearly a year ago and wound down manufacturing activities in its Portsmouth and Syracuse facilities during 1985. Would Volvo executives soon echo the GE decision? As Rabe reviewed activities of the past several months, he pondered whether the Chesapeake bus operations had effectively implemented the corporate philosophy and global strategy.

Corporate Management Philosophy

6   In Volvo's quest for development of production technology and quality products, top management had adopted a guiding philosophy: to adapt the industrial environment to humans rather than mold human behavior to fit the work environment. Based

Case developed by Robert P. Vichas of Florida Atlantic University and Betty R. Ricks of Old Dominion University.

upon this philosophy, corporate objectives were to allow employees an opportunity for more self-determination, increased responsibility (job depth), and greater influence in deciding how their work should be performed (autonomy).

7   Nevertheless, quality goals had always prevailed as the corporation's overriding principle. Assar Gabrielsson, one of Volvo's founders, wrote in the company's first sales manual in the 1930s: "Our pride, as manufacturers, is that Volvo's quality and performance are the base upon which we are building our popularity."

8   Management practices did not change quickly at Volvo. In the 1960s, people-handling discussions were largely theoretical. Management examined many theories, such as motivational models, participative management, and then quality circles in the 1970s. Lars Christen Jonson, a personnel manager, said, "The aim was never to try to influence moral or ideological values, but rather to create a work environment that provides social reward."

9   Beginning in 1971, employee representatives were given seats on AB Volvo's board of directors. Establishment of the Volvo Group Works Council provided a vehicle for cooperation between management and employee representatives in Sweden. In more recent years employee representatives had participated in all significant management acquisition and policy decisions.

10   By the mid-1970s, Volvo had experimented with sociotechnical innovations, which mainly amounted to a team approach on the shop floor. The purposes were to enable workers to develop skills using recent technology, increase motivation, raise productivity, and, above all, reduce the myriad personnel management problems the company had been experiencing for some time. In summarizing those 10-year-old efforts, Jonson said, "While we changed the situation on the shop floor, we didn't change anywhere else, and this led to the discovery that it's necessary to change the entire organization to achieve the expected results on the shop floor."

11   The leadership challenge for organizational revitalization was met by 50-year-old Pehr Gyllenhammar. Currently AB Volvo's chairman of the board and chief executive officer, he had been a board member and managing director since 1971. In developing a new kind of people management, CEO Gyllenhammar said:

> Volvo has done quite a lot of work in upgrading its quality and productivity through working with people. However, it's difficult to be proud of achievements when it comes to people because many still feel they could do and offer more. Their aspirations are often greater than can be met through us as leaders and employers. Such demands show there is enormous loyalty and willingness to achieve more. It is only due to our poor leadership that this potential isn't exploited in a sensible way.
>
> What we should be concerned about is our own leadership in defining our skills and technologies clearly so that the people both within and outside the organization understand what we want to achieve.
>
> People and their aspirations are important, and that's why Volvo is now investing heavily in a corporationwide program geared to informing every employee about the overall activities of the group in order to start a dialogue with them.

12   In 1983, AB Volvo signed a development agreement with unions to signal increased cooperation between management and labor. In part, the agreement stated,

Efficiency, profitability, and competitiveness are created through active participation on the part of the men and women in the organization. Through cooperation based on trust, and by giving employees greater influence with respect to their work and assignments, the know-how and experience of employees can be used more effectively for the good of the entire company.

Corporate Growth and Strategy

13 The Swedish Volvo Group (Volvo means "I roll"), probably best known for its automobiles, manufactures not only cars, trucks, and buses but also marine, industrial, and aircraft engines. It has invested in oil and gas exploration and owns food-processing companies.

14 Truly multinational, AB Volvo, with plants in Sweden, Belgium, the Netherlands, France, Great Britain, Australia, Thailand, Malaysia, Iran, Peru, Brazil, Canada, and the United States, employs nearly 68,000 people.

15 Corporatewide sales in 1985 exceeded SEK86 billion (down from SEK100 billion in 1983, and SEK87 billion in 1984); 80 percent of sales originated outside of Sweden. World truck and bus sales accounted for SEK18 billion. (Approximately one U.S. dollar equals seven Swedish kronor.) Income as a percent of equity reached 7.3 percent in 1978, 18.3 percent in 1983, 28.2 percent in 1984, and 23.7 percent in 1985.

16 The tables and charts below, as well as data in Appendixes A through G, summarize financial characteristics of AB Volvo. Exhibit 1 breaks down sales and income by operating groups for 1984 and 1985; the four line graphs in Exhibit 2 describe key corporate variables over the most recent 10 years.

17 Having built its reputation on quality motor vehicles, Volvo increased automotive sales during the stable growth period of the 1960s, which, by 1971, had accounted for 75 percent of total revenue. About 70 percent of automotive revenue originated outside of Sweden; Volvo contributed 8 to 9 percent to Sweden's total exports. Nevertheless, Volvo's world share of the automotive market amounted to little more than 1 percent.

18 Economic imbalance, increased competition, and weaker profits characterized the 1970s. Volvo adapted to a changing environment with a strategy aimed at creating conditions for improved profitability through growth of its traditional products and with market and product diversification.

19 Management initiated a plan to broaden product line in its transport vehicle sector, including automobiles, to widen product lines in its other activities, and to diversify in order to reduce dependency on automobile sales. After 1973 most of Volvo's profits arose from nonautomobile activities. It further engaged in risk diversification by spreading market activities to more than 100 countries. The firm began investing in energy, especially oil exploration and trading. It diversified into food processing and marketing of brand name food products and soft drinks.

20 To implement this broad strategy of growth through diversification, Volvo improved production technology and adopted a new management philosophy aimed at raising productivity and providing a more satisfying work environment. Beginning in 1972, the corporation restructured its organization along product lines. Each line became

Exhibit 1
Data by group company

SEK M	Sales		Income before allocations, taxes and minority interests		Employees December 31	
	1985	1984	**1985**	1984	**1985**	1984
AB Volvo	**5,504**	4,737	**885**	1,541	**2,425**	2,196
Subsidiaries in Sweden						
Volvo Car Corporation	**23,951**	20,914	**4,415**	4,333	**24,037**	22,212
Volvo Truck Corporation	**9,229**	9,161	**608**	438	**7,416**	6,610
Volvo Bus Corporation	**889**	852	**(11)**	61	**742**	750
Volvo BM AB	**–**	2,615	**–**	66	**–**	5,112
AB Volvo Penta	**1,772**	1,898	**131**	173	**1,031**	1,020
Volvo Flygmotor AB	**1,608**	1,345	**224**	143	**3,463**	3,326
Volvo Components Corporation	**6,339**	5,816	**(2)**	92	**9,818**	9,072
Volvo Svenska Bil AB	**6,709**	5,369	**197**	243	**777**	695
Försäkringsaktiebolaget Volvia (insurance company)	**342**	273	**1**	21	**–**	–
Volvo Data AB	**425**	340	**28**	12	**660**	612
Volvo Transport AB	**4,054**	3,378	**36**	31	**250**	205
AB Fortos	**188**	–	**58**	–	**130**	–
Kockums Jernverksaktiebolag	**184**	321	**(20)**	(52)	**300**	756
Centro-Morgårdshammar AB	**442**	383	**(126)**	4	**778**	772
Volvo Energy Corporation	**6**	39	**(31)**	164	**8**	8
STC Scandinavian Trading Company AB .	**21,757**	27,698	**50**	(330)	**316**	427
Provendor Food AB	**5,393**	4,947	**154**	131	**4,989**	4,946
Subsidiaries outside Sweden						
Nordic area, excluding Sweden	**5,148**	4,057	**181**	119	**1,066**	1,049
Europe, excluding Nordic area	**7,012**	6,518	**144**	227	**2,618**	2,652
North America	**22,757**	19,860	**1,070**	1,084	**4,657**	4,567
Other markets	**2,925**	2,277	**297**	203	**2,285**	1,499
Other companies and intra-Group transactions	**(40,438)**	(35,746)	**(687)**	(1,057)	**91**	100
Group total	**86,196**	87,052	**7,602**	7,647	**67,857**	68,586

The table above shows the sales, income before allocations, taxes and minority interests, and the number of employees in AB Volvo and its subsidiaries. Figures for company subsidiaries are included, where applicable.

In the table above, figures for "Subsidiaries in Sweden" include the operations of their subsidiaries in other countries.

Intra-Group transactions pertain mainly to sales between Group companies, to profits arising from these sales, and to dividends from subsidiaries.

The information is broken down by *legal entities*. This differs from the presentations dealing with *operating sectors* that appear on pages 14 through 30, since many Group companies have operations in more than one operating sector.

Exhibit 2
Key corporate variables

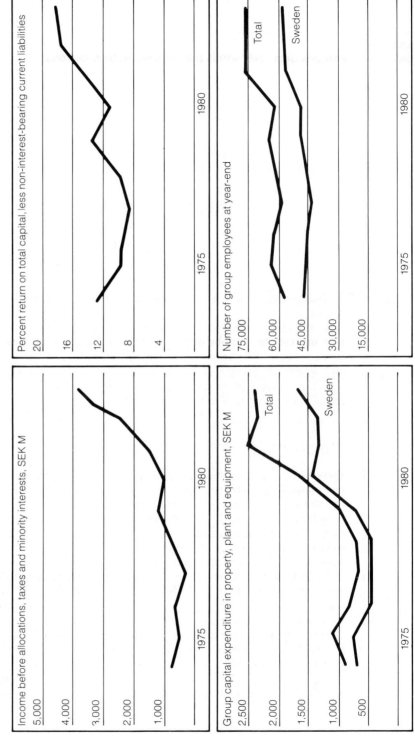

Exhibit 3
Volvo Bus operations data, 1984–1985 (all markets, in SEK millions)

Item	1985	1984
Bus sales	SEK1,672	SEK1,336
Operating income	60	114
Capital expenditures	48	47
Return on capital (percent)	8%	17%
Number of employees (December 31)	1,750	1,600

Source: Volvo, *1985 Annual Report.*

an independent division. Corporate headquarters reduced its staff from 1,800 to 100 persons.

21   By the 1980s, Volvo strengthened its corporate position in traditional areas, entered new markets by establishing a presence in various countries with assembly plants, created a worldwide sales organization, and consolidated its market position in important western European markets. Although the Nordic countries still constituted its sales base, especially in vehicle sales, by 1983 automobile sales accounted for only 25 percent of corporate revenue.

Volvo Bus Corporation

22   Volvo's bus operating sector develops, manufactures, and markets buses, bus chassis, and components. Although Sweden accounts for most production, assembly and limited manufacture take place in 10 countries.

23   Volvo had developed a number of systems for use in mass transit, which included route networks, scheduling, staffing, computerized control, and other functions. The chassis program covered the range of 12- to 27-ton buses for use in all types of service from city traffic to tourist transportation.

24   In 1983, Volvo introduced a completely new tourist bus of its own design, which was manufactured in Italy. In September 1985, an energy-efficient double-decker bus was delivered to London Transport, the world's largest bus operator, for test operations.

25   Because of reduction in market size since 1981, Volvo's growth of worldwide bus sales was achieved mostly by increasing market shares at the expense of its competition. During 1985, the bus market stabilized; Volvo's global bus sales registered a larger increase. (See Exhibit 3 for bus operations data for 1984–85.) In terms of unit sales, the delivery of bus chassis was virtually unchanged: 3,240 units in 1985; 3,220 units in 1985. The kronor-value increase in sales in 1985 mainly resulted from the larger

Exhibit 4
Volvo Bus sales, 1981–1985 (in SEK millions)

Market	1981	1982	1983	1984	1985
Sweden	192	341	308	303	318
Nordic area, except Sweden	196	199	215	262	236
Europe, except Nordic area	201	272	350	363	379
Other markets	441	216	258	408	739
Totals	1,030	1,028	1,131	1,336	1,672

Source: Volvo, *1985 Annual Report.*

percentage of delivery of completed buses during the year. About 81 percent of all bus sales originated outside of Sweden.

26   Volvo recently accounted for approximately 7 percent of heavy buses and bus chassis (over 12 tons) manufactured in Organization for Economic Cooperation and Development (OECD) countries. OECD countries comprise Australia, Austria, Belgium, Canada, Denmark, Finland, France, West Germany, Greece, Iceland, Ireland, Italy, Japan, Luxembourg, the Netherlands, New Zealand, Norway, Portugal, Spain, Sweden, Switzerland, Turkey, the United Kingdom, and the United States.

27   However, in western Europe the market for heavy buses decreased by 6 percent during 1985. Despite lower demand, Volvo retained market share in Great Britain, Belgium, the Netherlands, and other countries. In mid-1985, AB Volvo completed its US $4.6 million purchase of Nebim Bedrijfswagens BV, a Dutch importer of Swedish trucks and buses.

28   Nevertheless, bus market shares declined in Finland from 48 to 45 percent, in Norway from 42 to 36 percent, and in Denmark from 29 to 26 percent. On the other hand, market shares rose in Sweden from 58 to 63 percent and in Brazil from 14 to 16 percent. Higher sales in Australia, Morocco, and Algeria were due to slight market growth. By contrast, the U.S. subsidiary, Volvo Bus of North America, experienced large losses in 1984 and 1985. Exhibit 4 summarizes world bus sales, 1981–85, by geographic area.

29   Cooperation between management and labor resulted in improvements in production technology, work environments, job content, and personal development opportunities within the bus manufacturing group.

30   For example, the Boras bus plant, located in western Sweden, boasted self-paced production lines and an automated carrier system, where assembly work was performed on vehicles in a stationary position. To move work stations, platforms glided on compressed air over a smooth floor surface, which relieved workers of heavy, monotonous tasks and eliminated air and noise pollution.

The U.S. Operation

31   Volvo Bus of North America is headquartered in Chesapeake, Virginia. Chesapeake comprises part of the Hampton Roads market area, which includes Norfolk, Virginia Beach, Portsmouth, and several satellite cities in southeast Virginia.

Initial Decisions

32   With initial plans to construct an automobile assembly plant, Volvo began construction on its 520-acre Chesapeake facility in 1974. The Tidewater location had met company criteria of location, cost, and labor supply. Volvo desired an East Coast harbor site near its main markets, one accessible to an efficient highway system. Not only were land and construction costs important, but Volvo also preferred to locate in a community eagerly courting new businesses and industry. Of course, Volvo required availability of skilled labor plus a surplus pool of trainable workers to permit expansion. The Hampton Roads area provided the right environment for establishment of the automobile plant in Chesapeake as well as for Volvo Penta in Norfolk, producer of marine engines.

33   When auto sales dropped precipitously following the first oil crisis, plant construction was halted. The incompleted facility first functioned as an auto service center (1976–78) for 30,000 to 40,000 automobiles. Then, in 1979–80, it served as a job shop for light trucks imported from Belgium at the rate of 2,500 vehicles per year. Volvo bought the White Motor Corporation, a U.S. truck manufacturer, in 1981, and set up the Volvo White Truck Corporation in Greensboro, North Carolina. However, the Chesapeake plant still customized light trucks imported for the U.S. market.

Bus Manufacture

34   Also, in 1981, Volvo began market research on city mass transit buses in the United States and Canada. During 1983, bus prototypes were manufactured in Chesapeake, and, by 1984, the Chesapeake facility housed yet its third operation, the US$25 million Volvo bus manufacturing and offices complex. Full-scale bus manufacture and assembly were under way by early 1984.

35   In March 1985, Jan-Olof Rabe became the new president and chief executive officer of Volvo Bus of North America in Chesapeake. For a time prior to 1969, he and his family had lived in the United States. Then, with an engineering degree in hand, he joined the economics department of AB Volvo's Swedish auto division. Between 1969 and 1980, he remained in Sweden. As general manager of Volvo's Indonesian plant from 1980 to 1985, he directed the manufacture of all types of vehicles. Then, in March 1985, he signed a three-year contract to become top executive for U.S. bus manufacturing.

36   Volvo Bus of North America is a division of Volvo North America Corporation, headquartered in Rockleigh, New Jersey. Corporate headquarters, AB Volvo in Goteborg, Sweden, establishes worldwide corporate policy and global strategies. Consequently, an executive committee decides or approves both expansion and closures. Although AB Volvo makes policy and strategic decisions that affect Volvo Bus of North America, the divisional president, Jan-Olof Rabe, reports to Rockleigh, New Jersey, and is responsible for developing operational plans necessary to implement corporate decisions.

37   The decision to establish a U.S. bus assembly division grew out of a lagged corporate response to proposals and policies of the Carter administration. President Carter favored federal subsidies to create public transportation systems in key cities. Helped by two oil crises in the 1970s, which produced sharp increases in retail gasoline prices, President Carter initially mustered congressional support for funding a mass transit program.

Statistical studies conducted in selected major cities appeared to demonstrate the need for, and public acceptance of, massive public funding of rapid transit and ground transportation systems. Potential creation of a lucrative articulated (i.e., long, customized) bus market subsidized with federal money, coupled with higher tariffs applied to imported foreign vehicles designed to provide limited protection to American manufacturers and labor unions, did not go unnoticed by AB Volvo. H.R. 3129 had already promulgated a 50 percent local content requirement.

38   In response to higher U.S. tariffs and federal financing, Volvo acted to strengthen its U.S. presence. Around the end of the 1970s, corporate management had projected a total U.S. and Canadian bus market of 10,000 units per year. Since Volvo already owned the Chesapeake property and other fixed assets, a bus assembly venture would require a lower initial capital outlay. Besides, a plant and service facility located within the United States allowed Volvo direct access to U.S. markets, rather than having to contend with DOT, tariffs, and similar restrictions affecting imported, completely assembled, buses.

Production and Labor

39   The bus plant in Chesapeake utilized 16 workstations to assemble 40-foot transit coaches and 60-foot articulated buses. At peak employment, more than 360 plant and office workers enjoyed above-market wages and salaries at the carefully maintained facility. In fact, the entire complex was designed as an architectural expression of management's open-door policy. Mrs. Joan Richards, personnel manager, pointed out that a clean and open work environment was an important factor in achieving the high productivity and quality standards insisted upon by the company. Cleanliness pervaded the offices, plant, rest rooms, and even the parking areas.

40   Volvo paid attention to details. Phyllis Wilson, a production line worker, said, "I've been with Volvo for more than eight years and am truly impressed with the care that a company this large puts into the small details. I install seats, and, at Volvo, my job is as important as anyone else's." Of course, paying attention to details was not without cost.

41   Much like General Electric, Volvo demanded quality goods and quality performance from its employees; and both paid quality wages. At Volvo, in Chesapeake, the average wage earner received $10 per hour; hourly wages ranged between $9.94 and $13.48 by the end of 1985. Although Virginia is a right-to-work state, employees were unionized. Volvo paid wages above local and state labor markets. Joan Richards said that the wage scale was based on U.S. industry data, unrelated to local conditions.

42   Direct labor per manufactured bus typically added up to 1,500 hours. However, due to learning curve effects, manufacture time on large orders might decline to as low as 1,000 hours of direct labor per bus.

43   Exhibit 5 compares various local, state, and national wage figures for 1984 (the latest date for which comparative figures are available). Wages at GE and Volvo exceeded local and statewide rates as well as the national average in all manufacturing activities. However, workers of the heavily unionized transportation and motor vehicle industries obtained basic wages about 50 percent above the typical worker in manufacturing across the United States. These wages were exclusive of fringe benefits (some of which are nontaxable), which typically added another 25 to 50 percent equivalent in wages to unionized workers.

Exhibit 5
Comparative wage data, 1984–1985 (average rates in U.S. dollars per hour)

Volvo (Chesapeake, Virginia, 1985)	$10.00
General Electric (Portsmouth, Virginia, June 25, 1984)	9.97
Hampton Roads, Virginia area (May 1984)	8.60
Virginia—statewide (May 1984)	8.03
All U.S. manufacturing (June 1984)	8.77
Transportation equipment manufacturing (1984)	12.15
Motor vehicle and equipment manufacturing (1984)	12.65

Competitors and Market Size

44 By contrast, Volvo's chief U.S. competitors—Neoplan and MAN, both subsidiaries of German corporations—had located U.S. production facilities in lower-wage areas—in Lamar, Colorado, and near Charlotte, North Carolina, respectively. Aggressive marketers, Neoplan often underbid Volvo on city government contracts. The German-owned plants paid workers according to local, not national, scale.

45 Both competitors were U.S. subsidiaries of foreign-headquartered multinationals; both survived severe price competition; and both had engaged in deep discounting on bus bids during 1984 and 1985. Volvo management refused to compromise quality, which also meant no compromise on wages and salaries.

46 Although increasing global sales were profitable business for the Volvo Bus Corporation, Volvo Bus of North America suffered large losses in 1984 as the U.S. market for mass transit buses continued to shrink. In the face of fierce competition, operating results continued to worsen throughout 1985. In the early 1980s, a large bus in the United States would sell for $275,000 to $300,000. By the end of 1985, that same bus would yield only $225,000 in revenue, despite higher production costs.

47 The total market had shrunk to an estimated 2,000 to 3,000 buses per year; four new competitors appeared on the scene; federal subsidies sharply declined; and Volvo could not underbid competitors. Annual demand for long (articulated) buses (Volvo's specialty) would not exceed 300 units in Canada and 300 in today's U.S. market. Including those on order, the Chesapeake facility had generated sales for 230 buses, 112 of which were delivered during 1985.

48 Bus prices had dropped by 25 percent in fewer than five years. Due to reductions of federal government subsidies for public transportation, by 1985 the U.S. bus market had declined approximately 50 percent compared to 1980 figures.

49 Poor divisional performance and environmental changes favored a closure decision, on one hand. A physical presence in major markets—driven by a global strategy—favored staying in the United States, on the other hand. Although Volvo could export its buses into the United States and Canada from its Swedish production facilities, local regulations, bid requirements, and customizing necessitated that work be done in reasonable proximity to the market to ensure customer confidence. Additionally, Volvo had long ago committed itself to quality and service. It had already manufactured over 100 buses, had orders exceeding another 100 in the United States by the end of 1985, and had to maintain, at a minimum, a spare parts inventory and training facilities for technicians as a condition of its contracts with purchasers.

At a Crossroads

50   Nevertheless, by October 1985, due to heavy financial losses, corporate management reviewed its options. At its executive meeting, management asked for an assessment of the U.S. bus market.

51   Rabe observed that projected programs of the Carter administration had highly favored expansion of a public transportation system. Volvo management, in 1979, had forecast a total bus market of 10,000 units per year. At $300,000 1980 dollars per bus, this would have generated very profitable business. Management had committed itself to enter the U.S. market. Volvo funded those plans; but the Chesapeake plant did not deliver its first bus until five years later.

52   "What are the market projections and total bus sales today?"

53   "This is a difficult question," replied Rabe. "Buses purchased for public use are funded by local communities. Realistically, U.S. demand probably ranges between 200 and 400 articulated buses a year. Canada accounts for another 300 buses a year.

54   "We have a more difficult problem forecasting our competitors' activities. We don't have accurate cost data. Sales vary considerably each year. One manufacturer reports sales figures on number of buses produced; another adds delivered buses to work in progress or even adds contracts signed. There is double counting. The information is unreliable."

55   "Where do we stand in the U.S. market?"

56   "We have most of the articulated bus market," said Rabe, "as much as 50 percent of the market."

57   The main issue was that federal funding of a public bus system virtually disappeared under the Reagan administration, and renewed interest by Congress was unlikely for the rest of the decade. Since 1980 demand had decreased, potential supply had increased due to new competitors, and nominal prices decreased. Added to these environmental factors were inflation and higher labor and material costs. Also, cities usually awarded contracts on the basis of lowest bids coupled with specs that drove up production costs. Volvo had to implement a plan that would allow the firm to compete profitably and still maintain high standards of safety and quality.

58   Internal discussions continued throughout October. In November management asked Rabe to summarize the key problems. Rabe said that decreased demand, largely brought about by reduced funding, aggressive German competitors, bid prices well below the break-even point, and the threat of legislation that might raise the local content requirement from 50 to 85 percent were the chief challenges. Furthermore, because Volvo was already exporting more than 15 percent of bus components from its Swedish plants to Chesapeake, the proposed legislation would adversely affect divisional profits.

59   "What can we do to help you turn around the American bus business?"

60   One manager said that he believed some of the problems stemmed from company assessments made seven or eight years ago, because Europeans did not fully understand the American political system. From Watergate to Ford to Carter, it appeared to Europeans there had been a major shift in attitudes of the American public. Because the company had been accustomed to dealing with central governments and President Carter encouraged public funding of mass transit, the Americans were sending mixed signals. Then they confused the world even further with the election of Reagan.

61   Rabe said, "We didn't fully understand the low-bid process. Or the politics of bidding." He then explained how the low-bid system affected Volvo Bus's ability to compete:

After a city would request bids on transit buses, Volvo would analyze the requirements and submit a competitive bid. Neoplan, MAN, Grumann, and others submitted bids as well. The political process mandated that the manufacturer with the lowest bid would be awarded the contract. Many specs were often incompatible with the Volvo bus design.

62   "We know we have a superior design, but that doesn't enter into discussions. To meet customer specs raises manufacturing costs. A customer wants a fuel tank here instead of there, or orders a modification in the frame or body. If we move the fuel tank from the center to the left side, for instance, then everything else underneath must be redesigned. It takes workers longer to learn a new production routine. If the bid is for a few buses, our per-unit costs are higher. With a big order we can recapture some of those learning costs.

63   "Politics dictate buying the cheapest. The approach is strictly short run. They don't consider maintenance costs, fuel economy, comfort, safety, durability—none of these important elements that through many years of experience we have incorporated into our buses. Our buses last longer. They're efficient.

64   "In most other countries we work with negotiated bids. They consider fuel economy, availability of replacement parts, service, maintenance costs. They have a long-term approach. Our experience has been predominately with negotiated bids, and we didn't understand the American decision process."

65   By December 1985, continuing losses pressed hard on management. They had to act to stem financial losses. If retrenchment or, worse yet, closure was the best option, management could not just walk away from its Chesapeake operations. Closure required a carefully implemented strategy. There were many stakeholders to consider.

66   High-paid employees would not be able to find work with comparable salaries locally, especially after the GE layoff. The labor union apparently had not anticipated the possibility of retrenchment or closure and, consequently, had not negotiated termination benefits. Previous customers depended on Volvo Bus to supply parts and training, and pending orders might be canceled should Volvo decide to pull out. Volvo had to maintain good relationships with its suppliers because of its other operations—Volvo Penta of America, also located in Hampton Roads, Virginia, supplied marine engines; the truck operation in Greensboro, North Carolina; Volvo BM, the oldest heavy-equipment manufacturer in the world; and the recreational products division—and, of course, automobile sales as well as the good name of Volvo North America Corporation in Rockleigh, New Jersey, had to be maintained. The Hampton Roads area would lose an employer; the city of Chesapeake and the state of Virginia would lose tax revenues. Finally, competitors would quickly fill any vacuum left by Volvo Bus. Volvo currently had 110 buses on order for delivery during 1986.

67   Rabe had said, "A Volvo bus is a truly remarkable product. It's an accumulation of thousands of hours of designing, producing, and inspecting by hundreds of people. And what's so amazing is that each person puts forth an effort as if the bus they [sic] were building was their very own."

68   Rabe loved Volvo and was proud of its high standards and quality products. To surrender the North American market to competitors meant that Americans and Canadians would no longer have the option of riding in a safe, well-constructed Volvo bus.

69   The night watchman softly tapped on his door and called out, "Mr. Rabe?" Rabe put some papers into his briefcase and left his office.

70 Once the decision had been made to penetrate the U.S. and Canadian markets in the 1970s, corporate momentum continued to drive the plan, long after market conditions had changed. A recognition lag and lack of belief that the environment had shifted locked the decision into place.

71 Rabe walked confidently to his car. He now knew what he must recommend to the board.

Appendix A: Consolidated Statements of Income

SEK M except per share amounts		1985		1984
Sales		**86,196**		87,052
Costs and expenses (Note 3)				
Cost of sales	**70,388**		72,062	
Selling, general and administrative expenses	**7,608**	**77,996**	6,960	79,022
Depreciation and amortization (Note 4)		**1,725**		1,402
Operating income		**6,475**		6,628
Financial income (expense)				
Dividends received	**113**		42	
Gain (loss) on sale of securities—net	**(3)**		96	
Interest income	**2,223**		2,052	
Interest expense	**1,802**		1,803	
Foreign exchange gain (loss) (Note 5)	**759**	**1,290**	(551)	(164)
Income after financial income (expense)		**7,765**		6,464
Extraordinary income (expense) (Note 6)		**–**		1,363
Provision for employee bonus (Note 7)		**(163)**		(180)
Income before allocations, taxes and minority interests		**7,602**		7,647
Allocations to untaxed reserves (Note 8)		**(3,330)**		(4,384)
Income before taxes and minority interests		**4,272**		3,263
Taxes (Note 9)		**1,713**		1,624
Minority interests (Note 10)		**(13)**		(74)
Net income		**2,546**		1,565
Income per share, SEK (See calculation on page 7)		**49.20**		46.50
Approximate net income in accordance with U.S. generally accepted accounting principles (Note 26)		**4,478**		4,100
Approximate net income per share in accordance with U.S. generally accepted accounting principles (Note 26), SEK		**57.70**		52.90

In the financial statements and the tables in the Notes, parentheses are used to indicate negative figures. In the narrative text, parentheses enclose figures related to 1984 operations.

Appendix B: Consolidated Balance Sheets

SEK M	December 31, 1985		December 31, 1984	
Assets				
Current assets				
Cash in banks (Note 11)	**4,202**		5,713	
Temporary investments (Note 12)	**10,192**		6,187	
Receivables, etc. (Note 13)	**11,244**		13,265	
Inventories (Note 14)	**16,044**	**41,682**	15,462	40,627
Restricted deposits in Bank of Sweden (Note 15)		**2,823**		1,762
Other assets				
Property, plant and equipment—net (Note 16)	**9,565**		8,199	
Investments (Note 2)	**6,894**		5,409	
Long-term receivables and loans	**1,209**		1,213	
Intangible assets (Note 17).........................	**620**	**18,288**	419	15,240
Total assets		**62,793**		57,629
Liabilities and shareholders' equity				
Current liabilities				
Accounts payable	**6,340**		6,510	
Advances from customers	**1,024**		1,015	
Bank loans (Note 18)	**6,595**		6,074	
Other loans (Note 18)	**3,674**		3,757	
Other current liabilities (Note 18)	**9,223**	**26,856**	8,710	26,066
Long-term liabilities				
Notes and mortgages payable (Note 19)	**4,032**		4,566	
Bond loans (Note 19)	**2,710**		1,871	
Subordinated loans (Note 19)	**677**		673	
Provision for pensions (Note 20)	**1,866**	**9,285**	1,895	9,005
Untaxed reserves (Note 8)		**17,738**		14,973
Minority interests (Note 10)		**116**		229
Shareholders' equity (Note 21)				
Restricted equity				
Share capital	**1,940**		1,940	
Reserves	**2,585**		2,854	
	4,525		4,794	
Unrestricted equity				
Retained earnings	**1,727**		997	
Net income for year	**2,546**		1,565	
	4,273		2,562	
Total shareholders' equity.............................		**8,798**		7,356
Total liabilities and shareholders' equity		**62,793**		57,629
Assets pledged (Note 23)		**3,033**		3,516
Contingent liabilities (Note 24)		**2,106**		2,620
Capital expenditures approved		**5,000**		4,100

Appendix C: Statements of Changes in Consolidated Financial Position

SEK M		1985		1984
Operations				
Net income		**2,546**		1,565
Depreciation and amortization		**1,725**		1,402
Allocations to untaxed reserves		**3,330**		4,384
Increase in restricted deposits in Bank of Sweden		**(1,061)**		(1,498)
Funds provided by year's operations		**6,540**		5,853
Changes in working capital components				
Decrease (increase) in current assets:				
Receivables, etc	**2,021**		(2,559)	
Inventories	**(582)**		(47)	
Increase (decrease) in current operating liabilities:				
Accounts payable	**(170)**		410	
Advances from customers	**9**		(37)	
Other current liabilities	**513**	**1,791**	47	(2,186)
Net financing from year's operations		**8,331**		3,667
Investments (increase)				
Investments in shares and participations—net	**(1,485)**		(2,215)	
Property, plant and equipment, etc.:				
Capital expenditures	**(3,506)**		(2,589)	
Disposals	**228**		348	
Acquisitions and sales of companies	**(233)**		2,934	
Long-term receivables and loans—net	**4**	**(4,992)**	457	(1,065)
Remaining after net investments		**3,339**		2,602
External financing, dividends, etc.				
Increase (decrease) in short-term bank loans and other loans	**438**		(985)	
Increase (decrease) in long-term liabilities	**280**		(701)	
Share issue	**—**		237	
Decrease in minority interests	**(113)**		(528)	
Changes in composition of Group, translation differences, etc.	**(1,039)**		49	
Dividends paid	**(411)**	**(845)**	(399)	(2,327)
Increase in cash in banks and temporary investments		**2,494**		275

Appendix D: AB Volvo Statements of Income

SEK M		1985		1984
Sales		**5,504**		4,737
Costs and expenses				
Cost of sales	4,394		3,858	
Selling, general and administrative expenses	874	5,268	692	4,550
Depreciation (Note 1)		48		30
Operating income		**188**		157
Financial income (expense)				
Dividends received	703		872	
Gain on sale of securities (Note 2)	64		10	
Interest income	1,049		767	
Interest expense	1,392		1,038	
Foreign exchange gain (loss) (Note 3)	340	764	(319)	292
Income after financial income (expense)		**952**		449
Extraordinary income (expense) (Note 4)		**(60)**		1,101
Provision for employee bonus		**(7)**		(9)
Income before allocations and taxes		**885**		1,541
Allocations (Note 5)		**393**		(499)
Income before taxes		**1,278**		1,042
Taxes (Note 6)		**317**		43
Net income		**961**		999

In the financial statements and the tables in the Notes, parentheses are used to indicate negative figures in the narrative text, parentheses enclose figures related to 1984 operations.

Appendix E: Statements of Changes in Financial Position

SEK M	1985		1984	
Operations				
Net income	**961**		999	
Depreciation	**48**		30	
Allocations	**(393)**		499	
Increase in restricted deposits in Bank of Sweden	**(1,978)**		(195)	
Funds provided by year's operations	**(1,362)**		1,333	
Changes in working capital components				
Decrease (increase) in current assets:				
Receivables, etc.	3,274		(3,646)	
Inventories	(203)		(161)	
Increase (decrease) in current operating liabilities:				
Accounts payable	23		(480)	
Advances from customers	51		–	
Amounts due to subsidiaries	923		2,809	
Other current liabilities	73	**4,141**	(97)	(1,575)
Net financing from year's operations		**2,779**		(242)
Investments (increase)				
Investments in shares and participations—net	**(2,992)**		(316)	
Property, plant and equipment—net	**(131)**		(124)	
Long-term receivables—net	**(576)**	**(3,699)**	652	212
Net after investments		**(920)**		(30)
External financing, dividends, etc.				
Increase in short-term bank loans and other loans	**199**		531	
Increase in long-term liabilities	**1,162**		99	
Share issue	**–**		237	
Group contribution	**2,323**		1,895	
Transfers of assets and liabilities to Group companies	**(278)**		320	
Dividends paid	**(411)**	**2,995**	(399)	2,683
Increase in cash in banks and temporary investments . .		**2,075**		2,653

Appendix F: Balance Sheets

SEK M	December 31, **1985**		December 31, 1984	
Assets				
Current assets				
Cash in banks (Note 7)	**801**		2,350	
Temporary investments placed with subsidiaries (Note 7) ..	**4,286**		1,322	
Other temporary investments (Note 7)	**3,356**		2,696	
Accounts receivable from subsidiaries (Note 8)	**403**		1,026	
Other receivables (Note 8)	**993**		3,644	
Inventories (Note 9)	**1,176**	**11,015**	973	12,011
Restricted deposits in Bank of Sweden (Note 10)		**2,031**		103
Other assets				
Property, plant and equipment (Note 11)	**545**		462	
Shares and participations in subsidiaries (Note 12)	**7,827**		6,494	
Shares and participations—other (Note 12)	**3,250**		1,591	
Long-term loans to subsidiaries	**1,047**		776	
Other long-term loans	**440**	**13,109**	135	9,458
Total assets		**26,155**		21,572
Liabilities and shareholders' equity				
Current liabilities (Note 13)				
Accounts payable	**370**		347	
Advances from customers	**102**		51	
Amounts due to subsidiaries	**6,686**		5,763	
Bank loans......................................	**100**		58	
Other loans	**1,266**		1,109	
Other current liabilities	**814**	**9,338**	741	8,069
Long-term liabilities				
Amounts due to subsidiaries (Note 14)	**2,727**		1,148	
Notes and mortgages payable (Note 14)	**517**		697	
Bond loans (Note 14)	**1,411**		1,647	
Subordinated loans................................	**632**		673	
Provision for pensions (Note 15)	**420**	**5,707**	380	4,545
Untaxed reserves (Note 16)		**4,961**		3,359
Shareholders' equity (Note 17)				
Restricted equity				
Share capital (77,605,009 shares, par value SEK 25 each)	**1,940**		1,940	
Reserves	**1,242**		1,242	
	3,182		3,182	
Unrestricted equity				
Retained earnings................................	**2,006**		1,418	
Net income for year	**961**		999	
	2,967		2,417	
Total shareholders' equity.............................		**6,149**		5,599
Total liabilities and shareholders' equity		**26,155**		21,572
Assets pledged (Note 18)		**287**		383
Contingent liabilities (Note 19)		**2,487**		2,047
Capital expenditures approved		**256**		177

Appendix G: The Volvo Group, 1981–1985

Condensed Consolidated Statements of Income	1981	1982	1983	1984	1985
Sales	48,017	75,624	99,460	87,052	**86,196**
Operating income	1,966	3,335	4,502	6,628	**6,475**
Foreign exchange gain (loss)	(246)	(721)	(226)	(551)	**759**
Other financial income (expense)	(295)	(369)	(331)	387	**531**
Income after financial income (expense)	1,425	2,245	3,945	6,464	**7,765**
Extraordinary income (expense)	–	235	–	1,363	**–**
Provision for employee bonus	–	(40)	(166)	(180)	**(163)**
Income before allocations, taxes and minority interests	1,425	2,440	3,779	7,647	**7,602**
Allocations to untaxed reserves	704	1,348	2,981	4,384	**3,330**
Taxes	222	508	752	1,624	**1,713**
Minority interests in (income) losses	(46)	(88)	158	(74)	**(13)**
Net income	453	496	204	1,565	**2,546**
Income per share, SEK	11.00	15.70	24.30	46.50	**49.20**

Condensed Consolidated Balance Sheets					
Cash in banks and temporary investments	5,476	7,250	11,625	11,900	**14,394**
Receivables and inventories	20,126	24,869	26,121	28,727	**27,288**
Restricted deposits in Bank of Sweden	208	221	264	1,762	**2,823**
Other assets	10,835	13,935	15,496	15,240	**18,288**
Total assets	36,645	46,275	53,506	57,629	**62,793**
Current liabilities	17,388	21,484	26,631	26,066	**26,856**
Long-term liabilities	8,535	10,904	9,706	9,005	**9,285**
Untaxed reserves	6,458	7,846	10,832	14,973	**17,738**
Minority interests	451	732	757	229	**116**
Shareholders' equity	3,813	5,309	5,580	7,356	**8,798**
Total liabilities and shareholders' equity	36,645	46,275	53,506	57,629	**62,793**
Capital expenditures	2,514	2,346	2,397	2,589	**3,506**
Research and development expenses	1,617	2,002	2,508	3,304	**3,817**
Number of employees, year-end	76,085	75,136	76,206	68,586	**67,857**
Wages, salaries and social costs	7,547	9,021	10,348	10,509	**11,359**
Share capital	1,394	1,698	1,735	1,940	**1,940**
Dividends to shareholders	251[1]	340	399	411	**660[2]**
Dividend per share, SEK	3.88	4.55	5.23	5.30	**8.50[2]**

Approximate amounts as adjusted to conform with U.S. GAAP

	1981	1982	1983	1984	1985
Net income	687	850	1,496	4,100	**4,478[3]**
Net income per share, SEK	11.90	12.70	19.80	52.90	**57.70[3]**
Total assets	36,762	46,365	53,273	58,343	**64,233**
Shareholders' equity	6,547	8,381	9,871	13,496	**17,804**

[1] Including dividends from Beijerinvest AB.
[2] Proposed by the Board of Directors.
[3] Includes extraordinary income of SEK 744 M, equal to SEK 9.60 per share.

Amounts in SEK millions unless otherwise noted.

Case 34

Mack Truck and the UAW

Overview

1 Due to economic pressures and the need for more efficient facilities, Mack Truck Corporation decided that it would build a substitute plant in another city if the United Auto Workers International, which was negotiating a new agreement on behalf of Mack Truck's Allentown, Pennsylvania, workers, did not agree to a new contract with reduced wages for 1986. A direct result of this decision would be that 1,800 Mack Truck employees in Allentown could lose their jobs.

Mack Truck Corporation in the 1980s

2 In the 1980s, Mack Truck experienced lackluster performance. Following the closing of its Haywood, California, plant in 1980, Mack had a loss for the year of $20 million. Interpreting the significance of this loss was complicated by the layoffs of 2,000 Mack workers nationwide in that same year. In 1981, earnings were just under $10 million. In 1982 and 1983, the company had losses of $32 million and $26 million, respectively.

3   The company's management began taking a hard look at costs in 1983, after Renault Holding Company acquired 45 percent of Mack Truck's stock from the Signal Company. Mack Truck management began cutting the salaries of employees by 25 percent, followed by a policy of reducing inventories by "outsourcing," that is, by cutting the number of parts made by suppliers. These policies paid off, and the company had earnings of $75 million on sales of $2.1 billion in the industry boom year of 1984.

4   The company was simultaneously involved in a campaign to modernize its operations and reduce costs. In 1980, it took the company 60 cents of working capital to produce a dollar of sales. By 1984, the company was producing a dollar of sales with only 30 cents of working capital.

5   In 1985, the company showed a loss of $59 million, but this figure included a $62 million write-off due to a reserve fund set up to relocate an assembly plant and the expenses incurred in closing the number 3 and 4 plants in Allentown. Exhibit 1 reviews the highlights of Mack Truck's history, while Exhibit 2 provides financial data on the company for the years 1982–85.

6   Despite its periodic reversals, Mack Truck remained one of the largest U.S. makers of class 8 trucks, meaning those of more than 33,000 pounds vehicle weight. In 1986, the company made and sold heavy-duty trucks, truck tractors, and replacement parts. It was also the sole distributor for the United States, Canada, and some Central American countries of Renault-built, lighter, class 6 trucks, which were marketed under the Mack Mid-Liner trademark. It owned 5 used-truck centers, 27 new truck sales and service branches, and 1 parts store. The company also supervised 765 service and sales outlets, which included 241 sales and service distributors and 524 independently owned service dealerships. The company also supplied parts for Rockway Trucks through 58 independent parts and service outlets.

This case was prepared by John A. Pearce II of George Mason University with the assistance of Julio De Castro of the University of South Carolina. Copyright © 1987 by John A. Pearce II.

Exhibit 1
Noteworthy dates in the 85-year history of the Mack Truck Corporation

1901	Brooklyn wagonmakers William, Augustus, and John Mack are incorporated as Mack Brothers Company in New York.
1905	Mack Brothers Motor Company registers at the LeHigh County Courthouse as a business on January 2.
1909	The first motor-driven hook-and-ladder truck is produced as Mack branches out into the fire apparatus field.
1914	Production of the AB model truck begins and is followed a short time later by the famous AC truck, which is nicknamed the "Bulldog."
1925	Mack opens plants 3 and 4.
1926	Production begins at plant 5C in Allentown, Pennsylvania.
1932	The Bulldog is officially adopted as the company's trademark.
1940	The United Auto Workers union is chosen by a vote of 1,688 to 855 to represent Mack's workers.
1953	Mack introduces diesel engines in its trucks.
1956	Mack acquires Brockway Trucks.
1960	Bus production ends.
1965	Construction begins on a plant in Toronto.
1966	Hayward, California, production plant opens.
1967	Mack becomes part of Signal Oil and Gas Company.
1970	Mack opens its world headquarters building in Allentown.
1975	Mack opens its $7 million development and test center in Allentown.
1976	Mack opens a $25 million plant in Lower Macungie Township to build cab-over engine trucks.
1977	The Brockway plant in Cortland, New York, is closed as Mack decides to get out of assembling trucks from purchased parts.
1979	Renault, Inc., acquires a 20 percent interest.
1980	Layoffs hit 2,600 workers in Mack Truck plants throughout the nation. The UAW calls it the worst year ever for layoffs at Mack. The Hayward, California, plant closes, and production is shifted to Mack's then-underutilized and more efficient Macungie plant.
1983	Mack spins off from Signal. Renault increases its stock holdings in Mack from 20 percent to 45 percent.
1985	Allentown plants 3 and 4 close.

---

7   Mack shared second place among heavy truck manufacturers with Paccar (under tradenames Peterbilt and Kenworth) with an 18 percent market share, while Navistar (formerly International Harvester) held first place with a 22 percent market share. Other competitors were Freightliner with 13 percent, Ford Motor and General Motors with a 10 percent market share each, and Volvo-White with 7 percent.

8   On the negative side, Mack Truck faced heavy competition. The main reason was that the market for class 8 trucks was shrinking. The eight domestic truck makers had a capacity to build more than 230,000 class 8 trucks annually, which was almost twice the 125,000 class 8 trucks sold in 1985. Makers also faced the threat of a new wave of class 7 trucks imported from Japan, Brazil, and Europe that could make inroads into the class 8 market.

9   To remain competitive, if not dominant in its markets, Mack Truck believed that it needed to have a modern production facility—one more beneficial to operations than was the current 5C plant in Allentown. Although an upgrading and retooling of

Exhibit 2

MACK TRUCK CORPORATION
Consolidated Statements of Income (Loss)
For the Years Ended December 31
(in thousands except per share amounts)

	1985	1984	1983	1982
Net sales	$2,063,312	$2,105,458	$1,216,830	$1,291,552
Costs and expenses:				
Cost of sales	1,934,649	1,885,065	1,134,121	1,189,464
Depreciation and amortization of property (principally applicable to cost of sales)	29,663	27,981	26,199	24,306
Selling, general, and administrative expenses	99,058	105,355	89,500	91,241
Provision (credit) for doubtful accounts and notes receivable	2,044	(330)	7,527	8,646
Total	$2,065,414	$2,020,071	$1,257,347	$1,313,657
Income (loss) from operations	(2,102)	85,387	(40,517)	(22,105)
Other income (deductions):				
Interest expense (including $3,595,000 to an affiliate in 1982)	(20,534)	(19,727)	(25,983)	(45,665)
Provision for terminated operations	(68,294)	(11,539)	(1,000)	
Transactions with financial subsidiaries:				
Interest income on long term	2,388	1,457		
Charges from financial subsidiaries on customer accounts and wholesale (floorplan) notes	(21,202)	(24,601)	(10,712)	(16,150)
Adjustment with respect to receivables sold			(6,400)	(12,800)
Interest income (including amounts from an affiliate of $2,108,000 and $1,268,000 in 1984 and 1983, respectively)	6,077	11,521	15,233	6,323
Miscellaneous—net	(103)	253	3,568	3,607
Total	$ (101,668)	$ (42,636)	$ (25,294)	$ (64,685)
Income (loss) before income taxes, equity in net income (loss) of unconsolidated subsidiaries and extraordinary item	(103,770)	42,751	(65,811)	(86,790)
Provision (credit) for income taxes:				
Current	(17,999)	16,985	(23,317)	(41,448)
Deferred	(4,739)	(11,539)	(3,118)	3,297
Total	$ (22,738)	$ 4,546	$ (26,435)	$ (38,151)
Income (loss) before equity in net income (loss) of unconsolidated subsidiaries and extraordinary income	(81,032)	38,205	(39,376)	(48,639)
Equity in net income (loss) of unconsolidated subsidiaries:				
Financial subsidiaries	21,249	26,377	13,201	17,601
Other				(1,256)
Total	$ 21,249	$ 26,377	$ 13,201	$ 16,345
Income (loss) before extraordinary item	(59,783)	64,582	(26,175)	(32,294)
Extraordinary item (tax benefits)	567	10,371		
Net income (loss)	$ (59,216)	$ 74,953	$ (26,175)	$ (32,294)
Earnings (loss) per common share and common equivalent share:				
Income (loss) before extraordinary item	(2.09)	1.96	(.97)	(1.26)
Extraordinary item (tax benefits)	.02	.33		
Net income (loss)	$ (2.07)	$ 2.29	$ (.97)	$ (1.26)

Exhibit 2 *(concluded)*

	1985	1984	1983	1982
Earnings (loss) per common share—assuming full dilution:				
Income (loss) before extraordinary item	(2.09)	1.93	(.97)	(1.26)
Extraordinary item (tax benefits)	.02	.31		
Net income (loss)	$ (2.07)	$ 2.29	$ (.97)	$ (1.26)
Average number of common and common equivalent shares outstanding	30,056	30,993	28,388	25,530
Average number of common shares outstanding— assuming full dilution	30,056	33,049	28,388	25,530

Source: Mack Truck, *Annual Report 1984.*

the existing plant was possible, the company seemed to be leaning toward the option of building a new facility. In fact, Mack Truck appeared to favor a new location as well.

10   The main reasons the company gave for considering an alternative location for the 5C plant were the needs for increased productivity and reduced labor costs. The company alleged that (1) a remodeling of the 5C plant would be more costly than building a new plant, (2) a new plant would produce 70 trucks a year with 1,200 employees versus 52 trucks a year with 1,800 workers in the old plant, and (3) a location in the South would bring about a reduction of labor costs. For example, in the state of South Carolina, the average 1985 wage for a worker was $7.62 per hour, as opposed to a national average of $9.54 per hour. The company had hinted that in the event that the plant was located in South Carolina, the hourly wage would be around $11. It was estimated that fringe benefits would add 35 percent to the labor cost. UAW members working at the Allentown plant made $23 per hour, including fringe benefits, in 1985.

UAW and Mack Trucks

11   The wholly unionized company and the union were negotiating under conditions established by a three-year contract negotiated in 1984 following a brief strike. For several months the company had insisted that it needed substantial wage cuts for the Allentown location of a new plant to be economically feasible, while the union resisted that notion. Specifically, in January 1986, the company proposed a $2.04-per-hour cut in the $23-per-hour wage plus benefits the workers earned. The UAW rejected this offer and stipulated that it would only consider wage cuts if they applied to union and management employees equally.

12   The union countered with a proposal by which the workers would invest up to 6 percent of their pay in Mack securities to help finance a new plant in Allentown and to help renovate the company's Hagerstown, Maryland, facility. The company rejected this proposal and set a Friday, January 17, 1986, deadline to decide on the location of the new plant. Also of importance during the negotiations were 100 job classifications of union workers at the Allentown plant, which the company wanted to reduce and the union steadfastly refused to consider.

13   With the negotiations between Mack and the UAW International deadlocked, plant workers picketed outside the plant, calling for a chance to vote on the company's

proposal. UAW Local 677 President Eugene McCafferty said on Saturday, January 18, 1986, that the workers at the plant should be allowed to make their own decisions. But on the following Monday he said that since the company's offer included a plan to hire outside firms to make some of the parts currently made at the Hagerstown plant, under union bylaws all Mack plants would have to vote on the issue. He added that it was the international union's place to consider the proposals because some of the company's plans would affect all UAW Mack locals, not just the Allentown workers. On the Tuesday and Wednesday after the company's deadline, Allentown union leaders circulated petitions asking the company and union to resume talks in order to save jobs in the area.

Allentown and Mack

14   Allentown, Pennsylvania, housed the Mack Truck headquarters. By 1986 the company employed 5,000 workers at its plants in Macungie and Allentown and its headquarter offices. The company opened its first plant in Allentown in 1925 and continued building plants in the area. In 1970, it opened its world headquarters building in the city. In 1975, the company opened a $7 million research and development center, again in Allentown.

15   It was estimated that a move of the plant would result in lost wages of about $60 million annually to the Allentown community. This estimate was based on the vote of many UAW workers to follow the plant if it was moved. Under the current contract, plant workers had the opportunity to move if the plant was relocated, and a large group of surveyed workers had indicated that if the plant was moved, they would move with it.

16   Another source of concern for the Allentown residents was the fact that there were 40 local plants that existed to supply parts to the Mack plant. In the event of a Mack plant relocation, these firms and their more than 1,000 employees were also likely to move. It was estimated that hundreds of businesses would be directly or indirectly affected by the relocation of the plant.

17   For the past decade the city had followed a transition from an economy based on manufacturing jobs to one based on service sector jobs. According to the area's Bureau of Employment Security, employment in the manufacturing segment fell 28 percent (from 115,000 workers in 1974 to 90,000 workers in 1985). However, during the same period employment in the nonmanufacturing segment rose 25 percent (from 140,000 to 175,000). Overall employment had risen 8 percent during the period. Those new jobs would be jeopardized if the Mack plant moved, and the impact on the city would be especially hard if a Mack move occurred near the time of feared layoffs by the area's other big employer, Bethlehem Steel Company. City officials were confident that they could cope with the Mack move alone, but if it coincided with big layoffs from Bethlehem, they admitted that the city would be in economic turmoil.

Mack and Winnsboro

18   The city that appeared to be the most likely alternative location for the Mack plant was Winnsboro, South Carolina. The company had been scouting locations in the area as early as the summer of 1985. The South seemed a likely location for the plant because a score of Mack competitors had already moved south to plants with no unions

Exhibit 3

State-Provided Incentives Lure Mack Trucks

The State Development Board met Friday with representatives of various state agencies to put together a final inducement package for Mack Trucks, Inc. The package, combined with the Fairfield County inducement package and one from local utility companies, was enough to persuade Mack to move south.

The package from the state included:

A five-year abatement of county property taxes, excluding school taxes, for new industry and future industrial expansions, which is expected to amount to more than $2.5 million over five years.

Exempting pollution control devices and fixtures from property taxes.

Exempting inventory taxes on manufacturer's stocks, which could save more than $218,000.

Depreciation rates of at least 11 percent a year for property tax purposes.

Exempting of all manufacturing equipment, machinery, and replacement parts from sales taxes.

Exempting the purchase of raw material for a manufacturing process and wholesale sales and purchases from the sales tax.

Including Fairfield County in a special category of less developed counties to create a corporate income tax credit of $500 for each new job created. If 1,200 jobs were created, the credit could amount to a savings of $3 million over five years.

Providing vocational training for a pool of workers for Mack. The schools will provide preemployment recruitment, screening, and training according to Mack's requirements and all necessary training materials. The program is totally state funded and will depend on the requirements set by Mack.

The Displaced Worker program will provide a reimbursement for half of the pay of any worker hired by Mack and undergoing displaced worker job training. It also can pay for worker relocation. If 400 employees were to qualify, it would mean a $500,000 investment from the state.

The state highway department has committed, at a cost of at least $2.75 million, to improve Highway 34 from the plant site to Interstate 77, including strengthening the road and adding, as needed, a third lane. The work is to be completed before the plant opens.

Grants of up to $500,000 can be made available to pay for site improvements, roads, sewers, water, and other necessities to make the project possible.

A one-year, $5 million, low-rate construction loan can be made available if need by the company is demonstrated.

Source: This article appeared in the Friday edition of *The State* newspaper of Columbia, South Carolina, January 24, 1986.

or with company unions. These plants also enjoyed sharply fewer job classifications than the 100 that Mack had in its Allentown plant. South Carolina offered the further advantage of being one of the least unionized states in the United States. It did not have a single UAW local and had a pattern of industry wages that were well below the national average.

19   The state of South Carolina offered other cost-reduction possibilities for Mack. It was estimated that the company would save $50,000 a month on its nuclear-power-generated electric bill on usage of 5,000 megawatts/hour of 10,000 kilowatts of electricity, or 18.2 percent of its electric bill. It was also estimated that construction costs were 17.6 percent lower in South Carolina than in Pennsylvania. Other savings would come from cheaper inland transportation, lower docking costs, and a lower overall cost of living. South Carolina also boasted the lowest work stoppage rate in the country.

20   Once Mack made it known that it was looking for a location for its plant, South Carolina's public and business leaders developed a campaign to try to get the company to locate the plant in the state. The state offered a package of incentives, tax breaks, and other inducements that were believed to be worth over $5 million in savings to the company over a five-year period. Exhibit 3 gives a breakdown of the package.

The Decision

21   On Wednesday, January 22, 1986, Mack Truck announced its decision to locate the new plant in Fairfield County, in Winnsboro, South Carolina, as reported in the newspaper account shown in Exhibit 3. In justifying the move, the company expressed its expectation of annual pre-tax savings of $80 million or $47 million after taxes from a more favorable business climate in South Carolina. It was clear, however, that the move would have less favorable long-range implications for the future of the company's labor relations. Following the announcement, UAW officials vowed to continue the fight and said that the war had only begun over the plant relocation.

General Index

Case Index